Jimmy Swaggart Bible Commentary

I Chronicles
II Chronicles

JIMMY SWAGGART BIBLE COMMENTARY

- Genesis [639 pages 11-201]
- Exodus [639 pages 11-202]
- Leviticus [435 pages 11-203]
- Numbers
  Deuteronomy [493 pages 11-204]
- Joshua
  Judges
  Ruth [329 pages 11-205]
- I Samuel
  II Samuel [528 pages 11-206]
- I Kings
  II Kings [560 pages 11-207]
- I Chronicles
  II Chronicles [528 pages 11-226]
- Ezra
  Nehemiah
  Esther [288 pages 11-208]
- Job [320 pages 11-225]
- Psalms [672 pages 11-216]
- Proverbs [311 pages 11-227]
- Ecclesiastes
  Song Of Solomon [238 pages 11-228]
- Isaiah [688 pages 11-220]
- Jeremiah
  Lamentations [456 pages 11-070]
- Ezekiel [508 pages 11-223]
- Daniel [403 pages 11-224]
- Hosea
  Joel
  Amos [496 Pages 11-229]
- Obadiah
  Jonah
  Micah
  Nahum
  Habakkuk
  Zephaniah [545 pages 11-230]
- Haggai
  Zechariah
  Malachi [449 pages 11-231]
- Matthew [888 pages 11-073]
- Mark [606 pages 11-074]
- Luke [626 pages 11-075]
- John [532 pages 11-076]
- Acts [697 pages 11-077]
- Romans [536 pages 11-078]
- I Corinthians [632 pages 11-079]
- II Corinthians [589 pages 11-080]
- Galatians [478 pages 11-081]
- Ephesians [550 pages 11-082]
- Philippians [476 pages 11-083]
- Colossians [374 pages 11-084]
- I Thessalonians
  II Thessalonians [498 pages 11-085]
- I Timothy
  II Timothy
  Titus
  Philemon [687 pages 11-086]
- Hebrews [831 pages 11-087]
- James
  I Peter
  II Peter [730 pages 11-088]
- I John
  II John
  III John
  Jude [377 pages 11-089]
- Revelation [602 pages 11-090]

For prices and information please call: 1-800-288-8350
Baton Rouge residents please call: (225) 768-7000
Website: www.jsm.org • E-mail: info@jsm.org

Jimmy Swaggart Bible Commentary

I Chronicles
II Chronicles

World Evangelism Press

ISBN 978-1-934655-67-2
11-226 • COPYRIGHT © 2011 World Evangelism Press®
P.O. Box 262550 • Baton Rouge, Louisiana 70826-2550
Website: www.jsm.org • E-mail: info@jsm.org
(225) 768-8300
17 18 19 20 21 22 23 24 25 26 27 28 29 30 31 32 33 34 / EBM / 19 18 17 16 15 14 13 12 11 10 9 8 7 6 5 4 3 2
All rights reserved. Printed and bound in U.S.A.
No part of this publication may be reproduced in any form or by any means
without the publisher's prior written permission.

TABLE OF CONTENTS

1. I Chronicles Introduction 1
2. I Chronicles 2
3. II Chronicles Introduction 199
4. II Chronicles 200
Index 505

THE BOOK OF I CHRONICLES

INTRODUCTION

It is Saturday, September 1, 2007, as I begin commentary on I Chronicles.

According to Jewish tradition, Ezra is considered the author of the Chronicles. One thing is certain, both the Books of I and II Chronicles were written after the dispersion. Understanding that, it is more than likely that the Jewish tradition is correct as it regards Ezra as the instrument through which the Holy Spirit worked to bring us this tremendous history, in fact, the most important in the history of man.

HISTORICAL SIGNIFICANCE

At first glance it may seem to be a stretch of the imagination to chronicle these two Books as the single most important historical narrative ever written, but it happens to be true.

Chapters 1 through 9 consist of the genealogies of particular families, all with one focal point in mind, the coming of Christ. While these genealogies may be looked at in different ways, still, the all-important conclusion, the overriding principal, the purpose and reason are one, and that is that these families in some way had something to do with the coming of the Redeemer. That within itself is so outsized as to defy all description.

When we speak of the coming Redeemer, we are speaking of Redemption, without which there would be no Salvation.

If it is to be noticed in these genealogies, David is picked up as the King of Israel, with Saul little noticed. In fact, I think the evidence is clear that it was the Will of God

NOTES

that David be the first King of Israel. Saul was demanded by the people, which was premature. The Lord gave them what they demanded, but it fell out exactly as He said it would, as a great hindrance to the formation of Israel as a cohesive people. Saul was a work of the flesh, and that which is of the flesh cannot please God (Rom. 8:8). David was a Work of the Spirit, meaning that He was God's Choice; consequently, virtually the entirety of I Chronicles is given over to the history of David.

It was through the lineage of David that the Messiah would come; hence, Jesus would be referred to as the *"Son of David."* So, in retrospect, no higher honor could ever be paid to any family in history, or the present, or the future, than that which was accorded the *"sweet singer of Israel,"* in that the Messiah, the Son of the Living God, would come to this world in human form, and do so through the family of David. In fact, Joseph, Jesus' foster father, went back to David in his lineage through Solomon. Mary, the mother of our Lord, went back to David through another son, Nathan. So, the genealogy of our Lord was perfect in every respect as it regarded the Prophecy and prediction that through David's family would be the Incarnation. So, these genealogies are of utmost significance in that they culminate, in some manner, with Christ. That is why they are the most important genealogies, the most important histories, on the face of the Earth, past, present, or future.

Now, this doesn't mean that all of these individuals named were godly. In fact, many of them were very ungodly and died eternally lost; still, they had the opportunity, which was the greatest opportunity ever afforded to man, to be something more than just a mere name in history. Some few took advantage of that high and gracious honor, but most, sadly, didn't!

A MOST PROFITABLE STUDY

If you have purchased this Commentary, or it has been placed in your hands by other means, and if you will take advantage of the material given therein, I think as you conclude your study of these two great Books of the Bible, I and II Chronicles, you will have a greater appreciation for Christ, a greater understanding of our Lord, and the price that He paid for the Redemption of humanity, of which nothing could be more important.

A DIARY KEPT BY GOD

The name *"Chronicles"* is from the Hebrew, *"Dibrei Hayyamim,"* which means *"words of the days,"* or in modern language, *"the diary."* But, how intensely interesting — a Diary kept by God!

The two Books, like I and II Kings, were only one originally. The division was the work of the Septuagint translators and was adopted by Jerome, then by various branches of the western church.

The two Books of Chronicles are not new history; they cover many things written before. They belong, however, to quite another part of the Old Testament because they do not follow in sequence after the Books of Kings. They are, according to the Jewish Canon, the conclusion of the Old Testament, and the genealogies here lead to those of the New Testament. They begin with the first Adam and conclude looking forward to the Last Adam (Christ). They deal primarily with the kingdom of Judah because Christ was to be the successor of David on an Eternal Throne. As compared with I and II Kings, which give the history from the human standpoint, the two Books of Chronicles give the history from the Divine standpoint.

MAN RULES AND GOD OVERRULES

The former records of I and II Kings, at least to a measure, as man ruled history;

NOTES

the latter, I and II Chronicles, as God overruled it. Only four Verses, for instance, are devoted to Hezekiah's reformation in II Kings; whereas, three whole Chapters are given to it in Chronicles. The Books of Chronicles give God's Standpoint, pointing to the moral side and giving reasons for both Judgments and Mercies.

CHRONOLOGY

The Books of Kings are chronological in order, whereas, in Chronicles, chronology is sometimes ignored in order to bring out causes or consequences for the purpose of comparison and contrast between records.

In Kings we have the complete history of both houses of Israel. In Chronicles we have only that which pertains to the House of David and of Judah as being founded on the Covenant God made with David, of the Tribe of Judah, found in II Samuel, Chapter 7 and I Chronicles, Chapter 17. The Chronicles are entirely independent of the Books of Samuel and Kings, and the differences between them are designed to be so. Many critics create their own difficulties by first assuming that all the Books should be alike, which they are not, so they conclude that there are many discrepancies and corruptions in the Text, when actually the writings are full of Divine instruction containing additions for our learning.

CHAPTER 1

(1) "ADAM, SHETH, ENOSH,
(2) "KENAN, MAHALALEEL, JERED,
(3) "HENOCH, METHUSELAH, LAMECH,
(4) "NOAH, SHEM, HAM, AND JAPHETH."

The construction is:

1. (Vs. 1) The writer of Chronicles began abruptly with *"Adam,"* supposing that his readers would understand from the First Book of the Bible about the origin of Adam, the first man from whom all other men have their beings (Gen. 1:26-31; 2:7).

This Divine Diary, for Chronicles is a Diary kept by God, begins with the first Adam and carries on the story of Grace, in essence, to the Last Adam; in fact, this Book is placed as the last in the Hebrew Bible, and the reader passes at once to the First Chapter of Matthew.

2. (Vs. 3) Methuselah lived longer than any other human being, 969 years.

3. (Vs. 4) From Shem, Ham, and Japheth came all the descendants of Planet Earth.

ADAM

Adam, as the first man, was created by God. The Scripture says: *"So God created man in His Own Image* (the word *'man'* should have the definite article and should read *'the man,'* that is, Adam — the same man Adam spoken of in Gen. 2:7; these are not, therefore, two accounts of the creation of man but one Divine Statement). The Scripture then says, *"in the Image of God created He him* (the Image of God was lost at the Fall; however, the restoration of the Image was carried out at the Cross, but the completion of that restoration will not take place until the First Resurrection); *male and female created He them.* (represents, at least as far as we know, the first time that God has created the female gender, at least as it regards intelligent beings. There is no record of any female Angels)" (Gen. 1:27).

And then the Scripture adds to the first Passage: *"And the LORD God formed man of the dust of the ground* (proclaims the physical body made of clay), *and breathed into his nostrils the breath of life* (the *'breath of life,'* which comes from God, pertains to the soul and spirit of man; this was done with the first man, Adam, God breathing the soul and the spirit into man, and thereafter, it comes automatically at conception); *and man became a living soul* (man is a soul, has a spirit, both which reside in the physical body; the soul addresses the body; the spirit addresses God; the physical body addresses the world)" (Gen. 2:7).

THE CREATION OF EVE

Concerning the creation of the woman, the Bible says: *"And the LORD God caused a deep sleep to fall upon Adam, and he slept* (records the first anesthesia): *and He took one of his ribs* (the word *'rib'* here actually means *'side'*), *and closed up the flesh instead thereof* (the woman is not merely of a rib, but actually of one side of man);

"And the rib (side), *which the LORD God had taken from man, made He a woman* (the Hebrew says, *'built He a woman'*; Horton says, *'When God created the man, the word "form" was used, which is the same word used of a potter forming a clay jar; but the word "build" here seems to mean God paid even more attention to the creation of the woman'*), *and brought her unto the man* (presents a formal presentation, with God, in essence, performing the first wedding; thus He instituted the bonds of the Marriage Covenant, which is actually called the *'Covenant of God'* [Prov. 2:17], indicating that God is the Author of this sacred institution; this is the marriage model and was instituted by God; any other model, such as the homosexual marriages, so-called, can be constituted as none other than an abomination in the Eyes of God [Rom. 1:24-28])" (Gen. 2:21-22).

THE FALL OF ADAM AND EVE

The Scripture says: *"And the LORD God planted a Garden eastward in Eden* (it was actually planted before Adam was created; the area is believed by some Scholars to be the site where the city of Babylon would ultimately be built); *and there He put the man whom He had formed* (the Garden of Eden was to be the home place of man).

"And out of the ground made the LORD God to grow every tree that is pleasant to the sight (beautiful trees), *and good for food* (every fruit tree imaginable, even those which bear nuts); *the Tree of Life also in the midst of the Garden* (evidently contained a type of fruit; Gen. 3:22 says as much! the Tree of Life had the power of so renewing man's physical energies that his body, though formed of the dust of the ground and, therefore, naturally mortal, would, by its continual use, live on forever; Christ is now to us the *'Tree of Life'* [Rev. 2:7; 22:2]; and the *'Bread of Life'* [Jn. 6:48, 51]), *and the Tree of Knowledge of Good and Evil* (presents the tree of death)" (Gen. 2:8-9).

Then the Scripture says: *"And the LORD God took the man, and put him into the Garden of Eden to dress it and to keep it.*

"And the LORD God commanded the

man, saying, *Of every tree of the Garden you may freely eat* (as stated, before the Fall, man was vegetarian)*:*

"But of the tree of the Knowledge of Good and Evil, you shall not eat of it (as for the *'evil,'* that was obvious; however, it is the *'good'* on this tree that deceives much of the world; the *'good'* speaks of religion; the definition of religion pertains to a system devised by men in order to bring about Salvation, to reach God, or to better oneself in some way; because it is devised by man, it is unacceptable to God; God's answer to the dilemma of the human race is *'Jesus Christ and Him Crucified'* [I Cor. 1:23])*: for in the day that you eat thereof you shall surely die* (speaks of spiritual death, which is separation from God; let it be understood that the Tree of the Knowledge of Good and Evil was not the cause of Adam's Fall; it was a failure to heed and obey the Word of God, which is the cause of every single failure; spiritual death ultimately brought on physical death, and has, in fact, filled the world with death, all because of the Fall)" (Gen. 2:15-17).

The Scripture then says, and we continue to quote from THE EXPOSITOR'S STUDY BIBLE: *"Now the serpent was more subtle than any beast of the field which the LORD God had made* (the word *'subtle,'* as used here, is not negative, but rather positive; everything that God made before the Fall was positive; it describes qualities such as quickness of sight, swiftness of motion, activity of self-preservation, and seemingly intelligent adaptation to its surroundings). *And he said unto the woman* (not a fable; the serpent before the Fall had the ability of limited speech; Eve did not seem surprised when he spoke to her!), *Yes, has God said, You shall not eat of every tree of the Garden?* (The serpent evidently lent its faculties to Satan, even though the Evil One is not mentioned. That being the case, Satan spoke through the serpent, and questioned the Word of God.)

"And the woman said unto the serpent (proclaims Satan leveling his attack against Eve instead of Adam; his use of Eve was only a means to get to Adam), *We may eat of the fruit of the trees of the Garden* (the trial of our first parents was ordained by God because probation was essential to their spiritual development and self-determination; but as He did not desire that they should be tempted to their Fall, He would not suffer Satan to tempt them in a way that would surpass their human capacity; the tempted might, therefore, have resisted the tempter)*:*

"But of the fruit of the tree which is in the midst of the Garden, God has said, You shall not eat of it, neither shall you touch it, lest you die (Eve quoted what the Lord had said about the prohibition but then added, *'neither shall you touch it'*).

"And the serpent said unto the woman, You shall not surely die (proclaims an outright denial of the Word of God; as God had preached to Adam, Satan now preaches to Eve; Jesus called Satan a liar, which probably refers to this very moment [Jn. 8:44])*:*

"For God does know that in the day you eat thereof, then your eyes shall be opened (suggests the attainment of higher wisdom), *and you shall be as gods, knowing good and evil.* (In effect says, *'You shall be Elohim.'* It was a promise of Divinity. God is Omniscient, meaning that His Knowledge of evil is thorough, but not by personal experience. By His very Nature, He is totally separate from all that is evil. The knowledge of evil that Adam and Eve would learn would be by moral degradation, which would bring wreckage. While it was proper to desire to be like God, it is proper only if done in the right way, and that is through Faith in Christ and what He has done for us at the Cross.)

"And when the woman saw that the tree was good for food (presents the lust of the eyes), *and that it was pleasant to the eyes* (the lust of the flesh), *and a tree to be desired to make one wise* (the pride of life), *she took of the fruit thereof, and did eat* (constitutes the Fall), *and gave also unto her husband with her; and he did eat* (refers to the fact that evidently Adam was an observer to all these proceedings; some claim that he ate of the forbidden fruit which she offered him out of love for her; however, no one ever sins out of love; Eve submitted to the temptation out of deception, but *'Adam was not deceived'* [I Tim. 2:14]; he fell because of unbelief; he simply didn't believe what God

had said about the situation; contrast Verse 6 with Luke 4:1-13; both present the three temptations, *'the lust of the flesh,' 'the lust of the eyes,'* and *'the pride of life'*; the first man falls, the Second Man conquers).

"And the eyes of them both were opened (refers to the consciousness of guilt as a result of their sin), *and they knew that they were naked* (refers to the fact that they had lost the enswathing light of purity, which previously had clothed their bodies); *and they sewed fig leaves together, and made themselves aprons* (sinners clothe themselves with morality, sacraments, and religious ceremonies; they are as worthless as Adam's apron of fig leaves)" (Gen. 3:1-7).

How it must have hurt the Heart of God for Adam and Eve to fall.

WHAT IF ADAM HAD NOT JOINED EVE IN PARTAKING OF THE FORBIDDEN FRUIT?

The fall of Eve alone would not have constituted the Fall of mankind. She would have suffered, but her suffering would have been confined basically to herself. She could have asked the Lord to forgive her, which forgiveness would have been instantly granted.

But when Adam also partook of the forbidden fruit, due to the fact that he was the federal head of all who would follow, in other words, every human being that would be born thereafter, his fall would drag down the entirety of the human race.

When God created Adam and Eve, it seems that their creation was totally different than any other creation by God. For instance, when God created the Angels, every evidence is that they were all created at the same time and were created fully mature. In other words, there has never been such a thing as a baby Angel. As well, Angels were not given the power of procreation, as was mankind.

But when God created Adam and Eve, He gave them the ability to procreate, meaning to bring offspring into the world. So, in a sense, every human being who would ever live thereafter would bear the result of what Adam, the federal head, would do, and in fact, did do. In other words, his fall was, in effect, the Fall of the entirety of the human race. Concerning this, Paul said:

"But now is Christ risen from the dead (so says the Holy Spirit), *and become the Firstfruits of them who slept.* (The Resurrection of Christ guarantees the Resurrection of all Saints.)

"For since by man came death (refers to Adam and the Fall in the Garden of Eden, and speaks of spiritual death, separation from God), *by Man came also the Resurrection of the dead.* (This refers to the Lord Jesus Christ Who atoned for all sin, thereby, making it possible for man to be united once again with God, which guarantees the Resurrection.)

"For as in Adam all die (spiritual death, separation from God), *even so in Christ shall all be made alive.* (In the first man, all died. In the Second Man, all shall be made alive, at least all who will believe [Jn. 3:16])" (I Cor. 15:20-22).

The great Apostle then said:

"And so it is written (Gen. 2:7), *The first man Adam was made a living soul* (the natural body); *the last Adam* (Christ) *was made a quickening Spirit.* (The word *'last'* is used. No other will ever be needed. *'Quickening'* refers to making all alive who trust Him.)

"Howbeit that was not first which is spiritual, but that which is natural (Adam came first); *and afterward that which is spiritual.* (Christ, as the Last Adam, came second in order to undo that which occurred at the Fall.)

"The first man (Adam) *is of the earth, earthy* (materialistic): *the Second Man* (Christ) *is the Lord from Heaven* (a vast difference between the *'first man'* and the *'Second Man'*).

"As is the earthy, such are they also who are earthy (it is the body and its present condition to which Paul points with the term *'earthy'*): *and as is the Heavenly, such are they also who are Heavenly.* (Christ is *'the Heavenly One,'* and all who are *'the Heavenly ones'* are like Him. Paul is continuing to speak of the Resurrection, and what it will be like.)

"And as we have borne the image of the earthy (refers to the fact that as our first father, we are frail, decaying, and dying), *we shall also bear the image of the Heavenly.*

(This tells us what we will be like in the Resurrection, i.e., *'like Him.'*)

"Now this I say, Brethren, that flesh and blood cannot inherit the Kingdom of God (pertains to our present physical bodies as they are now)*; neither does corruption inherit incorruption.* (*'Flesh and blood'* comes under *'corruption,'* while *'the Kingdom of God'* comes under *'incorruption'*)" (I Cor. 15:45-50).

The time frame from Adam, the first man, to Noah, the time of the flood, was about sixteen hundred years.

(5) "THE SONS OF JAPHETH; GOMER, AND MAGOG, AND MADAI, AND JAVAN, AND TUBAL, AND MESHECH, AND TIRAS.

(6) "AND THE SONS OF GOMER, ASHCHENAZ, AND RIPHATH, AND TOGARMAH.

(7) "AND THE SONS OF JAVAN; ELISHAH, AND TARSHISH, KITTIM, AND DODANIM."

The diagram is:

1. (Vs. 5) The descendants of Japheth populated Europe, some parts of the Far East, the United Kingdom, and eventually the United States and Canada.

2. Concerning Japheth, Noah's son, the Scripture says: *"God shall enlarge Japheth, and he shall dwell in the tents of Shem."*

3. The Prophecy just mentioned, as given by Noah, in brief, refers to the following: Israel, the descendants of Shem, would reject Christ, while the descendants of Japheth would accept Him, which means that the Blessing intended for Shem, i.e., Israel, would instead go to the descendants of Japheth, i.e., the Gentiles. And so it has!

(8) "THE SONS OF HAM; CUSH, AND MIZRAIM, PUT, AND CANAAN.

(9) "AND THE SONS OF CUSH; SEBA, AND HAVILAH, AND SABTA, AND RAAMAH, AND SABTECHA. AND THE SONS OF RAAMAH; SHEBA, AND DEDAN.

(10) "AND CUSH BEGAT NIMROD: HE BEGAN TO BE MIGHTY UPON THE EARTH.

(11) "AND MIZRAIM BEGAT LUDIM, AND ANAMIM, AND LEHABIM, AND NAPHTUHIM,

(12) "AND PATHRUSIM, AND CASLUHIM, (OF WHOM CAME THE PHILISTINES,) AND CAPHTHORIM.

(13) "AND CANAAN BEGAT ZIDON HIS FIRSTBORN, AND HETH,

(14) "THE JEBUSITE ALSO, AND THE AMORITE, AND THE GIRGASHITE,

(15) "AND THE HIVITE, AND THE ARKITE, AND THE SINITE,

(16) "AND THE ARVADITE, AND THE ZEMARITE, AND THE HAMATHITE."

The construction is:

1. Ham, another son of Noah, is here addressed. Also, Canaan was one of the grandsons of Noah.

2. The Scripture says concerning Canaan, *"Cursed be Canaan; a servant of servants shall he be unto his brethren."* What was this curse?

It had absolutely nothing to do with the skin of some people being black. In fact, all the descendants of Ham and Canaan were not black; some were white, and we speak of those who occupied the land of Canaan. The evidence is, it was only upon those, and because they opposed Israel, hence the statement being *"Cursed be Canaan."* Even then, Canaanites who placed their Faith in God could escape the curse. Rahab, a Canaanite and a harlot, is an excellent example. She placed her Faith in God and after a period of purification, was brought into Israel's camp. She married an Israelite and became an ancestress of David, and even the greater Son of David, the Lord Jesus Christ (Josh. 6:25; Mat. 1:5; Heb. 11:31).

The Canaanites in Israel were defeated by David and became the servants of Israel.

3. (Vs. 10) It is believed that Nimrod led the first organized rebellion against God (Gen. 10:8-10).

THE TRIBES OF CANAAN

Several of the tribes listed under the descendants of Ham occupied the land of Canaan and greatly opposed Israel. The four listed are the *"Jebusite, the Amorite, the Girgashite, and the Hivite."* There were several others, as well, not here listed.

In the taking of the land of Canaan, Israel opposed most of these Tribes. It was because of their great evil that they were allowed by God to be driven out. Regrettably, just as we have studied in II Kings, Israel herself, because of great sin, was also driven out, and made captives of the Babylonians, where they remained for some seventy years before finally being allowed to come back into the land of Israel.

In fact, Israel literally ceased to be a Nation in A.D. 70 when Titus, Commander of the mighty Roman Tenth Legion, completely destroyed the city of Jerusalem. Over a million Jews were killed in that catastrophe, with other hundreds of thousands sold as slaves all over the world of that day. While Jews continued to maintain a presence in the land of Israel all through the centuries, the majority of Jews, in fact, were scattered all over the world. In 1948, the Lord brought them back and established the Nation, but with the contention with the Muslim world continuing. In fact, the problem will not be settled until the Second Coming of the Lord Jesus Christ.

NIMROD

The Scripture says concerning this man: *"And Cush begat Nimrod: he began to be a mighty one in the Earth.* (The word *'begat'* speaks of the lineage. The great figure of Genesis, Chapter 10, is Nimrod, and the great city of that same Chapter is Babylon. He and his city foreshadow the coming Antichrist and his city. He may be assumed to have counseled and built the Tower of Babel illustrated in Chapter 11 of Genesis. In fact, and as stated, he led the first organized rebellion against God.)

"He was a mighty hunter before the LORD (has nothing to do with hunting animals, but rather refers to opposition to the Lord)*: wherefore it is said, Even as Nimrod the mighty hunter before the LORD.* (As stated, Nimrod instituted the first organized rebellion against the Lord, and thereby the Ways of the Lord, and thereby those who followed the Lord. He *'hunted'* them down, possibly even killing those who worshipped Jehovah; consequently, Babylon has always stood for every false religion, every false doctrine, and every false way. That's why it is referred to as *'the great whore . . . the mother of harlots and abominations of the Earth'* [Rev. 17:1, 5].)

"And the beginning of his kingdom was Babel (Babylon: Nimrod founded that city), *and Erech, and Accad, and Calneh, in the land of Shinar.*

"Out of that land went forth Asshur, and built Nineveh, and the city Rehoboth, and Calah (should be translated, *'out of that land went forth Nimrod in Assyria and built Nineveh,'* which means he founded both Babylon and Nineveh; Asshur was the son of Shem, and not Ham)" (Gen. 10:8-11).

(17) "THE SONS OF SHEM; ELAM; AND ASSHUR, AND ARPHAXAD, AND LUD, AND ARAM, AND UZ, AND HUL, AND GETHER, AND MESHECH.

(18) "AND ARPHAXAD BEGAT SHELAH, AND SHELAH BEGAT EBER.

(19) "AND UNTO EBER WERE BORN TWO SONS: THE NAME OF THE ONE WAS PELEG; BECAUSE IN HIS DAYS THE EARTH WAS DIVIDED: AND HIS BROTHER'S NAME WAS JOKTAN.

(20) "AND JOKTAN BEGAT ALMODAD, AND SHELEPH, AND HAZARMAVETH, AND JERAH,

(21) "HADORAM ALSO, AND UZAL, AND DIKLAH,

(22) "AND EBAL, AND ABIMAEL, AND SHEBA,

(23) "AND OPHIR, AND HAVILAH, AND JOBAB. ALL THESE WERE THE SONS OF JOKTAN."

The overview is:

1. *"Uz"* listed in Verse 17 is where Job resided (Job 1:1). Exactly as to where the land of Uz was is not known; however, it is believed that it may have been at the northern end of the Gulf of Aqaba.

2. (Vs. 19) The Scripture says: *"The name of the one was Peleg; because in his days the Earth was divided."*

It is believed that at one time in the distant past all the continents of the Earth were joined together; but during the days of Peleg, which was about four thousand years ago, the continents were divided; this upheaval seemed to follow the Tower of Babel episode with the confusion of tongues, which scattered the people over the face of the Earth (Gen. 11:7-9).

3. The Holy Spirit emphasizes these descendants simply because they represent the entirety of humanity. The emphasis will

change with the next heading.

(24) "SHEM, ARPHAXAD, SHELAH,
(25) "EBER, PELEG, REU,
(26) "SERUG, NAHOR, TERAH,
(27) "ABRAM; THE SAME IS ABRAHAM."

The exegesis is:

1. Abraham, who is one of the prominent individuals of all time, is now brought into the picture.

2. He is a descendant of Shem, Noah's son, through whom the Messiah would ultimately come.

3. To Abraham was given the great means of Salvation, *"Justification by Faith."* The Scripture says:

"And he (Abraham) *believed in the LORD* (exercised Faith, believing what the Lord told him)*; and He* (the Lord) *counted it to him* (Abraham) *for Righteousness.* (This is one of the single most important Scriptures in the entirety of the Word of God. In this simple term, *'Abraham believed the LORD,'* we find the meaning of Justification by Faith. Abraham was Saved by Grace through Faith, not by his good works. There is no other way of Salvation anywhere in the Bible.

God demands Righteousness; however, it is the Righteousness afforded strictly by Christ and Christ Alone. Anything else is self-righteousness, and totally unacceptable to God. Directly the sinner believes God's Testimony about His Beloved Son, he is not only declared righteous, but he is made a son and an heir)" (Gen. 15:6).

(28) "THE SONS OF ABRAHAM; ISAAC, AND ISHMAEL."

The structure is:

1. (Vs. 28) Isaac, although younger than Ishmael, is placed first as the legitimate heir, since Sarah was the only true wife of Abraham.

2. (Vs. 28) But in the genealogy which follows, the sons of Ishmael and of Abraham's second wife are put first, so that the true line of the Messiah might be dealt with more fully, for that is the real purpose of all the genealogies.

3. Now the Holy Spirit, and beginning with Abraham, places the emphasis on Israel as it concerns the entirety of the human race. This is because Israel was raised up from the loins of Abraham and the womb of Sarah in order to give the world the Word of God, which they did, and as well, to serve as the womb, so to speak, of the Messiah, which they also did.

4. This concerns the Redemption of the fallen sons of Adam's lost race.

ISAAC THE LEGITIMATE HEIR

Even though Ishmael was the Firstborn, he was not recognized as such by God simply because Sarah wasn't the mother. The Scripture plainly says concerning Isaac: *"And God said unto Abraham . . . for in Isaac shall your seed be called"* (Gen. 21:12).

(29) "THESE ARE THEIR GENERATIONS: THE FIRSTBORN OF ISHMAEL, NEBAIOTH; THEN KEDAR, AND ADBEEL, AND MIBSAM,
(30) "MISHMA, AND DUMAH, MASSA, HADAD, AND TEMA,
(31) "JETUR, NAPHISH, AND KEDEMAH. THESE ARE THE SONS OF ISHMAEL."

The construction is:

1. (Vs. 31) Ishmael, Abraham's son through Hagar, had twelve sons, as did Jacob.

2. (Vs. 31) These twelve sons were also the heads of Twelve Tribes, making twenty-four Tribes, which descended from Abraham through two of his sons.

3. All because of Abraham and Sarah getting ahead of the Lord, a contention began which has lasted for nearly four thousand years, no doubt more heated presently than ever.

ISHMAEL

As stated, Ishmael had twelve sons, which fathered the Arab people. But Ishmael was not the Will of God, being a work of the flesh. By that I mean that Abraham and Sarah tried to fulfill the Promises of God, as it regarded them having an heir, by means of their own devisings. As a result, this was something God could not accept, and which has caused problems from then until now. In fact, the problems are, no doubt, worse presently than they ever have been.

Ahmadinejad, the President of Iran, which nation is furiously working to develop an Atomic Bomb, has sworn the destruction of Israel. Jerusalem is the hot spot of the world, even to a greater degree than Baghdad, etc. In fact, Israel sits in a sea of Arabs. The little spit of land they occupy is about the size of the state of New Jersey. As well, it constitutes approximately one tenth of one percent of all the land area of the Middle East.

Most people in the world, and I think I exaggerate not, think if Israel would just go away, peace would reign.

Not so!

The ancient land of Israel is the homeland of the Jews, originally given to them by the Lord. That's the area they occupy presently, at least part of it. And please understand, where the Lord is involved, whatever He says is going to happen, one can be doubly certain that's exactly what will take place.

The Muslim world will not take the land of Israel and will not destroy the Jews, even though under the Antichrist, who is soon to burst upon the world scene; they will come close. But when they think they have finally arrived at the final solution, that's when the most cataclysmic event the world has ever known will take place, and I speak of the Second Coming of the Lord. And to be certain, when He comes back, it will not be as He came the first time. The first time He was beaten, cursed, reviled, lampooned, and finally hung on a Cross. The second time He comes, it will be with such Power as the world has never known, Power, which will literally stagger the imagination. He will come back crowned King of kings, and Lord of lords (Rev., Chpt. 19).

(32) "NOW THE SONS OF KETURAH, ABRAHAM'S CONCUBINE: SHE BORE ZIMRAN, AND JOKSHAN, AND MEDAN, AND MIDIAN, AND ISHBAK, AND SHUAH. AND THE SONS OF JOKSHAN; SHEBA, AND DEDAN.

(33) "AND THE SONS OF MIDIAN; EPHAH, AND EPHER, AND HENOCH, AND ABIDA, AND ELDAAH. ALL THESE ARE THE SONS OF KETURAH."

The construction is:

1. Now the Holy Spirit through the sacred penman deals with the second wife of Abraham, after the death of Sarah.

2. The Holy Spirit deals with it now, and then Israel can be taken up, which will be in detail.

3. The tribes that came from this union turned almost totally to be enemies of Israel.

(34) "AND ABRAHAM BEGAT ISAAC. THE SONS OF ISAAC; ESAU AND ISRAEL."

The overview is:

1. (Vs. 34) Now, the author, under the Divine Guidance of the Holy Spirit, comes back to Isaac and his seed, Esau and Jacob.

2. (Vs. 34) The Holy Spirit follows the main purpose of His Writing, dealing briefly with the seed of Esau first before going into the more lengthy genealogies of the seed of Jacob or Israel.

3. (Vs. 34) After this, He writes twelve Chapters recording the genealogies of Jacob's sons to the time of Saul and David.

4. If it is to be noticed, the Holy Spirit in Verse 34 refers to Jacob as *"Israel,"* which means, *"Prince with God."*

ESAU AND JACOB

The great appellative of the Old Testament is, *"the God of Abraham, of Isaac, and of Jacob."*

Due to the fact that Esau was the firstborn by minutes, had he registered Faith, that appellative would have been, *"the God of Abraham, Isaac, and Esau."* But Esau did not want or desire the things of the Lord, and Jacob did. So, despite Jacob's weaknesses, his Faith would ultimately see him through.

(35) "THE SONS OF ESAU; ELIPHAZ, REUEL, AND JEUSH, AND JAALAM, AND KORAH.

(36) "THE SONS OF ELIPHAZ; TEMAN, AND OMAR, ZEPHI, AND GATAM, KENAZ, AND TIMNA, AND AMALEK.

(37) "THE SONS OF REUEL; NAHATH, ZERAH, SHAMMAH, AND MIZZAH.

(38) "AND THE SONS OF SEIR; LOTAN, AND SHOBAL, AND ZIBEON, AND ANAH, AND DISHON, AND EZAR, AND DISHAN.

(39) "AND THE SONS OF LOTAN; HORI, AND HOMAM: AND TIMNA WAS LOTAN'S SISTER.

(40) "THE SONS OF SHOBAL; ALIAN, AND MANAHATH, AND EBAL, SHEPHI, AND ONAM. AND THE SONS OF ZIBEON; AIAH, AND ANAH.

(41) "THE SONS OF ANAH; DISHON. AND THE SONS OF DISHON; AMRAM, AND ESHBAN, AND ITHRAN, AND CHERAN.

(42) "THE SONS OF EZER; BILHAN, AND ZAVAN, AND JAKAN. THE SONS OF DISHAN; UZ, AND ARAN."

The overview is:

1. The *"Eliphaz"* listed in Verse 35 was the Eliphaz of the Book of Job, who was a Temanite (Job 2:11; 4:1).

2. Amalek of Verse 36, a descendant of Esau, was noted for his opposition to Israel.

3. (Vs. 36) The Amalekites were the first to attack Israel as they came out of Egypt. For this God swore that Israel would have war from generation to generation with the Amalekites, ultimately with them destroyed. This was true; they were finally destroyed by Saul — all but a few. One of the reasons Saul was cut off was because he spared some of the Amalekites, which the Lord had sworn to destruction. The Amalekites were a symbol of the flesh ever at war with the Spirit (I Sam., Chpt. 15).

AMALEK

Flesh begets flesh! Therefore, Esau, the epitome of the flesh, would bring forth Amalek, who would be bitterly opposed to Israel, just as the flesh is opposed to the Spirit.

Concerning Amalek, the Bible says:

"Then came Amalek, and fought with Israel in Rephidim. (The reception of the Holy Spirit, of which the water was a Type, immediately causes war. It's the war between the *'flesh'* and the *'Holy Spirit'* [Gal. 5:17].)

"And Moses said unto Joshua, Choose us out men, and go out, fight with Amalek: tomorrow I will stand on the top of the hill with the Rod of God in my hand. (Up to this point God had fought for them. Then, Israel was to stand still and see His Salvation [Ex. 14:13-14]; but the command now is to go out and fight.

There is an immense difference between Justification and Sanctification. The one is Christ fighting *'for'* us; the other, the Holy Spirit fighting *'in'* us. The entrance of the new nature is the beginning of warfare with the old.)

"So Joshua did as Moses had said to him, and fought with Amalek: and Moses,

NOTES

Aaron, and Hur went up to the top of the hill. (Amalek pictures the old carnal nature. He was the grandson of Esau, who before and after birth tried to murder Jacob, and who preferred the mess of pottage to the birthright. This carnal nature wars against the Spirit; *'it is not subject to the Law of God, neither indeed can be'* [Rom. 8:7]. *'Hur'* means *'light'* — the emblem of Divine Holiness, and so points to the Holy Spirit. *'Joshua'* was a Type of Christ.)

"And it came to pass, when Moses held up his hand, that Israel prevailed: and when he let down his hand, Amalek prevailed. (The hands *'upheld'* signified total dependence on the Lord. When the Believer is totally depending on the Lord, and what He did for us at the Cross, the Victory of Christ belongs to us; otherwise, it doesn't!)

"But Moses' hands were heavy; and they took a stone, and put it under him, and he sat thereon; and Aaron and Hur stayed up his hands, the one on the one side, and the other on the other side; and his hands were steady until the going down of the sun. (The *'Stone,'* as well, is symbolic of Christ. Moses' exhaustion portrays the fact that our own efforts soon result in spiritual burnout. But once we are in God's glorious Way [sitting on the Stone], the Victory is ours. *'Aaron'* was a Type of Christ as our Great High Priest, and *'Hur,'* whose name means *'light,'* speaks to us of the Holy Spirit. This is the help afforded the Child of God. But unfortunately, most Christians are trying to hold up their hands [trusting in God] by their own personal strength, which is doomed to failure.)

"And Joshua discomfited Amalek and his people with the edge of the sword. (The *'sword'* here is a Type of the Word of God [Eph. 6:17]. The Word of God holds the answer to every single problem which pertains to *'Life and Godliness'* [II Pet. 1:3-4].)

"And the LORD said unto Moses, Write this for a memorial in the Book (this Verse presents the birth of the Bible as a written Book; the command was *'Write this in "the" Book,'* not in *'a'* book), *and rehearse it in the ears of Joshua: for I will utterly put out the remembrance of Amalek from under Heaven.* (It is remarkable that the first mention of

the Bible should be in connection with the hostility of the natural man [Amalek] to the Spiritual Man [Israel].)

"And Moses built an Altar, and called the name of it Jehovah-nissi (the Lord my Banner; the *'Altar,'* of course, is a Type of Calvary; Christ is our Banner only through the Cross)*:*

"For he said, because the LORD has sworn that the LORD will have war with Amalek from generation to generation. (Amalek was to dwell in the land, but not to reign in it. Rom. 6:12 says, *'Let not sin therefore reign in your mortal bodies.'* The command would be unmeaning if the sin nature were not existing in the Christian. The sin nature dwells in a Believer, but dwells and reigns in an unbeliever)" (Ex. 17:8-16).

(43) "NOW THESE ARE THE KINGS THAT REIGNED IN THE LAND OF EDOM BEFORE ANY KING REIGNED OVER THE CHILDREN OF ISRAEL; BELA THE SON OF BEOR: AND THE NAME OF HIS CITY WAS DINHABAH.

(44) "AND WHEN BELA WAS DEAD, JOBAB THE SON OF ZERAH OF BOZRAH REIGNED IN HIS STEAD.

(45) "AND WHEN JOBAB WAS DEAD, HUSHAM OF THE LAND OF THE TEMANITES REIGNED IN HIS STEAD.

(46) "AND WHEN HUSHAM WAS DEAD, HADAD THE SON OF BEDAD, WHICH SMOTE MIDIAN IN THE FIELD OF MOAB, REIGNED IN HIS STEAD: AND THE NAME OF HIS CITY WAS AVITH.

(47) "AND WHEN HADAD WAS DEAD, SAMLAH OF MASREKAH REIGNED IN HIS STEAD.

(48) "AND WHEN SAMLAH WAS DEAD, SHAUL OF REHOBOTH BY THE RIVER REIGNED IN HIS STEAD.

(49) "AND WHEN SHAUL WAS DEAD, BAAL-HANAN THE SON OF ACHBOR REIGNED IN HIS STEAD.

(50) "AND WHEN BAAL-HANAN WAS DEAD, HADAD REIGNED IN HIS STEAD: AND THE NAME OF HIS CITY WAS PAI; AND HIS WIFE'S NAME WAS MEHETABEL, THE DAUGHTER OF MATRED, THE DAUGHTER OF MEZAHAB."

The overview is:

1. If it is to be noticed, all of these Tribes, which sprang from Abraham and Ishmael, which were works of the flesh, all and without exception, greatly opposed Israel.

2. Anything that is born of the flesh, even from the Godliest, such as Abraham, will always and without exception, oppose the Spirit.

3. The name *"Edom"* denotes either the name of Esau, given in memory of the red pottage for which he exchanged his birthright (Gen. 25:30; 36:1, 8, 19); or the Edomites, descendants of Esau, collectively (Num. 20:18, 20-21; Mal. 1:4), or the land of Esau's descendants, formerly the land of Seir (Gen. 32:3; 36:20-21, 30; Num. 24:18).

4. The descendants of Esau were far ahead of Israel at the beginning, actually having a settled government long before the formation of Israel as a Nation.

Why?

The flesh is always dominant at the beginning. In the life of the individual Christian, the Seventh Chapter of Romans must be passed through, in one way or the other, before the Victory of Romans, Chapter 6, is finally put into practice, which then gives us the place and position of Romans, Chapter 8.

As someone has well said, Romans, Chapter 6 proclaims to us the Mechanics of the Holy Spirit, which tells us how He does what He does. Romans, Chapter 8 proclaims to us the Dynamics of the Holy Spirit, which tells us what He does after we learn how He does it.

The Holy Spirit, I think one can say, never gains the ascendancy at the beginning. He does so only after a lengthy struggle with the flesh. So, this would prove in type what takes place in reality.

(51) "HADAD DIED ALSO. AND THE DUKES OF EDOM WERE; DUKE TIMNAH, DUKE ALIAH, DUKE JETHETH,

(52) "DUKE AHOLIBAMAH, DUKE ELAH, DUKE PINON,

(53) "DUKE KENAZ, DUKE TEMAN, DUKE MIBZAR,

(54) "DUKE MAGDIEL, DUKE IRAM. THESE ARE THE DUKES OF EDOM."

The pattern is:

1. The word *"Dukes"* here listed probably denotes places instead of persons.

2. In fact, the genealogies of this Chapter, with their parallels in Genesis, are notable also for standing unique in all the world's writing.

3. We now come to the Jews, the principal theme of all of this, and because through them the Son of the Living God, the Messiah, would come.

Matthew Henry said, *"Since Christ came, the Jews have lost all their genealogies, even the most sacred of them, the building is reared, the scaffold is removed; the Seed is come, the line that led to Him is broken off."*[1]

"Praise ye the Lord, the Almighty, the King of creation!
"O my soul, praise Him, for He is thy health and salvation!
"All ye who hear, now to His Temple draw near;
"Join me in glad adoration!"

"Praise ye the Lord, Who o'er all things so wondrously reigneth,
"Shelters thee under His Wings, yea, so gently sustaineth!
"Hast thou not seen how thy desires e'er been granted,
"In what He ordaineth?"

"Praise ye the Lord, Who with marvelous Wisdom hath made thee!
"Decked thee with health, and with loving hand guided and stayed thee;
"How oft in grief has not He brought you relief,
"Spreading His Wings for to shade you!"

"Praise ye the Lord! O let all that is in me adore Him!
"All that has life and breath, come now with praises before Him!
"Let the Amen sound from His People again:
"Gladly for ay we adore Him."

CHAPTER 2

(1) "THESE ARE THE SONS OF ISRAEL; REUBEN, SIMEON, LEVI, AND JUDAH, ISSACHAR, AND ZEBULUN,

(2) "DAN, JOSEPH, AND BENJAMIN, NAPHTALI, GAD, AND ASHER."

The construction is:

1. Verses 1 and 2 list the twelve sons of Jacob (Israel). These sons, as obvious, are not listed in rank of birth. The six sons of Leah are given first, then the four sons of Rachel and her maid, with Joseph and Benjamin, the sons of Rachel, between the two sons of her maid.

After that came the two sons of Leah's maid. Why this was done in this manner, we aren't told; however, it is for certain that the Holy Spirit had something in mind. Perhaps the following might give a clue.

2. Taking the six sons of Leah first, the names of these boys spell out the great Plan of Salvation. The names epitomize Christ as it regards His Work on our behalf, and the names as well epitomize the Believer's walk with God. It is as follows:

• Reuben: his name means *"a son is born."* Likewise, it speaks of the human being born into the world.

• Simeon: the name means *"hearing."* The son is born, and then he is to *"hear"* the Word of God.

• Levi: the name means *"joined."* The son is born, he hears the Word of God, and he is then *"joined"* to the Father.

• Judah: the name means *"praises."* The child is born, he hears the Word of God, he is then joined to the Father, and *"praises"* the Lord.

• Issachar: the name means *"reward."* The son is born, he hears the Word of the Lord, he is joined to the Father, he praises the Lord, and he receives *"reward."*

• Zebulun: the name means *"to dwell."* The son is born, he hears the Word of the Lord, he is joined to the Father, he praises the Lord, he receives reward, and he is made to *"dwell in the House of the Lord forever."* As stated, the sons of Leah, totaling six, proclaim the entirety of the Plan of Redemption for the Believer.

3. The next name mentioned is *"Dan,"* and it means *"judgment."* So, why is Dan placed at this juncture?

The idea is, if the Plan of God is neglected, which is outlined in the meaning of the six sons of Leah, *"judgment"* will be the result.

4. *"Joseph"* and *"Benjamin"* are next in the line up, as here given. Joseph's name means *"adding,"* while Benjamin means *"strong right hand."* So, if the Plan of God is accepted, everything will be added with nothing subtracted, and the position will be a *"strong right hand,"* which speaks of power, which should characterize every Spirit-filled Child of God. In a sense, Benjamin has to do with this Spirit-filled Age.

5. The last three names added are: *"Naphtali, Gad, and Asher,"* meaning respectively, *"wrestling"* and *"truth,"* meaning that Jesus is the *"truth,"* Who has fought on our behalf, with *"Asher"* meaning *"happy."*

The last three have to do with the journey of the Believer in our living for God, in other words, our everyday walk before God.

There is the constant *"wrestling"* between the flesh and the spirit, the availability of the Army of the Lord, symbolized by the word *"truth,"* and then the *"happiness"* that we have, providing we follow God's Order of Life and Living. That Order of Life and Living is *"Jesus Christ and Him Crucified,"* with such ever being the Object of our Faith (I Cor. 1:23).

So, we have before us in the order of these names, God's Plan of Redemption, i.e., manner of living and pronounced Judgment, should that Plan be rejected, and then the place and position in Christ symbolized by Joseph and Benjamin, with the Believer's walk given in Naphtali, Gad, and Asher. Thus, there is a method that the Holy Spirit has in all of this.

(3) "THE SONS OF JUDAH; ER, AND ONAN, AND SHELAH: WHICH THREE WERE BORN UNTO HIM OF THE DAUGHTER OF SHUA THE CANAANITESS. AND ER, THE FIRSTBORN OF JUDAH, WAS EVIL IN THE SIGHT OF THE LORD; AND HE KILLED HIM.

(4) "AND TAMAR HIS DAUGHTER IN LAW BORE HIM PHAREZ AND ZERAH. ALL THE SONS OF JUDAH WERE FIVE.

(5) "THE SONS OF PHAREZ; HEZRON, AND HAMUL.

(6) "AND THE SONS OF ZERAH; ZIMRI, AND ETHAN, AND HEMAN, AND CALCOL, AND DARA: FIVE OF THEM IN ALL.

NOTES

(7) "AND THE SONS OF CARMI; ACHAR, THE TROUBLER OF ISRAEL, WHO TRANSGRESSED IN THE THING ACCURSED.

(8) "AND THE SONS OF ETHAN; AZARIAH.

(9) "THE SONS ALSO OF HEZRON, THAT WERE BORN UNTO HIM; JERAHMEEL, AND RAM, AND CHELUBAI.

(10) "AND RAM BEGAT AMMINADAB; AND AMMINADAB BEGAT NAHSHON, PRINCE OF THE CHILDREN OF JUDAH."

The construction is:

1. (Vs. 3) As is obvious here, Judah is dealt with first. In fact, he was to be the chief and ruling Tribe of the twelve, and the Messiah was to come through him (Gen. 49:8-12).

2. (Vs. 3) The evil thing that caused the Lord to slay Er was not recorded either in Genesis, Chapter 38, where this account is given, or elsewhere in Scripture. It could have been the same sin for which God killed Onan, as also in Genesis 38:8-10 — that of refusing to have offspring.

3. (Vs. 3) Incorporated in that, Er was the firstborn of Judah and, thereby, in the lineage of the coming Messiah. The evidence is he cared not at all for that, and Satan endeavored to use him to stop the Plan of God; therefore, the reason for the actions of the Lord.

4. (Vs. 5) The line of the Messiah (Isa. 7:14) came through Pharez (Ruth 4:18; Lk. 3:23-38); the kingly line also came through him (Mat. 1:1-17).

5. The *"Achar"* of Verse 7 is the *"Achan"* of Joshua 7:1.

(11) "AND NAHSHON BEGAT SALMA, AND SALMA BEGAT BOAZ,

(12) "AND BOAZ BEGAT OBED, AND OBED BEGAT JESSE,

(13) "AND JESSE BEGAT HIS FIRSTBORN ELIAB, AND ABINADAB THE SECOND, AND SHIMMA THE THIRD,

(14) "NETHANEEL THE FOURTH, RADDAI THE FIFTH,

(15) "OZEM THE SIXTH, DAVID THE SEVENTH:

(16) "WHOSE SISTERS WERE ZERUIAH AND ABIGAIL. AND THE SONS OF ZERUIAH; ABISHAI, AND JOAB, AND

I CHRONICLES 2:11-55

ASAHEL, THREE.

(17) "AND ABIGAIL BORE AMASA: AND THE FATHER OF AMASA WAS JETHER THE ISHMEELITE.

(18) "AND CALEB THE SON OF HEZRON BEGAT CHILDREN OF AZUBAH HIS WIFE, AND OF JERIOTH: HER SONS ARE THESE: JESHER, AND SHOBAB, AND ARDON.

(19) "AND WHEN AZUBAH WAS DEAD, CALEB TOOK UNTO HIM EPHRATH, WHICH BORE HIM HUR.

(20) "AND HUR BEGAT URI, AND URI BEGAT BEZALEEL.

(21) "AND AFTERWARD HEZRON WENT IN TO THE DAUGHTER OF MACHIR THE FATHER OF GILEAD, WHOM HE MARRIED WHEN HE WAS THREESCORE YEARS OLD; AND SHE BORE HIM SEGUB.

(22) "AND SEGUB BEGAT JAIR, WHO HAD THREE AND TWENTY CITIES IN THE LAND OF GILEAD.

(23) "AND HE TOOK GESHUR, AND ARAM, WITH THE TOWNS OF JAIR, FROM THEM, WITH KENATH, AND THE TOWNS THEREOF, EVEN THREESCORE CITIES. ALL THESE BELONGED TO THE SONS OF MACHIR THE FATHER OF GILEAD."

The pattern is:

1. (Vs. 15) Actually, we know that Jesse, David's father, begat eight sons (I Sam. 16:6-11; 17:12-14); here, only seven are numbered and named. David was the youngest (I Sam. 16:11), so the eighth may have died while young and without offspring. While it was proper to mention eight sons in the history, it was unnecessary to do so in the genealogy.

2. The sons named in Verse 16 are three nephews of David, who played important roles in David's kingdom, especially Joab, who was Captain of the Host until the death of David.

3. All of these names may seem to the unspiritual eye to be tedious and without significance; however, in some way, all of these individuals played a part, as minor as it may have been, in the coming of the Messiah, even though almost all of them were unaware of such at the time. And

NOTES

anything that is connected with Christ in any way, no matter how distant, is of utmost significance.

(24) "AND AFTER THAT HEZRON WAS DEAD IN CALEBEPHRATAH, THEN ABIAH HEZRON'S WIFE BORE HIM ASHUR THE FATHER OF TEKOA.

(25) "AND THE SONS OF JERAHMEEL THE FIRSTBORN OF HEZRON WERE, RAM THE FIRSTBORN, AND BUNAH, AND OREN, AND OZEM, AND AHIJAH.

(26) "JERAHMEEL HAD ALSO ANOTHER WIFE, WHOSE NAME WAS ATARAH; SHE WAS THE MOTHER OF ONAM.

(27) "AND THE SONS OF RAM THE FIRSTBORN OF JERAHMEEL WERE, MAAZ, AND JAMIN, AND EKER.

(28) "AND THE SONS OF ONAM WERE, SHAMMAI, AND JADA. AND THE SONS OF SHAMMAI; NADAB AND ABISHUR.

(29) "AND THE NAME OF THE WIFE OF ABISHUR WAS ABIHAIL, AND SHE BORE HIM AHBAN, AND MOLID.

(30) "AND THE SONS OF NADAB; SELED, AND APPAIM: BUT SELED DIED WITHOUT CHILDREN.

(31) "AND THE SONS OF APPAIM; ISHI. AND THE SONS OF ISHI; SHESHAN. AND THE CHILDREN OF SHESHAN; AHLAI.

(32) "AND THE SONS OF JADA THE BROTHER OF SHAMMAI; JETHER, AND JONATHAN: AND JETHER DIED WITHOUT CHILDREN.

(33) "AND THE SONS OF JONATHAN; PELETH, AND ZAZA. THESE WERE THE SONS OF JERAHMEEL.

(34) "NOW SHESHAN HAD NO SONS, BUT DAUGHTERS. AND SHESHAN HAD A SERVANT, AN EGYPTIAN, WHOSE NAME WAS JARHA.

(35) "AND SHESHAN GAVE HIS DAUGHTER TO JARHA HIS SERVANT TO WIFE; AND SHE BORE HIM ATTAI.

(36) "AND ATTAI BEGAT NATHAN, AND NATHAN BEGAT ZABAD,

(37) "AND ZABAD BEGAT EPHLAL, AND EPHLAL BEGAT OBED,

(38) "AND OBED BEGAT JEHU, AND JEHU BEGAT AZARIAH,

(39) "AND AZARIAH BEGAT HELEZ, AND HELEZ BEGAT ELEASAH,

(40) "AND ELEASAH BEGAT SISAMAI,

AND SISAMAI BEGAT SHALLUM,

(41) "AND SHALLUM BEGAT JEKAMIAH, AND JEKAMIAH BEGAT ELISHAMA.

(42) "NOW THE SONS OF CALEB THE BROTHER OF JERAHMEEL WERE, MESHA HIS FIRSTBORN, WHICH WAS THE FATHER OF ZIPH; AND THE SONS OF MARESHAH THE FATHER OF HEBRON.

(43) "AND THE SONS OF HEBRON; KORAH, AND TAPPUAH, AND REKEM, AND SHEMA.

(44) "AND SHEMA BEGAT RAHAM, THE FATHER OF JORKOAM: AND REKEM BEGAT SHAMMAI.

(45) "AND THE SON OF SHAMMAI WAS MAON: AND MAON WAS THE FATHER OF BETH-ZUR.

(46) "AND EPHAH, CALEB'S CONCUBINE, BORE HARAN, AND MOZA, AND GAZEZ: AND HARAN BEGAT GAZEZ.

(47) "AND THE SONS OF JAHDAI; REGEM, AND JOTHAM, AND GESHAM, AND PELET, AND EPHAH, AND SHAAPH.

(48) "MAACHAH, CALEB'S CONCUBINE, BORE SHEBER, AND TIRHANAH.

(49) "SHE BORE ALSO SHAAPH THE FATHER OF MADMANNAH, SHEVA THE FATHER OF MACHBENAH, AND THE FATHER OF GIBEA: AND THE DAUGHTER OF CALEB WAS ACHSA.

(50) "THESE WERE THE SONS OF CALEB THE SON OF HUR, THE FIRSTBORN OF EPHRATAH; SHOBAL THE FATHER OF KIRJATH-JEARIM,

(51) "SALMA THE FATHER OF BETHLEHEM, HAREPH THE FATHER OF BETH-GADER.

(52) "AND SHOBAL THE FATHER OF KIRJATH-JEARIM HAD SONS; HAROEH, AND HALF OF THE MANAHETHITES.

(53) "AND THE FAMILIES OF KIRJATH-JEARIM; THE ITHRITES, AND THE PUHITES, AND THE SHUMATHITES, AND THE MISHRAITES; OF THEM CAME THE ZARE-ATHITES, AND THE ESHTAULITES.

(54) "THE SONS OF SALMA; BETHLEHEM, AND THE NETOPHATHITES, ATAROTH, THE HOUSE OF JOAB, AND HALF OF THE MANAHETHITES, THE ZORITES.

(55) "AND THE FAMILIES OF THE SCRIBES WHICH DWELT AT JABEZ; THE TIRATHITES, THE SHIMEATHITES, AND SUCHATHITES. THESE ARE THE KENITES THAT CAME OF HEMATH, THE FATHER OF THE HOUSE OF RECHAB."

The exegesis is:

1. Even though all of these individuals were connected with Christ in some way as it regards His Incarnation, God becoming man, still, this didn't mean they were righteous or holy. In fact, most were very unrighteous.

2. The *"Kenites"* of Verse 55 were the descendants of Jethro, father-in-law of Moses [Judges 1:16; 4:11-17].

3. (Vs. 55) It is unusual that the Kenites should be alluded to as the descendants of Judah; this was because they were attached to the Tribe of Judah, and had become intermixed with them for so many centuries.

CHAPTER 3

(1) "NOW THESE WERE THE SONS OF DAVID, WHICH WERE BORN UNTO HIM IN HEBRON; THE FIRSTBORN AMNON, OF AHINOAM THE JEZREELITESS; THE SECOND DANIEL, OF ABIGAIL THE CARMELITESS:

(2) "THE THIRD, ABSALOM THE SON OF MAACHAH THE DAUGHTER OF TALMAI KING OF GESHUR: THE FOURTH, ADONIJAH THE SON OF HAGGITH:

(3) "THE FIFTH, SHEPHATIAH OF ABITAL: THE SIXTH, ITHREAM BY EGLAH HIS WIFE.

(4) "THESE SIX WERE BORN UNTO HIM IN HEBRON; AND THERE HE REIGNED SEVEN YEARS AND SIX MONTHS: AND IN JERUSALEM HE REIGNED THIRTY AND THREE YEARS.

(5) "AND THESE WERE BORN UNTO HIM IN JERUSALEM; SHIMEA, AND SHOBAB, AND NATHAN, AND SOLOMON, FOUR, OF BATH-SHUA THE DAUGHTER OF AMMIEL:

(6) "IBHAR ALSO, AND ELISHAMA, AND ELIPHELET,

(7) "AND NOGAH, AND NEPHEG, AND JAPHIA,

(8) "AND ELISHAMA, AND ELIADA,

AND ELIPHELET, NINE.

(9) "THESE WERE ALL THE SONS OF DAVID, BESIDE THE SONS OF THE CONCUBINES, AND TAMAR THEIR SISTER."

The structure is:

1. (Vs. 1) The whole of this Chapter is occupied with the descendants of David, because through his family the Messiah would ultimately be born (II Sam., Chpt. 7).

2. (Vs. 4) David reigned over the Tribe of Judah for seven and a half years, and over the entirety of Israel for thirty-three years, making a total of a little bit more than forty years.

3. (Vs. 5) Mary's family line, the Mother of our Lord, came through the lineage of Nathan (Lk. 3:23-38).

4. (Vs. 5) Joseph, Mary's husband, was of the kingly line through Solomon; so, the lineage of Christ was perfect, as it regards Him being the Son of David, for both Mary and Joseph went back to David in their lineage.

5. The *"Bathshua"* of Verse 5 is *"Bathsheba."*

6. It if is to be noticed, at times, the mother of the particular son is named. That is because some of these people, David being one of them, had several wives.

DAVID

If one would ascribe greatness to any individual of the Old Testament, that signal honor would have to go to David. There would be only one reason for that, and that is because through his family the Messiah was born. That is the only reason, but that is reason enough.

Any connection with Christ spells greatness, and to be connected as closely as was David, meaning that the Son of God would actually be referred to as the *"Son of David,"* affords an honor that is unmatched.

While in many things, others were greater than David, still, that one link, and we continue to speak of Christ, sets him apart from all others.

While he wrote over half of the Psalms, while he was given the plans for the Temple, while his position as the father of worship through music and singing causes him to stand out, and while he was, no doubt, intended to be the first king of Israel, still, it is his personal connection with Christ that causes his greatness to soar above the place and position of all others.

Regrettably, he wasn't blessed with a godly family. In fact, most of his sons turned out very poorly. Even Solomon, who was God's choice for the throne of Israel, drifted and strayed, but hopefully, came back to the Lord before his death. In fact, while great things can be said of him, still, it must also be noted that David committed some of the most dastardly sins, sins so awful that David, in a measure, was a type of Israel, her blessing, her terrible failure, and her future restoration. The great Fifty-first Psalm bears out all of this. And yet, despite the checkered life, the Son of God was not ashamed to be referred to as the *"Son of David."* Such gives us a portrait, if you will, as probably nothing else, of the Grace of God, i.e., *"Justification by Faith."* Nothing else could explain David's dilemma, as nothing else could explain our dilemma.

(10) "AND SOLOMON'S SON WAS REHOBOAM, ABIA HIS SON, ASA HIS SON, JEHOSHAPHAT HIS SON,

(11) "JORAM HIS SON, AHAZIAH HIS SON, JOASH HIS SON,

(12) "AMAZIAH HIS SON, AZARIAH HIS SON, JOTHAM HIS SON,

(13) "AHAZ HIS SON, HEZEKIAH HIS SON, MANASSEH HIS SON,

(14) "AMON HIS SON, JOSIAH HIS SON.

(15) "AND THE SONS OF JOSIAH WERE, THE FIRST BORN JOHANAN, THE SECOND JEHOIAKIM, THE THIRD ZEDEKIAH, THE FOURTH SHALLUM.

(16) "AND THE SONS OF JEHOIAKIM: JECONIAH HIS SON, ZEDEKIAH HIS SON.

(17) "AND THE SONS OF JECONIAH; ASSIR, SALATHIEL HIS SON,

(18) "MALCHIRAM ALSO, AND PEDAIAH, AND SHENAZAR, JECAMIAH, HOSHAMA, AND NEDABIAH.

(19) "AND THE SONS OF PEDAIAH WERE, ZERUBBABEL, AND SHIMEI: AND THE SONS OF ZERUBBABEL; MESHULLAM, AND HANANIAH, AND SHELOMITH THEIR SISTER:

(20) "AND HASHUBAH, AND OHEL, AND BERECHIAH, AND HASADIAH,

JUSHAB-HESED, FIVE.

(21) "AND THE SONS OF HANANIAH; PELATIAH, AND JESAIAH: THE SONS OF REPHAIAH, THE SONS OF ARNAN, THE SONS OF OBADIAH, THE SONS OF SHECHANIAH.

(22) "AND THE SONS OF SHECHANIAH; SHEMAIAH: AND THE SONS OF SHEMAIAH; HATTUSH, AND IGEAL, AND BARIAH, AND NEARIAH, AND SHAPHAT, SIX.

(23) "AND THE SONS OF NEARIAH; ELIOENAI, AND HEZEKIAH, AND AZRIKAM, THREE.

(24) "AND THE SONS OF ELIOENAI WERE, HODAIAH, AND ELIASHIB, AND PELAIAH, AND AKKUB, AND JOHANAN AND DALAIAH, AND ANANI, SEVEN."

The construction is:

1. (Vs. 10) There were twenty-one royal descendants of David through Solomon who occupied the throne of Judah.

2. (Vs. 17) *"Jehoiakim"* of Verse 16, was also called *"Jehoiachin"* or *"Coniah."* Though Jehoiachin had eight sons, not one of them, nor any descendant of any one of them, could ever sit on the throne of David and rule in Jerusalem over Israel, for God had cursed him and his seed forever, cutting them off from kingship.

3. (Vs. 17) The next king of Judah was not of his seed; he was an uncle.

4. (Vs. 17) All of these kings of Judah led up to the Messiah, and were intended to do so. This is the Incarnation, God becoming Man.

5. (Vs. 17) Jesus did not come through the kingly line, yet He had to obtain the throne rights through the kingly line to fulfill the Davidic Covenant regarding an eternal king of David's seed. However, this requirement was totally satisfied in Mary, the virgin mother of the Messiah, who came through Nathan, the son of David, who was not of the kingly line, and in Joseph, who was the legal heir to the throne through Solomon, the son of David.

When Joseph and Mary were married, Jesus, being the Firstborn of the family, therefore, became the legal heir to the throne of David. And yet, He did not come through Jehoiachin (Coniah), so that the curse of Jeremiah 22:4-30 was literally fulfilled.

CHAPTER 4

(1) "THE SONS OF JUDAH; PHAREZ, HEZRON, AND CARMI, AND HUR, AND SHOBAL.

(2) "AND REAIAH THE SON OF SHOBAL BEGAT JAHATH; AND JAHATH BEGAT AHUMAI, AND LAHAD. THESE ARE THE FAMILIES OF THE ZORATHITES.

(3) "AND THESE WERE OF THE FATHER OF ETAM; JEZREEL, AND ISHMA, AND IDBASH: AND THE NAME OF THEIR SISTER WAS HAZELELPONI:

(4) "AND PENUEL THE FATHER OF GEDOR, AND EZER THE FATHER OF HUSHAH. THESE ARE THE SONS OF HUR, THE FIRSTBORN OF EPHRATAH, THE FATHER OF BETH-LEHEM.

(5) "AND ASHUR THE FATHER OF TEKOA HAD TWO WIVES, HELAH AND NAARAH.

(6) "AND NAARAH BORE HIM AHUZAM, AND HEPHER, AND TEMENI, AND HAAHASHTARI. THESE WERE THE SONS OF NAARAH.

(7) "AND THE SONS OF HELAH WERE, ZERETH, AND JEZOAR, AND ETHNAN.

(8) "AND COZ BEGAT ANUB, AND ZOBEBAH, AND THE FAMILIES OF AHARHEL THE SON OF HARUM.

(9) "AND JABEZ WAS MORE HONOURABLE THAN HIS BRETHREN: AND HIS MOTHER CALLED HIS NAME JABEZ, SAYING, BECAUSE I BORE HIM WITH SORROW.

(10) "AND JABEZ CALLED ON THE GOD OF ISRAEL, SAYING, OH THAT YOU WOULD BLESS ME INDEED, AND ENLARGE MY COAST, AND THAT YOUR HAND MIGHT BE WITH ME, AND THAT YOU WOULD KEEP ME FROM EVIL, THAT IT MAY NOT GRIEVE ME! AND GOD GRANTED HIM THAT WHICH HE REQUESTED."

The exegesis is:

1. Let us say it again: all of these names are important because in some way, ever how distant, they were in the lineage of Christ.

Sadly, most of the individuals listed in these nine Chapters died lost. They were so close, but yet, so far away. The truth is, most of them had little or no knowledge at all of the honored place and position, as it regards Christ, in which they had been placed.

2. (Vs. 9) The Holy Spirit began the notation concerning Jabez by making the statement concerning him being more honorable. The reason was the trust in God and hunger for God which Jabez had.

3. (Vs. 9) In Hebrew culture, the mother, with some few exceptions, always named the child. In that culture, the name was very important. If the Holy Spirit did not impress upon her the name that was to be given, as He sometimes did, she would name the child according to what she wanted him to be, or because of something that had happened in the family that was either a blessing or a curse (especially the boys).

4. (Vs. 9) This lady, in naming her little boy *"Jabez,"* which means *"he makes sorrow,"* either did not want him, or else felt she could not properly care for him; therefore, the child, by being given this name, would always be reminded of the negative circumstances of his birth. This severe hindrance could have turned him toward bitterness, which would have destroyed him, as it has many, or toward God. Jabez allowed it to turn him toward God.

5. (Vs. 9) Every difficulty in the life of any person who knows the Lord, irrespective of its severity, can be turned into a blessing. In fact, God specializes in turning the curse into a blessing.

6. (Vs. 10) Every Believer should ask the Lord for *"the blessing,"* exactly as did Jabez, for God is a Blessing God.

7. (Vs. 10) The last entreaty of the prayer of Jabez, *"that You would keep me from evil, that it may not grieve me,"* is the largest and most far-seeing. It referred to *"evil"* in general but, more than that, it referred to evil which had evidently plagued his family in the past.

8. (Vs. 10) The conclusion is that the Lord will do the same for all who will dare to believe Him, exactly as He did for Jabez.

MEANT TO BE NOTICED

In the middle of this long litany of genealogies, we find a most refreshing intersection, all supplied by the Holy Spirit. This most interesting note is meant to be noticed, and for purpose.

It should be understood from all of this how much the Lord savors the consecration of His People, and especially their dedication to His Cause and His Purpose, of which was Jabez.

The very fact that the Holy Spirit inserted this little treasure presents that which is meant to be a lesson to us. The Lord is telling us by including this beautiful example that what was done for Jabez will be done for anyone who will humble themselves, as did this man of so long ago. We should read it and study it with that in mind.

HONORABLE

The short phrase, *"And Jabez was more honorable than his brethren,"* proclaims the fact that the Holy Spirit labeled him as such. In this capacity, there could be no higher honor than that.

Inasmuch as the Holy Spirit used this word to describe Jabez, and especially the context in which it was used, sets the stage for all that happened to this man. In other words, it speaks volumes.

THE NAME JABEZ

The Scripture says, *"And his mother called his name 'Jabez,' saying, Because I bear him with sorrow."*

As we have previously stated, in Hebrew culture, the mother normally named the child. The name she would give him was dictated to her by the Lord, or else a name was chosen as to what she wanted him to be, especially a boy, or because of some event, whether good or bad, which had taken place in the family. Inasmuch as the mother bore this child *"with sorrow"* tells us why she named him what she did.

The name *"Jabez"* means, *"he makes sorrow."* So, either she did not want him, or else her circumstances were such that she felt she could not properly care for him. At any rate, the name his mother gave him would have a tendency to drag him down, to breed bitterness, to put the proverbial chip on his shoulder, etc.

Children are marked, whether good or bad, as it regards things happening in their family. If it's negative, and according to how negative it is, some never pull out over the situation. In other words, they are scarred soul and spirit. As a result, they shortchange themselves or form an erroneous conclusion of themselves.

If the truth be known, millions of children feel unloved, and in truth, millions are unloved. As a result, there is a seething anger in their hearts against society, and in many cases, against they know not what. They just know they bear this curse, so to speak, of which there seems to be no relief.

Jabez could have easily succumbed to the circumstance, whatever it may have been. But he didn't, rather, allowing this thing to turn him toward God.

A TESTIMONY

One of our singers at Family Worship Center, B.J. Vavasseur, who, incidentally, has been with us at the time of this writing, about twenty years, related the following to me:

As a little girl she was molested, molestation incidentally, which lasted for a number of years. That within itself destroys almost anyone and everyone so unfortunate to suffer such.

Because of this terrible thing, she was taken out of her home and placed in a foster home. Immediately upon being placed in the home in question, she was told that she was not wanted and, therefore, she could expect nothing good.

When she told me that, I made the statement to her, *"This completely destroys most, and with many, has the effect of driving them away from the Lord."* In other words, in some cases, and hers definitely would have fit this description, the child blames God.

How many letters has this Ministry received over the years from ladies saying, *"I prayed to the Lord that it would stop, but it didn't."* And then they would go on to say, *"Because the Lord didn't answer my prayer, I grew resentful."* In other words, they blamed God!

B.J. said to me when I spoke to her, *"But Brother Swaggart, it didn't drive me away from the Lord; it drove me to the Lord."*

What a tremendous testimony!

This young lady now blesses millions all over the world with her beautiful voice, and because she did not allow an extremely traumatic experience to destroy her. It could easily have done so, but the Lord was her refuge, just as He will be the refuge for any and all who will seek His Face.

Jabez did not allow his negative circumstances to mark him. He rose above it.

THE PRAYER OF JABEZ

The secret of this great Victory, even as it is the secret of every Victory, is that *"Jabez called on the God of Israel."* That is your answer! In fact, that is the only answer!

The reader should understand, irrespective of the problem, irrespective of the difficulty, no matter the circumstances, and no matter how bad it may seem to be, if the person will turn to the Lord, and it's never too late to do so, the Lord, to be certain, can turn a curse into a blessing, and no matter how bad the curse might be. In fact, He Alone can do such. The world has no answer, no solution to this problem. But the Lord most definitely does have a solution.

What does it mean to *"call on God?"*

It means to trust Him completely. It means that one puts the problem, whatever the problem might be, into the Hands of the Lord. It means that one looks to Him exclusively for the answer, which He Alone can give.

Sadly and regrettably, far too many Christians presently call on everything except the Lord. But let it be understood, this is not only the answer, it is the only answer.

THE BLESSING

The Holy Spirit is careful to enumerate exactly what Jabez said. His prayer was, *"Oh that You would bless me indeed."*

Let it be understood that God is a Blessing God! He wants to bless His Children! And what does that mean, to be blessed?

The word, *"blessing,"* at least as it refers to the Lord, means, *"increase."* While one could fill up volumes explaining this word, perhaps that one word, *"increase,"* explains it more so than all.

Furthermore, it means an increase in things which are good, an increase in that which is healthy, and an increase in that which is positive.

Everyone wants this, but the Lord Alone can provide it. Please understand the following:

That which the world gives, which many think are blessings, turns out to be anything but that. The fame corrupts! The money buys anything and everything except happiness! The notoriety turns to dust! In fact, many in Hollywood at this very moment who fit the bill of the so-called *"stars,"* are quick to make the statement, *"life has no meaning."* That's why Jesus said, *"For a man's life consisteth not in the abundance of the things which he possesses"* (Lk. 12:15).

But that which the Lord gives is far and away above mere *"things."* While He definitely does give things, at the same time, He also gives that which is far more and far better, and I speak of *"peace of mind"* and *"inner joy,"* which money can never buy.

Is there a price tag to God's Blessings?

Only that we *"first of all seek the Kingdom of God and His Righteousness"* (Mat. 6:33).

ENLARGE MY COAST

The request would probably be better translated, *"enlarge my borders."*

What did Jabez mean by that request?

It could have referred to that which had been stolen from him by being stolen from his parents, hence, his mother naming him as she did. As well, it could have referred to the place and position in which he now found himself as a result of what had happened to his family, whatever that may have been. In other words, he felt that God did not mean for him to be confined to the place and position which circumstances had forced upon him. Whatever those circumstances and whatever the difficulties and problems, he must not dwell there. So, he goes to the only One Who can solve the problem and asks Him to *"enlarge his borders."*

It wasn't up to Jabez to know or understand as to exactly how the Lord would do this, or how it would be possible. That was the business of the Lord. He made the

NOTES

request, and he made it in Faith, and the Holy Spirit recorded it.

Again let us state, as the Lord did for this man so long ago, He will do the same for you, that is, if you will humble yourself and seek the Face of the Lord exactly as did Jabez.

THE HAND OF THE LORD

The man of our illustration, which can be typical of you and me, said to the Lord, *"And that Your Hand might be with me."*

This speaks of the *"Hand of strength,"* of which the Lord Alone was capable. With that Hand, that unseen Hand, leading us, guiding us, sustaining us, and upholding us, we cannot fail.

This particular part of his request insinuates that there would be some who would try to stop him, as there always are. But with the Hand of the Lord with him, the truth is, he could not fail. As then, so now, if we will only believe.

KEEP ME FROM EVIL

The phrase, *"And that You would keep me from evil, that it may not grieve me,"* proclaims an excellent Spiritual Foresight.

Many times Blessings tend to corrupt, but Jabez looks ahead and believes that the Lord has heard his petition, and that He will grant his request. As such, he knows the pitfalls that such could bring. In fact, prosperity often destroys. It doesn't have to, but so oftentimes, it does. So, Jabez asks the help of the Lord in this very important part of his request.

AN ANSWERED PRAYER

The Scripture says, *"And God granted him that which he requested."*

Simple, and to the point, the Holy Spirit tells us that the Lord heard the petition of Jabez, approved of the petition, and *"granted him that which he requested."* What a beautiful statement!

Once again, let me remind the reader that the Lord had this beautiful example given to us, and in a most unlikely place, right in the middle of endless genealogies.

He is telling us that we have access to the Lord just as much as did Jabez, and because of the Cross, even to a greater degree. As well, if we will trust the Lord and believe Him, He will *"grant us that which we request."*

We must believe that, even as the Holy Spirit desires that we believe that. We serve the same God that Jabez served, and to be sure, the Lord is the same now as He was then.

(11) "AND CHELUB THE BROTHER OF SHUAH BEGAT MEHIR, WHICH WAS THE FATHER OF ESHTON.

(12) "AND ESHTON BEGAT BETH-RAPHA, AND PASEAH, AND TEHINNAH THE FATHER OF IR-NAHASH. THESE ARE THE MEN OF RECHAH.

(13) "AND THE SONS OF KENAZ; OTHNIEL, AND SERAIAH: AND THE SON OF OTHNIEL; HATHATH.

(14) "AND MEONOTHAI BEGAT OPHRAH: AND SERAIAH BEGAT JOAB, THE FATHER OF THE VALLEY OF CHARASHIM; FOR THEY WERE CRAFTSMEN.

(15) "AND THE SONS OF CALEB THE SON OF JEPHUNNEH; IRU, ELAH, AND NAAM: AND THE SONS OF ELAH, EVEN KENAZ.

(16) "AND THE SONS OF JEHALELEEL; ZIPH, AND ZIPHAH, TIRIA, AND ASAREEL.

(17) "AND THE SONS OF EZRA WERE, JETHER, AND MERED, AND EPHER, AND JALON: AND SHE BORE MIRIAM, AND SHAMMAI, AND ISHBAH THE FATHER OF ESHTEMOA.

(18) "AND HIS WIFE, JEHUDIJAH BORE JERED THE FATHER OF GEDOR, AND HEBER THE FATHER OF SOCHO, AND JEKUTHIEL THE FATHER OF ZANOAH. AND THESE ARE THE SONS OF BITHIAH THE DAUGHTER OF PHARAOH, WHICH MERED TOOK."

The diagram is:

1. The Eighteenth Verse proclaims Bithiah, the daughter of Pharaoh, immortal! She was an Egyptian and, as well, the daughter of the king of Egypt. She joined the people of God, thereby, forsaking Egypt and, as well, the high state and position she could have occupied in that culture, with the Lord giving her a new name, *"Bithiah,"* which means *"the daughter of Jehovah!"*

2. (Vs. 18) The proud daughter of the Egyptian monarch degrades herself (in Egypt's eyes) by becoming the wife of a Hebrew slave. No doubt, her name was, therefore, with ignominy, erased from the royal genealogy of Egypt, but — what Eternal Glory — engraved among the daughters of the Royal Family of Heaven!

3. All of this tells us that one cannot have Egypt and Israel at the same time, i.e., *"the world and the Lord."* One or the other must go. Thank God, in this case, Bithiah said goodbye to Egypt, but in doing so, she forever inscribed her name in the hallowed halls of Glory. To be sure, and by far, she got the best of the trade.

(19) "AND THE SONS OF HIS WIFE HODIAH THE SISTER OF NAHAM, THE FATHER OF KEILAH THE GARMITE, AND ESHTEMOA THE MAACHATHITE.

(20) "AND THE SONS OF SHIMON WERE, AMNON, AND RINNAH, BEN-HANAH, AND TILON. AND THE SONS OF ISHI WERE, ZOHETH, AND BEN-ZOHETH.

(21) "THE SONS OF SHELAH THE SON OF JUDAH WERE, ER THE FATHER OF LECAH, AND LAADAH THE FATHER OF MARESHAH, AND THE FAMILIES OF THE HOUSE OF THEM WHO WROUGHT FINE LINEN, OF THE HOUSE OF ASHBEA,

(22) "AND JOKIM, AND THE MEN OF CHOZEBA, AND JOASH, AND SARAPH, WHO HAD THE DOMINION IN MOAB, AND JASHUBI-LEHEM. AND THESE ARE ANCIENT THINGS.

(23) "THESE WERE THE POTTERS, AND THOSE WHO DWELT AMONG PLANTS AND HEDGES: THERE THEY DWELT WITH THE KING FOR HIS WORK.

The overview is:

1. Verse 23 records the potters who dwelt among plants and hedges with the king for his work. Like Ruth and Naomi (Ruth 1:19), they returned from Moab to Beth-lehem and were employed on the royal estate in a very humble position. The Holy Spirit seems to add with exquisite Grace that the work, though lowly, was work *"for the king,"* and they dwelt there *"with the king!"*

2. (Vs. 23) Such is Grace that today points to some hidden ministries, and ennobles them by recording that *"they dwell with the king for his work."* To be sure, all Work for the Lord Jesus Christ, irrespective as to what it might be, is of profound significance,

even as brought out in these Passages.

3. Let us again state that all of these individuals are important, even though most of them, regrettably, died lost, simply because of their connection with the Lord Jesus Christ as it regards lineage, ever how distant that connection may have been.

(24) "THE SONS OF SIMEON WERE, NEMUEL, AND JAMIN, JARIB, ZERAH, AND SHAUL:

(25) "SHALLUM HIS SON, MIBSAM HIS SON, MISHMA HIS SON.

(26) "AND THE SONS OF MISHMA; HAMUEL HIS SON, ZACCHUR HIS SON, SHIMEI HIS SON.

(27) "AND SHIMEI HAD SIXTEEN SONS AND SIX DAUGHTERS; BUT HIS BRETHREN HAD NOT MANY CHILDREN, NEITHER DID ALL THEIR FAMILY MULTIPLY, LIKE TO THE CHILDREN OF JUDAH.

(28) "AND THEY DWELT AT BEER-SHEBA, AND MOLADAH, AND HAZAR-SHUAL,

(29) "AND AT BILHAH, AND AT EZEM, AND AT TOLAD,

(30) "AND AT BETHUEL, AND AT HORMAH, AND AT ZIKLAG,

(31) "AND AT BETH-MARCABOTH AND HAZAR-SUSIM, AND AT BETH-BIREI, AND AT SHAARAIM. THESE WERE THEIR CITIES UNTO THE REIGN OF DAVID.

(32) "AND THEIR VILLAGES WERE, ETAM, AND AIN, RIMMON, AND TOCHEN, AND ASHAN, FIVE CITIES:

(33) "AND ALL THEIR VILLAGES THAT WERE ROUND ABOUT THE SAME CITIES, UNTO BAAL. THESE WERE THEIR HABITATIONS, AND THEIR GENEALOGY.

(34) "AND MESHOBAB, AND JAMLECH, AND JOSHAH THE SON OF AMAZIAH,

(35) "AND JOEL, AND JEHU THE SON OF JOSIBIAH, THE SON OF SERAIAH, THE SON OF ASIEL,

(36) "AND ELIOENAI, AND JAAKOBAH, AND JESHOHAIAH, AND ASAIAH, AND ADIEL, AND JESIMIEL, AND BENAIAH,

(37) "AND ZIZA THE SON OF SHIPHI, THE SON OF ALLON, THE SON OF JEDAIAH, THE SON OF SHIMRI, THE SON OF SHEMAIAH;

(38) "THESE MENTIONED BY THEIR NAMES WERE PRINCES IN THEIR FAMILIES: AND THE HOUSE OF THEIR FATHERS INCREASED GREATLY.

(39) "AND THEY WENT TO THE ENTRANCE OF GEDOR, EVEN UNTO THE EAST SIDE OF THE VALLEY, TO SEEK PASTURE FOR THEIR FLOCKS.

(40) "AND THEY FOUND FAT PASTURE AND GOOD, AND THE LAND WAS WIDE, AND QUIET, AND PEACEABLE; FOR THEY OF HAM HAD DWELT THERE OF OLD.

(41) "AND THESE WRITTEN BY NAME CAME IN THE DAYS OF HEZEKIAH KING OF JUDAH, AND SMOTE THEIR TENTS, AND THE HABITATIONS THAT WERE FOUND THERE, AND DESTROYED THEM UTTERLY UNTO THIS DAY, AND DWELT IN THEIR ROOMS: BECAUSE THERE WAS PASTURE THERE FOR THEIR FLOCKS.

(42) "AND SOME OF THEM, EVEN OF THE SONS OF SIMEON, FIVE HUNDRED MEN, WENT TO MOUNT SEIR, HAVING FOR THEIR CAPTAINS PELATIAH, AND NEARIAH, AND REPHAIAH, AND UZZIEL, THE SONS OF ISHI.

(43) "AND THEY SMOTE THE REST OF THE AMALEKITES WHO WERE ESCAPED, AND DWELT THERE UNTO THIS DAY."

The synopsis is:

1. The Fortieth Verse says, *"For they of Ham had dwelt there of old."* This tells us that the descendants of Ham (Noah's son) possessed these parts in ancient times. When and by whom they were driven out is not fully known.

2. We know that from then to the conquest of Canaan by Israel giants ruled that section and might have driven out the sons of Ham.

3. The reason the Simeonites conquered it was to possess the pastureland, which they did. Of course, these were only a small portion of the Simeonites, inasmuch as the Tribe had its inheritance in the possession of Judah.

"Love Divine, all loves excelling, Joy of Heaven, to Earth come down;
"Fix in us Your humble Dwelling; all Your faithful Mercies crown.

"Jesus, You are all compassion, pure, unbounded Love You are;

"Visit us with Your Salvation; enter every trembling heart."

"Breathe, O breathe Your loving Spirit into every troubled breast!

"Let us all in You inherit, let us find that perfect rest.

"Take away our bent to sinning, Alpha and Omega be;

"End of Faith, as its beginning, set our hearts at liberty."

"Come, Almighty to deliver, let us all Your Life receive;

"Suddenly return, and never, nevermore Your Temples leave:

"Thee we would be always blessing, serve You as Your Host above,

"Pray, and praise Thee without ceasing, Glory in Your Perfect Love."

CHAPTER 5

(1) "NOW THE SONS OF REUBEN THE FIRSTBORN OF ISRAEL, (FOR HE WAS THE FIRSTBORN; BUT, FORASMUCH AS HE DEFILED HIS FATHER'S BED, HIS BIRTHRIGHT WAS GIVEN UNTO THE SONS OF JOSEPH THE SON OF ISRAEL: AND THE GENEALOGY IS NOT TO BE RECKONED AFTER THE BIRTHRIGHT.

(2) "FOR JUDAH PREVAILED ABOVE HIS BRETHREN, AND OF HIM CAME THE CHIEF RULER; BUT THE BIRTHRIGHT WAS JOSEPH'S:)

(3) "THE SONS, I SAY, OF REUBEN THE FIRSTBORN OF ISRAEL WERE, HANOCH, AND PALLU, HEZRON, AND CARMI.

(4) "THE SONS OF JOEL; SHEMAIAH HIS SON, GOG HIS SON, SHIMEI HIS SON,

(5) "MICAH HIS SON, REAIA HIS SON, BAAL HIS SON,

(6) "BEERAH HIS SON, WHOM TILGATH-PILNESER KING OF ASSYRIA CARRIED AWAY CAPTIVE: HE WAS PRINCE OF THE REUBENITES.

(7) "AND HIS BRETHREN BY THEIR FAMILIES, WHEN THE GENEALOGY OF THEIR GENERATIONS WAS RECKONED,

NOTES

WERE THE CHIEF, JEIEL, AND ZECHARIAH,

(8) "AND BELA THE SON OF AZAZ, THE SON OF SHEMA, THE SON OF JOEL, WHO DWELT IN AROER, EVEN UNTO NEBO AND BAAL-MEON:

(9) "AND EASTWARD HE INHABITED UNTO THE ENTERING IN OF THE WILDERNESS FROM THE RIVER EUPHRATES: BECAUSE THEIR CATTLE WERE MULTIPLIED IN THE LAND OF GILEAD.

(10) "AND IN THE DAYS OF SAUL THEY MADE WAR WITH THE HAGARITES, WHO FELL BY THEIR HAND: AND THEY DWELT IN THEIR TENTS THROUGHOUT ALL THE EAST LAND OF GILEAD."

The synopsis is:

1. The *"birthright"* consisted of the family name and titles passing through the line of the eldest son. And yet, it was more than a title to the family inheritance; the eldest son was to receive a double portion. It involved, as well, a Spiritual Position, the High Priest, so to speak, of the family. The place of the individual in the Covenant status of Israel was part of the birthright, which pointed to Christ, and why it was so important.

2. (Vs. 1) Reuben, being the firstborn of Jacob, should have had the birthright, but he forfeited it due to sin on his part (Gen. 35:22). This is why his genealogy was not given first.

3. (Vs. 1) In the place of Reuben, Judah inherited the kingly rights (Gen. 49:10), and Joseph inherited the other blessings of the birthright. (Jesus would be born of the Tribe of Judah.)

The Patriarch had the privilege of following custom according to the bestowal of the birthright, or changing it, which change, if any, would be dictated by events.

THE BIRTHRIGHT

While birthrights were always important as it regarded the families of that era, still, they were of singular significance with the family of Jacob, and because whoever held the birthright in this family, and we speak of the kingly line, through him would ultimately come the Messiah. Nothing in the world, in fact, in time or eternity, could be more important than that.

Reuben was the Firstborn of Jacob, therefore, was supposed to have the birthright but, as stated, he forfeited it through sin. The Scripture says:

"And it came to pass, when Israel dwelt in that land, that Reuben went and lay with Bilhah his father's concubine: and Israel heard it. Now the sons of Jacob were twelve (with this sin, Reuben, the firstborn, forfeited the birthright; Jesus would not be born through that line, but rather through the Tribe of Judah):

"The sons of Leah; Reuben, Jacob's firstborn, and Simeon, and Levi, and Judah, and Issachar, and Zebulun:

"The sons of Rachel; Joseph, and Benjamin:

"And the sons of Bilhah, Rachel's handmaid; Dan, and Naphtali:

"And the sons of Zilpah, Leah's handmaid: Gad, and Asher: these are the sons of Jacob, which were born to him in Padanaram." (The twelve sons of Jacob are listed here, who would head up the Tribes of Israel, with Manasseh and Ephraim, Joseph's sons, taking the place of Joseph, making the total thirteen. There would actually be thirteen Tribes, counting Levi, which was the Priestly Tribe)" (Gen. 35:22-26).

JOSEPH

Jacob was instructed by the Lord to give the birthright to Joseph, who was the firstborn of Rachel, who should have been, but for subterfuge, Jacob's true wife (Gen. 29:21-27). In giving the birthright to Joseph, in essence, Jacob gave it to his two sons, Manasseh and Ephraim. Concerning this the Scripture says:

"And it came to pass after these things (Heb. 11:21 throws much light on the beautiful Forty-eighth Chapter of Genesis; in fact, in Chapters 48 and 49, Jacob shines as never before; if it is to be noticed, the Holy Spirit refers to him again and again as 'Israel'; this is the great Faith action of his life; feeble and dying, and having nothing except the staff on which he leaned and worshipped, he yet bestowed vast and unseen possessions on his grandsons — Williams), *that one told Joseph, Behold, your father is sick: and he took with him his two sons, Manasseh and Ephraim* (these boys must have been about 18 or 20 years old at the time).

"And one told Jacob, and said, Behold, your son Joseph comes unto you: and Israel strengthened himself, and sat upon the bed. (Joseph wants his two grandsons to know and realize that even though they have been born in Egypt, and all they have ever known is Egypt, still, they aren't Egyptians, but rather of the house of Jacob, i.e., Israelites. Such is a portrayal of Believers born in this present world, but nevertheless not of this world, but rather of the world to come.

"And finally, the significance of the change of name from 'Jacob' to 'Israel' is not to be overlooked. By Faith [it is always Faith], the great Patriarch, moved upon by the Lord, will claim the Promises, and chart the course of Israel. Though the eyes of the Patriarch are, in the natural, very dim, even as we shall see, his Faith burns brightly, actually brighter than ever; hence, he is called 'Israel.')

"And Israel beheld Joseph's sons, and said, Who are these? (That Jacob did not at first discern the presence of the sons of Joseph shows that his adoption of them into the number of the theocratic family was prompted, not by the accidental impulse of a natural affection excited through beholding these young men, but by the inward prompting of the Spirit of God.)

"And Joseph said unto his father, They are my sons, whom God has given me in this place. And he said, Bring them, I pray you, unto me, and I will bless them. (The 'blessing' consisted of Joseph's double portion, which was the privilege of the one holding the birthright, with a portion being given to each of these sons, which, as stated, contained a significance all out of proportion to natural thinking.)

"And Joseph took them both, Ephraim in his right hand toward Israel's left hand (because Ephraim was the younger), and Manasseh in his left hand toward Israel's right hand (because he was the older), and brought them near unto him.

"And Israel stretched out his right hand, and laid it upon Ephraim's head, who was the younger (signifying by his right hand that the greater part of the blessing would go to Ephraim, even though he was the younger), *and his left hand upon Manasseh's head, guiding his hands wittingly* (guided by the Holy Spirit); *for Manasseh was the firstborn* (but for the Spirit of God would have received the greater portion).

"And he blessed them that day, saying, In you shall Israel bless, saying, God make you as Ephraim and as Manasseh: and he set Ephraim before Manasseh" (Gen. 48:1, 8, 13-14, 20).

And then Jacob bestowed the kingly part of the birthright upon Judah. The Scripture says:

"Judah, you are he whom your brethren shall praise (the name Judah means 'praise,' and it is from this Tribe that the Messiah would come): *Your hand shall be in the neck of Your enemies* (speaks of the great Victory that Christ would win over Satan and all the powers of darkness at the Cross [Col. 2:14-15]); *your father's children shall bow down before You* (Israel will do this at the Second Coming).

"Judah is a lions whelp (refers to a young lion, in the power of its youth, absolutely invincible; this represented Christ in the flower of His manhood, full of the Holy Spirit, healing the sick, casting out demons, raising the dead, and doing great and mighty things, with every demon spirit trembling at His Feet): *from the prey* (the lion is always seeking the prey, never the prey seeking the lion), *My Son* (Jesus is the Son of God), *You are gone up* (meaning that Christ is always on the offensive): *He stooped down, He couched as a lion* (a rampant lion, standing on his hind feet, ready to pounce, which, in fact, was the emblem of the Tribe of Judah), *and as an old lion* (referring to one ripening into its full strength and ferocity); *who shall rouse Him up?* (Who would be so foolish as to contest the absolute invincibility of Christ?)

"The sceptre shall not depart from Judah (the 'sceptre' is defined as 'a staff of office and authority as King,' which pertains to Christ), *nor a Lawgiver from between His Feet* (refers to the fact that Judah was meant to be a guardian of the Law, which they were; the Temple was in Jerusalem, which was a part of the Tribe of Judah, and which had to

NOTES

do with the Law), *until Shiloh come* (when Jesus came, typified by the name 'Shiloh,' Who, in fact, was, and is, the True Lawgiver, He fulfilled the Law in totality by His Life and His Death, thereby satisfying all of its just demands); *and unto Him shall the gathering of the people be* (the only way to God the Father is through Christ the Son; the only way to Christ the Son is through the Cross; the only way to the Cross is through an abnegation of self [Lk. 9:23-24].)

"Binding his foal unto the vine (the 'Vine' speaks of fruit, and, in fact, 'the blood of grapes,' which speaks of what He did on the Cross in the shedding of His Life's Blood, in order to bring forth this fruit [Jn. 15:1]), *and his animal's colt unto the choice vine; He washed His Garments in wine, and His clothes in the blood of grapes* (all of this speaks of the Cross, and Him washing His Garments in wine, i.e., 'in blood'):

"His Eyes shall be red with wine (His eyes ever toward the Cross), *and His Teeth white with milk."* (Speaks of the Righteousness of Christ; it is Righteousness which He has always had, but now is made possible to us, due to what He did in His Sufferings, i.e., 'the blood of grapes')" (Gen. 49:8-12).

SIMEON AND LEVI

Simeon and Levi were next in line after Reuben, and before Judah, who was born fourth, so why were they overlooked as it regards the birthright?

After coming from Syria, Jacob with his family settled in a place called Succoth (Gen. 33:17).

A young prince of the area by the name of *"Shechem the son of Hamor the Hivite,"* saw the daughter of Jacob, Dinah, and the Scripture says *"he took her, and lay with her, and defiled her"* (Gen. 34:2).

Dinah's two brothers, Simeon and Levi, swore vengeance. They killed Shechem and his father, Hamor, and furthermore, all the men of that small village. The account is given in Genesis, Chapter 34.

Because of this, Jacob had to uproot his family and flee to Bethel (Gen. 35:1).

Regarding the last days of the great Patriarch Jacob, and as it regards the Prophecies given concerning all of his sons and what they would be, he said of both Simeon and Levi:

"Simeon and Levi are brothers (guilty of the same sin)*; instruments of cruelty are in their habitations.*

"Oh my soul, do not come into their secret (secret plottings to murder the Shechemites)*; unto their assembly* (preparation for the slaughter)*, my honor, with them do not be united* (Jacob had no part in the slaughter of the Shechemites)*: for in their anger they killed a man, and in their self-will they dug down a wall* (in their taking matters into their own hands, instead of following the Lord, they greatly hindered the protective wall of the Lord around Jacob).

"Cursed be their anger, for it was fierce; and their wrath, for it was cruel: I will divide them in Jacob, and scatter them in Israel. (The Tribe of Simeon, when coming into the Land of Israel several centuries into the future, would have no inheritance, but, in fact, would have their part in the inheritance of Judah. As well, Levi would have no inheritance at all, but would have their curse turned into a blessing as they became the Priestly Tribe of Israel, but yet scattered over the nation, fulfilling the Prophecy)" (Gen. 49:5-7).

So, the next in line was Judah, and to him the kingly part of the birthright was given. Through the lineage of Judah, Jesus would be born.

HOW WAS JUDAH ANY BETTER THAN REUBEN, OR SIMEON OR LEVI?

That's a good question!

Morally, Judah was no better than the other three.

First of all, he married a Canaanite, which he knew was not the Will of God (Gen. 38:2).

As is obvious, that union was ill conceived, with two sons born, who were so evil that the Lord killed them (Gen. 38:3-10).

Then, he proposed to go in to a harlot, which he thought she was, but who, in fact, was his disguised daughter-in-law, Tamar, who had been married to his firstborn, Er. In fact, she became pregnant by him. She had twins, of which the firstborn was *"Pharez,"* who was in the direct lineage of Christ (Mat. 1:3).

NOTES

So, we come again to the question as to why the Lord would accept Judah but refuse Reuben, Simeon, and Levi?

As well, inasmuch as the birthright, and according to the Holy Spirit, was given to Joseph, why wasn't he chosen as the direct lineage of the Messiah? In truth, Joseph was one of the greatest Types of Christ found in the entirety of the Old Testament — perhaps the greatest. Even though we know that Joseph was a sinner, simply because all men are, still, not one single sin was recorded against him in the Word of God. So, in the natural, and even in the Spiritual, at least as far as we know, Joseph would most definitely have seemed to be the greatest choice. Yet, the Holy Spirit chose Judah.

While it is certain that there were untold reasons of which we are not privileged to know, the one thing we do know is:

The Lord does all things well. He never makes a mistake. What He does is right, not just because He does it, but because it is right. The choosing of Judah to be in the direct lineage of the coming Messiah, the greatest privilege afforded anyone on Earth, was the right choice. Perhaps some of the reasons are as follows:

GOD'S CHOICE

• The choice of Judah by the Holy Spirit is a direct blow given by the Holy Spirit against self-righteousness.

• Every evidence is that despite his checkered past, Judah ultimately turned out well.

• It was Judah who pleaded the case of his brother Benjamin, before Joseph, whom he did not recognize as his brother. In fact, he offered himself as a slave in the place of Benjamin. His answer was:

"For how shall I go up to my father, and the lad be not with me? lest peradventure I see the evil that shall come on my father" (Gen. 44:34). There is forgiveness for all who will humbly come to the Lord.

• God does not choose on the basis of merit, but rather, Grace.

• While the Lord never condones wrongdoing, He, at times, does use it for His Purpose.

For instance, Judah marrying a Canaanite, who, as is obvious, was a Gentile, proclaims, by natural right, Gentiles as brothers, mothers, and sisters to our Lord; in other words, the Word of Salvation is a Word for the whole world.

(11) "AND THE CHILDREN OF GAD DWELT OVER AGAINST THEM, IN THE LAND OF BASHAN UNTO SALCAH:

(12) "JOEL THE CHIEF, AND SHAPHAM THE NEXT, AND JAANAI, AND SHAPHAT IN BASHAN.

(13) "AND THEIR BRETHREN OF THE HOUSE OF THEIR FATHER'S WERE, MICHAEL, AND MESHULLAM, AND SHEBA, AND JORAI, AND JACHAN, AND ZIA, AND HEBER, SEVEN.

(14) "THESE ARE THE CHILDREN OF ABIHAIL THE SON OF HURI, THE SON OF JAROAH, THE SON OF GILEAD, THE SON OF MICHAEL, THE SON OF JESHISHAI, THE SON OF JAHDO, THE SON OF BUZ;

(15) "AHI THE SON OF ABDIEL, THE SON OF GUNI, CHIEF OF THE HOUSE OF THEIR FATHERS.

(16) "AND THEY DWELT IN GILEAD IN BASHAN, AND IN HER TOWNS, AND IN ALL THE SUBURBS OF SHARON, UPON THEIR BORDERS.

(17) "ALL THESE WERE RECKONED BY GENEALOGIES IN THE DAYS OF JOTHAM KING OF JUDAH, AND IN THE DAYS OF JEROBOAM KING OF ISRAEL."

The exegesis is:

1. Who these people were and where they dwelt was of great significance, but only because of their attachment to the Lord Jesus Christ, i.e., *"the Incarnation."*

2. It is sad when one realizes that most of these people listed in all of these genealogies died eternally lost. They were so close but at the same time, so far away. One could say that every person living in the United States falls into that same category. The opportunity is ever present, but sadly, most ignore that opportunity, going on in their rebellious ways.

3. Could these individuals, whomever they may have been, had even one thought that thousands of years later people would read their names, and because they were placed into the Holy Writ? Whatever else they did, and however so great it may have looked at the time, has so long, long ago

NOTES

faded into insignificance, that is, if it had any duration at all. Their names are here, once again, because of the Lord Jesus Christ.

(18) "THE SONS OF REUBEN, AND THE GADITES, AND HALF THE TRIBE OF MANASSEH, OF VALIANT MEN, MEN ABLE TO BEAR BUCKLER AND SWORD, AND TO SHOOT WITH BOW, AND SKILLFUL IN WAR, WERE FOUR AND FORTY THOUSAND SEVEN HUNDRED AND THREESCORE, WHO WENT OUT TO THE WAR.

(19) "AND THEY MADE WAR WITH THE HAGARITES, WITH JETUR, AND NEPHISH, AND NODAB.

(20) "AND THEY WERE HELPED AGAINST THEM, AND THE HAGARITES WERE DELIVERED INTO THEIR HAND, AND ALL THAT WERE WITH THEM: FOR THEY CRIED TO GOD IN THE BATTLE, AND HE WAS INTREATED OF THEM; BECAUSE THEY PUT THEIR TRUST IN HIM.

(21) "AND THEY TOOK AWAY THEIR CATTLE; OF THEIR CAMELS FIFTY THOUSAND, AND OF SHEEP TWO HUNDRED AND FIFTY THOUSAND, AND OF ASSES TWO THOUSAND, AND OF MEN AN HUNDRED THOUSAND.

(22) "FOR THERE FELL DOWN MANY KILLED, BECAUSE THE WAR WAS OF GOD. AND THEY DWELT IN THEIR STEADS UNTIL THE CAPTIVITY.

(23) "AND THE CHILDREN OF THE HALF TRIBE OF MANASSEH DWELT IN THE LAND: THEY INCREASED FROM BASHAN UNTO BAAL-HERMON AND SENIR, AND UNTO MOUNT HERMON.

(24) "AND THESE WERE THE HEADS OF THE HOUSE OF THEIR FATHERS, EVEN EPHER, AND ISHI, AND ELIEL, AND AZRIEL, AND JEREMIAH, AND HODAVIAH, AND JAHDIEL, MIGHTY MEN OF VALOUR, FAMOUS MEN, AND HEADS OF THE HOUSE OF THEIR FATHERS.

(25) "AND THEY TRANSGRESSED AGAINST THE GOD OF THEIR FATHERS, AND WENT A WHORING AFTER THE GODS OF THE PEOPLE OF THE LAND, WHOM GOD DESTROYED BEFORE THEM.

(26) "AND THE GOD OF ISRAEL STIRRED UP THE SPIRIT OF PUL KING OF ASSYRIA, AND THE SPIRIT OF TILGATH-PILNESER KING OF ASSYRIA,

AND HE CARRIED THEM AWAY, EVEN THE REUBENITES, AND THE GADITES, AND THE HALF TRIBE OF MANASSEH, AND BROUGHT THEM UNTO HALAH, AND HABOR, AND HARA, AND TO THE RIVER GOZAN, UNTO THIS DAY."

The overview is:

1. (Vs. 20) The simple words, *"They put their trust in Him,"* is the key to all Victory.

2. Sadly, the Twenty-fifth Verse records the fact that Israel went into idolatry exactly as those who had been dispossessed centuries before. Consequently, the Lord drove out the Children of Israel exactly as He had done the heathen, and because they were committing the same sin.

3. (Vs. 26) The heathen nation of *"Assyria"* was God's Rod of chastisement. As it regards God's People, the methods that God chooses may vary, but it is still God.

TRUST IN THE LORD

What a wonderful statement as given to us in Verse 20, *"And they were helped against them, and the Hagarites were delivered into their hand, and all who were with them: for they cried to God in the battle, and He was intreated of them; because they put their trust in Him."*

Here is, as stated, the key to all Victory.

What does it mean for one to put one's trust in the Lord?

It means to look exclusively to Him, to trust Him, to believe Him, and to expect Him to give guidance and leading, which He Alone can do.

The Child of God, who is mature, will desire only the Will of God, and the Perfect Will of God. He knows that outside of that Perfect Will, there is trouble. So, understanding that the Will of God is paramount, and that it is all together desired, such a Believer is to look at situations with the good sense that God gave him, and then, if he feels it's right for the Kingdom of God, he should claim the thing. If it's not the Will of God, the Lord, knowing that such a Believer desires and, in fact, demands the Perfect Will of God, the Lord will then step in and stop the situation. So, that means that such a Believer, the mature Believer, does not have to say, *"Lord, give me this or that, if it be Your Will."* Such a position only weakens one's Faith. As plainly stated, the mature Believer at all times wants, desires, and strives for the Perfect Will of God, and will be satisfied with nothing less.

A PERSONAL EXPERIENCE

In the year 2000, the Lord directed my attention to radio, actually, to what is now *"SonLife Radio."*

The Lord told me how to program the stations, and that I was to fill this land with stations, which we have set out to do.

At any rate, an FM station became available for purchase in Palm Springs, California. We tried every way to work it out but to no avail. We simply didn't have the money; therefore, we had to let it pass.

Nearly a year went by, and then, all of a sudden, that station came back to my mind. I couldn't shake it. I look back now, and I know this was the Lord dealing with me about the situation.

At any rate, immediately upon getting back to Baton Rouge, for we were away at the time, I called the party in question, asking the status of the station. The answer was not encouraging.

The owner said, *"Brother Swaggart, we just sold the station to another party."*

Of course, I was disappointed, but what else could I do?

Yet, the Lord kept dealing with me about the situation. I had David Whitelaw to call the man again. David was told that the buyer had not seemingly been able to come through with the agreed upon stipulations, and that so much time would be given to him, and then, if he could not produce, if we wanted the station, it would be available.

I remember telling David that I knew we were going to get that station. I did not know how it was going to happen, but in my spirit, I knew that it would happen.

PRAYER

I remember the afternoon very specifically. I had gone to prayer and then began to pray about the station. I was telling the Lord that I very much wanted this station, if it were His Will.

Then the Spirit of the Lord spoke to my

heart and stated, *"Do not make that statement again. When you say, 'if it be Your Will,' you're hindering your Faith. I know that you want My Will, and only My Will. So, what I want you to do is this:*

"I want you to claim that station. Do so in no uncertain terms, so that your Faith can work as it should. And do not again say, 'if it be Your Will.'"

I can remember this time as though it happened yesterday. I began to importune the Lord exactly as He had spoken to my heart.

And, oh yes, He also told me that everything I prayed about was to be addressed in the same manner. He said to me, *"I know that you want My Will, and only My Will. So, if you look at something, and it seems to be right for the Ministry, claim it, and don't waver in your claim. If it's not My Will, I will step in and stop it. Otherwise, it will go through."*

That evening I knew in my spirit that this station was ours.

THE MONEY

It was the next day, if I remember correctly, when the owner of the station called us and stated, *"The other man has fallen down on his contract. If you want the station, it's yours."* We immediately accepted it, but there was one more problem — a major problem.

We didn't have any money!

I had run into this same problem a year before, so what were we going to do now to get this station?

I went back to prayer, stating to the Lord our difficulties and problems. How could we get the station when no money was available?

The Lord again spoke to my heart and said, *"I'm going to show you how that you can raise the funds for this station."*

We had to have $300,000 for a down payment, and at that stage, we didn't have a single dollar.

I don't remember exactly how many stations we had at that time, but it was less than now. At any rate, the Lord spoke to my heart and stated, *"Tell the people what I've told you to do and ask for their help."*

That's exactly what we did, and the $300,000 was raised almost immediately. The station is now ours, broadcasting the Gospel, the Message of the Cross, 24 hours a day, seven days a week, covering the entirety of the Coachella Valley in California.

There have been other times that we have gone before the people asking for help for stations, and we've always received help, but not like it was the time we asked for help for California.

Why?

For reasons known only to the Lord, He wanted that station in Palm Springs. I do not exactly know the reason, meaning that I cannot state as to why that would be more important to Him than stations elsewhere; however, I do know that it was. But the lesson that I desire to teach, and because it's a lesson that the Lord taught me, is the manner and way that we as Believers, and I speak of mature Believers, should importune the Lord as it regards things for the Kingdom.

MATURE BELIEVERS

We should be mature Believers, meaning that we are not novices. As such, we should want and, in fact, settle only for the Perfect Will of God in all matters. Maturity demands that!

In that case, our wills will be closely aligned with His, and then we do not have to quibble as it regards what His Will actually is. We should then claim whatever it is for which we are asking, which releases our Faith.

FAITH

I've learned this in living for God. Faith is the coin of the realm. In other words, that's the coin, so to speak, which spends in God's Economy.

The Lord doesn't work from the premise of merit or from the premise of works, even though those things have their place. He works strictly from the premise of Faith. He wants us to believe Him, to trust Him, and to place our confidence in His Word, and His Word alone.

THE OBJECT OF FAITH

The only way, and this is very, very important, that the Believer can fully know and understand what trust in the Lord actually is, and what Faith actually is, is that we have the correct Object of Faith. And, what is the correct Object of Faith?

The correct Object of Faith has always been, is now, and ever shall be, *"the Cross of Christ."*

We learn that from the first page of human history (Gen., Chpt. 4). Everyone in the world has faith, at least faith in something. But it's only Faith in the Cross of Christ, which translates into the Word of God, that God will honor. We hear it constantly that Believers must have Faith in the Word, and that is exactly right; however, one must understand that the Story of the Bible is the Story of Jesus Christ and Him Crucified (I Cor. 1:23). In fact, that short statement, *"Jesus Christ and Him Crucified,"* will sum up the entirety of the understanding of the Word of God. That's what the Bible is all about; that's what the Word of God is all about. So, if the Believer is going to fully trust the Lord, he must first of all understand that everything must be based fully and totally on the premise of the Cross of Christ. The Lord will honor nothing else (Rom. 6:1-14; 8:1-2,11; I Cor. 1:17-18, 21, 23; 2:2; Gal. 1:8; Ch. 5; 6:14; Eph. 2:13-18; Col. 2:14-15).

Some 3,300 years ago, the people of God put their trust in the Lord, and the Lord gave them great victories. He is still doing the same today.

THE WAR IS OF GOD

Due to acute idol worship, which incorporated human sacrifice, and especially that of little children, the cup of iniquity for the individuals who occupied this land had long since run over. As a result, it was the Will of God that they be exterminated, and the Lord would use the Israelites to do so.

While war then and war now were both Spiritual, still, it normally played out then in the physical. Now, it is entirely in the spiritual.

Paul plainly told us, even as it regards the New Covenant: *"For we wrestle not against flesh and blood* (our foes are not human; however, Satan constantly uses human beings to carry out his dirty work), *but against principalities* (rulers or beings of the highest rank and order in Satan's kingdom), *against powers* (the rank immediately below the 'Principalities'), *against the rulers of the darkness of this world* (those who carry out the instructions of the 'Powers'), *against spiritual wickedness in high places."* (This refers to demon spirits [Eph. 6:12].)

All of these designations listed by Paul are fallen Angels or demon spirits. None, as he stated, are human, which makes this warfare totally different than that under the Old Covenant.

The tragedy is, due to the modern church abandoning the Cross, it knows very little as to how to fight this war.

Paul said to the Church at Corinth: *"For though we walk in the flesh* (refers to the fact that we do not yet have Glorified Bodies), *we do not war after the flesh* (after our own ability, but rather by the Power of the Spirit):

"For the weapons of our warfare are not carnal (carnal weapons consist of those which are man devised), *but mighty through God* (the Cross of Christ [I Cor. 1:18]) *to the pulling down of strongholds;*

"Casting down imaginations (philosophic strongholds; every effort man makes outside of the Cross of Christ), *and every high thing that exalts itself against the Knowledge of God* (all the pride of the human heart), *and bringing into captivity every thought to the obedience of Christ.* (Can be done only by the Believer looking exclusively to the Cross, where all Victory is found; the Holy Spirit will then perform the task)" (II Cor. 10:3-5).

Paul then said to Timothy: *"This charge I commit unto you, son Timothy* (refers to a command or injunction), *according to the Prophecies which went before on you* (probably refers to the time frame of Acts 16:1-3), *that you by them might war a good warfare.* (We aren't told exactly what the Prophecies were, but that they spoke of an assignment to leadership in the army of King Jesus)" (I Tim. 1:18).

HOW WE ARE TO FIGHT THIS WAR

Unfortunately, this is where most modern Christians drown, Spiritually speaking.

They simply don't know how to fight this war. Virtually the entirety of the effort of the modern church is in the arena of the flesh.

What do we mean by the flesh?

This speaks of any effort to overcome sin, for that's what Satan uses, other than by the Means of the Cross. Any Christian, who tries to fight this war by the means of the flesh, is going to lose, and it doesn't matter how good his effort may be. He is doomed to failure!

The manner and way in which this war is to be fought, and the only manner and way, is for the Believer to understand that everything we receive from the Lord comes through Christ as the Source and the Cross as the Means. The Holy Spirit is involved in all of this and, in fact, that is the key.

The Holy Spirit, Who Alone can bring about in our lives that which needs to be brought about, works exclusively within the parameters of the Finished Work of Christ, i.e., *"the Cross."* That's what gives the Holy Spirit the legal right to do all the things that He does. In fact, it is so legal that it is referred to as a *"Law."* The Scripture says:

"For the Law of the Spirit of Life in Christ Jesus has made me free from the Law of Sin and Death" (Rom. 8:2).

The only thing, really, that the Holy Spirit demands of us is that the Cross of Christ ever be the Object of our Faith. We are to simply place our Faith in Christ, understanding that every victory was won at the Cross, and it was all done on our behalf.

HOW IS THIS WAR OF THE LORD?

This war is necessary that we might learn how to overcome. We have to learn that we can do nothing by and through the flesh.

The flesh pertains to our own personal abilities, strengths, efforts, education, intellectualism, talent, and ability. These things within themselves aren't necessarily wrong; it's just that it's impossible for us to win the victory by their use. That's what Paul was talking about when he mentioned *"the flesh."*

No matter how hard we try in this arena, we're going to lose. We have to learn that, and unfortunately, we have to learn it the hard way.

If it's learned correctly, we learn how to

NOTES

trust; we learn how to have Faith; and, we learn how to believe God. In other words, we learn God's Prescribed Order of Victory (Rom. 6:14).

Unfortunately, the modern church has no understanding at all as it regards the Cross of Christ concerning our Sanctification.

THE CROSS OF CHRIST

What little understanding of the Cross there is presently pertains to Salvation. In fact, one of the greatest statements made by Christians is, *"Jesus died for me."* To be sure, there is, in fact, no greater statement than that. But unfortunately, that's about as far as most Believers understand, as it regards the Cross.

The Christian must learn that as there is no Salvation for the sinner outside of the Cross of Christ (Jn. 3:16), likewise, there is no Victory for the Saint outside of the Cross. The latter part is not understood at all by the modern Believer; consequently, Satan is wreaking havoc with most Believers.

We must ever understand that Jesus Christ is the Source of all things (Jn. 1:1-5). As well, the Cross of Christ is the Means and, in fact, the only Means, by which all these things are given to us (Rom. 6:3-14; I Cor. 1:17-18, 23; 2:2; Gal. 6:14).

That's what Jesus was addressing when He said: *"If any man will come after Me, let him deny himself, and take up his cross daily, and follow Me"* (Lk. 9:23).

When Jesus used the term *"let him deny himself,"* he was not speaking of asceticism, which is the denial of all things that are pleasurable or comfortable, in other words, things we enjoy. He was rather speaking of one denying one's own ability and strength, i.e., *"the flesh."*

What must have been the thoughts of His Disciples when He said to them, *"and take up his cross daily, and follow Me?"*

Then to seal the statement, He also said, *"And whosoever does not bear his Cross, and come after Me, cannot be My Disciple"* (Lk. 14:27).

TWO STATEMENTS BY CHRIST

Our Lord says two things in these two Passages. They are:

• He, in essence, says that it's impossible for the Believer to live the life he ought to live, and to be what he ought to be, unless he bears the Cross, i.e., *"take to himself its benefits."*

• If one doesn't do such, bear the Cross, plain and simple, our Lord stated that such a person cannot be His Disciple. That's pretty ironclad!

WHY IS THE CROSS SO IMPORTANT?

As stated, what Jesus did at the Cross is what gives the Holy Spirit the legal means, in essence, the legal right, to do all that He does for us. At the Cross, Jesus atoned for all sin, past, present, and future, at least for all who believe. In doing that, this defeated Satan and all of his cohorts, simply because it is sin that gives Satan the legal right to hold people captive. With that means removed, and I speak of sin, then Satan has no more legal right to hold anyone captive (Col. 2:14-15).

So, it was the Cross that effected all of this. There, the sin debt was completely settled, meaning that it's paid in full. Man now has the opportunity to be totally reconciled to God. Inasmuch as the sin debt has been paid, the Holy Spirit can now come into our hearts and lives and abide there permanently (I Cor. 3:16).

That's why the Cross is so very, very important. In fact, there is nothing in the world more important. That's the reason that Paul referred to the Cross as the *"Everlasting Covenant"* (Heb. 13:20).

BOASTING IN THE CROSS

What did Paul mean when he said: *"But God forbid that I should glory* (boast), *save in the Cross of our Lord Jesus Christ* (what the opponents of Paul sought to escape at the price of insincerity is the Apostle's only basis of exultation), *by Whom the world is crucified unto me, and I unto the world.* (The only way we can overcome the world, and I mean the only way, is by placing our Faith exclusively in the Cross of Christ and keeping it there)" (Gal. 6:14).

When Paul spoke of the Cross, and when we speak of the Cross, we aren't speaking of a wooden beam. That's not the idea at all!

NOTES

We are speaking of the event, what transpired there.

Donnie explained this very well over Son-Life Radio when he asked a caller, *"When you think of Pearl Harbor, what comes into your mind? Do you think of a bay, or an inlet, or do you think of what the Japanese did there in their attack?"*

Of course, the listener then knew what he was saying.

When we speak of the Cross of Christ, we are speaking of the event, what transpired there, and what did transpire?

Jesus gave Himself in His Perfection as a Sacrifice, which God accepted, and which atoned for all sin. Due to having broken the Law of God, every human being was guilty; therefore, Jesus had to pay the price for that (Col. 2:14-15).

When He paid that price, Satan was then defeated and in totality. As we've already stated, sin is the legal right that Satan had to hold men in bondage. With sin removed, which it was at the Cross, which only Christ could do, Satan lost his legal right to hold anyone in bondage.

SO WHY IS MOST OF THE WORLD STILL IN SPIRITUAL CAPTIVITY?

In fact, most of the world still is in spiritual captivity, including Christians, simply because they do not avail themselves of that which Christ has done for us. It is just that simple!

The person who is unsaved will not allow the Lord to come into his heart. That being the case, Satan continues to have a legal right to place that person in captivity, which he does with all who do not know the Lord. While the captivities may differ, meaning that the bondages differ, still, every single person without the Lord is in spiritual captivity.

In fact, there are approximately 20 million alcoholics in this nation. There are about 30 million drug addicts, whether street drugs or prescription pills; nevertheless, the bondage is just as real. Over 20 million are hooked on gambling. Only the Lord knows the tens upon tens of millions who are hooked on pornography, etc.

And yet, all bondages do not take that

course. There are many who aren't alcoholics, etc., but are in bondage to fear, which takes away their peace, and which robs them of correct life and living. Let us say it again:

Outside of Christ, there is not real joy in living; no real peace of mind, and that lack robs one of true life and living.

Someone asked the question the other day as to why many of the young actors and actresses in Hollywood, and some of the older ones as well, wreck their lives with alcohol and drugs, etc. One of them answered it herself. She said, *"Our lives are miserable; that's why we do what we do!"*

Despite the fact that she was making tens of millions of dollars a year, living in a mansion, driving the best automobiles that money can buy, and wearing the finest of clothes, still, all the things in the world, including money, could not fill the emptiness that's in the heart. That's why Jesus said: *"A man's life consists not in the abundance of the things which he possesses"* (Lk. 12:15).

Unfortunately, most Christians are in bondage, as well.

Why?

It's because, as we've already stated, they do not understand how to fight this war and, therefore, attempt to do it in the wrong way. They fail, as fail they must (Rom. 7:15).

Unfortunately, the church comes up with one fad, one scheme, after the other. Regrettably, the church falls for it hook, line, and sinker. But the end result is, as all the other fads and schemes, zero.

And yet, when the Cross is introduced as the answer and, in fact, the only answer, most in the modern church have little interest.

Why?

First of all, the Cross of Christ is not very romantic. As well, it eliminates every single thing about the individual except Faith. That's not appealing either!

In fact, the Cross of Christ lays waste all of man's efforts, and man doesn't like that, and especially, Christian man. We like to think that all of this hard work that we put into our efforts is the right way. And to be told that it isn't, is an offense (Gal. 5). So, religious man continues to reject the only

NOTES

means of Victory there is, and sadly, remains in bondage.

IDOLATRY

Unfortunately, after being used by God, and after being rewarded in a tremendous way, even as Verse 21 brings out, still, there came a time that the people of God *"transgressed against the God of their fathers, and went a whoring after the gods of the people of the land, whom God destroyed before them."*

In other words, they were committing the same identical sins as the people who had been expelled those centuries before. As a result, the Lord vomited them out of the land also.

He used, at least in this case, Pul, king of Assyria, and the spirit of Tilgath-Pilneser, to carry out that which needed to be done.

This could have been avoided, this terrible destruction which Israel suffered. And the Lord tried. Oh, how hard He tried! But they resisted Prophet after Prophet until, as the Scripture says, *"there was no remedy."*

Let the Believer clearly understand the following:

If the Believer rejects the Message of the Cross (I Cor. 1:18), if the Believer ignores the Message of the Cross (Gal. 6:14), if the Believer only pays lip service to the Cross, the end result will be with each Believer individually as it was with Israel of old — sold into captivity.

We may think of idolatry as something that took place thousands of years ago and has no bearing on our present circumstances. But, please understand the following:

Anything that we place ahead of the Cross of Christ, anything in which we place our faith other than the Cross of Christ, anything, and I mean anything of this nature, is constituted by the Lord as *"idolatry."* Unfortunately, religion is the greatest idolatry of all.

"Rejoice, ye pure in heart, rejoice, give thanks, and sing:
"Your festal banner wave on high, the Cross of Christ your King."

"With all the Angel choirs, with all the Saints on Earth,

"Pour out the strains of joy and bliss,
true rapture, noblest mirth!"

"Still lift your standard high, still
march in firm array;
"As warriors through the darkness toil
till dawns the golden day."

"Yes, on through life's long path, still
chanting as you go;
"From youth to age, by night and day,
in gladness and in woe."

"Then on, ye pure in heart rejoice,
give thanks, and sing.
"Your festal banner wave on high, the
Cross of Christ your King."

CHAPTER 6

(1) "THE SONS OF LEVI; GERSHON, KOHATH, AND MERARI.

(2) "AND THE SONS OF KOHATH; AMRAM, IZHAR, AND HEBRON, AND UZZIEL.

(3) "AND THE CHILDREN OF AMRAM; AARON, AND MOSES, AND MIRIAM. THE SONS ALSO OF AARON; NADAB, AND ABIHU, ELEAZAR, AND ITHAMAR.

(4) "ELEAZAR BEGAT PHINEHAS, PHINEHAS BEGAT ABISHUA,

(5) "AND ABISHUA BEGAT BUKKI, AND BUKKI BEGAT UZZI,

(6) "AND UZZI BEGAT ZERAHIAH, AND ZERAHIAH BEGAT MERAIOTH,

(7) "MERAIOTH BEGAT AMARIAH, AND AMARIAH BEGAT AHITUB,

(8) "AND AHITUB BEGAT ZADOK, AND ZADOK BEGAT AHIMAAZ,

(9) "AND AHIMAAZ BEGAT AZARIAH, AND AZARIAH BEGAT JOHANAN,

(10) "AND JOHANAN BEGAT AZARIAH, (HE IT IS WHO EXECUTED THE PRIEST'S OFFICE IN THE TEMPLE THAT SOLOMON BUILT IN JERUSALEM:)

(11) "AND AZARIAH BEGAT AMARIAH, AND AMARIAH BEGAT AHITUB,

(12) "AND AHITUB BEGAT ZADOK, AND ZADOK BEGAT SHALLUM,

(13) "AND SHALLUM BEGAT HILKIAH, AND HILKIAH BEGAT AZARIAH,

NOTES

(14) "AND AZARIAH BEGAT SERAIAH, AND SERAIAH BEGAT JEHOZADAK,

(15) "AND JEHOZADAK WENT INTO CAPTIVITY, WHEN THE LORD CARRIED AWAY JUDAH AND JERUSALEM BY THE HAND OF NEBUCHADNEZZAR."

The overview is:

1. The three sons of Levi given in Verse 1 represent the three branches of the Levites, who were responsible for various services to the Tabernacle, and then to the Temple.

2. As we have repeatedly stated, these people were important only because of their connection with the Lord Jesus Christ, albeit that connection was ever so distant.

3. Aaron was the first High Priest of Israel. All following High Priests were to be in his lineage. Unfortunately, the Lord had to kill two of his sons who were Priests, *"Nadab and Abihu."*

TABERNACLE SERVICE

It should be remembered that everything about the Tabernacle in the wilderness, and I mean everything, pointed to the Lord Jesus Christ in His Atoning Work, His Mediatorial Work, or His Intercessory Work. As a result, and it should be overly obvious, this means that all of it was extremely important.

This is at least one of the reasons that Believers should make a life-long study of the Old Testament. All of it in some way points to Christ. And, if one doesn't understand what is being said in the Old Testament, then one is going to misunderstand much of what is said in the New Covenant.

THE GERSHONITES

The Gershonites were to be responsible for the Tabernacle proper. The Scripture says concerning them:

"And the LORD spoke unto Moses, saying,

"Take also the sum of the sons of Gershon, throughout the houses of their fathers, by their families;

"From thirty years old and upward until fifty years old shall you number them; all who enter in to perform the service, to do the work in the Tabernacle of the congregation.

"This is the service of the families of the Gershonites, to serve, and for burdens:

"And they shall bear the curtains of the

Tabernacle, and the Tabernacle of the congregation, his covering, and the covering of the badgers' skins that is above upon it (the roof), *and the hanging for the door of the Tabernacle of the congregation,*

"And the hangings of the Court, and the hanging for the door of the gate of the Court (the entrance into the Court), *which is by the Tabernacle and by the Altar round about, and their cords, and all the instruments of their service, and all that is made for them: so shall they serve.*

"This is the service of the families of the sons of Gershon in the Tabernacle of the congregation: and their charge shall be under the hand of Ithamar the son of Aaron the Priest (the Gershonites carried all the hangings belonging to the Tabernacle and to the Outer Court, with the single exception of the *'Veil,'* which was wrapped around the Ark of the Covenant; as well, Ithamar, the son of Aaron, was in charge of the Gershonites)" (Num. 4:21-26, 28).

Incidentally, at the time that Moses gave these instructions, there were 2,630 Gershonites, who were employed in this particular service.

THE KOHATHITES

Concerning this group, the Scriptures say: *"And the LORD spoke unto Moses and unto Aaron, saying,*

"Take the sum of the sons of Kohath from among the sons of Levi, after their families, by the house of their fathers,

"From thirty years old and upward even until fifty years old, all who enter into the host, to do the work in the Tabernacle of the congregation.

"This shall be the service of the sons of Kohath in the Tabernacle of the congregation, about the most holy things.

They were responsible for the Sacred Vessels inside the Tabernacle. They were given implicit instructions as to exactly how these Vessels were to be handled when they were moved. Notes from THE EXPOSITOR'S STUDY BIBLE tell us:

"After the Priests had prepared all the Sacred Vessels for transportation, then, and then only, could the Kohathites come in to take them away. They were not for a moment to go in and look upon the holy things, lest they die (II Sam. 6:7). Concerning this, Williams says:

"'When God dwells in power in the camp, it is as when a wire is charged with electricity. Hence, when He withdrew, men could look on, and handle, these holy things with impunity. The carnal curiosity which would analyze Christ's Human Nature brings death unto the soul.'

"Consequently, the Kohathites had to be especially careful in the handling of the Sacred Vessels that they not die; that's how critical the situation was, and that's how critical the situation still is; spiritual death is the end result of mishandling the Word of God.

"The idea is that the Kohathites could go into the Tabernacle and carry these things out after they had been properly covered and attended to by the Priests" (Num. 4:1-20).

There were at the time of Moses and Aaron 2,750 Kohathites who attended to the service of the Sacred Vessels when they were to be moved.

THE MERARITES

Concerning this group the Scripture says: *"And under the custody and charge of the sons of Merari shall be the boards of the Tabernacle, and the bars thereof, and the pillars thereof, and the sockets thereof, and all the vessels thereof, and all that serves thereto,"* etc.

"(The charge of the Merarites consisted of everything not included in that of the Gershonites and the Kohathites. It must be understood that there was a greater dignity in carrying a lowly *'pin'* of the Tabernacle than in wielding the mighty scepter of Egypt)" (Num. 3:33-39).

There were 3,200 Merarites at that particular time.

Let us say it again:

To the unspiritual heart, all of these tedious instructions given in the Book of Numbers concerning these various groups and what they were to do, seem to be dull and uninteresting. Even worse than that, to most, it would seem as if though these things have no meaning or bearing on our everyday life and living now. But, they do!

Inasmuch as all of the Tabernacle, and every single Vessel in it, even down to the smallest pin, pictured Christ, whether in His Atoning Work, His Mediatorial Work, or His Intercessory Work, I would certainly hope, considering that, that we at least begin to realize how significant all of this is. In fact, there is absolutely nothing in the Word of God that is not vastly significant. If it doesn't seem to be such, it is because we, as Believers, do not really understand what we are reading. That's the reason that every Believer should avail himself or herself of every tool possible that will enable one to understand the Word of God more fully. Those of you who have purchased, or else you have been given this Commentary, would fall into the category of those who do understand the preciousness of the Word of God. You are to be commended.

FAILURE TO HEED THE WORD

The Fifteenth Verse says, *"And Jehozadak went into captivity, when the LORD carried away Judah and Jerusalem by the hand of Nebuchadnezzar."*

All of this was a failure to know the Word and to heed the Word. Those failures were brought about simply because of a lack of interest as it regarded the Word. As a result, Israel went into captivity and to a degree of suffering that beggars description, all because of disobeying the Word.

How important is the Bible to you?

Let it be understood, as a Believer, if you don't have a word for word translation of the Bible, such as the King James Version, then you really don't have a Bible, but rather a collection of religious thoughts, which will do you no good whatsoever.

Satan is attacking the Word of God today perhaps as never before. He is not denying its veracity, as he once did, but is rather seeking to pervert it, and doing so by the plethora of Versions, which are being released to the Christian public, such as the Message Bible, which, in reality, is no Bible at all. Please understand the following: many claim they cannot understand the King James Version, so they opt for a version, such as the Message Bible and others similar, because they claim to be able to understand it. But please note this: if what you think you understand is incorrect, and please believe me, these paraphrases are, then you haven't helped yourself, but rather have hurt yourself.

That's the reason we strongly recommend that you secure for yourself a copy of THE EXPOSITOR'S STUDY BIBLE. It will, we believe, help you to understand the Word of God as nothing else that's ever been placed into your hands.

(16) "THE SONS OF LEVI; GERSHOM, KOHATH, AND MERARI.

(17) "AND THESE BE THE NAMES OF THE SONS OF GERSHOM; LIBNI, AND SHIMEI.

(18) "AND THE SONS OF KOHATH WERE, AMRAM, AND IZHAR, AND HEBRON, AND UZZIEL.

(19) "THE SONS OF MERARI; MAHLI, AND MUSHI. AND THESE ARE THE FAMILIES OF THE LEVITES ACCORDING TO THEIR FATHERS.

(20) "OF GERSHOM; LIBNI HIS SON, JAHATH HIS SON, ZIMMAH HIS SON,

(21) "JOAH HIS SON, IDDO HIS SON, ZERAH HIS SON, JEATERAI HIS SON.

(22) "THE SONS OF KOHATH; AMMINADAB HIS SON, KORAH HIS SON, ASSIR HIS SON,

(23) "ELKANAH HIS SON, AND EBIASAPH HIS SON, AND ASSIR HIS SON,

(24) "TAHATH HIS SON, URIEL HIS SON, UZZIAH HIS SON, AND SHAUL HIS SON.

(25) "AND THE SONS OF ELKANAH; AMASAI, AND AHIMOTH.

(26) "AS FOR ELKANAH: THE SONS OF ELKANAH; ZOPHAI HIS SON, AND NAHATH HIS SON,

(27) "ELIAB HIS SON, JEROHAM HIS SON, ELKANAH HIS SON.

(28) "AND THE SONS OF SAMUEL; THE FIRSTBORN VASHNI, AND ABIAH.

(29) "THE SONS OF MERARI; MAHLI, LIBNI HIS SON, SHIMEI HIS SON, UZZA HIS SON,

(30) "SHIMEA HIS SON, HAGGIAH HIS SON, ASAIAH HIS SON.

(31) "AND THESE ARE THEY WHOM DAVID SET OVER THE SERVICE OF SONG IN THE HOUSE OF THE LORD, AFTER THAT THE ARK HAD REST.

(32) "AND THEY MINISTERED BEFORE THE DWELLING PLACE OF THE TABERNACLE OF THE CONGREGATION WITH SINGING, UNTIL SOLOMON HAD BUILT THE HOUSE OF THE LORD IN JERUSALEM: AND THEN THEY WAITED ON THEIR OFFICE ACCORDING TO THEIR ORDER.

(33) "AND THESE ARE THEY THAT WAITED WITH THEIR CHILDREN. OF THE SONS OF THE KOHATHITES: HEMAN A SINGER, THE SON OF JOEL, THE SON OF SHEMUEL,

(34) "THE SON OF ELKANAH, THE SON OF JEROHAM, THE SON OF ELIEL, THE SON OF TOAH,

(35) "THE SON OF ZUPH, THE SON OF ELKANAH, THE SON OF MAHATH, THE SON OF AMASAI,

(36) "THE SON OF ELKANAH, THE SON OF JOEL, THE SON OF AZARIAH, THE SON OF ZEPHANIAH,

(37) "THE SON OF TAHATH, THE SON OF ASSIR, THE SON OF EBIASAPH, THE SON OF KORAH,

(38) "THE SON OF IZHAR, THE SON OF KOHATH, THE SON OF LEVI, THE SON OF ISRAEL.

(39) "AND HIS BROTHER ASAPH, WHO STOOD ON HIS RIGHT HAND, EVEN ASAPH THE SON OF BERACHIAH, THE SON OF SHIMEA,

(40) "THE SON OF MICHAEL, THE SON OF BAASEIAH, THE SON OF MALCHIAH,

(41) "THE SON OF ETHNI, THE SON OF ZERAH, THE SON OF ADAIAH,

(42) "THE SON OF ETHAN, THE SON OF ZIMMAH, THE SON OF SHIMEI,

(43) "THE SON OF JAHATH, THE SON OF GERSHOM, THE SON OF LEVI.

(44) "AND THEIR BRETHREN THE SONS OF MERARI STOOD ON THE LEFT HAND: ETHAN THE SON OF KISHI, THE SON OF ABDI, THE SON OF MALLUCH,

(45) "THE SON OF HASHABIAH, THE SON OF AMAZIAH, THE SON OF HILKIAH,

(46) "THE SON OF AMZI, THE SON OF BANI, THE SON OF SHAMER,

(47) "THE SON OF MAHLI, THE SON OF MUSHI, THE SON OF MERARI, THE SON OF LEVI.

NOTES

(48) "THEIR BRETHREN ALSO THE LEVITES WERE APPOINTED UNTO ALL MANNER OF SERVICE OF THE TABERNACLE OF THE HOUSE OF GOD."

The construction is:

1. (Vs. 31) We learn somewhat from these Passages the great part that music plays in worship, and that, by and large, it had its beginning with David and the choirs.

2. As it regards Verse 32, it is said that often, with some saying that it occurred every day, the various choirs, under three lead singers [Heman, Asaph, and Ethan], gathered at the Tabernacle, or at the site where the Temple would be built, and ministered in worship and singing. Some even said that this was done each day at the rising of the sun.

This greeted Jerusalem at the beginning of each new day with worship and praise unto the Lord. Incidentally, Heman was Samuel's grandson (Verse 33).

3. Of the seven great religions of the world, Christianity is the only one that has a songbook. The truth is, Biblical Christianity is that alone, which has something to sing about.

THE MINISTRY OF MUSIC

Music and singing, which glorify the Lord and lift up the Name of Jesus, which extol the tremendous price that was paid for our Redemption, present the highest forms of praise and worship there is. They incorporate petition; they incorporate praise; and, they incorporate Prophecy. In other words, they are the vocal expressions of our relationship with Christ, and nothing could be higher than that.

Now, what is the concrete basis on which we base our claim that music and singing glorify the Lord and are the highest expressions and the highest forms of substance, as it regards worship of the Lord?

The Word of God is the foundation for what we say.

The longest Book in the Bible is Psalms. It contains 150 songs, all inspired by the Holy Spirit, with the Divine Spirit using various instrumentations, such as David, who penned at least half and, no doubt, more of the Psalms. Inasmuch as the Holy

Spirit devoted the longest Book in the Bible to this form of praise and worship tells us of the value placed therein by Heaven.

THE BAROMETER OF SPIRITUALITY

When the church begins to lose its way spiritually, the first thing that it loses is its song. In that atmosphere, an atmosphere of spiritual poverty, the music and the singing become stilted, formal, without meaning, because the Holy Spirit is no longer present.

As well, Satan has done everything within his power to corrupt the music and the singing of the church, and has been very successful in doing so. As a result, music and singing which glorifies Christ, which extols the precious shed Blood of Jesus Christ, and which has the Cross as its foundation, is little heard in most churches presently. Of course, the reasons are obvious; the very purpose of the Evil One is to pull the church away from the Cross, and he has, by and large, succeeded.

THE CREATION OF MUSIC

The Holy Spirit in the beginning created music in three parts, one might say.

1. Melody: this pertains to the tune of the song.
2. Harmony: this pertains to the various parts of music, such as lead, alto, tenor, bass.
3. Rhythm: this pertains to the measured beats.

Satan has attempted to interrupt this ordered flow and, as stated, has been very successful in doing so.

In much of the music in modern day churches, the melody is so perverted that it has neither rhyme nor reason. As a result, it can little be followed. Along with that, the words are garbled because they have no meaning. In fact, they aren't meant to have any meaning.

As well, the harmony for modern contemporary music is so disordered and disjointed that it cannot be followed. This stops all worship, which is Satan's intention.

As it regards *"rhythm,"* some have mistakenly thought that if the song had rhythm, it was worldly. The truth is, irrespective of the style, there is rhythm in every song.

NOTES

Inasmuch as God created rhythm, it's not wrong for it to be used, as should be obvious. In fact, it is impossible for music to be presented unless there is rhythm. While the beats or the measures might be different and, in fact, are different in songs, still, every song contains a form of rhythm. But, if the rhythm is the main attraction of the song, then it is of the flesh and not the Spirit.

DAVID AND MUSIC

It was to David, who was the greatest Type of Christ found in the Old Testament that was given the form of music and singing, which constitutes all praise and worship. In other words, whether it's the soloist glorifying the Lord through song, or great choirs, they all had their origin in David, given to him by the Holy Spirit.

The truth is Israel was very demonstrative in their praise and worship, in other words, extremely emotional. Oftentimes, when they would sing the Psalms, and at times there would be several choirs, all at the same time, answering one another, all meant to praise the Lord. In this setting, at times there would be scores of young men and young ladies, most of the time with tambourines, who would be whirling about in a dancing mode, glorifying the Lord. It is doubtful that it was structured, but mostly in the realm of spontaneity. In other words, as they would play their musical instruments, and the people would be singing, joy would fill the hearts of scores, and young people would begin to give vent to this emotion by dancing, but never with each other. As well, and as stated, it was not an orchestrated thing, but that which was spontaneous, from the heart, and meant to glorify the Lord.

Such has attempted to be imitated in many church circles in the last few years, but without much success. While there definitely has to be orchestration, as it regards the music and the singing, still, there cannot be orchestration, as it regards worship. Please understand that for it is very important.

When we try to orchestrate worship, it ceases to be of the Spirit and begins to be of the flesh, and will be a blessing to no one.

THE LORD JESUS CHRIST AND THE PSALMS

There are in many Study Bibles that which is noted as Messianic Psalms. In other words, it is claimed that these particular Psalms speak directly of Christ.

That is correct; however, the truth is, every single Psalm in the Bible glorifies Christ, speaks of Christ, pertains to Christ, and does so in His Atoning Work, His Mediatorial Work, or His Intercessory Work. The reason we do not understand some Psalms falling into that category is simply because we do not understand certain aspects of the Work of our Saviour.

As someone has rightly said, the four Gospels portray the Acts of our Lord, while the Psalms portray His Heart.

Concerning this, Williams says, and rightly so: *"The Book of the Psalms is a volume of prophecy; its principle predictions concern the perfections, the sufferings, and the succeeding glories of the Messiah.*

"God having been dishonored by human unbelief and disobedience, it was necessary that a man should be born who would perfectly love, trust, and serve Him; and Who would be the True Adam, Noah, Abraham, Israel, Moses, and David, etc.

"God's moral glory demanded that sin should be judged; that sinners should repent, confess and forsake sin and worship and obey Him; and being God His nature required perfection in these emotions of the heart and will.

"Such perfection was impossible to fallen man, and it was equally out of his power to provide a Sacrifice that could remove his guilt and restore his relationship with God.

"The Psalms reveal Christ as satisfying in these relationships all the Divine requirements. He, though Himself sinless, declares Himself in these Psalms to be the sinner; and He expresses to God the abhorrence of sin accompanied by the repentance and sorrow which man ought to feel and express but will not and cannot. Similarly the faith, love, obedience, and worship which man fails to give He perfectly renders.

"Thus as the High Priest of His people He, the True Advocate, charges Himself with the guilt of our sins; declares them to be His Own; confesses them, repents of them, declaring at the same time His Own sinlessness; and atones for them. Thus though Psalms in which the Speaker declares his sinfulness and his sinlessness become quite clear of comprehension when it is recognized Who the Speaker is.

"Messiah's other Offices and Ministries as Son of God and Son of Man, as King and Priest, as Servant of Jehovah, as Angel of Jehovah, as the Word of God, and as the Burnt Offering, the Meal Offering, the Peace Offering, the Sin Offering, and the Trespass Offering; and as the Resurrection and the Life, are all sung of, together with the sufferings or the glories appropriate to each office.

"The Gospels record the fact that He prayed; the Psalms furnish the words of the prayer.

"Only the sinless Messiah can sing the Psalms in their fullness. It deeply affects the heart to listen to Him as He sings; especially when, as the Representative and Sinbearer of His people, He declares that sins, sorrows, sufferings, and chastisement to be His Own."[1]

(49) "BUT AARON AND HIS SONS OFFERED UPON THE ALTAR OF THE BURNT OFFERING, AND ON THE ALTAR OF INCENSE, AND WERE APPOINTED FOR ALL THE WORK OF THE PLACE MOST HOLY, AND TO MAKE AN ATONEMENT FOR ISRAEL, ACCORDING TO ALL THAT MOSES THE SERVANT OF GOD HAD COMMANDED.

(50) "AND THESE ARE THE SONS OF AARON; ELEAZAR HIS SON, PHINEHAS HIS SON, ABISHUA HIS SON,

(51) "BUKKI HIS SON, UZZI HIS SON, ZERAHIAH HIS SON,

(52) "MERAIOTH HIS SON, AMARIAH HIS SON, AHITUB HIS SON,

(53) "ZADOK HIS SON, AHIMAAZ HIS SON."

The composition is:

1. The work of the Sacrifices was done only by the Priests, simply because they were Types of Christ. Christ Alone would be the supreme Sacrifice.

2. (Vs. 49) Only the Priests, as stated,

were allowed to do this work, not the kings or Prophets, unless they were of the Tribe of Levi. Kings were never of this Tribe, being of the Tribe of Judah, but sometimes a Prophet, as Ezekiel, would also be a Levite.

3. (Vs. 49) All the Levites, whether Priests or choir directors, etc., came from one of the branches of *"Gershon, Kohath, and Merari."* The term *"Levite"* refers to the descendants of Levi.

(54) "NOW THESE ARE THEIR DWELLING PLACES THROUGHOUT THEIR CASTLES IN THEIR COASTS, OF THE SONS OF AARON, OF THE FAMILIES OF THE KOHATHITES: FOR THEIRS WAS THE LOT.

(55) "AND THEY GAVE THEM HEBRON IN THE LAND OF JUDAH, AND THE SUBURBS THEREOF ROUND ABOUT IT.

(56) "BUT THE FIELDS OF THE CITY, AND THE VILLAGES THEREOF, THEY GAVE TO CALEB THE SON OF JEPHUNNEH.

(57) "AND TO THE SONS OF AARON THEY GAVE THE CITIES OF JUDAH, NAMELY, HEBRON, THE CITY OF REFUGE, AND LIBNAH WITH HER SUBURBS, AND JATTIR, AND ESHTEMOA, WITH THEIR SUBURBS,

(58) "AND HILEN WITH HER SUBURBS, DEBIR WITH HER SUBURBS,

(59) "AND ASHAN WITH HER SUBURBS, AND BETH-SHEMESH WITH HER SUBURBS:

(60) "AND OUT OF THE TRIBE OF BENJAMIN; GEBA WITH HER SUBURBS, AND ALEMETH WITH HER SUBURBS, AND ANATHOTH WITH HER SUBURBS. ALL THEIR CITIES THROUGHOUT THEIR FAMILIES WERE THIRTEEN CITIES.

(61) "AND UNTO THE SONS OF KOHATH, WHICH WERE LEFT OF THE FAMILY OF THAT TRIBE, WERE CITIES GIVEN OUT OF THE HALF TRIBE, NAMELY, OUT OF THE HALF TRIBE OF MANASSEH, BY LOT, TEN CITIES.

(62) "AND TO THE SONS OF GERSHOM THROUGHOUT THEIR FAMILIES OUT OF THE TRIBE OF ISSACHAR, AND OUT OF THE TRIBE OF ASHER, AND OUT OF THE TRIBE OF NAPHTALI, AND OUT OF THE TRIBE OF MANASSEH IN BASHAN, THIRTEEN CITIES.

NOTES

(63) "UNTO THE SONS OF MERARI WERE GIVEN BY LOT, THROUGHOUT THEIR FAMILIES, OUT OF THE TRIBE OF REUBEN, AND OUT OF THE TRIBE OF GAD, AND OUT OF THE TRIBE OF ZEBULUN, TWELVE CITIES.

(64) "AND THE CHILDREN OF ISRAEL GAVE TO THE LEVITES THESE CITIES WITH THEIR SUBURBS.

(65) "AND THEY GAVE BY LOT OUT OF THE TRIBE OF THE CHILDREN OF JUDAH, AND OUT OF THE TRIBE OF THE CHILDREN OF SIMEON, AND OUT OF THE TRIBE OF THE CHILDREN OF BENJAMIN, THESE CITIES, WHICH ARE CALLED BY THEIR NAMES.

(66) "AND THE RESIDUE OF THE FAMILIES OF THE SONS OF KOHATH HAD CITIES OF THEIR COASTS OUT OF THE TRIBE OF EPHRAIM.

(67) "AND THEY GAVE UNTO THEM, OF THE CITIES OF REFUGE, SHECHEM IN MOUNT EPHRAIM WITH HER SUBURBS; THEY GAVE ALSO GEZER WITH HER SUBURBS,

(68) "AND JOKMEAM WITH HER SUBURBS, AND BETH-HORON WITH HER SUBURBS,

(69) "AND AIJALON WITH HER SUBURBS, AND GATH-RIMMON WITH HER SUBURBS:

(70) "AND OUT OF THE HALF TRIBE OF MANASSEH; ANER WITH HER SUBURBS, AND BILEAM WITH HER SUBURBS, FOR THE FAMILY OF THE REMNANT OF THE SONS OF KOHATH.

(71) "UNTO THE SONS OF GERSHOM WERE GIVEN OUT OF THE FAMILY OF THE HALF TRIBE OF MANASSEH, GOLAN IN BASHAN WITH HER SUBURBS, AND ASHTAROTH WITH HER SUBURBS:

(72) "AND OUT OF THE TRIBE OF ISSACHAR; KEDESH WITH HER SUBURBS, DABERATH WITH HER SUBURBS,

(73) "AND RAMOTH WITH HER SUBURBS, AND ANEM WITH HER SUBURBS:

(74) "AND OUT OF THE TRIBE OF ASHER; MASHAL WITH HER SUBURBS, AND ABDON WITH HER SUBURBS,

(75) "AND HUKOK WITH HER SUBURBS, AND REHOB WITH HER SUBURBS:

(76) "AND OUT OF THE TRIBE OF

NAPHTALI; KEDESH IN GALILEE WITH HER SUBURBS, AND HAMMON WITH HER SUBURBS, AND KIRJATHAIM WITH HER SUBURBS.

(77) "UNTO THE REST OF THE CHILDREN OF MERARI WERE GIVEN OUT OF THE TRIBE OF ZEBULUN, RIMMON WITH HER SUBURBS, TABOR WITH HER SUBURBS:

(78) "AND ON THE OTHER SIDE JORDAN BY JERICHO, ON THE EAST SIDE OF JORDAN, WERE GIVEN THEM OUT OF THE TRIBE OF REUBEN, BEZER IN THE WILDERNESS WITH HER SUBURBS, AND JAHZAH WITH HER SUBURBS,

(79) "KEDEMOTH ALSO WITH HER SUBURBS, AND MEPHAATH WITH HER SUBURBS:

(80) "AND OUT OF THE TRIBE OF GAD; RAMOTH IN GILEAD WITH HER SUBURBS, AND MAHANAIM WITH HER SUBURBS,

(81) "AND HESHBON WITH HER SUBURBS, AND JAZER WITH HER SUBURBS."

The construction is:

1. As is obvious, the inheritance of the Levites was scattered all over Israel. In other words, they were given particular cities in the midst of other Tribes all over the nation. This fulfilled the Prophecy given by Jacob, which stated, *"I will divide them in Jacob, and scatter them in Israel"* (Gen. 49:7).

2. The Prophecy, of course, was a curse but, in essence, it was turned into a Blessing when *"Phinehas, the son of Eleazar, the son of Aaron the Priest, turned away the Wrath of God"* (Num. 25:11-18).

3. Israel had sinned by joining with the Moabites and the Midianites in the worship of Baal (Num. 25:1-3).

Phinehas took a stand, a bold stand, against the Israelites and the Moabites, both who were engaged in these acts, and by his act, became a Type of Christ, Who would defeat Satan at the Cross. The *"Everlasting Priesthood"* belongs to Christ and will belong to Him forever (Heb. 7:21-24). Phinehas, and all who make Christ their Lord and Saviour, as well, become a part of this *"Everlasting Priesthood."* John the Beloved wrote and stated:

"And has made us kings and priests unto God and His Father (made possible by what Christ did at the Cross, and only by what

NOTES

Christ did at the Cross)*; to Him be Glory and Dominion forever and ever. Amen."* (Christ is the Redeemer, so He deserves the *'Glory and Dominion,'* which will be His forever and ever)" (Rev. 1:6).

*"Sun of my soul, Thou Saviour Dear,
"It is not night if You be near;
"Oh may no Earthborn cloud arise,
"To hide You from Your Servant's eyes."*

*"When the soft dews of kindly sleep,
"My weary eyelids gently steep,
"Be my last thought, how sweet to rest,
"Forever on my Saviour's Breast."*

*"Abide with me from morn till eve,
"For without You I cannot live;
"Abide with me when night is nigh,
"For without You I dare not die."*

*"Come near and bless us when we wake,
"Ere through the world our way we take;
"Till, in the ocean of Your Love,
"We lose ourselves in Heaven above."*

CHAPTER 7

(1) "NOW THE SONS OF ISSACHAR WERE, TOLA, AND PUAH, JASHUB, AND SHIMROM, FOUR.

(2) "AND THE SONS OF TOLA; UZZI, AND REPHAIAH, AND JERIEL, AND JAHMAI, AND JIBSAM, AND SHEMUEL, HEADS OF THEIR FATHER'S HOUSE, TO WIT, OF TOLA: THEY WERE VALIANT MEN OF MIGHT IN THEIR GENERATIONS; WHOSE NUMBER WAS IN THE DAYS OF DAVID TWO AND TWENTY THOUSAND AND SIX HUNDRED.

(3) "AND THE SONS OF UZZI; IZRAHIAH: AND THE SONS OF IZRAHIAH; MICHAEL, AND OBADIAH, AND JOEL, ISHIAH, FIVE: ALL OF THEM CHIEF MEN.

(4) "AND WITH THEM, BY THEIR GENERATIONS, AFTER THE HOUSE OF THEIR FATHERS, WERE BANDS OF SOLDIERS FOR WAR, SIX AND THIRTY THOUSAND MEN: FOR THEY HAD MANY WIVES AND SONS.

(5) "AND THEIR BRETHREN AMONG ALL THE FAMILIES OF ISSACHAR WERE VALIANT MEN OF MIGHT, RECKONED IN ALL BY THEIR GENEALOGIES FOURSCORE AND SEVEN THOUSAND."

The overview is:

1. Chapter 7 denotes the generations or the genealogy of the Tribes of *"Issachar, Benjamin, Naphtali, Manasseh, Ephraim, and Asher."*

2. It should be understood that only partial genealogies of most of the Tribes of Israel are given.

3. The Tribe of Dan is not mentioned in these genealogies. The reason is not known.

Some have suggested that Dan went into idol worship; therefore, was omitted here and in Revelation, Chapter 7. However, all of the Tribes went into idol worship.

As well, it has been suggested that Dan may possibly be the Tribe from which the Antichrist will come. Genesis 49:17 does lend some credence to this theory. One thing is certain: the Holy Spirit left out Dan for a purpose and a reason. It definitely was not an oversight.

(6) "THE SONS OF BENJAMIN; BELA, AND BECHER, AND JEDIAEL, THREE.

(7) "AND THE SONS OF BELA; EZBON, AND UZZI, AND UZZIEL, AND JERIMOTH, AND IRI, FIVE; HEADS OF THE HOUSE OF THEIR FATHERS, MIGHTY MEN OF VALOUR; AND WERE RECKONED BY THEIR GENEALOGIES TWENTY AND TWO THOUSAND AND THIRTY AND FOUR.

(8) "AND THE SONS OF BECHER; ZEMIRA, AND JOASH, AND ELIEZER, AND ELIOENAI, AND OMRI, AND JERIMOTH, AND ABIAH, AND ANATHOTH, AND ALAMETH. ALL THESE ARE THE SONS OF BECHER.

(9) "AND THE NUMBER OF THEM, AFTER THEIR GENEALOGY BY THEIR GENERATIONS, HEADS OF THE HOUSE OF THEIR FATHERS, MIGHTY MEN OF VALOUR, WAS TWENTY THOUSAND AND TWO HUNDRED.

(10) "THE SONS ALSO OF JEDIAEL; BILHAN: AND THE SONS OF BILHAN; JEUSH, AND BENJAMIN, AND EHUD, AND CHENAANAH, AND ZETHAN, AND THARSHISH, AND AHISHAHAR.

NOTES

(11) "ALL THESE THE SONS OF JEDIAEL, BY THE HEADS OF THEIR FATHERS, MIGHTY MEN OF VALOUR, WERE SEVENTEEN THOUSAND AND TWO HUNDRED SOLDIERS, FIT TO GO OUT FOR WAR AND BATTLE.

(12) "SHUPPIM ALSO, AND HUPPIM, THE CHILDREN OF IR, AND HUSHIM, THE SONS OF AHER."

The pattern is:

1. Concerning the Tribes, several times the Word of God says, *"They were valiant men of might in their generations"* (Vs. 2). And then, in the Seventh Verse it says, *"mighty men of valour."*

The might and glory of Israel, when they were actually serving God, is almost beyond our comprehension. During the latter half of David's reign and the entirety of Solomon's reign, Israel was the mightiest nation on the Earth of that day.

2. The degree of intelligence possessed by these people so far eclipsed any other people or nation in the world that there was no comparison. No wonder when the Queen of Sheba saw the glory of Israel, the Scripture says, *"there was no spirit left in her"* (I Ki. 10:5). And then she said that what she had heard was not exaggeration, *"it was a true report"* (I Ki. 10:6). Israel only lost her way when she turned her back on God.

3. The Apostle Paul would ask the question, *"What advantage then has the Jew?"* (Rom. 3:1). And then he would answer, *"much every way"* (Rom. 3:2).

4. One day the glory of Israel will be reestablished. Paul, in effect, says, *"if, in consequence of their rebellion, the riches of God's Grace have come to the Gentile world, how much more will the world be blessed when Israel comes to her fullness of blessing again"* (Rom. 11:12)?

(13) "THE SONS OF NAPHTALI; JAHZIEL, AND GUNI, AND JEZER, AND SHALLUM, THE SONS OF BILHAH."

The overview is:

1. The Holy Spirit only gave this brief account, one Verse, concerning the descendants of Naphtali. According to Numbers 26:58-60, it was a large Tribe. So, we'll have to leave the reason for the brevity up to the Holy Spirit.

2. The Tribe of Naphtali later on covered the district called Galilee, referred to by some as *"the cradle of the Christian Faith."*

3. In fact, this area was the native home of most of the Apostles, and also, the home of our Lord.

4. Matthew said concerning this Tribe, and I quote from THE EXPOSITOR'S STUDY BIBLE:

"Now when Jesus had heard that John was cast into prison (John's Ministry was now finished; he had properly introduced Christ), *He* (Jesus) *departed into Galilee* (where the central core of His Ministry would be);

"And leaving Nazareth (refers to His rejection there [Lk. 4:16-30]), *He came and dwelt in Capernaum* (made this city His Headquarters), *which is upon the sea coast* (refers to the Sea of Galilee), *in the borders of Zabulon and Nephthalim* (refers to these two Tribes bordering the Sea of Galilee):

"That it might be fulfilled which was spoken by Isaiah the Prophet, saying (Isaiah prophesied of Christ more than any other Prophet),

"The land of Zabulon, and the land of Nephthalim, by the way of the sea (Sea of Galilee), *beyond Jordan, Galilee of the Gentiles* (the great Roman Road ran near the Sea of Galilee from Damascus; almost all Gentiles traveling in this direction did so on this road; the Headquarters of Christ was within the confines of the Tribe of Naphtali);

"The people which sat in darkness (implies a settled acceptance of this darkness; the moral darkness was even greater than the national misery) *saw great Light* (Christ is the Light of the world, and the only True Light); *and to them which sat in the region and shadow of death* (spiritual death is the result of this spiritual darkness) *Light* (Spiritual Illumination in Christ) *is sprung up.*

"From that time (the move to Capernaum) *Jesus began to preach* (the major method of the proclamation of the Gospel), *and to say, Repent* (beginning His Ministry, the first word used by Christ, as recorded by Matthew, was 'Repent'); *for the Kingdom of Heaven is at hand* (the Kingdom from Heaven, headed up by Christ, for the purpose of reestablishing the Kingdom of God

NOTES

over the Earth; the Kingdom was rejected by Israel)" (Mat. 4:12-17).

(14) "THE SONS OF MANASSEH; ASHRIEL, WHOM SHE BORE: (BUT HIS CONCUBINE THE ARAMITESS BORE MACHIR THE FATHER OF GILEAD:

(15) "AND MACHIR TOOK TO WIFE THE SISTER OF HUPPIM AND SHUPPIM, WHOSE SISTER'S NAME WAS MAACHAH;) AND THE NAME OF THE SECOND WAS ZELOPHEHAD: AND ZELOPHEHAD HAD DAUGHTERS.

(16) "AND MAACHAH THE WIFE OF MACHIR BORE A SON, AND SHE CALLED HIS NAME PERESH; AND THE NAME OF HIS BROTHER WAS SHERESH; AND HIS SONS WERE ULAM AND RAKEM.

(17) "AND THE SONS OF ULAM; BEDAN. THESE WERE THE SONS OF GILEAD, THE SON OF MACHIR, THE SON OF MANASSEH.

(18) "AND HIS SISTER HAMMOLEKETH BORE ISHOD, AND ABIEZER, AND MAHALAH.

(19) "AND THE SONS OF SHEMIDAH WERE, AHIAN, AND SHECHEM, AND LIKHI, AND ANIAM."

The overview is:

1. (Vs. 15) Zelophehad is mentioned here, with his fame being derived from the Faith of his daughters (Num. 26:33).

2. (Vs. 15) God always honors Faith. Tragically, doubt never dies, unless washed by the Blood of Jesus; and, gloriously, Faith never dies, but extends its influence forever.

3. In a sense, the daughters of Zelophehad were able, by their Faith, to cause an extension to the Law to be added by the Lord.

FAITH

A man by the name of Zelophehad of the Tribe of Manasseh had five daughters. Their names were *"Mahlah, Noah, Hoglah, Milcah, and Tirzah."*

Their father died in the wilderness, and now, when Moses began to speak of the land of Canaan being divided up among the Tribes, that is when the Children of Israel arrived there, these five daughters of Zelophehad posed this question to the great Lawgiver. They said:

"Why should the name of our father be

done away from among his family, because he has no son? Give unto us therefore a possession among the brethren of our father.

"*And Moses brought their cause before the LORD. ('The Faith of the daughters of Zelophehad presents a striking contrast to the unbelief of those who fell in the desert. While yet in the wilderness, they claim by Faith the unseen fields of Canaan; and, further, their Faith leaped a barrier, which both nature and Law set before them.*

"'*This was precious and refreshing to the Heart of God; and, accordingly, special legislation was given to meet their Faith'* — Williams.)

"*And the LORD spoke unto Moses, saying,*

"*The daughters of Zelophehad speak right: you shall surely give them a possession of an inheritance among their father's brethren; and you shall cause the inheritance of their father to pass unto them*" (Num. 27:4-7).

We must ever understand that God delights in Faith. In fact, that is the only way that we can receive anything from God. He rewards nothing on the basis of merit, of works, etc., but all on the basis of Faith. We Believers, it seems, have a hard time in understanding that.

(20) "AND THE SONS OF EPHRAIM; SHUTHELAH, AND BERED HIS SON, AND TAHATH HIS SON, AND ELADAH HIS SON, AND TAHATH HIS SON,

(21) "AND ZABAD HIS SON, AND SHUTHELAH HIS SON, AND EZER, AND ELEAD, WHOM THE MEN OF GATH WHO WERE BORN IN THAT LAND KILLED, BECAUSE THEY CAME DOWN TO TAKE AWAY THEIR CATTLE.

(22) "AND EPHRAIM THEIR FATHER MOURNED MANY DAYS, AND HIS BRETHREN CAME TO COMFORT HIM.

(23) "AND WHEN HE WENT IN TO HIS WIFE, SHE CONCEIVED, AND BORE A SON, AND HE CALLED HIS NAME BERIAH, BECAUSE IT WENT EVIL WITH HIS HOUSE.

(24) "(AND HIS DAUGHTER WAS SHERAH, WHO BUILT BETH-HORON THE NETHER, AND THE UPPER, AND UZZEN-SHERAH.)

(25) "AND REPHAH WAS HIS SON, ALSO RESHEPH, AND TELAH HIS SON, AND TAHAN HIS SON,

(26) "LAADAN HIS SON, AMMIHUD HIS SON, ELISHAMA HIS SON,

(27) "NON HIS SON, JEHOSHUAH HIS SON.

(28) "AND THEIR POSSESSIONS AND HABITATIONS WERE, BETH-EL AND THE TOWNS THEREOF, AND EASTWARD NAARAN, AND WESTWARD GEZER, WITH THE TOWNS THEREOF; SHECHEM ALSO AND THE TOWNS THEREOF, UNTO GAZA AND THE TOWNS THEREOF:

(29) "AND BY THE BORDERS OF THE CHILDREN OF MANASSEH, BETH-SHEAN AND HER TOWNS, TAANACH AND HER TOWNS, MEGIDDO AND HER TOWNS, DOR AND HER TOWNS. IN THESE DWELT THE CHILDREN OF JOSEPH THE SON OF ISRAEL."

The exegesis is:

1. Understanding that the Holy Spirit went into great detail to give us an account of these various families, we are led to know and understand just how important that Christ actually is; for all of these individuals in some way are in the lineage of Christ in His Incarnation.

2. From this we should understand that the Lord presently is keeping records of all that we say and do as Believers. We must never forget that.

3. All of this tells us how important that Believers are as it regards the Work of God.

(30) "THE SONS OF ASHER; IMNAH, AND ISUAH, AND ISHUAI, AND BERIAH, AND SERAH THEIR SISTER.

(31) "AND THE SONS OF BERIAH; HEBER, AND MALCHIEL, WHO IS THE FATHER OF BIRZAVITH.

(32) "AND HEBER BEGAT JAPHLET, AND SHOMER, AND HOTHAM, AND SHUA THEIR SISTER.

(33) "AND THE SONS OF JAPHLET; PASACH, AND BIMHAL, AND ASHVATH. THESE ARE THE CHILDREN OF JAPHLET.

(34) "AND THE SONS OF SHAMER; AHI, AND ROHGAH, JEHUBBAH, AND ARAM.

(35) "AND THE SONS OF HIS BROTHER HELEM; ZOPHAH, AND IMNA, AND SHELESH, AND AMAL.

(36) "THE SONS OF ZOPHAH; SUAH, AND HAR-NEPHER, AND SHUAL, AND BERI, AND IMRAH,

(37) "BEZER, AND HOD, AND SHAMMA, AND SHILSHAH, AND ITHRAN, AND BEERA.

(38) "AND THE SONS OF JETHER; JEPHUNNEH, AND PISPAH, AND ARA.

(39) "AND THE SONS OF ULLA; ARAH, AND HANIEL, AND REZIA.

(40) "ALL THESE WERE THE CHILDREN OF ASHER, HEADS OF THEIR FATHER'S HOUSE, CHOICE AND MIGHTY MEN OF VALOUR, CHIEF OF THE PRINCES. AND THE NUMBER THROUGHOUT THE GENEALOGY OF THEM WHO WERE APT TO THE WAR AND TO BATTLE WAS TWENTY AND SIX THOUSAND MEN."

The overview is:

1. As Israel was the Glory of the Lord, at least when they were serving the Lord, one day they shall occupy this position again.

2. Two conspicuous features are presented in these Chapters — *"genealogy and warfare."* Only those are numbered who were found in the registers, and these are all soldiers and *"mighty men of valor."*

3. They are described in the Seventh Chapter (Vss. 11-40) as *"fit to go out for war"* and *"apt to the war."* Thus it is with all of God's People.

Every Believer is a light of God to the world, or at least, we should be. As well, we *"war"* against the flesh and against the powers of darkness.

4. The name of every Believer is inscribed in the *"Lamb's Book of Life,"* of which these genealogies are somewhat of an example. We know our genealogy, and we can trace our pedigree. We are *"sons and daughters of the Lord God Almighty."* Christ is our Elder Brother. We are all *"soldiers."* And to this end we should function as *"good soldiers of Jesus Christ"* and, therefore, *"war a good warfare."*

CHAPTER 8

(1) "NOW BENJAMIN BEGAT BELA HIS FIRSTBORN, ASHBEL THE SECOND, AND AHARAH THE THIRD,

(2) "NOHAH THE FOURTH, AND RAPHA THE FIFTH.

(3) "AND THE SONS OF BELA WERE, ADDAR, AND GERA, AND ABIHUD,

(4) "AND ABISHUA, AND NAAMAN, AND AHOAH,

(5) "AND GERA, AND SHEPHUPHAN, AND HURAM.

(6) "AND THESE ARE THE SONS OF EHUD: THESE ARE THE HEADS OF THE FATHERS OF THE INHABITANTS OF GEBA, AND THEY REMOVED THEM TO MANAHATH:

(7) "AND NAAMAN, AND AHIAH, AND GERA, HE REMOVED THEM, AND BEGAT UZZA, AND AHIHUD.

(8) "AND SHAHARAIM BEGAT CHILDREN IN THE COUNTRY OF MOAB, AFTER HE HAD SENT THEM AWAY; HUSHIM AND BAARA WERE HIS WIVES.

(9) "AND HE BEGAT OF HODESH HIS WIFE, JOBAB, AND ZIBIA, AND MESHA, AND MALCHAM,

(10) "AND JEUZ, AND SHACHIA, AND MIRMA. THESE WERE HIS SONS, HEADS OF THE FATHERS.

(11) "AND OF HUSHIM HE BEGAT ABITUB, AND ELPAAL.

(12) "THE SONS OF ELPAAL; EBER, AND MISHAM, AND SHAMED, WHO BUILT ONO, AND LOD, WITH THE TOWNS THEREOF:

(13) "BERIAH ALSO, AND SHEMA, WHO WERE HEADS OF THE FATHERS OF THE INHABITANTS OF AIJALON, WHO DROVE AWAY THE INHABITANTS OF GATH:

(14) "AND AHIO, SHASHAK, AND JEREMOTH,

(15) "AND ZEBADIAH, AND ARAD, AND ADER,

(16) "AND MICHAEL, AND ISPAH, AND JOHA, THE SONS OF BERIAH;

(17) "AND ZEBADIAH, AND MESHULLAM, AND HEZEKI, AND HEBER,

(18) "ISHMERAI ALSO, AND JEZLIAH, AND JOBAB, THE SONS OF ELPAAL;

(19) "AND JAKIM, AND ZICHRI, AND ZABDI,

(20) "AND ELIENAI, AND ZILTHAI, AND ELIEL,

(21) "AND ADAIAH, AND BERAIAH, AND SHIMRATH, AND SONS OF SHIMHI;

(22) "AND ISHPAN, AND HEBER, AND ELIEL,

(23) "AND ABDON, AND ZICHRI, AND HANAN,

(24) "AND HANANIAH, AND ELAM, AND ANTOTHIJAH,

(25) "AND IPHEDEIAH, AND PENUEL, THE SONS OF SHASHAK;

(26) "AND SHAMSHERAI, AND SHEHARIAH, AND ATHALIAH,

(27) "AND JARESIAH, AND ELIAH, AND ZICHRI, THE SONS OF JEROHAM.

(28) "THESE WERE HEADS OF THE FATHERS, BY THEIR GENERATIONS, CHIEF MEN. THESE DWELT IN JERUSALEM.

(29) "AND AT GIBEON DWELT THE FATHER OF GIBEON; WHOSE WIFE'S NAME WAS MAACHAH:

(30) "AND HIS FIRSTBORN SON ABDON, AND ZUR, AND KISH, AND BAAL, AND NADAB,

(31) "AND GEDOR, AND AHIO, AND ZACHER.

(32) "AND MIKLOTH BEGAT SHIMEAH. AND THESE ALSO DWELT WITH THEIR BRETHREN IN JERUSALEM, OVER AGAINST THEM."

The overview is:

1. The phrase of Verse 28, *"these dwelt in Jerusalem,"* proves that the Tribe of Benjamin adhered to the worship of the True God and remained loyal to Judah.

2. (Vs. 28) As well, it seems that Simeon, whose inheritance was within the inheritance of Judah, had remained loyal also. We speak of the division of the kingdom, with Judah being the southern kingdom, and Israel the northern kingdom.

3. The Tribe of Benjamin has already been partly dealt with. It is addressed again because of Saul, the first king of Israel, who came from this Tribe.

(33) "AND NER BEGAT KISH, AND KISH BEGAT SAUL, AND SAUL BEGAT JONATHAN, AND MALCHI-SHUA, AND ABINADAB, AND ESH-BAAL.

(34) "AND THE SON OF JONATHAN WAS MERIB-BAAL; AND MERIB-BAAL BEGAT MICAH.

NOTES

(35) "AND THE SONS OF MICAH WERE, PITHON, AND MELECH, AND TAREA, AND AHAZ.

(36) "AND AHAZ BEGAT JEHOADAH; AND JEHOADAH BEGAT ALEMETH, AND AZMAVETH, AND ZIMRI; AND ZIMRI BEGAT MOZA,

(37) "AND MOZA BEGAT BINEA: RAPHA WAS HIS SON, ELEASAH HIS SON, AZEL HIS SON:

(38) "AND AZEL HAD SIX SONS, WHOSE NAMES ARE THESE, AZRIKAM, BOCHERU, AND ISHMAEL, AND SHEARIAH, AND OBADIAH, AND HANAN. ALL THESE WERE THE SONS OF AZEL.

(39) "AND THE SONS OF ESHEK HIS BROTHER WERE, ULAM HIS FIRSTBORN, JEHUSH THE SECOND, AND ELIPHELET THE THIRD.

(40) "AND THE SONS OF ULAM WERE MIGHTY MEN OF VALOUR, ARCHERS, AND HAD MANY SONS, AND SONS' SONS, AN HUNDRED AND FIFTY. ALL THESE ARE OF THE SONS OF BENJAMIN."

The pattern is:

1. From the Tribe of Benjamin would come the first king of Israel, *"Saul."* As well, from the Tribe of Benjamin would come Saul's namesake, *"Saul"* (Paul of the New Testament, one of the greatest men of God who ever lived).

2. It is ironic that Saul, the first king of Israel, was thought to have brought fame and glory to the Tribe of Benjamin, but instead, brought disgrace. Yet, Saul of Tarsus (Paul), who was thought to have brought only disgrace to the Tribe of Benjamin, instead, brought the Tribe everlasting glory.

3. Israel will recognize this when once again they are restored in the coming great Kingdom Age. That which man chooses has no merit with God. That which God chooses, sadly, has no merit with man.

CHAPTER 9

(1) "SO ALL ISRAEL WERE RECKONED BY GENEALOGIES; AND, BEHOLD, THEY WERE WRITTEN IN THE BOOK OF THE KINGS OF ISRAEL AND JUDAH,

WHO WERE CARRIED AWAY TO BABYLON FOR THEIR TRANSGRESSION.

(2) "NOW THE FIRST INHABITANTS WHO DWELT IN THEIR POSSESSIONS IN THEIR CITIES WERE, THE ISRAELITES, THE PRIESTS, LEVITES, AND THE NETHINIMS.

(3) "AND IN JERUSALEM DWELT OF THE CHILDREN OF JUDAH, AND OF THE CHILDREN OF BENJAMIN, AND OF THE CHILDREN OF EPHRAIM, AND MANASSEH;

(4) "UTHAI THE SON OF AMMIHUD, THE SON OF OMRI, THE SON OF IMRI, THE SON OF BANI, OF THE CHILDREN OF PHAREZ THE SON OF JUDAH.

(5) "AND OF THE SHILONITES; ASAIAH THE FIRSTBORN, AND HIS SONS.

(6) "AND OF THE SONS OF ZERAH; JEUEL, AND THEIR BRETHREN, SIX HUNDRED AND NINETY.

(7) "AND OF THE SONS OF BENJAMIN; SALLU THE SON OF MESHULLAM, THE SON OF HODAVIAH, THE SON OF HASENUAH,

(8) "AND IBNEIAH THE SON OF JEROHAM, AND ELAH THE SON OF UZZI, THE SON OF MICHRI, AND MESHULLAM THE SON OF SHEPHATHIAH, THE SON OF REUEL, THE SON OF IBNIJAH;

(9) "AND THEIR BRETHREN, ACCORDING TO THEIR GENERATIONS, NINE HUNDRED AND FIFTY AND SIX. ALL THESE MEN WERE CHIEF OF THE FATHERS IN THE HOUSE OF THEIR FATHERS."

The construction is:

1. The book mentioned in Verse 1 is a book we do not now have, but which, no doubt, contained a complete record of the genealogies of every family in Israel. From this, the author of Chronicles took only a part to serve his purpose of identifying certain key men in the history of the nation, by giving their background, so that something could be known of the ancestors of the coming Messiah.

2. (Vs. 1) During the time of Christ, the genealogy of every Tribe, and also of every family in Israel, was kept in the Temple. This was very important for several reasons:

• Each family in Israel could trace their ancestry all the way back to Abraham.

NOTES

• Each family could know to which Tribe they belonged.

• As well, Israel knew that the Messiah was to come through the Tribe of Judah (Gen. 49:10), and that, if the kingly line of David from the Tribe of Judah had continued, Jesus would now be the king of Israel. So, there was no excuse for Israel not to know His identity.

3. (Vs. 2) It is believed that the *"Nethinims"* were the descendants of the Gibeonites who deceived Joshua at the beginning of the occupation of Canaan, and who were made *"hewers of wood and drawers of water unto all the congregation"* (Josh. 9:21). This referred to wood and water for the sacrifices at the Tabernacle, and then the Temple.

4. (Vs. 3) Those of the two Tribes of Ephraim and Manasseh were representative of the ten Tribes, for the northern ten-Tribe kingdom was often called *"Ephraim."*

(10) "AND OF THE PRIESTS; JEDAIAH, AND JEHOIARIB, AND JACHIN,

(11) "AND AZARIAH THE SON OF HILKIAH, THE SON OF MESHULLAM, THE SON OF ZADOK, THE SON OF MERAIOTH, THE SON OF AHITUB, THE RULER OF THE HOUSE OF GOD;

(12) "AND ADAIAH THE SON OF JEROHAM, THE SON OF PASHUR, THE SON OF MALCHIJAH, AND MAASIAI THE SON OF ADIEL, THE SON OF JAHZERAH, THE SON OF MESHULLAM, THE SON OF MESHILLEMITH, THE SON OF IMMER;

(13) "AND THEIR BRETHREN, HEADS OF THE HOUSE OF THEIR FATHERS, A THOUSAND AND SEVEN HUNDRED AND THREESCORE; VERY ABLE MEN FOR THE WORK OF THE SERVICE OF THE HOUSE OF GOD.

(14) "AND OF THE LEVITES; SHEMAIAH THE SON OF HASSHUB, THE SON OF AZRIKAM, THE SON OF HASHABIAH, OF THE SONS OF MERARI;

(15) "AND BAKBAKKAR, HERESH, AND GALAL, AND MATTANIAH THE SON OF MICAH, THE SON OF ZICHRI, THE SON OF ASAPH;

(16) "AND OBADIAH THE SON OF SHEMAIAH, THE SON OF GALAL, THE SON OF JEDUTHUN, AND BERECHIAH THE SON OF ASA, THE SON OF ELKANAH,

THAT DWELT IN THE VILLAGES OF THE NETOPHATHITES.

(17) "AND THE PORTERS WERE, SHALLUM, AND AKKUB, AND TALMON, AND AHIMAN, AND THEIR BRETHREN: SHALLUM WAS THE CHIEF;

(18) "WHO HITHERTO WAITED IN THE KING'S GATE EASTWARD: THEY WERE PORTERS IN THE COMPANIES OF THE CHILDREN OF LEVI.

(19) "AND SHALLUM THE SON OF KORE, THE SON OF EBIASAPH, THE SON OF KORAH, AND HIS BRETHREN, OF THE HOUSE OF HIS FATHER, THE KORAHITES, WERE OVER THE WORK OF THE SERVICE, KEEPERS OF THE GATES OF THE TABERNACLE: AND THEIR FATHERS, BEING OVER THE HOST OF THE LORD, WERE KEEPERS OF THE ENTRY.

(20) "AND PHINEHAS THE SON OF ELEAZAR WAS THE RULER OVER THEM IN TIME PAST, AND THE LORD WAS WITH HIM.

(21) "AND ZECHARIAH THE SON OF MESHELEMIAH WAS PORTER OF THE DOOR OF THE TABERNACLE OF THE CONGREGATION.

(22) "ALL THESE WHICH WERE CHOSEN TO BE PORTERS IN THE GATES WERE TWO HUNDRED AND TWELVE. THESE WERE RECKONED BY THEIR GENEALOGY IN THEIR VILLAGES, WHOM DAVID AND SAMUEL THE SEER DID ORDAIN IN THEIR SET OFFICE.

(23) "SO THEY AND THEIR CHILDREN HAD THE OVERSIGHT OF THE GATES OF THE HOUSE OF THE LORD, NAMELY, THE HOUSE OF THE TABERNACLE, BY WARDS.

(24) "IN FOUR QUARTERS WERE THE PORTERS, TOWARD THE EAST, WEST, NORTH, AND SOUTH.

(25) "AND THEIR BRETHREN, WHICH WERE IN THEIR VILLAGES, WERE TO COME AFTER SEVEN DAYS FROM TIME TO TIME WITH THEM.

(26) "FOR THESE LEVITES, THE FOUR CHIEF PORTERS, WERE IN THEIR SET OFFICE, AND WERE OVER THE CHAMBERS AND TREASURIES OF THE HOUSE OF GOD.

NOTES

(27) "AND THEY LODGED ROUND ABOUT THE HOUSE OF GOD, BECAUSE THE CHARGE WAS UPON THEM, AND THE OPENING THEREOF EVERY MORNING PERTAINED TO THEM.

(28) "AND CERTAIN OF THEM HAD THE CHARGE OF THE MINISTERING VESSELS, THAT THEY SHOULD BRING THEM IN AND OUT BY TALE.

(29) "SOME OF THEM ALSO WERE APPOINTED TO OVERSEE THE VESSELS, AND ALL THE INSTRUMENTS OF THE SANCTUARY, AND THE FINE FLOUR, AND THE WINE, AND THE OIL, AND THE FRANKINCENSE, AND THE SPICES.

(30) "AND SOME OF THE SONS OF THE PRIESTS MADE THE OINTMENT OF THE SPICES.

(31) "AND MATTITHIAH, ONE OF THE LEVITES, WHO WAS THE FIRSTBORN OF SHALLUM THE KORAHITE, HAD THE SET OFFICE OVER THE THINGS THAT WERE MADE IN THE PANS.

(32) "AND OTHER OF THEIR BRETHREN, OF THE SONS OF THE KOHATHITES, WERE OVER THE SHEWBREAD, TO PREPARE IT EVERY SABBATH.

(33) "AND THESE ARE THE SINGERS, CHIEF OF THE FATHERS OF THE LEVITES, WHO REMAINING IN THE CHAMBERS WERE FREE: FOR THEY WERE EMPLOYED IN THAT WORK DAY AND NIGHT.

(34) "THESE CHIEF FATHERS OF THE LEVITES WERE CHIEF THROUGHOUT THEIR GENERATIONS; THESE DWELT AT JERUSALEM.

The exegesis is:

1. Verses 1 through 34 pertained to those who came back to the land of Israel from Babylonian captivity.

2. The phrase of Verse 13, *"Very able men for the work of the service of the House of God,"* was spoken by the Holy Spirit. Evidently this pertained to the consecration of these individuals, whomever they may have been.

3. Concerning *"Phinehas"* of Verse 20, the Scripture says, *"And the LORD was with him."* What a wonderful thing to be said of anyone.

4. Verse 22 proclaims the fact that Samuel

and David counseled together and received Revelations of the coming Temple worship.

5. The phrase of Verse 27, *"The charge was upon them,"* means, among other things, that they took this charge very, very seriously. We should understand that the charge most definitely is upon us presently as well!

6. Those of Verse 29 who were *"appointed to oversee the vessels, and all the instruments of the Sanctuary, and the fine flour, and the wine, and the oil, and the frankincense, and the spices,"* all had to do with worship, which was so very, very important. How many of us under the New Covenant have been *"appointed,"* but have not discharged that appointment nearly as we should have?

7. We find in Verse 33 that the *"singers"* were very important to the worship of God, as should be obvious. The Scripture says of them, *"for they were employed in that work day and night."*

(35) "AND IN GIBEON DWELT THE FATHER OF GIBEON, JEHIEL, WHOSE WIFE'S NAME WAS MAACHAH:

(36) "AND HIS FIRSTBORN SON ABDON, THEN ZUR, AND KISH, AND BAAL, AND NER, AND NADAB,

(37) "AND GEDOR, AND AHIO, AND ZECHARIAH, AND MIKLOTH.

(38) "AND MIKLOTH BEGAT SHIMEAM. AND THEY ALSO DWELT WITH THEIR BRETHREN AT JERUSALEM, OVER AGAINST THEIR BRETHREN.

(39) "AND NER BEGAT KISH; AND KISH BEGAT SAUL; AND SAUL BEGAT JONATHAN, AND MALCHI-SHUA, AND ABINADAB, AND ESH-BAAL.

(40) "AND THE SON OF JONATHAN WAS MERIB-BAAL: AND MERIB-BAAL BEGAT MICAH.

(41) "AND THE SONS OF MICAH WERE PITHON, AND MELECH, AND TAHREA, AND AHAZ.

(42) "AND AHAZ BEGAT JARAH; AND JARAH BEGAT ALEMETH, AND AZMAVETH, AND ZIMRI; AND ZIMRI BEGAT MOZA;

(43) "AND MOZA BEGAT BINEA; AND REPHAIAH HIS SON, ELEASAH HIS SON, AZEL HIS SON.

NOTES

(44) "AND AZEL HAD SIX SONS, WHOSE NAMES ARE THESE, AZRIKAM, BOCHERU, AND ISHMAEL, AND SHEARIAH, AND OBADIAH, AND HANAN: THESE WERE THE SONS OF AZEL.

The construction is:

1. Those listed in Verses 35 through 44 are in some way related to Saul, the first king of Israel.

2. If it is to be noticed, only a tiny bit of information is given as it regards Saul, but with basically the entirety of the Book of I Chronicles given over to David.

3. As it regards those who live a life of disobedience to the Lord, there is very little that one can say. As it regards those who strive to serve the Lord, even as did David, there is much to say, because everything then becomes important.

"Come, we who love the Lord and let our joys be known;
"Join in a song with sweet accord, and thus surround the Throne."

"Let those refuse to sing, who never knew our God;
"But Children of the Heavenly King may speak their joys abroad."

"The Hill of Zion yields a thousand sacred sweets,
"Before we reach the Heavenly fields or walk the golden streets."

"Then let our songs abound and every tear be dry;
"We're marching through Emmanuel's ground to fairer worlds on high."

CHAPTER 10

(1) "NOW THE PHILISTINES FOUGHT AGAINST ISRAEL; AND THE MEN OF ISRAEL FLED FROM BEFORE THE PHILISTINES, AND FELL DOWN KILLED IN MOUNT GILBOA.

(2) "AND THE PHILISTINES FOLLOWED HARD AFTER SAUL, AND AFTER HIS SONS; AND THE PHILISTINES KILLED JONATHAN, AND ABINADAB, AND MALCHI-SHUA, THE SONS OF SAUL.

(3) "AND THE BATTLE WENT SORE AGAINST SAUL, AND THE ARCHERS HIT HIM, AND HE WAS WOUNDED OF THE ARCHERS.

(4) "THEN SAID SAUL TO HIS ARMOURBEARER, DRAW YOUR SWORD, AND THRUST ME THROUGH THEREWITH; LEST THESE UNCIRCUMCISED COME AND ABUSE ME. BUT HIS ARMOURBEARER WOULD NOT; FOR HE WAS SORE AFRAID. SO SAUL TOOK A SWORD, AND FELL UPON IT.

(5) "AND WHEN HIS ARMOURBEARER SAW THAT SAUL WAS DEAD, HE FELL LIKEWISE ON THE SWORD, AND DIED.

(6) "SO SAUL DIED, AND HIS THREE SONS, AND ALL HIS HOUSE DIED TOGETHER."

The exegesis is:

1. (Vs. 1) The Holy Spirit, in the last ten Verses of the Ninth Chapter, recites the pedigree of King Saul, and then, in Chapter 10, repeats the circumstances of that monarch's death, which thus presents an introduction to the kingdom of David.

2. The sons of Saul listed in Verse 2 were the ones who accompanied him into the battle. There were other sons who stayed at home, and did not die. The Holy Spirit places Jonathan's name first. Of all of these, Jonathan was the only one who was godly, at least, that is known.

3. (Vs. 4) Saul committed suicide! He began so well, and concluded so poorly. He failed to defeat the enemies within, which were self-will, jealousy, and pride; therefore, the enemy without, *"the Philistines,"* ultimately defeated him. This should be a lesson to us!

DISOBEDIENCE

On one of our trips to Israel, we were coming back from the city of Tiberias, located on the western shore of the Sea of Galilee, journeying to Jerusalem. We were paralleling the Jordan River on the Israeli side.

That early morning, with the weather absolutely beautiful, we had traveled about 25 miles, I suppose, from Tiberias, when the guide spoke to me and motioned to his right. He said, *"There is Mt. Gilboa where Saul and Jonathan were killed."*

NOTES

Having visited Israel many times, and always interested in the sites of Biblical happenings, I couldn't take my eyes from this small mountain. Located in the valley of Jezreel, it is small, as mountains go, only about 600 feet high at its summit. Its slopes were gentle, as I viewed it from about a mile away. As stated, I could not take my eyes from it until we were out of sight.

My mind raced to the happenings recorded here in I Chronicles and also in the last Chapter of I Samuel.

I'm certain it was my imagination, but it seemed that I could hear the clash of armor, the neighing of the horses, and the din of battle. And so, this was where king Saul died!

That day, as these thoughts filled my mind, and I watched the mountain slip out of view, a great sadness filled my heart, even as it does attempting to write this account.

It didn't have to be this way. Saul in many ways was a great champion for Israel. One thing one can say about him is that he fought the battles of the Lord even to the end. So, what happened?

As always, it was a matter of disobedience.

And, what causes disobedience as it regards the heart of the Child of God, and as it pertains to the Word of God?

Probably the best answer is self-will!

The Lord loved Saul, and at the beginning, there is some evidence that Saul may have loved the Lord. But his life is chronicled by disobedience. He didn't want to consecrate to the Lord, thereby desiring to do things his own way, which, as always, spells disaster.

He could have been so blessed by the Lord, with his house and his family increasing greatly so, but despite the fact that the Lord dealt with him again and again, his situation steadily deteriorated.

At the first he loved David, but that love, which obviously was not the God-kind of love, quickly deteriorated until he came to hate the *"sweet singer of Israel,"* and without a cause. And now he dies, and for all we know, without God.

Perhaps at the very last he cried to God for Mercy, and if he did, the Lord most definitely would have granted it; however, the evidence is to the contrary.

If that, in fact, is the case, at this moment

Saul is in Hell and will be there forever and forever.

THE INNER FOES AND THE OUTER FOES

Saul was never able to defeat his demons, and inasmuch as he was not able to defeat the inner foes, the outer foes, i.e., *"Philistines,"* ultimately destroyed him. We should not allow this lesson to be lost on us.

Satan seeks to destroy the Believer first of all by the means of the flesh. What do we mean by that?

The *"flesh"* constitutes our own personal ability, strength, fortitude, courage, intellectualism, education, talent, knowledge, etc. Those things are not necessarily wrong within themselves. But, where the wrong comes in is when we depend on them to try to live this Christian life. Due to the Fall, man is incapable, at least within himself, of being what he ought to be before the Lord and doing what he ought to do. But unfortunately, that's the way, by the flesh, that most Christians attempt to live this life.

As a result, problems such as lust, jealousy, envy, malice, pride, etc., begin to hold sway within our lives, with, in fact, the situation becoming worse and worse, no matter how hard we try otherwise. In fact, this is what the entirety of the Seventh Chapter of Romans is all about. It proclaims the personal experience of the Apostle Paul after he was Saved, baptized with the Holy Spirit, called to preach the Gospel, and serving as a Minister, and actually, as an Apostle. But despite all of that, he found he could not live victoriously.

To Paul's credit, there was no one else in the world at that particular time who understood God's Prescribed Order of Victory. That great Truth, which is the meaning of the New Covenant, had not yet been given. In fact, it was given to the Apostle Paul, and he gave it to us.

THE CROSS OF CHRIST

When the Lord revealed this great Truth to the Apostle, which he gave to us in his fourteen Epistles, we find that the central focus is the Cross of Christ. While everything that Christ did was of the utmost significance, still, it was at the Cross that the Victory was won, and the Cross alone.

Some would argue that it's the Resurrection which proclaims the meaning of the New Covenant; however, Paul never said that. While the Resurrection, of course, was and is of extreme significance, as ought to be overly obvious, still, the Resurrection was not the focal point of Redemption, neither, in a sense, did it contribute anything toward that Finished Work. One could say that the Resurrection ratified what had already been done, but that's as far as one can go, at least Scripturally.

Everything was done at the Cross. If anything had been left lacking, then Jesus could not have said, *"It is finished."*

Due to the fact that Jesus atoned for all sin at the Cross, past, present, and future, at least for all who will believe, this means that the Resurrection was not in doubt. Actually, if He had failed to atone for even one sin, He could not have been raised from the dead (Rom. 6:23). One might say it this way:

The efficaciousness of the Cross did not depend on the Resurrection; the truth is, the Resurrection depended on the Cross. So, Paul would say: *"Christ sent me not to baptize, but to preach the Gospel, not with wisdom of words, lest the Cross of Christ be made of none effect"* (I Cor. 1:17).

If it is to be noticed, he didn't say, *"Lest the Resurrection be of none effect."*

Likewise, he said: *"For the preaching of the Cross is to them who perish foolishness, but to we who are Saved, it is the Power of God* (I Cor. 1:18). He did not say, *"For the preaching of the Resurrection...."*

He also said, *"God forbid that I should glory, save in the Cross of our Lord Jesus Christ..."* (Gal. 6:14). He did not say, *"But God forbid that I should glory save in the Resurrection...."*

This in no way is meant to minimize the veracity of the Resurrection, as should be obvious. But, it is meant to understand it correctly and, as well, that the emphasis be placed where it is placed Scripturally, and that is the Cross.

As another example, in the writing of the great Book of Hebrews, Paul mentioned (and I believe Paul wrote Hebrews), the

Resurrection only once, and that was in connection with the Cross (Heb. 13:20). The balance of that great Book has to do exclusively with Who Jesus was, and what Jesus did, with the latter speaking of the Cross.

Understanding all of this, the only way the Believer can live a victorious life, can be what he ought to be in Christ, and can grow in Grace and the Knowledge of the Lord, is that his Faith be placed exclusively in Christ and what Christ did at the Cross, which then gives the Holy Spirit latitude to work within his life. In brief, that is God's Prescribed Order of Victory. He has no other, because no other is needed.

Getting back to the original thought, unless the Believer understands how to overcome the flesh, which is always through the Cross, outer foes will ultimately drag him down. It did so with Saul; it's done so with untold millions of others; and, it will do the same for you.

(7) "AND WHEN ALL THE MEN OF ISRAEL THAT WERE IN THE VALLEY SAW THAT THEY FLED, AND THAT SAUL AND HIS SONS WERE DEAD, THEN THEY FORSOOK THEIR CITIES, AND FLED: AND THE PHILISTINES CAME AND DWELT IN THEM.

(8) "AND IT CAME TO PASS ON THE MORROW, WHEN THE PHILISTINES CAME TO STRIP THE SLAIN, THAT THEY FOUND SAUL AND HIS SONS FALLEN IN MOUNT GILBOA.

(9) "AND WHEN THEY HAD STRIPPED HIM, THEY TOOK HIS HEAD, AND HIS ARMOUR, AND SENT INTO THE LAND OF THE PHILISTINES ROUND ABOUT, TO CARRY TIDINGS UNTO THEIR IDOLS, AND TO THE PEOPLE.

(10) "AND THEY PUT HIS ARMOUR IN THE HOUSE OF THEIR GODS, AND FASTENED HIS HEAD IN THE TEMPLE OF DAGON.

(11) "AND WHEN ALL JABESH-GILEAD HEARD ALL THAT THE PHILISTINES HAD DONE TO SAUL,

(12) "THEY AROSE, ALL THE VALIANT MEN, AND TOOK AWAY THE BODY OF SAUL, AND THE BODIES OF HIS SONS, AND BROUGHT THEM TO JABESH, AND BURIED THEIR BONES UNDER THE OAK IN JABESH, AND FASTED SEVEN DAYS.

(13) "SO SAUL DIED FOR HIS TRANSGRESSION WHICH HE COMMITTED AGAINST THE LORD, EVEN AGAINST THE WORD OF THE LORD, WHICH HE KEPT NOT, AND ALSO FOR ASKING COUNSEL OF ONE WHO HAD A FAMILIAR SPIRIT, TO ENQUIRE OF IT;

(14) "AND ENQUIRED NOT OF THE LORD: THEREFORE HE KILLED HIM, AND TURNED THE KINGDOM UNTO DAVID THE SON OF JESSE."

The exegesis is:

1. (Vs. 7) That which the Lord gave to Israel is now occupied by the Philistines. It is the same with us presently. Satan desires to inhabit that which God has given us; therefore, the battle ever rages, with the enemy trying to mar our inheritance.

2. (Vs. 8) The evidence is obvious that Satan wants the last drop of blood. There can be no compromise with the evil one. We destroy him or he destroys us.

3. (Vs. 9) It was customary to take the heads of conquered kings and make sport with them in the houses of the gods, and in the cities of their own people. But this was a tragedy, because these were God's People who were being so maltreated.

4. (Vs. 12) I Samuel, Chapter 31, records the fact of Saul's death. I Chronicles, Chapter 10, records the reason. Men could see the outward historic event, but only the Spirit of God could reveal the cause of this event. Verse 13 proclaims that cause.

5. (Vs. 14) In fact, Saul did enquire of the Lord (I Sam. 28:6); however, it was an enquiry with no thought in mind of truly repenting. Had Saul truly repented at that time, the Lord definitely would have heard him and helped him. But man seems determined to insist upon his stubbornness and rebellion, even to his own death.

THE WILL OF GOD

The Second Verse says, *"And the Philistines followed hard after Saul, and after his sons; and the Philistines killed Jonathan, and Abinadab, and Malchi-shua, the sons of Saul."*

The Sixth Verse says, *"So Saul died, and his three sons...."*

The Seventh Verse says, "... *and that Saul and his sons were dead....*"

And then the Eighth Verse says, "... *that they found Saul and his sons fallen in Mount Gilboa.*"

The Twelfth Verse says, *"They arose, all the valiant men, and took away the body of Saul, and the bodies of his sons...."*

The great question looms large, *"Was it the Will of God for Jonathan to die in this battle?"*

I think it can be said without fear of contradiction that Jonathan was one of the godliest men on record in the Old Testament.

Jonathan, the son of Saul, is first mentioned in I Samuel 13:2.

The Philistines had attacked Israel, and this battle will see a tremendous exploit, even a Miracle, on the part of Jonathan and the victory there won. So, the first glimpse we have of this man is momentous indeed!

When Saul began to lose his way, and it was known that the Lord had anointed David to be the king of Israel, at least when that time would come, Jonathan said to David: "... *fear not: for the hand of Saul my father shall not find you; and you shall be king over Israel, and I shall be next to you; and that also Saul my father knows*" (I Sam. 23:17).

Actually, the record says: "... *that the soul of Jonathan was knit with the soul of David, and Jonathan loved him as his own soul*" (I Sam. 18:1).

Jonathan was in line for the throne, but he gave that up in favor of the Will of God, for he knew that David was the one who was chosen.

Not many men would have done this!

The last thing said in Scripture concerning Jonathan before his death pertains to the Covenant made before the Lord between David and Jonathan. The Scripture says:

"And they two made a covenant before the LORD: and David abode in the wood, and Jonathan went to his house" (I Sam. 23:18).

Even though the Holy Spirit gave very little enlightenment upon the subject, still, it seems from what was said that the Spirit of God dealt with Jonathan concerning a total alignment with David. To do this, he would have had to have broken with his father once and for all.

It seems from the little information given that this is what he should have done. In that case, he would have been a tremendous blessing to David and to Israel. As well, he would not have died in the battle with the Philistines, but could have been of more years of service and use for the Kingdom of God and for Israel.

One thing is certain; irrespective that Jonathan died with his father Saul, every evidence is, as stated, that he was one of the godliest men who ever lived. Truly his loss was felt keenly by David and, as well, by Israel. In the family of Saul, not much good can be said or shown; however, Jonathan was that bright and shining light.

POSSESSIONS LOST

The Scripture says: "... *then they forsook their cities, and fled: and the Philistines came and dwelt in them.*"

How many cities were forsaken is not stated, but it appears that all of them on the west side of Jordan and in this particular battle section became Philistine cities for a time, perhaps ten or twelve years. When David became king over all Israel, these cities were recovered, and the kingdom of Israel for the first time became truly great. In fact, it extended to the river of Egypt and the Gulf of Akabah, and north to the Euphrates, taking in all of Philistia, Amalek, Edom, Moab, Syria, and other countries. "... *This is the Victory that overcomes the world, even our Faith*" (I Jn. 5:4).

Satan hated Israel, as should be obvious; therefore, he took the occasion of Saul's death to occupy a number of the cities of Israel. In fact, he wanted the entirety of the country, and most definitely would have taken it had it not been for the Power of God.

That for which Jesus paid such a price at Calvary's Cross, Satan doesn't want us to have. In fact, he will do everything within his power to keep us from having and enjoying the great Victories won by our Lord. Unfortunately, he all too often succeeds.

THE PROVISION MADE AT CALVARY

Even though the following illustration is known by almost every Believer, still, it bears repeating. The story is true.

A young couple who lived in Ireland saved and scrimped for many months in order to buy a ticket and, thereby, immigrate to the United States. Even then, they could only afford the least expensive passage. At any rate, they were looking forward with great anticipation to making a new home, whatever the difficulties might be, in the land of the brave and the home of the free.

A couple of days before reaching New York harbor, one of the stewards happened to walk past their little cabin. The door was open, and seeing the man and woman standing there, he stopped to chat for a few moments.

They had just finished eating their lunch, such as it was, and there were some crumbs scattered over the bed. The steward casually asked them about the crumbs.

The young man spoke up and stated, *"We had money only for the cheapest fare, so we packed all the food we could to bring with us."* He then went on to add as to how stale it had become, hence, the cracker crumbs on the bed.

The steward stood there for a few moments looking at them and then finally asked, *"You mean you have been eating food that you prepared for the entirety of this journey?"*

The young man nodded his head in the affirmative and again stated, *"We didn't have money for anything except the fare."*

The steward once again stood there for a few moments, taken aback by what he had heard, and then said, *"Don't you realize that your ticket paid for your meals as well?"*

They both looked at him and said, *"You mean our ticket paid for the meals?"*

He shook his head in the affirmative and said, *"Yes! In fact, you could have had any number of meals each day that you wanted, all the food that you desired to eat. Several restaurants are at your disposal, all paid for in your ticket."* The young man and his wife stood there, shaking their heads and said, *"And you mean that we've eaten this stale food for the entirety of the journey, when we could have had excellent meals?"*

"That's exactly what I mean," the steward said.

JESUS PAID IT ALL

Many Christians and, in fact, most are doing exactly as that young couple did so long, long ago. Through a lack of knowledge, or even unbelief, they do not have and, thereby, do not enjoy all that Christ has done for us. And to be sure and as stated, Satan takes full advantage of that.

Everything that man lost in the Fall, Jesus answered at Calvary's Cross. In other words, our Lord purchased back, and did so with His Own Precious Blood, everything that was lost, meaning that everything is now available to the Child of God. Jesus Himself said: *"The thief comes not but for to steal and to kill, and to destroy, but I am come that they might have life and that they might have it more abundantly"* (Jn. 10:10).

The truth is that every single Believer has *"more abundant life."* But the facts are that most Believers aren't enjoying their *"more abundant life."*

MORE ABUNDANT LIFE

The only way the fullness of Christ's Victory at Calvary can be obtained and maintained is by the Believer placing his Faith exclusively in Christ and what Christ did at the Cross.

Many, upon reading these words, that is, if they have followed our teaching for very long, might retort and say, *"You claim the Cross as the answer for everything!"*

Now, you are beginning to hear what we are saying. You are exactly right! The Cross of Christ, what Jesus there did, is the answer for everything. It alone holds the answer, the solution, for that which we seek, whatever it might be. If our Faith is not based entirely in the Cross of Christ, we can never have all for which Jesus died. This is the only way that His Victory, which is meant to be our Victory, can truly be that which the Lord intends.

It sounds simple enough! Anyone, even a child, can place his Faith in Christ and the Cross. That is true; however, to have the great Victory afforded by Christ at Calvary, our Faith cannot be divided, in other words, we have to let go of everything else, and above all, deny ourselves (Lk. 9:23). Let us say it this way:

• The only way to God is through Jesus Christ (Jn. 14:6).

- The only way to Jesus Christ is through the Cross (Lk. 9:23; 14:27).
- The only way to the Cross is a denial of self (Lk. 9:23; Rom. 6:3-14).

Christ is the Source of all things, while the Cross is the Means by which it is done. That being the case, the Holy Spirit superintends everything else. Only then can we have all that Calvary affords; otherwise, even though the person may be Saved, and I pray to God they are, the simple fact is, they are miserably Saved.

THE TRANSGRESSION

The Eighth Verse says: *"... when the Philistines came to strip the dead, that they found Saul and his sons fallen in Mount Gilboa."*

The Ninth Verse says, *"... they took his head...."*

Taking *"his head"* is something additional to I Samuel 31:9-10, and *"his body,"* as referred to there, is something additional to this Passage. This shows that I and II Chronicles were not copies made by men of I and II Samuel and I and II Kings, but that the two accounts given in Samuel, Kings, and Chronicles were written by the Spirit of God. The different information given in both accounts shows an independent composition by an infallible Author.

Verse 12 says: *"... and buried their bones under the oak in Jabesh...."* I Samuel 31:12 says that they burned them first and then buried them. They did the burning at night and then buried the bones under a tree.

The city of *"Jabesh"* was where Saul had won his first military victory. The name *"Jabesh"* means, *"hill of witnessing."* There he had fought *"Nahash the Ammonite"* (I Sam., Chpt. 11) whose name means, *"bright shining serpent."*

So, Saul defeated the *"bright shining serpent"* at first, but was defeated by the *"bright shining serpent"* at the last.

As we have stated, I Samuel records the fact of Saul's death. I Chronicles, Chapter 10 records the reason.

The Thirteenth Verse says, *"So Saul died for his transgression which he committed against the LORD."* There were two reasons:

1. *"Even against the Word of the LORD, which he kept not."*

2. *"And also for asking counsel of one who had a familiar spirit, and to enquire of it."*

Some may possibly read the words in I Samuel, *"And when Saul enquired of the LORD, the LORD answered him not, neither by dreams, nor by Urim, nor by Prophets"* (I Sam. 28:6), and think there is a contradiction with I Chronicles 10:14.

It should be noted, however, that Hebrew scholars point out that the verb *"to enquire"* used in I Samuel is a different verb from that used in I Chronicles where it says, *"... and enquired not of the LORD"* (Vs. 14). The verb recorded in I Samuel records an outward and formal action; the other, referred to in I Chronicles, records an inward and deep emotion. Had Saul inquired of the Lord with the same intense earnestness with which he inquired of the witch, how prompt and gracious would have been the response!

FAMILIAR SPIRITS

The Text plainly tells us that the Lord was very angry that Saul *"asked counsel of one who had a familiar spirit."*

What are familiar spirits?

They are demon spirits which pretend to be a person deceased. They learn things about that individual, and using a medium, such as this witch of Endor, or even appearing in a vision in the form of the deceased, make people believe they are actually speaking to the deceased.

So, the question must be asked, *"Was it really Samuel to whom Saul spoke, as recorded in I Samuel 28?"*

There is much controversy by Bible scholars as to whether Samuel actually came up, or whether it was a demon spirit impersonating Samuel. Looking at the circumstances, it might be said that either could have been possible; however, this truth should be made known:

Saul received absolutely no help whatsoever from trying to communicate with the dead; likewise, all others seeking such will receive the same — nothing.

Pope John Paul II claimed that many years ago he saw a vision of Mary, and that she told him that he would be Pope; consequently, he took the Catholic church deeper into Mary worship than it had previously known. In fact, he attempted to have Mary looked at as a co-redemptress with Christ. Fortunately, wiser heads prevailed and stopped the effort.

Was it really Mary that appeared to this man?

No!

I have no doubt that he had a vision. I have no doubt that he saw an apparition that seemed to be Mary; however, it was not Mary that he saw, but rather a familiar spirit impersonating Mary.

Some may claim that it must have been Mary simply because he did become Pope.

We learn from Job, Chapters 1 and 2, that Satan, at times having access to the Throne of God, learns some things and, no doubt, oftentimes well in advance. In fact, he uses such to make people think things which are wrong.

Just because something comes to pass that has been prophesied doesn't necessarily mean that it is Scriptural. The Word says:

"If there arise among you a prophet, or a dreamer of dreams, and gives you a sign or a wonder,

"And the sign or wonder come to pass, whereof he spoke unto you, saying, Let us go after other gods, which you have not known, and let us serve them (no matter the signs or the wonders, if what is being said is not Scriptural, it must not be heeded);

"You shall not hearken unto the words of that prophet, or that dreamer of dreams: for the LORD your God proves you, to know whether you love the LORD your God with all your heart and with all your soul. (The Lord allows false preachers and false teachers to succeed for awhile in order to test His People. To be sure, He already knows what His People will do, or won't do. The test is for our benefit)" (Deut. 13:1-3).

The final word is never to be a Prophecy, dreams, or whatever of that nature, but rather the Word of God.

The doctrines of the Catholic church aren't Scriptural. In fact, they are anything but Scriptural. So, anything claimed in this capacity, whether it comes to pass or not, is not to be taken as from the Lord.

There is no such thing Scripturally as a pope. Jesus Christ is the Head of the Church, not some man. As well, there is no such thing as priests, at least, since the Cross. Jesus is our great High Priest, and no other is needed. John Paul II was a priest. So, his position was unscriptural; his office was unscriptural; and, his claims were unscriptural. As such, what he saw, as stated, was not Mary, but rather a familiar spirit impersonating Mary.

"Brethren, we have met to worship and adore the Lord our God;
"Will you pray with all your power, while we try to preach the Word?
"All is vain unless the Spirit of the Holy One comes down;
"Brethren, pray, and Holy Manna will be showered all around."

"Brethren, see poor sinners round you slumbering on the brink of woe;
"Death is coming, Hell is moving, can you bear to let them go?
"See our fathers and our mothers, and our children sinking down;
"Brethren, pray, and Holy Manna will be showered all around."

"Sisters, will you join and help us? Moses' sister aided him;
"Will you help the trembling mourners who are struggling hard with sin?
"Tell them all about the Saviour, tell them that He will be found;
"Sisters pray and Holy Manna will be showered all around."

"Let us love our Lord supremely, let us love each other too;
"Let us love and pray for sinners, till our God makes all things new.
"Then He'll call us home to Heaven, at His Table we'll sit down;
"Christ will gird Himself, and serve us with manna all around."

CHAPTER 11

(1) "THEN ALL ISRAEL GATHERED THEMSELVES TO DAVID UNTO HEBRON, SAYING, BEHOLD, WE ARE YOUR BONE AND YOUR FLESH.

(2) "AND MOREOVER IN TIME PAST, EVEN WHEN SAUL WAS KING, YOU WERE HE WHO LED OUT AND BROUGHT IN ISRAEL: AND THE LORD YOUR GOD SAID UNTO YOU, YOU SHALL FEED MY PEOPLE ISRAEL, AND YOU SHALL BE RULER OVER MY PEOPLE ISRAEL.

(3) "THEREFORE CAME ALL THE ELDERS OF ISRAEL TO THE KING TO HEBRON; AND DAVID MADE A COVENANT WITH THEM IN HEBRON BEFORE THE LORD; AND THEY ANOINTED DAVID KING OVER ISRAEL, ACCORDING TO THE WORD OF THE LORD BY SAMUEL."

The pattern is:

1. (Vs. 2) It was the Will of God that David be the first king of Israel, and not Saul. It is just as wrong to get ahead of God as it is to lag behind.

2. (Vs. 2) We find that Israel, despite the problems with Saul, and even though they knew that David had been anointed by the Lord to be king over Israel, did not, in fact, make him king until they thought it was in their best interest to do so.

Very few Believers, likewise, will carry out the Will of God, if they erroneously feel that it's not in their best interests. The truth is, the Will of God, no matter what the circumstances may seem to be, is always the far better place for the Believer to be. There is no loss, never any loss, by abiding by the Will of God, and great loss by not doing so.

3. One can literally sense the Presence of God in reading the words of Verse 3. It had taken some time, and much suffering and sorrow, but Israel had finally come around to God's Way.

4. (Vs. 3) Thus, David, the commanding figure of the First Book of Chronicles, is introduced. He is a Type of his greater Son, the Lord Jesus Christ. Characteristically, the first event of the Book is the deliverance of Jerusalem from the Jebusites, and David's ascension to the Throne of Jehovah on Zion. Such will be the happy action of Israel's great King in a future happy day.

THE WILL OF GOD

It took Israel a long time to realize that the Will of God, and not her own personal will, was the key to all prosperity, freedom, and blessing. Regrettably, it seems to take us the same amount of time.

All the sorrow and heartache that Israel went through under Saul was totally unnecessary. It was God's Will that David be the first king. All Israel had to do was to wait for a few years; however, they didn't want to wait, despite the fact that the Lord told them that they were inviting trouble, and trouble they had!

WAITING ON THE LORD

Why was it so hard for Israel to wait on the Lord? And, why is it so hard for us to wait on the Lord?

The Believer should desire in his heart above all, the Perfect Will of God above everything else, and he should be willing to wait on the Lord for that Perfect Will to be brought to pass.

We should know and understand that God has a Perfect Will, a Perfect Plan, for every single Believer. None is left wandering aimlessly. If we get into trouble, most of the time, it's because we attempt to force the Will of God by devising our own plans and acting thereon.

At the same time, we must understand that Satan will do everything within his power to keep the Perfect Will of God from coming to pass in the Believer's life. Look at David as an example.

For several years, the *"sweet singer of Israel"* had no home, was running for his life and, at times, even bereft of the common, simple necessities of life. This was Satan trying to cause David to quit, or to take matters into his own hands, which always proves to be catastrophic.

So, in ascertaining that Will, don't get it in your mind that it's a bed of roses, proverbially speaking. Be prepared for Satan to hinder, to obstruct, etc. But, please understand the following:

Ever how long we have to wait, that which the Lord will do is always, and without exception, well worth the wait, and then some!

We find that David never took matters into his own hands. He had many opportunities to kill Saul and, to be frank, most in Israel would have agreed with him; however, the Lord would not have agreed with him. David waited on the Lord, allowing the Lord to handle the situation, which He did. If we will wait, God's Perfect Will will be brought to pass in our lives also.

There is one more thing as it regards the *"waiting."*

Wherever it is that the Lord has placed you, even though you may think that you have better things ahead, never demean your present circumstances. Understand that the Lord has placed you there; therefore, you should make the very best of your present place and position. As well, you should not seek to move from that position until you are absolutely positive that you have the Mind of God in the matter.

As another example, David went over to the Philistines for some 16 months. During that time, he was out of the Will of God. His actions showed a lack of trust, a lack of faith. Growing weak in his faith, he thought the Lord could no longer protect him; therefore he stated, *". . . shall now perish one day by the hand of Saul: there is nothing better for me than that I should speedily escape into the land of the Philistines. . . ."* (I Sam. 27:1).

The truth is, there was no way that Saul could kill David, or anyone else, for that matter. But, David lost faith, and so have we at times; however, it always leads to trouble!

A TEST OF FAITH

In effect, anything the Lord does with us, whatever it might be, is a test of Faith. As someone has well said, Faith must be tested, and great Faith must be tested greatly. And, so it is!

How much do we really believe the Lord? How much Faith do we have in Him? How much do we trust Him? Are we fearful that we aren't going to make it, as David of old when he went over to the Philistines? Do circumstances cause us to fear?

All of us, even the Bible greats, faced these questions, which I have posed. The Lord allows such, all in order to test our Faith.

Of course, the Lord knows what our Faith is, knowing exactly as to how strong or weak that it is. All of this, our test of Faith, is that we may know. Always, and I think I can say, without exception, we will find that our faith is not quite as strong as we thought it was.

But, the test, which the Lord allows our way, is not meant to wash us out. It's meant to do the very opposite.

Living for the Lord is not like baseball, *"three strikes and you are out."* The Lord will never call anyone out. If we stumble and fall, He will pick us up, dust us off, and start us back on our way, that is, if we will allow Him to do so. The Holy Spirit, to be sure, is there for the long haul. And, if we will give Him even a little latitude, He will see us through, and of that, there is no doubt.

HEBRON

At the time of our text, Hebron was the capital of Judah. In fact, David had been king over Judah for some seven and a half years. No mention is here made of his intermediate partial rule. Nor, is any mention made of the temporary rule of Ishbosheth, Saul's son, over Benjamin and Israel proper.

No mention is made simply because none of this was the Will of God.

Ishbosheth had been promoted by Abner, and not the Lord. As well, the Lord did not call David to be king over Judah, but rather, the entirety of the nation.

This is not meant to imply that David was wrong by serving Judah these seven and a half years, but it is meant to say that Israel was wrong in waiting all of this time before the Will of God would be carried out.

David being a Type of Christ, it was the Will of God that he become king over the entirety of Israel, and not just Judah, at 30 years of age. Jesus began His public Ministry when he was 30 years old.

So, thousands from all over Israel came to Hebron in order to make David king.

Incidentally, Hebron was probably the oldest city in Israel. It was the first home of Abraham and the Patriarchs. In fact, it was the city of Arba, the old Canaanite chief, with his three giant sons, under whose walls the trembling spies stole through the land by the adjacent Valley of Eshcol. Here Caleb chose his portion when, at the head of his valiant Tribe, he drove out the old inhabitants, and called the whole surrounding territory after his own name (Pulpit).[1]

THE ANOINTING

When the Elders of Israel anointed David to be *"king over Israel,"* and *"according to the Word of the LORD by Samuel,"* in effect, this was the third anointing.

As a young boy, David had first been anointed by Samuel to be king (I Sam. 16:1, 13). David, at the time, was probably about 15 years old. The second time was when the *"men of Judah"* anointed him king over *"the House of Judah"* (II Sam. 2:4). In fact, David should have then become king over the whole of Israel. His third anointing, which is the present time, is over all of Israel.

Regrettably, it seems that most will not obey the Lord until they think it's in their best interest to do so.

What do we mean by that statement?

The truth is, and as already stated, irrespective of circumstances, and irrespective as to how things may look, obeying the Lord is always, and without exception, our very best interest.

Most will not obey the Lord if the crowd is going in the other direction. Most will not obey the Lord if it's not popular to do so. Most will not obey the Lord if they think it's going to cost them something. In truth, precious few seek to obey the Lord and, thereby, carry out His Will within their lives, irrespective of circumstances. But, thank God for the few!

Israel knew what the Lord had said concerning David. So why were they so long in their waiting to act?

They made the following statements:

• *"Behold, we are your bone and your flesh."* In other words, *"You are ours."*

• You are *"He who led out and brought in Israel."* In other words, he was and, in fact, had always been their Spiritual Leader.

• They admitted that the *"LORD God had said unto him, You shall feed My People Israel"* (II Sam. 5:1-2).

• They also admitted that the Lord had said, *"You shall be ruler over My People Israel"* (II Sam. 7:8). Yet, they were very slow to act! But finally, they did.

"Oh happy day, oh happy day!"

(4) "AND DAVID AND ALL ISRAEL WENT TO JERUSALEM, WHICH IS JEBUS; WHERE THE JEBUSITES WERE, THE INHABITANTS OF THE LAND.

(5) "AND THE INHABITANTS OF JEBUS SAID TO DAVID, YOU SHALL NOT COME HITHER. NEVERTHELESS DAVID TOOK THE CASTLE OF ZION, WHICH IS THE CITY OF DAVID.

(6) "AND DAVID SAID, WHOSOEVER SMITES THE JEBUSITES FIRST SHALL BE CHIEF AND CAPTAIN. SO JOAB THE SON OF ZERUIAH WENT FIRST UP, AND WAS CHIEF.

(7) "AND DAVID DWELT IN THE CASTLE; THEREFORE THEY CALLED IT THE CITY OF DAVID.

(8) "AND HE BUILT THE CITY ROUND ABOUT, EVEN FROM MILLO ROUND ABOUT: AND JOAB REPAIRED THE REST OF THE CITY.

(9) "SO DAVID WAXED GREATER AND GREATER: FOR THE LORD OF HOSTS WAS WITH HIM."

The exposition is:

1. (Vs. 4) As a type, the Jebusites symbolize a stronghold that Satan erects within our hearts and lives. Saul never did defeat the Jebusites, who were within; consequently, the Philistines, who were without, eventually defeated him.

2. (Vs. 4) Likewise, if we do not defeat the strongholds that are within our lives, strongholds of Satan, those without will ultimately overcome us. In connection with this, Paul said: *"For the weapons of our warfare are not carnal, but mighty through God to the pulling down of strongholds"* (II Cor. 10:4).

3. (Vs. 4) This is done, as it only can be done, by the Believer placing his Faith exclusively in Christ and what Christ has done for us at the Cross. That being the case, the Holy Spirit will then mightily help us, without Whom these great battles cannot be won (Rom. 8:1-2, 11).

4. As it regards Verse 5, Satan will ever taunt us, declaring that since he has established this stronghold for so long, he cannot be dislodged. Through Christ and the Cross, every stronghold of Satan, in fact, can be dislodged! (I Cor. 1:17-18).

5. (Vs. 7) At least one of the reasons that

Satan attempts to erect strongholds in our lives is because he knows that God intends for this area, so to speak, to be our strong point; so David, by the help of the Lord, took this, which had been inhabited by the enemy, and made it his Capital, i.e., *"the city of David."*

PULLING DOWN STRONGHOLDS

Jebus was an ancient name for Jerusalem because the Jebusites, a very fierce and warlike tribe, dwelt there. Jerusalem had long been a stronghold of the Jebusites, ever since the conquest of Canaan, except for a short time when it was in the hands of Judah (Josh. 10:1-5).

It is said that Jerusalem is the *"navel of the world,"* meaning that it sits in the exact center of the planet. It is also said that the Jebusites were so strong that even mighty Egypt would not come against them.

Saul, during his forty-year reign, did not defeat the Jebusites; actually, there is no record that he even attacked them.

As a type, the Jebusites symbolize a stronghold that Satan erects within our hearts and lives. Saul never did defeat the Jebusites, as stated, who were within; consequently, the Philistines, who were without, eventually defeated him; likewise, if we do not defeat the strongholds that are within our lives, those without will ultimately overcome us.

So, the very first thing that David did after becoming king was to come against this stronghold of Zion, this place of the Jebusites. In fact, II Samuel 5:7, calls it a *"stronghold."*

THE WEAPONS OF OUR WARFARE

Jebus was in the very midst of Israel, something that could not continue to exist, that is, if Israel were to be the nation that God intended. The Jebusites had to be defeated and removed. So, this was the very first thing that David did upon becoming king of Israel. No doubt, he was moved upon by the Holy Spirit to do this thing. This shows us how important it was that this stronghold of the enemy be removed, and forthwith.

The main part of this stronghold of the Jebusites was actually on the very site where the Temple later would be built. Of course, David did not know it at that time, but the Lord knew.

This tells us that the very thing the Lord intends in our lives to be our strong suit, in a sense, the Capital of the Holy Spirit, so to speak, is what Satan will attempt to greatly hinder. In other words, he attempts to build a stronghold in the very place where the Holy Spirit desires to occupy and use.

In addressing this very thing, Paul said, and I quote from THE EXPOSITOR'S STUDY BIBLE:

"For though we walk in the flesh (refers to the fact that we do not yet have Glorified Bodies), *we do not war after the flesh* (after our own ability, but rather by the Power of the Spirit):

"(For the weapons of our warfare are not carnal (carnal weapons consist of those which are man-devised), *but mighty through God* (the Cross of Christ [I Cor. 1:18]) *to the pulling down of strongholds;)*

"Casting down imaginations (philosophic strongholds; every effort man makes outside of the Cross of Christ), *and every high thing that exalts itself against the Knowledge of God* (all the pride of the human heart), *and bringing into captivity every thought to the obedience of Christ.* (Can be done only by the Believer looking exclusively to the Cross, where all Victory is found; the Holy Spirit will then perform the task)" (II Cor. 10:3-5).

What are the weapons of our warfare? Paul gave us the answer to that, as well.

THE WHOLE ARMOR OF GOD

Paul tells us that our conflict is not with flesh and blood, but rather, against the demon powers of darkness. He said:

"Finally, my Brethren, be strong in the Lord (be continually strengthened, which one does by constant Faith in the Cross), *and in the power of His Might.* (This Power is at our disposal. The Source is the Holy Spirit, but the Means is the Cross [I Cor. 1:18]).

"Put on the whole Armour of God (not just some, but all), *that you may be able to stand against the wiles of the Devil.* (This refers to the *'stratagems'* of Satan.)

*"For we wrestle not against flesh and

blood (our foes are not human; however, Satan constantly uses human beings to carry out his dirty work), *but against principalities* (rulers or beings of the highest rank and order in Satan's kingdom), *against powers* (the rank immediately below the 'Principalities'), *against the rulers of the darkness of this world* (those who carry out the instructions of the *'Powers'*), *against spiritual wickedness in high places.* (This refers to demon spirits)" (Eph. 6:10-12).

After telling us what we are facing, in other words, that which we are up against, he then tells us how it is to be done. He says:

"Wherefore take unto you the whole Armour of God (because of what we face), *that you may be able to withstand in the evil day* (refers to resisting and opposing the powers of darkness), *and having done all, to stand.* (This refers to the Believer not giving ground, not a single inch.)

"Stand therefore, having your loins gird about with Truth (the Truth of the Cross), *and having on the Breastplate of Righteousness* (the Righteousness of Christ, which comes strictly by and through the Cross);

"And your feet shod with the preparation of the Gospel of Peace (peace comes through the Cross as well);

"Above all, taking the Shield of Faith (ever making the Cross the Object of your Faith, which is the only Faith God will recognize, and the only Faith Satan will recognize), *wherewith you shall be able to quench all the fiery darts of the wicked.* (This represents temptations with which Satan assails the Saints.)

"And take the Helmet of Salvation (has to do with the renewing of the mind, which is done by understanding that everything we receive from the Lord, comes to us through the Cross), *and the Sword of the Spirit, which is the Word of God* (the Word of God is the Story of Christ and the Cross)" (Eph. 6:13-17).

If it is to be noticed, all of the *"Armour of God,"* in some way, is connected with the Cross of Christ, because that is where Satan was totally and completely defeated (Col. 2:14-15).

THE AUTHORITY OF THE BELIEVER

Every Believer has authority given to us by the Word of God and the Holy Spirit, actually, the moment we get Saved. In fact, that authority should grow and develop as we mature in the Lord.

But, the Believer should understand that the authority that we have is never over other human beings. It is always, and without fail, over demon spirits and even Satan himself. We are given this in Ephesians 6:12, that which we have just quoted. Unfortunately, some misguided Christians have attempted to use this authority against other Believers. It won't work, even as it is not supposed to work, at least, not in that fashion.

Pure and simple, the Apostle said: *"For we wrestle not against flesh and blood, but against principalities, against powers, against the rulers of the darkness of this world, against spiritual wickedness in high places"* (Eph. 6:12).

The authority we have is given to us totally and completely by the Lord Jesus Christ. It's not something we earn or merit but is ours as a free gift. And yet, we must remember that even though Christ is most definitely the Source, it is the Cross that is the Means by which everything comes to us.

THE CROSS AS THE MEANS

Anything and everything that we as Believers are to be in Christ, and I mean everything, can only be done one way, and that is by Faith in Christ and what He did for us at the Cross. While Jesus Christ is the Source of all things that we need, it is the Cross that is the Means by which He gives these things to us, whatever they might be. And, in relationship to that, the Holy Spirit superintends all, whatever it might be.

Jesus addressed this when He said: *". . . If any man thirst, let him come unto Me, and drink* (presents the greatest invitation ever given to mortal man).

"He who believes on Me (it is *'not doing,'* but rather, *'believing'*), *as the Scripture has said* (refers to the Word of God being the Story of Christ and Him Crucified; all the Sacrifices pointed to Christ and what He would do at the Cross, as well as the entirety of the Tabernacle and Temple and all their appointments), *out of his belly* (innermost being) *shall flow rivers of Living Water*

(speaks of Christ directly, and Believers indirectly).

"(But this spoke He of the Spirit (Holy Spirit)*, which they who believe on Him should receive* (it would begin on the Day of Pentecost)*: for the Holy Spirit was not yet given* (He has now been given)*; because that Jesus was not yet glorified.)* (The time of which John wrote was shortly before the Crucifixion. When Jesus died on the Cross and was resurrected three days later, He was raised with a Glorified Body, which was one of the signs that all sin had been atoned, now making it possible for the Holy Spirit to come in a new dimension)" (Jn. 7:37-39).

The idea is, everything that Christ now does is done by and through the Holy Spirit. In fact, the Holy Spirit is the only Member of the Godhead functioning on this Earth and, in fact, ever has been, other than the glorious Redemption plan carried out by our Lord at Calvary's Cross.

WHY DOES THE CHURCH HAVE A PROBLEM WITH THE CROSS?

The Church, at least the part of the Church which still believes the Word of God, has no problem whatsoever with the Cross as it refers to Salvation; however, when it comes to our everyday walk before God, in other words, how we order our behavior, that's where many in the modern church have a problem.

When the church says, *"Jesus died for me,"* basically, they are limiting that to Salvation and Salvation alone. And how do I know that?

If you like, you can go to basically any Christian bookstore and pick up any one of the many titles which are carried, and if you have the time, read them through, and you'll find that most all of them are relating to people how to have a better life, or something of that nature. You will be hard put to find one that points people to the Cross. There is a reason for that.

In the first place, precious few preachers know anything about the Cross as it regards our Sanctification. And furthermore, not many are interested in learning.

Why?

The Cross presents Christ as having done it all, leaving only Faith in what He did as our part. Except for Faith, that cuts man out.

The truth is, if most preachers preached the Cross, they would have to give up their schemes that they have perfected, which claim to bring victory, but don't. These schemes appeal to the flesh and, as such, preachers gain a large following. As well, many of them are making a lot of money out of these schemes, whatever they might be, and to be told they've got to give all of that up doesn't set too well. In other words, it's exactly as Paul said, *"the offence of the Cross"* (Gal. 5:11).

But the sad fact is, despite all the ballyhoo about these schemes put forth in untold numbers of books, etc., they simply don't work. In fact, there is nothing that will work except the Cross of Christ.

Again, if it is to be noticed, preachers of today are writing precious few books which explain the Bible. While paying lip service to the Word of God, still, the major theme of almost all of these books, whatever they might be, is something other than the Cross of Christ. As such, it's not worth the paper it's written on.

Now, please understand that!

If the preacher is not preaching the Cross, then whatever it is he is preaching is not truly the Gospel. Paul said:

"For Christ sent me not to baptize (presents to us a Cardinal Truth)*, but to preach the Gospel* (the manner in which one may be Saved from sin)*: not with wisdom of words* (intellectualism is not the Gospel)*, lest the Cross of Christ should be made of none effect.* (This tells us in no uncertain terms that the Cross of Christ must always be the emphasis of the Message, or else it's not the Gospel)" (I Cor. 1:17).

The Scripture says, *"So David waxed greater and greater: for the LORD of Hosts was with him."*

This can only be done by the means of the Cross!

(10) "THESE ALSO ARE THE CHIEF OF THE MIGHTY MEN WHOM DAVID HAD, WHO STRENGTHENED THEMSELVES WITH HIM IN HIS KINGDOM, AND WITH ALL ISRAEL, TO MAKE HIM

KING, ACCORDING TO THE WORD OF THE LORD CONCERNING ISRAEL.

(11) "AND THIS IS THE NUMBER OF THE MIGHTY MEN WHOM DAVID HAD; JASHOBEAM, AN HACHMONITE, THE CHIEF OF THE CAPTAINS: HE LIFTED UP HIS SPEAR AGAINST THREE HUNDRED KILLED BY HIM AT ONE TIME.

(12) "AND AFTER HIM WAS ELEAZAR THE SON OF DODO, THE AHOHITE, WHO WAS ONE OF THE THREE MIGHTIES.

(13) "HE WAS WITH DAVID AT PASDAMMIM, AND THERE THE PHILISTINES WERE GATHERED TOGETHER TO BATTLE, WHERE WAS A PARCEL OF GROUND FULL OF BARLEY; AND THE PEOPLE FLED FROM BEFORE THE PHILISTINES.

(14) "AND THEY SET THEMSELVES IN THE MIDST OF THAT PARCEL, AND DELIVERED IT, AND KILLED THE PHILISTINES; AND THE LORD SAVED THEM BY A GREAT DELIVERANCE.

(15) "NOW THREE OF THE THIRTY CAPTAINS WENT DOWN TO THE ROCK TO DAVID, INTO THE CAVE OF ADULLAM; AND THE HOST OF THE PHILISTINES ENCAMPED IN THE VALLEY OF REPHAIM.

(16) "AND DAVID WAS THEN IN THE HOLD, AND THE PHILISTINES' GARRISON WAS THEN AT BETH-LEHEM.

(17) "AND DAVID LONGED, AND SAID, OH THAT ONE WOULD GIVE ME DRINK OF THE WATER OF THE WELL OF BETH-LEHEM, THAT IS AT THE GATE!

(18) "AND THE THREE BROKE THROUGH THE HOST OF THE PHILISTINES, AND DREW WATER OUT OF THE WELL OF BETH-LEHEM, THAT WAS BY THE GATE, AND TOOK IT, AND BROUGHT IT TO DAVID: BUT DAVID WOULD NOT DRINK OF IT, BUT POURED IT OUT TO THE LORD,

(19) "AND SAID, MY GOD FORBID IT ME, THAT I SHOULD DO THIS THING: SHALL I DRINK THE BLOOD OF THESE MEN WHO HAVE PUT THEIR LIVES IN JEOPARDY? FOR WITH THE JEOPARDY OF THEIR LIVES THEY BROUGHT IT. THEREFORE HE WOULD NOT DRINK IT. THESE THINGS DID THESE THREE MIGHTIEST."

The synopsis is:

NOTES

1. (Vs. 10) The Holy Spirit refers to these individuals as *"mighty men;"* however, they were *"mighty"* only because they came under the anointing of David, whom God had called for a particular task — to be the king of Israel. In fact, there would have been no *"might,"* had they not functioned under David's anointing.

To be sure, they also had an anointing all of their own, but it was predicated on them being in the Will of God, as it regarded David. Regrettably, far too many Christians don't understand this.

2. (Vs. 10) As a Believer, one should seek the Lord ardently about whom you are to follow, as it regards Preachers. If you guess wrong, or follow after the flesh, it will prove to be destructive. If you find the Mind of God, and it's not hard to find, He will lead you to that which you should follow, and then the anointing that's on that particular Ministry will also, in some way, the way God wants, be on you, as well.

3. As it regards Verse 11, I think it should be obvious that this man had to have the Anointing of the Holy Spirit to perform such a mighty deed against God's enemies. However, had he and all the others not followed David, they would have never been used by God in any capacity.

4. (Vs. 12) Also, it must ever be understood that God places His Anointing only upon a man or a woman. He does not anoint denominations, church officials (just because they are church officials), committees, boards, or groups. There definitely may be individuals occupying these particular positions who are definitely called of God and perform a mighty service, but it's not because of that position.

5. (Vs. 13) Barley, being the least of all the grains, many, perhaps, would have thought it not worthy to defend. However, God desires that Satan be rooted out of every part of our inheritance, no matter how seemingly insignificant. The reason? Little matters quickly grow into large matters!

6. (Vs. 14) The people of God labored intensely to plant and cultivate these crops. And when they were ready to be harvested, the Philistines would swoop down and take what rightly belonged to Israel.

This is a perfect example of what Satan attempts to do to the Believer. He attempts to rob you of your inheritance, and will do so, if you do not know how to properly follow the Lord, which is always by having Faith in Christ and the Cross, which then gives the Holy Spirit power to work on our behalf.

7. (Vs. 14) To be sure, the Holy Spirit, Who is God, can do anything. But He is hindered so much of the time, simply because we are not following the Word of God. This refers to the fact that we are serving Christ, or claiming to do so, while eliminating the Cross, or ignoring it. If the Cross is ignored, then, pure and simple, we are serving *"another Jesus,"* whom God can never recognize (Rom. 6:3-14; 8:1-2, 11; I Cor. 1:17-18, 21, 23; 2:2; Gal. 6:14; Col. 2:14-15).

8. (Vs. 18) Beth-lehem was where Jesus was born. The water being poured out by David was symbolic of Christ pouring out His Life on the Cross of Calvary, which guaranteed Salvation for all of mankind, at least all who will believe (Jn. 3:16). How much David understood of this, we do not know; however, he probably understood far more than we presently realize.

9. Verse 19 proclaims the fact that the Sacrifice of Christ at Calvary's Cross is to never be used for personal aggrandizement, but always for what it was intended, which is the Salvation of souls, gained only by Christ pouring out His Life.

10. (Vs. 19) This is, at least in part, what makes the *"Word of Faith"* doctrine, so-called, so wrong and false. It attempts to use Christ for personal gain, i.e., *"riches."* While it is certainly true that God does bless, and bless abundantly, He does so only on the basis of our Faith exclusively being in Christ and the Cross. The truth is, in that particular false doctrine, the only ones getting rich are the preachers, and that by subterfuge, and the perversion of Scripture.

THE WORD OF THE LORD

Several things are said in the Tenth Verse, things which are of extreme significance as it regards the great Work of God on Earth. They are:

• *"The mighty men whom David had, who strengthened themselves with him in his kingdom."*

• As stated, these men were *"mighty"* simply because they were with David whom the Lord had called. If they had chosen any other way, they would not have been mighty.

• They were there *"to make him king,"* and it is our business presently to make Jesus King in our lives and, as well, to eagerly anticipate the coming day when He will be King over all the Earth.

• All of this was *"according to the Word of the LORD."* This pertains to the *"Word"* which the Lord gave to Samuel many years before. It says:

"And the LORD said unto Samuel (interrupts the great Prophet's negative thoughts), *How long will you mourn for Saul* (Samuel was mourning and, at the same time, God was planning the greatest moment in Israel's history; the truth is, we have nothing to mourn, for, at this moment, God is planning great things for us; we must remember that!), *seeing I have rejected him from reigning over Israel?* (The Lord rejects all who will not obey His Word.) *fill your horn with oil* (a Type of the Holy Spirit), *and go* (if the Holy Spirit is present, it is always in order that a mission be accomplished), *I will send you to Jesse the Beth-lehemite: for I have provided Me a king among his sons* (of course, that was David, but, above all, the provision was the Greater Son of David)" (I Sam. 16:1).

THE ANOINTING

There are 52 mighty men who are listed in this Chapter. This is at the beginning of David's reign. At the conclusion of his reign, and just before he died, only 37 mighty men are listed (II Sam. 23:8-39). Evidently, some 15 of them died or proved unfaithful during the reign, and were, therefore, not counted with the 37 at the close of David's rule.

Among these 52 mighty men, Joab is not listed.

It should be understood, even to which we have eluded, that the *"might"* of these *"mighty men"* did not come from their own prowess but, instead, from David's anointing.

Also, it must ever be understood that God places His Anointing only upon a man or a woman. He does not anoint denominations, church officials (just because they are church officials), committees, boards, or groups.

The Bible method is for God to anoint a man (or a woman), and for other individuals to gather around that person and draw from that anointing. This was so with Abraham, with Moses, with Joshua, with the Apostle Paul and, above all, with the Lord Jesus Christ. Instead, the church has attempted to substitute denominations, committees, or positions. There is no anointing in these.

THE THREE MIGHTIES

In this Chapter, only two are listed, *"Jashobeam the Hachmonite,"* and *"Eleazar the son of Dodo, the Ahohite."*

The third one is listed in II Samuel 23:11, and his name was *"Shammah the son of Agee the Hararite."*

These were the three mightiest. The first one is *"Jashobeam,"* and the Scripture says that *"he lifted up his spear against three hundred killed by him at one time."* II Samuel 23:8 reads 800 men. What seems like a discrepancy may be as follows:

• The incident in question is not the same account as that of II Samuel 23:8.

• Some of the old Manuscripts became marred through use, and copyists were, thereby, faced with difficulty. The fault is not with the original as inspired by God. All mistakes are from copyists or marred Manuscripts and not from the Lord giving contradictory statements in the Inspired Records.

Verses 13 and 14 speak of a *"parcel of ground full of barley."* It says that *"Eleazar"* and *"David"* faced the Philistines *"and delivered it, and killed the Philistines."*

Barley, being the least of all the grains, many, perhaps, would have thought it not worthy to defend; however, God desires that Satan be rooted out of every part of our inheritance, no matter how seemingly insignificant.

And then it says of Shammah in II Samuel, *"And the Philistines were gathered together into a troop, where was a piece of ground full of lentils: and the people fled from the Philistines."*

"But Shammah stood in the midst of the ground, and defended it, and killed the Philistines: and the LORD wrought a great victory" (II Sam. 23:11-12).

NOTES

I'VE LEFT THIS PEA PATCH MY LAST TIME

"Lentils" are peas.

Years ago, I preached a Message entitled, *"I've Left This Pea Patch My Last Time."* It's a Message, I think, that every Believer ought to hear.

Whether it was the barley, or whether it was the pea patch, these things belonged to God's People and not the Philistines.

Anything and everything given to us by the Lord is special. There is nothing small in His Sight. We must not allow Satan to have anything that is ours, and I mean anything, because everything we have as Believers has been given to us by the Lord. Considering that He has given it to us, whatever it might be, it must be very special in our sight. That means that Satan cannot have anything.

Satan is a past master at robbing the harvest.

Far too many Christians, and if it were even one, it would be too many, labor and work over that which the Lord has called us to do, and then Satan comes down and robs it, exactly as the Philistines were doing during the time of David.

The indication is that the Philistines and other idol worshippers had been doing this for a period of time, possibly even during the entire reign of Saul. It's not very pleasant to work hard and then see it all stolen by the enemy, but that's exactly what was happening.

The indication is that the moment that David became king, everything changed in Israel. The Anointing of the Holy Spirit was flowing, and flowing like a river. Men who had once been merely ordinary, now become *"mighty."* In effect, the Holy Spirit is serving notice on the Philistines that there is *"a new sheriff in town."* The days of them robbing the harvest are now over. But, please notice the following:

These men did not become mighty until they joined with David and joined in the fight. Paul told Timothy to *"war a good warfare."*

HE STOOD IN THE MIDST OF THE GROUND, AND DEFENDED IT

As stated, the Philistines had been

accustomed to coming down and robbing the harvest, even after the people of God had labored long and hard to bring it to the place that it was to be gathered. It seems, as also stated, that they had been doing this for quite some years.

But, this year was different. When the Philistines came charging down, ready to do the same thing they had been doing all along, Shammah got mad.

The Scripture says that all the other people there *"fled from the Philistines."* But Shammah might have looked at the situation, and said, *"Lord, I'm tired of running. I'm tired of these Philistines robbing that for which we've worked so very hard to have. I've left this pea patch my last time."*

That's exactly what you, reading this book, need to say right now. You need to tell the Devil, *"I'm tired of running. I'm tired of you stealing everything that I've worked for. I'm going to stand my ground and defend that which the Lord has given unto me."*

Please notice; Shammah *"stood his ground."*

You must stand your ground. God has given every single Believer an inheritance. It is our *"Israel,"* so to speak. It is not meant to be robbed by the Philistines, or taken over by the Hivites or the Hittites, or anyone else for that matter. Everything we have was paid for at Calvary's Cross. We must not allow the Evil One to take it, not one ounce of it, not one foot of ground. Listen to Paul:

". . . that you may be able to withstand in the evil day (refers to resisting and opposing the powers of darkness), *and having done all, to stand.* (This refers to the Believer not giving ground, not a single inch. It refers to the Believer actually saying to Satan, 'Here I am, and here I stand. That which the Lord has given unto me, I will not yield one single inch of it to Satan. I will not give one iota of ground')" (Eph. 6:13).

A DRINK OF THE WATER OF THE WELL OF BETHLEHEM

The Sixteenth Verse says, *"And David was then in the hold, and the Philistines' garrison was then at Beth-lehem."*

Beth-lehem was David's home, and even more than that, much more, it was to be the birthplace of the Lord of Glory; consequently, it was very important.

And that's exactly where Satan wants to build a garrison, the very place that God desires to use.

To be sure, and even as we have previously discussed it, Satan will attempt to erect a stronghold in the very area of your life that God desires to singularly use.

I don't know how much the Devil knew about the coming Redeemer, whether he knew that Jesus would be born in Beth-lehem or not, but he probably did. So, he would station a Philistine garrison there, which in essence, made a mockery of Israel.

What happened then with David has great Scriptural connotations. It says:

• *"And David longed"*: The Holy Spirit, I believe, created this thirst in David, and a thirst for water that would come from a particular well at a particular place. Maybe David's thoughts were no higher than the fact that Beth-lehem was his home, and the water from that well was sweet and cool to him. But the Holy Spirit had something far greater in mind.

• *"The water of the well of Beth-lehem"*: As stated, about 1,000 years later, this is where Jesus, the Son of the Living God, would be born. The *"water"* that He would give to all who would believe Him, and unto this very hour, would slake the thirst, as it alone can slake the thirst. No other well can produce this *"water of life"*.

• *"Three broke through the host of the Philistines, and drew water out of the well of Beth-lehem, that was by the gate, and took it, and brought it to David"*: As these three men braved the enemy in order to obtain this water to give it to David, likewise, we must take this *"water of life"* to others.

• In the Scripture: *"But David would not drink of it, but poured it out to the LORD."* This was a drink offering to the Lord. It pictured the pouring out of Himself on Calvary's Cross, which would provide a life-giving flow of this *"water of life"* to any and all, and would slake their Spiritual Thirst.

• Concerning these three men who brought the water, David said: *"For with the jeopardy of their lives they brought it"*: Are we sacrificing anything to take this Gospel to others? They risked their lives, while untold numbers of others have given their lives. What are we doing?

(20) "AND ABISHAI THE BROTHER OF JOAB, HE WAS CHIEF OF THE THREE: FOR LIFTING UP HIS SPEAR AGAINST THREE HUNDRED, HE KILLED THEM, AND HAD A NAME AMONG THE THREE.

(21) "OF THE THREE, HE WAS MORE HONOURABLE THAN THE TWO; FOR HE WAS THEIR CAPTAIN: HOWBEIT HE ATTAINED NOT TO THE FIRST THREE.

(22) "BENAIAH THE SON OF JEHOIADA, THE SON OF A VALIANT MAN OF KABZEEL, WHO HAD DONE MANY ACTS; HE KILLED TWO LIONLIKE MEN OF MOAB: ALSO HE WENT DOWN AND KILLED A LION IN A PIT IN A SNOWY DAY.

(23) "AND HE KILLED AN EGYPTIAN, A MAN OF GREAT STATURE, FIVE CUBITS HIGH; AND IN THE EGYPTIAN'S HAND WAS A SPEAR LIKE A WEAVER'S BEAM; AND HE WENT DOWN TO HIM WITH A STAFF, AND PLUCKED THE SPEAR OUT OF THE EGYPTIAN'S HAND, AND KILLED HIM WITH HIS OWN SPEAR.

(24) "THESE THINGS DID BENAIAH THE SON OF JEHOIADA, AND HAD THE NAME AMONG THE THREE MIGHTIES.

(25) "BEHOLD, HE WAS HONOURABLE AMONG THE THIRTY, BUT ATTAINED NOT TO THE FIRST THREE: AND DAVID SET HIM OVER HIS GUARD.

(26) "ALSO THE VALIANT MEN OF THE ARMIES WERE, ASAHEL THE BROTHER OF JOAB, ELHANAN THE SON OF DODO OF BETH-LEHEM,

(27) "SHAMMOTH THE HARORITE, HELEZ THE PELONITE,

(28) "IRA THE SON OF IKKESH THE TEKOITE, ABIEZER THE ANTOTHITE,

(29) "SIBBECAI THE HUSHATHITE, ILAI THE AHOHITE,

(30) "MAHARAI THE NETOPHATHITE, HELED THE SON OF BAANAH THE NETOPHATHITE,

(31) "ITHAI THE SON OF RIBAI OF GIBEAH, THAT PERTAINED TO THE CHILDREN OF BENJAMIN, BENAIAH THE PIRATHONITE,

(32) "HURAI OF THE BROOKS OF GAASH, ABIEL THE ARBATHITE,

(33) "AZMAVETH THE BAHARUMITE, ELIAHBA THE SHAALBONITE,

(34) "THE SONS OF HASHEM THE GIZONITE, JONATHAN THE SON OF SHAGE THE HARARITE,

(35) "AHIAM THE SON OF SACAR THE HARARITE, ELIPHAL THE SON OF UR,

(36) "HEPHER THE MECHERATHITE, AHIJAH THE PELONITE,

(37) "HEZRO THE CARMELITE, NAARAI THE SON OF EZBAI,

(38) "JOEL THE BROTHER OF NATHAN, MIBHAR THE SON OF HAGGERI,

(39) "ZELEK THE AMMONITE, NAHARAI THE BEROTHITE, THE ARMOURBEARER OF JOAB THE SON OF ZERUIAH,

(40) "IRA THE ITHRITE, GAREB THE ITHRITE,

(41) "URIAH THE HITTITE, ZABAD THE SON OF AHLAI,

(42) "ADINA THE SON OF SHIZA THE REUBENITE, A CAPTAIN OF THE REUBENITES, AND THIRTY WITH HIM,

(43) "HANAN THE SON OF MAACHAH, AND JOSHAPHAT THE MITHNITE,

(44) "UZZIA THE ASHTERATHITE, SHAMA AND JEHIEL THE SONS OF HOTHAN THE AROERITE,

(45) "JEDIAEL THE SON OF SHIMRI, AND JOHA HIS BROTHER, THE TIZITE,

(46) "ELIEL THE MAHAVITE, AND JERIBAI, AND JOSHAVIAH, THE SONS OF ELNAAM, AND ITHMAH THE MOABITE,

(47) "ELIEL, AND OBED, AND JASIEL THE MESOBAITE."

The pattern is:

1. (Vs. 21) Nowhere in the world were there men like these, and all because of the Anointing of the Holy Spirit which was upon them.

2. (Vs. 23) The Egyptian was seven and half feet tall.

3. (Vs. 24) For time and eternity, their names are forever inscribed in the Word of God. What an honor! What a privilege! There is not one single Believer in the world today who cannot, in God's Way, attain to the same energy of power, if they will only truly follow the Lord.

4. There is a great spiritual meaning in Verse 25 concerning the *"guard."*

Demon spirits, of which the defeated represent, will attempt to destroy the Child of God. We must *"guard"* ourselves from their encroachment, as *"Benaiah did."* In the *"Name of Jesus,"* it can be done, and only in that mighty Name!

5. (Vs. 41) Uriah is listed here. He was listed in II Samuel, Chapter 23, although dead. An exception in listing him, even though dead, perhaps, was because of his connection with David, as the husband of the woman with whom David sinned; how tragic!

"Praise, my soul, the King of Heaven,
"To His Feet your tribute bring;
"Ransom, heal, restored, forgiven,
"Who like me, His Praise should sing?"

"Praise Him for His Grace and Favor,
"To our fathers in distress;
"Praise Him, still the same forever,
"Slow to chide, and swift to bless."

"Father-like He tends and spares us,
"Well our feeble frame He knows,
"In His Hands He gently bears us,
"Rescues us from all our foes."

"Angels, help us to adore Him,
"Ye behold Him face-to-face;
"Sun and moon, bow down before Him,
"Dwellers all in time and space."

CHAPTER 12

(1) "NOW THESE ARE THEY WHO CAME TO DAVID TO ZIKLAG, WHILE HE YET KEPT HIMSELF CLOSE BECAUSE OF SAUL THE SON OF KISH: AND THEY WERE AMONG THE MIGHTY MEN, HELPERS OF THE WAR.

(2) "THEY WERE ARMED WITH BOWS, AND COULD USE BOTH THE RIGHT HAND AND THE LEFT IN HURLING STONES AND SHOOTING ARROWS OUT OF A BOW, EVEN OF SAUL'S BRETHREN OF BENJAMIN.

(3) "THE CHIEF WAS AHIEZER, THEN JOASH, THE SONS OF SHEMAAH THE GIBEATHITE; AND JEZIEL, AND PELET, THE SONS OF AZMAVETH; AND BERACHAH, AND JEHU THE ANTOTHITE,

(4) "AND ISMAIAH THE GIBEONITE, A MIGHTY MAN AMONG THE THIRTY, AND OVER THE THIRTY; AND JEREMIAH, AND JAHAZIEL, AND JOHANAN, AND JOSABAD THE GEDERATHITE,

(5) "ELUZAI, AND JERIMOTH, AND BEALIAH, AND SHEMARIAH, AND SHEPHATIAH THE HARUPHITE,

(6) "ELKANAH, AND JESIAH, AND AZAREEL, AND JOEZER, AND JASHOBEAM, THE KORHITES,

(7) "AND JOELAH, AND ZEBADIAH, THE SONS OF JEROHAM OF GEDOR.

(8) "AND OF THE GADITES THERE SEPARATED THEMSELVES UNTO DAVID INTO THE HOLD TO THE WILDERNESS MEN OF MIGHT, AND MEN OF WAR FIT FOR THE BATTLE, WHO COULD HANDLE SHIELD AND BUCKLER, WHOSE FACES WERE LIKE THE FACES OF LIONS, AND WERE AS SWIFT AS THE ROES UPON THE MOUNTAINS;"

The pattern is:

1. (Vs. 1) This is a glorious Chapter, as Israel finally begins to do God's Will. It begins with David's darkest days. It closes with unimaginable victory. The present need is *"helpers of the war,"* for we are engaged in a war (II Cor. 10:3; I Tim. 1:18, 6:12; I Pet. 2:11). However, this war must be fought God's Way, and it is a war of Faith, and that exclusively.

2. As it regards Verse 2, even though these were Benjamites and, consequently, from Saul's Tribe, still, they knew the Anointing of God rested on David, and not on Saul. How much faith does it take for these men to forsake Saul and come to David? How much faith does it take today for men to forsake man's religion and come to David, even though he is a fugitive, but has the Anointing of the Holy Spirit?

3. As it regards the Eighth Verse, in the spirit world, these men were so anointed by the Holy Spirit that their faces looked like *"lions,"* and their swiftness was as *"deer."* What do we look like to the spirit world?

HELPERS OF THE WAR

Ziklag was David's last encampment as an exile from Saul before becoming king of Judah. It had been a place of great defeat with the Amalekites smiting Ziklag and burning it with fire while David and his men were away. All of their families were taken captive. So, it was a time of great distress (I Sam. 30:6). But, as well, the Lord gave David a great victory here because he defeated the Amalekites and recovered all, plus much spoil.

It is easy to see that, despite the discouragement of the hour while David was at Ziklag, the Spirit of God began to move upon individuals all over the land of Israel that they might come to David. As stated, it was God's Time. The First Verse also says, *"Mighty men, helpers of the war."*

There are several things I want the reader to see as it regards the first phrase of the First Verse where it says, *"Now these are they who came to David to Ziklag."*

TO SEE BY FAITH

David's time at Ziklag, which was approximately 16 months, was anything but positive, at least on the outward. In fact, and to be perfectly honest, all of this time, David was outside of the Will of God. He had gone over to the Philistines, with his fear of Saul having driven him there. While the Philistines thought that he was invading Israel and killing Israelites, he was invading towns inhabited by the Geshurites, the Gezrites, and the Amalekites (I Sam. 27:8). In fact, in these towns and villages that David attacked, the Scripture says that he *"saved neither man nor woman alive,"* so that none would be able to inform the Philistines as to what he was actually doing (I Sam. 27:11). As stated, it was not exactly a high point in David's life and living. In effect, he lied to Achish, who was the leader of the Philistines.

And then, there was the occasion of the Amalekites raiding Ziklag while he and his men were away, taking all the wives and children captives, and then burning the city with fire. David recovered all without loss, but still, this was not exactly a happy time.

But, in spite of all this, the Lord knew that David was going to come back to his Faith and would, therefore, ultimately do what was right, and so the Lord at this time, even in David's darkest days, was working for him.

NOTES

This tells us, even as it should, that irrespective of the circumstances, the Lord is still in control, and He is guiding things for our good, if, as Believers, our hearts are set fully toward Him.

During this time, the most hurtful time in David's life, at least to date, individuals from all over Israel were beginning to come to the *"sweet singer of Israel."* This was all at the behest of the Holy Spirit. Even though it would be over seven years before David would become king over all of Israel, still, the Holy Spirit had already begun to deal with the hearts of individuals that the Will of God be carried out as it regarded David being king.

THE GREAT SIGNIFICANCE OF ALL THIS

While David becoming king was of extreme significance, even as should be obvious, still, the Plan of the Lord was of far greater magnitude than meets the eye.

Even though at that time David had no idea of such, the Lord knew that He would choose this man through whose family the Messiah would come. There could be nothing in the world greater than that. As David was to be king, Christ, the Greater Son of David, will one day be King over the entirety of this world, as well. David was the Type and, therefore, in a sense, as the people treated David, they were treating the Lord.

MEN OF WAR

If it is to be noticed, the Holy Spirit describes these individuals who came to David as *"men of war."*

Why?

It was a tremendous Spiritual conflict then, carried out in the physical realm, and it is a tremendous Spiritual conflict now. The war is with the spirit world, and what do we mean by that?

Because of the manner of government, which the Lord instituted at that time, Israel was attacked constantly by surrounding nations, and even remnants of heathen tribes still left in the land of Israel. They were constantly attempting to destroy Israel, and were used of Satan to do such. So, those who came to David were described as *"helpers of the war."*

Presently, even though there are many foes, the greatest physical opposition to the True Work of God in the world is the apostate church.

THE APOSTATE CHURCH

While the world is most definitely not the friend of True Believers, to be sure, it is the apostate church, however, that is the greatest enemy. It was basically that way in the Early Church; it has been that way from then until now; and, it is most definitely the greatest danger presently.

What is the apostate church?

While volumes could be written on that question, suffice to say, which I think will sum it up, the apostate church constitutes that which does not subscribe to the simple message of *"Jesus Christ and Him Crucified"* (I Cor. 1:23). It refers to anything that is projected as the answer to man's dilemma other than the Cross of Christ.

The Bible teaches that the Gospel is what Jesus did at the Cross. Paul said:

"Christ sent me not to baptize, but to preach the Gospel, not with wisdom of words, lest the Cross of Christ should be made of none effect" (I Cor. 1:17). In simple words, the Holy Spirit through the Apostle Paul tells us in this one Verse as to exactly what the Gospel of Jesus Christ actually is. Please understand the following:

Every single thing that we have from the Lord, whether Salvation, the Baptism with the Holy Spirit, Divine Healing, Gifts of the Spirit, Fruit of the Spirit, or Blessings of every nature, all, and without exception, are made possible by what Jesus Christ did at the Cross. As we say repeatedly, *"Jesus Christ is the Source while the Cross is the Means."*

While the Conception of Christ in the womb of Mary by the Holy Spirit, which was done by decree, was absolutely necessary, still, had it stopped with the virgin birth, as necessary as that was, no one would have been redeemed.

Even though it was absolutely necessary that His Life and Living be absolutely perfect, meaning without sin, still, had it stopped there, no one would have been Saved.

Even though His Healings and Miracles were absolutely necessary, as well, had it stopped there, as wonderful as those Miracles were, still, no one would have been Saved.

In order for the Plan of Redemption to be carried out, Jesus Christ had to go to the Cross. In fact, that was His primary Purpose for coming to this world. As stated, even though everything He did was of the utmost importance and played a great part in all that was done, still, it was the Cross, and the Cross alone, which atoned for all sin, meaning that the sin debt was forever lifted, that is, for all who will believe (Jn. 3:16).

Regarding the Cross, the Lord spoke through the great Prophet Isaiah and said: *"I gave My Back to the smiters, and My Cheeks to them who plucked off the hair: I hid not My Face from shame and spitting.* (This Verse addresses itself to the hours before the Crucifixion. Mat. 26:67 and 27:26 fulfilled this Passage.)

"That our Lord, of such Power as is described in Verse 3, could contain Himself, when His Own People would treat Him thusly, is beyond comprehension! Their response to His Love was their hate. They whipped Him, pulled His Beard from His Face, and spit on Him.

"Their doing it was no surprise. By His Omniscience, He knew before He came what the results would be. And yet, He came anyway!)

"For the Lord GOD will help Me; therefore shall I not be confounded: therefore have I set My Face like a flint, and I know that I shall not be ashamed." (Lk. 9:31, 51, fulfilled this Verse. The *'help'* that His Father gave Him was that He might finish the task of redeeming mankind. The idea of redeeming someone who responds only with hate cannot be comprehended by the mortal mind, especially, when one considers what that Redemption cost!

"The phrase, *'I set My Face like a flint,'* refers to the resolve of accomplishing a certain thing despite all the scorn and hatred. Such was our Lord!)" (Isa. 50:6-7).

The Cross of Christ is where the great Plan of Redemption was finished. It took the Cross, which personified the great Sacrifice of Christ in offering up Himself, to satisfy the demands of a thrice-Holy God.

God could not allow sin to go unpunished. His Nature demanded that the full payment be made.

While it was impossible for man to pay what was owed, the only way it could be paid was for God to pay the debt, which He did in the most open, undeniable manner — the Cross. There He satisfied the claims of Divine Justice. There a thrice-Holy God and wicked men met, all in the Person of Jesus Christ, Who was both God and man. But, while He was man, very man, He never one time sinned, never one time failed, and never one time disobeyed the Word in any manner. And we must remember that everything He did, and I mean everything, was done solely for us, i.e., *"for sinners."* Our Faith in Him and what He did for us guarantees us His Victory, His Power, and above all, His More Abundant Life (Jn. 10:10).

Without the Cross, there is no Salvation, no Victory, and no Holy Spirit; in fact, without the Cross, we can receive nothing from God. As repeatedly stated, Christ is the Source while the Cross is the Means.

(9) "EZER THE FIRST, OBADIAH THE SECOND, ELIAB THE THIRD,

(10) "MISHMANNAH THE FOURTH, JEREMIAH THE FIFTH,

(11) "ATTAI THE SIXTH, ELIEL THE SEVENTH,

(12) "JOHANAN THE EIGHTH, ELZABAD THE NINTH,

(13) "JEREMIAH THE TENTH, MACHBANAI THE ELEVENTH.

(14) "THESE WERE OF THE SONS OF GAD, CAPTAINS OF THE HOST: ONE OF THE LEAST WAS OVER AN HUNDRED, AND THE GREATEST OVER A THOUSAND.

(15) "THESE ARE THEY WHO WENT OVER JORDAN IN THE FIRST MONTH, WHEN IT HAD OVERFLOWN ALL HIS BANKS; AND THEY PUT TO FLIGHT ALL THEM OF THE VALLEYS, BOTH TOWARD THE EAST, AND TOWARD THE WEST."

The pattern is:

1. (Vs. 15) The Bible says, back up in the Eighth Verse, that the *"Gadites* (from the Tribe of Gad) *there separated themselves unto David."* There has to be a separation from man's way to God's Way.

2. (Vs. 15) There were hindrances, as it regards them joining with David, such as the Jordan overflowing its banks; however, they did not allow this to stop them, and neither must we allow hindrances to stop us.

THE SPIRIT WORLD

The Scripture says that these Gadites were *"men of war fit for the battle."* It goes on to say that their *"faces were like the faces of lions, and were as swift as the roes upon the mountains."* This tells us what these men looked like in the spirit world.

When demon spirits came against them, these spirits did not see ordinary men, but rather mighty men of Faith, with such being characterized by the Holy Spirit.

These Gadites, whomever they may have been, would never have characterized themselves in this fashion, but the Holy Spirit did, and we have the record here before us.

What is the Holy Spirit saying about us? What do we look like in the spirit world? Do we have *"faces like lions,"* and are we *"swift as the deer upon the mountains?"* Evidently, these men terrorized the spirit world of darkness. In other words, the Devil knew when they got up each morning. Instead of saying, *"Good Lord, morning,"* they said, *"Good morning, Lord!"*

As a Believer, you must conduct yourself in a certain way. And what might that way be?

• Never complain.
• Hold your head high at all times.
• Praise the Lord anyhow!
• Refuse to look at circumstances.
• Place your confidence strictly in the Word of God.
• Make the Cross of Christ the Object of your Faith, and ever the Object of your Faith!
• Conduct yourself as one who is *"more than a conqueror."*

SEPARATION

The Scripture is emphatic to say that these Gadites *"separated themselves unto David into the hold to the wilderness."*

Please understand, at this particular time when David was in the wilderness, there was nothing outwardly that would attract anyone. In fact, it was the very opposite. But, despite circumstances and outward appearances, these Gadites knew that the Touch of God was on David's life, and that was enough for them.

Every Believer is going to have to separate himself unto our Heavenly David, the Lord Jesus Christ. This means that while we are in the world, we are to never be a part of the world.

But, while the Bible, even as here proclaims, definitely teaches separation, it does not teach isolation. We are in this world in order to be a Light in the midst of its darkness. We can only be that Light by separating ourselves exclusively unto Christ. Having done that, our responsibility there ends. He will then shine through us.

Separation involves being separated from something to something. In this case, it is being separated from the world and unto Christ.

We speak of the world system, the way it operates, the way it conducts itself. It has no place for the Child of God, as far as its operation is concerned, and we have no place for it within our lives. As stated, we are in it but not of it.

HINDRANCES

The Scripture is careful to point out that when the Gadites came to David, it was not the most opportune time. The Jordan River lay between them and David, and this river was normally only about 30 feet wide and four or five feet deep. But now, it was springtime, and as it did every year, it had flooded its banks, actually now approximately a mile a half wide and some 40 feet deep.

(Such does not transpire with the Jordan presently because of constant irrigation. In other words, so much water is now siphoned out of the river that it has no opportunity to flood. But, in those years of long ago, conditions were different.)

The idea is, even though the Jordan lay between them and David, even though it had flooded its banks, and even though this presented a problem, the Holy Spirit evidently moved upon these Gadites that they knew it was now time to join the *"sweet singer of Israel."* So, they did not allow anything to hinder them or to stop them.

If the Believer is looking for perfect circumstances without any hindrances before he will do what he ought to do for God, that time will never come.

The flooding of the Jordan was normal at that time of year. So, there are normal hindrances, and then there are hindrances caused by the spirit world of darkness. Irrespective, if the Lord has said to do something, hindrances must not stop us. There will be giants to hinder our victory and obstacles to hinder our advance. We are to expect it; however, that which is with us, the Lord Jesus Christ and the Power of the Holy Spirit, is more than be with them.

(16) "AND THERE CAME OF THE CHILDREN OF BENJAMIN AND JUDAH TO THE HOLD UNTO DAVID.

(17) "AND DAVID WENT OUT TO MEET THEM, AND ANSWERED AND SAID UNTO THEM, IF YOU BE COME PEACEABLY UNTO ME TO HELP ME, MY HEART SHALL BE KNIT UNTO YOU: BUT IF YOU BE COME TO BETRAY ME TO MY ENEMIES, SEEING THERE IS NO WRONG IN MY HANDS, THE GOD OF OUR FATHERS LOOK THEREON, AND REBUKE IT.

(18) "THEN THE SPIRIT CAME UPON AMASAI, WHO WAS CHIEF OF THE CAPTAINS, AND HE SAID, YOURS ARE WE, DAVID, AND ON YOUR SIDE, YOU SON OF JESSE: PEACE, PEACE BE UNTO YOU, AND PEACE BE TO YOUR HELPERS; FOR YOUR GOD HELPS YOU. THEN DAVID RECEIVED THEM, AND MADE THEM CAPTAINS OF THE BAND."

The construction is:

1. Perhaps David suspected them because some of them were *"of the Children of Benjamin,"* the Tribe of Saul; nevertheless, he was to find that they were true men.

2. The Holy Spirit revealed to him through Amasai that there was no subterfuge about these men, but rather sincerity.

3. (Vs. 18) The phrase, *"Yours are we, David, and on your side,"* must ever be the statement of any Child of God concerning the Lord Jesus Christ. As Amasai burned his bridges behind him, so to speak, we, as Children of the Living God, must do the same in our service for Jesus Christ. Amasai was not looking back; we must not look back either.

THE MOVING OF THE HOLY SPIRIT

We must understand that these men coming to David was not done at the most opportune time. As stated, this was when he was still in the wilderness, running from Saul, thereby, looking suspiciously at everyone. Some of these men were from the Tribe of Benjamin, the Tribe of Saul, so what did David think? But the Spirit of the Lord quickly put his mind to rest.

When David questioned them, the Scripture says, *"Then the Spirit came upon Amasai, who was chief of the captains...."*

We know what Amasai then said, but we do not know what else took place, if anything. At any rate, David detected the Moving and the Operation of the Holy Spirit, and that was enough.

This, the Moving of the Holy Spirit, is a must within our hearts and lives, that is, if we are to be anything for the Lord, and do anything for the Lord.

Without the Holy Spirit, the church is no more than any other earthly meeting or gathering; however, with the Holy Spirit, it becomes a living dynamo.

A PERSONAL EXPERIENCE

As I dictate these notes on September 19, 2007, for the past two days we have been raising funds over the SonLife Radio Network, and doing so for the support of the radio operation. At this time, the Ministry owns 78 stations. All are FM stations with the exception of three.

At any rate, the Network is totally supported by the listeners. In fact, we devote two days each month for the raising of funds.

The two days of this particular fund raising were not turning out too well. In fact, on the second day, at about 10:00 a.m., the phones had all but stopped ringing.

At noon I left the studio and went over to the Church in order to seek the Lord. Donnie was left in charge, and he always does an excellent job at raising funds, even better than I can do. But that day, nothing was happening.

As I began to pray at the noon hour, at first, the Heavens seemed as brass. In other words, I couldn't seem to get through. I began to importune the Lord to give me an answer. What were we to do?

I believe that the Lord has a Perfect Will for everything. Nothing is left to chance as far as He is concerned.

And then, all of a sudden, it happened! The Spirit of God instantly began to move upon me. Strangely enough, the Lord did not tell me anything. He gave me no Word, no direction, just the Moving and Operation of His Spirit. But that was enough.

When I finished seeking the Lord, Frances and I went out to get a bite of lunch. Because of the Moving and Operation of the Holy Spirit, in other words, the Presence of God, it seemed like 100 pounds had lifted off of my shoulders.

I hurried through the short lunch in order to get back to the studio. I knew that things would turn around.

And, so they did!

The Lord gave us what we needed, and all because of the Holy Spirit.

As Believers, all of us have the Holy Spirit, but the question is, *"How much is He allowed to do within our lives?"*

IS HIS OPERATION AUTOMATIC?

I think most Believers think His Operation is automatic; however, it isn't.

If the Work of the Holy Spirit in our lives were automatic, there would never be another failure on the part of the Child of God. There would never be another wrong direction; there would never be another sin. But the truth is, the Working and Operation of the Spirit are not automatic. He is limited, or else given access, according to certain things.

If the Believer wants to be led and guided by the Spirit, wants the empowerment of the Spirit, wants the Fruit of the Spirit, and wants all the help of the Holy Spirit which we are intended to have, the following must be done:

The Believer must place his Faith exclusively in the Cross of Christ (Rom. 6:3-14; 8:1-2, 11; I Cor. 1:17-18, 23; 2:2; Gal., Chpt. 5; 6:14; Col. 2:14-15).

We must remember that it is the Holy Spirit Who inspired all of these Passages; Passages, incidentally, which lead us strictly to the Cross of Christ. In fact, the Holy

Spirit works entirely within the framework of the Cross of Christ. We are told this in Romans 8:2. It says:

"For the Law of the Spirit of Life in Christ Jesus has made me free from the Law of Sin and Death."

Whenever Paul uses the term, *"in Christ Jesus,"* or one of its many derivatives, without fail, he is speaking of what Christ did at the Cross.

This is the way the Holy Spirit works. While He doesn't demand much of us, He most definitely does demand that our Faith be properly placed, and be properly maintained, and we speak of the Cross of Christ as ever being its Object.

If we make anything other than the Cross of Christ the Object of our Faith, we grieve the Holy Spirit. The Scripture says:

"Let no corrupt communication proceed out of your mouth (let no slander or faithlessness proceed out of your mouth), *but that which is good to the use of edifying* (does what we are saying build up or tear down?), *that it may Minister Grace unto the hearers* (a Blessing).

"And grieve not the Holy Spirit of God (proclaims the fact that the utterance of evil or worthless words is repugnant to the Holiness of the Spirit), *whereby you are sealed unto the Day of Redemption.* (This should have been translated, *'In Whom you are sealed unto the Day of Redemption.'* The Holy Spirit is Himself the Seal God has placed on us)" (Eph. 4:29-30).

(19) "AND THERE FELL SOME OF MANASSEH TO DAVID, WHEN HE CAME WITH THE PHILISTINES AGAINST SAUL TO BATTLE: BUT THEY HELPED THEM NOT: FOR THE LORDS OF THE PHILISTINES UPON ADVISEMENT SENT HIM AWAY, SAYING, HE WILL FALL TO HIS MASTER SAUL TO THE JEOPARDY OF OUR HEADS.

(20) "AS HE WENT TO ZIKLAG, THERE FELL TO HIM OF MANASSEH, ADNAH, AND JOZABAD, AND JEDIAEL, AND MICHAEL, AND JOZABAD, AND ELIHU, AND ZILTHAI, CAPTAINS OF THE THOUSANDS WHO WERE OF MANASSEH.

(21) "AND THEY HELPED DAVID AGAINST THE BAND OF THE ROVERS: FOR THEY WERE ALL MIGHTY MEN OF VALOUR, AND WERE CAPTAINS IN THE HOST.

(22) "FOR AT THAT TIME DAY BY DAY THERE CAME TO DAVID TO HELP HIM, UNTIL IT WAS A GREAT HOST, LIKE THE HOST OF GOD."

The construction is:

1. (Vs. 19) Some of Manasseh coming to David implies, at the same time, that some did not come. Regrettably, that seems to always be the case!

2. (Vs. 22) This was God's Time for Israel. David was His man; consequently, all who were in the Will of God came to David; otherwise, they were out of the Will of God.

3. The phrase of the Twenty-second Verse, *"like the Host of God,"* means that this host of men who came to David were of God. This was God's Will, His Time, His Place, and His Operation.

A GREAT HOST

As the time drew near when David would be crowned king, at the same time, the Lord began to move on the hearts of many men throughout Israel. They too sensed that this was God's Time. So, they would be used of God to make it happen. This was all orchestrated by God.

A lot of these individuals began to come to David even before he became king of Judah, even when he was in the wilderness. As we've already stated, there was nothing outwardly at this particular time that would draw them, but they felt something in their spirit, and that something they felt was the Lord.

I suppose the question must be asked as to how many men that the Lord moved upon, but did not favorably respond.

Knowing human nature, there must have been some, and possibly many.

It's not always easy to ascertain God's Man, in other words, as to exactly who he might be. Unfortunately, many look outwardly, and they see what they want to see. But the Ways of the Lord are seldom found in that capacity. One thing is certain; it's almost never popular to go with that which is of the Lord. As well, the majority will probably be in the opposite direction. At the same time, David did virtually nothing in order to point to himself as God's Man. He left that up to the Lord, and to be sure, the Lord carried out the operation as only He can do. He brought forth *"a great host, like the Host of God,"* to see this thing through.

Let me ask this question!

I believe the Lord is forming a *"great host"* at the present time. Are you a part of that great host?

To be sure, you can be, even if you aren't already.

(23) "AND THESE ARE THE NUMBERS OF THE BANDS WHO WERE READY ARMED TO THE WAR, AND CAME TO DAVID TO HEBRON, TO TURN THE KINGDOM OF SAUL TO HIM, ACCORDING TO THE WORD OF THE LORD.

(24) "THE CHILDREN OF JUDAH WHO BORE SHIELD AND SPEAR WERE SIX THOUSAND AND EIGHT HUNDRED, READY ARMED TO THE WAR.

(25) "OF THE CHILDREN OF SIMEON, MIGHTY MEN OF VALOUR FOR THE WAR, SEVEN THOUSAND AND ONE HUNDRED.

(26) "OF THE CHILDREN OF LEVI FOUR THOUSAND AND SIX HUNDRED.

(27) "AND JEHOIADA WAS THE LEADER OF THE AARONITES, AND WITH HIM WERE THREE THOUSAND AND SEVEN HUNDRED;

(28) "AND ZADOK, A YOUNG MAN MIGHTY OF VALOUR, AND OF HIS FATHER'S HOUSE TWENTY AND TWO CAPTAINS.

(29) "AND OF THE CHILDREN OF BENJAMIN, THE KINDRED OF SAUL, THREE THOUSAND: FOR HITHERTO THE GREATEST PART OF THEM HAD KEPT THE WARD OF THE HOUSE OF SAUL."

The pattern is:

1. The individuals of Verse 23 were not coming to be armed; they were *"ready armed."* So many today in modern Christendom are not armed and, therefore, are of no consequence to the Work of God.

2. (Vs. 23) As well, they knew their mission. They were called of God. So many in the Church presently do not know their mission. Our mission is to take this *"kingdom of Saul"* (the world) and turn it over to our Heavenly David, because it is *"according to the Word of the LORD."*

3. Many of the Tribe of Benjamin came to David, even though this was the Tribe of Saul. Some of them, it seems, had even been employed by Saul; however, they left their good jobs, whatever that may have been, in order to come to David, even though it was a hardship, at least at the beginning, to do so.

THE WORD OF THE LORD

The vision and burden that these men had were actually the same as that of David. In other words, they did not have a separate agenda. When they came to David, they came *"armed to the war,"* and their purpose was that which God gave them, *"to turn the kingdom of Saul to David, according to the Word of the LORD."*

In other words, they knew in their hearts what the *"Word of the LORD"* was, at least as it regarded David, and they wanted to be a part of what the Lord was doing.

That, *"the Word of the LORD,"* is the key to everything. What does the Lord want and desire? What is His Will?

The Believer is to understand several things. They are:

1. Everything must be according to the Word of the Lord.

2. As well, God has a specific Word for each and every situation, whatever that situation might be.

3. The Lord cannot bless anything that's not exactly according to His Word. So, no matter what something may look like on the surface, if it's not according to the Word of the Lord, then it's not of God, but rather of man.

There were a goodly number who came to David from the Tribe of Benjamin, which was the Tribe of Saul, and it seems that some of these individuals had once been close to Saul. But they saw that the Lord was not with Saul, and they ascertained that the Lord was with David. So, they came to David, which is exactly what they should have done.

There are many Christians who are trying to swim in a river that no longer has any water. There are many who are trying to remain in a boat that is, in fact, sinking. Saul's house is going down, and David's house is going up. Irrespective as to what

Satan might do, and irrespective as to what circumstances might look like, that's the way it's going to be because it is *"the Word of the LORD."*

(30) "AND OF THE CHILDREN OF EPHRAIM TWENTY THOUSAND AND EIGHT HUNDRED, MIGHTY MEN OF VALOUR, FAMOUS THROUGHOUT THE HOUSE OF THEIR FATHERS.

(31) "AND OF THE HALF TRIBE OF MANASSEH EIGHTEEN THOUSAND, WHICH WERE EXPRESSED BY NAME, TO COME AND MAKE DAVID KING.

(32) "AND OF THE CHILDREN OF ISSACHAR, WHICH WERE MEN WHO HAD UNDERSTANDING OF THE TIMES, TO KNOW WHAT ISRAEL OUGHT TO DO; THE HEADS OF THEM WERE TWO HUNDRED; AND ALL THEIR BRETHREN WERE AT THEIR COMMANDMENT.

(33) "OF ZEBULUN, SUCH AS WENT FORTH TO BATTLE, EXPERT IN WAR, WITH ALL INSTRUMENTS OF WAR, FIFTY THOUSAND, WHICH COULD KEEP RANK: THEY WERE NOT OF DOUBLE HEART.

(34) "AND OF NAPHTALI A THOUSAND CAPTAINS, AND WITH THEM WITH SHIELD AND SPEAR THIRTY AND SEVEN THOUSAND.

(35) "AND OF THE DANITES EXPERT IN WAR TWENTY AND EIGHT THOUSAND AND SIX HUNDRED.

(36) "AND OF ASHER, SUCH AS WENT FORTH TO BATTLE, EXPERT IN WAR, FORTY THOUSAND.

(37) "AND ON THE OTHER SIDE OF JORDAN, OF THE REUBENITES, AND THE GADITES, AND OF THE HALF TRIBE OF MANASSEH, WITH ALL MANNER OF INSTRUMENTS OF WAR FOR THE BATTLE, AN HUNDRED AND TWENTY THOUSAND.

(38) "ALL THESE MEN OF WAR, WHO COULD KEEP RANK, CAME WITH A PERFECT HEART TO HEBRON, TO MAKE DAVID KING OVER ALL ISRAEL: AND ALL THE REST ALSO OF ISRAEL WERE OF ONE HEART TO MAKE DAVID KING.

(39) "AND THERE THEY WERE WITH DAVID THREE DAYS, EATING AND DRINKING: FOR THEIR BRETHREN HAD PREPARED FOR THEM.

NOTES

(40) "MOREOVER THEY WHO WERE NEAR THEM, EVEN UNTO ISSACHAR AND ZEBULUN AND NAPHTALI, BROUGHT BREAD ON ASSES, AND ON CAMELS, AND ON MULES, AND ON OXEN, AND MEAT, MEAL, CAKES OF FIGS, AND BUNCHES OF RAISINS, AND WINE, AND OIL, AND OXEN, AND SHEEP ABUNDANTLY: FOR THERE WAS JOY IN ISRAEL."

The pattern is:

1. Those mentioned in Verse 31 were individuals who were *"expressed by name,"* and wanted everyone to know that they had *"come to make David king."* They were not ashamed of their mission. They wanted all to know their purpose. These are the type who make a full consecration.

2. (Vs. 32) If we follow the Holy Spirit like these men were then doing, we will, as well, have *"understanding of the times."* Only those who truly follow the Lord will *"know what the Church ought to do."*

3. (Vs. 33) Far too many Christians cannot keep rank simply because their hearts are divided between the world and the Lord Jesus Christ, or else between denominational religion and the Lord Jesus Christ. No matter the danger in battle, these men from Zebulun could keep rank.

4. (Vs. 33) The *"double heart"* is also the bane of all of Christendom. The heart is divided between Christ and other pursuits. Our hearts must be single, meaning that all its devotion must be to Christ.

5. (Vs. 34) How is it that only 6,800 of Judah came (Vs. 24), and 50,000 of the Tribe of Zebulun came? Maybe Judah was not actually remiss. David being king of Judah, possibly most in that Tribe concluded themselves to already be with him.

6. (Vs. 38) Israel, at this time, is finally marching in tune with the Holy Spirit.

7. (Vs. 40) Now there is *"fellowship,"* there is *"plenty,"* and there is *"joy,"* all because Israel is now in the Will of God. It should be noted that in the entirety of this Chapter, the seven-and-a-half year reign in Hebron of David over Judah is not referred to once. The truth is, it was God's Will for David to be king over all Israel, not just Judah. Likewise, the Lord must be king over all our lives, not just part.

FAMOUS

The Scripture says of the Tribe of Ephraim that they were *"famous throughout the house of their fathers."*

Whatever they were in the past, the truth is, they are famous now because of their siding with David. Everything the world has is temporal and, thereby, fleeting. It is only that which is locked to the Lord Jesus Christ that is eternal and, thereby, lasting.

These individuals made a decision to follow the Lord. So, their names are forever linked with eternity, and all because of what their decision represented. In essence, they were following Christ!

EXPRESSED BY NAME

All that the Holy Spirit meant as it regards this half Tribe of Manasseh being *"expressed by name,"* is known only to the Lord; however, the indication is that they wanted to *"make David king,"* and they wanted everyone to know that this was their ambition, their determination, and their goal. In other words, they would settle for nothing less.

The old song says:

"I'm not ashamed to speak for Jesus,
"I'm not ashamed to praise His Name,
"I'm not ashamed to own His Blessings,
"Oh, Praise the Lord, I'm not ashamed."

The Holy Spirit would forever enshrine their boldness and their determination. What is He saying about us?

UNDERSTANDING OF THE TIMES

The statement, *"And of the children of Issachar, which were men who had understanding of the times, to know what Israel ought to do,"* presents a beautiful proclamation. Evidently, these were men of wisdom.

Whatever they were, and whatever it was in which they excelled, the main thing was that they approved wholeheartedly of the elevation of David to the throne.

Wisdom, unless it's in the Will of God and, thereby, ordained solely for His Service, is of little good. It must ever be understood that the whole of human capacity must be for Divine use. Every faculty and power must be laid on the Divine Altar. No man can be said to be truly wise and to be truly of understanding unless that man knows the Lord, and knows Him in a personal way of relationship. To be frank, that's one of the reasons for so many of the problems in the world. Men try to make decisions without God and without His Approval.

AN ILLUSTRATION

At the dawn of this great country of the United States of America, men of wisdom gathered to endeavor to draw up a Constitution. They labored for days, but to no avail. In fact, they were at the place that they had decided to call it off and go back to their respective homes, which could very well have destroyed what this nation became, that of freedom and prosperity for all.

At a moment of great exasperation, even after many efforts had been made, but all to no avail, it is said that Benjamin Franklin stood to his feet, asked for permission to speak, and then said the following to the assembled gathering:

"Gentlemen, I propose that we get on our knees and ask Divine Favor for our undertaking. Without the help of the Lord, our efforts will be useless. The truth is, unless the Lord build the house, they labor in vain who build it."

My words are not exact, but they are close.

That assemblage did exactly as Franklin said, got on their knees and asked guidance and help from the Lord as it regarded the drawing up of the Constitution of the United States.

In a short time, the Constitution was completed, which is, no doubt, one of the greatest documents, other than the Holy Bible, devised by men, but aided by God.

Our problems presently in Iraq are because those who are in positions of power do not know or understand, whether we admit it or not, that this is a religious war we are fighting. Refusing to believe that, we stagger from one mistake to the other. To be frank, those in this nation who are truly Born-Again, through intercessory prayer, can bring this thing to a successful conclusion to a far greater degree than our armed forces, or all the political sagacity of our leaders in question.

KEEPING RANK

Hard on the heels of the previous statement, the Holy Spirit gives us another tremendous statement. He said:

"Of Zebulun, such as went forth to battle, expert in war, with all instruments of war, fifty thousand, which could keep rank: they were not of double heart."

What a statement, *"which could keep rank: they were not of double heart."* This is a most searching statement.

The idea is that these individuals had no personal agenda. They were after only one purpose, and that was to do what the Lord wanted, which was to make David king.

Jesus mentioned the impossibility of *"serving God and Mammon."* The Apostle James speaks of the *"double-minded man."*

The idea is, these men of Zebulun had but one determination, one thought, and one purpose, and that was to carry out the Will of God. They were not looking back and were not looking at circumstances, for their hearts and their minds were fully made up. They were there to do the Will of God, and that alone!

How so much this is needed presently in the Work of God.

A PERFECT HEART

When the Bible uses the *"heart"* as an example, it is not speaking of the physical organ in the body of the individual. It is speaking of the inner being, including soul and spirit, the very passions of the person.

It must be remembered that the word *"perfect"* was sanctioned here by the Holy Spirit. It speaks of a heart that is perfect toward God in the matter of making David king. It is not meaning that the individuals themselves were sinless or perfect in that respect, for they were not. It is speaking of the Will of God, and in this instance, that of making David king, which the Holy Spirit was grandly promoting at that time.

What a wonderful thing to have said of a person or a group of people, as it regards the Will of God, and according to whatever matter at hand is addressed, that the heart is perfect toward that effort. Such is not often the case. But this was God's Time, and whenever the Holy Spirit Moved on the many thousands in Israel at that time, there were many, if not most, who responded favorably.

FELLOWSHIP, PLENTY, JOY

The particular occasion respecting Verses 39 and 40 presents one of the greatest moments in human history.

Israel was raised up for the specific purpose of giving the world the Word of God, of serving as the womb of the Messiah and, in essence, of evangelizing the world. They succeeded as it regards the first two, but failed miserably regarding the latter.

Israel was the only monotheistic nation in the world, meaning that they worshipped one God, i.e., *"Jehovah."* All the other nations of the world were polytheistic, meaning they worshipped many gods, in essence, demon spirits. This means there was no Spiritual Light in the world at that time except in Israel.

Even though they were raised up for this very purpose, still, Israel did not often conduct herself as God desired. In fact, the time would come, which would be several hundreds of years later, that Israel would have to be vomited out of the land exactly as the heathen were before her, because of her great sin. In fact, the religious leaders of Israel would crucify their Messiah, the Lord Jesus Christ, when He did come. As a result, they would be destroyed and scattered all over the world, and they remained in that scattered condition for about 1,900 years, only becoming a Nation once again in 1948.

When Jesus addressed the Samaritan woman at Jacob's well, he bluntly said to her, *"You worship you know not what* (He minced no words, telling her plainly that the Samaritan way of worship held no validity with God; regrettably it is the same with most presently)*: we know what we worship: for Salvation is of the Jews* (meaning that through the Jewish people, came the Word of God and, as well, the Son of God, Who Alone brought Salvation, and did so by going to the Cross)" (Jn. 4:22).

Of course, Satan would do everything within his power to hinder the Jewish people from carrying out their intended task, even as he had done with attempting to stop David from becoming king. He did not succeed, although he did cause tremendous problems. But, despite his efforts of destruction, David is now about to become king, and in actuality, through the family of this shepherd boy, will come the Messiah, which is the greatest thing ever known to the whole of humanity. On this glad day, the following was evident:

• Fellowship: Union with the Lord always denotes glorious fellowship, for whenever we are of *"one heart,"* there will be glorious fellowship.

• Plenty: There is never lack when the Spirit of the Lord has His Way. The word that is used concerning this *"plenty"* is *"abundantly."*

• Joy: The joy of the Lord will always follow *"fellowship"* and *"plenty."*

"Come, thou Fount of every Blessing,
tune my heart to sing Your Grace.
"Streams of Mercy, never ceasing, call
for songs of loudest praise.
"Teach me some melodious sonnet,
sung by Flaming Tongues above;
"Praise the Mount I'm fixed upon it,
Mount of Your Redeeming Love."

"Here I raise my Ebenezer; hither by
Your Help I'm come;
"And I hope, by Your Good Pleasure,
safely to arrive at home.
"Jesus sought me when a stranger,
wandering from the Fold of God;
"He to rescue me from danger, interposed His Precious Blood."

"Oh to Grace how great a debtor daily
I'm constrained to be!
"Let Your Goodness, like a fetter, bind
my wandering heart to Thee:
"Prone to wander, Lord I feel it, Prone
to leave the God I love;
"Here's my heart, O take and seal it;
seal it for Your Courts above."

CHAPTER 13

(1) "AND DAVID CONSULTED WITH THE CAPTAINS OF THOUSANDS AND HUNDREDS, AND WITH EVERY LEADER.

(2) "AND DAVID SAID UNTO ALL THE CONGREGATION OF ISRAEL, IF IT SEEM GOOD UNTO YOU, AND THAT IT BE OF THE LORD OUR GOD, LET US SEND ABROAD UNTO OUR BRETHREN EVERYWHERE, WHO ARE LEFT IN ALL THE LAND OF ISRAEL, AND WITH THEM ALSO TO THE PRIESTS AND LEVITES WHICH ARE IN THEIR CITIES AND SUBURBS, THAT THEY MAY GATHER THEMSELVES UNTO US:

(3) "AND LET US BRING AGAIN THE ARK OF OUR GOD TO US: FOR WE ENQUIRED NOT AT IT IN THE DAYS OF SAUL.

(4) "AND ALL THE CONGREGATION SAID THAT THEY WOULD DO SO: FOR THE THING WAS RIGHT IN THE EYES OF ALL THE PEOPLE.

(5) "SO DAVID GATHERED ALL ISRAEL TOGETHER, FROM SHIHOR OF EGYPT EVEN UNTO THE ENTERING OF HEMATH, TO BRING THE ARK OF GOD FROM KIRJATH-JEARIM.

(6) "AND DAVID WENT UP, AND ALL ISRAEL, TO BAALAH, THAT IS, TO KIRJATH-JEARIM, WHICH BELONGED TO JUDAH, TO BRING UP THENCE THE ARK OF GOD THE LORD, WHO DWELLS BETWEEN THE CHERUBIMS, WHOSE NAME IS CALLED ON IT.

(7) "AND THEY CARRIED THE ARK OF GOD IN A NEW CART OUT OF THE HOUSE OF ABINADAB: AND UZZA AND AHIO DROVE THE CART.

(8) "AND DAVID AND ALL ISRAEL PLAYED BEFORE GOD WITH ALL THEIR MIGHT, AND WITH SINGING, AND WITH HARPS, AND WITH PSALTERIES, AND WITH TIMBRELS, AND WITH CYMBALS, AND WITH TRUMPETS."

The pattern is:

1. (Vs. 1) While David did consult with many individuals, it doesn't say that he consulted with God; the results of such action would be disastrous.

2. (Vs. 2) There was much religious activity at this point, but very little, if any, leading of the Holy Spirit.

3. (Vs. 3) It is ironic that the entire motive for the bringing of the Ark was to *"enquire of it,"* yet David did not enquire of the

Lord concerning this all-important task.

4. (Vs. 4) While the bringing of the Ark was right in the Eyes of God, still, it was not right in the way it was done, and such a direction would bring forth death.

5. (Vs. 5) How many times does the church, with great fanfare, rush forward to carry out its bold plans, when, in reality, those plans will not bring life, but death? Great religious activity never denotes great Spiritual Depth; nevertheless, the clatter of religious machinery, combined with the noise of great religious profession, completely fools most people.

6. (Vs. 6) During the time of Saul, who was a work of the flesh, the Ark of God was ignored, because Spiritual things had no value to Saul; I'm afraid the modern church, at least for all practical purposes, is following the same course of ignoring the Will of God.

7. (Vs. 7) The Ark of God, by the Command of God, was to be carried on the shoulders of Priests, and not on a cart of any kind. The Priests were Types of Christ; the symbolism portrayed the fact that the Presence of God rested solely on Christ, and within Christ.

8. (Vs. 7) It must be clearly noted that anything and everything instituted by man is always, and without exception, a *"new cart."* It is doomed to failure. All directions for all things are laid down in the Word of God (II Pet. 1:3). Any deviation will always bring death (Ex. 37:5; Num. 4:15; Deut. 10:8; Josh. 3:8-14). Regrettably, the church presently is full of *"new carts"*!

9. How much does the Eighth Verse characterize our modern day church? It is all very religious, but very wrong! It is all very loud, but very lost! It is all with great activity, but not by the Holy Spirit. If it's not according to the Word of God, then all the religious activity will not make it right, and death will be the result.

CONSULTING MAN

The First Verse says, *"And David consulted with the captains of thousands and hundreds, and with every leader;"* however, it doesn't say that David consulted with God. In fact, he didn't!

How so often we assume that we know

NOTES

what God wants, when, in reality, we don't. The modern church is so quick to seek the advice of frail humans, and this statement in no way is meant to demean the counsel of godly brethren, still, there are two things that must always be done concerning the Work of God:

1. We always must go to God first, seeking His Counsel and His Direction.

2. Whatever counsel or advice that we receive from men, even though they may be ever so godly, must coincide perfectly with the Word of God. If it doesn't, it must be rejected out of hand.

David's failure to consult with the Lord is amazing, especially when we consider that David's strength was in being led by the Holy Spirit. Also, if the student will observe carefully David's life, he will easily notice how the Holy Spirit observed David's seeking the Will of God regarding direction. It should also be noted how carefully the Holy Spirit portrays David's actions when he did not inquire of the Lord. Every time this happened, David brought upon himself great difficulties. This time would be no exception. What a lesson this should be for us today.

What David proposed to do, the bringing of the Ark into Jerusalem, was right and noble. It was what the Lord wanted, with the Holy Spirit, no doubt, impressing upon him to do this thing; however, David never looked in the Word of God to see how the Ark should be handled, but rather just assumed that he knew what to do.

He didn't!

We will find that what he didn't know caused his actions to violate the Word of God, and to do so in a very serious way. The Word of God must be the criteria for all things, and not merely the advice of men.

No doubt, this occasion was celebrated with great zeal. All of Israel was involved. Because of ignoring the Word of God, it would end in disaster.

THE ARK OF GOD

The plans are great. There are great festivities. The action is noble. For the Third Verse says, *"And let us bring again the Ark of our God to us."*

Men think that because their plans are

noble and their motivations correct, God will bless their efforts without fail, nevertheless, He is sorely displeased when we attempt to do *"good things our way."* God has no interest in man's ways. Our ways, regardless of our great show of religion, are not God's Ways.

Perhaps, the boldest task of the Holy Spirit in our lives is to bring us from our own ways to God's Ways. Unfortunately, God's Ways cannot be learned easily or quickly.

The Ark of God had not been consulted in approximately 70 years.

After it was brought back from the land of the Philistines to a place called Kirjath-jearim, the time was given as 20 years (I Sam. 7:1-2).

Also, it remained there during the 40-year reign of Saul. David would reign approximately ten years (seven years in Judah and three years over the whole of Israel) before the Ark would be brought to Jerusalem. This is a total of approximately 70 years.

Furthermore, when the Ark was finally found by David, it seems that it had been discarded and was standing alone out in a field next to the woods. The Psalm of David says, *"Lo, we heard of it at Ephratah: we found it in the fields of the wood"* (Ps. 132:6). Whether that can be taken literally or not, we cannot say; yet, I wonder if the Glory of God has not been abandoned in the modern church even more so than it was with Israel?

At any rate, the Ark of the Covenant is being brought into Jerusalem, its rightful place, but sadly, brought in the wrong way.

A NEW CART

The Scripture says, *"And they carried the Ark of God in a new cart out of the house of Abinadab"* (Vs. 7).

Why not?

It seemed the proper thing to do. The Philistines had sent the Ark of God back to Israel in this manner (I Sam. 6:7). There is a slim possibly that it could have even been the same *"new cart."*

Unfortunately, the modern church is full of *"new carts,"* or *"the ways of the world."* It must be clearly noted that any and everything instituted by man is always, and without exception, a *"new cart."* It is doomed to failure.

The Ark of God, as stated, was not to be transported on any type of contrivance of this sort, but rather on the shoulders of Priests (Ex. 37:5; Num. 4:15; Deut. 10:8; Josh. 3:8-14).

Why Priests?

Priests, under the old economy of God, served as mediators between God and men, i.e., *"between God and Israel."* As such, they were Types of Christ. Even though they were men and, thereby, very much imperfect, still, they served as Types; consequently, they were the only ones who were qualified, so to speak, to bear the Ark of the Covenant.

David should have known this, and above all, the High Priest should have known it, but it seems that he didn't. They put the Ark of God on a *"new cart"* because that seemed to be the thing to do.

As stated, the church today is full of new carts; therefore, let us make a statement that will make all of this abundantly clear.

THE CROSS OF CHRIST

If whatever we do for the Lord, or in the Name of the Lord, is not based squarely on the Cross of Christ, then pure and simple, it is a *"new cart,"* that which God will never honor. This means that all worship must be based on the Cross of Christ. Our giving of money to the Work of God must be based entirely upon the Cross of Christ. The Message we heed must be 100 percent the Cross of Christ. In other words, the Cross of Christ must ever be the Object of our Faith, and the Cross of Christ alone!

Now, I'll ask the question, *"Is that what is taking place presently in the modern church?"*

I think not!

Consequently, two things will happen:

1. Individually, each Believer subscribing to that which is really not the Gospel, which means it's not the Cross, will experience a spiritual leanness in their souls, with many even losing their way completely.

2. Not only will the leanness take place individually, but, as well, the major institutions, i.e., denominations, will begin to lose their way, more and more looking to things of the world instead of that which is solidly

the Word of God. For instance, the *"Purpose Driven Life"* scheme is a *"new cart."* So were the Promise Keepers and so is the Word of Faith message. Let's say it again:

Any doctrine, any plan, or any proposal that purports to come from the Lord, which is not based solely on the Cross of Christ, pure and simple, is false. It is a *"new cart."*

GREAT RELIGIOUS FERVOR

The Scripture says, *"And David and all Israel played before God with all their might, and with singing, and with harps, and with psalteries, and with timbrels, and with cymbals, and with trumpets"* (Vs. 8).

It doesn't matter what religious show of emotion is presented, it doesn't matter the fervor and intensity, it doesn't matter the ceremonial, religious setting, if it's not the Cross, it can never be accepted by God, and will ultimately bring death.

The modern church all too often is trying to cover up the barrenness of its possession with the loudness of its profession. There is nothing wrong with fervor or intensity or excitement, etc. But, at the same time, such doesn't necessarily mean that things are right. Things looked right during this time of David, but they were all together wrong, which wrong would suddenly show itself very shortly.

Remember this, that which God recognizes, and the only thing He recognizes, is Faith; however, the Object of that Faith must always be the Cross of Christ. This means that the Lord is not looking for ostentatiousness, ceremony, ritual, works, performance, etc., but rather, *"Faith"* (Rom., Chpts. 4-5).

Probably there are more books being written presently about the Gospel than ever before. Most of them are worthless. Oh yes, all of them say some good things, but it's good things to which the reader will never attain, and neither has the person attained who has written the book.

I say that because most all of these books, as they relate to the Gospel telling people how to exercise their faith, how to receive from God, how to be the champion you really are, how to reach your maximum, how to improve yourself, how to make yourself what you ought to be, etc., present that

NOTES

which cannot be done. Paul nailed it when he said:

"For if Righteousness come by the Law, then Christ is dead in vain" (Gal. 2:21).

In other words, if all of these things can be done by means other than Christ and the Cross, then Jesus unnecessarily died on the Cross. But we know that Jesus did not needlessly die on the Cross.

THE POTENTIAL OF THE BELIEVER

While the Believer, irrespective as to whom he might be, or his circumstances, most definitely can rise to a place and position far, far beyond what he may ask or think, it can only be done in one way. Before I relate the way, please note carefully the following:

If the individual will totally consecrate to the Lord, seek to know and understand the Word of God, place his Faith entirely in Christ and the Cross, and not allow it to be moved elsewhere, the potential is literally unlimited as to what the Lord can make of you, can do for you, and can do with you.

The foolishness that is presented outside of the Cross, even if attained, which it will not be, will amount to precious little.

The reason?

The reason is simple! Whatever it is that I need to be, that I ought to be, or that I can be, no matter how clever the proposals may be, I cannot better myself, neither can anyone else. Sometimes we may think that particular things constitute a betterment; however, the betterment is mostly temporary, or else it never addresses the true things of life.

That which the Lord does with a person and for a person addresses every facet and every capacity of our being. In other words, the growth is never abnormal but always well-rounded.

THE CROSS OF CHRIST

All of this can be attained by anyone, and is meant to be attained by anyone, at least those who are Believers, providing they understand several things. Those things are:

• Whatever it is that needs to be done, it simply cannot be accomplished within our own strength and ability. In other words, self cannot improve self. We must understand that, which means that most all of the books written will be discarded, and most of the sermons heard will be laid aside.

• It is the Holy Spirit Alone Who can make us what we ought to be. The Holy Spirit is God. As such, He can do anything. We must understand that, that is, if we are to be what we ought to be.

• To have the Work of the Holy Spirit carried out within our lives, we must understand, first of all, that He functions entirely within the framework of the Finished Work of Christ. In other words, it is the Cross of Christ, which has given the Holy Spirit latitude to do all that He does (Rom. 8:2).

• We must ever know that God is looking for Faith on our part. He does not work from the premise of performance or merit, only Faith (Rom. 5:1-2).

• The type of Faith that God recognizes, and the only type of Faith that God will recognize, is that which ever has the Cross of Christ as its Object. This is absolutely imperative! Our Faith being anchored firmly in the Cross of Christ is an absolute requirement in order for the Holy Spirit to Work within our lives. We must never forget that (Rom. 6:3-5, 11).

• This is so critical that, in a sense, we must renew our Faith in the Cross of Christ even on a daily basis. If this is not done, Jesus firmly stated that we cannot be His Disciple. That's how important the correct Object of our Faith must be (Lk. 9:23; 14:27).

• Having properly placed our Faith in the Cross of Christ, and maintaining it in the Cross of Christ, is where the *"good fight of Faith"* begins. Just because our Faith is correctly placed doesn't mean that Satan is going to strike his tent and leave. In truth, he will do everything within his power to move our Faith from the Cross of Christ to something else. That's the reason the Holy Spirit referred to this through the Apostle Paul as *"a fight."* Yet, it is a *"good fight,"* because it is the *"right fight"* (I Tim. 6:12).

• Functioning in this manner, we are guaranteed that sin will no longer have dominion over us in any fashion (Rom. 6:14).

(9) "AND WHEN THEY CAME UNTO THE THRESHINGFLOOR OF CHIDON, UZZA PUT FORTH HIS HAND TO HOLD THE ARK; FOR THE OXEN STUMBLED.

NOTES

(10) "AND THE ANGER OF THE LORD WAS KINDLED AGAINST UZZA, AND HE SMOTE HIM, BECAUSE HE PUT HIS HAND TO THE ARK: AND THERE HE DIED BEFORE GOD.

(11) "AND DAVID WAS DISPLEASED, BECAUSE THE LORD HAD MADE A BREACH UPON UZZA: WHEREFORE THAT PLACE IS CALLED PEREZ-UZZA TO THIS DAY.

(12) "AND DAVID WAS AFRAID OF GOD THAT DAY, SAYING, HOW SHALL I BRING THE ARK OF GOD HOME TO ME?

(13) "SO DAVID BROUGHT NOT THE ARK HOME TO HIMSELF TO THE CITY OF DAVID, BUT CARRIED IT ASIDE INTO THE HOUSE OF OBED-EDOM THE GITTITE.

(14) "AND THE ARK OF GOD REMAINED WITH THE FAMILY OF OBED-EDOM IN HIS HOUSE THREE MONTHS. AND THE LORD BLESSED THE HOUSE OF OBED-EDOM, AND ALL THAT HE HAD."

The exposition is:

1. (Vs. 9) There is always *"a threshingfloor"*; the threshingfloor was where the grain was separated from the husk; on this memorable day, the Spiritual Grain would be separated from the husk as well (Mat. 3:11-12).

2. (Vs. 10) Of all people, Uzza should have known better. The Ark had been at his place, for he was a son of Abinadab, where the Ark had been left many years before (I Sam. 7:1); however, it seems he had not bothered to check out the Word of God, as to exactly what the disposition of the Ark should be.

3. (Vs. 10) As well, millions presently think, as Uzza evidently did at that time, that David would be responsible, because he had delegated the responsibility to Uzza. Uzza was to find out differently.

4. (Vs. 10) Millions are in Hell presently, because they left responsibility up to a preacher or a Priest. God demands that each individual know and understand the Word of God, and be responsible accordingly. So, the idea that Believers are to obey someone in authority, and do so without question, irrespective as to whether it's right or wrong, is not taught in the Bible. In fact, the very opposite is taught (Ezek. 18:4).

5. (Vs. 11) The word *"displeased"* means *"saddened"*; David had a right to be sad, because he definitely was mostly to blame.

6. (Vs. 12) David's sadness was quickly turned into acute fear. He realized how close he personally had come to death on this day. Sadly, most of the modern church is only *"displeased."* There is very little *"fear of God"* left! Consequently, David's heart sobbed, *"How shall I bring the Ark of God home to me?"* All must be done God's Way.

7. (Vs. 13) Undoubtedly, David was led by the Lord in leaving the Ark with Obed-edom; as the facts will prove, this man had a great heart for God, and knew how to treat the Ark, so to speak, even to a greater extent, it seems, than did David.

8. (Vs. 14) One man died because of ignoring the Word of God, and one man and his house are greatly blessed because of obeying the Word of God. That was the criteria then, obedience to the Word, and it is the criteria now!

THE THRESHINGFLOOR

For a period of time, everything went well in this procession. The singers were singing, and the musicians were playing their instruments. There were many praises that went up to the Lord. The Ark was coming home; however, there was a *"threshingfloor"* just ahead.

A wrong direction may seem like the right direction, at least for a period of time. But, as it regards the Work of the Lord, sooner or later, if situations are unscriptural, things are going to have to be made right. In other words, we are going to have to be brought in line with the Word of God, that is, if we are to remain a Child of God.

It is the business of the Holy Spirit to get us in line with the Word of God. That is one of His Responsibilities and, to be sure, one way or the other, He will get done what He is assigned to do. The only way that such will not be, and which, sadly, is mostly the case, is that the Believer will refuse direction from the Lord and insist upon his own way.

If such a way continues, which means that faith is sadly misplaced, at a point in time, a time known only to the Lord, such

NOTES

a person ceases to be a Child of God and becomes a *"bastard."* Paul said:

"But if you be without chastisement, whereof all (all true Believers) *are partakers, then are you bastards, and not sons.* (Many claim to be Believers while continuing in sin, but the Lord never chastises them. Such shows they are illegitimate sons, meaning they are claiming faith on a basis other than the Cross. The true son, without doubt, will be chastised at times)" (Heb. 12:8).

The threshingfloor is the place where the husk is separated from the grain. Almost always, it is a violent process. Yet, inasmuch as the husk must be separated, the threshingfloor is absolutely necessary. As well, this goes for every Believer. None are excluded, and from time to time, all need the threshingfloor.

John the Baptist, in speaking of Christ, said: *"I indeed baptize you with water unto Repentance* (Water Baptism was an outward act of an inward work already carried out)*: but He* (Christ) *Who comes after me is mightier than I, Whose Shoes I am not worthy to bear: He shall baptize you with the Holy Spirit, and with fire* (to burn out the sinful dross [Acts 2:2-4])*:*

"Whose fan is in His Hand (the ancient method for winnowing grain)*, and He will thoroughly purge His Floor* ('purging it, that it may bring forth more fruit' [Jn. 15:2])*, and gather His Wheat into the garner* (the end product as developed by the Spirit)*; but He will burn up the chaff with unquenchable fire* (the wheat is symbolic of the Work of the Spirit, while the chaff is symbolic of the work of the flesh)" (Mat. 3:11-12).

DEATH

The Scripture says, *"And the anger of the LORD was kindled against Uzza, and He smote him, because he put his hand to the Ark: and there he died before God"* (Vs. 10).

As we have already stated, Uzza, of all people, should have known better.

When the oxen pulling the cart, which held the Ark, came to the threshingfloor, evidently, there was something there uneven about it, and the oxen stumbled. Afraid that the Ark would fall off the cart, Uzza reached up and put his hand on it to steady it. When he did this, the Scripture says, *"The anger of the LORD was kindled against Uzza."* Because the Ark had been at the house of Abinadab for many years, David apparently thought that the two sons of this man, Uzza and Ahio, should be put in charge of the procession, at least, to watch over the Ark. These two men had no idea whatsoever as to what they were facing.

Untold numbers of religious men are presently being appointed by other religious men to places of position, which, if the truth be known, will bring death to them, and we speak of spiritual death.

The Ark of God was not to be touched under any circumstances, except in a prescribed way. Considering that it should have been on the shoulders of Priests, but was rather on a new cart, such provided fertile ground for death and destruction. We must ever understand that the things of God are never to be taken lightly. The Lord says what He means and means what He says. David should have known better, as well, the Priests should have known better, and Uzza should have known better.

When the oxen stumbled, and evidently the Ark wavered, Uzza, no doubt thinking he was doing right, reached up to steady the Ark, and when he touched it, he was instantly stricken dead by the Lord.

WAS GOD CRUEL FOR DOING SUCH A THING?

Many, if not most, would think God was cruel for doing this; however, He would have been cruel not to have done so.

In fact, the very existence of man, and above all, the Salvation of man, at least those who will be Saved, is dependent on God adhering strictly to His Word. Otherwise, all is lost!

Uzza touching the Ark, and being stricken dead instantly, should be a warning to all that God means what He says about the place called Hell. Jesus Christ, God's Only Son, is the Way of Salvation, and the only Way. What He did at the Cross makes it possible for the fallen sons of Adam's lost race to be Saved.

Man is a free moral agent and, as such,

NOTES

he can refuse that which God has provided; however, if he does so, and most, regrettably, do, eternal Hell will be the result. It has to be that way; it can be no other!

Some time ago I preached a Message entitled, *"Can God Condemn A Man To Hell, Burn Him There Forever And Forever, And Justify Himself In Doing So?"* It is quite a question!

First of all, Hell is not merely a figment of someone's imagination; it is a place, a place, incidentally, located in the heart of the Earth (Mat. 12:40).

Secondly, Hell is a place of torment (Lk. 16:20-31). As well, the fire of Hell is real (Lk. 16:24).

Last of all, Hell was not really prepared for man, but rather, for Satan and his Angels (Mat. 25:41). So, if man goes there, it will be because he preferred Satan and his evil over God and His Righteousness, of which the latter can only be received by one accepting Jesus Christ. If sinful, wicked man were allowed into Heaven, meaning that he rejected Christ, God's Answer for man's dilemma, then Heaven would soon be turned into a Hell. So, God has no choice but to condemn all to Hell who will not accept Christ. The truth is, the Lord has done everything, even to the giving of His Only Son, in order that man might be Saved.

Yes, God is fully justified in condemning man to Hell forever and forever if man refuses that which He has provided regarding Salvation (Rev. 20:11-15).

Yes, the Lord was also fully justified in striking Uzza dead!

THE SADNESS OF DAVID

The phrase, *"And David was displeased,"* as we have previously stated, would have probably been better translated *"saddened."*

At this stage, it is obvious, I think, that David did not really know why the Lord was angered and, thereby, had stricken Uzza dead. But, at the same time, he most definitely knew that the Lord had done this thing, and that after a measure, the fault was his. The idea is this:

When leadership goes wrong, as should be obvious, even though what we've said is correct, still, every single Believer in the world, irrespective as to whom that Believer might be, is to study the Word of God himself, so that he will have a firm grasp on that which the Lord wants and desires. While leadership is most definitely to be respected, no Believer is ever absolved of blame, as it regards the right and responsibility to know. Let us say it again:

SPIRITUAL AUTHORITY

Let me state that Spiritual Authority never refers to authority over other people. Always, and without exception, it refers to authority over the spirit world, i.e., demon spirits, fallen Angels, and even Satan himself. That's where the Spiritual Authority begins, and that's where the Spiritual Authority ends. Let me say it again, Spiritual Authority never pertains to authority over other human beings; unfortunately, some have tried to claim such, thereby, demanding that they be obeyed, irrespective as to what the demand would be. The idea is, the person is supposed to obey without question regardless of the demand being Scriptural or not Scriptural. The idea continues that if someone is to be accountable, it's the one in authority. Denominational heads are bad about such attitudes. So are many so-called Charismatic leaders. In fact, this problem is far more widespread than meets the eye. Religious men love to control other men and believe it or not, many Christians love to be controlled. They think this absolves them of responsibility. It doesn't!

The Scripture says, *"The soul that sins, it shall die. The son shall not bear the iniquity of the father, neither shall the father bear the iniquity of the son: the righteousness of the righteous shall be upon him, and the wickedness of the wicked shall be upon him"* (Ezek. 18:20).

If any Believer acquiesces to the demands of a spiritual leader, so-called, who is demanding that they do something that's unscriptural, they must not obey such a demand. If they do, they sin, and sin grievously!

It is certain that David did not know what should be done with the Ark when this procession began. It is also certain that Uzza did not know what should be done, as well; however, two things must be said here.

NOTES

1. Ignorance did not stop the Judgment of God. We must never forget that.

2. As well, let's say for the sake of argument that David did not know, but, that Uzza did know. Just because David was king and demanded that Uzza serve in this capacity, had this man known what was right, that he must do. In other words, even though it's the king commanding something, if it's wrong, it should not be obeyed.

Of course, it must be quickly added, the one who would take such a position, even as they ought to do so, will have to suffer the consequences. With David, there would not have been any negative consequences; however, down through the ages, there have been many consequences, with many having to give up their lives, simply because they would not obey what they were demanded to do, because they knew it to be wrong.

Again we state, David had a right to be saddened because he knew that he was at least partly to blame for the death of Uzza. Wrongdoing has a spreading effect. It does not merely begin and end with the perpetrator.

"HOW SHALL I BRING THE ARK OF GOD TO ME?"

In connection with the Ark, the Scripture says, *"And David was afraid of God that day."* In essence, his displeasure was turned into acute fear. He realized how close he had come to death on this day.

Sadly, most of the modern church is only *"displeased."* There is very little *"fear of God"* left. It is bad enough to do wrong, as David did. It is even worse still to not tremble at our wrongdoing. But, with impunity, millions think nothing of placing their polluted, religious hands on the Ark of God; nevertheless, it must be remembered that it brought death then, and it will bring death now.

For Israel to be what she should be, for David to do what he should do, and for the Blessings of God to come upon this people, the Ark of God must be in its rightful place. But, considering the recent events which have brought death to one man and cast a pall of gloom over the entirety of the procession, David realizes that the entire situation must be re-thought. He must ascertain as to what the Lord desires in such a situation. In other words, he must go to the Word of God, which he should have done at the beginning, to ascertain the rightful handling of the most Holy Object on the face of the Earth, the Ark of the Covenant.

I wish I could presently say that the modern church wants and desires the Ark of God, i.e., *"the Presence of God."* I wish I could say that at the moment it is re-evaluating its situation, attempting to ascertain exactly what the Lord wants. I wish I could say that it is going to the Word of God and, thereby, intently studying its contents to ascertain what the Lord desires. But, I'm afraid that's not the case.

With the exception of the few hearts, which truly hunger and thirst after Righteousness, and there are some, tragically, the far greater majority of the modern church doesn't even really want the Presence of God. Let me make the following statement:

WE HAVE NEED OF NOTHING

When Christ addressed the church at Laodicea which, incidentally, was His last Message to the Church, and which characterizes the modern church, they were saying, *"I am rich, and increased with goods, and have need of nothing."* His answer to them was blunt and to the point. He said:

"And knowest not that you are wretched, and miserable, and poor, and blind, and naked."

He then said, *"I counsel you to buy of Me gold tried in the fire, that you may be rich; and white raiment, that you may be clothed, and that the shame of your nakedness do not appear; and anoint your eyes with eyesalve, that you may see"* (Rev. 3:17-18).

THREE THINGS SAID BY OUR LORD

Three things are said here by our Lord as it regards what is needed by the modern church, and He is speaking of the modern church. Those things are:

1. *"Buy of Me gold tried in the fire, that you may be rich."*

Gold in the Bible, at least when used in this fashion, signifies Deity. In essence, He is saying that the church must quit looking to man and look to Him.

As well, it is only that which is anchored in Christ, i.e., *"gold,"* that will stand the test of fire. Everything else will burn up.

2. White raiment: This speaks of the Righteousness, which Christ Alone can give, and which is made possible by the Cross.

3. *"Anoint your eyes with eyesalve, that you may see:"* The modern church is spiritually blind because the modern church has ignored or even repudiated the Cross of Christ. Unless one's Faith is anchored solely in Christ and the Cross, one cannot really Spiritually see as one should.

THE PRESENCE OF GOD

As stated, the Ark of the Covenant was a Type of the Presence of God presently. This is the only thing that counts. Our beautiful new buildings will not set one captive free. Our educational degrees will not set one captive free. All of our religious programs will not set one captive free. It is the Presence of God, typified by the Ark of long ago, which is what the church desperately needs, and which will set the captive free.

It must be understood that the Presence of God is made possible solely by Christ and what He did for us at the Cross. How shall the Ark of God come to me? Jesus told us. He said:

"Be zealous therefore, and repent."

He then said: *"Behold, I stand at the door, and knock (presents Christ outside the church): if any man hear My Voice (so much religious racket is going on that it is difficult to 'hear His Voice') and open the door (Christ is the True Door, which means the church has erected another door), I will come in to him, and will sup with him, and he with Me. (Having been rejected by the church, our Lord now appeals to individuals, and He is still doing so presently)"* (Rev. 3:19-20).

THE BLESSING OF THE LORD

The Scripture says, *"So David brought not the Ark home to himself to the city of David, but carried it aside into the house of Obed-edom the Gittite.*

"And the Ark of God remained with the family of Obed-edom in his house three

months. *And the LORD blessed the house of Obed-edom, and all that he had"* (Vss. 13-14).

There is a difference of opinion as to exactly who Obed-edom the Gittite actually was. Some think that because the name *"Gittite"* was attached, this meant that he was a Gentile and, thereby, a proselyte to Jehovah. That may have been possible, but it is unlikely.

More than likely, the attachment *"Gittite"* only specified the home of his family. There is little doubt that this Obed-edom was a Levite, of the Kohathite family. There is no evidence that he was a Priest, but he was most definitely qualified to care for the Ark.

Whenever the Lord struck Uzza dead, stopping this procession, David did not know exactly what to do. One thing was certain, they could not proceed. In fact, they dare not proceed. They were out of the Will of God because they were violating the Word of God and, above all, it concerned a matter so important as the Ark of the Covenant.

While the Scripture doesn't say, no doubt, David cried to the Lord as to exactly what he should do and maybe, as well, he inquired of the High Priest, who quite possibly was present. At any rate, it was ascertained that the domicile of Obed-Edom, a Levite, was nearby, and it was deemed desirable that the Ark of the Covenant be left at this man's house.

OBED-EDOM

We aren't told exactly as to what Obed-edom thought as it regards the Ark being left with him. No doubt, he quickly learned of the death of Uzza, but despite all of that, every indication is that this man knew exactly how the Ark of God should be treated and, thereby, welcomed it gladly.

As to exactly how he handled it, we aren't told, but this we do know: inasmuch as *"The LORD blessed the house of Obed-edom, and all that he had,"* and did so for the three month's duration that the Ark was there, this tells us that whatever Obed-edom did, the Lord was very pleased.

THE MANNER OF THE ARK

When the Ark was moved, the beautiful Veil, which separated the Holy Place from the Holy of Holies, was to be taken down and placed first over the Ark. Above that was to be *"a covering of badgers' skins,"* and then, over that, *"a cloth wholly of blue"* (Num. 4:5-6).

The *"covering Veil"* symbolized the Righteousness of Christ, portrayed in the white, with the scarlet of the Veil symbolizing the Cross, and the blue symbolizing that it was all from Heaven and, thereby, none of man.

The *"badgers' skins"* symbolized Christ as the great High Priest of His People. The blue cloth that went on last, and was the only part actually seen, once again, symbolized, and in no uncertain terms, that Salvation is totally from Heaven, which means that man has no part in this great Work, except to obey.

While the Bible is silent in regard to what Obed-edom did as it pertained to the Ark, the possibility definitely existed that he did what he could to obey the Scripture regarding the coverings. He would not have had access to the *"covering Veil,"* but he could have had access to the other two coverings. At any rate, whatever it is that he did, it pleased the Lord tremendously so, and great Blessings followed.

THE BLESSING AND THE CURSE

We have here in perfect relief a perfect example of what brings the curse of God, and what brings Blessings. David ignored the Word of God, and death followed. Obed-edom adhered strictly to the Word of God, and he was blessed accordingly. Is it any different presently?

The Lord cannot change. If we obey His Word, great Blessings will always follow. If we disobey, judgment will follow. Either one or the other may not happen immediately, but ultimately, the Law of Divine Blessing, or Divine retribution, will go into effect.

"A Mighty Fortress is our God, a Bulwark never failing;
"Our Helper He, amid the flood of mortal ills prevailing,
"For still our ancient foe does seek to work us woe;
"His craft and power are great,
"And armed with cruel hate, on Earth

is not His equal."

*"Did we in our own strength confide,
our striving would be losing,*
*"Were not the Right Man on our side,
the Man of God's Own choosing.*
*"Dost ask who that may be? Christ
Jesus it is He; Lord Sabaoth His
Name,*
*"From age to age the same, and He
must win the battle."*

*"And though this world with devils
filled, should threaten to undo us,*
*"We will not fear, for God has willed
His Truth to triumph through us.*
*"The prince of darkness grim we
tremble not for him; His rage we
can endure,*
*"For lo! His doom is sure; one little
Word shall fell him."*

*"That Word above all earthly powers
no thanks to them abideth;*
*"The Spirit and the Gifts are ours
through Him who with us sideth.*
*"Let goods and kindred go, this mortal
life also; the body they may kill;*
"God's Truth abideth still, His Kingdom is forever."

CHAPTER 14

(1) "NOW HIRAM KING OF TYRE SENT MESSENGERS TO DAVID, AND TIMBER OF CEDARS, WITH MASONS AND CARPENTERS, TO BUILD HIM AN HOUSE.

(2) "AND DAVID PERCEIVED THAT THE LORD HAD CONFIRMED HIM KING OVER ISRAEL, FOR HIS KINGDOM WAS LIFTED UP ON HIGH, BECAUSE OF HIS PEOPLE ISRAEL."

The construction is:

1. (Vs. 2) The first two Verses picture the coming day when Christ, the Great Shepherd of His People, shall be confirmed by God the Father as King over Israel, and when the Gentile princes, represented here by Hiram, shall bring their offerings to His Feet.

2. (Vs. 2) David perceived that the Lord had established his kingdom because of this fact, but more so that Israel was the flock of God. Grace had elected that flock and had chosen David as its shepherd.

3. God had chosen David, through whom the Messiah would ultimately come. There could be no greater honor than that; hence, our Lord would be referred to in some cases as the *"Son of David."*

4. The time frame of the happenings of this Chapter is between the unsuccessful attempt to bring home the Ark and then, some three months later, the successful bringing of it. As well, it followed the taking of the fort of Zion, which information is given to us in Chapter 11.

LEBANON AND ISRAEL

"Hiram," king of Tyre, i.e., *"Lebanon,"* was David's friend. In fact, he seems to be the only friend that David had as it regarded the surrounding nations. Consequently, it was Hiram who supplied all the timber and workmen for construction of various buildings under David.

As well, the son of Hiram, also called *"Hiram,"* helped Solomon build the Temple. In fact, while Israel was an agricultural nation, Tyre was a nation of commerce; consequently, the craftsmen needed, which were scarce in Israel, were abundant in Tyre.

The construction here mentioned, even as it concerned a house for David, proclaimed the establishment of the kingdom. Nothing is said of such as it regarded Saul because, in the Mind of God, Saul most definitely was not God's Choice. But now, the one chosen by God, David, is fully reigning over all of Israel, and this construction shows God's pleasure. While Hiram would help David build the *"house,"* the truth is, this house, of whatever state, was a symbol of something far greater. From this *"house"* would come the Messiah of Israel, the Son of the Living God, the Saviour of the world. So, what we are seeing here is so much bigger than meets the eye.

THE CONFIRMATION OF THE LORD

The Scripture says, *"And David perceived that the LORD had confirmed him king over Israel."* The word *"confirmed"* in the Hebrew means *"to establish, to prepare, to appoint, to fashion, to fix, to make prosperous."* As we've already stated, David was God's Choice and, in fact, was meant to be the first king of Israel. Regrettably, Israel jumped the gun, demanding a king before it was time, and brought upon themselves untold trouble and difficulty, which has been the story of man from the very beginning, even redeemed man.

It is so easy to get ahead of the Lord or fall behind the Lord. We seem prone to do one or the other. This means that Israel wasted 40 years, the length of Saul's reign.

But, as the Lord always does, He uses failures as teaching tools. While it was hard on David, still, the Lord used the animosity of Saul to teach David trust, obedience, and faithfulness, which David, one way or the other, had to learn.

As we will find in the balance of this Chapter and succeeding Chapters, the Lord lifted David up in the eyes of the people, and did so by giving him victories over the enemy on every hand.

In the meantime, Israel would be brought to the place of a cohesive nation, and not just a polyglot of tribes. Under David and, actually, under the Lord, government would be firmly established. As well, one military victory after the other would follow, even over armies which were much stronger than that of Israel. But, if God be for something, who can be against it?

As then, so now, the confirmation of the Lord upon any person, any Ministry, is proven by the Presence of the Lord. God's Presence cannot abide with false doctrine or with sin. The latter doesn't speak of sinless perfection, because such does not exist. However, it does refer to individuals who are fully trusting the Lord and believing Him in order that Victory may be theirs, and that Victory can come from no other source. All of it is in the Force and Work of the Holy Spirit, without Whom, we cannot have all that for which Christ has paid such a price.

THE WAY OF THE SPIRIT

The Holy Spirit works entirely within the framework, or one might say, the parameters, of the Finished Work of Christ, i.e., *"the Cross."* The Cross is what gave and gives the Holy Spirit the latitude to do all things that He does. It was there that Jesus atoned for all sin, thereby, lifting the sin debt for mankind, at least for those who will believe, which gives the Holy Spirit latitude to work. That's why Paul wrote:

"For the Law of the Spirit of Life in Christ Jesus has made me free from the Law of Sin and Death" (Rom. 8:2). In fact, the Eighth Chapter of Romans tells us what the Holy Spirit will do in our lives, after we come to the place that we understand how He does it, of which the latter information is given to us in Romans, Chapter 6. In one way or the other in the Bible, and I speak of the entirety of the Bible, everything points to the Lord Jesus Christ and what He would do with us and for us at the Cross. In fact, the entirety of the system of Law given to Moses in the Old Testament pointed to Christ in either His Atoning Work, His Mediatorial Work, or His Intercessory Work.

While the confirmation of David was glorious during that time, it is even more glorious at present, as the Lord confirms those upon whom He has laid His Hand, and does so, as stated, by the Moving and Operation of the Holy Spirit, which portrays the Presence of God.

(3) "AND DAVID TOOK MORE WIVES AT JERUSALEM: AND DAVID BEGAT MORE SONS AND DAUGHTERS.

(4) "NOW THESE ARE THE NAMES OF HIS CHILDREN WHICH HE HAD IN JERUSALEM; SHAMMUA, AND SHOBAB, NATHAN, AND SOLOMON,

(5) "AND IBHAR, AND ELISHUA, AND ELPALET,

(6) "AND NOGAH, AND NEPHEG, AND JAPHIA,

(7) "AND ELISHAMA, AND BEELIADA, AND ELIPHALET."

The diagram is:

1. (Vs. 3) Even though David taking more wives was tolerated by the Lord, still, such was not the Will of God.

2. (Vs. 4) Mary, the mother of Christ, went back to David through Nathan, while Joseph went back to David through Solomon.

3. Even though David was a Type of Christ, still, he was not a perfect Type, even as there could be no perfect Type. What a fall

there is from the Second Verse to the Third! Yet, the Holy Spirit faithfully records facts.

Nathan and Solomon were both born in Jerusalem, becoming, thereby, entitled to the throne, and the Verse establishes their connection with Christ.

POLYGAMY

It was the custom in those days for kings to take many wives, thereby, having many children, and thus, guaranteeing the succession of the throne. Even though the Holy Spirit places no sin to the account of David, yet, by this very thing, the *"sweet singer"* of Israel was undermining the peace and unity of his own family. This would come back to haunt him, and severely so, in the following years.

Pulpit says, *"The less necessitated we are to regard David's polygamy in the light of individual sin, the more emphatic in the light of history does the tendency of the practice proclaim itself as thoroughly and irredeemably bad."*[1]

The ideal model was Adam and Eve, created purposely in this manner by God. It was to be one man for one woman. Any other type of arrangement spells trouble. We speak of polygamy, and above all, homosexual marriages, so-called!

This latter thing is an insult to God of the highest order and will ultimately guarantee the Wrath of God, that is, if the practice is not stopped (Rom. 1:18-28).

There are many types of sins, and all sins are bad; however, some sins are worse, much worse, than others. Homosexuality and homosexual marriages fall into that category. They are an abomination. The Scripture says:

"You shall not lie with mankind, as with womankind: it is abomination" (Lev. 18:22).

The Scripture then says: *"For whosoever shall commit any of these abominations, even the souls who commit them shall be cut off from among their people"* (Lev. 18:29).

The Law of Moses then said: *"If a man also lie with mankind, as he lies with a woman, both of them have committed an abomination: they shall surely be put to death; their blood shall be upon them"* (Lev. 20:13).

The Lord speaks here of homosexuality

NOTES

as *"an abomination"*; the word *"abomination"* in the Hebrew is *"towebh,"* and means *"something disgusting, an abhorrence."*

As it regards the reason that God destroyed Sodom and Gomorrah, and did so in a moment's time, the Scripture says: *"Behold, this was the iniquity of your sister Sodom, pride, fullness of bread, and abundance of idleness was in her and in her daughters, neither did she strengthen the hand of the poor and needy.*

"And they were haughty, and committed abomination before Me: therefore I took them away as I saw good. (The 'abomination' they committed was the sin of homosexuality, i.e., 'sodomy')" (Ezek. 16:49-50).

Concerning this very sin, Paul said:

"Wherefore God also gave them up to uncleanness through the lusts of their own hearts (not merely permissive, but God judicially delivered them over), *to dishonour their own bodies between themselves* (speaks of every type of immorality):

"Who changed the Truth of God into a lie (refers back to Verse 23, which speaks of spiritual and sexual uncleanness), *and worshipped and served the creature more than the Creator* (this refers to man worshiping the creation of his own hands, which means that he is worshiping something less than himself), *Who is blessed forever. Amen* (should have been translated 'Bless-ed' [two syllables], because it refers to the One doing the blessing, in this case the Lord).

"For this cause God gave them up unto vile affections (the Lord removed His restraints and, therefore, gave them unimpeded access to their desires): *for even their women did change the natural use into that which is against nature* (in short speaks of Lesbianism):

"And likewise also the men (homosexuality), *leaving the natural use of the woman* (speaks of the sex act which is performed between the man and his wife), *burned in their lust one toward another* (raging lust); *men with men working that which is unseemly* (specifies its direction, which is total perversion), *and receiving in themselves that recompence of their error which was meet* (refers to the penalty attached to wrongdoing).

"And even as they did not like to retain God in their knowledge (carries the idea of the human race putting God to the test for the purpose of approving or disapproving Him), *God gave them over to a reprobate mind* (Light rejected is Light withdrawn), *to do those things which are not convenient* (which are not fitting)" (Rom. 1:24-28).

The Scripture then says, *"Who knowing the Judgment of God* (in essence, saying 'do Your worst, and it will not stop us'), *that they which commit such things are worthy of death* (Divine Judgment is implied), *not only do the same, but have pleasure in them who do them* (proclaims the result of the 'reprobate mind')" (Rom. 1:32).

In closing out the Canon of Scripture, the Holy Spirit through the Apostle John telling us as to those who will not be in the New Jerusalem, said, *"for without are dogs."* This refers to homosexuals (Rev. 22:15).

HOMOSEXUALITY

The idea that homosexuals are born that way carries no validity, whether scientifically, or by experience.

It is definitely true that babies are born with different proclivities, meaning that some will have a proclivity toward the direction of homosexuality more than others, which could be said for thieves, the criminal mind, alcoholism, etc. All of that, however, is a result of the Fall, which is referred to as original sin.

The answer for that, irrespective as to what man's condition might be, is the Cross of Christ. In fact, there is no other answer (Rom. 6:1-14; 8:1-2, 11; I Cor. 1:17-18, 21, 23; 2:2; Gal., Chpt. 5; 6:14; Eph. 2:13-18; Col. 2:14-15).

It doesn't matter what the law of the land may do, and I speak of legalizing homosexual marriages, etc. The fact is, the guilt of such action is not removed. That's the reason that thirty percent of homosexuals attempt suicide, which is nine times more than heterosexuals. As we've tried to bring out, there is a glaring reason for that.

Sin carries with it its own guilt, and some sins carry a much greater guilt than others, and homosexuality is such a sin. The powers that be aren't doing homosexuals a service by legalizing this abomination, and an abomination it is!

As we've already stated, the only answer for homosexuality, and it must be said the same for every other sin, is the Cross of Christ. As well, my statements are not meant to be homophobic. In other words, it is not right for a Christian or anyone, for that matter, to demean a person because he is homosexual. He must be treated with the same dignity and respect as all others, at least as far as such will be allowed. Our Lord loves the homosexual as He loves all sinners, but He hates the sin of homosexuality, as He hates all sin. We should conduct ourselves in the same manner.

AMERICA AND THE BIBLE

This nation, sadly and regrettably, is fast turning its back on the very thing that has made us great, and I speak of the Bible. Our Founding Fathers used the Word of God as the basis, the foundation, of all its government and laws. Actually, the constitution and bylaws of the United States are based on the Word of God. That and that alone is the reason for the blessing.

One might say that it began with abortion, and now it has extended to the legalization, and in every capacity, of homosexuality. Someone has said, and I'm afraid it just might be correct, that the religion of America presently is *"atheism."* In other words, it is disavowing the existence and, therefore, the belief in God and His Word. Its gospel is abortion, homosexuality, and pleasure — the more sordid, the better!

What is to blame for all of this?

Regrettably, the blame must be laid at the doorstep of the church.

THE CHURCH AND AMERICA

If the spirituality of a nation sinks, so does everything else, and we speak of the economy of the country, its military, and its freedoms. In other words, if God is lost, then everything is lost.

The church is to blame for this, inasmuch as it too has abandoned the Word of God. It's not a case of being on a road to such a position, the truth is, the church has already apostatized.

Sin is no longer in its vocabulary. In other words, the pulpit is now silent as it regards sin. The preaching against sin just might offend people, so it's never mentioned. As a result, the true problem of the human race is not recognized at all. And, if we don't know what the problem actually is, how can we come by the cure.

Speaking of the cure, which is the Cross of Christ, this has fallen by the wayside as well. Once again, the Cross may offend people, so the Cross is not mentioned anymore, which means the Blood is not mentioned, which means the Finished Work of Christ is not mentioned, which means that whatever it is that's being preached is not the Gospel, but rather the concoctions of men. That is the reason that our nation, our great nation, a nation that has influenced the world for good, is, proverbially speaking, losing its way, and fast!

(8) "AND WHEN THE PHILISTINES HEARD THAT DAVID WAS ANOINTED KING OVER ALL ISRAEL, ALL THE PHILISTINES WENT UP TO SEEK DAVID. AND DAVID HEARD OF IT, AND WENT OUT AGAINST THEM.

(9) "AND THE PHILISTINES CAME AND SPREAD THEMSELVES IN THE VALLEY OF REPHAIM.

(10) "AND DAVID ENQUIRED OF GOD, SAYING, SHALL I GO UP AGAINST THE PHILISTINES? AND WILL YOU DELIVER THEM INTO MY HAND? AND THE LORD SAID UNTO HIM, GO UP; FOR I WILL DELIVER THEM INTO YOUR HAND.

(11) "SO THEY CAME UP TO BAAL-PERAZIM; AND DAVID SMOTE THEM THERE. THEN DAVID SAID, GOD HAS BROKEN IN UPON MY ENEMIES BY MY HAND LIKE THE BREAKING FORTH OF WATERS: THEREFORE THEY CALLED THE NAME OF THAT PLACE BAAL-PERAZIM.

(12) "AND WHEN THEY HAD LEFT THEIR GODS THERE, DAVID GAVE A COMMANDMENT, AND THEY WERE BURNED WITH FIRE."

The pattern is:

1. The word *"seek"* in Verse 8 means *"to kill him,"* speaking of David. The moment there is an *"Anointing of the Spirit,"* Satan will come against it, and powerfully so!

NOTES

2. *"Rephaim"* of Verse 9 was the valley of the giants. It must be clearly understood that the *"flesh"* cannot overcome these *"giants."* They can be overcome only by *"the Spirit of God."* The Philistines dwelt in the land; they illustrate the energies of sin that dwell in the Christian (Rom. 7:17). Whenever Christ is enthroned as King over the whole life, these energies gather themselves together to oppose Him in the Believer's heart, where Divine Faith and a child-like obedience have the upper hand; there will be complete victory over them (Rom. 8:1-2, 11).

3. (Vs. 10) It seems that David now had learned his lesson well, concerning a lack of inquiry regarding the bringing up of the Ark; now, he would take nothing for granted; consequently, he would experience victory.

4. Concerning *"Baal-perazim"* of Verse 11, the prefix Baal, speaks of heathen gods. So, in effect, David is saying, *"The Lord has broken through and defeated these idol gods."* How many idol gods are in our lives?

5. The *"waters,"* also mentioned in Verse 11, typify the Word of God, which sweeps away these idol gods, and which must be swept away in our lives also. But we must remember they cannot be destroyed by human ingenuity, only by the Spirit of God!

6. (Vs. 12) David burned these idol gods. The Fire of the Spirit is to burn the dross out of our lives as well (Mat. 3:11-12).

THE ANOINTING

The Eighth Verse says, *"And when the Philistines heard that David was anointed king over all Israel...."*

Satan is little concerned about our ability, money, education, or prestige. He is concerned about *"the anointing."* The church, sadly, never seems to learn this. It, by and large, encourages things which God ignores, and too often, opposes that which Gods honors.

Likewise, Satan is little bothered by our beautiful buildings, educational institutions, degrees conferred upon ministers, pride, place, and position. But, he is greatly stirred up over *"the anointing."*

WHAT IS THE ANOINTING?

The anointing is when God has laid His

Hand upon a Believer to help him perform a certain task, and then the Holy Spirit gives him the help to carry out that task, whatever it might be.

Unfortunately, we presently have far too many preachers who God has never called, and who went where they were never sent, at least, not by God.

The Holy Spirit is the One, and the only One, Who signals the Call and then gives the Power for that Call to be carried out. Jesus said, *"For the Spirit of the Lord is upon Me, because He has anointed Me. . . ."* (Lk. 4:18).

In effect, this means that the Anointing belongs to Christ. He now gives it to whomsoever He wills.

Unfortunately, far too many claim *"the anointing"*, when in reality, there is no anointing there.

The Spirit of God carries out that which the Lord wants and desires. Concerning this very thing, Jesus said, *"Howbeit when He, the Spirit of Truth, is come* (which He did on the Day of Pentecost), *He will guide you into all Truth* (if our Faith is properly placed in Christ and the Cross, the Holy Spirit can then bring forth Truth to us; He doesn't guide into some truth, but rather 'all Truth')*: for He shall not speak of Himself* (tells us not only What He does, but Whom He represents)*; but whatsoever He shall hear, that shall He speak* (doesn't refer to lack of knowledge, for the Holy Spirit is God, but rather He will proclaim the Work of Christ only)*: and He will show you things to come* (pertains to the New Covenant, which would shortly be given).

"He shall glorify Me (will portray Christ and what Christ did at the Cross for dying humanity)*: for He shall receive of Mine* (the benefits of the Cross), *and shall show it unto you* (which He did, when He gave these great Truths to the Apostle Paul [Rom., Chpts. 6-8, etc.]).

"All things that the Father has are Mine (has always been the case; however, due to the Cross, all these things can now be given to the Believer as well)*: therefore said I, that He shall take of Mine, and shall show it unto you* (the foundation of all the Holy Spirit reveals to the Church is what Christ did at the Cross [Rom. 6:1-14; 8:1-2, 11; Eph. 2:13-18])*"* (Jn. 16:13-15).

THE WORK OF THE HOLY SPIRIT

The Holy Spirit Who superintends the anointing, which comes from Christ, is the only Person of the Godhead Who functions on this Earth on a Personal basis. Even though God the Son and God the Father are present as well, and because they are Omnipresent, still, They function by and through the Holy Spirit. There is only one thing the Holy Spirit did not do on this Earth, and that was the Redemption of mankind, which was carried out solely by the Lord Jesus Christ. Of course, God was in Christ at all times and, especially, when He died on the Cross, reconciling the world unto Himself (II Cor. 5:19). The Holy Spirit being God falls into the same category.

And yet, even though it was not the Holy Spirit Who carried out the Atonement on Calvary's Cross, He most definitely was involved, and graphically so, in every aspect of our Lord's Life and Ministry. In fact, the Holy Spirit by decree brought about the Conception of Christ in the womb of Mary, and never left Him from then until He ascended to Glory.

In fact, every Miracle carried out by Christ, even though He was Deity, and never ceased to be Deity, was carried out rather as a man anointed by the Holy Spirit. Concerning this, the Scripture says:

"How God anointed Jesus of Nazareth with the Holy Spirit and with Power (as a Man, Christ needed the Holy Spirit, as we certainly do as well! in fact, everything He did was by the Power of the Spirit)*: Who went about doing good* (everything He did was good), *and healing all who were oppressed of the Devil* (only Christ could do this, and Believers can do such only as Christ empowers them by the Spirit)*; for God was with Him* (God is with us only as we are *'with Him'*)*"* (Acts 10:38).

SATAN'S RESPONSE TO THE ANOINTING

The Evil One fears little in our Christian claims, with the exception of the Holy Spirit. The Scripture says, *"And when the*

Philistines heard that David was anointed . . ." then they came against him, and did so to seek to kill him.

The Anointing of the Holy Spirit, which most definitely was upon David, and can be upon any and every Believer, is that alone which will give us Victory over the powers of darkness and help us put the enemy to flight. Unfortunately, the Anointing of the Holy Spirit upon modern preachers is about as scarce as the proverbial hen's teeth. But that is what makes the Church what the Church ought to be. Without the Anointing of the Spirit, the church is no more than any other club or gathering, but with the Holy Spirit, it becomes a living, a flaming, a burning dynamo, which gives Satan fits, and takes this glorious Gospel to the furthest corners of the Earth.

The truth is, the Devil bothers most churches and most ministries very little because there is no anointing there; consequently, he knows that whatever it is they do will cause him precious little trouble. But, the moment the Anointing of the Holy Spirit comes upon anyone at any time, then the enemy will oppose, and oppose greatly. The sad part about it is that the Evil One will mostly use professing Christians to do his dirty work. In other words, while they claim to know the Lord, the truth is, they have a Philistine heart, so they oppose that which is truly of God, while at the same time, professing Christ.

THE VALLEY OF THE GIANTS

The Scripture says, *"And the Philistines came and spread themselves in the valley of Rephaim."* The word *"Rephaim,"* means *"giants,"* hence, *"the valley of the giants."*

When Satan comes against God's Man, even as he came against David, to be sure, he comes with powerful forces.

The Child of God should know and understand that what he is facing in the spirit world is far beyond his personal strength and ability; unfortunately, the modern church does not seem to realize that. If it did, it would not propose the foolishness that it does in order to face the powers of darkness. Please understand, Satan laughs at humanistic psychology. As well, he laughs at our machinations and efforts, which we propose, although religious, but which he knows will have no effect on him.

Please understand that you are not *"wrestling against flesh and blood, but against principalities, against powers, against the rulers of the darkness of this world, against spiritual wickedness in high places"* (Eph. 6:12). As such, these beings are far more powerful than you are in any sense. But, to be sure, they aren't more powerful than the Holy Spirit.

IS THE HELP OF THE HOLY SPIRIT AUTOMATIC?

No, the help of the Holy Spirit isn't automatic!

If the help of the Holy Spirit, which we've already addressed, were automatic, there would never be another failure on the part of any Christian. The Holy Spirit would just automatically take charge and do what has to be done; however, we know that isn't true.

Unfortunately, Christians, even preachers, are failing, and in every capacity. So, how can we stop these failures? How can we have the help of the Holy Spirit, Who is God, and Who can do anything?

As we've said repeatedly in this Volume, the Holy Spirit works entirely within the framework of the Finished Work of Christ. In other words, it's the Cross which has given Him, and does give Him, the legal right to do all of the great things that He can do, and desires to do, within our hearts and lives. Understand that, it is the Cross! The Cross! The Cross! That's the reason the great Apostle said: *"God forbid that I should glory save in the Cross of the Lord Jesus Christ, by Whom I was crucified to the world and the world unto me"* (Gal. 6:14).

Understanding that, for us to have His Help, His Power, His Leading, and His overcoming Victory, all of it spread abroad within our lives, and on a constant basis, our Faith, correspondingly, must ever be in the Cross of Christ (Rom. 6:1-14; 8:1-2, 11; I Cor. 1:17-18, 21, 23; 2:2; Gal. 2:20-21; Chpt. 5; 6:14; Eph. 2:13-18; Col. 2:14-15).

With Faith properly placed in the Cross of Christ (Rom. 5:1-2), and ever remaining in the Cross of Christ, the Holy Spirit will then begin to work in our lives, and do so until sin no longer has dominion over us (Rom. 6:14).

SINLESS PERFECTION?

The Bible doesn't teach sinless perfection. Anyone who knows anything about the Lord, His Word, and themselves, would not even think of referring to themselves as sinlessly perfect. Yet, the Lord does not save in sin, but rather from sin. So, how is the sin question handled?

If the Believer doesn't understand the Cross as it refers to Sanctification, in other words, our everyday living for God, which is the single most important thing there is to the Believer, then the Believer is going to find the sin nature once again ruling and reigning in his heart and life. This means that there will be a certain type of sin or sins, which will begin to rule and dominate the Believer, in fact, getting worse and worse, despite all the Believer does otherwise to try to stop it. In other words, if the Believer doesn't place his Faith exclusively in Christ and the Cross, he will be dominated in some way by sin. That means that the sin nature will rule in his life in some way, despite the fact that he's Saved and even Spirit-filled.

Unfortunately, the world thinks that Salvation can come by means other than the Cross. Sadder still, the church thinks that Sanctification can come by means other than the Cross. Both efforts are doomed to failure. All hinges on the Cross of Christ, which, in effect, is the Story of the Bible.

As you hold this Volume in your hand, I would ask you a question, *"Is there some type of sin in your life that's dominating you?"*

Now, be honest about it! It is something that you have fought and struggled with; however, sadly and regrettably, it is not only continuing to be active in your life, but the situation is getting worse and worse. In fact, with some, it has been there for years.

At times you have wondered if you are really Saved. Yes, you are Saved! So, if you are Saved, and if Jesus Christ is Lord, why is it that you are bound by this power of darkness despite the fact that you have done everything within your power to stop this situation?

You are bound by this sin, whatever it might be, even though you are a Christian, and even though you are Spirit-filled, possibly, even though you are a preacher and even being used by God, simply because your Faith has been in something other than Christ and the Cross. You have not understood firmly and fully that Christ is the Source, and the Cross is the Means. You may go as far as to believe that Christ is the Source of all things and, more than likely, you do, but your faith stops there. You've never thought of the Cross of Christ as the Means by which all the great things of God are given to you. Consequently, you have placed your faith in your church, your denomination, particular manifestations, or one scheme or fad after the other, which the church is always promoting, all to no avail. Let me say it again! It is the Cross! The Cross! The Cross! And, the Cross alone enables the Grace of God to be given to you.

FRUSTRATING THE GRACE OF GOD

Concerning this, Paul said: *"I do not frustrate the Grace of God* (if we make anything other than the Cross of Christ the Object of our Faith, we frustrate the Grace of God, which means we stop its action, and the Holy Spirit will no longer help us)*: for if Righteousness come by the Law* (any type of religious law), *then Christ is dead in vain.* (If I can successfully live for the Lord by any means other than Faith in Christ and the Cross, then the Death of Christ was a waste)" (Gal. 2:21).

First of all, what is the *"Grace of God?"*

In simple terminology, it is the Goodness of God given freely to undeserving Saints.

God has no more Grace today than He did 3,000 years ago, etc. The situation is, the Cross of Christ has made it possible for God to give His Goodness to us, and to do so in an unprecedented manner. To be sure, we need that Goodness, and need it constantly. The only requirement that God demands of us to receive such Goodness, and to do so in an uninterrupted flow, is for us to have our Faith in Christ and what Christ did at the Cross. That's what Paul meant by the statement, *"then Christ is dead in vain."*

In other words, if you and I could receive this Grace in any other manner, then Jesus didn't have to die on the Cross.

THE LAW!

What did Paul mean by the statement, *"For if Righteousness come by the Law...?"*

He is speaking here of the Law of Moses, but it could refer to any kind of law. What do we mean by any type of law?

That refers to any law made up by churches, religious denominations, preachers, or that we make up ourselves.

These are laws, whether they are referred to that as such, designed to help us realize our full potential, or to overcome sin, etc.

For instance, the *"Purpose Driven Life"* scenario is law. The *"confession message"* is law. Rules and regulations made up by churches constitute law. In other words, if it's not Faith placed exclusively in Christ and the Cross, whatever label is placed upon it, in the Mind of God, it is law. In fact, every Believer is under either Grace or law. The Grace of God is available to all and is achieved by Faith in Christ and the Cross, but, if that is not understood, or is ignored, or denied, then the only thing left is law. And Paul plainly tells us here that Righteousness cannot come by the Law. Such is impossible, not on the part of law, but on the part of the individual. In other words, we cannot live up to the demands.

Everything that Jesus did in His Coming to this Earth was to address law. In His Life and Living, He kept the Law perfectly, and in every respect, not failing even one time. He did it all for us. In other words, He was our Substitute, and our identification with Him gives us that for which He paid such a price.

And then He had to address the broken Law, of which, all were guilty, and which carried the penalty of death. To address that Law, He had to go to the Cross, which He did, and there give Himself in Sacrifice. This satisfied the demands of a thrice-Holy God and set man free from Law's dominion. Due to what Christ did at the Cross, the Law of God has no more claim on me. I am not subject to its demands, nor am I subject to its penalty. Concerning this, Paul also wrote:

NOTES

"Blotting out the handwriting of Ordinances that was against us (pertains to the Law of Moses, which was God's Standard of Righteousness that man could not reach), *which was contrary to us* (Law is against us, simply because we are unable to keep its precepts, no matter how hard we try), *and took it out of the way* (refers to the penalty of the Law being removed), *nailing it to His Cross* (the Law with its decrees was abolished in Christ's Death, as if Crucified with Him)" (Col. 2:14).

Once again, we are here plainly told that it was at the Cross that this great Work of satisfying the demands of the Law was carried out and, once again, we state that it was all on our behalf. That's at least one of the many, many reasons, that the Cross is so very, very important! That's the reason Paul said that if we try to attain to the things of God by means of Law, then we fail. It is a gross insult to Christ, considering the price that He paid.

The giants which we face in this life that are determined to destroy us, can be overcome, and they can be overcome completely. However, they can be overcome in only one way, and that way is by Faith in Christ and the Cross, and by maintaining our Faith in that Finished Work. This is the Means by which the Holy Spirit works, and which, in essence, contains the entirety of the Story of the Bible. In other words, when your Faith is properly placed, you are adhering to the Word and, in fact, that's the only way that one can adhere to the Word.

INQUIRING OF GOD

The Scripture says, *"And David enquired of God, saying, Shall I go up against the Philistines? and will You deliver them into my hand?"*

Just as to exactly how David inquired of the Lord, we aren't told; however, more than likely, from the way the questions are framed, he inquired of the Urim and the Thummim, which were contained by the High Priest. The two words mean *"Lights"* and *"Perfections."* They were contained in a pouch on the underside of the breastplate worn by the High Priest.

No information is given in the Bible as

to what these objects were. It is thought by some that they were two flat stones with the word *"no"* on the first one, and the word *"yes"* on the second. But that, at best, is only conjecture.

At any rate, it seems that they were inquired of mostly in the form of questions, even as we see here. In fact, they seemed to be in use more in the time of Saul and David than any other time (I Sam. 14:18, 41; 23:9-12; 28:6).

It also seems that they were consulted in Ezra 2:63 and Nehemiah 7:65.

While some may read this and think, *"Wouldn't it be wonderful if we had such presently?"*

No! We have something presently far greater.

THE CROSS AND THE HOLY SPIRIT

Before the Cross, due to the sin debt continuing to abide, the Lord was limited as to how He could converse with His People. Now that the Cross is history, meaning that the terrible sin debt has been lifted, at least for all who will believe, the Holy Spirit, Who is God, and in Whom all knowledge resides, now lives constantly within the hearts and lives of all Believers. That's at least one of the reasons that Paul said, *". . . by how much also He is the Mediator of a Better Covenant, which was established upon better Promises"* (Heb. 8:6).

Now the Holy Spirit lives constantly within our hearts and lives and has done so since conversion. Concerning this, Paul also said:

"Know you not that you are the Temple of God, and that the Spirit of God dwells in you?" (I Cor. 3:16).

Concerning the Work of the Spirit within our lives, Jesus addressed this. He said:

"Howbeit when He, the Spirit of Truth, is come, He will guide you into all Truth: for He shall not speak of Himself; but whatsoever He shall hear, that shall He speak: and He will show you things to come."

He then said, *". . . that He shall take of Mine, and shall show it unto you"* (Jn. 16:13, 15).

So, what we presently have is so much better than what they had in those years of long ago. As well, if we will earnestly seek the Lord about direction, He has promised that He will give such to us.

And yet, unless the Believer understands the Cross of Christ as it regards our Sanctification, i.e., our everyday living before God and for God, at the same time, such a Believer will not properly understand the Work of the Holy Spirit within his life. In fact, everything hinges on the Cross of Christ and our understanding of that great Work, which is really the Foundation of the Gospel.

VICTORY

As to exactly how David won this victory over the Philistines, we aren't here told. He merely said, *"God has broken in upon my enemies by my hand like the breaking forth of waters."*

The latter phrase carries the idea of a dam breaking, with the waters rushing forth through the breach; therefore, it seems that the Lord made a breach in the Philistine army, which gave David and his army the means to divide the company and easily defeat them, which they did.

Victories given by the Lord mean that precious little or virtually no losses are sustained by the victor. Victories that we win by our own ingenuity, most of the time, occasion great loss.

It is said that Napoleon won a particular victory and was congratulated by certain individuals. His answer was revealing. He said, *"Yes, we won, but if we win many more like that, we won't be here to tell the story."* In other words, he was meaning that while he did win, he suffered tremendous losses in doing so.

But, if we follow the course of events through the Bible, we find that Israel, at least when the Lord led the fight, suffered no losses. Whenever a person is in the Will of God, as was David, and whenever such a person inquires diligently of the Lord as to what should be done, the victory is complete. That was true not only of David, but it is true of us as well.

At the same time, we find in David's experience that when he failed to consult the Lord, even as with the bringing of the

Ark of the Covenant into Jerusalem, there is always great loss.

THE BURNING OF THE IMAGES

Evidently the Philistines had carried images of their god Dagon into the battle. They obviously felt that this would give them some type of advantage. They should have remembered the debacle of a little over 100 years before, when they took the Ark of the Covenant in battle and placed it in the Temple of their god Dagon. Their god suffered terrible reproach, while the people were plagued as well. But, as then, so now, we forget so easily! Up beside Jehovah, they were to find that their gods were no more than a figment of their imagination.

Whenever Israel was functioning in Faith, there was no nation on the face of the Earth that could have remotely defeated them. If God be for us, who can be against us?!

The idea seems to be that they were put out with their images, seeing they had been of no help whatsoever. As such, they discarded them, with David giving instructions that they were to be *"burned with fire."*

It is the same presently with America. With the Lord's Help being sought, and decisions made on the Authority of the Word of God, no nation in the world can defeat us. However, the sad fact is, our nation is leaving the Bible, going deeper and deeper into immorality, and unless there is a revival, which must begin at the church, Judgment will ultimately come!

(13) "AND THE PHILISTINES YET AGAIN SPREAD THEMSELVES ABROAD IN THE VALLEY.

(14) "THEREFORE DAVID ENQUIRED AGAIN OF GOD; AND GOD SAID UNTO HIM, GO NOT UP AFTER THEM; TURN AWAY FROM THEM, AND COME UPON THEM OVER AGAINST THE MULBERRY TREES.

(15) "AND IT SHALL BE, WHEN YOU SHALL HEAR A SOUND OF GOING IN THE TOPS OF THE MULBERRY TREES, THAT THEN YOU SHALL GO OUT TO BATTLE: FOR GOD IS GONE FORTH BEFORE YOU TO SMITE THE HOST OF THE PHILISTINES.

(16) "DAVID THEREFORE DID AS GOD COMMANDED HIM: AND THEY SMOTE THE HOST OF THE PHILISTINES FROM GIBEON EVEN TO GAZER.

(17) "AND THE FAME OF DAVID WENT OUT INTO ALL LANDS; AND THE LORD BROUGHT THE FEAR OF HIM UPON ALL NATIONS."

The construction is:

1. (Vs. 13) Our mistake is large, if we think Satan will not return; he probes for an opportunity. Just because there has been great victory does not mean that he will not come *"yet again."* However, the victory of the first day, and the methods which Grace counseled for the winning of it, are not to be rested upon in order to secure victory for the next day.

2. (Vs. 14) Had David thought it unnecessary to pray previous to the second battle, he would, no doubt, have been defeated. He learned that God cannot give victories to the *"flesh."* Flesh must be humbled! So David is commanded to run away from the Philistines, which was very humbling to so brave a warrior, who then learns to hide, wait, and listen for the Power and Leading of the Holy Spirit.

3. (Vs. 14) No two victories are alike; hence, there must be definite exercises of heart and prayer, if the Philistine is to be defeated, not only the first time, but the second time as well.

4. (Vs. 15) The *"sound"* which David heard was the coming of the Holy Spirit. He came to stay on the Day of Pentecost (Acts 2:2).

5. Verse 17 proclaims that which will be when the Greater Son of David rules over the entirety of the Planet, which will take place after the Second Coming.

THE ENEMY COMES YET AGAIN

The Scripture says, *"And the Philistines yet again spread themselves abroad in the valley."*

This is a perfect picture as to how Satan works. Never mind that he was defeated before, and maybe many times before, he will keep coming, portraying his persistence.

Why does the Lord allow such?

He allows such in order to teach us many things. Some of those things are:

- Faith and trust.

• No two spiritual battles are alike; each conflict must have the Leading of the Spirit.

• We must never take anything for granted. Just because a conflict was won by a particular method, it doesn't mean the Lord wants to use it again. He demands that we look to Him for each situation.

• As stated, the Lord told David to actually retreat from before the Philistines. This was hard on the flesh, considering he had soundly defeated them a short time before; however, the flesh has to be humbled, meaning that we understand that our own efforts and ability are insufficient. We have to look to the Lord, hear what He tells us, and then do what the Spirit desires. Then and only then will we experience Victory.

TAKE UP THE CROSS DAILY

Inasmuch as the Cross of Christ is God's Prescribed Order of Victory (Rom. 6:1-14), Satan, to be sure, will do everything within his power to move our Faith from the Cross to something else. He doesn't too much care what the something else is, just as long as it's away from the Cross. He knows that the Cross is his death knell, so to speak.

That's the reason Jesus told us that we had to deny ourselves and take up the Cross daily in following Him (Lk. 9:23). In fact, He said in Luke 14:27, that if we do not take up the Cross in our following Him, simply put, *"we cannot be His Disciple."*

If it is to be noticed, He used the word *"daily,"* meaning that this is something that must be reinforced every day and reinvigorated every day, meaning that we must renew our Faith even on a daily basis. That's how critical all of this is.

Living for the Lord is the greatest thing, the grandest thing, in which one could ever begin to engage. To say that such a life is fruitful is a gross understatement. In fact, it is the only type of life that is fruitful.

But, despite what some say, it is a most difficult life to live. It is very simple in its approach. We are to simply place our Faith in Christ and the Cross, and maintain our Faith in Christ and the Cross, and the Holy Spirit will do the rest. It sounds simple, and it is simple! Yet, the difficulty comes because this is what Satan will fight as nothing else.

He will do everything within his power to move your Faith from the Cross to something else, which requires constant vigilance and constant Faith and trust, always making certain that the Cross of Christ is the Object of our Faith.

THE SOUND

The Lord, basically, told David, at this stage of the game, to do the very opposite of that which he had done in the previous battle. As stated, he was now to retreat *"from them,"* and of all things, to focus his attention on the grove of mulberry trees that, evidently, was near the Philistines.

This being done, the great warrior just waited; waited for the *"sound of going in the tops of the mulberry trees."*

What was that sound?

The Hebrew word here used actually means, *"the sound of steps."* In fact, it was the sound of the Lord coming to the aid of David. What it sounded like to the Philistines, that is, if they heard any sound at all, we aren't told. At any rate, David knew this was the Lord and obeyed exactly as demanded. Once again, a great victory would be his, much to the chagrin of the Philistines.

If we do exactly what the Lord tells us to do, and if we seek His Face, He will reveal Himself to us, and the victory will be ours, and on a grand scale.

THE FAME OF DAVID

The Scripture says, *"And the fame of David went out into all lands; and the LORD brought the fear of him upon all nations."*

The news of these great victories spread to all the surrounding nations, which was all designed by the Lord, and *"brought the fear of David upon all nations."* To be sure, this will happen in the coming Kingdom Age when the Greater Son of David will sit as the Governor of the entire world.

"Almighty Father, strong to save,
Whose Arm has bound the restless wave,
"Who bids the mighty ocean deep its own appointed limits keep;
"O hear us when we cry to You for those in peril on the sea."

"O Christ, the Lord of hill and plain,
O'er which our traffic runs amain;
"By mountain pass or valley low;
wherever, Lord, Your Brethren go,
"Protect them by Your guarding Hand
from every peril on the land."

CHAPTER 15

(1) "AND DAVID MADE HIM HOUSES IN THE CITY OF DAVID, AND PREPARED A PLACE FOR THE ARK OF GOD, AND PITCHED FOR IT A TENT.

(2) "THEN DAVID SAID, NONE OUGHT TO CARRY THE ARK OF GOD BUT THE LEVITES: FOR THEM HAS THE LORD CHOSEN TO CARRY THE ARK OF GOD, AND TO MINISTER UNTO HIM FOR EVER.

(3) "AND DAVID GATHERED ALL ISRAEL TOGETHER TO JERUSALEM, TO BRING UP THE ARK OF THE LORD UNTO HIS PLACE, WHICH HE HAD PREPARED FOR IT.

(4) "AND DAVID ASSEMBLED THE CHILDREN OF AARON, AND THE LEVITES:

(5) "OF THE SONS OF KOHATH; URIEL THE CHIEF, AND HIS BRETHREN AN HUNDRED AND TWENTY:

(6) "OF THE SONS OF MERARI; ASAIAH THE CHIEF, AND HIS BRETHREN TWO HUNDRED AND TWENTY:

(7) "OF THE SON OF GERSHOM; JOEL THE CHIEF, AND HIS BRETHREN AN HUNDRED AND THIRTY:

(8) "OF THE SONS OF ELIZAPHAN; SHEMAIAH THE CHIEF, AND HIS BRETHREN TWO HUNDRED:

(9) "OF THE SONS OF HEBRON; ELIEL THE CHIEF, AND HIS BRETHREN FOURSCORE:

(10) "OF THE SONS OF UZZIEL; AMMINADAB THE CHIEF, AND HIS BRETHREN AN HUNDRED AND TWELVE.

(11) "AND DAVID CALLED FOR ZADOK AND ABIATHAR THE PRIESTS, AND FOR THE LEVITES, FOR URIEL, ASAIAH, AND JOEL, SHEMAIAH, AND ELIEL, AND AMMINADAB,

(12) "AND SAID UNTO THEM, YOU ARE THE CHIEF OF THE FATHERS OF THE LEVITES: SANCTIFY YOURSELVES, BOTH YOU AND YOUR BRETHREN, THAT YOU MAY BRING UP THE ARK OF THE LORD GOD OF ISRAEL UNTO THE PLACE THAT I HAVE PREPARED FOR IT.

(13) "FOR BECAUSE YOU DID IT NOT AT THE FIRST, THE LORD OUR GOD MADE A BREACH UPON US, FOR THAT WE SOUGHT HIM NOT AFTER THE DUE ORDER.

(14) "SO THE PRIESTS AND THE LEVITES SANCTIFIED THEMSELVES TO BRING UP THE ARK OF THE LORD GOD OF ISRAEL.

(15) "AND THE CHILDREN OF THE LEVITES BORE THE ARK OF GOD UPON THEIR SHOULDERS WITH THE STAVES THEREON, AS MOSES COMMANDED ACCORDING TO THE WORD OF THE LORD."

The pattern is:

1. According to Verse 1, evidently the Lord instructed David to place the Ark in a tent. He would later give David the plans for the Temple, which would be built by his son Solomon, and would be the most expensive structure ever built.

2. (Vs. 2) David searched the Scriptures and learned how the Ark should be carried (Num. 4:15); had he done that previously, a man would not have died. Priests were Types of Christ, hence, they were ordained to carry the Ark.

3. Verse 13 speaks of David admitting his sin of some three months earlier. He was speaking of the manner in which the Ark of God was to be transported.

PREPARATION FOR THE ARK OF GOD

Of all the sacred vessels, of which the plans for their design were given by the Lord to Moses, the Ark of the Covenant would be considered the most Holy. One might say that the Ark had three components: the chest, which contained the two tables of stone on which were inscribed the Ten Commandments; the Mercy Seat, which was the lid over the chest on which the blood was applied once a year on the Great Day of Atonement; and then, the Cherubim, which were all actually a part of the Mercy Seat, with one at either end and with both of them looking down on the Mercy Seat. One could say that due to the fact that God dwelt between the Mercy Seat and the Cherubim, the Ark was a type of the Throne of God.

Some 500 years later, Nebuchadnezzar, the Babylonian monarch, destroyed Jerusalem, sacked the Temple, and took all the Sacred Vessels in the Temple to Babylon; however, when his soldiers went into the Holy of Holies, no Ark of the Covenant was there. In fact, no one knows exactly what happened to it. Tradition says that Jeremiah the Prophet took the Ark and hid it in a cave, or somewhere, yet, it has never been found.

Even if, in some manner, it were presently found, it would not have the meaning now that it had then. Due to the Cross, where the sin debt was forever paid, the Lord has changed His Dwelling Place from the Ark of the Covenant to the hearts and lives of Believers (I Cor. 3:16). As an aside, it was undoubtedly the Third Person of the Godhead, the Holy Spirit, Who occupied the Ark, and Who lives in the hearts and lives of Believers presently.

The question might be asked, *"As David prepared a place for the Ark when it was finally brought into Jerusalem, have we prepared a place in our hearts, as well, for Him to reside and to perform His Work?"*

THE WORK OF THE HOLY SPIRIT IN OUR HEARTS

As we have repeatedly stated in this Volume and will continue to do so, the Holy Spirit works entirely within the framework, or the parameters, one might say, of the Cross of Christ. This means that what Jesus did at the Cross provides the legal Means for the Holy Spirit to do all that He does. In fact, that's the reason the Holy Spirit referred to this as a *"Law"* (Rom. 8:2). It only remains for the Believer to understand that it is the Cross which makes all of this possible, and I speak of the Holy Spirit living within our hearts and lives, and given the latitude to do what He Alone can do. That being the case, we are to make the Cross of Christ the Object of our Faith and do so on a constant basis. This and this alone gives the Holy Spirit latitude to work. He doesn't demand much of us, but He does demand that the Cross of Christ be the Object of our Faith (Rom. 6:1-14; 8:1-2, 11; I Cor. 1:17-18, 23; 2:2; Gal. 6:14; Col. 2:14-15).

ACCORDING TO THE WORD OF THE LORD

The first effort to bring the Ark into Jerusalem met with disaster because it was not done according to the Word of the Lord. A man died because of it, which caused tremendous consternation in Israel, and especially with David, as well it should. Now the *"sweet singer"* of Israel consults the Word of God, knows exactly as to how the Ark should be transported, and functions accordingly.

Is the Lord cruel for demanding that we abide by His Word, and if we don't, the results can be catastrophic?

No! In fact, He would be cruel for not demanding such.

If there is a minefield before one with bombs planted all over it, which will blow off one's legs, or even kill the person, and there is a path of safety through that field, wouldn't the person in charge be cruel if he did not demand that the path be followed?

I think the answer is obvious!

While the Lord can do anything, the truth is, He will do nothing that conflicts with His Nature of Perfect Righteousness and Perfect Holiness. If He is to be honest and true, He must adhere to these principles, as should be understood!

The Word of the Lord is given to us, and is meant to be a road map for life and a blueprint for eternity. It is the single most important thing in the world. And, the second most important thing is the Believer's proper understanding of the Word. Regrettably, at this particular time (2010), there aren't many helps being given to the Christian public that will help them to properly understand the Word. Rather, superficial religious pabulum is served up, which caters strictly to the flesh.

One could say, I think, without any fear of contradiction, that all of this is because of the rejection of the Cross of Christ. The world tries to obtain Salvation without the Cross and, regrettably, the church tries to obtain Sanctification without the Cross. Both are doomed to failure!

(16) "AND DAVID SPOKE TO THE CHIEF OF THE LEVITES TO APPOINT THEIR BRETHREN TO BE THE SINGERS WITH INSTRUMENTS OF MUSIC, PSALTERIES AND HARPS AND CYMBALS, SOUNDING, BY LIFTING UP THE VOICE WITH JOY.

(17) "SO THE LEVITES APPOINTED HEMAN THE SON OF JOEL; AND OF HIS BRETHREN, ASAPH THE SON OF BERECHIAH; AND OF THE SONS OF MERARI THEIR BRETHREN, ETHAN THE SON OF KUSHAIAH;

(18) "AND WITH THEM THEIR BRETHREN OF THE SECOND DEGREE, ZECHARIAH, BEN, AND JAAZIEL, AND SHEMIRAMOTH, AND JEHIEL, AND UNNI, ELIAB, AND BENAIAH, AND MAASEIAH, AND MATTITHIAH, AND ELIPHELEH, AND MIKNEIAH, AND OBED-EDOM, AND JEIEL, THE PORTERS.

(19) "SO THE SINGERS, HEMAN, ASAPH, AND ETHAN, WERE APPOINTED TO SOUND WITH CYMBALS OF BRASS;

(20) "AND ZECHARIAH, AND AZIEL, AND SHEMIRAMOTH, AND JEHIEL, AND UNNI, AND ELIAB, AND MAASEIAH, AND BENAIAH, WITH PSALTERIES ON ALAMOTH;

(21) "AND MATTITHIAH, AND ELIPHELEH, AND MIKNEIAH, AND OBED-EDOM, AND JEIEL, AND AZAZIAH, WITH HARPS ON THE SHEMINITH TO EXCEL.

(22) "AND CHENANIAH, CHIEF OF THE LEVITES, WAS FOR SONG: HE INSTRUCTED ABOUT THE SONG, BECAUSE HE WAS SKILLFUL.

(23) "AND BERECHIAH AND ELKANAH WERE DOORKEEPERS FOR THE ARK.

(24) "AND SHEBANIAH, AND JEHOSHAPHAT, AND NETHANEEL, AND AMASAI, AND ZECHARIAH, AND BENAIAH, AND ELIEZER, THE PRIESTS, DID BLOW WITH THE TRUMPETS BEFORE THE ARK OF GOD: AND OBED-EDOM AND JEHIAH WERE DOORKEEPERS FOR THE ARK."

The pattern is:

1. (Vs. 16) This time it will not be an empty profession; the joy will be real, because they are now abiding by the Word of God.

2. (Vs. 24) The great processional that will go into Jerusalem with the Ark of God in its midst will be designed by the Holy Spirit. David seemingly wrote Psalm 68 to commemorate this great event. There were 862 Priests and Levites, plus others consecrated to bear the Ark and to offer sacrifices.

3. (Vs. 24) Three choirs accompanied the Ark. The first choir was led by the Levites. The second choir was made up of maiden singers (Vs. 20). The third choir was made up of the men singers (Vs. 21).

4. (Vs. 24) All three choirs are referred to in Psalms 68:25. The men's choir seemingly went before the musicians, who were following the maidens playing timbrels among or in-between the men singers and the musicians.

MUSIC AND SINGING

It was to David that the Lord gave the manner of worship as it regards music and singing. Considering that the Holy Spirit delegated the Book of Psalms as the longest in the Bible, constituting 150 songs, over half of them authored by David, this lets us know that music and singing make up the highest form of worship there is. If it's anointed by the Holy Spirit, music and singing incorporate praise, prayer, and Prophecy. In fact, some of the greatest Prophecies of all are found in the Book of Psalms.

Considering that the Holy Spirit instituted the procession of the Ark of the Covenant into Jerusalem, we must also conclude that the music and singing, which accompanied this most important event, were, as well, stipulated by the Spirit.

All of this is one reason that Satan has done everything within Hell's power to pervert music and, especially, in the church. Regrettably, he has, by and large, succeeded. Music is meant to illicit worship and praise of the Lord and most definitely will do so, if it's the right type of music.

The Holy Spirit originally perfected music in three parts. They are:

1. Rhythm: this constitutes the measured beats.

2. Melody: this is the tune or the melody line of the song.

3. Harmony: this pertains to lead, alto, tenor, and bass.

If the melody line is confused, which modern contemporary music often does, and/or the words are unscriptural or meaningless, then it's impossible for people to worship to such a sound. I believe I speak, at least, with some authority.

When I was eight years old, I asked the Lord to give me the talent to play the piano. I promised Him that I would never use it in the world but always for His Service. I've kept that promise and, above all, the Lord did exactly that which I asked, and even much more.

He did give me that talent, plus He gave me a talent also to understand what the Holy Spirit wants and desires as it regards music and singing. Concerning this, the Lord has helped us to touch this world with music, for which we give Him all the praise and all the glory.

In harmony with the Word of God, this procession led by David incorporated praise and worship as the nation had not previously seen or known. It was the beginning of an era, which would catapult Israel into prominence among the nations. It was accompanied by a song.

OBED-EDOM

If it is to be noticed, Obed-edom is among the leaders as it regards this procession of praise and worship. If it is to be remembered, the Ark of the Covenant, after the disastrous results of the first effort, was left at the home of this man. The Scripture says, *"And the LORD blessed Obed-edom, and all his household"* (II Sam. 6:11).

The Scripture is silent as it regards the place and position of Obed-edom before this occasion. But, this one thing is sure, knowing and having the Blessings of God during the three months specified, and in a way that he had never known before, evidently, he resolved in his heart that wherever the Ark of the Covenant was, there he would be as well. So, now we find him in this procession playing a harp along with others, worshipping the Lord.

His name is mentioned some 20 times in the Sacred Writ. Furthermore, the Scripture indicates that his sons followed him in the Service of the Lord (I Chron. 26:4, 8, 15; II Chron. 25:24).

What an honor to have one's name mentioned this many times in the Word of God, and always in a positive sense.

(25) "SO DAVID, AND THE ELDERS OF ISRAEL, AND THE CAPTAINS OVER THOUSANDS, WENT TO BRING UP THE ARK OF THE COVENANT OF THE LORD OUT OF THE HOUSE OF OBED-EDOM WITH JOY.

(26) "AND IT CAME TO PASS, WHEN GOD HELPED THE LEVITES WHO BORE THE ARK OF THE COVENANT OF THE LORD, THAT THEY OFFERED SEVEN BULLOCKS AND SEVEN RAMS.

(27) "AND DAVID WAS CLOTHED WITH A ROBE OF FINE LINEN, AND ALL THE LEVITES WHO BORE THE ARK, AND THE SINGERS, AND CHENANIAH THE MASTER OF THE SONG WITH THE SINGERS: DAVID ALSO HAD UPON HIM AN EPHOD OF LINEN.

(28) "THUS ALL ISRAEL BROUGHT UP THE ARK OF THE COVENANT OF THE LORD WITH SHOUTING, AND WITH SOUND OF THE CORNET, AND WITH TRUMPETS, AND WITH CYMBALS, MAKING A NOISE WITH PSALTERIES AND HARPS."

The exegesis is:

1. (Vs. 26) The sacrifices typified that all were based upon the shed Blood of the Lamb.

2. (Vs. 27) The *"linen"* represents the *"Righteousness of the Saints,"* and, once again, a Righteousness that did not come from the merit of David, but from the merit of the slain Lamb — hence, the sacrifices.

3. (Vs. 28) We find here, as is obvious, all types of musical instruments, and all used for the Glory of God. In fact, the Book of Psalms is the longest Book in the Bible, showing us the emphasis that the Holy Spirit puts upon worship, as it regards music and singing.

THE JOY OF THE LORD

Verse 25 says that the procession of bringing the Ark of the Covenant into Jerusalem now is done with joy. Three months earlier, when they attempted to bring the Ark into Jerusalem, while noise is mentioned

(I Chron. 13:8), nothing is said about joy. Rightly so, a man died in that attempt! But now, it is with joy because they are adhering to the Word of God, and doing so in totality and, thereby, can expect the Blessings of God.

The Word of God is everything. The entirety of the Believer's life and existence is coming to a proper understanding of the Word, and then making it the center point of his life. Everything for life and living is found in the Word of God, and found only in the Word of God.

Peter said: *"According as His Divine Power has given unto us all things* (the Lord with large-handed generosity has given us all things) *that pertain unto life and godliness* (pertains to the fact that the Lord Jesus has given us everything we need regarding life and living), *through the knowledge of Him Who has called us to Glory and Virtue* (the *'knowledge'* addressed here speaks of what Christ did at the Cross, which alone can provide *'Glory and Virtue'*):

"Whereby are given unto us exceeding great and Precious Promises (pertains to the Word of God, which alone holds the answer to every life problem)*: that by these* (Promises) *you might be partakers of the Divine Nature* (the Divine Nature implanted in the inner being of the believing sinner becomes the source of our new life and actions; it comes to everyone at the moment of being *'Born-Again'*), *having escaped the corruption that is in the world through lust.* (This presents the Salvation experience of the sinner, and the Sanctification experience of the Saint)" (II Pet. 1:3-4).

THE SACRIFICES

At the beginning of the procession bringing the Ark from the house of Obed-edom, it seems that the Levites offered up *"seven bullocks and seven rams."* This typified that Israel's security and prosperity were based on the shed Blood of the Lamb. This was the foundation of their protection, of their prosperity, of their power, in fact, of all that they were and had, as it regards Blessings. All were founded on the Cross of Christ.

It has not changed from then until now. The Church is blessed only as long as the Cross of Christ is the Object of our Faith. In fact, I think it would be impossible for anyone to overemphasize the validity and the veracity of the Cross of Christ.

It was to the Apostle Paul that the Lord gave the meaning of the New Covenant. In effect, the meaning is the Cross of Christ. That's the reason that Paul was as adamant as he was as it regarded the Cross. In fact, he was so adamant that he basically began his Epistle to the Galatians by saying, *"But though we* (Paul and his associates), *or an Angel from Heaven, preach any other gospel unto you than that which we have preached unto you* (Jesus Christ and Him Crucified), *let him be accursed* (eternally condemned; the Holy Spirit speaks this through Paul, making this very serious)" (Gal. 1:8).

THE PROBLEM WITH THE MODERN CHURCH

The world tries to save itself without the Cross and, sadly and regrettably, the church tries to sanctify itself without the Cross. There can be no success in either direction.

The problem with the modern church is that it's not preaching the Cross. It is preaching, in fact, everything but the Cross.

Man's problem is sin. That's what it has been from the time of the Fall. But the modern church ignores man's problem, in effect, stating that the problem is something else. It's bad habits, they say! Or it's improper education, they say! Or it's improper environment, they say! So, whatever it is they claim the problem to be, they, at the same time, present their solution and, to be sure, the solution is definitely not the Cross. So, the modern church ignores the real problem plaguing mankind and, thereby, denies the only solution for that problem. This means that the modern church is pretty well a waste of time. Let us say it again:

SIN

Man's problem is sin, and once he comes to Christ, it continues to be his problem. When the Holy Spirit gave to Paul the blueprint for life and living, in other words, how to live this Christian experience, which, in fact, is given to us in the Sixth Chapter of Romans, first of all, he stated the problem, which is sin!

He asked the question: *"What shall we say then?"* (This is meant to direct attention to Rom. 5:20.) *Shall we continue in sin, that Grace may abound?* (Just because Grace is greater than sin doesn't mean that the Believer has a license to sin.)

"God forbid (presents Paul's answer to the question, *'Away with the thought, let not such a thing occur'*). *How shall we, who are dead to sin* (dead to the sin nature), *live any longer therein?* (This portrays what the Believer is now in Christ)" (Rom. 6:1-2).

And then immediately he tells us the answer for sin. It is the Cross of Christ. He said:

"Know you not, that so many of us as were baptized into Jesus Christ (plainly says that this Baptism is into Christ and not water [I Cor. 1:17; 12:13; Gal. 3:28-29; Eph. 4:5; Col. 2:11-13]) *were baptized into His Death?* (When Christ died on the Cross, in the Mind of God, we died with Him; in other words, He became our Substitute, and our identification with Him in His Death gives us all the benefits for which He died; the idea is that He did it all for us!)

"Therefore we are buried with Him by baptism into death (not only did we die with Him, but we were buried with Him as well, which means that all the sin and transgression of the past were buried; when they put Him in the Tomb, they put all of our sins into that Tomb as well): *that like as Christ was raised up from the dead by the Glory of the Father, even so we also should walk in Newness of Life* (we died with Him, we were buried with Him, and His Resurrection was our Resurrection to a *'Newness of Life'*).

"For if we have been planted together (with Christ) *in the likeness of His Death* (Paul proclaims the Cross as the instrument through which all Blessings come; consequently, the Cross must ever be the Object of our Faith, which gives the Holy Spirit latitude to work within our lives), *we shall be also in the likeness of His Resurrection* (we can have the *'likeness of His Resurrection,'* i.e., *'live this Resurrection Life,'* only as long as we understand the *'likeness of His Death,'* which refers to the Cross as the Means by which all of this is done)" (Rom. 6:3-5).

NOTES

If one takes the Cross out of Christianity, all that one has left is a social gospel which, in reality, even as Paul also said, *"is no Gospel at all"* (Gal. 1:7).

THE ARK OF THE COVENANT

The action here is the setting up of the Throne of Jehovah, that is, the Ark, in Zion. David is the central figure. The High Priest is not seen. David, as king and priest — likened to Melchizedek distributing bread and wine — appears in connection with the throne, and blesses the people. Grace is the foundation upon which all is here established.

The Tabernacle and the Brazen Altar are at a distance in Gibeon. They represent the First Covenant (now passed away), and the Holy Spirit carries David and Israel forward into the liberty of the New Covenant. The whole scene is prophetic of the day when the Son of David will establish His Throne in Zion and reign gloriously thereon as King and Priest before His Ancients.

There will be in that day the remembrance of the One Great Sacrifice once accomplished at Calvary, just as upon this day, the Blood, once sprinkled upon the Mercy Seat of the Ark, was the memorial of the Atonement consummated at the Brazen Altar.

Calvary will not be repeated in the day when Israel's King appears in Zion, which will be at the Second Coming, but its remembrance as being the foundation of all blessing will be extremely prominent.

So it is in this Chapter. The Brazen Altar and the Tabernacle are at Gibeon; the Ark is not brought there by David but, instead, by design, which he was, no doubt, instructed to do by the Lord.

Thus, prophetically, the placing of the Ark in Zion and not at Gibeon was a setting aside of the First Covenant and a setting up of the Second, at least in type.

As the Ark is taken into Jerusalem, it is borne on the shoulders of Priests. That God would ordain His Mighty Glory to be transported on the shoulders of frail Priests must ever be understood that it was not because of any merit or personal holiness on the part of these Priests, but on the part of God; likewise, God anoints those He calls to take His great and glorious Gospel; however, the Call is not because the Lord saw any merit in the ones called, but only because of the Grace of God.

THE DIVINE PROCESSION

There will be three special choirs that will lead the procession. The first choir will be led by *"the Levites,"* of whom the leaders are *"Heman,"* incidentally, Samuel's grandson, *"Asaph,"* and *"Ethan."* It should be noticed that *"Obed-edom"* is with the Ark. Actually, the Twenty-fourth Verse says, *"Obed-edom and Jehiah were doorkeepers for the Ark."*

Some three months earlier David had left the Ark at the house of *"Obed-edom."* He had been so blessed by God that when David came to remove the Ark from his house, he resolved to go with it and remain forever. He had tasted the Glory of God, and nothing else would ever satisfy.

So many today have little interest in the things of God because they have little tasted of the Glory of God. Once we have seen, felt, witnessed, and experienced His great *"Glory,"* nothing else will ever satisfy again. Jesus said, *"If you drink of this water, you'll thirst again, but if you drink of the water that I shall give, you shall never thirst"* (Jn. 4:13-14).

As the first choir was made up of *"the Levites,"* the second choir was made up of *"the Alamoth,"* who were the maiden singers (Vs. 20).

The third choir was made up of the *"men singers"* (Vs. 21).

THE ROBE OF RIGHTEOUSNESS

The Twenty-seventh Verse says, *"And David was clothed with a robe of fine linen. . . ."*

This represents the *"Righteousness of the Saints"* and, once again, a Righteousness that did not come from the merit of David, but from the merit of the slain Lamb — hence, the sacrifices.

The Scripture, as well, says, *"David also had upon him an Ephod of linen."* This was the garment for Priests and Levites, not kings, but since he was a Type of Christ, who was to be a Priest-King (Zech. 6:12-13),

NOTES

David was allowed by God to use it as a type on this occasion.

Jesus Christ Alone can furnish a Perfect, Pure Righteousness. He is able to give that Perfect Righteousness instantly and freely due to what He did at the Cross and our Faith in that Finished Work.

Paul wrote: *"Even the Righteousness of God which is by Faith of Jesus Christ* (concerns Imputed Righteousness, and tells how it is obtained) *unto all and upon all them who believe* (the criteria is believing, and believing in Christ and Him Crucified)*: for there is no difference* (Salvation is by Faith, whether the person is a Jew or a Gentile)*"* (Rom. 3:22).

As we've already stated, David was allowed to wear this Ephod of linen, which normally was worn exclusively by the Priests, for two reasons.

1. David was a Type of Christ, Who is our Great High Priest.

2. This episode, as we have stated, was a portrayal of the coming New Covenant that we now have, which means that all Believers are now kings and priests unto the Lord (Rev. 1:6).

What a wonder and what a blessing, which have been afforded by the Cross of Christ. Let us say it again:

Christ is the Source of all things that we receive from God, and the Cross is the Means by which these things are received, all superintended by the Holy Spirit (Gal., Chpt. 5).

(29) "AND IT CAME TO PASS, AS THE ARK OF THE COVENANT OF THE LORD CAME TO THE CITY OF DAVID, THAT MICHAL THE DAUGHTER OF SAUL LOOKING OUT AT A WINDOW SAW KING DAVID DANCING AND PLAYING: AND SHE DESPISED HIM IN HER HEART."

The construction is:

1. (Vs. 29) The *"flesh"* can never understand things of the *"Spirit."* Actually, the *"flesh"* despises all that which is of the *"Spirit."* II Samuel 6:20-23 states that *"she was childless to the day of her death."* Likewise, if the church disobeys the Word of God, there will be no joy and, as well, the church will also be barren.

2. The reason this lady *"despised David in her heart"* can only be found in the heart

itself. It was a heart that did not know God!

The phrase, *"David dancing and playing,"* should have been translated, *"dancing and leaping."*

THE HEART OF THE UNREDEEMED

The idea is that the spirit of Saul was alive and well in his daughter. She did not know the things of God and had no desire for the things of God, therefore, that which was truly of the Lord, as most certainly was this procession into Jerusalem, meant absolutely nothing to her. All she saw was her husband, David, the king of Israel, leaping and dancing, and the meaning of it totally escaped her. Tragically, her attitude, which resulted in her being barren (II Sam. 6:23), happens to be the attitude of most of the modern church.

God's Ways are not the ways of the world, and neither are they the ways of the apostate church. The only way that one can fully understand the Ways of the Lord is through and by the Cross of Christ. Any other direction will lead one further and further away.

> *"Now thank we all our God with heart and hands and voices,*
> *"Who wondrous things has done, in Whom His World rejoices;*
> *"Who, from our mother's arm, has blessed us on our way,*
> *"With countless gifts of love, and still is ours today."*
>
> *"O may this Bounteous God, through all our life be near us,*
> *"With ever joyful hearts and blessed peace to cheer us;*
> *"And keep us in His Grace, and guide us when perplexed,*
> *"And free us from all ills in this world and the next."*
>
> *"All praise and thanks to God the Father now be given,*
> *"The Son, in Him Who reigns with them in highest Heaven,*
> *"The one Eternal God, Whom Earth and Heaven adore;*
> *"For thus it was, is now, and shall be evermore."*

CHAPTER 16

(1) "SO THEY BROUGHT THE ARK OF GOD, AND SET IT IN THE MIDST OF THE TENT THAT DAVID HAD PITCHED FOR IT: AND THEY OFFERED BURNT SACRIFICES AND PEACE OFFERINGS BEFORE GOD.

(2) "AND WHEN DAVID HAD MADE AN END OF OFFERING THE BURNT OFFERINGS AND THE PEACE OFFERINGS, HE BLESSED THE PEOPLE IN THE NAME OF THE LORD.

(3) "AND HE DEALT TO EVERYONE OF ISRAEL, BOTH MAN AND WOMAN, TO EVERYONE A LOAF OF BREAD, AND A GOOD PIECE OF FLESH, AND A FLAGON OF WINE.

(4) "AND HE APPOINTED CERTAIN OF THE LEVITES TO MINISTER BEFORE THE ARK OF THE LORD, AND TO RECORD, AND TO THANK AND PRAISE THE LORD GOD OF ISRAEL:

(5) "ASAPH THE CHIEF, AND NEXT TO HIM ZECHARIAH, JEIEL, AND SHEMIRAMOTH, AND JEHIEL, AND MATTITHIAH, AND ELIAB, AND BENAIAH, AND OBEDEDOM: AND JEIEL WITH PSALTERIES AND WITH HARPS; BUT ASAPH MADE A SOUND WITH CYMBALS;

(6) "BENAIAH ALSO AND JAHAZIEL THE PRIESTS WITH TRUMPETS CONTINUALLY BEFORE THE ARK OF THE COVENANT OF GOD."

The pattern is:

1. (Vs. 1) Once again, the Holy Spirit calls attention to the sacrifices, which typified Calvary. We aren't told where these sacrifices were offered, whether at Gibeon, where the Brazen Altar was located, or whether a makeshift Altar was constructed nearby the Ark of the Covenant. At any rate, wherever they were offered at this time, everything seemed to be in the Will of God.

2. We find from Verse 2 that everything was built and ordered on the basis of the Cross, which the sacrifices typified.

3. (Vs. 3) It is very difficult to explain to the reader the significance of this moment in Israel's history. The *"Ark of God"* was

symbolic of all of Israel's power, strength, and glory. With the *"Ark,"* she was the most powerful Nation on Earth; without the *"Ark,"* she was nothing. David understood this; sadly, most of the kings who were to later come did not understand it.

4. (Vs. 3) Likewise, the Presence of God in our Churches is the only thing of any real value. But sadly, most churches are little more than a business. There is no Presence of God and, in fact, there never has been. The sacrificial meal denoted fellowship, joy, and communion.

5. The word *"continually,"* as used in Verse 6, means both morning and evening, and at the time of the morning and evening sacrifices. This means that the choirs would worship the Lord by singing the Psalms each day at 9 a.m. (the time of the morning sacrifice) and 3 p.m. (the time of the evening sacrifice). This would be done each day, with the exception of the Sabbath, which was the day of rest. The sacrifices were offered on the Sabbath day as well, but, were actually doubled (Num. 28:9).

BURNT SACRIFICES AND PEACE OFFERINGS

These were, no doubt, *"Whole Burnt Offerings"* and, as stated, *"Peace Offerings."*

As it regards the Whole Burnt Offering, it was consumed totally on the Altar. The Peace Offering was different, with very little of it burned upon the Altar, basically, just the fat. A portion of the animal was eaten by the Priests, and the remainder was eaten by the family that had brought the Offering in the first place. Actually, those who brought the Offering were encouraged to invite others in for a feast. The idea was:

The Whole Burnt Offering, burnt wholly on the Altar, signified the Lord giving His All for humanity, meaning that He gives us His Perfection.

In the Whole Burnt Offering, the sinner receives the Perfection of Christ, while in the Sin Offering, Christ receives the sin of the sinner.

With Atonement being made for sin in the Whole Burnt Offering, peace is now restored between God and the sinner, thereby, the cause of the celebration, and rightly so.

NOTES

David had sinned, and sinned greatly, by mishandling the Ark of the Covenant when he attempted to bring it to Jerusalem some three months earlier. This sin included the High Priest plus, no doubt, all the Priests, ever how many there were. They all should have known better.

As well, on the first occasion of attempting to bring the Ark in, there is no mention of sacrifices (II Sam. 6:1-11). That was a grievous sin within itself.

Israel's prosperity, her freedom, her blessing and, in fact, every blessing, was predicated solely on the shed Blood of the Lamb, which was typified by the offering of sacrifices in the Levitical system. That being ignored, which evidently it was the first time, was an invitation for disaster.

If it is to be noticed, the moment the Ark was ensconced within the tent prepared for it, sacrifices were offered. Let it be understood, everything depends on the Cross, of which all of this was a Type.

I'm afraid it would have to be said that the modern church has all but totally dispensed with the Cross. Oh yes, there is much religious fervor but, let it be understood, as Israel of old, none of that forestalled the judgment that came with the death of Uzza. It will bring about the same judgment presently.

The Cross of Christ is the central core of Biblical Christianity. That removed, Christianity becomes only another philosophy. The Power is in the Cross because it was there that Jesus defeated the powers of darkness and did so by atoning for all sin. That being done, meaning that the sin debt was forever lifted, at least for all who will believe, the Holy Spirit, Who is actually the Power Source, can now exert that Power on behalf of the Believer (I Cor. 1:17; Rom. 8:2).

THE BLESSING

The Scripture says, *"And when David had made an end of offering the Burnt Offerings and the Peace Offerings, he blessed the people in the name of the LORD."*

All of this tells us that all blessings, and we mean all blessings, come to the Believer solely by the Means of the Cross of Christ. In other words, it was there that the price was paid, which satisfied the demands of a thrice-Holy God. Now, all blessings are made possible because of what Jesus did at the Cross, and only because of what Jesus did at the Cross.

All types of blessings are presently promised in the modern religious climate in which we live. Please remember the following: unless they are preaching the Cross, their promises are empty. God will honor nothing that bypasses the Cross of Christ.

It is not so much an arbitrary rule laid down by the Lord, but rather, because of what Jesus did at the Cross.

In fact, the Incarnation, God becoming man, was solely for the purpose of the Cross, for there the price would be paid. While everything that Jesus did was of utmost significance, as should be obvious, still, the central core of His Ministry on this Earth, the very reason He came, was and is the Cross. He had to do for man what man could not do for himself. To be sure, the price demanded by God was so high that man could not hope to pay that which he owed. So, if it were to be paid, God would have to pay it Himself, which He did, by becoming man and going to the Cross. In fact, this thing is so important, of such consequence, that it was all decided in the councils of Heaven, even before the world was created (I Pet. 1:18-20). In other words, through foreknowledge, God knew that He would make man, and that man would Fall. It was determined by the councils of Heaven that man would be redeemed by God becoming man and going to the Cross. In fact, the very first Prophecy that was given took place immediately after the Fall when the Lord addressed Satan through the serpent. He said:

"And I will put enmity (animosity) *between you and the woman* (presents the Lord now actually speaking to Satan, who had used the serpent; in effect, the Lord is saying to Satan, 'You used the woman to bring down the human race, and I will use the woman as an instrument to bring the Redeemer into the world, Who will save the human race'), *and between your seed* (mankind which follows Satan) *and her Seed* (the Lord Jesus Christ); *it* (Christ) *shall bruise your head* (the Victory that Jesus won at the Cross [Col. 2:14-15]), *and you shall bruise His Heel* (the sufferings of the Cross)" (Gen. 3:15).

So, when man attempts to bring about that which he, in effect, cannot do, thereby, ignoring Christ, in the Eyes of God, such a sin is wicked. Whether the perpetrator realizes it or not, such an act actually proclaims to Christ that what He did was insufficient, and that our grandiose effort must be added to that *"Finished Work."* That's the reason the Lord said through Paul, *"So then they who are in the flesh cannot please God"* (Rom. 8:8).

THE BREAD, THE FLESH, THE WINE

The Scripture says, *"And he dealt to everyone of Israel, both man and woman, to everyone a loaf of bread, and a good piece of flesh, and a flagon of wine."*

In a sense, this was a type of the Lord's Supper, which we celebrate presently. At any rate, the Lord, no doubt, impressed upon David to do this. Once again, it all points to the Cross and the price that Jesus would there pay.

As we have previously stated, every blessing of Israel was predicated solely on the Shed Blood of the Lamb. And, we must not forget, as it was then, so it is now. Without the Cross, there is no blessing, only death. With the Cross, we have access to the very Throne of God.

THREE CHOIRS

The first choir, in essence, had three leaders, Heman, who was Samuel's grandson, and Asaph, who was actually the principal leader, and then, Ethan. There could well have been other singers with them.

They were followed by the maiden singers accompanied by Zechariah and other musicians.

The third band of singers and musicians contained six men.

It could be said that the first choir was accompanied by cymbals, the second by psalteries, and the third by harps.

It seems that the three different choirs sang different portions of the Psalm, which is included in this Chapter.

The first choir sang about Israel in

connection with Jehovah and His Throne in Zion. These are Verses 8 through 22.

The second choir, that is the maiden chorus, sang Verses 23 through 33, the subject being the Gentiles in connection with Jehovah in Zion.

The third choir sang Verses 34 through 36, the subject here being the Redemption of Israel from the great captivity, then still future, and predicted in Leviticus and Deuteronomy (Williams).[1]

As well, this Psalm will be sung by Israel in a future day, and we speak of the Second Coming when our Lord returns to Zion.

There are some who believe that these singers and musicians, who were appointed by David, functioned not only at the installation of the Ark but, as well, did so on a daily basis and, in fact, continued throughout the reign of David.

The Sixth Verse says, "*. . . continually before the Ark of the Covenant of God."*

This means both morning and evening and at the time of the morning and evening sacrifices.

So, every morning and every evening, those who were near the site of the Ark of the Covenant witnessed the worship that went up before the Lord *"continually."*

MUSIC AND SINGING

I think it can be said with Scriptural validation that music and singing constitute the highest form of worship as it regards the Lord. We know this because of the length of the Book of Psalms, which is actually 150 songs, constituting the longest Book in the Bible. For the Holy Spirit to relegate that much time and space to this form of worship tells us of its validity.

To be frank, music in the church is the Spiritual barometer of the church. If the music is merely entertainment, as so much of it is, there is no true worship. If it's of the contemporary type, with disordered harmony and melody, likewise, there can be no worship. But, if the songs glorify the Lord, Who He is, and What He has done, then the Holy Spirit will definitely make Himself known, with the people being greatly blessed. If the music and singing are as they ought to be, it will include prayer, praise, petition, and

NOTES

Prophecy. It was to David that the foundation of this great form of worship was given to Israel and, thereby, to the Church.

(7) "THEN ON THAT DAY DAVID DELIVERED FIRST THIS PSALM TO THANK THE LORD INTO THE HAND OF ASAPH AND HIS BRETHREN.

(8) "GIVE THANKS UNTO THE LORD, CALL UPON HIS NAME, MAKE KNOWN HIS DEEDS AMONG THE PEOPLE.

(9) "SING UNTO HIM, SING PSALMS UNTO HIM, TALK YOU OF ALL HIS WONDROUS WORKS.

(10) "GLORY YOU IN HIS HOLY NAME: LET THE HEART OF THEM REJOICE WHO SEEK THE LORD.

(11) "SEEK THE LORD AND HIS STRENGTH, SEEK HIS FACE CONTINUALLY.

(12) "REMEMBER HIS MARVELOUS WORKS THAT HE HAS DONE, HIS WONDERS, AND THE JUDGMENTS OF HIS MOUTH."

The overview is:

1. (Vs. 7) There are five great words which make up the entirety of this Psalm, which comprise praise and worship in our living for God. They are: *"Give," "Sing," "Glory," "Seek,"* and *"Remember."*

2. (Vs. 9) We are to sing to Him, and the song should be about His wondrous Works.

3. (Vs. 10) Our *"Glory"* is to be in *"His Holy Name,"* which incorporates His Character and Power. We then have the assurance that He will hear our prayers.

THE FIVE WORDS

If it is to be noticed, Asaph, David's Praise and Worship Director, is mentioned in the Seventh Verse. This particular position, the position of Praise and Worship Director, is probably the most important position in the Church other than that of the Senior Pastor, and for all of the obvious reasons. As the music goes, so goes the Church! And yet, while Asaph was the Praise and Worship Leader, still, he was always under the leadership of David. In fact, and as we've already stated, it was to David that the Lord gave the rudiments of worship as it regarded music and singing. If the truth be known, all of the praise and worship that's truly touched by the Holy Spirit presently, stems from that which was originally given to the *"sweet singer of Israel."*

GIVE THANKS

The very first word is *"Give,"* and it refers to *"giving thanks unto the LORD."*

Most of our prayer time should be given over to thanking the Lord for what He has done for us, and for what He is doing for us. Inasmuch as the Holy Spirit placed this first, this tells us of its significance. In fact, the Psalmist also wrote: *"Enter into His Gates with thanksgiving, and into His Courts with praise: be thankful unto Him, and bless His Name"* (Ps. 100:4).

Properly giving thanks to the Lord portrays the fact that we know and understand what He has done for us. It portrays our gratitude, which should be abundant. So, whatever it is we want from the Lord and, to be sure, there is much that we want; we should begin by *"giving thanks unto the LORD."*

SING UNTO HIM

The Holy Spirit here tells us that the Lord actually desires that we *"sing unto Him."* The idea is not that we have a beautiful voice, but rather, that, once again, we understand His Nature and His Character. Even in natural life, people who perform great feats of service have songs sung about them and to them. That's exactly what we are to do with the Lord. We are to sing *"of all His wondrous Works."*

GLORY IN HIS HOLY NAME

To what are we to glory? The Scripture is clear. We are to *"glory in His Holy Name."*

We presently have a greater privilege even than David had under the Old Covenant. The Name now is *"Jesus,"* and He is Lord. All the things to which those of old looked forward, now is a reality. So, if they could glory in His Name in those years of long ago, since the Cross, we have much more in which to glory.

SEEK THE LORD

The Scripture plainly says, *"Seek His Face continually."* This means to seek Him about everything.

He alone holds the answer to all of life's problems. He is the Source of all that we need, and we must quickly add, the Cross is the Means by which these things are given unto us.

The term is somewhat strange. The Psalmist said, *"Seek the LORD and His Strength."*

This tells us that whatever the needs are, and the needs are many, we do not have the power or the strength to get done what needs to be done. That lies in the domain of the Holy Spirit. He alone can make us what we ought to be, and do with us that which needs to be done; however, we must learn that the Holy Spirit works exclusively within, by, and through the Finished Work of Christ. In fact, this is so much a standard that it is referred to in the Scriptures as a *"Law"* (Rom. 8:2). It remains for the Believer to place his Faith exclusively in Christ and the Cross, and not allow it to be moved elsewhere, which will then give the Holy Spirit latitude to Work, with His Strength expended on our behalf. This is the only way that one can have Victory over the world, the flesh, and the Devil.

REMEMBER HIS MARVELOUS WORKS

Last of all, we are told to *"remember."* Remember what?

The Scripture is emphatic; we are to *"remember His marvelous Works."* We are also to remember *"the Judgments of His Mouth,"* which speaks of His Glorious Word.

So, we are to *"Give," "Sing," "Glory," "Seek,"* and *"Remember."*

(13) "O YOU SEED OF ISRAEL HIS SERVANT, YOU CHILDREN OF JACOB, HIS CHOSEN ONES.

(14) "HE IS THE LORD OUR GOD; HIS JUDGMENTS ARE IN ALL THE EARTH.

(15) "BE YOU MINDFUL ALWAYS OF HIS COVENANT; THE WORD WHICH HE COMMANDED TO A THOUSAND GENERATIONS;

(16) "EVEN OF THE COVENANT WHICH HE MADE WITH ABRAHAM, AND OF HIS OATH UNTO ISAAC;

(17) "AND HAS CONFIRMED THE SAME TO JACOB FOR A LAW, AND TO ISRAEL FOR AN EVERLASTING COVENANT,

(18) "SAYING, UNTO YOU WILL I GIVE THE LAND OF CANAAN, THE LOT OF YOUR INHERITANCE;

(19) "WHEN YOU WERE BUT FEW, EVEN A FEW, AND STRANGERS IN IT.

(20) "AND WHEN THEY WENT FROM NATION TO NATION, AND FROM ONE KINGDOM TO ANOTHER PEOPLE;

(21) "HE SUFFERED NO MAN TO DO THEM WRONG: YES, HE REPROVED KINGS FOR THEIR SAKES,

(22) "SAYING, TOUCH NOT MY ANOINTED, AND DO MY PROPHETS NO HARM."

The pattern is:

1. (Vs. 18) The Bible is the greatest title deed known to man. Pure and simple, it allots here the *"land of Canaan"* to Israel, and not the so-called Palestinians, as claimed by the Muslims.

2. The Lord watches extensively over that which is His, and if we will but obey, the Blessing will be ours.

3. As should be obvious, the Lord loves Israel. Long before this Psalm was written, the Lord promised Abraham that He would bless those who blessed Israel and, at the same time, He would curse those who curse Israel (Gen. 12:1-3).

ISRAEL

The Lord plainly says, *"O you seed of Israel His Servant, you Children of Jacob, His chosen Ones."* All of this tells us several things about these people referred to in the Bible as *"Israelites."* It says:

1. The Lord raised up the Nation of Israel out of the loins of Abraham and the womb of his wife Sarah, for the express purpose of giving the world the Word of God and, as well, to serve as the womb of the Messiah, the Saviour of mankind. He also intended for them to evangelize the world. They succeeded with the first two, but with great difficulty, and failed miserably with the third. However, in the coming Kingdom Age, they will yet fulfill this demand, as well, evangelizing the whole of mankind, in other words, telling the world about Jesus.

2. Israel was the only Nation on Earth that was monotheistic, meaning that they worshipped one God, Whose Name was and

NOTES

is Jehovah. All the other nations of the world were polytheistic, meaning that they worshipped many gods, i.e., demon spirits. But the Scripture plainly says in the Fourteenth Verse, *"He is the LORD our God; His Judgments are in all the Earth."* This tells us that the Lord, despite the fact that the balance of the world rejected Him, still, was the Lord of all the Earth, and for all the obvious reasons. He is the Creator of this Earth, as well as mankind.

3. Israel is cautioned to always be mindful of His Covenant, which He *"commands to a thousand generations."* This is a term that is indicative of eternity. In other words, there will be no end to His Covenant and, thereby, no end to demanded obedience.

4. This Covenant, His Law, was not made with generalities, but rather, with *"Abraham, Isaac, and Jacob."* It was *"confirmed to Jacob for a Law, and to Israel for an Everlasting Covenant."* And, what is the Covenant of which He speaks?

5. He emphatically states in this Psalm, *"Unto you will I give the land of Canaan, the lot of your inheritance."* This means that the land area formerly referred to as *"Israel,"* and presently referred to as *"Israel,"* belongs to the Jews. This also means it doesn't belong to the Palestinians or to the Muslims. So, when the Jews are opposed, as it regards the ownership of this land, it must be remembered that it, first of all, belongs to the Lord, and He has given it to Israel. Thereby, woe to any people or nation that would seek to usurp authority over the Word of God.

6. The Holy Spirit some 3,000 years ago plainly stated, *"He suffered no man to do them wrong: yes, He reproved kings for their sakes."* The world should take notice of this statement. The world is not to *"touch the Lord's anointed, and they must not do His Prophets any harm."* While the Lord might punish Israel and, in fact, did do so, and while He might use other nations to be His Instrument of punishment, still, these nations, whoever they might be, will be unwitting instruments.

A PERSONAL EXPERIENCE

On one of our trips to Israel, on the day in

question, we were standing on top of Masada. The guide had given some explanation as to what had transpired here, and now the people were told they could wander about and investigate the premises.

I was standing and talking with the guide, with no one else present, and we were looking down at the fortifications that had been built by the Romans nearly 2,000 years ago. These fortifications were constructed for the purpose of dislodging the Israelites who had garrisoned themselves on top of this strategic mount of Masada.

I said to him, *"When Rome built these fortifications, and ultimately took the heights where the Jews had fortified themselves, Rome was the mightiest power on the face of the Earth, hands down."* I then said, *"But, where is Rome today?"* I then added, *"Israel is a vibrant, growing Nation, in fact, one of the strongest in the world, and despite its small size, while Rome, with its imperial legions and its mighty Caesars, is no more."*

He stood there looking at me for a moment, and finally said, *"I've never thought of that."*

Yes, the Lord had to punish Israel greatly at times, and He will have to do so in the very near future once again; nevertheless, the Antichrist, who will try to destroy them and, in fact, will come close to succeeding, will himself, however, be totally and completely destroyed. It must be understood, the Lord means what He says, and says what He means. When He said, *"Touch not My anointed, and do My Prophets no harm,"* He meant that! The Palestinians, the Muslims and, in fact, the entirety of the world, had better take note.

(23) "SING UNTO THE LORD, ALL THE EARTH; SHOW FORTH FROM DAY TO DAY HIS SALVATION.

(24) "DECLARE HIS GLORY AMONG THE HEATHEN; HIS MARVELOUS WORKS AMONG ALL NATIONS.

(25) "FOR GREAT IS THE LORD, AND GREATLY TO BE PRAISED: HE ALSO IS TO BE FEARED ABOVE ALL GODS.

(26) "FOR ALL THE GODS OF THE PEOPLE ARE IDOLS: BUT THE LORD MADE THE HEAVENS.

NOTES

(27) "GLORY AND HONOUR ARE IN HIS PRESENCE; STRENGTH AND GLADNESS ARE IN HIS PLACE.

(28) "GIVE UNTO THE LORD, YOU KINDREDS OF THE PEOPLE, GIVE UNTO THE LORD GLORY AND STRENGTH.

(29) "GIVE UNTO THE LORD THE GLORY DUE UNTO HIS NAME: BRING AN OFFERING, AND COME BEFORE HIM: WORSHIP THE LORD IN THE BEAUTY OF HOLINESS.

(30) "FEAR BEFORE HIM, ALL THE EARTH: THE WORLD ALSO SHALL BE STABLE, THAT IT BE NOT MOVED.

(31) "LET THE HEAVENS BE GLAD, AND LET THE EARTH REJOICE: AND LET MEN SAY AMONG THE NATIONS, THE LORD REIGNS.

(32) "LET THE SEA ROAR, AND THE FULLNESS THEREOF: LET THE FIELDS REJOICE, AND ALL THAT IS THEREIN.

(33) "THEN SHALL THE TREES OF THE WOOD SING OUT AT THE PRESENCE OF THE LORD, BECAUSE HE COMES TO JUDGE THE EARTH.

(34) "O GIVE THANKS UNTO THE LORD; FOR HE IS GOOD; FOR HIS MERCY ENDURES FOR EVER.

(35) "AND SAY YOU, SAVE US, O GOD OF OUR SALVATION, AND GATHER US TOGETHER, AND DELIVER US FROM THE HEATHEN, THAT WE MAY GIVE THANKS TO YOUR HOLY NAME, AND GLORY IN YOUR PRAISE.

(36) "BLESSED BE THE LORD GOD OF ISRAEL FOR EVER AND EVER. AND ALL THE PEOPLE SAID, AMEN, AND PRAISED THE LORD."

The pattern is:

1. Israel is told in the Twenty-fourth Verse to evangelize the world, which they miserably failed to do. As stated, they will yet carry out this command in the coming Kingdom Age (Isa. 66:19-20).

2. The Twenty-sixth Verse proclaims the fact that there is One God, and only One, and He is the Creator of all things.

3. The Twenty-eighth Verse declares the fact that we are to give Him the credit He is due.

4. The Thirty-first Verse plainly tells us that there is coming a time, which will be in

the Kingdom Age, when the entirety of the world will say, *"The LORD reigns."*

5. (Vs. 36) The entirety of this Psalm, given by the Holy Spirit and written by David, and used at the time of the Ark of the Covenant being brought back to Jerusalem, can be summed up in the great phrase of Verse 25, *"For great is the LORD, and greatly to be praised."*

GREAT IS THE LORD

Some of the things said in the remainder of this Psalm are:

1. Every Believer is to, day-by-day, *"sing unto the LORD."* And, there is coming a day, this Twenty-third Verse tells us, that all of the entire Earth will *"show forth from day to day His Salvation."* That day is coming as surely as God lives.

2. We are to *"declare His Glory among the heathen,"* which tells us that the world must be evangelized, exactly that which Jesus said (Mk. 16:15). We must tell the world how great our Lord is, and what *"marvelous Works"* that He will perform for those who will love Him and believe Him.

3. There is only one God, and that is the Lord of Glory, *"Who made the heavens."* Every other supposed god is nothing but an idol, meaning that it is an evil spirit, at best.

4. His Presence brings *"glory and honour,"* while *"strength and gladness are in His Place."* This means that He has the Strength and the Power to help us to be what we ought to be, which will always bring forth *"gladness of heart."* The Believer receives this *"strength and gladness"* by placing his Faith exclusively in Christ and the Cross, which then gives the Holy Spirit latitude to Work within his life, thereby, developing His Fruit. In turn, even as the Twenty-eighth Verse proclaims, we are to give the Lord praise for all of these great things, and do so constantly.

5. Every Believer must *"Give unto the LORD the glory due unto His Name."* As well, we are to *"bring an Offering, and come before Him."*

This referred to a lamb that was to be brought in sacrifice, which typified the coming Redeemer, Who would give Himself on the Cross of Calvary. So, we are told here

NOTES

that all of this, Who the Lord is, and what He will do, and our part in all that He is, is predicated solely upon the Cross of Christ. In other words, Jesus Christ is the Source of all things, and the Cross is the Means by which these things are given to us, all superintended by the Holy Spirit.

6. The Twenty-ninth Verse also proclaims the fact that we must *"worship the LORD in the beauty of Holiness."*

This can only be done by our Faith being placed exclusively in Christ and the Cross. Regrettably, most people, even preachers, know little about the Cross beyond *"Jesus died for me."* While that is possibly the greatest statement ever made, still, that, as wonderful and great as it is, is only the beginning. The Cross of Christ has as much to do with our Sanctification, that is, how we live for God, and on a daily basis, as it does our initial Salvation.

HOLINESS

Holiness, which refers to one being totally set apart unto God, and totally for His Purpose, can only be brought about by the Holy Spirit. Unfortunately, almost every time the church has attempted to address holiness, it has tried to do so through rules and regulations. Such cannot be.

We must understand as Believers that holiness is a state that is demanded of us by the Lord. The Scripture plainly tells us:

"Follow peace with all men, and Holiness, without which no man shall see the Lord" (Heb. 12:14). So, how can a Believer be holy? I think it is clear from Hebrews 12:13 that without holiness, a person cannot be Saved.

As stated, man cannot develop holiness by rules, by regulations, by laws, etc. It simply cannot be done in this fashion. All that will tend to be done in such cases, which the church has ever tried to do, is to develop self-righteousness, which is abhorrent to God.

There is really nothing that man can do to develop holiness within his life, other than providing a willing mind and an obedient heart. Holiness can be brought about in our lives only by the Holy Spirit, and He does such through what Jesus did at the Cross, which demands our Faith. And now, we have touched upon the keyword — Faith.

The Holy Spirit is sent into our hearts and lives immediately at conversion and takes up abode there in order to do many things. One of those things and, no doubt, the greatest, is to rid us of all sin. No, that doesn't mean sinless perfection but most definitely does mean that the sin nature is no longer to rule over us (Rom. 6:14).

But, the Holy Spirit demands cooperation on our part. And, what type of cooperation does He demand?

He wants us to know and understand that whatever it is we need, we cannot do, we cannot be, we cannot have, at least, by our own machinations and ability. It simply cannot be done, despite the fact that we keep trying.

Holiness and, in fact, everything the Lord does for us, as stated, is brought about solely by Christ, and the Means by which He gives all of this to us is by and through the Cross, where He paid the price. This means that our Faith is to be placed exclusively in Christ and what He did for us at the Cross, and to keep our Faith there and not allow it to be moved. In fact, this is so important that Jesus, in essence, stated that we must do this, even on a daily basis (Lk. 9:23).

Faith properly placed doesn't mean perfection. It doesn't even mean that the Believer will not fail again, but it does mean that the Believer is now on the right path and, ultimately, the Holy Spirit will be able to pull the Believer in line with the Word of God. That is God's Way, God's Method, and His only Way.

With our Faith properly placed, trusting totally in Him and what He has done for us at the Cross, the Holy Spirit, Who Works exclusively within the confines and parameters of the Finished Work of Christ, can then begin to work within our lives, carrying out that which He Alone can do. Unfortunately, the church keeps trying to do what the Holy Spirit only can do, which is impossible.

To be sure, with our Faith properly placed, the Holy Spirit will most definitely begin to develop holiness within our hearts and lives. He will give us Victory over the works of the flesh. He will ever draw us closer to the Lord. He will develop His Fruit within our lives, which can be developed no other way.

So, one might well say that holiness is not so very much what we do, but it's altogether what He has done, with our Faith ever placed in that Finished Work. This is the reason the Cross of Christ is so very, very important. This is the reason that Paul said, *"We preach Christ Crucified"* (I Cor. 1:23). Unfortunately, all too many Christians have their faith in their particular church, their particular religious denomination, in preachers, in manifestations, or whatever, all of which are worthless. That's the reason that Paul also said:

"For Christ sent me not to baptize (presents to us a Cardinal Truth), *but to preach the Gospel* (the manner in which one may be Saved from sin)*: not with wisdom of words* (intellectualism is not the Gospel), *lest the Cross of Christ should be made of none effect.* (This tells us in no uncertain terms that the Cross of Christ must always be the emphasis of the Message)" (I Cor. 1:17).

In fact, this Seventeenth Verse tells us what the Gospel actually is. It is the preaching of the Cross (I Cor. 1:18).

Paul is not belittling Water Baptism, as should be obvious, but is rather telling us that the emphasis must always be on the Cross of Christ, exactly as we have just said, and not on other things. While the other things may be important in their own right, they are important only in the area in which the Lord intends. The Cross of Christ is the central core of the Gospel. Nothing must take its place, even as nothing can take its place.

(37) "SO HE LEFT THERE BEFORE THE ARK OF THE COVENANT OF THE LORD ASAPH AND HIS BRETHREN, TO MINISTER BEFORE THE ARK CONTINUALLY, AS EVERY DAY'S WORK REQUIRED:

(38) "AND OBED-EDOM WITH THEIR BRETHREN, THREESCORE AND EIGHT; OBED-EDOM ALSO THE SON OF JEDUTHUN AND HOSAH TO BE PORTERS:

(39) "AND ZADOK THE PRIEST, AND HIS BRETHREN THE PRIESTS, BEFORE THE TABERNACLE OF THE LORD IN THE HIGH PLACE THAT WAS AT GIBEON,

(40) "TO OFFER BURNT OFFERINGS UNTO THE LORD UPON THE ALTAR OF

THE BURNT OFFERING CONTINUALLY MORNING AND EVENING, AND TO DO ACCORDING TO ALL THAT IS WRITTEN IN THE LAW OF THE LORD, WHICH HE COMMANDED ISRAEL;

(41) "AND WITH THEM HEMAN AND JEDUTHUN, AND THE REST WHO WERE CHOSEN, WHO WERE EXPRESSED BY NAME, TO GIVE THANKS TO THE LORD, BECAUSE HIS MERCY ENDURES FOR EVER;

(42) "AND WITH THEM HEMAN AND JEDUTHUN WITH TRUMPETS AND CYMBALS FOR THOSE WHO SHOULD MAKE A SOUND, AND WITH MUSICAL INSTRUMENTS OF GOD. AND THE SONS OF JEDUTHUN WERE PORTERS.

(43) "AND ALL THE PEOPLE DEPARTED EVERY MAN TO HIS HOUSE: AND DAVID RETURNED TO BLESS HIS HOUSE."

The pattern is:

1. (Vs. 37) The great celebration of worship was not to be discontinued after the installation of the Ark; it was to be *"continually."* Too often those who name the Name of Christ worship the Lord only on selected days or times. The Holy Spirit is saying here, *"Every day, continually."*

2. (Vs. 38) This man, Obed-edom, in whose house the Ark of God had been left by David for some three months, would forsake all that he had in order to be near the *"Ark"*. He would be associated with the singers and musicians. The Holy Spirit would be so pleased with his actions, dedication, and service that He would mention his name some 20 times throughout the Word of God, and always in a positive way. What an honor!

3. (Vs. 40) The Ark was in Jerusalem, while the Brazen Altar was at Gibeon, about five miles northwest of Jerusalem. Evidently, the Table of Shewbread, Golden Lampstand, and Altar of Incense were at Gibeon, as well! They would remain separated until the Temple was built, some years later.

4. (Vs. 42) Under David, the great worship of God regarding musical instrumentation and choirs actually began. Of course, he was led by the Lord to do so. The Book of Psalms was Earth's First Songbook. David wrote at least half of those that are recorded, and possibly others that do not bear his name. In fact, some parts of the Psalm given in this Chapter are incorporated into Psalm 105.

TO MINISTER CONTINUALLY

There is a great Spiritual Truth in the command given by David that worship must be carried on before the Ark continually. More than likely, this was at set times each day, most probably at 9:00 a.m. in the morning and at 3:00 p.m. in the afternoon. This was referred to as the morning and the evening sacrifices. This was done every day.

Worship is what we are, while praise is what we do. The idea is, every single thing, as it involves the Child of God, must be labeled as worship. In other words, we are to do everything as unto the Lord, thereby, doing our very best.

Praise and worship should be a common aspect of our lives, and on a continual basis. Unfortunately, all too many who refer to themselves as *"Christians,"* park the Lord at the door of the church when they leave, meaning they spend an hour a week in church, etc. The other time, the Lord is forgotten.

One who is truly Born-Again, truly Spirit-filled and, thereby, Spirit-led, should function in the realm of praise and worship continually. This is the answer, and to be sure, for nervous disorders, emotional disturbances, fear, unbelief, etc.

This doesn't mean that Christians should be praising the Lord out loud at all times. That's not the meaning at all. We're speaking of the heart of the Believer. In one's heart, there should be continual praise and worship, which will brighten the day, make problems seem less, and, in fact, allow the Holy Spirit to glorify the Lord in one's life. This is the way it ought to be, and the symbol of this is what the Lord told David to do as it regarded *"ministering before the Ark."*

BURNT OFFERINGS

As stated, during the time of David, and the first years of Solomon, the Ark of the Covenant was in Jerusalem, while the Altar of Sacrifice and, obviously, the other instruments were in Gibeon.

Why the separation?

We have to assume that the Lord instructed

David as it regards the placement of these Vessels. I cannot imagine, especially after the first debacle of bringing the Ark into Jerusalem, that David would now take anything for granted.

The Tabernacle and the Brazen Altar with the other Vessels were away from Jerusalem, thereby, representing the First Covenant, now passed away. The Ark of the Covenant represents the Throne of God that will, in essence, be typified in the reign of the Lord Jesus Christ in Jerusalem. David was that Type, as well.

Williams says, *"The whole scene is prophetic of the day when the Son of David will establish His Throne in Zion and reign thereon as King and Priest before His ancients gloriously."*

He went on to say, *"There will be in that day the remembrance of the One Great Sacrifice once accomplished at Calvary, just as upon this day the blood once sprinkled upon the Mercy Seat of the Ark was the memorial of the Atonement consummated at the Brazen Altar. Calvary will not be repeated in the day when Israel's King appears in Zion, and because its repetition is unnecessary, but its remembrance as being the foundation of all blessing, will be overly prominent."*²

THE WORSHIP

Not only was there to be music and singing each day before the Ark of the Covenant but, as well, the same was to be carried forth before the great Altar, typifying the Cross.

This is new, the worship of the Lord in this fashion before the Brazen Altar.

But, why not? As gruesome as the Sacrificial system was, and understandably so, still, what it represented was so glorious, so wonderful, even so eternal as to defy all description. Understanding it in that fashion, the symbolic act of the Redemption of humanity, such would present itself as the occasion of great joy.

Calvary is said by the Word of Faith preachers to be the greatest defeat in human history. These preachers need to read these Verses. Such doesn't sound like defeat to me.

The Truth is, Calvary was the greatest Victory that this world has ever known or ever shall know, eclipsing everything that preceded it, and everything that follows it. It was there that the price was paid, and that satisfaction for sin was guaranteed, all by the Precious Blood of the Lord Jesus Christ. This act of Redemption was so complete, so total, so absolute, that the Holy Spirit referred to it through the Apostle Paul as *"the Everlasting Covenant"* (Heb. 13:20).

"Crown Him with many crowns, the Lamb upon His Throne;
"Hark! How the Heavenly anthem drowns all music but its own.
"Awake, my soul, and sing, of Him Who died for thee,
"And hail Him as your matchless King through all eternity."

"Crown Him the Lord of Life. Who triumphed o'er the grave,
"And rose Victorious in the strife for those He came to save;
"His Glories now we sing Who died, and rose on high,
"Who died Eternal Life to bring, and lives, that death may die."

"Crown Him the Lord of Peace, Whose Power a scepter sways,
"From pole to pole, that wars may cease, and all be prayer and praise:
"His Reign shall know no end, and round His pierced Feet,
"Fair flowers of Paradise extend their fragrance ever sweet."

"Crown Him the Lord of Love; behold His Hands and Side,
"Those wounds, yet visible above, in beauty glorified:
"All hail Redeemer, hail! For You have died for me:
"Your Praise and Glory shall not fail throughout eternity."

CHAPTER 17

(1) "NOW IT CAME TO PASS, AS DAVID SAT IN HIS HOUSE, THAT DAVID SAID TO NATHAN THE PROPHET, LO, I DWELL IN AN HOUSE OF CEDARS, BUT THE ARK OF THE COVENANT OF THE LORD

REMAINS UNDER CURTAINS.

(2) "THEN NATHAN SAID UNTO DAVID, DO ALL THAT IS IN YOUR HEART; FOR GOD IS WITH YOU."

The pattern is:

1. (Vs. 1) David is here a Type of the Lord Jesus Christ residing in Jerusalem in the glories of the Kingdom Age. All enemies are defeated.

2. (Vs. 1) David desires to build a house for the Lord. This pictures the beginning of the Kingdom Age, when the Lord Jesus, as a *"greater than Solomon"* will begin to build His *"House."*

3. (Vs. 2) While the Lord definitely was with David, it was not the Will of God that David build the House. This tells us that irrespective as to who the person might be, even a Prophet such as Nathan, we must not assume that we know what God wants. We must seek His Face about everything, which Nathan did not then do.

THE KINGDOM AGE

Everything pertaining to the Temple speaks of the coming Kingdom Age, which will portray God's Glory. The Tabernacle portrays God's Grace; the Temple portrays God's Glory; therefore, as stated, the Tabernacle at this particular time would be separated from the Ark of the Covenant, with it residing at Gibeon and the Ark residing in Jerusalem.

Both David and Solomon were Types of Christ. David subduing all his enemies, casting the Jebusites out of Zion, and setting up there the Throne of Jehovah, is a Type of the Messiah, when He will come back to this Earth and overthrow the Antichrist. In fact, the Messiah is stated in Exodus, Chapter 15, to be Jehovah, the Man of War. In Revelation, Chapter 19, it states that He makes war righteously. As the Great Captain of the Host, He will overcome all His Enemies, establish His Throne in Zion, redeem Israel, and make the Gentiles subject to His Scepter. Having accomplished all this, He will then, as the Divine Solomon, display the Glory of His Millennial Reign. The building of the Temple was designed to symbolize that Glory.

The Tabernacle, given to Moses in the wilderness, foretold the first Advent of Christ in humility; the Temple of Solomon foretold His Second Advent in Power and great Glory.

Hence, David could not build that Temple, for he typified Messiah as a Man of War, destroying His Enemies and setting up His Throne.

Solomon, typifying Christ as the Prince of Peace, which he did, built the glorious palace of Jehovah, and in doing so, gave a forepicture of the time when the kingdoms of this world shall become the Kingdom of our Lord and of His Christ, the Son of David, Who shall reign forever and ever.

TYPES OF CHRIST

David's heart was to build a structure for the Ark. To be sure, the Lord most definitely did place it in the heart of David that this structure be built, but it was not to be built by the *"sweet singer of Israel."*

Why?

The Temple, which would house the Ark, was a type of the coming Kingdom Age when Christ would reign supremely in peace, with the world then knowing prosperity and freedom as it has never known before. To be sure, that day is just ahead. But, the Rapture of the Church and the Great Tribulation must precede this coming event.

At any rate, the Temple was to portray that coming grand time, a time of such glory and splendor as to defy all description. Though David was a Type of Christ, and perhaps one of the greatest Types who ever existed, still, he could not portray Christ in this posture. David was a Type of Christ, as we have stated, as it regards Redemption's Plan, pertaining to the defeat of Satan and all his cohorts (Col. 2:14-15). As such, David was not a man of peace, even as he could not be a man of peace.

Solomon, David's son by Bath-sheba, would be a Type of Christ as it regards peace, thereby, the Kingdom Age. In fact, under Solomon, Israel knew peace and prosperity as the Nation had not known before, and would not know again, at least until the Second Advent of Christ.

So, we have in both David and Solomon Types of Christ, the former portraying the

Redemption Plan that was purchased at great cost, and the latter as a victory that is totally won. David was the Type of the conquering Christ, while Solomon was a Type of the Victorious Christ. So, David could not build the Temple, and for the obvious reasons. But he was given the plans in totality, which we shall see.

PROPHETS AND APOSTLES

Concerning the construction of the Temple, the Scripture says, *"Then Nathan said unto David, Do all that is in your heart; for God is with you."*

Now, without fanfare, without introduction, we have Nathan the Prophet who comes on the scene.

Under Old Testament guidelines, the Prophet, in effect, was used by the Lord to guide Israel. Presently, the Office of the Prophet is used of the Lord very similarly to Old Testament times, with one great exception. Now, the Apostle, and not the Prophet, is the titular leader of the Church. This Office was inaugurated by the Saviour in the choosing of Twelve Apostles who would be witnesses of His Life, Ministry, Death, and Resurrection, as well as His Ascension. While there could never be another twelve like those originally chosen by Christ, with Matthias taking the place of Judas, still, this Office is set firmly in the Church, meaning that the Lord is still appointing Apostles. Counting the Twelve, there were approximately twenty-four named as such in the New Testament.

WHAT ARE THE EARMARKS OF AN APOSTLE?

The word *"Apostle"* in the Greek is *"Apostolos,"* and means, *"a messenger, he that is sent."* It actually refers to one sent with a particular message. In fact, the particular message is the greatest earmark of the Apostle.

What do we mean by that?

The Holy Spirit, knowing what the Church needs, will lay it on the heart of a man (there is no record of a woman being called to be an Apostle) to stress a particular message, whatever that might be. Of course, it will always coincide perfectly with the Word of God, not deviating at all from that Word.

All of this means that Apostles aren't appointed by men, and aren't selected by men, with the fact remaining that men have absolutely nothing to do with those whom God calls for such an Office. As stated, these are the titular leaders of the Church, whether recognized as such or not.

As the Lord sees that the Church needs healing emphasized, or Prophecy emphasized, or Faith emphasized, or the Message of the Cross emphasized, the Holy Spirit will then appoint certain ones to emphasize the Message desired. As well, there could be two or more emphases at the same time. Yet, and I think history will prove me correct, there will always be a greater emphasis on one aspect of the Ministry and the Work of God.

We see this greater emphasis in the Book of Acts and the Epistles, as it regards the Cross of Christ. While the Holy Spirit emphasized other things, this was the primary emphasis of that time, and the Apostle Paul was the titular leader as it regards that Message. As well, if it is to be noticed, other than the original Twelve, most of the Apostles of that time fell into that category. In other words, their emphasis was the Cross of Christ.

Down through history, the Lord has emphasized other things. For instance, during the time of Martin Luther, He emphasized Justification by Faith. At the turn of the Twentieth Century the Holy Spirit was emphasized, and rightly so. At approximately the mid-time of the Twentieth Century, Divine Healing was emphasized. Now, I believe, it is the Message of the Cross.

COUNTERFEITS

To be sure, during the time of the Early Church, Satan endeavored to hinder the true Message of the Cross, which was the Message of Grace, by attempting to institute the message of Law. In fact, this was Paul's greatest nemesis. False apostles from Jerusalem and elsewhere were continually trying to overthrow the Message of Grace and, thereby, substituting Law. Inasmuch as flesh appeals to flesh, they were successful at times. Presently, false apostles are attempting to institute other types of emphasis, such as the *"Purpose Driven Life"* scheme, or the *"Government of Twelve"* scheme, or the *"Confession Message"* scheme, etc. But, as Satan did not succeed in the Early Church, he will not succeed presently.

Yes, he will draw many aside after these false apostles, whom Paul referred to as *"grievous wolves,"* but for those who truly love the Lord, who truly hunger and thirst after Righteousness, the great Message of the Cross, which is the present emphasis by the Holy Spirit, will be paramount (Acts 20:29-30).

PRESUMPTION

We should take a lesson from this which Nathan said to David. Both were great men of God; however, Nathan was wrong in telling David to *"do all that is in your heart."* Neither one had prayed about the matter. They were presuming this is what the Lord wanted; however, presumption is never the thing to do.

We must pray about everything, whether it's little or large. God is omniscient, meaning that He knows all things, past, present, and future. We, as human beings, are very much limited. We know very little about the past, very little about the present, and very little, if anything, about the future. So, we need to pray about everything, asking the Lord's Leading and Guidance, never presuming that we know what He wants and desires. The example given us here proclaims the fact that even the godliest cannot know what the Lord wants without ardently seeking His Face. Let us say it again, and because it is so very, very important.

We must never presume that we know what the Lord wants. We must seek His Face about everything. And to be sure, He has a Perfect Will as it regards every single thing, whether it be small or large. God's Ways are right, and they are right not simply because they are His Ways but, in fact, because they are right. He knows the way through the wilderness, we don't!

(3) "AND IT CAME TO PASS THE SAME NIGHT, THAT THE WORD OF GOD CAME TO NATHAN, SAYING,

(4) "GO AND TELL DAVID MY SERVANT, THUS SAYS THE LORD, YOU SHALL NOT BUILD ME AN HOUSE TO DWELL IN:

(5) "FOR I HAVE NOT DWELT IN AN HOUSE SINCE THE DAY THAT I BROUGHT UP ISRAEL UNTO THIS DAY; BUT HAVE GONE FROM TENT TO TENT, AND FROM ONE TABERNACLE TO ANOTHER.

(6) "WHERESOEVER I HAVE WALKED WITH ALL ISRAEL, SPOKE I A WORD TO ANY OF THE JUDGES OF ISRAEL, WHOM I COMMANDED TO FEED MY PEOPLE, SAYING, WHY HAVE YOU NOT BUILT ME AN HOUSE OF CEDARS?

(7) "NOW THEREFORE THUS SHALL YOU SAY UNTO MY SERVANT DAVID, THUS SAYS THE LORD OF HOSTS, I TOOK YOU FROM THE SHEEPCOTE, EVEN FROM FOLLOWING THE SHEEP, THAT YOU SHOULD BE RULER OVER MY PEOPLE ISRAEL:

(8) "AND I HAVE BEEN WITH YOU WHERESOEVER YOU HAVE WALKED, AND HAVE CUT OFF ALL YOUR ENEMIES FROM BEFORE YOU, AND HAVE MADE YOU A NAME LIKE THE NAME OF THE GREAT MEN WHO ARE IN THE EARTH.

(9) "ALSO I WILL ORDAIN A PLACE FOR MY PEOPLE ISRAEL, AND WILL PLANT THEM, AND THEY SHALL DWELL IN THEIR PLACE, AND SHALL BE MOVED NO MORE; NEITHER SHALL THE CHILDREN OF WICKEDNESS WASTE THEM ANYMORE, AS AT THE BEGINNING,

(10) "AND SINCE THE TIME THAT I COMMANDED JUDGES TO BE OVER MY PEOPLE ISRAEL. MOREOVER I WILL SUBDUE ALL YOUR ENEMIES. FURTHERMORE I TELL YOU THAT THE LORD WILL BUILD YOU AN HOUSE."

The pattern is:

1. (Vs. 3) As to how the Lord spoke to Nathan, we aren't told; however, the main thing is, Nathan was in such a Spiritual condition that God could speak to him. Regrettably, that isn't the case with most.

2. The Hebrew marks the personal pronoun, *"you,"* in Verse 4, as emphatic; *"you"* shall not build.

3. In Verse 5 the Lord reminds David how surely and faithfully He had shared the pilgrim lot and unsettledness of His People.

4. Verse 7 records the price of admission

into this house. It is trust in the *"slain Lamb,"* by the route of humility. As well, David was a shepherd, and the Lord Jesus Christ also would be a Shepherd (Heb. 13:20).

5. Verse 9 proclaims God's unconditional Covenant with Israel; however, it must be stated that this unconditional Covenant is unconditional only in the sense that God will bring the Promises to pass irrespective. The only thing that is unconditional is the Covenant itself. To come into the blessing of the Covenant, one must meet its conditions, which is Faith in Christ and what Christ has done at the Cross. Those Jews who do this will definitely dwell in the place ordained for them, which is the land of Israel. This includes all Jews who have accepted Christ before death, and all those who will accept Him at the Second Coming.

6. (Vs. 10) The more complete fulfillment of this great Promise awaits the coming of the Messiah (Isa. 9:6-7; Rom. 11:25-27).

A PLACE FOR ISRAEL

What did the Lord mean when He spoke to David saying, *"I tell you that the LORD will build you an house?"*

As we have already stated, while a house most definitely was to be built, David was not the one who would build it. Emphatically, the Lord stated, *". . . you shall not build Me an house to dwell in."*

The idea of Verses 5 and 6 is that the Lord had suffered whatever dwelling He had, and we speak of the time during the wilderness and, as well, the time of the Judges, and through the reign of Saul.

The idea is, Israel, during that time, was very unsettled. They had little sense of purpose or direction, a time frame, incidentally, which lasted several hundreds of years. So, to epitomize Israel's condition during that time, the Ark of the Covenant was moved *"from tent to tent,"* and *"from one tabernacle to another."* In other words, whatever it was in which the Ark of the Covenant was placed was indicative of what Israel was at that time. For most of that particular time, Israel was out of the Will of God. In fact, the time frame of the Judges is fraught with rebellion against the Lord. And then, they jumped the gun, demanding a king when it was not time, and the result was Saul. Basically, they treated the Ark of God with disdain, simply because they were not functioning right; they were not functioning in the Will of God; and, they were not functioning as Believers should function.

WHAT TYPE OF HOUSE DOES
THE LORD HAVE NOW?

We should take a lesson from this. When you came to Christ, the Holy Spirit came into your heart and life to abide permanently. Concerning this, Paul said:

"Know you not that you are the Temple of God (where the Holy Spirit abides), *and that the Spirit of God dwells in you?"* (I Cor. 3:16).

Is the Temple in which He abides obedient? Is it subservient to the Lord? Is it, God forbid, filled with pollution?

The Lord didn't leave Israel during those times of acute failure, and neither will He leave you; however, as is His Dwelling Place, so will be you!

It must be understood that the modern Believer cannot make a fit house for the Lord without his Faith being entirely in Christ and what Christ has done at the Cross. That sounds like a simple statement and, in fact, it is; however, that simple statement, Faith in Christ and what He did for us at the Cross, and that exclusively, lays waste all of man's concoctions, schemes, efforts, and futile plans. Man doesn't like that, so it is not easy for him to fully accept the Message of the Cross. But, if the Believer is to have a proper house in which the Holy Spirit is to dwell, he can do so only by his Faith in Christ and the Cross (Rom. 6:1-14; 8:1-2, 11; I Cor. 1:17-18, 23; 2:2; Gal., Chpt. 5; 6:14; Eph. 2:13-18; Col. 2:14-15).

THE SHEPHERD

As we have stated, David, although at times failing miserably, still, was a Type of Christ. Perhaps as a shepherd, his Type did show greater than all. Jesus was and is the Great Shepherd, the Great Shepherd of the sheep. In fact, David learned how to be a *"ruler over My People Israel,"* by being a shepherd. The Lord made David a name, by linking the Name of Christ to David. In fact, our Lord would be referred to as the *"Son of David,"* and there could be no higher honor shown to David than that of which we speak. Nothing is greater than being linked to Christ!

What kind of house would the Lord build David?

This house would be his link to Christ. It will finally be realized in the coming Kingdom Age, when Israel will finally accept Jesus as Saviour, Messiah, Lord, and Master. Then, this House of Israel will function under Christ as it was always intended to be.

While the Kingdom was offered to Israel at the First Advent of Christ, as is obvious, they rejected it. They wanted the Kingdom, but they didn't want the King, i.e., *"the Lord Jesus Christ."* In fact, millions today want the Kingdom, but they don't want the King. Let the following be understood:

It is impossible to have the Kingdom, or any part of the Kingdom, unless one, first of all, has the King, and that King is the Lord Jesus Christ.

The truth is, we don't build the Lord much of anything. He builds us a house.

THE BUILDING OF THE HOUSE

The major problem with Believers is that we try to build the house which, in fact, we cannot do. Actually, it is impossible! Any yet, the house must be built.

Abraham tried to build the house through Ishmael. Jacob tried to build the house through his schemes. In fact, all of us have tried to build this house and found to our dismay that we were unable to do so. If the house is to be built, the Lord must build it.

What do I mean by building the house?

I mean that we try to build righteousness and holiness within our hearts and lives. We try to effect our Spiritual Growth by our religious machinations. But, let it ever be understood, religious flesh is still flesh and is totally unacceptable to God (Rom. 8:8).

The Believer cannot build his own house. In other words, he cannot make himself righteous and holy, no matter what he does. We cannot effect the growth of the Fruit of the Spirit. Actually, as it regards living for God, i.e., *"building this house,"* we cannot do anything except provide to the Lord

NOTES

a willing mind and an obedient heart. The Lord Alone can build the house.

And how does He do such?

He does it by us placing our Faith simply, clearly, and completely in Christ and the Cross, which then gives the Holy Spirit latitude to Work within our lives, thereby, building the house. Otherwise, it will be built on sand and will topple with the first difficulty that arises.

(11) "AND IT SHALL COME TO PASS, WHEN YOUR DAYS BE EXPIRED THAT YOU MUST GO TO BE WITH YOUR FATHERS, THAT I WILL RAISE UP YOUR SEED AFTER YOU, WHICH SHALL BE OF YOUR SONS; AND I WILL ESTABLISH HIS KINGDOM.

(12) "HE SHALL BUILD ME AN HOUSE, AND I WILL ESTABLISH HIS THRONE FOR EVER.

(13) "I WILL BE HIS FATHER, AND HE SHALL BE MY SON: AND I WILL NOT TAKE MY MERCY AWAY FROM HIM, AS I TOOK IT FROM HIM WHO WAS BEFORE YOU:

(14) "BUT I WILL SETTLE HIM IN MY HOUSE AND IN MY KINGDOM FOR EVER: AND HIS THRONE SHALL BE ESTABLISHED FOR EVERMORE.

(15) "ACCORDING TO ALL THESE WORDS, AND ACCORDING TO ALL THIS VISION, SO DID NATHAN SPEAK UNTO DAVID."

The construction is:

1. Verse 11 has a double application. Solomon is spoken of in the immediate present, but far more so in the Lord Jesus Christ as the *"Son of David."*

2. As it regards the building of the house as described in Verse 12, the total fulfillment will be in Christ, Who will occupy this Throne in the coming Kingdom Age, and then forever.

3. The Muslims should read the words of Verse 14, and consider them carefully. In fact, the entirety of the world needs to read them, and to consider them carefully.

SPIRITUAL CONSTRUCTION

While the Lord Alone can build the house, the facts are, He uses human instrumentation to do so. The Scripture says: *"Except the LORD build the house, they labour in vain who build it"* (Ps. 127:1).

In the building of this house, in fact, the single most important thing in the history of man, which pertains to the Incarnation of our Lord, the Lord is the One Who chose the family through which the Redeemer would come. It would be the family of David. Through his line, which would be an unfailing line of descendants, the Messiah would ultimately come.

This Eleventh Verse is probably that to which Peter referred in his statement respecting Acts 2:29-30.

While the first part of Verse 11 refers to David, the latter part refers to his son, Solomon.

In fact, the lineage of David followed all the way to Christ, which it was intended to do. Mary went back to David in her lineage through Nathan, another son of David. Joseph went back to David through Solomon. So, the lineage of Christ was perfect in every respect, just as here promised.

The phrase in Verse 14, *"And his throne shall be established for evermore,"* in effect, has a double meaning. Most of all, it refers to Christ Who will occupy this throne *"for evermore."* Yet, the Scriptural indication is that David will reign upon this throne under Christ and, in essence, do so forever.

(16) "AND DAVID THE KING CAME AND SAT BEFORE THE LORD, AND SAID, WHO AM I, O LORD GOD, AND WHAT IS MY HOUSE, THAT YOU HAVE BROUGHT ME HITHERTO?

(17) "AND YET THIS WAS A SMALL THING IN YOUR EYES, O GOD; FOR YOU HAVE ALSO SPOKEN OF YOUR SERVANT'S HOUSE FOR A GREAT WHILE TO COME, AND HAVE REGARDED ME ACCORDING TO THE ESTATE OF A MAN OF HIGH DEGREE, O LORD GOD.

(18) "WHAT CAN DAVID SPEAK MORE TO YOU FOR THE HONOUR OF YOUR SERVANT? FOR YOU KNOW YOUR SERVANT.

(19) "O LORD, FOR YOUR SERVANT'S SAKE, AND ACCORDING TO YOUR OWN HEART, HAVE YOU DONE ALL THIS GREATNESS, IN MAKING KNOWN ALL THESE GREAT THINGS.

NOTES

(20) "O LORD, THERE IS NONE LIKE YOU, NEITHER IS THERE ANY GOD BESIDE YOU, ACCORDING TO ALL THAT WE HAVE HEARD WITH OUR EARS.

(21) "AND WHAT ONE NATION IN THE EARTH IS LIKE YOUR PEOPLE ISRAEL, WHOM GOD WENT TO REDEEM TO BE HIS OWN PEOPLE, TO MAKE YOU A NAME OF GREATNESS AND TERRIBLENESS, BY DRIVING OUT NATIONS FROM BEFORE YOUR PEOPLE, WHOM YOU HAVE REDEEMED OUT OF EGYPT?

(22) "FOR YOUR PEOPLE ISRAEL DID YOU MAKE YOUR OWN PEOPLE FOR EVER; AND YOU, LORD, BECAME THEIR GOD.

(23) "THEREFORE NOW, LORD, LET THE THING THAT YOU HAVE SPOKEN CONCERNING YOUR SERVANT AND CONCERNING HIS HOUSE BE ESTABLISHED FOR EVER, AND DO AS YOU HAVE SAID.

(24) "LET IT EVEN BE ESTABLISHED, THAT YOUR NAME MAY BE MAGNIFIED FOR EVER, SAYING, THE LORD OF HOSTS IS THE GOD OF ISRAEL, EVEN A GOD TO ISRAEL: AND LET THE HOUSE OF DAVID YOUR SERVANT BE ESTABLISHED BEFORE YOU.

(25) "FOR YOU, O MY GOD, HAVE TOLD YOUR SERVANT THAT YOU WILL BUILD HIM AN HOUSE: THEREFORE YOUR SERVANT HAS FOUND IN HIS HEART TO PRAY BEFORE YOU.

(26) "AND NOW, LORD, YOU ARE GOD, AND HAVE PROMISED THIS GOODNESS UNTO YOUR SERVANT:

(27) "NOW THEREFORE LET IT PLEASE YOU TO BLESS THE HOUSE OF YOUR SERVANT, THAT IT MAY BE BEFORE YOU FOR EVER: FOR YOU BLESS, O LORD, AND IT SHALL BE BLESSED FOR EVER."

The pattern is:

1. (Vs. 16) David now knows fully and beyond the shadow of a doubt that the Messiah will come through his lineage.

2. (Vs. 17) Even though it is not recorded in this Chapter, still, in II Samuel 7:19, David says, *"And is this the manner of man, O LORD God?"* This refers to the Promise that the Seed of the woman shall bruise the serpent's head (Gen. 3:15); that is, from David's line the Messiah will come, bringing

eternal Salvation and reigning as the eternal King of the Earth. This would be the highest honor that God could show any man, i.e., *"high degree."*

3. Verse 18 proclaims the fact that David in no way could merit this great and high honor, even as no Child of God can merit the high honor of Salvation freely given by the Lord Jesus Christ.

4. (Vs. 19) Once again, David exclaims the Glory of God, which is so much greater than what he at first thought. He wanted to build a house for the Lord; instead, the Lord tells David that He will build him a house, and it will be eternal.

5. (Vs. 21) Israel constituted the only people on Earth who knew Jehovah, the Creator of the ages.

6. (Vs. 23) The establishment of this house forever has only been partially fulfilled to date, but definitely will be fulfilled in the coming Kingdom Age.

7. As it regards Verse 24, hence, Jesus would say to the woman at Jacob's well, *"For Salvation is of the Jews"* (Jn. 4:22). It was through Israel that Jesus, the Saviour of the world, came!

8. (Vs. 25) When prayers are found in the heart, they are the result of gratitude or the overflow of some desperate need.

9. (Vs. 26) God keeps His Promises!

10. In Verse 27, the Lord pronounces Israel *"blessed for ever."* This means that Israel will ultimately be restored. It also means that what God has blessed, nothing can curse (Num. 23:8, 20).

THE INCARNATION OF CHRIST

What the Lord had spoken to David was, in a sense, beyond comprehension. The remainder of this Chapter records his response. And yet, his answer also records the fact that he little understood the implication of that which had been given to him.

For man to be redeemed, God would have to become man, simply because that which was required was beyond the pale of man's ability. So, if Redemption were to be brought forth, which would be by the Cross, God would have to become man and carry out this great Work Himself.

Angels could not do this thing because they were of another creation. And man couldn't do so simply because of his fallen, polluted condition. God would have to carry out the act and, in order to do so, He would have to become man. In effect, He would become the *"last Adam,"* or as Paul also referred, the *"Second Man"* (I Cor. 15:45-47). This was done for the purpose of going to the Cross. As well, a Perfect Sacrifice had to be offered, and God Alone could provide such, which He did, in the form of His Son and our Saviour, the Lord Jesus Christ.

This is the reason that man is so foolish when he attempts to place Christ in the category of a mere man. While He most definitely was a man, and in every respect, still, He was not only a man. He was, as well, God! One might say that He was the God-Man, the Lord Jesus Christ. All of this means that He was Very Man and Very God. He was God manifest in the flesh. Concerning all of this, Paul said:

"For what the Law could not do, in that it was weak through the flesh (those under Law had only their willpower, which is woefully insufficient; so despite how hard they tried, they were unable to keep the Law then, and the same inability persists presently; any person who tries to live for God by a system of laws is doomed to failure, because the Holy Spirit will not function in that capacity), *God sending His Own Son* (refers to man's helpless condition, unable to save himself and unable to keep even a simple law and, therefore, in dire need of a Saviour) *in the likeness of sinful flesh* (this means that Christ was really human, conformed in appearance to flesh which is characterized by sin, but yet sinless), *and for sin* (to atone for sin, to destroy its power, and to save and sanctify its victims), *condemned sin in the flesh* (destroyed the power of sin by giving His Perfect Body as a Sacrifice for sin, which made it possible for sin to be defeated in our flesh; it was all through the Cross)" (Rom. 8:3).

BLESSED FOREVER

Emphatically, and even dogmatically, the Holy Spirit through David says, and concerning Israel, *"O LORD, and it shall be blessed forever."*

All of this means, as stated, that the Lord will ultimately and eventually restore Israel. In fact, this will be done at the Second Coming, which will be the most cataclysmic event the world has ever known. Then Israel will understand that the One they crucified was and is their Messiah. They will then accept Him, and then be restored to their rightful place and position in the family of nations.

In fact, Israel, in that coming day, the Kingdom Age, will be the greatest Nation on the face of the Earth, all under Christ.

So, the Muslim world has about as much chance of destroying Israel as Mohammad has of getting out of Hell, where he is presently, and ever shall be.

Something that is blessed may have difficulties and problems but, to be sure, that which the Lord has promised most definitely will come to pass, and without fail.

"Oh for a thousand tongues to sing,
"My Great Redeemer's praise,
"The glories of my God and King,
"The triumphs of His Grace."

"My gracious Master and my God,
"Assist me to proclaim,
"To spread through all the Earth abroad,
"The honors of Your Name."

"Jesus! The Name that charms our fears,
"That bids our sorrows cease;
"Tis music in the sinners' ears,
"Tis life, and health, and peace."

"He breaks the power of cancelled sin,
"He sets the prisoner free;
"His Blood can make the foulest clean;
"His Blood availed for me."

"Hear Him, you deaf; His Praise, you dumb,
"Your loosened tongues employ;
"You blind, behold your Saviour come;
"And leap, you lame, for joy."

CHAPTER 18

(1) "NOW AFTER THIS IT CAME TO PASS, THAT DAVID SMOTE THE PHILISTINES, AND SUBDUED THEM, AND TOOK GATH AND HER TOWNS OUT OF THE HAND OF THE PHILISTINES.

(2) "AND HE SMOTE MOAB; AND THE MOABITES BECAME DAVID'S SERVANTS, AND BROUGHT GIFTS.

(3) "AND DAVID SMOTE HADAREZER KING OF ZOBAH UNTO HAMATH, AS HE WENT TO STABLISH HIS DOMINION BY THE RIVER EUPHRATES.

(4) "AND DAVID TOOK FROM HIM A THOUSAND CHARIOTS, AND SEVEN THOUSAND HORSEMEN, AND TWENTY THOUSAND FOOTMEN: DAVID ALSO HOUGHED ALL THE CHARIOT HORSES, BUT RESERVED OF THEM AN HUNDRED CHARIOTS.

(5) "AND WHEN THE SYRIANS OF DAMASCUS CAME TO HELP HADAREZER KING OF ZOBAH, DAVID KILLED OF THE SYRIANS TWO AND TWENTY THOUSAND MEN.

(6) "THEN DAVID PUT GARRISONS IN SYRIA-DAMASCUS; AND THE SYRIANS BECAME DAVID'S SERVANTS, AND BROUGHT GIFTS. THUS THE LORD PRESERVED DAVID WHITHERSOEVER HE WENT.

(7) "AND DAVID TOOK THE SHIELDS OF GOLD THAT WERE ON THE SERVANTS OF HADAREZER, AND BROUGHT THEM TO JERUSALEM.

(8) "LIKEWISE FROM TIBHATH, AND FROM CHUN, CITIES OF HADAREZER, BROUGHT DAVID VERY MUCH BRASS, WHEREWITH SOLOMON MADE THE BRASEN SEA, AND THE PILLARS, AND THE VESSELS OF BRASS."

The pattern is:

1. Verses 1 and 2 illustrate the moral fact, always true, that when Christ is set upon the throne of the heart, victory over both inward and outward enemies is assured; but the inward is always first conquered, as in the case of David and the Philistines in this Chapter, and then the outward will be conquered.

2. *"Hadarezer"* of Verse 3 means *"my demon helper"*; so, despite demon spirits helping this man, David, who was greater, *"smote"* them.

3. (Vs. 3) The River Euphrates was the

northeastern extremity of the kingdom promised to Abraham by the Lord (Gen. 15:18). Through our *"Heavenly David,"* the Lord Jesus Christ, we can conquer and, in fact, must conquer, every part of our inheritance.

4. Verse 4 proclaims the fact that Israel's strength was not chariots, but rather the Lord!

5. (Vs. 5) All of this is a Type of Christ, Who will defeat every enemy at the Cross (Col. 2:14-15). When our Faith and trust are placed exclusively in Him and the Cross, His Victory then becomes our victory!

6. (Vs. 6) It is the Will of God, and even the insistence of the Lord, that we subdue not just some of our spiritual enemies, but all. We must rule the sin nature, or else the sin nature will rule us (Rom. 6:3-14).

7. (Vs. 7) The wealth of Zobah was illustrated by the shields of gold. Now this wealth belongs to the people of God, stipulating the coming Kingdom Age.

8. All of this material of Verse 8, formerly used for heathen idols, will now be used for God, as it regards the building of the Temple. This symbolizes the Believer, who is brought out of sin and darkness, brought to the Family of God, and made to be *"a pillar in the Temple of My God"* (Rev. 3:12).

THE INWARD AND OUTWARD ENEMIES

This Chapter is freighted with victory and the reasons such victories are afforded. With Christ as a Type of the Ark being now enthroned in Zion, the center of the kingdom, David soon enjoys complete victory over all enemies, both at home and foreign. The Philistines, internal enemies, are first bridled, and then, the external foes are brought into subjection; however, before the external foes can be defeated, the internal foes must be defeated, here illustrated by the Philistines. They were within the sacred borders of Israel.

How many Christians still have Philistines within their lives? This is a question that should be looked at very carefully, and simply because this is so very, very important. External foes, whatever those foes might be, can never be defeated until the inward enemies are subdued. As it regards the modern Believer, I speak of uncontrollable temper, jealousy, envy, malice, unforgiveness, and immorality of various stripes, plus many we haven't named, which are described as inward hindrances, and great hindrances at that, of our Christian walk.

If it is to be noticed, the very first thing that David did when he became king of Israel was to subdue the Jebusites, who occupied the very area where the Temple would be built years later. This was in the very heart of Israel, and most certainly constituted an inward foe (II Sam. 5:6-10). Then he conquered the Philistines, another inward foe (I Chron. 13:8-17). We will now find that the outward foes, those outside the borders of Israel, but promised by the Lord to Israel, will now be subdued.

This lesson must not be lost on us!

THE MANNER OF VICTORY

The Believer will find, and without exception, that the greatest foes of all are those which are inward foes. Satan knows that if he can keep his strongholds within our hearts and lives, this will greatly hinder our walk and progress with the Lord. So, these things, whatever they might be, must be defeated. There is only one way they can be defeated. Now, understand that, read those words carefully, and believe what is said.

Satan will also come up with every type of means and way that one can think to overcome these foes, and will use preachers and entire denominations to carry out his work. But, no matter how religious it might be, there is only one way that Victory can be assured in one's heart and life, and that is the Way of the Cross. The answer is found in the Cross. The solution is found in the Cross. And, the answer and the solution are found only in the Cross! Now, understand that. There is no victory over sin outside of the Cross! There is no victory over inward foes or outward foes outside of the Cross! There is no victory over the world, the flesh, and the Devil outside of the Cross. That is God's Way, and a Way, we might quickly add, that is stamped on every page of the Bible. So, there is no excuse for us to misunderstand.

Unfortunately, at this particular time, and I speak of the modern church, the Devil is very slickly parading his wares of so-called solutions, all propagated by the church. Too many Believers have itching ears, desiring to hear something that sounds pleasing to the flesh, and which will not bother their sin. Regrettably, the nation and the world are full of such sermons. But, let us say it again:

There is no answer to the sin problem, no answer to the life and living problem, and no answer to the victory problem, other than the Cross of Christ. We must ever understand that Christ is the Source of all things that we receive from God, and the Cross is the Means by which these things are given to us, all superintended by the Holy Spirit (Rom. 6:1-14; 8:1-2, 11; I Cor. 1:17-18, 21, 23; 2:2; Gal., Chpt. 5; 6:14; Eph. 2:13-18; Col. 2:14-15). And these Scriptures I've just given are only a tiny fraction of the Word of God, which actually deals with this very subject.

It is the Cross! The Cross! The Cross!

DOMINION

Concerning David's victories, the Scripture says: *"And David smote Hadarezer king of Zobah unto Hamath, as he went to stablish his dominion by the river Euphrates."*

The upshot of this statement is, we either establish dominion over Satan and his powers of darkness, or he establishes dominion over us. In fact, the very name *"Hadarezer,"* means, *"my demon helper."*

As we've already stated, before David could defeat the enemy without, he had to first of all defeat the enemy within, which was the Philistines.

I think I can say without fear of exaggeration that every single modern Believer falls into the category of dominating Satan or being dominated by Satan. There is no in-between. There is only one way that the Believer can establish dominion over the powers of darkness, and in whatever capacity they may come against us, and that is by the Cross of Christ. Whatever else the Believer attempts to do, no matter how religious it might be, and no matter how right it might be in its own way and manner, those things, whatever they might be, cannot be used to overcome the Powers of Darkness. Let me explain further!

NOTES

I heard a preacher over television the other day stating that if Believers would take the Lord's Supper every day, or some such time frame, this would defeat all enemies, guarantee health and prosperity, etc. There is nothing like that in the Bible. While the Lord's Supper is most definitely Scriptural, still, to try to use it in the wrong way will not bring about the desired results. If that were the case, Jesus needlessly came down here and died on a Cross.

I heard another preacher say that if a Believer were experiencing bondage of any kind, he should establish a time that he would pray so much each day, and read so many Chapters in the Bible. Now, in fact, the Believer's prayer life and Bible Study are two of the most important things in one's life. Without a proper prayer life, one simply cannot have a proper relationship with the Lord. And, if one doesn't know the Word, then one is drifting without any direction. But at the same time, as helpful as it may be in other means and ways, the idea that doing such will rid one of bondage is not Biblical. Again, if one could overcome powers of darkness by praying so much each day and reading so many Chapters, then again, Jesus didn't need to come down here and die on a Cross.

While all of these things we have named are very, very important, when we try to use them to establish dominion over the powers of darkness, we turn them into law, which God can never honor. Paul said it well:

"I do not frustrate the Grace of God (if we make anything other than the Cross of Christ the Object of our Faith, we frustrate the Grace of God, which means we stop its action, and the Holy Spirit will no longer help us)*: for if Righteousness come by the Law* (any type of law), *then Christ is dead in vain.* (If I can successfully live for the Lord by any means other than Faith in Christ and the Cross, then the Death of Christ was a waste)*"* (Gal. 2:21).

FRUSTRATING THE GRACE OF GOD

When the Believer places his Faith in anything, and no matter how good it might be, other than the Cross of Christ, this frustrates the Grace of God, which means that the good things the Lord desires to do for us are halted.

The *"Grace of God"* is simply the Goodness of God extended to undeserving Saints. The truth is, God has no more Grace today than He did under Law. The difference is, due to the fact that animal blood was insufficient to remove sin, this hindered God from extending His Goodness, as He desired, to the Saints of that time. Now, since the Cross, where every debt was paid, every sin cleansed, at least for all who will believe, God can pour Grace upon any individual who will dare to believe Him. But, the trouble is, most of the modern church is frustrating the Grace of God, and doing so by placing their faith in something other than the Cross of Christ.

In connection with the statement, as it regards frustrating the Grace of God, the great Apostle said: *"I am Crucified with Christ* (as the Foundation of all Victory; Paul, here, takes us back to Rom. 6:3-5): *nevertheless I live* (have new life); *yet not I* (not by my own strength and ability), *but Christ lives in me* (by virtue of me dying with Him on the Cross, and being raised with Him in Newness of Life): *and the life which I now live in the flesh* (my daily walk before God) *I live by the Faith of the Son of God* (the Cross is ever the Object of my Faith), *Who loved me, and gave Himself for me* (which is the only way that I could be Saved)" (Gal. 2:20).

Two times in this one Verse, Paul takes us straight to the Cross. This tells us that the Cross alone gives us Victory. What Jesus did there, which was to offer Himself as a Perfect Sacrifice, satisfied the demands of a thrice-Holy God, which refers to our Faith in that Finished Work, and on an unending basis. Let us say it again:

Christ is the Source of all things we receive from God, and the Cross is the Means by which these things are done, all superintended by the Holy Spirit (Eph. 2:13-18).

All of this means that the Believer can have dominion over the powers of darkness only by exercising Faith in Christ and the Cross and, as stated, doing such on an unending, even daily, basis (Lk. 9:23). If the Believer tries to live for God by any other manner, failure will be the guaranteed result.

NOTES

The following is an article written some years ago by the late Oswald Chambers. It is a truth that needs to be read most carefully. It is entitled:

IT IS FINISHED

"I have finished the Work which You gave Me to do (Jn. 17:4).

"The Death of Jesus Christ is the performance in history of the very Mind of God. There is no room for looking on Jesus Christ as a martyr; His Death was not something that happened to Him which might have been prevented: His Death was the very reason why He came.

"Never build your preaching of forgiveness on the fact that God is our Father and He will forgive us because He loves us. It is untrue to Jesus Christ's Revelation of God; it makes the Cross unnecessary, and the Redemption 'much ado about nothing.' If God does forgive sin, it is because of the Death of Christ. God could forgive men in no other way than by the Death of His Son, and Jesus is exalted to be Saviour because of His Death. 'We see Jesus because of the suffering of death, crowned with glory and honor.' The greatest note of triumph that ever sounded in the ears of a startled universe was that sounded on the Cross of Christ — 'it is finished.' That is the last word in the Redemption of man.

"Anything that belittles or obliterates the Holiness of God by a false view of the Love of God, is untrue to the Revelation of God given by Jesus Christ. Never allow the thought that Jesus Christ stands with us against God out of pity and compassion; that He became a curse for us out of sympathy with us. Jesus Christ became a curse for us by the Divine Decree. Our portion of realizing the terrific meaning of the curse is conviction of sin, the guilt of shame and penitence is given us — this is the great mercy of God. Jesus Christ hates the wrong in man, and Calvary is the estimate of His hatred.'"[1]

PILLARS IN THE TEMPLE OF GOD

In defeating the enemies of Israel, which included various countries, the Scripture says that David *"took the shields of gold...."*

and, as well, *". . . very much brass, wherewith Solomon made the Brasen Sea, and the Pillars, and the vessels of brass."*

Jesus, in addressing the Church in Philadelphia said, *"Him who overcomes will I make a pillar in the Temple of My God"* (Rev. 3:12). When He said this, He, no doubt, had in mind the two Pillars, which graced the front of the Temple built by Solomon. Incidentally, this is the only building on Planet Earth that was designed by God, and done so in totality. In fact, God was to reside between the Mercy Seat and the Cherubim in the Holy of Holies in the Temple, which He did for several centuries.

The two Pillars in front of the Temple did not function as pillars normally do. In fact, the two Pillars in front of the Temple did not hold up anything. In other words, there was no porch or portico in front of the Temple. The two Pillars made of brass were strictly for ornamentation. In fact, one was named *"Jachin,"* which means, *"He shall establish,"* and the second was named *"Boaz,"* which means, *"in it is strength."*

The two Pillars were fifty-two and a half feet high, each with a chapter on top of each Pillar seven and a half feet high, making each Pillar a total of sixty feet tall.

There were chains at the top of the Pillars, which typifies our union with Christ. Also, there were pomegranates carved into the brass, typifying the Fruit of the Spirit.

The Pillars faced the east, actually the rising of the sun.

It is said that travelers, in coming to Jerusalem, would at times camp out at night on Mt. Olivet, so they could watch the sun come up over the mountain. When it did each morning, with its rays striking the Pillars, the burnished brass would throw off reflections of light that, it is said, was a sight to behold.

These Pillars, Jesus, in essence, said, typify the Child of God. This means that we aren't really needed in the Great Plan of God; therefore, one might as well refer to all Believers as ornamentation. And we must always remember, the beautiful reflection that comes from the *"Son"* is that of His Light, and not ours. We are only, as stated, a reflection of that Light.

NOTES

(9) "NOW WHEN TOU KING OF HAMATH HEARD HOW DAVID HAD SMITTEN ALL THE HOST OF HADAREZER KING OF ZOBAH;

(10) "HE SENT HADORAM HIS SON TO KING DAVID, TO ENQUIRE OF HIS WELFARE, AND TO CONGRATULATE HIM, BECAUSE HE HAD FOUGHT AGAINST HADAREZER, AND SMITTEN HIM; (FOR HADAREZER HAD WAR WITH TOU;) AND WITH HIM ALL MANNER OF VESSELS OF GOLD AND SILVER AND BRASS.

(11) "THEM ALSO KING DAVID DEDICATED UNTO THE LORD, WITH THE SILVER AND THE GOLD THAT HE BROUGHT FROM ALL THESE NATIONS; FROM EDOM, AND FROM MOAB, AND FROM THE CHILDREN OF AMMON, AND FROM THE PHILISTINES, AND FROM AMALEK.

(12) "MOREOVER ABISHAI THE SON OF ZERUIAH KILLED OF THE EDOMITES IN THE VALLEY OF SALT EIGHTEEN THOUSAND.

(13) "AND HE PUT GARRISONS IN EDOM; AND ALL THE EDOMITES BECAME DAVID'S SERVANTS. THUS THE LORD PRESERVED DAVID WHITHERSOEVER HE WENT.

(14) "SO DAVID REIGNED OVER ALL ISRAEL, AND EXECUTED JUDGMENT AND JUSTICE AMONG ALL HIS PEOPLE.

(15) "AND JOAB THE SON OF ZERUIAH WAS OVER THE HOST; AND JEHOSHAPHAT THE SON OF AHILUD, RECORDER.

(16) "AND ZADOK THE SON OF AHITUB, AND ABIMELECH THE SON OF ABIATHAR, WERE THE PRIESTS; AND SHAVSHA WAS SCRIBE;

(17) "AND BENAIAH THE SON OF JEHOIADA WAS OVER THE CHERETHITES AND THE PELETHITES; AND THE SONS OF DAVID WERE CHIEF ABOUT THE KING."

The pattern is:

1. (Vs. 11) If the Lord does see fit to bless us with worldly riches, it must, without fail, be *"dedicated unto the LORD,"* and not to our own selfish desires.

2. (Vs. 12) Those who were with David experienced David's anointing.

3. Verse 13 is repeated from Verse 6, and

with purpose. It is meant to impress upon all that the Lord was the Source of David's victories, and the Lord Alone.

4. Verse 14 means that no enemy occupied any part of the land of Israel. How many of us can say that we *"reign over all the possession that God has given us"*? It can be done only through Faith expressed in Christ and what Christ has done for us at the Cross, which then gives us the help of the Holy Spirit, without Whom nothing can be done (Rom. 8:1-2, 11).

5. The last two groups listed in Verse 17 were probably Philistines who served as David's bodyguards. They had, thereby, thrown in their lot with David, consequently forsaking their past, in effect, symbolic of all Believers.

THE PRESERVATION OF THE LORD

The Scripture says, *"Thus the LORD preserved David whithersoever he went."*

When one is in the Will of God, as obviously David was at this time, the Lord works for such a person, even as He worked for David. As a result, David won every conflict in which he was engaged, and besides that, took into the coffers of Israel *"all manner of vessels of gold and silver and brass."* The Lord is with Israel and, as such, the Nation will quickly rise to ascendancy. Every enemy will be defeated. Every power of darkness will be put down. The Nation is now on the march.

Concerning this succession of victories, Williams says: *"The affection of David's heart for the people and House of God is evidenced by his consecrating the entire spoil of these victories to Jehovah's treasury. He kept nothing for himself. It shows rich spiritual experience on the part of Christian people when all the glory and profit of spiritual victories are denied to self and willingly given to the enrichment of others, whether physically or spiritually."*²

"Oh, worship the King, all-glorious above;
"Oh, gratefully sing His Power and His Love:
"Our Shield and Defender, The Ancient of Days,

NOTES

"Pavilioned in splendor and girded with praise."

"Oh, tell of His Might, Oh sing of His Grace,
"Whose Robe is the Light, Whose Canopy Space;
"His Chariots of wrath the deep thunderclouds form,
"And dark is His Path on the wings of the storm."

"The Earth, with its store of wonders untold,
"Almighty, Your Power has founded of old;
"Has stablished it fast, by a changeless decree,
"And round it has cast, like a mantle, the sea."

"Your Bountiful Care what tongue can recite?
"It breathes in the air, It shines in the light;
"It streams from the hills, It descends to the plain,
"And sweetly distills in the dew and the rain."

"Frail children of dust, and feeble as frail,
"In Thee do we trust, nor find Thee to fail;
"Your Mercies how tender, how firm to the end,
"Our Maker, Defender, Redeemer, and Friend."

—■—

CHAPTER 19

(1) "NOW IT CAME TO PASS AFTER THIS, THAT NAHASH THE KING OF THE CHILDREN OF AMMON DIED, AND HIS SON REIGNED IN HIS STEAD.

(2) "AND DAVID SAID, I WILL SHOW KINDNESS UNTO HANUN THE SON OF NAHASH, BECAUSE HIS FATHER SHOWED KINDNESS TO ME. AND DAVID SENT MESSENGERS TO COMFORT HIM CONCERNING HIS FATHER. SO THE SERVANTS OF DAVID CAME INTO THE

LAND OF THE CHILDREN OF AMMON TO HANUN, TO COMFORT HIM.

(3) "BUT THE PRINCES OF THE CHILDREN OF AMMON SAID TO HANUN, THINK YOU THAT DAVID DOES HONOUR YOUR FATHER, THAT HE HAS SENT COMFORTERS UNTO YOU? ARE NOT HIS SERVANTS COME UNTO YOU FOR TO SEARCH, AND TO OVERTHROW, AND TO SPY OUT THE LAND?

(4) "WHEREFORE HANUN TOOK DAVID'S SERVANTS, AND SHAVED THEM, AND CUT OFF THEIR GARMENTS IN THE MIDST HARD BY THEIR BUTTOCKS, AND SENT THEM AWAY.

(5) "THEN THERE WENT CERTAIN, AND TOLD DAVID HOW THE MEN WERE SERVED. AND HE SENT TO MEET THEM: FOR THE MEN WERE GREATLY ASHAMED. AND THE KING SAID, TARRY AT JERICHO UNTIL YOUR BEARDS BE GROWN, AND THEN RETURN."

The construction is:

1. (Vs. 1) The name *"Nahash"* means, *"shining serpent."*

2. Verse 2 presents a perfect Type of our Heavenly David sending godly preachers and teachers to the world to comfort them with the Gospel. This comfort alone is valid!

3. (Vs. 3) Evil cannot discern Righteousness, but rather sees evil in everything.

KINDNESS REWARDED?

This Chapter is a perfect example of God's Love for this world and His Efforts to save mankind. It is also a picture of man's rejection of such love, graciousness, and kindness extended by the Lord of Glory.

David said, *"I will show kindness unto Hanun the son of Nahash."*

These individuals were heathen and, thereby, aliens to the commonwealth of Israel and strangers to the Promise. Their right and just desert was Judgment.

This, as well, typifies the whole of the human race. Mankind is filled with Satan and can, thereby, lay no claim on the Grace and Glory of God through its own merit. The extended hand to the sons of Satan, which characterizes the entirety of the human race, is only because of the *"kindness"* of our Heavenly David. Seldom, incidentally,

NOTES

is that hand properly accepted!

David's servants were shamefully treated, which means that David's kindness was thrown back in his face. This is the lot, seemingly, of almost all who attempt to take the great Message of Redemption to a lost and dying world.

The manner in which these men were treated was designed especially to humiliate them; likewise, the world will greatly humiliate anyone who attempts to bring the great and glorious Gospel of Jesus Christ to the hardened heart. Jesus would say of the system of this world, *"If it loved Me, it will love you."* It did not love Him, as is obvious, so it will not love us. By and large, there will be a total rejection of the *"comfort"* of the great Message of Redemption. But some few, thankfully, will accept.

WHY THE ANIMOSITY TOWARD THE LORD?

Strangely enough, there was very little animosity toward the world of Islam even after September 11, 2001, snuffed out nearly 3,000 lives.

Why?

Most of the animosity of this world, at least as it regards the Lord, is registered against that which is truly Biblical. There is almost no animosity whatsoever toward Islam, Buddhism, Hinduism, Confucianism, etc.

These religions are of Satan, meaning they were formulated by the Prince of Darkness. As a result, the followers of Satan, which include almost all the world, simply do not see the evil in these religions.

As it regards Christianity, and we speak of Biblical Christianity, great animosity is, in fact, registered toward the Lord Jesus Christ and those who follow Him. The reason is simple:

This animosity began in the Garden of Eden at the time of the Fall. Jehovah Alone is Lord, so, the anger of the world of darkness is registered against Him, and all who follow Him.

These other religions are all figments of men's imaginations, and at the most, as it regards the spirit world, they were begun by demons. So, the animosity of the world is always against the Lord Jesus Christ.

ISLAM

It would seem, would it not, that people in this nation and other democratic nations of the world, could easily see the intent of Islam. But seemingly, that intent is not easily observed.

The religion of Islam is the cause of all the terrorist activity. This means that the blame cannot be laid at the feet of only a few malcontents which, in fact, is the policy of most of the world. The problem is the religion itself. And to be sure, this religion will not change. It will continue to hate America, and with a passion. As a result, it will do everything within its power to destroy this nation, and yet, we are so blind that we cannot see what is happening, even though it's under our very nose. The powers that be in this nation still cling to the stupid idea that the religion of Islam is loving, peaceful, and kind, and again, it's the few malcontents who are causing the problem. This is believed despite overwhelming evidence to the contrary. None are so blind as those who will not see.

As a result of this blindness, it is not *"politically correct"* to point out the true intent of the religion of Islam. As a result, we keep inviting rattlesnakes into our house.

If the powers that be in this nation had any sense at all, they would bug every single mosque in this country. This is where the plans are fomented as it regards destruction respecting this nation. As well, they would not allow any more Muslims into this country, period.

Also, every Muslim student in our universities should be sent back to their respective countries. It all boils down to the effect that we are training them to destroy us.

In thousands of Muslim schools all over the world, even here in the U.S.A., little children are taught to hate Israel and to hate America. And please understand, this is not merely a casual mention, but rather a steady stream of hate-filled rhetoric that fills the hearts and minds of children. They grow up with this thing; grow up hating Israel and America.

In the last few decades the Muslims have quickly learned, that if they hit us, we in turn shower them with aid, thereby, asking them as to what we can do to show them how much we care for them. So, there's not much fear of the U.S.A. As it regards Russia, if Muslims hit them, they know what to expect — acute retaliation, and done swiftly. So, guess who they are going to hit.

America is asleep politically simply because America is asleep spiritually. In fact, if the nation doesn't have Revival, and soon, the America, as we know it, will be no more.

(6) "AND WHEN THE CHILDREN OF AMMON SAW THAT THEY HAD MADE THEMSELVES ODIOUS TO DAVID, HANUN AND THE CHILDREN OF AMMON SENT A THOUSAND TALENTS OF SILVER TO HIRE THEM CHARIOTS AND HORSEMEN OUT OF MESOPOTAMIA, AND OUT OF SYRIA-MAACHAH, AND OUT OF ZOBAH.

(7) "SO THEY HIRED THIRTY AND TWO THOUSAND CHARIOTS, AND THE KING OF MAACHAH AND HIS PEOPLE; WHO CAME AND PITCHED BEFORE MEDEBA. AND THE CHILDREN OF AMMON GATHERED THEMSELVES TOGETHER FROM THEIR CITIES, AND CAME TO BATTLE.

(8) "AND WHEN DAVID HEARD OF IT, HE SENT JOAB, AND ALL THE HOST OF THE MIGHTY MEN.

(9) "AND THE CHILDREN OF AMMON CAME OUT, AND PUT THE BATTLE IN ARRAY BEFORE THE GATE OF THE CITY: AND THE KINGS WHO WERE COME WERE BY THEMSELVES IN THE FIELD.

(10) "NOW WHEN JOAB SAW THAT THE BATTLE WAS SET AGAINST HIM BEFORE AND BEHIND, HE CHOSE OUT OF ALL THE CHOICE OF ISRAEL, AND PUT THEM IN ARRAY AGAINST THE SYRIANS.

(11) "AND THE REST OF THE PEOPLE HE DELIVERED UNTO THE HAND OF ABISHAI HIS BROTHER, AND THEY SET THEMSELVES IN ARRAY AGAINST THE CHILDREN OF AMMON.

(12) "AND HE SAID, IF THE SYRIANS BE TOO STRONG FOR ME, THEN YOU SHALL HELP ME: BUT IF THE CHILDREN OF AMMON BE TOO STRONG FOR YOU, THEN I WILL HELP YOU.

(13) "BE OF GOOD COURAGE, AND

LET US BEHAVE OURSELVES VALIANTLY FOR OUR PEOPLE, AND FOR THE CITIES OF OUR GOD: AND LET THE LORD DO THAT WHICH IS GOOD IN HIS SIGHT.

(14) "SO JOAB AND THE PEOPLE WHO WERE WITH HIM DREW NEAR BEFORE THE SYRIANS UNTO THE BATTLE; AND THEY FLED BEFORE HIM.

(15) "AND WHEN THE CHILDREN OF AMMON SAW THAT THE SYRIANS WERE FLED, THEY LIKEWISE FLED BEFORE ABISHAI HIS BROTHER, AND ENTERED INTO THE CITY. THEN JOAB CAME TO JERUSALEM."

The exegesis is:

1. Verses 6 and 7 speak in prophetic tones of the Antichrist, who will attempt, once and for all, to overthrow Christ and to destroy Israel. However, let the axis hosts be ever so strong, for they cannot overcome the Divine energy which offered Grace and, that being rejected, now decrees Judgment.

2. In Verse 8, the Holy Spirit is quick to emphasize the fact that some of these men who were in the army of Israel were *"mighty."*

3. (Vs. 14) As the Syrians fled before Joab, likewise, when Believers resist Satan, and do so in the Name of Jesus, he will also flee (James 4:7).

TO STEAL, TO KILL, AND DESTROY

Jesus said, *"The thief comes not, but for to steal, and to kill, and to destroy"* (Jn. 10:10).

The Ammonites treated the kindness extended to them by David with disdain. In effect, they declared war on him. Knowing that he would come against them, which he had no choice but to do, the Scripture says, *"And when the children of Ammon saw that they had made themselves odious to David, Hanun and the children of Ammon sent a thousand talents of silver to hire them chariots and horsemen out of Mesopotamia, and out of Syria-maachah, and out of Zobah."*

It then said, *"So they hired thirty and two thousand chariots, and the king of Maachah and his people; who came and pitched before Medeba. And the children of Ammon gathered themselves together from their cities, and came to battle."*

The quote, *"Thirty two thousand chariots,"* is probably a miscopy.

NOTES

The Hebrew language did not have numbers, but rather letters for numbers. So, it was easy for certain letters to be miscopied, as here it no doubt was. It was probably about a thousand chariots that were hired. In the first place, it is almost certain that no country of that day had thirty-two thousand chariots. As well, that many chariots, even if possessed, could not be hired for a mere thousand talents of silver. Yet, even a thousand chariots would have presented a formidable force against David.

All of this is an example in the physical of what takes place against us presently in the Spiritual. Satan, coming against us, will always do so with a formidable force determined to destroy us.

From this we should know and understand that in order to defeat him, and defeat him we must, we have to do things God's Way. That Way is the Cross of Christ and our Faith in that Finished Work (Rom. 6:1-14; 8:1-2, 11; I Cor. 1:17-18, 23; 2:2; Col. 2:14-15).

Christian man is foolish to think that he can defeat the powers of darkness by using his own stratagems and machinations. It makes no difference how cleverly designed these stratagems may be, they are no match for the powers of darkness; consequently, the modern church turning to humanistic psychology is the sure road to spiritual failure. There is no help from that source. All of this presents several things as it regards the modern church.

• Modern Christians simply do not know or understand that which is arrayed against them from the spirit world. If they did, they would understand how helpless and hopeless their efforts are against these forces. Paul plainly told us: *"Put on the whole Armour of God* (not just some, but all), *that you may be able to stand against the wiles of the Devil.* (This refers to the *'stratagems'* of Satan.)

"For we wrestle not against flesh and blood (our foes are not human; however, Satan constantly uses human beings to carry out his dirty work), *but against principalities* (rulers or beings of the highest rank and order in Satan's kingdom), *against powers* (the rank immediately below the

'Principalities'), against the rulers of the darkness of this world (those who carry out the instructions of the *'Powers'), against spiritual wickedness in high places.* (This refers to demon spirits)" (Eph. 6:11-12).

• The Cross of Christ is the only answer to these powers of darkness. It was at the Cross that Jesus atoned for all sin, which took away the legal right that Satan had to hold men in captivity (Col. 2:14-15).

Sin is what gave Satan the right, and still does, to hold men in bondage. So, the way that Jesus defeated Satan at Calvary's Cross was to atone for all sin, which means that He atoned for all past sins, present sins, and future sins, at least for all who will believe. This done, the legal right that the Evil One has to hold men in bondage is removed. So, that being the case, why is it that men are still in bondage to Satan?

They are in bondage because they will not trust Christ and what He did at the Cross of Calvary. That goes for the unredeemed and it, as well, goes for the Redeemed. Regrettably, most Christians have their faith in anything and everything except the Cross of Christ. In fact, most Christians have no knowledge whatsoever as to the part the Cross plays in our Sanctification, which refers to our everyday life and living for the Lord. Let's look at it further.

• To walk in Victory, and that means Victory over the world, the flesh, and the Devil, the Believer must exercise Faith. That is the ingredient through which the Lord works, Faith; however, the correct Object of one's Faith must be the Cross of Christ and nothing else. And that's the problem with the modern church.

The church talks about faith constantly; however, virtually all of the understanding of faith is apart from the Cross of Christ. God will honor Faith in Christ and the Cross alone. He will not honor faith in anything else (Rom. 6:1-14; I Cor. 1:17-18, 23; 2:2; Gal., Chpt. 5; 6:14; Col. 2:14-15).

Please allow me to give a little formula that we have previously used; however, it explains this subject very well, hence, us using it quite often.

FOCUS: The Lord Jesus Christ (Jn. 14:6).
OBJECT OF FAITH: The Cross of Christ (Rom. 6:3-5; I Cor. 1:17-18; 2:2).
POWER SOURCE: The Holy Spirit (Rom. 8:1-2, 11).
RESULTS: Victory (Rom. 6:14).

Now, in an extremely abbreviated manner, what we've just given to you, one might say, is God's Prescribed Order of Victory.

Now, let's turn it around using the same formula, but in the wrong way.
FOCUS: Works.
OBJECT OF FAITH: One's performance.
POWER SOURCE: Self.
RESULTS: Defeat!

(16) "AND WHEN THE SYRIANS SAW THAT THEY WERE PUT TO THE WORSE BEFORE ISRAEL, THEY SENT MESSENGERS, AND DREW FORTH THE SYRIANS WHO WERE BEYOND THE RIVER: AND SHOPHACH THE CAPTAIN OF THE HOST OF HADAREZER WENT BEFORE THEM.

(17) "AND IT WAS TOLD DAVID; AND HE GATHERED ALL ISRAEL, AND PASSED OVER JORDAN, AND CAME UPON THEM, AND SET THE BATTLE IN ARRAY AGAINST THEM. SO WHEN DAVID HAD PUT THE BATTLE IN ARRAY AGAINST THE SYRIANS, THEY FOUGHT WITH HIM.

(18) "BUT THE SYRIANS FLED BEFORE ISRAEL; AND DAVID KILLED OF THE SYRIANS SEVEN THOUSAND MEN WHO FOUGHT IN CHARIOTS, AND FORTY THOUSAND FOOTMEN, AND KILLED SHOPHACH THE CAPTAIN OF THE HOST.

(19) "AND WHEN THE SERVANTS OF HADAREZER SAW THAT THEY WERE PUT TO THE WORSE BEFORE ISRAEL, THEY MADE PEACE WITH DAVID, AND BECAME HIS SERVANTS: NEITHER WOULD THE SYRIANS HELP THE CHILDREN OF AMMON ANY MORE."

The construction is:

1. It is the Will of God, as should be obvious, that the Christian gain and maintain total Victory over the powers of darkness that would destroy his soul.

2. That Victory is gained solely by our Faith in Christ and what He did for us at the Cross.

3. (Vs. 19) In a sense, these Passages come to us as a type of the great Battle of

Armageddon, when Jesus Christ will defeat the Antichrist and all the powers of darkness, and then will be the reigning Lord of Heaven and Earth. At that time, the world will make peace with our Heavenly David and, in effect, will become His Servant.

VICTORY!

As David defeated these enemies, irrespective as to how strong they were, and did so by the Power of God, likewise, it is the Will of God for every Believer to experience Victory in every capacity of our life and living.

How can we do that?

As we've stated repeatedly, there is only one Way it can be done. That one Way is Christ and the Cross.

As also stated, most Christians have at least a modicum of understanding as it respects the Cross referring to our Salvation; however, most Christians have no understanding at all as it regards the Cross in our Sanctification. In fact, most modern Christians don't even know what Sanctification actually means.

SANCTIFICATION

The Greek word for Sanctification is *"hagiasmos,"* and means, *"to purify, to consecrate, to make holy."* It means to be completely set apart unto God.

For all of this to be brought about, every vestige of sin must be put out of our lives. No, I'm not speaking of sinless perfection because the Bible doesn't teach such. But I am teaching, even as the Bible teaches, that sin is not to have dominion over us, which actually means that the sin nature is not to have dominion over us (Rom. 6:14).

WHAT IS THE SIN NATURE?

The sin nature refers to the nature of the human being given over to sin, to disobedience, to transgression, and to iniquity, on a constant, non-ending basis. When Adam and Eve fell in the Garden of Eden, they fell from the position of total God-consciousness, down to the far, far lower level of total self-consciousness. Their very nature became that of sin, that of iniquity, etc.

In fact, before any person comes to Christ,

NOTES

they are ruled 24 hours a day, totally and completely, by the sin nature. Understandably, some are ruled worse than others, but the fact remains that all are ruled in this manner. In other words, their very nature is that of sin and disobedience to God.

When the Believer comes to Christ, while the sin nature is not removed, it is made dormant in his heart and life. In other words, it is made ineffective (Rom. 6:6). It is like an appliance that has been unplugged. Without the source of electricity coming to that appliance, it will not function. Likewise, when the believing sinner comes to Christ, his sin nature is unplugged, so to speak.

But then, very shortly the Believer in some way fails the Lord. Startled and shocked at the failure, the Believer sets about to keep from doing such again. Invariably, the Believer will place his faith in some religious work, whatever it might be. While what he is doing may be good, still, it will not keep him from defeat. In fact, he will find himself committing the same sin over and over again, with other sins beginning to be committed, as well. This is what Paul was talking about when he said, *"For that which I do* (the failure) *I allow not* (should have been translated, *'I understand not'*)*"* (Rom. 7:15).

Of course, when Paul wrote this, he very well understood the situation; however, he is going back in his life, after he was Saved on the road to Damascus, and giving us a page from his experience. At that time, and possibly for several years, he did not know or understand God's Prescribed Order of Victory. So, he tried to live for the Lord by the keeping of Commandments (Rom. 7:9). He found to his dismay that despite the fact that he was Saved, baptized with the Holy Spirit, and called to preach the Gospel, and actually preaching the Gospel, still, he could not live a life of victory. That's why he said: *"Oh wretched man that I am! Who shall deliver me from the body of this death"* (Rom. 7:24)?

Every single Believer, more or less, has to go through the Seventh Chapter of Romans.

THE SEVENTH CHAPTER OF ROMANS

While it is true that every Believer has to

go through the Seventh Chapter of Romans, as stated, still, the tragedy is, most Christians remain there all of their Christian experience. This is an extremely unpleasant way to try to live for God. While such a person, and all of us have been there at one time or the other, is still Saved, and thank God for that, the fact remains, they are living far beneath that for which Jesus paid such a price. The idea is, the sin nature is ruling such a person, and doing so constantly.

THE CROSS OF CHRIST

The only answer for the sin nature is the Cross of Christ, even as we've already explained in previous paragraphs. Then and only then, with the Believer placing his Faith exclusively in Christ and the Cross, and maintaining his Faith exclusively in Christ and the Cross, can Victory be obtained over the sin nature, which refers to every single power of darkness.

Satan little cares about our efforts in any capacity, and no matter how religious those efforts might be, just as long as our faith is in something other than the Cross. He knows that the Victory is in the Cross and the Cross alone. By our Faith in that Finished Work alone, we can defeat the powers of the enemy.

Unfortunately, most Christians have never heard this of which we are presently teaching. They understand the Cross of Christ not at all as it regards Sanctification. As a result, they place their faith in other things, which brings nothing but frustration. Please understand, the answer is the Cross! The Cross! The Cross!

"You Servants of God, your Master proclaim,
"And publish abroad His Wonderful Name;
"The Name all-victorious of Jesus extol;
"His Kingdom is glorious, and rules over all."

"God rules on High, Almighty to save;
"And still He is nigh, His Presence we have.
"The great congregation His Triumph shall sing,

"Ascribing Salvation to Jesus our King."

"Let children acclaim their Saviour and Friend;
"In songs to His Name their praises ascend:
"In such a Salvation how great is their joy;
"In true adoration how blest their employ."

"Salvation to God, Who sits on the Throne;
"Let all cry aloud, and honor the Son:
"The Praises of Jesus all Angels proclaim,
"Fall down on their faces, and worship the Lamb."

CHAPTER 20

(1) "AND IT CAME TO PASS, THAT AFTER THE YEAR WAS EXPIRED, AT THE TIME THAT KINGS GO OUT TO BATTLE, JOAB LED FORTH THE POWER OF THE ARMY, AND WASTED THE COUNTRY OF THE CHILDREN OF AMMON, AND CAME AND BESIEGED RABBAH. BUT DAVID TARRIED AT JERUSALEM. AND JOAB SMOTE RABBAH, AND DESTROYED IT.

(2) "AND DAVID TOOK THE CROWN OF THEIR KING FROM OFF HIS HEAD, AND FOUND IT TO WEIGH A TALENT OF GOLD, AND THERE WERE PRECIOUS STONES IN IT; AND IT WAS SET UPON DAVID'S HEAD: AND HE BROUGHT ALSO EXCEEDING MUCH SPOIL OUT OF THE CITY.

(3) "AND HE BROUGHT OUT THE PEOPLE WHO WERE IN IT, AND CUT THEM WITH SAWS, AND WITH HARROWS OF IRON, AND WITH AXES. EVEN SO DEALT DAVID WITH ALL THE CITIES OF THE CHILDREN OF AMMON. AND DAVID AND ALL THE PEOPLE RETURNED TO JERUSALEM."

The exegesis is:

1. (Vs. 1). This Chapter coincides with II Samuel, Chapter 11, but with a glaring difference. David's sin with Bath-sheba and

the sin concerning her husband are totally omitted. Why?

I and II Samuel and I and II Kings give these accounts from the human standpoint; I and II Chronicles, from God's standpoint.

2. (Vs. 1) David had repented of these terrible sins (Ps. 51). So now, as far as the Lord was concerned, it is as if David had never committed these sins, and so it is with all who place their sins at the foot of the Cross (I Jn. 1:7, 9).

3. (Vs. 2) As the crown was taken from the head of the Ammonite king, so at Calvary, Jesus defeated Satan, and took the crown from his head. This victory is now ours (Col. 2:14-15).

4. The phrase of Verse 3, *"cut them with saws,"* etc., would have been better translated, *"appointed them certain tasks."* The Hebrew word for *"cut"* is *"sur,"* and does not literally mean to cut with something material.

JUSTIFICATION BY FAITH

As already stated, the two Books of Chronicles give the history from the Divine standpoint. The Books of I and II Samuel and I and II Kings give these accounts from the human standpoint. There is a tremendously valuable lesson here to be learned. God does not see things as man sees them and vice versa; consequently, one of the great works in the heart and life of the Believer by the Holy Spirit is to help him *"see"* as God sees. This Spiritual Place and Position is not easily arrived at. There must be a complete submissiveness to the Will of God, which will always adhere totally to the Word of God. As well, all of this is actually an account of *"Justification by Faith,"* of which the Believer cannot understand as he or she should, unless such a Believer understands the Cross, which makes Justification possible.

FORGIVENESS

When a Christian is forgiven, God, true to His Promise, forgets the sin and, as well, omits it from the later Books of His Remembrance. As stated, this is called *"Justification by Faith."* Sanctification *"makes"* one not guilty; whereas, Justification *"declares"* one not guilty. So, in effect, by the lack of any mention of David's sin, the Lord has declared him not guilty of such.

How can this be?

It can be such with David, as with every single Believer who has ever lived, because God has placed the penalty of the broken Law on His Son, Jesus Christ. Our Lord at Calvary took upon Himself the penalty, which was death, of every person who has ever lived; in fact, that price to be paid was death. He offered up the Perfect Sacrifice at Calvary, which was His Sinless Body; therefore, He satisfied all claims that Satan had against the human race. And now, *"whosoever believes in Him, shall not perish, but have Everlasting Life"* (Jn. 3:16). Before Calvary, men were Saved by looking forward to that event. After Calvary, men are Saved by looking backward to that event.

When David repented (the Fifty-first Psalm), the Lord washed him, cleansed him, forgave him, and redeemed him. The sin was not only put away, but David was exonerated as if he never committed the sin.

That is the reason the Holy Spirit could come to this particular time frame concerning David's history and never even mention the terrible sin with Bath-sheba and Uriah. The sin was gone; likewise, for every single Child of God who has ever lived, every sin they have ever committed before conversion or after, if properly confessed and put away, is totally forgotten by God.

The church should do the same, but, regrettably, it little does so. That's the reason Paul said to the Church at Corinth concerning someone who had sinned and repented, *"For to this end also did I write, that I might know the proof of you, whether you be obedient in all things"* (II Cor. 2:9). Paul wanted to make certain that the Church had forgiven this individual. It is ironic that after the individual sinned and before Repentance, the person was on trial (I Cor., Chpt. 5). Now, after the person's Repentance, the Church is on trial.

Justification by Faith is the Foundation, the capstone, so to speak, of the great Work of Redemption. Remove that, weaken that, disregard that, or even attempt to change that, and the whole of Christianity becomes meaningless. And, please remember, Justification by Faith is all wrapped up in the Cross of Christ, in other words, what Jesus there did in order to redeem the lost sons of Adam's fallen race.

WHO WILL WEAR THE CROWN?

The Scripture says, *"And David took the crown of their king from off his head . . . and it was set upon David's head: and he brought also exceeding much spoil out of the city."*

This *"crown"* is a picture of our Spiritual Life in Christ Jesus. Satan endeavors to reign as king in some part of our Spiritual Inheritance. The Holy Spirit demands that we destroy his kingdom and take the crown from his head—and in every part of our lives.

As the Second Verse says, *"And it was set upon David's head,"* Revelation 1:6 says, *"And has made us kings and priests unto God."* The Lord demands that we be king over all the possession that He has given us and that Satan have no place in it. Concerning any part of our Spiritual Possession, does the crown sit on Satan's head or some part of it on our heads?

The only way that the Believer can know Victory, can have Victory, can walk in Victory, and I mean perpetual Victory, is by placing one's Faith exclusively in Christ and the Cross, which then gives the Holy Spirit latitude to Work within his heart and life. All too often, victory is attempted in other ways. And let the reader understand, it really doesn't matter how righteous the *"other ways"* may seem to be. The truth is, there is only one answer, one solution, and that is the Cross of Christ. The Holy Spirit, Who Alone can carry out in our lives that which needs to be carried out, works exclusively within the parameters of the Finished Work of Christ (Rom. 8:2). In other words, the Cross of Christ, that is what Jesus there did, gives the Spirit the legal Means to do all that He does. That's the reason it's referred to as a *"Law"* (Rom. 8:2).

The Lord doesn't require much of Believers; however, He does require that we have the correct Object of Faith, and that correct Object is the Cross, and the Cross alone!

NOTES

(4) "AND IT CAME TO PASS AFTER THIS, THAT THERE AROSE WAR AT GEZER WITH THE PHILISTINES; AT WHICH TIME SIBBECHAI THE HUSHATHITE KILLED SIPPAI, WHO WAS OF THE CHILDREN OF THE GIANT: AND THEY WERE SUBDUED.

(5) "AND THERE WAS WAR AGAIN WITH THE PHILISTINES; AND ELHANAN THE SON OF JAIR KILLED LAHMI THE BROTHER OF GOLIATH THE GITTITE, WHOSE SPEAR STAFF WAS LIKE A WEAVER'S BEAM.

(6) "AND YET AGAIN THERE WAS WAR AT GATH, WHERE WAS A MAN OF GREAT STATURE, WHOSE FINGERS AND TOES WERE FOUR AND TWENTY, SIX ON EACH HAND, AND SIX ON EACH FOOT: AND HE ALSO WAS THE SON OF THE GIANT.

(7) "BUT WHEN HE DEFIED ISRAEL, JONATHAN THE SON OF SHIMEA DAVID'S BROTHER KILLED HIM.

(8) "THESE WERE BORN UNTO THE GIANT IN GATH; AND THEY FELL BY THE HAND OF DAVID, AND BY THE HAND OF HIS SERVANTS."

The exegesis is:

1. (Vs. 8) In I Samuel, Chapter 17; II Samuel, Chapter 21; and, I Chronicles, Chapter 20, some five giants are spoken of. It seems they were brothers (II Sam. 21:19-22).

2. (Vs. 8) These were the last of the mighty races of giants, who were the offspring of fallen Angels and women, in Satan's efforts to pollute the human race, so that the Seed of the woman, the Lord Jesus Christ, might not be able to come into the world in order to redeem Adam's fallen race (Gen. 6:4).

3. (Vs. 8) These also represent hindrances in our particular Christian lives, which seek to usurp authority over God's Rule. Every Satanic *"giant"* in our lives must be destroyed. There is no room for compromise. The *"flesh"* must die, and the *"Spirit"* must reign supreme.

This can be done only by the Believer placing his Faith exclusively in Christ and the Cross, which then gives the Holy Spirit latitude to Work in his heart and life, bringing forth complete Victory (Rom. 6:3-14; 8:1-2, 11).

THE GIANTS

Verses 4 through 8 record the last mention of giants, with the first mention being in Genesis 6:4. In this last account of the giants, some five are addressed. They are as follows:
- Goliath—he was most probably the oldest of the giants and was killed by David (I Sam., Chpt. 17).
- Sippai (Vs. 4). Called Saph (II Sam. 21:18).
- Lahmi—brother of Goliath (Vs. 5; II Sam. 21:19).
- The giant with six fingers and six toes on each hand and foot (Vs. 6; II Sam. 21:20-22).
- Ishbi-benob (II Sam. 21:16-17).

It seems these five giants were brothers (II Sam. 21:19-22). They were the last of the mighty races of giants. These were the offspring of fallen Angels and women, which was Satan's effort to do away with the pure Adamic race, so that the Seed of the woman (the Lord Jesus Christ) might not come into the world to redeem Adam's race (Gen. 6:4).

In a spiritual sense, of which all of these situations are types, they also represent hindrances in our particular Christian lives that seek to usurp authority over God's Rule. Every Satanic *"giant"* in our lives must be destroyed. They cannot be reasoned with, nor can we come to terms with such. There is no room for compromise.

Paul said, *"Let not sin* (the sin nature—a giant) *therefore reign in your mortal body"* (Rom. 6:12).

As there were giants in Israel (the God-given possession), likewise, there are, or desire to be, giants in every Christian's life. As the giants were destroyed by David and his mighty men, likewise, the giants can only be destroyed by our *"Heavenly David,"* Who is the Lord Jesus Christ. Within our own strength and power we cannot destroy these giants, but through Christ, all can and will be destroyed.

THAT WHICH THE CHILD OF GOD FACES

The Believer must understand as to what he is facing in the spirit world. The great Apostle wrote: *"For we wrestle not against flesh and blood* (our foes are not human; however, Satan constantly uses human beings to carry out his dirty work), *but against principalities* (rulers or beings of the highest rank and order in Satan's kingdom), *against powers* (the rank immediately below the *'Principalities'*), *against the rulers of the darkness of this world* (those who carry out the instructions of the *'powers'*), *against spiritual wickedness in high places.* (This refers to demon spirits)" (Eph. 6:12).

So, the Believer must understand that which he is facing, that which opposes him, in fact, that which is determined to destroy him. If he properly understands the spirit world, he then understands that he is no match for the powers of darkness, at least within himself.

This means that any effort that we might make against this world of darkness, no matter how good it may seem to be on the surface, will come out to no avail. It is a shame when the modern church has adopted and, in fact, is adopting the ways of the world to try to combat these evils. The effort is doomed before it begins. And yet, that's where most modern Believers are. They are attempting to oppose the spirit world of darkness by human means, which is impossible.

THE WAY TO VICTORY

There is only one Way to Victory, and that is the Cross of Christ. There, the Lord Jesus Christ, in the offering of Himself as a Sacrifice, a Perfect Sacrifice, that which was accepted by God, to be sure, atoned for all sin, past, present, and future, at least for those who will believe. This, the Cross, is where Satan was defeated. This, the Cross, is where every demon spirit was defeated. This, the Cross, is where all powers of darkness were laid waste (Col. 2:14-15).

The Believer overcomes these powers of darkness, irrespective as to what they might be, by simply evidencing Faith in Christ and what Christ has done at the Cross. But, let it ever be understood, faith within itself will bring about no victory. Faith, for it to do its mighty thing, must have the correct Object.

That Object must be, and without exception, the Cross of Christ (Lk. 9:23; 14:27).

> *"Great is Thy Faithfulness, O God my Father,*
> *"There is no shadow of turning with Thee;*
> *"Thou changest not, Thy Compassions, they fail not;*
> *"As Thou has been Thou forever will be."*
>
> *"Great is Thy Faithfulness! Great is Thy Faithfulness!*
> *"Morning by morning new Mercies I see.*
> *"All I have needed Your Hand has provided;*
> *"Great is Thy Faithfulness, Lord, unto me!"*
>
> *"Summer and winter, and springtime and harvest,*
> *"Sun, moon, and stars in their courses above,*
> *"Join with all nature in manifold witness,*
> *"To Thy Great Faithfulness, Mercy and Love."*
>
> *"Pardon for sin and a peace that endures,*
> *"Thy Own Dear Presence to cheer and to guide;*
> *"Strength for today and bright hope for tomorrow,*
> *"Blessings all mine, with ten thousand beside!"*

CHAPTER 21

(1) "AND SATAN STOOD UP AGAINST ISRAEL, AND PROVOKED DAVID TO NUMBER ISRAEL.

(2) "AND DAVID SAID TO JOAB AND TO THE RULERS OF THE PEOPLE, GO, NUMBER ISRAEL FROM BEER-SHEBA EVEN TO DAN; AND BRING THE NUMBER OF THEM TO ME, THAT I MAY KNOW IT.

(3) "AND JOAB ANSWERED, THE LORD MAKE HIS PEOPLE AN HUNDRED TIMES SO MANY MORE AS THEY BE: BUT, MY LORD THE KING, ARE THEY NOT ALL MY LORD'S SERVANTS? WHY THEN DOES MY LORD REQUIRE THIS THING? WHY WILL HE BE A CAUSE OF TRESPASS TO ISRAEL?

(4) "NEVERTHELESS THE KING'S WORD PREVAILED AGAINST JOAB. WHEREFORE JOAB DEPARTED, AND WENT THROUGHOUT ALL ISRAEL, AND CAME TO JERUSALEM.

(5) "AND JOAB GAVE THE SUM OF THE NUMBER OF THE PEOPLE UNTO DAVID. AND ALL THEY OF ISRAEL WERE A THOUSAND THOUSAND AND AN HUNDRED THOUSAND MEN WHO DREW SWORD: AND JUDAH WAS FOUR HUNDRED THREESCORE AND TEN THOUSAND MEN WHO DREW SWORD.

(6) "BUT LEVI AND BENJAMIN COUNTED HE NOT AMONG THEM: FOR THE KING'S WORD WAS ABOMINABLE TO JOAB."

The exegesis is:

1. (Vs. 1) II Samuel 24:1 says, *"God moved David"* to do such. Is there a contradiction? No. We learn from these Passages that Satan can do nothing against a Child of God, but that God allows it. He permits Satan a limited power in bringing merited judgment upon men. Why did the Lord allow this against David? The following Passages will tell us.

2. (Vs. 2) What the Philistines, Ammonites, and Syrians failed to effect, this mental weapon of subtle temptation accomplished. It was *"pride"*!

3. (Vs. 2) What could be more laudable than to verify the truthfulness of the Promise made to Abraham that his children should exceed the stars in multitude? However, to seek to carnally verify a Divine Promise brings deadness to the soul! And such a desire leads not to the Bible, but from the Bible.

4. (Vs. 3) It was not wrong to take a census; however, to do so, Exodus 30:12 demanded a half-shekel of silver be paid for each individual. It was referred to as *"ransom money,"* meaning, in essence, that all the Children of Israel were purchased by the Blood of the Lamb, for *"silver"* was a type of Redemption in Old Testament terminology. In ignoring

this Command of the Lord to pay the ransom money, David was bypassing the Cross, which God can never allow!

5. (Vs. 4) It is doubtful that Joab would have known of the admonition of the payment of the half-shekel, but he felt that what David was doing was wrong, which it was. It seems, as well, that David never bothered to consult the Word, even as he didn't bother to consult the Word concerning the transportation of the Ark (Chpt. 13). God cannot abide a violation of the Word, even in His most choice Servants, as David. The results will never be pleasant!

6. (Vs. 5) The numbers do not tally with II Samuel, Chapter 24. The explanation is: Chronicles says, *"All Israel were 1,100,000 men who drew sword,"* while II Samuel says, *"800,000 valiant men who drew sword."* Evidently, 300,000 were young soldiers who could not justly be deemed as *"valiant."* Similar details appear respecting Judah. II Samuel states that *"the men of Judah were 500,000"*; Chronicles records the number as *"470,000."* Evidently, therefore, the remaining 30,000 were either untrained men or non-combatants.

7. (Vs. 6) Joab was a man of the world. He had not the Spiritual insight of David; and yet, at times, such will have a better Spiritual insight than a self-willed Believer. Such is the case here!

THE PROVOCATION OF SATAN

The first account of this is given in II Samuel, Chapter 24, Verse 1. It says: *"And again the Anger of the LORD was kindled against Israel, and He* (the Lord) *moved David against them to say, Go, number Israel and Judah."*

The same statement in I Chronicles 21:1 says, *"And Satan stood up against Israel, and provoked David to number Israel."*

Is there a contradiction?

No!

The truth is Satan can do nothing against a Child of God unless given permission by the Lord to do so. In other words, the Lord has the last word in everything. Satan can only do what he is allowed to do, and as he is allowed to do such. Job, Chapters 1 and 2 verify this. The answer is, God allowed Satan to do what was done; therefore, the Lord, at times, is said to do what He allows the Evil One to do. In fact, Satan is used by the Lord constantly, and in many and varied capacities. But, let it ever be understood, anything and everything that happens to the Child of God is either caused or allowed by the Lord. While the Lord definitely does not cause Believers to sin, He does allow such, that is, if Believers insist upon doing so, which will always reap bitter circumstances.

THE NUMBERING OF ISRAEL

There is nothing in the Word of God that actually prohibits the numbering of Israel, and yet, it must be done in a certain way, even as we shall see. Concerning this, the Scripture says:

"And the LORD spoke unto Moses, saying,

"When you take the sum (census) *of the Children of Israel after their number, then shall they give every man a ransom for his soul unto the LORD, when you number them; that there be no plague among them, when you number them.* (Vss. 11-16 portray the ransom or Redemption money. The money was a special tax of registration in Israel, as a memorial or reminder of God's provision of Redemption, and of their obligation under the terms of the Mosaic Covenant. Christ died on the Cross; *'He gave Himself a ransom for all'* [I Tim. 2:6].)

"This they shall give, everyone who passes among them who are numbered, half a shekel after the shekel of the sanctuary: (a shekel is twenty gerahs:) an half shekel shall be the Offering of the LORD (equal to about $40 in 2004 money).

"Everyone who passes among them who are numbered, from twenty years old and above, shall give an Offering unto the LORD.

"The rich shall not give more, and the poor shall not give less than half a shekel, when they give an Offering unto the LORD, to make an Atonement for your souls. (All gave the same whether *'rich'* or *'poor,'* placing every man on an equal footing in relation to God and obligation to the Law. It should be noted that the money did not actually redeem the soul. Not even the blood of bulls and other animals did this [Heb. 10:4; I Pet. 1:18-23], but rather Faith in the Blood of the coming Redeemer, of which the blood

of sacrifices was a Type. It was strictly for a *'memorial,'* even as the next Verse proclaims. Incidentally, this shekel was of silver; hence, silver is a type of Redemption.)

"And you shall take the Atonement money of the Children of Israel, and shall appoint it for the service of the Tabernacle of the congregation; that it may be a memorial unto the Children of Israel before the LORD, to make an Atonement for your souls. (A *'census'* taken of the Children of Israel was important, because they belonged to God, and they belonged to Him by virtue of the slain lamb, and their Faith in that Sacrifice [Gen. 15:6; Rom. 4:3])" (Ex. 30:11-16).

A TYPE OF REDEMPTION

The ransom money was silver, which in Old Testament typology was a type of Redemption. This portrayed the fact to Israel that, irrespective as to their numbers, or their riches, or their supposed power, their safety and protection were totally and completely in the shed Blood of the Lamb, and not in that which was thought to be observable power. In other words, the Cross of Christ is typified in all of this, and proclaimed in type, the security, protection, and power of Israel.

The modern church should understand that our victory, our prosperity, in other words, everything, is all predicated on the Cross. Take the Cross away from modern Christianity, and there is nothing left but a hollow shell. It doesn't matter what else might be, the money, the fame, the acceptance by the world, the power, or the prestige. It is only the shed Blood of the Lamb that makes us what we are, that gives us what we are, that helps us to be what we are, that is, if we even come close to that which the Lord demands.

David ignored the ransom money. He did not consult with the Priests, and neither did he consult with the Word of God. So, why did he want to take a census?

PERSONAL PRIDE?

Who knows what was in David's heart! And yet, we definitely do know from his action concerning this thing that there were things there that were wrong.

NOTES

As far as we know, every other census taken by Israel always was at the Command of the Lord, and was carried out with the payment of the half-shekel of silver. As it regards this census, there is nothing in the Word of God that indicates the Lord had a purpose for the census to be taken. In fact, Verse 2 says, *"... that I may know it,"* speaking of David.

When Satan fails to break down a Servant of God by one plan, he tries another, and too often succeeds. As a rule, his first plan is violent; his second plan is usually subtle. He lays a semi-religious trap for the foot of the Christian, thus causing him to fail. So it was here with David! What the Philistines, the Ammonites, and the Syrians failed to effect, this mental weapon of subtle temptation accomplished.

Had David obeyed the Word of God, the foundation of the Temple, which was shortly to be built, would have been laid just as the foundation of the Tabernacle was with the Redemption money of the thousands of Israel, instead of the blood of the 70,000 who perished.

After a victory, there is always a secret temptation in the heart of a Christian to search for a personal and carnal cause. How guilty we all are. A preacher is tempted to think that the conversions reported during his ministry resulted from the clearness, the force, or the eloquence of his preaching. Thus it was with David.

Conqueror over all his enemies, he wished to find out for himself the strength of the weapon, his standing army, which was his glory, and with which he gained his victories. So, he took his eyes off the Strength of God from Whom Alone the victories came. This sin, and it is a great one, brings famine, defeat, or death to the soul.

THE WORLD, THE FLESH, AND THE DEVIL

All of these things of the heading constitute the work of darkness, and yet, at times, it seems the world, as Joab, has a keener insight into the things of God than even the Believer.

Why?

If the Believer allows self to intrude into

the things of God, spiritual deadness is the result.

The Believer, at least within himself, has nothing that God can use. His entrance into the very Throne of God, and all of us have that privilege, is brought about simply because of the shed Blood of the Lamb. In other words, everything is predicated on the Cross. When the Cross is ignored, even as David did such, and which it is being ignored presently, all discernment on the part of the Child of God is lost.

David got his census, but it would not bring forth that which he thought. As presently, failure to abide by the Word of God places the Believer in the same position.

(7) "AND GOD WAS DISPLEASED WITH THIS THING; THEREFORE HE SMOTE ISRAEL.

(8) "AND DAVID SAID UNTO GOD, I HAVE SINNED GREATLY, BECAUSE I HAVE DONE THIS THING: BUT NOW, I BESEECH YOU, DO AWAY THE INIQUITY OF YOUR SERVANT; FOR I HAVE DONE VERY FOOLISHLY.

(9) "AND THE LORD SPOKE UNTO GAD, DAVID'S SEER, SAYING,

(10) "GO AND TELL DAVID, SAYING, THUS SAYS THE LORD, I OFFER YOU THREE THINGS: CHOOSE YOU ONE OF THEM, THAT I MAY DO IT UNTO YOU.

(11) "SO GAD CAME TO DAVID, AND SAID UNTO HIM, THUS SAYS THE LORD, YOU CHOOSE

(12) "EITHER THREE YEARS' FAMINE; OR THREE MONTHS TO BE DESTROYED BEFORE YOUR FOES, WHILE THAT THE SWORD OF YOUR ENEMIES OVERTAKES YOU; OR ELSE THREE DAYS THE SWORD OF THE LORD, EVEN THE PESTILENCE, IN THE LAND, AND THE ANGEL OF THE LORD DESTROYING THROUGHOUT ALL THE COAST OF ISRAEL. NOW THEREFORE ADVISE YOURSELF WHAT WORD I SHALL BRING AGAIN TO HIM WHO SENT ME.

(13) "AND DAVID SAID UNTO GAD, I AM IN A GREAT STRAIT: LET ME FALL NOW INTO THE HAND OF THE LORD; FOR VERY GREAT ARE HIS MERCIES: BUT LET ME NOT FALL INTO THE HAND OF MAN.

NOTES

(14) "SO THE LORD SENT PESTILENCE UPON ISRAEL: AND THERE FELL OF ISRAEL SEVENTY THOUSAND MEN.

(15) "AND GOD SENT AN ANGEL UNTO JERUSALEM TO DESTROY IT: AND AS HE WAS DESTROYING, THE LORD BEHELD, AND HE REPENTED HIM OF THE EVIL, AND SAID TO THE ANGEL WHO DESTROYED, IT IS ENOUGH, STAY NOW YOUR HAND. AND THE ANGEL OF THE LORD STOOD BY THE THRESHINGFLOOR OF ORNAN THE JEBUSITE.

(16) "AND DAVID LIFTED UP HIS EYES, AND SAW THE ANGEL OF THE LORD STAND BETWEEN THE EARTH AND THE HEAVEN, HAVING A DRAWN SWORD IN HIS HAND STRETCHED OUT OVER JERUSALEM. THEN DAVID AND THE ELDERS OF ISRAEL, WHO WERE CLOTHED IN SACKCLOTH, FELL UPON THEIR FACES.

(17) "AND DAVID SAID UNTO GOD, IS IT NOT I WHO COMMANDED THE PEOPLE TO BE NUMBERED? EVEN I IT IS WHO HAS SINNED AND DONE EVIL INDEED; BUT AS FOR THESE SHEEP, WHAT HAVE THEY DONE? LET YOUR HAND, I PRAY YOU, O LORD MY GOD, BE ON ME, AND ON MY FATHER'S HOUSE; BUT NOT ON YOUR PEOPLE, THAT THEY SHOULD BE PLAGUED."

The construction is:

1. (Vs. 7) The Lord was displeased because David, among other things, had ignored, when taking the census, the payment of the ransom money of silver, which typified Redemption, which, of course, also typified Calvary. The Lord will *"smite"* all who follow this course. In fact, He has no choice. It is the Judgment of God on Christ, which speaks of the Cross, or it's Judgment on the people. If the Cross is ignored, Judgment is the inevitable result.

2. (Vs. 8) Let all know and understand, to treat the Cross with disdain is a *"great sin."* All who ignore the Cross do so *"foolishly"*!

3. (Vs. 9) The Lord presently is speaking to His Prophets, at least what precious few there presently are. Regrettably, the modern church is not hearing and obeying the Message, as David did.

4. (Vs. 12) Sin has to be addressed, whether

in Christ and what He did for us at the Cross, or Judgment upon men. Let all understand, the only answer for sin is the Cross of Christ (Heb. 10:12).

5. (Vs. 14) In Exodus 30:12, the Lord said there would be a *"plague among them,"* if the *"half-shekel"* were not paid as ransom money for each person. It should be understood here that God means what He says. What type of *"pestilence"* it was, we aren't told.

6. (Vs. 15) The word *"repented,"* as used of the Lord, doesn't mean that God changes, for, in fact, He never changes (Mal. 3:6); however, His Direction may vary according to the obedience or disobedience of man.

It was not coincidental that the Angel *"stood by the threshingfloor."* As always, the wheat must be separated from the chaff, and it takes a threshingfloor to do that (Mat. 3:12).

We find from this Text that the sin of ignoring the Cross is at least one of the worst sins, if not the worst sin, that can be committed. The degree of punishment, 70,000 men dying, guarantees that fact.

7. (Vs. 16) The *"sackcloth"* denoted humility and Repentance. God has promised to look with favor at such (Isa. 66:2).

8. (Vs. 17) In a sense, David stood here similar to Moses, when the Lord was about to destroy them, as it regards the golden calf (Ex. 32:11-14). As well, and even more importantly, David is here a Type of Christ, Who, at this moment, is interceding for all Believers (Heb. 7:25-26).

THE DISPLEASURE OF GOD

This displeasure was, no doubt, caused by many things; however, the greatest cause of all was that David had ignored the Cross of Christ. His failure to pay the half-shekel of silver for each man counted proclaimed any one of several things:

- Silver was a type of Redemption in the Old Testament. Therefore, the half-shekel of silver demanded for each man counted signified that Israel's power and prestige rested solely upon the Cross of Christ, typified by the silver. Perhaps David didn't know that, but, if he had only asked the Lord, the information would have been instantly forthcoming.
- If David did have at least some knowledge of the silver payment, and that it

represented the coming Redeemer and what He would do in the giving of Himself, then this made the matter all the worse. In fact, this is the sin of the modern church. It knows, but it seeks to ignore what it does know.

- The only thing standing between mankind and the Judgment of God is the Cross of Christ. We must never forget that.

THE FOOLISHNESS OF SIN

As David prayed to the Lord, actually repenting, he related to the Lord, *"For I have done very foolishly."* All sin is foolish, and sin makes fools out of men!

One of the major churches in the *"Purpose Driven Life"* scheme, I'm told, took a poll among their many members. Evidently, the people filling out the forms didn't have to sign their names; consequently, they told the truth.

The leadership was shocked at what they found in their church; adultery, incest, homosexuality, stealing, gambling, alcohol, drugs, etc., in other words, about every vile sin of which one could think.

Their conclusion was that what they had been teaching evidently wasn't working.

"The Purpose Driven Life" scheme ignores the Cross. As such, they are an open target for the powers of darkness. No, what they had been teaching wasn't working because they were not teaching the Cross.

There is only one answer for sin, and that is the Cross of Christ. To ignore that one answer, is foolishness indeed!

THE PROPHET

The meanings of the two words *"Seer"* and *"Prophet"* are so close that it would probably be pointless to try to point out what little difference there would be in these words. Other than *"king,"* of which these men were to be Types of Christ, at least as it regarded Israel, and finally Judah, the God-called Prophet constituted the Spiritual Leadership of Israel. Regrettably, there were not many godly kings, and there were not many godly Prophets, but an abundance of false prophets. Gad, as should be obvious, was as true Prophet of God.

There is no background on the man. He just suddenly comes upon the scene and his first message to the king, at least that which is recorded, is that of judgment and woe. It would not be a pleasant message to deliver. It was the Office of the Prophet which led and guided Israel.

True Prophets of God were not exactly appreciated by Israel, and neither are they appreciated so very much presently. The news they bring is mostly negative, just as the message that would be given by Gad to David.

The true Prophet is more a Preacher of Righteousness than one who foretells the future. In fact, John the Baptist, referred to by Christ as the greatest Prophet of them all, said almost nothing about the future, and everything about the present.

THE MESSAGE

Sin, even if it is properly repented of, put away, and forsaken, still, carries with it extremely negative consequences; however, it is always God who levels the punishment and not man. There is no man who is qualified to punish another. Concerning such, James, the Lord's Brother, said:

"*Speak not evil one of another, brethren* (refers to self-appointed Judges [Mat. 7:1-5]). *He who speaks evil of his Brother, and judges his brother, speaks evil of the Law, and judges the Law* (pertains to the Law of Moses, to which James is pointing; when a Believer judges another, he has taken himself out from under Grace and placed himself under Law, where he will only find condemnation): *but if you judge the Law, you are not a doer of the Law, but a Judge.* (In other words, such a person has placed himself in the position of God.)

"*There is one Lawgiver, Who is able to save and to destroy* (presents God as the only One Who can fill this position): *who are you who judges another?* (The Greek actually says, 'But you—who are you?' In other words, 'who do you think you are?')" (James 4:11-12).

As it regards true Children of God, it is not really punishment ladled out by the Lord against such when wrong is committed, but rather chastisement (Heb. 12:5-11). In fact, Jesus took the punishment at Calvary's Cross. The facts are, if we took the punishment for our failures and wrongdoings that

NOTES

should be ladled out to us, none of us would be alive. Sin is an awful business, so awful, in fact, that it can be correctly addressed by the Cross of Calvary and the Cross of Calvary alone!

David was given one of three choices by the Lord:

1. Three years famine;
2. Three months to be destroyed by the enemies of Israel; or,
3. Three days pestilence by the Sword of the Lord.

WHY ISRAEL AND NOT DAVID ALONE?

The evidence is, Israel had gone into deep sin, even the worship of idols. If, in fact, this were the case, David had not taken the position he should have taken against these terrible sins. In effect, both David and the majority of Israel were guilty. So, the Lord would use this man to punish Israel for their terrible disobedience. And, as we have stated, David was definitely not without guilt himself.

It would be somewhat similar to the wars fought by America. We would like to think they were all justified; however, as is obvious, America suffered in these wars, as well. This means that, even though God may have used this nation as He, no doubt, did in a number of conflicts, still, America was not without sin herself; consequently, there was always a modicum of judgment visited upon us, and rightly so.

The question begs to be asked that if God blotted out David's terrible sin with Bath-sheba and to Uriah, recording it in II Samuel, Chapter 11, but not recording it in I Chronicles, Chapter 20, why was this sin of II Samuel, Chapter 24 not treated thusly in I Chronicles, Chapter 21 (the sin of numbering the people)? Does God treat all sin alike? Could this sin of numbering the people even have been worse than David's sin with Bath-sheba and to Uriah? And, if so, doesn't God treat all sin alike according to the Precious Blood of Jesus?

TWO TYPES OF SIN

1. There are sins of passion (Gal. 5:19-21), of which David sinned with Bath-sheba and to Uriah. These sins are so bad that Paul

wrote, *"That they which do such things shall not inherit the Kingdom of God,"* meaning to continue in these types of sins.

2. We have the sin of pride. This sin is just as deadly as the sins of the flesh but far more subtle. The sin of pride is the foundation sin of the universe. It is what caused Satan's Fall (Isa., Chpt. 14 – Ezek., Chpt. 28) and man's Fall in the Garden of Eden (Gen., Chpt. 3).

The sin of pride is the sin of *"playing God."* Satan said, *"And you shall be as gods"* (Gen. 3:5). This sin is subtle because it is deceptive. This is actually the sin that nailed Christ to the Cross.

It was not the thieves, harlots, or publicans who killed Christ. It was the church leaders (Pharisees) of the day. The *"sin of pride"* actually says in its spirit, *"I know more than God knows and can guide my destiny far better."* That's the reason the sin of the modern day church of the *"psychological way"* is so deadly. In effect, it is saying, *"we know more about the human need than God knows, and we can cure man of his psychological maladjustments."*

It is fairly simple to get someone to confess and repent of the *"sin of passion."* It is almost impossible to get someone to confess and repent of the *"sin of pride."* This is the sin that characterizes all religion. It is the most deadly sin of all. Of the sins that God hates, *"pride"* leads the list (Prov. 6:16).

The *"sins of passion"* pretty well incorporate themselves according to individuals. The *"sin of pride"* incorporates itself in an entire house, a church, or the entirety of a religious denomination. Even though all sin is directly against God, still, the *"sin of pride"* spreads like a cancer to cover an entire people. There is evidence that David repented (I Chron. 21:8). There is no evidence that the *"70,000 men"* repented. Regrettably, most never do repent!

A GREAT STRAIT

The Scripture says, *"And David said unto Gad, I am in a great strait."*

Sin places people, even the most consecrated, as David, in *"a great strait."*

In such a situation, the only place for the person to turn is to the Lord, which is exactly what David did. The *"sweet singer of Israel"* said, *"Let me fall now into the Hand of the LORD; for very great are His Mercies: but let me not fall into the hand of man."*

So David made his choice, and 70,000 men of Israel died, actually, only in a three-day period of time. No doubt, had David chosen otherwise, many more would have died.

What was the pestilence sent by the Lord?

We aren't told, but, evidently, it was instigated by an Angel.

How many similar incidents have occurred down through history, and even occur presently, but are labeled otherwise? One thing is certain:

Whatever happens in this world, and to whomever it happens, whatever it might be, little or large, is either caused by the Lord or allowed by the Lord. And to be frank, were it not for the Cross of Christ, this world would have been destroyed a long time ago. It is the Cross alone, and what it represents, that stands between mankind and the Judgment of God.

At that time, Israel was probably a Nation of about 5,000,000 people. Of these 5,000,000, there were probably about 2,000,000 men. Of that number of men, 70,000 were killed. At this time, this would be the equivalent of America losing in one three-day period of time approximately 6,000,000 men. So, it is obvious that the judgment wasn't small.

JERUSALEM

The Scripture says, *"And God sent an Angel unto Jerusalem to destroy it."* But the Scripture says that the Angel was stopped by the Lord at a point in time. The answer was, *"It is enough, stay now your hand."*

It is remarkable that the Angel stopped *"by the threshingfloor of Ornan the Jebusite."* He is referred to in II Samuel as *"Araunah"* (II Sam. 24:18).

Where the Angel stopped is where the great Temple would be built by David's son, Solomon. The site for the Temple belonging to a Gentile, and the men employed in the building of the Temple, for the most part being Gentiles, accord with the Lord's declaration that the House was to be a House of Prayer for all nations; and such will it be in the coming Millennial Days. So, the

Lord would turn this extremely hurtful time into a time of great blessing. That's what the Lord will do with all who turn totally to him, as David did. While sin is never overlooked, and while no one gets by with sin, even the greatest Type possibly of Christ found in the Bible, and we continue to speak of David, still, if one turns totally to the Lord, Mercy will always be granted, even as it was here.

(18) "THEN THE ANGEL OF THE LORD COMMANDED GAD TO SAY TO DAVID, THAT DAVID SHOULD GO UP, AND SET UP AN ALTAR UNTO THE LORD IN THE THRESHINGFLOOR OF ORNAN THE JEBUSITE.

(19) "AND DAVID WENT UP AT THE SAYING OF GAD, WHICH HE SPOKE IN THE NAME OF THE LORD.

(20) "AND ORNAN TURNED BACK, AND SAW THE ANGEL; AND HIS FOUR SONS WITH HIM HID THEMSELVES. NOW ORNAN WAS THRESHING WHEAT.

(21) "AND AS DAVID CAME TO ORNAN, ORNAN LOOKED AND SAW DAVID, AND WENT OUT OF THE THRESHINGFLOOR, AND BOWED HIMSELF TO DAVID WITH HIS FACE TO THE GROUND.

(22) "THEN DAVID SAID TO ORNAN, GRANT ME THE PLACE OF THIS THRESHINGFLOOR, THAT I MAY BUILD AN ALTAR THEREIN UNTO THE LORD: YOU SHALL GRANT IT ME FOR THE FULL PRICE: THAT THE PLAGUE MAY BE STAYED FROM THE PEOPLE.

(23) "AND ORNAN SAID UNTO DAVID, TAKE IT TO YOU, AND LET MY LORD THE KING DO THAT WHICH IS GOOD IN HIS EYES: LO, I GIVE YOU THE OXEN ALSO FOR BURNT OFFERINGS, AND THE THRESHING INSTRUMENTS FOR WOOD, AND THE WHEAT FOR THE MEAT OFFERING; I GIVE IT ALL.

(24) "AND KING DAVID SAID TO ORNAN, NO; BUT I WILL VERILY BUY IT FOR THE FULL PRICE: FOR I WILL NOT TAKE THAT WHICH IS YOURS FOR THE LORD, NOR OFFER BURNT OFFERINGS WITHOUT COST.

(25) "SO DAVID GAVE TO ORNAN FOR THE PLACE SIX HUNDRED SHEKELS OF GOLD BY WEIGHT.

NOTES

(26) "AND DAVID BUILT THERE AN ALTAR UNTO THE LORD, AND OFFERED BURNT OFFERINGS AND PEACE OFFERINGS, AND CALLED UPON THE LORD; AND HE ANSWERED HIM FROM HEAVEN BY FIRE UPON THE ALTAR OF BURNT OFFERING.

(27) "AND THE LORD COMMANDED THE ANGEL; AND HE PUT UP HIS SWORD AGAIN INTO THE SHEATH THEREOF.

(28) "AT THAT TIME WHEN DAVID SAW THAT THE LORD HAD ANSWERED HIM IN THE THRESHINGFLOOR OF ORNAN THE JEBUSITE, THEN HE SACRIFICED THERE.

(29) "FOR THE TABERNACLE OF THE LORD, WHICH MOSES MADE IN THE WILDERNESS, AND THE ALTAR OF THE BURNT OFFERING, WERE AT THAT SEASON IN THE HIGH PLACE AT GIBEON.

(30) "BUT DAVID COULD NOT GO BEFORE IT TO ENQUIRE OF GOD: FOR HE WAS AFRAID BECAUSE OF THE SWORD OF THE ANGEL OF THE LORD."

The exegesis is:

1. (Vs. 18) The threshingfloor of Ornan the Jebusite would be the exact place where the Temple would be built. So, *"where sin abounded, Grace did much more abound"* (Rom. 5:20).

That which David had ignored in taking the census, the *"Altar,"* which typified the Cross, must be erected here. This is why Paul said, *"We preach Christ Crucified"* (I Cor. 1:23). The modern church presently casts about in its dilemma, trying to find a solution. The only solution is the Cross. The church must go back to the Cross.

2. (Vs. 19) The true Prophets of God are saying the same thing presently to the modern church, *"Build an Altar,"* i.e., go back to the Cross, but, regrettably, they are little heeded.

3. (Vs. 20) Regarding the entirety of this episode, the picture is striking: the wrath of God about to fall upon the city, the guilty king confessing his sin, the spotless sacrifice slain, the Judgment of God vindicated and honored.

4. (Vs. 20) This Grace is the more apparent and all-embracing, when it is noticed that the ground upon which this most satisfactory

sacrifice was offered up belonged to a Gentile, Araunah, the Jebusite.

5. From Verse 23, it seems that this Jebusite was well acquainted with the various Offerings of Israel.

6. (Vs. 24) Sin can never be atoned for without the *"full price"* of the Blood of Calvary. The problem with the church is bloodless altars and a cross-less salvation; in fact, such do not exist. Man cannot be redeemed by half measures. As stated, it has to be the *"full price"*—the Precious shed Blood of the Lord Jesus Christ (Jn. 3:16).

7. (Vs. 26) The lightning coming from Heaven and striking the sacrifice is a picture of God's Judgment on sin—the Judgment, we may quickly add, that should have fallen on David, and on us, for that matter, but, instead, fell upon Christ. The choice belongs to man! Man can accept the Judgment that fell on Christ, and do so by accepting Christ, which sets the sinner free. Or he can rebel against Christ, and suffer the lightning-strike of Judgment upon himself. There is no alternative!

8. (Vs. 27) The only thing, as previously stated, that stands between Judgment of the entirety of this Planet and God Almighty is the Cross of Christ.

9. Verses 28-29 proclaim to us that the Lord told David that this site would now become the site of the Temple, soon to be constructed.

THE ALTAR

The Scripture says, *"Then the Angel of the LORD commanded Gad to say to David, that David should go up, and set up an Altar unto the LORD in the threshingfloor of Ornan the Jebusite."*

The Altar, which represented the coming Lord, Who would give His Life on the Cross of Calvary, was absolutely necessary if this Judgment could be held in check. This is a powerful picture.

God must judge sin, irrespective as to where the sin might be, even in one such as David, a man after His Own Heart. While the Lord could give the command that the death Angel would stop in his destructive powers, still, the ceasing of the judgment was predicated solely upon the sacrifice that would be offered on the Altar to be built. In fact, this is the reason for the urgency of David in getting it all done, and rightly so!

The world understands the Cross not at all, but the tragedy is, and what a tragedy it is, the church little understands it, as well. How many preachers presently are preaching the Cross? In fact, the Cross is repudiated in some circles, namely by the Word of Faith people, so-called! It is almost altogether ignored by the balance of the church.

If the Cross of Christ is removed from Christianity, Christianity is left only as a meaningless philosophy. And yet, despite the fact that the Cross of Christ is the answer, and the only answer, the church continues to ignore the very heartbeat of the Plan of Redemption.

A PERSONAL REVELATION

After some six years of two prayer meetings a day, the Lord gave to me a Revelation, straight from the Word of God, that was to revolutionize my life, my Ministry and, in fact, everything and anything that I might be. The year was 1997.

The first thing the Lord showed me, as to the problem of sin as it regards Believers, was the meaning of the sin nature. He took me straight to Romans, Chapter 6. I found out later that this was the very first thing shown to the Apostle Paul, as well. The great Apostle proclaims to us in Romans, Chapter 7, his futile task at attempting to live a victorious life in the Lord, no matter how hard he tried. But, then the Lord gave the great Apostle the meaning of the New Covenant which, in effect, is the meaning of the Cross. In this great Revelation, the meaning of the sin nature is the first thing given to the Apostle, which he gave to us in Romans, Chapter 6.

For a full account of this Revelation, I would advise the reader to secure for yourself a copy of the Study Guide, "The Revelation Of The Cross, What The Lord Gave To Me In 1997, *The Cross Of Christ Series*". It will go into much greater detail, and I think will be a tremendous blessing.

A few days later, the Lord showed me the answer to the dilemma of the sin nature, and that answer was and is the Cross of Christ.

The Lord made it emphatically clear to me that the Cross of Christ was the only solution to this problem, meaning that there aren't other solutions.

The problem is sin. No matter what label it may be given otherwise, no matter what schemes or stratagems may be proposed, the problem is sin, and the only answer for this problem is the Cross of Christ.

Some weeks later, the Lord then portrayed to me how the Holy Spirit functions in all of this, in effect, taking me to Romans 8:2.

Then David had to build an Altar. The Altar presently has already been built. It was built 2,000 years ago, and there the Great Sacrifice in the Person of Christ was forever offered, and the finality was complete. *"It is finished,"* and to be sure, the Lord meant exactly what He said.

Unless the preacher preaches the Cross, he's not really preaching the Gospel.

WHAT DOES IT MEAN TO PREACH THE CROSS?

In brief, *"to preach the Cross"* means that Jesus Christ is the Source of all things that we receive from God, but the Cross is the Means by which these things are received, all superintended by the Holy Spirit (Rom. 6:1-14; 8:1-2, 11; I Cor. 1:17-18, 21, 23; 2:2; Gal., Chpt. 5; 6:14; Col. 2:14-15).

Preaching the Cross refers to the fact that man can be Saved only by having Faith in Christ and what Christ did at the Cross. Admittedly, the believing sinner understands nothing about Christ and what He did at the Cross when Salvation is effected. In fact, in order to be Saved, the only thing the believing sinner has to do is to furnish the sinner, and to be sure, the Lord will furnish the Saviour.

But after one comes to Christ, successfully living for God is now the great achievement. This can only be done by the Believer placing his faith exclusively in Christ and the Cross, understanding that the Cross not only pertains to our Salvation but, as well, pertains to our Sanctification. In other words, the Holy Spirit operates solely and completely in the parameters of the Finished Work of Christ. He demands that our faith conclusively be in Christ and the Cross, and that it be in nothing else.

The preacher must understand that our everyday living for God, our daily walk before God, in other words, our Sanctification, all depends upon our Faith in the Cross of Christ. Most preachers understand at least something about the Cross as it regards Salvation, but almost nothing at all as it regards Sanctification. Consequently, the church lurches from one scheme to the other, trying to find a solution to the sin problem.

There is only one solution, only one! That solution is, *"Jesus Christ and Him Crucified"* (I Cor. 1:23).

There are only two places for the Believer to be as it regards our life and living for the Lord. Those two places are law and Grace. One can function in Grace only as one understands the Cross of Christ regarding our Sanctification. Otherwise, by default, the Believer will be immersed in law, whether he understands such or not. Let us say it this way:

If our Faith as Believers is not exclusively in the Cross of Christ, which then enables the Holy Spirit to work mightily within our lives, automatically, such a Believer will be in law. Admittedly, such law is not the Law of Moses, but rather law made up and devised of our own stratagem, or laws made up by other preachers or religious denominations, etc. Nevertheless, it is law, and it is that which the Lord can never bless.

Man cannot keep the law, no matter how hard he tries, and no matter who he might be. Therefore, the Lord Jesus Christ came to this world, took upon himself the rudiments of sinful flesh, even though He never sinned, and then kept the Law perfectly, all on our behalf. In other words, it was all done for you and me. He then addressed the broken Law by going to the Cross of Calvary and there offering Himself as a Sacrifice, which appeased the demands of a thrice-Holy God. Of course, the Law of which we speak concerning Christ was the Law of Moses. At the present time, due to the Cross, in order to enjoy the fullness of the Spirit, and all that the Lord has done for us, we need only to place our Faith exclusively in Christ and the Cross, and maintain our Faith in Christ and the Cross even on a daily basis.

WHY ISN'T THE CROSS RELATIVE TO OUR DAILY WALK BEFORE GOD TAUGHT IN MOST CHURCHES?

That's a good question!

Actually, there are two reasons.

1. The first reason is ignorance. I do not mean that unkindly, and I certainly do not mean for it to be sarcastic, but the fact is, most preachers have no understanding at all regarding the Cross as it regards Sanctification. Therefore, they lumber from one scheme to the other, trying to find a solution to the problem of sin.

The church tries to change the definition of the problem, borrowing heavily from the world, but irrespective as to what is done in this capacity, the problem is sin. And the only solution to the problem, and I mean the only solution, is the Cross of Christ. As we've already stated, most preachers have at least a modicum of understanding as it regards the Cross respecting Salvation, but none at all as it regards Sanctification.

The Bible plainly tells us that *"Faith comes by hearing and hearing by the Word of God"* (Rom. 10:17). So, if the Word of God is not heard in this respect, there can be no Faith to believe. Regrettably, the modern church is heavily laden with ignorance as it regards this all-important aspect of life and living—in fact, the most important of all!

2. We have the problem of unbelief. If the problem were only a problem of ignorance, then light being shown on the Word of God, as it regards this difficulty, would solve the problem; however, the sad fact is, most of the ignorance of the modern church is a willful ignorance. In other words, it doesn't know anything about the Cross as it regards Sanctification, and it doesn't want to know anything about the Cross as it regards Sanctification. It is unbelief!

WHY DOESN'T THE MODERN CHURCH WANT TO KNOW ABOUT THE CROSS REGARDING SANCTIFICATION?

Paul said that there is an offense to the Cross (Gal. 5:11).

The offense is, the Cross lays waste all of man's ideas, stratagems, schemes, and proposed solutions, etc. As Abraham did not enjoy giving up Ishmael, even though the boy was a work of the flesh, likewise, most are loath to give up that which they have conceived out of their own minds. And, if there is anything the Cross accomplishes, it is the laying waste of all of man's ideas and schemes. Everything is out, with the Cross of Christ left, and that alone. That means that all the faith we have in our stratagems and schemes has got to go. That means that everything else pales into insignificance, and man does not like that. That's the reason the great Apostle said, *"And I, Brethren, if I yet preach Circumcision, why do I yet suffer persecution? then is the offence of the Cross ceased"* (Gal. 5:11).

The Early Church from the Jewish sector did not want to give up the Law, i.e., *"Circumcision."* They wanted to demand that of Gentiles, along with accepting Christ. Paul said it cannot be. Circumcision, and anything that relates to the Law, or our own stratagems, must go. The Cross does that, so it is an offense.

And, at the same time, most preachers in the modern church simply don't believe that what Jesus did at the Cross answers the dilemma of the human problem. Therefore, they turn to humanistic psychology, etc.

In the meantime, Christians lurch from one failure to the other, realizing only a small portion of that for which Jesus paid such a price. The great Prophet Hosea said: *"My People are destroyed for lack of knowledge: because you have rejected knowledge, I will also reject you, that you shall be no Priest to Me: seeing you have forgotten the Law of your God, I will also forget your children"* (Hos. 4:6).

While Israel was plagued with ignorance, still, as stated, it was a willful ignorance. In other words, they had no desire to know what the Lord wanted, so their place and position was rather a willful rejection of the Law of God. They didn't know, but it was because they didn't want to know!

I'm concerned that this fits the modern church perfectly!

THE PRICE

David had been told by the Lord that he was to build an Altar on the threshingfloor of the Jebusite. Now, the *"sweet singer of Israel"* proceeds forward to obey what the Lord has told him to do, and rightly so.

When David proposes buying the piece of ground, he was told by the Jebusite that nothing would be charged for the ground, and besides that, he would give David the oxen for burnt offerings and the threshing instruments for wood, etc. David's answer was as follows, even though I am positive he appreciated the kindness of the Jebusite. The Scripture says:

"And king David said to Ornan, No; but I will verily buy it for the full price: for I will not take that which is yours for the LORD, nor offer Burnt Offerings without cost."

David paid the Jebusite *"six hundred shekels of gold by weight,"* for the piece of ground.

We have far too many Believers presently trying to offer things to the Lord which costs them nothing. I hardly think that the Lord could be pleased with such, especially considering the price that He paid in order that we might be Saved.

What are you as a Believer giving as it regards the Work of the Lord?

Are you giving of your financial means? Are you giving of your time?

While it is definitely true that Jesus paid it all, and there is nothing that we can earn as it regards any price that we might pay, still, we dare not offer to the Lord that which costs us nothing. To do so, in effect, demeans the price that Jesus paid. And nothing must be done to demean that for which He has paid such a price.

FIRE FROM HEAVEN

Even though it is not mentioned in II Samuel as the account of this incident is given, the writer here tells us that the Lord honored the sacrifice offered on the hastily built Altar by sending fire from Heaven.

This typified the Judgment of God that would come upon Christ in our stead. In other words, Christ would take the Judgment that you and I should have taken. But, had we taken such Judgment, the conclusion would have only been the total annihilation of our person and being. We deserve such Judgment! On the other hand, Jesus was a Perfect Sacrifice, meaning that He was born without sin, and lived without sin; consequently, in the offering up of Himself, the Judgment that He took did not consume Him, but rather served as the penalty paid on behalf of all who will believe.

The statement of Verse 28, which says, *"Then he sacrificed there,"* means that he *"thenceforward sacrificed there."* He established there the service of sacrifices.

Concerning this, Pulpit says: *"David was so impressed by the answer given in fire from Heaven, that he began systematically to sacrifice on the site of this threshing-floor instead of going to the high place at Gibeon, where the Altar of Burnt Offering still stood."*[1]

As we have stated, the site of the Jebusite purchased by David would be the site where the Temple would be built by Solomon. It would be where God would dwell between the Mercy Seat and the Cherubim. Consequently, out of this terrible sin of David and Israel, Grace would shine forth even as Grace always shines forth.

The Lord Alone has the Solution, and that Solution is the Cross of Calvary. We must never, never forget that.

> *"Thine be the glory, risen, conquering Son,*
> *"Endless is the Victory over death You have won;*
> *"Angels in bright raiment roll the stone away,*
> *"Kept the folded grave clothes, where Your Body lay."*

> *"Lo! Jesus meets us risen from the tomb;*
> *"Lovingly He greets us, scatters fear and gloom;*
> *"Let the Church with gladness hymns of triumph sing,*
> *"For her Lord now lives, death has lost its sting."*

> *"No more we doubt You, glorious Prince of Life;*
> *"Life is naught without You: aid us in our strife;*
> *"Make us more than conquerors, through Your deathless Love:*

"Bring us safe through Jordan to Your Home above."

CHAPTER 22

(1) "THEN DAVID SAID, THIS IS THE HOUSE OF THE LORD GOD, AND THIS IS THE ALTAR OF THE BURNT OFFERING FOR ISRAEL.

(2) "AND DAVID COMMANDED TO GATHER TOGETHER THE STRANGERS WHO WERE IN THE LAND OF ISRAEL; AND HE SET MASONS TO HEW WROUGHT STONES TO BUILD THE HOUSE OF GOD.

(3) "AND DAVID PREPARED IRON IN ABUNDANCE FOR THE NAILS FOR THE DOORS OF THE GATES, AND FOR THE JOININGS; AND BRASS IN ABUNDANCE WITHOUT WEIGHT;

(4) "ALSO CEDAR TREES IN ABUNDANCE: FOR THE ZIDONIANS AND THEY OF TYRE BROUGHT MUCH CEDAR WOOD TO DAVID.

(5) "AND DAVID SAID, SOLOMON MY SON IS YOUNG AND TENDER, AND THE HOUSE THAT IS TO BE BUILT FOR THE LORD MUST BE EXCEEDING MAGNIFICENT, OF FAME AND OF GLORY THROUGHOUT ALL COUNTRIES: I WILL THEREFORE NOW MAKE PREPARATION FOR IT. SO DAVID PREPARED ABUNDANTLY BEFORE HIS DEATH."

The structure is:

1. (Vs. 1) The site has now been selected as to where the Temple will be built. It was all done totally by the Lord and none at all by the hand of man.

2. The *"strangers"* mentioned in Verse 2 pertained to Gentiles, who were craftsmen and, thereby, could provide skills not available among the Israelites.

3. In Verse 3, we have the beginning of gathering the materials for the Temple—not counted in the 7 1/2 years of the actual construction by Solomon.

4. (Vs. 5) This *"House"* was to be *"in type"* the Millennial Glory of the Messiah, just as the Tabernacle had set forth His Mediatorial Glory.

THE HOUSE OF THE LORD

This one Verse of Scripture (I Chron. 22:1), among other similar Scriptures, is the cause of much conflict in the Middle East and, more particularly, in Jerusalem. This is the site where Solomon, David's son, did build the great Temple. It is, as would be obvious, the most holy site in Judaism.

As of now, the Muslim world controls this site, and yet, in the very near future Israel must rebuild her Temple on this site.

Some have claimed that Prophecy would be fulfilled even if the Temple were built on another site, or even next door to the Dome of the Rock; however, that is highly unlikely. Every indication is, when the Temple is rebuilt in the future, it must be built on the same site that Solomon's Temple was constructed.

As stated, at the present it is controlled by the Muslims. As well, they have no intention whatsoever of giving up this site, claiming it as the third most holy site in the world of Islam.

Islam claims that Ishmael was the promised seed instead of Isaac. They believe in God; however, it is a god of their own making. They claim that Mohammed is God's Prophet. They also believe and teach that Jesus Christ was a great Prophet, but not the Son of God. They believe the only way to God is through Mohammed. Christianity and the Bible teach that the only way to God is through Jesus Christ (Jn. 14:6).

All of this means, at least for Bible Prophecy to be fulfilled, that the Dome of the Rock will have to be moved in order for the new Jewish Temple to be built. How it will be done, especially at this time, no one knows, but it will be done. Once again, sacrifices will be offered up on the great Altar, which will, as well, be placed in front of the Temple, just as it was with Solomon's. However, at the mid-point of the Great Tribulation the Antichrist, who will enable Israel to rebuild her Temple, will show his true colors and actually invade Israel. At that time Israel will be defeated for the first time since becoming a Nation in 1948. Were it not for the intervention of the Lord, she would be totally destroyed; however, she will be preserved.

The Antichrist will take over the Temple, making it his religious headquarters, and will, thereby, stop the sacrifices. For all of this to happen, even as the Prophet Daniel proclaimed, the Temple, as would be obvious, will have to be rebuilt (Dan. 9:27).

One thing is certain. Whatever the Bible says will happen, that is exactly what will happen. The Bible is the Word of God. And when we speak of *"the Bible,"* we are speaking of a word for word translation, such as the King James. Unfortunately, there are untold numbers of religious books which go under the name of *"Bible,"* but which actually aren't. They are just merely a collection of religious thoughts and should in no fashion be looked at as the Word of God. I speak of those such as the *"Message Bible."*

PREPARATION

As it regards the Temple, the Scripture says, *"And David prepared. . . ."*

The preparation that David made as it regards the Temple, which was a monumental undertaking, was almost as detailed as the actual building of the structure.

In some way, any and every great Work of God must be preceded by proper preparation. As well, even as the Great Work, whatever it might be, is prepared by the Holy Spirit, and the Holy Spirit Alone, likewise, the Holy Spirit will conduct the preparation, but using men and women as instruments.

I was reading the other day the remarks of one particular preacher as it regarded David in his later years. He made the statement that because of the sin of David with Bath-sheba and the murder of her husband Uriah, which sins were dastardly indeed, David, in those later years, accomplished little for the Lord.

The truth is, David probably accomplished more for the Lord after this terrible incident than before. Several of the Psalms were written at this particular time and, as well, the preparation for the Temple was, without doubt, one of the most important works in which any individual could engage himself. And, we must quickly add, the Lord chose David to accomplish this most important task. For the Lord to choose a person, even as He did David, to gather the materials with which the Temple would be built, actually, the place where God would dwell, the only place on Earth, incidentally, was monumental indeed.

None of my statements are meant to minimize the effect of the terrible sin committed by the *"sweet singer of Israel."* To be sure, David paid dearly for that which he did; however, it did not stop the Lord from using him, and it was because David properly repented of this foul deed.

Preachers, or anyone, for that matter, who suggest that a person cannot be used because of failure in the past, whether they realize it or not, have just eliminated the entirety of the Body of Christ. In other words, God wouldn't be able to use anyone. Anyone who doesn't know that fact does not know the Bible as he should, does not know himself as he should, and, above all, doesn't know the Lord as he should. It all comes under *"Justification by Faith."*

The only thing that disqualifies a person from being used of the Lord is lack of Repentance and unbelief. When the Lord forgives a person, even as He forgave David and has forgiven everyone of us, we are forgiven totally and completely. In other words, Justification demands that in the Mind of God, the terrible sin, whatever it may have been, no longer even exists. The Lord has no black marks beside the name of any Believer. We should understand that! When we as Believers are forgiven and cleansed, the action is blotted out as if it never existed. What a wonderful Lord we serve!

But, again I state, this in no way is meant to minimize sin. Because the Lord will forgive and cleanse doesn't mean there isn't payment. Sin is so awful, so bad, so destructive, and so degrading that it must never be looked at with any degree of impunity. It is so bad, in fact, that it took the Cross with all of its implications to eliminate this mad monster.

But, thank God there was and is a Cross. There the matter was settled and settled forever!

Satan is a master at telling Believers that if they have done something wrong, even though they have properly repented, they are on God's blacklist. Don't believe it! The sad fact is, Satan uses preachers to peddle his lies. Irrespective, you must not believe it.

WHAT TYPE OF PREPARATION?

I'm sure the *"type"* would be as different as the individuals involved. Regarding something so delicate, even as the Lord allowed David to use his own personal experience, I will use mine, as well.

In 1991, with the Ministry in shambles and not knowing what to do, and knowing, as well, that the fault was mine, but yet, not knowing quite how it was mine, despite the pain and suffering, this was the beginning of the preparation for the great Revelation of the Cross, which the Lord ultimately would give me.

At that time, almost the entirety of the church world was screaming, and screaming loudly, that I not preach anymore. I must stop all Ministry, etc.

I did have the presence of mind to know and understand that at this time, especially, I must have the leading of the Lord. If I missed it here, I would be destroyed forever.

At the very heart of sorrow and heartache, a pain so unimaginable that it defies description, eight or ten of us gathered for prayer that night. If I remember it correctly, it was a Thursday night in October, 1991.

In that prayer session, the Holy Spirit came down in such a way that I have seldom seen or witnessed. There was a Word of Prophecy given. And this is what it was:

"I'm not a man that I should lie, neither the son of man that I should repent. What I have blessed, nothing can curse!"

I had my answer. The Lord had Called me to preach. He had not lied about it, and neither had He changed His Mind. It didn't matter what men said, I was to do what He said that I had to do. And thank God for that Moving of the Spirit that Thursday night in 1991, and thank God that I had the Presence of the Holy Spirit to know exactly what the Lord was saying. As stated, it was the beginning of the preparation time.

The next morning, that is, if I remember correctly, on my way to the office, the Lord spoke to my heart and told me to begin two prayer meetings a day, morning and night.

The very first prayer meeting we conducted was at the office. There must have been about 15 or 20 at that particular meeting, and the Spirit of God, once again, Moved in a mighty, mighty way.

I knew the Lord had told me to continue preaching, but I wondered if that meant I was to stay on television. There is no greater medium for reaching people with the Gospel than television. And even though in the aggregate, it is probably the least expensive of presentations, still, it costs a lot of money to make and air the programming. Untold numbers of people are reached, but it costs much money to do it.

That morning, as I began to importune the Lord as to what I should do as it regarded television, once again, the Lord spoke to my heart. He said:

"I have called you for Media Ministry, and I have not lifted that Call."

My next thought was, *"How can we pay for the Telecast?"*

THE ANSWER OF THE LORD

In answer to my question, the Lord took me to Matthew, Chapter 17. The incident there recorded is found only in Matthew, but answered my question readily.

The tax collectors came to Peter, in effect, stating that taxes were owed.

Peter went to the Lord and asked Him if, in fact, the taxes were owed.

In essence, Jesus said *"no,"* but then stated, *"Notwithstanding, lest we should offend them, you go to the sea, and cast a hook, and take up the fish that first comes up; and when you have opened his mouth, you shall find a piece of money: that take, and give unto them from Me and you"* (Mat. 17:27).

The Lord then spoke to my heart, saying, *"In the manner that I met the need that day regarding the taxes, in like manner I will meet the need of the telecast and the Ministry as a whole."*

I knew it was the Lord Who had spoken to me. His Presence was undeniable; however, I also knew this was the most unorthodox manner of raising funds that anyone has ever known.

How unorthodox—catching a fish, looking in its mouth, finding a piece of money, and with that paying the taxes.

But that's exactly the way the Lord has provided for this Ministry. He has performed

Miracle after Miracle in order that the finances be met.

There have been countless times that I didn't see how we could make it, but every time, sometimes at the last moment, the Lord would always come through.

In all of this, as should be obvious, He was and is teaching me trust. It all had to do, and has to do, with the preparation.

THE REVELATION

And then in 1997, the Lord opened up to me Truths from His Word that I had not previously known, which would revolutionize my life and Ministry. To be sure, and as stated, it was not new, but that which had actually been given to the Apostle Paul.

He, first of all, showed me why Christians fail, despite the fact of trying so very hard not to fail. He took me to the Sixth Chapter of Romans and there explained the sin nature to me. However, that morning, even though the Revelation He gave me was of such magnitude as to be beyond compare, still, He didn't tell me the solution to the problem of the sin nature. That would come several days later.

In prayer meeting a week or so later, the Lord again moved upon my heart greatly and told me, *"The answer for which you seek is found in the Cross."* He then said with a slight variation, *"The solution for which you seek is found in the Cross."* He then said, *"The answer and the solution for which you seek are found only in the Cross."* He once again took me to the great Sixth Chapter of Romans.

THE HOLY SPIRIT

If the answer were found solely in the Cross, where did that leave the Holy Spirit?

I knew beyond the shadow of a doubt that the Holy Spirit plays a tremendous part in all that is done as it regards the Work of God on Earth, but I was left that day not really knowing or understanding just how He Works as it regards the Cross and its involvement in our lives.

A few weeks later, the Lord gave me the answer to that, taking me to Romans 8:2, which says: *"For the Law of the Spirit of Life in Christ Jesus has made me free from the Law of Sin and Death."*

I knew then that the Holy Spirit Works entirely within the framework of the Finished Work of Christ. In other words, it is the Cross which gives Him the legal right to do all that He does in our hearts and lives. The Cross has made it all possible.

To be sure, I'm only touching the high spots of this Revelation. And, as I've already stated some pages back, I would strongly recommend that the reader secure for yourself the Study Guide entitled, "The Revelation Of The Cross, What The Lord Gave To Me In 1997, *The Cross Of Christ Series*".

This Study Guide, about 70 or 80 pages long, will go into much greater detail, and I feel will be a great blessing to you. I would strongly advise that you secure a copy for yourself.

THE REVELATION OF THE CROSS

I was to find out that this Revelation given to me was of far greater degree than I could even begin to imagine. In fact, I believe that it is a Word from the Lord for the entirety of the church world at this hour. I believe this is what the Holy Spirit is saying to the churches.

During the some six years of conducting two prayer meetings a day, the Lord never really told me why He directed me to do this, with one exception. He said to me at the outset, *"Do not seek Me so much for what I can do, but rather for Who I am."* In other words, it was relationship of which He was speaking. It took much preparation for that Revelation to be given. And to be frank, the preparation has not ceased from then until now, and I suspect it will never cease.

(6) "THEN HE CALLED FOR SOLOMON HIS SON, AND CHARGED HIM TO BUILD AN HOUSE FOR THE LORD GOD OF ISRAEL.

(7) "AND DAVID SAID TO SOLOMON, MY SON, AS FOR ME, IT WAS IN MY MIND TO BUILD AN HOUSE UNTO THE NAME OF THE LORD MY GOD:

(8) "BUT THE WORD OF THE LORD CAME TO ME SAYING, YOU HAVE SHED BLOOD ABUNDANTLY, AND HAVE MADE GREAT WARS: YOU SHALL NOT BUILD AN HOUSE UNTO MY NAME, BECAUSE YOU HAVE SHED MUCH BLOOD UPON

THE EARTH IN MY SIGHT.

(9) "BEHOLD, A SON SHALL BE BORN TO YOU, WHO SHALL BE A MAN OF REST; AND I WILL GIVE HIM REST FROM ALL HIS ENEMIES ROUND ABOUT: FOR HIS NAME SHALL BE SOLOMON, AND I WILL GIVE PEACE AND QUIETNESS UNTO ISRAEL IN HIS DAYS.

(10) "HE SHALL BUILD AN HOUSE FOR MY NAME; AND HE SHALL BE MY SON, AND I WILL BE HIS FATHER; AND I WILL ESTABLISH THE THRONE OF HIS KINGDOM OVER ISRAEL FOR EVER.

(11) "NOW, MY SON, THE LORD BE WITH YOU; AND PROSPER YOU, AND BUILD THE HOUSE OF THE LORD YOUR GOD, AS HE HAS SAID OF YOU.

(12) "ONLY THE LORD GIVE YOU WISDOM AND UNDERSTANDING, AND GIVE YOU CHARGE CONCERNING ISRAEL, THAT YOU MAY KEEP THE LAW OF THE LORD YOUR GOD.

(13) "THEN SHALL YOU PROSPER, IF YOU TAKE HEED TO FULFILL THE STATUTES AND JUDGMENTS WHICH THE LORD CHARGED MOSES WITH CONCERNING ISRAEL: BE STRONG, AND OF GOOD COURAGE; DREAD NOT, NOR BE DISMAYED.

(14) "NOW, BEHOLD, IN MY TROUBLE I HAVE PREPARED FOR THE HOUSE OF THE LORD AN HUNDRED THOUSAND TALENTS OF GOLD, AND A THOUSAND THOUSAND TALENTS OF SILVER; AND OF BRASS AND IRON WITHOUT WEIGHT; FOR IT IS IN ABUNDANCE: TIMBER ALSO AND STONE HAVE I PREPARED; AND YOU MAY ADD THERETO.

(15) "MOREOVER THERE ARE WORKMEN WITH YOU IN ABUNDANCE, HEWERS AND WORKERS OF STONE AND TIMBER, AND ALL MANNER OF CUNNING MEN FOR EVERY MANNER OF WORK.

(16) "OF THE GOLD, THE SILVER, AND THE BRASS, AND THE IRON, THERE IS NO NUMBER. ARISE THEREFORE, AND BE DOING, AND THE LORD BE WITH YOU.

(17) "DAVID ALSO COMMANDED ALL THE PRINCES OF ISRAEL TO HELP SOLOMON HIS SON, SAYING,

(18) "IS NOT THE LORD YOUR GOD WITH YOU? AND HAS HE NOT GIVEN YOU REST ON EVERY SIDE? FOR HE HAS GIVEN THE INHABITANTS OF THE LAND INTO MY HAND; AND THE LAND IS SUBDUED BEFORE THE LORD, AND BEFORE HIS PEOPLE.

(19) "NOW SET YOUR HEART AND YOUR SOUL TO SEEK THE LORD YOUR GOD; ARISE THEREFORE, AND BUILD YOU THE SANCTUARY OF THE LORD GOD, TO BRING THE ARK OF THE COVENANT OF THE LORD, AND THE HOLY VESSELS OF GOD, INTO THE HOUSE THAT IS TO BE BUILT TO THE NAME OF THE LORD."

The construction is:

1. According to Verse 6, Solomon was chosen by the Lord (I Ki. 1:30, 37, 39).

2. (Vs. 8) David typifies Christ as a Man of war, destroying His enemies; Solomon, as Christ, the Prince of Peace, reigning over a kingdom free from these enemies.

3. (Vs. 9) This Verse proclaims that Solomon was named before he was born. He was one of the seven men in the Bible named before birth.

4. The complete fulfillment of Verse 10 will be in Christ, and will take place in the coming Kingdom Age (Isa., Chpt. 11).

5. (Vs. 12) These words said by David may have been the germ of Solomon's own prayer, which *"pleased the Lord"* (I Ki. 3:5-14; II Chron. 1:7-12).

6. Basically, David, in Verse 13, quotes the very words given by the Lord to Joshua, which were given about 500 years earlier; however, a general Promise given by the Lord is applicable to anyone who will dare to believe!

7. The hundred thousand talents of gold of Verse 14 would be worth approximately a hundred billion dollars or more in 2008 currency.

8. (Vs. 14) All that David said in his admonishment to Solomon confirmed what so often appears in the character of this man, that all through his stormy life of warfare, his heart was true to one great purpose, the establishment of the House of God, and the Peace of God in the midst of the people of God.

9. The command of Verse 16, *"Arise . . .*

and be doing," should be the criteria for every Believer, as well!

10. (Vs. 18) At long last, every enemy has been defeated, and the great Promises of God have been brought to fulfillment. What a time!

DAVID AND SOLOMON, BOTH TYPES OF CHRIST

David was a Type of Christ as it regards the Mediatorial Glory of our Lord. Solomon was a Type of Christ as it regards the Millennial Glory of the Messiah.

Regarding the Mediation of Christ, many enemies had to be defeated, and which were defeated at the Cross. The Millennial Glory is yet to come, and will proclaim a time with all enemies defeated, a time of peace and prosperity such as the world has never known before. As stated, David typifies the former, while his son Solomon typifies the latter.

Concerning this, Williams says: *"David typifies Christ as a man of war destroying his enemies, and Solomon as Christ, the Prince of Peace, reigning over a kingdom made free from these enemies."*[1]

And yet, all types are imperfect, as should be overly obvious. Consequently, many might ask the question as to how David could be a Type of Christ, especially considering the terrible sins he committed. Others may point to Solomon, asking the same question, especially considering that he lost his way in his older years, hopefully, coming back at the end.

JUSTIFICATION BY FAITH

Once again, Justification by Faith is the answer and, in fact, the only answer.

There are no perfect human beings. In fact, there has never been a perfect human being, with one exception, and that is our Lord and Saviour, Jesus Christ. He Alone was Perfect, Pure, and without corruption of any nature. Therefore, when the believing sinner says, *"yes"* to Christ, the sin of the sinner is loaded onto the Saviour, while the Perfection of the Redeemer is given freely to the believing sinner. Two of the sacrifices of old typified this perfectly.

In the Sin Offering, the sin of the individual, whatever it may have been, was

NOTES

loaded on Christ. The whole Burnt Offering represented the very opposite. It presented the totality of the Perfection of Christ given to the sinner. Even as I dictate these notes, I sense the Presence of God. My sins are no more because they've all been given to Him, and He atoned for them on the Cross. And on top of that, He has given me His Glorious Perfection. What a Mighty God we serve!

David typified Redemption, while Solomon typified Peace.

PROSPERITY

Pure and simple, the Holy Spirit through David tells his son, *"The LORD be with you; and prosper you, and build the House of the LORD your God, as He has said of you.*

"Only the LORD give you wisdom and understanding, and give you charge concerning Israel, that you may keep the Law of the LORD your God.

"Then shall you prosper, if you take heed to fulfill the Statutes and Judgments which the LORD charged Moses with concerning Israel: be strong, and of good courage; dread not, nor be dismayed."

Several things were demanded of Solomon. They were:

- Solomon was not to fail in the building of the House of the Lord.
- He was to keep the Law of the Lord his God.
- He must take heed to fulfill the Statutes and Judgments, which the Lord charged Moses with concerning Israel.
- He was to be strong, and of a good courage. As well, he must not fear, nor be dismayed.

I don't think there is much difference in these commands than those given to us presently.

But yet, given the weakness of humanity, even the best of Believers, how can these Commandments be kept?

Paul addressed this over and over. In fact, most of his teaching centered up in this very question, as to how the Believer can live an overcoming, victorious life, victorious over the world, the flesh, and the Devil. It was to Paul that the meaning of the New Covenant was given, and actually, that Meaning is the Cross.

THE APOSTLE PAUL

Paul could be quoted in many capacities regarding this, but please notice the following:

"And if Christ be in you (He is in you through the Power and Person of the Spirit [Gal. 2:20]), *the body is dead because of sin* (means that the physical body has been rendered helpless because of the Fall; consequently, the Believer trying to overcome by willpower presents a fruitless task)*; but the Spirit is life because of Righteousness* (only the Holy Spirit can make us what we ought to be, which means we cannot do it ourselves; once again, He performs all that He does within the confines of the Finished Work of Christ)*"* (Rom. 8:10).

The phrase, *"The body is dead because of sin,"* proclaims the fact that physically we are unable to do what is demanded of us. It may seem so simple, but the sad fact is, the Believer cannot keep the Commandments of the Lord by his own strength, ability, power, education, intellect, motivation, etc. So, how are the Commandments to be kept?

HOW THE COMMANDMENTS ARE KEPT

Jesus Christ, as our Substitute, Who Paul referred to as the *"Last Adam"* and the *"Second Man,"* has already kept all the Commandments on our behalf. He lived a Perfect Life, never failing even one time in thought or deed. And then, as He kept the Law of God and did so perfectly in His Life and Living, He addressed the broken Law by going to the Cross and giving Himself in Sacrifice. The thing is, He did it all for us. And he did it for us simply because we could not do it ourselves.

That seems to be difficult for most Believers to comprehend, to understand, or to accept. Once we are Saved and Spirit-filled, we tend to think that we can do anything. In fact, one of the most oft quoted Scriptures is, *"I can do all things through Christ Who strengthens me"* (Phil. 4:13).

While, of course, the Word of God is most certainly true, still, we must understand what Paul is talking about as he mentions *"all things."*

It's not *"all things"* that we want, but rather *"all things"* that He wants and desires. He will never strengthen us to disobey Him, to circumvent His Will, or to dishonor His Word, which should be obvious. He will only strengthen us to carry out His Will, whatever that Will might be.

The way and, in fact, the only way that the Commandments of the Lord can be kept, and this goes for all Believers, is for the Believer to understand that within himself, he cannot hope to please the Lord in doing what he must do. We fall short and, in fact, woefully short!

It is the Holy Spirit Alone Who can carry out the Will of God in our lives, developing His Fruit, and helping us to grow in Grace and the Knowledge of the Lord. The Holy Spirit Alone can accomplish this.

And yet, we don't see Him carrying out all of these great things in the hearts and lives of most Believers. Why?

The Holy Spirit doesn't require very much of us. If He did, none of us would make it; however, He does require one thing and, in fact, demands it, and that is that our Faith must be exclusively in Christ and the Cross. We must ever understand that Christ is the Source of all things we receive from the Lord, and the Cross is the Means by which these things are received, with the Holy Spirit superintending it all (Rom. 6:1-14; 8:1-2, 11; I Cor. 1:17-18, 21, 23; 2:2; Gal., Chpt. 5; 6:14; Eph. 2:13-18; Col. 2:14-15). We must ever know and understand that the Cross of Christ plays just as abundantly in our life and living as it did in our initial Salvation. We are to look to Christ and what Christ did at the Cross for everything. The Holy Spirit will not tolerate anything else. In other words, the Cross of Christ must ever be the Object of our Faith.

This being done, and maintained, we might quickly add, the Holy Spirit, Who Works strictly within the parameters of the Finished Work of Christ, will then work mightily on our behalf, doing what only He can do. The Commandments will then be kept and, in fact, without us even thinking about it.

BUILD THE HOUSE OF THE LORD

The command given to Solomon by David

so long, long ago, as it regards building the House of the Lord, is just as apropos presently as it was then. Of course, there is a great difference now, but, in essence, the command is the same.

Then, it was a physical house, as is overly obvious. Now, it is a Spiritual House.

This Spiritual House, referred to as the *"New Covenant,"* concerns our life and living. Concerning this, Paul said:

"Know you not that you are the Temple of God (where the Holy Spirit abides), *and that the Spirit of God dwells in you?* (That makes the Born-Again Believer His permanent Home)" (I Cor. 3:16).

Then, it was a corporate situation, while now, it is a personal affair.

The Spirit of God was to dwell between the Mercy Seat and the Cherubim in the house that Solomon built. Due to the Cross, where the price was paid, the Holy Spirit, just as we have quoted, now resides within our hearts and lives, and does so forever.

But yet, the Lord warns us by saying, *"If any man defile the Temple of God* (our physical bodies must be a living sacrifice, which means that we stay Holy by ever making the Cross the Object of our Faith [Rom. 12:1]), *him shall God destroy* (to fail to function in God's Prescribed Order [the Cross], opens the Believer up to Satan, which will ultimately result in destruction); *for the Temple of God is Holy, which Temple you are.* (We are 'Holy' by virtue of being 'in Christ.' We remain Holy by the Work of the Holy Spirit, Who demands that our Faith ever be in the Cross, which has made all of this possible)" (I Cor. 3:17).

Israel of old ultimately defiled their Temple, and even as the Prophet Ezekiel portrays the fact, the Lord destroyed it. He had no alternative or choice!

The same is said for the Temple of our body, which houses the Spirit of God. Please understand the following:

To guarantee against destruction of this Temple, our Faith must ever be in the Cross of Christ. God will always honor that Faith and, in fact, He will honor no other type of faith. This is the only manner in which our bodies, our life and living, etc., can be kept free, pure, and clean. It is Faith in Christ, ever Faith in Christ, and what Christ has done for us at the Cross.

Some have claimed that we make too much of the Cross!

How can this be? How is it possible for one to make too much of the great Plan of Redemption? Please understand, the Cross is not just one of many steps as it regards Redemption. It is the entirety of the Plan of God. That's the reason that every doctrine must be built squarely upon the Foundation of the Cross of Christ. If it is built otherwise, every single time, it will fall out to false doctrine.

We are to continue to build the House, which means to grow in Grace and the Knowledge of the Lord. Every Believer ought to be closer to the Lord today than they were yesterday. This Spiritual Growth can only be brought about by the Believer ever understanding more and more about the Cross, which the Holy Spirit will bring to fruition in our lives, if we will only walk a path of obedience respecting the great Plan of God.

It is ever the Cross! The Cross! The Cross!

"Give to our God immortal praise!
"Mercy and Truth are all His Ways;
"Wonders of Grace to God belong,
"Repeat His Mercies in your song."

"Give to the Lord of lords renown,
"The King of kings with glory crown;
"His Mercies ever shall endure,
"When lords and kings are known no more."

"He saw the Gentiles dead in sin,
"And felt His Pity work within;
"His Mercies ever shall endure,
"When death and sin shall reign no more."

"He sent His Son with Power to save,
"From guilt, and darkness, and the grave;
"Wonders of Grace to God belong,
"Repeat His Mercies in your song."

CHAPTER 23

(1) "SO WHEN DAVID WAS OLD AND FULL OF DAYS, HE MADE SOLOMON

HIS SON KING OVER ISRAEL.

(2) "AND HE GATHERED TOGETHER ALL THE PRINCES OF ISRAEL, WITH THE PRIESTS AND THE LEVITES.

(3) "NOW THE LEVITES WERE NUMBERED FROM THE AGE OF THIRTY YEARS AND UPWARD: AND THEIR NUMBER BY THEIR POLLS, MAN BY MAN, WAS THIRTY AND EIGHT THOUSAND.

(4) "OF WHICH, TWENTY AND FOUR THOUSAND WERE TO SET FORWARD THE WORK OF THE HOUSE OF THE LORD; AND SIX THOUSAND WERE OFFICERS AND JUDGES:

(5) "MOREOVER FOUR THOUSAND WERE PORTERS; AND FOUR THOUSAND PRAISED THE LORD WITH THE INSTRUMENTS WHICH I MADE, SAID DAVID, TO PRAISE THEREWITH.

(6) "AND DAVID DIVIDED THEM INTO COURSES AMONG THE SONS OF LEVI, NAMELY, GERSHON, KOHATH, AND MERARI.

(7) "OF THE GERSHONITES WERE, LAADAN, AND SHIMEI.

(8) "THE SONS OF LAADAN; THE CHIEF WAS JEHIEL, AND ZETHAM, AND JOEL, THREE.

(9) "THE SONS OF SHIMEI; SHELOMITH, AND HAZIEL, AND HARAN, THREE. THESE WERE THE CHIEF OF THE FATHERS OF LAADAN.

(10) "AND THE SONS OF SHIMEI WERE, JAHATH, ZINA, AND JEUSH, AND BERIAH. THESE FOUR WERE THE SONS OF SHIMEI.

(11) "AND JAHATH WAS THE CHIEF, AND ZIZAH THE SECOND: BUT JEUSH AND BERIAH HAD NOT MANY SONS; THEREFORE THEY WERE IN ONE RECKONING, ACCORDING TO THEIR FATHER'S HOUSE.

(12) "THE SONS OF KOHATH; AMRAM, IZHAR, HEBRON, AND UZZIEL, FOUR.

(13) "THE SONS OF AMRAM; AARON AND MOSES: AND AARON WAS SEPARATED, THAT HE SHOULD SANCTIFY THE MOST HOLY THINGS, HE AND HIS SONS FOR EVER, TO BURN INCENSE BEFORE THE LORD, TO MINISTER UNTO HIM, AND TO BLESS IN HIS NAME FOR EVER.

(14) "NOW CONCERNING MOSES THE MAN OF GOD, HIS SONS WERE NAMED OF THE TRIBE OF LEVI.

(15) "THE SONS OF MOSES WERE, GERSHOM, AND ELIEZER.

(16) "OF THE SONS OF GERSHOM, SHEBUEL WAS THE CHIEF.

(17) "AND THE SONS OF ELIEZER WERE, REHABIAH THE CHIEF. AND ELIEZER HAD NONE OTHER SONS; BUT THE SONS OF REHABIAH WERE VERY MANY.

(18) "OF THE SONS OF IZHAR; SHELOMITH THE CHIEF.

(19) "OF THE SONS OF HEBRON; JERIAH THE FIRST, AMARIAH THE SECOND, JAHAZIEL THE THIRD, AND JEKAMEAM THE FOURTH.

(20) "OF THE SONS OF UZZIEL; MICAH THE FIRST, AND JESIAH THE SECOND.

(21) "THE SONS OF MERARI; MAHLI AND MUSHI. THE SONS OF MAHLI; ELEAZAR, AND KISH.

(22) "AND ELEAZAR DIED, AND HAD NO SONS, BUT DAUGHTERS: AND THEIR BRETHREN THE SONS OF KISH TOOK THEM.

(23) "THE SONS OF MUSHI; MAHLI, AND EDER, AND JEREMOTH, THREE."

The composition is:

1. (Vs. 1) As previously stated, David was a Type of Christ defeating all His enemies, and putting down Satan and all the minions of darkness, which Christ did at the Cross. Solomon is a Type of Christ resting in splendor and glory, victorious and triumphant over all enemies, reigning in the coming Kingdom Age, such as the world has never known.

2. (Vs. 2) All of this is a foretype of the glorious day when the Lord Jesus Christ will reign supreme in Jerusalem, and will, as outlined by Ezekiel, Chapters 40 through 48, gather the worship classes (Priests and Levites) together to establish the worship of God in Israel, and for the entire world, for that matter.

3. (Vs. 3) The age of the Levites, when they could perform service, was changed to 25 years in Numbers 8:24 and to 20 years by David in Verse 27. The reason for the lowering of the age was because of the need for greater numbers to service the Temple in

the great Work for God.

4. As it regards Verses 4 and 5, it is interesting to note that the workers and the worshippers are equal in number; consequently, we have here the tremendous emphasis placed by the Holy Spirit on worship. As well, the worship consisted of singing and music, which constitutes the greatest forms of praise and worship there is.

5. (Vs. 6) All the many thousands of Levites who served in the Work of God came under one of the three designations of Gershonites, Kohathites, and Merarites.

KING SOLOMON

The normal procedure for advancement to the throne in those times was that the eldest son would replace his father. The oldest living son at this time regarding David was Adonijah. To be sure, he very much wanted the throne and tried to take it, even without the permission of his father (I Ki. 1:5-9). It was not God's Will that Adonijah reign as king. Had he been successful in his efforts, in a short time Israel would, more than likely, have been destroyed. If not destroyed, it most definitely would not have functioned in the Will of God.

Israel was raised up for a specific purpose. They were totally unlike any other nation on the face of the Earth. This Nation came from the loins of Abraham and the womb of Sarah. They were the only people on the face of the Earth who knew Jehovah, with every other nation worshipping demon spirits.

God raised them up that His Word would be given to the world, which it ultimately was, and even above that, if possible, they would serve as the womb of the Messiah, the Son of God, the Redeemer of mankind, the Lord Jesus Christ. They also were to evangelize the world, in that, regrettably, failing miserably; however, they will yet fulfill that destiny in the coming Kingdom Age. They ultimately lost their way when they rejected the Lord Jesus Christ as their Messiah and Saviour. The Holy Spirit through the Apostle Paul tells us why, and I quote from THE EXPOSITOR'S STUDY BIBLE:

"For they being ignorant of God's Righteousness (spells the story not only of ancient Israel, but almost the entirety of the world, and for all time; *'God's Righteousness'* is that which is afforded by Christ, and received by exercising Faith in Him and what He did at the Cross, all on our behalf; Israel's ignorance was willful!), *and going about to establish their own righteousness* (the case of anyone who attempts to establish Righteousness by any method other than Faith in Christ and the Cross), *have not submitted themselves unto the Righteousness of God* (God's Righteousness is ensconced in Christ and what He did at the Cross, and is given freely to all who will place their Faith and trust in Him)" (Rom. 10:3).

ESTABLISHING THEIR OWN RIGHTEOUSNESS

This, the establishing of their own righteousness, was not only the cause of the destruction of Israel as a Nation, but, it is the cause of the fall of the church as well.

The only Righteousness that God will recognize is that which is afforded by His Son and our Saviour, the Lord Jesus Christ, through what He did for us at the Cross. Any believing sinner can have this Righteousness instantly, if he will only place his Faith and trust in the Lord Jesus Christ, and what He did for us at the Cross. As we constantly affirm, Christ is the Source of all things from God, and the Cross is the Means by which He gives us these things, all superintended by the Holy Spirit (Rom. 8:1-2, 11).

Is the modern church looking to Christ and the Cross exclusively?

The truth is, the modern church knows precious little about the Cross of Christ as it refers to our Sanctification. That's the reason for the vast popularity of the *"Purpose Driven Life"* scheme, or the *"Government of Twelve"* scheme, or the *"Word of Faith"* scheme, or a hundred and one other stratagems devised by men that we might name.

To be what we ought to be in Christ, the church lurches from one scheme after the other, anything and everything, however, but the Cross.

IS IT WHO HE IS OR WHAT HE DID?

Anyone who would ask that question is, for the most part, attempting to belittle the Message of the Cross.

This question is very easily answered.

Of course, for the Lord to do what He did for us on the Cross, He had to be Who He was, namely the Son of God. But I remind the reader that He was always God. And, if that alone were enough to redeem mankind, then why did He have to come down here and die on a Cross?

He had to come down here and die on a Cross simply because Who He was, as important as that is, was simply not enough. In fact, the very reason that God became man, and we speak of the Incarnation, was to go to the Cross. While everything that Jesus did was of supreme significance, as should be obvious, still, His Purpose for coming to this Earth, the Purpose for His Ministry, all, and in totality were for His destination, the Cross. It was there that He would redeem the fallen sons of Adam's lost race.

So, to properly answer the question, it most definitely was Who He was, but more specifically, what He did, and we speak of the Cross. The Holy Spirit through the Word of God places the emphasis, however, on what He did (Gen. 3:15; 15:6; Isa., Chpt. 53; Jn. 3:16; Rom. 5:1-2; 6:1-14; 8:1-2, 11; Gal., Chpt. 5; 6:14; Eph. 2:13-18; Col. 2:14-15).

THE CHURCH AND THE CROSS

The church lurches, as stated, from one scheme to the other.

Why?

They do so simply because whatever it is they are doing doesn't work. So, when something new comes out, or proposes to be new, it becomes all the rage, at least, for a period of time.

Why is the *"Purpose Driven Life"* scheme so popular? It's popular because whatever the church was doing previously didn't work. Something else will come out shortly to take the place of the *"Purpose Driven Life"* debacle because it doesn't work either. There's only one thing that does work, and that is the Cross of Christ.

GOD'S PRESCRIBED ORDER OF VICTORY

Virtually the entirety of the Bible is given over to telling people how to live for God. Now, that's quite a statement, but it happens to be true. Maybe one hundredth of one percent of the information given relates to the sinner finding Christ, but everything else deals with the Believer successfully living for the Lord.

So, I will try to condense the teaching of some 66 Books, which took some 1,600 years to be written, down to a few paragraphs. But yet, that's not as difficult as it seems, considering that we are now dealing with a finished product.

God has a Prescribed Order of Victory given to us in His Word, in fact, that which was given to the Apostle Paul. This Prescribed Order of Victory is the meaning of the New Covenant, which, in essence, is the meaning of the Cross.

Everything under the Old Covenant strained toward the New Covenant. In fact, the Old Covenant was meant to be temporary. Everything in that Covenant pointed to Christ in one way or the other, whether in His Atoning Work, His Mediatorial Work, or His Intercessory Work. All of that is now a reality because of the Cross. Paul referred to the New Covenant, i.e., *"The Cross,"* as *"The Everlasting Covenant"* (Heb. 13:20). This means that this New Covenant will never have to be amended or replaced. It is forever because it is all in Christ.

God's Prescribed Order of Victory, as given to the Apostle Paul, is found in all of his writings, with all the balance of the Word of God, in one form or the other, pointing to that Finished Work.

• It is all wrapped up in Jesus Christ. In fact, the entirety of the Story of the Bible is the Lord Jesus Christ and Him Crucified (Jn. 1:1-2).

• The Work that Jesus Christ performed at the Cross, which was to atone for all sin, past, present, and future, at least for all who will believe, presents the culminating effect of the great Plan of God, in fact, that which was perfected from before the foundation of the world (I Pet. 1:18-20).

• The believing sinner must then exercise Faith in Christ and what Christ did for us at the Cross in order to be Saved. That's the reason the little simple phrase, *"Jesus died for me,"* is perhaps the most beautiful statement ever made. As it regards Faith, the believing sinner, after coming to Christ, must maintain his Faith in Christ and the Cross, always understanding that it is through the Cross that all Victory was won. While most of the church has at least a modicum of understanding as it regards the Cross of Christ respecting Salvation, it has almost no understanding at all as it regards the Cross and our Sanctification, in other words, how we live for God. But that is God's Prescribed Order of Victory, and we speak of the Cross and our Faith in that Finished Work.

• We must ever understand that, as Believers, everything we need has to be accomplished by the Holy Spirit. Within ourselves, no matter our zeal, we cannot make ourselves holy or righteous. We cannot grow in Grace and the Knowledge of the Lord. We cannot develop the Fruit of the Spirit. All of this is the Work of the Holy Spirit.

His Work is carried out in our hearts and lives, solely and completely, according to our Faith in the Cross of Christ. He works exclusively within the parameters of the Finished Work of Christ, and will not work outside of those parameters. In fact, the Cross of Christ is what gave and gives the Holy Spirit the legal right to do all that He does. That's the reason it is referred to as a *"Law."* It is *"the Law of the Spirit of Life in Christ Jesus, which has made us free from the Law of Sin and Death"* (Rom. 8:2). The Holy Spirit doesn't demand much of us, but He does demand one thing, and that is that the Cross of Christ ever be the Object of our Faith. That being done, He will begin His Work within our lives, bringing us to the place where we should be, which He Alone can do (I Cor. 1:17-18, 23; 2:2).

That which I have given above, in brief, is God's Prescribed Order of Victory. As stated, He has no other means or method simply because nothing else is needed. But, when we try to insert something else, no matter how religious it might be, such presents the efforts of man to establish his own righteousness, which God can never accept. It destroyed Israel of old and, in fact, it is destroying the modern church as well. Concerning this, Paul continued to say:

"Well; because of unbelief they (Israel) *were broken off* (unbelief respecting Christ and the Cross), *and you stand by Faith* (proclaims that the Church was brought in because of Faith and not merit, and stands in its present position by Faith and not merit). *Be not highminded, but fear* (the reason is given in the next Verse)*:*

"For if God spared not the natural branches (Israel), *take heed lest He also spare not you* (again refers to the Church, as is obvious).

"Behold therefore the Goodness and Severity of God (don't mistake the Goodness of God for license)*: on them which fell, severity* (speaks of Judgment which came on Israel, God's chosen People)*; but toward you, goodness, if you continue in His Goodness* (proclaims the condition; the continuing of that *'Goodness'* pertains to continued Faith in Christ and the Cross)*: otherwise you also shall be cut off* (is the modern church on the edge of that even now? Rev. 3:15-22 tells us this is the case!)*"* (Rom. 11:20-22).

But, as it regards the Passages of our study, we are now looking at the glory days of Israel and thankful that David could not see what would happen in the future. But yet, even though there was a dark future ahead, still, the Scripture bears out the fact that Israel will ultimately come home. And then they will be what God originally intended. It will be during the coming Kingdom Age, which will immediately follow the Second Coming.

THE WILL OF GOD

It was the Will of God for Solomon to be king, and not Adonijah, despite the fact that in normal circumstances the latter had first claim on the throne.

The truth is, most in the modern church, had they been placed in Israel of that time, would have voted for Adonijah instead of Solomon.

How do I know that?

Solomon was the son of David and Bathsheba; consequently, due to that fact, most modern day Christians placed in that time frame of so long ago would not have even remotely considered accepting Solomon as the great king of Israel. But God did! In the first place, the Lord didn't hold Solomon accountable for what David and his mother had done. He had no part in that, which should be overly obvious. As well, he had a heart toward God, which Adonijah had the very opposite. The problem with the church, which, evidently, has always been a problem, is that it looks on the outward instead of the inward. Consequently, all too often, it chooses Adonijah and not Solomon. The end results will always be obvious!

LABOR AND LOVE

If it is to be noticed, while there were 4,000 Levites who served as porters, as well, there were 4,000 who *"praised the Lord with the instruments which David had made."*

We learn here the value of praise. As well, we learn the value of praise as gendered by music and singing. In fact, considering that the Psalms constitute the longest Book in the Bible, we learn the great significance that the Holy Spirit places on music and singing as it regards praising the Lord. This is at least one of the reasons and, in reality, the primary reason, that Satan has fought so hard to pervert music and singing as it regards that which is anointed by the Holy Spirit. Regrettably, he has been very successful in many quarters.

As well, we must remember that it is the Holy Spirit Who gave to David the direction of the care for the Temple and all that pertained to it.

WORK FOR THE LORD AND PRAISE TO THE LORD

All of these Passages tell us just how important that the Work of God actually is. It is so important, in fact, that the Lord left nothing to chance, giving implicit instructions to David as to how every facet of this Work be carried forth in the Temple. Nothing was left to chance, nothing was left to man's ideas; all were given directly by the Holy Spirit.

At the same time, we learn, as previously stated from Verse 5, that the Lord places our praise and worship to Him on the same par as He does our work for Him. In fact, if the proper praise and worship to Him are not tendered, and done so on a constant basis, very little true work for the Lord will be carried out. While there might be much religious activity, the sad truth will be that it ceases to be a work for God and becomes a work of man.

There are two problems with the modern church:

1. All the religious activity is by and large man-made and man-directed. In other words, the Holy Spirit did not give birth to what is happening.

How do I know that?

I know it because the Cross of Christ has been either repudiated or totally ignored in most modern religious circles. It becomes overly obvious, as it regards the Temple, just as with the Tabernacle, that the Sacrifice was at the very heart of the judicial system, and rightly so. It pictured and proclaimed the coming Redeemer Who would give Himself on the Cross in order that man might be redeemed.

Is the Cross at the center of what is presently being done in the modern church?

I think not!

Man's schemes, whatever they might be, and they change almost daily, are at the center, and not the Cross; consequently, what is being done is not of the Lord.

2. There is very little true Praise and Worship going up to the Lord at this present time. Once again, let me direct attention to the Cross.

All praise and worship must have as its foundation the Cross of Christ. If that is not the case, then it's praise and worship that God will not honor. And sadly, the modern church does not have the Cross of Christ as its foundation as it regards Praise and Worship, or anything else for that matter.

In the Tabernacle of old, which would be carried forth in the Temple when it would be built, the Priests had to go in at least twice a day and trim the wicks on the Golden Lampstand and offer up Incense on the Golden Altar. However, to offer up Incense, they had to get coals of fire from the Brazen Altar, which Altar was a Type of the Cross. Those coals of fire could not come from any other ignition, even under pain of death. They had to come from the Brazen Altar, i.e., the Cross.

The coals of fire were placed on the Golden Altar, incense was poured over those coals, and the aroma filled the Holy Place.

The incense burned twice a day on the Golden Altar was a Type of the Intercession of Christ, all on our behalf. As well, the Intercession opened the door for us to come into the very Presence of the Throne of God and there make our case, whatever it might be. It includes prayer, petition, praise, and worship, all made possible by the Intercession of Christ, and all made possible by the Cross.

So, we have *"work"* which is formulated by man and not God and, as well, *"praise"* that is orchestrated by man and not God, all because it does not center up in the Cross.

(24) "THESE WERE THE SONS OF LEVI AFTER THE HOUSE OF THEIR FATHERS; EVEN THE CHIEF OF THE FATHERS, AS THEY WERE COUNTED BY NUMBER OF NAMES BY THEIR POLLS, WHO DID THE WORK FOR THE SERVICE OF THE HOUSE OF THE LORD, FROM THE AGE OF TWENTY YEARS AND UPWARD.

(25) "FOR DAVID SAID, THE LORD GOD OF ISRAEL HAS GIVEN REST UNTO HIS PEOPLE, THAT THEY MAY DWELL IN JERUSALEM FOR EVER:

(26) "AND ALSO UNTO THE LEVITES; THEY SHALL NO MORE CARRY THE TABERNACLE, NOR ANY VESSELS OF IT FOR THE SERVICE THEREOF.

(27) "FOR BY THE LAST WORDS OF DAVID THE LEVITES WERE NUMBERED FROM TWENTY YEARS OLD AND ABOVE:

(28) "BECAUSE THEIR OFFICE WAS TO WAIT ON THE SONS OF AARON FOR THE SERVICE OF THE HOUSE OF THE LORD, IN THE COURTS, AND IN THE CHAMBERS, AND IN THE PURIFYING OF ALL HOLY THINGS, AND THE WORK OF THE SERVICE OF THE HOUSE OF GOD;

(29) "BOTH FOR THE SHEWBREAD, AND FOR THE FINE FLOUR FOR MEAT OFFERING, AND FOR THE UNLEAVENED CAKES, AND FOR THAT WHICH IS BAKED IN THE PAN, AND FOR THAT WHICH IS FRIED, AND FOR ALL MANNER OF MEASURE AND SIZE;

(30) "AND TO STAND EVERY MORNING TO THANK AND PRAISE THE LORD, AND LIKEWISE AT EVENING;

(31) "AND TO OFFER ALL BURNT SACRIFICES UNTO THE LORD IN THE SABBATHS, IN THE NEW MOONS, AND ON THE SET FEASTS, BY NUMBER, ACCORDING TO THE ORDER COMMANDED UNTO THEM, CONTINUALLY BEFORE THE LORD:

(32) "AND THAT THEY SHOULD KEEP THE CHARGE OF THE TABERNACLE OF THE CONGREGATION, AND THE CHARGE OF THE HOLY PLACE, AND THE CHARGE OF THE SONS OF AARON THEIR BRETHREN, IN THE SERVICE OF THE HOUSE OF THE LORD."

The construction is:

1. Verse 24 and Verse 27 proclaim the lowering of the age for the Priests and the Levites to 20 years old and upward.

2. (Vs. 25) Regrettably, the children of Israel did not dwell in Jerusalem forever. Because of sin, they were driven from Jerusalem and, in fact, all the Holy Land; but in the future, they will be restored, and then will fulfill God's original Purpose (Isa. 11:1-12).

3. Verse 29 proclaims work that had to go on constantly, meaning all these things were a constant necessity, and also meaning that the work of the Priests and Levites never ended. It did end when Jesus went to the Cross, thereby, fulfilling all rudiments of the Law, plus its ceremonies and rituals.

4. According to Verse 30, it seems that the choir met every morning at 9 a.m., and every evening at 3 p.m., at the time of the morning and evening sacrifices, which was done every day.

5. In Verse 32 the Priests are reminded of their representative character and position, and of the solemn responsibility which rested on them.

THE WORK OF THE PRIESTS

Their work, as should be obvious, never ended. Twenty-four hours a day, seven days a week, these functions were carried forth, centering up on the Burnt Sacrifices, which typified the Cross. Even on the Sabbath, which was supposed to be a day of rest, the fact is, the sacrifices were not only to be carried forth on that day but actually doubled. In other words, whereas one lamb was offered each morning and each afternoon on the other days, that number was doubled on the Sabbath.

This was done so because it typified the *"rest"* which Christ would bring, of which the Sabbath was a type, all made possible by the Cross. In other words, every one of these rituals, whether the *"Shewbread,"* the *"Meat Offering,"* the *"Unleavened Cakes,"* the *"Burnt Sacrifices,"* the *"New Moons,"* or the *"set feasts,"* etc., all, and without exception, pointed to Christ in His Atoning Work, Mediatorial Work, or Intercessory Work. Consequently, when Christ came and then went to the Cross, all of the Mosaic Law, and without exception, was fulfilled. So, every duty, every work, all of the courses, all of the thousands of Priests who were necessary, all of the Levites, thousands of them that carried forth the duties of the Temple proper, all and without exception were fulfilled in Christ, making them no more necessary whatsoever.

THE FINISHED WORK OF CHRIST

Perhaps one of the greatest faults of all Believers, myself included, is that we do not properly understand all that Christ did for us at the Cross. We limit His Great Work there, and on the other end of the spectrum, it is impossible to overstate the case as it regards all that He did. That's the reason that Paul referred to it as *"The Everlasting Covenant"* (Heb. 13:20). It is all in Christ, so it will never have to be amended, deleted, or changed. This Covenant is perfect!

One of the reasons, I believe, that the church little understands the great price paid at Calvary is because we keep ignoring it, or else we try to add to what has already been done, as if what He did were insufficient.

His Work on the Cross of Calvary satisfied the Law of Moses in every respect. It also defeated every demon spirit, even Satan himself (Col. 2:14-15). What He did at the Cross makes it possible for Believers to live a Holy life and to have Victory over the world, the flesh and the Devil. In fact, the Cross is the only Means by which these things are done. And that's where the great problem comes in.

The church, at least as a whole, doesn't seem to understand this and rather tries to insert its own schemes and machinations in order to overcome sin. Such is not to be.

GOD'S PRESCRIBED ORDER OF VICTORY

The Believer is to understand that everything we receive from God the Father comes to us through His Son and our Saviour, the Lord Jesus Christ. In other words, Christ is the Source. But, we must also understand that everything we receive from Him comes to us by the Means of the Cross of Christ. It is the Cross, which has made everything possible. That's the reason the Cross of Christ must ever be the Object of our Faith.

But that is, one might say, only half the issue. Where does the Holy Spirit come in regarding all of this?

THE HOLY SPIRIT AND THE CROSS OF CHRIST

Everything that we as Believers need to have done within our hearts and lives is done solely and completely by the Holy Spirit. In fact, whatever it is that's needed, victory over sin, Spiritual Growth, Fruit of the Spirit, etc., all, and without exception, are accomplished by the Holy Spirit. We within ourselves cannot bring about anything. Paul addressed this by saying:

"And if Christ be in you (He is in you through the Power and Person of the Spirit [Gal. 2:20]), *the body is dead because of sin* (means that the physical body has been rendered helpless because of the Fall; consequently, the Believer trying to overcome by willpower presents a fruitless task); *but the Spirit is life because of Righteousness* (only the Holy Spirit can make us what we ought to be, which means we cannot do it ourselves; once again, He performs all that He does within the confines of the Finished Work of Christ)" (Rom. 8:10).

Even though the Believer is Saved and Spirit-filled, he cannot live for God by the means of the flesh, due to the fact that the *"body is dead because of sin."* This refers to what happened at the Fall, which made the physical body unable to be what God originally intended. This pertains to the physical body and even the mental ability of the Believer. Once again, whatever needs to be done within our lives, can only be done by the Power of the Holy Spirit.

So, how does He do what He does? Or, what can we do to insure that He carries out His Great Work within our lives?

The Holy Spirit functions entirely within the parameters of the Finished Work of Christ. Paul also said:

"For the Law of the Spirit of Life in Christ Jesus has made me free from the Law of Sin and Death" (Rom. 8:2).

What we are discussing here is actually a *"Law,"* which was devised by the Godhead even from before the foundation of the world (I Pet. 1:18-20). It is the Cross of Christ which has given the Holy Spirit the legal right to do all that He does.

Understanding that, our Faith is to be placed exclusively in Christ and the Cross. As previously stated, the Holy Spirit doesn't demand much of us, but He does demand that. Our Faith must ever be in Christ and what Christ did for us at the Cross (Lk. 9:23; 14:27; Rom. 6:1-14; 8:1-2, 11; I Cor. 1:17-18, 21, 23; 2:2; Gal., Chpt. 5; 6:14; Eph. 2:13-18; Col. 2:14-15).

Our Faith placed in the Cross of Christ, and the Cross of Christ exclusively, gives the Holy Spirit the latitude to function and work within our lives, to bring about His Work, which He has been sent to do, and which He Alone can do.

In a nutshell, that is God's Prescribed Order of Victory.

If we do not follow that course, placing our Faith exclusively in Christ and the Cross, which gives the Holy Spirit latitude to Work, then, in some way, the sin nature is going to rule us, which will make life miserable. Regrettably, that's the state of most of the modern church, and it's simply because they do not understand the Cross of Christ.

"The strife is over, the battle is done;
"The victory of life is won;
"The song of triumph has begun.
"Hallelujah!"

"The powers of death have done their
  worst,
"But Christ their legions has dispersed;
"Let shouts of holy joy outburst.
"Hallelujah!"

"The three sad days have quickly sped;

NOTES

"He rises glorious from the dead:
"All glory to our risen Head!
"Hallelujah!"

"Lord, by the stripes which wounded
  Thee,
"From death's dread sting Your Servants free,
"That we may live and sing to Thee.
"Hallelujah!"

CHAPTER 24

(1) "NOW THESE ARE THE DIVISIONS OF THE SONS OF AARON. THE SONS OF AARON; NADAB, AND ABIHU, ELEAZAR, AND ITHAMAR.

(2) "BUT NADAB AND ABIHU DIED BEFORE THEIR FATHER, AND HAD NO CHILDREN: THEREFORE ELEAZAR AND ITHAMAR EXECUTED THE PRIEST'S OFFICE.

(3) "AND DAVID DISTRIBUTED THEM, BOTH ZADOK OF THE SONS OF ELEAZAR, AND AHIMELECH OF THE SONS OF ITHAMAR, ACCORDING TO THEIR OFFICES IN THEIR SERVICE.

(4) "AND THERE WERE MORE CHIEF MEN FOUND OF THE SONS OF ELEAZAR THAN OF THE SONS OF ITHAMAR; AND THUS WERE THEY DIVIDED. AMONG THE SONS OF ELEAZAR THERE WERE SIXTEEN CHIEF MEN OF THE HOUSE OF THEIR FATHERS, AND EIGHT AMONG THE SONS OF ITHAMAR ACCORDING TO THE HOUSE OF THEIR FATHERS.

(5) "THUS WERE THEY DIVIDED BY LOT, ONE SORT WITH ANOTHER; FOR THE GOVERNORS OF THE SANCTUARY, AND GOVERNORS OF THE HOUSE OF GOD, WERE OF THE SONS OF ELEAZAR, AND OF THE SONS OF ITHAMAR.

(6) "AND SHEMAIAH THE SON OF NETHANEEL THE SCRIBE, ONE OF THE LEVITES, WROTE THEM BEFORE THE KING, AND THE PRINCES, AND ZADOK THE PRIEST, AND AHIMELECH THE SON OF ABIATHAR, AND BEFORE THE CHIEF OF THE FATHERS OF THE PRIESTS AND LEVITES: ONE PRINCIPAL HOUSEHOLD

BEING TAKEN FOR ELEAZAR, AND ONE TAKEN FOR ITHAMAR.

(7) "NOW THE FIRST LOT CAME FORTH TO JEHOIARIB, THE SECOND TO JEDAIAH,

(8) "THE THIRD TO HARIM, THE FOURTH TO SEORIM,

(9) "THE FIFTH TO MALCHIJAH, THE SIXTH OF MIJAMIN,

(10) "THE SEVENTH TO HAKKOZ, THE EIGHTH TO ABIJAH,

(11) "THE NINTH TO JESHUAH, THE TENTH TO SHECANIAH,

(12) "THE ELEVENTH TO ELIASHIB, THE TWELFTH TO JAKIM,

(13) "THE THIRTEENTH TO HUPPAH, THE FOURTEENTH TO JESHEBEAB,

(14) "THE FIFTEENTH TO BILGAH, THE SIXTEENTH TO IMMER,

(15) "THE SEVENTEENTH TO HEZIR, THE EIGHTEENTH TO APHSES,

(16) "THE NINETEENTH TO PETHAHIAH, THE TWENTIETH TO JEHEZEKEL,

(17) "THE ONE AND TWENTIETH TO JACHIN, THE TWO AND TWENTIETH TO GAMUL,

(18) "THE THREE AND TWENTIETH TO DELAIAH, THE FOUR AND TWENTIETH TO MAAZIAH.

(19) "THESE WERE THE ORDERINGS OF THEM IN THEIR SERVICE TO COME INTO THE HOUSE OF THE LORD, ACCORDING TO THEIR MANNER, UNDER AARON THEIR FATHER, AS THE LORD GOD OF ISRAEL HAD COMMANDED HIM."

The exegesis is:

1. The First Verse proclaims the four sons of Aaron. In fact, all the High Priests of Israel came from the lineage of Eleazar and Ithamar, or were supposed to. Under the Romans, the office became political, which means the lineage was corrupted.

2. (Vs. 2) Nadab and Abihu were stricken dead by the Lord for offering *"strange fire"* (Lev. 10:1-2). They died before they had any children.

3. (Vs. 2) From the two remaining sons, as stated, the order of High Priests would derive their office.

4. (Vs. 4) Eleazar had sixteen sons, and Ithamar had eight sons. From this total of 24 came the names that would be applied to the 24 courses or orders.

5. (Vs. 7) The first order of Priests, consisting actually of many Priests, would have been the *"Jehoiarib order or division."* The second, third, and so forth, would have been after their own respective names given in these Passages. The 24 chief men, who went by their respective names given, were governors of the House of the Lord in their own turn, one week at a time. Each Priest would serve from Sabbath to Sabbath. Zechariah (Lk. 1:5), the father of John the Baptist, belonged to the 8th course, which is the course of Abijah (Vs. 10). It is interesting to learn from Luke 1:5 how the Divine Son of David, through all the changes of Israel's history, watched over and maintained these courses of the Priests.

THE ORDER OF EVENTS

Verse 1 says, *"Now these are the divisions of the sons of Aaron."* The Temple was not yet built and, in fact, would not be built until constructed by Solomon; however, every part about it was already in David's heart, designed there by the Holy Spirit. All of its activities concerning the Levites and the Priests were given to David by the Holy Spirit, even down to the most minute detail. Nothing was left to chance or to guess.

The *"divisions"* or *"orders"* were designed by the Holy Spirit concerning the services of the Priests. Aaron, Moses' brother, was the very first High Priest. He had four sons, *"Nadab, Abihu, Eleazar, and Ithamar."*

The Second Verse says, *"But Nadab and Abihu died before their father, and had no children."* Actually, they were stricken dead by God with fire from the Holy of Holies because of offering *"strange fire"* before the Lord (Lev., Chpt. 10). Therefore, all of the order of High Priests would derive from the two remaining sons, as stated, *"Eleazar and Ithamar."*

The reason they were so very important is because they were Types of Christ.

If every Christian were as skillful in the Word of Righteousness as they should be, they would never find these lists of names dull, but, on the contrary, full of Spiritual Wealth. The Holy Spirit wrote these lists and, in so doing, designed the profit of God's People.

The Fifth Verse says, *"Thus were they divided by lot."* This refers to the Urim and Thummim. Absolutely nothing about the Temple, its furnishings, fixtures, design, the order of the Priests, or the Levites, was left to chance. Everything was ordered, guided, and directed by the Holy Spirit.

It might also be quickly added that whenever the Temple was to be built by Solomon, every single thing concerning its order, its worship, and its purpose would have been previously prepared.

WHAT WAS THE SIN OF NADAB AND ABIHU?

Nadab and Abihu's sin was ignoring the Cross. They proposed to enter into the Presence of God by means other than the Cross. Concerning this, the Scripture proclaims the following:

"And Nadab and Abihu, the sons of Aaron (they were Priests), *took either of them, his censer, and put fire therein, and put incense thereon, and offered strange fire before the LORD, which He commanded them not.* (This was 'fire' which came from something other than the Brazen Altar. As such, it was not a type of Christ and Him Crucified and, therefore, could not be recognized by God. It was the sin of Cain.)

"They attempted to put the *'strange fire'* on the Altar of Incense, situated immediately in front of the Veil. All false doctrine falls into this same category and, thereby, presents a fearful spectacle.)

"And there went out fire from the LORD (from the Ark of the Covenant, which passed through the Veil without burning it), *and devoured them, and they died before the LORD.* (A short time earlier, fire had come out from this same place and consumed the sacrifice on the Altar [Lev. 9:24]. Inasmuch as the Cross of Christ was ignored here, that same fire came upon the sinner instead of the sacrifice)" (Lev. 10:1-2).

In fact, the offering up of *"strange fire"* is the sin of the modern church.

THE DISPENSATION OF GRACE

Many assume, wrongfully, I might quickly add, that because this is the Dispensation of Grace, the Judgment of God is withheld, with individuals suffering no ill effects.

While this is most definitely the Dispensation of Grace, it doesn't mean that God looks at sin any differently than He did 3,000 years ago, or anytime, for that matter.

As it regards this Dispensation of Grace, all made possible by the Cross, the Scripture also says: *"And the times of this ignorance God winked at* (does not reflect that such ignorance was Salvation, for it was not! before the Cross, there was very little Light in the world, so God withheld Judgment); *but now commands all men everywhere to repent* (but since the Cross, the 'Way' is open to all; it's up to us Believers to make that 'Way' known to all men)" (Acts 17:30).

It, no doubt, can be said that presently the Judgment of God is poured out on this world to a greater degree than ever before. When Light is given, even as an abundance of Light is given as it regards the Cross, and that Light is rejected, then there remains nothing but the Judgment of God. I speak of inclement weather; I speak of diseases run rampant; and, I speak of wars and rumors of wars.

These things are prompted by two particulars:

1. The situation in which the world now finds itself due to the Fall, which in reality is the cause of most of these things.

2. And then, the Judgment of God being poured out at times because of sin.

A reporter asked me once if AIDS were the result of the Judgment of God?

The answer to that question is twofold, just as given. Due to the Fall, which propelled men toward constant sin, such becomes the seedbed of such-like diseases. And then again, the Lord very well could have brought on AIDS as a result of sin.

The Cross of Christ is the only thing standing between man and the Judgment of God. We must never forget that. Nadab and Abihu did forget it and suffered disastrous consequences. Please do not make the mistake of thinking that God is any different now than He was then. He feels the same presently over sin as He did then! His Judgment is just as sure now as it was then, and because of the Cross, even more so. In other words, the world today should know better, considering that some 2,000 years of Gospel have gone out.

(20) "AND THE REST OF THE SONS OF LEVI WERE THESE: OF THE SONS OF AMRAM; SHUBAEL: OF THE SONS OF SHUBAEL; JEHDEIAH.

(21) "CONCERNING REHABIAH: OF THE SONS OF REHABIAH, THE FIRST WAS ISSHIAH.

(22) "OF THE IZHARITES; SHELOMOTH: OF THE SONS OF SHELOMOTH; JAHATH.

(23) "AND THE SONS OF HEBRON; JERIAH THE FIRST, AMARIAH THE SECOND, JAHAZIEL THE THIRD, JEKAMEAM THE FOURTH.

(24) "OF THE SONS OF UZZIEL; MICHAH: OF THE SONS OF MICHAH; SHAMIR.

(25) "THE BROTHER OF MICHAH WAS ISSHIAH: OF THE SONS OF ISSHIAH; ZECHARIAH.

(26) "THE SONS OF MERARI WERE MAHLI AND MUSHI: THE SONS OF JAAZIAH; BENO.

(27) "THE SONS OF MERARI BY JAAZIAH; BENO, AND SHOHAM, AND ZACCUR, AND IBRI.

(28) "OF MAHLI CAME ELEAZAR, WHO HAD NO SONS.

(29) "CONCERNING KISH: THE SON OF KISH WAS JERAHMEEL.

(30) "THE SONS ALSO OF MUSHI; MAHLI, AND EDER, AND JERIMOTH. THESE WERE THE SONS OF THE LEVITES AFTER THE HOUSE OF THEIR FATHERS.

(31) "THESE LIKEWISE CAST LOTS OVER AGAINST THEIR BRETHREN THE SONS OF AARON IN THE PRESENCE OF DAVID THE KING, AND ZADOK, AND AHIMELECH, AND THE CHIEF OF THE FATHERS OF THE PRIESTS AND LEVITES, EVEN THE PRINCIPAL FATHERS OVER AGAINST THEIR YOUNGER BRETHREN."

The synopsis is:

1. (Vs. 31) The words *"cast lots"* refer to the Urim and the Thummim. The word *"Urim"* means *"lights,"* while the word *"Thummim"* means *"perfection."* As to exactly what these items were, we aren't told. They were kept in a pouch underneath the breastplate worn by the High Priest. Some think they were two stones with the word *"yes"* on one and the word *"no"* on the other. At any rate, it was of the Holy Spirit.

2. (Vs. 31) As stated, absolutely nothing about the Temple, its furnishings, fixtures, design, the order of the Priests, as well as the Levites, was left to chance. Everything was ordered, guided, and directed by the Holy Spirit.

3. Verses 20 through 31 give the order or courses of the Levites. They were 24 courses, as well. Whereas the Priests had to do with the sacrifices (the Priests were also Levites), the balance of the Levites had to do with the worship, which concerned music and singing, along with maintenance of the Temple.

THE LIST OF NAMES

Regrettably, most Believers find these lists of names dull. Actually, most wonder as to why they are even in the Bible.

The truth is, the listing of these names is full of moral wealth. The Holy Spirit, we must remember, wrote these lists, and in doing so, designed the profit of God's People.

So, how are they profitable to us in our everyday walk before God presently?

• The Holy Spirit chose these individuals, and that mere fact alone is of tremendous note.

• As to how they acquitted themselves is something else all together. The truth is, the Holy Spirit chooses many who do not give very good account of themselves. The fault is definitely not that of the Lord but that of the individual.

• All of this shows us that the Lord keeps a record of everything that is done, and who does it.

• Somewhere in the Portals of Glory at this moment, your name, if you are a Believer, is on the Roll. As well, your faithfulness, or the lack thereof, is duly noted.

• Our Lord, as evidenced by these names, is a personal Lord. In other words, He deals with us individually.

• The Holy Spirit designed the task and the person to accomplish the task, even to the place of listing the name. He is doing no less presently.

"Jesus, wondrous Saviour! Christ, of kings the King!
"Angels fall before Thee prostrate, worshipping;
"Fairest they confess Thee in the Heaven above.
"We would sing Thee fairest here in hymns of love."

"All Earth's flowing pleasures were a wintry sea,
"Heaven itself without Thee dark as night would be.
"Lamb of God! Thy Glory is the Light above.
"Lamb of God! Thy Glory is the Life of love."

"Life is death, if severed from Your throbbing Heart.
"Death with life abundant at Your Touch would start.
"Worlds and men and Angels all consist in Thee:
"Yet You came to us in humility."

"Jesus! All perfections rise and end in Thee;
"Brightness of God's Glory Thou eternally.
"Favored beyond measure they Your Face who see;
"May we, gracious Saviour, share this ecstasy."

CHAPTER 25

(1) "MOREOVER DAVID AND THE CAPTAINS OF THE HOST SEPARATED TO THE SERVICE OF THE SONS OF ASAPH, AND OF HEMAN, AND OF JEDUTHUN, WHO SHOULD PROPHESY WITH HARPS, WITH PSALTERIES, AND WITH CYMBALS: AND THE NUMBER OF THE WORKMEN ACCORDING TO THEIR SERVICE WAS:

(2) "OF THE SONS OF ASAPH; ZACCUR, AND JOSEPH, AND NETHANIAH, AND ASARELAH, THE SONS OF ASAPH UNDER THE HANDS OF ASAPH, WHICH PROPHESIED ACCORDING TO THE ORDER OF THE KING.

(3) "OF JEDUTHUN: THE SONS OF JEDUTHUN; GEDALIAH, AND ZERI, AND JESHAIAH, HASHABIAH, AND MATTITHIAH, SIX, UNDER THE HANDS OF THEIR FATHER JEDUTHUN, WHO PROPHESIED WITH A HARP, TO GIVE THANKS AND TO PRAISE THE LORD.

(4) "OF HEMAN: THE SONS OF HEMAN; BUKKIAH, MATTANIAH, UZZIEL, SHEBUEL, AND JERIMOTH, HANANIAH, HANANI, ELIATHAH, GIDDALTI, AND ROMAMTI-EZER, JOSHBEKASHAH, MALLOTHI, HOTHIR, AND MAHAZIOTH:

(5) "ALL THESE WERE THE SONS OF HEMAN THE KING'S SEER IN THE WORDS OF GOD, TO LIFT UP THE HORN. AND GOD GAVE TO HEMAN FOURTEEN SONS AND THREE DAUGHTERS.

(6) "ALL THESE WERE UNDER THE HANDS OF THEIR FATHER FOR SONG IN THE HOUSE OF THE LORD, WITH CYMBALS, PSALTERIES, AND HARPS, FOR THE SERVICE OF THE HOUSE OF GOD, ACCORDING TO THE KING'S ORDER TO ASAPH, JEDUTHUN, AND HEMAN.

(7) "SO THE NUMBER OF THEM, WITH THEIR BRETHREN WHO WERE INSTRUCTED IN THE SONGS OF THE LORD, EVEN ALL WHO WERE CUNNING, WAS TWO HUNDRED FOURSCORE AND EIGHT.

(8) "AND THEY CAST LOTS, WARD AGAINST WARD, AS WELL THE SMALL AS THE GREAT, THE TEACHER AS THE SCHOLAR."

The composition is:

1. (Vs. 1) We are now told of the division of the 4,000 singers into 24 courses or weekly periods.

2. (Vs. 1) There was no such provision for song and worship in the Tabernacle in the wilderness, as in the Temple of Solomon. This was because the former spoke of a provided Redemption, the latter of an accomplished Salvation.

3. (Vs. 1) Musical instrumentation, according to this Word, which accompanies Spirit-led singing is constituted as *"prophecy"* (I Cor. 14:3).

4. (Vs. 6) The overseership of this service of worship, as it regards music and singing, seems to be divided among the sons of Asaph, Jeduthun, and Heman.

5. These 4,000 singers would have been divided into 24 choirs, with a little bit over 150 members to the choir, except, no doubt, for special occasions, when several of the choirs, or even all of the singers, would have joined together. Also, according to Verse 7, these choirs were helped by the 288 skilled musicians and skilled singers.

MUSIC, SINGING, WORSHIP, AND PROPHECY

The reader should well note the volume of praise that was to fill the Temple area and all of Jerusalem. It was symbolic of that which will fill not only the Temple area and Jerusalem during the Kingdom Age, but the entirety of the Earth. The great Prophet Isaiah said: *"For the Earth shall be full of the Knowledge of the LORD, as the waters cover the sea"* (Isa. 11:9). As well, in our present-day churches, volumes of praise should fill the sanctuary constantly. And, inasmuch as we are now the Temple of the Holy Spirit (I Cor. 3:16), a volume of praise to the Lord should fill our hearts constantly. Surely, by now the Bible student has learned the premium that God places on praise. Jesus came from the Tribe of Judah, which means *"praise."*

THE OVERSEERSHIP

The overseership of this Service seemed to be divided under the following:
- The sons of Asaph (Vs. 2).
- The sons of Jeduthun (Vs. 3).
- The sons of Heman (Vss. 4-7).

They were given charge of the great choirs and the musicians with a Spiritual term being attached to such, *"Who would prophesy with harps, with psalteries, and with cymbals."* The *"songs of the LORD"* (Vs. 7) were basically the same as that which would be given in I Corinthians 14:3, which speak to men to edification, to exhortation, and comfort. This was accomplished by the singing and the music and is, as well, accomplished thusly today.

In other words, when anyone sings *"the songs of the LORD,"* which will always glorify God, they are, in effect, *"prophesying."* We would do well to note that the Holy Spirit is the One Who used the word *"prophesy."* For such to be, the *"flesh"* must have no place, only the *"Spirit."* Sadly, too much of that which passes for Christian music emphasizes the *"flesh"* instead of the *"Spirit."*

MUSIC HAS THREE CHARACTERISTICS

1. Melody;
2. Harmony; and,
3. Rhythm.

All three coordinate with each other to produce the worship that the Holy Spirit intends. So-called Contemporary Christian music destroys the harmony and the melody; consequently, it neither produces nor elicits praise and worship. Efforts to worship thusly are fruitless.

Likewise, rhythm is legitimate and Scriptural providing measures of accompaniment according to the cymbal, etc.— unless it is rhythm for the sake of rhythm, thereby, catering solely to the *"flesh"*. Then it becomes spiritually illegitimate.

As we read this particular Chapter, we are actually reading the formation of music given by the Holy Spirit to David, which formed the foundation of all Spiritual Music from then until now. To show how important music and singing are as it regards worship, the Psalms, which are songs (150), constitute the longest Book in the Bible. The fact that the Holy Spirit delegated the longest Book in the Bible to the worship of music and singing lets us know how important it actually is.

Concerning the singers and the musicians, the Scripture says, *"Who were instructed in the songs of the LORD."* What a beautiful statement! These *"songs of the LORD"* made up at this particular time at least part of the Psalms, as we now know them.

The Holy Spirit takes special note, as the Fourth Verse says, *"Of Heman and his fourteen sons."* In the Hebrew it seems that the names of his sons form a sentence, and this sentence glorifies God for *"lifting up the horn."* The Holy Spirit specifically says, *"And God gave to Heman fourteen sons and three daughters,"* meaning that these were especially used in the Service of the Lord. How blessed Heman was!

These choirs were very lively in their worship, hence, the different types of percussion instrumentation used.

Tradition says that at times the choirs of Israel would be divided into two sections, with the men on one side and the ladies on the other. A phrase or a stanza would be sung by one group and then answered by the other. Thus, the Temple was to be filled with song. As well, praise will characterize the great Kingdom Age soon to come. So, today, an accomplished Salvation fills the Believer's mouth with singing and with praise.

(9) "NOW THE FIRST LOT CAME FORTH FOR ASAPH TO JOSEPH: THE SECOND TO GEDALIAH, WHO WITH HIS BRETHREN AND SONS WERE TWELVE:

(10) "THE THIRD TO ZACCUR, HE, HIS SONS, AND HIS BRETHREN, WERE TWELVE:

(11) "THE FOURTH TO IZRI, HE, HIS SONS, AND HIS BRETHREN, WERE TWELVE:

(12) "THE FIFTH TO NETHANIAH, HE, HIS SONS, AND HIS BRETHREN, WERE TWELVE:

(13) "THE SIXTH TO BUKKIAH, HE, HIS SONS, AND HIS BRETHREN, WERE TWELVE:

(14) "THE SEVENTH TO JESHARELAH, HE, HIS SONS, AND HIS BRETHREN, WERE TWELVE:

(15) "THE EIGHTH TO JESHAIAH, HE, HIS SONS, AND HIS BRETHREN, WERE TWELVE:

(16) "THE NINTH TO MATTANIAH, HE, HIS SONS, AND HIS BRETHREN, WERE TWELVE:

(17) "THE TENTH TO SHIMEI, HE, HIS SONS, AND HIS BRETHREN, WERE TWELVE:

(18) "THE ELEVENTH TO AZAREEL, HE, HIS SONS, AND HIS BRETHREN, WERE TWELVE:

(19) "THE TWELFTH TO HASHABIAH, HE, HIS SONS, AND HIS BRETHREN, WERE TWELVE:

(20) "THE THIRTEENTH TO SHUBAEL, HE, HIS SONS, AND HIS BRETHREN, WERE TWELVE:

(21) "THE FOURTEENTH TO MATTITHIAH, HE, HIS SONS, AND HIS BRETHREN, WERE TWELVE:

(22) "THE FIFTEENTH TO JEREMOTH, HE, HIS SONS, AND HIS BRETHREN, WERE TWELVE:

(23) "THE SIXTEENTH TO HANANIAH, HE, HIS SONS, AND HIS BRETHREN, WERE TWELVE:

(24) "THE SEVENTEENTH TO JOSHBEKASHAH, HE, HIS SONS, AND HIS BRETHREN, WERE TWELVE:

(25) "THE EIGHTEENTH TO HANANI, HE, HIS SONS, AND HIS BRETHREN, WERE TWELVE:

(26) "THE NINETEENTH TO MALLOTHI, HE, HIS SONS, AND HIS BRETHREN, WERE TWELVE:

(27) "THE TWENTIETH TO ELIATHAH, HE, HIS SONS, AND HIS BRETHREN, WERE TWELVE:

(28) "THE ONE AND TWENTIETH OF HOTHIR, HE, HIS SONS, AND HIS BRETHREN, WERE TWELVE:

(29) "THE TWO AND TWENTIETH TO GIDDALTI, HE, HIS SONS, AND HIS BRETHREN, WERE TWELVE:

(30) "THE THREE AND TWENTIETH TO MAHAZIOTH, HE, HIS SONS, AND HIS BRETHREN, WERE TWELVE:

(31) "THE FOUR AND TWENTIETH TO ROMAMTI-EZER, HE, HIS SONS, AND HIS BRETHREN, WERE TWELVE."

The pattern is:

1. All of these 24 courses added up to 288 skilled singers and musicians (Vs. 7).

2. The number *"twelve"* was chosen by the Lord because it is His Number of government. This tells us that music and singing, as it regards worship, is not random as far as the Lord is concerned, but is a part of His Government, meaning that it must be done His Way.

3. An individual was chosen to head up the group, and evidently the group went under that particular name from then on.

"Praise Him! Praise Him! Jesus, our Blessed Redeemer!
"Sing, O Earth, His Wonderful Love proclaim!

"Hail Him! Hail Him! Highest Archangels in Glory;
"Strength and honor give to His Holy Name!
"Like a Shepherd Jesus will guard His Children,
"In His Arms He carries them all day long:"

"Praise Him! Praise Him! Jesus, our Blessed Redeemer!
"For our sins He suffered, and bled and died;
"He our Rock, our Hope of Eternal Salvation,
"Hail Him! Hail Him! Jesus the Crucified.
"Sound His Praises! Jesus Who bore our sorrows;
"Love unbounded, wonderful, deep and strong:"

"Praise Him! Praise Him! Jesus, our Blessed Redeemer!
"Heavenly portals loud with Hosannas ring!
"Jesus, Saviour, reigns forever and ever,
"Crown Him! Crown Him! Prophet and Priest and King!
"Christ is coming! Over the world victorious,
"Power and Glory unto the Lord belong."

CHAPTER 26

(1) "CONCERNING THE DIVISIONS OF THE PORTERS: OF THE KORHITES WAS MESHELEMIAH THE SON OF KORE, OF THE SONS OF ASAPH.

(2) "AND THE SONS OF MESHELEMIAH WERE, ZECHARIAH THE FIRSTBORN, JEDIAEL THE SECOND, ZEBADIAH THE THIRD, JATHNIEL THE FOURTH,

(3) "ELAM THE FIFTH, JEHOHANAN THE SIXTH, ELIOENAI THE SEVENTH.

(4) "MOREOVER THE SONS OF OBED-EDOM WERE, SHEMAIAH THE FIRSTBORN, JEHOZABAD THE SECOND, JOAH THE THIRD, AND SACAR THE FOURTH, AND NETHANEEL THE FIFTH,

(5) "AMMIEL THE SIXTH, ISSACHAR THE SEVENTH, PEULTHAI THE EIGHTH: FOR GOD BLESSED HIM.

(6) "ALSO UNTO SHEMAIAH HIS SON WERE SONS BORN, WHO RULED THROUGHOUT THE HOUSE OF THEIR FATHER: FOR THEY WERE MIGHTY MEN OF VALOUR.

(7) "THE SONS OF SHEMAIAH; OTHNI AND REPHAEL, AND OBED, ELZABAD, WHOSE BRETHREN WERE STRONG MEN, ELIHU, AND SEMACHIAH.

(8) "ALL THESE OF THE SONS OF OBED-EDOM: THEY AND THEIR SONS AND THEIR BRETHREN, ABLE MEN FOR STRENGTH FOR THE SERVICE, WERE THREESCORE AND TWO OF OBED-EDOM.

(9) "AND MESHELEMIAH HAD SONS AND BRETHREN, STRONG MEN, EIGHTEEN.

(10) "ALSO HOSAH, OF THE CHILDREN OF MERARI, HAD SONS; SIMRI THE CHIEF, (FOR THOUGH HE WAS NOT THE FIRSTBORN, YET HIS FATHER MADE HIM THE CHIEF;)

(11) "HILKIAH THE SECOND, TEBALIAH THE THIRD, ZECHARIAH THE FOURTH: ALL THE SONS AND BRETHREN OF HOSAH WERE THIRTEEN.

(12) "AMONG THESE WERE THE DIVISIONS OF THE PORTERS, EVEN AMONG THE CHIEF MEN, HAVING WARDS ONE AGAINST ANOTHER, TO MINISTER IN THE HOUSE OF THE LORD."

The exegesis is:

1. (Vs. 1) There were 4,000 porters (23:5). They were Levites, as well. They were divided into 24 courses and were ruled by 93 chiefs. They were workers and helpers of the Temple service.

2. The *"son of Korah,"* mentioned in Verse 1, constituted the descendants of Korah, who had led the rebellion against Moses, over 500 years before (Num., Chpt. 16).

We find from this that where sin abounded, Grace did much more abound. The sons of Korah are first chosen as doorkeepers, their duty being to prevent the presumption of which their father was guilty. Such are the Ways of God! The sinful sons of a rebellious father are set on high by Him, and heavenly things are committed to their hands. Such is Grace!

3. As it regards Verse 8, it is remarkable that the Holy Spirit will mention Obed-edom's name some 20 times throughout the Word of God, and it was all because of his love for the things of God (II Sam. 6:10-11).

THE BLESSINGS OF THE LORD

Once again, the name of Obed-edom is mentioned and, as well, the Blessings of the Lord are attached to it. What a tremendous statement, *"For God blessed him."*

Why?

The reason goes back some 27 years. It pertains to the time that David was planning to bring the Ark of God into Jerusalem. Through ignorance and lack of seeking direction from the Lord, he sought to bring in the Ark in an unscriptural manner. It resulted in the death of one by the name of Uzzah.

Staring Judgment in the face, David did not quite know what to do. So, he took the Ark to *"the house of Obed-edom,"* where it remained for three months. The Scripture says, as it regards this time, *"And the LORD blessed Obed-edom, and all his household"* (II Sam. 6:1-11).

Now, as to exactly what Obed-edom did as it regards his care for the Ark, we aren't told. But evidently, he must have functioned toward this most Holy Vessel exactly in the manner in which the Lord desired because the Lord greatly blessed him, even with that blessing remaining forever.

So, now these years later, we see the descendants of Obed-edom functioning in the maintenance of the Temple, at least, they would do so when it would be built a few years later.

The Scriptures are replete with all types of evidences of the Blessings of the Lord upon those who seek to obey Him. The Lord, to be truthful, doesn't demand much of us. But He does demand loyalty, and that we try our best, as frail as that might be, to live a life of obedience to His Word. That being the case, He will always firmly bless the individual involved.

The very word *"blessing,"* in a sense,

NOTES

means *"increase."* To have the Blessings of the Lord is to have everything. To not have those blessings is to have nothing!

The Sixth Verse mentions the first son of Obed-edom, *"Shemaiah."* Speaking of the sons who were born to him, it says, *"For they were mighty men of valour."* These would have been the grandsons of Obed-edom.

Then the Eighth Verse uses the words, *"able men for strength,"* and then it says, *"were threescore and two (62) of Obed-edom."*

Whatever Obed-edom was, it filtered through to his sons, and even his grandsons. What a legacy!

(13) "AND THEY CAST LOTS, AS WELL THE SMALL AS THE GREAT, ACCORDING TO THE HOUSE OF THEIR FATHERS, FOR EVERY GATE.

(14) "AND THE LOT EASTWARD FELL TO SHELEMIAH. THEN FOR ZECHARIAH HIS SON, A WISE COUNSELLOR, THEY CAST LOTS; AND HIS LOT CAME OUT NORTHWARD.

(15) "TO OBED-EDOM SOUTHWARD; AND TO HIS SONS THE HOUSE OF ASUPPIM.

(16) "TO SHUPPIM AND HOSAH THE LOT CAME FORTH WESTWARD, WITH THE GATE SHALLECHETH, BY THE CAUSEWAY OF THE GOING UP, WARD AGAINST WARD.

(17) "EASTWARD WERE SIX LEVITES, NORTHWARD FOUR A DAY, SOUTHWARD FOUR A DAY, AND TOWARD ASUPPIM TWO AND TWO.

(18) "AT PARBAR WESTWARD, FOUR AT THE CAUSEWAY, AND TWO AT PARBAR.

(19) "THESE ARE THE DIVISIONS OF THE PORTERS AMONG THE SONS OF KORE, AND AMONG THE SONS OF MERARI."

The overview is:

1. The short phrase of Verse 13, *"And they cast lots,"* pertains to the Urim and the Thummim. This shows that David was instructed by the Lord that he was to do nothing of his own accord, but rather, have the Mind of God, even for every minute detail as it regarded the Temple.

2. Consequently, the Holy Spirit decided the direction of each individual.

3. How so much we as Believers should know the Mind of the Lord in all things and not move until we have His Perfect Will.

GUARDING THE GATES

As should be obvious, the gates to the Temple had to be guarded, and done so day and night. This is the type of the gates of the True Gospel of Jesus Christ and Him Crucified that must be guarded as well.

The cry today is unity. The so-called principle on which this is built is called *"love."* However, let it be understood, there is no such thing as unity or love at the expense of truth.

Satan is attacking the Gospel Message today as never before. He's doing it with *"another gospel"* (Gal. 1:6), and *"another Jesus"* (II Cor. 11:4).

Let's state what the Gospel of Jesus Christ actually is. Paul gave it to us in a nutshell, so to speak. He said: *"For Christ sent me not to baptize* (presents to us a Cardinal Truth), *but to preach the Gospel* (the manner in which one may be Saved from sin)*: not with wisdom of words* (intellectualism is not the Gospel), *lest the Cross of Christ should be made of none effect."* (This tells us in no uncertain terms that the Cross of Christ must always be the emphasis of the Message [I Cor. 1:17].)

Unequivocally, and as stated, we are told in this simple Passage as to exactly what the Gospel of Christ actually is. In brief, it is *"the Cross of Christ."*

Was Paul opposed to Water Baptism?

Of course not!

Paul was merely telling the Corinthians and all of us, as well, that the emphasis must always be the Cross of Christ, for that is the Gospel, and not the other things, as true and right as they may be in their own way.

The truth is, the Truth of the Gospel cannot be known, had, or understood without a correct knowledge of the Cross of Christ. And, what is that correct knowledge?

THE CORRECT KNOWLEDGE OF THE CROSS OF CHRIST

The Believer must understand that Jesus Christ, even as we have related any number of times, is the Source of all things from God, while the Cross is the Means (Rom. 6:1-14).

This means that the Believer must understand that the Cross has made his Salvation possible, and the Cross alone made it possible. But, as well, the Believer must understand that in our daily living for God, our daily walk before God, it is the Cross of Christ, as well, that makes it possible for the Holy Spirit to function within our lives and bring about the desired Spiritual Growth. In other words, the Cross of Christ must ever be the Object of our Faith (Lk. 9:23; 14:27).

Understanding that the Cross of Christ is the Means by which the Holy Spirit works within our hearts and lives (Rom. 8:2), means that everything else must go as it regards whatever it is in which we are placing our faith. That's the reason that Paul chose Water Baptism. As viable and as Scriptural as that Ordinance is, it must be understood that it holds absolutely no place whatsoever in our Salvation or Sanctification, the Cross of Christ being the principal of that great work.

ALL SHOULD BE GUARDIANS

I think we should understand just how important the True Gospel of Jesus Christ actually is. It must not be diluted, compromised, or watered down in any respect. If it is, even to the slightest degree, ultimately, a little leaven will leaven the whole lump.

Men have forever tried to figure out a way to defend the Gospel without defending it. Such is impossible.

There come times that the Preacher has to say that certain doctrines are wrong. He must do it with love, but it must be done. If it makes people angry, it must be done. The gates must be guarded at any cost. As there were watchmen at the gates of the Temple, there must be watchmen respecting the Gospel presently. In fact, every Believer should be a guardian of the gate.

Satan can little deny the Gospel, that being a worldwide fact, but he can pollute the Gospel and pervert the Gospel, and that's exactly what he attempts to do. Listen again to Paul:

"I marvel that you are so soon removed from Him (the Holy Spirit) *Who called you into the Grace of Christ* (made possible by

the Cross) *unto another gospel* (anything which doesn't have the Cross as its Object of Faith)*:*

"Which is not another (presents the fact that Satan's aim is not so much to deny the Gospel, which he can little do, as to corrupt it)*; but there be some who trouble you, and would pervert the Gospel of Christ* (once again, to make the object of Faith something other than the Cross)*"* (Gal. 1:6-7).

Whenever the Gospel is perverted, when it is changed to something else altogether, such removes the Believer from the Holy Spirit. No, the Holy Spirit, thank God, doesn't leave us, but He is greatly hindered in the help that He Alone can render to us. That's the reason Paul said, *"I marvel that you are so soon removed from Him."* The pronoun *"Him"* refers to the Holy Spirit. And please understand the following:

Whatever needs to be done in our lives, the Holy Spirit Alone can do it. He works exclusively within the parameters of the Finished Work of Christ. In fact, He will not work outside of those parameters. He only demands of us that our Faith be placed explicitly in the Cross of Christ and in nothing else. In that manner alone can He work. So, whenever the Devil moves us *"unto another gospel,"* this deprives us of the help of the Holy Spirit which, in effect, leaves the Believer helpless against the onslaught of Satan. In fact, this is the reason for the failure and the fall of all Believers. This is the reason the Message of the Cross, which, in effect, is the Message of Redemption, and which, in effect, is the meaning of the New Covenant, is so very, very important. In fact, there is nothing in the world more important.

(20) "AND OF THE LEVITES, AHIJAH WAS OVER THE TREASURES OF THE HOUSE OF GOD, AND OVER THE TREASURES OF THE DEDICATED THINGS.

(21) "AS CONCERNING THE SONS OF LAADAN; THE SONS OF THE GERSHONITE LAADAN, CHIEF FATHERS, EVEN OF LAADAN THE GERSHONITE, WERE JEHIELI.

(22) "THE SONS OF JEHIELI; ZETHAM, AND JOEL HIS BROTHER, WHICH WERE OVER THE TREASURES OF THE HOUSE OF THE LORD.

(23) "OF THE AMRAMITES, AND THE IZHARITES, THE HEBRONITES, AND THE UZZIELITES:

(24) "AND SHEBUEL THE SON OF GERSHOM, THE SON OF MOSES, WAS RULER OF THE TREASURES.

(25) "AND HIS BRETHREN BY ELIEZER; REHABIAH HIS SON, AND JESHAIAH HIS SON, AND JORAM HIS SON, AND ZICHRI HIS SON, AND SHELOMITH HIS SON.

(26) "WHICH SHELOMITH AND HIS BRETHREN WERE OVER ALL THE TREASURES OF THE DEDICATED THINGS, WHICH DAVID THE KING, AND THE CHIEF FATHERS, THE CAPTAINS OVER THOUSANDS AND HUNDREDS, AND THE CAPTAINS OF THE HOST, HAD DEDICATED.

(27) "OUT OF THE SPOILS WON IN BATTLES DID THEY DEDICATE TO MAINTAIN THE HOUSE OF THE LORD.

(28) "AND ALL THAT SAMUEL THE SEER, AND SAUL THE SON OF KISH, AND ABNER THE SON OF NER, AND JOAB THE SON OF ZERUIAH, HAD DEDICATED; AND WHOSOEVER HAD DEDICATED ANYTHING, IT WAS UNDER THE HAND OF THE SHELOMITH, AND OF HIS BRETHREN."

The overview is:

1. The Twenty-seventh Verse proclaims the fact of the oft-forgotten lesson that the Spiritual Temple of Jehovah must be built up with *"spoils won in battle."*

2. (Vs. 27) There must be labor and prayer, battling with wicked spirits in Heavenly Places, and sharp encounters with the Devil and his human servants, if spoil, that is, souls, are to be won for Jesus Christ.

3. (Vs. 28) The doorkeepers were to exclude evil, and treasure-keepers were to guard the Spiritual Wealth. This implies warfare. Paul told Timothy to *"war a good warfare."* He was a *"doorkeeper"* and a *"treasure-keeper"* (I Tim. 1:3; 4:20).

THE TREASURES OF
THE DEDICATED THINGS

These treasures were, no doubt, silver and gold plus other particular things, all dedicated to the Lord.

We find at particular times in history, Israel, actually Judah, would give these dedicated things to heathen kings, trying to buy off their threats (II Ki. 12:18; 18:14-16). In fact, not long after Solomon died, when his son Rehoboam took the throne, Shishak, king of Egypt, came up against Jerusalem, and the Scripture says, *"And took away the treasures of the House of the LORD"* (II Chron. 12:9). This was less than 40 years after the Temple was built.

How would this terminology fit the modern church as it regards treasures?

Without a doubt, I think that we would label *"treasures"* in the modern vernacular as the great Biblical Doctrines of the Faith.

Concerning this, Jude said, *"Beloved, when I gave all diligence* (a compulsion generated by the Holy Spirit) *to write unto you of the common Salvation* (he had at first thought to write an Epistle similar to Romans, but the Holy Spirit, although the Author of the compulsion, did not lead in this direction), *it was needful for me to write unto you* (the implication is that whatever was to be written had to be written at once, and could not be prepared for at leisure), *and exhort you that you should earnestly contend for the Faith* (refers to the fact that the Saints must defend the Doctrines of Christianity with intense effort) *which was once delivered unto the Saints* (refers to the fact that no other Faith will be given; the idea is that God gave the Christian Doctrines to the Saints as a deposit of Truth to be guarded)" (Jude 3).

The Holy Spirit through the Apostle further warns as to why this is necessary. He said:

"For there are certain men crept in unawares (false teachers had crept into the church), *who were before of old ordained to this condemnation, ungodly men* (they came in by stealth and dishonesty; however, their methods were by no means new; they would assume an outward expression of light), *turning the Grace of our God into lasciviousness* (refers to the fact that 'Grace' had been turned to license), *and denying the only Lord God, and our Lord Jesus Christ* (if we deny the Cross, which is God's Plan of Redemption, we are at the same time denying both the Father and the Son)" (Jude 4).

It is not easy or simple to *"guard these treasures!"* The current is always in the other direction. In guarding the treasures, almost invariably, one is accused of destroying the unity, etc. But, let it ever be understood, there is no true unity without Truth. To base unity on anything other than Truth presents such based on a false foundation.

THE FOUNDATION

The Foundation of Truth, i.e., the Gospel, is the Cross of Christ, which was formulated in the Mind of the Godhead from before the foundation of the world (I Pet. 1:18-20). This means that every single Doctrine in the Bible must be built, and without exception, on the Cross of Christ. If the Cross of Christ is eliminated, sidestepped, ignored, or refused in any fashion, the end result will always be catastrophic. In fact, that's where every false doctrine has made its debut. For instance, look at the doctrine of *"Word of Faith"*, so-called! It repudiates the Cross in totality, referring to it as *"the worst defeat in human history,"* and *"past miseries."* In other words, according to their teaching, the Cross of Christ was just another incident. They teach that Salvation was effected by Jesus becoming a sinner on the Cross, going to the burning side of Hell as all sinners do, there being tormented three days and nights by the powers of darkness, and then, with God saying, *"It's enough,"* Jesus was Born-Again. That is how Salvation was effected, they say!

There is not a shred of that in the Word of God. In fact, it borders on blasphemy, if not outright.

In my estimation, the *"Word of Faith"* doctrine is *"another gospel"* in totality. It has grossly perverted the Gospel of Christ (Gal. 1:6-7).

Of course, there are scores of other proposed gospels which fall into the same category, or near so, but greater damage to the True Gospel has been afforded by *"Word of Faith"*, I think, than anything else. It is a perfect example as to what happens when the Cross is repudiated.

The major emphasis of that particular doctrine, which has taken the world by storm, is money. It is not righteousness and holiness, but rather, money! There is no way that one can Biblically label that doctrine as anything but grossly unscriptural. The end result for its adherence will not be peace and prosperity, but rather the opposite. In fact, many will lose their souls simply because they aren't seeking first the Kingdom of God and His Righteousness.

SPOILS WON IN BATTLE

Those battles then were physical against heathen enemies. These enemies were bent on destroying the People of God. But, whenever Israel totally followed the Lord, the Lord gave them victory, in fact, astounding victories over the enemy, and in every capacity. As a result, much spoil would be taken.

That spoil consisted of gold, silver, precious stones, and many other things.

Presently, the conflict is the same with one major exception. Now, it is Spiritual instead of physical.

Whenever we as Believers lose a bout with Satan, our loss almost always is much greater than at first realized. Conversely, when we win a battle, the spoils are great. It is increased Faith, increased confidence in the Lord, greater liberty in prayer, a greater understanding of the Word of God, Divine Healing and, as well, material Blessings and prosperity. All of us have lost some battles, and all of us have won some battles. Let's go back to the Cross.

THE WAY OF THE CROSS

The Child of God can know Victory, and I speak of perpetual Victory over the powers of the enemy, only on one basis. That is the principal of the Cross of Christ. It was there that every Victory was won by our Lord Jesus Christ. It was there that all sin was atoned, which defeated all demon spirits, every fallen Angel, and Satan himself. In other words, every single thing that man lost in the Fall was addressed at the Cross of Calvary, and one might quickly add, bought back in totality.

While it is true that we presently only have the *"firstfruits"* of that which Jesus did

NOTES

(Rom. 8:23), still, and to be certain, that is enough for us to walk in perpetual Victory.

By perpetual Victory, I am not speaking of sinless perfection, because the Bible doesn't teach such. But it most definitely does teach that sin, i.e., *"the sin nature,"* is not to have dominion over us (Rom. 6:14). And to be sure, this is a Victory of unprecedented proportions.

Satan will do everything within his power to erect strongholds within our lives, which means that the sin nature in some way is dominating us as a Child of God. There is only one way that victory can be attained as it regards the sin nature. That is the Believer placing his Faith exclusively in Christ and the Cross, not allowing it to be moved elsewhere, which then gives the Holy Spirit latitude to work within his heart and life (Rom. 8:2).

The Christian placing his Faith in the Cross of Christ, and maintaining his Faith in the Cross of Christ, will guarantee every battle won, with much, much *"spoils."*

Incidentally, at the Trump of God, which is the First Resurrection of Life, each Believer, which will include every Believer who has ever lived, will receive all that was purchased at the Cross of Calvary. I speak of the Glorified Body, which every Saint will have with all of its attendant wonders and glory. But once again, let me state that the *"firstfruits,"* which we presently have, are far and away enough for us to live the life of Victory that we ought to live.

(29) "OF THE IZHARITES, CHENANIAH AND HIS SONS WERE FOR THE OUTWARD BUSINESS OVER ISRAEL, FOR OFFICERS AND JUDGES.

(30) "AND OF THE HEBRONITES, HASHABIAH AND HIS BRETHREN, MEN OF VALOUR, A THOUSAND AND SEVEN HUNDRED, WERE OFFICERS AMONG THEM OF ISRAEL ON THIS SIDE JORDAN WESTWARD IN ALL THE BUSINESS OF THE LORD, AND IN THE SERVICE OF THE KING.

(31) "AMONG THE HEBRONITES WAS JERIJAH THE CHIEF, EVEN AMONG THE HEBRONITES, ACCORDING TO THE GENERATIONS OF HIS FATHERS. IN THE FORTIETH YEAR OF THE REIGN

OF DAVID THEY WERE SOUGHT FOR, AND THERE WERE FOUND AMONG THEM MIGHTY MEN OF VALOUR AT JAZER OF GILEAD.

(32) "AND HIS BRETHREN, MEN OF VALOUR, WERE TWO THOUSAND AND SEVEN HUNDRED CHIEF FATHERS, WHOM KING DAVID MADE RULERS OVER THE REUBENITES, THE GADITES, AND THE HALF TRIBE OF MANASSEH, FOR EVERY MATTER PERTAINING TO GOD, AND AFFAIRS OF THE KING."

The overview is:

1. (Vs. 32) Terms such as *"mighty men of valor"* and *"men of valor"* were used in connection with the appointment of these officers by David, as it regarded the administrative offices of the kingdom.

2. (Vs. 32) This shows that God honors and rewards proper business activity as a dedication to His Service. It is to be carried on with the same consecration and dedication to God, even as the Temple worship and service. We must conduct ourselves thusly today, as well!

3. All of this was in the Work of God. There had to be workers and there had to be worshippers. All were extremely important. It has not changed presently.

MIGHTY MEN OF VALOR

What a wonderful thing for the Holy Spirit to say about the individuals addressed in these particular Verses.

What is the Holy Spirit saying about us presently? Are we a man or woman of valor? Could, as well, the word *"mighty"* be attached also to that which the Holy Spirit says of us?

To be sure, the Holy Spirit is constantly evaluating Believers presently just as he did then. The times may be different, but the principal is the same. In fact, this Chapter closes with the words, *"for every matter pertaining to God, and affairs of the king."* The King presently is the Lord Jesus Christ.

If the truth be known, most of those given such accolades by the Lord, as *"mighty men of valour,"* are seldom recognized by the world or even the church. In fact, all too often, the church places its seal of approval on those whom God ignores.

Believers should take note of what God is blessing and, as well, make doubly certain that what they see is really the Blessing of the Lord and not the mere accomplishments of man. Ascertaining such, those are the ones who should be followed.

"Look, you Saints, the sight is glorious:
"See the 'Man of Sorrows' now;
"From the fight return victorious:
"Every knee to Him shall bow!
"Crown Him! Crown Him! Crown Him! Crown Him!
"Crowns become the Victor's Brow."

"Crown the Saviour! Angels, crown Him!
"Rich the trophies Jesus brings;
"In the seat of power enthrone Him,
"While the vault of Heaven rings!
"Crown Him! Crown Him! Crown Him! Crown Him!
"Crown the Saviour 'King of kings.'"

"Sinners in derision crowned Him,
"Mocking thus the Saviour's Claim;
"Saints and Angels crowd around Him,
"Own His Title, praise His Name.
"Crown Him! Crown Him! Crown Him! Crown Him!
"Spread abroad the Victor's Fame."

"Hark, the burst of acclamation!
"Hark those loud triumphant chords!
"Jesus takes the high station,
"Oh, what joy the sight affords!
"Crown Him! Crown Him! Crown Him! Crown Him!
"King of kings, and Lord of lords."

CHAPTER 27

(1) "NOW THE CHILDREN OF ISRAEL AFTER THEIR NUMBER, TO WIT, THE CHIEF FATHERS AND CAPTAINS OF THOUSANDS AND HUNDREDS, AND THEIR OFFICERS WHO SERVED THE KING IN ANY MATTER OF THE COURSES, WHICH CAME IN AND WENT OUT MONTH BY MONTH THROUGHOUT ALL THE MONTHS OF THE YEAR,

OF EVERY COURSE WERE TWENTY AND FOUR THOUSAND.

(2) "OVER THE FIRST COURSE FOR THE FIRST MONTH WAS JASHOBEAM THE SON OF ZABDIEL: AND IN HIS COURSE WERE TWENTY AND FOUR THOUSAND.

(3) "OF THE CHILDREN OF PEREZ WAS THE CHIEF OF ALL THE CAPTAINS OF THE HOST FOR THE FIRST MONTH.

(4) "AND OVER THE COURSE OF THE SECOND MONTH WAS DODAI AN AHOHITE, AND OF HIS COURSE WAS MIKLOTH ALSO THE RULER: IN HIS COURSE LIKEWISE WERE TWENTY AND FOUR THOUSAND.

(5) "THE THIRD CAPTAIN OF THE HOST FOR THE THIRD MONTH WAS BENAIAH THE SON OF JEHOIADA, A CHIEF PRIEST: AND IN HIS COURSE WERE TWENTY AND FOUR THOUSAND.

(6) "THIS IS THAT BENAIAH, WHO WAS MIGHTY AMONG THE THIRTY, AND ABOVE THE THIRTY: AND IN HIS COURSE WAS AMMIZABAD HIS SON.

(7) "THE FOURTH CAPTAIN FOR THE FOURTH MONTH WAS ASAHEL THE BROTHER OF JOAB, AND ZEBADIAH HIS SON AFTER HIM: AND IN HIS COURSE WERE TWENTY AND FOUR THOUSAND.

(8) "THE FIFTH CAPTAIN FOR THE FIFTH MONTH WAS SHAMHUTH THE IZRAHITE: AND IN HIS COURSE WERE TWENTY AND FOUR THOUSAND.

(9) "THE SIXTH CAPTAIN FOR THE SIXTH MONTH WAS IRA THE SON OF IKKESH THE TEKOITE: AND IN HIS COURSE WERE TWENTY AND FOUR THOUSAND.

(10) "THE SEVENTH CAPTAIN FOR THE SEVENTH MONTH WAS HELEZ THE PELONITE, OF THE CHILDREN OF EPHRAIM: AND IN HIS COURSE WERE TWENTY AND FOUR THOUSAND.

(11) "THE EIGHTH CAPTAIN FOR THE EIGHTH MONTH WAS SIBBECAI THE HUSHATHITE, OF THE ZARHITES: AND IN HIS COURSE WERE TWENTY AND FOUR THOUSAND.

(12) "THE NINTH CAPTAIN FOR THE NINTH MONTH WAS ABIEZER THE ANETOTHITE, OF THE BENJAMITES: AND IN HIS COURSE WERE TWENTY AND FOUR THOUSAND.

(13) "THE TENTH CAPTAIN FOR THE TENTH MONTH WAS MAHARAI THE NETOPHATHITE, OF THE ZARHITES: AND IN HIS COURSE WERE TWENTY AND FOUR THOUSAND.

(14) "THE ELEVENTH CAPTAIN FOR THE ELEVENTH MONTH WAS BENAIAH THE PIRATHONITE, OF THE CHILDREN OF EPHRAIM: AND IN HIS COURSE WERE TWENTY AND FOUR THOUSAND.

(15) "THE TWELFTH CAPTAIN FOR THE TWELFTH MONTH WAS HELDAI THE NETOPHATHITE, OF OTHNIEL: AND IN HIS COURSE WERE TWENTY AND FOUR THOUSAND."

The pattern is:

1. Verses 1 through 15 pertain to David's standing army, which numbered 288,000. These were divided into twelve monthly courses of 24,000 each. In other words, all 288,000 were not on duty at all times.

2. (Vs. 15) Only 24,000, in their respective month, would stand duty, with the others going about their business at their homes, etc. Counting all the officers, leaders, and personal guard, the total number would have been approximately 300,000. Of course, during times of emergency, larger numbers than that could easily be marshaled.

3. (Vs. 15) It is interesting to note the exact manner in which the Holy Spirit appointed the army, as well as the exact manner in which it would stand guard.

THE GOVERNMENT OF GOD

If one will carefully notice, the Holy Spirit appointed the affairs of the Nation of Israel in all capacities, which would have included the worship, with all the Temple duties, the civil government, as well as the military appointments. Nothing was left to chance; nothing was left to the wisdom or the ability of man. All was designated by the Holy Spirit.

Likewise, the Holy Spirit desires to guide every facet of our being, be it physical, domestic, financial, or Spiritual. In other words, the Holy Spirit desires control in every single facet of our lives; however, control will never be taken; it must be given.

If the Holy Spirit has His Perfect Way, prosperity is guaranteed; nevertheless, prosperity will be God's Prosperity and not man's.

(16) "FURTHERMORE OVER THE TRIBES OF ISRAEL: THE RULER OF THE REUBENITES WAS ELIEZER THE SON OF ZICHRI: OF THE SIMEONITES, SHEPHATIAH THE SON OF MAACHAH:

(17) "OF THE LEVITES, HASHABIAH THE SON OF KEMUEL: OF THE AARONITES, ZADOK:

(18) "OF JUDAH, ELIHU, ONE OF THE BRETHREN OF DAVID: OF ISSACHAR, OMRI THE SON OF MICHAEL:

(19) "OF ZEBULUN, ISHMAIAH THE SON OF OBADIAH: OF NAPHTALI, JERIMOTH THE SON OF AZRIEL:

(20) "OF THE CHILDREN OF EPHRAIM, HOSHEA THE SON OF AZAZIAH: OF THE HALF TRIBE OF MANASSEH, JOEL THE SON OF PEDAIAH:

(21) "OF THE HALF TRIBE OF MANASSEH IN GILEAD, IDDO THE SON OF ZECHARIAH: OF BENJAMIN, JAASIEL THE SON OF ABNER:

(22) "OF DAN, AZAREEL THE SON OF JEROHAM. THESE WERE THE PRINCES OF THE TRIBES OF ISRAEL.

(23) "BUT DAVID TOOK NOT THE NUMBER OF THEM FROM TWENTY YEARS OLD AND UNDER: BECAUSE THE LORD HAD SAID HE WOULD INCREASE ISRAEL LIKE TO THE STARS OF THE HEAVENS.

(24) "JOAB THE SON OF ZERUIAH BEGAN TO NUMBER, BUT HE FINISHED NOT, BECAUSE THERE FELL WRATH FOR IT AGAINST ISRAEL; NEITHER WAS THE NUMBER PUT IN THE ACCOUNT OF THE CHRONICLES OF KING DAVID."

The exegesis is:

1. The wrath mentioned against Israel in Verse 24 was all because of David disobeying the Word of God, and not supplying the half-shekel of silver of the Sanctuary, as he was commanded to do. This was failure to recognize that Israel's prosperity and protection depended solely upon the shed Blood of the Lamb (Ex. 30:11-16).

2. (Vs. 24) Unfortunately, the modern church is in the same position presently as was Israel at that time. The Cross is being ignored, or openly repudiated. As then, so now, judgment will be the ultimate result.

NOTES

THE WRATH OF GOD

Verses 23 and 24 show how conscious David was of his sin in numbering the people.

Verses 23 and 24 also portray the displeasure of God when man attempts to take matters into his own hands. The Twenty-third Verse says, *"But David took not the number of them from twenty years old and under: because the LORD had said He would increase Israel like the stars of the heavens."*

No census was taken of any in the Tribes under the age of 20 for, by this time, the new age limit for entering some service was in force (I Chron. 23:27).

The Lord had promised that Israel would be as the sand, dust, and stars—innumerable, and somehow, it stirred His Wrath for David to undertake any counting of the people, whether in doubt of the Promise being fulfilled or in plans for future conquest.

On top of all that, for the *"sweet singer of Israel"* to forget or to ignore the paying of the half shekel of silver for each man counted guaranteed the Wrath of God. As a result of that wrath, 70,000 men of Israel died, and did so suddenly.

(25) "AND OVER THE KING'S TREASURES WAS AZMAVETH THE SON OF ADIEL: AND OVER THE STOREHOUSES IN THE FIELDS, IN THE CITIES, AND IN THE VILLAGES, AND IN THE CASTLES, WAS JEHONATHAN THE SON OF UZZIAH:

(26) "AND OVER THEM WHO DID THE WORK OF THE FIELD FOR TILLAGE OF THE GROUND WAS EZRI THE SON OF CHELUB:

(27) "AND OVER THE VINEYARDS WAS SHIMEI THE RAMATHITE: OVER THE INCREASE OF THE VINEYARDS FOR THE WINE CELLARS WAS ZABDI THE SHIPHMITE:

(28) "AND OVER THE OLIVE TREES AND THE SYCOMORE TREES THAT WERE IN THE LOW PLAINS WAS BAAL-HANAN THE GEDERITE: AND OVER THE CELLARS OF OIL WAS JOASH:

(29) "AND OVER THE HERDS THAT FED IN SHARON WAS SHITRAI THE SHARONITE: AND OVER THE HERDS THAT

WERE IN THE VALLEYS WAS SHAPHAT THE SON OF ADLAI:

(30) "OVER THE CAMELS ALSO WAS OBIL THE ISHMAELITE: AND OVER THE ASSES WAS JEHDEIAH THE MERONOTHITE:

(31) "AND OVER THE FLOCKS WAS JAZIZ THE HAGERITE. ALL THESE WERE THE RULERS OF THE SUBSTANCE WHICH WAS KING DAVID'S.

(32) "ALSO JONATHAN DAVID'S UNCLE WAS A COUNSELLOR, A WISE MAN, AND A SCRIBE: AND JEHIEL THE SON OF HACHMONI WAS WITH THE KING'S SONS:

(33) "AND AHITHOPHEL WAS THE KING'S COUNSELLOR: AND HUSHAI THE ARCHITE WAS THE KING'S COMPANION:

(34) "AND AFTER AHITHOPHEL WAS JEHOIADA THE SON OF BENAIAH, AND ABIATHAR: AND THE GENERAL OF THE KING'S ARMY WAS JOAB."

The overview is:

1. Verses 33 and 34 mention *"Ahithophel"* and *"Joab."* This illustrates the sad truth that it is possible to have a very high official position in the Spiritual Household of the King of kings, and yet at heart be a rebel to the Lord Jesus Christ!

2. These men, Ahithophel and Joab, were indicative of so many in the modern church. The opportunity was given to them, in fact, an opportunity of unprecedented proportions; however, they allowed self-will to guide them instead of the Will of God. As a result, they lost their lives, and they lost their souls.

3. What a blessing it is to note that the Lord observes all things, with even each administrative position listed, irrespective of its seeming importance in the Kingdom. The idea is, nothing is insignificant in the Kingdom of God.

"All hail the Power of Jesus' Name!
"Let Angels prostrate fall,
"Bring forth the royal diadem,
"And crown Him Lord of all."

"Ye chosen seed of Israel's race;
"Ye ransomed from the Fall,
"Hail Him Who saves you by His Grace,
"And crown Him Lord of all."

NOTES

"Sinners, whose love can never forget,
"The wormwood and the gall,
"Go, spread your trophies at His Feet,
"And crown Him Lord of all."

"Let every kindred, every tribe,
"On this terrestrial ball,
"To Him all majesty ascribe,
"And crown Him Lord of all."

"Oh that with yonder sacred throng,
"We at His Feet may fall,
"We'll join the everlasting song,
"And crown Him Lord of all."

CHAPTER 28

(1) "AND DAVID ASSEMBLED ALL THE PRINCES OF ISRAEL, THE PRINCES OF THE TRIBES, AND THE CAPTAINS OF THE COMPANIES WHO MINISTERED TO THE KING BY COURSE, AND THE CAPTAINS OVER THE THOUSANDS, AND CAPTAINS OVER THE HUNDREDS, AND THE STEWARDS OVER ALL THE SUBSTANCE AND POSSESSION OF THE KING, AND OF HIS SONS, AND WITH THE OFFICERS, AND WITH THE MIGHTY MEN, AND WITH ALL THE VALIANT MEN, UNTO JERUSALEM.

(2) "THEN DAVID THE KING STOOD UP UPON HIS FEET, AND SAID, HEAR ME, MY BRETHREN, AND MY PEOPLE: AS FOR ME, I HAD IN MY HEART TO BUILD AN HOUSE OF REST FOR THE ARK OF THE COVENANT OF THE LORD, AND FOR THE FOOTSTOOL OF OUR GOD, AND HAD MADE READY FOR THE BUILDING:

(3) "BUT GOD SAID UNTO ME, YOU SHALL NOT BUILD AN HOUSE FOR MY NAME, BECAUSE YOU HAVE BEEN A MAN OF WAR, AND HAVE SHED BLOOD.

(4) "HOWBEIT THE LORD GOD OF ISRAEL CHOSE ME BEFORE ALL THE HOUSE OF MY FATHER TO BE KING OVER ISRAEL FOR EVER: FOR HE HAS CHOSEN JUDAH TO BE THE RULER; AND OF THE HOUSE OF JUDAH, THE HOUSE OF MY FATHER; AND AMONG THE SONS OF MY FATHER HE LIKED ME TO MAKE ME KING OVER ALL ISRAEL:

(5) "AND OF ALL MY SONS, (FOR THE

LORD HAS GIVEN ME MANY SONS,) HE HAS CHOSEN SOLOMON MY SON TO SIT UPON THE THRONE OF THE KINGDOM OF THE LORD OVER ISRAEL.

(6) "AND HE SAID UNTO ME, SOLOMON YOUR SON, HE SHALL BUILD MY HOUSE AND MY COURTS: FOR I HAVE CHOSEN HIM TO BE MY SON, AND I WILL BE HIS FATHER.

(7) "MOREOVER I WILL ESTABLISH HIS KINGDOM FOR EVER, IF HE BE CONSTANT TO DO MY COMMANDMENTS AND MY JUDGMENTS, AS AT THIS DAY.

(8) "NOW THEREFORE IN THE SIGHT OF ALL ISRAEL THE CONGREGATION OF THE LORD, AND IN THE AUDIENCE OF OUR GOD, KEEP AND SEEK FOR ALL THE COMMANDMENTS OF THE LORD YOUR GOD: THAT YOU MAY POSSESS THIS GOOD LAND, AND LEAVE IT FOR AN INHERITANCE FOR YOUR CHILDREN AFTER YOU FOR EVER."

The construction is:

1. The assembly mentioned in Verse 1 would constitute David's last gathering for Israel.

2. (Vs. 2) This address will show that David, in his dying hour, was more concerned with the House of God than with anything else in his kingdom.

3. The expression found in Verse 5, not found in its entirety elsewhere, is an emphatic statement of the true theocracy, which should have ever prevailed among the people of Israel, but was set aside because of failure on the part of Israel. It is now paralleled by the Kingship of our Lord in His Own Church.

4. The provision of Verse 7 is emphatically presented again to the attention of Solomon, when the time comes for the direct appeal of God to him (I Ki. 3:14; 8:61; 9:4).

5. (Vs. 8) For a time, Solomon was a Child of God. He loved the Lord and walked in all His Statutes (I Ki. 3:3), and the Lord loved him (II Sam. 12:24). However, in later life, Solomon grew cold toward Jehovah and loved many strange women, who turned his heart away from God (I Ki. 11:1-8). The Lord then became angry with Solomon and turned against him in his backslidings (I Ki. 11:9-40). The Lord then took his kingdom from him and finally destroyed it, all because of sin. The Kingdom will be renewed again when Israel comes to Repentance, which she will immediately after the Second Coming (Zech. 12:10). Under the Messiah, the true David and, in fact, the true Solomon, this Kingdom shall continue eternally.

THE LAST ASSEMBLY

It must have taken several weeks, and possibly even several months, for the message to go out all over Israel concerning this assembly, which David called. It will be his last one.

Israel is now at the height of power. Every enemy is defeated. Solomon, God's Will as the titular leader of this great people, has already been enthroned.

The people of Israel constituted the only people on Earth who had a knowledge of Jehovah. Every other nation in the world was polytheistic, meaning they worshipped many gods, in effect, demon spirits. Israel alone knew the Lord and knew His Ways which, in effect, placed them light years ahead of anyone else on Earth.

And yet, they were not raised up to become an empire, but rather, their mission was threefold:

1. They were to give the world the Word of God, which they did. All the writers of every Book of the Bible were Jewish, with possibly the exception of Luke; however, it is my belief that Luke was Jewish as well.

2. They were to serve as the womb of the Messiah. The Lord, the Prince of Glory, would be born to these people, actually born of a virgin, which was a Miracle of Miracles within itself, all prophesied by Isaiah (Isa. 7:14). Tragically, when Christ was born, Israel did not recognize their Messiah and ultimately crucified Him. This problem will have to be rectified before certain things can be done, and it most certainly will at the Second Coming. Then Israel will see the terrible mistake they made, a mistake that caused them untold suffering and sorrow, and will then truly engage in Repentance. They will then be able to carry out that which the Lord originally intended for them.

3. They were raised up to evangelize the world, meaning to show the world the One

True God. In this, they miserably failed, but will one day carry out worldwide evangelization. This will occur after the Second Coming of our Lord.

There have been many trying times for Israel to be brought to the place of our Text of study.

The question must be asked as to how much delay was brought about by Israel's self-will and tremendous failures respecting her walk with the Lord.

That question, I think, is impossible to answer. Unfortunately, every single Believer on the face of the Earth, more or less, falls into the same category. How much do we hinder the Lord by our unbelief? How much do we miss the mark by going astray because of self-will? How much is the Lord hindered by these wild actions on our part?

Disobedience does definitely hinder, and hinder greatly; however, I think the Lord takes everything into consideration, and works everything out accordingly, and according to His Timetable.

THE TEMPLE OF THE LORD

As we have stated in previous notes, as David comes down to the end of his life's journey, his mind and heart are totally on that which the Lord has ordained that he do. Were there regrets?

There are always regrets; however, the regrets are behind, and David is now preparing for the construction of the Temple, and to a degree that you and I cannot comprehend.

He had desperately wanted to build the Temple himself; however, the Lord bluntly told him that he would not build the house, *"because he had been a man of war, and had shed blood."* So, his son Solomon would build the Temple, and it would be the grandest building on the face of the Earth. It is the only building, per se, where the Lord actually dwelt. In fact, the great Prophet Ezekiel tells us in his writings as to exactly when the Lord left the Temple (Ezek. 11:23). The great Prophet also saw the Spirit of the Lord return, but that is yet future. It will be during the time of the coming Kingdom Age when Jesus Christ will rule Personally from Jerusalem, and after the Millennial Temple is built (Ezek. 43:1-7). This means that the Lord did not actually dwell in Zerubabel's Temple, which was constructed after the dispersion, nor did the Lord dwell in Herod's Temple.

The reason is clear. In either case, Israel was no longer her own, but rather a vassal state ruled by another, and all because of sin.

In Verse 4, David makes the statement, *"For He has chosen Judah to be the Ruler."*

What did this mean?

Of course, David is speaking of the Tribe of Judah, which was the largest of all the Tribes. It was the Tribe from which he came, and from which our Lord would come, with the latter referring most of all to the meaning of the phrase. Everything centered around the Lord Jesus Christ, and we speak of the Temple and its entirety, with all of its rituals and ceremonies. In some way, every part and parcel of the Temple and every Ceremony spoke of Christ in His Atoning Work, Mediatorial Work, or Intercessory Work. As well, the Temple proper was in Jerusalem, which, of course, was in the area of the Tribe of Judah. But, the boundary for the Tribe of Benjamin ran very close to Jerusalem, if not actually within the city itself. At any rate, Judah was the main Tribe, and more specifically, because the Lord Jesus Christ, the very reason for the existence of Israel, came from that Tribe.

KEEP AND SEEK THE COMMANDMENTS OF THE LORD

This was the condition for the Blessings of God upon Israel. They were to keep the Commandments of the Lord and to seek understanding of these Commandments.

These *"Commandments"* included the entirety of the Law of Moses, but more specifically, were centered up in that which we refer to as the Ten Commandments (Ex., Chpt. 20).

To be sure, the Law of Moses did not save them, as the Law cannot save. In fact, it was what the Sacrificial system represented that brought Salvation. They were to understand that the Sacrificial system pointed to One Who was to come, Who would pay the full price, and Jesus was that One.

The Ten Commandments' part of the Law was the Standard of the Righteousness of

God. It was what He demanded of men, and rightly so. As we look at these Commandments, they seem simple enough, but the truth is, man, in his fallen state, has been rendered helpless in the face of obedience. In other words, he simply cannot keep these Commandments, no matter how hard he tries. Yet, the Lord placed great stock in the sincere trying.

The Law covered every aspect of life and living as it regarded the people of Israel. It included everything and excluded nothing. This was the only Law on the face of the Earth which was given by Jehovah. All other laws in all other nations in the world were man-devised and, therefore, terribly uneven. This put Israel light years, so to speak, ahead of the balance of the nations of the world.

It was when Israel ceased to *"keep and seek"* that she ultimately lost it all.

THE LAW AND THE MODERN CHRISTIAN

Of course, and as is surely known, Jesus fulfilled the Law in every capacity when He came. He kept the Law perfectly in His Life and Living, never failing even one time in thought, word, or deed. In fact, He did it all for us, even as our Substitutionary Man.

He satisfied, as well, every aspect of the broken Law by giving Himself in Perfect Sacrifice on the Cross in the pouring out of His Precious Blood, a Sacrifice, incidentally, which God readily accepted as payment for all sin, at least for all who will believe (Jn. 3:16).

So, where does that leave the modern Christian and the Law? Are the Ten Commandments, the Moral Law of God, still incumbent upon us as Believers?

It certainly is simply because Moral Law cannot change.

Considering that, does that mean that modern Believers should set about to keep the Commandments?

To be sure, these Commandments must be kept, but not in the way as normally suggested.

The truth is, modern Christians, even Spirit-filled Christians, cannot keep the Law of God any better than our Jewish friends of so long ago. We may think we can because we live under the Dispensation of Grace, and because we have the Holy Spirit, but, if the truth be known, we are quick to find out that we simply cannot do what is demanded of us. As someone has well said, *"The Law is like a mirror, which shows man what he is but gives no power to change what he sees."*

So, what is the answer?

The Believer is to approach the Law in this manner. We are first to understand that Jesus fulfilled the Law in every capacity. He is the end of the Law! Considering that, we are to place our Faith exclusively in Him and what He did for us at the Cross. That being the case, the Holy Spirit, Who works completely within the parameters of the Finished Work of Christ, will work mightily on our behalf, in effect, keeping the Law for us.

In other words, keeping the Law should not be a bother for the Child of God. It is not the Law on which we dwell, but rather Faith (Rom. 5:1-2). And to be sure, the Object of that Faith must always be the Cross of Christ because it was there that all Victory was won.

THE HOLY SPIRIT

Whatever is done in the heart and life of the Believer, it is the Holy Spirit Alone Who can carry out the task. In other words, the Believer, and no matter that he is Spirit-filled or not, cannot make himself holy, cannot make himself righteous, and cannot initiate Spiritual Growth within his heart and life. All of these things must be done by the Holy Spirit.

The key to Him doing all of these things is our Faith, but more than all, the correct Object of our Faith, which is the Cross.

Regrettably, most modern Christians don't have the faintest idea as to how the Holy Spirit works. And please believe me, without Him, we cannot do anything. Christ through the Holy Spirit lives within our hearts and our lives, and works within our hearts and our lives (Gal. 2:20). But never forget, the Cross of Christ is the very center of circumference. This is where the Victory was won, and this is how the Holy Spirit works.

For the Believer to place his Faith exclusively in the Cross of Christ, and maintain his Faith in that Finished Work, will garner the action of the Holy Spirit within one's life, with the Commandments being kept without any thought given as it regards how it is done. Please remember, what is impossible for us, is nothing with the Holy Spirit. He is God!

(9) "AND YOU, SOLOMON MY SON, KNOW YOU THE GOD OF YOUR FATHER, AND SERVE HIM WITH A PERFECT HEART AND WITH A WILLING MIND: FOR THE LORD SEARCHES ALL HEARTS, AND UNDERSTANDS ALL THE IMAGINATIONS OF THE THOUGHTS: IF YOU SEEK HIM, HE WILL BE FOUND OF YOU; BUT IF YOU FORSAKE HIM, HE WILL CAST YOU OFF FOR EVER.

(10) "TAKE HEED NOW; FOR THE LORD HAS CHOSEN YOU TO BUILD AN HOUSE FOR THE SANCTUARY: BE STRONG, AND DO IT.

(11) "THEN DAVID GAVE TO SOLOMON HIS SON THE PATTERN OF THE PORCH, AND OF THE HOUSES THEREOF, AND OF THE TREASURIES THEREOF, AND OF THE UPPER CHAMBERS THEREOF, AND OF THE INNER PARLOURS THEREOF, AND OF THE PLACE OF THE MERCY SEAT,

(12) "AND THE PATTERN OF ALL THAT HE HAD BY THE SPIRIT, OF THE COURTS OF THE HOUSE OF THE LORD, AND OF ALL THE CHAMBERS ROUND ABOUT, OF THE TREASURIES OF THE HOUSE OF GOD, AND OF THE TREASURIES OF THE DEDICATED THINGS:

(13) "ALSO FOR THE COURSES OF THE PRIESTS AND THE LEVITES, AND FOR ALL THE WORK OF THE SERVICE OF THE HOUSE OF THE LORD, AND FOR ALL THE VESSELS OF SERVICE IN THE HOUSE OF THE LORD."

The pattern is:

1. (Vs. 9) Actually, the only thing that one can give to the Lord is *"a perfect heart with a willing mind."*

2. Verse 9 also proclaims the fact that the Lord sees all things and knows all things, past, present, and future.

3. In Verse 9 is also one of the greatest Promises found in the entirety of the Word of God. Irrespective of the disposition of the individual involved, if the person seeks the Lord with all his heart, the Lord will be found. What a consolation! Conversely, if we turn our backs on the Lord, He will turn His Back on us. Consequently, this completely refutes the unscriptural doctrine of Unconditional Eternal Security.

4. (Vs. 13) These Verses declare that the Temple of Solomon was wholly planned by God, and an absolutely full pattern of it and its vessels given to David—nothing was left to his or to Solomon's imagination.

THE GREAT PROMISE OF GOD

Beautiful is the promise, *"If you seek Him, He will be found of you."* That is the Word of the Lord, and it is just as true today as it was when it was uttered some 3,000 years ago.

About 400 years later, the great Prophet Jeremiah said something very similar: *"And you shall seek Me, and find Me, when you shall search for Me with all your heart"* (Jer. 29:13).

What a Word!

This is an unlimited invitation, in effect, saying, *"Whosoever will."* If anyone wants the Lord and all the things that He Alone can do, this Passage tells us, and in no uncertain terms, that we can find Him, that is, if we will *"seek Him."*

Why will men lean on the frail arm of other men when they have the Lord to Whom they can turn? It is understandable that the world would do such, but not at all understandable as it regards the church. Yet, so few presently seek the Lord, with almost all seeking that which is constituted by man.

THE PATTERN OF ALL THAT
HE HAD BY THE SPIRIT

This was not David's spirit, but rather *"The Holy Spirit."*

All of this means that the Holy Spirit guided David in every aspect of the Temple, even down to the most minute detail. In other words, none of the pattern was out of David's mind or that of his son Solomon. All of it was of the Lord.

Even the weight of the gold and silver was measured out for the various instruments and sacred Vessels.

Everything done on this Earth, as it pertains to the Work of God, is done, without exception, through the Person, Office, and Ministry of the Holy Spirit.

Before the Cross, the Holy Spirit was greatly limited as to what He could do. The reason is that the sin debt, which was on the head of every person, could not be removed by the blood of bulls and goats. Therefore, the Holy Spirit could not come into the hearts and lives of Believers during Old Testament times except for short periods of time, and then, to enable the person to carry out a particular task.

Since the Cross, which atoned for all sin, past, present, and future, at least for all who will believe, the Holy Spirit now comes into the heart and life of the Believer at conversion, and there to remain forever (Jn. 14:16-17).

Before the Cross, the Holy Spirit dwelt with Believers. Now, He dwells in Believers (Jn. 14:17).

The Holy Spirit will now help David draw the plans for the Temple, and in total detail. Those plans will be given to Solomon for him to construct this edifice. It will be the grandest building ever constructed because it will be the only building in which the Lord will dwell.

(14) "HE GAVE OF GOLD BY WEIGHT FOR THINGS OF GOLD, FOR ALL INSTRUMENTS OF ALL MANNER OF SERVICE; SILVER ALSO FOR ALL INSTRUMENTS OF SILVER BY WEIGHT, FOR ALL INSTRUMENTS OF EVERY KIND OF SERVICE:

(15) "EVEN THE WEIGHT FOR THE CANDLESTICKS OF GOLD, AND FOR THEIR LAMPS OF GOLD, BY WEIGHT FOR EVERY CANDLESTICK, AND FOR THE LAMPS THEREOF: AND FOR THE CANDLESTICKS OF SILVER BY WEIGHT, BOTH FOR THE CANDLESTICK, AND ALSO FOR THE LAMPS THEREOF, ACCORDING TO THE USE OF EVERY CANDLESTICK.

(16) "AND BY WEIGHT HE GAVE GOLD FOR THE TABLES OF SHEWBREAD, FOR EVERY TABLE; AND LIKEWISE SILVER FOR THE TABLES OF SILVER:

(17) "ALSO PURE GOLD FOR THE FLESHHOOKS, AND THE BOWLS, AND THE CUPS: AND FOR THE GOLDEN BASONS HE GAVE GOLD BY WEIGHT FOR EVERY BASON; AND LIKEWISE SILVER BY WEIGHT FOR EVERY BASON OF SILVER:

(18) "AND FOR THE ALTAR OF INCENSE REFINED GOLD BY WEIGHT; AND GOLD FOR THE PATTERN OF THE CHARIOT OF THE CHERUBIMS, THAT SPREAD OUT THEIR WINGS, AND COVERED THE ARK OF THE COVENANT OF THE LORD.

(19) "ALL THIS, SAID DAVID, THE LORD MADE ME UNDERSTAND IN WRITING BY HIS HAND UPON ME, EVEN ALL THE WORKS OF THIS PATTERN.

(20) "AND DAVID SAID TO SOLOMON HIS SON, BE STRONG AND OF GOOD COURAGE, AND DO IT: FEAR NOT, NOR BE DISMAYED: FOR THE LORD GOD, EVEN MY GOD, WILL BE WITH YOU; HE WILL NOT FAIL YOU, NOR FORSAKE YOU, UNTIL YOU HAVE FINISHED ALL THE WORK FOR THE SERVICE OF THE HOUSE OF THE LORD.

(21) "AND, BEHOLD, THE COURSES OF THE PRIESTS AND THE LEVITES, EVEN THEY SHALL BE WITH YOU FOR ALL THE SERVICE OF THE HOUSE OF GOD: AND THERE SHALL BE WITH YOU FOR ALL MANNER OF WORKMANSHIP EVERY WILLING SKILLFUL MAN, FOR ANY MANNER OF SERVICE: ALSO THE PRINCES AND ALL THE PEOPLE WILL BE WHOLLY AT YOUR COMMANDMENT."

The pattern is:

1. (Vs. 19) David says that this Divine Pattern was communicated to him by him being compelled by the Hand, or the Spirit, of Jehovah, to record it all in writing, which he did!

2. (Vs. 21) Nothing was left, as stated, to Solomon's or David's genius or taste. All was *"by the Spirit"*; all was Divine!

3. David's words to Solomon, as it regards the charge given to him, were very similar to the charge given to Joshua by none other than the Lord (Josh. 1:9).

I CHRONICLES 29:1-9

INSPIRATION

The closing Verses of this Chapter are most important, not only because they declare that the Temple of Solomon was wholly planned by God, and an absolutely full pattern of it and its Vessels given to David—nothing was left to his or to Solomon's imagination—but it throws a great light upon the mode of Inspiration.

This appears in Verses 12 and 19. Here, David says that this Divine Pattern was communicated to him by him being compelled by the Hand, or the Spirit of Jehovah, to record it all in writing.

These Passages, therefore, picture David drawing the pattern of every portion of the Temple, great or small, and of every article of its varied ministry, and writing notes explanatory of the drawings, and dividing the woods and metals to be used, and the weight of the several metals. He is seen to do this all when under the Inspiration of the Holy Spirit. As well, from this explanation we are given a view as to how the Bible in its entirety was written.

"O the deep, deep Love of Jesus,
"Vast, unmeasured, boundless, free;
"Rolling as a mighty ocean, in its fullness over me.
"Underneath me, all around me, is the current of Your Love;
"Leading onward, leading onward, to my glorious rest above."

"O the deep, deep Love of Jesus,
"Spread His Praise from shore to shore;
"How He loves, ever loves, changes never, never more,
"How He watches o'er His Loved Ones,
"Died to call them all His Own;
"How for them He intercedeth, watches o'er them from the Throne."

"O the deep, deep Love of Jesus,
"Love of every love the best;
"Tis an ocean vast of blessing, tis a haven sweet of rest,
"O the deep, deep Love of Jesus,
"Tis a Heaven of heavens to me;
"And it lifts me up to Glory, for it lifts me up to Thee."

NOTES

CHAPTER 29

(1) "FURTHERMORE DAVID THE KING SAID UNTO ALL THE CONGREGATION, SOLOMON MY SON, WHOM ALONE GOD HAS CHOSEN, IS YET YOUNG AND TENDER, AND THE WORK IS GREAT: FOR THE PALACE IS NOT FOR MAN, BUT FOR THE LORD GOD.

(2) "NOW I HAVE PREPARED WITH ALL MY MIGHT FOR THE HOUSE OF MY GOD THE GOLD FOR THINGS TO BE MADE OF GOLD, AND THE SILVER FOR THINGS OF SILVER, AND THE BRASS FOR THINGS OF BRASS, THE IRON FOR THINGS OF IRON, AND WOOD FOR THINGS OF WOOD; ONYX STONES, AND STONES TO BE SET, GLISTERING STONES, AND OF DIVERS COLOURS, AND ALL MANNER OF PRECIOUS STONES, AND MARBLE STONES IN ABUNDANCE.

(3) "MOREOVER, BECAUSE I HAVE SET MY AFFECTION TO THE HOUSE OF MY GOD, I HAVE OF MY OWN PROPER GOOD, OF GOLD AND SILVER, WHICH I HAVE GIVEN TO THE HOUSE OF MY GOD, OVER AND ABOVE ALL THAT I HAVE PREPARED FOR THE HOLY HOUSE,

(4) "EVEN THREE THOUSAND TALENTS OF GOLD, OF THE GOLD OF OPHIR, AND SEVEN THOUSAND TALENTS OF REFINED SILVER, TO OVERLAY THE WALLS OF THE HOUSES WITHAL:

(5) "THE GOLD FOR THINGS OF GOLD, AND THE SILVER FOR THINGS OF SILVER, AND FOR ALL MANNER OF WORK TO BE MADE BY THE HANDS OF ARTIFICERS. AND WHO THEN IS WILLING TO CONSECRATE HIS SERVICE THIS DAY UNTO THE LORD?

(6) "THEN THE CHIEF OF THE FATHERS AND PRINCES OF THE TRIBES OF ISRAEL, AND THE CAPTAINS OF THOUSANDS AND OF HUNDREDS, WITH THE RULERS OF THE KING'S WORK, OFFERED WILLINGLY,

(7) "AND GAVE FOR THE SERVICE OF THE HOUSE OF GOD OF GOLD FIVE THOUSAND TALENTS AND TEN THOUSAND DRAMS, AND OF SILVER TEN

THOUSAND TALENTS, AND OF BRASS EIGHTEEN THOUSAND TALENTS, AND ONE HUNDRED THOUSAND TALENTS OF IRON.

(8) "AND THEY WITH WHOM PRECIOUS STONES WERE FOUND GAVE THEM TO THE TREASURE OF THE HOUSE OF THE LORD, BY THE HAND OF JEHIEL THE GERSHONITE.

(9) "THEN THE PEOPLE REJOICED, FOR THAT THEY OFFERED WILLINGLY, BECAUSE WITH PERFECT HEART THEY OFFERED WILLINGLY TO THE LORD: AND DAVID THE KING ALSO REJOICED WITH GREAT JOY."

The pattern is:

1. (Vs. 1) These Verses continue the account of what David said to the whole congregation respecting his son Solomon.

2. (Vs. 2) David's preparation was never for himself, but for God; however, if the Lord is put first, then blessings will come to such an individual (Mat. 6:33).

3. (Vs. 3) In today's inflationary dollar, 2008, David would have personally given over $30 billion for the construction of the Temple (the cost of the Temple would be over $1 trillion in 2008 currency, with much of the cost going to labor).

4. (Vs. 5) Our service to God is to always be on a voluntary basis. As well, the Lord accepts the consecration of all, both small and great. As God has freely given to us, will we freely give to Him?

5. (Vs. 9) The words *"perfect heart"* specify that their motivation was not one of greed. Proper giving always elicits *"great joy!"*

"AFFECTION TO THE HOUSE OF MY GOD"

David uttered the words of the heading, and the Holy Spirit sanctioned them.

This is David's love, even though the Temple was not yet built. He understood that God would dwell in this Temple, making it the most unique building on the face of the Earth.

Since the Cross, which settled the sin debt, at least for all who will believe, the Holy Spirit now dwells in the hearts and lives of all Believers, and does so permanently. What a blessing!

NOTES

The Second Verse says, *"Now I have prepared with all my might for the House of my God."*

The Third Verse says, *"Moreover, because I have set my affection to the House of my God."*

The Third Verse also says, *"Which I have given to the House of my God."* So, there are three things which David here did. They are:

1. He prepared;
2. He loved; and,
3. He gave.

If one properly prepares himself toward God, he at the same time will greatly love the Lord and, as well, will always give to the Work of God.

WHO IS WILLING TO CONSECRATE?

The Fifth Verse proclaims David asking this question, *"And who then is willing to consecrate his service this day unto the LORD?"*

Several things must be noted about this question:

• Our service to God is always on a voluntary basis.

• God accepts the consecration of all, both small and great.

• This question is a test of Faith because God is the One Who gave it to us in the first place.

• As God has freely given to us, will we freely give to Him?

OFFERED WILLINGLY

The Ninth Verse says, *"Then the people rejoiced."*

The tremendous offering given by the people and listed in these Passages proclaims that which was given by a willing heart to the Lord. Such always elicits tremendous joy. The Holy Spirit says: *"Because with perfect heart they offered willingly to the LORD."*

The word *"perfect heart"* specifies that their motivation was not one of greed. Too often the Christian gives in order to receive. This is not really giving. It is more of an investment or even a gamble. God will have none of it. The Apostle Paul and his tremendous treatment of the Grace of giving in

II Corinthians, Chapters 7 and 8, extols the abundance of God's Blessings that come to the liberal giver. However, he also says that our giving is *"to prove the sincerity of our love"* (II Cor. 8:8). God will accept giving on no other basis.

(10) "WHEREFORE DAVID BLESSED THE LORD BEFORE ALL THE CONGREGATION: AND DAVID SAID, BLESSED BE YOU, LORD GOD OF ISRAEL OUR FATHER, FOR EVER AND EVER.

(11) "YOURS, O LORD, IS THE GREATNESS, AND THE POWER, AND THE GLORY, AND THE VICTORY, AND THE MAJESTY: FOR ALL THAT IS IN THE HEAVEN AND IN THE EARTH IS YOURS; YOURS IS THE KINGDOM, O LORD, AND YOU ARE EXALTED AS HEAD ABOVE ALL.

(12) "BOTH RICHES AND HONOUR COME OF YOU, AND YOU REIGN OVER ALL; AND IN YOUR HAND IS POWER AND MIGHT; AND IN YOUR HAND IT IS TO MAKE GREAT, AND TO GIVE STRENGTH UNTO ALL.

(13) "NOW THEREFORE, OUR GOD, WE THANK YOU, AND PRAISE YOUR GLORIOUS NAME.

(14) "BUT WHO AM I, AND WHAT IS MY PEOPLE, THAT WE SHOULD BE ABLE TO OFFER SO WILLINGLY AFTER THIS SORT? FOR ALL THINGS COME OF YOU, AND OF YOUR OWN HAVE WE GIVEN YOU.

(15) "FOR WE ARE STRANGERS BEFORE YOU, AND SOJOURNERS, AS WERE ALL OUR FATHERS: OUR DAYS ON THE EARTH ARE AS A SHADOW, AND THERE IS NONE ABIDING.

(16) "O LORD OUR GOD, ALL THIS STORE THAT WE HAVE PREPARED TO BUILD YOU AN HOUSE FOR YOUR HOLY NAME COMES OF YOUR HAND, AND IS ALL YOUR OWN.

(17) "I KNOW ALSO, MY GOD, THAT YOU TRY THE HEART, AND HAVE PLEASURE IN UPRIGHTNESS. AS FOR ME, IN THE UPRIGHTNESS OF MY HEART I HAVE WILLINGLY OFFERED ALL THESE THINGS: AND NOW HAVE I SEEN WITH JOY YOUR PEOPLE, WHICH ARE PRESENT HERE, TO OFFER WILLINGLY UNTO YOU.

NOTES

(18) "O LORD GOD OF ABRAHAM, ISAAC, AND OF ISRAEL, OUR FATHERS, KEEP THIS FOR EVER IN THE IMAGINATION OF THE THOUGHTS OF THE HEART OF YOUR PEOPLE, AND PREPARE THEIR HEART UNTO YOU:

(19) "AND GIVE UNTO SOLOMON MY SON A PERFECT HEART, TO KEEP YOUR COMMANDMENTS, YOUR TESTIMONIES, AND YOUR STATUTES, AND TO DO ALL THESE THINGS, AND TO BUILD THE PALACE, FOR THE WHICH I HAVE MADE PROVISION.

(20) "AND DAVID SAID TO ALL THE CONGREGATION, NOW BLESS THE LORD YOUR GOD. AND ALL THE CONGREGATION BLESSED THE LORD GOD OF THEIR FATHERS, AND BOWED DOWN THEIR HEADS, AND WORSHIPPED THE LORD, AND THE KING.

(21) "AND THEY SACRIFICED SACRIFICES UNTO THE LORD, AND OFFERED BURNT OFFERINGS UNTO THE LORD, ON THE MORROW AFTER THAT DAY, EVEN A THOUSAND BULLOCKS, A THOUSAND RAMS, AND A THOUSAND LAMBS, WITH THEIR DRINK OFFERINGS, AND SACRIFICES IN ABUNDANCE FOR ALL ISRAEL."

The exegesis is:

1. (Vs. 10) The majesty of this prayer includes adoration, acknowledgment of the inherent nature of human dependence, self-humiliation, confession, dedication of all the offerings, and prayer both for the whole people in general, and for Solomon in particular.

2. (Vs. 14) Even though the people gave liberally to the Work of God, it was what God had given to them in the first place, as it is with all of us.

3. It may very well be possible that the stress with which David says in Verse 17, *"I know,"* has its special cause. The thought of God as One Who *"tries the heart"* is one often brought out in David's Psalms.

4. Most probably, the sacrifices listed in Verse 21 were offered on the threshingfloor of Araunah, the Jebusite, where the Temple would be built. All is ever anchored in Calvary.

All the gold and silver given on this memorable occasion could not purchase

Redemption of even one soul. This could only be brought about by the precious shed Blood of the Lord Jesus Christ. The giving of the people pointed toward Calvary; the Temple site pointed toward Calvary; and, the construction of the Temple itself would point toward Calvary.

In fact, the entirety of the Temple site must have been saturated with blood. To the unspiritual eye, this would have been a gruesome and unacceptable sight. To those who know their Lord and His Love for lost mankind, it would speak of Redemption so glorious that it would beggar description.

THINE IS THE KINGDOM

This prayer prayed by David, even after he had addressed the people, was most surely inspired by the Holy Spirit.

He begins the prayer by saying, *"Blessed be You, LORD God of Israel our Father, forever and ever."*

In our petitions to the Lord, we should carefully consider what David did here. He entered into this prayer blessing the Lord.

How ill-mannered it is for Believers to begin their petition before the Lord with a shopping list, so to speak, of wants and desires. Such completely ignores the Majesty of the Lord, and the goodness that He has already given unto us. That's the reason the Psalmist said:

"Enter into His Gates with thanksgiving, and into His Courts with praise: be thankful unto Him, and bless His Name" (Ps. 100:4).

The Eleventh Verse is very similar to the prayer prayed by our Lord:

"Our Father Who is in Heaven, Hallowed be Your Name. Your Kingdom come, Your Will be done in Earth, as it is in Heaven. Give us this day our daily bread and forgive us our debts, as we forgive our debtors. And lead us not into temptation, but deliver us from evil: for Yours is the Kingdom, and the Power, and the Glory forever. Amen" (Mat. 6:9-13).

In the Twelfth Verse, David proclaims the fact that *"riches and honor"* come from the Lord, and that *"He reigns over all."* He is the One Who *"makes great, and gives strength unto all,"* meaning that everything is in His Hands.

WHO AM I?

David now puts himself in a place and position of subservience, which is where he most definitely should have been, and all others as well. Humility is the hallmark of the true Child of God. And, please allow me to say the following:

It is not possible, I think, for any Believer to know and understand humility without first having an understanding of the Cross. Not understanding the Cross as it refers to our everyday life and living before the Lord, and the total place and position that it plays in our hearts and lives, a Believer is then going to resort to Law, whether he or she understands it or not. That being the case, humility will not be the end result of such action, but rather self-righteousness. The only cure for pride, self-righteousness, etc., is the Cross of Christ. As someone has well said, *"All ground is level at the foot of the Cross."*

David knew what he was. He knew that everything he had from the Lord was given because of the Grace of God. He knew that he merited nothing as far as blessings were concerned and, in fact, merited stern judgment. But, because of the Love and Grace of God, which were available to David and are available to all others, as well, the *"sweet singer of Israel"* had been blessed supremely. So have we!

David plainly says that *"riches and honour come of the Lord, and He reigns over all."* Also, all *"power and might"* are in the Hand of the Lord. The Lord, David says, has the power to *"make great,"* and *"to give strength unto all."* In that one Verse, Verse 12, we have the secret of all prosperity, riches, and advancement. It is all in the Lord, even as all things are always all in the Lord.

PROSPERITY

Every Believer, at least those who understand the secret of all things, which is Christ and the Cross, ought to believe God for prosperity, ought to believe God for Blessings, ought to believe God for advancement, and ought to believe God for beautiful, good, and wonderful things to happen to each of us as a Child of God. I think we do not expect great things to happen as we should. Please understand, the Economy of the Lord is not tied to Wall Street or the economy of the world in any fashion. God's Economy is dependent on nothing!

In view of all of this, the *"sweet singer of Israel"* said, *"Now therefore, our God, we thank You, and praise Your glorious Name."*

MAKE THE MOST OF THE TIME WE HAVE

The king said, *"But we are strangers before You, and sojourners, as were all our fathers: our days on the Earth are as a shadow, and there is none abiding."*

In other words, we don't have long on this Earth, and we should make the most of what we have.

Everything should be for the Lord; everything should be from the Lord; and, everything should be by the Lord. He should be our life and living, 24 hours a day, 7 days a week, and that not only for preachers, but also for all who speak His Name.

THE TRYING OF THE HEART

In the Psalms a number of times David speaks of the heart being tried by God.

The greater the Call of God on a heart and life, the greater will be the trial of the heart. It's not that God may know, for He already knows, but that we may know.

Concerning the heart, the great Prophet Jeremiah said: *"The heart is deceitful above all things, and desperately wicked: who can know it?* (God knows the hopeless corruption of the natural heart, and so He said to Nicodemus that no one, however cultured and moral, could either see or enter into the Kingdom of God. There must be a new birth.)

"I the LORD search the heart, I try the reins, even to give every man according to his ways, and according to the fruit of his doings. (The phrase, *'I the LORD search the heart,'* refers to the fact that only God knows the heart. The phrase, *'I try the reins,'* refers to the Lord allowing certain particulars to take place, according to the disposition of the individual involved, in order to bring out what is actually there. The Lord,

NOTES

as stated, through Omniscience already knows all things, in other words, what is in the heart of man, even before man knows it. But in order that man not be able to say that he is unjustly judged, the Lord allows events to transpire, uncaused or caused by Him, which always reveal exactly what is in the heart, whether good or bad. This is done in order that the Judgment Day will be fair and impartial, and that the record of such actions can be shown in black and white to the individual, who, at that time, will be without argument. Therefore, his judgment will be *'according to his ways, and according to the fruit of his doings')"* (Jer. 17:9-10).

THE CROSS OF CHRIST

The Twenty-first Verse says, *"And they sacrificed sacrifices unto the LORD, and offered Burnt Offerings unto the LORD, on the morrow after that day, even a thousand bullocks, a thousand rams, and a thousand lambs, with their Drink Offerings, and sacrifices in abundance for all Israel:*

"(These multitudinous sacrifices evidently were offered on the threshingfloor of Araunah, the Jebusite, where the Temple would be built.

"All of this tells us that all is ever anchored in Calvary. All the gold and silver given on this memorable occasion could not purchase the Redemption of even one soul. This could only be brought about by the precious shed Blood of the Lord Jesus Christ. All of this means that everything here done pointed toward Calvary.

"Considering the number of sacrifices offered, the entirety of the Temple site must have been saturated with blood. To the unspiritual eye, this would have been a gruesome and unacceptable sight. To those who knew their Lord and His Love for lost mankind, it would speak of Redemption so glorious that it would beggar description.)"

Whenever our worship is anchored in Calvary as the Twenty-second Verse says, there will always be *"great gladness."*

It is ever the Cross! The Cross! The Cross!

(22) "AND DID EAT AND DRINK BEFORE THE LORD ON THAT DAY WITH GREAT GLADNESS. AND THEY MADE

SOLOMON THE SON OF DAVID KING THE SECOND TIME, AND ANOINTED HIM UNTO THE LORD TO BE THE CHIEF GOVERNOR, AND ZADOK TO BE PRIEST.

(23) "THEN SOLOMON SAT ON THE THRONE OF THE LORD AS KING INSTEAD OF DAVID HIS FATHER, AND PROSPERED; AND ALL ISRAEL OBEYED HIM.

(24) "AND ALL THE PRINCES, AND THE MIGHTY MEN, AND ALL THE SONS LIKEWISE OF KING DAVID, SUBMITTED THEMSELVES UNTO SOLOMON THE KING.

(25) "AND THE LORD MAGNIFIED SOLOMON EXCEEDINGLY IN THE SIGHT OF ALL ISRAEL, AND BESTOWED UPON HIM SUCH ROYAL MAJESTY AS HAD NOT BEEN ON ANY KING BEFORE HIM IN ISRAEL."

The pattern is:

1. (Vs. 22) The *"second anointing"* has reference to the first anointing, as is outlined in I Kings, Chapter 1. However, this anointing is before the entirety of Israel.

2. The Twenty-fifth Verse speaks of Solomon, but more particularly of the Greater than Solomon, the Lord Jesus Christ, all of which will come to pass in the coming Kingdom Age.

3. The Lord magnifies that which He chooses. He does not magnify that which is chosen by man.

SOLOMON

Concerning Solomon on this occasion, Williams says, *"This double consecration, Solomon being anointed twice, was necessary because he was Divinely designed to be a type of the Greater than Solomon. Two key-words unlock the significance of these two crownings.*

"The key words are 'The Altar of Burnt-Offering' (Chpt. 22:1), and the 'Throne of Jehovah' (Chpt. 29:23).

"The first symbolizes Grace; the second, Glory. The first is connected with Calvary; the second with the Millennium. The setting up of the Altar of Burnt-Offering on the threshingfloor of Araunah the Jebusite, was followed by the first coronation of Solomon. The completion of the material for the Temple occasioned the second crowning. So *with Christ's Sacrifice upon Calvary, He is crowned in the Heavens; His spiritual Temple completed, He will ascend the Throne of Jehovah at Jerusalem in the crowning day that will mark the beginning of the Kingdom Age."*[1]

(26) "THUS DAVID THE SON OF JESSE REIGNED OVER ALL ISRAEL.

(27) "AND THE TIME THAT HE REIGNED OVER ISRAEL WAS FORTY YEARS; SEVEN YEARS REIGNED HE IN HEBRON, AND THIRTY AND THREE YEARS REIGNED HE IN JERUSALEM.

(28) "AND HE DIED IN A GOOD OLD AGE, FULL OF DAYS, RICHES, AND HONOUR: AND SOLOMON HIS SON REIGNED IN HIS STEAD.

(29) "NOW THE ACTS OF DAVID THE KING, FIRST AND LAST, BEHOLD, THEY ARE WRITTEN IN THE BOOK OF SAMUEL THE SEER, AND IN THE BOOK OF NATHAN THE PROPHET, AND IN THE BOOK OF GAD THE SEER,

(30) "WITH ALL HIS REIGN AND HIS MIGHT, AND THE TIMES THAT WENT OVER HIM, AND OVER ISRAEL, AND OVER ALL THE KINGDOMS OF THE COUNTRIES."

The exegesis is:

1. (Vs. 28) So concluded the life of one of the greatest men of God who ever lived.

2. (Vs. 28) David wrote over half the Psalms, and he was given the plans for the Temple, which would be the grandest building ever constructed by the hand of man. Above all, he would be the ancestor of the Incarnation, of Whom the Son of David would be named. His name is the first human name in the New Testament (Mat. 1:1). It is, as well, the last human name in the New Testament (Rev. 22:16).

3. (Vs. 30) And yet, David's greatest time is yet to come. I speak of the coming Kingdom Age, when he will rule and reign over all of Israel, directly under the Lord Jesus Christ (Ezek. 37:24-25).

"And can it be that I should gain an interest in the Saviour's Blood?
"Died He for me, who caused His Pain? For me, who Him to death pursued?

"Amazing love! How can it be that You, my God, should die for me?
"Amazing love! How can it be that You, my God, should die for me?"

"'Tis as mystery all! Th' immortal dies: who can explore His strange Design?
"In vain the firstborn Seraph tries to sound the depths of Love Divine.
"'Tis Mercy all! Let Earth adore, let Angel minds inquire no more.
"'Tis Mercy all! Let Earth adore, let Angel minds inquire no more."

"He left His Father's Throne above, so free, so infinite His Grace,
"Emptied Himself of all but love, and bled for Adam's helpless race.
"'Tis Mercy all, immense and free; For O my God, it found out me!
"'Tis Mercy all, immense and free; For O my God, it found out me!"

"Long my imprisoned spirit lay, fast bound in sin and nature's night;
"Thine Eye diffused a quickening ray, I woke, the dungeon flamed with light;
"My chains fell off, my heart was free, I arose, went forth, and followed Thee.
"My chains fell off, my heart was free, I arose, went forth, and followed Thee."

"No condemnation now I dread; Jesus, and all in Him, is mine!
"Alive in Him, my living Head, and clothed in Righteousness Divine,
"Bold I approach the Eternal Throne, and claim the crown, through Christ my own.
"Bold I approach the Eternal Throne, and claim the crown, through Christ my own."

BIBLIOGRAPHY

CHAPTER 1

Matthew Henry, *Matthew Henry Commentary on the Holy Bible*, Nashville, Thomas Nelson Inc., Publishers, 1979, pg. 377.

CHAPTER 6

George Williams, *The Student's Commentary on the Holy Scriptures*, Grand Rapids, Kregel Publications, 1949, pg. 297.

CHAPTER 11

H.D.M Spence, *The Pulpit Commentary: Vol. 6*, Grand Rapids, Eerdmans Publishing Company, 1978, pg. 143.

CHAPTER 14

H.D.M Spence, *The Pulpit Commentary: Vol. 6*, Grand Rapids, Eerdmans Publishing Company, 1978, pg. 215.

CHAPTER 16

George Williams, *The Student's Commentary on the Holy Scriptures*, Grand Rapids, Kregel Publications, 1949, pg. 230.
Ibid.

CHAPTER 18

Oswald Chambers, *My Utmost for His Highest*, Uhrichsville, Ohio, Barbour Publishing, 2000, pg. 326.
George Williams, *The Student's Commentary on the Holy Scriptures*, Grand Rapids, Kregel Publications, 1949, pg. 233.

CHAPTER 21

H.D.M Spence, *The Pulpit Commentary: Vol. 6*, Grand Rapids, Eerdmans Publishing Company, 1978, pg. 331.

CHAPTER 22

George Williams, *The Student's Commentary on the Holy Scriptures*, Grand Rapids, Kregel Publications, 1949, pg. 232.

CHAPTER 29

George Williams, *The Student's Commentary on the Holy Scriptures*, Grand Rapids, Kregel Publications, 1949, pg. 239.

REFERENCE BOOKS

Atlas Of The Bible — Rogerson
Matthew Henry Commentary On The Holy Bible — Matthew Henry
My Utmost For His Highest — Oswald Chambers
New Bible Dictionary — Tyndale
Notes On Exodus — C.H. Mackintosh
Strong's Exhaustive Concordance Of The Bible
The Complete Word Study Dictionary
The Interlinear Greek — English New Testament — George Ricker Berry
The International Standard Bible Encyclopedia
The Pulpit Commentary — H.D.M. Spence
The Student's Commentary On The Holy Scriptures — George Williams
The Zondervan Pictorial Encyclopedia Of The Bible
Vine's Expository Dictionary Of New Testament Words
Webster's New Collegiate Dictionary
Word Studies In The Greek New Testament, Volume I — Kenneth S. Wuest
Young's Literal Translation Of The Holy Bible

NOTES

THE BOOK OF II CHRONICLES

INTRODUCTION

The major emphasis of the Book of II Chronicles centers upon Judah's history to the exile and the Lord's gracious dealing with the Davidic house. Because of that emphasis, little attention is given to the Northern Kingdom. Solomon is also presented as king in this Book. Only David was more important in connection with the Temple and its services.

Actually, the first nine Chapters deal with Solomon's reign and his building of the Temple. He had a Vision at Gibeon, where he asked God for wisdom, which prayer was gloriously answered.

STEPPINGSTONES TO THE FINISHED WORK

Everything that we read in the Old Testament presents itself as steppingstones toward the final Work that would be carried out on the Cross by Christ. Everything in all of these incidents was important. Some may wonder as to how all of this, and we speak of the Old Testament kings, etc., has a bearing on our life and living presently? It is vastly important because everything said and done, and we continue to speak of that recorded in the Word of God, presents itself as a steppingstone toward Redemption's Plan being totally and completely fulfilled, which it was at the Cross. Consequently, if we look at the Old Testament in that light, then it takes on a brand-new perspective. We must never forget that while the Holy Spirit used human instrumentation as it regards the writing of the various Books of the Bible, in essence, the Spirit is the

NOTES

Author; consequently, every single thing in the Bible, due to the fact that it is the Word of God, is of vast significance. While some parts of it may not present themselves as immediately clear in that respect, still, it's because we fail to understand what the Holy Spirit is saying. That's the reason that Jesus said, *"Man shall not live by bread alone, but by every Word that proceeds out of the Mouth of God"* (Mat. 4:4).

PERSONAL

It is January 14, 2008, as I begin work on this Commentary regarding II Chronicles. I pray that when it's done, it will have accomplished its purpose, which is to glorify our Blessed Lord. I pray it will be as much a blessing to you as it has been to me in the studying of its Chapters, its Verses, and even the very words of the Text.

"To God be the glory, great things He has done,
"So loved He the world that He gave us His Son,
"Who yielded His Life an Atonement for sin,
"And opened the Life Gate that all may go in."

"Oh, Perfect Redemption, the purchase of Blood,
"To every Believer the Promise of God;
"The vilest offender who truly believes,
"That moment from Jesus a pardon receives."

"Great things He has taught us, great things He has done,
"And great our rejoicing through

Jesus the Son!
"But purer, and higher, and greater will be,
"Our wonder, our transport when Jesus we see."

"Praise the Lord, praise the Lord, let the Earth hear His Voice;
"Praise the Lord, praise the Lord, let the people rejoice;
"Oh come to the Father, through Jesus the Son,
"And give Him the glory; great things He has done."

CHAPTER 1

(1) "AND SOLOMON THE SON OF DAVID WAS STRENGTHENED IN HIS KINGDOM, AND THE LORD HIS GOD WAS WITH HIM, AND MAGNIFIED HIM EXCEEDINGLY.

(2) "THEN SOLOMON SPOKE UNTO ALL ISRAEL, TO THE CAPTAINS OF THOUSANDS AND OF HUNDREDS, AND TO THE JUDGES, AND TO EVERY GOVERNOR IN ALL ISRAEL, THE CHIEF OF THE FATHERS.

(3) "SO SOLOMON, AND ALL THE CONGREGATION WITH HIM, WENT TO THE HIGH PLACE THAT WAS AT GIBEON; FOR THERE WAS THE TABERNACLE OF THE CONGREGATION OF GOD, WHICH MOSES THE SERVANT OF THE LORD HAD MADE IN THE WILDERNESS.

(4) "BUT THE ARK OF GOD HAD DAVID BROUGHT UP FROM KIRJATH-JEARIM TO THE PLACE WHICH DAVID HAD PREPARED FOR IT: FOR HE HAD PITCHED A TENT FOR IT AT JERUSALEM.

(5) "MOREOVER THE BRASEN ALTAR, THAT BEZALEEL THE SON OF URI, THE SON OF HUR, HAD MADE, HE PUT BEFORE THE TABERNACLE OF THE LORD: AND SOLOMON AND THE CONGREGATION SOUGHT UNTO IT.

(6) "AND SOLOMON WENT UP THITHER TO THE BRASEN ALTAR BEFORE THE LORD, WHICH WAS AT THE TABERNACLE OF THE CONGREGATION, AND OFFERED A THOUSAND BURNT OFFERINGS UPON IT."

The pattern is:

1. (Vs. 1) For a time, Solomon, as well, magnified the Lord, and then would close his life, sadly and regrettably, by magnifying himself.

2. Regarding Verse 2, Solomon wanted the leaders of Israel to know and realize that their prosperity was based solely on the Blood of the Lamb, symbolized by the sacrifices.

3. (Vs. 3) The *"Tabernacle"* was a type of the wilderness struggle. Even though the wilderness struggle was long and hard, still, the Tabernacle remained. Likewise, the Lord Jesus, of which the Tabernacle is a Type, will *"never leave us nor forsake us."*

4. (Vs. 4) The *"Ark"* was a type of the *"land possessed."* It represents the Throne of God and victory in the inheritance. The *"Temple"* represents the glorious Kingdom Age to come; therefore, both mentioned in Chapters 1 and 2 portray the Christian life.

5. (Vs. 6) The first instance of the Whole Burnt Offering is Genesis 8:20. Of the five Levitical Offerings, it was the chief, and was usually preceded by a *"Sin Offering"* (Ex. 29:36-38; Lev. 8:14). How long it took to offer up a thousand Burnt Offerings, we aren't told!

THE LORD HIS GOD WAS WITH HIM

Solomon was the third king of Israel. He began reigning 81 years after the kingdom was established.

He was the first of David's descendants to reign in unbroken succession for the next 513 years. From the end of that time until today, the Israelites have not had a kingdom, and they will not have one until the Messiah comes to reign. He will rebuild the Tabernacle of David, re-establish the kingdom, and sit on the Throne of David forever (Isa. 9:6-7; Zech. 14:5-9; Rev. 20:1-10). Christ was the last Son of David in the Bible genealogies, and He will be the next King, as stated, on the Throne of David (Lk. 3:23-38).

Solomon was *"magnified exceedingly"* because *"God was with him."* Nothing greater could be said of a man than, *"God is with Him."*

THE CROSS OF CHRIST

The first act of Solomon was to confess without shame to the whole world that he and all Israel owed everything to the Blood of the Lamb, which was typified in the offering of the clean animals. He sought to set out something of the infinite preciousness of the Blood by offering 1,000 Burnt Offerings upon the Brazen Altar made by Bezaleel nearly 600 years before. But 10,000 times 10,000 Offerings could never worthily exhibit the preciousness of that Blood! It was, however, a glorious testimony on the part of Solomon at the commencement of his reign. How glorious it would have been had Solomon maintained this testimony without fault to the close of his reign!

If one studies the Bible honestly, one cannot fail to see that the Cross of Christ, in essence, is the Story of the Bible. One might say the following:

• The only way to God the Father is through Jesus Christ (Jn. 14:6).
• The only way to Jesus Christ is by the Way of the Cross (Lk. 9:23).
• The only way to the Cross is by a denial of self (Lk. 9:23). If the Cross is removed, Christianity becomes little more than another meaningless philosophy. Regrettably and sadly, the Cross is being removed in far too many modern church circles. If it's not completely removed, it is all but ignored. Please understand the following:

GOD'S PRESCRIBED ORDER OF VICTORY

The only way that people can be Saved is because of what Jesus did at the Cross.

The only way that Believers can live a victorious life is by making the Cross exclusively the Object of their Faith, which then gives the Holy Spirit latitude to work within their lives, thereby, bringing about the Victory that one must have (Rom. 1:3-14; 8:1-2, 11; I Cor. 1:17-18, 21, 23; 2:2).

Does the reader realize that virtually all of the Bible is given over, in one way or the other, to telling people how to live for God? Only a small part is given over to telling people how to be Saved. The central core of the Word of God, as it regards living for the Lord, is found in Romans, Chapters 6, 7, and 8. To fail to understand those three Chapters is to fail to understand God's Prescribed Order of Victory.

Everything in the Old Testament strains toward the Cross, while everything in the New Testament strains back to the Cross. It is the Foundation of all Doctrine, and to misunderstand the Cross is to misunderstand the Word of God in totality.

THE TABERNACLE

The Tabernacle was at Gibeon. This small place was about five miles northwest of Jerusalem.

As to exactly why the Tabernacle was at Gibeon, we aren't told. While all the sacred Vessels were with the Tabernacle at Gibeon, there was one exception, and that was the Ark of the Covenant. When David brought the Ark to Jerusalem, he pitched a tent for it there, undoubtedly on the threshingfloor of Araunah the Jebusite, where the Temple would be built by Solomon. In fact, the Ark would never occupy a place in the Tabernacle while it was at Gibeon.

The Tabernacle was a Type of Christ in every capacity, and I speak of His Atoning Work, His Mediatorial Work, and His Intercessory Work. In fact, every part and parcel of the Tabernacle, including the material with which it was made, the manner in which it was made, as well as the sacred Vessels, all, and without exception, pointed to Christ. As we have previously stated, the Tabernacle was a Type of the conquering Work of Christ, which pertains to Redemption, while the Temple was a Type of Christ as it pertains to His Glory, and as it regards the coming Millennium. They were all of Christ, but in different capacities.

WHOLE BURNT OFFERINGS

After Solomon was made king, one of the first acts that he committed was to go to Gibeon, and there at the Brazen Altar, which sat immediately in front of the Tabernacle, the Scripture says that he *"offered a thousand Burnt Offerings upon it."*

Generally, Sin Offerings were offered in conjunction with the Whole Burnt Offerings. Both had a tremendous meaning attached to their purpose.

The Sin Offering represented the fact that all the iniquities of the sinner were loaded upon Christ. The Whole Burnt Offering signified the Perfection of Christ, and that He would give for us His All. The idea is, we give Him our sins, and He gives us His Perfection. As the old song says, *"I Got The Best Of The Trade"*.

But the principal meaning behind all that Solomon did was the fact that the Holy Spirit was telling Israel, through these many *"Offerings,"* that Israel's power and strength were built, not upon military prowess, but rather on the shed Blood of the Lamb. That was the strength of the nation, and it is the strength of the church today.

Regrettably, the church is abandoning the Cross, thereby, looking to other things. Jeremiah spelled it out perfectly. The weeping Prophet said:

"For My People have committed two evils; they have forsaken Me the Fountain of Living Waters, and hewed them out cisterns, broken cisterns, that can hold no water" (Jer. 2:13).

Anything that is looked to as the answer to man's dilemma, other than the Cross of Christ, must be labeled a *"broken cistern that can hold no water."*

God's Plan has never changed and, in fact, will never change. At the dawn of time, the Lord told the First Family that through the virtue of the slain lamb, which was an innocent victim, they could have forgiveness of sins and communion with Him. This was in spite of their having been driven from the Garden and in a terrible, fallen state. Regrettably, Cain did not believe the Lord and, consequently, offered up the fruit of his own hands, which God could never accept. The Lord most graciously did accept the offering of Abel because it was a slain lamb, which typified the Redeemer Who was to come. Unfortunately, Cain, jealous and angry because God accepted Abel's offering and rejected his, murdered his brother in cold blood. That spirit has not changed from then until now.

The modern church does not deny the fact that there is a God, and does not even deny the fact of the need for an Altar, but instead of Christ, wants to produce its own offering, which God can never accept. Please understand, if the offering is rejected, the offerer is rejected out of hand. If the Offering is accepted, and the only Offering that can be accepted is the Sacrifice of Christ, then the offerer is accepted also. Would to God that Solomon had remained as he began.

(7) "IN THAT NIGHT DID GOD APPEAR UNTO SOLOMON, AND SAID UNTO HIM, ASK WHAT I SHALL GIVE YOU.

(8) "AND SOLOMON SAID UNTO GOD, YOU HAVE SHOWED GREAT MERCY UNTO DAVID MY FATHER, AND HAVE MADE ME TO REIGN IN HIS STEAD.

(9) "NOW, O LORD GOD, LET YOUR PROMISE UNTO DAVID MY FATHER BE ESTABLISHED: FOR YOU HAVE MADE ME KING OVER A PEOPLE LIKE THE DUST OF THE EARTH IN MULTITUDE.

(10) "GIVE ME NOW WISDOM AND KNOWLEDGE, THAT I MAY GO OUT AND COME IN BEFORE THIS PEOPLE: FOR WHO CAN JUDGE THIS YOUR PEOPLE, WHO IS SO GREAT?

(11) "AND GOD SAID TO SOLOMON, BECAUSE THIS WAS IN YOUR HEART, AND YOU HAVE NOT ASKED RICHES, WEALTH, OR HONOR, NOR THE LIFE OF YOUR ENEMIES, NEITHER YET HAVE ASKED LONG LIFE; BUT HAVE ASKED WISDOM AND KNOWLEDGE FOR YOURSELF, THAT YOU MAY JUDGE MY PEOPLE, OVER WHOM I HAVE MADE YOU KING:

(12) "WISDOM AND KNOWLEDGE IS GRANTED UNTO YOU; AND I WILL GIVE YOU RICHES, AND WEALTH, AND HONOR, SUCH AS NONE OF THE KINGS HAVE HAD WHO HAVE BEEN BEFORE YOU, NEITHER SHALL THERE ANY AFTER YOU HAVE THE LIKE."

The pattern is:

1. The Seventh Verse seems to indicate that the night in question was that which followed the days of sacrifices.

2. (Vs. 10) Many criticize Solomon for making the request he did as it regards *"wisdom and knowledge,"* claiming that he should have asked for other things. What does the Word say?

3. (Vs. 12) I Kings 3:10 proclaims the Holy Spirit saying, *"And the speech pleased*

the LORD, that Solomon had asked this thing." If the Holy Spirit said that God was pleased with it, and He did, surely it should be good enough for us.

ASK WHAT I SHALL GIVE YOU

I Kings 3:15 states that the Lord appeared to Solomon in a Dream.

As well, let it be understood that this great appearance of the Lord to the king took place almost immediately after the sacrifice of 1,000 Burnt Offerings. This should tell us something.

Every single thing the Lord does for us is done by the Means of the Cross. While the Lord Jesus Christ is always the Source, the Cross is always the Means by which He does these things. In other words, it is the Cross that made it possible for the Lord to come near us, even to dwell in us in the Person of the Holy Spirit (I Cor. 3:16).

If the Cross of Christ is ignored, and in whatever fashion, we close the door to all the things the Lord can give us and, in fact, desires to give us.

It is not that Solomon earned anything by offering up all these sacrifices, but that this was the door through which the Lord moved and did. It is the same with us presently!

What an open-ended invitation to the king as given by the Lord, *"Ask what I shall give you."* That's a wide open door. And yet, is He saying any less to us presently?

Jesus said the following:
• Ask and you shall receive (Mat. 7:7).
• Nothing shall be impossible unto you (Mat. 17:20).
• All things, whatsoever you shall ask in prayer, believing, you shall receive (Mat. 21:21-22).
• All things are possible to him who believes (Mk. 9:23).

And these are just a few of the many given in the New Testament, and by none other than the Lord Himself!

Under the New Covenant, we have much greater Promises than even the Old Testament Saints had under the Old Covenant. And yet, we must ever understand that God deals with us according to that which He has called us to do. A mature Believer will ask the Lord first of all for His Leading and Guidance in all things. In other words, the mature Believer will not set the agenda, this always being left in the Hands of the Holy Spirit. Then, as we ascertain what God has called us to do, we will ask for our needs to be met in that capacity. Please remember the following:

THE LORD WILL NEVER ALLOW HIS WORD TO BE USED AGAINST HIMSELF

Now, what do we mean by that statement?

When Jesus said, *"All things, whatsoever you shall ask in prayer, believing, you shall receive,"* He was referring to His Will for our lives. In that context we can ask for whatever we need.

Selfish agendas are never promoted by the Lord, or even acknowledged by Him. Our Lord personally set the standard in the Garden of Gethsemane when He said, *"Not My Will, but Thy Will be done"* (Lk. 22:42).

In the last few decades the modern church has been led by some to believe that we have a franchise on anything we want. Such constitutes the road to disaster.

WISDOM AND KNOWLEDGE

"Knowledge" pertains to information. Just how the Lord imparted such, as it regards all types of subjects, is beyond the pale of human understanding. But it is obvious that this is exactly what the Lord did.

"Wisdom" is the application of *"knowledge."*

So, the king was given a vast resource of knowledge about almost every category of God's Creation, and was given by the Lord the wisdom as to how to use that knowledge.

As we have stated, some have said that Solomon should have asked for other things; however, it was a Dream that Solomon had, and as such, I'm not sure as to how much in charge he was of his own faculties. And yet, before the Lord appeared to him in a Dream, it's quite possible that he had prayed for wisdom and knowledge; however, this is something about which we can only speculate.

At any rate, the Lord graciously acceded to his request and then added, *"And I will give you riches, and wealth, and honor, such as none of the kings have had who have been* before you, neither shall there any after you have the like." And that's exactly what the Lord did.

(13) "THEN SOLOMON CAME FROM HIS JOURNEY TO THE HIGH PLACE THAT WAS AT GIBEON TO JERUSALEM, FROM BEFORE THE TABERNACLE OF THE CONGREGATION, AND REIGNED OVER ISRAEL.

(14) "AND SOLOMON GATHERED CHARIOTS AND HORSEMEN: AND HE HAD A THOUSAND AND FOUR HUNDRED CHARIOTS, AND TWELVE THOUSAND HORSEMEN, WHICH HE PLACED IN THE CHARIOT CITIES, AND WITH THE KING AT JERUSALEM.

(15) "AND THE KING MADE SILVER AND GOLD AT JERUSALEM AS PLENTEOUS AS STONES, AND CEDAR TREES MADE HE AS THE SYCOMORE TREES THAT ARE IN THE VALE FOR ABUNDANCE.

(16) "AND SOLOMON HAD HORSES BROUGHT OUT OF EGYPT, AND LINEN YARN: THE KING'S MERCHANTS RECEIVED THE LINEN YARN AT A PRICE.

(17) "AND THEY FETCHED UP, AND BROUGHT FORTH OUT OF EGYPT A CHARIOT FOR SIX HUNDRED SHEKELS OF SILVER, AND AN HORSE FOR AN HUNDRED AND FIFTY: AND SO BROUGHT THEY OUT HORSES FOR ALL THE KINGS OF THE HITTITES, AND FOR THE KINGS OF SYRIA, BY THEIR MEANS."

The exegesis is:

1. The Fifteenth Verse is a type of the coming Kingdom Age, when prosperity will rule the Earth, completely ridding the world of all hunger and want, because our Lord will be reigning supreme from Jerusalem.

2. This Chapter begins with Solomon offering up great numbers of sacrifices to the Lord and ends with him serving as a horse trader.

3. (Vs. 17) The Holy Spirit doesn't comment on these things, but merely mentions them, and for a reason.

PROSPERITY

When we think of gold and silver in Jerusalem *"as plenteous as stones,"* and realize that the Holy Spirit verifies this, then we must come to the conclusion as to how prosperous Israel was at that time.

It is because of the great wisdom and knowledge that the Lord gave to Solomon. As well, Solomon's reign was a type of how the entirety of the world will be in the coming Kingdom Age when the Lord Jesus Christ will rule supreme from Jerusalem. In other words, there will be prosperity such as the world has never remotely known before, eliminating all poverty, all hunger, and want, over the entirety of the globe.

"The sands of time are sinking, the dawn of Heaven breaks,
"The summer morn I've sighed for, the fair sweet morn awakes.
"Dark, dark has been the midnight, but dayspring is at hand,
"And glory, glory dwells in Emmanuel's Land."

"The King there in His Beauty, without a veil is seen;
"It were a well-spent journey, though seven deaths lay between;
"The Lamb, with His fair Army, does on Mt. Zion stand,
"And glory, glory dwells in Emmanuel's Land."

"Oh! Christ He is the Fountain, the deep sweet Well of Love!
"The streams on Earth I've tasted, more deep I'll drink above:
"There to an ocean fullness, His Mercy does expand,
"And glory, glory dwells in Emmanuel's Land."

"Oh, I am my Beloved's, and my Beloved's mine!
"He brings a poor vile sinner into His 'House of Wine':
"I stand upon His Merit, I know no other stand,
"Not e'en where Glory dwells in Emmanuel's Land."

"The bride eyes not her garment, but her dear Bridegroom's Face;
"I will not gaze at Glory, but on my King of Grace:
"Not at the crown He gives, but on His pierced Hands;

"The Lamb is all the Glory of Emmanuel's Land."

CHAPTER 2

(1) "AND SOLOMON DETERMINED TO BUILD AN HOUSE FOR THE NAME OF THE LORD, AND AN HOUSE FOR HIS KINGDOM.

(2) "AND SOLOMON TOLD OUT THREESCORE AND TEN THOUSAND MEN TO BEAR BURDENS, AND FOURSCORE THOUSAND TO HEW IN THE MOUNTAIN, AND THREE THOUSAND AND SIX HUNDRED TO OVERSEE THEM.

(3) "AND SOLOMON SENT TO HURAM THE KING OF TYRE, SAYING, AS YOU DID DEAL WITH DAVID MY FATHER, AND DID SEND HIM CEDARS TO BUILD HIM AN HOUSE TO DWELL THEREIN, EVEN SO DEAL WITH ME.

(4) "BEHOLD, I BUILD AN HOUSE TO THE NAME OF THE LORD MY GOD, TO DEDICATE IT TO HIM, AND TO BURN BEFORE HIM SWEET INCENSE, AND FOR THE CONTINUAL SHEWBREAD, AND FOR THE BURNT OFFERINGS MORNING AND EVENING, ON THE SABBATHS, AND ON THE NEW MOONS, AND ON THE SOLEMN FEASTS OF THE LORD OUR GOD. THIS IS AN ORDINANCE FOR EVER TO ISRAEL.

(5) "AND THE HOUSE WHICH I BUILD IS GREAT: FOR GREAT IS OUR GOD ABOVE ALL GODS.

(6) "BUT WHO IS ABLE TO BUILD HIM AN HOUSE, SEEING THE HEAVEN AND HEAVEN OF HEAVENS CANNOT CONTAIN HIM? WHO AM I THEN, THAT I SHOULD BUILD HIM AN HOUSE, SAVE ONLY TO BURN SACRIFICE BEFORE HIM?

(7) "SEND ME NOW THEREFORE A MAN CUNNING TO WORK IN GOLD, AND IN SILVER, AND IN BRASS, AND IN IRON, AND IN PURPLE, AND CRIMSON, AND BLUE, AND WHO CAN SKILL TO GRAVE WITH THE CUNNING MEN WHO ARE WITH ME IN JUDAH AND IN JERUSALEM, WHOM DAVID MY FATHER DID PROVIDE.

(8) "SEND ME ALSO CEDAR TREES, FIR TREES, AND ALGUM TREES, OUT OF LEBANON: FOR I KNOW THAT YOUR SERVANTS CAN SKILL TO CUT TIMBER IN LEBANON; AND, BEHOLD, MY SERVANTS SHALL BE WITH YOUR SERVANTS,

(9) "EVEN TO PREPARE ME TIMBER IN ABUNDANCE: FOR THE HOUSE WHICH I AM ABOUT TO BUILD SHALL BE WONDERFUL GREAT.

(10) "AND, BEHOLD, I WILL GIVE TO YOUR SERVANTS, THE HEWERS WHO CUT TIMBER, TWENTY THOUSAND MEASURES OF BEATEN WHEAT, AND TWENTY THOUSAND MEASURES OF BARLEY, AND TWENTY THOUSAND BATHS OF WINE, AND TWENTY THOUSAND BATHS OF OIL."

The exegesis is:

1. (Vs. 1) In essence, Solomon wanted to build two structures, the Temple, and a royal residence for himself.

2. The wording of Verse 1 proclaims to us that Solomon's determination was even more than the prompting to do so by his father David. The Holy Spirit is, in fact, now helping him.

3. (Vs. 2) A total of 153,600 men are pressed into service for the construction of the Temple. These were all foreigners, Gentiles, actually prisoners of war, justly condemned to hard labor for life. David could easily have put these men to death, as he might justly have done; for when they were captured, they had been attempting to kill David, destroy Israel, and the God of Israel. So, David allowing these people to remain alive was an act of mercy on his part.

4. (Vs. 2) As well, any one of these individuals could have subscribed to the God of Abraham, Isaac, and Jacob, by submitting to the Law of Moses and to circumcision. They would have then become free men. Possibly, some of them did this.

5. The Hiram of Verse 3 was not the same Hiram of David's day, but the son of the Hiram of II Samuel 5:11.

6. (Vs. 4) The mention of these three particulars portray Christ. The *"Sweet Incense"* speaks of His glorious Presence. The *"continual Shewbread"* speaks of His continual Life, for Jesus is the *"Bread of*

Life". The *"Burnt Offerings"* speak of His glorious Sacrifice at Calvary that would forever atone for the sins of man in their Redemption.

7. (Vs. 5) The testimony of Solomon, as to the greatness of God above the heathen entities of surrounding nations, is a witness to his boldness of testimony. He did not flinch from proclaiming the greatness of God over the insignificance of the god of Tyre, which was the capital of Lebanon, the realm over which king Hiram reigned.

8. Solomon's statement of Verse 6 actually refers back to the time that David desired to build a house for the Lord (I Chron., Chpt. 17), and the Lord, in effect, told David, *"I do not want or need your house, and furthermore, I will build you a house"* (I Chron. 17:10). The major problem of the church is that it tries to build the Lord a house. We are the ones who need the house, and that House is Jesus.

9. (Vs. 7) It is remarkable that in Solomon's letter nearly two-thirds extols the God of Glory, with only about one-third itemizing his request.

10. (Vs. 9) This house would be *"wonderful great,"* only because the Lord would occupy the structure; otherwise, it would be just another house.

11. (Vs. 10) A *"measure"* equals about 3 gallons, while a *"bath"* equals about 6 gallons.

BUILDING THE HOUSE

Previously stated in the Commentary of I Chronicles, the Lord gave the plans in toto to David as it regarded what the Temple would be. Nothing was left to chance or to guess, with every single part of the structure designed by the Holy Spirit and then given to David, who was to give it to Solomon for the Temple to be built. David was instructed that he could not build the Temple, and for a variety of reasons. His son Solomon would put up this structure.

It would be the only building in the world where God would dwell, in fact, in the Holy of Holies, between the Mercy Seat and the Cherubim. To be sure, the building within itself was not large, but considering the way that it was to be constructed, even as we shall see, the cost would probably be in the neighborhood of a trillion dollars, if tabulated according to 2008 currency.

Considering that not even the sound of a hammer was to be heard on the Temple site while construction was taking place, several things were demanded.

Every single part of the Temple, whatever it was, whether hewed stones, or whether things much smaller, all, and without exception, had to be prepared off the Temple site. This catapulted the cost to an astronomical level, as would be obvious.

The manner of construction was because of the Holy Spirit. This would be where God would dwell and, in fact, it would be occupied by the Third Person of the Trinity, the Holy Spirit. Even presently, when the Spirit of God Moves in certain ways, one does not want to make a sound for fear of offending the Lord. Of course, the Holy Spirit Moves in many and varied ways, but at least one of those ways pertains to all human activity stopping, especially, if it generates noise of any kind.

A PERSONAL EXPERIENCE

In our Thanksgiving Campmeeting conducted at Family Worship Center in Baton Rouge, Louisiana, a most thrilling thing took place on the Saturday night of that meeting. It was in November, 2007.

The Service concluded, and we had experienced a mighty Moving of the Holy Spirit in various ways. I stepped up to the pulpit and dismissed the people, but strangely enough, no one left. Then, it was like a Holy Hush settled down over the Sanctuary.

I sat down in a chair on the platform and began to lead the people in worship choruses.

For over an hour, no one moved, with the exception of getting out of their seats and coming to the Altar. The Holy Spirit was present in such a way that no one wanted to make a sound for fear of offending Him. Some few of you know what I mean. In a sense, this is what was happening at the Temple site where the building would ultimately come under construction. It was to be a house in which the Holy Spirit would dwell. Due to the Cross, He now dwells within our hearts and lives and does so permanently (I Cor. 3:16).

THE THREE PARTICULARS OF THE TEMPLE

Those three are:
1. Sweet Incense;
2. Shewbread; and,
3. Burnt Offerings.

The Incense had to do with the Golden Altar, which sat immediately in front of the Veil, which led to the Holy of Holies. Other than the side rooms of the Temple, the main Temple itself only had two rooms, the Holy Place, where the Tables of Shewbread were placed, five to each side, and the Lampstands, five to each side. There was only one Golden Altar.

Twice a day, the Priests would come into the Holy Place, bringing coals of fire from the Brazen Altar, with these coals deposited on the Golden Altar. Over those coals was poured the Incense, which filled the Holy Place with a cloud. This was a Type of the Intercession of Christ, which is carried on presently in Heaven on behalf of every Saint, and has been carried on since the time of the Ascension of Christ. The Intercession of Christ, needed by every Believer, and carried on for every Believer, makes possible our prayers and our petitions.

As it regards the *"Shewbread,"* there were ten Tables in the Holy Place, as stated, each carrying twelve loaves, which were consumed by the Priests every Sabbath, with fresh loaves taking their place. This was a Type of Christ as the Bread of Life.

The Golden Lampstands were a Type of Christ as the Light of the world. As stated, there were ten of these Lampstands, five to each side.

Every morning at 9 a.m., the Priests would come in and trim the wicks on the lamps and replenish the oil. They would do the same thing at 3 p.m. These are the times, as well, that coals of fire were brought from the Brazen Altar and placed on the Golden Altar of Incense.

Incidentally, no sacrifices were to be offered on this Golden Altar, only the Incense. To have done so would have repudiated what the Brazen Altar represented, which was the Cross of Christ.

As should be obvious, every ceremony and every ritual, as it regarded the Temple, as with the Tabernacle which preceded the Temple, represented Christ in His Atoning Work, His Mediatorial Work, or His Intercessory Work. When Christ came, neither the Temple nor its appointments were needed anymore.

The *"Burnt Offerings"* were actually the core of all that the Temple represented. Most of the time, when Burnt Offerings were offered, they were preceded by a Sin Offering.

As previously stated, the Sin Offering portrayed Christ taking all the sins of the sinner, while the Whole Burnt Offering portrayed Christ giving His Perfection to the sinner.

The *"Burnt Offerings"* were a Type of Christ and what He would do in the giving of Himself on the Cross of Calvary. This was the heartbeat of the Temple, the very reason for its existence.

While, of course, the Holy of Holies, one might say, was the most important part of the Temple, because it was where God dwelt, still, the Holy of Holies could not be reached, except by sacrifice, with the blood applied to the Mercy Seat. Likewise presently, the Lord cannot be reached in any capacity unless it's by and through Jesus Christ and what He did at the Cross. The Temple is a perfect example of that.

Once a year, which was the Great Day of Atonement, the High Priest went into the Holy of Holies. He had to go in alone. He would take the blood of the sacrifice and apply it to the Mercy Seat, actually doing such twice, once for himself and then the second time for Israel.

This portrays in perfect Type that the Throne of God, of which the Holy of Holies was a Type, could not be reached and, in fact, cannot be reached, except by the Means of the Cross. That's the reason we constantly state that Christ is the Source of all things we receive from God, while the Cross is the Means by which these things are done, all superintended by the Holy Spirit (Eph. 2:13-18).

(11) "THEN HURAM THE KING OF TYRE ANSWERED IN WRITING, WHICH HE SENT TO SOLOMON, BECAUSE THE LORD HAS LOVED HIS PEOPLE, HE HAS

MADE YOU KING OVER THEM.

(12) "HURAM SAID MOREOVER, BLESSED BE THE LORD GOD OF ISRAEL, WHO MADE HEAVEN AND EARTH, WHO HAS GIVEN TO DAVID THE KING A WISE SON, ENDUED WITH PRUDENCE AND UNDERSTANDING, WHO MIGHT BUILD AN HOUSE FOR THE LORD, AND AN HOUSE FOR HIS KINGDOM.

(13) "AND NOW I HAVE SENT A CUNNING MAN, ENDUED WITH UNDERSTANDING, OF HURAM MY FATHER'S,

(14) "THE SON OF A WOMAN OF THE DAUGHTERS OF DAN, AND HIS FATHER WAS A MAN OF TYRE, SKILLFUL TO WORK IN GOLD, AND IN SILVER, IN BRASS, IN IRON, IN STONE, AND IN TIMBER, IN PURPLE, IN BLUE, AND IN FINE LINEN, AND IN CRIMSON; ALSO TO GRAVE ANY MANNER OF GRAVING, AND TO FIND OUT EVERY DEVICE WHICH SHALL BE PUT TO HIM, WITH YOUR CUNNING MEN, AND WITH THE CUNNING MEN OF MY LORD DAVID YOUR FATHER.

(15) "NOW THEREFORE THE WHEAT, AND THE BARLEY, THE OIL, AND THE WINE, WHICH MY LORD HAS SPOKEN OF, LET HIM SEND UNTO HIS SERVANTS:

(16) "AND WE WILL CUT WOOD OUT OF LEBANON, AS MUCH AS YOU SHALL NEED: AND WE WILL BRING IT TO YOU IN FLOATS BY SEA TO JOPPA; AND YOU SHALL CARRY IT UP TO JERUSALEM.

(17) "AND SOLOMON NUMBERED ALL THE STRANGERS WHO WERE IN THE LAND OF ISRAEL, AFTER THE NUMBERING WHEREWITH DAVID HIS FATHER HAD NUMBERED THEM; AND THEY WERE FOUND AN HUNDRED AND FIFTY THOUSAND AND THREE THOUSAND AND SIX HUNDRED.

(18) "AND HE SET THREESCORE AND TEN THOUSAND OF THEM TO BE BEARERS OF BURDENS, AND FOURSCORE THOUSAND TO BE HEWERS IN THE MOUNTAIN, AND THREE THOUSAND AND SIX HUNDRED OVERSEERS TO SET THE PEOPLE A WORK."

The pattern is:

1. Verse 11 presents a testimony to the indirect influences on surrounding nations of the knowledge of the One True Creator-God and Ruler-God, Who was domiciled by special Revelation and Oracle with Israel (Rom. 3:2). Even when nations near were bitter foes, they often feared Israel's God.

2. (Vs. 12) Two buildings were to be constructed, a palace for Solomon, which, in essence, would be the center of government, and the Temple.

3. (Vs. 12) There is no doubt that the Lord greatly blessed Hiram and the kingdom of Tyre for their willingness to help as it regards this work for the Lord.

4. As it regards Verse 16, the distance from Joppa to Jerusalem was about 34 miles.

HIRAM, THE KING OF TYRE

It is spelled *"Hiram"* in II Samuel, Chapter 5 and I Kings, and is probably the better spelling. As we have seen in the first part of this Chapter, Solomon has written Hiram a beautiful letter portraying the Glory of Christ. Hiram now answers him.

It should be understood that this is not the Hiram of David's day, but rather his son.

The Twelfth Verse has this heathen king proclaiming the greatness of the Lord by saying, *"Blessed be the LORD God of Israel, Who made Heaven and Earth."* This heathen had more Spiritual sense than the majority of so-called Christianized America and Canada, who claim evolution as the maker of such. In effect, Hiram states that he is honored to have a part in this *"House of God"* that is to be built. Hiram and the kingdom of Tyre will, no doubt, as stated, be greatly blessed because of their participation in this great Work for God.

Anything that is truly of the Lord carries with it great Blessing. If this heathen prince had enough sense to understand the Blessing of such participation, surely modern Christians can understand the same.

The truth is, and sadly so, the majority of modern Christendom supports that which is really not of God, which means that no blessing accompanies such efforts.

In all of the Earth of that day, what Solomon was doing was of God; consequently, any participation in that Work brought Blessing.

For instance, when Solomon allowed the Gentiles, who were prisoners of war, to help in the building of the Temple, in essence, he made them fellow-workers with himself in the building of this great structure. This forms a picture of Christ, Who saves men and makes them captives, allowing us to be fellow-laborers in the building of His great Spiritual Temple. What an honor to be able to work for the Lord in the construction of this Holy Edifice in any capacity.

WHAT IS THE TRUE WORK OF GOD PRESENTLY?

Pure and simple, it is the Message of the Cross. In effect, that has always been the True Work of God and, in fact, there has never been any other, as there cannot be any other. So, the question presently poses itself:

How many modern preachers are preaching the Cross?

Paul said, *"For after that in the Wisdom of God the world by wisdom knew not God* (man's puny wisdom, even the best he has to offer, cannot come to know God in any manner), *it pleased God by the foolishness of preaching* (preaching the Cross) *to save them who believe.* (Paul is not dealing with the art of preaching here, but with what is preached.)

"For the Jews require a sign (the sign of the Messiah taking the Throne and making Israel a great Nation once again), *and the Greeks seek after wisdom* (they thought that such solved the human problem; however, if it did, why were they ever seeking after more wisdom?):

"But we preach Christ Crucified (this is the Foundation of the Word of God and, thereby, of Salvation), *unto the Jews a stumblingblock* (the Cross was the stumblingblock), *and unto the Greeks foolishness* (both found it difficult to accept as God a dead Man hanging on a Cross, for such Christ was to them);

"But unto them who are called (refers to those who accept the Call, for the entirety of mankind is invited [Jn. 3:16; Rev. 22:17]), both Jews and Greeks (actually stands for both *'Jews and Gentiles'*), *Christ the Power of God* (what He did at the Cross atoned for all sin, thereby, making it possible for the Holy Spirit to exhibit His Power within our lives), *and the Wisdom of God.* (This Wisdom devised a Plan of Salvation which pardoned guilty men and at the same time vindicated and glorified the Justice of God, which stands out as the wisest and most remarkable Plan of all time)" (I Cor. 1:21-24).

Paul admits that the Preaching of the Cross is foolishness to the world; nevertheless, the Cross must be preached because this is the only manner in which men can be Saved. In other words, and as we have repeatedly stated, Christ is the Source of all things that come from God, and the Cross is the Means by which these things are given to us, all superintended by the Holy Spirit (Rom. 8:2; I Cor. 1:17-18; Gal. 6:14).

The sad truth is, not many preachers are preaching the Cross. There are a few who preach the Cross as it regards Salvation, and thank God for that; however, there are almost none who are preaching the Cross as it regards our Sanctification, in other words, how we live for God.

Why?

THE PREACHING OF THE CROSS AS IT REGARDS OUR LIFE AND LIVING

The modern church, and I speak of those who claim to truly believe the Bible, knows next to nothing about the Cross of Christ as it regards our daily living for God. After Salvation, in the thinking of most preachers, the Cross is forgotten. As a result, the church stumbles from one scheme to the other, trying to find victory. As there is no Salvation outside of the Cross, likewise, there is no victory outside of the Cross. Regrettably, as the world tries to save itself outside of the Cross of Christ, the church tries to sanctify itself outside of the Cross of Christ. Neither is successful, as neither can be successful.

What does it mean to preach the Cross as it regards Sanctification?

Paul said, *"Christ sent me not to baptize, but to preach the Gospel: not with wisdom of words, lest the Cross of Christ should be made of none effect"* (I Cor. 1:17).

As we've already stated in previous study, in this one verse the Apostle tells us what the Gospel actually is, and please understand, the great Apostle is not addressing Salvation in this statement, but rather Sanctification.

To preach the Cross, as it regards Sanctification, simply means that the Preacher of the Gospel is to proclaim the fact that the Cross of Christ must ever be the Object of our Faith, meaning that the Cross alone is the Means by which we receive all things from the Lord. Sadly, however, there is an argument regarding that.

IS IT WHO JESUS WAS OR WHAT HE DID?

Generally, those who ask this question are denigrating the Cross. In other words, they do not want to make the Cross the sole Object of their Faith. So, they try to divide Christ from the Cross, claiming that the Cross is of little consequence and that the emphasis must be placed on Who Christ was and is, namely the Son of God.

The answer to that is simple!

It was both Who He was and what He did!

No one else but Jesus Christ, the Son of the Living God, could have carried out this great Work of Redemption. No Angel could have done so; no human being could have done so, only Christ. John addressed this by saying:

"In the beginning was the Word, and the Word was with God, and the Word was God" (Jn. 1:1).

This plainly tells us that Jesus Christ was and is God from eternity past to eternity future.

The great Apostle then said, *"And the Word was made flesh, and dwelt among us, (and we beheld His Glory, the Glory as of the Only Begotten of the Father,) full of Grace and Truth"* (Jn. 1:14).

Why was the Word made flesh, which speaks of the Incarnation of Christ, God becoming man?

We are given that answer when John the Baptist introduced Christ. He said:

"Behold the Lamb of God, which takes away the sin of the world" (Jn. 1:29).

This tells us that God became man, and did so for the purpose of going to the Cross, hence, John addressing Jesus as *"the Lamb of God."*

The short phrase, *"Lamb of God,"* had reference to the untold millions of lambs that had been offered up in sacrifice even from the first page of human history, all symbolic of Christ and what He would do for us at the Cross. Hence, the Holy Spirit through John the Baptist referred to Christ as *"the Lamb of God."*

In other words, God became man for the express purpose of going to the Cross and, thereby, redeeming mankind from the terrible bondage of sin. He would give Himself as a Perfect Sacrifice, which God the Father would accept, thereby, atoning for all sin, past, present, and future, at least for those who will believe (Jn. 3:16).

Jesus Christ has always been God. He did not suddenly become God in the Incarnation. As John 1:1 states, He was God from eternity past and will be God to eternity future. But the answer to the great question is this:

The mere fact of Him being God, in other words, *"Who He was,"* did not save anyone. While it was absolutely necessary that He be God, which He was, in order for men to be redeemed, still, that mere fact alone was insufficient for Salvation. For Salvation to be carried out, which includes Sanctification, in other words, all that we receive from the Lord, and all that we are in the Lord, it was absolutely necessary that God would become man and for the sole purpose of going to the Cross. That was why He came. So, it was not only Who He was but, as well, what He did, which refers to the Cross!

It is absolutely impossible, at least with any degree of honesty, to read the Bible and not see that the central core of the Word of God is, *"Jesus Christ and Him Crucified."* Therefore, to denigrate the Cross in any capacity is to misunderstand the entire scope of the Word of God and the Plan of Redemption. When the Cross is taken out of Christianity, there is nothing left but a vapid philosophy. And regrettably, that is exactly what is presently being done. Christianity is being degenerated to the mere whims of man.

"Oh Jesus, King most wonderful,
"Thou Conqueror renowned;
"Thou Sweetness most ineffable,
"In Whom all joys are found;"

"When once You visit the heart,
"Then Truth begins to shine;
"Then earthly vanities depart,

"Then kindles Love Divine."

"Jesus! Your Mercies are untold,
"Through each returning day;
"Your Love exceeds a thousand fold,
"Whatever we can say."

"May every heart confess Your Name,
"And ever You adore;
"And, seeking You itself inflame,
"And seek You more and more."

"You may our tongues forever bless,
"You may we love alone:
"And ever in our lives express,
"The Image of Your Own."

CHAPTER 3

(1) "THEN SOLOMON BEGAN TO BUILD THE HOUSE OF THE LORD AT JERUSALEM IN MOUNT MORIAH, WHERE THE LORD APPEARED UNTO DAVID HIS FATHER, IN THE PLACE THAT DAVID HAD PREPARED IN THE THRESHINGFLOOR OF ORNAN THE JEBUSITE.

(2) "AND HE BEGAN TO BUILD IN THE SECOND DAY OF THE SECOND MONTH, IN THE FOURTH YEAR OF HIS REIGN."

The exegesis is:

1. (Vs. 1) This is the first mention of Mount Moriah since Genesis 22:2. It is never mentioned after this. It is where Abraham, it is believed, was to offer up Isaac.

2. (Vs. 1) *"The threshingfloor of Ornan the Jebusite"* presents a place of judgment, which speaks of the destroying Angel (II Sam. 24:16). It is now turned into a place of Blessing, all by the Grace of God.

3. It is believed that Solomon was 20 years old when he began to reign, and that he reigned 40 years, dying at 60 years of age.

THE BEGINNING OF CONSTRUCTION

I Kings 6:1 states that the beginning of the construction of the Temple was some 480 years from the time of the Exodus.

Some say this is a corrupted Text, with some of the older manuscripts omitting the time frame. In fact, it has never been settled as to exactly how long the period of the Judges actually was; however, it is my opinion that the number given in I Kings 6:1 (480 years) is correct.

Their beginning to build constituted the greatest building project in the history of man. In this building God would dwell, and yet, even as Solomon had said, *"The heaven and heaven of heavens could not contain the Lord,"* much less this building. Nevertheless, this building was designed by the Lord with its design, down to the minutest detail, being given to David, and then David giving the design to his son Solomon, and now the structure is beginning to take shape.

Israel was the only Nation at this time on the face of the Earth who knew Jehovah. This means they were monotheistic, the worshipper of one God. All the other nations of the world were polytheistic, meaning they worshipped many gods, in reality, demon spirits. In view of the fact that God was with Israel, this means that they were light years ahead of every other nation on Earth. It was sin that brought them down, and it is sin that will bring anyone down, if it remains unconfessed and, thereby, unforgiven.

(3) "NOW THESE ARE THE THINGS WHEREIN SOLOMON WAS INSTRUCTED FOR THE BUILDING OF THE HOUSE OF GOD. THE LENGTH BY CUBITS AFTER THE FIRST MEASURE WAS THREESCORE CUBITS, AND THE BREADTH TWENTY CUBITS.

(4) "AND THE PORCH THAT WAS IN THE FRONT OF THE HOUSE, THE LENGTH OF IT WAS ACCORDING TO THE BREADTH OF THE HOUSE, TWENTY CUBITS, AND THE HEIGHT WAS AN HUNDRED AND TWENTY: AND HE OVERLAID IT WITHIN WITH PURE GOLD.

(5) "AND THE GREATER HOUSE HE CIELED WITH FIR TREE, WHICH HE OVERLAID WITH FINE GOLD, AND SET THEREON PALM TREES AND CHAINS.

(6) "AND HE GARNISHED THE HOUSE WITH PRECIOUS STONES FOR BEAUTY: AND THE GOLD WAS GOLD OF PARVAIM.

(7) "HE OVERLAID ALSO THE HOUSE, THE BEAMS, THE POSTS, AND THE WALLS THEREOF, AND THE DOORS THEREOF, WITH GOLD; AND GRAVED CHERUBIMS ON THE WALLS."

The pattern is:

1. (Vs. 3) The length and width of the house here given pertained to the Holy Place and the Holy of Holies. The entire length was 90 feet, and the width was 30 feet; however, this pertained only to the Temple proper. Many rooms were also built on each side.

2. (Vs. 4) The height is definitely a copyist error in one of the old manuscripts. This would make the Temple 180 feet high—twice as high as it was long. In I Kings 6:2, it states that the height was 30 cubits, or 45 feet, counting 18 inches to the cubit. This would be normal for the highest part of the Temple, and for the three stories of chambers (I Ki. 6:8).

3. (Vs. 4) The *"gold"* signified the Deity of Christ, with every part of the Temple, in fact, portraying Christ, in His Atoning, Mediatorial, or Intercessory Work.

4. (Vs. 5) Everything about the house was designed by the Holy Spirit, even down to the minutest detail. It must be adhered to strictly.

5. (Vs. 7) The *"Cherubims"* speak of God's Holiness. The *"palm trees"* of Verse 5 speak of the perfect rest found only in Christ, with the *"chains"* of that Verse speaking of the never-ceasing link of the Child of God with the Lord Jesus Christ.

THE DIMENSIONS OF THE HOUSE

As stated, the structure was 90 feet long. The first room, the Holy Place, was 60 feet long, while the smaller room, which was the Holy of Holies where the Ark of the Covenant was kept and where God dwelt, was 30 feet long and 30 feet wide.

It should be observed that the great Brazen Altar, which was a Type of Christ and what He would do at the Cross, was, as well, 30 feet wide and 30 feet long. This means that the Grace of God through the Sacrifice was just as great as the Power of God, as it pertained to the Holy of Holies.

PURE GOLD

As is here obvious, there was gold in abundance in Solomon's Temple. Oddly enough, in the Millennial Temple described in Ezekiel, Chapters 40 through 48, there is no record that there is any gold whatsoever in that particular Temple.

Why the difference?

Gold in the Old Testament, at least as it regards the Tabernacle and the Temple, refers to Deity. In the coming Kingdom Age, Christ will be present personally, so there will be no need for gold in the Millennial Temple.

The Temple of Solomon was a fore picture of the Millennial Glory of Christ as Melchizedek, but only a fore picture. The Tabernacle in the Wilderness set out our Lord's Grace as Saviour.

Nothing was left to the imagination of Moses in the building of the Tabernacle or of Solomon in the building of the Temple. Grace was expressed by the Tabernacle; Glory by the Temple. As silver is resplendent of Grace; therefore, it was prominent in the Tabernacle. Gold, as stated, speaks of Deity and Glory, hence, was prominent in the Temple. The Tabernacle spoke of access to God; the Temple, of fellowship with God.

The first building (the Tabernacle) pictures Christ in His First Advent; the latter building, the Temple, pictures Christ in His Second Advent. The first building had sand for a floor; the second, gold. The first is a Tent; the second, a Temple. But whether a Tent or a Temple, the materials, the Vessels, and all the gathered wealth of each are precious and utter His Praise.

THE GLORY OF GOD

Both the Tabernacle and the Temple speak of fellowship with God, which can only come through the Atonement of Christ.

Both Solomon and the Temple picture Christ's glorious Kingdom over the Earth. Solomon in his glory, riches, and wisdom sets out the Person of Christ. The Temple symbolizes the Nature of Christ—gold prefiguring His Deity and cedar His Humanity, but all has Grace and Atonement as its Foundation, for this building of Glory was built upon the threshingfloor of Araunah, the Jebusite.

PRECIOUS STONES

The Sixth Verse says, *"And he garnished the house with precious stones for beauty."*

This explains what was done with the

many precious stones and gems of various colors, which David had gathered to beautify the Temple (I Chron. 29:2). This must have been a beautiful sight to behold. The *"precious stones"* speak of the Redeemed. *"And they shall be Mine, says the LORD of Hosts, in that day when I make up My Jewels"* (Mal. 3:17).

The Seventh Verse says, *". . . And graved Cherubims on the walls."* The *"Cherubims"* speak of God's Holiness. The *"palm trees"* speak of a perfect climate. The *"chains"* speak of the never-ceasing link of the Child of God to the Lord Jesus Christ.

God is a thrice-Holy God; consequently, the Cherubims are Living Creatures, which stand before the Throne of God in Heaven continually, and cry unceasingly, *"Holy, Holy, Holy, Lord God Almighty, which was, and is, and is to come"* (Rev. 4:8).

"What a mighty God we serve,
"What a mighty God we serve,
"Angels bow before Him,
"Heaven and Earth adore Him,
"What a mighty God we serve!"

(8) "AND HE MADE THE MOST HOLY HOUSE, THE LENGTH WHEREOF WAS ACCORDING TO THE BREADTH OF THE HOUSE, TWENTY CUBITS, AND THE BREADTH THEREOF TWENTY CUBITS: AND HE OVERLAID IT WITH FINE GOLD, AMOUNTING TO SIX HUNDRED TALENTS.

(9) "AND THE WEIGHT OF THE NAILS WAS FIFTY SHEKELS OF GOLD. AND HE OVERLAID THE UPPER CHAMBERS WITH GOLD.

(10) "AND IN THE MOST HOLY HOUSE HE MADE TWO CHERUBIMS OF IMAGE WORK, AND OVERLAID THEM WITH GOLD.

(11) "AND THE WINGS OF THE CHERUBIMS WERE TWENTY CUBITS LONG: ONE WING OF THE ONE CHERUB WAS FIVE CUBITS, REACHING TO THE WALL OF THE HOUSE: AND THE OTHER WING WAS LIKEWISE FIVE CUBITS, REACHING TO THE WING OF THE OTHER CHERUB.

(12) "AND ONE WING OF THE OTHER CHERUB WAS FIVE CUBITS, REACHING TO THE WALL OF THE HOUSE: AND THE OTHER WING WAS FIVE CUBITS ALSO, JOINING TO THE WING OF THE OTHER CHERUB.

(13) "THE WINGS OF THESE CHERUBIMS SPREAD THEMSELVES FORTH TWENTY CUBITS: AND THEY STOOD ON THEIR FEET, AND THEIR FACES WERE INWARD.

(14) "AND HE MADE THE VEIL OF BLUE, AND PURPLE, AND CRIMSON, AND FINE LINEN, AND WROUGHT CHERUBIMS THEREON."

The pattern is:

1. (Vss. 8, 10) *"The most Holy House,"* was actually the *"Holy of Holies,"* which contained the Ark of the Covenant.

2. (Vs. 9) It seems that even the nails were made of pure gold.

3. As it regards the word *"inward"* used in Verse 13, there is some indication in the Hebrew, as used here, that it means *"toward the house,"* in other words, outward.

In Moses' Tabernacle, the Cherubim looked down upon the blood-sprinkled Mercy Seat, for only there could their eyes rest with satisfaction all around, being under the reign of sin and death. But here the new Cherubim looked *"outward"* upon a kingdom governed in Righteousness by the King of Righteousness.

4. (Vs. 14) The *"Veil of blue"* signified that Christ came from Heaven.

5. (Vs. 14) The *"purple"* signified that Christ is the King.

6. (Vs. 14) The *"crimson"* signified His shed Blood on the Cross of Calvary, which was necessary in order that man be redeemed.

7. (Vs. 14) The *"fine linen"* signified the Perfect Righteousness of Christ.

8. (Vs. 14) The *"Cherubims,"* as stated, signified the Holiness of our Lord. The Veil of the Temple is described here as being like that in the Tabernacle of Moses. It is not mentioned in I Kings at all. In I Kings 6:31, the Holy Spirit records the fact that there were doors made of olive wood between the Most Holy Place and the Holy Place. It does not mention the Veil. In this Passage, it mentions *"the Veil,"* but does not mention the doors. Quite possibly, the Veil hung immediately behind the doors; therefore, when the doors were opened, the Veil would

remain, and continue to hide the Holy of Holies from inquisitive stares.

THE HOLY OF HOLIES

"The most Holy House" refers to the *"Holy of Holies"* where the Ark of the Covenant was kept. It was the smaller of the two rooms of the main part of the Temple, and was where the Ark of the Covenant was placed.

It was 30 feet square and was overlaid with pure gold (I Ki. 6:20). The Scripture says the amount of gold was *"six hundred talents."* As it regards the price of gold in 2008, there would have been nearly 10 billion dollars worth of gold in this one room.

The flooring, the ceiling, the walls, the ornamentation, the costly stones, the precious wood, the gold, the brass, the carved Cherubim, the Veils, the two pillars and all the vessels of the house, together with its golden doors, and the dedicated treasures—all picture the Glories, the Perfections, the Graces, the Ministries, the Activities, and the Offices of Christ in His Second Advent and Millennial Reign.

Upon entering either chamber of the Sanctuary (the Holy Place or the Most Holy Place), nothing was seen above, beneath, or on either side but the purest gold, wrought by Divine Inspiration into exquisite ornamentation—Palm Trees and Wreathen work and Cherubim.

The Ninth Verse says, *"And the weight of the nails was fifty shekels of gold."*

This means that each nail, as it regards the price of gold in 2008, cost nearly $200,000 each.

It is so beautiful as to how the Grace of the Holy Spirit drew attention to the nails used in the construction of this great Temple. He does not overlook such small and simple things when detailing all these dazzling splendors. He Alone saw them, for they were hidden, but they held everything together and are remembered and named by God.

Were a golden lampstand to speak slightingly of the little golden nail, as some great preachers are tempted so to treat a junior Sunday School Teacher, the nail could reply that it was also formed of pure gold and had an indispensable office in the structure of this great House of God.

THE CHERUBIM

Verse 10 says, *"And in the Most Holy House he made two Cherubims of image work, and overlaid them with gold."*

These two Cherubim were very large, their wings reaching across the width of the Most Holy Place—30 feet. Each wing was 5 cubits or 7 and one half feet long. The outer ones touched the wall of the house while the inner ones touched each other. Thus, the two Cherubim with their four wings outstretched took the whole width of the room. These were completely covered with gold, and they stood on their feet, which were like those of a calf (Ezek. 1:7).

The latter portion of the Thirteenth Verse says, *"And their faces were inward."*

The word *"inward,"* as it is here used, in the Hebrew means, *"toward the house,"* in other words, outward.

There is no way that the mind of man can grasp what the Holy of Holies must have looked like with these huge Cherubim with their outstretched wings covering the entirety of the room. Even though this was only symbolic of the reality, which was in Heaven, still, it must have been an awesome sight.

How wonderful will it be when at long last we stand before the Throne of God and hear the Cherubim and the Seraphim (Isa. 6:1-8) cry *"Holy, Holy, Holy, Lord God Almighty, which was, and is, and is to come"* (Rev. 4:8).

The Cherubim in Moses' Tabernacle looked down on the Mercy Seat and the Shed Blood because the work was not yet finished. Now, and we speak of Solomon's Temple, the Cherubim look outward upon a Finished Work of the Grace and Glory of God.

(15) "ALSO HE MADE BEFORE THE HOUSE TWO PILLARS OF THIRTY AND FIVE CUBITS HIGH, AND THE CHAPTER THAT WAS ON THE TOP OF EACH OF THEM WAS FIVE CUBITS.

(16) "AND HE MADE CHAINS, AS IN THE ORACLE, AND PUT THEM ON THE HEADS OF THE PILLARS; AND MADE AN HUNDRED POMEGRANATES, AND PUT THEM ON THE CHAINS.

(17) "AND HE REARED UP THE PILLARS BEFORE THE TEMPLE, ONE ON THE RIGHT HAND, AND THE OTHER ON THE LEFT; AND CALLED THE NAME OF THAT ON THE RIGHT HAND JACHIN, AND THE NAME OF THAT ON THE LEFT BOAZ."

The exegesis is:

1. (Vs. 15) Counting the Chapiters, the pillars were 60 feet tall.

2. (Vs. 16) The *"chains"* typified our union with Christ.

3. (Vs. 16) The *"pomegranates"* typified the Fruit of the Spirit.

4. (Vs. 17) Actually, the two pillars did not hold up anything. They were strictly for ornamentation, and signified Believers (Rev. 3:12).

5. (Vs. 17) The name *"Jachin"* means *"He shall establish."* The name *"Boaz"* means *"in it is strength."* The actual meaning is *"Believers shall be established in the Strength of the Lord."*

THE TWO PILLARS

Jesus said, as it regards His Message to the church at Philadelphia, *"Him who overcomes will I make a pillar in the Temple of My God* (the *'overcomer'* is the one who trusts explicitly in Christ and what He did for us at the Cross), *and he shall go no more out* (refers to a constant position in the Presence of God): *and I will write upon him the Name of My God, and the Name of the City of My God, which is New Jerusalem, which comes down out of Heaven from My God: and I will write upon him My new Name.* (At the Cross, Christ identified with our sin by suffering its penalty. Now He identifies with our most excellent Blessing, as He is the Source of all.)

"He who has an ear, let him hear what the Spirit says unto the Churches. (The Spirit is saying we must be ready for the Rapture, which can only be done by Faith constantly exhibited in Christ and His Finished Work)" (Rev. 3:12-13).

As we've already stated, these pillars sat right in front of the Temple; however, they did not uphold anything, as pillars usually do. They were made of bronze, or one might say, copper. In effect, these pillars were strictly for ornamentation. They served no purpose otherwise. They did not hold up anything, did not support anything, and did not figure at all into the structure of the building. As stated, they were for ornamentation only.

By our Lord using *"overcomers"* as *"pillars,"* He was telling us several things:

• The names given the pillars simply means, *"Believers shall be established in the Strength of the Lord."*

• The pillars were for ornamentation only, meaning that Believers are not actually needed in the Kingdom of God, and that our presence is constituted as ornamentation.

• Copper is beautiful if it is regularly scrubbed and honed; however, it corrodes very easily. If Believers are what we ought to be, the beauty will be apparent, otherwise, not so!

• Inasmuch as the Temple faced the east, when the sun would rise each morning over Mount Olivet, it would strike those pillars first, creating a beautiful light display. We must understand that as Believers, our beauty is only in Christ. Otherwise, there is no beauty. We are merely a reflection of His Glory; at least that's what we are supposed to be. This means we have no glory of our own; all is in Christ.

"Fairest Lord Jesus, Ruler of all nature,
"Oh Thou of God and Man the Son;
"You will I cherish, You will I honor,
"You my soul's glory, joy and crown."

"Fair are the meadows, fairer still the woodlands,
"Robed in the blooming garb of spring;
"Jesus is Fairer, Jesus is Purer,
"Who makes the woeful heart to sing."

"Fair is the sunshine, fairer still the moonlight,
"And fair the twinkling starry host;
"Jesus shines brighter, Jesus shines purer,
"Than all the Angels Heaven can boast."

"All fairest beauty, heavenly and earthly,

"Wondrously, Jesus is found in Thee;
"None can be nearer, fairer, or dearer,
"Than You my Saviour are to me."

CHAPTER 4

(1) "MOREOVER HE MADE AN ALTAR OF BRASS, TWENTY CUBITS THE LENGTH THEREOF, AND TWENTY CUBITS THE BREADTH THEREOF, AND TEN CUBITS THE HEIGHT THEREOF.

(2) "ALSO HE MADE A MOLTEN SEA OF TEN CUBITS FROM BRIM TO BRIM, ROUND IN COMPASS, AND FIVE CUBITS THE HEIGHT THEREOF; AND A LINE OF THIRTY CUBITS DID COMPASS IT ROUND ABOUT.

(3) "AND UNDER IT WAS THE SIMILITUDE OF OXEN, WHICH DID COMPASS IT ROUND ABOUT: TEN IN A CUBIT, COMPASSING THE SEA ROUND ABOUT. TWO ROWS OF OXEN WERE CAST, WHEN IT WAS CAST.

(4) "IT STOOD UPON TWELVE OXEN, THREE LOOKING TOWARD THE NORTH, AND THREE LOOKING TOWARD THE WEST, AND THREE LOOKING TOWARD THE SOUTH, AND THREE LOOKING TOWARD THE EAST: AND THE SEA WAS SET ABOVE UPON THEM, AND ALL THEIR HINDER PARTS WERE INWARD.

(5) "AND THE THICKNESS OF IT WAS AN HANDBREADTH, AND THE BRIM OF IT LIKE THE WORK OF THE BRIM OF A CUP, WITH FLOWERS OF LILIES; AND IT RECEIVED AND HELD THREE THOUSAND BATHS."

The exegesis is:

1. (Vs. 1) The dimensions given concerning the Brazen Altar were, as stated, the same dimensions as the Most Holy Place. The Altar portrayed God's Judgment on sin. The Holy of Holies portrayed His Mercy and Grace; therefore, God's Mercy and Grace are as large as His Judgment.

2. As it regards the *"twelve oxen"* of Verse 4, the number *"twelve"* signifies God's Government, while *"oxen"* symbolize the Word of God. So, God's Government is built entirely upon His Word, from which we must not deviate at all.

3. The latter portion of the Fourth Verse signifies that God's Government is the same throughout the entirety of the Earth. In other words, there is no such thing as a white man's gospel, or a black man's gospel, etc. It is one Gospel for the entirety of mankind.

4. (Vs. 4) As it regards the oxen holding up the Great Laver, considering that the oxen represent the Word of God, this tells us the Power of the Word.

5. Three thousand baths of Verse 5 constitute approximately 18,000 gallons. I Kings 7:27 says, *"two thousand baths."* There is no contradiction. The three thousand baths were the maximum amount of water that the molten sea would hold. Two thousand baths were the amount it generally held.

THE BRAZEN ALTAR

The Brazen Altar sat immediately in front of the Temple. One might say, I think, that this Altar constituted the core of all for which the Temple stood. As well, I think one might say, and without fear of contradiction, that it was the single most important Vessel of the entirety of the Temple structure. While every Vessel, of course, served a distinct purpose, all pointing to Christ, still, everything was dependent upon what took place at the Brazen Altar, namely the sacrifices.

As most know, the Brazen Altar was a portrayal, a Type, if you will, of the Cross of Calvary, of God's Judgment upon sin, carried out in the form of the Sacrifice of His Only Son, given for our sins. As we continue to say, Christ is the Source of all things from God, while the Cross is the Means by which those things are given to us, all superintended by the Holy Spirit.

Even the Holy of Holies, which represented the great Throne of God, where God actually dwelt between the Mercy Seat and the Cherubim, in an obvious way, depended upon the Brazen Altar, and what was there done.

The High Priest, who alone could come into the Holy of Holies, and then only once a year on the Great Day of Atonement, dared not come in without blood, which, of course, pertained to the sacrifice offered up on the

Brazen Altar.

THE GOLDEN ALTAR

As well, the Priests came into the Holy Place constantly, twice a day, at the time of the morning and the evening sacrifices. They were to take coals of fire from the Brazen Altar, place those coals on the Golden Altar, and then pour Incense on that, which filled the Holy Place with a fragrance. All of this typified Christ in His Intercessory Work. This was a Type, a Shadow, if you will, of that which makes possible our prayers, our petitions, our praise, and our worship. None could be accepted were it not for the Intercessory Work of Christ, of which the Golden Altar was a Type. So, we must never forget that all of this was made possible by the Cross.

THE BRAZEN LAVER

This apparatus, which had five smaller lavers on each side, held, as stated, about 18,000 gallons of water. The huge laver was for the Priests to wash when they went into the Holy Place. The smaller lavers were used to wash the parts of the sacrifices which were to be offered. It was all a Type of the Word of God, and failure to comply with the demands of the washings could well bring about the penalty of death. It signified the cleansing of the Word of God, which is incumbent upon every modern Believer.

The giant Laver sat upon twelve oxen, all made of copper. Three of the oxen looked toward the north, three toward the west, three toward the south, and three toward the east. This signified that the Word of God, of which these oxen were a Type, was the same all places and everywhere, in other words, every point of the compass. It is the Gospel for the entirety of mankind.

As it regards the whole of humanity, irrespective of class, culture, or race, the problem with all is sin. The solution to that problem, and there is only one solution, is the Cross of the Lord Jesus Christ. Around the top of the great Brazen Laver, and more than likely, the smaller ones, as well, were carved into the copper *"flowers of lilies."* This signified the Righteousness of Christ, all made possible by the Word, for Jesus is the Living Word (Jn. 1:1).

The giant Brazen Laver was 15 feet from brim to brim; 7 and a half feet high, and 45 feet all the way around. Incidentally, it was about 4 inches thick. It weighed anywhere from 15 to 20 tons. Having its 7 and a half foot depth filled would have taken approximately 18,000 gallons of water. Completely filled, it would have weighed about 75 tons.

The ten small Lavers were supposed to contain about 300 gallons of water each, which made each one weigh about two tons. Jewish writers say that the water was changed daily so as to be always fresh and pure for use in the ceremonial worship.

The entirety of the apparatus of the Brazen Laver was a Type of the Word of God. As the Priest would look into the water, he would see his reflection as in a mirror; likewise, when we read and study the Word of God, we see our reflection in the Word proclaiming to us what we are. The *"oxen"* stand for the indestructibility, power, and strength of the Word of God.

When Jesus came and went to the Cross, His Life, Living, and Death satisfied every demand of the Law, meaning that all of this we are studying came to an end. Why would one want the Shadow when one could have the substance?

All of this was ever meant to be temporary. It was all meant to point to Christ, Who would fulfill all the requirements when He came, which He did!

And please understand, as important as all of this was, and no matter how zealous the Priests were in carrying out all the demands of the Law, and even as much as they should have done this, still, none of it Saved anyone. Men have always been Saved in the same way. Before the Cross, they were Saved by looking forward to that which would ultimately come, and now that it is a fact, men are Saved by looking back to that Finished Work. This means that the Cross of Christ stands at the apex of humanity, with everything straining toward that Finished Work.

To make too much of the Cross is impossible. To make too little of the Cross is to invite spiritual disaster.

(6) "HE MADE ALSO TEN LAVERS, AND

PUT FIVE ON THE RIGHT HAND, AND FIVE ON THE LEFT, TO WASH IN THEM: SUCH THINGS AS THEY OFFERED FOR THE BURNT OFFERING THEY WASHED IN THEM; BUT THE SEA WAS FOR THE PRIESTS TO WASH IN."

The pattern is:

1. (Vs. 6) These were used to wash the sacrifices before they were offered.

2. (Vs. 6) The Priests, as we have stated, had to wash both their hands and feet every time they went into the Temple, with the giant Laver for this purpose.

3. If it is to be noticed, the Law demanded a constant doing.

THE WASHING OF THE HANDS AND THE FEET

The Scripture says, even as it regards the Brazen Laver, *"For Aaron and his sons shall wash their hands and their feet thereat:*

"When they go into the Tabernacle of the congregation, they shall wash with water, that they die not; or when they come near to the Altar to minister, to burn offerings made by fire unto the LORD:

"So they shall wash their hands and their feet, that they die not: it shall be a Statute forever to them, even to him and to his seed throughout their generations" (Ex. 30:19-21).

All of this meant that every time the Priests went into the Tabernacle (or the Temple) they were to wash both their hands and their feet. When they offered up the sacrifices on the great Altar, they were, as well, to wash their hands and their feet before it was carried out. This meant they were washing constantly, *"that they die not."* All of this meant, and we continue to speak of the washing, that everything be done according to the Word of God, of which the water was a Type.

THE WASHING OF THE FEET

As it regards the last Passover, the Scripture says that Jesus, *"After that He poured water into a basin* (spiritually, it referred to the Holy Spirit, which would pour from Him like a River [7:38-39]), *and began to wash the Disciples' feet* (presenting the servant principle which we are

NOTES

to follow, but even more particularly the cleansing guaranteed by the Holy Spirit concerning our daily walk, which comes about according to our Faith in Christ and what He did for us at the Cross), *and to wipe them with the towel wherewith He was girded* (refers to the Incarnation, which made possible His Death on Calvary that atoned for all sin and made cleansing possible for the human race).

"Then comes He to Simon Peter (seems to indicate it was Peter to whom He first approached): *and Peter said unto Him, Lord, do you wash my feet?* ('The flesh' cannot understand spiritual realities; it is too backward or too forward, too courageous or too cowardly; it is incapable of ever being right, and it is impossible to improve, consequently, it must *'die.'*)

"Jesus answered and said unto him, What I do you know not now; but you shall know hereafter (when Peter was filled with the Spirit, which he was on the Day of Pentecost).

"Peter said unto Him, You shall never wash my feet (the Greek Text actually says, 'Not while eternity lasts'; Calvin said, 'With God, obedience is better than worship'). *Jesus answered him, If I wash you not, you have no part with Me* (the statement as rendered by Christ speaks to the constant cleansing needed regarding our everyday walk before the Lord, which the washing of the feet [our walk], at least in part, represented).

"Simon Peter said unto Him, Lord, not my feet only, but also my hands and my head (Chrysostom said, 'In His deprecation He was vehement, and His yielding more vehement, but both came from His love').

"Jesus said to him, he who is washed needs not save to wash his feet (as stated, pertains to our daily walk before God, which means that the Believer doesn't have to get Saved over and over again; the *'head'* refers to our Salvation, meaning that we do not have to be repeatedly Saved, while the *'hands'* refer to our *'doing,'* signifying that this doesn't need to be washed because Christ has already done what needs to be done; all of this is in the Spiritual sense), *but is clean every whit.* (Refers to Salvation, and pertains to the

Precious Blood of Jesus that cleanses from all sin; the infinite Sacrifice needs no repetition) . . ." (Jn. 13:5-10).

The Priests of old had to wash both their hands and their feet, and do so constantly, because the Law could not save and neither could it cleanse. This means that not only did their walk at times become polluted, but their doing as well.

Since the Cross, while our *"walk"* needs attending constantly, even as Jesus here portrayed, the doing doesn't have to be done anymore. It has already been done in Christ.

OUR WALK BEFORE GOD

The Holy Spirit through the Apostle Paul used the word *"walk"* constantly, as it describes our everyday life and living, in other words, our walk before God and our fellowman (Rom. 8:1).

How is the Believer to look to this constant need? Should there be foot washing services each week at church?

No!

What Jesus did was an example and carried out to teach the Disciples, you, and me a lesson.

There is nothing that we can personally do, no matter how consecrated to the Lord, at least within our own capabilities, that will cleanse our walk. So, how do we walk correctly before the Lord, and do so on a constant basis?

WALKING AFTER THE SPIRIT

The Holy Spirit through Paul said:

"There is therefore now no condemnation (guilt) *to them which are in Christ Jesus* (refers back to Rom. 6:3-5 and our being baptized into His Death, which speaks of the Crucifixion), *who walk not after the flesh* (depending on one's personal strength and ability or great religious efforts in order to overcome sin), *but after the Spirit*. (The Holy Spirit works exclusively within the legal confines of the Finished Work of Christ; our Faith in that Finished Work, i.e., 'the Cross,' guarantees the help of the Holy Spirit which guarantees Victory)" (Rom. 8:1).

So, what does it mean to *"walk after the Spirit?"*

Unfortunately, most people think the explanation of this question is that we do spiritual things. In other words, we are faithful to attend church, faithful in our giving of our tithe to the Work of the Lord, faithful in witnessing to souls, faithful in our prayer life and Bible study, etc.

While all of these things are very, very important, actually Christian disciplines, which should be a part of all Christian life and living, still, that's not what Paul is talking about.

"Walking after the Spirit" simply means that we place our Faith exclusively in Christ and what Christ has done for us at the Cross and not allow it to be moved elsewhere (Rom. 8:2, 11).

The Spirit of God works exclusively within the parameters of the Finished Work of Christ, i.e., the Cross. It is the Cross of Christ which gave and gives the Holy Spirit the legal right to do all that He does. That's the reason that it is referred to as *"the Law."* And please understand, when Paul used that word in Romans 8:2, he wasn't speaking of the Law of Moses, but rather a Law that was devised by the Godhead in eternity past.

In the modern Christian climate, Jesus Christ is held up, at least to some extent, but the Cross is all but ignored. Please understand, if the Believer tries to separate Christ from the Cross, he is left with *"another Jesus"* (II Cor. 11:4). That's the reason that Paul also said, *"We preach Christ Crucified"* (I Cor. 1:23). He did not say, *"We preach Christ,"* but rather, *"we preach Christ Crucified."* In other words, he never separated Christ from the Cross, i.e., what Christ did for us at the Cross, the victories there won.

So, to walk after the Spirit, is simply to place our Faith exclusively in Christ and what Christ did for us at the Cross, which then gives the Holy Spirit latitude to work within our lives.

WALKING AFTER THE FLESH

What did Paul mean by *"walking after the flesh?"*

He is referring to the natural strength, power, motivation, intellect, education, talents, and ability of the individual. Within themselves, these things aren't necessarily wrong. But it's impossible to please the Lord, in other words, to successfully live for God, by human means, as dedicated as those human means may very well be. When we look to these particular means within ourselves, no matter how dedicated we might be, no matter how consecrated we might be, no matter how sincere we might be, and no matter how much we load up the flesh with Scriptures, still, the Scripture bluntly says, *"they who are in the flesh cannot please God"* (Rom. 8:8).

In other words, the Believer within himself, by his own ability, strength, machinations, talent, etc., cannot develop Righteousness and Holiness within his life. It is impossible. These are Works that the Holy Spirit Alone can bring about in our lives. And he does so by us placing our Faith exclusively in Christ and the Cross.

WHY ARE OUR PERSONAL EFFORTS INSUFFICIENT?

Paul answered that as well. He said: *"And if Christ be in you* (He is in you through the Power and Person of the Spirit [Gal. 2:20]), *the body is dead because of sin* (means that the physical body has been rendered helpless because of the Fall; consequently, the Believer trying to overcome by willpower presents a fruitless task); *but the Spirit is life because of Righteousness.* (Only the Holy Spirit can make us what we ought to be, which means we cannot do it ourselves; once again, He performs all that He does within the confines of the Finished Work of Christ)" (Rom. 8:10).

This, looking totally to Christ and what He did for us at the Cross, instead of looking to our own strength and ability, is the great struggle facing every Child of God. In fact, because of this great struggle, most of that which is given to us by the Apostle Paul, which was inspired by the Holy Spirit, deals with this very subject. When we depend totally on Christ and the Cross, it gives the Holy Spirit latitude to work in our lives. And yet, we find so little preaching and teaching from the modern pulpit regarding this which is so very, very important.

Jesus bluntly and plainly told us, *"If any man will come after Me* (the criteria for Discipleship), *let him deny himself* (not asceticism as many think, but rather that one denies one's own willpower, self-will, strength, and ability, depending totally on Christ), *and take up his Cross* (the benefits of the Cross, looking exclusively to what Jesus did there to meet our every need), *daily* (this is so important, our looking to the Cross; that we must renew our Faith in what Christ has done for us, even on a daily basis, for Satan will ever try to move us away from the Cross as the Object of our Faith, which always spells disaster), *and follow Me.* (Christ can be followed only by the Believer looking to the Cross, understanding what it accomplished, and by that means alone [Rom. 6:3-5, 11, 14; 8:1-2, 11; I Cor. 1:17-18, 21, 23; 2:2; Gal. 6:14; Eph. 2:13-18; Col. 2:14-15])" (Lk. 9:23).

The Lord then followed up by saying, *"And whosoever does not bear his Cross* (this doesn't speak of suffering as most think, but rather ever making the Cross of Christ the Object of our Faith; we are Saved and we are victorious not by suffering, although that sometimes will happen, or any other similar things, but rather by our Faith, but always with the Cross of Christ as the Object of that Faith), *and come after Me* (one can follow Christ only by Faith in what He has done for us at the Cross; He recognizes nothing else), *cannot be My Disciple.* (The statement is emphatic! If it's not Faith in the Cross of Christ, then it's faith that God will not recognize, which means that such people are refused)" (Lk. 14:27). The Word of God must always be the criteria.

THE WORD OF GOD

The Word of God, i.e., the Bible, is the single most important thing in the world. I know that's quite a statement, but it is true.

The second most important thing is that the Believer understands what is said in the Word. Admittedly, some parts of the Bible, especially some of the Prophecies given in the Old Testament, and even some of the teaching of Paul, are not easy to understand; therefore, every Believer ought to set himself to study the Word, asking the Lord to help him understand the Word, in effect, making it a lifelong project. It will be the most rewarding and the most fruitful thing in which anyone could ever begin to engage.

Presently, Satan is attacking the Word of God maybe as never before; however, he is doing it in a very subtle way.

When I was just a boy, Satan, of course, made his efforts at that time as well. But in those days it was a frontal attack, mostly generated by the modernists, so-called. Today, scores of versions of the Bible are being brought out, such as the Message Bible, for instance.

Please understand, unless your Bible is a word for word translation, then you really do not have a Bible but only a religious book. The Message Bible, plus scores of others like that particular version, are really not Bibles. It is Satan's way of diluting, perverting, and ultimately destroying the Word of God.

WHAT IS A WORD FOR WORD TRANSLATION?

The term, *"word for word translation,"* simply means that the translators did their very best to translate from the original Hebrew and Greek Text into the language at hand, in this case, English.

There are no original manuscripts of the Bible left. However, there are thousands of copies which do remain, some of them going back to within 300 years of the original. The Dead Sea Scrolls are a case in point.

The Old Testament was originally written in Hebrew with the New Testament originally written in Greek. Not having printing presses in those days, Scribes were used to make copies of the original manuscript, and there were, as stated, thousands made.

We believe that the Lord inspired the writers in that they wrote exactly what He wanted and desired, meaning that every word is important.

WHAT IS INSPIRATION?

Inspiration simply means, at least in this case, that the Lord gave to the writers that which He wanted, and consequently, it is error free. This means there are no contradictions, and all because it is the Word of God.

The details of Inspiration mean that the Lord searched through the vocabulary of every writer and, thereby, chose the exact word out of their vocabulary that He wanted as it regarded what was being said.

These men knew what they were writing. They did not go into a trance as some teach, but rather wrote as the Holy Spirit gave them the very words they were to use. It would be somewhat like a computer searching for particular words, as the Lord searched through their vocabulary, as stated, and then had them to write what He so desired. That's the reason Jesus said, *"Man shall not live by bread alone, but by every Word that proceeds out of the Mouth of God"* (Mat. 4:4).

This is what makes it so wrong for people to change the words given by the Holy Spirit, thereby, substituting their own words to take their place. But, there is something else that needs to be said about that.

I use the King James Version of the Bible, believing that it is still the very best Version that's in the world today, at least as it regards English.

However, the reader must understand, that the King James Version has been edited two or three times.

I have a copy of one of the pages of the original King James Version. The Elizabethan English at that time was so different than what we now speak that it's very difficult to even read what was printed. So, the King James Version has been edited two or three times because of the change of language.

This doesn't mean that the words were changed, but that the Elizabethan English was changed to more accommodating English for the present time, and rightly so.

For instance, there are still some words in the modern King James Version which are antiquated, meaning that we do not use them anymore. Words such as *"hast,"* etc. Consequently, when the Lord helped us to put together THE EXPOSITOR'S STUDY BIBLE, we changed some of those words to modern English, which mean the same thing.

The reader must understand that when the original writers wrote the Text, and we speak of Moses, David, Isaiah, Peter, Paul, etc., they didn't use Elizabethan English. So, the idea is, a word for word translation must be just that, meaning that the translators have done everything within their power to bring the original Hebrew and Greek Text over into the language at hand, and as already stated, in this case, English.

The Bible is the road map for eternity, the blueprint for life. There is no other. There are many other books that claim to be holy, but they aren't. The Bible alone fits that Standard. It is the Word of God, and there is only one Word of God.

I have said many times, and continue to say, personally, I only have one desire, and that is to understand the Word of God, whatever it teaches. I have no personal preference regarding what the Bible teaches. I just want to know what it does teach and, prayerfully, that I understand it correctly and deliver it to the public.

(7) "AND HE MADE TEN CANDLESTICKS OF GOLD ACCORDING TO THEIR FORM, AND SET THEM IN THE TEMPLE, FIVE ON THE RIGHT HAND, AND FIVE ON THE LEFT.

(8) "HE MADE ALSO TEN TABLES, AND PLACED THEM IN THE TEMPLE, FIVE ON THE RIGHT SIDE, AND FIVE ON THE LEFT. AND HE MADE AN HUNDRED BASONS OF GOLD."

The exegesis is:

1. (Vs. 7) The word *"candlesticks"* should have been translated *"lampstands."*

2. (Vs. 7) The Lampstands typify the fact that Christ is the Light of the world.

3. (Vs. 8) The *"ten tables"* were tables that held *"Shewbread."*

4. (Vs. 8) There was only one Lampstand and one Table in the Tabernacle, but here there are ten of each.

5. (Vs. 8) The *"tables"* each held twelve loaves of bread, which had to be eaten by the Priests every Sabbath, with new loaves taking their place. The bread was a Type of Christ as the *"Bread of Life"* (Jn. 6:48).

THE LAMPSTANDS

These Lampstands provided light for the Holy Place in order that the Priests could carry out their work. They were Types of Christ, as stated, as the Light of the world.

Every morning at 9 a.m. and every afternoon at 3 p.m., the Priests were to trim the wicks on each lamp in order that soot would not develop, thereby, polluting the Holy Place. As well, the oil was to be replenished at that time also.

The Lampstands, in a sense, typify the Lord Jesus Christ, the Holy Spirit, and Believers.

The golden part of the stand, and all of it was of pure gold, typified Christ in His Deity.

The oil typified the Holy Spirit, as would be obvious.

The wicks that had to be trimmed twice a day, typified Believers. That was the only part of the Lampstand that could be polluted and, thereby, not burn brightly as it should, therefore, typifying Believers. As Believers, we constantly need trimming, all in order that we function as we should function. How many Believers are burning brightly, and how many Believers are smoking up the Holy Place?

The three prongs to the side of the main stem, as it regards the Lampstand, are, in a sense, types of Believers. Christ is the Main Stem, as would be obvious. Believers are *"in Christ,"* exactly as the three stems from each side are in the main stem. But, here is the thing about the joining of the side stems with the main stem.

These stems were not welded to the main stem or fixed in any manner. When the goldsmith fashioned the Lampstand, he fashioned it, as stated, out of one piece of gold. Consequently, each stem is a part of the main stem exactly as a limb is the part of a tree.

This portrays the fact that we, as Believers, are more than merely being attached to Christ, inasmuch as we are *"in Christ."* Jesus said:

"At that day you shall know that I am in My Father, and you in Me, and I in you" (Jn. 14:20).

As well, Paul used the term, *"in Christ Jesus,"* or one of its derivatives, such as *"in Him,"* over a hundred times in his fourteen Epistles.

We are *"in Christ"* by virtue of His Atoning Death on the Cross. The Scripture says:

"Know you not, that so many of us as were baptized into Jesus Christ (plainly says that this Baptism is into Christ and not water [I Cor. 1:17; 12:13; Gal. 3:28-29;

Eph. 4:5; Col. 2:11-13]) *were baptized into His Death?* (When Christ died on the Cross, in the Mind of God, we died with Him; in other words, He became our Substitute, and our identification with Him in His Death gives us all the benefits for which He died; the idea is that He did it all for us!)

"Therefore we are buried with Him by baptism into death (not only did we die with Him, but we were buried with Him as well, which means that all the sin and transgression of the past were buried; when they put Him in the Tomb, they put all of our sins into that Tomb as well)*: that like as Christ was raised up from the dead by the Glory of the Father, even so we also should walk in Newness of Life* (we died with Him, we were buried with Him, and His Resurrection was our Resurrection to a 'Newness of Life').

"For if we have been planted together (with Christ) *in the likeness of His Death* (Paul proclaims the Cross as the instrument through which all Blessings come; consequently, the Cross must ever be the Object of our Faith, which gives the Holy Spirit latitude to work within our lives), *we shall be also in the likeness of His Resurrection.* (We can have the 'likeness of His Resurrection,' i.e., 'live this Resurrection Life,' only as long as we understand the 'likeness of His Death,' which refers to the Cross as the Means by which all of this is done)" (Rom. 6:3-5).

IS IT POSSIBLE FOR THE BELIEVER TO BE TAKEN OUT OF CHRIST?

The word *"Believer"* proclaims the fact that the individual has Faith in Christ and what Christ has done for us at the Cross. As such, no, the Believer cannot be removed from Christ.

It is Faith that gets the Believer into Christ, which refers to Faith in Christ and what He did at the Cross. Even though the believing sinner may understand little of Christ when He first comes to the Lord, still, it is his Faith supplied by the Holy Spirit, which is tendered upon the Word of God that's been delivered to the believing sinner in some way that makes all of this possible. The Holy Spirit supplies the Faith, and the believing sinner then believes, at least, if he does. At that moment he is Saved.

NOTES

So, Faith gets one in (Rom. 5:1-2), and it is Faith that keeps one in (Rom. 6:1-14). But, if the Believer ceases to believe, thereby, ceasing to be a Believer, then such a person is put in the category of being lost. Listen again to Paul:

"For it is impossible for those who were once enlightened (refers to those who have accepted the Light of the Gospel, which means accepting Christ and His great Sacrifice), *and have tasted of the Heavenly Gift* (pertains to Christ and what He did at the Cross), *and were made partakers of the Holy Spirit* (which takes place when a person comes to Christ),

"And have tasted the good Word of God (is not language that is used of an impenitent sinner, as some claim; the unsaved have no relish whatsoever for the Truth of God, and see no beauty in it), *and the powers of the world to come* (refers to the Work of the Holy Spirit within hearts and lives, which the unsaved cannot have or know),

"If they shall fall away (should have been translated, 'and having fallen away'), *to renew them again unto Repentance* ('again' states they had once repented, but have now turned their backs on Christ); *seeing they crucify to themselves the Son of God afresh* (means they no longer believe what Christ did at the Cross, actually concluding Him to be an imposter; the only way any person can truly repent is to place his Faith in Christ and the Cross; if that is denied, there is no repentance), *and put Him to an open shame.* (Means to hold Christ up to public ridicule; Paul wrote this Epistle because some Christian Jews were going back into Judaism, or seriously contemplating doing so)" (Heb. 6:4-6).

Christ and what He did at the Cross is the only way a person can be Saved, and continued Faith in that Sacrifice is the only thing that keeps us *"in Christ."* That being lost, which means that a person of his own free will makes a conscious decision to cease to believe, then that individual is lost. As stated, it's Faith that got us in, and it's Faith that keeps us in. As long as Faith is maintained in Christ and what He did at the Cross, Salvation is maintained, as well, irrespective of the state of the individual otherwise.

WHAT DO WE MEAN BY THE TERM *"FAITH"*?

Always and without exception, when the word *"Faith"* is used in the Bible, at least as it refers to the individual and the Lord, it is referring to Faith in Christ and what He did for us at the Cross. In other words, the Cross of Christ must always be the Object of our Faith.

The truth is, every person in the world has faith, but it is only Faith in Christ and the Cross which is recognized by the Lord. So, to merely have faith is not enough. It must be Faith in Christ and the Cross, meaning that the Cross of Christ, as stated, is the Object of one's Faith, and is always the Object of one's Faith.

Paul said: *"Therefore being justified by Faith* (this is the only way one can be justified; refers to Faith in Christ and what He did at the Cross [I Cor. 1:17-18, 23; 2:2]), *we have peace with God* (justifying peace) *through our Lord Jesus Christ* (what He did at the Cross)*:*

"By Whom also we have access by Faith into this Grace (we have access to the Goodness of God by Faith in Christ) *wherein we stand* (wherein alone we can stand), *and rejoice in hope* (a hope that is guaranteed) *of the Glory of God* (our Faith in Christ always brings Glory to God; anything else brings glory to self, which God can never accept)" (Rom. 5:1-2).

CHRIST AND THE CROSS

Christ is to never be separated from the Cross. And by that, we are not referring to the wooden beam, but rather to what He did there.

At the Cross, which refers to His Atoning Death, the Sacrifice of Himself, He atoned for all sin, past, present, and future, at least for all who will believe. In the atoning for all sin, this removed the legal right that Satan had to hold man in bondage. Sin was that which gave him that right, and with all sin atoned, *"taken away,"* that legal right the Evil One had has now been removed. So, if Satan is able to hold a Believer in bondage, it is because the Believer has placed his faith in something else other than Christ and the Cross. This gives Satan the consent to place such a one in bondage. That's why Paul also said:

"Stand fast therefore in the liberty wherewith Christ has made us free (we were made free, and refers to freedom to live a Holy Life by evidencing Faith in Christ and the Cross), *and be not entangled again with the yoke of bondage.* (To abandon the Cross and go under Law of any kind guarantees bondage once again to the sin nature)" (Gal. 5:1).

The modern church is big to laud Christ, most of the time as a Miracle Worker, or a great Example, or a great Teacher, etc., while conveniently forgetting that while He definitely was all of these things, most of all, however, He is Saviour. That's what He came to this world to do, to free man from the bondage of sin. He did it by the Cross, a Plan of Redemption which, in essence, was formulated in the Mind of the Godhead from before the foundation of the world (I Pet. 1:18-20).

So, when the Believer thinks *"Christ,"* it always must be in conjunction with His Sacrificial, Atoning Death on the Cross of Calvary. That's the reason that Paul said, *"We preach Christ Crucified"* (I Cor. 1:23).

That's the reason the great Apostle said, *"Christ sent me not to baptize, but to preach the Gospel: not with wisdom of words, lest the Cross of Christ should be made of none effect"* (I Cor. 1:17).

That's the reason that he also stated, *"For I determined not to know anything among you, save Jesus Christ, and Him Crucified"* (I Cor. 2:2).

Paul never separated Christ from the Cross because, while Jesus was most definitely the Source of all things that we receive from God, it was the Cross that provided the Means for these things to be done. We must never forget that!

TABLES OF SHEWBREAD

Everything in the Tabernacle, and everything in the Temple that would be built, portrayed Christ in some way. It pictured Who He was, what He would do, and how He would do it, which is what makes the Old Testament so important. Anything that pertains to Christ is of utmost significance, as should be obvious.

The Tables of Shewbread pictured Christ as the *"Bread of Life."* In fact, He mentioned this in John 6:35. He said:

"I am the Bread of Life (proclaims Him dropping all disguise, and gathering up into one burning Word all the previous teaching which they might have fathomed, but did not)*: he who comes to Me shall never hunger* (pertains to Spiritual hunger)*; and he who believes on Me shall never thirst.* (Pertains to Spiritual thirst; Christ satisfies all Spiritual desire)."

Our Lord then said: *"I am the Living Bread which came down from Heaven* (now proclaims Jesus presenting Himself as God ['*I am*'], while in the previous Verse He presented Himself as Man; and so He is the God-Man Jesus Christ)*: if any man eat of this Bread, he shall live forever* (says the same thing as in the previous Verse, but in a different way; there He said, '*and not die,*' now He says, '*shall live forever*'; the latter adds to the former)*: and the Bread that I will give is My flesh, which I will give for the life of the world.* (This speaks of Him giving Himself on the Cross as a Sacrifice, which would guarantee Salvation for all who would believe)" (Jn. 6:51).

EATING THE BREAD

On the Sabbath, the Priests had to eat all of the loaves of bread on the ten tables. Counting 12 loaves to the table, there would have been 120 loaves. These were replaced by fresh loaves.

The eating of the Bread, in essence, portrays the partaking of Christ, and doing so by placing Faith in Him and what He did at the Cross.

When the believing sinner accepts Christ, in the Mind of God, that believing sinner is actually placed into Christ, which includes His Death, His Burial, and His Resurrection (Rom. 6:3-5).

Jesus was and is the Last Adam, the Second Man (I Cor. 15:45-47), and as such is our Substitute, i.e., *"our representative Man."*

Being *"in Christ,"* means that whatever He is, that we are as well. In fact, everything He did was done in totality for us. He did nothing for Heaven, for Angels, for God the Father, or for Himself, rather, it was all done for us, i.e., *"for sinners."*

Did the Priests understand the symbolism in their eating the bread? It is doubtful! Quite possibly some few did, but more than likely, that number was small.

To prove my point, Israel came to believe that engaging in the ritual, i.e., the ceremony, granted them some type of dispensation with God. They even finally came to the place that they believed in a nationalistic Salvation, hence, being a Jew was sufficient enough, unless some of their rules were broken. That's why John the Baptist said when He came, *"And think not to say within yourselves, We have Abraham to our father: for I say unto you, that God is able of these stones to raise up children unto Abraham"* (Mat. 3:9).

(9) "FURTHERMORE HE MADE THE COURT OF THE PRIESTS, AND THE GREAT COURT, AND DOORS FOR THE COURT, AND OVERLAID THE DOORS OF THEM WITH BRASS.

(10) "AND HE SET THE SEA ON THE RIGHT SIDE OF THE EAST END, OVER AGAINST THE SOUTH."

The construction is:

1. (Vs. 9) The *"Doors"* also typified Christ; He said, *"I am the Door"* (Jn. 10:9).

2. (Vs. 9) The *"brass"* signified the Humanity of Christ.

3. (Vs. 10) The Brazen Laver, i.e., *"the Sea,"* had its position as the Tabernacle Laver of old, which was between the Altar and the porch.

THE COURTS

As is obvious, very little information is given here as it regards the Courts proper. The emphasis seems to be on the material used, such as the doors covered with brass.

Actually, there were three Courts in front of the Temple. The first one was nearest the Temple and was referred to as the *"Court of men,"* or *"the Court of Israel."* This means that only men and, of course, Priests could come into this Court.

The Court immediately behind the Court of Israel was the *"Court of women."* As well, only women were allowed here.

The last Court was the *"Court of Gentiles,"* which was separated from the Court of Women by a barrier. The height of the barrier was not given, but it is believed that it was about four feet high. For Gentiles to Cross that barrier, they could be stoned to death.

The women were placed in a secondary position, as is obvious, because of Eve who failed the Lord first of all.

As it regards the Gentiles, they had no Covenant with the Lord whatsoever; however, Gentiles, if they so chose, could become a proselyte Jew, which some did. To be Saved, this would have to be their course of action.

When Jesus came, all of this was addressed. Paul said:

"Wherefore remember, that you being in time past Gentiles in the flesh, who were called Uncircumcision (referred to the Gentiles not being in Covenant with God; physical circumcision under the old economy was its external sign) *by that which is called the Circumcision in the flesh made by hands* (is said by Paul in this manner, regarding the Jews, in contradistinction from the Circumcision of the heart);

"That at that time you were without Christ (describes the former condition of the Gentiles, who had no connection with Christ before the Cross), *being aliens from the commonwealth of Israel, and strangers from the Covenants of Promise, having no hope, and without God in the world* (all of this argues a darkened and perverted heart; the Gentiles had no knowledge of God at that time):

"But now in Christ Jesus (proclaims the basis of all Salvation) *you who sometimes* (times past) *were far off* (far from Salvation) *are made nigh* (near) *by the Blood of Christ.* (The Sacrificial Atoning Death of Jesus Christ transformed the relations of God with mankind. In Christ, God reconciled not a Nation, but 'a world' to Himself [II Cor. 5:19].)

"For He (Christ) *is our peace* (through Christ and what He did at the Cross, we have peace with God), *Who has made both one* (Jews and Gentiles), *and has broken down the middle wall of partition between us* (between Jews and Gentiles);

"Having abolished in His Flesh (speaking of His Death on the Cross, by which He Redeemed humanity, which also means He didn't die spiritually, as some claim) *the enmity* (the hatred between God and man, caused by sin), *even the Law of Commandments contained in Ordinances* (pertains to the Law of Moses, and more particularly the Ten Commandments); *for to make in Himself of twain* (of Jews and Gentiles) *one new man, so making peace* (which again was accomplished by the Cross);

"And that He (Christ) *might reconcile both* (Jews and Gentiles) *unto God in one body* (the Church) *by the Cross* (it is by the Atonement only that men ever become reconciled to God), *having slain the enmity thereby* (removed the barrier between God and sinful man):

"And came and preached peace to you which were afar off (proclaims the Gospel going to the Gentiles), *and to them who were nigh.* (This refers to the Jews. It is the same Message for both.)

"For through Him (through Christ) *we both* (Jews and Gentiles) *have access by One Spirit unto the Father.* (If the sinner comes by the Cross, the Holy Spirit opens the door, otherwise it is barred [Jn. 10:1].)

"Now (speaks of the present state of Believers) *therefore you are no more strangers and foreigners* (pertains to what Gentiles once were), *but fellowcitizens with the Saints* (speaks of Gentiles now having access the same as Jews, all due to the Cross), *and of the Household of God* (a progressive relationship with God in Christ);

"And are built upon the Foundation (the Cross) *of the Apostles and Prophets* (Apostles serve as leadership under the New Covenant, with Prophets having served in that capacity under the Old), *Jesus Christ Himself being the Chief Corner Stone.* (Presents the part of the Foundation which holds everything together; Jesus Christ is the 'Chief Corner Stone' by virtue of what He did at the Cross)" (Eph. 2:11-20).

Now, all are one in Christ, whether Jew or Gentile, whether male or female, irrespective of race or color. As someone has said, all is level at the foot of the Cross.

NOTES

Thank God, Jesus opened the door that whosoever will may come and drink of the Water of Life freely (Rev. 22:17).

Now, and due to Christ and what He did at the Cross, there are no more various or different Courts. There is still a Holy of Holies in the Spiritual sense, and thank God. Paul also wrote concerning that. He said:

Let us therefore come boldly unto the Throne of Grace (presents the Seat of Divine Power, and yet the Source of boundless Grace), *that we may obtain Mercy* (presents that which we want first), *and find Grace to help in time of need.* (Refers to the Goodness of God extended to all who come, and during any *'time of need'*; all made possible by the Cross)" (Heb. 4:16).

This means that every Believer, irrespective as to who they might be, has access to the very Throne of God and can come to that Throne any time, providing we do so in the Name of Jesus.

(11) "AND HURAM MADE THE POTS, AND THE SHOVELS, AND THE BASONS. AND HURAM FINISHED THE WORK THAT HE WAS TO MAKE FOR KING SOLOMON FOR THE HOUSE OF GOD;

(12) "TO WIT, THE TWO PILLARS, AND THE POMMELS, AND THE CHAPITERS WHICH WERE ON THE TOP OF THE TWO PILLARS, AND THE TWO WREATHS TO COVER THE TWO POMMELS OF THE CHAPITERS WHICH WERE ON THE TOP OF THE PILLARS;

(13) "AND FOUR HUNDRED POMEGRANATES ON THE TWO WREATHS; TWO ROWS OF POMEGRANATES ON EACH WREATH, TO COVER THE TWO POMMELS OF THE CHAPITERS WHICH WERE UPON THE PILLARS.

(14) "HE MADE ALSO BASES, AND LAVERS MADE HE UPON THE BASES;

(15) "ONE SEA, AND TWELVE OXEN UNDER IT.

(16) "THE POTS ALSO, AND THE SHOVELS, AND THE FLESHHOOKS, AND ALL THEIR INSTRUMENTS, DID HURAM HIS FATHER MAKE TO KING SOLOMON FOR THE HOUSE OF THE LORD OF BRIGHT BRASS.

(17) "IN THE PLAIN OF JORDAN DID THE KING CAST THEM, IN THE CLAY GROUND BETWEEN SUCCOTH AND ZEREDATHAH.

(18) "THUS SOLOMON MADE ALL THESE VESSELS IN GREAT ABUNDANCE: FOR THE WEIGHT OF THE BRASS COULD NOT BE FOUND OUT.

(19) "AND SOLOMON MADE ALL THE VESSELS THAT WERE FOR THE HOUSE OF GOD, THE GOLDEN ALTAR ALSO, AND THE TABLES WHEREON THE SHEWBREAD WAS SET;

(20) "MOREOVER THE CANDLESTICKS WITH THEIR LAMPS, THAT THEY SHOULD BURN AFTER THE MANNER BEFORE THE ORACLE, OF PURE GOLD;

(21) "AND THE FLOWERS, AND THE LAMPS, AND THE TONGS, MADE HE OF GOLD, AND THAT PERFECT GOLD;

(22) "AND THE SNUFFERS, AND THE BASONS, AND THE SPOONS, AND THE CENSERS, OF PURE GOLD: AND THE ENTRY OF THE HOUSE, THE INNER DOORS THEREOF FOR THE MOST HOLY PLACE, AND THE DOORS OF THE HOUSE OF THE TEMPLE, WERE OF GOLD."

The diagram is:

1. (Vs. 11) In a very limited sense, Huram may be said to be a Type of the Holy Spirit, Who will finish the work regarding the Church, thereby presenting us faultless before the Throne of God (Jude, Vs. 24).

2. (Vs. 13) The *"Pomegranates"* were typical of the Fruit of the Spirit.

3. (Vs. 13) The *"chains,"* or *"wreaths,"* typified our union with Christ.

4. Verse 17 represents death and Resurrection. In a sense, there must be a death to the old self, with the new self raised in the identification of Christ. This means that all former identity for the Believer must be lost. What we were before Salvation is of no consequence.

5. (Vs. 17) Truly, the Holy Spirit is making a *"new creature,"* which can only be carried out by our understanding that we are *"baptized into His Death, buried with Him by baptism into death, and raised with Him in Newness of Life"* (Rom. 6:3-4).

6. (Vs. 17) So, all of these heathen gold idols, along with the silver and the brass, had to be melted, which means they lost their old identity, and then fashioned into a new

mold, in order to be of fit use for the Temple. This is a picture of what the Spirit of God does with us, which is carried out by and through the Cross (I Cor. 1:17-18, 23; 2:2).

7. The *"Golden Altar"* of Verse 19 actually was the Altar of Incense, which stood immediately in front of the Holy of Holies.

8. The *"pure gold"* of Verse 20, and, actually, all the gold that was used in the Temple, and to whatever degree, typified the Deity of Christ. The term *"pure gold"* meant that it contained no alloy whatsoever.

9. As it regards Verse 22, there is no way into this *"House of God"* except through the Lord Jesus Christ, Who is the *"Door"* (Jn. 10:9).

DEATH AND RESURRECTION

All of this abundance of brass, silver, and gold, which was taken from the heathen in battles fought by David, will now be used for the Temple.

No doubt, the brass, gold and silver, to a great degree, had been used in all types of vessels as it regards idol worship. There were, no doubt, altars to idols made of gold, with silver and brass used in this capacity as well. There would have been doors made of this material in these heathen temples, as stated, altars, altar rails, and actually idols themselves, all taken by David, carried to Jerusalem, and there deposited in warehouses awaiting the construction of the Temple.

All of this is a perfect example of what we were before coming to Christ. And let it be understood, it really doesn't matter what the person was before conversion, whatever it was they were, whatever type of talent they had, or whatever it was that made them great in the world, holds no weight with the Lord whatsoever. In fact, every vestige of the world has to be eradicated, and there is only one way it can be done.

At a point in time, when the Temple was under construction, all of these heathen altar rails, or golden doors, or whatever they may have been, were taken to the plain of Jordan. Now, the real Work of the Spirit would begin.

According to the Seventeenth Verse, all of the gold, and whatever it represented, was put in one pile, with the silver in another, and the brass in another. In succession, it was all placed into a furnace and melted. In other words, all identity with what it was before was now being erased.

No matter how beautiful it may have been in a heathen temple, all of that had to be eliminated. The fire of the furnace would attend to that. The molten material would then be poured into molds designed for the use of the Temple.

THE WORK OF THE SPIRIT WITHIN OUR LIVES

It is not an easy thing, a simple thing, or a quick thing for the Holy Spirit to bring us to the place He desires that we be.

The Believer must learn to *"walk after the Spirit,"* instead of *"walking after the flesh."* It is not nearly as simple as it sounds.

Simon Peter addressed this when he said: *"Beloved, think it not strange concerning the fiery trial which is to try you* (trials do not merely happen; they are designed by wisdom and operated by love; Job proved this), *as though some strange thing happened unto you.* (Your trial, whatever it is, is not unique; many others are experiencing the same thing!)*"* (I Pet. 4:12).

We as Believers do not give up works of the flesh easily, especially considering that most of them are so very religious. These are *"our works,"* and, as such, we are proud of them and part with them very reluctantly.

Abraham is an excellent example.

He and Sarah attempted to help God bring about the Promise. The result was Ishmael, a work of the flesh.

Ultimately Isaac was born, who was a Work of the Holy Spirit in every capacity; however, the effect of the birth of Isaac was to make manifest the character of Ishmael. Ishmael hated him and so did his mother. Prompted by her, he sought to murder Isaac (Gal. 4:29), and with his mother, was justly expelled. Both merited the severer sentence. Thus, the birth of Isaac, which filled Sarah's heart with mirth, filled Hagar's with murder.

Isaac and Ishmael symbolized the new and the old nature in the Believer. Sarah and Hagar typified the two covenants of works and Grace, of bondage and liberty

(Gal., Chpt. 4). The birth of the new nature demands the expulsion of the old. It is impossible to improve the old nature. The Holy Spirit says in Romans, Chapter 8 that *"it is enmity against God, that it is not subject to the Law of God, neither indeed can be."* If it cannot be subject to the Law of God, how can it be improved? How foolish, therefore, appears the doctrine of moral evolution!

The Divine way of Holiness is to *"put off the old man"* just as Abraham *"put off"* Ishmael. Man's way of holiness is to improve the *"old man,"* that is, to improve Ishmael. The effort is both foolish and hopeless.

Of course, the casting out of Ishmael was *"very grievous in Abraham's sight,"* because it always causes a struggle to cast out this element of bondage, that is, Salvation or Sanctification by works. For legalism is dear to the heart. Ishmael was the fruit, and to Abraham, the fair fruit of his own energy and planning. But Ishmael had to go, and likewise, the flesh in our hearts and lives has to go as well.

(The material regarding Abraham was derived from the work of George Williams.)[1]

THE EXAMPLE GIVEN BY OUR LORD

The Scripture says, *"And He commanded the multitude to sit down on the grass, and took the five loaves, and two fishes, and looking up to Heaven, He blessed, and brake, and gave the loaves to His Disciples, and the Disciples to the multitude"* (Mat. 14:19).

Please notice the order:
- He took;
- He blessed;
- He broke; and,
- He gave.

If it is to be noticed, when a person comes to Christ, generally, great Blessings follow. But, we find that it does not stop there.

Then comes the *"breaking."* It's not pleasant, which means it's certainly not enjoyable; however, it is so very, very necessary.

Only after one has been *"broken,"* can one then be *"given"* to the world.

We have far too many Christians who are trying to give themselves to the Cause of Christ without being properly broken. The only thing that can be given in such a circumstance is *"self,"* which cannot help anyone.

It's difficult for us to realize that after we are Born-Again and Spirit-filled, still, there is a lot of work for the Spirit to do within our hearts and lives in order to bring us to the place we ought to be. In fact, and I think one can say without fear of contradiction, the *"breaking"* is something that is a lifelong project. Once we think the *"breaking"* has achieved its purpose, we then find that there are other areas of *"the flesh"* which need to be addressed.

I mentioned to our congregation at Family Worship Center Sunday night that the closer we get to the Lord, the more we see how Wonderful the Lord is, but at the same time, we see how lacking that we actually are. In fact, the closer we get to the Lord, the more the light shines upon us and reveals the flaws, which, otherwise, may have been somewhat hidden. And make no mistake about it, every one of us is riddled with flaws, which the Holy Spirit Alone can address.

That's the reason Jesus said that if we are to come after Him, we must deny ourselves, and take up the Cross daily and follow Him (Lk. 9:23). In fact, until the Believer properly understands the Cross or, at least, has a modicum of understanding regarding this great Work, there is no way the flesh can be subdued within our lives. The Holy Spirit works entirely within the framework of the Cross of Christ. He doesn't demand much of us, but He does demand that our Faith be implicitly, and even explicitly, in the Cross of Christ (Gal., Chpt. 5; 6:14).

"A wonderful Saviour is Jesus my Lord,
"A wonderful Saviour to me;
"He hides my soul in the cleft of the rock,
"Where rivers of pleasure I see."

"A wonderful Saviour is Jesus my Lord,
"He takes my burden away;
"He holds me up, and I shall not be moved,
"He gives me strength as my day."

"With numberless Blessings each

moment He crowns,
"And, filled with His Fullness Divine,
"I sing in my rapture, oh Glory to God,
"For such a Redeemer as mine!"

"When clothed in His Brightness transported I rise,
"To meet Him in clouds of the sky,
"His Perfect Salvation, His Wonderful Love,
"I'll shout with the millions on high."

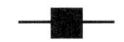

CHAPTER 5

(1) "THUS ALL THE WORK THAT SOLOMON MADE FOR THE HOUSE OF THE LORD WAS FINISHED: AND SOLOMON BROUGHT IN ALL THE THINGS THAT DAVID HIS FATHER HAD DEDICATED; AND THE SILVER, AND THE GOLD, AND ALL THE INSTRUMENTS, PUT HE AMONG THE TREASURES OF THE HOUSE OF GOD."

The construction is:

1. (Vs. 1) Solomon was seven years in building the Temple (I Ki. 6:38). Now it is time for the dedication.

2. All the sacred vessels which had been in the Tabernacle, such as the Altar of Incense, the Golden Lampstand, etc., were now brought to the Temple and *"put among the treasures of the House of God."*

3. The dedication of the Temple was approximately a year after it was finished.

THE WORK OF THE HOUSE OF THE LORD IS FINISHED

The Lord would dwell in this House, actually in the Holy of Holies, between the Mercy Seat and the Cherubim. It would be His only abiding Place on Earth; consequently, Israel was blessed indeed! No other nation in the world had the privilege of Jehovah being in their midst.

Today, due to what Christ has done at the Cross, the Holy Spirit, Who once occupied that House of so long ago, now occupies our physical bodies. Paul said:

"Know you not that you are the Temple of God (where the Holy Spirit abides), *and that the Spirit of God dwells in you?* (That makes the Born-Again Believer His permanent Home)" (I Cor. 3:16).

Let us state it again:

This wonderful privilege, of having the Holy Spirit abide with us permanently (Jn. 14:16), came about at great price—a price paid by our Redeemer, the Lord Jesus Christ. It took the offering of Himself in Sacrifice, which He did on the Cross, thereby, satisfying the terrible penalty of sin that was leveled at all of humanity, at least for all who will believe (Jn. 3:16).

The Holy Spirit is God. He is, as one might say, the Third Person of the Triune Godhead, of *"God the Father, God the Son, and God the Holy Spirit."*

He occupies this physical frame, and even our soul and spirit, at least for those who are Born-Again, in order to carry out a particular work in our lives. At least a part of that work is:

• He will reprove of sin and of Righteousness and of Judgment (Jn. 16:8). In other words, it is the business of the Holy Spirit to rid us of all sin. This does not mean sinless perfection because the Bible doesn't teach such. But it does mean that the sin nature is to no longer have dominion over us (Rom. 6:14). This can be done, ridding us of all sin, only by the Believer placing his Faith exclusively in Christ and the Cross.

• He is to guide us into all Truth (Jn. 16:13).

• He is to show us things to come (Jn. 16:13).

• He is to glorify Christ within our hearts and lives (Jn. 16:14).

• He is to show us all things for which Christ has paid such a price (Jn. 16:14).

• He is to give us power to carry out the Work of God (Acts 1:8).

• He quickens our mortal bodies that we might be able to live for God as we should live, which He Alone can do (Rom. 8:11).

• We have access by the Holy Spirit unto the Father (Eph. 2:18).

(2) "THEN SOLOMON ASSEMBLED THE ELDERS OF ISRAEL, AND ALL THE HEADS OF THE TRIBES, THE CHIEF OF THE FATHERS OF THE CHILDREN OF ISRAEL, UNTO JERUSALEM, TO BRING

UP THE ARK OF THE COVENANT OF THE LORD OUT OF THE CITY OF DAVID, WHICH IS ZION.

(3) "WHEREFORE ALL THE MEN OF ISRAEL ASSEMBLED THEMSELVES UNTO THE KING IN THE FEAST WHICH WAS IN THE SEVENTH MONTH."

The overview is:

1. (Vs. 3) The time of this great gathering, the dedication of the Temple, was the time of the Feast of Tabernacles, which convened in October (Lev. 23:33).

2. This could probably be said to be the greatest assembly that Israel had ever had. It was the dedication of the Temple.

3. The Ark of the Covenant had probably been placed at the beginning, which was before construction began on the Temple, on the threshingfloor of Araunah the Jebusite. No doubt, when construction began, the Ark had to be moved to another place in Jerusalem. Now it will be brought to the Temple, and ensconced in the Holy of Holies.

THE ARK OF THE COVENANT

Out of all the sacred Vessels, and we speak of those that had been made for the Tabernacle, the only one of those Vessels now used in the Temple seems to be the Ark of God.

It was placed, no doubt, in the center of the Holy of Holies, with the Cherubim at either end looking down on the Mercy Seat; however, filling the room were the huge Cherubim made of olive wood and overlaid with gold. Their wings touched in the middle with the back wings touching the back wall on either side. In other words, the wings of both Cherubim touched each outer wall. Also, as stated, whereas the Cherubim on the Ark of the Covenant looked down on the Mercy Seat, the faces of the giant Cherubim looked outward, which signified Redemption accomplished. Such portrayed these Cherubim looking out on a world that is now absent of Satan and his minions of darkness, with the whole world, in one way or the other, serving God, whether by free will or of necessity. They look out on a world that is at peace, which is the first time such has ever happened. It will be during the coming Millennial Reign.

NOTES

(4) "AND ALL THE ELDERS OF ISRAEL CAME; AND THE LEVITES TOOK UP THE ARK.

(5) "AND THEY BROUGHT UP THE ARK, AND THE TABERNACLE OF THE CONGREGATION, AND ALL THE HOLY VESSELS THAT WERE IN THE TABERNACLE, THESE DID THE PRIESTS AND THE LEVITES BRING UP.

(6) "ALSO KING SOLOMON, AND ALL THE CONGREGATION OF ISRAEL WHO WERE ASSEMBLED UNTO HIM BEFORE THE ARK, SACRIFICED SHEEP AND OXEN, WHICH COULD NOT BE TOLD NOR NUMBERED FOR MULTITUDE.

(7) "AND THE PRIESTS BROUGHT IN THE ARK OF THE COVENANT OF THE LORD UNTO HIS PLACE, TO THE ORACLE OF THE HOUSE, INTO THE MOST HOLY PLACE, EVEN UNDER THE WINGS OF THE CHERUBIMS:

(8) "FOR THE CHERUBIMS SPREAD FORTH THEIR WINGS OVER THE PLACE OF THE ARK, AND THE CHERUBIMS COVERED THE ARK AND THE STAVES THEREOF ABOVE.

(9) "AND THEY DREW OUT THE STAVES OF THE ARK, THAT THE ENDS OF THE STAVES WERE SEEN FROM THE ARK BEFORE THE ORACLE; BUT THEY WERE NOT SEEN WITHOUT. AND THERE IT IS UNTO THIS DAY.

(10) "THERE WAS NOTHING IN THE ARK SAVE THE TWO TABLES WHICH MOSES PUT THEREIN AT HOREB, WHEN THE LORD MADE A COVENANT WITH THE CHILDREN OF ISRAEL, WHEN THEY CAME OUT OF EGYPT."

The pattern is:

1. As it regards Verse 4, these were Priests, who also were Levites, who were the only ones who could carry the Ark. They were Types of Christ, Who Alone is the Door to the Throne of God, of which the Ark was a Type.

2. All of the *"holy vessels"* of Verse 5 were by now a little over 600 years old. They, no doubt, were put *"among the treasures of the House of God"* in a separate chamber.

3. (Vs. 6) All the gold and precious stones in this magnificent Temple could not redeem one precious soul; only the Blood

of Jesus could do such. Consequently, the thousands of animals slaughtered, which soaked the ground with blood, were an eternal Type of the great price that would be paid at Calvary's Cross.

4. The staves being drawn out of the Ark of Verse 9 signify that it was to be moved no more. While Israel was in the wilderness, they were constantly moving. Now that is over.

5. The phrase of Verse 9, *"And there it is unto this day,"* proves that this section of II Chronicles was written before the destruction of the Temple by Nebuchadnezzar.

6. (Vs. 10) When Paul, in Hebrews 9:4, mentioned the golden pot of Manna and Aaron's rod being in the Ark, he was speaking of the Ark while in the Tabernacle instead of the Temple. It is not known when these two things were removed.

THE SACRIFICE OF SHEEP AND OXEN WITHOUT NUMBER

The sacrifice of this tremendous number of animals proclaimed the fact that, as important as the Temple was, still, the strength of Israel always had been, was, and ever would be, the shed Blood of the Lamb. Likewise, it is the strength of the Church presently, at least for those who will believe.

Of course, the Holy Spirit knew exactly as to how many animals were offered in sacrifice; however, so many were offered that the number was not known as far as Solomon and others were concerned. There was a reason for this.

This great number offered signified the price that would be paid at Calvary, and that it would be a Finished Work. In other words, the Sacrifice of Christ would be complete, meaning that there would never be the need for another sacrifice.

It is impossible for one to honestly study the Bible and not come to the conclusion of the veracity of the Cross of Christ. It is the central theme of the entirety of the Word of God. That being the case, it most definitely must be the central theme of the Church.

Everything we receive from God comes through Jesus Christ by the Means of the Cross. The Cross has made everything possible. If we do not understand this, then we do not really understand the Word of God.

All Victory is found in the Cross! All Prosperity is found in the Cross! All Operation of the Holy Spirit is found in the Cross!

(11) "AND IT CAME TO PASS, WHEN THE PRIESTS WERE COME OUT OF THE HOLY PLACE: (FOR ALL THE PRIESTS WHO WERE PRESENT WERE SANCTIFIED, AND DID NOT THEN WAIT BY COURSE:

(12) "ALSO THE LEVITES WHICH WERE THE SINGERS, ALL OF THEM OF ASAPH, OF HEMAN, OF JEDUTHUN, WITH THEIR SONS AND THEIR BRETHREN, BEING ARRAYED IN WHITE LINEN, HAVING CYMBALS AND PSALTERIES AND HARPS, STOOD AT THE EAST END OF THE ALTAR, AND WITH THEM AN HUNDRED AND TWENTY PRIESTS SOUNDING WITH TRUMPETS:)

(13) "IT CAME EVEN TO PASS, AS THE TRUMPETERS AND SINGERS WERE AS ONE, TO MAKE ONE SOUND TO BE HEARD IN PRAISING AND THANKING THE LORD; AND WHEN THEY LIFTED UP THEIR VOICE WITH THE TRUMPETS AND CYMBALS AND INSTRUMENTS OF MUSIC, AND PRAISED THE LORD, SAYING, FOR HE IS GOOD; FOR HIS MERCY ENDURES FOR EVER: THAT THEN THE HOUSE WAS FILLED WITH A CLOUD, EVEN THE HOUSE OF THE LORD;

(14) "SO THAT THE PRIESTS COULD NOT STAND TO MINISTER BY REASON OF THE CLOUD: FOR THE GLORY OF THE LORD HAD FILLED THE HOUSE OF GOD."

1. (Vs. 11) When the Priests had placed the Ark in the Most Holy Place, they left, never to enter this place again, except for the visit of the High Priest once a year, which was on the Great Day of Atonement.

2. The *"Altar"* of Verse 12 pertained to the Brazen Altar, which sat in front of the Temple.

3. The phrase of Verse 14, *"could not stand to minister by reason of the Cloud,"* meant that their knees buckled under them, and they fell to the floor, because of the magnitude of the Power of God being manifested.

4. (Vs. 14) *"The Glory of the LORD filled*

that House," but now, Paul says that we are the Temple of God (I Cor. 3:16), and that the Spirit of God dwells in us. The next question is, *"Is He allowed to have His Perfect Way within our lives?"* If He is, then *"the Glory of the LORD will fill this House of God,"* as well.

WORSHIP

When the Ark was finally placed in the Holy of Holies, then the scores of singers and musicians began to worship and praise the Lord.

All music and singing began, in essence, with David as the Holy Spirit gave him the fundamentals of this most excellent way of worship. In fact, as it regards music and singing, at least that which is anointed by the Holy Spirit, such constitutes the highest form of worship and praise. We know this from the fact that the Book of Psalms, which constitutes 150 songs, all written by the Holy Spirit, presents the longest Book in the Bible. In other words, for the Lord to devote this much time and space to this form of worship tells us of its vast significance. In fact, that's the reason that Satan comes against music and singing in the church as he does. If he can pervert that form of worship, he has greatly succeeded in wrecking the Gospel. Actually, the Spiritual temperature of a church can be gauged by its worship, as it regards music and singing, or the lack thereof.

THE TEN COMMANDMENTS

The Scripture bears out that there were *"two tables in the Ark of the Covenant,"* which refers to the two stone tablets which contained the Ten Commandments.

At other times the Ark of the Covenant also contained a pot of Manna and Aaron's rod that budded (Heb. 9:4).

What happened to these two?

What happened we have no way of knowing; however, there was a reason that the two tablets containing the Ten Commandments were in the Ark at that time.

The Temple represented the Millennial Reign, which is to come, when Jesus will be ruling and reigning Personally from Jerusalem over the entirety of the world.

NOTES

Inasmuch as He will be Personally present, there will be no need for the pot of Manna, which represented Christ as the Bread of Life, or Aaron's rod that budded, because that represented the Resurrection of Christ, which was future when that Rod was placed in the Ark. Of course, it is obvious that the Resurrection has long since taken place, making unnecessary that particular item.

However, the two Tables containing the Ten Commandments present moral laws, which never change. They will be just as much incumbent upon the world during the time of the Kingdom Age as they were when they were first given. The Ten Commandments, which constitute the moral part of the Law of Moses, actually present the central core of that Law. Even though the entirety of the Law was fulfilled in Christ, still, it is the Ten Commandments which constitute the Righteousness of God and, as well, His Standard, by which all men will be judged.

Even though the unredeemed do not know of such and, in fact, if it is brought to their attention, they express little concern. Still, all will answer to the Law of God, whether it is answered in Jesus Christ by one giving one's heart to the Lord, or at the Great White Throne Judgment (Rev. 20:11-15). Its demands are inescapable!

THE GLORY OF THE LORD

The *"Glory of the LORD filling the House"* constitutes the Power of God.

Most people, sadly, do not understand the Power of God. Most churches have no idea as to what the Power of God actually is.

One must understand that the Power of the Lord was so present that, as the Priests went about their duties, their knees would buckle under them, and they would fall to the floor. This is what our churches desperately need. This will bring conviction of sin as nothing else will. This is what the preacher needs; this is what every Christian needs.

We should call to our attention, once again, the fact that all of this great celebration, the dedication of the Temple, and the glory thereof, all began with the offering of the sacrifices, which were without number. This means that all of the proceedings were based on the shed Blood of the Lamb. This and this alone is the strength of the Church, and we speak of the Cross.

The Power of God cannot be manifested unless the Cross of Christ is the Object of Faith. There may be that which disguises itself as the Power of God, but unless it's based on the Cross, i.e., the shed Blood of the Lamb, it is not really the Power of God.

"I will sing of my Redeemer,
"And His wondrous Love to me;
"On the cruel Cross He suffered,
"From the curse to set me free."

"I will tell the wondrous Story,
"How my lost estate to save,
"In His boundless Love and Mercy,
"He the ransom freely gave."

"I will praise my dear Redeemer,
"His triumphant Power I'll tell,
"How the Victory He gives,
"Over sin, and death, and Hell."

"I will sing of my Redeemer,
"And His heavenly Love to me;
"He from death to life has brought me,
"Son of God, with Him to be."

"Sing, Oh, sing of my Redeemer,
"With His Blood He purchased me,
"On the Cross He sealed my pardon,
"Paid the debt, and made me free."

CHAPTER 6

(1) "THEN SAID SOLOMON, THE LORD HAS SAID THAT HE WOULD DWELL IN THE THICK DARKNESS.

(2) "BUT I HAVE BUILT AN HOUSE OF HABITATION FOR YOU, AND A PLACE FOR YOUR DWELLING FOREVER.

(3) "AND THE KING TURNED HIS FACE, AND BLESSED THE WHOLE CONGREGATION OF ISRAEL: AND ALL THE CONGREGATION OF ISRAEL STOOD.

(4) "AND HE SAID, BLESSED BE THE LORD GOD OF ISRAEL, WHO HAS WITH HIS HANDS FULFILLED THAT WHICH HE SPOKE WITH HIS MOUTH TO MY FATHER DAVID, SAYING,

NOTES

(5) "SINCE THE DAY THAT I BROUGHT FORTH MY PEOPLE OUT OF THE LAND OF EGYPT I CHOSE NO CITY AMONG ALL THE TRIBES OF ISRAEL TO BUILD AN HOUSE IN, THAT MY NAME MIGHT BE THERE; NEITHER CHOSE I ANY MAN TO BE A RULER OVER MY PEOPLE ISRAEL:

(6) "BUT I HAVE CHOSEN JERUSALEM, THAT MY NAME MIGHT BE THERE; AND HAVE CHOSEN DAVID TO BE OVER MY PEOPLE ISRAEL.

(7) "NOW IT WAS IN THE HEART OF DAVID MY FATHER TO BUILD AN HOUSE FOR THE NAME OF THE LORD GOD OF ISRAEL.

(8) "BUT THE LORD SAID TO DAVID MY FATHER, FORASMUCH AS IT WAS IN YOUR HEART TO BUILD AN HOUSE FOR MY NAME, YOU DID WELL IN THAT IT WAS IN YOUR HEART:

(9) "NOTWITHSTANDING YOU SHALL NOT BUILD THE HOUSE; BUT YOUR SON WHICH SHALL COME FORTH OUT OF YOUR LOINS, HE SHALL BUILD THE HOUSE FOR MY NAME.

(10) "THE LORD THEREFORE HAS PERFORMED HIS WORD THAT HE HAS SPOKEN: FOR I AM RISEN UP IN THE ROOM OF DAVID MY FATHER, AND AM SET ON THE THRONE OF ISRAEL, AS THE LORD PROMISED, AND HAVE BUILT THE HOUSE FOR THE NAME OF THE LORD GOD OF ISRAEL.

(11) "AND IN IT HAVE I PUT THE ARK, WHEREIN IS THE COVENANT OF THE LORD, THAT HE MADE WITH THE CHILDREN OF ISRAEL."

The construction is:

1. (Vs. 1) As it regards the Lord *"dwelling in thick darkness,"* Solomon may have taken this idea from the fact of God's Appearance in darkness at Sinai (Ex. 20:21).

2. (Vs. 5) For approximately 500 years God had not chosen any particular place in Israel where a House should be built for Himself, nor had He chosen any man to be a permanent ruler over Israel. Now, He makes it clear that He has chosen Jerusalem as the place of His Headquarters on Earth, and David as the one through whom all the future kings of Israel should come (II Sam.,

Chpt. 7; I Chron., Chpt. 17). This makes it clear that God did not choose Saul as he chose David.

3. The Lord was pleased with David's motives, as it regards Verse 8.

THE LORD CHOSE JERUSALEM THAT HIS NAME MIGHT BE THERE AND DAVID TO BE OVER HIS PEOPLE

The entirety of this Chapter is broken into two parts:

1. The sermon of Solomon – Vss. 1-11 and
2. The prayer of Solomon – Vss. 14-42.

In all of this, we see the manner and the way in which the Lord works. First of all, the Lord chose David to be over His People, Israel. The people didn't choose David; the Lord did. In fact, before David finally gained the throne, there was much difficulty. Satan always opposes, and does so greatly, that which is of God. Nevertheless, if the individual so Called will maintain his Faith in Christ and what Christ has done at the Cross, the Will of God will ultimately be brought about. It may be and, no doubt, will be, even as John Newton wrote:

"Through many dangers, toils, and snares,
"I have already come,
"But Grace has brought me safe thus far,
"And Grace will lead me on."

The Lord then chose Jerusalem as the city where He would place His Name.

He then gave to David the plans for the Temple that was to be built, plans that included every detail. In other words, neither David nor Solomon added anything to what the Lord gave. He gave David the plans as to how the building was to be constructed, and then the manner in which it was to be constructed. Nothing was left to chance or to the imagination of man.

The Lord then chose the exact spot where He wanted the Temple erected. It was on the threshingfloor of Araunah the Jebusite, a part of the range of Mt. Moriah. So, we see in all of this that everything was of God, and nothing was of man.

This is the manner and the way that God must work. In fact, He cannot use anything that originates with man, even the godliest of men, and for all the obvious reasons. It must be all of God, or it cannot be at all accepted by God.

THE MUSLIM WORLD

As is obvious and well-known, the Muslim world claims Jerusalem and, in fact, all of Israel, and above all, the Temple mount where, presently, the Dome of the Rock now occupies. Of course, this is Satan making his effort to thwart the Plan of God.

But, let it ever be understood that whatever the Lord says, and especially, when the statement is unconditional, even as His Choice of Jerusalem, etc., most definitely is, ultimately it's going to come out exactly as the Lord has said. The Muslims need to understand that. It doesn't matter what the nations of the world try to do, what the Muslims try to do, or what the United States does, the land referred to as *"Israel"* belongs to the Jews. As well, the Temple site belongs to the Jews. And ultimately, despite all the efforts of the Muslims, Israel will occupy it all.

Those who set themselves against the Lord will ultimately be defeated.

(12) "AND HE STOOD BEFORE THE ALTAR OF THE LORD IN THE PRESENCE OF ALL THE CONGREGATION OF ISRAEL, AND SPREAD FORTH HIS HANDS:

(13) "FOR SOLOMON HAD MADE A BRASEN SCAFFOLD, OF FIVE CUBITS LONG, AND FIVE CUBITS BROAD, AND THREE CUBITS HIGH, AND HAD SET IT IN THE MIDST OF THE COURT: AND UPON IT HE STOOD, AND KNEELED DOWN UPON HIS KNEES BEFORE ALL THE CONGREGATION OF ISRAEL, AND SPREAD FORTH HIS HANDS TOWARD HEAVEN,

(14) "AND SAID, O LORD GOD OF ISRAEL, THERE IS NO GOD LIKE YOU IN THE HEAVEN, NOR IN THE EARTH; WHICH KEEPS COVENANT, AND SHOWS MERCY UNTO YOUR SERVANTS, WHO WALK BEFORE YOU WITH ALL THEIR HEARTS:

(15) "YOU WHO HAVE KEPT WITH YOUR SERVANT DAVID MY FATHER THAT WHICH YOU HAVE PROMISED HIM; AND SPOKE WITH YOUR MOUTH, AND HAVE FULFILLED IT WITH YOUR HAND, AS IT IS THIS DAY.

(16) "NOW THEREFORE, O LORD GOD OF ISRAEL, KEEP WITH YOUR SERVANT DAVID MY FATHER THAT WHICH YOU HAVE PROMISED HIM, SAYING, THERE SHALL NOT FAIL YOU A MAN IN MY SIGHT TO SIT UPON THE THRONE OF ISRAEL; YET SO THAT YOUR CHILDREN TAKE HEED TO THEIR WAY TO WALK IN MY LAW, AS YOU HAVE WALKED BEFORE ME.

(17) "NOW THEN, O LORD GOD OF ISRAEL, LET YOUR WORD BE VERIFIED, WHICH YOU HAVE SPOKEN UNTO YOUR SERVANT DAVID.

(18) "BUT WILL GOD IN VERY DEED DWELL WITH MEN ON THE EARTH? BEHOLD, HEAVEN AND THE HEAVEN OF HEAVENS CANNOT CONTAIN YOU; HOW MUCH LESS THIS HOUSE WHICH I HAVE BUILT!

(19) "HAVE RESPECT THEREFORE TO THE PRAYER OF YOUR SERVANT, AND TO HIS SUPPLICATION, O LORD MY GOD, TO HEARKEN UNTO THE CRY AND THE PRAYER WHICH YOUR SERVANT PRAYS BEFORE YOU:

(20) "THAT YOUR EYES MAY BE OPEN UPON THIS HOUSE DAY AND NIGHT, UPON THE PLACE WHEREOF YOU HAVE SAID THAT YOU WOULD PUT YOUR NAME THERE; TO HEARKEN UNTO THE PRAYER WHICH YOUR SERVANT PRAYS TOWARD THIS PLACE.

(21) "HEARKEN THEREFORE UNTO THE SUPPLICATIONS OF YOUR SERVANT, AND OF YOUR PEOPLE ISRAEL, WHICH THEY SHALL MAKE TOWARD THIS PLACE: HEAR YOU FROM YOUR DWELLING PLACE, EVEN FROM HEAVEN; AND WHEN YOU HEAR, FORGIVE.

(22) "IF A MAN SIN AGAINST HIS NEIGHBOUR, AND AN OATH BE LAID UPON HIM TO MAKE HIM SWEAR, AND THE OATH COME BEFORE YOUR ALTAR IN THIS HOUSE;

(23) "THEN HEAR YOU FROM HEAVEN, AND DO, AND JUDGE YOUR SERVANTS, BY REQUITING THE WICKED, BY RECOMPENSING HIS WAY UPON HIS OWN HEAD; AND BY JUSTIFYING THE RIGHTEOUS, BY GIVING HIM ACCORDING TO HIS RIGHTEOUSNESS.

NOTES

(24) "AND IF YOUR PEOPLE ISRAEL BE PUT TO THE WORSE BEFORE THE ENEMY, BECAUSE THEY HAVE SINNED AGAINST YOU; AND SHALL RETURN AND CONFESS YOUR NAME, AND PRAY AND MAKE SUPPLICATION BEFORE YOU IN THIS HOUSE;

(25) "THEN HEAR YOU FROM THE HEAVENS AND FORGIVE THE SIN OF YOUR PEOPLE ISRAEL, AND BRING THEM AGAIN UNTO THE LAND WHICH YOU GAVE TO THEM AND TO THEIR FATHERS.

(26) "WHEN THE HEAVEN IS SHUT UP, AND THERE IS NO RAIN, BECAUSE THEY HAVE SINNED AGAINST YOU; YET IF THEY PRAY TOWARD THIS PLACE, AND CONFESS YOUR NAME, AND TURN FROM THEIR SIN, WHEN YOU DO AFFLICT THEM;

(27) "THEN HEAR YOU FROM HEAVEN, AND FORGIVE THE SIN OF YOUR SERVANTS, AND OF YOUR PEOPLE ISRAEL, WHEN YOU HAVE TAUGHT THEM THE GOOD WAY, WHEREIN THEY SHOULD WALK; AND SEND RAIN UPON YOUR LAND, WHICH YOU HAVE GIVEN UNTO YOUR PEOPLE FOR AN INHERITANCE.

(28) "IF THERE BE DEARTH IN THE LAND, IF THERE BE PESTILENCE, IF THERE BE BLASTING, OR MILDEW, LOCUSTS, OR CATERPILLERS; IF THEIR ENEMIES BESIEGE THEM IN THE CITIES OF THEIR LAND; WHATSOEVER SORE OR WHATSOEVER SICKNESS THERE BE:

(29) "THEN WHAT PRAYER OR WHAT SUPPLICATION SOEVER SHALL BE MADE OF ANY MAN, OR OF ALL YOUR PEOPLE ISRAEL, WHEN EVERYONE SHALL KNOW HIS OWN SORE AND HIS OWN GRIEF, AND SHALL SPREAD FORTH HIS HANDS IN THIS HOUSE:

(30) "THEN HEAR YOU FROM HEAVEN YOUR DWELLING PLACE, AND FORGIVE, AND RENDER UNTO EVERY MAN ACCORDING UNTO ALL HIS WAYS, WHOSE HEART YOU KNOW; (FOR YOU ONLY KNOW THE HEARTS OF THE CHILDREN OF MEN:)

(31) "THAT THEY MAY FEAR YOU, TO WALK IN YOUR WAYS, SO LONG AS THEY LIVE IN THE LAND WHICH YOU GAVE

UNTO OUR FATHERS.

(32) "MOREOVER CONCERNING THE STRANGER, WHICH IS NOT OF YOUR PEOPLE ISRAEL, BUT IS COME FROM A FAR COUNTRY FOR YOUR GREAT NAME'S SAKE, AND YOUR MIGHTY HAND, AND YOUR STRETCHED OUT ARM; IF THEY COME AND PRAY IN THIS HOUSE;

(33) "THEN HEAR YOU FROM THE HEAVENS, EVEN FROM YOUR DWELLING PLACE, AND DO ACCORDING TO ALL THAT THE STRANGER CALLS TO YOU FOR; THAT ALL PEOPLE OF THE EARTH MAY KNOW YOUR NAME, AND FEAR YOU, AS DOES YOUR PEOPLE ISRAEL, AND MAY KNOW THAT THIS HOUSE WHICH I HAVE BUILT IS CALLED BY YOUR NAME.

(34) "IF YOUR PEOPLE GO OUT TO WAR AGAINST THEIR ENEMIES BY THE WAY THAT YOU SHALL SEND THEM, AND THEY PRAY UNTO YOU TOWARD THIS CITY WHICH YOU HAVE CHOSEN, AND YOUR HOUSE WHICH I HAVE BUILT FOR YOUR NAME;

(35) "THEN HEAR YOU FROM THE HEAVENS THEIR PRAYER AND THEIR SUPPLICATION, AND MAINTAIN THEIR CAUSE.

(36) "IF THEY SIN AGAINST YOU, (FOR THERE IS NO MAN WHICH SINS NOT,) AND YOU BE ANGRY WITH THEM, AND DELIVER THEM OVER BEFORE THEIR ENEMIES, AND THEY CARRY THEM AWAY CAPTIVES UNTO A LAND FAR OFF OR NEAR;

(37) "YET IF THEY BETHINK THEMSELVES IN THE LAND WHERE THEY ARE CARRIED CAPTIVE, AND TURN AND PRAY UNTO YOU IN THE LAND OF THEIR CAPTIVITY, SAYING, WE HAVE SINNED, WE HAVE DONE AMISS, AND HAVE DEALT WICKEDLY;

(38) "IF THEY RETURN TO YOU WITH ALL THEIR HEART AND WITH ALL THEIR SOUL IN THE LAND OF THEIR CAPTIVITY, WHITHER THEY HAVE CARRIED THEM CAPTIVES, AND PRAY TOWARD THEIR LAND, WHICH YOU GAVE UNTO THEIR FATHERS, AND TOWARD THE CITY WHICH YOU HAVE CHOSEN, AND TOWARD THE HOUSE WHICH I HAVE BUILT FOR YOUR NAME:

(39) "THEN HEAR YOU FROM THE HEAVENS, EVEN FROM YOUR DWELLING PLACE, THEIR PRAYER AND THEIR SUPPLICATIONS, AND MAINTAIN THEIR CAUSE, AND FORGIVE YOUR PEOPLE WHO HAVE SINNED AGAINST YOU.

(40) "NOW, MY GOD, LET, I BESEECH YOU, YOUR EYES BE OPEN, AND LET YOUR EARS BE ATTENT UNTO THE PRAYER THAT IS MADE IN THIS PLACE.

(41) "NOW THEREFORE ARISE, O LORD GOD, INTO YOUR RESTING PLACE, YOU, AND THE ARK OF YOUR STRENGTH: LET YOUR PRIESTS, O LORD GOD, BE CLOTHED WITH SALVATION, AND LET YOUR SAINTS REJOICE IN GOODNESS.

(42) "O LORD GOD, TURN NOT AWAY THE FACE OF YOUR ANOINTED: REMEMBER THE MERCIES OF DAVID YOUR SERVANT."

The pattern is:

1. The Fourteenth Verse says as it regards the Lord, *"which keeps Covenant."*

No man will ever be able to say, in all eternity, that God has not kept His Part of every agreement with men or that He has not fulfilled every Promise to them.

2. (Vs. 16) Regrettably, Solomon himself, even after praying this prayer, did not *"take heed to walk in God's Law."*

3. As it regards God dwelling on this Earth, with this question asked in Verse 18, most definitely, the Lord will indeed dwell with men on this Earth, and do so forever. Revelation, Chapters 21 and 22 proclaim this fact.

4. (Vs. 19) Prayer includes every thought and word from the heart that is Godward.

5. (Vs. 25) In this prayer, Solomon seems to sense the future of Israel prophetically. *"Sin"* is the only reason that Israel was ever defeated. In fact, sin is to blame for all the troubles among men. As well, the Lord gave the land of Canaan to Israel, and not the Arabs, even as this Verse proclaims.

6. (Vs. 27) Praying toward the Temple, Jerusalem, and this land is referred to eight times in this prayer. It was done so because, at that particular time, that is where God dwelt. Today, in this great Dispensation of

Grace, it doesn't really matter which direction a person faces while praying. The reason is that the Lord, through the Power of the Holy Spirit, now lives in the heart of Born-Again man (I Cor. 3:16), wherever such a man is, and not in some particular temple or building. This was all made possible by the Cross.

7. (Vs. 27) As well, the land between the River Euphrates and the Mediterranean, and from the Red Sea on the south to Hamath on the north, is the only land promised in all Scripture for all the Tribes of Israel. Theories which teach that America and England are new Promised Lands for Israel are all error. There is no hint of such in Scripture.

8. (Vs. 33) Solomon, in his wisdom, did not forget the Gentiles, whom God had in mind to bless from the very beginning of His calling Abraham, Isaac, and Jacob. All nations were to be blessed through Israel and her seed.

As well, this would imply the preaching of the Gospel, for how could individuals come to the God of Israel, if they do not hear (Rom. 10:9-17; I Cor. 1:18-24)?

In fact, in the Millennium and the New Earth, all nations will go up to Jerusalem to pray and to worship, exactly as they do now (Isa. 2:2-4; Zech. 8:23).

9. (Vs. 36) Solomon was right; all have sinned and come short of the Glory of God (Rom. 3:23).

10. (Vs. 41) The word *"Saints"* in the Hebrew reads *"men of Grace,"* that is, those who are subjects of the Grace of God.

This plainly shows that those in Old Testament times were under Grace, as well as we are in New Testament times. Actually, everyone who has been Saved has been Saved by Grace, for there is no other way that an individual can be Saved (Eph. 2:8).

And yet, Grace, as we know it under the New Dispensation, which came by Jesus Christ, means that it was all made possible by the Cross. Christ is always the Source, while the Cross is the Means.

11. (Vs. 42) God's Anointed is the Messiah. Every blessing that we receive comes through the Lord Jesus Christ, and what He has done for us at the Cross.

NOTES

THE ALTAR

As Solomon begins his prayer, he does so *"before the Altar of the LORD."* This speaks of the great Brazen Altar, on which sacrifices were offered constantly, which sat immediately in front of the Temple.

Solomon praying his prayer at this particular place was not by accident. It was designed by the Holy Spirit.

This should be a lesson to us as to the value of the Cross of Christ. Regrettably, the modern church tends to think it can live this life by devising its own means and ways. Failure is the guaranteed result.

Solomon knew that his prayer would be heard because of the sacrifices which had been offered upon the great Altar. In fact, the Lord could be approached in no other way. As a result, he prays this prayer of dedication very near the Altar.

THE LORD GOD OF ISRAEL

In Verse 14, Solomon extols *"the LORD God of Israel."* He went on to state, *"there is no God like You in the heaven, or in the Earth; which keeps Covenant, and shows Mercy unto Your Servants, who walk before You with all their hearts."*

The truth is, of all the nations on the Earth at that time, Israel was the only one who knew the Lord of Glory. And, to be sure, Jehovah Alone is the Lord. There is no other.

Many nations referred to their *"god,"* but, in reality, they had no God, only demon spirits. So, this made Israel, in a sense, the Lord of the Earth. In fact, there was no other nation like these people.

As long as they served God, they could not be defeated by their enemies, and they knew nothing but freedom and prosperity. But, when they sinned and refused to repent, such was the ruin of these people, as sin is the ruin of any and all people.

DAVID

Some nine times in this Chapter, Solomon refers to his father David. Those nine times are:

1. He says the Lord *"spoke with His Mouth to David"* (Vs. 4).

2. He *"chose David to be over His People Israel"* (Vs. 6).

3. He maintains, and rightly so, that it was *"in the heart of David to build the House of the LORD God"* (Vs. 7).

4. The Lord said to David, *"You shall not build the house, but your son which shall come forth out of your loins, he shall build the House for My Name"* (Vs. 9).

5. Solomon proclaims the fact that he was chosen by the Lord to occupy the throne when David died (Vs. 10).

6. He proclaims the fact that the Lord kept every promise that He had given to David (Vs. 15).

7. The Lord promised David that his lineage would sit on the throne of Israel, unless they failed to *"walk in God's Law"* (Vs. 16).

8. Solomon implores the Lord that every Promise made to David be kept (Vs. 17).

9. The Holy Spirit through Solomon uses the term *"Your Anointed."* Whether he knew it or not, this spoke of the coming Messiah. It is attached to the request, *"remember the mercies of David Your Servant."* This refers to the fact that the Anointed One, the Messiah, would come from the lineage of David and, in fact, would be referred to as *"The Son of David"* (Vs. 42).

WILL GOD DWELL ON THE EARTH?

When Solomon asked the question of Verse 18, *"But will God in very deed dwell with men on the Earth?"*, He had in mind the Lord dwelling between the Mercy Seat and the Cherubim regarding this Temple just finished. He knew that God would have to condescend to dwell in this building, considering *"The heaven of heavens cannot contain You; how much less this house which I have built!"*

In Truth, God will dwell with men on the Earth and will do so forever. Chapters 21 and 22 of Revelation bear this out. John said: *"And I heard a great Voice out of Heaven saying, Behold, the Tabernacle of God is with men, and He will dwell with them, and they shall be His People, and God Himself shall be with them, and be their God"* (Rev. 21:3).

This will be in the coming Perfect Age, when the Lord will actually transfer His Headquarters from Heaven to Earth. Concerning that, John the Beloved said: *"And I John saw the Holy City, New Jerusalem, coming down from God out of Heaven, prepared as a Bride adorned for her husband"* (Rev. 21:2).

TOWARD JERUSALEM

In essence, all Jews were admonished to pray toward Jerusalem irrespective as to where they were in the world, which many do unto this day.

That was correct at that time, inasmuch as God dwelt in the Temple in Jerusalem, in the Holy of Holies.

Now, due to what Jesus did at the Cross, the Holy Spirit can dwell in the hearts and lives of Believers wherever they might be; consequently, when prayer is offered now, no direction is specified, and for all the obvious reasons.

SIN

The Holy Spirit through Solomon proclaims the fact that *"sin"* is the problem and that which causes so much difficulty and destruction. It is the same presently as it was then.

Every problem, in one way or the other, can be traced back to *"sin."* While the person undergoing the difficulty may not have sinned at all, still, the cause of all trouble and heartache in this world, and the cause of all problems and difficulties can be traced back to sin. As we say over and over, sin is the problem, and the solution is Jesus Christ and Him Crucified.

As well, Solomon implores the Lord to *"forgive the sin of Your People Israel,"* considering that they have *"confessed His Name, and prayed and made supplication before the Lord in this House"* (Vss. 24-25). In other words, Repentance will turn away the Judgment of God.

It must be ever understood that God is unalterably opposed to sin. And, to be sure, there is no one who gets by with sin.

Any and every human being can allow Jesus Christ to serve as their Mediator, which He will do by virtue of the Cross, which means that He took the penalty of sin, or else such people are subject to the

Judgment of God. We can accept what Jesus did on our behalf at the Cross, or else, we will feel the Wrath of God. The Scripture says, and unequivocally so:

"For the Wrath of God is revealed from Heaven against all ungodliness and unrighteousness of men, who hold the truth in unrighteousness" (Rom. 1:18).

Unfortunately, sin is hardly mentioned in the modern church, and because to do so, it is said, such may offend the congregation.

Telling a person who has cancer that everything is all right, when, in reality, the individual is dying, is not doing that person a favor. Let's say it again:

The problem is sin! The solution is Jesus Christ and what He did at the Cross. There is no other solution simply because there need not be any other solution.

GENTILES

Solomon refers to Gentiles as *"strangers"* (Vs. 32).

No doubt, the Holy Spirit moved upon Solomon to pray this prayer and its content. The Lord is quick to include the *"stranger"* in the blessings that can come from seeking His Face at this *"House."* In other words, Gentiles are encouraged to come. In fact, there was an entire court set aside for the Gentiles to which they could come and pray to the Lord.

It was in this Court, the Court of the Gentiles, that Jesus ran out the money changers. In essence, the Jews had taken over this Court and had set up all types of stalls to change money, and to do other things. In other words, it was almost impossible for any Gentile to come to this place and pray due to the activity. Jesus ran them all out (Jn. 2:13-17).

Israel was raised up by the Lord for three major purposes. They are:

1. To give the world the Word of God. Every writer in the Bible is Jewish, with the possible exception of Luke. Israel succeeded in this all-important task.

2. To serve as the womb of the Messiah, which refers to the Coming of the Lord Jesus Christ. This was brought about, as well, but, sadly and regrettably, Israel crucified her Messiah. They have suffered untold agony from that day until this because of that action.

3. Israel was also ordained by God to serve as a missionary to the Gentile world. In this they failed miserably but will yet fulfill this requirement. However, it will be in the coming Kingdom Age (Isa. 66:18-20).

THE ANOINTED

When the word *"Anointed"* is used in the manner in which it has been used in Verse 42, it is speaking of the coming Redeemer, the Lord Jesus Christ. Christ would come through the lineage of David exactly as He had promised the King of Israel (II Sam., Chpt. 7).

So, Solomon begins his prayer at the Altar, i.e., *"the Cross,"* and closes it with the coming Messiah, the Lord Jesus Christ. How fitting!

"I stand all amazed at the love Jesus offers me,
"Confused at the Grace that so fully He proffers me;
"I tremble to know that for me He was crucified,
"That for me, a sinner, He suffered, He bled, and died."

"I marvel that He would descend from His Throne Divine,
"To rescue a soul so rebellious and proud as mine;
"That He should extend His great Love unto such as I;
"Sufficient to own, to redeem, and to justify."

"I think of His Hands pierced and bleeding to pay that debt!
"Such Mercy, such love and devotion can I forget?
"No! I will praise and adore at the Mercy Seat,
"Until at the glorified Throne I kneel at His Feet."

CHAPTER 7

(1) "NOW WHEN SOLOMON HAD MADE

AN END OF PRAYING, THE FIRE CAME DOWN FROM HEAVEN, AND CONSUMED THE BURNT OFFERING AND THE SACRIFICES; AND THE GLORY OF THE LORD FILLED THE HOUSE.

(2) "AND THE PRIESTS COULD NOT ENTER INTO THE HOUSE OF THE LORD, BECAUSE THE GLORY OF THE LORD HAD FILLED THE LORD'S HOUSE.

(3) "AND WHEN ALL THE CHILDREN OF ISRAEL SAW HOW THE FIRE CAME DOWN, AND THE GLORY OF THE LORD UPON THE HOUSE, THEY BOWED THEMSELVES WITH THEIR FACES TO THE GROUND UPON THE PAVEMENT, AND WORSHIPPED, AND PRAISED THE LORD, SAYING, FOR HE IS GOOD; FOR HIS MERCY ENDURES FOR EVER."

The overview is:

1. Verse 1 is additional to I Kings 8:63-64, and shows the Divine acceptance by the Lord of the sacrifices, until Christ should come to offer Himself as the one great eternal Sacrifice for all of humanity.

2. (Vs. 1) The Fire of God from Heaven has fallen several times on such occasions (Gen. 4:4; 15:17; Lev. 9:24; I Chron. 21:26; I Ki. 18:38).

3. (Vs. 2) As it regards all the sacrifices being offered, we should learn from this that the *"Glory of the LORD"* can only come through Calvary.

4. (Vs. 3) On the Day of Pentecost, approximately 1,000 years later, the Fire fell from Heaven in a way that it had never fallen previously.

In Old Testament Times, it fell upon the sacrifice. Now that the Sacrifice, the Lord Jesus Christ, has been offered, this same Fire can now accompany the Holy Spirit into the heart and life of the Believer, but not with judgment, for the judgment has been expended on Christ. But yet, this *"Pentecostal Fire"* will definitely correct the Believer (Mat. 3:11-12; Acts 2:3).

FIRE CAME DOWN FROM HEAVEN

Williams says, *"The fire that consumed the Burnt Offering at the dedication of the Temple 'came down from Heaven,' but the fire that consumed the Burnt Offering— Offering at the dedication of the Tabernacle 'came out from before the Lord,' that is, came out from between the Cherubim within the Most Holy Place. But in coming out from, and passing through the Tabernacle, it did not burn it, for that tent was Christ.*

"This is characteristic. The fire from the Tabernacle is Christ in His First Advent; the fire from Heaven, Christ in His Second Advent."[1] The Fire that came down from Heaven also showed the Divine acceptance of sacrifices until the Messiah should come to offer Himself as the One, great, Eternal Sacrifice for all men.

The scene of this Chapter is one of grandeur and awe. The king, with uplifted hands, kneeling in royal robes upon the brazen platform; the vast multitude prostrate upon the ground; the Fire from Heaven consuming the sacrifice upon the Brazen Altar; and the Cloud of the Glory of Jehovah filling the House of Jehovah—all formed a scene of mysterious splendor such as the world has never witnessed.

THE DWELLING PLACE OF GOD

The fact that this was the only Temple in the whole world in which the One True God was worshipped adds to the moral grandeur of the scene.

The Spiritual Knowledge that Solomon possessed and the visible fire that burned upon the Altar came from Heaven; both originated there, both were Divine. Man could not have created that miraculous Fire or that equally miraculous Knowledge. The fact of the existence of God was attested by the Fire. No other nation possessed this knowledge of God, or could any nation by reason or culture obtain such knowledge. It could only be had by Revelation. Thus, both the Fire and the teaching of the prayer came from Heaven.

THE BURNT OFFERING

The *"Burnt Offering"* on the Altar signifies that God gives His All in the Person of Jesus Christ. The fire upon that sacrifice signifies the Judgment of God that should have come upon us, but instead, would fall upon the Perfect Offering for sin, the Christ of Calvary.

Does one think that all of these sacrifices

were merely for the act of ceremony or ritual? Hardly!

First of all, the voluminous amount of sacrifices pictured and portrayed the coming Redeemer; therefore, they were of utmost significance.

Secondly, all of this portrayed the fact that Israel's safety and protection, and her freedom and prosperity, rested solely upon the shed Blood of the Lamb. When can we see this as it regards the modern church?

The cross in the modern church is little more than a good luck charm, little more than a part of the whole, and a small part at that. Cannot we see from the Word of God that all Blessing, all prosperity, all the Leading and Guidance of the Holy Spirit, in fact, everything that we receive from God, comes to us through Jesus Christ and by the Means of the Cross? If we can't see that, it's simply because we willfully do not desire to see it.

THE GLORY OF THE LORD FILLED THE HOUSE

The *"Glory of the LORD"* can only come through Calvary. In too many churches, Calvary has been relegated to second or even third place, or completely ignored all together. Let it ever be understood that God's Glory cannot rest upon anything except the precious shed Blood of Jesus Christ. If we want the *"Glory of the LORD to fill the House,"* we must place the preeminence on Calvary. Paul said, *"Glory in the Cross."* He also said, *"I determined to know nothing among you save Christ, and Him Crucified"* (I Cor. 2:2).

The *"house"* presently is our physical body, our hearts, and our lives. Paul said concerning this:

"Know you not that you are the Temple of God (where the Holy Spirit abides), *and that the Spirit of God dwells in you?* (That makes the Born-Again Believer His permanent Home.)"

The Apostle went on to say, *"If any man defile the Temple of God* (our physical bodies must be a living sacrifice, which means that we stay Holy by ever making the Cross the Object of our Faith [Rom. 12:1]), *him shall God destroy* (to fail to function in God's Prescribed Order [the Cross], opens the Believer up to Satan, which will ultimately result in destruction); *for the Temple of God is Holy, which Temple you are.* (We are *'Holy'* by virtue of being *'in Christ.'* We remain Holy by the Work of the Holy Spirit, Who demands that our Faith ever be in the Cross, which has made all of this possible)" (I Cor. 3:16-17).

The fact that the Holy Spirit now abides permanently within the hearts and lives of all Believers was all made possible by the Cross of Christ. Before the Cross, which pictures and proclaims the shed Blood of Christ, which atoned for all sin, past, present and future, at least for those who believe, animal blood served as a stopgap measure, so to speak. However, animal blood was and is woefully insufficient. It could cover sin, or serve as an atoning factor as it regards the principal of substitution, because animal blood was only a substitute. That being the case, the sin debt was not lifted, meaning that man was still under that dread plague, even the godliest among those of Old Testament times. Actually, whenever Believers died in those times, their soul and spirit did not go to Heaven, but rather down into Paradise, referred to as Abraham's bosom, which was actually a part of Hell itself. True, there was a great gulf, Jesus said, between Paradise and the burning side of Hell, but still, all the Believers before the Cross were, in a measure, held captive by Satan. That's the reason that Paul said concerning Jesus, *"When He ascended up on high* (the Ascension), *He led captivity captive* (liberated the souls in Paradise; before the Cross, despite being Believers, they were still held captive by Satan because the blood of bulls and goats could not take away the sin debt; but when Jesus died on the Cross, the sin debt was paid, and now He makes all of these His Captives), *and gave Gifts unto men.* (These *'Gifts'* include all the Attributes of Christ, all made possible by the Cross.)

"Now that He ascended (mission completed)], *what is it but that He also descended first into the lower parts of the earth?* (Immediately before His Ascension to Glory, which would be done in total triumph, He first went down into Paradise to deliver all

the believing souls in that region, which He did!)" (Eph. 4:8-9).

As it should be understood, everything hinged on the Cross of Christ. This means that every single Believer who was in Paradise was dependent solely on the great Work that Jesus would carry out at the Cross, which would release them from this place, and give them access to Heaven, which Christ afforded Himself.

The phrase, *"He led captivity captive,"* is strange. But what it means is this:

These people in Paradise, ever how many there were, and quite possibly there were millions, due to the fact that animal blood was insufficient to rid them of the sin debt, as stated, were actually captives of Satan. While he could not harm them and could not take them over into the burning side of Hell, still, due to the fact that the sin debt remained, this meant that they were in the domain of Satan himself. When Jesus died on the Cross, thereby, atoning for all sin, past, present, and future, in effect, this liberated them in totality. And to make certain they were liberated, He went into this place Himself and made each one of them His Captives and took them with Him to Glory.

Now, when a Believer dies, due to the Cross, in that the sin debt is paid, such a Believer instantly goes to be with Christ in the Portals of Glory (Phil. 1:23).

THE LORD IS GOOD, HIS MERCY ENDURES FOREVER

The Lord is Good! Every Believer knows that, and the whole world should know that as well.

If one wants to know Who and what God the Father is like, one only has to look at the Lord Jesus Christ in the four Gospels. Jesus said: *"If you had known Me, you should have known My Father also* (means, 'If you had learned to know Me Spiritually and experientially, you should have known that I and the Father are One' i.e., One in essence and unity, and not in number)*: and from henceforth you know Him, and have seen Him* (when one truly sees Jesus, one truly sees the Father; as stated, they are 'One' in essence).

"Philip said unto Him, Lord, show us

NOTES

the Father, and it suffices us (like Philip, all, at least for the most part, want to see God, but the far greater majority reject the only manner and way to see Him, which is through Jesus).

"Jesus said unto Him, Have I been so long with you, and yet have you not known Me, Philip? (Reynolds says, 'There is no right understanding of Jesus Christ until the Father is actually seen in Him.') *He who has seen Me has seen the Father* (presents the very embodiment of Who and what the Messiah would be; if we want to know what God is like, we need only look at the Son)*; and how do you say then, Show us the Father?*

"Do you believe not that I am in the Father, and the Father in Me? (The key is 'believing.') *the words that I speak unto you I speak not of Myself* (the words which came out of the mouth of the Master are, in fact, those of the Heavenly Father)*: but the Father Who dwells in Me, He does the works* (the Father does such through the Holy Spirit).

"Believe Me that I am in the Father, and the Father in Me (once again places Faith as the vehicle and Jesus as the Object)*: or else believe Me for the very works' sake.* (Presents a level which should be obvious to all, and includes present observation as well)" (Jn. 14:7-11).

WHAT IS MERCY?

In the Hebrew, the word *"Mercy"* could probably be expressed best by the word *"loving-kindness."*

It denotes devotion to a covenant, and so, of God, His Covenant-love (Ps. 89:28). But God's Faithfulness to a graciously established relationship with Israel or an individual, despite human unworthiness and defection, readily passes over into His Mercy. In fact, this steady, persistent refusal of God to wash His Hands of wayward Israel is the essential meaning of the Hebrew word, which is translated, *"loving-kindness."*

In the New Testament, *"Mercy"* could probably be defined as *"compassion to one in need or helpless distress, or in debt and without claim to favorable treatment."* God is referred to as *"the Father of Mercies"* (II Cor. 1:3; Ex. 34:6; Neh. 9:17; Ps. 86:15;

103:8-14; Joel 2:13; Jonah 4:2).

His Compassion is over all that He has made (Ps. 145:9), and it is because of His Mercy that we are Saved (Eph. 2:4; Titus 3:5). Jesus was often *"moved with compassion,"* and He bids us to be *"merciful, as your Father also is merciful"* (Lk. 6:36; Mat. 18:21, 27).

The Scripture says *"The merciful are blessed, and will receive mercy"* (Mat. 5:7; James 2:13).

(The above material on Mercy was derived from the New Bible Dictionary.)[2]

RECIPIENTS OF MERCY

Mercy is afforded the undeserving, as no one deserves God's Mercy, strictly by and through the Cross of Christ. In fact, everything comes to the Believer by the Means of the Cross, with our Lord as the Source.

The Holy Spirit gave over the entirety of the 136th Psalm to the Mercy of God, *"For His Mercy endures forever."* It is not known who wrote this Psalm, but more than likely, the author was David. In fact, the people of Israel basically quote the First Verse of the 136th Psalm in their praises. So, this means it was written by the time they quoted it and, as stated, more than likely by David. I quote from THE EXPOSITOR'S STUDY BIBLE:

"O give thanks unto the LORD; for He is good: for His Mercy endures forever. (We must never forget that *'God is good!'* Therefore, He is merciful.)

"O give thanks unto the God of gods: for His Mercy endures forever. (The Hebrew for *'God of gods'* is *'Elohim of the Elohim.'* He is speaking here of the Trinity of which all are equal. In the Trinity, *'His Mercy endures forever.'*)

"O give thanks to the Lord of lords: for His Mercy endures forever. (The Hebrew is *'Adonim of the adonim,'* which means *'Sovereign of the sovereigns; Master of the masters; Ruler of the rulers.'*)

"To Him Who Alone does great wonders: for His Mercy endures forever. (God Alone can perform constructive Miracles.)

"To Him Who by wisdom made the heavens: for His Mercy endures forever. (This ascribes to God all the planetary systems.)

"To Him Who stretched out the Earth above the waters: for His Mercy endures forever (who separated the land and the seas; the attention which the Holy Spirit gives to the Mercy of God in all of these Verses is beautifully amazing, and rightly so!).

"To Him Who made great lights: for His Mercy endures forever (God is *'Light,'* so the creation of Light is a natural result of His Divine Person):

"The sun to rule by day: for His Mercy endures forever:

"The moon and stars to rule by night: for His Mercy endures forever. (The Holy Spirit is telling us here that all of Creation, and its ordered existence, is a result of the Mercy of God.)

"To Him Who smote Egypt in their firstborn: for His Mercy endures forever (this tells us that all Judgments poured out on Egypt were a result of Mercy; the Lord could have smitten Egypt at the beginning; however, He sent Judgments, including the death of the firstborn, all in order to get them to repent, but to no avail):

"And brought out Israel from among them: for His Mercy endures forever (to bring Israel out was not only an act of Mercy for Israel, but for Egypt as well):

"With a strong hand, and with a stretched out arm: for His Mercy endures forever (The *'strong hand'* and the *'stretched out arm,'* which God used to deliver Israel, were all because of Mercy.)

"To Him Who divided the Red Sea into parts: for His Mercy endures forever (this Passage destroys the myth that the Red Sea, at the place of the crossing, was only a few inches deep):

"And made Israel to pass through the midst of it: for His Mercy endures forever (it took Faith for Israel to pass through; they had to believe that God, Who had made this path through the Sea, would, as well, continue to defy the laws of gravity by holding the water up like two walls on either side):

"But overthrew Pharaoh and his host in the Red Sea: for His Mercy endures forever. (The indication here is that Pharaoh drowned along with his army.)

"To Him Who led His People through the wilderness: for His Mercy endures forever (God intended for the stay in the wilderness to be of short duration—a few months to

two years at the most. The forty years was because of Israel's unbelief and rebellion.)

"*To Him Who smote great kings: for His Mercy endures forever* (this speaks of Pharaoh as well as the kings mentioned in the following Verses):

"*And killed famous kings: for His Mercy endures forever:*

"*Sihon king of the Amorites: for His Mercy endures forever:*

"*And Og the king of Bashan: for His Mercy endures forever* (tradition says that Sihon was the brother of king Og; both were Amorites; they were giants of the race of the Rephaim at the time of the conquest of Palestine):

"*And gave their land for an heritage: for His Mercy endures forever:*

"*Even an heritage unto Israel His Servant: for His Mercy endures forever.* (Og's territory was given to the half-Tribe of Manasseh [Deut. 3:13]. Sihon's territory was given to the Tribes of Reuben and Gad [Num. 32:23-38; Josh. 13:10]).

"*Who remembered us in our low estate: for His Mercy endures forever* (God remembers His Mercy and Grace and forgets our sins; man forgets God's Mercy and Grace and remembers our sins):

"*And has redeemed us from our enemies: for His Mercy endures forever.* (The word 'redeemed' means to rescue and to break the power of the one who has us bound, namely Satan. This Redemption is so powerful that it not only redeems us, but also destroys our enemies.)

"*Who gives food to all flesh: for His Mercy endures forever.* (The 'food' addressed here pertains not only to spiritual food, but also to natural food.)

"*O give thanks unto the God of Heaven: for His Mercy endures forever.* (As '*His Mercy endures forever,*' likewise, our '*thanks unto Him*' should endure forever)" (Ps. 136:1-26).

(4) "THEN THE KING AND ALL THE PEOPLE OFFERED SACRIFICES BEFORE THE LORD.

(5) "AND KING SOLOMON OFFERED A SACRIFICE OF TWENTY AND TWO THOUSAND OXEN, AND AN HUNDRED AND TWENTY THOUSAND SHEEP: SO THE KING AND ALL THE PEOPLE DEDICATED THE HOUSE OF GOD.

(6) "AND THE PRIESTS WAITED ON THEIR OFFICES: THE LEVITES ALSO WITH INSTRUMENTS OF MUSIC OF THE LORD, WHICH DAVID THE KING HAD MADE TO PRAISE THE LORD, BECAUSE HIS MERCY ENDURES FOR EVER, WHEN DAVID PRAISED BY THEIR MINISTRY; AND THE PRIESTS SOUNDED TRUMPETS BEFORE THEM, AND ALL ISRAEL STOOD.

(7) "MOREOVER SOLOMON HALLOWED THE MIDDLE OF THE COURT THAT WAS BEFORE THE HOUSE OF THE LORD: FOR THERE HE OFFERED BURNT OFFERINGS, AND THE FAT OF THE PEACE OFFERINGS, BECAUSE THE BRASEN ALTAR WHICH SOLOMON HAD MADE WAS NOT ABLE TO RECEIVE THE BURNT OFFERINGS, AND THE MEAT OFFERINGS, AND THE FAT.

(8) "ALSO AT THE SAME TIME SOLOMON KEPT THE FEAST SEVEN DAYS, AND ALL ISRAEL WITH HIM, A VERY GREAT CONGREGATION, FROM THE ENTERING IN OF HAMATH UNTO THE RIVER OF EGYPT.

(9) "AND IN THE EIGHTH DAY THEY MADE A SOLEMN ASSEMBLY: FOR THEY KEPT THE DEDICATION OF THE ALTAR SEVEN DAYS, AND THE FEAST SEVEN DAYS.

(10) "AND ON THE THREE AND TWENTIETH DAY OF THE SEVENTH MONTH HE SENT THE PEOPLE AWAY INTO THEIR TENTS, GLAD AND MERRY IN HEART FOR THE GOODNESS THAT THE LORD HAD SHOWN UNTO DAVID, AND TO SOLOMON, AND TO ISRAEL HIS PEOPLE.

(11) "THUS SOLOMON FINISHED THE HOUSE OF THE LORD, AND THE KING'S HOUSE: AND ALL THAT CAME INTO SOLOMON'S HEART TO MAKE IN THE HOUSE OF THE LORD, AND IN HIS OWN HOUSE, HE PROSPEROUSLY EFFECTED."

The exposition is:

1. (Vs. 5) The tremendous number of sacrifices offered portrayed the fact to Israel that her great blessing was built on the

Foundation of the shed Blood of Christ. Even though the number of sacrifices offered was staggering, still, it could not begin to portray Calvary. The blood of bulls and goats can never take away sin (Heb. 10:4); nevertheless, those sacrifices did point to the Lamb of God, Who would take away all sin (Jn. 1:29).

2. (Vs. 6) The worship, heavily anchored in the sacrifices, portrays the fact that Spirit-led music and singing accompany the Cross and, in fact, are made possible by the Cross.

3. (Vs. 7) The *"Burnt Offerings"* typified the perfection of Christ being given to the sinner.

4. (Vs. 7) The *"fat"* typified the very best that God has in the offering up of His Son.

5. (Vs. 7) The *"Peace Offerings"* typified that peace had been restored, as a result of the Burnt Offering.

6. (Vs. 7) The middle Court, which was the Court of women, had to also be used for sacrifices, because the area around the Brazen Altar was too small, considering the great number of sacrifices being offered.

7. (Vs. 9) There was a Feast of Dedication of the Temple which was seven days long, and then Solomon also kept the Feast of Tabernacles for an additional seven days, making altogether fourteen days of feasting at this time.

8. (Vs. 10) Joy always follows proper worship, which is always anchored in the Cross, typified by the sacrifices.

THE SACRIFICES

The Fifth Verse says, speaking of the number of sacrifices, *"Twenty and two thousand oxen, and an hundred and twenty thousand sheep."* The brook Kidron that ran between the Mount of Olives and the Temple site ran red with blood, showing Israel that her great blessing was built on the Foundation of the shed Blood of Christ.

Even though the number of sacrifices offered was staggering, still, it could not even begin to portray Calvary. While the blood of bulls and goats could not take away sins, still, they served as a Type, a Symbol, of the One, the Lamb of God, Who would and, in fact, did take away all sin (Jn. 1:29).

It has been asked as to why Solomon offered this many sacrifices. The Law of Moses did not require such. Even the Scripture doesn't say. I believe that Solomon was led by the Lord in this which he did. He was so very much aware of the true strength of Israel, which was, as stated, the shed Blood of the Lamb, all typified by the sacrificial offerings of these clean animals, that the staggering number offered typified several things:

• No number offered, no matter how high it would have been, could have even remotely compared with the One Offering of Calvary.

• Even the staggering number offered could not take away sins (Heb. 10:4), still, the number involved did serve as a Symbol that the Blood shed by the One Sacrifice of Calvary would suffice for all of mankind, and for all of time, at least for all who would believe.

• The tremendous number of sacrifices offered, as well, speaks of the preciousness of the Blood that would be shed on Calvary's Cross. Precious in that it serves as the price paid for every single soul who will believe, which places its worth beyond the comprehension of man.

• Incidentally, the value in 2008 money, regarding the number of sacrifices offered, would have been not much short of 50 million dollars.

BURNT OFFERINGS, PEACE OFFERINGS, AND MEAT OFFERINGS

The *"Whole Burnt Offerings"* were probably the most common type of offerings presented. As we have previously stated, this particular Offering represented Christ giving His All, even as the Sin Offering represented the sinner giving Christ the totality of his sin.

Whenever Whole Burnt Offerings or Sin or Trespass Offerings were presented, almost always they were followed by Peace Offerings.

The *"Peace Offering"* was the one offering of which very little was burnt on the Altar (the fat), with the bulk being eaten by the Priests and especially by the one who presented the Offering. The idea was, inasmuch as the matter of sin had been settled between God and the individual as a result of the Offering, which typified Christ, now there could be rejoicing in the eating of the Peace Offering inasmuch as Peace is now restored.

The scene at the dedication of the Temple must have been beautiful to behold. Tens of thousands of people partaking of the *"Peace Offerings,"* in other words, holding a feast for their family and friends, as the Scripture provided for them to do, was a Perfect Type of what Christ would do in the hearts and lives of those who trust Him.

THE EATING OF THE PEACE OFFERING

The Priests eating portions of the Offerings, which they were commanded to do, and now as it regards the Peace Offering, the people themselves able to participate, and this was the only Offering in which they could participate in this manner, all have a great Scriptural meaning in Christ.

In essence, this is what Jesus was talking about when He said to Israel: *"Except you eat the Flesh of the Son of Man, and drink His Blood, you have no life in you."* The notes from The Expositor's Study Bible says: *"This terminology addresses the Cross; Christ would give Himself on the Cross for the Salvation of mankind; to fully believe in Him and what He did for us is what He means here; however, this Verse tells us the degree of believing that is required; it refers to the Cross being the total Object of one's belief; failing that, there is no Life in you.*

"Whoso eats My Flesh, and drinks My Blood, has Eternal Life (once again, Christ reiterates the fact that if the Cross is the total Object of one's Faith, such a person has *'Eternal Life'*); *and I will raise him up at the last day* (constitutes the fourth time this is spoken by Christ; consequently, the Believer has a fourfold assurance of the Resurrection).

"For My Flesh is meat indeed, and My Blood is drink indeed (the idea is that one must continue eating and drinking even on a daily basis, which speaks of bearing the Cross daily [Lk. 9:23]).

"He who eats My Flesh, and drinks My Blood, dwells in Me, and I in Him. (The only way that one can dwell in Christ and Christ in him, which guarantees a victorious, overcoming life, is for the Cross to ever be the Object of Faith and, as stated, on a daily basis)" (Jn. 6:53-56).

The idea is, when one fully believes in Christ and what He did at the Cross, in the Mind of God, one literally is placed in Christ, which means that whatever Christ is, that we are as well. The union is to be so total, so close, and so complete, hence, Jesus praying, *"That they may be one, as We are"* (Jn. 17:11).

The eating of the Flesh of the Son of God and the drinking of His Blood was not meant, as should be obvious, to be taken literally. The terminology is used in this fashion to emphasize the validity of the Cross. It speaks of the Crucifixion of Christ, and one's Faith in that Finished Work (Rom. 6:3-5). It was typified, as stated, in the eating of the *"Peace Offerings."*

MEAT OFFERINGS

The *"Meat Offerings"* probably would have been better translated *"Thank Offerings."* In fact, they were the only Offering of the fivefold Offerings, which contained no flesh. It was bread which was made in a certain way. No leaven or honey was permitted (Lev. 2:11) on the cakes being offered.

The offerer was responsible for bringing the prepared loaves or wafers to the Sanctuary. The Priests burned one handful on the Altar, and the rest was his to eat (Lev. 2:2).

The *"Meat Offering"* or *"Cereal Offering"* normally accompanied every *"Burnt Offering."* The quantities of fine flour and oil were fixed according to the animal being sacrificed. It is believed that *"Peace Offerings"* were always accompanied by *"Cereal Offerings."* The Priests ate a part of these offerings, with the rest being eaten by the offerer with the flesh of the sacrificial animal. All of this was a Type of Christ, totally fulfilled when He came to this world and gave Himself on the Cross as a complete and total Sacrifice for the sins of man.

As much as it being a Type of Christ, it must be emphasized, it was a Type of Christ as it regarded what He would do for us at the Cross.

GLAD AND MERRY IN HEART

When the Cross of Christ, i.e., *"the Sacrifice of Christ,"* is the Foundation of all that we are and all that we do, to be sure, it will produce that which is *"glad and merry in heart."* This is something that money cannot buy, secular education cannot give, and that is beyond the pale of human endeavor, that is, as we look at personal ability. And yet, it is an automatic place and position when the Cross of Christ becomes the Foundation of all that we are.

Presently, the spirit of depression among Christians is at an all time high. This is not the way that it is supposed to be.

Sometime back, while preaching on a Sunday morning at Family Worship Center, I was dealing with oppression, which is the first cousin, if not the twin brother, of depression. While Satan cannot posses a Believer, he most definitely can oppress a Believer. The difference is, possession is within, while oppression is without.

OPPRESSION

I think I can say without fear of contradiction or exaggeration that every single Believer at one time or the other has experienced satanic oppression. The Scripture says concerning oppression: *"How God anointed Jesus of Nazareth with the Holy Spirit and with Power: Who went about doing good, and healing all who were oppressed of the Devil; for God was with Him"* (Acts 10:38).

Oppression causes emotional disturbance, which, within itself, can cause a raft of problems with the individual. It causes nerve disorders, as well, certain types of sicknesses, and as would be obvious, destroys the peace, the security, and the assurance of the individual.

As I was preaching that Sunday morning at Family Worship Center and, as stated, dealing with this very subject, all of a sudden something dawned on me that had not previously come to my attention.

The Lord gave me the Revelation of the Cross in 1997. Whereas I was troubled with demonic oppression quite often before that time, I suddenly realized, even while I was preaching, that I had not experienced one single solitary moment of oppression since my Faith had been anchored securely in the Cross of Christ. In other words, the Lord Jesus Christ and what He did for us at the Cross had become my Object of Faith in totality. No more oppression.

Why?

OPPRESSION AND THE CROSS OF CHRIST

It was at the Cross that every demon spirit was defeated, along with Satan himself. The Scripture says concerning this:

"Buried with Him in Baptism (does not refer to Water Baptism, but rather to the Believer baptized into the Death of Christ, which refers to the Crucifixion and Christ as our substitute [Rom. 6:3-4]), *wherein also you are risen with Him through the Faith of the operation of God, Who has raised Him from the dead.* (This does not refer to our future physical Resurrection, but to that Spiritual Resurrection from a sinful state into Divine Life. We died with Him, we are buried with Him, and we rose with Him [Rom. 6:3-5], and herein lies the secret to all Spiritual Victory.)

"And you, being dead in your sins and the uncircumcision of your flesh (speaks of Spiritual death [i.e., 'separation from God'], which sin does!), *has He quickened together with Him* (refers to being made Spiritually alive, which is done through being 'Born-Again'), *having forgiven you all trespasses* (the Cross made it possible for all manner of sins to be forgiven and taken away);

"Blotting out the handwriting of Ordinances that was against us (pertains to the Law of Moses, which was God's Standard of Righteousness that man could not reach), *which was contrary to us* (Law is against us, simply because we are unable to keep its precepts, no matter how hard we try), *and took it out of the way* (refers to the penalty of the Law being removed), *nailing it to His Cross* (the Law with its decrees was abolished in Christ's Death, as if Crucified with Him);

"And having spoiled principalities and powers (Satan and all of his henchmen were defeated at the Cross by Christ atoning for all sin; sin was the legal right Satan had to

hold man in captivity; with all sin atoned, he has no more legal right to hold anyone in bondage), *He* (Christ) *made a show of them openly* (what Jesus did at the Cross was in the face of the whole universe), *triumphing over them in it.* (The triumph is complete, and it was all done for us, meaning we can walk in power and perpetual Victory due to the Cross)" (Col. 2:12-15).

It was at the Cross where Satan and all his minions of darkness were defeated; consequently, the Holy Spirit works entirely within the framework of the Finished Work of Christ. In other words, He works entirely within those boundaries and will not work outside of those boundaries. It is the Cross which provides the legal means for the Holy Spirit to abide within our hearts and lives, and to do with us and for us what He Alone can do. In fact, this is such an ironclad Truth that the Holy Spirit refers to it as a *"Law."* Listen to Paul:

"For the Law (that which we are about to give is a Law of God, devised by the Godhead in eternity past [I Pet. 1:18-20]; this Law, in fact, is *'God's Prescribed Order of Victory'*) *of the Spirit* (Holy Spirit, i.e., *'the way the Spirit works'*) *of Life* (all life comes from Christ, but through the Holy Spirit [Jn. 16:13-14]) *in Christ Jesus* (any time Paul uses this term or one of its derivatives, he is, without fail, referring to what Christ did at the Cross, which makes this *'life'* possible) *has made me free* (given me total Victory) *from the Law of Sin and Death* (these are the two most powerful Laws in the universe; the *'Law of the Spirit of Life in Christ Jesus'* alone is stronger than the *'Law of Sin and Death'*; this means that if the Believer attempts to live for God by any manner other than Faith in Christ and the Cross, he is doomed to failure)" (Rom. 8:2).

RESURRECTION LIFE

The secret to living for God, to this *"more abundant life,"* and to enjoying all of that for which Christ paid such a price at Calvary's Cross, is *"Resurrection Life."*

What is Resurrection Life?

Listen again to Paul:

"For if we have been planted together (with Christ) *in the likeness of His Death* (Paul proclaims the Cross as the instrument through which all Blessings come; consequently, the Cross must ever be the Object of our Faith, which gives the Holy Spirit latitude to work within our lives), *we shall be also in the likeness of His Resurrection* (we can have the *'likeness of His Resurrection,'* i.e., *'live this Resurrection Life,'* only as long as we understand the *'likeness of His Death,'* which refers to the Cross as the Means by which all of this is done)" (Rom. 6:5).

Coming up as a young Preacher in a particular Full Gospel denomination, from time to time Frances and I would hear Preachers talking about *"living the Resurrection Life."*

I found out later that none of these Preachers really knew or understood what that term actually meant. If you had asked them, they would have referred to works of the law of some kind that the Believer is supposed to carry out, which would enable such a Believer to live the Resurrection Life. Nothing could be further from the truth.

In this Fifth Verse of Romans 6, the Holy Spirit through Paul emphatically states, *"For if we have been planted together in the likeness of His Death,"* which refers to the fact that all Victory is in the Cross. That's where we go wrong; we try to place the center and circumference of victory in other things. And it really doesn't matter what the other things are, or how valuable they are in their own right, the Believer must understand that all Victory, and we mean all Victory, is found exclusively in the Cross of Christ. In other words, before we can enjoy *"Resurrection Life,"* or as Paul put it, *"Newness of Life,"* we have to first understand that it was all made possible by the Death of Christ at Calvary's Cross.

Most definitely, the Resurrection of Christ is of supreme significance, as should be obvious and well understood; however, it was not at the Resurrection where our victory was won, but rather the Cross of Christ.

THE ATTACK AGAINST THE CROSS

I personally feel that a greater attack is being made presently against the Cross of Christ than ever before.

To be sure, Satan has always attacked the

Cross, and for all the obvious reasons; however, heretofore, it has mostly been done by and through those who are unbelievers, such as the modernists, etc. But this attack presently is from those who claim to be Spirit-filled, and I speak of the Word of Faith people, etc.

They refer to the Cross as *"past miseries."* They also call it *"the greatest defeat in human history."*

They claim that if the Preacher preaches the Cross, he is preaching death, etc. They then go on and encourage their people to place their faith in the Resurrection or the Exaltation of Christ. But what does the Bible say?

Paul said, *"For Christ sent me not to baptize, but to preach the Gospel: not with wisdom of words, lest the Cross of Christ should be made of none effect"* (I Cor. 1:17).

He did not say, *"Lest the Resurrection or the Exaltation of Christ should be made of none effect."*

The great Apostle also said, *"For the preaching of the Cross is to them who perish foolishness; but unto us who are Saved it is the Power of God"* (I Cor. 1:18).

He did not say, *"For the preaching of the Resurrection. . . ."*

He also said, *"But we Preach Christ Crucified . . ."* (I Cor. 1:23).

He did not say, at least as it regards Salvation and Sanctification, *"But we preach Christ resurrected."*

He also said, *"For I determined not to know anything among you, save Jesus Christ and Him Crucified"* (I Cor. 2:2).

He did not say, *"For I determined not to know anything among you, save Jesus Christ and Him Resurrected."*

He also said, *"But God forbid that I should glory, save in the Cross of our Lord Jesus Christ"* (Gal. 6:14).

He did not say, *"But God forbid that I should glory, save in the Resurrection of our Lord Jesus Christ. . . ."*

No, the great Apostle was not denigrating the Resurrection or the Exaltation of Christ in any way, and neither are we. Those things mentioned are of tremendous significance, as should be obvious; however, the Resurrection of Christ and the Exaltation of Christ before the Father were all made possible by what He did at the Cross. If Christ had not carried out a full Atonement and, thereby, defeating all the powers of darkness, and for all time, there would have been no Resurrection, etc.

Now, you can believe the Word of God, of which we have just given you ample proof, or you can believe these preachers who are denigrating the Cross. And there is one other thing that the Apostle Paul said about those who would denigrate the Cross:

"But though we, or an Angel from Heaven, preach any other gospel unto you than that which we have preached unto you, let him be accursed" (Gal. 1:8).

THE FORMULA

The following is a short formula that might help the Believer to understand the Message of the Cross a little better. It is:

- FOCUS: The Lord Jesus Christ (Jn. 14:6).
- OBJECT OF FAITH: The Cross of Christ (Rom. 6:3-5; I Cor. 1:17-18, 23; 2:2; Gal., Chpt. 5; 6:14; Eph. 2:13-18; Col. 2:14-15).
- POWER SOURCE: The Holy Spirit (Rom. 8:1-2, 11).
- RESULTS: Victory (Rom. 6:14).

Now, let's use the same formula, but turn it around the way it is mostly being used at this particular time.

- FOCUS: Works.
- OBJECT OF FAITH: One's performance.
- POWER SOURCE: Self.
- RESULTS: Failure.

(12) "AND THE LORD APPEARED TO SOLOMON BY NIGHT, AND SAID UNTO HIM, I HAVE HEARD YOUR PRAYER, AND HAVE CHOSEN THIS PLACE TO MYSELF FOR AN HOUSE OF SACRIFICE.

(13) "IF I SHUT UP HEAVEN THAT THERE BE NO RAIN, OR IF I COMMAND THE LOCUSTS TO DEVOUR THE LAND, OR IF I SENT PESTILENCE AMONG MY PEOPLE;

(14) "IF MY PEOPLE, WHO ARE CALLED BY MY NAME, SHALL HUMBLE THEMSELVES, AND PRAY, AND SEEK MY FACE, AND TURN FROM THEIR WICKED WAYS; THEN WILL I HEAR FROM HEAVEN, AND WILL FORGIVE THEIR SIN, AND WILL HEAL THEIR LAND.

(15) "NOW MY EYES SHALL BE OPEN, AND MY EARS ATTENT UNTO THE PRAYER THAT IS MADE IN THIS PLACE.

(16) "FOR NOW HAVE I CHOSEN AND SANCTIFIED THIS HOUSE, THAT MY NAME MAY BE THERE FOREVER: AND MY EYES AND MY HEART SHALL BE THERE PERPETUALLY.

(17) "AND AS FOR YOU, IF YOU WILL WALK BEFORE ME, AS DAVID YOUR FATHER WALKED, AND DO ACCORDING TO ALL THAT I HAVE COMMANDED YOU, AND SHALL OBSERVE MY STATUTES AND MY JUDGMENTS;

(18) "THEN WILL I STABLISH THE THRONE OF YOUR KINGDOM, ACCORDING AS I HAVE COVENANTED WITH DAVID YOUR FATHER, SAYING, THERE SHALL NOT FAIL YOU A MAN TO BE RULER IN ISRAEL.

(19) "BUT IF YOU TURN AWAY, AND FORSAKE MY STATUTES AND MY COMMANDMENTS, WHICH I HAVE SET BEFORE YOU, AND SHALL GO AND SERVE OTHER GODS, AND WORSHIP THEM;

(20) "THEN WILL I PLUCK THEM UP BY THE ROOTS OUT OF MY LAND WHICH I HAVE GIVEN THEM; AND THIS HOUSE, WHICH I HAVE SANCTIFIED FOR MY NAME, WILL I CAST OUT OF MY SIGHT, AND WILL MAKE IT TO BE A PROVERB AND A BYWORD AMONG ALL NATIONS.

(21) "AND THIS HOUSE, WHICH IS HIGH, SHALL BE AN ASTONISHMENT TO EVERYONE WHO PASSES BY IT; SO THAT HE SHALL SAY, WHY HAS THE LORD DONE THUS UNTO THIS LAND, AND UNTO THIS HOUSE?

(22) "AND IT SHALL BE ANSWERED, BECAUSE THEY FORSOOK THE LORD GOD OF THEIR FATHERS, WHICH BROUGHT THEM FORTH OUT OF THE LAND OF EGYPT, AND LAID HOLD ON OTHER GODS, AND WORSHIPPED THEM, AND SERVED THEM: THEREFORE HAS HE BROUGHT ALL THIS EVIL UPON THEM."

The exegesis is:

1. (Vs. 12) The Lord not only answered Solomon's prayer by a manifestation of the Fire falling from Heaven, but, as well, He portrayed what He will do, as it regards Solomon's petition, and in no uncertain terms.

2. (Vs. 12) As well, we find here that the Lord referred to the Temple as a *"House of Sacrifice."* We should take note that the modern church should fall into the same category, inasmuch as our Message should be, *"Jesus Christ and Him Crucified"* (I Cor. 1:23). The Cross must be the primary Message (Rom. 6:3-14; I Cor. 2:2). Verse 14 constitutes a prayer of Repentance and, thereby, proclaims the manner of true Repentance.

3. (Vs. 15) Prayer from a distance being made toward the Temple would be answered.

Due to what Christ did at the Cross, the Lord no longer resides in a building, but rather in the hearts and lives of Believers (I Cor. 3:16). Now we pray to the Father up in Heaven, and do so in the Name of Jesus (Jn. 16:23).

4. (Vs. 22) Verses 19-22 portray the Solomonic Covenant, which is conditional. In other words, if Solomon or his sons forsake the Lord, the Lord will forsake them.

5. (Vs. 22) These two Covenants basically proclaim the correct scriptural teaching on predestination. It is predestined that God would have a Nation called Israel (the Davidic Covenant). Man's acceptance, rejection, failure, or otherwise does not alter the fact; however, who will actually be a part of the Israel which is Saved (the Solomonic Covenant) will depend on obedience. Actually, Paul said only a remnant would be Saved (Rom. 9:27).

HOUSE OF SACRIFICE

Despite the fact that the Temple was the most costly structure in the world, still, the Holy Spirit alludes to it rather as a *"House of Sacrifice."*

Despite the fact that there was more gold in this building than any other structure in the world, still, the Holy Spirit now makes no mention of that whatsoever, again referring to the Temple as a *"House of Sacrifice."*

Despite the fact that everything carried on in this House was of supreme significance, still, the Holy Spirit refers to it as a *"House of Sacrifice,"* which refers to the real purpose of this structure.

As we have said, and will continue to say, the Cross of Christ is the Foundation of the entirety of the Plan of God, actually formulated in the Mind of the Godhead from before the foundation of the world (I Pet. 1:18-20). While all other things that pertain to the Lord are vastly significant, as should be obvious, still, it is the Cross of Christ that is at the very center and circumference of the Plan of God. In other words, every other doctrine, every other principal, and every other premise, all and without exception, must be built upon the Foundation of the Cross. If that is not the case, error will be the result, which means that God cannot bless it. He can only bless that which has the Cross of Christ as its Foundation, and its Foundation alone!

All of this means that the great Brazen Altar, thirty feet long and thirty feet wide, which sat immediately in front of the Temple, was in use 24 hours a day. Actually, the fires on that Altar were to never go out. As well, the four horns that protruded on the Altar, and did so from each corner, pointed to all points of the compass, telling us that what Jesus would do at the Cross would be for the entirety of the world (Jn. 3:16). This means that this great Gospel is for the entirety of mankind. It shows no preference or prejudice as it regards skin color, nationality, or creed. Jesus died for all! In fact, in the Mind of God there are only two races of people in this world, those who are Saved, and those who aren't.

If it is to be noticed, the answer that the Lord gave to Solomon began with the Cross of Christ, i.e., *"the House of Sacrifice."*

THE ELEMENTS

In Verse 13, the Holy Spirit plainly portrays to us that God rules all. He has the Power to shut up Heaven that there be no rain, and the Power to open Heaven that there be copious showers. He can command the insects to *"devour the land,"* or He can give abundant crops.

As well, He can send pestilence and sickness among the people, or He can stop it from coming to the people.

All of this means that anything and everything that happens to a Child of God is either caused or allowed by the Lord. While, of course, the Lord never causes sin, if a person is dead set upon committing sin, the Lord will allow such, but as always, the end result of sin is never pretty. Even though the Lord will forgive and do so instantly, still, there is a price to pay for disobedience.

THE PRAYER OF REPENTANCE

- *"If My People"*: Even though this is an Old Testament prayer, still, it is just as valid presently as it was then. Sadly and unfortunately, at times, God's People stray from the Word of God. When they do, all types of problems occur.
- *"Humble themselves"*: How hard is it for one to humble oneself before the Lord? It's not hard at all, but yet, it seems to be an overwhelming factor in the lives of many, if not most. Pride is the problem, and that's why the Lord demands humility. We have to humble ourselves before Him and admit that we are wrong, and that He Alone holds the solution and, in fact, is the Solution.
- *"Pray and seek My Face"*: The Believer, and we are speaking of Believers here, should know how to pray. If it is to be noticed, the Lord did not tell us to consult a psychologist or even to seek counseling. He told us to *"pray and seek His Face."*
- *"Turn from your wicked ways"*: That is what Repentance is all about. It is turning from something, in this case sin, and turning to something, which is presently the Lord Jesus Christ.

Since the Cross, the Believer is to repent not only of the evil that he or she has done but, as well, even of the good. What do we mean by that?

We tend to think that doing good will solve the problem, whatever the good might be. It won't! That's what Jesus meant when He told us to *"deny ourselves"* (Lk. 9:23). He was referring to denying our ability, our strength, our intellect, our power, our talent, our education, our motivation, etc. We are to look exclusively to Him and what He did for us at the Cross. In other words, we are to depend totally on Christ and His Sacrificial, Atoning Work.

- *"Then will I hear from Heaven"*: If we do it God's Way, He has promised to hear us. To be sure, if He promised such under the Old Covenant, don't you think that He most definitely will do the same under the New Covenant, especially considering that we now have even better Promises (Heb. 8:6)?

- *"I will forgive their sin, and will heal their land"*: That's about as simple as it can get. If we will do what the Lord says do, to be sure, He most definitely will keep His Promise without fail.

THE EYES AND EARS OF GOD

The Lord here said that He would be careful to *"see"* and to *"hear"* the *"prayer that is made in this place,"* referring to the Temple. To those who truly desire to carry out the Will of God, such presents itself as a great Blessing. To know that the Lord is watching us and listening for our prayers and petitions should be a tremendous consolation to all true Believers. His Eyes are open to see and to do, while His Ears are open to be attentive to our praise, our prayer, and our petitions.

SANCTIFICATION OF THE HOUSE

"Sanctification" refers to being set apart, and in this case, totally for the Lord. In other words, this House was to be separated from the world unto God. It is the same presently with Believers.

If the Believer is totally given over to the Lord, which refers more than anything else to his Faith being placed entirely and totally within the Cross of Christ, then we have the Promise that the *"eyes and heart of the Lord would be on us perpetually"* (I Cor. 3:16).

THE CONDITIONS

David was ever used, as here, as the example.

Why?

How?

Considering the terrible sins that David committed, adultery with Bath-sheba and then murdering her husband in cold blood, how could this be?

While David definitely committed these terrible sins, the truth is, he paid dearly for what he did, in fact, suffering an agony that was unimaginable. But David's position with the Lord was not because of such suffering but because he truly repented of his actions, and as he always did, truly tried to follow the Lord as far as *"His Statutes and Judgments were concerned."*

If Solomon would follow the Lord as did David, his father, the Lord most definitely would keep His Promises, with the Throne of Israel being established and, as well, the lineage of David continuing until the Messiah. Those were the conditions!

DESTRUCTION

But if Solomon and those who followed him would turn away from God and *"serve other gods, and worship them,"* the Lord also stated that He would decimate the Throne of Israel and would, as well, destroy *"this House."*

Unfortunately, with some few exceptions, the kings of Israel, although in the lineage of David, turned their backs on God and did exactly what the Lord told them not to do, which was to worship idols. To be sure, the Lord sent Prophet after Prophet unto them, seeking to turn them from their wicked ways, all to no avail. So, the time finally came that the Lord was forced to do exactly what He said he would do, which was to forsake the Nation, thereby, allowing the heathen to take it over, which Nebuchadnezzar did.

It was all, *"Because they forsook the LORD God of their fathers, which brought them forth out of the land of Egypt, and laid hold on other gods, and worshipped them, and served them."*

Let it be understood that the Lord, even under this Dispensation of Grace, can abide sin no more now than He could then. In fact, I think it can be said that He can abide it even less. The reasons ought to be obvious.

Concerning this, Paul said, and I continue to quote from THE EXPOSITOR'S STUDY BIBLE:

"And the times of this ignorance God winked at (does not reflect that such ignorance was Salvation, for it was not! before the Cross, there was very little Light in the world, so God withheld Judgment); *but now commands all men everywhere to repent* (but since the Cross, the 'Way' is open to all; it's up to us Believers to make that 'Way' known to all men):

"Because He has appointed a day (refers to the coming of the Great White Throne

Judgment [Rev. 20:11-15]), *in the which He will judge the world in Righteousness by that Man Whom He has ordained* (this Righteousness is exclusively in Christ Jesus and what He has done for us at the Cross, and can be gained only by Faith in Him [Eph. 2:8-9; Rom. 10:9-10, 13; Rev. 22:17]); *whereof He has given assurance unto all men, in that He has raised Him from the dead.* (Refers to the Resurrection ratifying that which was done at Calvary, and is applicable to all men, at least all who will believe)" (Acts 17:30-31).

In other words, due to the Cross, the world has much less excuse now than at any time in human history. So, I think it can be said that even though the Lord promises much more under the New Covenant, at the same time, He expects more out of the Church.

> "Hark! Ten thousand harps and voices sound the note of praise above;
> "Jesus reigns and Heaven rejoices, Jesus reigns, the God of Love:
> "See, He sits on yonder Throne; Jesus rules the world Alone."
>
> "King of Glory, reign forever, Thine an everlasting Crown;
> "Nothing from Your Love shall sever those whom You have made Your Own:
> "Happy objects of Your Grace, destined to behold Your Face."
>
> "Saviour, hasten Your Appearing; bring, O bring the glorious day,
> "When, the awful summons hearing, Heaven and Earth shall pass away:
> "Then, with golden harps we'll sing, Glory, Glory to our King!"

─■─

CHAPTER 8

(1) "AND IT CAME TO PASS AT THE END OF TWENTY YEARS, WHEREIN SOLOMON HAD BUILT THE HOUSE OF THE LORD, AND HIS OWN HOUSE,

(2) "THAT THE CITIES WHICH HURAM HAD RESTORED TO SOLOMON, SOLOMON BUILT THEM, AND CAUSED THE CHILDREN OF ISRAEL TO DWELL THERE.

(3) "AND SOLOMON WENT TO HAMATH-ZOBAH, AND PREVAILED AGAINST IT.

(4) "AND HE BUILT TADMOR IN THE WILDERNESS, AND ALL THE STORE CITIES, WHICH HE BUILT IN HAMATH.

(5) "ALSO HE BUILT BETH-HORON THE UPPER, AND BETH-HORON THE NETHER, FENCED CITIES, WITH WALLS, GATES, AND BARS;

(6) "AND BAALATH, AND ALL THE STORE CITIES THAT SOLOMON HAD, AND ALL THE CHARIOT CITIES, AND THE CITIES OF THE HORSEMEN, AND ALL THAT SOLOMON DESIRED TO BUILD IN JERUSALEM, AND IN LEBANON, AND THROUGHOUT ALL THE LAND OF HIS DOMINION.

(7) "AS FOR ALL THE PEOPLE WHO WERE LEFT OF THE HITTITES, AND THE AMORITES, AND THE PERIZZITES, AND THE HIVITES, AND THE JEBUSITES, WHICH WERE NOT OF ISRAEL,

(8) "BUT OF THEIR CHILDREN, WHO WERE LEFT AFTER THEM IN THE LAND, WHOM THE CHILDREN OF ISRAEL CONSUMED NOT, THEM DID SOLOMON MAKE TO PAY TRIBUTE UNTIL THIS DAY.

(9) "BUT OF THE CHILDREN OF ISRAEL DID SOLOMON MAKE NO SERVANTS FOR HIS WORK; BUT THEY WERE MEN OF WAR, AND CHIEF OF HIS CAPTAINS, AND CAPTAINS OF HIS CHARIOTS AND HORSEMEN.

(10) "AND THESE WERE THE CHIEF OF KING SOLOMON'S OFFICERS, EVEN TWO HUNDRED AND FIFTY, WHO BORE RULE OVER THE PEOPLE.

(11) "AND SOLOMON BROUGHT UP THE DAUGHTER OF PHARAOH OUT OF THE CITY OF DAVID UNTO THE HOUSE THAT HE HAD BUILT FOR HER: FOR HE SAID, MY WIFE SHALL NOT DWELL IN THE HOUSE OF DAVID KING OF ISRAEL, BECAUSE THE PLACES ARE HOLY, WHEREUNTO THE ARK OF THE LORD HAS COME."

The overview is:

1. (Vs. 1) This Chapter in small measure

pictures the peace and plenty, which will characterize the Millennial Earth.

2. (Vs. 2) Likewise, the coming Millennial Reign, of which all of this is a type, will see the greatest construction boom the world has ever known.

3. The conflict mentioned in Verse 3 presents the only war that was fought in the entirety of Solomon's reign. This typifies the scarcity of such in the coming Kingdom Age.

4. (Vs. 6) So much of the world as designed by man has specialized in destruction instead of construction. However, during the coming Kingdom Age, when Jesus will reign supreme from Jerusalem and over the entirety of the Earth, there will be no destruction except of that which is evil. Rather, there will be construction. For the first time, the world will see what the Earth could really be like under God's Government instead of man's flawed and faulty government.

5. (Vs. 8) Likewise, in the coming Kingdom Age, the Gentile world will pay tribute to the Lord of Glory; but yet, it will not be in the form of ruinous taxation. In fact, it will gladly be paid because of the great prosperity that will fill the entirety of the Earth.

6. Verses 9 and 10 typify redeemed Israel and the Blood-washed Saints of God in the coming Kingdom Age, who, under Christ, will carry out the Plan of God over the entirety of the Earth.

7. With such a Gentile wife, as recorded in Verse 11, Solomon was starting out the wrong way, and he did not learn the lesson he should have learned. In fact, he later loved many foreign women, who turned his heart away from God (I Ki. 11:1-9). Solomon, like all the other Types, was a broken figure of Him Who is to come; nevertheless, the Antitype, Who is Christ, will be Perfect.

THE COMING KINGDOM AGE

This Chapter portrays the coming Kingdom Age when Christ will reign supreme from Jerusalem and, in fact, will reign over the entirety of the world.

Solomon was a Type of Christ, although as all, a very unworthy Type. Yet, we get a dim picture of what it's going to be like in that coming day with Satan and all of his henchmen locked away in the bottomless pit and, as well, Christ Ruling supreme. In fact, it will be the grandest time the world has ever known in its history. For the first time, mankind will see what life could be like, but only under Christ.

RESTORATION

What happened as it regards these cities that once belonged to Hiram, but are now restored to Solomon, we do not actually know; however, this we do know:

Israel then will realize the entirety of her borders as originally promised. In other words, the Nation's boundaries will include modern Lebanon, Syria, and part of Iraq. In fact, the border on the eastern side will go all the way to the Euphrates River.

On the south, it will include the entirety of the Arabian Peninsula. That area now is nothing but desert and, in fact, one of the largest deserts in the world; however, during the coming Kingdom Age, the entirety of the Arabian Peninsula will be brought back to fertility and will become a verdant garden. That's when the *"desert will blossom as the rose"* (Isa. 35:1). In fact, Israel will at that time be the leading Nation on the Earth, fulfilling all the Promises that God made to her, even beginning with Abraham. But, all of it will be because of the Lord Jesus Christ, as all blessing and prosperity are always because of Christ.

WAR?

The Scripture says, *"And Solomon went to Hamath-zobah, and prevailed against it."*

This area was in northwestern Syria, probably about 300 miles north of Jerusalem. In fact, this was the only conflict fought by Solomon during his time as the king of Israel.

Likewise, in the coming Kingdom Age, the world will not know war because those who may oppose the Government of our Lord will be quick to hide their feelings. After all, who could defeat One with Almighty Power?

During the coming Kingdom Age, the Scripture says: *"And He shall judge among the nations, and shall rebuke many people: and they shall beat their swords into plowshares, and their spears into pruninghooks: nation shall not lift up sword against nation, neither shall they learn war anymore.* (The words, *'judge among,'* should read *'arbitrate between,'* and *'rebuke'* would have been better translated *'decide the disputes of.'* Man's courts of arbitration are doomed to failure, but, to Messiah's Court, success is here promised)" (Isa. 2:4).

When Jesus came at His First Advent, He offered the Kingdom to Israel, but they refused it; consequently, this subjected the world to what is now some 2,000 years of war and brutality. The Scripture says:

"For nation shall rise against nation, and kingdom against kingdom: and there shall be famines, and pestilences, and earthquakes, in divers places" (Mat. 24:7).

All of this is because Israel rejected her Lord. Thankfully, at the Second Coming, Israel will accept Jesus Christ as her Lord, her Saviour, and her Messiah, but only after first realizing that the One she crucified was in reality the Lord of Glory, in fact, the same One Who will save her during the coming Battle of Armageddon.

CONSTRUCTION

As Israel experienced a tremendous construction boom under Solomon, likewise, the entirety of the world will experience the same under Christ. In fact, under Christ during the Kingdom Age, the entirety of the world will be developed and modernized, with no country left in the lurch. All will come under the Blessing of the Lord Jesus Christ. It will be peace and prosperity as the world has never known before. Satan, who steals, kills, and destroys, will be locked away, which means that temptation and evil are, in effect, no more!

THE GENTILES

The Seventh Verse speaks of the *"Hittites, the Amorites, the Perizzites, the Hivites, and the Jebusites,"* all Gentiles. Under Solomon, these individuals were made to pay tribute; however, at the same time, they were afforded the luxury of living in a land of peace and prosperity, with them enjoying that prosperity. Under such a government, it was not a hardship to pay tribute.

During the coming Kingdom Age, there will be similar taxation by the Gentile world,

NOTES

but, in a sense, gladly so. There will be such prosperity that what few taxes that are paid will be done so willingly and gladly.

As stated, Israel will be the leading Nation in the world of that day, all under Christ. All the great Promises made to Abraham and the Prophets of old will now be realized. But yet, the Gentile nations will not envy Israel. In fact, the population of every country will encourage strongly their leadership to bless Israel because from this source, all Blessings will come.

THE DAUGHTER OF PHARAOH

And yet, there is a fly in this ointment, at least as far as Solomon is concerned. While he did all within his power to follow the Lord through most of his reign, striving to obey the Law of Moses in every respect, even as we shall see, still, this *"daughter of Pharaoh"* was the beginning of that which would cause him untold difficulties and problems.

While he did isolate her, still, every indication is that she continued to worship idols, and he permitted her to do so. In fact, he would become drawn away by many strange women, and in his later years, would lose his way.

For all of his wisdom, actually the wisest man who ever lived, with his great Gift coming from God, still, sin took its deadly toll. In fact, there is no defense against sin except the Cross of Christ. How hard it is for us to learn that. Education is no defense, money is no defense, intelligence is no defense; only the Cross! The Cross! The Cross!

Regrettably, all Types, as Solomon, break down; however, the reign of our Lord and Saviour, Jesus Christ, will have no flaws because everything, the government and all rulership, all and without exception, will be in His Hands, or as the Bible says:

"For unto us a Child is born, unto us a Son is given: and the Government shall be upon His Shoulder: and His Name shall be called Wonderful, Counsellor, The Mighty God, The Everlasting Father, The Prince of Peace. (This glorious Promise pertains not only to the First Advent, but to the Second Advent, as well.

"The pronoun *'us'* refers to Israel. From

the Seed of Abraham, which spawned the Jewish people and, hence, ultimately the Messiah, the greatest Promise of all time would finally be fulfilled.

"The phrase, *'Government on His Shoulder,'* refers to the coming Kingdom Age, when Christ will rule and reign over the entirety of the Earth [Dan. 7:13-14; I Cor. 15:24-28; Rev. 11:15; 20:4-10])" (Isa. 9:6).

"Of the increase of His Government and peace there shall be no end, upon the throne of David, and upon His Kingdom, to order it, and to establish it with judgment and with justice from henceforth even forever. The zeal of the LORD of Hosts will perform this. (The last phrase guarantees that what the Lord has promised, He will perform.

"The first part of this Verse has reference to the fact that there will not be an immediate subjugation of the Earth upon the Lord's return, but that the Messiah's Kingdom shall ever increase more and more until it ultimately fills the world)" (Isa. 9:7).

(12) "THEN SOLOMON OFFERED BURNT OFFERINGS UNTO THE LORD ON THE ALTAR OF THE LORD, WHICH HE HAD BUILT BEFORE THE PORCH,

(13) "EVEN AFTER A CERTAIN RATE EVERY DAY, OFFERING ACCORDING TO THE COMMANDMENT OF MOSES, ON THE SABBATHS, AND ON THE NEW MOONS, AND ON THE SOLEMN FEASTS, THREE TIMES IN THE YEAR, EVEN IN THE FEAST OF UNLEAVENED BREAD, AND IN THE FEAST OF WEEKS, AND IN THE FEAST OF TABERNACLES.

(14) "AND HE APPOINTED, ACCORDING TO THE ORDER OF DAVID HIS FATHER, THE COURSES OF THE PRIESTS TO THEIR SERVICE, AND THE LEVITES TO THEIR CHARGES, TO PRAISE AND MINISTER BEFORE THE PRIESTS, AS THE DUTY OF EVERY DAY REQUIRED: THE PORTERS ALSO BY THEIR COURSES AT EVERY GATE: FOR SO HAD DAVID THE MAN OF GOD COMMANDED.

(15) "AND THEY DEPARTED NOT FROM THE COMMANDMENT OF THE KING UNTO THE PRIESTS AND LEVITES CONCERNING ANY MATTER, OR CONCERNING THE TREASURES.

(16) "NOW ALL THE WORK OF SOLOMON WAS PREPARED UNTO THE DAY OF THE FOUNDATION OF THE HOUSE OF THE LORD, AND UNTIL IT WAS FINISHED. SO THE HOUSE OF THE LORD WAS PERFECTED."

The synopsis is:

1. (Vs. 13) The *"Feast of Unleavened Bread"* was conducted in April. The *"Feast of Weeks,"* which was in reality the Feast of Pentecost, was conducted in June. The *"Feast of Tabernacles"* was conducted in October. All the males of Israel were supposed to gather three times a year on these special Feasts (Ex. 23:14; Deut. 16:16).

2. Verse 14 pertains to the appointment of the 24 courses of the Priests in their services (I Chron., Chpt. 24), the 24 courses of the Levites to sing and play music regarding praise and worship (I Chron., Chpt. 25), and the 24 courses of the porters (I Chron., Chpt. 26). All this had been revealed to David by the Holy Spirit, and now it is being obeyed as he had left instructions.

3. (Vs. 16) This is the desire and the Work of the Holy Spirit—that He may *"perfect the House of the LORD,"* that House now being our physical and spiritual persons, which are Temples of the Holy Spirit (I Cor. 3:16). This is done by the Believer constantly exhibiting Faith in Christ and what Christ has done at the Cross. The Holy Spirit, Who works exclusively within the parameters of the Finished Work of Christ, will then carry out the work within our lives (Rom. 8:1-2, 11).

THE ALTAR OF THE LORD

Every evidence is that Solomon was extremely faithful in carrying out the Command of the Lord that had been given to David his father, as it regarded Temple worship, with all its proceedings, ceremonies, and rituals. All of it was of extreme significance because all of it in one way or the other portrayed Christ in either His Atoning Work, His Mediatorial Work, or His Intercessory Work. But let it be understood, even though the Word of the Lord is carried out, even as it must be, still, that gives no license to sin.

It is ironic, every evidence is, Solomon continued faithful as it regarded the Temple rituals, but, at the same time, at least in his later years, he also built heathen temples for his Gentile wives that they may worship their idol gods.

The liberty had by the Believer is liberty to live a holy life, which can only be done by our Faith being placed exclusively in Christ and the Cross. There is never liberty to sin.

Faith must properly be placed, and we speak of the Cross. If it degenerates to a mere ceremony, it will provide no power. The Holy Spirit cannot work under such circumstances. Jesus addressed this when He said:

"*Not everyone who says unto Me, Lord, Lord, shall enter into the Kingdom of Heaven* (the repetition of the word *'Lord'* expresses astonishment, as if to say: *'Are we to be disowned?'*); *but he who does the Will of My Father which is in Heaven* (what is the Will of the Father? Verse 23 tells us).

"*Many will say to Me in that day, Lord, Lord, have we not Prophesied in Your Name? and in Your Name have cast out devils? and in Your Name done many wonderful works?* (These things are not the criteria, but rather Faith in Christ and what Christ has done for us at the Cross, which then gives us the liberty to live a holy life [Eph. 2:8-9, 13-18]. The Word of God alone is to be the judge of doctrine.)

"*And then will I profess to them, I never knew you* (again we say, the criteria alone is Christ and Him Crucified [I Cor. 1:23]): *depart from Me, you who work iniquity* (we have access to God only through Christ, and access to Christ only through the Cross, and access to the Cross only through a denial of self [Lk. 9:23]; any other Message is judged by God as *'iniquity,'* and cannot be a part of Christ [I Cor. 1:17]).

"*Therefore whosoever hears these sayings of Mine, and does them, I will liken him unto a wise man, who built his house upon a rock.* (The *'Rock'* is Christ Jesus, and the Foundation is the Cross [Gal. 1:8-9])" (Mat. 7:21-24).

So there will be no misunderstanding, let us say it again:

Even though the Believer does have his Faith exclusively in Christ and the Cross, that gives him no license to sin. Willful sin carries with it a willful rejection by the Lord.

NOTES

PASSOVER, PENTECOST, AND TABERNACLES

These three Feasts commanded by Israel to be kept every year actually incorporated four other Feasts, with a total of seven.

The first Feast was Passover, which included the Feast of Unleavened Bread, which typified the Perfection of Christ's Perfect Body. Firstfruits typified His Resurrection. Passover, which incorporated all three of these Feasts, portrayed the price that Christ would pay at Calvary's Cross.

The *"Feast of Weeks,"* or better known as *"Pentecost,"* took place 50 days after the Passover. This featured Christ as the Baptizer with the Holy Spirit. Actually, it was on this particular day that the Holy Spirit, due to the Cross, came to the world in a new dimension. The *"Feast of Tabernacles"* was conducted in October and portrays the coming Kingdom Age when Christ will rule and reign on this Earth, and do so for 1,000 years. At this particular Feast, two other Feasts were celebrated also.

The Great Day of Atonement was not actually a Feast. In a sense, it was the very opposite, being the only fast day of the year included in the Law of Moses. It was the day that the High Priest went into the Holy of Holies and there applied blood to the Mercy Seat, which served as Atonement for the entirety of Israel, at least all who would believe. But, immediately after this particular day, there was a great Feast.

And then, associated with Tabernacles was, as well, the Feast of Trumpets. In one sense of the word, this speaks of the coming Rapture of the Church, but even more than that, it is when the great push will be made to bring Israel back to God. The trumpets in Heaven will announce this. All of this will lead to the Second Coming, which will take place some seven years after the initial Rapture of the Church. At that time Israel will accept Christ as her Lord, her Saviour and her Messiah.

THE COURSES OF THE PRIESTS

Hundreds of Priests, and even thousands, officiated, actually serving around the clock, 24 hours a day, 7 days a week, in order that everything be done and done as it should be done.

Sacrifices were offered every morning at 9 a.m. and every afternoon at 3 p.m. On the Sabbath, this was doubled, with two lambs offered instead of one at each appointed time. Besides that, the Priests had to go into the Holy Place constantly, and especially at the two times designated, when they would take coals of fire from the Brazen Altar, place those coals on the Golden Altar of worship, and then pour incense on those coals, which would fill the Holy Place, typifying the Intercession of Christ on our behalf. They would, as well, trim the wicks in the ten golden lampstands, five to the side, and replenish with oil.

On the Sabbath, they would eat all the loaves of bread that were on the ten tables, with the tables then being replaced with fresh loaves, twelve to the table.

And besides all of that, there were people coming constantly, even day and night, bringing animals for sacrifice for their own particular sins and transgressions. In fact, the altar fires were never to go out.

With each sacrifice, the animal had to be attended in a certain way, actually, some of it being eaten by the Priests, of course, after it was properly prepared and cooked.

But all of this, down to the most minute detail, was designated by the Holy Spirit and given to David, who then gave it to Solomon, with Solomon carrying it out as David had demanded.

THE PERFECTION OF THE HOUSE OF THE LORD

The phrase, *"So the House of the LORD was perfected,"* has to do with all the rituals and ceremonies being carried out and conducted exactly as the Lord had originally commanded. Solomon saw to it that it was done and done right.

Presently, it is the business of the Holy Spirit to perfect our House, that House being our personal and physical being (I Cor. 3:16). He can do this in only one way.

The Believer must place his Faith in Christ and the Cross exclusively. As well, it must be maintained in Christ and the Cross with it not allowed to be moved elsewhere.

NOTES

To be sure, the Evil One will do everything within his power to move our faith to other things. We must fight this good fight of Faith, never giving an inch, always understanding that *"we overcome by the Blood of the Lamb, and by the word of our testimony"* (Rev. 12:11).

Whatever needs to be done in our hearts and lives, and to be sure, much needs to be done, only the Holy Spirit can carry it out. He works on only one premise, and that is the Cross of Christ (Rom. 8:2). This means that the Believer must anchor his Faith, as stated, in Christ and the Cross, which then gives the Holy Spirit latitude to work. Only then can *"the House of the LORD be perfected."*

(17) "THEN WENT SOLOMON TO EZION-GEBER, AND TO ELOTH, AT THE SEA SIDE IN THE LAND OF EDOM.

(18) "AND HURAM SENT HIM BY THE HANDS OF HIS SERVANTS SHIPS, AND SERVANTS THAT HAD KNOWLEDGE OF THE SEA; AND THEY WENT WITH THE SERVANTS OF SOLOMON TO OPHIR, AND TOOK THENCE FOUR HUNDRED AND FIFTY TALENTS OF GOLD, AND BROUGHT THEM TO KING SOLOMON."

The composition is:

1. (Vs. 18) In fact, the entirety of the world, even as we shall see, beat a path to Solomon's door, exactly as the entirety of the world will come to Christ, availing themselves of His Perfect Wisdom, in the coming Kingdom Age, of which Solomon was a Type.

2. The Kingdom Age will see freedom and prosperity as no other age in human history. This particular time will be unparalleled.

3. It will be unparalleled simply because the Lord Jesus Christ Reigns supreme in all the world. The world will then see what it could have had and could have been all along. But thank God, even though it's been a long night, the Daystar is about to rise, and that Daystar is Christ.

THE PROSPERITY OF SOLOMON

The Kingdom Age will see prosperity as it has never been known on this Earth before.

The great problem of humanity is that the majority of the world is abjectly poor, while a few are obscenely rich. Probably the United States has gone further to rectify this problem than any other nation. But still, the problem remains.

When Jesus comes back and sets up His Kingdom, this problem will be addressed, and addressed in totality. The idea is, every person on the face of the Earth at that time will be rich. There will be no more want and no more poverty; whatever is needed will be available, and in abundance.

In the 2008 presidential election here in the States, each candidate seemed to constantly state how he was going to change America and change the world. The truth is, these poor individuals cannot change anything. Only the Lord Jesus Christ can effect change in the hearts and lives of individuals. He has changed the hearts and lives of untold millions, and He is going to effect a change in this world as it has never known before, which will commence at His Second Coming.

"Majestic sweetness sits enthroned,
"Upon the Saviour's Brow;
"His Head with radiant glories crowned,
"His Lips with Grace overflows."

"No mortal can with Him compare,
"Among the sons of men;
"Fairer is He than all the fair,
"That fill the heavenly train."

"He saw me plunged in deep distress,
"He flew to my relief;
"For me He bore the shameful Cross,
"And carried all my grief."

"To Him I owe my life and breath,
"And all the joys I have;
"He makes me triumph over death,
"And saves me from the grave."

"Since from His Bounty I receive,
"Such proofs of Love Divine,
"Had I a thousand hearts to give,
"Lord, they should all be Thine."

CHAPTER 9

(1) "AND WHEN THE QUEEN OF SHEBA HEARD OF THE FAME OF SOLOMON,

NOTES

SHE CAME TO PROVE SOLOMON WITH HARD QUESTIONS AT JERUSALEM, WITH A VERY GREAT COMPANY, AND CAMELS THAT BORE SPICES, AND GOLD IN ABUNDANCE, AND PRECIOUS STONES: AND WHEN SHE WAS COME TO SOLOMON, SHE COMMUNED WITH HIM OF ALL THAT WAS IN HER HEART.

(2) "AND SOLOMON TOLD HER ALL HER QUESTIONS: AND THERE WAS NOTHING HID FROM SOLOMON WHICH HE TOLD HER NOT.

(3) "AND WHEN THE QUEEN OF SHEBA HAD SEEN THE WISDOM OF SOLOMON, AND THE HOUSE THAT HE HAD BUILT,

(4) "AND THE MEAT OF HIS TABLE, AND THE SITTING OF HIS SERVANTS, AND THE ATTENDANCE OF HIS MINISTERS, AND THEIR APPAREL; HIS CUPBEARERS ALSO, AND THEIR APPAREL; AND HIS ASCENT BY WHICH HE WENT UP INTO THE HOUSE OF THE LORD; THERE WAS NO MORE SPIRIT IN HER.

(5) "AND SHE SAID TO THE KING, IT WAS A TRUE REPORT WHICH I HEARD IN MY OWN LAND OF YOUR ACTS, AND OF YOUR WISDOM:

(6) "HOWBEIT I BELIEVED NOT THEIR WORDS, UNTIL I CAME, AND MY EYES HAD SEEN IT: AND, BEHOLD, THE ONE HALF OF THE GREATNESS OF YOUR WISDOM WAS NOT TOLD ME: FOR YOU EXCEED THE FAME THAT I HEARD.

(7) "HAPPY ARE YOUR MEN, AND HAPPY ARE THESE YOUR SERVANTS, WHICH STAND CONTINUALLY BEFORE YOU, AND HEAR YOUR WISDOM.

(8) "BLESSED BE THE LORD YOUR GOD, WHICH DELIGHTS IN YOU TO SET YOU ON HIS THRONE, TO BE KING FOR THE LORD YOUR GOD: BECAUSE YOUR GOD LOVED ISRAEL, TO ESTABLISH THEM FOREVER, THEREFORE MADE HE YOU KING OVER THEM, TO DO JUDGMENT AND JUSTICE.

(9) "AND SHE GAVE THE KING AN HUNDRED AND TWENTY TALENTS OF GOLD, AND OF SPICES GREAT ABUNDANCE, AND PRECIOUS STONES: NEITHER WAS THERE ANY SUCH SPICE AS THE QUEEN OF SHEBA GAVE KING SOLOMON.

(10) "AND THE SERVANTS ALSO OF HURAM, AND THE SERVANTS OF SOLOMON, WHICH BROUGHT GOLD FROM OPHIR, BROUGHT ALGUM TREES AND PRECIOUS STONES.

(11) "AND THE KING MADE OF THE ALGUM TREES TERRACES TO THE HOUSE OF THE LORD, AND TO THE KING'S PALACE, AND HARPS AND PSALTERIES FOR SINGERS: AND THERE WERE NONE SUCH SEEN BEFORE IN THE LAND OF JUDAH.

(12) "AND KING SOLOMON GAVE TO THE QUEEN OF SHEBA ALL HER DESIRE, WHATSOEVER SHE ASKED, BESIDE THAT WHICH SHE HAD BROUGHT UNTO THE KING. SO SHE TURNED, AND WENT AWAY TO HER OWN LAND, SHE AND HER SERVANTS."

The structure is:

1. (Vs. 1) Solomon was a Type of Christ, albeit an imperfect Type, as all Types are. Jesus would say of Himself, *"A greater than Solomon is here."*

2. (Vs. 1) The Glory of the Lord having now risen upon Israel, the kings of the Gentiles come to that light, bringing their riches with them, and find there a glory and a wisdom such as the world had never seen. None of these monarchs are mentioned particularly except the queen of Sheba, the Holy Spirit reserving that dignity for a woman. She is further honored by the Lord Himself in Matthew 12:42, where He predicts her reappearance in the Resurrection.

3. (Vs. 1) Sheba communed with Solomon. Until one *"communes with Christ,"* they can never know the glory and the splendor of all that Christ is and has. For anyone who cares to investigate, the Lord is waiting.

4. According to Verse 2, if the honest heart will earnestly seek, that which it desires will be revealed by the Lord Jesus Christ. The Word of God is His Voice.

5. (Vs. 4) The splendor of Solomon was, in fact, greater than anything in the world. This is a comparison, at least as much as a comparison can be in the natural realm, of the coming reign of the Lord Jesus Christ, in the coming Kingdom Age. As grand as that was of Solomon, still, even though a Type of that coming day, it will be nothing by comparison to that which will be of Christ. In Solomon's day, the great blessing pertained only to Israel. In the coming Kingdom Age, the Blessing will cover the entirety of the world.

6. (Vs. 5) Everything the Word of God says about the Lord Jesus Christ is *"a true report."*

7. (Vs. 6) The Lord Jesus invites inspection. His appeal to the hungry heart is, *"Come...."*

8. (Vs. 7) The only true happiness in the world is that which has been provided by the *"Greater than Solomon."* It is a happiness that is based on the Fruit of the Spirit, which is *"joy."*

9. (Vs. 8) Due to the fact that the queen spoke of the Lord as being Solomon's God, some have claimed that she really did not accept the Lord. However, the same terminology also suggests, at the same time, that she very well may have accepted the Lord, and no doubt did!

10. (Vs. 9) What the queen of Sheba gave to Solomon could be measured; what he gave to her could not be measured.

11. (Vs. 12) Our *"Greater than Solomon"* admonishes us to ask of Him accordingly, and He will give (Lk., Chpt. 11).

THE QUEEN OF SHEBA AND THE FAME OF SOLOMON

How the queen of Sheba heard of the fame of Solomon, no one knows, but she did hear. As well, the whole world must hear of the fame of the Lord Jesus Christ. It is incumbent upon us, the church, to take this great and glorious Gospel to the ends of the Earth. They must hear! Of all of God's Work, this is priority. And yet, so little attention is presently given to World Evangelism.

The world of Islam, which has no message to tell, spends approximately a hundred times more to propagate their false message of Islam than we do our great Message of Christ. Why are we so lax in carrying out Christ's last Command (Mk. 16:15)?

THE QUEEN OF SHEBA CAME

- She came to prove Solomon with hard questions.
- She came with a very great company.

• She came with a great offering of spices, gold, and precious stones.

• She came in order to tell him her heart's desire.

The Scripture says, *"And Solomon told her all her questions: and there was nothing hid from Solomon which he told her not."*

If people would come to the Lord with the same demeanor, the same character, and the same plea, as did the queen of Sheba to Solomon, to be sure, they would have every need met, even to a far greater degree than did the queen of Sheba. When one communes with the Lord, which means to tell the Lord all of one's heart, such a petition the Lord will always answer.

THE TRUE REPORT

Evidently when this woman heard of Solomon's riches and prosperity, she hardly believed her ears. Yet, the stories came to her thick and fast, so much, in fact, that she undertook this long, long voyage in order to see for herself.

When she came into Jerusalem, what she witnessed was even far greater than that which she had heard. Her response was, *"It was a true report which I heard...."*

Please understand, everything in the Word of God as it extols Christ, is a *"true report."* In fact, it's not possible to exaggerate the Glory, the Greatness, and the Grandeur of the Lord Jesus Christ. To live for God, to walk with Him, and to have Him abide in one's heart, is the greatest thing that man could ever begin to know, that which money cannot buy, and that which the world cannot give.

No matter how big and no matter how grand that one might make it, one will find when he comes to Christ that it's even greater than he had been told, far greater. It is a *"true report."*

Is this great and glorious Salvation real? Yes, *"it is a true report."* Does it change men's lives? Yes, *"it is a true report."* Does it truly bring abiding peace? Yes, *"it is a true report."* Are we, in fact, given Eternal Life? Yes, *"it is a true report."*

"MY EYES HAVE SEEN IT"

The Sixth Verse says, *"Howbeit I believed not their words, until I came, and my eyes had seen it."*

The Lord Jesus Christ invites inspection. His appeal to the hungry heart is, *"Come unto Me, all you who labor and are heavy laden, and I will give you rest."* For all who come, they will say, *"For you exceed the thing that I heard."* In other words, as the Sixth Verse continues to say, *"the one half of the greatness of your wisdom was not told me."*

If it's that great, some may ask, why is it that only a few respond favorably?

It is the problem of deception!

DECEPTION

The Gospel of Jesus Christ is somewhat like the Tabernacle of old. Outwardly, there was nothing attractive or inviting about it. But, if one had walked into the Tabernacle, what would have met one's eyes would have been glorious, to say the least.

The walls were covered in gold, and the sacred vessels were also made out of gold. Thus is Bible Christianity.

When men look at it from the outward, they do not understand why anyone would want this. Going to church to them is like being sentenced to a penal institution. They cannot imagine anyone desiring to do such a thing.

But, if they come in, as the Tabernacle of old, what is inward is altogether different than that which is outward.

They do not understand, *"If any man be in Christ, he is a new creature: old things are passed away; behold, all things are become new"* (II Cor. 5:17).

HAPPY!

And then the queen of Sheba says in the Seventh Verse concerning the subjects of Solomon, *"Happy are your men, and happy are your servants."*

The only true happiness in the world is that which has been provided by the *"Greater than Solomon."* It is a happiness, as stated, that is based on the Fruit of the Spirit, which is *"joy."*

In this woman observing all of this, she had to admit that it was different than anything that she had ever known, seen, witnessed, or experienced. She then sees the Source of all this, which her eyes behold.

She then says, *"Blessed be the LORD your God."*

"BLESSED BE THE LORD YOUR GOD"

The queen of Sheba now worships and praises the Lord. As well, anyone who feasts upon the *"Greater than Solomon"* will likewise praise the Lord. A people who called themselves Christians, of which praise is foreign to them, actually do not know the Lord. Churches that claim to worship the Lord and never praise Him and, in fact, are ashamed by praise, really do not know Him. To know Him is to truly worship and praise Him.

Under the New Covenant, all worship and praise must be anchored in Calvary, even as it was under the Old Covenant. While the understanding of such then was very limited, understanding presently should be more open and obvious. Types, by their very nature, as was the Brazen Altar, constitute that which is limited, as far as knowledge is concerned, because it's before the fact. After the fact, as it is now, and because the Cross is history, everything is much more open, obvious, and understandable, or at least it should be.

Everything about Christianity, at least if it's totally Biblical, has its Foundation in the Cross, including praise and worship, and especially praise and worship. The problem with the modern church, and it's a problem that has always existed, is that the world thinks it can save itself without the Cross of Christ, and the church thinks it can sanctify itself without the Cross of Christ.

THE QUEEN OF SHEBA GAVE . . .

Whenever a person comes to Christ, the first thing that happens is that they want to give to God.

Why would the queen of Sheba want to give Solomon a hundred and twenty talents of gold, and spices in great abundance, and precious stones? Solomon already had an abundance of such.

That was not the idea. Actually, Solomon already had more of this than the queen of Sheba. The idea was and is, Solomon had given so much to her, she felt she had to reciprocate, at least as best she could. No doubt, her gifts seemed to be miniscule beside the riches of Solomon, but that was not the point.

Our gifts to the Lord fall into the same category. In effect, the Lord needs nothing, as should be obvious. But, we give to support His Work because we love Him. Actually, Paul said that we give *"to prove the sincerity of our love"* (II Cor. 8:8).

To be sure, the Lord could finance His Work in any number of ways; however, He has chosen the manner in which we function, which is to give to the Work of God, not for His Sake, but rather for our sakes. Giving builds Faith, assurance, and confidence within our hearts. In other words, our giving is for us and really not for the Lord. He allows us to participate, and what a privilege that is.

So, the queen of Sheba will give to Solomon because she desires to do so. He has been so good to her and so wonderful to her, she feels she can do no less, and rightly so.

ALL HER DESIRE

The Twelfth Verse says, *"And king Solomon gave to the queen of Sheba all her desire, whatsoever she asked. . . ."*

Undoubtedly, Solomon was the only man in the world at that time who could function in such capacity. He had this great wisdom given to him by God, which superceded any individual in the entirety of the world. In other words, there was no human being alive at that time or since that had the wisdom of Solomon, and the queen of Sheba was privileged to be a recipient of that wisdom.

Even in a greater way presently, we have a greater privilege now than ever before.

We who know the Lord are privileged to tap into resources that literally boggle the mind. Our great problem is that we do not do such as we should. Too often we resort to the counsel of men, which most of the time is wrong. We have a *"Greater than Solomon"* in our midst, but all too often, and sadly so, He is ignored. What a travesty!

(13) "NOW THE WEIGHT OF GOLD THAT CAME TO SOLOMON IN ONE YEAR

WAS SIX HUNDRED AND THREESCORE AND SIX TALENTS OF GOLD;

(14) "BESIDE THAT WHICH CHAPMEN AND MERCHANTS BROUGHT. AND ALL THE KINGS OF ARABIA AND GOVERNORS OF THE COUNTRY BROUGHT GOLD AND SILVER TO SOLOMON.

(15) "AND KING SOLOMON MADE TWO HUNDRED TARGETS OF BEATEN GOLD: SIX HUNDRED SHEKELS OF BEATEN GOLD WENT TO ONE TARGET.

(16) "AND THREE HUNDRED SHIELDS MADE HE OF BEATEN GOLD: THREE HUNDRED SHEKELS OF GOLD WENT TO ONE SHIELD. AND THE KING PUT THEM IN THE HOUSE OF THE FOREST OF LEBANON.

(17) "MOREOVER THE KING MADE A GREAT THRONE OF IVORY, AND OVERLAID IT WITH PURE GOLD.

(18) "AND THERE WERE SIX STEPS TO THE THRONE, WITH A FOOTSTOOL OF GOLD, WHICH WERE FASTENED TO THE THRONE, AND STAYS ON EACH SIDE OF THE SITTING PLACE, AND TWO LIONS STANDING BY THE STAYS:

(19) "AND TWELVE LIONS STOOD THERE ON THE ONE SIDE AND ON THE OTHER UPON THE SIX STEPS. THERE WAS NOT THE LIKE MADE IN ANY KINGDOM.

(20) "AND ALL THE DRINKING VESSELS OF KING SOLOMON WERE OF GOLD, AND ALL THE VESSELS OF THE HOUSE OF THE FOREST OF LEBANON WERE OF PURE GOLD: NONE WERE OF SILVER; IT WAS NOT ANY THING ACCOUNTED OF IN THE DAYS OF SOLOMON.

(21) "FOR THE KING'S SHIPS WENT TO TARSHISH WITH THE SERVANTS OF HURAM: EVERY THREE YEARS ONCE CAME THE SHIPS OF TARSHISH BRINGING GOLD, AND SILVER, IVORY, AND APES, AND PEACOCKS.

(22) "AND KING SOLOMON PASSED ALL THE KINGS OF THE EARTH IN RICHES AND WISDOM.

(23) "AND ALL THE KINGS OF THE EARTH SOUGHT THE PRESENCE OF SOLOMON, TO HEAR HIS WISDOM, THAT GOD HAD PUT IN HIS HEART.

(24) "AND THEY BROUGHT EVERY MAN HIS PRESENT, VESSELS OF SILVER, AND VESSELS OF GOLD, AND RAIMENT, HARNESS, AND SPICES, HORSES, AND MULES, A RATE YEAR BY YEAR.

(25) "AND SOLOMON HAD FOUR THOUSAND STALLS FOR HORSES AND CHARIOTS, AND TWELVE THOUSAND HORSEMEN; WHOM HE BESTOWED IN THE CHARIOT CITIES, AND WITH THE KING AT JERUSALEM.

(26) "AND HE REIGNED OVER ALL THE KINGS FROM THE RIVER EVEN UNTO THE LAND OF THE PHILISTINES, AND TO THE BORDER OF EGYPT.

(27) "AND THE KING MADE SILVER IN JERUSALEM AS STONES, AND CEDAR TREES MADE HE AS THE SYCOMORE TREES THAT ARE IN THE LOW PLAINS IN ABUNDANCE."

The diagram is:

1. (Vs. 13) Six hundred and sixty-six talents of gold; Solomon, as well, had six steps to his throne. Inasmuch as the number "6" is the number of man, and always, of course, comes short of "7," which is the number of perfection, we find imperfection upon all his glory. Man was created on the sixth day. Despite all the glory given to Solomon, still, he was but a man, hence, the number "6." Perfection comes only in and through the Lord Jesus Christ.

2. Each shield of beaten gold would cost in 2008 currency, approximately $400,000.00.

3. Verse 20 symbolizes the great prosperity that will characterize the entirety of the Planet when Jesus Christ comes back.

4. (Vs. 22) Likewise, Jesus Christ, of Whom Solomon was a Type, when reigning from Jerusalem in the days of the coming Kingdom Age, will be the wisest King Who has ever lived and, thereby, will bring riches and prosperity to the entirety of the Planet.

5. (Vs. 24) In fact, Israel, at the time of Solomon, was the most powerful Nation on the face of the Earth; however, it was not because of a mighty armed force, but because of the Grace of God.

RICHES AND PROSPERITY

When we read this Chapter, it portrays the great prosperity that will characterize this Planet when Jesus Christ comes back, and as previously stated, prosperity which will cover the entirety of the Earth. In other words, no nation at that time will be poor.

Much of the world presently goes to bed hungry each night. Every day hundreds or even thousands of little children fall down from hunger and are too weak to rise. It is called *"the silent death."* And this, despite the fact that Planet Earth, even now in its cursed state, has the capacity to feed one hundred billion people. It is sin that causes all the present problems and, in fact, has been the cause of all problems from the beginning of time. When Jesus comes back, there will be no more *"silent death."*

SPIRITUALITY

There will be many things in the coming Kingdom Age that will be prevalent and present, which Israel under Solomon did not have.

Material prosperity is one thing, but if the Spiritual part is neglected, then the material part is of little consequence.

In the coming Kingdom Age, Righteousness will rule the Earth, and the greater privilege, and one might say, the greater Blessing, will be the Spirit of God which moves in the hearts and lives of untold millions. That will be the great strength of the world of that coming day.

Solomon had the material benefits, but especially in his latter years, the spirituality was lacking. He lost his way, and we could only hope that he came back at the end.

All of this should be a lesson to us.

With all the wisdom in the world, and Solomon had it all, greater than any human being has ever had, all a Gift from God, and all the money and wealth in the world, and Israel had it all at that time, and because of the Blessings of God, still, as we will see, this did not stop Solomon from losing his way, or Israel from losing her way, for she most definitely foundered almost immediately after the death of Solomon. What a shame!

This only proves that the heart of man is so vile and so wicked that, irrespective of the climate, the environment, the association, or the participation in the things of God, still, man fails at every turn. There's only one Man Who has not failed, and cannot fail, and His Name is the Lord Jesus Christ. That's the reason our Faith must reside in Him and what He did for us at the Cross. Let us say it another way:

The only thing standing between mankind and eternal Hell is the Cross of Christ!

SIX STEPS TO THE THRONE

Please look at the number *"6,"* of which the Holy Spirit did not comment, but it most definitely was noted.

• There were *"666"* talents of gold each year that came to Solomon.
• He had *"6"* steps to his Throne.
• Man was created on the *"6th"* day.
• Goliath had *"6"* pieces of armor.
• Nebuchadnezzar's great image also presented the number *"6."*
• And finally, *"666" appears* as the number of the Antichrist.

"Seven" is God's number. A perfect example of this is found in the taking of Jericho by Joshua. The Scripture says:

• Joshua was instructed by the Lord to encompass Jericho for *"7"* days.
• *"Seven"* Priests were to walk before the Ark of the Covenant.
• They were to blow *"7"* trumpets of ram's horns.
• On the *"7th"* day they were to compass the city *"7"* times.
• The *"7th"* time when they marched around Jericho on the *"7th"* day, the *"7"* Priests blew the *"7"* trumpets, and then the people were to shout, *"For the LORD has given you the city."*
• *"Seven"* is God's Number of totality, completion, universality, and above all, perfection. Only God reaches that number. Man always stops short of perfection, in other words, he can never quite get it right, hence, the number *"6"* is the number of man.

The greatest effort by man to usurp authority over God will be by the Antichrist whose number is *"666."* He will fail, as all others before him have failed. No matter how you look at it, one cannot make *"6"* more than *"7."*

ALL THE KINGS OF THE EARTH

There was a constant parade of kings coming from various different countries to test the wisdom of Solomon, still, only one of these potentates was mentioned by name, and that was and is the queen of Sheba.

Why did the Holy Spirit single her out?

I think the reasons are obvious.

I believe that she came to Solomon out of a heart's desire to know the real cause of Solomon's great wisdom, which and Who was the Lord. I think the evidence is there that she accepted the Lord and His Grace. In a sense, I think that Jesus said so. His exact words were:

"The queen of the south shall rise up in the judgment with the men of this generation, and condemn them: for she came from the utmost parts of the Earth to hear the wisdom of Solomon; and, behold, a Greater than Solomon is here" (Lk. 11:31).

Inasmuch as the queen of Sheba will condemn the generation of Jesus' day, I think this tells us of her Salvation. She wanted many things when she came to Solomon, but most of all, I think she wanted to know about Solomon's God, the Source of his wisdom.

As it regarded all the other kings who came to Solomon and, no doubt, there were many hundreds, their interest, it seems, was altogether in things of material value, and not at all that which was Spiritual; consequently, the Holy Spirit only mentioned their coming without giving any specifics whatsoever.

(28) "AND THEY BROUGHT UNTO SOLOMON HORSES OUT OF EGYPT, AND OUT OF ALL LANDS.

(29) "NOW THE REST OF THE ACTS OF SOLOMON, FIRST AND LAST, ARE THEY NOT WRITTEN IN THE BOOK OF NATHAN THE PROPHET, AND IN THE PROPHECY OF AHIJAH THE SHILONITE, AND IN THE VISIONS OF IDDO THE SEER AGAINST JEROBOAM THE SON OF NEBAT?

(30) "AND SOLOMON REIGNED IN JERUSALEM OVER ALL ISRAEL FORTY YEARS.

(31) "AND SOLOMON SLEPT WITH HIS FATHERS, AND HE WAS BURIED IN THE CITY OF DAVID HIS FATHER: AND REHOBOAM HIS SON REIGNED IN HIS STEAD."

NOTES

The exposition is:

1. (Vs. 31) The fact that God did not record the great sins of Solomon in his latter years, at least in this account, is some indication that Solomon asked for and received Mercy, Forgiveness, and Grace.

2. (Vs. 31) If so, these sins would have been washed away and, thereby, unrecorded. This is about the only indication that we have that Solomon may have made things right with God before he died.

3. It is said that the last thing the Holy Spirit says about Solomon, the wisest man who ever lived, the man who was greatly beloved of the Lord, was the fact that he was a horse trader. That speaks volumes!

SOLOMON, THE HORSE TRADER

In Verses 24, 25, and 28, the Holy Spirit sorrowfully calls attention to Solomon as a horse trader. In essence, this was forbidden him by the Word of God. Williams says, *"Later on, they were instruments in the Devil's hand for destroying Judah"*[1] (II Chron. 12:3-4, 9; Ps. 33:17).

Desires forbidden by the Word of God, if indulged, afterwards return, like Solomon's horses, as instruments of captivity to the soul.

We find in Verse 29 that Solomon was warned as it regarded the ambition of Jeroboam; however, Solomon evidently did not listen.

THE DEATH OF SOLOMON

It is believed that Solomon became king when he was some 20 years of age. He reigned for 40 years and died at 60 years old. Had he faithfully followed the Lord, he could have lived to have been 100, or even more.

This man was used by the Holy Spirit to pen three Books of the Bible; Proverbs, Ecclesiastes, and the Song of Solomon. If he died lost, he is the only one used by the Holy Spirit to write the Sacred Text and then to die without God.

The account of his last years is given in I Kings, Chapter 11, and I quote from *"THE EXPOSITOR'S STUDY BIBLE"*:

"But king Solomon loved many strange women, together with the daughter of Pharaoh, women of the Moabites, Ammonites, Edomites, Zidonians, and

Hittites (we have already heard of the multiplication of silver and gold [I Ki. 10:14-25], in defiance of Deuteronomy 17:17, and of the multiplication of horses [I Ki. 10:27-29], in disregard of Deuteronomy 17:16; we now read how the ruin of this great prince was completed by the multiplication of wives, and heathen wives at that);

"*Of the nations concerning which the LORD said unto the Children of Israel, You shall not go in to them, neither shall they come in unto you: for surely they will turn away your heart after their gods: Solomon clave unto these in love* (to disobey the Word of God is to invite disaster).

"*And he had seven hundred wives, princesses, and three hundred concubines: and his wives turned away his heart.* (Why? Past Blessings from God, even though of tremendous import at the time, will not suffice for today's journey. There must ever be fresh revelations. Due to Solomon's backsliding, there were no fresh revelations.

"The great gift of wisdom did not deter Solomon's transgression. Such cannot take the place of a constant day-by-day walk of holiness and humility before the Lord.

"As well, pride played its part, and probably the biggest part.

"All of this shows us that Believers do not fare too very well in a life of blessings only. These tend to take their eyes off of God, and onto themselves.)

"*For it came to pass, when Solomon was old, that his wives turned away his heart after other gods: and his heart was not perfect with the LORD his God, as was the heart of David his father.* (Self-righteousness could never understand this statement, especially due to the fact of the horrid sin of David with Bath-sheba and then the murder of her husband, Uriah. David failed in many other areas, as well; however, his heart was perfect toward God, because he always took these terrible sins to God [Ps. 51]; moreover, David suffered terribly for these sins, which is always the case with sin.)

"*For Solomon went after Ashtoreth the goddess of the Zidonians, and after Milcom the abomination of the Ammonites.* (The words '*and served them*' should be added. There is no sadder picture in the Bible than

NOTES

that of Solomon's fall. His extraordinary gift of wisdom did not save him from disobedience to the Law of God. His neglect of that Law, and his loss of the fellowship of God which gives power to it, opened the door wide to the entrance of every form of evil. Had he clung to the Sacred Scriptures, how bright would have been his life! He was probably about 50 years of age when he apostatized.)

"*And Solomon did evil in the sight of the LORD, and went not fully after the LORD, as did David his father.* (David was always held up as the example, because, as stated, he always turned to the Lord. The ironical thing was, Solomon continued to worship the Lord, at least after a fashion, while at the same time worshipping idols. How so indicative of the modern church!)

"*Then did Solomon build an high place for Chemosh, the abomination of Moab, in the hill that is before Jerusalem* (the Mount of Olivet), *and for Molech, the abomination of the children of Ammon* (with some of these, human sacrifice was offered up, most of the time that of little children; however, we have no record of Jewish children being sacrificed to idols before the time of Ahaz, which was a little over 200 years after Solomon).

"*And likewise did he for all his strange wives, which burnt incense and sacrificed unto their gods.*

"*And the LORD was angry with Solomon, because his heart was turned from the LORD God of Israel, which had appeared unto him twice,* (there is a special Hebrew verb used in the Bible for '*to be angry*'; it is only used of Divine anger; it occurs fourteen times; here, and in five other passages, a form of the verb is used expressing the forcing of oneself to be angry with a person who is loved; in other words, the Lord, because of His Nature, and despite Solomon's spiritual declension, had to force Himself to be angry with Solomon; He loved him that much!)

"*And had commanded him concerning this thing, that he should not go after other gods: but he kept not that which the LORD commanded.* (The idea is: the Lord dealt with him over and over again about this matter)" (I Ki. 11:1-10).

We see from the Sacred Text that Solomon sinned terribly so in his later years. We see also that the Lord evidently warned him time and time again, but to no avail. So, the great question looms large, did he at the last moment cry to God for Mercy? He most definitely could have, and I would like to think that he did; however, the Scripture doesn't say.

What a sad way for the wisest man who ever lived, and so beloved of the Lord, to end his days in this fashion!

I'll say again what was previously said:

The fact that God did not record these great sins of Solomon in this last account of II Chronicles is some indication that Solomon may have asked for and received Mercy, Forgiveness, and Grace. If so, all of his sins would have been washed away and, thereby, unrecorded. As also stated, this is about the only indication that we have that Solomon may have made things right with God before he died.

"Joyful, joyful, we adore Thee,
"God of Glory, Lord of Love;
"Hearts unfold like flowers before Thee,
"Praising Thee their Son above.
"Melt the clouds of sin and sadness,
"Drive the dark of doubt away;
"Giver of immortal gladness,
"Fill us with the light of day!"

"All Your Works with joy surround You,
"Earth and Heaven reflect Your Rays,
"Stars and Angels sing around You,
"Center of unbroken praise:
"Field and forest, vale and mountain,
"Blooming meadow, flashing sea,
"Chanting bird and flowing fountain,
"Call us to rejoice in Thee."

"You are Giving and Forgiving,
"Ever Blessing, ever Blessed,
"Wellspring of the joy of living,
"Ocean depth of happy rest!
"You our Father, Christ our Brother,
"All who live and love are Thine,
"Teach us how to love each other,
"Lift us to the joy Divine."

"Mortals join the mighty chorus,

NOTES

"Which the morning stars began;
"Father-love is reigning o'er us,
"Brother-love binds man to man.
"Ever singing march we onward,
"Victors in the midst of strife;
"Joyful music lifts us sunward
"In the triumph song of life."

CHAPTER 10

(1) "AND REHOBOAM WENT TO SHECHEM: FOR TO SHECHEM WERE ALL ISRAEL COME TO MAKE HIM KING.

(2) "AND IT CAME TO PASS, WHEN JEROBOAM THE SON OF NEBAT, WHO WAS IN EGYPT, WHERE HE HAD FLED FROM THE PRESENCE OF SOLOMON THE KING, HEARD IT, THAT JEROBOAM RETURNED OUT OF EGYPT.

(3) "AND THEY SENT AND CALLED HIM. SO JEROBOAM AND ALL ISRAEL CAME AND SPOKE TO REHOBOAM, SAYING,

(4) "YOUR FATHER MADE OUR YOKE GRIEVOUS: NOW THEREFORE EASE YOU SOMEWHAT THE GRIEVOUS SERVITUDE OF YOUR FATHER, AND HIS HEAVY YOKE THAT HE PUT UPON US, AND WE WILL SERVE YOU.

(5) "AND HE SAID UNTO THEM, COME AGAIN UNTO ME AFTER THREE DAYS. AND THE PEOPLE DEPARTED.

(6) "AND KING REHOBOAM TOOK COUNSEL WITH THE OLD MEN WHO HAD STOOD BEFORE SOLOMON HIS FATHER WHILE HE YET LIVED, SAYING, WHAT COUNSEL GIVE YOU ME TO RETURN ANSWER TO THIS PEOPLE?

(7) "AND THEY SPOKE UNTO HIM, SAYING, IF YOU BE KIND TO THIS PEOPLE, AND PLEASE THEM, AND SPEAK GOOD WORDS TO THEM, THEY WILL BE YOUR SERVANTS FOR EVER.

(8) "BUT HE FORSOOK THE COUNSEL WHICH THE OLD MEN GAVE HIM, AND TOOK COUNSEL WITH THE YOUNG MEN WHO WERE BROUGHT UP WITH HIM, WHO STOOD BEFORE HIM.

(9) "AND HE SAID UNTO THEM, WHAT ADVICE DO YOU GIVE THAT WE MAY

RETURN ANSWER TO THIS PEOPLE, WHICH HAVE SPOKEN TO ME, SAYING, EASE SOMEWHAT THE YOKE THAT YOUR FATHER DID PUT UPON US?

(10) "AND THE YOUNG MEN WHO WERE BROUGHT UP WITH HIM SPOKE UNTO HIM, SAYING, THUS SHALL YOU ANSWER THE PEOPLE WHO SPOKE UNTO YOU, SAYING, YOUR FATHER MADE OUR YOKE HEAVY, BUT YOU MAKE IT SOMEWHAT LIGHTER FOR US; THUS SHALL YOU SAY UNTO THEM, MY LITTLE FINGER SHALL BE THICKER THAN MY FATHER'S LOINS.

(11) "FOR WHEREAS MY FATHER PUT A HEAVY YOKE UPON YOU, I WILL PUT MORE TO YOUR YOKE: MY FATHER CHASTISED YOU WITH WHIPS, BUT I WILL CHASTISE YOU WITH SCORPIONS."

The pattern is:

1. (Vs. 1) Jerusalem was where the Lord had placed His Name, and yet, for political purposes, and without consulting the Lord, Rehoboam would go to Shechem. So much of what is today called *"Christianity"* is operated on the rudiments of political expediency, and not according to the Word of the Lord.

2. (Vs. 2) Jeroboam heard that Solomon had died. It is instructive to point out the dissatisfaction of the Nation with the glorious reign of Solomon, with all of its prosperity. In fact, much of Israel would elect Solomon's enemy as king. This is a perfect picture of Revelation, Chapter 20.

3. (Vs. 2) In Revelation 20, it is foretold that although Christ will maintain an absolutely perfect and prosperous government over the entirety of the Earth for 1,000 years, yet some of the world will be dissatisfied with that reign of Glory and Righteousness, and will, in effect, call back Satan from exile, as Israel called back Jeroboam and, for a short time, will enthrone Satan as prince over at least a part of the Earth. However, his tenure will not last long.

4. As it regards the grievous yoke of Verse 4, there is no Scriptural evidence of such!

5. (Vs. 6) While Rehoboam took counsel with the old men and then with the young men, still, there is no place that it says that he took counsel with God. In fact, there

NOTES

seemed to be little desire for the Will of God. All was political expediency.

6. (Vs. 7) He should have taken the counsel of the old men!

7. (Vs. 11) The advice that Rehoboam received from the young men was the worst possible advice he could have gotten! Regrettably, he followed that advice, which brought about the ruin of the Nation.

GOD'S PEOPLE GOING ASTRAY

Whatever Rehoboam was at present, for the most part, Solomon could be blamed for that. He did not raise his son in the fear of God; consequently, Rehoboam, as the record will show, had precious little fear.

Under David in the first years of Solomon, we saw how the Blessings of God came upon Israel, and supremely so. There was a reason for that. David earnestly sought the Lord, and Solomon in his first years did as well. Rehoboam, as stated, although the grandson of David and the son of Solomon had little or no knowledge of the Lord. His thoughts were secular entirely, and the Nation would go into ruin, despite it having been the greatest kingdom on the face of the Earth.

As it regards Rehoboam being made king, he would choose Shechem for the place of enthronement. Jerusalem was where the Lord had placed His Name, and yet, for political purposes and without consulting the Lord at all, Rehoboam strikes out on his own and goes to Shechem. It is a shame, but so much of the modern church is political as well. In fact, it is even more political many times than civil government, which means it's not being led by the Lord. As Rehoboam's efforts were not of God, likewise, the political nature of the church is not of God either.

JUDAH

We will find that the Nation will soon break apart, with the northern kingdom being referred to as Israel, Ephraim, or Samaria. The southern kingdom was referred to as *"Judah."*

The time frame from the present to the end of II Chronicles will cover a period of about 450 years. The account will ignore almost altogether the Nation of Israel because the northern kingdom was not the Will of God. There were 20 kings that graced the throne of Judah, beginning with Rehoboam and ending with Zedekiah.

This lineage of kings, beginning with David, was very, very important because through this particular lineage the Messiah would come. While it is true that most of these kings were ungodly, as important as that was, still, it did not mar the lineage per se.

The following is a list of the kings who could be labeled as godly, or who served the Lord diligently, at least for a period of time:

Abijah, Asa, Jehoshaphat, Joash, Amaziah, Uzziah, Jotham, Hezekiah, and Josiah.

Some of the kings listed began correctly and then ended poorly. It could probably be said that the godliest were Jehoshaphat, Hezekiah, and Josiah. Of Jehoshaphat, it is said, *"And the LORD was with Jehoshaphat, because he walked in the first ways of his father David, and sought not unto Baalim; but sought to the LORD God of his father, and walked in His Commandments, and not after the doings of Israel"* (II Chron. 17:3-4). Concerning Hezekiah it is said, *"And he did that which was right in the sight of the LORD, according to all that David his father had done"* (II Chron. 29:2). Regarding Josiah it is said, *"And he did that which was right in the sight of the LORD, and walked in the ways of David his father, and declined neither to the right hand, nor to the left"* (II Chron. 34:2).

DAVID

If it is to be noticed, David was always used as the example of Righteousness.

How could this be, especially considering his sin with Bath-sheba, and worse yet, his murder of her husband, Uriah?

To be sure, David paid dearly for those sins.

Despite these terrible sins, David's heart was ever right with God, at least in the sense of always going to Him to make things right. In other words, he had a repentant heart.

While these things, as wonderful as they might be, are so necessary, still, that doesn't make up for any sin committed. But it does show the true heart and the true direction of the individual.

And we must remember, if true Repentance is engaged, as it regards any sin, and no matter how heinous it might be, the Lord will always be quick to show Mercy and to forgive. It is called *"Justification by Faith."* And when the Lord forgives, that means as far as He is concerned, the sins never took place.

And yet, despite the fact of what the Lord does, which is always glorious and wonderful, still, the aftereffects of sin, many times, even most of the time, remain. This we must ever understand.

It's not so much that the person pays for sin, or can pay for sin, for such cannot be done, but it is that sin sets into motion a series of events that must be played out. It was that way with David, despite the fact that God forgave him fully, and it is that way with every other Believer also.

COUNSEL

Jeroboam seems to be the spokesman for the people. He implores Rehoboam to serve the people, instead of the people serving Rehoboam.

We find Rehoboam taking counsel from the old men, and finally from the young men. He did not consult the Lord and seemingly had no desire to consult the Lord. For all practical purposes, God is forgotten!

We find a comedy of errors that makes one want to weep. The greatest Nation on the face of the Earth is soon to be reduced to splinters. That which had taken so long to build will now be destroyed in a very short period of time.

Is it possible that the modern church is operating pretty much in the same manner as did Rehoboam? Despite the fact of what Jesus did at Calvary, despite the tremendous Victory there won, despite the fact that this Covenant is so secure and so Perfect that it is referred to as the *"Everlasting Covenant,"* still, church leaders seek counsel of men instead of God (Heb. 13:20).

THE WORD OF THE LORD

The Word of the Lord, i.e., *"the Bible,"* implores us to seek the advice and counsel of the Lord regarding anything and everything we do. Nothing is too little and nothing is too large! The Lord, as should be obvious, desires this and is very upset when Believers ignore Him. But now, all too often, the Lord has been ignored with humanistic psychologists taking His Place.

Why do we desire the counsel of mere men when we can have the Leading of the Holy Spirit?

I think the reason lies in the fact that relationship with the Lord has grown thin, if it exists at all. That being the case, the Lord is like a stranger; therefore, other directions are pursued. In most modern churches, seeking the Face of the Lord for Leading, for Guidance, for Help, and yes, for Counsel, is almost a thing of the past. In fact, most modern churches do not even believe that the Lord speaks to people presently.

The truth is He will speak to any of us through His Word if we will only take the time to peruse and study His Word. As well, He at times will speak through Prophecy or Tongues and Interpretation, but, I forget that most of the modern churches don't even believe in the Gifts of the Spirit anymore. And in the churches which claim to believe in the Gifts, the Holy Spirit oftentimes is so little present that the Gifts aren't in Operation. What a tragedy!

And then the Lord can speak through Dreams or Visions, as He often has done. The truth is, the Lord will be as close to a person as that person desires the Lord to be. Considering that counsel from mere mortals is almost altogether sought at the present time, we have to conclude from this that the modern church is not too very close to the Lord.

(12) "SO JEROBOAM AND ALL THE PEOPLE CAME TO REHOBOAM ON THE THIRD DAY, AS THE KING BADE, SAYING, COME AGAIN TO ME ON THE THIRD DAY.

(13) "AND THE KING ANSWERED THEM ROUGHLY; AND KING REHOBOAM FORSOOK THE COUNSEL OF THE OLD MEN,

(14) "AND ANSWERED THEM AFTER THE ADVICE OF THE YOUNG MEN, SAYING, MY FATHER MADE YOUR YOKE HEAVY, BUT I WILL ADD THERETO: MY FATHER CHASTISED YOU WITH WHIPS, BUT I WILL CHASTISE YOU WITH SCORPIONS.

(15) "SO THE KING HEARKENED NOT UNTO THE PEOPLE: FOR THE CAUSE WAS OF GOD, THAT THE LORD MIGHT PERFORM HIS WORD, WHICH HE SPOKE BY THE HAND OF AHIJAH THE SHILONITE TO JEROBOAM THE SON OF NEBAT."

The structure is:

1. (Vs. 15) Solomon, although dead, bears his full share of the responsibility of what Rehoboam was, and shortly came to show he was.

2. (Vs. 15) The Lord did not instigate Rehoboam's direction arbitrarily, but did so because of Judah's terrible idol-worship, which now characterized the country, and was instigated by Solomon.

3. If we sow to the wind, we will always reap the whirlwind.

THE CAUSE WAS OF GOD

What was the word spoken by Ahijah the Prophet?

The answer is given to us in I Kings 11:29. It says:

"And it came to pass at that time when Jeroboam went out of Jerusalem, that the Prophet Ahijah the Shilonite found him in the way; and he had clad himself with a new garment; and they two were alone in the field:

"And Ahijah caught the new garment that was on him, and rent it in twelve pieces:

"And he said to Jeroboam, You take ten pieces: for thus says the LORD, the God of Israel, Behold, I will rend the kingdom out of the hand of Solomon, and will give ten Tribes to you:

"(But he shall have one Tribe for my servant David's sake, and for Jerusalem's sake, the city which I have chosen out of all the Tribes of Israel:)

"Because that they have forsaken Me, and have worshipped Ashtoreth the goddess of the Zidonians, Chemosh the god of the Moabites, and Milcom the god of the children of Ammon, and have not walked in My Ways, to do that which is right in My Eyes,

and to keep My Statutes and My Judgments, as did David his father.

"Howbeit I will not take the whole kingdom out of his hand: but I will make him prince all the days of his life for David My Servant's sake, whom I chose, because he kept My Commandments and My Statutes:

"But I will take the kingdom out of his son's hand, and will give it unto you, even ten Tribes.

"And unto his son will I give one Tribe, that David My Servant may have a light always before me in Jerusalem, the city which I have chosen Me to put My Name there.

"And I will take you, and you shall reign according to all that your soul desires, and shall be king over Israel.

"And it shall be, if you will hearken unto all that I command you, and will walk in My Ways, and do that which is right in My Sight, to keep My Statutes and My Commandments, as David My Servant did; that I will be with you, and build you a sure house, as I built for David, and will give Israel unto you.

"And I will for this afflict the seed of David, but not forever" (I Ki. 11:29-39).

Solomon had instituted idol worship into Israel during the last years of his reign, with the account given to us in I Kings, with such idol worship continuing under his son Rehoboam. In effect, Israel had gone into deep sin.

The fulfillment of the prediction of Ahijah affords an instance similar to many others in the Scriptures of Prophecies being accomplished by the operation of human passions and, seemingly, in the natural course of events. Men think they are obeying their own wills and carrying out their own plans, unconscious that the matter is of God and permitted and overruled by Him for the performance of His Word.

And this is exactly what happened with Jeroboam as it regards his decisions. He wants evil, so the Lord will allow him to steer a course of events that will bring about more evil. The following can be said:

If a person wills Righteousness, Righteousness will be willed to him. If he wills evil, to be sure, evil will also be willed to him.

(16) "AND WHEN ALL ISRAEL SAW

NOTES

THAT THE KING WOULD NOT HEARKEN UNTO THEM, THE PEOPLE ANSWERED THE KING, SAYING, WHAT PORTION HAVE WE IN DAVID? AND WE HAVE NO INHERITANCE IN THE SON OF JESSE: EVERY MAN TO YOUR TENTS, O ISRAEL: AND NOW, DAVID, SEE TO YOUR OWN HOUSE. SO ALL ISRAEL WENT TO THEIR TENTS.

(17) "BUT AS FOR THE CHILDREN OF ISRAEL WHO DWELT IN THE CITIES OF JUDAH, REHOBOAM REIGNED OVER THEM.

(18) "THEN KING REHOBOAM SENT HADORAM WHO WAS OVER THE TRIBUTE; AND THE CHILDREN OF ISRAEL STONED HIM WITH STONES, THAT HE DIED. BUT KING REHOBOAM MADE SPEED TO GET HIM UP TO HIS CHARIOT, TO FLEE TO JERUSALEM.

(19) "AND ISRAEL REBELLED AGAINST THE HOUSE OF DAVID UNTO THIS DAY."

The construction is:

1. (Vs. 16) This was the beginning of over 250 years of division and strife between Israel, the northern kingdom, and Judah, the southern kingdom. This rupture would result in untold numbers of deaths.

2. (Vs. 17) The northern kingdom under Jeroboam would be called by several names—Israel, Samaria, and Ephraim. Some ten tribes would be loyal to the northern confederacy. The southern confederacy, called Judah, would have some three Tribes that would remain loyal—Judah, Benjamin, and Levi. Shechem, and then Samaria, would be the capital of the northern confederacy, with Jerusalem being the capital of the southern confederacy.

3. God gives a Vision, and then He makes possible Provision, in order that the Vision might be carried out. Unfortunately, Satan comes along with Division in order to destroy the Vision. The Evil One does everything within his power to cause the Vision to die. This is what was happening to the People of God. The Vision was being destroyed!

WHAT PORTION HAVE WE IN DAVID?

This was the beginning of 250 years of division and strife between the two nations, Israel and Judah. Wars, bloodshed, and intrigue became the program of a once united and godly people. God's Plan for a united nation being a blessing to all other nations of the Earth had now come to a definite standstill, and both kingdoms faced ruin and dispersion among the Gentiles.

Little did these rebels realize what they were doing when the Bible said, *"So all Israel went to their tents."* When people rebel against God, they seldom think of the results but only of the present.

Their question, *"What portion have we in David?"* in essence, said that they had no more desire for the things of God. They didn't want the Promises that had been given to David, as it regarded the coming Messiah. They had no desire for the worship of the Lord, as it regarded the sacrifices and the Temple. While their question at that time, at least in their minds, may have been political, above all, whether they realized it or not, it was spiritual. They were severing themselves from the Promises of God.

How does that relate to us presently?

WHAT PORTION HAVE WE IN THE WORD OF GOD?

For the last two decades, the new church model has taken the church world by storm. Preaching is out while counseling is in. The Bible is out, except only as window dressing, while new thought prevails. What the Holy Spirit wants and desires is out because we must be sensitive to what the seeker desires. The Cross and the Blood are no more simply because those things might be offensive. Sin is not to be mentioned because, as well, it may offend people. Everything is seeker sensitive. In other words, what does the person want? Whatever it is they want, that's what we will give them. It's the *"feel-good"* gospel, the *"I'm okay and you're okay"* gospel that is predominant.

This is the new gospel; it is the new way. But the great question must be asked, does it work?

DOES THE NEW GOSPEL PRODUCE DESIRED RESULTS?

Paul said to the Church at Corinth, *"But I fear, lest by any means, as the serpent beguiled Eve through his subtilty* (the strategy of Satan), *so your minds should be corrupted from the simplicity that is in Christ.* (The Gospel of Christ is simple, but men complicate it by adding to the Message.)

"For if he who comes preaching another Jesus (a Jesus who is not of the Cross), *whom we have not preached* (Paul's Message was *'Jesus Christ and Him Crucified'*; anything else is *'another Jesus'*), *or if you receive another spirit* (which is produced by preaching another Jesus), *which you have not received* (that's not what you received when we preached the True Gospel to you), *or another gospel, which you have not accepted* (anything other than *'Jesus Christ and Him Crucified'* is *'another gospel'*), *you might well bear with him.* (The Apostle is telling the Corinthians they have, in fact, sinned because they tolerated these false apostles who had come in, bringing *'another gospel'* which was something other than Christ and the Cross)" (II Cor. 11:3-4).

That's exactly what is being preached presently. It is *"another Jesus"* produced by *"another spirit,"* which presents *"another gospel."*

As it regards this new church model, this new gospel, one of the leading proponents of this message, who pastors a church running many thousands (deceived people), a poll was taken among these many thousands a short time ago. The results were not surprising, yet, they were a surprise to the proponents of this new church model.

They found that this new gospel had not affected, at least in a positive sense, their people at all. Adultery, fornication, drunkenness, alcoholism, gambling, and drugs, the whole gamut of vices, sins, iniquities, and bondages were rife among the people and getting worse.

To their credit, I will have to applaud their honesty. They printed the results of the poll that was taken, admitting that what they had been doing had failed. The lives of the people had not changed for the better, but rather for the worse.

In their words, they were going to have to *"rethink"* their position. And please understand, this is not something that was relegated to a local church somewhere, but rather something that has influenced the church all over the world. In other words, untold thousands of preachers hung on every word this particular pastor uttered because he was the great church growth guru.

They don't need to rethink their position; they just need to go back to the Bible.

THE ANSWER IS THE CROSS OF CHRIST

There is only one answer for dying humanity, one answer for the fallen sons of Adam's lost race, and one answer for sin and bondage, and that answer is, *"Jesus Christ and Him Crucified."* There is no other answer because there doesn't need to be another answer. A tremendous price was paid for this solution, and it was paid at Calvary's Cross and by none other than the Son of the Living God.

Why is it so difficult for preachers to *"preach the Cross?"* Why is it so difficult for our Faith to be placed exclusively in Christ and what He did at the Cross? Why is the Cross such an offense?

THE FLESH AND THE SPIRIT

The Cross is difficult for most simply because they don't want to give up their works of the flesh. Men love to devise their own means of victory and deliverance. But the problem is, there is no victory and there is no deliverance in their schemes. It doesn't matter how religious it might be, or how many Scriptures they may load upon their efforts, if their Message is not *"Jesus Christ and Him Crucified,"* then whatever it is, is a waste of time.

The flesh loves what it produces, and religious flesh loves what it religiously produces most of all! And please understand, anything, and it doesn't matter what it is, other than Christ and Him Crucified, is pure and simple, a work of the flesh.

WHAT IS THE FLESH?

The *"flesh,"* as the Holy Spirit through Paul used the term, and did so repeatedly, pertains to the ability, talent, education, intellect, power, and motivation of the individual. In essence, these things within themselves aren't wrong. Where the wrong comes in is according to the following:

NOTES

Whatever it is that man needs from God, whether Salvation or Sanctification, he, within himself, cannot produce. But he is loath to admit that truth. The unredeemed man wants to think he can produce his own Salvation, and the redeemed man wants to think he can produce his own Sanctification. Both are wrong.

Let's say it again:

The growing in Grace and the Knowledge of the Lord that I must have as a Believer, I cannot carry out by my own stratagems, ability, and strength. No matter how dedicated I might be, how consecrated I might be, and how zealous I might be, it cannot be done. Whatever has to be done can only be done by the Holy Spirit. If I try to do it any other way than God's Way, God constitutes it as *"flesh,"* meaning that it is man-conceived, man-birthed, man-instituted, and man-devised, a stratagem that can never be accepted by the Lord. It is all constituted as *"flesh."*

GOD'S PRESCRIBED ORDER OF VICTORY

God's Way is for the Believer to place his Faith and trust exclusively in Christ and what Christ did at the Cross. The Believer must understand that Jesus is the Source of all things we receive from the Lord, and the Cross is the Means by which these things are received, all superintended by the Holy Spirit. In this, we must ever understand that Christ must never be separated from the Cross, or the Cross from Christ. And by that, we are not speaking of the wooden beam, but rather what Jesus there did, the benefits of the Cross, the great Victories there won.

With our Faith placed exclusively in Christ and what He did for us at the Cross, and not allowing it to be moved elsewhere, ever fighting this good fight of Faith, the Holy Spirit, Who works exclusively within the parameters of the Finished Work of Christ, will then go to work on our behalf, producing what He Alone can produce, which is whatever it is that we need.

The Holy Spirit is God. As such, there is nothing that He cannot do. But for Him to work in our lives as He Alone can work, our

Faith must be solidly placed in the Cross of Christ, and it must not be moved.

Paul said, *"For the Law of the Spirit of Life in Christ Jesus has made me free from the Law of Sin and Death"* (Rom. 8:2).

The particular Passage just quoted gives one the Ways and the Means the Holy Spirit works, and to be sure, He will not be deviated from that course.

The Nineteenth Verse of this Tenth Chapter says, *"And Israel rebelled against the house of David unto this day."*

The idea is, they rebelled against God, and it would bring untold suffering and heartache. But sin always does that.

"Praise ye the Lord, the Almighty, the King of Creation!
"O my soul, praise Him, for He is your Health and Salvation!
"All ye who hear, now to His Temple draw near;
"Join me in glad adoration!"

"Praise ye the Lord, Who over all things so wondrously Reigns,
"Shelters you under His Wings, yea, so gently sustaineth!
"Have you not seen how your desires e'er have been,
"Granted in what He Ordains?"

"Praise ye the Lord, Who with marvelous Wisdom has made thee!
"Decked thee with health, and with loving hand guided and stayed thee;
"How oft in grief has not He brought thee relief,
"Spreading His Wings for to shade thee!"

"Praise ye the Lord! O let all that is in me adore Him!
"All that has life and breath, come now with praises before Him!
"Let the Amen sound from His People again:
"Gladly for aye we adore Him."

CHAPTER 11

(1) "AND WHEN REHOBOAM WAS COME TO JERUSALEM, HE GATHERED OF THE HOUSE OF JUDAH AND BENJAMIN AN HUNDRED AND FOURSCORE THOUSAND CHOSEN MEN, WHICH WERE WARRIORS, TO FIGHT AGAINST ISRAEL, THAT HE MIGHT BRING THE KINGDOM AGAIN TO REHOBOAM.

(2) "BUT THE WORD OF THE LORD CAME TO SHEMAIAH THE MAN OF GOD, SAYING,

(3) "SPEAK UNTO REHOBOAM THE SON OF SOLOMON, KING OF JUDAH, AND TO ALL ISRAEL IN JUDAH AND BENJAMIN, SAYING,

(4) "THUS SAYS THE LORD, YOU SHALL NOT GO UP, NOR FIGHT AGAINST YOUR BRETHREN: RETURN EVERY MAN TO HIS HOUSE: FOR THIS THING IS DONE OF ME. AND THEY OBEYED THE WORDS OF THE LORD, AND RETURNED FROM GOING AGAINST JEROBOAM."

The exegesis is:

1. (Vs. 1) Once again, Rehoboam did this thing without consulting the Lord; nevertheless, the Lord would consult him!

2. The word of the Prophet Shemaiah was, in effect, *"cease-and-desist."* True Prophets of God were the titular leaders of Israel under the Old Covenant.

3. (Vs. 4) To Rehoboam's credit, he obeyed the Word of the Lord. The idea was, Israel could not be forced to serve God. As God would not force Israel to serve Him then, likewise, He will not force men to serve Him today. Salvation must always be from a *"willing heart"* (Rev. 22:17).

PLANS WHICH WERE NOT OF GOD

Rehoboam and Judah were slowly slipping away from God's Direction. Had it not been for the Prophet Shemaiah, and to Rehoboam's credit that he listened to him, a river of blood on both sides would have been spilled. Even though the Lord will continue to deal with both nations, the northern kingdom of Israel seemingly had no inclination toward God whatsoever. They did not have one godly king. Actually, in the year 722 B.C., after a three year siege by the Assyrians, Israel fell. About 133 years after the Fall of Israel, Judah, as well, would go into captivity, all because of sin. It began with the last years of Solomon and would conclude with total destruction, even though the Lord pleaded with both Israel and Judah to repent, all to no avail.

The great temptation, as with Rehoboam, is to follow the wisdom of man instead of seeking the Lord for His Leading and Guidance. Plainly and clearly, Jesus said that the Holy Spirit would *"guide us into all Truth"* (Jn. 16:13).

A PERSONAL EXPERIENCE

Back in 1975, when we first went on television, we had a 30-minute program. After a period of time, I felt that the Lord spoke to my heart, telling me to increase the program to one hour, to show the Altar Calls from the Crusades over television and, as well, to give the viewing audience an opportunity to accept Christ. Also, we were to show the Holy Spirit services over television and pray for the viewers to be baptized with the Spirit, at least those who were Born-Again.

When I announced what we were going to do and, as stated, because I felt led of the Lord to do so, a barrage of advice came from preachers from all quarters, telling me that if I did this, I would destroy my Ministry, etc. I cannot recall one single preacher telling me that what I was doing was correct. All advised me strongly against that which the Lord had told me to do.

Why did they do this?

They did it because the conventional wisdom was that a 30 minute program was about the time limit of keeping the viewer's interest. As well, making a strong appeal to get people Saved by television, or so they seemed to think, was something that should not be done. And above all, I must not preach on the Baptism with the Holy Spirit with the evidence of speaking with other Tongues and then pray for people to be filled. What would people think?

Well, I didn't really care too much what people thought. I only wanted to know what the Lord desired, and I knew, after much prayer, that He had told me to do what I was doing.

We tried our best to do exactly what the Lord told us to do. We increased the program to one hour, gave Altar Calls for the viewing audience to be Saved and, as well, prayed for Believers to be baptized with the Holy Spirit with the evidence of speaking with other Tongues.

We did not lose our audience. In fact, it doubled, tripled, quadrupled, possibly even up to a tenfold increase. Untold thousands from all over the world, for we were translating the program into several languages, were brought to a Saving Knowledge of Jesus Christ. Also, thousands were baptized with the Holy Spirit, and I exaggerate not.

While it's not always easy to get Guidance from the Lord, to be sure, if we will persevere, such Guidance will most definitely be afforded us.

ARGENTINA

Another example of what I speak took place in the beautiful city of Buenos Aires, Argentina. If I remember correctly, the year was 1985. We were to conduct a crusade in the giant stadium in the capital city.

Our people made arrangements with the customs officials as it regarded bringing in the equipment that we had to have, such as sound, television, etc. Everything was taken care of, or so we thought.

When we arrived, incidentally, with a Cargo 747 filled to the brim, we were told that we were going to have to pay a large sum of money for custom fees, some $40,000, if I remember correctly, in order to bring the equipment into the country. Never mind that the arrangements had already been made. The equipment was to be brought in and then taken out with no charge. So, somebody was trying to rip off the Ministry.

Our people worked tirelessly for two days trying to get the equipment released but to no avail.

We were to have a Thursday morning breakfast with the Crusade scheduled to begin Friday night. To say I was concerned would be a gross understatement. We could not have a Crusade unless this equipment was released, but our people seemed to be making no headway whatsoever. The demand was, if we were to get the equipment in, we had to pay $40,000. We refused to do so!

In praying about the Thursday morning

breakfast, at which I was to speak, I felt that the Lord wanted me to preach on the Baptism with the Holy Spirit. But my mind was so troubled over the Customs situation that I could not settle on anything. In fact, I didn't think too very much about that particular breakfast.

That Thursday morning when Frances and I arrived at the banquet hall in the hotel, to our surprise, hundreds and hundreds of people were present, and also to our surprise, among them, some of the most noted dignitaries in the country. Actually, the Ambassador from the United States to Argentina was present.

As I sat by the interpreter on the platform with a host of other Preachers, I became very unsettled about my Message I was to bring. My mind raced ahead thinking, what will these people know about the Holy Spirit? But yet, I kept feeling it strongly that this was what the Lord wanted. It was not that I didn't want to obey the Lord, rather, I wanted to make sure it was the Lord.

About five minutes before I was to take the podium, I turned to my interpreter and told him that the Message had been changed and gave him the Scripture I was to use. I would preach on the Baptism with Holy Spirit.

To say that the Lord Moved that morning would be a gross understatement. The Spirit of God fell like rain as I began to minister on this all-important aspect of Christianity, the Baptism with the Holy Spirit.

When I called people to the front to pray, scores came weeping and sobbing as the Spirit of God touched their hearts.

As I was praying with people, a very stylishly dressed woman came up and introduced herself, speaking perfect English.

I looked up at her. She had wept so much that mascara had streaked down her face as the Spirit of God had moved mightily upon her. She introduced herself and stated that she was Saved and Spirit-filled. I had no way of knowing who she was, but then she surprised me by stating, *"I understand that you are having some difficulty getting your equipment out of customs."*

I quickly turned to her and said, *"Yes, we are."*

NOTES

I wondered as to how she knew!

And then she said, *"I think I can help you. You see, the President of Argentina is my brother."* She did not need to say more.

That afternoon the equipment was released.

I don't know how much that dear lady had to do with that release, but I do know that if we do things God's Way, great and wonderful things happen.

Yes, we had a tremendous Crusade in Buenos Aires, Argentina. And the Lord once again showed me that whatever the situation and problems may have been, He knew best.

THE MAN OF GOD

Shemaiah was that man. How fortunate was Judah to have such a person in their midst, and to their credit, they listened to him, at least this time.

The Bible does refer to Shemaiah as a Prophet and, as well, as *"a man of God,"* and there could be precious little greater than that.

The role of the true Prophet of God, whether of the northern kingdom of Israel, or the southern kingdom of Judah, was to serve as Spiritual Leadership. When either nation drifted, it was the business of the true Prophet to whip the people back in line according to the Word of God. As it regarded the northern kingdom, they little listened at all. As it regarded the southern kingdom, it depended on whether the king was godly or not.

Under the New Covenant, the role of the Prophet remains the same, with one exception. The Spiritual Leadership of the church is to be effected by the office of the Apostle. These are men who are called of God for that particular office (Eph. 4:11).

An Apostle is known by the Message the Lord has given him for the Church. In other words, there will be heavy emphasis on a certain part of the Word of God which the Apostle is to deliver. This is simply because the Holy Spirit, Who Guides and Directs all these things, knows exactly what the Church needs.

Even though true Apostles of God are seldom recognized by the modern church, still, the Lord has a way of getting His Word delivered to His People. Unfortunately, the true Apostle (there are many fake apostles), is treated about the same presently as true Prophets were treated under the old economy of God. Nevertheless, the Word of the Lord, in some way, prevails.

THUS SAYS THE LORD . . .

If it is the Lord Who has truly spoken, there is no greater word. The *"man of God"* told Rehoboam, *"You shall not go up, nor fight against your brethren: return every man to his house: for this thing is done of Me. And they obeyed the Words of the LORD, and returned from going against Jeroboam."*

As we have previously stated, to their credit, they obeyed. Sadly, not many do!

Strangely enough, as it regards the modern church, there probably are more saying, *"thus says the LORD,"* than ever before; however, almost all of these are in the realm of personal Prophecies, with only a small percentage actually being from the Lord.

In the final analysis, there has never been a greater need than presently for the Word to truly be from the Lord, and we speak mostly as it regards the modern pulpit.

(5) "AND REHOBOAM DWELT IN JERUSALEM, AND BUILT CITIES FOR DEFENCE IN JUDAH.

(6) "HE BUILT EVEN BETH-LEHEM, AND ETAM, AND TEKOA,

(7) "AND BETH-ZUR, AND SHOCO, AND ADULLAM,

(8) "AND GATH, AND MARESHAH, AND ZIPH,

(9) "AND ADORAIM, AND LACHISH, AND AZEKAH,

(10) "AND ZORAH, AND AIJALON, AND HEBRON, WHICH ARE IN JUDAH AND IN BENJAMIN FENCED CITIES.

(11) "AND HE FORTIFIED THE STRONGHOLDS, AND PUT CAPTAINS IN THEM, AND STORE OF VICTUAL, AND OF OIL AND WINE.

(12) "AND IN EVERY SEVERAL CITY HE PUT SHIELDS AND SPEARS, AND MADE THEM EXCEEDING STRONG, HAVING JUDAH AND BENJAMIN ON HIS SIDE.

(13) "AND THE PRIESTS AND THE LEVITES WHO WERE IN ALL ISRAEL RESORTED TO HIM OUT OF ALL THEIR COASTS."

The diagram is:

1. Rehoboam went into a defensive posture. His enemy on the south was Egypt, and his enemy on the north was Israel. He little realized that the Lord was his True Defense.

2. It is obvious that the Lord is little sought for Leading and Guidance in all of these things, if at all. The end result would ultimately be catastrophic.

3. (Vs. 13) All worship of God had been discontinued in the northern confederacy; consequently, many Priests and Levites moved to Jerusalem.

DEFENSE

The portrayal of Rehoboam, regrettably, is the portrayal of the modern church. He will defend himself against the enemy by conventional means, and as we have stated, the end result will be catastrophic. The modern church does the same.

Then the opposition was physical which, of course, translated into the Spiritual, as all things do regarding that which belongs to the Lord. Presently, however, *"We wrestle not against flesh and blood* (our foes are not human; however, Satan constantly uses human beings to carry out his dirty work), *but against principalities* (rulers or beings of the highest rank and order in Satan's kingdom), *against powers* (the rank immediately below the *'Principalities'*), *against the rulers of the darkness of this world* (those who carry out the instructions of the *'Powers'*), *against spiritual wickedness in high places.* (This refers to demon spirits)" (Eph. 6:12).

In addition, the modern church needs to really understand the true source of its opposition. It either underplays that opposition or overplays it.

THE CROSS OF CHRIST AND
THE POWERS OF DARKNESS

Understanding that Satan comes at us *"as a roaring lion, walking about, seeking whom he may devour,"* we must realize several things (I Pet. 5:8).

As Believers, understanding our opposition

from the spirit world of darkness, we must also understand that we, at least in a personal sense, are no match for these beings. And that's the major problem with the modern church. It tries to face the powers of darkness by man-devised means which, of course, have no bearing whatsoever on the spirit world of darkness. What in the world can humanistic psychology do as it regards demon spirits? The answer is nothing! In fact, the world of psychology little believes in the spirit world of darkness, and if they do, it's in a convoluted sense, which has no bearing on the true application. There is only one way that the Believer can properly defend himself against this evil. That way is the Cross of Christ and it ever being the Object of our Faith, which then gives the Holy Spirit latitude to Work in our lives. The Holy Spirit is God, and as such, the powers of darkness have no chance against Him whatsoever. The only answer they give to the Holy Spirit is when He tells them to jump, they immediately answer, *"How high?"* But, the tragedy is, most Christians do not have the help of the Holy Spirit very much simply because the object of their faith is something else other than the Cross of Christ.

THE CROSS OF CHRIST, SATAN'S PLACE OF DEFEAT

When the Believer places his Faith exclusively in Christ and the Cross, understanding that the Cross is the Means by which the Lord gives us all things and, as well, understanding that the Holy Spirit works exclusively within the perimeters of the Finished Work of Christ, such a Believer will see great and wonderful things begin to take place within his heart and life.

When Jesus died on the Cross, shedding His Life's Blood, thereby, giving Himself in Sacrifice, He atoned for all sin, past, present, and future, at least for all who will believe (Jn. 3:16). This means the sin debt was completely lifted, making the person a fit habitation for the Holy Spirit.

The Sacrifice of Christ on the Cross, thereby, atoning for all sin, removed Satan's ability to hold mankind in bondage, once again, at least for those who will believe.

NOTES

This is how Satan was defeated.

Many Christians have the idea that there was some type of physical combat that went on between Jesus and Satan. Such thinking is foolish! There is nothing in the Bible that even hints at such.

Satan knows totally and completely that Jesus Christ is God. He, as well, knows that he (Satan) is a created being and is no match for the Lord. The only way that he can function with his stealing, killing, and destroying (Jn. 10:10), is by the power of the lie. What do we mean by that?

THE MANNER IN WHICH SATAN KEEPS BELIEVERS IN BONDAGE

Sin was the legal right that Satan had to hold man in captivity. With the sin debt removed, which it was at the Cross, this left Satan with no legal right whatsoever, actually leaving him and all of his minions of darkness totally defeated (Col. 2:14-15).

So, that being the case, how can Satan hold a Believer captive?

The sad fact is Satan is presently holding almost all Believers in a state of captivity.

THE HOMEBORN SLAVE

The Prophet Jeremiah said: *"Is Israel a servant? is he a homeborn slave? why is he spoiled?* (Israel was a son, not a slave, yet they were about to become slaves! In fact, Israel had become a *'servant,'* i.e., slave, to the heathenistic gods. As a result, they would soon become a slave to a foreign power.

"The question, *'Is he a homeborn slave?'*, is interesting indeed! It has reference to an animal in a zoo. An animal was made by God to be free and unfettered. However, if born in a zoo and knowing nothing but the confines of such, it is a slave without really knowing it. Such was Israel, and such are so many modern Believers!)" (Jer. 2:14).

All too often, modern Believers, after giving their hearts to the Lord and being truly Born-Again and, thereby, a Child of God, little know and understand, if at all, how to successfully live for the Lord. In other words, they don't understand the Cross of Christ and the great part it plays in our Sanctification. As a result, they resort to measures that they devise of themselves, or most probably, are devised by preachers or other Christians, all wrong, and very quickly the sin nature in some way begins to rule them. Not knowing the way to victory, they tend to think that this is normal Christianity. They are like the animal in the zoo born in those confines and really never knowing true freedom.

Sadly, the modern church, at least as a whole, has little or no knowledge at all of the victorious, overcoming, Christian life.

Why?

They don't know simply because they do not understand God's Prescribed Order of Victory, which is the Cross of Christ (Rom. 6:1-14; I Cor. 1:17-18, 23; 2:2; Gal. 5; 6:14; Eph. 2:13-18; Col. 2:14-15).

THE MESSAGE OF THE CROSS

The question may be quickly asked, *"If the Message of the Cross is Scriptural, and if it is the answer to the Believer's dilemma, why isn't it more readily accepted?"*

That's a good question!

I think probably at least one of the greatest reasons is, when one mentions the Cross, automatically, Believers, and especially preachers, assume that they know all about the Cross. The truth is, they don't!

While they do know something about the Cross as it refers to Salvation, they know absolutely nothing about the Cross as it refers to Sanctification. But in assuming they do and, thereby, passing it off with a shrug of the shoulders, they completely miss what the Lord is trying to tell them. As a result, they actually continue to function as *"a homeborn slave."* They don't know they are a slave, and, in fact, they constantly talk about being free. But, the truth is, they aren't free. In fact, it is impossible for the Believer, preacher, or otherwise, to be free unless his Faith is exclusively in Christ and the Cross. That must be understood!

And then we have the problem of pride. Many preachers, upon hearing the Message of the Cross, even though they understand at least some part of it, refuse to admit as to what it is, and that's because of pride. They don't want to admit that there is something there, in fact, the most important aspect of their Christian experience, and they do not

NOTES

know or understand it. They are loath to admit that.

And then there is the great problem of unbelief. In fact, it just might be the greatest problem of all.

Many, if not most, simply do not believe that what Jesus did at the Cross of Calvary is the answer to man's dilemma, and actually, the only answer. There is no other!

I read where one very popular preacher was being interviewed, and the Cross was mentioned.

He readily claimed that he believed in the Cross, but that it would never be mentioned in the church or in his sermons. The reason?

He said that it might offend people.

The truth is, and glaringly so, that preacher, despite his statement, doesn't believe in the Cross. If one truly knows that sin is the problem, and the only answer for sin is the Cross of Christ, one is going to say something about it. No, I think that unbelief is probably the greatest problem of all. When Paul said:

"We preach Christ Crucified (this is the Foundation of the Word of God and, thereby, of Salvation), *unto the Jews a stumblingblock* (the Cross was the stumblingblock), *and unto the Greeks foolishness* (both found it difficult to accept as God a dead Man hanging on a Cross, for such Christ was to them)" (I Cor. 1:23).

I'm afraid the statement, *"Unto the Greeks, foolishness,"* regrettably and sadly, applies to many in the modern church, and especially preachers. While many, if not most, will pay lip service to the Cross, that's about as far as it goes. They keep promoting man's stratagems, schemes, efforts, abilities and talents as the answer to man's dilemma. As it was with Israel of the day of Christ, it is the same presently. He said of Israel, *"And you will not come to Me, that you might have Life.* (All Life is in Christ; to have that Life, one must accept what Christ has done at the Cross)" (Jn. 5:40).

Satan respects our man-made schemes not at all. Conversely, he fears Calvary more than anything else, and for all the obvious reasons. It was there that he was defeated, including all of his minions of darkness, and defeated completely. So, if Satan presently holds a Believer captive, it is, in a sense, by the consent of the captive. While such a Believer may not look at it in that fashion, in effect, that's what it is. The Believer is trying to find victory by means other than Christ and the Cross. There is no victory outside of the Cross.

ANOTHER JESUS

If Jesus is proclaimed, preached, taught, and held up in any way other than by and through the Cross, the Holy Spirit labels such direction as *"another Jesus"* (II Cor. 11:4).

In other words, if the preacher preaches Jesus but ignores the Cross, in the Mind of God, such a preacher is proclaiming *"another Jesus,"* incidentally, a Jesus that God will not honor. Regrettably, this is the way that Jesus is presently preached, by and large.

Jesus is held up as a Great Teacher, a Great Miracle Worker, a Great Example, etc., but little held up as the Saviour. In fact, it is virtually impossible to preach Him as the great Saviour, and at the same time, ignore the Cross. It was by and through the Cross that He became the Saviour, and did so by giving Himself as a Sacrifice, which satisfied the demands of a thrice-Holy God. In other words, God was satisfied with the price that was paid at Calvary's Cross and, thereby, accepted it fully. Jesus is Saviour by that Means and that Means only.

Let us say it again, the tragedy is, the Jesus that is being presently preached is mostly *"another Jesus,"* meaning it's not the Jesus of the Bible. It is a Jesus of man's own concoctions. Let us say the following, which we have also previously stated:

• The only way to God is through Jesus Christ (Jn. 14:6).

• The only way to Jesus is through the Cross (Rom. 6:3-5).

• The only way to the Cross is by a denial of self (Lk. 9:23).

Many do not want to believe that the only way to Jesus is through the Cross, so, at the same time, they also refuse to deny themselves. That is the state of the modern church!

(14) "FOR THE LEVITES LEFT THEIR SUBURBS AND THEIR POSSESSION, AND CAME TO JUDAH AND JERUSALEM:

NOTES

FOR JEROBOAM AND HIS SONS HAD CAST THEM OFF FROM EXECUTING THE PRIEST'S OFFICE UNTO THE LORD:

(15) "AND HE ORDAINED HIM PRIESTS FOR THE HIGH PLACES, AND FOR THE DEVILS, AND FOR THE CALVES WHICH HE HAD MADE.

(16) "AND AFTER THEM OUT OF ALL THE TRIBES OF ISRAEL SUCH AS SET THEIR HEARTS TO SEEK THE LORD GOD OF ISRAEL CAME TO JERUSALEM, TO SACRIFICE UNTO THE LORD GOD OF THEIR FATHERS.

(17) "SO THEY STRENGTHENED THE KINGDOM OF JUDAH, AND MADE REHOBOAM THE SON OF SOLOMON STRONG, THREE YEARS: FOR THREE YEARS THEY WALKED IN THE WAY OF DAVID AND SOLOMON."

The overview is:

1. Verse 14 refers to the fact that living for God means forsaking all. It would seem farfetched to the carnal mind for individuals to leave their home, friends, and even family to go where God is moving; nevertheless, this is what the Levites did, which has characterized true followers of the Lord from the very beginning.

2. (Vs. 15) Because of worshipping Satan, the northern confederacy would be destroyed as a nation about 749 B.C. (II Sam., Chpt. 17). A little over 130 years later (616 B.C.), Judah was also destroyed for her sins (I Ki., Chpts. 24-25). Seventy years later (546 B.C.), the godly of all the thirteen Tribes returned to make a Nation again in the land of Israel.

3. (Vs. 16) The Temple and Altar were at Jerusalem, and this was the place that God had chosen. So, for all in the northern kingdom who truly wanted to serve God, they had to come to Judah to do so.

4. Verse 17 speaks of the southern kingdom of Judah. It says, *"For three years they walked in the way of David and Solomon,"* but only for three years. It is amazing how the Holy Spirit delineated the time, down to almost the day. After this time, Rehoboam and Judah went into deep sin. As a result, God permitted Egypt to conquer them and take away all their treasures (II Chron. 12:2-12). If Rehoboam had continued in

the godly Way, no kingdom or combination of kingdoms could have overcome him.

THE PRIESTS AND THE LEVITES

When the nation split apart, there were thousands of Priests and Levites who found themselves living in the northern kingdom of Israel. There was no way they could function in that climate, and besides that, the Temple was at Jerusalem. And for the Priests to officiate, they had to be at Jerusalem and the Temple. So, the evidence is that most *"left their suburbs and their possession, and came to Judah and Jerusalem,"* even as they should have done. They couldn't live in that idol worshipping climate of the northern confederacy, and above all, they were cut off from the Temple. So, they had to come to Jerusalem.

While, of course, under the New Covenant, there is no more Temple or Sacrifices, etc., and, as well, no particular site that is more holy than the next, still, the modern church is reaching a declining spiritual place to where that many Believers are having to leave their respective churches. And please understand, where the Believer attends church is very, very important. While the name on the door may be of little significance, what is taught behind the pulpit is of tremendous significance.

THE WORD OF GOD

There are many thousands of people all over the world who tune in by the Internet, as it regards each of the Services which come from Family Worship Center. In fact, they receive virtually all of their Spiritual Instruction and their learning of the Word of God from Family Worship Center. This is where they are fed, and by this means they grow in Grace and the knowledge of the Lord.

If I remember correctly, it was 2005. The Lord spoke to my heart about organizing FAMILY WORSHIP CENTER MEDIA CHURCH. The Lord, I felt, instructed me to give an invitation for those who were truly Born-Again, irrespective as to where they might live in the world, to join FAMILY WORSHIP CENTER MEDIA CHURCH.

Of course, this was speaking of people who join us regularly by the Internet to watch the Services at Family Worship Center and, thereby, worship the Lord with us. We have had many hundreds to join and, in fact, continue to do so even up to this hour.

This doesn't mean that we do not greatly support the local church. We most definitely do. But the truth is, most churches are not preaching the Cross, and if they aren't preaching the Cross, whatever it is they are preaching is really not the Gospel (I Cor. 1:17). So, by means of modern communications, it is possible now for the Services at Family Worship Center to be aired all over the world, which they are on a constant basis. And please understand, Church is really not four walls and a steeple. Church is actually those who are Born-Again, which automatically makes them members of the Body of Christ. Church is wherever they are.

If Believers, wherever they might be, have a good Church to attend which preaches the Cross, they should most definitely attend and support that Church; however, if that is not the case, the next best thing is FAMILY WORSHIP CENTER MEDIA CHURCH.

DEVIL WORSHIP

Jeroboam devised his own type of religion for the northern kingdom. He *"ordained him priests"* to carry out the religious functions, whatever they were. But, whatever those functions were, actually, through their idols, the northern kingdom was worshipping Satan.

It was to the Apostle Paul that the Lord gave the meaning of the New Covenant, which was the meaning of the Cross. In fact, the New Covenant is in totality that to which the Old Covenant pointed. The Old Covenant was meant to be temporary, while the New Covenant, all in Christ, is eternal. In fact, Paul called it *"the Everlasting Covenant"* (Heb. 13:20).

In the meaning of this New Covenant, the Holy Spirit told Paul to *"preach the Cross,"* which, in effect, is the embodiment of the New Covenant (Rom. 6:1-14; 8:1-2, 11; I Cor. 1:17-18, 23; 2:2).

The Holy Spirit was so adamant, as it regarded the Message that had been given to Paul, that the Holy Spirit through the Apostle stated, *"For though we, or an Angel from Heaven, preach any other gospel unto you than that which we have preached unto you, let him be accursed"* (Gal. 1:8).

WHAT WAS THE GOSPEL THAT PAUL PREACHED?

He tells us. He said:

"For Christ sent me not to baptize, but to preach the Gospel: not with wisdom of words, lest the Cross of Christ should be made of none effect" (I Cor. 1:17).

In this one Verse the Apostle plainly tells us what the Gospel actually is. It is *"the Cross of Christ."* That's why he also said: *"But we preach Christ Crucified"* (I Cor. 1:23).

He also stated, *"For I determined not to know anything among you, save Jesus Christ, and Him Crucified"* (I Cor. 2:2).

While many other proof Texts could be given, I think what we have given is enough to make it abundantly clear as to the Gospel that Paul preached.

This is so serious that the Holy Spirit said to the Apostle, even as we have already stated, that if one did not preach the same Gospel that was given to Paul, and that he gave to us, that such a preacher would be *"accursed,"* which means to be eternally lost.

Where does that leave the modern ministry?

There aren't enough preachers truly preaching the Cross to even count. So, is the modern church, at least in a sense, the same as Judah and Israel of long ago? In other words, is there a division?

There definitely is a division, but the difference is this, and it is a great difference. It has to do with numbers.

It can be said that the Gospel is divided. There are those who are preaching another gospel, whatever it might be, and there are those who are preaching the Cross. But the truth is, there are so few preaching the Cross as to be almost non-existent. So, where does that leave the modern church?

THE MODERN CHURCH

I personally believe that the modern church is in worse spiritual condition than it ever has been since the Reformation. Sadly, there are fewer people being Saved today than at any time since Martin Luther. To be sure, there are millions who have become religious and joined churches, but who have never been truly Born-Again.

As well, there are fewer Believers presently being baptized with the Holy Spirit than at any time since the beginning of the Twentieth Century. In fact, many Pentecostal or Full Gospel churches, so-called, have not seen anyone baptized with the Holy Spirit in their ranks in the proverbial month of Sundays. In fact, the Baptism with the Spirit with the evidence of speaking with other Tongues is not even preached anymore in many modern Pentecostal churches, again, so-called! In other words, they really aren't Pentecostal.

When it comes to preaching *"another gospel,"* the statement of Paul, *"Let him be accursed,"* is strong indeed! As to all the nuances of what it exactly means, we'll have to leave to the Lord; however, it should be taken very, very seriously.

THE WAY OF DAVID AND SOLOMON

What was that way?

David and Solomon, at least for the first approximate 30 years of Solomon's reign, adhered strictly to the Word of God as it regarded the Sacrificial system and, in effect, all Temple activities. There is even evidence that Solomon continued such the last 10 years of his life, even though he wasn't living right otherwise.

No doubt, when the Lord gave to David the plans for the Temple, plus all the courses for the Priests, he explained to the *"sweet singer of Israel"* what all of this meant. I believe that David knew that it all pointed to the coming Redeemer, the One Who would be referred to as the *"Son of David."* I can't imagine that the Lord would give him this tremendous information regarding the building of the Temple, even how it was to be constructed, and not give him the meaning of what it was all about.

And then, David gave this information to Solomon, so, the wisest man who ever lived knew what the Temple service was all about, and especially, the Sacrificial system. When it came to Rehoboam, however, it seems he adhered to the Word of God only for the first three years. Then the nation of Judah went into deep apostasy, i.e., *"idol worship."*

I think one can say without fear of exaggeration that the modern church is doing the same thing. It is forsaking the old paths, and I speak of the Word of God, the Cross of Calvary, and the Blood of Jesus, in other words, the very Fundamentals of Christianity. The Holy Spirit in many modern circles is little referred to, actually taken for granted, if thought about at all. Sadly, this is happening even in churches which label themselves as Full Gospel, etc. It is amazing as to how the Holy Spirit delineated the time down almost to the day as it regarded the three years. This portrays His constant Observation, as should be obvious.

(18) "AND REHOBOAM TOOK HIM MAHALATH THE DAUGHTER OF JERIMOTH THE SON OF DAVID TO WIFE, AND ABIHAIL THE DAUGHTER OF ELIAB THE SON OF JESSE;

(19) "WHICH BORE HIM CHILDREN; JEUSH, AND SHAMARIAH, AND ZAHAM.

(20) "AND AFTER HER HE TOOK MAACHAH THE DAUGHTER OF ABSALOM; WHICH BORE HIM ABIJAH, AND ATTAI, AND ZIZA, AND SHELOMITH.

(21) "AND REHOBOAM LOVED MAACHAH THE DAUGHTER OF ABSALOM ABOVE ALL HIS WIVES AND HIS CONCUBINES: (FOR HE TOOK EIGHTEEN WIVES, AND THREESCORE CONCUBINES; AND BEGAT TWENTY AND EIGHT SONS, AND THREESCORE DAUGHTERS.)

(22) "AND REHOBOAM MADE ABIJAH THE SON OF MAACHAH THE CHIEF, TO BE RULER AMONG HIS BRETHREN: FOR HE THOUGHT TO MAKE HIM KING.

(23) "AND HE DEALT WISELY, AND DISPERSED OF ALL HIS CHILDREN THROUGHOUT ALL THE COUNTRIES OF JUDAH AND BENJAMIN, UNTO EVERY FENCED CITY: AND HE GAVE THEM VICTUAL IN ABUNDANCE. AND HE DESIRED MANY WIVES."

This synopsis is:

1. (Vs. 21) According to Deuteronomy 17:17, Rehoboam was clearly wrong as it regards the taking of many wives. Sadly, he followed the example of his father Solomon.

2. The words in the Hebrew, *"wise*

NOTES

dealing," of Verse 23, are an indication that the conscience of Rehoboam was not quite at ease, and that he knew he was wrong. Nothing is so liable to blind judgment as personal affection.

3. A departure from the Word of God is always the road to disaster. As someone has well said, *"I don't really care what the Bible teaches, I have no personal preferences."* I only want to interpret it correctly and preach it accordingly.

4. Maachah was the granddaughter of Absalom. In the Hebrew there is no word for granddaughter or grandson, etc.

"Bright King of Glory, Glorious God!
"Our spirits bow before Your Seat,
"To You we lift a humble thought,
"And worship at Your Blessed Feet."

"A thousand Seraphs, strong and bright,
"Stand around the glorious Deity;
"But who among the sons of light
"Pretends comparison with Thee?"

"Yet there is One of human frame,
"Jesus, arrayed in flesh and bone,
"Thinks it no robbery to claim,
"A full equality with God."

"There Glory shines with equal beams;
"There essence is forever won,
"Though They are known by different Names,
"The Father God, and God the Son."

"Then let the Name of Christ our King,
"With equal honors be adored;
"His Praise let every Angel sing,
"And all the nations own their Lord."

CHAPTER 12

(1) "AND IT CAME TO PASS, WHEN REHOBOAM HAD ESTABLISHED THE KINGDOM, AND HAD STRENGTHENED HIMSELF, HE FORSOOK THE LAW OF THE LORD, AND ALL ISRAEL WITH HIM."

The composition is:

1. (Vs. 1) Judah prospered. Regrettably, prosperity sometimes is not a blessing. Too

many times when Believers are blessed, they do exactly as Rehoboam did. They *"forsake the Law of the LORD."*

2. The name *"Israel"* is sometimes used to describe either the southern kingdom of Judah or the northern kingdom of Israel, or both.

3. Judah being referred to in Verse 1 as *"Israel"* is by no means a mistake. The idea is, Judah under Rehoboam is now following the example of the northern confederation of Israel regarding idol worship, etc.

PROSPERITY

Prosperity can be a Blessing from the Lord and, in fact, is meant to be a Blessing; however, prosperity can be the undoing of many Christians, even as it was the undoing of Rehoboam so long, long ago.

Why?

• When Believers suddenly come into money, some cannot properly handle the situation. In the process they lose their way with the Lord.

• When some Believers suddenly come into money, they tend to trust the money instead of trusting the Lord.

• Some Believers are very faithful to give to the Work of the Lord when their income is small. But, at times, when that income grows, sometimes greatly so, they find it difficult to increase their giving.

• Some Believers, regrettably, find it very difficult to put God first when prosperity comes. They do not seem to realize that the Blessings of God are given for two purposes:

1. That their families may be taken care of, with provision made for whatever is needed.

2. To bless the Work of God. The latter oftentimes goes lacking.

In all of our years of being engaged in the Work of God, we have seen many people who expressed a great interest in helping to get this work done. And to be sure, whatever gifts are given, whether little or large, we are so appreciative. However, for the few whom the Lord has blessed with goodly sums of money, only a few, according to our experience, truly put the Lord first. Thank the Lord for that few, but the truth is, it should be many more.

(2) "AND IT CAME TO PASS, THAT IN THE FIFTH YEAR OF KING REHOBOAM SHISHAK KING OF EGYPT CAME UP AGAINST JERUSALEM, BECAUSE THEY HAD TRANSGRESSED AGAINST THE LORD,

(3) "WITH TWELVE HUNDRED CHARIOTS, AND THREESCORE THOUSAND HORSEMEN: AND THE PEOPLE WERE WITHOUT NUMBER WHO CAME WITH HIM OUT OF EGYPT; THE LUBIMS, THE SUKKIIMS, AND THE ETHIOPIANS.

(4) "AND HE TOOK THE FENCED CITIES WHICH PERTAINED TO JUDAH, AND CAME TO JERUSALEM.

(5) "THEN CAME SHEMAIAH THE PROPHET TO REHOBOAM, AND TO THE PRINCES OF JUDAH, WHO WERE GATHERED TOGETHER TO JERUSALEM BECAUSE OF SHISHAK, AND SAID UNTO THEM, THUS SAYS THE LORD, YOU HAVE FORSAKEN ME, AND THEREFORE HAVE I ALSO LEFT YOU IN THE HAND OF SHISHAK.

(6) "WHEREUPON THE PRINCES OF ISRAEL AND THE KING HUMBLED THEMSELVES; AND THEY SAID, THE LORD IS RIGHTEOUS.

(7) "AND WHEN THE LORD SAW THAT THEY HUMBLED THEMSELVES, THE WORD OF THE LORD CAME TO SHEMAIAH, SAYING, THEY HAVE HUMBLED THEMSELVES; THEREFORE I WILL NOT DESTROY THEM, BUT I WILL GRANT THEM SOME DELIVERANCE; AND MY WRATH SHALL NOT BE POURED OUT UPON JERUSALEM BY THE HAND OF SHISHAK.

(8) "NEVERTHELESS THEY SHALL BE HIS SERVANTS; THAT THEY MAY KNOW MY SERVICE, AND THE SERVICE OF THE KINGDOMS OF THE COUNTRIES.

(9) "SO SHISHAK KING OF EGYPT CAME UP AGAINST JERUSALEM, AND TOOK AWAY THE TREASURES OF THE HOUSE OF THE LORD, AND THE TREASURES OF THE KING'S HOUSE; HE TOOK ALL: HE CARRIED AWAY ALSO THE SHIELDS OF GOLD WHICH SOLOMON HAD MADE.

(10) "INSTEAD OF WHICH KING REHOBOAM MADE SHIELDS OF BRASS, AND COMMITTED THEM TO THE

NOTES

HANDS OF THE CHIEF OF THE GUARD, WHO KEPT THE ENTRANCE OF THE KING'S HOUSE.

(11) "AND WHEN THE KING ENTERED INTO THE HOUSE OF THE LORD, THE GUARD CAME AND FETCHED THEM, AND BROUGHT THEM AGAINST INTO THE GUARD CHAMBER.

(12) "AND WHEN HE HUMBLED HIMSELF, THE WRATH OF THE LORD TURNED FROM HIM, THAT HE WOULD NOT DESTROY HIM ALTOGETHER: AND ALSO IN JUDAH THINGS WENT WELL."

The exposition is:

1. (Vs. 2) Shishak king of Egypt invading Judah was allowed by the Lord because of Judah's backsliding. The Lord allows such in order to cause people to appeal to Him. Sometimes it works, and sometimes it doesn't!

2. (Vs. 4) The only way that Shishak could have taken Judah, and especially Jerusalem, was because Judah had forsaken the Lord. The Lord was their power and strength. As long as they kept His Commandments and Statutes, no nation in the world, or confederation of nations, could defeat them; however, when they *"forsook the Law of the LORD,"* defeat was inevitable.

3. (Vs. 5) The Lord, in His Mercy, gives Judah warning. No warning could be clearer than this. If we follow the Lord, we will receive His Blessing; if we forsake the Lord, He will allow enemies to intrude upon us. Our Blessings are tied totally to Him.

4. (Vs. 6) Regrettably, the Repentance of Rehoboam and those with him was not very deep; nevertheless, the Lord would honor it. When they said, *"The LORD is Righteous,"* this means that they knew that He was justified in what He had done, and that they deserved it.

5. Notice the words of Verse 7, *"some deliverance."* They would not have a complete Deliverance, only partial. The reason? Their Repentance was partial; therefore, their Deliverance was partial.

6. (Vs. 8) The Lord allowing Judah to be under this heathen potentate was done in order that Judah would learn to obey and know the difference between serving God and serving ungodly nations. If they persisted in their ungodly ways, they would serve ungodly nations, which is what ultimately happened!

7. (Vs. 9) To be sure, considering the riches that Solomon had amassed, what Shishak took must have been astronomical. Let the reader understand:

Satan desires to take away our spiritual treasures, plus everything else. And he will definitely do so, unless we minutely follow the Lord, which means to minutely follow His Word.

8. (Vs. 10) The world robs the church of Divine realities and public worship, and the church tries to hide the loss by substituting imitation. How many churches presently have *"shields of brass"* instead of *"shields of gold"*? The *"shields of gold"* represent Deity. They are symbolic of God's Glory, Protection, and Power. *"Shields of brass"* are symbolic of man and man's ways.

9. Humility, as expressed in Verse 12, is the only coin that will spend in God's Economy (Isa. 66:2).

BECAUSE THEY HAD TRANSGRESSED AGAINST THE LORD

Less than five years after the death of Solomon, the whole kingdom of Israel was divided into two kingdoms. The northern confederacy had gone into apostasy. Now the southern confederacy of Judah has experienced both apostasy and military defeat by a foreign king, who even robbed the treasuries of Judah and disgraced the whole nation—this after only three years of Righteousness.

Thus, through sin, such a wonderful kingdom that had ruled many kings and countries from the Euphrates to Egypt, and whose king had all the other kings coming to him to hear his wisdom and present him with gifts, was now in complete humiliation before these same kings and countries.

The Holy Spirit is very explicit as it regards the call; he says, *"Because they had transgressed against the LORD."*

The Fourth Verse says of Shishak, *"And he took. . . ."* Shishak was founder of the Twenty-second Egyptian Dynasty. He was powerful, but in no way could he have taken the cities of Judah unless Judah had *"transgressed against the LORD."*

The Lord was Judah's Power and Strength. There was only one condition for them to retain His Power and Strength, and that was to keep His Commandments and His Statutes. As long as they did that, no nation in the world could defeat them; however, when they *"forsook the Law of the LORD,"* defeat was inevitable.

THE PROPHET SHEMAIAH

The Fifth Verse proclaims the Lord in His Mercy giving Judah warning. It says: *"Then came Shemaiah the Prophet to Rehoboam."* The Lord speaks to them, *"You have forsaken Me, and therefore have I also left you in the hand of Shishak."*

No warning could be clearer than this. If we follow the Lord, we receive His Blessing. If we forsake the Lord, He allows enemies to intrude upon us. Our Blessings are tied totally to Him.

HUMILITY

To Rehoboam's credit, he and the *"princes of Israel humbled themselves."* Their answer to what the Lord was doing is revealing. They said, *"The LORD is Righteous."*

The idea is, they admitted that the Lord was justified in what He was doing in allowing Shishak the liberty to do what he did.

There is some indication that their Repentance was halfhearted, but, at best, that is only speculation.

Is it possible, even if their Repentance was sincere and total, that a price had to be enacted? Every evidence is that Judah had gone into deep sin. The Scripture says concerning this:

"And Judah did evil in the sight of the LORD, and they provoked Him to jealousy with their sins which they had committed, above all that their fathers had done.

"For they also built them high places, and images, and groves, on every high hill, and under every green tree.

"And there were also sodomites in the land: and they did according to all the abominations of the nations which the LORD cast out before the Children of Israel" (I Ki. 14:22-24).

It is impossible for one to sin without it having its effect. Repentance always brings about the Mercy and Grace of God, with His Forgiveness; however, proverbially speaking, wheels are set in motion, which are inevitable. In other words, *"What we sow, we reap!"*

The Lord could soften the blow as it regarded Shishak, which He most definitely did; however, that's as far as He would go and, in fact, could go.

SIN AND ITS CONSEQUENCES

Every Believer should understand the terribleness of sin and the consequences of sin. We should know that it's not merely an aberration, a misdirection, or a bad habit. It is the epitome of selfishness. Sin is the ruination of everything good in the Universe. It has been the cause of a million battlefields. It has soaked the Earth with blood and is the cause of every heartache, every grief, and every sorrow. It is the blight of the Universe, and, as stated, it is disobedience of the Word of God.

Admittedly, there is pleasure in sin, but only for a season. The Scripture says:

"By Faith Moses, when he was come to years (refers to him coming to the age of 40 [Ex. 2:11]), *refused to be called the son of Pharaoh's daughter* (in effect, he refused the position of Pharaoh of Egypt, for which he had been trained because he had been adopted by Pharaoh's daughter);

"Choosing rather to suffer affliction with the people of God (proclaims the choice Moses made; he traded the temporal for the Eternal), *than to enjoy the pleasures of sin for a season* (presents the choice which must be made, affliction or the pleasures of sin)" (Heb. 11:24-25).

Even though there are pleasures in sin, we must remember, as the Scripture states, that it is only for a *"season."* Then comes the *"bondage,"* which *"steals, kills, and destroys"* (Jn. 10:10). One must also remember, the bondage is inescapable. That's when the hell starts!

THE CHRISTIAN AND SIN

I'm going to make a statement up front that many, if not most, Believers have never heard regarding the problem of sin as it concerns the Believer.

If the Believer doesn't understand the Message of the Cross, in other words, the part the Cross plays in our everyday life and living, Satan can force such a Believer into a place and position of spiritual failure, despite that Believer's efforts to not fail.

In other words, if the Believer doesn't understand God's Prescribed Order of Victory, no matter how hard that Believer struggles, no matter how hard he may fight, the truth is, he will not succeed. Satan will force him into a course of action he doesn't want to take and is trying not to take. Let me prove it to you from the Word of God.

Paul said: *"For the good that I would I do not: but the evil which I would not, that I do"* (Rom. 7:19).

Now, please understand. When Paul wrote these words, he full well understood God's Prescribed Order of Victory and, in fact, he was the very one to whom this great Word was given (Gal. 1:12). So, Paul is speaking of the time frame between his Conversion and the time that the Lord opened up to him the meaning of the New Covenant. How long that time was, we aren't told; however, it probably was two or more years.

At any rate, during that period of time, Paul was trying to live for God, even as all other Believers at that time were trying to live for God, in all the wrong ways. They were trying to do it by the keeping of Commandments and by the means of willpower. The end result was obvious:

The victory that Paul wanted and desired, and struggled intensely to have, he plainly says, *"I do not."*

The sin, and he referred to it as *"evil,"* which he did not want to do and was struggling not to do, his exact words were, *"that I do."*

The idea is, even though most Christians don't want to hear it, Satan was forcing the man's will, even as he is forcing the wills of untold millions of Christians presently.

No Christian, that is, if that person is truly Saved, desires to sin. Sin is abhorrent. So, the idea that Believers want to sin is simply unscriptural. Paul said concerning this, as well:

"Therefore, if any man be in Christ, he is a new creature (a new creation)*: old things are passed away; behold all things are become new"* (II Cor. 5:17).

WILLPOWER!

Most Christians are trying to live for God by the means of willpower. In other words, they erroneously think that before they were Saved, Satan could force their will. But now that they have come to Christ, or so they think, their willpower has increased in strength greatly, and they can now say *"no"* to the Devil, whereas, they once could not do so. They could not be more wrong. Listen again to Paul. He said:

"For I know that in me, (that is, in my flesh,) dwells no good thing (speaks of man's own ability, or rather the lack thereof in comparison to the Holy Spirit, at least when it comes to spiritual things)*: for to will is present with me* (Paul is speaking here of his willpower; regrettably, most modern Christians are trying to live for God by means of willpower, thinking falsely that since they have come to Christ, they are now free to say 'no' to sin; that is the wrong way to look at the situation; the Believer cannot live for God by the strength of willpower; while the will is definitely important, it alone is not enough; the Believer must exercise Faith in Christ and the Cross, and do so constantly; then he will have the ability and strength to say 'yes' to Christ, which automatically says 'no' to the things of the world)*; but how to perform that which is good I find not* (outside of the Cross, it is impossible to find a way to do good)*"* (Rom. 7:18).

HOW TO LIVE FOR GOD

If it is to be noticed, most all of Paul's writings are given over to telling Believers how to live for God. While he has a small amount of information as it regards the sinner coming to Christ, virtually all is given over to information for the Believer.

It must be understood that it was to Paul that the meaning of the New Covenant was given, which, in effect, is the meaning of the Cross (Gal. 1:11-12).

The Lord gave to Paul the meaning of the sin nature, and how it affects the Child of God, and how to have victory over this difficulty. It is found in Romans, Chapter 6.

Some 17 times in that one Chapter the word *"sin"* is used. Fifteen of those times, in the original Text, the Apostle put in front of the word *"sin"* what is referred to as the definite article, making it read *"the sin,"* which means that Paul is not speaking of acts of sin, but rather the sin principle, or the fact of sin itself.

WHAT IS THE SIN NATURE?

The sin nature is that which took place in the hearts and lives of both Adam and Eve at the Fall. In other words, their very nature became one of transgression, of evil, of sin, and of disobeying the Word of the Lord. The entire gamut of their lives and living was turned over to sin. Due to the fact that Adam was the federal head of the human race, this means that everyone born thereafter would be controlled by the sin nature. To every Believer reading these words, if you will look back at your life before you came to Christ, you will have to admit that you were controlled completely by the sin nature, in other words, that your very nature was that of sin and disobedience of the Word of the Lord.

When you got Saved, however, the sin nature was made dormant or ineffective (Rom. 1:6).

Unfortunately, immediately after getting Saved, we all too often set about to try to live for God in all the wrong ways. We do it by means of the *"flesh,"* in other words, by the strength of our own ability, talent, education, etc. Considering that's the wrong way to try to live for God, we immediately fail the Lord in some way. While the failure itself has no bearing on the sin nature, what follows next most definitely does.

To overcome that failure, whatever it may have been, we set out to make sure it doesn't happen again, but do so in all the wrong ways. In other words, instead of placing our Faith exclusively in Christ and the Cross at this juncture, we again make something else the object of our faith. Most of the time it is done in ignorance, but still, it is done. And when this happens, the sin nature then revives and begins to control us in some way, which makes life miserable for the Child of God.

THE SIN NATURE AND THE CHILD OF GOD

At this particular time, virtually the entirety of all Believers is controlled in some way by the sin nature. Now, how do I know that?

I know it simply because most modern Believers have little or no understanding at all as to how the Holy Spirit works. This means they have no understanding as to the part the Cross plays in our everyday life and living as Believers. So, not knowing God's Prescribed Order of Victory, which is the Cross of Christ and our Faith in that Finished Work, which gives the Holy Spirit latitude to work within our lives, this means that the sin nature is going to rule us in some way. It is inevitable!

Such a Believer now finds himself in a situation of perpetual failure. He is struggling not to fail, fighting with all his strength not to fail, but finds that he is failing anyway.

Unfortunately, the modern church, seeing the problem, has no solution. It doesn't understand the Cross, so its supposed solution is humanistic psychology, or else one fad or scheme after the other, which we might quickly add, contains no victory. Please understand the following:

THE CROSS

• There is no Salvation for the sinner outside of the Cross of Christ (Jn. 3:16).

• There is no Sanctification for the Saint outside of the Cross of Christ (Rom. 6:1-14).

• The only thing standing between mankind and eternal Hell is the Cross of Christ (Gal. 6:14).

• There is no victory over Satan and his cohorts of darkness outside of the Cross of Christ (Col. 2:14-15).

• The Believer must make the Cross of Christ the Object of his Faith, and that alone as the Object of his Faith (I Cor. 1:17).

• The Holy Spirit works entirely within the parameters of the Finished Work of Christ. He will not work any other way. Understanding this, we must place our Faith exclusively in Christ and the Cross and not allow it to be moved elsewhere. The Holy

Spirit will then do great and mighty things within our hearts and lives (Rom. 8:2).

• The Believer is to *"deny himself* (deny his own ability, strength, power, talent, education, etc.), *and take up the Cross* (which means to take up its benefits, all for which Jesus paid such a price, which is the key to all Blessing) *daily* (this is so important, and because it is so important, it must be something that we renew even on a daily basis) *and follow Me"* (Lk. 9:23).

Jesus then said, *"If you don't do this, take up the Cross, you cannot be My Disciple"* (Lk. 14:27).

SERVANTS OF SATAN

Judah was to now become servants of Egypt. In other words, instead of being ruled exclusively by the Lord, they were now being ruled, at least partially, by Egypt. The Lord decreed it so, and because of many reasons.

They had turned to idols, and now they were to see what these nations were like which were ruled by these idols.

How many modern Christians are ruled, in some way, by evil spirits?

While Believers cannot be demon possessed, they most definitely can be demon oppressed.

Without going into great dialogue, let's once again go back to the Cross.

If the Believer doesn't have his faith placed exclusively in Christ and the Cross, and maintain it constantly in Christ and the Cross, even *"fighting this good fight of Faith,"* then in some way, the sin nature is going to rule that Believer, and he will be a servant of Satan. That's tragic, but it is true!

The only way to have Victory, to walk in Victory, to be Victorious, and to do so perpetually, is by one's Faith being placed exclusively in Christ and the Cross, which then gives the Holy Spirit latitude to work in one's life, Who Alone can bring about the Victory that we need (Rom. 8:1-2, 11; Col. 2:14-15).

The Apostle said: *"Knowing this, that our old man is crucified with Him, that the body of sin might be destroyed* (made ineffective), *that henceforth we should not serve sin"* (Rom. 6:6).

Being the servant of sin is the same thing as being the servant of the Devil, which, regrettably and sadly, is the plight of most modern Christians. Satan is a hard taskmaster.

So, Judah, who had known nothing but freedom, will now become the servant of Shishak king of Egypt.

THE TREASURES OF THE HOUSE OF THE LORD

The Scripture says that Shishak *"took away the treasures of the House of the LORD,"* and what did that mean?

Did it mean that he took away copious amounts of gold and silver, which no doubt he did? Did it mean that he, as well, took away the sacred Vessels in the Holy Place, such as the Golden Lampstand, etc., which were made of pure gold?

We have no way of knowing; however, this we do know. The Holy Spirit purposely delineated the *"treasures,"* meaning that these things, whatever they were, were very special to the Lord and should have been very special to Judah.

The question is, is it possible that Satan is presently taking away your treasures, which refers to your victory?

Those things, during the time of Rehoboam, were material; now they are spiritual, but can very well translate into the material also. To be sure, Shishak was a type of Satan taking that which rightly belongs to the Child of God. The Believer must understand the following, however:

SATAN CAN DO NOTHING TO THE CHILD OF GOD BUT THAT WHICH IS ALLOWED BY THE LORD

The Lord allowed Shishak to come into Judah. He allowed Shishak to take over these *"treasures."* In other words, the Lord was in control completely, and not Shishak, whatever this heathen potentate may have thought!

Every Believer, irrespective of their Spiritual status, belongs to the Lord. As such, Satan has no latitude with that Believer unless the Lord allows such.

But, at the same time, the Lord has set up a System of Laws, and if those Laws are broken, Satan is then allowed certain latitude by the Lord. That's when he causes us great problems.

While there are a number of these Laws, the two major ones are:

1. The Law of the Spirit of Life in Christ Jesus (Rom. 8:2).

2. The Law of Sin and Death (Rom. 8:2).

These two Laws are the most powerful Laws in the Universe, and, *"the Law of the Spirit of Life in Christ Jesus"* alone is stronger than *"the Law of Sin and Death."* If we do not follow *"the Law of the Spirit of Life in Christ Jesus,"* which is the Cross, and the way the Holy Spirit Works, Satan will be allowed by the Lord to take certain liberties in our lives, and the end result will not be pleasant.

There is, in fact, a hedge built around every Child of God, exactly as given to us in Job, Chapters 1 and 2. That hedge can be taken down by our failing to subscribe to God's Way, or it can remotely be taken down by the Lord decreeing such, exactly as He did with Job. The latter would be very rare, however!

Everything that happens to a Believer is either caused or allowed by the Lord. This we must understand.

While the Lord most definitely does not cause the Believer to sin, as ought to be obvious, still, He does allow it, even though the consequences will not be pleasant.

While Satan seeks to destroy us, the Lord, in whatever He allows or causes, seeks to bring us to a place of victory. Far too many of us have allowed Satan to take away our *"treasures,"* and mostly because of self-will.

The wonderful thing is, those *"treasures"* can be restored. The Scripture says:

"And I will restore to you the years that the locust has eaten, the cankerworm, and the caterpillar, and the palmerworm" (Joel 2:25).

"SHIELDS OF GOLD"

Shishak took away to Egypt the *"shields of gold,"* which Solomon had made.

The Tenth Verse then says, *"Instead of which king Rehoboam made shields of brass."* He had to make these *"shields of brass"* simply because all the gold had been taken by Shishak.

The world robs the church of Divine realities and the church tries to hide the loss by substituting imitations. How many churches today have *"shields of brass"* instead of *"shields of gold"*?

The *"shields of gold"* represent Deity. They are symbolic of God's Glory, Protection, and Power. The *"shields of brass"* are symbolic of man and man's ways. The church world has substituted virtually all of its *"shields of gold"* for *"shields of brass."*

(13) "SO KING REHOBOAM STRENGTHENED HIMSELF IN JERUSALEM, AND REIGNED: FOR REHOBOAM WAS ONE AND FORTY YEARS OLD WHEN HE BEGAN TO REIGN, AND HE REIGNED SEVENTEEN YEARS IN JERUSALEM, THE CITY WHICH THE LORD HAD CHOSEN OUT OF ALL THE TRIBES OF ISRAEL, TO PUT HIS NAME THERE. AND HIS MOTHER'S NAME WAS NAAMAH AN AMMONITESS.

(14) "AND HE DID EVIL, BECAUSE HE PREPARED NOT HIS HEART TO SEEK THE LORD.

(15) "NOW THE ACTS OF REHOBOAM, FIRST AND LAST, ARE THEY NOT WRITTEN IN THE BOOK OF SHEMAIAH THE PROPHET, AND OF IDDO THE SEER CONCERNING GENEALOGIES? AND THERE WERE WARS BETWEEN REHOBOAM AND JEROBOAM CONTINUALLY.

(16) "AND REHOBOAM SLEPT WITH HIS FATHERS, AND WAS BURIED IN THE CITY OF DAVID: AND ABIJAH HIS SON REIGNED IN HIS STEAD."

The pattern is:

1. Rehoboam strengthened himself in Jerusalem but not in the Lord. The results would be catastrophic!

2. (Vs. 14) The Scripture says, *"And he did evil, because he prepared not his heart to seek the LORD."* What an indictment!

3. There were continuous wars between Rehoboam and Jeroboam because Rehoboam did not seek the Lord, but rather sought evil.

STRENGTH

Rehoboam strengthened himself but not in the Lord. It doesn't matter how strong one may be otherwise; if one is not strong in the Lord, then pure and simple, one is not strong. And, if one is strong in the Lord and poor otherwise, the Lord judges such a person as strong, irrespective as to what others might think or say.

Strength in the Lord is predicated solely upon one's Faith, and above all, the correct Object of Faith, which is the Cross of Christ. Of course, as one studies this Commentary, one may come to the conclusion that we propose the Cross for everything. You are exactly right!

The whole of Bible Christianity, the whole of the Plan of Redemption, and the whole of this New Covenant is wrapped up totally and completely in the Cross of Christ. Everything must be built upon that Foundation, the Foundation of the Cross, or else in some way, it will be specious.

Strength in the Lord is not that which the flesh can produce, but rather that which Faith can produce, but yet, it must be Faith in the correct Object, which is, *"Jesus Christ and Him Crucified."*

PREPARATION OF THE HEART

Once again, we go back to the Cross.

It is impossible for the Believer, within his own ability, strength, education, intellect, knowledge, talent, power, or ability, to prepare his heart to seek the Lord, no matter how consecrated he may be, how dedicated he may be, how zealous for the Lord he may be, or how sincere he may be. In other words, the flesh cannot prepare Spiritual things. Anything that originates with man, no matter how good it may seem to be on the surface, is always and without exception unacceptable to God.

The Holy Spirit Alone can properly prepare the heart. And he does so, as we have repeatedly stated, by and through what Jesus did at the Cross. In other words, it is the Cross that has given the Holy Spirit the legal right and the legal Means to do all that He does within our hearts and lives (Rom. 8:2).

THE FLESH

As we have said in this Volume, the Holy Spirit through Paul uses the word *"flesh"* quite often. It refers to the person's own ability and strength, etc. Anything conceived by that means, God cannot use. And yet, it is so easy for man, even consecrated man, to gravitate toward the flesh. We load it up with Scriptures, use the Name of Jesus, and try to make ourselves believe that what we're doing is spiritual. It isn't! Flesh is flesh, irrespective as to how it's handled, and *"they who are in the flesh cannot please God"* (Rom. 8:8). But that's where the problem comes in.

Abraham did not desire to give up Ishmael. This young man was the result of the scheming and planning of Abraham and Sarah, in other words, a work of the flesh. We are still suffering today from this terrible mistake.

It is so natural to resort to the flesh. We are human beings, so that's what we do; however, it is not God's Way. To be sure, He has made His Way very simple and very easy. Even a child can understand it, so the problem that we have for not placing our faith exclusively in Christ and the Cross is not theological but rather moral. What do I mean by that?

MORAL, NOT THEOLOGICAL

What do I mean by the statement, *"The problem is not theological but rather moral?"*

We are speaking of placing one's Faith exclusively in Christ and the Cross. The reason that most do not do this is not a theological problem. By using the term *"theological,"* we are referring to the fact that it is difficult or beyond the capacity to understand. The truth is, the Cross of Christ is about the simplest Doctrine that one could ever address, so simple, in fact, that it is within the scope of anyone and everyone, even a child. The problem is moral! And what do we mean by that?

There is a problem of self-will, of pride, of arrogance, of stubbornness, etc., all of which constitutes a moral problem.

Untold Victory lies in the path of the Believer who functions according to the Word of God, and that Word is the Cross of Christ. As well, this Victory lies within the reach of every grasp.

"There's not a place in Earth's vast round,
"In ocean deep, or air,
"Where skill and wisdom are not found,

"For God is everywhere."

"Around, within, below, above,
"Wherever space extends,
"There Heaven displays its boundless love,
"And Power with Mercy blends."

"Then rise, my soul, and sing His Name,
"And all His Praise rehearse,
"Who spread abroad Earth's wondrous frame,
"And built the Universe."

"Wherever your earthly lot is cast,
"His Power and Love declare;
"Nor think the mighty theme too vast,
"For God is everywhere."

CHAPTER 13

(1) "NOW IN THE EIGHTEENTH YEAR OF KING JEROBOAM BEGAN ABIJAH TO REIGN OVER JUDAH.

(2) "HE REIGNED THREE YEARS IN JERUSALEM. HIS MOTHER'S NAME ALSO WAS MICHAIAH THE DAUGHTER OF URIEL OF GIBEAH. AND THERE WAS WAR BETWEEN ABIJAH AND JEROBOAM."

The structure is:

1. Abijah began to reign in the eighteenth year of Jeroboam, four years before Jeroboam died (I Ki. 14:20).

2. The wars that have continued off and on during the reigns of Rehoboam and Jeroboam now continue when Abijah is made king, but God gave him a great victory from which Jeroboam never did fully recover.

The Holy Spirit changed Abijah's name from Abijam, which means *"the tumult of the sea."* Abijah means *"Jehovah is my Father."*

3. It says in I Kings, Chapter 15 that Abijah *"walked in all the sins of his father."* Those sins are not mentioned here in II Chronicles, giving some hint that he may have repented.

4. In the Second Verse the Holy Spirit is careful to say, *"His mother's name also was Michaiah,"* which means, *"who is like Jehovah."* It was changed from Maachah, which means, *"oppression."* I Kings 15:13 says that she had been an idol-worshipper. Perhaps she repented as well.

5. The Second Verse also says, *"And there was war between Abijah and Jeroboam."* Once again, we see the People of God fighting each other, and all because of sin.

(3) "AND ABIJAH SET THE BATTLE IN ARRAY WITH AN ARMY OF VALIANT MEN OF WAR, EVEN FOUR HUNDRED THOUSAND CHOSEN MEN: JEROBOAM ALSO SET THE BATTLE IN ARRAY AGAINST HIM WITH EIGHT HUNDRED THOUSAND CHOSEN MEN, BEING MIGHTY MEN OF VALOUR.

(4) "AND ABIJAH STOOD UP UPON MOUNT ZEMARAIM, WHICH IS IN MOUNT EPHRAIM, AND SAID, HEAR ME, YOU JEROBOAM, AND ALL ISRAEL;

(5) "OUGHT YOU NOT TO KNOW THAT THE LORD GOD OF ISRAEL GAVE THE KINGDOM OVER ISRAEL TO DAVID FOREVER, EVEN TO HIM AND TO HIS SONS BY A COVENANT OF SALT?

(6) "YET JEROBOAM THE SON OF NEBAT, THE SERVANT OF SOLOMON THE SON OF DAVID, IS RISEN UP, AND HAS REBELLED AGAINST HIS LORD.

(7) "AND THERE ARE GATHERED UNTO HIM VAIN MEN, THE CHILDREN OF BELIAL, AND HAVE STRENGTHENED THEMSELVES AGAINST REHOBOAM THE SON OF SOLOMON, WHEN REHOBOAM WAS YOUNG AND TENDERHEARTED, AND COULD NOT WITHSTAND THEM.

(8) "AND NOW YOU THINK TO WITHSTAND THE KINGDOM OF THE LORD IN THE HAND OF THE SONS OF DAVID; AND YOU BE A GREAT MULTITUDE, AND THERE ARE WITH YOU GOLDEN CALVES, WHICH JEROBOAM MADE YOU FOR GODS.

(9) "HAVE YOU NOT CAST OUT THE PRIESTS OF THE LORD, THE SONS OF AARON, AND THE LEVITES, AND HAVE MADE YOU PRIESTS AFTER THE MANNER OF THE NATIONS OF OTHER LANDS? SO THAT WHOSOEVER COMES TO CONSECRATE HIMSELF WITH A YOUNG BULLOCK AND SEVEN RAMS, THE SAME MAY BE A PRIEST OF THEM THAT ARE NO GODS.

(10) "BUT AS FOR US, THE LORD IS OUR GOD, AND WE HAVE NOT FORSAKEN HIM; AND THE PRIESTS, WHICH MINISTER UNTO THE LORD, ARE THE SONS OF AARON, AND THE LEVITES WAIT UPON THEIR BUSINESS:

(11) "AND THEY BURN UNTO THE LORD EVERY MORNING AND EVERY EVENING BURNT SACRIFICES AND SWEET INCENSE: THE SHEWBREAD ALSO SET THEY IN ORDER UPON THE PURE TABLE; AND THE CANDLESTICK OF GOLD WITH THE LAMPS THEREOF, TO BURN EVERY EVENING: FOR WE KEEP THE CHARGE OF THE LORD OUR GOD; BUT YOU HAVE FORSAKEN HIM.

(12) "AND, BEHOLD, GOD HIMSELF IS WITH US FOR OUR CAPTAIN, AND HIS PRIESTS WITH SOUNDING TRUMPETS TO CRY ALARM AGAINST YOU. O CHILDREN OF ISRAEL, FIGHT YOU NOT AGAINST THE LORD GOD OF YOUR FATHERS; FOR YOU SHALL NOT PROSPER."

The construction is:

1. (Vs. 3) A few years before, Rehoboam could muster only 180,000 chosen men (11:1). This indicates that many thousands of the northern confederacy had come down to become a part of the kingdom of Judah. The Holy Spirit wants us to note that even though these troops of Jeroboam were *"mighty men of valor,"* still, they could not overcome what God had decreed otherwise!

2. (Vs. 5) A *"Covenant of Salt"* is mentioned two other times in the Word of God (Lev. 2:13; Num. 18:19). This Covenant became a symbol of the incorruptibility of God's Covenant, and the perpetuity of man's obligation to Him. This Covenant refers to the solemnizing of any inviolable covenant. In other words, Abijah is telling Jeroboam that he is attempting to destroy what God has ordained. All of this shows that Abijah had a tremendous knowledge of the Word of God.

3. (Vs. 8) Abijah reminds Jeroboam of his worship of the *"golden calves,"* which, in some measure, was the same as the religion of Egypt, and was totally detrimental to the Ways of the Lord.

4. (Vs. 9) Jeroboam had substituted his own priesthood for God's Priesthood.

A COVENANT OF SALT

Even though the term, *"Covenant of Salt,"* is mentioned only two times in the Word of God (Lev. 2:13; Num. 18:19), Abijah mentions it here to Jeroboam, portraying an excellent knowledge of the Word of God. *"Salt,"* as the word is used in the Old Testament, portrays the incorruptibility of the Word of God. In other words, it symbolizes the Word of God and does so because of its preservative factor.

As an example, when Elisha took the mantle of Elijah, he went, it seems, from the translation of the great Prophet, to Jericho. The Scripture says concerning this visit:

"And the men of the city said unto Elisha, Behold, I pray you, the situation of this city is pleasant, as my lord sees: but the water is naught (poisoned), *and the ground barren* (because of the poisoned water. Jericho is the city of the curse, and by God at that, simply because of its heathen worship in the days of Joshua. As well, the world is cursed, because of sin. In fact, it could be, as Jericho, a pleasant place; but instead, the water is poisoned and the ground barren).

"And he said, Bring me a new cruse (this is symbolic of the sinless Body of the Lord Jesus Christ, because the cruse was made of clay), *and put salt therein* (the 'salt' in it—a Type of the incorruptible Word of God, that in its plenitude dwelt in Him—was the vehicle of this great healing power). *And they brought it to him.*

"And he went forth unto the spring of the waters, and cast the salt in there (the Word of God must be cast into the poisoned spring; there is no other answer; that's the reason that it is imperative that this great Gospel of Jesus Christ be taken to the whole world [Mk. 16:15]), *and said, Thus says the LORD, I have healed these waters; there shall not be from thence any more death or barren land* (Christ Alone can heal the broken heart, can set the captive free [Lk. 4:18-19]).

"So the waters were healed unto this day, according to the saying of Elisha which he spoke (it was not a mere temporary, but a permanent, benefit which Elisha bestowed upon

the town; when Christ comes in, there is *'no more death or barren land'*)" (II Ki. 2:19-22).

A PERSONAL EXPERIENCE

This passage concerning Elisha healing the poisoned waters of Jericho by the Power of God is very dear to me personally.

It was in the month of October, 1991. We had just begun the daily prayer meetings, which incidentally, we were to continue in that fashion for some ten years.

At any rate, I read this Passage concerning Elisha and Jericho that night as I stood before the small group that had gathered for prayer. It was a Friday night.

I commented on it for a few moments, and then we went to prayer.

The Spirit of God moved upon me that night as I have seldom experienced. To be frank, I awakened about midnight, and the Spirit of the Lord was still prevalent. In fact, it lingered until nearly noon the next day.

At any rate, while praying, the Lord impressed heavily upon me the Scriptures I had just read concerning Elisha and the healing of the poison waters of Jericho. And then the Lord spoke to my heart so graphically so that I will never forget it. He said:

"As I healed the poisoned waters of Jericho, I will heal you, and I will heal this Ministry." I knew it was the Lord, of that I had no doubt.

During the intervening years, I have witnessed the Lord as He has Worked within my life and Worked within this Ministry in miraculous Ways. I speak of the Church, Family Worship Center; I speak of the Telecast and SonLife Radio; I speak of the Bible College; and, I speak of the Expositor's Study Bible, which the Lord has helped us to develop; in fact, every part and parcel of this Ministry, which the Lord is using to touch the world. But, probably more than all, I speak of the great Revelation of the Cross, which the Lord gave me in 1997. It changed my life, my Ministry, my understanding of the Word of God, and, in fact, my entire world. That Revelation is the foundation of everything else that has taken place, is taking place, and shall take place. And yet, it's not something new, but that which was originally given to the Apostle Paul (Gal. 1:12).

NOTES

As salt is a Type of the Word of God, and as Elisha was given instructions by the Holy Spirit to pour the salt into the poisoned water, this presents itself as the answer to man's dilemma. The Word of God alone, of which the salt was a Type, is the answer. It was my answer, it is your answer, and, in fact, is the only answer.

THE WORD OF GOD AND THE CROSS OF CHRIST

The Word of God is the Story of Jesus Christ and Him Crucified. This is given to us in beautiful prose in the Gospel according to St. John. The great Apostle said, and I quote from THE EXPOSITOR'S STUDY BIBLE: *"In the beginning* (does not infer that Christ as God had a beginning, because as God He had no beginning, but rather refers to the time of Creation [Gen. 1:1]) *was the Word* (the Holy Spirit through John describes Jesus as *'the Eternal Logos'*), *and the Word was with God* (*'was in relationship with God,'* and expresses the idea of the Trinity), *and the Word was God* (meaning that He did not cease to be God during the Incarnation; He *'was'* and *'is'* God from eternity past to eternity future)."

And then it says: *"And the Word was made flesh* (refers to the Incarnation, *'God becoming man'*), *and dwelt among us* (refers to Jesus, although Perfect, not holding Himself aloft from all others, but rather lived as all men, even a peasant), *(and we beheld His Glory, the Glory as of the Only Begotten of the Father,)* (speaks of His Deity, although hidden from the eyes of the merely curious; while Christ laid aside the expression of His Deity, He never lost the possession of His Deity) *full of Grace and Truth* (as *'flesh,'* proclaimed His Humanity, *'Grace and Truth'* His Deity)."

And then we are told: *"The next day* (refers to the day after John had been questioned by the emissaries from the Sanhedrin) *John sees Jesus coming unto him* (is, no doubt, after the Baptism of Jesus, and the temptation in the wilderness), *and said, Behold the Lamb of God* (proclaims Jesus as the Sacrifice for sin, in fact, the Sin-Offering, Whom all the multiple millions of offered lambs had represented), *which takes away the sin of the world* (animal blood could only cover sin, it could not take it away; but Jesus offering Himself as the Perfect Sacrifice took away the sin of the world; He not only cleansed acts of sin, but, as well, addressed the root cause [Col. 2:14-15]).

"*This is He of Whom I said* (proclaims John making a positive identification; it is the One Who '*takes away the sin of the world*'), *After me comes a Man which is preferred before me* (affirms His essential Humanity): *for He was before me* (affirms His essential Deity)" (Jn. 1:1, 14, 29-30).

It is impossible for the Believer to properly understand the Bible unless first of all that Believer has a proper understanding of the Cross of Christ. While any Believer can definitely have correct understanding about certain parts of the Bible, to understand it as it should be understood, which means to place it in its proper perspective, an understanding of the Cross of Christ is an absolute necessity. It is this way simply because the entirety of the Bible, in one way or the other, is the Story of Jesus Christ and that which He did to redeem fallen humanity. In fact, the very first Prophecy given after the Fall of man was that which the Lord spoke to Satan through the serpent. He said:

"*And I will put enmity* (animosity) *between you and the woman* (presents the Lord now actually speaking to Satan, who had used the serpent; in effect, the Lord is saying to Satan, '*You used the woman to bring down the human race, and I will use the woman as an instrument to bring the Redeemer into the world, Who will save the human race*'), *and between your seed* (mankind which follows Satan) *and her Seed* (the Lord Jesus Christ); *it* (Christ) *shall bruise your head* (the Victory that Jesus won at the Cross [Col. 2:14-15]), *and you shall bruise His Heel* (the sufferings of the Cross)" (Gen. 3:15).

So, the very first Prophecy given was about the Cross of Christ!

THE LORD IS OUR GOD

Abijah claims the sovereignty of the Lord and of Judah's total dependence on Him. He said, "*... and we have not forsaken Him; and the Priests, which minister unto the LORD, are the sons of Aaron, and the Levites wait upon their business.*"

He went on to say, "*And, behold, God Himself is with us for our Captain.*" This was true!

The idea is, even though Judah only had 400,000 fighting men, and the northern kingdom of Israel had 800,000 fighting men, still, the Lord was with Judah, and He wasn't with Israel.

Abijah seems to be somewhat of an enigma. First of all, he seemed to have great knowledge of the Word of God, which means that he made a study of the Word, and at times sought to do right, even as here. However, at other times, "*he walked in all the sins of his father, which he had done before him: and his heart was not perfect with the LORD his God, as the heart of David his father*" (I Ki. 15:3). These sins are not mentioned in the Chronicles account.

Why?

The account in Kings is as man saw the situation, with the account in Chronicles as the Lord saw the situation.

What do we mean by that?

The account of his sins being omitted in II Chronicles could be because Abijah repented of these sins, and in the Eyes of God they were no more. If, in fact, that was the case, this would be the reason the Lord did not mention them.

Also, in I Kings, this king is referred to as "*Abijam,*" while in II Chronicles he is referred to as "*Abijah.*" As we have previously stated, Abijam means "*the sea,*" that is, "*tumult is my father.*" Abijah means "*Jehovah is my Father.*"

Williams says as it regards this man, "*Any prosperity he enjoyed was for the sake of David his father.*"[1] That is true; however, that does not prevent the possibility that the king repented. Of course, we certainly hope that he did so.

At any rate, the Holy Spirit refers to him in II Chronicles as "*Abijah,*" instead of "*Abijam.*" That tells us something within itself.

(13) "BUT JEROBOAM CAUSED AN AMBUSHMENT TO COME ABOUT BEHIND THEM: SO THEY WERE BEFORE JUDAH, AND THE AMBUSHMENT WAS

BEHIND THEM.

(14) "AND WHEN JUDAH LOOKED BACK, BEHOLD, THE BATTLE WAS BEFORE AND BEHIND: AND THEY CRIED UNTO THE LORD, AND THE PRIESTS SOUNDED WITH THE TRUMPETS.

(15) "THEN THE MEN OF JUDAH GAVE A SHOUT: AND AS THE MEN OF JUDAH SHOUTED, IT CAME TO PASS, THAT GOD SMOTE JEROBOAM AND ALL ISRAEL BEFORE ABIJAH AND JUDAH.

(16) "AND THE CHILDREN OF ISRAEL FLED BEFORE JUDAH: AND GOD DELIVERED THEM INTO THEIR HAND.

(17) "AND ABIJAH AND HIS PEOPLE KILLED THEM WITH A GREAT SLAUGHTER: SO THERE FELL DOWN SLAIN OF ISRAEL FIVE HUNDRED THOUSAND CHOSEN MEN.

(18) "THUS THE CHILDREN OF ISRAEL WERE BROUGHT UNDER AT THAT TIME, AND THE CHILDREN OF JUDAH PREVAILED, BECAUSE THEY RELIED UPON THE LORD GOD OF THEIR FATHERS.

(19) "AND ABIJAH PURSUED AFTER JEROBOAM, AND TOOK CITIES FROM HIM, BETH-EL WITH THE TOWNS THEREOF, AND JESHANAH WITH THE TOWNS THEREOF, AND EPHRAIN WITH THE TOWNS THEREOF.

(20) "NEITHER DID JEROBOAM RECOVER STRENGTH AGAIN IN THE DAYS OF ABIJAH: AND THE LORD STRUCK HIM, AND HE DIED."

The exegesis is:

1. (Vs. 13) Jeroboam, king of the northern kingdom of Israel, because of having twice as many soldiers as Abijah, thinks his victory is certain; consequently, he ignores Abijah's message. In fact, he surrounded the army of Judah, thinking his victory was sure.

2. (Vs. 14) The army of Judah, however, cried unto the Lord. Man's only hope is to *"cry unto the LORD!"* But sadly, few do.

3. (Vs. 15) The Holy Spirit is careful to denote the cause of the great victory as being of God. In the natural there was no way that Abijah's 400,000 men could even hope to defeat Jeroboam's army of 800,000 men; but with God all things are possible!

4. (Vs. 17) The word *"slain"* in the Hebrew can also mean *"wounded,"* which it, no doubt, means here. At any rate the victory was gargantuan!

5. Over and over again, even as Verse 18 brings out, the Holy Spirit makes it known that it is God Who is the Author of this victory. Obedience brings blessing, while disobedience brings defeat.

6. (Vs. 20) The Lord terminated the life of Jeroboam, because he had set himself to do evil. How many others fall into the same category?

THEY CRIED UNTO THE LORD

The idea is, Jeroboam had the army of Judah surrounded. In the natural, there was no way that Judah could escape this trap. But the Scripture says that *"Judah . . . cried unto the Lord."*

As someone has well said, *"When we seek the help of men, we get the help that man gives, which is little or nothing. When we seek the help that God gives, we receive the help which He Alone can give, which is everything."*

Please understand, Satan is still in the ambushment business. And please understand, as well, the only answer to such a situation is the Lord. Regrettably, the modern church is little seeking the Lord presently, but rather the help that man gives.

As Judah began to cry unto the Lord, the Scripture also says, *"and the Priests sounded with the trumpets."*

Concerning this, the Scripture continues, *"And if you go to war in your land against the enemy who oppresses you, then you shall blow an alarm with the trumpets; and you shall be remembered before the LORD your God, and you shall be saved from your enemies"* (Num. 10:9).

The Priests began to blow the trumpets in obedience to the Word of the Lord. He had promised to remember them, and had promised to save them from their enemies. This was the sound that Judah heard.

THE SOUND

To be sure, Satan is declaring war presently upon the people of God, even as he always has, and possibly now, even to a greater degree; however, what type of sound are we hearing out of the modern church?

To be sure, it is not a certain sound, and it is not a sure sound, but something else altogether.

Some few Preachers of the Gospel blow the trumpet presently by proclaiming the Gospel without fear and without compromise. But precious few are engaged in such Ministry.

Satan can little deny the great Gospel of Jesus Christ for that is a forgone conclusion; however, he can pervert it, and that's exactly what he is doing.

The Cross of Christ is where Satan was totally defeated (Col. 2:14-15). That's why Paul, to whom was given the meaning of the New Covenant, which is the meaning of the Cross, proclaimed as his basic Message, the Cross of Christ. He said:

"For the preaching of the Cross is to them who perish foolishness, but to we who are Saved it is the Power of God" (I Cor. 1:18).

If the Church preaches the Cross, it has power, because this is the manner in which the Holy Spirit works. He will not work, in fact, outside of the Cross (Rom. 8:2).

But the modern church, sadly and regrettably, is little preaching the Cross, and the modern church, sadly and regrettably, has precious little power.

THE SHOUT OF VICTORY

The Scripture says, *"When the Priests sounded with the trumpets, the men of Judah gave a shout."* It was a shout of victory!

In other words, they believed that God said what He meant and meant what He said. He had promised that when the Priests blew those trumpets, and did so in Faith and confidence, victory would be theirs, and on that basis, they *"shouted."*

And at the sound of that shout the Scripture then says, *"God smote Jeroboam and all Israel before Abijah and Judah."*

As to exactly what the Lord did, we aren't told, but whatever it was, the ambushment that Israel had brought about against Judah was to no avail. The Scripture further says, *"So there fell down slain of Israel 500,000 chosen men."*

As previously stated, the word *"slain"* in the Hebrew also means *"wounded."* So, it could read and is, no doubt, the case, *"so there fell down killed and wounded of Israel 500,000 chosen men."*

At any rate, the victory was so complete that Jeroboam never did recover his strength, and at a point in time, *"the LORD struck him, and he died."*

And yet, all of this great victory, the Scripture says, was *"for David's sake"* (I Ki. 15:4).

One could say, and be Scripturally right, that it is all *"for Jesus' sake,"* inasmuch as our Lord is the *"Son of David."*

Everything the Lord does for us is, without exception, *"for Jesus' sake."* We must never forget that. He is the One Who paid the price on Calvary's Cross. He is the One Who shed His Life's Blood in order that we might be Saved. He is the One Who has satisfied the demands of the broken Law and atoned for all sin. He is the One Who has defeated Satan and done so completely. So, make no mistake about it:

Everything the Lord does for us, every Blessing, every victory, is all, and without exception, *"for Jesus' sake."*

(21) "BUT ABIJAH WAXED MIGHTY, AND MARRIED FOURTEEN WIVES, AND BEGAT TWENTY AND TWO SONS, AND SIXTEEN DAUGHTERS.

(22) "AND THE REST OF THE ACTS OF ABIJAH, AND HIS WAYS, AND HIS SAYINGS, ARE WRITTEN IN THE STORY OF THE PROPHET IDDO."

The construction is:

1. It is our prayer that Abijah made things right with God before his demise.

2. The Scripture does say of him, *"but Abijah waxed mighty,"* which, in a sense, refers to the Blessings of God.

3. The Scripture also says that, *"his heart was not perfect with the LORD his God"* (I Ki. 15:3). However, the Lord most definitely could have changed his heart.

"The Eye of God is everywhere,
"To watch the sinner's ways;
"He sees who joins in humble prayer,
"And who in solemn praise."

"One glance of Thine, Eternal Lord,
"Can pierce and search us through;
"Nor Heaven, nor Earth, nor Hell afford,
"A shelter from Your View!"

"The Universe, in every part,
"At once before Thee lies;
"And every thought of every heart,
"Is open to Your Eyes."

"Prepare us, Lord, to pray and praise,
"With fervent, Holy Love,
"And fit us by the Word of Grace,
"To worship Thee above."

CHAPTER 14

(1) "SO ABIJAH SLEPT WITH HIS FATHERS, AND THEY BURIED HIM IN THE CITY OF DAVID: AND ASA HIS SON REIGNED IN HIS STEAD. IN HIS DAYS THE LAND WAS QUIET TEN YEARS.

(2) "AND ASA DID THAT WHICH WAS GOOD AND RIGHT IN THE EYES OF THE LORD HIS GOD:

(3) "FOR HE TOOK AWAY THE ALTARS OF THE STRANGE GODS, AND THE HIGH PLACES, AND BROKE DOWN THE IMAGES, AND CUT DOWN THE GROVES:

(4) "AND COMMANDED JUDAH TO SEEK THE LORD GOD OF THEIR FATHERS, AND TO DO THE LAW AND THE COMMANDMENT.

(5) "ALSO HE TOOK AWAY OUT OF ALL THE CITIES OF JUDAH THE HIGH PLACES AND THE IMAGES: AND THE KINGDOM WAS QUIET BEFORE HIM."

The structure is:

1. The *"ten years"* mentioned in Verse 1, referred to ten years without war, ten years of peace and prosperity.

2. Verse 2 gives the reason for this peace, quiet, and prosperity. It was that *"Asa did that which was good and right in the Eyes of the LORD his God."*

3. According to Verse 3, evidently, Judah, under Abijah, had been involved at least to some degree in idol worship, hence, the statement made about Abijah in I Kings, Chapter 15.

4. Verse 4 proclaims the fact that Asa pointed Judah to the Bible. How so badly we need Preachers presently who will, as well, point people to the Bible; but all too often the people are pointed in every direction except the Bible.

5. (Vs. 5) The lesson we should learn from these Passages should be plain to every Christian—that sin opens the door for strife, opposition, destruction, and all manner of turbulence, while seeking the Ways of God and following the Word of God ensure serenity, rest, and peace. This doesn't mean that Satan will cease to oppose the true Child of God; however, it does mean victory and then peace when Satan does oppose.

GOOD AND RIGHT IN THE EYES OF THE LORD

Notice the terminology, *"in the Eyes of the LORD his God."* Too many attempt to do that which is right in the eyes of others. Asa wanted to do that which was *"right in the Eyes of the LORD his God."*

This is the reason for the peace, prosperity, and serenity. Pure and simple, it pays to serve God, it pays to obey God, and it pays to please the Lord.

How many presently can say that they are doing that which is *"good and right in the Eyes of the LORD?"*

What does it mean to do such?

Does it mean sinless perfection?

No, it doesn't! In fact, the Bible doesn't teach sinless perfection; however, it does teach that sin is not to have dominion over us, which means that we are not to be ruled in any way by the sin nature (Rom. 6:14). So, what does it mean?

All of us must realize that within ourselves, within our capabilities, our talent, our motives, our education, our intellect, our zeal, etc., pure and simple, we cannot do what needs to be done within our hearts and lives, no matter how dedicated we might be. While Believers are quick to state that the sinner cannot get Saved other than by trusting the Lord, the same Believer, all too often, will then attempt to sanctify himself by his own strength and ability. There is no greater example of what I'm endeavoring to teach than that of Paul.

He was Saved on the road to Damascus and actually saw Jesus. Three days later he was baptized with the Holy Spirit as Ananias prayed for him. He was called to preach and immediately began to preach the Gospel;

however, despite having a Vision of Jesus, despite being baptized with the Holy Spirit, and despite the Call to be an Apostle, he found to his dismay that he simply could not live right. Listen to what he said:

"For the good that I would I do not (if I depend on self, and not the Cross)*: but the evil which I would not* (don't want to do), *that I do* (which is exactly what every Believer will do no matter how hard he tries to do otherwise, if he tries to live this life outside of the Cross [Gal. 2:20-21])*"* (Rom. 7:19).

The great Apostle then said, *"O wretched man that I am!* (Any Believer who attempts to live for God outside of God's Prescribed Order, which is *'Jesus Christ and Him Crucified,'* will, in fact, live a wretched and miserable existence. This life can only be lived in one way, and that way is the Cross.) *Who shall deliver me from the body of this death?* (The minute the Apostle cries *'Who,'* he finds the path to Victory, for he is now calling upon a Person for help, and that Person is Christ; actually, the Greek Text is masculine, indicating a Person)*"* (Rom. 7:24).

Of course, when Paul wrote these words, he full well knew God's Prescribed Order of Victory, and was walking therein. However, he is reaching back in his life after he was Saved and explaining what took place with him, and how he tried to live for God in all the wrong ways. To Paul's credit, no one else at that time knew God's Prescribed Order of Victory. That great Revelation would be given to Paul and, actually, given to him by the Lord Jesus Christ (Gal. 1:12).

SPIRITUAL DEFEAT

Sadly and regrettably, the far greater majority of the modern church, and we are speaking here of those who are truly Saved and who truly love God, nevertheless, are living lives of spiritual defeat. In other words, the modern church simply does not know how to live for God. As a result, the sin nature more or less rules almost every Believer in some way. As stated, despite being truly Saved, such is not exactly a happy time of Spiritual Rest, but rather the very opposite.

GOD'S PRESCRIBED ORDER OF VICTORY

He has but one Order of Victory, and that is the Cross of Christ. In other words, the Believer must place his Faith exclusively in Christ and the Cross, never separating the two (I Cor. 2:2), which will then give the Holy Spirit latitude to work in his life. It is all a matter of Faith.

Probably one of the most, if not the most, salient Scriptures in the entirety of the Bible is found in Genesis 15:6, and allow me to quote from the EXPOSITOR'S STUDY BIBLE:

"And he (Abraham) *believed in the LORD* (exercised Faith, believing what the Lord told him)*; and He* (the Lord) *counted it to him* (Abraham) *for Righteousness.* (This is, as stated, one of the single most important Scriptures in the entirety of the Word of God. In this simple term, *'Abraham believed the LORD,'* we find the meaning of Justification by Faith. Abraham was Saved by Grace through Faith, not by his good works. There is no other way of Salvation anywhere in the Bible. God demands Righteousness; however, it is the Righteousness afforded strictly by Christ and Christ Alone. Anything else is self-righteousness, and totally unacceptable to God. Directly the sinner believes God's Testimony about His Beloved Son, he is not only declared righteous, but he is made a son and an heir.)*"*

WHAT IS RIGHTEOUSNESS?

In simple terminology, *"it is that which is right."* It is right, however, according to God's Standard and not man's. Man's standard of righteousness, which God can never accept, only leads to self-righteousness, which is the blight of religion.

God's Standard of Righteousness cannot be achieved by man's ability, strength, efforts, religion, motives, intellect, education, etc. It is all referred to in the New Testament as *"the flesh."* It is always totally unacceptable to God.

The only Righteousness that God will accept is the Perfect Righteousness of His Son, the Lord Jesus Christ. The believing sinner can receive that Righteousness, and receive it instantly, by simply placing his Faith in Christ and the Cross (Rom. 5:1-2; 6:3-5). Upon simple Faith in Christ and what Christ did at the Cross, the believing sinner receives a perfect, pure, spotless Righteousness, the Righteousness afforded by Christ. It is not earned, as it cannot be earned. It is not merited, as it cannot be merited. It is freely given upon Faith.

If it is to be noticed, the Scripture simply says that Abraham believed in the Lord.

BELIEVE WHAT?

Did he merely believe there was a God?

Well, of course, he believed that; however, his Faith went much further. He believed, in essence, what God said as it regarded the coming of a Redeemer, Who would redeem the human race, at least all who would believe. Concerning this, Jesus said:

"Your father Abraham rejoiced to see My Day: and he saw it, and was glad (in the great Revelation of Justification by Faith given to Abraham by God, he was made to understand that this great Redemption Plan was wrapped up, not in a philosophy, but rather a Man, the Man Christ Jesus, and what He would do at the Cross; the Patriarch rejoiced in that)" (Jn. 8:56).

WHAT IS JUSTIFICATION BY FAITH?

Let's look at the word, *"Justification."*

Justification is the act of a thrice-Holy God declaring an obviously unrighteous man as totally and perfectly righteous.

How can God declare one as righteous who is obviously unrighteous and retain His Integrity?

Paul said concerning this: *"To declare, I say, at this time His Righteousness* (refers to God's Righteousness which must be satisfied at all times, and is in Christ and only Christ)*: that He* (God) *might be just* (not overlooking sin in any manner), *and the Justifier of him which believes in Jesus.* (God can justify a believing [although guilty] sinner, and His Holiness not be impacted, providing the sinner's Faith is exclusively in Christ; only in this manner can God be *'just'* and at the same time *'justify'* the sinner)" (Rom. 3:26).

FAITH!

We are justified by Faith (Rom. 5:1-2).

Now, what exactly does that mean?

It means that the believing sinner expresses Faith in Christ and what Christ did at the Cross. One must understand that Jesus is our Substitute Man. Paul referred to Him as *"the Last Adam,"* and *"the Second Man"* (I Cor. 15:45-47). The Victory that He won at Calvary's Cross becomes our Victory upon simple Faith in Him. In fact, it was all done for us at the very beginning. We simply believe in what He did, and God freely justifies us and grants us a perfect Righteousness. Again, Paul said, and I quote from THE EXPOSITOR'S STUDY BIBLE:

"Where is boasting then?" (This refers primarily to the Jews boasting of themselves as a result of the Law of God given to them, but the principle is true for modern Christians as well!) *It is excluded* (not only means that God will not accept such boasting [outside of Christ], but that it actually serves to keep one from Salvation). *By what Law? of works?* (In a sense, this tells us where and how the boasting, God will not accept, originates). *No: but by the Law of Faith* (refers to trust exclusively in Christ and what He did at the Cross; Faith in Christ and Him Crucified is more than a principle; it is a Law, meaning that God will not deviate at all from this proclamation).

"Therefore we conclude that a man is justified by Faith (and only by Faith, with the Cross ever being the Object of such Faith) *without the deeds of the Law* (faith in works is out)" (Rom. 3:27-28).

Salvation has ever been the same. In other words, there is no such thing as a different type of Salvation before the Cross and now another type of Salvation.

People were Saved before the Cross by looking forward to that coming event. Their Faith had to be placed in that which was to come, which the sacrifices represented. Now believing sinners are Saved by looking back to that which is now a fact, and we continue to speak of the Cross of Christ. The Cross has ever been the center point, the Foundation of all, as it regards the Redemption Plan. The Plan of Redemption now, and has been from the very beginning, is *"Jesus Christ and Him Crucified"* (Gen. 15:6; I Cor. 1:23).

(6) "AND HE BUILT FENCED CITIES IN JUDAH: FOR THE LAND HAD REST, AND HE HAD NO WAR IN THOSE YEARS; BECAUSE THE LORD HAD GIVEN HIM REST.

(7) "THEREFORE HE SAID UNTO JUDAH, LET US BUILD THESE CITIES, AND MAKE ABOUT THEM WALLS, AND TOWERS, GATES, AND BARS, WHILE THE LAND IS YET BEFORE US; BECAUSE WE HAVE SOUGHT THE LORD OUR GOD, WE HAVE SOUGHT HIM, AND HE HAS GIVEN US REST ON EVERY SIDE. SO THEY BUILT AND PROSPERED."

The construction is:

1. (Vs. 6) When one properly follows the Lord, *"rest"* is guaranteed (Mat. 11:28-30).

2. (Vs. 7) Five times in the first seven Verses of this Fourteenth Chapter, the Holy Spirit alludes to this great blessing of *"rest."*

3. All rest, and without exception, is found only in Christ (Mat. 11:28-30).

SO THEY BUILT AND PROSPERED

Because of the beauty and glory of the Sixth Verse, please permit us to quote it again: *"For the land had rest, and he had no war in those years; because the LORD had given him rest."* How beautiful is this statement! How so few enjoy such! Jesus Himself would say, *"Come unto Me, all ye who labor and are heavy laden, and I will give you rest."* The Lord of Glory is the only One Who can.

Again, let us quote, and because of its beauty, the Seventh Verse as well: *"Because we have sought the LORD our God, we have sought Him, and He has given us rest on every side."*

In this capacity, and only in this capacity, could they *"build and prosper."*

The enemies of Judah in those days were, of course, the surrounding nations which were idol worshippers and, thereby, had a built-in animosity against the People of God. In fact, Judah was the only monotheistic nation on the face of the Earth. This word means that they worshipped one God, namely, Jehovah. Due to the faithfulness of Judah at this time under King Asa, the Lord protected them from surrounding nations and gave the land quiet and rest. There could be no greater blessing!

The *"rest"* which we now have, and which Jesus briefly addressed in Matthew 11:28-30, is more so a Spiritual Rest than anything else. But, of course, when this Spiritual Rest is brought about, which can only be brought about in Christ, everything else goes well also. In other words, in such a climate, so to speak, the Believer is meant to *"build and prosper."*

HOW DO WE OBTAIN THIS REST?

Once again, we go back to the Cross. The reader must understand, everything is in the Atonement. All victory is in the Atonement; all power is in the Atonement; all Grace and Mercy are in the Atonement; all forgiveness and cleansing from sin are in the Atonement; and, all privileges in Christ are in the Atonement. What Jesus did at the Cross, which is the Atonement, meaning that He there atoned for all sin, presents the culmination of all that God has done for the human race as it regards Salvation. And, of course, when we speak of Salvation, we are speaking of the entirety of the Plan of God, which includes cleansing from sin, as well as the Sanctification of the Saint.

The opposite of rest is consternation, anxiety, fear, guilt, etc. All of these come about when we try to live our lives for God in all the wrong ways. To sum up, it refers to the Believer attempting to live for God by the means of works, thinking this somehow earns him something with God. Concerning all of this, Jesus said:

"Come unto Me (is meant by Jesus to reveal Himself as the Giver of Salvation), *all you who labor and are heavy laden* (trying to earn Salvation by works), *and I will give you rest* (this 'rest' can only be found by placing one's Faith in Christ and what He has done for us at the Cross [Gal. 5:1-6]).

"Take My Yoke upon you (the 'yoke' of the 'Cross' [Lk. 9:23]), *and learn of Me* (learn of His Sacrifice [Rom. 6:3-5]); *for I am meek and lowly in heart* (the only thing that our Lord Personally said of Himself): *and you shall find rest unto your souls* (the

soul can find rest only in the Cross).

"For My Yoke is easy, and My Burden is light (what He requires of us is very little, just to have Faith in Him, and His Sacrificial Atoning Work)" (Mat. 11:28-30).

The phrase, *"All you who labor and are heavy laden,"* is interesting indeed!

It means, *"To be fatigued, to be wearied."* Heavy laden means to *"be overburdened with ceremony and spiritual anxiety."* All of this relates to the Believer trying to live for God by means of *"doing,"* in other words, *"works."*

Or else, the Believer is trying to find victory in his life by employing wrong means, which is the plight of most modern Believers. They either do not know anything about the Cross as it refers to Sanctification, or else, they do not believe what they do know about the Cross and, therefore, resort to other things.

THE PROBLEM IS SIN

Even though the modern church claims many things, the truth is, the problem is sin. The sin may be *"overt,"* which refers to that which is outward, or it may be *"covert,"* which means hidden, but, still, the problem is sin.

The modern church doesn't seem to believe that, so it claims all types of difficulties and problems as the culprit.

Whenever the Holy Spirit gives us through Paul God's Prescribed Order of Victory, which is found in Romans, Chapter 6, the Chapter begins with the problem, which is sin. It says:

"What shall we say then? (This is meant to direct attention to Rom. 5:20.) *Shall we continue in sin, that Grace may abound?* (Just because Grace is greater than sin doesn't mean that the Believer has a license to sin.)

"God forbid (presents Paul's answer to the question, *'Away with the thought, let not such a thing occur'*). *How shall we, who are dead to sin* (dead to the sin nature), *live any longer therein?* (This portrays what the Believer is now in Christ)" (Rom. 6:1-2).

After telling us that the problem is sin, then the Holy Spirit through Paul emphatically tells us what the Solution is. It is the Cross of Christ. He said:

"Know you not, that so many of us as were baptized into Jesus Christ (plainly says that this Baptism is into Christ and not water [I Cor. 1:17; 12:13; Gal. 3:27; Eph. 4:5; Col. 2:11-13]) *were baptized into His Death?* (When Christ died on the Cross, in the Mind of God, we died with Him; in other words, He became our Substitute, and our identification with Him in His Death gives us all the benefits for which He died; the idea is that He did it all for us!)

"Therefore we are buried with Him by baptism into death (not only did we die with Him, but we were buried with Him as well, which means that all the sin and transgression of the past were buried; when they put Him in the Tomb, they put all of our sins into that Tomb as well): *that like as Christ was raised up from the dead by the Glory of the Father, even so we also should walk in Newness of Life* (we died with Him, we were buried with Him, and His Resurrection was our Resurrection to a *'Newness of Life'*).

"For if we have been planted together (with Christ) *in the likeness of His Death* (Paul proclaims the Cross as the instrument through which all Blessings come; consequently, the Cross must ever be the Object of our Faith, which gives the Holy Spirit latitude to work within our lives), *we shall be also in the likeness of His Resurrection* (we can have the *'likeness of His Resurrection,'* i.e., *'live this Resurrection Life,'* only as long as we understand the *'likeness of His Death,'* which refers to the Cross as the Means by which all of this is done)" (Rom. 6:3-5).

So, in those above Passages, we have the problem, which is sin, and the solution to that problem, which is *"Jesus Christ and Him Crucified."* In fact, Paul spells it out so succinctly as to how all of this is done that there is no excuse for the Believer looking elsewhere. It is the Cross where all Victory was won, which speaks of the Sacrificial, Atoning Death of the Lord Jesus Christ in the shedding of His Precious Blood, which atoned for all sin, past, present and future, at least for all who will believe (Jn. 3:16).

If the Believer attempts to come against sin by any means other than Faith in Christ and the Cross, the end result will be, *"labor and heavy laden."* If he comes against it with Faith in Christ and the Cross and not allow his Faith to be moved elsewhere but takes up the Cross daily, even as Jesus demanded, he will find peace and rest which passes all understanding. Once again, as always, it is in the Cross!

(8) "AND ASA HAD AN ARMY OF MEN WHO BORE TARGETS AND SPEARS, OUT OF JUDAH THREE HUNDRED THOUSAND; AND OUT OF BENJAMIN, WHO BORE SHIELDS AND DREW BOWS, TWO HUNDRED AND FOURSCORE THOUSAND: ALL THESE WERE MIGHTY MEN OF VALOUR."

The exegesis is:

1. (Vs. 8) The Holy Spirit here alludes to the power of Judah. When people are right with God, they have power over the enemy (Acts 1:8).

2. The cause and reason for this power is that Judah was right with God; consequently, Blessings upon Blessings followed.

3. These 580,000 men were *"mighty men of valor,"* and were labeled such by the Holy Spirit.

MIGHTY MEN OF VALOR

We must remember that it was the Holy Spirit Who labeled these soldiers as *"mighty men of valor."* In other words, it was the Lord Who was their strength.

As the evidence will show in the following Passages, Asa, as strong and powerful as his army was, did not depend upon that army but rather on the Lord.

That's the way the Lord works!

He blesses us, and sometimes abundantly, even as He did Judah; however, we are not to depend upon those Blessings, whatever they might be, and as wonderful as they are, but our dependence is always to be on the Lord.

The Lord is not predisposed to save by many or few. He is able to do whatever needs to be done, whenever it needs to be done, and however it needs to be done, and to be dependent on nothing or no one. In fact, the Lord is not dependent on anything or anybody. He is totally independent as it regards His Personal Ability.

(9) "AND THERE CAME OUT AGAINST THEM ZERAH THE ETHIOPIAN WITH AN HOST OF A THOUSAND THOUSAND, AND THREE HUNDRED CHARIOTS; AND CAME UNTO MARESHAH.

(10) "THEN ASA WENT OUT AGAINST HIM, AND THEY SET THE BATTLE IN ARRAY IN THE VALLEY OF ZEPHATHAH AT MARESHAH.

(11) "AND ASA CRIED UNTO THE LORD HIS GOD, AND SAID, LORD, IT IS NOTHING WITH YOU TO HELP, WHETHER WITH MANY, OR WITH THEM WHO HAVE NO POWER: HELP US, O LORD OUR GOD; FOR WE REST ON YOU, AND IN YOUR NAME WE GO AGAINST THIS MULTITUDE. O LORD, YOU ARE OUR GOD; LET NOT MAN PREVAIL AGAINST YOU.

(12) "SO THE LORD SMOTE THE ETHIOPIANS BEFORE ASA, AND BEFORE JUDAH; AND THE ETHIOPIANS FLED.

(13) "AND ASA AND THE PEOPLE WHO WERE WITH HIM PURSUED THEM UNTO GERAR: AND THE ETHIOPIANS WERE OVERTHROWN, THAT THEY COULD NOT RECOVER THEMSELVES; FOR THEY WERE DESTROYED BEFORE THE LORD, AND BEFORE HIS HOST; AND THEY CARRIED AWAY VERY MUCH SPOIL.

(14) "AND THEY SMOTE ALL THE CITIES ROUND ABOUT GERAR; FOR THE FEAR OF THE LORD CAME UPON THEM: AND THEY SPOILED ALL THE CITIES; FOR THERE WAS EXCEEDING MUCH SPOIL IN THEM.

(15) "THEY SMOTE ALSO THE TENTS OF CATTLE, AND CARRIED AWAY SHEEP AND CAMELS IN ABUNDANCE, AND RETURNED TO JERUSALEM."

The pattern is:

1. (Vs. 11) Even though Asa, in fact, did have a mighty army, still, he did not rely on such. He *"cried unto the LORD."*

2. (Vs. 11) All too often blessing and prosperity, even though from God, can turn the hearts and the heads of men away from God, but Asa seems, at least at this time, to have trusted solely in the Lord. If God does bless us with money and numbers, fine, well, and good; however, we must never look to these things, but always, and only, to the Lord.

3. The Holy Spirit in Verse 12 is quick to

proclaim the fact that it was the Lord Who brought about this great victory.

4. The *"very much spoil"* of Verse 13 is the Way of the Lord! Instead of Satan taking all that we have in the Lord, we are to take all that he has. It can be done only if the Believer will place his Faith exclusively in Christ and the Cross. Then the Holy Spirit will Work mightily on our behalf, even as He did here for Asa (Rom. 8:1-2, 11).

5. (Vs. 14) The area around Gerar constituted the extreme southern portion of Judah, in fact, that which bordered Egypt. If the Believer has forfeited any of his spiritual inheritance to Satan, it must be regained, and can be regained, and in totality.

6. (Vs. 15) This great victory dated the commencement of a period of comparative internal peace and reform for the kingdom of Judah, which lasted some 21 years, and all because of trust in God.

HELP US, O LORD OUR GOD

The Ninth Verse records the efforts of Satan to destroy the Blessing that God had given unto Judah, for it says concerning the Ethiopians, *"A thousand thousand, and three hundred chariots."* These one million men that came against Judah were the largest number of any army given to us in the Bible. We must always remember, Satan comes as a *"roaring lion."*

Asa said to the Lord as it regarded this mighty army, *"LORD, it is nothing with You to help, whether with many, or with them who have no power."* Ethiopia's one million men had no effect on God whatsoever. Asa is saying that God could use many or a few; numbers mean nothing to Him; obstacles mean nothing to Him. Asa says, *"For we rest on You, and in Your Name we go against this multitude."*

This is the secret of Victory for every Child of God. The authority of the Believer is the privilege of using the mighty *"Name of Jesus."* Jesus said, *"In My Name shall they cast out demons; they shall speak with new Tongues; they shall take up* (in the Greek, put away) *serpents; and if they drink any deadly thing, it shall not hurt them; they shall lay hands on the sick, and they shall recover"* (Mk. 16:17-18).

WHAT IS THE AUTHORITY OF THE BELIEVER?

The authority of the Believer pertains to authority over demon spirits and even Satan himself. It is never authority over other human beings.

The Believer has the right to use the Mighty Name of Jesus. And we must remember, the Power of that Name is not predicated on the power of the individual using it.

A PERSONAL EXPERIENCE

If I remember correctly, the year was 1953. Frances and I were married in 1952, and Donnie was born in 1954. This happened before Donnie was born.

Having just married, Frances and I lived in a tiny mobile home. In fact, it was parked next to the parsonage where my mother and dad resided. It was in the little town of Wisner in northeastern Louisiana.

My dad had built the church there in 1950, and for a country church, it was a thriving congregation, with hundreds of people who had been influenced by the Gospel, and with hundreds giving their hearts and lives to Christ. Frances and I, of course, were very much involved in the Church.

I was just beginning to preach the Gospel, with most of my Services conducted on street corners, as Frances and I would take a number of young people from the Church and conduct Services in surrounding towns.

At a particular time, which led up to the incident at hand, the oppressive powers of darkness seemed to be very severe. I don't remember the cause of the occasion; I just remember the night in question.

Frances had gone to bed, and I had stayed up, endeavoring to read my Bible. I couldn't read for it seemed like the words ran together. I remember leaving out of the little mobile home and walking up and down the street outside, trying to pray, but again, to no avail.

As stated, I don't remember the cause of the oppression, or what had taken place to bring me to this point. I only remember the night at hand and the powers of darkness that I was contesting.

I finally went to bed and drifted off into a

troubled sleep.

THE DREAM

It must have been sometime close to daylight when I had the dream, or else the dream lasted for several hours. At any rate, I dreamed that I was in a house, a house with which I was not familiar.

In the dream, I wondered as to why I was there. I didn't recognize anything in the house and, in fact, the room I was in, which was the front room, was barren of all furniture. There were no windows in the room, only a front door that led outside.

Surveying the situation, a tremendous fear came over me, and my thoughts were, *"I've got to get out of this place."* As stated, I did not know where I was, or why I was there. I just knew I had to leave.

I turned to go toward the door when, all of a sudden, I saw standing in the doorway the most hideous looking being that words could ever begin to describe. The thing standing before me seemed to stand about seven or eight feet tall and had the body of a bear and the face of a man. I will never forget it!

On the face or the countenance of this beast was the most horrid look of evil that anyone could ever surmise. But it was the eyes that seemed to be the most evil of all.

The thing said nothing but slowly began to lumber toward me as if to say, *"I have you now."*

As I looked at this thing slowly coming toward me, strength instantly seemed to drain from my body, and my legs simply would not hold me up. I fell to the floor, unable to stand.

In my weakened condition, I began to feel around over the floor, looking for something to try to defend myself, as if it would have done me any good, had there been anything there. But there was nothing there.

The Scripture plainly tells us, *"For the weapons of our warfare are not carnal, but mighty through God to the pulling down of strongholds"* (II Cor. 10:4).

THE NAME OF JESUS

Without premeditation, I screamed it as loud as I could, *"In the Name of Jesus."*

NOTES

Even though I exerted every effort, still, my voice was no more than a whisper. But I was to learn that the Power of that Name did not rest upon the power of the one using it. Thank God for that for I had no power or strength.

Even though my efforts were so weak, me lying flat on my back on the floor, unable to stand, still, when I uttered that Name, the beast screamed and clutched its head as if somebody had hit it with a ball bat.

It began to stagger around across the floor, continuing to scream in pain and clutching its head, and I began to gather strength by the moment.

I said it again, *"In the Name of Jesus."* This time, my voice carried more strength. When I said it the second time, the beast fell to the floor, and now, as I gathered strength, I was standing on my feet.

Actually, I was standing over this horrid thing, watching it writhe on the floor, still clutching its head. Before, it had been standing over me, and now I was standing over it.

I said it the third time, *"In the Name of Jesus."* This time, I exerted no strength whatsoever, but yet, my voice sounded like it was connected to a powerful P.A. system, with it literally vibrating off the walls.

When I said it the third time, *"In the Name of Jesus,"* I heard something coming toward me. It was the *"sound of the Mighty Rushing Wind."*

I did not see anything, but I heard it, and I will never forget it. That which they heard on the Day of Pentecost, I heard it that night in the dream. Unmistakably, it was the Holy Spirit.

Even though, as stated, I saw nothing, as the sound grew louder and louder, it came through that room, hit that thing on the floor, and blew it out the door as if it were a piece of tissue paper. I remember in the dream running to the door, looking outside as that thing wafted away like a leaf on the wind. And it was gone!

Just about daylight, I awakened. I literally woke myself up, speaking with other Tongues. I lay there for some time, worshipping the Lord, praying and praising in Tongues, as the Spirit of God filled my soul.

There is Power in that Mighty Name of Jesus. I know, for I have experienced it.

WHAT DID THE DREAM MEAN?

At the time I really did not know exactly what it meant. I knew the Lord was telling me of His great Power and especially the Power of His Name, but I did not know exactly as to how it related to me, except the situation at hand, as it regarded the present oppression. I believe I have come to understand what it meant as the years followed.

I believe the Lord was telling me that night that Satan would try to destroy me. He would come close to succeeding. And I believe he told me that night that the Power of the Name of Jesus would see me through, and Victory would be mine.

I also believe that He related to me in the dream that my Spiritual Strength after this terrible ordeal would be greater than ever, not through anything that I had done, but all because of the Lord Jesus Christ and His Power to save.

Yes, the Believer has authority, but, as stated, it is over the powers of darkness. We should use that Name more often in this realm, for in the spirit realm is where most difficulties begin.

VERY MUCH SPOIL

Of course, whenever the people of God, as Asa and Judah, begin to grow closer to the Lord, and the Lord begins to bless, Satan will always rear his ugly head, attempting to stop the Move of God. He did it this time with the Ethiopians coming against Asa with a million-man army. That's exactly the way that Satan works. He comes against us with what looks like an overwhelming force. But, it's exactly as Asa said:

"LORD, it is nothing with You to help, whether with many, or with them who have no power."

In other words, the Lord is not helped or hindered by whatever man does but according to what the Lord wants to do. He is Almighty, meaning that nothing is beyond His Ability.

But Asa did that which he should have done as he was faced with this overwhelming force. And yet, it was overwhelming only in the sense of looking at it in the natural. The truth is according to the following:

God and one man are a majority in any situation. While Asa did not have an army nearly as large as the Ethiopians, still, he had the majority of the power, simply because the Lord was on the side of Judah.

Whatever the individual does, he must make certain that he's on the Lord's Side. That means he is doing his very best to obey the Word of God. That being the case, Victory is assured.

What exactly the Lord did with the Ethiopians the Scripture doesn't say. It just merely states, "So, the LORD smote the Ethiopians before Asa, and before Judah; and the Ethiopians fled."

If we resist the Devil, and do so in the Name of Jesus, understanding that our Victory is in Christ and what He did at the Cross, the Evil One will flee. Now the upshot was this:

The Ethiopians were planning on taking a great spoil, but the facts were, they lost the battle and, as well, lost everything that was with them, whatever that may have been. And it was a lot!

The Scripture says, "And they (Judah) carried away very much spoil."

It also says, "They (Judah) spoiled all the cities." And then, "For there was exceeding much spoil in them."

And finally, "They smote also the tents of cattle, and carried away sheep and camels in abundance, and returned to Jerusalem."

But they returned in victory and about ten times richer than when they began.

You are reading in this Fourteenth Chapter of II Chronicles the Ways of the Lord, that is, when people truly trust Him. What He did for Asa, He will do for you and me. Believe Him, and prosper!

"Holy as Thou, O Lord, is none!
"Your Holiness is all Your Own;
"A drop of that unbounded sea,
"Is ours, a drop derived from Thee."

"And when Your Purity we share,
"Your only Glory we declare;
"And humbled into nothing own,
"Holy and Pure is God Alone."

"Sole, self-existing God and Lord,

"By all Your heavenly Hosts adored;
"Let all on Earth bow down to Thee,
"And own Your peerless Majesty:"

"Your Power unparalleled confessed,
"Established on the Rock of Peace;
"Thee Rock that never shall remove,
"Thee Rock of Pure, Almighty Love."

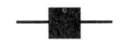

CHAPTER 15

(1) "AND THE SPIRIT OF GOD CAME UPON AZARIAH THE SON OF ODED:

(2) "AND HE WENT OUT TO MEET ASA, AND SAID UNTO HIM, HEAR YOU ME, ASA, AND ALL JUDAH AND BENJAMIN; THE LORD IS WITH YOU, WHILE YOU BE WITH HIM; AND IF YOU SEEK HIM, HE WILL BE FOUND OF YOU; BUT IF YOU FORSAKE HIM, HE WILL FORSAKE YOU.

(3) "NOW FOR A LONG SEASON ISRAEL HAS BEEN WITHOUT THE TRUE GOD, AND WITHOUT A TEACHING PRIEST, AND WITHOUT LAW.

(4) "BUT WHEN THEY IN THEIR TROUBLE DID TURN UNTO THE LORD GOD OF ISRAEL, AND SOUGHT HIM, HE WAS FOUND OF THEM.

(5) "AND IN THOSE TIMES THERE WAS NO PEACE TO HIM WHO WENT OUT, NOR TO HIM WHO CAME IN, BUT GREAT VEXATIONS WERE UPON ALL THE INHABITANTS OF THE COUNTRIES.

(6) "AND NATION WAS DESTROYED OF NATION, AND CITY OF CITY: FOR GOD DID VEX THEM WITH ALL ADVERSITY.

(7) "BE YOU STRONG THEREFORE, AND LET NOT YOUR HANDS BE WEAK: FOR YOUR WORK SHALL BE REWARDED."

The exegesis is:

1. Verse 1 is the only place in the Bible that the Prophet Azariah is mentioned.

2. (Vs. 2) Three things are here said:

• The Lord is with you while you are with Him.

• If you seek Him, He will be found of you.

• If you forsake Him, He will forsake you.

These eternal facts are true of an individual or a nation, Jews or Gentiles, people under Law or under Grace, in one age as well as another.

3. Verse 3 probably refers to the last years of Solomon, the fourteen years of Rehoboam's reign (II Chron. 11:17; 12:1), and the three years of Abijah's reign (I Ki. 15:1-4).

4. Verse 4 proclaims that the Promise is clear. God will not forsake those who turn to Him and seek Him. The Scripture is emphatic: *"He was found of them."*

5. (Vs. 6) Even though Israel constituted His chosen People, called of Him and loved of Him, still, when they turned their backs on Him, spiritually speaking, He would *"vex them with all adversity."* God desires to bless us, but, if we desire to oppose Him, He will, instead, *"vex us,"* and He does it in order to bring us to our spiritual senses.

6. (Vs. 7) The admonishment by the Holy Spirit was then and is now, *"Be strong"* (I Cor. 16:13; Eph. 6:10; II Tim. 2:1).

THE SPIRIT OF GOD

The *"Spirit of God,"* as should be obvious, pertains to the Holy Spirit.

If it is to be noticed, it says that *"the Spirit of God came upon Azariah the son of Oded."* In Old Testament times the Holy Spirit was limited as to what He could do, even in the godliest, because the blood of bulls and goats could not take away sins, which means that the sin-debt remained.

In fact, before the Cross, when Believers died, they were not taken to Heaven, but their soul and spirit went down into Paradise, or as Jesus referred to it, *"Abraham's bosom."* There are five parts to the underworld of departed spirits. The entirety of the region is referred to as *"Hades,"* or *"Hell."* The five different parts are:

1. Paradise or Abraham's bosom: This was where all Believers went before the Cross. Even though they were Saved by looking forward to the coming Redeemer, Who would be the Lord Jesus Christ, in a sense, they were still captives of Satan because the sin-debt remained. Animal blood was woefully insufficient to cleanse the slate, so to speak, that awaiting the Cross of Christ (Lk. 16:19-31). Actually, that place is now empty because, upon His Death at Calvary's

Cross, Jesus liberated all the multitudinous souls who were there. That's what Paul was talking about when he said, *"Wherefore He said* (Ps. 68:18), *When He* (Jesus) *ascended up on high* (the Ascension), *He led captivity captive"* (Eph. 4:8).

The strange statement, *"He led captivity captive,"* simply means that Jesus made all the Old Testament Saints His Captives, which means the captivity of Satan was broken. While in this place, Satan could not harm them, still, due to the sin-debt, they were not yet free. Jesus set them free. Now, when Believers die, which refers to all the time since the Cross, their soul and their spirit immediately go to be with Christ in Heaven (Phil. 1:23).

2. Hell: This is where every unbeliever has gone when they died, even from the time of Adam to this particular moment. It is a place of torment and is described in Luke 16:19-31.

3. Prison: According to the Word of God, there is a prison in this underworld where certain fallen Angels are incarcerated. The Scripture says: *"By which also He* (Jesus) *went* (between the time of His Death and Resurrection) *and preached* (announced something) *unto the spirits in prison* (does not refer to humans, but rather to fallen Angels; humans in the Bible are never referred to in this particular manner; these were probably the fallen Angels who tried to corrupt the human race by cohabiting with women [II Pet. 2:4; Jude, Vss. 6-7]; these fallen Angels are still locked up in this underworld prison);

"Which sometime (in times past) *were disobedient* (this was shortly before the Flood), *when once the longsuffering of God waited in the days of Noah* (refers to this eruption of fallen Angels with women taking place at the time of Noah; this was probably a hundred or so years before the Flood), *while the Ark was a preparing* (these fallen Angels were committing this particular sin while the Ark was being made ready, however long it took; the Scripture doesn't say!)" (I Pet. 3:19-20).

The word translated *"preached,"* as used by Peter, is not the normal Greek word used for preaching. The word he used actually means that Jesus announced something to these fallen Angels. What it was, we aren't told.

Incidentally, these were Angels who threw in their lot with Lucifer when he led his rebellion against God sometime in eternity past. This particular group, which participated in this particular sin, were, no doubt, powerful Angels but made the terrible mistake of throwing in their lot with the Evil One.

How large this prison is, we aren't told, or how many fallen Angels are there incarcerated, as well, we aren't told. One thing is certain, they will be cast into the Lake of Fire at the Great White Throne Judgment.

4. The bottomless pit: This is another part of the underworld, but which will play a great part in things to come. The Scripture says concerning this place:

"And I saw an Angel come down from Heaven (continues with the idea that Angels are very prominent in the Plan and Work of God), *having the key of the bottomless pit* (speaks of the same place recorded in Rev. 9:1; however, there the key is given to Satan, but this Angel of Rev. 20:1 *'has the key,'* implying that he has had it all along; more than likely, God allows this Angel to give the key to Satan in Rev. 9:1) *and a great chain in his hand* (should be taken literally).

"And he laid hold on the dragon, that old serpent, which is the Devil, and Satan (as a *'dragon,'* he shows his power; as a *'serpent,'* he shows his cunning; as the *'Devil,'* he is the accuser; and as *'Satan,'* he is the adversary), *and bound him a thousand years* (refers to being bound by the great chain carried by the Angel),

"And cast him into the bottomless pit, and shut him up, and set a seal upon him (speaks of the abyss being sealed to keep him there), *that he should deceive the nations no more, till the thousand years should be fulfilled: and after that he must be loosed a little season.* (At the end of the thousand-year period, Satan will be loosed out of his prison. He will make another attempt to deceive the nations, in which he will not succeed. We aren't told how long this *'little season'* will be. As well, more than likely, all fallen Angels and demon spirits will be incarcerated with him in this place)" (Rev. 20:1-3).

5. The Lake of Fire: Concerning this place, the Scripture says: *"And the Devil who deceived them was cast into the Lake of Fire and brimstone* (marks the end of Satan regarding his influence in the world and, in fact, in any part of the Creation of God), *where the Beast and the False Prophet are* (proclaims the fact that these two were placed in *'the Lake of Fire and brimstone'* some 1,000 years earlier [Rev. 19:20]), *and shall be tormented day and night forever and ever.* (This signifies the eternity of this place. It is a matter of interest to note that Satan's first act is recorded in Gen., Chpt. 3 [the Third Chapter from the beginning], whereas his last act on a worldwide scale is mentioned in Rev., Chpt. 20 [the Third Chapter from the end].)

"And whosoever was not found written in the Book of Life (refers to the record of all the Redeemed) *was cast into the Lake of Fire.* (This includes every single individual who isn't Redeemed, beginning with Adam and Eve, that is, if they didn't come back to God)" (Rev. 20:10, 15).

However, Jesus, the Son of the Living God, the Creator of the Ages, came down to this mortal coil for one purpose, and that was to go to the Cross, where man would be redeemed, at least those who would believe. This means that mankind doesn't have to go to Hell. That's why the Gospel is referred to as *"good news."* It's good news to the sinner who is lost that he can be Saved. It's good news to those bound by the terrible ravages of sin that that bondage can be broken. It's good news to the alcoholic and to the drug addict that they can be free. In fact, it's good news to all mankind, whoever they might be, and wherever they might be, that Jesus Saves, and His Blood washes whiter than snow.

The Lord did not devise Hell for mankind but rather for Satan and his Angels. If men go there, it will be because they have refused God's Answer to their dilemma and have chosen rather to follow Satan. That means the old adage is true, *"There is a Hell to shun and a Heaven to gain."* The Old Rugged Cross has made the difference.

THE WAYS OF GOD

The Spirit of the Lord said to the people of Judah and Benjamin, *"The LORD is with you, while you be with Him; and if you seek Him, He will be found of you; but if you forsake Him, He will forsake you."*

In this Passage we find three eternal and unchangeable facts, which are as apropos today as they were when they were uttered nearly 3,000 years ago. They are:

1. The Lord is with you while you are with Him.

2. If you seek Him, He will be found of you.

3. If you forsake Him, He will forsake you.

The Lord is with a person as that person is with Him. Now, what does that mean?

It does not mean sinless perfection, for the Bible does not teach such. But it does mean that the individual has a heart after God and, thereby, desires the things of God. It means that such a person wants to please God, that he takes his Salvation seriously, and he ever seeks to grow closer to the Lord. He loves the Lord, loves the Word of God, and loves the Ways of God. For that type of individual, the Lord will be with him.

Then we have the beautiful Promise which tells us that if we seek the Lord, He will be found of us. That's a Promise given by the Lord, and it pertains to any and every living soul, irrespective as to who they may be, or where they may reside, etc. Understanding this, that means there is no excuse for anyone to not find the Lord and His Ways, if they earnestly seek the Lord and His Ways. This is the key to all happiness, the key to all joy, the key to all fulfillment in life, and is available to all.

And then we have the warning that if we forsake Him, He, in turn, will forsake us. In fact, He has no choice. Can two walk together unless they be agreed?

If an individual doesn't want the Lord and, thereby, walks away from Him, there is nothing the Lord can do but allow that person that particular choice, which is the road to destruction. Let not the person think that he can forsake the Ways of the Lord, ignore the Word of God, go into sin, and still have the Lord with him. Such is not to be.

WITHOUT THE LORD

The Scripture says, *"Now for a long*

season Israel has been without the True God, and without a teaching Priest, and without Law." As to exactly what time the Spirit of the Lord through Azariah is speaking, we aren't told.

Some Hebrew scholars claim the translation is somewhat wrong, and that it should be translated, *"And many the days to Israel to not have the True God, and to not have teaching Priests, and to not have the Law."*

That translation is probably correct. It means for great periods of time, Israel walked away from the Lord and ignored the Law, with the Priests unable to teach the Law, or because the Priesthood was corrupt.

This was very much true oftentimes during the period of the Judges. It was also true during the time of Saul after Samuel the great Prophet died. It was true during the last years of Solomon and during the 14 years of Rehoboam's reign (II Chron. 11:17; 12:1), and could possibly include some three years of Abijah's reign (I Ki. 15:1-4).

During those times, even though the Lord gave warning after warning and extended Grace so very often, still, when the people would not turn, oftentimes, heathen nations were allowed to come in and to cause Israel great difficulties.

Believers should understand that we are not in the same league as the unredeemed. We are bought with a price, meaning that we actually aren't our own any longer. We belong to the Lord. If we stray, the Holy Spirit will use Mercy and Grace to try to bring us back. But, if that fails, ultimately, and because He loves us so much, He will bring judgment upon us, with Israel being the great example.

If, in fact, a Believer is straying and there is no judgment ever, meaning there is no chastisement, it can possibly be said of that person that he really isn't Saved.

CHASTISEMENT

The Scripture says concerning chastisement: *"And you have forgotten the exhortation which speaks unto you as unto children* (the Apostle's objective in introducing this here is to show that afflictions are designed, on the part of God, to produce positive effects in the lives of His People), *My son,*

NOTES

despise not you the chastening of the Lord, nor faint when you are rebuked of Him (everything that happens to a Believer is either caused or allowed by the Lord; consequently, we should learn the lesson desired to be taught):

"For whom the Lord loves He chastens (God disciplines those He loves, not those to whom He is indifferent), *and scourges every son whom He receives.* (This refers to all who truly belong to Him.)

"If you endure chastening, God deals with you as with sons (chastening from the Lord guarantees the fact that one is a Child of God); *for what son is he whom the father chastens not?* (If an earthly father truly cares for his son, he will use whatever measures necessary to bring the boy into line. If an earthly father will do this, how much more will our Heavenly Father do the same?)

"But if you be without chastisement, whereof all (all true Believers) *are partakers, then are you bastards, and not sons.* (Many claim to be Believers while continuing in sin, but the Lord never chastises them. Such shows they are illegitimate sons, meaning they are claiming faith on a basis other than the Cross. The true son, without doubt, will be chastised at times.)

"Furthermore we have had fathers of our flesh which corrected us, and we gave them reverence (earthly parents): *shall we not much rather be in subjection unto the Father of Spirits, and live?* ('Father of Spirits' is contrasted to 'Fathers of the flesh.' The latter concerns our earthly parents. Their relation to us is limited. His is universal and eternal.)

"For they verily for a few days chastened us after their own pleasure (the use of the word 'pleasure' indicates that the chastening may or may not have been proper, as it regards our earthly parents); *but He for our profit* (presents the difference between human liability of error and the perfect knowledge of our Heavenly Father; He seeks our profit, and cannot err in the means He employs), *that we might be partakers of His Holiness.* (This presents the objective of the chastening and correction of God.)

"Now no chastening for the present seems to be joyous, but grievous (presents the fact

that the trials we are at times exposed to do not give joy at that moment, and are often hard indeed to bear): *nevertheless afterward it yields the peaceable fruit of Righteousness unto them which are exercised thereby.* (All of this is carried out by the Holy Spirit for a specific purpose [Jn. 15:1-9])" (Heb. 12:5-11).

THE MODERN CHURCH

Even though the following words may seem to be strong, nevertheless, I believe them to be true.

The modern church, I believe, is in worse spiritual condition than it has been at any time since the Reformation. Fewer people are presently being Saved than at any time regarding this. Fewer Believers are being baptized presently with the Holy Spirit than at any time since the turn of the Twentieth Century. For all practical purposes, the modern church is without God and without godly Pastors who will teach them the True Word of God.

The modern church needs a reformation. That means a return to the Word of God, a return to the Ways of God, and, thereby, a return to the Lord. That means the modern church must return to the Cross. It has abandoned the Cross, replacing it instead with its own stratagems and schemes. All of it looks good to the eye, exactly as Cain's altar looked good to the eye. But God cannot accept anything that is birthed by man. And please understand, the modern way has been conceived by man, birthed by man, instituted by man, and carried out by man. As such, it is totally unacceptable to the Lord. The Lord can accept that alone which is conceived by the Holy Spirit. And that requires godly individuals through whom the Lord can work, of which there are precious few at present.

REPENTANCE

The Scripture says, *"But when they in their trouble did turn unto the LORD God of Israel, and sought Him, He was found of them."*

This was not only the case with Israel but is the case with anyone and everyone, whoever they may be, and wherever they may be. If they earnestly turn to the Lord God, which means that they confess their sins before Him, and their hearts are truly desirous of obeying the Lord, meaning that they sincerely seek Him, the Scripture emphatically and even dogmatically states, *"He was found of them,"* i.e., *"He will be found of them."*

WHAT IS TRUE REPENTANCE?

Please understand that God will honor any type of Repentance, irrespective of the fact that it might not be as Scriptural as it should be. I will explain momentarily. The Lord is not holding the standard so high that it's impossible for men to reach it. As well, He knows our weaknesses, the tendencies of the flesh, which means that we are prone to go in the wrong direction. So, if there is any type of Repentance that is forthcoming, irrespective that it's not quite what it ought to be, the Lord most definitely will honor it, at least as far as He can do so. Now, let's look at what true Repentance actually is, that which the Lord truly desires of us, and which will reap the greatest results.

The greatest sin of any individual is not so much the act of sin, whatever that might be, but rather what causes it in the first place. And what is it that causes us to sin as Believers?

It is when we resort to the flesh instead of the Spirit of God. Now, what does that mean?

No Believer is immune from temptation, meaning there is nothing we can do that will stop all temptation. The Lord allows Satan certain latitude, all in order for us to be strengthened.

The only way the Believer can successfully live for God, can overcome the Evil One, can throw aside temptation, and can be what one ought to be in the Lord, is that his Faith be exclusively in Christ and what Christ has done for us at the Cross. That gives the Holy Spirit, Who Alone can do that which is needed, latitude to work within our lives, and to bring forth the desired results, which is Victory upon Victory. When the Believer fails the Lord, it's because his faith has been shifted from the Cross of Christ to something else. To be sure, the something else, no doubt, looks very appealing and, in fact, may be correct and right in its own way. So, we load it up with Scriptures, use the Name of Jesus, and think we're on the right track when all the time, we're going in the opposite direction. Let us say it again:

It is the Cross of Christ through which the Holy Spirit works, without Whom we cannot do anything. He will not work outside of the benefits of the Cross, for, in fact, the Cross is a legal work, which gave Him, and gives Him, the latitude to do all the things which He can do.

Let's look at the proximity of the Holy Spirit and Christ, and above that, Christ as the slain Lamb. We are given a perfect example in the great Book of Revelation.

I'm going to quote directly from THE EXPOSITOR'S STUDY BIBLE:

"And I beheld, and, lo, in the midst of the Throne and of the four Beasts, and in the midst of the Elders, stood a Lamb as it had been slain (the Crucifixion of Christ is represented here by the word 'Lamb,' which refers to the fact that it was the Cross which redeemed mankind; the slain Lamb Alone has redeemed all things), *having seven horns* (horns denote dominion, and 'seven' denotes total dominion; all of this was done for you and me, meaning that we can have total dominion over the powers of darkness, and in every capacity; so there is no excuse for a lack of victory) *and seven eyes* (denotes total, perfect, pure, and complete illumination of all things spiritual, which is again made possible for you and me by the Cross; if the Believer makes the Cross the Object of his Faith, he will never be drawn away by false doctrine), *which are the Seven Spirits of God sent forth into all the Earth* (signifying that the Holy Spirit, in all His Perfection and Universality, functions entirely within the parameters of the Finished Work of Christ; in other words, it is required that we ever make the Cross the Object of our Faith, which gives the Holy Spirit latitude, and guarantees the 'dominion,' and the 'illumination' [Isa. 11:2; Rom. 8:2])" (Rev. 5:6).

In the Vision given to John as he wrote this Book of Revelation, the Lord made it very easy for the Apostle to understand what he was seeing. It is as follows:

NOTES

• It portrays Jesus Christ in the very midst of the Throne, meaning that the only way to the Throne of God is by and through the slain Lamb (Heb. 4:16).

• Jesus is presented as a *"Lamb as it had been slain,"* referring to the fact that without the Cross, there is no access to the Throne of God or anything pertaining to God. While Christ is the Source, the Cross is the Means.

• This Lamb had *"seven horns,"* which denotes dominion, in fact, total dominion, inasmuch as *"seven"* denotes perfection. In effect, this means that we can have total Victory within our hearts and lives as it regards living for God, but only as we place our Faith in the Cross of Christ, and maintain our Faith in the Cross of Christ.

• This slain Lamb also had *"seven eyes."* As we stated in the notes, this denotes illumination and, in fact, once again, due to the number *"seven,"* perfect illumination. This means that no Believer can properly understand the Word of God unless his Faith is properly placed in the Cross.

• And then we are told that these *"seven horns"* and *"seven eyes"* are the *"Seven Spirits of God sent forth into all the Earth."* This doesn't mean that there are seven Holy Spirits, but rather, it denotes the Perfection of the Holy Spirit, once again, proven by the word *"seven,"* which is God's Number of Perfection and Universality.

• This which the Lord has done is for all men everywhere, proven by the words *"sent forth into all the Earth."*

• It must be noticed that the *"Holy Spirit"* and the *"slain Lamb"* are so closely connected as to be indivisible, in other words, inseparable. That's how close the Spirit of God works with that which Christ has done on the Cross. As stated, the Work of Christ on the Cross was a legal work, satisfying the demands of a thrice-Holy God and, thereby, giving the Holy Spirit latitude to work. In fact, what Jesus did at the Cross alone gives the Holy Spirit the liberty to do what He Alone can do. That's why it is demanded of Believers that our Faith be placed in the Cross of Christ alone, and maintained in the Cross of Christ alone (Gen. 3:15; 4:4; 15:6; Isa., Chpt. 53; Mat. 1:1; Rom. 6:1-14; 8:1-2,

11; I Cor. 1:17-18, 21, 23; 2:2; Gal., Chpt. 5; 6:14; Eph. 2:13-18; Col. 2:14-15).

The idea of all of this, at least as it regards Repentance, is that the Believer must not only repent of the evil that's been done, but of the good as well. By the *"good"* we refer to the Believer depending on the good things he does to bring him Righteousness or closeness with God. It never has, and it never will.

It is easy for the Believer to repent of the evil but not so easy for the good. But the so-called good in the Eyes of God is just as evil as that which we think of as evil. Our so-called good is evil simply because we have placed our faith and trust in that instead of Christ and the Cross.

The other day I watched a preacher over television tell his audience that if they will take the Lord's Supper every day, or twice a week, or whatever he said, they will find victory over sin, prosperity, healing, etc.

Now, while the Lord's Supper is certainly Scriptural, and is a beautiful Ordinance of the Church, still, it is not to be used in that fashion whatsoever. To do so insults Christ and what He has done at the Cross and, in fact, is an insult to God. It is a shifting of faith from Christ and the Cross to something else. And no matter how good that something else might be in its own right, it then becomes wrong. Remember this:

All victory, all forgiveness, all prosperity, all blessings, all Grace, in fact, everything the Lord has comes from Jesus Christ as the Source and the Cross as the Means, all superintended by the Holy Spirit.

GREAT VEXATIONS

Verses 5 and 6 make it clear that spiritual declension happened to Israel many times, and that they had to seek the Lord in great distress. In *"those times"* there was *"no peace"* and there were *"great vexations."*

Then it says in the Sixth Verse, *". . . for God did vex them with all adversity."* Even though they were His chosen People, called of Him and loved of Him, still, in times of spiritual declension, God would *"vex them."* This should be a warning to every Believer. God desires to bless us, but if we desire to oppose Him, He will, instead, *"vex*

NOTES

us." In the New Testament, to which we have already addressed ourselves, it refers to *"chastisement"* (Heb. 12:5-11). We must understand, however, that the Lord's *"vexing"* is not meant to hurt us but rather to pull us back to the place where we ought to be.

The word *"vexations"* in the Hebrew is *"mhuwmah,"* and means *"confusion, uproar, destruction, discomfiture, trouble, tumult."*

All of this means that whatever happens to a Believer is either caused by God or allowed by God. While the Lord most definitely does not cause anyone to sin, He will allow it if the person insists. But then, the Lord will most definitely cause certain things to be brought about that will hopefully wake us up.

As it regards Israel of old, sometimes the entirety of their Nation was destroyed, and then at other times, the Lord only allowed a certain city to be destroyed. In other words, it was the Lord Who measured out what Satan could do. The Lord is always in control.

"YOUR WORK SHALL BE REWARDED"

Through the Prophet the Lord has just told of judgment that would come if Israel sinned and, thereby, forsook the Lord. He now says the opposite, *"Be you strong therefore, and let not your hands be weak: for your work shall be rewarded."*

Irrespective of the relentless attacks by Satan, irrespective of his efforts to steal, kill, and destroy, irrespective as to how things may look on the surface, the Believer is admonished by the Lord to *"be strong"* and to not *"allow our hands to be weak."* A great Promise is then given, *"your work shall be rewarded."*

This admonition is very real to me personally. It goes back to when Frances and I first began in Evangelistic Work in the late 1950's.

If I remember correctly, it was in the month of January, 1958. We were preaching a meeting in a small town in northeast Louisiana. In the midst of the meeting, I came down sick and was unable to continue, and actually had to be hospitalized. I had pneumonia.

My stay in the hospital, which was only

overnight, was not uneventful. The nurse that came into my room seemed to use one profanity after the other, with me deciding I would do better at home than there.

I didn't really check out of the hospital, I just left, and did so with this nurse cursing me and telling me that the hospital would no longer be responsible. I didn't feel they had been too very responsible anyway, and as quickly as I could get my clothes on, Frances and I left.

All of that is incidental to what took place next. At that particular time, I had three cousins in entertainment, and one of them, Jerry Lee Lewis, was competing with Elvis Presley for the number one song in the nation. In other words, Jerry Lee's song would be on top one week, and Elvis' would be number one the next. This went on for some time.

Jerry Lee and I were raised together, actually learning to play the piano on almost the same instrument. Our paths took different turns, as is obvious, with him going into entertainment and me going into the Ministry.

While his foray into entertainment seemed on the surface to be much more profitable than my efforts in the Ministry, in the midst of it all, the Lord was to teach me a valuable lesson.

After arriving home from the hospital, I was still too sick to get out of bed. I would try to read my Bible, but the words seemed to blur together because of the nausea.

Not having a television set at that particular time, I would turn on the radio occasionally, and almost invariably one of my cousins would be featured. The Devil was to use that mightily a couple of nights ahead.

THE LORD SPOKE TO ME

It was Wednesday evening, and Frances and Donnie had gone to prayer meeting. Donnie was four years old at the time.

That night, Satan entered that room, or at least one of his cohorts of darkness. He began to tell me what a fool I was. My cousin, he went on to illustrate to me, was making more money in one day than I was making all year. Even though Satan lies, he was pretty close to being right as it

NOTES

regards this account. He mocked me, telling me that I called myself a Preacher, but I had nowhere to preach, and besides that, I couldn't even put food on the table. How would I pay the car note? How would I pay the house note? While the amounts were very small, still, they loomed large if there was no money available whatsoever.

And then he taunted me even further, telling me that my God wasn't doing a very good job of taking care of me, considering that I was so sick I couldn't walk.

Few times in my life have I sensed the powers of darkness as I did that early evening.

I began to make every effort to pray and to seek the Face of the Lord, but it was like the heavens were brass.

My Bible was on the bed beside me, and I remember reaching for it hurriedly, pulling it to me. I didn't open it, the Lord did. He opened it to Joshua 1:9. And this is what He said:

"Have not I commanded you? Be strong and of a good courage; be not afraid, neither be thou dismayed: for the LORD your God is with you whithersoever you go."

Those words on the page seemed to be capitalized. They stood out so boldly, and I knew instantly that it was the Lord's Message to me personally.

He was telling me, no matter what it looked like on the surface, no matter what the circumstances were, that I was to *"be strong."* As well, I was to *"be of good courage and be not afraid, and neither be dismayed."* And then He said to me, and I've never forgotten it, *"The Lord your God is with you whithersoever you go."* All of a sudden, the powers of darkness left, and left immediately. The Spirit of God filled that room, as I began to worship and praise the Lord.

I remember sitting up in bed and placing my feet on the floor, thinking in my mind, *"It's no need me staying in this bed any longer. I am healed!"*

I slowly arose and then began to walk through the room praising the Lord.

When Frances and Donnie came home from prayer meeting a little bit later, they didn't find me in bed, but rather continuing to praise the Lord for the great Visitation that I had had.

There have been many, many times when Satan has made his efforts to steal, kill, and destroy; however, each time the Holy Spirit has brought me back to the great Promise which the Lord gave me in 1958. It is still just as viable today as it was then, *"Have not I commanded you? Be strong and of a good courage; be not afraid, neither be thou dismayed: for the LORD your God is with you whithersoever you go."*

(8) "AND WHEN ASA HEARD THESE WORDS, AND THE PROPHECY OF ODED THE PROPHET, HE TOOK COURAGE, AND PUT AWAY THE ABOMINABLE IDOLS OUT OF ALL THE LAND OF JUDAH AND BENJAMIN, AND OUT OF THE CITIES WHICH HE HAD TAKEN FROM MOUNT EPHRAIM, AND RENEWED THE ALTAR OF THE LORD, THAT WAS BEFORE THE PORCH OF THE LORD.

(9) "AND HE GATHERED ALL JUDAH AND BENJAMIN, AND THE STRANGERS WITH THEM OUT OF EPHRAIM AND MANASSEH, AND OUT OF SIMEON: FOR THEY FELL TO HIM OUT OF ISRAEL IN ABUNDANCE, WHEN THEY SAW THAT THE LORD HIS GOD WAS WITH HIM.

(10) "SO THEY GATHERED THEMSELVES TOGETHER AT JERUSALEM IN THE THIRD MONTH, IN THE FIFTEENTH YEAR OF THE REIGN OF ASA.

(11) "AND THEY OFFERED UNTO THE LORD THE SAME TIME, OF THE SPOIL WHICH THEY HAD BROUGHT, SEVEN HUNDRED OXEN AND SEVEN THOUSAND SHEEP.

(12) "AND THEY ENTERED INTO A COVENANT TO SEEK THE LORD GOD OF THEIR FATHERS WITH ALL THEIR HEART AND WITH ALL THEIR SOUL;

(13) "THAT WHOSOEVER WOULD NOT SEEK THE LORD GOD OF ISRAEL SHOULD BE PUT TO DEATH, WHETHER SMALL OR GREAT, WHETHER MAN OR WOMAN.

(14) "AND THEY SWORE UNTO THE LORD WITH A LOUD VOICE, AND WITH SHOUTING, AND WITH TRUMPETS, AND WITH CORNETS.

(15) "AND ALL JUDAH REJOICED AT THE OATH: FOR THEY HAD SWORN WITH ALL THEIR HEART, AND SOUGHT HIM WITH THEIR WHOLE DESIRE; AND HE WAS FOUND OF THEM: AND THE LORD GAVE THEM REST ROUND ABOUT.

(16) "AND ALSO CONCERNING MAACHAH THE MOTHER OF ASA THE KING, HE REMOVED HER FROM BEING QUEEN, BECAUSE SHE HAD MADE AN IDOL IN A GROVE: AND ASA CUT DOWN HER IDOL, AND STAMPED IT, AND BURNT IT AT THE BROOK KIDRON.

(17) "BUT THE HIGH PLACES WERE NOT TAKEN AWAY OUT OF ISRAEL: NEVERTHELESS THE HEART OF ASA WAS PERFECT ALL HIS DAYS.

(18) "AND HE BROUGHT INTO THE HOUSE OF GOD THE THINGS THAT HIS FATHER HAD DEDICATED, AND THAT HE HIMSELF HAD DEDICATED, SILVER, AND GOLD, AND VESSELS.

(19) "AND THERE WAS NO MORE WAR UNTO THE FIVE AND THIRTIETH YEAR OF THE REIGN OF ASA."

The exegesis is:

1. (Vs. 8) Evidently, Oded, the father of Azariah, prophesied to Asa, as well as his son.

2. (Vs. 8) Any time there is a true Move of God, the Lord will bring the people back to the Cross, symbolized here by the *"Altar."*

3. (Vs. 9) Tens of thousands from the northern kingdom of Israel moved to Judah when they saw that the Lord was with Asa.

4. The Tenth Verse probably refers to the Feast of Pentecost, conducted in June.

5. As it regards Verse 11, according to Numbers 31:25-54, the Lord's portion, concerning the spoil of war, was to be one animal out of every 500 from the half that belonged to the men of war, and one out of every 50 of the other half of the spoils that belonged to the congregation. On this basis (eleven animals for the Lord out of every 1,000 taken), the total spoil must have numbered approximately 63,000 oxen and 636,000 sheep. When the Fourteenth Verse of the last Chapter said *"exceeding much spoil,"* it meant exactly that.

6. The penalty of Verse 13 probably had to do with Exodus 22:20 and Deuteronomy 13:6-11.

7. What a great statement of Verse 15, *"And He was found of them"*. In fact, He can be found of anyone, if, with true sincerity,

8. (Vs. 16) *"Maachah"* was actually the grandmother of Asa. There is no word for grandmother or grandfather in the Hebrew language. She was a worshipper of the Asherah, an idol carved in the likeness of the male reproductive organ.

9. The word *"perfect"* of Verse 17 does not mean sinless perfection, but that his heart was perfect as far as idolatry was concerned. The *"high places,"* at least in this instance, would have been used to sacrifice to Jehovah. However, still, this was not in keeping with the Commandment of God that the sacrifices be offered only at the Temple at Jerusalem. Consequently, the Holy Spirit mentions the *"high places"* for a reason.

10. (Vs. 19) Asa had peace the first ten years of his reign (II Chron. 14:1); then came the Ethiopian invasion of Judah (II Chron. 14:9-15). After that, there was peace for 25 years (II Chron. 15:19); then came war with Baasha, king of the northern confederacy of Israel (II Chron. 16:1-6). Because he trusted in Syria at that time instead of God, wars were pronounced upon him for the balance of his reign—six more years (II Chron. 16:9).

PUT AWAY THE IDOLS

Asa heard the Prophecy of Oded, heeded the prophecy, and began to conduct himself accordingly. He did two things:

1. He *"put away the abominable idols out of all the land of Judah and Benjamin, and out of the cities which he had taken from Mount Ephraim."*

2. He *"renewed the Altar of the LORD, that was before the porch of the LORD."* Which one of these he did first, we aren't told; however, it is most probable that he *"renewed the Altar of the LORD"* first.

The word *"renewed"* means that he *"built the Altar."* Evidently, not being used as it should have been, it was in a state of disrepair. What a tragedy!

And yet, the same thing can probably be said of the modern church. It desperately needs to *"renew the Altar,"* which means to rebuild or repair the Altar, i.e., *"the Cross."*

The modern church has little idea as to the central position of the Cross of Christ. It has almost no knowledge at all as it regards the Cross concerning our daily lives and living. Some Preachers understand the Cross as it regards Salvation, but as it regards Sanctification, not at all! And yet, virtually the entirety of the teaching given by the Apostle Paul concerned itself with our living for God, not only being Saved. However, when the Cross is ignored as it regards our daily life and living, it will soon be ignored as it regards our Salvation, which it is in many circles presently.

When the Cross is in a state of disrepair, i.e., Faith is placed elsewhere, idols flourish. This was so whether under the Old Covenant or whether under the New.

What is the difference in idol worship then and idol worship now?

The spirit of idol worship is the same, whether under the Old Covenant or the New. In Israel, material figures were made of what some thought a particular god looked like. Most were made out of wood, but some were made out of silver and gold. They came in all sizes.

Presently, such material figures are seldom concocted. But idol worship continues to flourish.

How?

Anything in which one places one's faith other than the Cross of Christ is looked at by the Lord as idol worship (II Cor. 13:5).

John the Beloved in writing his first Epistle said, *"Little children, keep yourselves from idols."* The notes in THE EXPOSITOR'S STUDY BIBLE say, *"This does not refer here to the heathen worship of idol gods, but of the heretical substitutes for the Christian conception of God, or anything that pulls us away from Christ and the Cross"* (I Jn. 5:21).

When a Believer, so-called, thinks that Water Baptism constitutes Salvation, he has just made an idol out of that Biblical Ordinance, even though Water Baptism in its own right is perfectly Scriptural and desirable. The same can be done for the Lord's Supper or even the Church itself. Millions think that because they belong to a certain church or religious denomination, this affords them some type of spirituality. In such a case, they have just made that church an idol. Let us say it again:

The Faith of the Believer is supposed to be in the Cross of Christ entirely. Anything else constitutes spiritual adultery and is looked at by the Lord as idol worship. The Believer should consider this very carefully. That's why Paul said:

"But though we, or an Angel from Heaven, preach any other gospel unto you than that which we have preached unto you, let him be accursed" (Gal. 1:8).

In fact, it is possible to make an idol out of a false interpretation of Jesus. The great Apostle also said, *"For if he who comes preaching another Jesus, whom we have not preached . . ."* (II Cor. 11:4).

WHAT DID PAUL MEAN BY ANOTHER JESUS?

He also spoke of *"another spirit,"* which, as well, produced *"another gospel."*

In short, he was speaking of separating Jesus from the Cross. By that, we are speaking of the benefits of the Cross, which He there did. We aren't talking about the wooden beam.

If Jesus is held up as the great Healer, or the great Teacher, or the great Miracle Worker, etc., with the Cross being ignored, that constitutes *"another Jesus,"* which means we have made a false Jesus into an idol. Regrettably, millions in the modern church fall into this category.

DO WE MAKE TOO MUCH OF THE CROSS?

According to the Word of God, is it possible to make too much of the Cross?

I don't think so!

It was to Paul that the meaning of the New Covenant was given, which in actuality is the meaning of the Cross. One might say they are one and the same.

If one honestly reads the New Testament, understanding that this great Revelation was given to the Apostle Paul, and will read what he stated as it regards the Cross, I think it's impossible to make too much of the Cross (Rom. 6:1-14; 8:1-2, 11; I Cor. 1:17-18, 21, 23; 2:2; Gal., Chpt. 5; 6:14; Eph. 2:13-18; Col. 2:14-15). In fact, the entirety of the Bible is the Story of Jesus Christ and Him Crucified.

NOTES

At the very dawn of time, in fact, to the First Family, the Lord gave provision as to how they could have communication and fellowship with Him and forgiveness of sins. It would be by the means of the slain lamb, which would serve as an innocent victim and, thereby, a Type of the coming Redeemer, Who would be the Lord Jesus Christ.

The Fourth Chapter of Genesis bears this out in no uncertain terms. In fact, the Sacrificial system remained in vogue all the way to the coming of Christ. It was actually the central core of the Mosaic Law. Had it not been for the Sacrificial system ensconced in the Law, Israel would have been doomed.

That system portrayed Christ, symbolized Christ, and epitomized Christ and His Substitutionary Work on the Cross, and did so in no uncertain terms.

No, the sin of the modern church most definitely is not making too much of the Cross, but rather, the very opposite.

When Jesus *". . . began to show unto His Disciples, how that He must go unto Jerusalem, and suffer many things of the Elders and Chief Priests and Scribes, and be killed, and be raised again the third day,"* the Scripture says, *"Then Peter took Him, and began to rebuke Him. . . ."*

The Scripture then says, *"But He (Jesus) turned, and said unto Peter, Get thee behind Me, Satan: you are an offence unto Me: for you savor not the things that be of God, but those that be of men."*

The Master then said, *". . . If any man will come after Me, let him deny himself, and take up his Cross, and follow Me"* (Mat. 16:21-24).

Our Lord then said that if Believers didn't take up the Cross and follow Him, they *"could not be His Disciple"* (Lk. 14:27). All of this came from none other than the Lips of our Lord!

To ignore the Cross is a serious thing. To deny the Cross is blasphemy!

Due to the manner of Creation of the human race, God as God could not deliver man. And yet, we must say that with the proverbial grain of salt. God is Omnipotent, meaning all-powerful, therefore, He can do anything. However, the Lord will never violate His Nature or His Character. So, while

He can do anything, there are many things He won't do, and for the reason given.

God would have to become man, which He did as it regards the Incarnation. He did so for many reasons, but the overall primary reason was to go to the Cross. There He would redeem mankind and do so by the giving of Himself in Sacrifice. That was His Plan, is His Plan, and ever shall be His Plan.

THE LORD HIS GOD WAS WITH HIM

Thousands, and possibly even tens of thousands, began to come to Judah out of the northern kingdom of Israel, *"when they saw that the LORD his God was with him."* These people, whomever they might have been, didn't want to live in a land that had been given over totally to idol worship, even as the northern Kingdom was.

The name of *"Simeon"* mentioned in Verse 9 is interesting.

As is obvious, Simeon is one of the Twelve Tribes of Israel; however, their territory or inheritance was within the inheritance of Judah. In fact, the northernmost boundary of their Tribe was probably about 60 miles south of Jerusalem.

This had been brought about because hundreds of years before, actually previous to any Tribes, Simeon and Levi, sons of Jacob, had murdered the entire male population of *"... Shalem, a city of Shechem...."* They did so because *"... Shechem the son of Hamor the Hivite, prince of the country, saw her, took her, and lay with her, and defiled her"* (Gen. 33:18; 34:2, 25). Dinah, the sister of Simeon and Levi, was raped.

As it regards this crime committed by Simeon and Levi, Jacob, on his dying bed, prophesied and said: *"Cursed be their anger, for it was fierce; and their wrath, for it was cruel; I will divide them in Jacob, and scatter them in Israel"* (Gen. 49:7).

Consequently, as the Tribes of Israel began to grow, all from the sons of Jacob and Joseph, the time came for them to possess the land of Canaan, which was about 250 years later. The Scripture says as it concerns Simeon, and keeping in tune with the Prophecy given by Jacob, *"... and their inheritance was within the inheritance of the Children of Judah"* (Josh. 19:1). In other words, exactly as the Prophecy said, they had no inheritance of their own. So, why are they linked in Scripture with Ephraim and Manasseh, as recorded in Verse 9, regarding the Chapter of our study? This tells us two things:

1. In whatever capacity, they evidently had sided with the northern kingdom of Israel when the split of the nation took place. It is quite possible, as well, that the northern kingdom had given the Tribe of Simeon a place in their area. They, no doubt, as well, chafed at being under the domain of the Tribe of Judah. But yet, what we're saying is speculation at best. At any rate, many out of the Tribe of Simeon, wherever they were, threw in their lot with the Lord, which speaks so well of them.

2. Due to the curse resting upon the human race as a result of the Fall, this means that man has no spiritual inheritance. But our Heavenly Judah, the Lord Jesus Christ, allowed us to come into His Inheritance, which, in fact, is the greatest inheritance of all. So, Simeon is a type, in a sense, of the entirety of the human race.

THE COVENANT

Their Covenant was that they were to *"seek the LORD God of their fathers with all their heart and with all their soul."* This referred to them doing all they could do to abide by the Word of God, which meant, among other things, that all idol worship was out.

The great sin of that time was, in fact, idol worship.

In effect, they stated that if anyone in Judah would be found worshipping idols, they were to be *"put to death, whether small or great, whether man or woman."* No doubt, their thinking was derived from Exodus 22:20 and Deuteronomy 13:9; 17:2-6. In this context, and, no doubt, this is correct, they sought to follow the Lord, and rightly so! They were to *"seek the LORD God of Israel,"* and not idol gods.

THE LORD GAVE THEM REST

As Judah sought to obey the Lord, thereby, putting all idol worship away from them, and doing so with all their heart, the

Scripture plainly says, *"and He (the Lord) was found of them: and the LORD gave them rest round about."*

In fact, Asa was so sincere about this which he and all of Judah were doing that he removed his grandmother from being queen, *"because she had made an idol in a grove."*

Whenever Believers, any Believers, as it regards the Lord, *"seek Him with their whole desire,"* to be sure, *"He will be found."* *"Rest"* always accompanies the Blessings of God.

Rest from what?

In this case, it was rest from war. In a sense, it is the same presently. Most of the turbulence faced by the Child of God, which causes tremendous consternation in the individual and in the family, is because of a disobedience of the Word of God in some way. Probably, if the truth be known, that disobedience would be found in one's approach to the Cross of Christ. Correct that and most everything else will fall into place, and *"rest"* will be ours.

The heart of Asa was perfect all his days, which refers to his attitude toward idols. It did not mean sinless perfection.

THE HOUSE OF GOD

Asa brought into the House of God, *"silver, and gold, and vessels."* The *"House of God"* presently is our physical bodies (I Cor. 3:16). What are we putting into this House?

In the Old Testament, *"silver"* was a type of Redemption. *"Gold"* was a type of Deity. The *"sacred vessels"* were a type of worship. It should be the same presently in a Spiritual sense.

We are redeemed by none other than the Lord Jesus Christ, the Son of God; therefore, we *"worship,"* and gladly so!

"High in the Heavens, Eternal God,
"Your Goodness in full glory shines;
"Your Truths shall break through every cloud,
"That veils Your just and wise Designs."

"Forever firm Your Justice stands,
"As mountains their foundations keep;
"Wise are the wonders of Your Hands,
"Your Judgments are a mighty deep."

"O God, how excellent Your Grace!
"Whence all our hope, our comfort springs,
"The sons of Adam, in distress,
"Fly to the shadow of Your Wings."

"Life, like a fountain, rich and free,
"Springs from the Presence of my Lord;
"And in Your Light our souls shall see,
"The glories promised in Your Word."

CHAPTER 16

(1) "IN THE SIXTH YEAR OF THE REIGN OF ASA BAASHA KING OF ISRAEL CAME UP AGAINST JUDAH, AND BUILT RAMAH, TO THE INTENT THAT HE MIGHT LET NONE GO OUT OR COME IN TO ASA KING OF JUDAH.

(2) "THEN ASA BROUGHT OUT SILVER AND GOLD OUT OF THE TREASURES OF THE HOUSE OF THE LORD AND OF THE KING'S HOUSE, AND SENT TO BEN-HADAD KING OF SYRIA, WHO DWELT AT DAMASCUS, SAYING,

(3) "THERE IS A LEAGUE BETWEEN ME AND YOU, AS THERE WAS BETWEEN MY FATHER AND YOUR FATHER: BEHOLD, I HAVE SENT YOU SILVER AND GOLD; GO, BREAK YOUR LEAGUE WITH BAASHA KING OF ISRAEL, THAT HE MAY DEPART FROM ME.

(4) "AND BEN-HADAD HEARKENED UNTO KING ASA, AND SENT THE CAPTAINS OF HIS ARMIES AGAINST THE CITIES OF ISRAEL; AND THEY SMOTE IJON, AND DAN, AND ABEL-MAIM, AND ALL THE STORE CITIES OF NAPHTALI.

(5) "AND IT CAME TO PASS, WHEN BAASHA HEARD IT, THAT HE LEFT OFF BUILDING OF RAMAH, AND LET HIS WORK CEASE.

(6) "THEN ASA THE KING TOOK ALL JUDAH; AND THEY CARRIED AWAY THE STONES OF RAMAH, AND THE TIMBER THEREOF, WHEREWITH BAASHA WAS BUILDING; AND HE BUILT THEREWITH GEBA AND MIZPAH."

The construction is:

1. (Vs. 1) Tens of thousands of people from the northern kingdom of Israel were coming down to Judah, as previously stated, that they might worship God at the Temple. Baasha, king of Israel, was attempting to stop this flight by building this border city of Ramah.

2. (Vs. 1) One of the sure signs that a doctrine, or a so-called gospel, is wrong is when the propagators try to stop people from hearing anything else. One of Satan's greatest ploys is to place the true worship of God *"off limits,"* and to threaten by force anyone who would attempt to exceed those limits.

3. (Vs. 2) Rather than trust God to help him regarding Baasha, Asa hired the king of Syria. Asa's plan would succeed militarily, but fail spiritually. The success of self-made plans is always a spiritual disaster.

4. (Vs. 2) It must be remembered that new victories cannot be won by the remembrance of old faith. There must be fresh exercise of Faith in every crisis.

RESORTING TO THE WAYS OF THE WORLD

When Baasha king of Israel came up against Judah, Asa did not do as he had done some years earlier, that is, to seek the Lord as to what direction he should take. Rather, he succumbed to the ways of the world by seeking the help of Ben-hadad, king of Syria. It would prove to be a disastrous choice.

Why did Asa ignore the Lord in this situation, thereby, resorting to the ways of the world?

That's a good question!

Did he not remember the invasion by the Ethiopians when they came against Judah with a million men and three hundred chariots? Did he not remember how he *"cried unto the LORD his God,"* and then the Lord powerfully *"smote the Ethiopians?"*

Regrettably and sadly, Asa, at this particular time, had begun drifting, and I speak of a spiritual drift. We can think of any number of reasons this was happening. One thing is sure, he began well and ended poorly.

Did he die lost?

Only the Lord knows the answer to that; however, the Biblical evidence is not in his favor. What a tragedy! Regrettably, it happens all too often. Some preachers, in the sunset of their lives, compromise the Gospel.

A CARNAL PLAN SUCCEEDS!

The Lord has done us a great favor when our carnal plans fail; however, at times He will allow them to succeed. That being the case, deception takes over.

So, many think that because plans succeed, such constitutes the Blessings of God. They might, but again, they might not! One thing is certain, what Asa did, even though it succeeded, was not the Will of God. We should take a lesson from that!

(7) "AND AT THAT TIME HANANI THE SEER CAME TO ASA KING OF JUDAH, AND SAID UNTO HIM, BECAUSE YOU HAVE RELIED ON THE KING OF SYRIA, AND NOT RELIED ON THE LORD YOUR GOD, THEREFORE IS THE HOST OF THE KING OF SYRIA ESCAPED OUT OF YOUR HAND.

(8) "WERE NOT THE ETHIOPIANS AND THE LUBIMS A HUGE HOST, WITH VERY MANY CHARIOTS AND HORSEMEN? YET, BECAUSE YOU DID RELY ON THE LORD, HE DELIVERED THEM INTO YOUR HAND.

(9) "FOR THE EYES OF THE LORD RUN TO AND FRO THROUGHOUT THE WHOLE EARTH, TO SHOW HIMSELF STRONG IN BEHALF OF THEM WHOSE HEART IS PERFECT TOWARD HIM. HEREIN YOU HAVE DONE FOOLISHLY: THEREFORE FROM HENCEFORTH YOU SHALL HAVE WARS.

(10) "THEN ASA WAS WROTH WITH THE SEER, AND PUT HIM IN A PRISON HOUSE; FOR HE WAS IN A RAGE WITH HIM BECAUSE OF THIS THING. AND ASA OPPRESSED SOME OF THE PEOPLE THE SAME TIME.

(11) "AND, BEHOLD, THE ACTS OF ASA, FIRST AND LAST, LO, THEY ARE WRITTEN IN THE BOOK OF THE KINGS OF JUDAH AND ISRAEL."

The pattern is:

1. (Vs. 7) Is it possible that God makes plans for us which speak of great victory, and we forfeit those plans by our faithlessness? Rather than trusting Him, we trust man.

2. (Vs. 8) Why did Asa rely on the Lord

as it regards the Ethiopians and the Lubims, and not rely on Him now? As stated, yesterday's Faith will not suffice for today!

3. (Vs. 9) When one considers that the Lord is ardently looking for individuals who will believe Him, so that He might *"show Himself strong on their behalf,"* such should give us a very positive perspective on the Ways of the Lord. Our Lord desires to help people, but they must evidence Faith in Him, and it must be a continuous Faith.

4. (Vs. 10) This is the same Asa who instituted the great Revival of Chapter 15. How the mighty have fallen! If Asa had truly repented at this time, thereby heeding the Prophet, more than likely the diseases of Verse 12 would not have come upon him and shortened his life.

5. The statement, *"first and last,"* of Verse 11, signifies that there was a difference in Asa in his last years.

THE PROPHET OF GOD

It was not easy for Hanani the Prophet to take this message to Asa. In fact, it did not turn out well for him at all. But the facts are, he was faithful to hear from the Lord and to deliver that which he had heard without compromising the message at all.

Asa was very angry with Hanani and the Scripture says that he *"put him in a prison house; for he was in a rage with him because of this thing."* He did not like at all what the Lord had said through the Prophet.

The Scripture also says that *"Asa oppressed some of the people the same time."* Exactly as to what this means, we aren't told. However, it probably refers to the fact that some of the advisors to Asa, or whomever they may have been, agreed with the Prophet that he had heard from the Lord, and had delivered the Word of the Lord, which portrayed the fact that Asa had done wrong before God.

Regrettably, in a sense, Asa's story closes with this rebellion against God and against God's Prophet. That does not speak well at all of his last days.

What a tragedy to begin so well and then to end so poorly!

The duty of the Prophet is not always to bring forth pleasant news. Sometimes and, in fact, it seems that most of the time, what the true Prophet of God has to say is not pleasant to hear. So, there was always then and is always now a bevy of false prophets who are furiously willing to tell the people, whomever they might be, what they want to hear. Also, they will be paid well for their services. Israel always seemed to have plenty of false prophets and very few true Prophets, and likewise, the modern church, regrettably, follows the same path.

"THE EYES OF THE LORD"

The Prophet Hanani gave us a great Promise, but the Holy Spirit in other places gave similar Promises, also. *"For the Eyes of the LORD run to and fro throughout the whole Earth, to show Himself strong on behalf of them whose heart is perfect toward Him."*

It was first given in Job, *"For His Eyes are upon the ways of man, and He sees all his goings"* (Job 34:21).

He also said in Proverbs, *"For the ways of man are before the Eyes of the LORD, and He ponders all his goings"* (Prov. 5:21).

And then, *"The Eyes of the LORD are in every place, beholding the evil and the good"* (Prov. 15:3).

And then in Jeremiah, *"For My Eyes are upon all their ways: they are not hid from My Face, neither is their iniquity hid from My Eyes"* (Jer. 16:17).

And then, *"Great in counsel, and mighty in work: for Your Eyes are open upon all the ways of the sons of men: to give everyone according to his ways, and according to the fruit of his doings"* (Jer. 32:19).

And finally, *"For who has despised the day of small things? for they shall rejoice, and shall see the plummet in the hand of Zerubbabel with those seven; they are the Eyes of the LORD, which run to and fro through the whole Earth"* (Zech. 4:10).

But the greatest statement is probably by Hanani. Several things are said:

• *"The Eyes of the LORD"* see everything throughout the entirety of the world.

• *"The Eyes of the LORD run to and fro throughout the whole Earth,"* and do so looking for specific things.

• He is looking for individuals to whom

He might *"show Himself strong in the behalf of them."*

• He is looking for those *"whose heart is perfect toward Him."*

THE PERFECT HEART

The word *"perfect,"* as here used, in the Hebrew is *"Shalem,"* and means, *"to be complete, to be just, to be peaceable, to be whole."*

As it regards *"perfect,"* if we look at ourselves, what we will see will be anything but perfect, that is, if we are honest with ourselves.

As someone has well said, *"Look away from your ten thousand failures to the headband worn by the High Priest with the words inscribed, 'Holiness unto the Lord.'"*

There are no perfect Believers; there is only a Perfect Christ.

For one who has his Faith exercised totally and completely in Christ and what Christ has done at the Cross, the Perfection of Christ is automatically given to such an individual. In that capacity, and in that capacity only, can one lay claim to perfection.

It is wonderful to know, and have it said in such plain terminology, that the Lord desires to *"show Himself strong in behalf of them whose heart is perfect toward Him."*

What does that mean?

Of course, one could say that it means any number of things. However, I personally feel that there are two that are most important of all the things one could name. They are that the Lord desires to bless His people and, as well, that our relationship with Him might grow and become ever closer.

(12) "AND ASA IN THE THIRTY AND NINTH YEAR OF HIS REIGN WAS DISEASED IN HIS FEET, UNTIL HIS DISEASE WAS EXCEEDING GREAT: YET IN HIS DISEASE HE SOUGHT NOT TO THE LORD, BUT TO THE PHYSICIANS.

(13) "AND ASA SLEPT WITH HIS FATHERS, AND DIED IN THE ONE AND FORTIETH YEAR OF HIS REIGN.

(14) "AND THEY BURIED HIM IN HIS OWN SEPULCHRES, WHICH HE HAD MADE FOR HIMSELF IN THE CITY OF DAVID, AND LAID HIM IN THE BED WHICH WAS FILLED WITH SWEET ODOURS AND DIVERS KINDS OF SPICES PREPARED BY THE APOTHECARIES' ART: AND THEY MADE A VERY GREAT BURNING FOR HIM."

The exegesis is:

1. (Vs. 12) The Lord permitted this disease as a result of Asa's actions. I wonder how many presently fall into the same category?

2. The Scripture lends credence to the thought that the Lord, in allowing this disease to come upon the king, gave him another opportunity to seek the Face of the Lord. But regrettably, Asa sought otherwise.

3. (Vs. 12) The idea of this Verse is that if Asa had sought the Lord, the Lord would have forgiven him and healed him.

4. (Vs. 12) The *"physicians"* who are spoken of here were probably Egyptian physicians, who were in high repute at foreign courts in ancient times, and who pretended to expel diseases by charms, incantations, and mystic arts. In other words, they were Satanic!

5. (Vs. 13) Because of his faithlessness, Asa, no doubt, cut his life short!

SEEKING THE LORD OR MAN

The Lord is not opposed to physicians, inasmuch as Luke, who wrote two of the great Books of the Bible, was a physician. But the Lord was and is very much opposed to the type of physician that is here addressed, who, more than likely, was Egyptian.

These were individuals who were controlled by demon spirits, and were pretty much the same as that of the Native American medicine men. They sought to bring about healing by charms, incantations, etc. So, in essence, Asa had the privilege of seeking the Lord or demon spirits. Regrettably and sadly, he chose demon spirits and paid dearly for that particular move.

The implication of the Text is that the Lord brought this disease upon Asa, giving him an opportunity to seek the Lord, as he had once done. Regrettably, that would not be the case.

HUMANISTIC PSYCHOLOGY

While we do not at all mean to impugn those who truly are trying to help people, nevertheless, the foray of the church into humanistic psychology presents a direction that is not of God. The Holy Spirit refers to this as human wisdom and says it is *"earthly, sensual, devilish"* (James 3:15).

The Scripture then says, *"But the wisdom that is from above is first pure, then peaceable, gentle, and easy to be intreated, full of Mercy and good fruits, without partiality, and without hypocrisy"* (James 3:17).

It is sad when some in the modern church claim that modern man is facing problems that the Bible does not address and, thereby, needs the help of humanistic psychology. Nothing could be further from the truth. Concerning this, Peter said: *"According as His Divine Power has given unto us all things* (the Lord with large-handed generosity has given us all things) *that pertain unto life and godliness* (pertains to the fact that the Lord Jesus has given us everything we need regarding life and living), *through the knowledge of Him Who has called us to Glory and Virtue* (the 'knowledge' addressed here speaks of what Christ did at the Cross, which alone can provide 'Glory and Virtue'):

"Whereby are given unto us exceeding great and Precious Promises (pertains to the Word of God, which alone holds the answer to every life problem): *that by these* (Promises) *you might be partakers of the Divine Nature* (the Divine Nature implanted in the inner being of the believing sinner becomes the source of our new life and actions; it comes to everyone at the moment of being 'Born-Again'), *having escaped the corruption that is in the world through lust.* (This presents the Salvation experience of the sinner, and the Sanctification experience of the Saint)" (II Pet. 1:3-4).

So, either the Lord did give us all things that pertain to life and godliness, or else He didn't, and if the latter be the case, we should turn to the likes of Freud, etc. However, we who know our Bibles, know that the Scripture means exactly what it says and says exactly what it means. He has given us all things that pertain to life and godliness, and that covers every need of man.

The problems of the human race are not indicative to the age in which we live. Those problems began at the Fall and have continued from then until now. Emotional disturbances, stress, nervous disorders, depression, and oppression are problems that are common to man, because, as stated, of the Fall.

THE ONLY ANSWER IS, *"JESUS CHRIST AND HIM CRUCIFIED"*

Every problem of mankind, irrespective as to what it is, at least that which pertains to life and godliness, was handled at the Cross. Concerning the Cross, Paul said: *"Blotting out the handwriting of Ordinances that was against us* (pertains to the Law of Moses, which was God's Standard of Righteousness that man could not reach), *which was contrary to us* (Law is against us, simply because we are unable to keep its precepts, no matter how hard we try), *and took it out of the way* (refers to the penalty of the Law being removed), *nailing it to His Cross* (the Law with its decrees was abolished in Christ's Death, as if Crucified with Him);

"And having spoiled principalities and powers (Satan and all of his henchmen were defeated at the Cross by Christ atoning for all sin; sin was the legal right Satan had to hold man in captivity; with all sin atoned, he has no more legal right to hold anyone in bondage), *He* (Christ) *made a show of them openly* (what Jesus did at the Cross was in the face of the whole universe), *triumphing over them in it.* (The triumph is complete and it was all done for us, meaning we can walk in power and perpetual Victory due to the Cross)" (Col. 2:14-15).

The Believer must understand and register Faith in the fact that Christ addressed every single problem at the Cross, and did so by atoning for all sin, which also addressed the cause of sin, which are Satan and the sin nature.

IS THE CROSS THE ANSWER FOR EVERYTHING?

If one studies our Commentaries, sooner or later, he will come to the conclusion that we hold up the Cross as the answer to every life problem and every sin, irrespective as to what it might be. Some have claimed that we portray the Cross as the answer for everything. They are claiming exactly right.

The meaning of the New Covenant is the

meaning of the Cross. It was at the Cross that every Victory, as stated, was won. It was at the Cross that the New Covenant became viable. Without the Cross, everything else that Jesus did would have been of little consequence.

That's the reason the Believer is to place his Faith exclusively in Christ and the Cross and not allow it to be moved elsewhere (Rom. 6:1-14; 8:1-2, 11; I Cor. 1:17-18, 23; 2:2; Gal., Chpt. 5; 6:14; Eph. 2:13-18, etc.).

The idea is, Jesus must not be separated from the Cross. No, that doesn't mean that He is supposed to be placed back on the Cross, as our Catholic friends teach, for the truth is, Christ is seated by the right Hand of the Father. The Cross is a historic fact and will never have to be repeated. Neither are we trying to put you on the Cross. That would be a waste of time.

When we speak of the Cross, we are speaking of the benefits of the Cross, that which Jesus there did, the price that He paid, and the Victory that He there won. Those benefits come down to us according to our Faith in Christ and His Finished Work. In fact, the benefits of the Cross will never end. Paul referred to it as *"the Everlasting Covenant"* (Heb. 13:20). That's why Paul said, *". . . we preach Christ Crucified . . ."* (I Cor. 1:23). He did not say, *"We preach Christ,"* but rather, *"We preach Christ Crucified."* That's the reason he also told the Corinthian Church and us, as well, *"I determined to know nothing among you save Jesus Christ and Him Crucified"* (I Cor. 2:2).

Paul is the one to whom the meaning of the New Covenant was given, which is the meaning of the Cross. I certainly should think, considering that, that he knows what he's talking about. So, Jesus must not be separated from the Cross, ever! With the Cross removed from Christianity, there is nothing left but a vapid philosophy. But, with the Cross of Christ, it is that which has liberated untold millions.

So, Asa died, and the evidence is not good at all as it regards the Salvation of his soul.

"Give to the Lord, you sons of fame,
"Give to the Lord Renown and Power;
"Ascribe due honors to His Name,
"And His Eternal Might adore."

"The Lord proclaims His Power aloud,
"Over the ocean and the land;
"His Voice divides the watery cloud,
"And lightning's blaze at His Command."

"He speaks and tempest, hail, and wind,
"Lay the wide forest bare around;
"The fearful heart and frighted hind,
"Leap at the terror of the sound."

"To Lebanon He turns His Voice,
"And lo! The stately cedars break;
"The mountains tremble at the noise,
"The valleys roar, the deserts quake."

"The Lord sits Sovereign on the flood,
"The Thunderer reigns forever King;
"But make His Church His blessed Abode,
"Where we His awful Glories sing."

"In gentler language there the Lord,
"The counsels of His Grace impart;
"Amidst the raging storm His Word,
"Speaks peace and courage to our hearts."

CHAPTER 17

(1) "AND JEHOSHAPHAT HIS SON REIGNED IN HIS STEAD, AND STRENGTHENED HIMSELF AGAINST ISRAEL.

(2) "AND HE PLACED FORCES IN ALL THE FENCED CITIES OF JUDAH, AND SET GARRISONS IN THE LAND OF JUDAH, AND IN THE CITIES OF EPHRAIM, WHICH ASA HIS FATHER HAD TAKEN.

(3) "AND THE LORD WAS WITH JEHOSHAPHAT, BECAUSE HE WALKED IN THE FIRST WAYS OF HIS FATHER DAVID, AND SOUGHT NOT UNTO BAALIM;

(4) "BUT SOUGHT TO THE LORD GOD OF HIS FATHER, AND WALKED IN HIS COMMANDMENTS, AND NOT AFTER THE DOINGS OF ISRAEL.

(5) "THEREFORE THE LORD

STABLISHED THE KINGDOM IN HIS HAND; AND ALL JUDAH BROUGHT TO JEHOSHAPHAT PRESENTS; AND HE HAD RICHES AND HONOUR IN ABUNDANCE."

The overview is:

1. (Vs. 1) Jehoshaphat is a godly man, yet with one glaring weakness—forming alliances with heathenistic Israel. Strangely enough, he would fortify himself greatly in a military sense against Israel, but yet, he will compromise his spiritual stand by forming an alliance with the same people.

2. (Vs. 1) Far too often, the modern church begins by opposing evil and then compromises with evil.

3. The phrase, *"And the LORD was with Jehoshaphat,"* of Verse 3, presents the greatest thing that could ever be said of any man.

4. It is believed by some scholars that the name of David is wrongly inserted in Verse 3. As well, it is not in the Septuagint. Most probably, the reference is to Asa, the father of Jehoshaphat. Inasmuch as the terminology does not exactly fit David, it is my personal opinion also that the translation is incorrect here, with Asa being the correct name.

5. (Vs. 5) Blessings follow obedience!

"AND THE LORD WAS WITH JEHOSHAPHAT"

The name *"Jehoshaphat"* means *"whom God judges"* or *"for whom God pleads."*

The First Verse says that Jehoshaphat *"strengthened himself against Israel,"* but later on, the king formed an alliance with Israel, which proved to be his undoing. Alliance with the world prevents victory over the world.

Many church denominations *"strengthen themselves against evil"* in their early days; however, when God begins to bless, and they are no longer poverty-stricken and weak, then, sadly, too many compromise their convictions by their alliance with the world.

The Scripture says that the Lord was with Jehoshaphat.

The reasons?

• *"Because he walked in the first ways of his father Asa."* More than likely, as stated, *"David"* is a mistake regarding a copyist. The terminology is not similar concerning statements made about David. The first years of Asa, Jehoshaphat's father, were strong with the Lord. In fact, the Scripture says, as it concerns the first years of Asa, *"And Asa did that which was good and right in the Eyes of the LORD his God"* (II Chron. 14:2).

• The Scripture says that Jehoshaphat *"sought not unto Baalim,"* meaning that he gave no credence whatsoever to the various false gods of surrounding nations.

• He *"sought to the LORD God of his father."*

• He *"walked in the LORD God's Commandments, and not after the doings of Israel."*

• *"His heart was lifted up in the ways of the LORD."*

• *"He took away the high places and groves out of Judah."*

• *"In the third year of his reign"* he sent out teachers *"to teach the Law of God in the cities of Judah."*

How refreshing it is to read of this man seeking after the Lord and, thereby, greatly enjoying the Blessings of the Lord, instead of reading the opposite.

"RICHES AND HONOR IN ABUNDANCE"

The *"riches and honor"* were all the Blessings of God. While, of course, Jehoshaphat fell into this category himself, the statement actually pertains to the whole of Judah. The whole nation was blessed abundantly, even as the Lord actually intended to be the norm.

As it regards riches, how does such fit Scripturally with modern Believers?

The Bible teaches that God will abundantly bless those who look to Him, who serve Him, and who are faithful to His Cause and Work. In other words, every Believer should believe the Lord for Blessings, which, of course, includes material things. We should give to God, and do so with the understanding that *"He loves a cheerful giver"* (II Cor. 9:7).

The Word also says to us, *"But this I say, He who sows sparingly shall reap also sparingly; and he who sows bountifully shall reap also bountifully"* (II Cor. 9:6). Pure and simple, this is a Promise of the Lord.

As the Lord blesses the Believer, he should use such Blessings to provide adequately for his family, and then, he must, as well, understand that the Lord has blessed him that he, as well, may bless the Work of the Lord. Such a person must be a good steward, knowing where his money is going as it regards the Work of the Lord, and making certain that the Work definitely is of the Lord. Regrettably, about ninety-nine percent (probably more than that) of all money given to that which purports to be the Work of the Lord is anything but! So, it's the responsibility of the Believer to ascertain if the work he is supporting is actually Scriptural. To be frank, there is only one Work listed in the Bible, as it regards the Work of God, that we should support.

THE CROSS OF CHRIST

The Holy Spirit through the Apostle tells us who we should support, and what we should support. It is found in his Epistle to the Philippians.

Paul was in prison in Rome when this Epistle was written.

One of the men in the Church at Philippi, Epaphroditus by name, had made the journey of approximately 700 miles to Rome in order to bring Paul an offering plus necessities, which the Apostle desperately needed. Consequently, the Epistle to the Philippians is actually a *"thank you letter"* sent to them for the offering sent to him.

As he closes out the Epistle, the Holy Spirit has him say some things that let us know that which the Lord desires to be supported.

The great Apostle said, and I quote from THE EXPOSITOR'S STUDY BIBLE:

"Now you Philippians know also, that in the beginning of the Gospel (refers to the time when Paul first preached the Word to them, about ten years previously), *when I departed from Macedonia, no Church communicated with me as concerning giving and receiving, but you only* (proclaims the fact that the Philippians had always been generous).

"For even in Thessalonica (when he was starting the Church there) *you sent once and again unto my necessity* (proclaims

NOTES

their faithfulness).

"Not because I desire a gift (presents the Apostle defending himself against the slanderous assertion that he is using the Gospel as a means to make money): *but I desire fruit that may abound to your account.* (God keeps a record of everything, even our gifts, whether giving or receiving.)

"But I have all, and abound: I am full (proclaims the fact that the Philippian gift must have been generous), *having received of Epaphroditus the things which were sent from you* (Epaphroditus had brought the gift from Philippi to Rome), *an odour of a sweet smell* (presents the Old Testament odors of the Levitical sacrifices, all typifying Christ), *a sacrifice acceptable, well-pleasing to God.* (For those who gave to Paul, enabling him to take the Message of the Cross to others, their gift, and such gifts presently, are looked at by God as a part of the Sacrificial Atoning Work of Christ on the Cross. Nothing could be higher than that!)

"But my God shall supply all your need (presents the Apostle assuring the Philippians, and all other Believers, as well, that they have not impoverished themselves by giving so liberally to the Cause of Christ) *according to His Riches in Glory* (the measure of supply will be determined by the Wealth of God in Glory) *by Christ Jesus* (made possible by the Cross)" (Phil. 4:15-19).

Several things are said here, things which are of extreme significance:

• The Holy Spirit placed the gift sent by the Philippians to Paul in the category of the Finished Work of Christ.

• This means that when gifts are given to that which purports to be the Work of God, such a Work must fall into the category of the Message of the Cross. Otherwise, it will not be honored by God.

• The *"odour of a sweet smell"* pertained, as stated, to the Old Testament sacrifices being offered to the Lord. A perfect example is the sacrifice offered by Noah (Gen. 8:21).

If our giving in these modern times is not that which promotes the Message of the Cross, then it is not a sweet smell in the Nostrils of God.

• The gift of the Philippians was also

likened as *"a sacrifice acceptable, well-pleasing to God."* This tells us that the only gift that is *"well-pleasing to God"* is that which furthers the Message of the Cross.

• When the Philippians gave to Paul, they were helping him to proclaim this Message of the Cross to a hurting and dying world. The Message of the Cross is the Message of Grace, which is the Message of the New Covenant.

Regrettably, as stated, most of the giving which purports to be to the Work of God, definitely does not fall into the category of advancing the Message of the Cross but something else altogether.

If we want the Lord to *"supply all our needs according to His Riches in Glory by Christ Jesus,"* we must give to that which the Lord sanctions, and only that which the Lord sanctions.

The Message of the Cross is the Message of Grace and is actually, as stated, the meaning of the New Covenant. It is that which the Lord gave to the Apostle Paul (Gal. 1:11-12).

Satan cannot deny that Gospel because it is a fact. But yet, he can pervert it (Gal. 1:7), and that's exactly what he has done. He does so by subtly, and sometimes not so subtly, ignoring the Cross, and in some cases, actually repudiating the Cross. In fact, the Evil One doesn't care too very much what the preacher preaches just as long as it isn't the Cross.

R.A. Torrey, one of the great Preachers of some years back, spoke to the president of Harvard University, who was advocating a more modern gospel. He said, *"Unless you preach 'Jesus Christ and Him Crucified,' Christianity will soon be no more than another vapid philosophy."* How right R.A. Torrey was. Sadly and regrettably, the modern church, by and large, has abandoned the Cross, and exactly as Torrey said, Christianity in most circles is little more than another philosophy. The Cross of Christ is what makes the Gospel what it is. Eliminate the Cross and for all practical purposes, the Gospel has been eliminated. That's at least one of the reasons the Holy Spirit proclaimed that all giving must support the Message of the Cross (I Cor. 1:17-18,

NOTES

23; 2:2; Gal. 6:14; Col. 2:14-15).

And then again, the Holy Spirit gave us ample warning as Believers, as it regards money.

MONEY

Paul said that some preachers would use the Gospel for gain, and I quote from THE EXPOSITOR'S STUDY BIBLE:

"Perverse disputings of men of corrupt minds (should have been translated, 'of men corrupted in mind'), *and destitute of the Truth* (refers to the fact that they had once possessed the Truth, which is the Cross, but had turned away to other things), *supposing that gain is godliness* (should have been translated, 'supposing that godliness is a way or source of gain'): *from such withdraw yourself* (have no dealings with these preachers).

"But godliness with contentment (content with what we have, which means we are thankful to God for what we have) *is great gain* (true gain).

"For we brought nothing into this world, and it is certain we can carry nothing out. (This speaks of worldly possessions. The only thing a person can keep is his Faith, that is if it's true Faith, which refers to Faith in Christ and the Cross.)

"And having food and raiment let us be therewith content. (The Lord can never bless grasping greed.)

"But they who will be rich fall into temptation and a snare, and into many foolish and hurtful lusts (speaks of the sacrifice of principle), *which drown men in destruction and perdition.* (This refers to the wreck and ruin of the mind and body, but more particularly to the awful ruin of the eternal soul.)

"For the love of money is the root of all evil (there is no conceivable evil that can happen to the sons and daughters of men, which may not spring from covetousness—the love of gold and wealth): *which while some coveted after, they have erred from the Faith* (speaking of Believers who have lost sight of the True Faith, which is the Cross, and have ventured into a false faith, trying to use it to garner much money), *and have pierced themselves through with many sorrows* (the end result of turning in that

direction; let all understand that the Word of God is true, and what it says will happen!).

"But you, O man of God, flee these things (the Holy Spirit is unequivocally clear in His Command; we can follow the Lord, or we can follow other things; we can't follow both!); *and follow after Righteousness, godliness, Faith, Love, Patience, Meekness.* (In a sense, this is the Fruit of the Spirit, or at least that which the Spirit Alone can bring about in our lives, which He does by the Cross ever being the Object of our Faith)" (I Tim. 6:5-11).

(6) "AND HIS HEART WAS LIFTED UP IN THE WAYS OF THE LORD: MOREOVER HE TOOK AWAY THE HIGH PLACES AND GROVES OUT OF JUDAH.

(7) "ALSO IN THE THIRD YEAR OF HIS REIGN HE SENT TO HIS PRINCES, EVEN TO BEN-HAIL, AND TO OBADIAH, AND TO ZECHARIAH, AND TO NETHANEEL, AND TO MICHAIAH, TO TEACH IN THE CITIES OF JUDAH.

(8) "AND WITH THEM HE SENT LEVITES, EVEN SHEMAIAH, AND NETHANIAH, AND ZEBADIAH, AND ASAHEL, AND SHEMIRAMOTH, AND JEHONATHAN, AND ADONIJAH, AND TOBIJAH, AND TOB-ADONIJAH, LEVITES; AND WITH THEM ELISHAMA AND JEHORAM, PRIESTS.

(9) "AND THEY TAUGHT IN JUDAH, AND HAD THE BOOK OF THE LAW OF THE LORD WITH THEM, AND WENT ABOUT THROUGHOUT ALL THE CITIES OF JUDAH, AND TAUGHT THE PEOPLE."

The overview is:

1. (Vs. 6) The people were not sacrificing to idols at these *"high places and groves,"* but were sacrificing to Jehovah. Yet, this was against the Law of God inasmuch as they were supposed to sacrifice in Jerusalem. Almost invariably, the sacrifices to Jehovah would eventually degenerate into sacrifices to idols. The reason for the one place of sacrifice, and we speak of the Temple, is because there was to be but one Calvary.

2. Verse 7 proclaims Jehoshaphat doing something that had never been done before—the teaching of the Law throughout Judah.

3. (Vs. 9) This was the first great teaching

NOTES

mission instituted by any king of Israel. The Law of Moses was taken from city to city and taught to the people. The *"Law of the LORD"* was the Pentateuch—Genesis, Exodus, Leviticus, Numbers, and Deuteronomy. Fidelity to the Word of God is the key to all Blessing from God.

TEACHING THE PEOPLE THE WORD OF GOD

This was truly a red letter day in Judah. For the first time, as stated, the king of Judah would send Priests all over Judah with instructions that they were to teach the people the Law of the Lord. This consisted then of Genesis, Exodus, Leviticus, Numbers, and Deuteronomy.

The Princes of Judah were given instruction by Jehoshaphat that they were to see to it that this was done, in other words, that the Priests would carry out this mission and do so with diligence. They went from village to village, from town to town, and from city to city. The Scripture says, "*. . . And went about throughout all the cities of Judah, and taught the people.*"

The single most important thing in Judah was the Word of God, just as the single most important thing in the world today is the Word of God. Unfortunately, the world little recognizes such, and sadder still, the church oftentimes follows suit.

Satan, at this particular time, is probably making the greatest attack against the Word of God that he has ever made. While he has always opposed the Word of God, as would be obvious, still, his attack today, although subtle, is, I think, the most dangerous ever.

When I was a child, most of the attacks by Satan against the Word came from modernists. Satan has changed his tactics somewhat presently.

He has brought out and is bringing out scores of versions referred to as *"Bibles,"* but in reality are no more than religious books. I speak of that such as the *"Message Bible."*

Unless your Bible is a word for word translation, then you really don't have a Bible. And to be certain, even as it regards a word for word translation, you had best stick with the King James Version.

WHAT DO WE MEAN BY A WORD FOR WORD TRANSLATION?

The Old Testament was originally written in Hebrew with a few Verses written in Aramaic. The New Testament was written in Greek. A word for word translation simply means that the translators sought to give the identical word in the language in which it is being translated as was originally given in the Hebrew and the Greek. Translation at its best is not easy; however, as it regards English, I personally feel that the King James translation is by far the best translation. In other words, it comes closer to the original languages than any other effort, I think.

However, it should be understood, as it regards the King James, that it has been modified several times, and rightly so, from its original printing.

The original printing, of which I personally have one or two pages, was written with such an Elizabethan flare, and understandably so, that it really cannot be read presently. So, to bring the language up to date, which is proper, it has been revised two or three times.

The reader must understand that when Moses wrote the Pentateuch and other of the Old Testament Books and, as well, the Apostles having written the New Testament Books, they did not speak in Elizabethan English. And neither did they write the Words of Christ in red.

THE EXPOSITOR'S STUDY BIBLE

When we developed, by the admonition of the Holy Spirit, the EXPOSITOR'S STUDY BIBLE, we elected, to a small degree, to substitute modern words to take the place of some of the Elizabethan words in the King James which are no longer used. I speak of words such as *"ye,"* or *"hast,"* etc. And please let me again emphasize, when the original writers wrote the Sacred Text, which they did under the inspiration of the Holy Spirit, they did not write in Elizabethan English, but rather the language of their day. I personally feel, as also stated, that the King James translators did an excellent job in translating the Scriptures. However, they translated it according to the words in use in their day, and as we have again stated, the King James has been revised two or three times, without changing the meaning whatsoever, in order to make it more readable. This was proper that it be done simply because if it had been left the way that it was originally written, no one would be able to read it.

WHAT IS INSPIRATION?

Peter said, and concerning the writing of the Holy Scriptures, and I quote from THE EXPOSITOR'S STUDY BIBLE: *"We have also a more sure Word of Prophecy* (Peter is speaking here of the Old Testament, which is the Word of God, and even more sure than his personal experience); *whereunto you do well that you take heed, as unto a light that shines in a dark place* (in effect, states that the Word of God is the only True Light, which alone can dispel the spiritual darkness), *until the day dawn, and the Day Star arise in your hearts* (the 'Day Star' is Christ; 'arising in our hearts' pertains to the Rapture):

"Knowing this first (harks back, as stated, to the Old Testament, which, in effect, was the Bible of Peter's day), *that no Prophecy of the Scripture is of any private interpretation.* (This refers to the fact that the Word of God did not originate in the human mind.)

"For the Prophecy (the word 'Prophecy' is used here in a general sense, covering the entirety of the Word of God, which means it's not limited merely to predictions regarding the future) *came not in old time by the will of man* (did not originate with man): *but Holy men of God spoke as they were moved by the Holy Spirit.* (This proclaims the manner in which the Word of God was written and, thereby, given unto us)" (II Pet 1:19-21).

Inspiration refers to the fact that God moved upon the hearts of the individuals who wrote the Holy Scriptures, guiding them in their thoughts, and even going so far as to select each and every word.

Some teach that these individuals went into a trance, with the Holy Spirit guiding their hands as they wrote; however, according to Peter, that is not the case.

The Holy Spirit, in using the individuals

to write the Holy Scriptures, used their education, their culture, and their personality, while at the same time selecting, as stated, the very words out of their vocabulary that He desired to be used. Some of the men who wrote the Scriptures were well educated, and some were not. In giving them what He wanted written, He did not go beyond their education and their knowledge, at least as far as instruction was concerned.

If what they were writing concerned instruction and teaching, to be sure, they understood perfectly that of which they wrote. However, if it were Prophecy they were writing, many times they did not understand what was being said. In fact, Peter also said concerning this: *"Of which Salvation the Prophets have enquired and searched diligently* (Old Testament Prophets carefully and diligently sought the meaning of the things they were prophesying as it concerned Christ and what He would do to redeem humanity [Gen. 49:10; Isa., Chpt. 53]), *who prophesied of the Grace that should come unto you* (this 'Grace' was not for their day, but for the coming dispensation, all made possible by the Cross):

"Searching what (these men diligently searched their own Prophecies, and the Prophecies of other Prophets, so that they might know that of which was spoken), *or what manner of time* (what kind of time would usher in this particular unique Salvation? the time of Grace alone, which means the Law would be no more) *the Spirit of Christ which was in them did signify* (whatever the Spirit of God did in Old Testament times, all pertained to Christ, without exception), *when it testified beforehand the sufferings of Christ* (refers to the Message of the Old Testament, all given by the Holy Spirit, and all pointing to the coming Redemption of man, which would be brought about by the Cross of Christ), *and the Glory that should follow.* (This proclaims all the wonderful things made possible by the 'Sufferings of Christ.')

"Unto whom it was revealed (refers to the Church), *that not unto themselves, but unto us they did minister the things* (proclaims the entirety of the Old Testament), *which are now reported unto you by them*

NOTES

who have preached the Gospel unto you (refers to what Christ did at the Cross, which the Prophets predicted) *with the Holy Spirit sent down from Heaven* (the Holy Spirit verified what Christ did at the Cross by coming from Heaven in a new dimension, thereby, abiding in the hearts and lives of Believers, and doing so permanently [Jn. 14:16-17]); *which things the Angels desire to look into.* (In other words, the Church is the University for Angels)" (I Pet. 1:10-12).

THE BEGINNINGS OF THE EXPOSITOR'S STUDY BIBLE

In the early 1980's, the Lord began to quietly deal with me about developing a Study Bible. To be sure, I instantly put such out of my mind, reckoning that I was woefully inadequate for such a task, and of that, I was most definitely correct. But the Holy Spirit did not let up.

I tried to put it out of my mind, but all to no avail, with the Holy Spirit continuing to lean in that direction.

I looked at other Study Bibles, some few that I considered to be very good, but still, was unhappy with the way and the manner they were developed. In other words, at times, it was difficult to find the notes that were prepared for the Text.

In looking back, even though the Lord began to deal with me as it regarded this momentous project, still, He did not allow me to follow it through to completion until after the Revelation of the Cross was given to me in 1997.

I know now and I realize that without a proper understanding of the Cross of Christ, one's understanding of the Word of God will be somewhat deficient. That is certainly not to say that understanding cannot be had, even extensively so, but it is meant to say that the Cross of Christ is actually the Story of the Bible. Consequently, if one doesn't fully understand the Cross of Christ as it refers not only to Salvation but, as well, to Sanctification, of which almost all of Paul's writings dealt, then one cannot properly understand the Word of God. The Story of the Bible is the Story of Jesus Christ and Him Crucified.

THE HOLY SPIRIT

Even after the Revelation of the Cross was given to me, which was actually that given to the Apostle Paul, which he gave to us in his fourteen Epistles, it was not until 2003, if I remember correctly, that the Holy Spirit said, in effect, *"It is time."*

Feeling strongly that the Holy Spirit desired me to do this, but yet, not knowing how it was to be done, and I speak of the physical makeup of the Scriptures and the notes, the Holy Spirit brought that together as well.

While writing Commentaries, I began to dissect the Scriptures, and then one fine day, the Holy Spirit spoke to my heart and said, *"This is the way that I want you to do this Bible."*

Now I had the format that I felt the Lord wanted me to use, a format, incidentally, which I had never seen anywhere else.

I felt that the Lord would have me to attempt to develop the New Testament first of all, so this is what I did.

I will never forget the day, sitting behind my desk, when I was to begin the work on THE EXPOSITOR'S STUDY BIBLE. To be sure, at that time, we didn't even have a name for this particular Bible. That was to come later.

I sat there for a few moments behind my desk, realizing what I was about to attempt to do, and also, for a few moments at least, realizing the heavy responsibility that encumbered itself upon me. I knew and realized that many people would guide their lives by the notes that were placed in the Text. I thought for a few moments that I would not be able to even begin. But then, the Spirit of the Lord began to move upon my heart, as I began to dictate.

THE LORD HELPED ME

The Lord told me to carry forth this project, told me how to do it, and then helped me to do it. I would be less than honest if I did not relate it in that fashion. That's exactly the way it happened.

Some have commented on the voluminous amount of work involved. But when such comments were addressed to me, I had to think about it for a few moments, simply because it did not seem like work or labor to me. It was because the Lord was helping me.

When the first printing was done, I read it from Genesis 1:1 through Revelation 22:21. As I was reading the Text, I remarked to Frances, *"If I had to do this again, I don't believe that I could do such a thing."* Of course, I could if the Lord would help me, but otherwise, no!

WHY DID THE LORD HAVE ME TO DEVELOP THE EXPOSITOR'S STUDY BIBLE?

No doubt, the Lord has many more reasons than we could ever begin to contemplate. But, to name just a few, we must understand first of all that the Word of God is the single most important thing in the world. Second, proper understanding of the Word is the single most important thing to each individual. I believe THE EXPOSITOR'S STUDY BIBLE will help an individual understand the Word of God as possibly they have not understood it previously.

A Baptist Preacher wrote me a short time ago stating, and I paraphrase his words, *"THE EXPOSITOR'S STUDY BIBLE is the greatest tool that has ever been placed into the hands of the Christian public to help them more perfectly understand the Word of God."* I realize that's quite a statement, but, as well, I believe it to be true.

There is no Study Bible, at least to my knowledge, that develops the great Message of the Cross as this Bible. This means that, regarding this all-important subject, information can be found in this Bible that simply cannot be found, at least to date, elsewhere.

As well, I believe that THE EXPOSITOR'S STUDY BIBLE is at least one of the greatest bulwarks against false doctrine that can be presently found. In other words, if any Believer will read this Bible, he will not fall for much of what is being passed off as gospel presently.

Also, if the Holy Spirit, in fact, told me to do this and helped me to do it, then it is His Desire that this Bible be placed into the hands of every single Believer. That's the reason presently that we are doing everything within our power to translate this Bible into every major language.

As I dictate these notes, the Spanish and Portuguese versions of THE EXPOSITOR'S NEW TESTAMENT have been completed. The entirety of the Bible in these languages should be finished shortly as well. Russian is being worked on right now with French soon to follow.

THE FIRST PRINTING

The first printing was the New Testament only. We printed 10,000 copies, wondering if that would be too many. They were gone within a matter of days. People were writing and asking, *"When will the entire Bible be finished?"*

The completion of the entire Bible took place in 2004. It is now the best seller of its kind in the world today, for which we give the Lord all the praise and the glory. Incidentally, THE EXPOSITOR'S STUDY BIBLE is the King James Version.

(10) "AND THE FEAR OF THE LORD FELL UPON ALL THE KINGDOMS OF THE LANDS THAT WERE ROUND ABOUT JUDAH, SO THAT THEY MADE NO WAR AGAINST JEHOSHAPHAT.

(11) "ALSO SOME OF THE PHILISTINES BROUGHT JEHOSHAPHAT PRESENTS, AND TRIBUTE SILVER; AND THE ARABIANS BROUGHT HIM FLOCKS, SEVEN THOUSAND AND SEVEN HUNDRED RAMS, AND SEVEN THOUSAND AND SEVEN HUNDRED HE GOATS.

(12) "AND JEHOSHAPHAT WAXED GREAT EXCEEDINGLY; AND HE BUILT IN JUDAH CASTLES, AND CITIES OF STORE.

(13) "AND HE HAD MUCH BUSINESS IN THE CITIES OF JUDAH: AND THE MEN OF WAR, MIGHTY MEN OF VALOUR, WERE IN JERUSALEM.

(14) "AND THESE ARE THE NUMBERS OF THEM ACCORDING TO THE HOUSE OF THEIR FATHERS: OF JUDAH, THE CAPTAINS OF THOUSANDS; ADNAH THE CHIEF, AND WITH HIM MIGHTY MEN OF VALOUR THREE HUNDRED THOUSAND.

(15) "AND NEXT TO HIM WAS JEHOHANAN THE CAPTAIN, AND WITH HIM TWO HUNDRED AND FOURSCORE THOUSAND.

(16) "AND NEXT TO HIM WAS AMASIAH THE SON OF ZICHRI, WHO WILLINGLY OFFERED HIMSELF UNTO THE LORD; AND WITH HIM TWO HUNDRED THOUSAND MIGHTY MEN OF VALOUR.

(17) "AND OF BENJAMIN; ELIADA A MIGHTY MAN OF VALOUR, AND WITH HIM ARMED MEN WITH BOW AND SHIELD TWO HUNDRED THOUSAND.

(18) "AND NEXT TO HIM WAS JEHOZABAD, AND WITH HIM AN HUNDRED AND FOURSCORE THOUSAND READY PREPARED FOR WAR.

(19) "THESE WAITED ON THE KING, BESIDE THOSE WHOM THE KING PUT IN THE FENCED CITIES THROUGHOUT ALL JUDAH."

The pattern is:

1. (Vs. 10) All of this shows that the Lord was immensely pleased with this which Jehoshaphat was doing. This Passage shows that God can stop enemies from making war, or He can cause them to make war. All depends on our Faith and our consecration.

2. As it regards Verse 11, this is the way it should be! Instead of Satan taking what we have, we should take what he has.

3. (Vs. 19) If it is to be noticed, terminology used of Jehoshaphat and his mighty men was very similar to the terminology used regarding David and his *"mighty men."*

THE FEAR OF THE LORD

The Tenth Verse shows that God was immensely pleased with Jehoshaphat's teaching program, for it says, *"And the fear of the LORD fell upon all the kingdoms of the lands that were round about Judah."* The lesson is made clear over and over again that if we serve the Lord with humility, He will bless us immeasurably. He will work for us; He will fight for us. It says, *"So that they made no war against Jehoshaphat."*

The Eleventh Verse proclaims that which God intends for every Believer. It says, *"Also some of the Philistines brought Jehoshaphat presents...."* Then it says, *"... The Arabians brought him flocks...."*

How sad it is when we read conversely that these same nations would take by force that which belonged to the People of God, but here, they are bringing to Jehoshaphat *"presents"* and *"silver."*

The Twelfth Verse says, *"And Jehoshaphat waxed great exceedingly...."* His *"greatness"* was all the Blessings of God. Can we expect the same today? Yes, we can, but only if we adhere to the *"Ways of the Lord."*

In actuality, Satan fears Spirit-filled Believers who have made the Cross of Christ the Object of their Faith. He fears in no other capacity. He was defeated at Calvary's Cross, along with all fallen Angels and demon spirits (Col. 2:14-15).

Satan doesn't fear our churches per se, doesn't fear our denominations, doesn't fear our religiosity, etc. He fears only the Cross of Christ. So, when Believers place their Faith exclusively in Christ and the Cross, understanding that the Cross of Christ is the meaning of the New Covenant, and understanding that the Cross is the Means by which all Blessings are given to the Child of God, Satan knows that such a Believer truly understands the Gospel.

Incidentally, a great part of the Law of God, which Jehoshaphat was having taught to the people of Judah, was made up of the great Sacrificial system, which was a symbol, a substitute, if you will, for the Cross of Christ. Judah was learning that despite the fact that she had a mighty army, still, her strength, her prosperity, and her power were in the shed Blood of the Lamb. It is the same presently; however, today we have the substance whereas Judah of old had only the Shadow.

"All to Jesus I surrender,
"All to Him I freely give;
"I will ever love and trust Him,
"In His Presence daily live."

"All to Jesus I surrender,
"Humbly at His Feet I bow,
"Worldly pleasures all forsaken,
"Take me, Jesus, take me now."

"All to Jesus I surrender,
"Make me, Saviour, wholly Thine;
"Let me feel the Holy Spirit,
"Truly know that You are mine."

"All to Jesus I surrender,
"Lord, I give myself to Thee;

"Fill me with Your Love and Power,
"Let Your Blessing fall on me."

CHAPTER 18

(1) "NOW JEHOSHAPHAT HAD RICHES AND HONOUR IN ABUNDANCE, AND JOINED AFFINITY WITH AHAB.

(2) "AND AFTER CERTAIN YEARS HE WENT DOWN TO AHAB TO SAMARIA. AND AHAB KILLED SHEEP AND OXEN FOR HIM IN ABUNDANCE, AND FOR THE PEOPLE WHO HE HAD WITH HIM, AND PERSUADED HIM TO GO UP WITH HIM TO RAMOTH-GILEAD.

(3) "AND AHAB KING OF ISRAEL SAID UNTO JEHOSHAPHAT KING OF JUDAH, WILL YOU GO WITH ME TO RAMOTH-GILEAD? AND HE ANSWERED HIM, I AM AS YOU ARE, AND MY PEOPLE AS YOUR PEOPLE; AND WE WILL BE WITH YOU IN THE WAR."

The pattern is:

1. (Vs. 1) Oftentimes, riches and honor are more dangerous to the Spiritual life than contempt and poverty. It is much better for the Preacher if most are cursing him instead of praising him.

2. (Vs. 1) Probably the greatest danger to the Church is *"joining affinity with the world."* This leaven that Satan introduced into Judah would ultimately drench Jerusalem with blood.

3. Verse 2 says, *"And after certain years he went down to Ahab to Samaria."* When the Believer *"goes down"* to the world, he is received with great hospitality, but immediately is made a tool of the world.

4. As it regards Verse 3, Jehoshaphat answered falsely. He, in fact, was led by the Lord, while Ahab was led by Satan. The people of Judah were worshippers of the True God, with the people of Israel worshipping Baal. In fact, there was no similarity between the two. The Lord was grossly displeased with Jehoshaphat making affinity with Ahab.

The idea seems to be that Ahab courted Jehoshaphat because of his *"riches and honor in abundance."* At this time, Judah was one of the most powerful nations in the region, and more than likely, the most powerful. So, Ahab sought this affinity.

Satan only desires the company of the true Believer for one purpose and reason, and that is to compromise his Faith.

Any attack by Satan, and this most definitely was an attack against Jehoshaphat, although it came in a very disguised way, was to hinder his Faith, which it ultimately did. Any departure from the right way is a departure from true Faith. Satan desires to destroy our Faith, and if he is unsuccessful in that, he desires to at least seriously weaken it. Any attack, irrespective as to its design, is for that purpose.

WHAT IS FAITH?

Paul said, *"Examine yourselves, whether you be in the Faith* (the words, 'the Faith,' refer to 'Christ and Him Crucified,' with the Cross ever being the Object of our Faith); *prove your own selves.* (Make certain your Faith is actually in the Cross, and not other things.) *Know you not your own selves, how that Jesus Christ is in you* (which He can only be by our Faith expressed in His Sacrifice), *except you be reprobates?* (Rejected)" (II Cor. 13:5).

Faith is the act of believing something!

Regarding Biblical Faith, it pertains to the Believer making the Cross of Christ the sole Object of his Faith. Faith in anything else will not be recognized by God. He recognizes His Son, the Lord Jesus Christ, and what He did at the Cross, and that alone. That's the reason that the Holy Spirit through the great Apostle said, *"Examine yourselves, whether you be in the Faith."*

Satan does not so much mind you having faith, even all kinds of faith in religious things. He just doesn't want your Faith to be in the Cross of Christ (I Cor. 1:17-18, 23; 2:2).

THE CORRECT OBJECT OF FAITH

Every human being in the world has faith. In fact, that is the manner of our creation (Heb. 11:3). Even the scientist who claims that he doesn't operate by faith, in fact, operates only by faith. He has faith that his experiments in the laboratory will ultimately produce the results that are desired. If it weren't for faith, he would not do anything. In fact, every single invention the world has ever known has come about because someone had faith.

The capitalist system runs entirely upon faith. Entrepreneurs invest in something they think is going to pay dividends, which makes the capitalist wheel turn. That's the reason that communism will not work. It takes out the commodity of faith, which leaves man with no incentive.

But yet, all of the faith mentioned is not faith that God recognizes, but is rather faith according to the creation model. While it most definitely was originated by God, such faith has nothing to do with the Redemption process.

Such faith is carried over into the realm of religion. In fact, every religion in the world, whether they realize it or not, or whether they will even admit to it or not, is founded on the basis of faith. It cannot be otherwise. But, even though all of this is religious faith, it is not faith that God will recognize.

When the Muslim straps a bomb belt around his or her waist, intent upon blowing himself up, along with others, he is doing so with faith that he is going to be immediately ushered into paradise. Of course, it's faith based on a lie, but, still, it's faith.

Unfortunately, Christianity is riddled with improper faith. It's faith in religious objects, faith in religious works, or faith in religious efforts, but still, it's not faith that God will recognize.

The Lord recognizes Faith in His Son, the Lord Jesus Christ, and what He did at the Cross, and that alone. Always remember, for Faith to be proper, for it to be recognized by God, and acted upon by God, it must have the correct Object, and that correct Object is the Cross of Christ. As we say over and over again, Christ is the Source of all things that we receive from God, while the Cross is the Means by which those things are given to us, all superintended by the Holy Spirit (Eph. 2:13-18).

Satan's greatest attack against the true Church is against the correct Object of Faith. He doesn't care what type of faith the Church has, how it promotes such faith, or how religious it might be. He only cares that it's in something other than the Cross of Christ.

WHY IS THE CROSS OF CHRIST
SO IMPORTANT?

It is important only in one aspect, but what an aspect, and that is that the Cross is the place where the price was paid for man's Redemption. When we talk about the Cross, we really aren't speaking of the wooden beam, but rather, the benefits which were there afforded. It's what Jesus did there.

Man's problem is sin. It is the cause of all heartache, all bloodshed, all war, all broken hearts, all sickness, and disease, etc. It is the cause of most of the population of the human race going to Hell. It is sin.

Our Lord gave His Body as a Sacrifice for sin, a Perfect Sacrifice, and that which God would accept and, in fact, did accept. It was accepted as total payment for all sin, past, present, and future, at least for all who will believe (Jn. 3:16).

Sin is that which provides the legal right for Satan to hold man captive. When Jesus died on the Cross, it was a Sacrifice which paid for all sin, because the life of the flesh is in the blood.

At the Cross the total Victory for man's Redemption was won. When Jesus said, *"It is finished,"* that was it! What happened at the Cross did not await even the Resurrection for it to be complete. Actually, due to the fact that all sin was atoned at the Cross, the Resurrection was not in doubt. The wages of sin is death, but if there is no sin remaining, there is no death. Actually, if there had been one sin left unatoned, Jesus could not have risen from the dead. The fact that He was raised from the dead proves that all sin was atoned.

While the Resurrection was very important, as should be understood, this tremendous Miracle, one could say the greatest ever performed by God, was not the cause of Redemption but rather the result of Redemption.

Everything that Jesus now is, the Saviour of mankind, seated at the right Hand of the Father, Victorious in every capacity, is all because of the Cross. And furthermore, it was all done for us.

NOTES

Ahab will now pull Jehoshaphat deeper into this morass of compromise, which will prove to be very costly.

(4) "AND JEHOSHAPHAT SAID UNTO THE KING OF ISRAEL, ENQUIRE, I PRAY YOU, AT THE WORD OF THE LORD TODAY.

(5) "THEREFORE THE KING OF ISRAEL GATHERED TOGETHER OF PROPHETS FOUR HUNDRED MEN, AND SAID UNTO THEM, SHALL WE GO TO RAMOTH-GILEAD TO BATTLE, OR SHALL I FORBEAR? AND THEY SAID, GO UP; FOR GOD WILL DELIVER IT INTO THE KING'S HAND.

(6) "BUT JEHOSHAPHAT SAID, IS THERE NOT HERE A PROPHET OF THE LORD BESIDES, THAT WE MIGHT ENQUIRE OF HIM?

(7) "AND THE KING OF ISRAEL SAID UNTO JEHOSHAPHAT, THERE IS YET ONE MAN, BY WHOM WE MAY ENQUIRE OF THE LORD: BUT I HATE HIM; FOR HE NEVER PROPHESIED GOOD UNTO ME, BUT ALWAYS EVIL: THE SAME IS MICAIAH THE SON OF IMLA. AND JEHOSHAPHAT SAID, LET NOT THE KING SAY SO.

(8) "AND THE KING OF ISRAEL CALLED FOR ONE OF HIS OFFICERS, AND SAID, FETCH QUICKLY MICAIAH THE SON OF IMLA.

(9) "AND THE KING OF ISRAEL AND JEHOSHAPHAT KING OF JUDAH SAT EITHER OF THEM ON HIS THRONE, CLOTHED IN THEIR ROBES, AND THEY SAY IN A VOID PLACE AT THE ENTERING IN OF THE GATE OF SAMARIA; AND ALL THE PROPHETS PROPHESIED BEFORE THEM.

(10) "AND ZEDEKIAH THE SON OF CHENAANAH HAD MADE HIM HORNS OF IRON, AND SAID, THUS SAYS THE LORD, WITH THESE YOU SHALL PUSH SYRIA UNTIL THEY BE CONSUMED.

(11) "AND ALL THE PROPHETS PROPHESIED SO, SAYING, GO UP TO RAMOTH-GILEAD, AND PROSPER: FOR THE LORD SHALL DELIVER IT INTO THE HAND OF THE KING."

The diagram is:

1. (Vs. 4) If Jehoshaphat had inquired of the Lord previously, he would not even be

here with Ahab.

2. (Vs. 5) The modern church abounds presently with this type of *"prophet."* They prophesy continuously, but they prophesy out of their own minds, because precious few are actually from the Lord.

3. (Vs. 6) At least, Jehoshaphat knew that their prophesies did not ring true. Unfortunately, far too many of modern Christendom don't know the false from the true.

4. (Vs. 7) Sadly, the ratio of 400-to-1 would pretty well hold true today. Prophets abound on every corner, but precious few are actually from the Lord. The few who are from the Lord are *"hated"*. Of this, one can be certain.

5. (Vs. 9) If it is to be noticed, these false prophets were prophesying prosperity, exactly as is the modern brand.

6. (Vs. 10) The false prophets were just as quick to cry, *"Thus says the LORD,"* but the truth was, what they were saying was <u>not</u> from the Lord.

"INQUIRE OF THE LORD?"

Jehoshaphat was in the wrong place at the wrong time to inquire of the Lord. He was in the midst of unbelief, calf-worship, and false prophets.

So, in answer to the request of Jehoshaphat, Ahab gathered together some 400 prophets of the calves, and said unto them, *"Shall we go to Ramoth-gilead to battle, or shall I forbear?"* They answered quickly, saying, *"Go up; for God will deliver it into the king's hand."*

They were very accustomed to saying what the king wanted to hear, and furthermore, even though the name of *"God"* is used, this is a god of their own making!

Jehoshaphat quickly ascertains that this situation is not on the up-and-up.

FALSE PROPHETS!

As the northern kingdom of Israel was full of false prophets then, the church, sadly so, is full of false prophets now. Prophets and prophecies abound with all type of supposed revelations, which, incidentally, never come to pass. Yes, there are a few true Prophets of the Lord, but if the truth be known, they are not too very much appreciated, even as Micaiah was not appreciated, which presents itself as a gross understatement.

The tragedy of it is, at least at this particular time, while Jehoshaphat was close enough to the Lord to ascertain the falseness of these calf-prophets, it seems the modern church has precious little discernment. Statements are made by these so-called prophets with dates and specifics given, which do not come to pass, and no one is called to account. Instead, they are paid and paid handsomely.

Concerning this, the Scripture says, *"For the time will come when they will not endure sound Doctrine* ('sound Doctrine' pertains to overriding principles: the Salvation of the sinner, and the Sanctification of the Saint; the Cross is the answer for both, and is the only answer for both); *but after their own lusts shall they heap to themselves teachers, having itching ears* (refers to the people who have ears that 'itch' for the smooth and comfortable word, and are willing to reward handsomely the man who is sufficiently compromising to speak it; hearers of this type have rejected the Truth and prefer to hear the lie);

"And they shall turn away their ears from the Truth (those who follow false teachers not only turn away their ears from the Truth, but see to it that the ears are always in a position such that they will never come in contact with the Truth), *and shall be turned unto fables.* (If it's not the *'Message of the Cross,'* then it is *'fables'* [I Cor. 1:18])" (II Tim. 4:3-4).

A FALSE MESSAGE

Verse 11 says, *"And all the prophets prophesied so, saying, Go up to Ramoth-gilead, and prosper: for the LORD shall deliver it into the hand of the king."*

That is the message of a great part of the modern church, as well, *"prosperity," "get rich,"* etc. The idea is, *"I'm going to get my stuff!"* So, in those circles, Christianity has been reduced to the dollar bill, and many of the people seem to love to have it so.

(12) "AND THE MESSENGER WHO WENT TO CALL MICAIAH SPOKE TO HIM, SAYING, BEHOLD, THE WORDS OF THE PROPHETS DECLARE GOOD

TO THE KING WITH ONE ASSENT; LET YOUR WORD THEREFORE, I PRAY YOU, BE LIKE ONE OF THEIRS, AND YOU SPEAK GOOD.

(13) "AND MICAIAH SAID, AS THE LORD LIVES, EVEN WHAT MY GOD SAYS, THAT WILL I SPEAK.

(14) "AND WHEN HE WAS COME TO THE KING, THE KING SAID UNTO HIM, MICAIAH, SHALL WE GO TO RAMOTH-GILEAD TO BATTLE, OR SHALL I FORBEAR? AND HE SAID, YOU GO UP, AND PROSPER, AND THEY SHALL BE DELIVERED INTO YOUR HAND.

(15) "AND THE KING SAID TO HIM, HOW MANY TIMES SHALL I ADJURE YOU THAT YOU SAY NOTHING BUT THE TRUTH TO ME IN THE NAME OF THE LORD?

(16) "THEN HE SAID, I DID SEE ALL ISRAEL SCATTERED UPON THE MOUNTAINS, AS SHEEP THAT HAVE NO SHEPHERD: AND THE LORD SAID, THESE HAVE NO MASTER; LET THEM RETURN THEREFORE EVERY MAN TO HIS HOUSE IN PEACE.

(17) "AND THE KING OF ISRAEL SAID TO JEHOSHAPHAT, DID I NOT TELL YOU THAT HE WOULD NOT PROPHESY GOOD UNTO ME, BUT EVIL?

(18) "AGAIN HE SAID, THEREFORE HEAR THE WORD OF THE LORD; I SAW THE LORD SITTING UPON HIS THRONE, AND ALL THE HOST OF HEAVEN STANDING ON HIS RIGHT HAND AND ON HIS LEFT.

(19) "AND THE LORD SAID, WHO SHALL ENTICE AHAB KING OF ISRAEL, THAT HE MAY GO UP AND FALL AT RAMOTH-GILEAD? AND ONE SPOKE SAYING AFTER THIS MANNER, AND ANOTHER SAYING AFTER THAT MANNER.

(20) "THEN THERE CAME OUT A SPIRIT, AND STOOD BEFORE THE LORD, AND SAID, I WILL ENTICE HIM. AND THE LORD SAID UNTO HIM, WHEREWITH?

(21) "AND HE SAID, I WILL GO OUT, AND BE A LYING SPIRIT IN THE MOUTH OF ALL HIS PROPHETS. AND THE LORD SAID, YOU SHALL ENTICE HIM, AND YOU SHALL ALSO PREVAIL: GO OUT, AND DO EVEN SO.

NOTES

(22) "NOW THEREFORE, BEHOLD, THE LORD HAS PUT A LYING SPIRIT IN THE MOUTH OF THESE YOUR PROPHETS, AND THE LORD HAS SPOKEN EVIL AGAINST YOU.

(23) "THEN ZEDEKIAH THE SON OF CHENAANAH CAME NEAR, AND SMOTE MICAIAH UPON THE CHEEK, AND SAID, WHICH WAY WENT THE SPIRIT OF THE LORD FROM ME TO SPEAK UNTO YOU?

(24) "AND MICAIAH SAID, BEHOLD, YOU SHALL SEE ON THAT DAY WHEN YOU SHALL GO INTO AN INNER CHAMBER TO HIDE YOURSELF.

(25) "THEN THE KING OF ISRAEL SAID, YOU TAKE MICAIAH, AND CARRY HIM BACK TO AMON THE GOVERNOR OF THE CITY, AND TO JOASH THE KING'S SON;

(26) "AND SAY, THUS SAYS THE KING, PUT THIS FELLOW IN THE PRISON, AND FEED HIM WITH BREAD OF AFFLICTION AND WITH WATER OF AFFLICTION, UNTIL I RETURN IN PEACE.

(27) "AND MICAIAH SAID, IF YOU CERTAINLY RETURN IN PEACE, THEN HAS NOT THE LORD SPOKEN BY ME. AND HE SAID, HEARKEN, ALL YOU PEOPLE."

The diagram is:

1. (Vs. 12) The times have changed; the demand has not. The apostate church is still saying, *"You speak good."* As Israel of old could not tolerate the truth, the modern church cannot tolerate the truth, either.

2. (Vs. 13) The determination of Micaiah to speak only what *"Thus says the LORD,"* would earn him continued imprisonment, the bread and water of affliction, and without Jehoshaphat lifting a hand to help him.

3. (Vs. 14) Micaiah begins by answering a fool according to his folly. He answers in sarcasm, which is easily obvious.

4. (Vs. 15) As the facts will prove, Ahab didn't want the truth!

5. (Vs. 17) Unfortunately, there are many false prophets presently, who are ready and willing to prophesy *"good,"* irrespective of what the truth actually is.

6. (Vs. 18) We are now privy to one of the most astounding pictures of the Throne of God, and the manner in which Heavenly business is conducted.

7. If Ahab had repented, the scene of Verse 19 would not have taken place. But despite the warning of the Lord, he will carry out his own self-will. It would be to his doom!

8. (Vs. 20) We learn from this account, and from Job, Chapters 1 and 2, that Satan, along with evil spirits, presently have access, at least at times, to the Throne of God. There will come a time, and shortly, when all such will be cast out of Heaven, and allowed no more entrance (Rev. 12:9-10). In fact, just exactly why the Lord has allowed Satan and demon spirits such access is a mystery (Rev. 10:7).

9. (Vs. 21) Lying spirits still have access to the mouths of false prophets, even unto this hour.

10. The idea of Verse 21 is, if men will not have the truth, the Lord will aid and abet their believing a lie.

11. (Vs. 22) We learn from this account that God controls not only the Heavenly Host of Righteousness, but also the world of spiritual darkness. Satan can only do what God allows him to do.

12. (Vs. 23) Jehoshaphat saw Zedekiah the son of Chenaanah smite Micaiah upon the cheek, and yet did not lift his hand to help the Prophet of God. Judah would pay dearly for Jehoshaphat's sin.

13. (Vs. 27) Before Micaiah was led away to prison, he turned to all the people who were present, who had heard God's pronouncement, and warned them! Sadly, they did not hearken, and Ahab was killed.

THE MESSAGE OF THE TRUE PROPHET

It was not a message that Ahab desired to hear, but it was from the Lord, and it was true. The message was clear. It said, *"I did see all Israel scattered upon the mountains, as sheep that have no shepherd. . . ."* This meant that Ahab, the king of the northern confederacy of Israel, would be killed.

As stated, this was the very opposite of what the 400 false prophets had stated.

Despite the sin and rebellion of Ahab, this was the Lord showing Mercy to this man. If Ahab had listened and believed, his life would have been spared, at least at that time;

NOTES

however, he did not heed! He did not listen!

Most of the time, men hear what they want to hear. That's the reason that Jesus repeatedly stated, *"He who has ears to hear, let him hear"* (Mat. 11:15; 13:9, 43; Mk. 4:9; etc.).

JEHOSHAPHAT

So, what did Jehoshaphat believe as it regarded this Prophecy?

The evidence seems to be, and despite the clearness of the delivery, that Jehoshaphat did not know what to believe. Whenever a Believer is in the wrong place, a place, incidentally, which is captured by evil spirits, his judgment is almost always faulty. It was no less with Jehoshaphat. He should not have been there in the first place, and even now, it is not too late to turn around. But for reasons unknown to us, he seemed to not have the courage to take a stand.

THE VISION

At this particular time, the Prophet Micaiah, who, incidentally, is listed here only, sees a Vision which he relates to all present, even going into great detail, of the Throne of God, and the way that business is at times conducted. The following is what he saw:

• He saw the Throne of God with all of its splendor and glory.

• He then heard the Lord ask the question, *"Who shall entice Ahab king of Israel, that he may go up and fall at Ramoth-gilead?"* Evidently, these were Angels to whom the Lord was speaking.

• The Scripture then portrays the fact that an evil spirit came and stood before the Lord. Yes, in a limited way, evil spirits still have access to Heaven. Job, Chapters 1 and 2, also bear this out.

• The evil spirit said that he would be *"a lying spirit in the mouth of all his prophets,"* which is exactly what happened. In other words, the exact opposite of what they stated would take place would be what would happen. Ahab would be killed!

EVIL SPIRITS IN HEAVEN

It is very difficult for many Believers to understand evil spirits having access to the

Throne of God and, even at times, Satan himself, but the Bible bears it out that this is the case.

It also tells us that there is coming a time when Satan and his cohorts of darkness will no more have access to Heaven, but will be cast out. The Scripture says,

"*And there was war in Heaven* (pertains to the '*Mystery of God*' being finished [Rev. 10:7]): *Michael and his Angels fought against the dragon; and the dragon fought and his Angels* (this pertains to Satan and all the Angels who followed him being cast out of Heaven, which will take place at the midpoint of the Great Tribulation; why the Lord has allowed Satan and his minions to remain in Heaven all of this time, we aren't told; it is a '*Mystery,*' but it will now be finished),

"*And prevailed not* (Satan will then be defeated; incidentally, it is not Satan who instigates this war, but rather the Archangel Michael at the Command of God); *neither was their place found any more in Heaven* (joins with the close of the Book of Revelation, where the Evil One has no more place on Earth as well, but rather the place of torment forever and ever [Rev. 20:10]).

"*And the great dragon was cast out, that old serpent, called the Devil, and Satan* (he is referred to as '*the Great Dragon*' because of his propensity to '*steal, kill, and destroy*' [Jn. 10:10]; he is the '*old serpent*' because in his first appearance in the Bible, he chose to work through a serpent; therefore, he is what the curse caused the serpent to be, wryly subtle, and treacherous), *which deceives the whole world* (deception is his greatest weapon; he deceives, and is himself deceived): *he was cast out into the Earth, and his Angels were cast out with him* (pronounces the beginning of the end for this evil monster)" (Rev. 12:7-9).

As we said in the notes, just exactly as to why the Lord has allowed such to happen, and we continue to speak of demon spirits, and even Satan himself, having access to Heaven, and even the very Throne of God at times, is a mystery. The Lord has not chosen to inform us as to why He has allowed this, except for the scant information given. But this we do know, whatever the Lord has done, He has done it well, always having a

NOTES

reason for that which is carried out.

THE FATE OF MICAIAH

The last we hear of this faithful Prophet, he is being taken to prison and, as well, to be *"fed with the bread of affliction and the water of affliction."* That's one of the reasons true Prophets are in short supply.

Why didn't Jehoshaphat speak up at this time and demand different treatment for this Prophet?

That's a good question!

Ahab did not return in peace but returned as a corpse, so where did that leave Micaiah?

One would like to think that Jehoshaphat saw to him after this battle was complete, but the Scripture is silent.

What were the thoughts of Micaiah?

No doubt, he reasoned in his heart that surely Jehoshaphat would help him, but the king of Judah was silent.

One thing is certain, Micaiah was faithful to his calling. He did not compromise or trim the Message, even though the pressure was great for him to do so. Would to God there were more like him presently!

(28) "SO THE KING OF ISRAEL AND JEHOSHAPHAT THE KING OF JUDAH WENT UP TO RAMOTH-GILEAD.

(29) "AND THE KING OF ISRAEL SAID UNTO JEHOSHAPHAT, I WILL DISGUISE MYSELF, AND I WILL GO TO THE BATTLE; BUT YOU PUT ON YOUR ROBES. SO THE KING OF ISRAEL DISGUISED HIMSELF; AND THEY WENT TO THE BATTLE.

(30) "NOW THE KING OF SYRIA HAD COMMANDED THE CAPTAINS OF THE CHARIOTS WHO WERE WITH HIM, SAYING, FIGHT YOU NOT WITH SMALL OR GREAT, SAVE ONLY WITH THE KING OF ISRAEL.

(31) "AND IT CAME TO PASS, WHEN THE CAPTAINS OF THE CHARIOTS SAW JEHOSHAPHAT, THAT THEY SAID, IT IS THE KING OF ISRAEL. THEREFORE THEY COMPASSED ABOUT HIM TO FIGHT: BUT JEHOSHAPHAT CRIED OUT, AND THE LORD HELPED HIM; AND GOD MOVED THEM TO DEPART FROM HIM.

(32) "FOR IT CAME TO PASS, THAT, WHEN THE CAPTAINS OF THE CHARIOTS PERCEIVED THAT IT WAS NOT THE

KING OF ISRAEL, THEY TURNED BACK AGAIN FROM PURSUING HIM.

(33) "AND A CERTAIN MAN DREW A BOW AT A VENTURE, AND SMOTE THE KING OF ISRAEL BETWEEN THE JOINTS OF THE HARNESS: THEREFORE HE SAID TO HIS CHARIOT MAN, TURN YOUR HAND, THAT YOU MAY CARRY ME OUT OF THE HOST; FOR I AM WOUNDED.

(34) "AND THE BATTLE INCREASED THAT DAY: HOWBEIT THE KING OF ISRAEL STAYED HIMSELF UP IN HIS CHARIOT AGAINST THE SYRIANS UNTIL THE EVENING: AND ABOUT THE TIME OF THE SUN GOING DOWN HE DIED."

The pattern is:

1. (Vs. 28) Jehoshaphat was a foolish man, especially in the face of this Prophecy, to accompany Ahab.

2. As it regards Verse 29, one can only say *"stupid men!"* If men spent as much time trying to please God as they do trying to outwit God, how much better off they would be.

3. (Vs. 30) The Lord had put it in the mind of the king of Syria to seek only Ahab.

4. (Vs. 31) It was only by the Mercy and Grace of God that Jehoshaphat was spared. In fact, he had no business being here.

5. (Vs. 33) The *"certain man who drew a bow at venture"* means he just shot the arrow, not especially aiming at anything, but God guided the arrow straight toward Ahab.

6. The Thirty-fourth Verse says, *"And about the time of the sun going down he died."* The sun went *"down"* for Ahab in more ways than one. He not only lost his life; he lost his soul—despite the fact that God had attempted to show him Mercy and Grace. His death is a portrayal of rebellion—a rebellion that characterizes most of the human race. How many today are headed toward their doom, spurning the Love, Grace, and Mercy of God, along with repeated warnings? Their *"sun is going down."*

THE DISGUISE

How foolish are men. While Ahab most definitely was a long way from God, still, he knew enough about the Lord to know that he could not outwit God.

What was he thinking?

NOTES

The Lord had said that if he went into this battle, he was going to be killed.

This man had seen God perform some of the greatest Miracles through the Ministry of the great Prophet Elijah. So, he knew better. But, let the following be understood:

When an individual is in rebellion against God, as was Ahab, pure and simple, they don't think right. How foolish he was to think that he could disguise himself, and such would thwart the Will of God. But, evidently that's what he thought.

As well, how foolish was Jehoshaphat in participating in this battle. He had heard what the Prophet had said about the coming death of Ahab. He should not have wanted or desired to have been anywhere close. In fact, had it not been for the Mercy and Grace of God, Jehoshaphat would have been killed as well.

Even though the king of Judah was a Man of God and, in fact, one of the greatest kings that Judah had, still, at this time he was out of the Will of God, and we might say, as well, did not think correctly.

THE LORD HELPED HIM

Pure and simple, if the Lord had not helped Jehoshaphat, he would have been killed that day, as stated, along with Ahab.

The men manning the chariots of the nation of Syria saw Jehoshaphat, and because he was wearing kingly robes, thought it was Ahab, the king of the northern confederation of Israel. So, they went in to kill him. That's when he cried to the Lord.

Thank God that the Lord does not limit His Help to us only on the premise of perfect obedience. If He did, all of us would be in serious trouble.

Out of the Will of God, in a place he was not supposed to be, still, the Scripture plainly and beautifully says, *". . . and the LORD helped him."*

To carry out this maneuver, the Lord moved upon the charioteers, causing something else to grab their attention, and the Scripture says they *"departed from him."* It seems from Verse 32 that somehow they recognized Jehoshaphat and then realized that it wasn't Ahab. So, *"they turned back again from pursuing him."*

Due to the fact that Ahab had not worn his kingly robes and had put on the ordinary dress of all of the thousands of his other soldiers, there was really no way that the army of Syria could successfully seek him out; so, he, no doubt, felt very secure in his disguise.

But, *"A certain man drew a bow at a venture,"* meaning that he just merely shot an arrow into the sky. He wasn't shooting at Ahab simply because he did not know who Ahab was. But the Lord guided the arrow and it *"smote the king of Israel between the joints of the harness." "At about the time of the sun going down he died."*

At this moment, about 2,900 years after this event, Ahab is still in Hell. He will be there forever and forever. He has had time to think of all the Miracles he saw performed by Elijah. He has, no doubt, mulled it over in his mind countless times how the Lord, through the Prophet Micaiah, told him what would happen in this battle, but he didn't heed the words of the Man of God. He will think upon it forever and forever, because Hell is eternal.

What an opportunity he had, and what an opportunity untold millions have, all to no avail. The sun went down for him the last time, as it has gone down, and is going down, for millions of others—the last time.

"Holy Spirit, Truth Divine,
"Dawn upon this soul of mine;
"Word of God, an Inward Delight,
"Wait my spirit, clear my sight."

"Holy Spirit, Love Divine,
"Glow within this heart of mine,
"Kindle every high desire,
"Perish self in Your Pure Fire."

"Holy Spirit, Power Divine,
"Fill and nerve this will of mine;
"By You may I strongly live,
"Bravely bear, and nobly strive."

"Holy Spirit, Peace Divine,
"Still this restless heart of mine,
"Speak to calm this tossing sea,
"Stayed in Your Tranquility."

"Holy Spirit, Joy Divine,
"Gladden Thou this heart of mine;

"In the desert ways I'll sing:
"Spring, O Well, forever spring!"

CHAPTER 19

(1) "AND JEHOSHAPHAT THE KING OF JUDAH RETURNED TO HIS HOUSE IN PEACE TO JERUSALEM.

(2) "AND JEHU THE SON OF HANANI THE SEER WENT OUT TO MEET HIM, AND SAID TO KING JEHOSHAPHAT, SHOULD YOU HELP THE UNGODLY, AND LOVE THEM WHO HATE THE LORD? THEREFORE IS WRATH UPON YOU FROM BEFORE THE LORD.

(3) "NEVERTHELESS THERE ARE GOOD THINGS FOUND IN YOU, IN THAT YOU HAVE TAKEN AWAY THE GROVES OUT OF THE LAND, AND HAVE PREPARED YOUR HEART TO SEEK GOD."

The pattern is:

1. (Vs. 1) This Chapter proclaims rebuke and Repentance. Jehoshaphat returned in peace, only because the Lord was merciful to him.

2. (Vs. 1) The two kings, Ahab and Jehoshaphat, are perfect examples of rebellion against God, which brings death, and serving God, which brings life—and that despite Jehoshaphat's unfaithfulness.

3. (Vs. 2) The Lord was very displeased with Jehoshaphat's alliance with Ahab, and there would be repercussions, even as the word *"wrath"* proclaims, and which we shall see. Sin must never be taken lightly or with impunity. In fact, sin is so powerful that the only answer to this dilemma is the Cross (Heb. 10:12).

THE PROPHET OF GOD

Hanani is the Prophet, and he goes out to meet Jehoshaphat, who was returning from this conflict with Syria in which Ahab lost his life. He will give a Message from the Lord to the king, and part of it will be very negative.

Why didn't Jehoshaphat go to this Prophet before he formed an alliance with Ahab?

No doubt, Jehoshaphat made himself believe that what he was doing was right, despite the warning signs all along the way. He probably felt that he didn't need the counsel of Hanani. If, in fact, those were his thoughts, how wrong he was.

When we read these accounts in the Bible, even as we certainly should do so, it seems so easy to us as to what should have been done or what should not have been done. But, as we understand it from our own life and living, situations in retrospect are never as simple or as easy as they may seem to be. If they were that easy, and we were sincere, we would never make a mistake, taking our example from the Word of God.

To be sure, our example is the Word of God, and again, we should learn from that which is given to us, but as Jehoshaphat and all the other Bible greats, we seemingly do not learn quickly or easily.

The Message that Hanani gave was as follows. We will give the negative side first:
- *"Why do you help the ungodly?"*
- *"Why do you love them who hate the LORD?"*
- *"Therefore is wrath come upon you from before the LORD."*

The Third Verse records a positive side to the Message from the Lord. It is as follows:
- *"Nevertheless there are good things found in you."*
- *"You have taken away the groves out of the land."*
- *"You have prepared your heart to seek God."*

As should be obvious, the Lord knows all about us at all times, what we are doing, where we are going, and even what we are thinking.

THE SERIOUSNESS OF THE MATTER

One might tend to think that the Lord was being somewhat harsh with Jehoshaphat, specifying to him that *"wrath would come upon him from the LORD."* But the magnitude of his sin, as it regards his alliance with Ahab, was not a small thing.

In his *"helping the ungodly,"* namely Ahab and, in fact, the northern confederation of Israel, in effect, he was actually helping them to disobey God. Now think about that! Helping the ungodly to disobey the Lord is not exactly something that we desire to do. The Lord does not look upon it lightly.

And then the question, *"Why do you love them who hate the LORD?"* That's a good question!

While we love the souls of those who are opposed to the Lord, we certainly do not love their sinful actions. Neither do we do things for them that will aid and abet them in their wrongdoing and rebellion against God, for that's what Jehoshaphat was doing as it regarded Ahab.

COME OUT FROM AMONG THEM AND BE SEPARATE

Concerning Believers under the New Covenant, Paul said, *"Be you not unequally yoked together with unbelievers* (there are two fellowships in the world, and only two; all men belong either to one or the other; no one can belong to both and claim to be a Christian; one is with the world, and one is with the Lord): *for what fellowship has Righteousness with unrighteousness?* (None!) *and what communion has light with darkness?* (None!)

"And what concord has Christ with Belial? (This presents another name for Satan.) *or what part has he who believes with an infidel?* (Those who make a profession of Salvation should resolve to separate themselves from the world. However, it is separation and not isolation.)

"And what agreement has the Temple of God with idols? (God and idols cannot mix.) *for you are the Temple of the Living God* (speaking of all Believers); *as God has said* (Ex. 29:45; Lev. 26:12; Ezek. 37:27), *I will dwell in them, and walk in them; and I will be their God, and they shall be My People.* (The Believer is the Sanctuary of the Holy Spirit, all made possible by the Cross.)

"Wherefore come out from among them, and be you separate, says the Lord (as stated, the Word of God emphatically teaches separation from the world, but not isolation), *and touch not the unclean thing* (refers to Christians avoiding all unholy contact with a vain and polluted world); *and I will receive you* (at the same time, means if the person disobeys these injunctions, the Lord will not receive us; the Christian can walk clean

in this world only by constantly evidencing Faith in the Cross of Christ, which makes it possible for the Holy Spirit to do His Work within our lives),

"And will be a Father unto you (but only under the conditions mentioned in the above Scriptures), *and you shall be My Sons and Daughters, says the Lord Almighty.* (*'Lord Almighty'* in the Hebrew is *'Jehovah Shaddai.'* The Hebrew word *'Shad'* means a woman's breast. The title *'Shaddai'* suggests that we must never resort to the world, but rather draw all nourishment from the Lord Who can provide all things, which the world can never provide)" (II Cor. 6:14-18).

IN THE WORLD BUT NOT OF THE WORLD

Regrettably, some modern day churches, which, incidentally, claim to be Spirit-filled, have blurred the line, and badly, between the Believer and the world. They are encouraging Christians into occupations that by no means can be said to be Christlike.

But the question is, *"How could a preacher, who claims to believe the Bible, encourage someone to remain in that type of atmosphere?"*

Let the following be understood:

We cannot be a witness by becoming that to which we are opposed or most definitely should be opposed. In other words, one cannot win the drunkard by drinking with him or the gambler by gambling with him, etc. While we must love the sinner and do all that we can to be a blessing to them, it must ever be understood that their lifestyle is no longer ours.

GOOD THINGS FOUND IN YOU

The good things were:
- *"You have taken away the groves out of the land."*
- *"You have prepared your heart to seek God."*

All of this portrays the fact, as should be obvious, that the Lord knows all things. He sees that which is wrong, and He sees that which is right. He knows our hearts, and He Alone knows our hearts.

We must bear in mind, however, that there were great limitations as it regarded

NOTES

how the Holy Spirit could help those under the Old Covenant. For instance, while He was with all Believers, He definitely was not in all Believers as He is now. That's what Jesus was talking about when He said, ". . . *for He dwells with you* (before the Cross), *and shall be in you* (which would take place on the Day of Pentecost and forward, because the sin debt has been forever paid by Christ on the Cross, changing the disposition of everything)" (Jn. 14:17).

Before the Cross, the Holy Spirit did come into the hearts and lives of a select few, such as Prophets, etc., to help them carry out a particular task, but it was only for a period of time. The help of the Holy Spirit in this capacity had little or nothing to do with one's Sanctification, in other words, how they lived for God. It was only for the task at hand.

Since the Cross, every Believer has the Holy Spirit living within our hearts and lives, and doing so permanently. This gives us, as should be obvious, a tremendous advantage. But the tragedy is, most Believers simply do not know how the Holy Spirit works, which means that He is able to help not nearly as much as He would like. Let me explain.

HOW THE HOLY SPIRIT WORKS

The Holy Spirit works entirely within the framework of the Finished Work of Christ. In other words, it is the Cross of Christ which provides the legal means for the Spirit to do all the things that He Alone can do.

When Jesus died on the Cross, He atoned for all sin, past, present and future, at least for all who will believe. This made it possible for the Holy Spirit to come into the hearts and lives of Believers, which He does at conversion, and there to abide forever (Jn. 14:16).

Under the Old Testament economy, animal blood was woefully insufficient to remove sin, so that means the sin debt remained, which means the Holy Spirit was limited as to what He could do.

The Spirit does not demand much of us, but He does demand that our Faith be exclusively in Christ and the Cross. Then and then alone can He work in our lives, helping us to overcome sin and to be what we ought to be (Rom. 6:1-14; 8:1-2, 11; I Cor. 1:17-18, 23; 2:2; Gal., Chpt. 5; 6:14; Eph. 2:13-18; Col. 2:14-15).

If the Believer's Faith is in something other than Christ and the Cross, this greatly limits the Holy Spirit, which means that the sin nature is going to rule in the heart and life of such a Believer (Rom. 6:12).

Regrettably, most Believers have some knowledge of the Cross of Christ as it refers to Salvation, but almost none at all as it refers to our Sanctification or how we live for God. In other words, they draw a total blank on that score.

It must be understood that almost the entirety of the teaching given by the Apostle Paul concerned Believers and how we live for God. Virtually the entirety of his teaching on the Cross referred to our Sanctification, but most Believers do not seem to understand that.

HUMANISTIC PSYCHOLOGY AND THE CROSS OF CHRIST

In the late 1950's and the early 1960's, the church began to embrace humanistic psychology. When this happened, they began to abandon the Cross of Christ. At the present time, the church has, for all practical purposes, embraced humanistic psychology in totality. In fact, most preachers are preaching psychology and don't even know they are. As well, the preaching of the Cross is pretty much nonexistent.

One cannot have both, psychology and the Cross of Christ. One or the other must go. Unfortunately, and that's a gross understatement, the modern church has opted for humanistic psychology.

While they claim to believe in the Cross, the truth is, they don't. They have opted for worldly wisdom, which is sensual and devilish, and, thereby, have forsaken heavenly wisdom (James 3:15-17). As a result, fewer Believers are being delivered today than at any time since the Reformation. There desperately needs to be another Reformation, which will take the church back to the Cross. Please understand the following:

The only thing standing between mankind and eternal Hell is the Cross of Christ.

That should be enough said.

NOTES

(4) "AND JEHOSHAPHAT DWELT AT JERUSALEM: AND HE WENT OUT AGAIN THROUGH THE PEOPLE FROM BEER-SHEBA TO MOUNT EPHRAIM, AND BROUGHT THEM BACK UNTO THE LORD GOD OF THEIR FATHERS.
(5) "AND HE SET JUDGES IN THE LAND THROUGHOUT ALL THE FENCED CITIES OF JUDAH, CITY BY CITY,
(6) "AND SAID TO THE JUDGES, TAKE HEED WHAT YOU DO: FOR YOU JUDGE NOT FOR MAN, BUT FOR THE LORD, WHO IS WITH YOU IN THE JUDGMENT.
(7) "WHEREFORE NOW LET THE FEAR OF THE LORD BE UPON YOU; TAKE HEED AND DO IT: FOR THERE IS NO INIQUITY WITH THE LORD OUR GOD, NOR RESPECT OF PERSONS, NOR TAKING OF GIFTS.
(8) "MOREOVER IN JERUSALEM DID JEHOSHAPHAT SET OF THE LEVITES, AND OF THE PRIESTS, AND OF THE CHIEF OF THE FATHERS OF ISRAEL, FOR THE JUDGMENT OF THE LORD, AND FOR CONTROVERSIES, WHEN THEY RETURNED TO JERUSALEM.
(9) "AND HE CHARGED THEM, SAYING, THUS SHALL YOU DO IN THE FEAR OF THE LORD, FAITHFULLY, AND WITH A PERFECT HEART.
(10) "AND WHAT CAUSE SOEVER SHALL COME TO YOU OF YOUR BRETHREN WHO DWELL IN YOUR CITIES, BETWEEN BLOOD AND BLOOD, BETWEEN LAW AND COMMANDMENT, STATUTES AND JUDGMENTS, YOU SHALL EVEN WARN THEM THAT THEY TRESPASS NOT AGAINST THE LORD, AND SO WRATH COME UPON YOU, AND UPON YOUR BRETHREN: THIS DO, AND YOU SHALL NOT TRESPASS.
(11) "AND, BEHOLD, AMARIAH THE CHIEF PRIEST IS OVER YOU IN ALL MATTERS OF THE LORD; AND ZEBADIAH THE SON OF ISHMAEL, THE RULER OF THE HOUSE OF JUDAH, FOR ALL THE KING'S MATTERS: ALSO THE LEVITES SHALL BE OFFICERS BEFORE YOU. DEAL COURAGEOUSLY, AND THE LORD SHALL BE WITH THE GOOD."

The pattern is:

1. The word *"again"* in Verse 4 speaks

of Repentance on the part of Jehoshaphat and, as well, the second revival of teaching the Law of Moses and bringing the people back to God. The *"Word"* must always be set before the people. There is no other refuge!

2. (Vs. 6) Civil duties were to be carried out in Judah strictly according to the Word of the Lord.

3. The *"taking of gifts"* of Verse 7 speaks of bribery. Honest judgment by these Judges must be in the Name of the Lord, and all, as stated, according to God's Word.

4. Verse 8 concerned cases appealed to the higher court, actually the highest in Israel. There must be justice for the poor, and the rich must not be able to buy their way out of wrongdoing. All of this actually goes back to the Cross, in effect, stating that sin cannot be assuaged by any other manner than the Cross.

5. (Vs. 10) Jehoshaphat warns these Judges that if they do not abide by the Word of the Lord, they will be committing sin, and the Wrath of God will be the result.

6. *"The LORD being with the good,"* of Verse 11, at the same time states that the Lord cannot be with the bad.

BROUGHT THE PEOPLE BACK TO
THE LORD GOD OF THEIR FATHERS

The idea is, Jehoshaphat seemed to be doing all that he could to bring Judah to a place of surrender to the Lord, and that was according to the Law of God. He is to be greatly commended for that, especially considering that the Holy Spirit recorded this effort.

If the leadership will take the initiative, even as did Jehoshaphat, most of the time, many of the people will follow. Unfortunately, as it regards religious denominations presently, there aren't so very many leaders of these denominations who put the Lord first. Regrettably, most religious denominations are more political even than their secular counterparts. So, that which is politically expedient is that which is done instead of that which the Lord desires. Jehoshaphat, thankfully, was the exception.

BACK TO THE CROSS

In the late 1950's and the early 1960's, the Pentecostal Denominations in America and Canada began to drift toward humanistic psychology. The nominal denominations had long since gone in that direction. Embracing humanistic psychology means at the same time that the Cross of Christ is abandoned. One cannot have it both ways; either one cancels out the other.

At the present time, the modern church little preaches the Cross at all, and it is because, as stated, of the psychological direction. Men have traded the heavenly wisdom, which is peaceable and pure, for the wisdom of this world, which is *"earthly, sensual, and devilish"* (James 3:15-17).

I can personally remember when the drift began. In those days, I had no knowledge of humanistic psychology. If I had given any opinion on it at all, my thoughts were that those who had gone into this field were trying to help people, and there were most definitely people who needed help, so, more power to the effort.

When we began Family Worship Center in 1980 (I believe it was), my thoughts continued in the same vein, and, in fact, we hired two psychologists and put them on staff.

In those days, we had a 5,000 watt AM radio station over which we broadcast the Gospel every day. I gave these two psychologists, a man and his wife, a 30 minute program each day. Being busy, I really did not listen to the program.

One day one of my associates came to me and asked, *"Do you know what these people are teaching?"* I admitted that I did not, actually thinking that they were teaching what we were proclaiming, which, in effect, was the Lord Jesus Christ. I listened to the program and quickly ascertained that their message was not ours.

I called the brother in. I don't remember if his wife was with him or not. After questioning him for a period of time, I ascertained that we were not on the same wave length and terminated his employment, along with his wife's.

At that time I began to look into humanistic psychology, actually reading all the material I could find regarding psychology and the Bible. I found to my dismay that this philosophy was totally unscriptural.

A BELIEF SYSTEM

Humanistic psychology teaches that man is inherently good, and if he is placed in the right environment, the good will come out and will be exhibited for all to see. If men are bad, it's because of something that was done to them. In other words, they are victims.

The Bible teaches the very opposite of that. It teaches that the heart is desperately wicked, and that includes all (Jer. 17:9).

God knows the hopeless corruption of the natural heart, and so He said to Nicodemus that no one, however cultured and moral, can either see or enter into the Kingdom of God. There must be a New Birth.

Concerning man, the Holy Spirit through Paul said, *"As it is written* (Ps. 14:1-3), *There is none righteous, no, not one* (addresses the complaint of the Jews and clinches the argument with the Scriptures, which the Jews could not deny)*:*

"There is none who understands (proclaims total depravity), *there is none who seek after God* (man left on his own will not seek God and, in fact, cannot seek God; he is spiritually dead).

"They are all gone out of the Way (speaks of the lost condition of all men; the *'Way'* is God's Way), *they are together become unprofitable* (refers to the terrible loss in every capacity of wayward man); *there is none who does good, no, not one* (the Greek Text says, *'useless!'*).

"Their throat is an open sepulcher (the idea is of an open grave, with the rotting remains sending forth a putrid stench); *with their tongues they have used deceit* (speaks of guile, deception, hypocrisy, etc.); *the poison of asps is under their lips* (man cannot be trusted in anything he says)*:*

"Whose mouth is full of cursing (wishing someone evil or hurt) *and bitterness* (bitter and reproachful language)*:*

"Their feet are swift to shed blood (the world is filled with murder, killing, and violence)*:*

"Destruction and misery are in their ways (all brought about by sin)*:*

"And the way of peace have they not known (and cannot know until Christ returns)*:*

NOTES

"There is no fear of God before their eyes (there is no fear of God, because unbelieving man does not know God)*"* (Rom. 3:10-18).

So, if the Bible says such of man, which is diametrically opposed to that which psychology claims, how can the two be reconciled? That's what the so-called Christian psychologist attempts to do.

The truth is, the two cannot be reconciled. As stated, the Bible is of the Wisdom of God, while humanistic psychology is of the wisdom of this world.

As a result of this foray into humanistic psychology by the church, there are fewer people presently being Saved than at any time since the Reformation. There are fewer Believers being baptized with the Holy Spirit than at any time since the turn of the Twentieth Century. There are fewer people being healed by the Power of God, and fewer people being delivered, than at any time since the Reformation. But yet, the church spurns the Cross and embraces the wisdom of this world. How the mighty have fallen!

UNBELIEF

When the Lord opened up to me the Revelation of the Cross in 1997, the elation and joy which filled my soul were absolutely boundless. This event was the greatest in my Spiritual Life, other than when I was Saved by the Precious Blood of Christ. I now knew the problem, which was the sin nature, and the cure for that problem, which is the Cross of Christ and how the Holy Spirit works in all of this. I was so happy, so thrilled, and so overjoyed that I found some nights that it was difficult to sleep. I was that excited about what the Lord had done for me. Thankfully, I had the presence of mind during the very midst of this Revelation to request of the Lord that He keep revealing to me the great Truths of the Cross. I realized that what I had was absolutely revolutionary, but I also knew that I had just scratched the surface. Thankfully, the Lord took me at my word. From that day until now, He has continually opened this door wider and wider, showing me more and more as it regards the greatest Covenant the world has ever known, the New Covenant, all in Christ and what He did at the Cross.

In those days in 1997, my feelings were that if the church world knew and understood what the Lord had given to me, they would surely embrace it, and do so wholeheartedly. I was to find to my dismay that they were not very much interested.

Although the church most definitely was and is ignorant, by and large, of this great Truth, which is not new but actually that which was given to the Apostle Paul, I found that ignorance was not the problem even though it was very much prevalent. The problem was unbelief. In other words, the church is ignorant of the Truth of the New Covenant simply because it wants to be ignorant. Having embraced the world, it really has no desire for that which is of God. Listen to what the Prophet said, *"My People are destroyed for lack of knowledge: because you have rejected knowledge, I will also reject you, that you shall be no Priest to Me: seeing you have forgotten the Law of your God, I will also forget your children.* (The phrase, *'My People are destroyed for lack of knowledge,'* is the cause of all the problems in the church, and the world, for that matter! The *'knowledge'* spoken of is the Bible. This *'lack of knowledge'* was not ignorance, but rather a willful rejection of the Law of God. They didn't know, but it was because they didn't want to know!)" (Hos. 4:6). It is the same with the modern church. It has little desire to know!

Nevertheless, there are a few who do want to know, and who are hungry for the things of God. Mark my words, these few will see a mighty Move of God, possibly the greatest Move the world has ever known.

One Preacher whose life and ministry has been gloriously changed and, thereby, salvaged through and by the Message of the Cross, made the statement, *"They told me all my life what I had to do, but nobody told me how to do it, until I heard the Message of the Cross."* The tragedy is, and I mean no sarcasm by this statement, the fellow preachers who were telling him what he had to do but not telling him how to do it, in fact, did not know how. This means that whatever problems he was facing, they were facing as well. Salvation comes through the Cross Alone! Sanctification comes through the Cross Alone!

"Dying with Jesus, by Death reckoned mine;
"Living with Jesus a new life Divine;
"Looking to Jesus till Glory does shine,
"Moment by moment, O Lord, I am Thine."

"Never a battle with wrong for the right,
"Never a contest that He does not fight;
"Lifting above us His Banner so white,
"Moment by moment I'm kept in His Sight."

"Never a trial that He is not there,
"Never a burden that He does not bear;
"Never a sorrow that He does not share,
"Moment by moment, I'm under His Care."

"Never a heartache, and never a groan,
"Never a teardrop, and never a moan;
"Never a danger but there on the Throne,
"Moment by moment, He thinks of His Own."

"Never a weakness that He does not feel,
"Never a sickness that He cannot heal;
"Moment by moment, in woe or in weal,
"Jesus, my Saviour, abides with me still."

CHAPTER 20

(1) "IT CAME TO PASS AFTER THIS ALSO, THAT THE CHILDREN OF MOAB, AND THE CHILDREN OF AMMON, AND WITH THEM OTHER BESIDE THE AMMONITES, CAME AGAINST JEHOSHAPHAT TO BATTLE.

(2) "THEN THERE CAME SOME WHO TOLD JEHOSHAPHAT, SAYING, THERE COMES A GREAT MULTITUDE AGAINST YOU FROM BEYOND THE SEA ON THIS SIDE SYRIA; AND, BEHOLD, THEY BE IN HAZAZON-TAMAR, WHICH IS EN-GEDI."

The pattern is:

1. (Vs. 1) This invasion was probably allowed by the Lord because of Jehoshaphat's previous alliance with Ahab, which, as stated, greatly displeased the Lord (II Chron. 19:2).

2. (Vs. 2) This war was more than a mere skirmish. It was a concentrated effort by the powers of darkness to destroy Judah.

3. Everything that happens to a Believer is either caused by the Lord or allowed by the Lord.

THE OPPOSITION OF THE ENEMY

Concerning this, Williams says, *"Two foundation principles appear in this Chapter. First, God's fidelity to His Word, i.e., His wrath, and, second, His response to faith, i.e., His Love.*

"The Prophet announced the wrath of God because of Jehoshaphat's unholy alliance with Ahab, and the Ammonites and Moabites became the instruments of that wrath. But in response to Jehoshaphat's cry of distress and his song of faith, sung before the battle began, a complete victory, as we shall see, was granted to him."[1]

Sometimes the Lord allows such, not because we've done something wrong, but in order to increase our Faith. Efforts by the Evil One that are beyond our capacity to resist are meant to point us toward the Lord and total dependence on Him. He delights in showing us what He can do. So, tests and trials should be a cause of great rejoicing, but only the most mature in the Lord can accomplish such.

THE THORN IN THE FLESH

The Apostle Paul said, concerning this of which we speak, *"And lest I should be exalted above measure through the abundance of the Revelations* (presents the reasons for the thorn in the flesh), *there was given to me a thorn in the flesh* (I think it was all the difficulties of II Cor. 11:23-27), *the messenger of Satan to buffet me* (an Angel of Satan), *lest I should be exalted above measure.* (This has the Apostle concluding this sentence as it began.)

"For this thing I besought the Lord thrice, that it might depart from me. (The Apostle knew it was the Lord allowing this, but he didn't understand why.)

"And He said unto me (the Lord responded, but did not agree), *My Grace is sufficient for you* (speaks of enabling Grace, which is really the Goodness of God carried out by the Holy Spirit): *for My Strength is made perfect in weakness.* (All Believers are weak, but the Lord tends to make us weaker, with the intention being that we now depend solely upon Him, thereby, obtaining His Strength.) *Most gladly therefore will I rather glory in my infirmities* (because of the end result), *that the Power of Christ may rest upon me.* (If Paul needed so humbling and painful an experience of what the carnal nature is, it is evident that all Christians need it. Whatever weakens, belittles, and humiliates that proud and willful nature should be regarded by the Believer as most worthwhile.)

"Therefore I take pleasure in infirmities, in reproaches, in necessities, in persecutions, in distresses for Christ's Sake: for when I am weak, then am I strong (then the strength of Christ can be exhibited through me, but only when I know I am weak)" (II Cor. 12:7-10).

(3) "AND JEHOSHAPHAT FEARED, AND SET HIMSELF TO SEEK THE LORD, AND PROCLAIMED A FAST THROUGHOUT ALL JUDAH.

(4) "AND JUDAH GATHERED THEMSELVES TOGETHER, TO ASK HELP OF THE LORD: EVEN OUT OF ALL THE CITIES OF JUDAH THEY CAME TO SEEK THE LORD.

(5) "AND JEHOSHAPHAT STOOD IN THE CONGREGATION OF JUDAH AND JERUSALEM, IN THE HOUSE OF THE LORD, BEFORE THE NEW COURT,

(6) "AND SAID, O LORD GOD OF OUR FATHERS, ARE YOU NOT GOD IN HEAVEN? AND DO YOU NOT RULE OVER ALL THE KINGDOMS OF THE HEATHEN? AND IN YOUR HAND IS THERE NOT POWER AND MIGHT, SO THAT NONE IS

ABLE TO WITHSTAND YOU?

(7) "ARE YOU NOT OUR GOD, WHO DID DRIVE OUT THE INHABITANTS OF THIS LAND BEFORE YOUR PEOPLE ISRAEL, AND GAVE IT TO THE SEED OF ABRAHAM YOUR FRIEND FOREVER?

(8) "AND THEY DWELT THEREIN, AND HAVE BUILT YOU A SANCTUARY THEREIN FOR YOUR NAME, SAYING,

(9) "IF, WHEN EVIL COMES UPON US, AS THE SWORD, JUDGMENT, OR PESTILENCE, OR FAMINE, WE STAND BEFORE THIS HOUSE, AND IN YOUR PRESENCE, (FOR YOUR NAME IS IN THIS HOUSE,) AND CRY UNTO YOU IN OUR AFFLICTION, THEN YOU WILL HEAR AND HELP.

(10) "AND NOW, BEHOLD, THE CHILDREN OF AMMON AND MOAB AND MOUNT SEIR, WHOM YOU WOULD NOT LET ISRAEL INVADE, WHEN THEY CAME OUT OF THE LAND OF EGYPT, BUT THEY TURNED FROM THEM, AND DESTROYED THEM NOT;

(11) "BEHOLD, I SAY, HOW THEY REWARD US, TO COME TO CAST US OUT OF YOUR POSSESSION, WHICH YOU HAVE GIVEN US TO INHERIT.

(12) "O OUR GOD, WILL YOU NOT JUDGE THEM? FOR WE HAVE NO MIGHT AGAINST THIS GREAT COMPANY THAT COMES AGAINST US; NEITHER KNOW WE WHAT TO DO: BUT OUR EYES ARE UPON YOU."

The exegesis is:

1. The fear mentioned in Verse 3 is not the *"spirit of fear"* spoken of by Paul, but rather the type of fear that is supposed to drive us to the Lord, and which it did Jehoshaphat.

2. (Vs. 4) Regrettably, the modern church is teaching the people to seek the help of humanistic psychologists. Let it ever be known, there is no help whatsoever from that source. The Lord Alone can help!

3. (Vs. 6) These heathen powers could do nothing except that which the Lord allowed them to do. As well, while Satan may be mighty in some respects, God Alone is Almighty!

4. (Vs. 7) The Lord was Israel's God, and they were His Children. Now, Satan is attempting to take the possession and inheritance that were given by the Lord.

The word *"forever"* signifies the fact that our inheritance is never to be taken from us by the powers of darkness. God intends for us to keep it forever. In fact, it can be forfeited only by rebellion against the Lord.

5. The Sanctuary mentioned in Verse 8 was a House of Sacrifices, hence, the shed Blood of the Lamb being the defense, and the only true defense, of Israel (II Chron. 7:12).

6. (Vs. 9) Solomon had prayed this prayer many years before, now prayed by Jehoshaphat (II Chron., Chpt. 6). The Lord had promised to answer, that is, if certain conditions were met (II Chron. 7:14).

7. (Vs. 10) In reading this prayer, we must come to the conclusion that Jehoshaphat knew the Word of God.

8. (Vs. 12) Within ourselves, we have no might against Satan, and that we must ever learn. Our strength is totally in the Lord; as then, so now!

SEEKING THE LORD

Satan was coming against the People of God with a mighty army, intending to destroy them, even down to the last man. As well, in the natural, it seems that the force arrayed against Jehoshaphat was mightily superior to the force of Judah. So, Jehoshaphat did what every Believer ought to do. He *"set himself to seek the LORD, and proclaimed a fast throughout all Judah."*

In response to their king, the Scripture says, *"And Judah gathered themselves together, to ask help of the LORD: even out of all the cities of Judah they came to seek the LORD."* Jehoshaphat took the lead and Judah responded. This is exactly what the Lord wanted them to do.

Unfortunately, the modern church little seeks the Lord anymore. It turns to other means, means, we might quickly add, that, in effect, offer no help whatsoever.

THE CROSS OF CHRIST

I think the basic reason for the lack of faith in the modern church has to do with the Cross of Christ. If Faith is true, that is, Faith which God recognizes, it must ever have the Cross of Christ as its Object. If not, it is faith that the Lord will not recognize, which means that it degenerates into little more than human endeavor. The idea is, millions of Christians claim to have Faith in God, but they have no understanding of the Cross, so their Faith in God is, for the most part, a misplaced faith. In such a case, which is virtually all, true Faith in God is very limited.

I'll go back to that which I originally stated. In the early 1960's, when the church, and I speak of the part of the church that claims to be Spirit-filled, began to embrace humanistic psychology, that was the time they began, as well, to abandon the Cross. As a result, the modern church is almost wholly secular. Without the Cross of Christ, the Bible begins to be laid aside, the Promises of God are forgotten, and the world, instead of the Lord, becomes the source.

THE PRAYER

Jehoshaphat begins his prayer for deliverance by proclaiming the fact that the Lord *"rules over all the kingdoms of the heathen."* This is a tremendous truth that should be recognized by all. The Lord not only rules where His Name is held up, but, as well, He rules over the kingdoms of the Earth that do not recognize Him at all, but rather worship and serve other gods. In fact, the Lord rules over everything, and this should ever be understood.

It is true that Satan does a lot of things, and we speak of the realm of *"stealing, killing, and destroying"* (Jn. 10:10). But, at the same time, he can only do what the Lord allows him to do.

THE MANNER OF THE RULE OF GOD

God has established certain Laws by which He governs and rules the world.

Even though the Lord has established many Laws, I think it can be said without fear of contradiction that there are two major Laws established by the Godhead with all other laws being subject to these two. They are:

1. *"The Law of the Spirit of Life in Christ Jesus"* and
2. *"The Law of Sin and Death."*

The account of both of these Laws is found in Romans 8:2. Let's look at the latter one first.

"THE LAW OF SIN AND DEATH"

This Law has soaked the Earth with blood, has filled Hell to the brim, and is the cause of all heartache, pain, sickness, suffering, dying, and death. It is the cause of all poverty, all bondage, and all superstition in the world. It has made this Planet a place of Hell, and is the Law under which Satan operates, and does so legally.

In other words, that which Satan can do comes under the auspices of *"the Law of Sin and Death."* This Law was devised by the Godhead in eternity past.

In essence, this Law refers to the fact that sin, which is disobedience to the Word of God, gives Satan the right to hold men in bondage. That bondage ranks all the way from alcohol to drugs, to fear, to unbelief, etc. In fact, it covers every bondage known to man and is the cause, as stated, of all the pain and heartache in the world.

As to exactly when the Lord devised this Law, we aren't told, but we do know that it came into this world through the Fall of Adam and Eve. They fell from the highest plane of total God-consciousness down to the far, far lower level of total self-consciousness. At that time, their very nature became that of sin, which means that all they did, meaning every action and every direction, constituted sin. It is the same with the entirety of the fallen sons of Adam's lost race. They are governed by the sin nature in totality, with that bondage broken only when they come to the Lord Jesus Christ.

Sin gives Satan the legal right to do all the things that he does, and we speak of the realm of stealing, killing, and destroying (Jn. 10:10).

Man's efforts to try to assuage *"the Law of Sin and Death"* is futile to say the least. Irrespective as to what he does, it only makes the matter worse. There is only one answer for this terrible Law, and that is, *"the Law of the Spirit of Life in Christ Jesus."*

"THE LAW OF THE SPIRIT OF LIFE IN CHRIST JESUS"

The one Law and, in fact, the only Law that is stronger than *"the Law of Sin and*

Death," is *"the Law of the Spirit of Life in Christ Jesus."* This Law alone supersedes the other Law.

Regrettably, the world will not admit to that and keeps trying to address the terrible problem of *"the Law of Sin and Death"* by its own intellectualism and ability. All are doomed to failure with some 6,000 recorded years of proven failure. The Lord Alone can overcome the terrible Law of Sin.

What is the *"Law of the Spirit of Life in Christ Jesus?"*

It, as well, was devised by the Godhead in eternity past, even before the foundation of the world. In respect to this, Peter wrote,

"Forasmuch as you know that you were not redeemed with corruptible things, as silver and gold (presents the fact that the most precious commodities [silver and gold] could not redeem fallen man), *from your vain conversation* (vain lifestyle) *received by tradition from your fathers* (speaks of original sin that is passed on from father to child at conception);

"But with the Precious Blood of Christ (presents the payment, which proclaims the poured out Life of Christ on behalf of sinners), *as of a Lamb without blemish and without spot* (speaks of the lambs offered as substitutes in the Old Jewish economy; the Death of Christ was not an execution or assassination, but rather a Sacrifice; the Offering of Himself presented a Perfect Sacrifice, for He was Perfect in every respect [Ex. 12:5]):

"Who verily was foreordained before the foundation of the world (refers to the fact that God, in His Omniscience, knew He would create man, man would fall, and man would be redeemed by Christ going to the Cross; this was all done before the Universe was created; this means the Cross of Christ is the Foundation Doctrine of all Doctrine, referring to the fact that all Doctrine must be built upon that Foundation, or else it is specious), *but was manifest in these last times for you.* (Refers to the invisible God Who, in the Person of the Son, was made visible to human eyesight by assuming a human body and human limitations)" (I Pet. 1:18-20).

"The Law of the Spirit of Life in Christ Jesus" tells us what the Lord did to redeem

NOTES

humanity and how the Holy Spirit works within that Law. As Peter said to us, this was all done by the Godhead from before the foundation of the world.

The name *"Spirit"* in the Text refers to the Holy Spirit. He is referred to here as *"the Spirit of Life,"* meaning that all Life comes from Christ but through the Holy Spirit. In other words, it is the Holy Spirit Who superintends this life as it regards Believers. He does many things in our hearts and lives, as should be obvious, but His main Work is to ascertain if we have proper Faith, which is Faith in Christ and the Cross. In other words, we must make the Cross of Christ the Object of our Faith (Rom. 6:1-14; 8:1-2, 11; I Cor. 1:17-18, 23; 2:2; Gal., Chpt. 5; 6:14; Gen. 3:15; 15:6).

"IN CHRIST JESUS"

The latter part of this Law says, *"In Christ Jesus."* Every time Paul uses that term or one of its derivatives, such as *"in Christ,"* or *"in Him,"* or *"in the Lord,"* etc., he is speaking, and without exception, of what Christ did at the Cross. It's all wrapped up in the Cross of Christ. This means this great *"Law of the Spirit of Life in Christ Jesus,"* in effect, is the Cross. Christ is the Source, while the Cross is the Means.

That we do not misunderstand this, and that we do not make less of it than we should, it is referred to as *"a Law,"* which means that it will function exactly as God designed it.

The Holy Spirit is the One Who does all things within our hearts and lives as it pertains to Righteousness. In fact, He abides with us on a continual basis (I Cor. 3:16). But yet, everything He does, always and without exception, glorifies Christ. Jesus said, and concerning this, *"Howbeit when He, the Spirit of Truth, is come* (which He did on the Day of Pentecost), *He will guide you into all Truth* (if our Faith is properly placed in Christ and the Cross, the Holy Spirit can then bring forth Truth to us; He doesn't guide into some truth, but rather 'all Truth'): *for He shall not speak of Himself* (tells us not only What He does, but Whom He represents); *but whatsoever He shall hear, that shall He speak* (doesn't refer to a lack of knowledge, for the Holy Spirit is God, but rather He will proclaim the Work of Christ only): *and He will show you things to come* (pertains to the New Covenant, which would shortly be given).

"*He shall glorify Me* (will portray Christ and what Christ did at the Cross for dying humanity): *for He shall receive of Mine* (the benefits of the Cross), *and shall show it unto you* (which He did, when He gave these great Truths to the Apostle Paul [Rom., Chpts. 6-8, etc.]).

"*All things that the Father has are Mine* (has always been the case; however, due to the Cross, all these things can now be given to the Believer as well): *therefore said I, that He shall take of Mine, and shall show it unto you.* (The Foundation of all the Holy Spirit reveals to the Church is what Christ did at the Cross [Rom. 6:3-14; 8:1-2, 11])" (Jn. 16:13-15).

Pure and simple, it is the Cross of Christ which gives the Holy Spirit the legal right to do all the things He does in our hearts and lives. It's the Cross that can give the Believer Victory over sin, and the Cross Alone can give the Believer Victory over sin.

One could say that "*the Law of the Spirit of Life in Christ Jesus*" is, in effect, "*the Cross of Christ.*" That alone has defeated Satan and all of his minions of darkness (Col. 2:14-15).

So, the Lord rules the entirety of this Planet on the basis of those two Laws. As stated, while He has made many Laws, as should be obvious, still, all the Laws, at least in the Spiritual sense, are subject to these two Laws.

THE BLESSINGS OF THE LORD

Concerning the Blessings, Jehoshaphat said several things. They are:

• He said, "*O LORD God of our fathers,*" meaning that whatever the Lord did for them, He would do presently for Judah.

• He further said, "*Are You not God in Heaven?*" In other words, there is no God but You.

• "*You rule over all the kingdoms of the heathen,*" meaning that "*they can do nothing unless You allow it to be done.*"

• "*In Your Hand there is Power and Might.*" This refers to all Power and all Might. In other words, God can do anything.

• There is no power on Earth that can "*withstand You,*" meaning that You control all things.

• "*You drove out all the inhabitants of this land,*" who were most wicked and most vile.

• You gave this land of Judah "*to the seed of Abraham Your Friend forever.*"

If it is to be noticed, Jehoshaphat praises the Lord for Who He is and then lists a number of great things which the Lord has done. As it regards prayer, that should be a model for us as well.

THE PROMISE

He reminds the Lord of the "*Sanctuary,*" i.e., the Temple, actually, where the Lord dwelt between the Mercy Seat and the Cherubim. He brings to the Lord's Remembrance the Promise that He made to Solomon and to all of Israel, as it regarded trouble, and how that God's People should pray toward "*this house*" (II Chron. 6:34-35; 7:14).

Jehoshaphat reminds the Lord that if they "*cried unto Him in their affliction, that He would hear and help.*"

Every Believer should take a lesson from the way and the manner in which Jehoshaphat prayed.

THE POSSESSION OF THE CHILDREN OF GOD

Judah had a possession, actually, a possession given to them by God, even as Jehoshaphat has already mentioned. Now he tells the Lord that the enemy has come to "*cast us out of Your Possession, which You have given us to inherit.*" If it is to be noticed, Jehoshaphat said "*Your Possession,*" which the Lord had given unto Israel.

Every Child of God has a possession given to them by the Lord.

The Scripture says, "*And if children* (Children of God), *then heirs* (a privilege); *heirs of God* (the highest enrichment of all), *and joint-heirs with Christ* (everything that belongs to Christ belongs to us through the Cross, which was done for us)" (Rom. 8:17).

It is the business of Satan to attempt to take away this great possession, and unless we understand God's Prescribed Order of Victory, he will succeed, if not totally, then partially. To be sure, he definitely will not give up. The tragedy is, the Evil One succeeds in most cases, at least to the point that the Believer does not have all for which Christ paid such a price.

Doesn't it stand to reason, considering the price paid by our Lord on Calvary's Cross, that He wants us to have everything for which He has paid this great price? I think the answer to that is obvious. But the tragedy is, most Believers are not even coming close to that which the Lord desires that we have.

Our possession is that for which He has paid this great price. It includes:
- Salvation (Rom. 5:1-2).
- The Baptism with the Holy Spirit with the evidence of speaking with other Tongues (Acts 2:4).
- Victory over all sin that the sin nature not dominate us in any fashion (Rom. 6:1-14).
- Divine healing (James 5:14-15).
- Leading and guidance (Jn. 16:13).
- Economic prosperity (II Cor. 9:6).

I think it can be said without fear of contradiction that of all of these great possessions for which the Lord has paid such a price, Victory over the sin nature is probably the most difficult of all. The following presents God's Prescribed Order of Victory.

THE CROSS

Every one of these things we have named, and anything else that one might conceive, as it regards the Lord, has come to us by and through the Cross of Christ. As we repeatedly state, our Lord is the Source of all things that we receive from God, and the Cross is the Means by which those things are given unto us. We must understand that and understand it fully. Without the Cross, nothing could be given. That's why the Sacrificial system was instituted at the very dawn of time. It was done so that it might serve as a substitute for the Redeemer Who would ultimately come. The lamb was a Type of Christ, an innocent victim, which would give its life, typifying what Christ would do. The entire Sacrificial system,

NOTES

even under the Law of Moses, and especially under the Law of Moses, typified the Cross. In fact, that's the reason that Jesus came. While He did many things, and everything He did was of vast significance, still, His Destination was the Cross. It was there that all sin was atoned, which defeated Satan and all of his cohorts of darkness, and did so in totality, thereby, making it possible for the Holy Spirit to work mightily in our lives.

Everything the Spirit does is because of what Jesus did at the Cross. In other words, the Cross was a legal Work carried out by Christ that satisfied the demands of a thrice-Holy God, and which gave the Holy Spirit latitude to work within our lives. This requires constant, unending, never-ending Faith in the Cross by the Child of God, even as Christ related to us (Lk. 9:23).

All of this means that the only way that Satan can be defeated, thereby, keeping him from stealing our possession, is our Faith in Christ and what Christ has done for us at the Cross. It's just that simple. It's just that certain!

(13) "AND ALL JUDAH STOOD BEFORE THE LORD, WITH THEIR LITTLE ONES, THEIR WIVES, AND THEIR CHILDREN.

(14) "THEN UPON JAHAZIEL THE SON OF ZECHARIAH, THE SON OF BENAIAH, THE SON OF JEIEL, THE SON OF MATTANIAH, A LEVITE OF THE SONS OF ASAPH, CAME THE SPIRIT OF THE LORD IN THE MIDST OF THE CONGREGATION;

(15) "AND HE SAID, HEARKEN YOU, ALL JUDAH, AND YOU INHABITANTS OF JERUSALEM, AND THOU KING JEHOSHAPHAT, THUS SAYS THE LORD UNTO YOU, BE NOT AFRAID NOR DISMAYED BY REASON OF THIS GREAT MULTITUDE; FOR THE BATTLE IS NOT YOURS, BUT GOD'S.

(16) "TOMORROW YOU GO DOWN AGAINST THEM: BEHOLD, THEY COME UP BY THE CLIFF OF ZIZ; AND YOU SHALL FIND THEM AT THE END OF THE BROOK, BEFORE THE WILDERNESS OF JERUEL.

(17) "YOU SHALL NOT NEED TO FIGHT IN THIS BATTLE: SET YOURSELVES, STAND YOU STILL, AND SEE THE SALVATION OF THE LORD WITH YOU,

O JUDAH AND JERUSALEM: FEAR NOT, NOR BE DISMAYED; TOMORROW GO OUT AGAINST THEM: FOR THE LORD WILL BE WITH YOU.

(18) "AND JEHOSHAPHAT BOWED HIS HEAD WITH HIS FACE TO THE GROUND: AND ALL JUDAH AND THE INHABITANTS OF JERUSALEM FELL BEFORE THE LORD, WORSHIPPING THE LORD.

(19) "AND THE LEVITES, OF THE CHILDREN OF THE KOHATHITES, AND OF THE CHILDREN OF THE KORHITES, STOOD UP TO PRAISE THE LORD GOD OF ISRAEL WITH A LOUD VOICE ON HIGH."

The exegesis is:

1. (Vs. 14) The Spirit of the Lord is the answer, and the only answer (Zech. 4:6).

2. (Vs. 15) If we try to fight the battle on our terms, we will lose. If we fight the battle on His Terms, we will win. What are those Terms?

3. (Vs. 15) We have to trust in Christ, Who has already fought this battle and won, and did so at the Cross (Col. 2:14-15). Doing that, the Holy Spirit will then guarantee us the Victory of Christ (Rom. 8:1-2, 11).

4. (Vs. 17) *"Stand still"* refers to the ceasing and desisting of our own personal efforts, i.e., *"the flesh,"* and, thereby, trusting the Lord completely, and what He has done for us at the Cross.

5. (Vs. 17) If the Lord is with us, who can be against us?

THE SPIRIT OF THE LORD

The great Prophet Zechariah later on would say, *"Not by might* (human might), *nor by power* (human power), *but by My Spirit, says the LORD of Hosts"* (Zech. 4:6).

The Holy Spirit is the Strength of the Church. Without the Holy Spirit, the church is no more than any other human organization. Without the Holy Spirit, no one will be Saved, no one will be healed, no one will be delivered, and no one will be baptized in the Spirit. In fact, nothing for the Lord will take place. But with the Holy Spirit, lives are changed, bondages are broken, people are led to Christ and what He did at the Cross, and sick bodies are healed, making this Christ-filled life the greatest life and living on the face of the Earth.

It's not pleasant to be negative, but sad to say, sometimes we have no choice.

I, regrettably, feel that the modern church has less Moving and Operation of the Holy Spirit than it has known since the Reformation. Even the religious denominations, which claim to be Spirit-filled, have almost totally opted for the ways of the world, which means that the Holy Spirit is shut out.

THE HOLY SPIRIT AND THE CROSS OF CHRIST

When the Cross is abandoned, the Holy Spirit, for all practical purposes, is abandoned as well. When the Cross of Christ is held up as the Means by which our Saviour gives us all things, then the Holy Spirit is prominent (Rom. 8:2). Regrettably, the modern church no longer preaches the Cross as the answer for the perversions, the sins, and the ills of man, but rather something else altogether. Consequently, the Holy Spirit, sad to say, has long since departed.

Without the Holy Spirit, Christianity is little more than a vapid philosophy. It is the Holy Spirit Who makes all the difference.

As Jehoshaphat and Judah stood before the Lord, pleading for His Help against the enemy, the Scripture says, *"Then upon Jahaziel . . . came the Spirit of the LORD in the midst of the congregation."* He then had a Word of Prophecy to give to all of Judah. In fact, looking at it in New Testament terms, he operated in a *"Word of Knowledge"* and a *"Word of Wisdom,"* along with *"Prophecy."*

The *"Word of Knowledge"* pertains to people, places, and things regarding the present or the past. The *"Word of Wisdom"* pertains to people, places, or things relative to the future. It was a gracious Message. The Holy Spirit said, *"Thus says the LORD unto you, Be not afraid nor dismayed by reason of this great multitude; for the battle is not yours, but God's."*

"THE BATTLE IS NOT YOURS, BUT GOD'S"

The Spirit also said through Jahaziel, *"You shall not need to fight in this battle: set yourselves, stand you still, and see the Salvation of the LORD with you."*

These words are very similar to that given by the Lord to Moses and to Israel when He said, *"Fear you not, stand still, and see the Salvation of the LORD . . . The LORD shall fight for you, and you shall hold your peace"* (Ex. 14:13-14).

That Promise is given to us today exactly as it was given to Judah so long ago, *"The battle is not yours, but God's."*

HOW DO WE LET THE LORD FIGHT FOR US?

We must first ascertain what the Will of God is in the matter. In the case with Jehoshaphat, the Children of Israel were not to fight at all, but sometimes, the Lord would direct His People to fight. While He would tell them what to do and how to do it, still, they were to fill a particular role. So the idea is that, above all, we not assume but rather look to the Lord and seek His Guidance as to what we should do as it regards the matter at hand, whatever it might be.

And then there are occasions that sometimes arise to where we have to employ certain people and certain things as a matter of necessity. In other words, we have no choice.

For instance, if at times we are sued by someone, we cannot ignore such a thing, meaning that we have to hire a lawyer, no matter how right our cause may be. The idea is, irrespective of having to employ someone of this nature, we must look to the Lord, understanding that our help comes from above. The Lord is able to manipulate events, and He is able to move situations. In fact, there is nothing that He cannot do.

Having said that, the manner and the way in which the Lord comes to our rescue, helps us, and stands with us, are always and without exception, by and through the Cross. This means that our Faith must ever be in Christ and what He did for us at the Cross, understanding that our Lord is the Source of all good things, and the Cross is the Means by which these are given to us, and all superintended by the Holy Spirit.

The Believer is ever to place his Faith exclusively in Christ and the Cross, never allowing it to be moved to something else, although the Evil One will constantly seek to push us away from our Source of victory.

The fight in which we are engaged is referred to as the *"good fight of Faith"* (I Tim. 6:12).

In essence, it is the only fight we're called upon to engage. Every attack by Satan against the Believer, irrespective of its form, is to destroy or seriously weaken our Faith. He wants to push our Faith from the Cross to other things.

Every battle is fought and won at the Cross. In essence, every Victory was won by our Lord at the Cross. He is not fighting any more battles because no more battles need to be fought. Understanding that He did all of this for us, we are to rest completely in Him; however, this is where the fight comes in. As stated, Satan will move Heaven and Earth to push our Faith from that which alone gives us the Victory, i.e., *"the Cross of Christ"* (I Cor. 1:17-18, 21, 23; 2:2).

"STAND STILL, AND SEE THE SALVATION OF THE LORD"

"Standing still" just might be the most difficult thing for any Believer to do. We have to come to the understanding that Christ, as stated, has already fought and won the battle, having done so at Calvary's Cross. As also stated, we rest secure in His Victory, which is meant to become our Victory.

"Standing still" refers to the Believer not depending upon his own ability, strength, talent, education, intellect, knowledge, etc. That's what Jesus was talking about when He said, *"deny yourself"* (Lk. 9:23).

It took me 50 years to understand that my being an overcomer was not in what I did or didn't do, but rather in what He has done, which was done for us.

Believers must understand that everything Christ did in His earthly pilgrimage was for you and me. He did nothing for Himself, nothing for Heaven, nothing for God His Father, and nothing for the Angels. It was all for us. He was the *"Last Adam,"* and the *"Second Man"* (I Cor. 15:45-47).

Understanding what He did for us, our Faith is always to be in His Finished Work. I am an overcomer because of what He has done for me, and my Faith in Him and what He did at the Cross guarantees me all for which He has paid such a price.

As one Preacher said, *"Look away from

your 10,000 failures to our Great High Priest, and look at His Headband which says 'Holiness unto the Lord.'" My holiness is in Him, and it will always be in Him.

If I look at myself, I see nothing but imperfection, but if I look at Him, I see nothing but Perfection. If I look at myself, I see nothing but poverty; if I look at Him, I see the Riches of Glory. If I look at myself, I see nothing but weakness; if I look at Him, I see nothing but Strength. If I look at myself, I see nothing but death; if I look at Him, I see nothing but Life.

*"Hallelujah, what a thought, Jesus full
　Salvation brought;
"Victory, yes Victory,
"Let the powers of sin assail, Heaven's
　Grace shall never fail,
"Victory, yes Victory."*

No, my statements in no way are meant to provide a license to sin. As Paul said, *"God forbid!"* I am merely proclaiming the true nature of things as they really are, no matter how zealous, and no matter how consecrated or dedicated the Believer might be. All of us fall so very, very short, and no matter how hard we try otherwise. But, when such a Believer quits looking at himself, meaning, in a sense, that he *"stands still,"* and places his eyes upon the King of kings and the Lord of lords, and then keeps his Faith there, all for which Jesus paid such a price now becomes his.

In such a case, and in every case of such like, exactly as it was said of Judah of old, *"the LORD will be with you."*

"WORSHIPPING THE LORD"

Whenever the Lord gave this great Word to Judah, the Scripture says *"Jehoshaphat bowed his head with his face to the ground: and all Judah and the inhabitants of Jerusalem fell before the LORD, worshipping the LORD."*

This was Judah's strength! This was Judah's power! This was Judah's life! And it is the life of the True Church as well!

The Scripture says that they worshipped the Lord by *"standing up to praise the LORD God of Israel with a loud voice on high."*

Would that fit most modern churches? I think not!

I'm glad I can say, however, it fits Family Worship Center.

People who claim to be Saved but never worship the Lord and never show any exuberance, I personally feel have precious little relationship with the Lord, if any at all. When a person is truly Saved, *"praise the Lord"* becomes common on his lips. Praise becomes natural! If it's not natural, then again I state, the individual needs to get Saved.

I quote from THE EXPOSITOR'S STUDY BIBLE:

"Praise you the LORD. Praise God in His Sanctuary: praise Him in the firmament of His Power. (This is the fifth and, therefore, last Hallelujah Psalm. As well, it should be described as the *'Deuteronomy Psalm'* of the Deuteronomy Book.

"In this glad day of the Kingdom Age, with Christ reigning supreme in Jerusalem, praise will be offered unto God continually all over the world.

"The Divine titles in this Psalm are *'El'* and *'Jah.' 'El'* is essentially the Almighty, and *'Jah'* signifies the Ever-existing One, for example, Jesus Christ, the same yesterday, today, and forever.)

"Praise Him for His mighty Acts: praise Him according to His excellent Greatness. (The theme of praise will be twofold:

1. What He does – His mighty Acts.
2. What He is – His excellent Greatness.

"These express His Glory as Creator, as Redeemer, as the Lamb of God, and as the Son of God. The scene of worship in the Book of Revelation is Heaven; in this Psalm, it is the Earth in unison with Heaven.)

"Praise Him with the sound of the trumpet: praise Him with the psaltery and harp.

"Praise Him with the timbrel and dance: praise Him with stringed instruments and organs.

"Praise Him upon the loud cymbals: praise Him upon the high sounding cymbals. (These praises portray to us the fact that the worship is not only spontaneous, but orchestrated, exactly as it is now in praise and worship. By and large, the musicians of the world have formerly dedicated their talents to the Evil One. Now these talents

will be dedicated exclusively to God's Glory.)

"*Let everything that has breath praise the LORD. Praise you the LORD.* (The very first Psalm calls the Messiah *'the Blessed Man.'* In this last Psalm He is worshipped as *'the Blessed God.'* All of the 148 intervening Psalms sing of the countless perfections of His Nature and of His Actions, as both Son of Man and Son of God.

"The cry here is that everything that has breath must praise the Lord. In the coming Kingdom Age, this will be brought about. Men will have nothing but praise for Him.

"The Book of Psalms assures this. Its pages are wet with tears, and its music broken with sighs, but its last Song is a burst of satisfied rapture. Its five Volumes fitly close with a loud *'Hallelujah!')*" (Ps. 150:1-6).

(20) "AND THEY ROSE EARLY IN THE MORNING, AND WENT FORTH INTO THE WILDERNESS OF TEKOA: AND AS THEY WENT FORTH, JEHOSHAPHAT STOOD AND SAID, HEAR ME, O JUDAH, AND YOU INHABITANTS OF JERUSALEM; BELIEVE IN THE LORD YOUR GOD, SO SHALL YOU BE ESTABLISHED; BELIEVE HIS PROPHETS, SO SHALL YOU PROSPER.

(21) "AND WHEN HE HAD CONSULTED WITH THE PEOPLE, HE APPOINTED SINGERS UNTO THE LORD, AND THAT SHOULD PRAISE THE BEAUTY OF HOLINESS, AS THEY WENT OUT BEFORE THE ARMY, AND TO SAY, PRAISE THE LORD; FOR HIS MERCY ENDURES FOR EVER.

(22) "AND WHEN THEY BEGAN TO SING AND TO PRAISE, THE LORD SET AMBUSHMENTS AGAINST THE CHILDREN OF AMMON, MOAB, AND MOUNT SEIR, WHICH WERE COME AGAINST JUDAH; AND THEY WERE SMITTEN.

(23) "FOR THE CHILDREN OF AMMON AND MOAB STOOD UP AGAINST THE INHABITANTS OF MOUNT SEIR, UTTERLY TO KILL AND DESTROY THEM: AND WHEN THEY HAD MADE AN END OF THE INHABITANTS OF SEIR, EVERY ONE HELPED TO DESTROY ANOTHER.

(24) "AND WHEN JUDAH CAME TOWARD THE WATCH TOWER IN THE WILDERNESS, THEY LOOKED UNTO THE MULTITUDE, AND, BEHOLD, THEY WERE DEAD BODIES FALLEN TO THE EARTH, AND NONE ESCAPED.

(25) "AND WHEN JEHOSHAPHAT AND HIS PEOPLE CAME TO TAKE AWAY THE SPOIL OF THEM, THEY FOUND AMONG THEM IN ABUNDANCE BOTH RICHES WITH THE DEAD BODIES, AND PRECIOUS JEWELS, WHICH THEY STRIPPED OFF FOR THEMSELVES, MORE THAN THEY COULD CARRY AWAY: AND THEY WERE THREE DAYS IN GATHERING OF THE SPOIL, IT WAS SO MUCH.

(26) "AND ON THE FOURTH DAY THEY ASSEMBLED THEMSELVES IN THE VALLEY OF BERACHAH; FOR THERE THEY BLESSED THE LORD: THEREFORE THE NAME OF THE SAME PLACE WAS CALLED, THE VALLEY OF BERACHAH, UNTO THIS DAY.

(27) "THEN THEY RETURNED, EVERY MAN OF JUDAH AND JERUSALEM, AND JEHOSHAPHAT IN THE FOREFRONT OF THEM, TO GO AGAIN TO JERUSALEM WITH JOY; FOR THE LORD HAD MADE THEM TO REJOICE OVER THEIR ENEMIES.

(28) "AND THEY CAME TO JERUSALEM WITH PSALTERIES AND HARPS AND TRUMPETS UNTO THE HOUSE OF THE LORD.

(29) "AND THE FEAR OF GOD WAS ON ALL THE KINGDOMS OF THOSE COUNTRIES, WHEN THEY HAD HEARD THAT THE LORD FOUGHT AGAINST THE ENEMIES OF ISRAEL.

(30) "SO THE REALM OF JEHOSHAPHAT WAS QUIET: FOR HIS GOD GAVE HIM REST ROUND ABOUT."

The pattern is:

1. (Vs. 21) Praise and worship through singing and music constitute the highest form of worship, that is if it is Spirit-directed. To be sure, modern contemporary Christian music, so-called, definitely does not fall into this category, and any Christian who thinks it does is only fooling himself.

2. As it regards Verse 22, the Jewish Targums say that these ambushments were caused by Angels.

3. (Vs. 23) The children of Ammon and Moab became so confused that they began to destroy the Edomites instead of the Israelites. They then turned on each other—

all of this caused by the Lord.

4. (Vs. 24) All of this portrays to us, in type and shadow, the manner presently in which our battles must be fought and won. Paul said that these are examples for us (I Cor. 10:11).

5. (Vs. 25) The true position of the Child of God is that we take the spoil of Satan, instead of him robbing us.

6. (Vs. 26) The *"Valley of Berachah"* means the *"Valley of Blessing."*

7. (Vs. 27) The Lord will enable us to rejoice over our enemies, providing we look to Christ as our Source and the Cross as our Means.

8. (Vs. 28) When the Children of Israel came back into Jerusalem, they did not come in defeat, but rather playing their instruments and praising the Lord, a signification of great victory.

9. (Vs. 29) Such a miraculous defeat of the Moabites, Ammonites, and Edomites, was soon known by all nations round about. What a victory!

BELIEVE HIS PROPHETS AND PROSPER

It must be understood that it's the Lord's Prophets addressed here and not false prophets. Unfortunately, whether in Israel of old or the modern day church, for every one true Prophet, there are scores of false prophets.

How does one know if the prophet is true or false?

Our Lord gave us an excellent clue. He said, and I quote from THE EXPOSITOR'S STUDY BIBLE:

"Beware of false prophets, who come to you in sheep's clothing, but inwardly they are ravening wolves ('beware of false prophets' is said in the sternest of measures! there will be and are false prophets, and are some of Satan's greatest weapons).

"You shall know them by their fruits (this is the test as given by Christ as it regards identification of false prophets and false apostles). *Do men gather grapes of thorns, or figs of thistles?* (It is impossible for false doctrine, generated by false prophets, to bring forth good fruit.)

"Even so every good tree brings forth good fruit; but a corrupt tree brings forth evil fruit (the good fruit is Christlikeness, while the evil fruit is self-likeness).

"A good tree cannot bring forth evil fruit, neither can a corrupt tree bring forth good fruit (the 'good tree' is the Cross, while the 'corrupt tree' pertains to all of that which is other than the Cross).

"Every tree that brings not forth good fruit is hewn down, and cast into the fire (Judgment will ultimately come on all so-called gospel, other than the Cross [Rom. 1:18]).

"Wherefore by their fruits you shall know them." (The acid test) (Mat. 7:15-20).

And then our Lord said, *"Not everyone who says unto Me, Lord, Lord, shall enter into the Kingdom of Heaven* (the repetition of the word 'Lord' expresses astonishment, as if to say: 'Are we to be disowned?'); *but he who does the Will of My Father which is in Heaven* (what is the Will of the Father? Verse 24 tells us).

"Many will say to Me in that day, Lord, Lord, have we not prophesied in Your Name? and in Your Name have cast out devils? and in Your Name done many wonderful works? (These things are not the criteria, but rather Faith in Christ and what Christ has done for us at the Cross [Eph. 2:8-9, 13-18]. The Word of God alone is to be the judge of doctrine.)

"And then will I profess unto them, I never knew you (again we say, the criteria alone is Christ and Him Crucified [I Cor. 1:23]): *depart from Me, you who work iniquity* (we have access to God only through Christ, and access to Christ only through the Cross, and access to the Cross only through a denial of self [Lk. 9:23]; any other Message is judged by God as 'iniquity,' and cannot be a part of Christ [I Cor. 1:17])" (Mat. 7:21-23).

By coupling what our Lord said in Matthew with what He said in Luke, we have the answer as to how the Prophet, or any so-called Believer, for that matter, can be judged as to whether he is true or false.

He said in Luke, *"If any man will come after Me* (the criteria for Discipleship), *let him deny himself* (not asceticism as many think, but rather that one denies one's own willpower, self-will, strength, and ability, depending totally on Christ), *and take up his cross* (the benefits of the Cross, looking exclusively to what Jesus did there to meet our every need) *daily* (this is so important, our looking to the Cross; that we must renew our Faith in what Christ has done for us, even on a daily basis, for Satan will ever try to move us away from the Cross as the Object of our Faith, which always spells disaster), *and follow Me.* (Christ can be followed only by the Believer looking to the Cross, understanding what it accomplished, and by that means alone)" (Lk. 9:23).

Then Jesus said, *"And whosoever does not bear his Cross and come after Me, cannot be My Disciple"* (Lk. 14:27).

PRAISE THE BEAUTY OF HOLINESS

Judah went to war, so to speak, saying, *"Praise the LORD; for His Mercy endures forever."*

This Twenty-first Verse tells us that *"Holiness"* and *"Praise"* constitute the strength of the Believer, and not the might and power of man. They did deploy *"the army,"* but, actually, it would do very little except gather the spoil. Their victory was *"Holiness and Praise."* As well, it is our victory today.

Think about it. Judah's army was prepared, even though it was much smaller than the army of the enemy. But then, the Lord told Jehoshaphat to put the *"singers"* out in front of the army, and that they were to march to battle saying, *"Praise the LORD; for His Mercy endures forever."*

Please understand, this is what the Lord told them to do. Had they done it after their own planning and scheming, Judah would have been defeated.

The Lord very seldom works the same way twice, at least as it regards Miracles of this sort.

As an example, when David became king, the Philistines came against him, and he *"enquired of the LORD, saying, Shall I go up to the Philistines? will You deliver them into my hand? And the LORD said unto David, Go up: for I will doubtless deliver the Philistines into your hand."*

David did exactly what the Lord said to do, and victory was his.

A short time later, the Philistines came against Israel again, and again David sought the Lord, asking as to what he should do?

But this time, the Lord told him the very opposite, *"You shall not go up . . . but let it be, when you hear the sound of a going in the tops of the mulberry trees, that then you shall bestir yourself: for then shall the LORD go out before you, to smite the host of the Philistines"* (II Sam. 5:19-24).

In the second battle, had David assumed that he could do the very same thing as he did previously, he would have been defeated.

The Believer must understand that presumption is not Faith. We must never take the Lord for granted or assume that because He has done something for someone else, He will do the same for us. He might, but then again, He may want something else for us.

At this time, Jehoshaphat heard from the Lord, obeyed the Lord, and as strange as it was, went against the enemy even as the Lord directed. If the Lord has said do something, then it must be done exactly in that fashion.

The Lord doesn't do a lot of special things for many Believers because there is precious little relationship with Him. Jehoshaphat didn't start seeking the Lord merely when the problem reared its head but continuously sought the Lord, as all Believers ought to do. Then, if the problem comes, and sooner or later it will, such a relationship can ask direction and receive it, which will fall out to glorifying the Lord.

"AMBUSHMENTS"

The Scripture says, *"And when they began to sing and to praise, the LORD set ambushments against the children of Ammon, Moab, and Mount Seir, which were come against Judah; and they were smitten."*

It doesn't tell us here what the Lord did; however, the Jewish Targums say that the Lord sent Angels among the enemy, which is, no doubt, correct. The Angels made the Ammonites and the Moabites think that the Edomites of Mount Seir were the enemy; consequently, they *"utterly did kill and destroy them."* And then, when that was done, the Ammonites thought the Moabites were the enemy, with the Moabites thinking the Ammonites were the enemy, and they began to destroy each other, with what seems like the entire army of the enemy being destroyed. In other words, every last soldier was killed and *"none escaped."*

One can imagine what the countries of Ammon, Moab, and Edom must have thought when their armies did not return. I mean, not a single individual from those armies survived.

At the same time, not a single soldier in the army of Judah was killed or even wounded!

That's the reason that *"the fear of God was on all the kingdoms of those countries, when they had heard that the LORD fought against the enemies of Israel."* This was a victory of unimagined proportions!

THE SPOILS

The truth is, the spoil was so great, as it regarded *"precious jewels"* and, no doubt, much gold and silver, that *"they were three days in gathering of the spoil, it was so much."*

Would the Lord do more for the Children of Israel under the Old Covenant than He will do for modern Believers under the New?

I think not!

Actually, due to the fact that we now have *"a better Covenant established on better Promises,"* we should expect even more, much more (Heb. 8:6)!

I am persuaded that most Believers little ask the Lord at all for things we need, and then if we do ask, we don't ask big enough.

My grandmother taught me when I was a kid, and I still see her face even yet as she would tell me, *"Jimmy, God is a Big God, so ask big!"* I have never forgotten that, and it has helped me to touch this world for Christ.

We should believe God for great things! We should believe that He answers prayer, and does so today the same as He always has, and even greater for those who will dare to believe Him.

Our Lord addressed this by saying, and I continue to quote from THE EXPOSITOR'S STUDY BIBLE:

"Which of you shall have a friend, and shall go unto him at midnight, and say unto him, Friend, lend me three loaves (a meager request);

"For a friend of mine in his journey is come to me, and I have nothing to set before him? (We as Believers must give the Message of Eternal Life to all of mankind, but the truth is, within ourselves, we have nothing to give.)

"And he from within shall answer and say, Trouble me not: the door is now shut, and my children are with me in bed; I cannot rise and give to you (an obvious denial).

"I say unto you, Though he will not rise and give him, because he is his friend, yet because of his importunity he will rise and give him as many as he needs (the argument of this Parable is that if a sufficiency for daily need can, by importunity, i.e., 'persistence,' be obtained from an unwilling source, how much more from a willing Giver, which and Who is the Lord).

"And I say unto you (telling us how to approach the Lord for whatever we need), *Ask, and it shall be given you; seek, and you shall find; knock, and it shall be opened unto you* (all of this speaks of persistence and guarantees a positive answer, at least if it's in the Will of God).

"For everyone who asks receives; and he who seeks finds; and to him who knocks it shall be opened (he says 'everyone,' and that includes you!).

"If a son shall ask bread of any of you who is a father, will he give him a stone? or if he ask a fish, will he for a fish give him a serpent?

"Or if he shall ask an egg, will he offer him (an egg containing) *a scorpion?*

"If you then, being evil, know how to give good gifts unto your children (means that an earthly parent certainly would not give a child a stone who had asked for bread, etc.): *how much more shall your Heavenly Father give the Holy Spirit to them who ask Him?* (This refers to God's Goodness, and the fact that everything from the Godhead comes to us through the Person and Agency of the Holy Spirit; and all that He does for us is based upon the Cross of Christ, and our Faith in that Finished Work)" (Lk. 11:5-13).

THE VALLEY OF BLESSING

"The Valley of Berachah," means *"the Valley of Blessing,"* and so it was!

The enemy had set out to make it a valley

of death, but the Lord made it the very opposite.

When Jehoshaphat with the army of Judah, and accompanied, as well, by the *"singers"* and the *"praisers,"* returned to Jerusalem, they did so with *"joy."* It was truly a triumphant entry.

Satan had planned something else. He had planned to destroy Judah and, as well, to destroy Jerusalem. But instead, he suffered a defeat of gargantuan proportions. In fact, and as stated, every last soldier in the army of the enemy was killed. The evidence is that not one was left alive.

The Scripture says that Jehoshaphat and all those with him, *"came to Jerusalem with psalteries and harps and trumpets unto the House of the LORD."*

And then the Scripture says that all the surrounding nations became greatly fearful of Jehoshaphat and Judah because *"the fear of God was on all the kingdoms of those countries...."* They heard what the Lord had done for Israel, and how that the entirety of the armies of the Ammonites, the Moabites, and the Edomites were destroyed, to a man, and without one single soldier of Judah being killed. That would be enough to put the fear of God in anyone. So the Scripture then said, *"So the realm of Jehoshaphat was quiet: for his God gave him rest round about."*

(31) "AND JEHOSHAPHAT REIGNED OVER JUDAH: HE WAS THIRTY AND FIVE YEARS OLD WHEN HE BEGAN TO REIGN, AND HE REIGNED TWENTY AND FIVE YEARS IN JERUSALEM. AND HIS MOTHER'S NAME WAS AZUBAH THE DAUGHTER OF SHILHI.

(32) "AND HE WALKED IN THE WAY OF ASA HIS FATHER, AND DEPARTED NOT FROM IT, DOING THAT WHICH WAS RIGHT IN THE SIGHT OF THE LORD.

(33) "HOWBEIT THE HIGH PLACES WERE NOT TAKEN AWAY: FOR AS YET THE PEOPLE HAD NOT PREPARED THEIR HEARTS UNTO THE GOD OF THEIR FATHERS.

(34) "NOW THE REST OF THE ACTS OF JEHOSHAPHAT, FIRST AND LAST, BEHOLD, THEY ARE WRITTEN IN THE BOOK OF JEHU THE SON OF HANANI, WHO IS MENTIONED IN THE BOOK OF THE KINGS OF ISRAEL.

(35) "AND AFTER THIS DID JEHOSHAPHAT KING OF JUDAH JOIN HIMSELF WITH AHAZIAH KING OF ISRAEL, WHO DID VERY WICKEDLY:

(36) "AND HE JOINED HIMSELF WITH HIM TO MAKE SHIPS TO GO TO TARSHISH: AND THEY MADE THE SHIPS IN EZION-GABER.

(37) "THEN ELIEZER THE SON OF DODAVAH OF MARESHAH PROPHESIED AGAINST JEHOSHAPHAT, SAYING, BECAUSE YOU HAVE JOINED YOURSELF WITH AHAZIAH, THE LORD HAS BROKEN YOUR WORKS. AND THE SHIPS WERE BROKEN, THAT THEY WERE NOT ABLE TO GO TO TARSHISH."

The construction is:

1. (Vs. 33) Jehoshaphat had given instructions that the high places were to be taken away (II Chron. 17:6), but evidently, the people had not obeyed.

2. (Vs. 33) Despite the great Miracle which Judah experienced in the defeat of their enemies, still, Judah did not fully obey the Lord. This shows that Miracles do not necessarily turn one to God.

3. Verse 36 proves that an old sin is an easy sin.

4. (Vs. 37) The prosperity of Jehoshaphat was not to be found in wicked Ahaziah, but in the Lord, always in the Lord!

5. (Vs. 37) When it says in the Thirty-second Verse that Jehoshaphat departed not from doing that which was right in the sight of the Lord, it was speaking of idol-worship. Despite his sin regarding alliances with the northern kingdom of Israel, he never succumbed in any manner to idol-worship.

THE HIGH PLACES

There is no contradiction between Chapter 17, Verse 6 and Verse 33 of this Chapter. Jehoshaphat commanded the destruction of these high places, and, so far as he was individually responsible, he took them away; but the people failed to carry out his commands. Concerning this, the Scripture says, *"Howbeit the high places were not taken away: for as yet the people had not prepared their hearts unto the God of their fathers.*" Even after these great victories, still, the people's hearts were not after God. What a tragedy!

The problem of the *"high places"* continued through the entirety of the existence of Israel and Judah. Over and over again, the Scriptures say, *"the high places were not removed"* (I Ki. 15:14; 22:43; II Ki. 12:3; 14:4; 15:4, 35).

WHAT EXACTLY WERE THE HIGH PLACES?

As best as can be known, the high places were shrines or even altars built in elevated places, thinking that such placed one closer to God or gods.

Israel sometimes sacrificed to Jehovah in these places, but generally, when this was done, it eventually degenerated into idol-worship. At times, great immorality was carried on at these *"high places,"* as it regarded temple prostitutes, etc. Of course, this pertained to the worship of idol-gods.

The heathen did this repeatedly, and, in a sense, Israel was actually copying the heathen with her *"high places."*

Besides all of this, the Lord had commanded that when the Temple would be built, sacrifices would be offered there and there only (Deut. 16:6; II Chron. 7:12).

The reason?

There were many reasons, no doubt, that the Temple was to be the only place of sacrifice in Israel, but the most binding reason of all was that the Altar of Sacrifice at the Temple pictured Calvary. And there was to be only one Calvary, i.e., *"one Cross."* As there would be only one Sacrifice of the Cross, there would be only one place of sacrifice in Israel, namely Jerusalem.

AN OLD SIN IS AN EASY SIN

The short phrase, *"And after this,"* refers to the wonderful deliverance of this Chapter, which was a Miracle of astounding proportions.

This was Jehoshaphat's third alliance with the guilty house of Ahab. It was fellowship and commerce, even as had been the previous alliance, with the first one being that of the military.

Comparing Verses 36 and 37 with I Kings 22:48-49, two commercial expeditions appear. The first, ships to go to Tarshish, that is, Spain; the second, ships of Tarshish, i.e., Tarshish ships, that is, ocean-going vessels, to sail to Ophir for gold. The one fleet sailed to the west, the other to the east. God broke them both.

Jehoshaphat must have reasoned that an alliance of commerce with the northern kingdom of Israel would be permissible. Evidently he did not seek the Lord as it concerned this thing; consequently, *"Eliezer the son of Dodavah of Mareshah prophesied against Jehoshaphat, saying, Because you have joined yourself with Ahaziah, the LORD has broken your works."* As stated, an old sin is an easy sin.

We look at this and wonder why in the world that Jehoshaphat would do such a thing, especially three times? Evidently, in his mind, he thought it was the right thing to do. But we see that each time, he did not consult the Lord at all. Had he done so, these fiascos would have been avoided.

Jehoshaphat died at 60 years old. Quite possibly, his early death was because of this failure.

When the Thirty-second Verse says, *"And departed not from it, doing that which was right in the sight of the LORD,"* it is speaking of idol-worship. Jehoshaphat, despite his sin, regarding alliances with the northern kingdom of Israel, never succumbed in any manner to idol-worship.

"It is finished; what a Gospel!
"Nothing has been left to do,
"But to take with grateful gladness,
"What the Saviour did for you."

"It is finished; what a Gospel!
"Bringing news of Victory won,
"Telling us of peace and pardon,
"Through the Blood of God's dear Son."

"It is finished; what a Gospel!
"Here each weary laden breast,
"That accepts God's gracious Offer,
"Enters into perfect rest."

"It is finished; what a Gospel!
"Jesus died to save your soul;
"Have you taken His Salvation?
"Have you let Him make you whole?"

CHAPTER 21

(1) "NOW JEHOSHAPHAT SLEPT WITH HIS FATHERS, AND WAS BURIED WITH HIS FATHERS IN THE CITY OF DAVID. AND JEHORAM HIS SON REIGNED IN HIS STEAD.

(2) "AND HE HAD BRETHREN THE SONS OF JEHOSHAPHAT, AZARIAH, AND JEHIEL, AND ZECHARIAH, AND AZARIAH, AND MICHAEL, AND SHEPHATIAH: ALL THESE WERE THE SONS OF JEHOSHAPHAT KING OF ISRAEL.

(3) "AND THEIR FATHER GAVE THEM GREAT GIFTS OF SILVER, AND OF GOLD, AND OF PRECIOUS THINGS, WITH FENCED CITIES IN JUDAH: BUT THE KINGDOM GAVE HE TO JEHORAM; BECAUSE HE WAS THE FIRSTBORN.

(4) "NOW WHEN JEHORAM WAS RISEN UP TO THE KINGDOM OF HIS FATHER, HE STRENGTHENED HIMSELF, AND KILLED ALL HIS BRETHREN WITH THE SWORD, AND DIVERS ALSO OF THE PRINCES OF ISRAEL.

(5) "JEHORAM WAS THIRTY AND TWO YEARS OLD WHEN HE BEGAN TO REIGN, AND HE REIGNED EIGHT YEARS IN JERUSALEM.

(6) "AND HE WALKED IN THE WAY OF THE KINGS OF ISRAEL, LIKE AS DID THE HOUSE OF AHAB: FOR HE HAD THE DAUGHTER OF AHAB TO WIFE: AND HE WROUGHT THAT WHICH WAS EVIL IN THE EYES OF THE LORD.

(7) "HOWBEIT THE LORD WOULD NOT DESTROY THE HOUSE OF DAVID, BECAUSE OF THE COVENANT THAT HE HAD MADE WITH DAVID, AND AS HE PROMISED TO GIVE A LIGHT TO HIM AND TO HIS SONS FOREVER."

The overview is:

1. The word *"Israel"* being used in Verse 2 instead of Judah is not an error in transcription. It does show that God recognized the faithful remnant of Judah as His entire People.

2. Jehoram, Jehoshaphat's son, was one of the most wicked kings to sit on the throne of Judah. According to the last phrase of Verse 3, the implication is that Jehoshaphat did not have the mind of the Lord regarding the selection of Jehoram. Most of the time, the law of the firstborn held true even in throne rights, but not always. God overruled in some cases because the firstborn was not the suitable one for a position. To be sure, Jehoram was certainly not the suitable one here.

3. (Vs. 4) Jehoram strengthened himself by murder and ruthlessness, instead of doing it the way his godly father had done, by the Blessing of God.

4. Verse 6 proclaims to us the leaven that was in the life of Jehoshaphat concerning his alliance with Ahab. The awful thing about sin is that it breeds more sin and, in fact, can only be stopped by Faith in Christ and what Christ did at the Cross.

A CHOICE THAT WAS NOT THE WILL OF GOD

The choice of Jehoram was not the Will of God.

Evidently, Jehoshaphat did not pray about this selection, which would prove to be awful, to say the least. Jehoram would be one of the most ungodly kings to ever grace the throne of Judah. He was a murderer, a liar, a blasphemer, and an idol-worshipper. The situation regarding this man could not have been worse, and Judah suffered because of it. Jehoshaphat, as should go without saying, made a terrible choice!

These kings of Judah were all in the lineage of David, with ultimately the Messiah to be born in that particular lineage. Of course, when you understand this, you realize that this was the single most important family on the face of the Earth; however, some of them were godly, and some were ungodly! But due to what was to be brought about through their lineage, whatever they did, whether godly or ungodly, was of utmost significance, as should be obvious (II Sam., Chpt. 7).

In fact, the Nation of Israel, whether referred to as Judah or Israel, was actually the single most important Nation on the face of the Earth because they were a people having been raised up by God. They had been raised up for the purpose of giving the world the Word of God and, as well, serving as the womb of the coming Messiah, Who would be the Redeemer of the world. Of course, that Messiah would be the Lord Jesus Christ. They were also to evangelize the world but failed miserably in this latter responsibility. They will yet fulfill it in the coming Kingdom Age (Isa. 66:18-19).

Evidently, Jehoshaphat did not heed the words of Solomon which said, *"Train up a child in the way he should go: and when he is old, he will not depart from it"* (Prov. 22:6).

The words, *"train up,"* mean to *"hedge up"* or *"hedge in."* It is like building a fence around a child; however, what is to be fenced in must be two things, *"the child and the Bible."* This is the *"way he should go."*

I think it is obvious that Jehoram was not trained in the way that he should go.

THE HOUSE OF AHAB

Now we are able to see the leaven that was in the life of Jehoshaphat concerning his alliance with Ahab. For it says, *"And he walked in the way of the kings of Israel, like as did the house of Ahab: for he had the daughter of Ahab to wife: and he wrought that which was evil in the Eyes of the LORD."*

Despite this glut of evil, the Seventh Verse says, *"Howbeit the LORD would not destroy the House of David, because of the Covenant that He had made with David. . . ."*

The Lord has a reason for everything that He does. For Jehoshaphat to associate with Ahab was more than just a momentary lapse. The leaven would spread until it included his son, who would marry Ahab's daughter (or some say *"granddaughter"*), who, no doubt, was a party to his evil. So, when the Lord says, *"Thou shalt not . . . ,"* there is always more there than meets the eye.

WHY DIDN'T THE LORD STOP THE SITUATION?

The Lord will never violate the free moral agency of man. He will warn man, deal with man, speak to man, and use events to teach man, but, if man insists, the Lord will allow him to do whatever it is he desires to do, at least in most cases.

The Lord has the Power to do whatever is needed, for He is Almighty; however, He purposely limits Himself, and for good reason.

In the Creation of man, God gave the human race certain autonomy, among which is free moral agency. In other words, man is not a machine, some glorified computer, but rather has the power to reason and to make a choice. Due to the Fall, sadly and regrettably, the far greater majority of the time, that choice is not to his well-being or the well-being of others. The sin nature rules the unconverted man and does so 24 hours a day, 7 days a week. In other words, every single thing that the unconverted individual does is more or less in the realm of disobedience to the Word of God. In fact, it cannot be otherwise. The only answer for that state of wickedness, which, due to the Fall, covers every individual, is the acceptance of Jesus Christ as one's Lord and Saviour, ever looking to the Cross where the terrible sin debt was forever settled (Rom. 6:1-14; Gal., Chpt. 5; 6:14; Col. 2:14-15).

Jehoram had no heart for God but did most definitely have a heart for evil. As a result, to guarantee the throne, in other words, that there would be none that would lay claim to his place and position, he would murder all six of his brothers. As well, it seems that anyone who disagreed with his murderous action, even the *"princes of Israel,"* he murdered them also.

Due to the alliance of his father with Ahab, and the fact that he had married *"the daughter of Ahab,"* he now had the spirit of Ahab. As we shall see, he would die without God as Ahab did.

(8) "IN HIS DAYS THE EDOMITES REVOLTED FROM UNDER THE DOMINION OF JUDAH, AND MADE THEMSELVES A KING.

(9) "THEN JEHORAM WENT FORTH WITH HIS PRINCES, AND ALL HIS CHARIOTS WITH HIM: AND HE ROSE UP BY NIGHT, AND SMOTE THE EDOMITES WHICH COMPASSED HIM IN, AND THE CAPTAINS OF THE CHARIOTS.

(10) "SO THE EDOMITES REVOLTED FROM UNDER THE HAND OF JUDAH UNTO THIS DAY. THE SAME TIME ALSO DID LIBNAH REVOLT FROM UNDER HIS HAND; BECAUSE HE HAD FORSAKEN

THE LORD GOD OF HIS FATHERS."

The exposition is:

1. (Vs. 10) Over and over again, we see blessing coming because of adherence to the Word of God and, as well, judgment because of failure to adhere to the Word of God.

2. The Edomites did not succeed in killing Jehoram as they, no doubt, had desired to do. Still, they were able to throw off the yoke of Judah, and there was nothing that Judah could do to stop them. Libnah also revolted.

3. All of this happened, *"because he had forsaken the LORD God of his fathers."*

FORSAKING THE LORD

When the Lord is forsaken, that which He has given us is lost, as well, and to be sure, that which He has given us is the only Saving Grace in our lives.

The Edomites were trying to kill Jehoram and would have succeeded had it not been for the Mercy of God, Mercy which Jehoram did not recognize or admit.

The tragedy of America at this present time (2008) is that it is, as well, forsaking God. That which has made us great, the envy of the world, we are losing simply because we're losing the Blessings of the Lord.

The governmental leaders, or at least far too many of them, are insulting the Lord to His Face by advocating same-sex marriages, in other words, placing the seal of approval upon this abomination. To be sure, God will not allow the sanctioning of homosexuality. His Judgment upon this nation cannot be far removed and, in fact, has already begun.

The nation is faced with the problem of Islam, and it has no idea, because of its spiritual deadness, just how dangerous this abomination is. Islam, I believe, is Satan's final touch in this world, which will help usher in the Antichrist. This is Ishmael, the work of the flesh, and to be sure, he hates Isaac and all that pertains to Isaac.

I marvel at the senselessness of our politicians as it regards Israel. They keep thinking that if Israel will do this or do that, it will appease the Palestinians. What they do not seem to realize is the Palestinians, so-called, will not be satisfied until every Jew

NOTES

in Israel is dead, and they, the Palestinians, possess the entirety of the land, actually, every square inch. This is what they demand, and this is what they have openly stated any number of times. But yet, our politicians never seem to be able to understand the motives of these people.

Incidentally, there is really no such thing as Palestinians. The word comes from *"Philistines,"* and to be sure, there are no more Philistines in that part of the world, or anywhere, for that matter. Those who refer to themselves presently as Palestinians are actually Jordanians, Egyptians, Syrians, etc.

It is amazing, but I fear that if the truth be known, Bible Christianity is hated more in this nation even than Islam. In fact, Islam is tolerated, and tolerated to such an extent that it borders on idiocy.

If it is to be noticed, the Muslims do not hit the Russians.

Why?

They know the Russians will take stern measures against them and do so quickly.

But, what happens if they hit America?

We give them a billion dollars in foreign aid and then ask if we can do anything else for them. Not only will they not suffer for their efforts against this nation, they are actually rewarded. So, they have nothing to fear. What does the Bible say?

"Because sentence against an evil work is not executed speedily, therefore the heart of the sons of men is fully set in them to do evil" (Eccl. 8:11).

This means that government is morally and Spiritually obligated to put down all *"evil work,"* whether in the hearts and lives of individuals or in entire nations. To not do so will only increase the evil.

(11) "MOREOVER HE MADE HIGH PLACES IN THE MOUNTAINS OF JUDAH AND CAUSED THE INHABITANTS OF JERUSALEM TO COMMIT FORNICATION, AND COMPELLED JUDAH THERETO.

(12) "AND THERE CAME A WRITING TO HIM FROM ELIJAH THE PROPHET, SAYING, THUS SAYS THE LORD GOD OF DAVID YOUR FATHER, BECAUSE YOU HAVE NOT WALKED IN THE WAYS OF JEHOSHAPHAT YOUR FATHER, NOR IN THE WAYS OF ASA KING OF JUDAH,

(13) "BUT HAVE WALKED IN THE WAY OF THE KINGS OF ISRAEL, AND HAVE MADE JUDAH AND THE INHABITANTS OF JERUSALEM TO GO A WHORING, LIKE TO THE WHOREDOMS OF THE HOUSE OF AHAB, AND ALSO HAVE KILLED YOUR BRETHREN OF YOUR FATHER'S HOUSE, WHICH WERE BETTER THAN YOURSELF:

(14) "BEHOLD, WITH A GREAT PLAGUE WILL THE LORD SMITE YOUR PEOPLE, AND YOUR CHILDREN, AND YOUR WIVES, AND ALL YOUR GOODS:

(15) "AND YOU SHALL HAVE GREAT SICKNESS BY DISEASE OF YOUR BOWELS, UNTIL YOUR BOWELS FALL OUT BY REASON OF THE SICKNESS DAY BY DAY.

(16) "MOREOVER THE LORD STIRRED UP AGAINST JEHORAM THE SPIRIT OF THE PHILISTINES, AND OF THE ARABIANS, WHO WERE NEAR THE ETHIOPIANS:

(17) "AND THEY CAME UP INTO JUDAH, AND BROKE INTO IT, AND CARRIED AWAY ALL THE SUBSTANCE THAT WAS FOUND IN THE KING'S HOUSE, AND HIS SONS ALSO, AND HIS WIVES; SO THAT THERE WAS NEVER A SON LEFT HIM, SAVE JEHOAHAZ, THE YOUNGEST OF HIS SONS."

The pattern is:

1. The *"fornication"* of Verse 11 was mostly the worship of the *"Asherah."* It was the male sex organ, carved out of a tree trunk, and standing anywhere from 10 to 20 feet high. This, as the god of fertility, would be worshipped with all types of sexual sins being practiced. In other words, it was idol-worship!

2. (Vs. 15) Even though Elijah was a Prophet to the northern kingdom of Israel, which was sometimes referred to as Samaria, still, the Lord gave him this great word for Jehoram, King of Judah. Had the king repented, all of this could have been avoided. But regrettably, he ignored the Word of the Lord from the Lord through Elijah the Prophet. The end result would be exactly as Elijah prophesied.

3. The Sixteenth Verse proclaims the Lord's Hand in everything, be it negative or positive, all based on disobedience or obedience.

4. (Vs. 17) This was the first of two times in this period that the royal line was cut off except for one boy—the line that would be in the lineage of Christ (II Chron. 22:10).

FORNICATION

The word *"fornication,"* as it is here used, pertains to idol-worship. Jehoram, totally unlike his father Jehoshaphat, took Judah deep into idol-worship, which ultimately brought about the Judgment of God.

What was the attraction of idol-worship?

Well, of course, first and foremost, the powers of darkness functioned in idols and did so in varied ways.

In most idol-worship, irrespective of the so-called god being worshipped, there were extensive practices of immorality of every stripe, including homosexuality, incest, bestiality, and every other type of perversion.

One archeologist working in the Holy Land said, *"The God of the Bible Who gave instructions for entire tribes to be wiped out, even the children, did future generations an untold service."*

He was speaking of the gross immorality, including incest, to which they had submitted themselves, which brought about all types of diseases, and worse than that, brought about mental malignancy to such an extent that extermination was the only answer.

Sin always degrades, and, in fact, the degradation never stops. It is ever downward until everything is destroyed.

MODERN IDOLS

The sophistication of the world has increased to the extent that it very seldom sees idol-worship carried on presently as it was in those days of long ago; however, idol-worship is still rampant.

To be frank, religion is the greatest idol of all.

As an explanation, religion is that which is conceived by man, devised by man, carried out by man, and fabricated by man, which means it's not of God, and which means it's not accepted by God. It is that which is claimed by man to better one in some way or help one to reach God. As stated, anything devised by man cannot be accepted by God, as it regards things Spiritual.

In its purest sense, Christianity is not a religion but is rather a relationship, and more particularly, a relationship with a man, the Man Christ Jesus. As it regards Christianity, if Christ and the Cross are not the Object of our Faith, then whatever else it is in which we have placed our faith is looked at by God as an idol. In some senses of the word, it is no different than the idols of Old Testament times.

When John the Beloved said, *"Little children, keep yourselves from idols,"* he was not referring to the heathen worship of idol gods but of the heretical substitutes for the Christian conception of God, or anything that pulls us away from Christ and the Cross (I Jn. 5:21).

ELIJAH THE PROPHET

Some claim that the statement about Elijah is an error because he had already been translated. It is quite possible that by now he had, in fact, already been translated. If that were the case, then he wrote the letter to Jehoram before his Translation, which means that the Spirit of God revealed to him what he was to say.

And then again, with the chronology of these happenings not easy to ascertain, it is quite possible and probable that Elijah was most definitely alive at this point in Jehoram's reign. At any rate, it is absolutely certain that Elijah the Prophet sent this letter, irrespective as to when it was sent.

Elijah was a Prophet for the northern kingdom of Israel. As far as it is known, this is his only involvement in the southern kingdom of Judah.

Elijah was contemporary with Ahab and Ahaziah, both of the northern kingdom.

The following presents the terrible crimes and sins of Jehoram:
• Elijah claims his word to be from the *"LORD God of David your father,"* several times removed, we might quickly add.
• Jehoram did not walk in the ways of his father Jehoshaphat or in the ways of Asa king of Judah, his grandfather.
• He rather *"walked in the way of the kings of Israel."*

NOTES

• He *"made Judah and the inhabitants of Jerusalem to go a whoring, like to the whoredoms of the house of Ahab."*
• He murdered his six brothers, with all, Elijah said, *"better than yourself."*

The Judgment is now pronounced. It is:
• *"With a great plague will the LORD smite your people, and your children, and your wives, and all your goods."*
• *"You shall have great sickness by disease of your bowels, until your bowels fall out by reason of the sickness day by day."*

While this letter sent by Elijah was dire indeed, still, it was the Lord speaking to the king, seeking to get him to repent. Had he done so, much of this Judgment, and possibly all of it, could have been avoided.

But despite the fact that this letter came from one of the greatest Prophets who ever lived, and of whom Jehoram undoubtedly was well acquainted by reputation, still, he would not repent.

Why is it that man in the face of incontrovertible evidence will continue to rebel against the Lord?

Why?

How?

HOW CAN MAN RESIST GOD?

Of course, as is obvious, God, Who is All-powerful, could force man into any posture He so desired, but as we've already stated, the Lord will not violate the free moral agency of any individual.

Due to the Fall, there is a built-in animosity toward God in the hearts of all men, and we refer to the unconverted.

This is because God is the Creator of the Universe and of man, as well, and also, that God gave Adam instructions as to what he should and should not do. As is known, Adam disobeyed those instructions. While Eve was deceived into doing what she did, Adam was not deceived, thereby, doing what he did with eyes wide open, so to speak. So, the controversy is between God and man.

That's the reason there is a greater animosity in this nation, which some refer to as Christian, against Jesus Christ, to which we've already alluded, than it is Muhammad. That's strange when one considers that the religion of Muhammad caused the deaths of nearly 4,000 people on September 11, 2001 (9/11/01).

Conversely, untold thousands in this nation have been delivered from acute alcoholism, drug addiction, gambling, immorality, etc., and all by and through the Lord Jesus Christ and what He did at the Cross. But yet, the animosity is against Him and not Muhammad.

Strange, isn't it?

As well, the tremendous life-changing experiences which characterize so many in this nation because of Jesus Christ are the same, more or less, in virtually every nation in the world.

That animosity is there simply because Jesus Christ truly is God. Men do not want to admit that because if He truly is God, then they are in the position of resisting God and doing so in a very angry way.

JESUS CHRIST THE SON OF GOD

If the unconverted world thinks of Jesus Christ at all, they definitely do not think of Him as God, but rather, just another man. In fact, and to which we have already alluded, they don't want to think of Him as God because that would put a totally new complexion on the entirety of the situation. If Jesus Christ is only a man, that's one thing; if He, as well, is God, then that's something else entirely. Somehow, they think by claiming that He is only a man, this will absolve them of any type of responsibility. It won't!

Irrespective, Jesus Christ is very Man and very God, and as such, every human being on the face of the Earth will one day answer to Him. We will either answer to Him as it regards His Saving Grace and what He did for us at the Cross, or we will answer to Him at the *"Great White Throne Judgment"* (Rev. 20:11-15).

However, the world has become so psychologized that it no longer believes in a judgment of any kind. Psychology teaches that man is inherently good, and if, in fact, he does something bad, it is because of outside influences, etc. So, if a person is inherently good, and their wrongdoing is to be blamed on something else, then a judgment, according to the thinking of most, would not be in order.

NOTES

Irrespective as to how man may think and how he has been brainwashed by humanistic psychology, there is a Judgment that's coming for all unredeemed, and it's called the *"Great White Throne Judgment."*

THE GREAT WHITE THRONE JUDGMENT

Several things must be said about this Judgment, and they are as follows:

• The fact of this Judgment is revealed to us in Revelation 20:11-15.

• It is called, the *"Great White Throne Judgment."*

• Jesus Christ will be the Judge.

• Only the unredeemed will appear at this Judgment, which will include the soul and the spirit of every unredeemed person who has ever lived.

• No redeemed person will be at this Judgment because the sins of the Redeemed have already been judged in Christ according to what He did for us at the Cross.

• At that Judgment, the Books will be opened. In the first set of Books, every action of the unredeemed has been catalogued. As well, the *"Book of Life"* will also be brought out, containing the names of every person who has ever been redeemed. It will be shown to all the unredeemed that they may see their names are not there.

• Every unredeemed person who is now in Hell will be released from that place for a short period of time in order that they may stand at the *"Great White Throne Judgment."*

• This Judgment will be carried forth in order that the unredeemed will know and understand that their consignment to the Lake of Fire forever and forever is fully and totally justified.

The idea is, every human being on the face of the Earth must face Christ as Saviour, or they will face Him as Judge.

THE ACTIONS OF THE LORD

The Scripture says, *"The LORD stirred up against Jehoram the spirit of the Philistines, and of the Arabians, who were near the Ethiopians."* In other words, the Lord put it in their spirits that they were to invade Judah, which they did. They had no idea that this was the Lord moving upon them, but this is exactly what happened.

The Lord can stop such excursions, or He can cause such excursions to come to pass. He is in total control of everything, as should be obvious.

When they invaded Judah, they *"carried away all the substance that was found in the king's house, and his sons also, and his wives. . . ."* The Scripture says that one boy was left, *"Jehoahaz, the youngest of his sons."* He was also referred to as *"Ahaziah."*

When Jehoram became king and murdered his six brothers, leaving only himself, he was the only one left in the lineage of David, through which the Messiah had to come. So, if he had been killed or had died before he had a son, which, no doubt, was Satan's intention, this would have been a tragedy of unprecedented proportions.

Now, all the sons of Jehoram had been taken captive by the Philistines and the Arabians, *"save Jehoahaz,"* as stated, the *"youngest of his sons."* So now, the entire lineage hangs on this one young man.

A little later, Satan would attempt such again by having all the sons of Jehoahaz killed, except baby Joash, and on that one thread the hope of man's Redemption hung.

(18) "AND AFTER ALL THIS THE LORD SMOTE HIM IN HIS BOWELS WITH AN INCURABLE DISEASE.

(19) "AND IT CAME TO PASS, THAT IN PROCESS OF TIME, AFTER THE END OF TWO YEARS, HIS BOWELS FELL OUT BY REASON OF HIS SICKNESS: SO HE DIED OF SORE DISEASES. AND HIS PEOPLE MADE NO BURNING FOR HIM, LIKE THE BURNING OF HIS FATHERS.

(20) "THIRTY AND TWO YEARS OLD WAS HE WHEN HE BEGAN TO REIGN, AND HE REIGNED IN JERUSALEM EIGHT YEARS, AND DEPARTED WITHOUT BEING DESIRED. HOWBEIT THEY BURIED HIM IN THE CITY OF DAVID, BUT NOT IN THE SEPULCHRES OF THE KINGS."

The pattern is:

1. (Vs. 18) Exactly as the Prophet Elijah had predicted, because of his gross wickedness. All sickness in Believers cannot be traced to sin in their lives; however, most definitely, some can!

NOTES

2. (Vs. 19) In essence, the Lord gave this wicked monarch *"two years"* in which to repent; but he didn't!

3. This king was so wicked that Judah was glad to see him go!

WITHOUT BEING DESIRED

What an indictment!

And it's the Holy Spirit Who said this! Men were glad to see the last of him. And such is the conclusion of those who rebel against God, seeing how deep in sin that they can actually go. They would not engage a burning for him, as they did for his good father and pious grandfather when they died. His rotten carcass they buried in the city of David; they would not desecrate with it the sepulchers of the kings (Pulpit[1]).

"Open my eyes that I may see,
"Glimpses of Truth You have for me;
"Place in my hands the wonderful key,
"That shall unclasp and set me free."

"Open my ears that I may hear,
"Voices of Truth You sendest clear;
"And while the wave-notes fall on my ear,
"Everything false will disappear."

"Open my mouth and let me bear,
"Tidings of Mercy everywhere;
"Open my heart and let me prepare,
"Love with Your Children thus to share."

"Open my mind that I may read,
"More of Your Love in word and deed:
"What shall I fear while yet You do lead?
"Only for light from You I plead."

CHAPTER 22

(1) "AND THE INHABITANTS OF JERUSALEM MADE AHAZIAH HIS YOUNGEST SON KING IN HIS STEAD: FOR THE BAND OF MEN WHO CAME WITH THE ARABIANS TO THE CAMP HAD KILLED ALL THE ELDEST. SO AHAZIAH THE SON OF JEHORAM KING OF JUDAH REIGNED.

(2) "FORTY AND TWO YEARS OLD WAS AHAZIAH WHEN HE BEGAN TO REIGN, AND HE REIGNED ONE YEAR IN JERUSALEM. HIS MOTHER'S NAME ALSO WAS ATHALIAH THE DAUGHTER OF OMRI.

(3) "HE ALSO WALKED IN THE WAYS OF THE HOUSE OF AHAB: FOR HIS MOTHER WAS HIS COUNSELOR TO DO WICKEDLY.

(4) "WHEREFORE HE DID EVIL IN THE SIGHT OF THE LORD LIKE THE HOUSE OF AHAB: FOR THEY WERE HIS COUNSELORS AFTER THE DEATH OF HIS FATHER TO HIS DESTRUCTION.

(5) "HE WALKED ALSO AFTER THEIR COUNSEL, AND WENT WITH JEHORAM THE SON OF AHAB KING OF ISRAEL TO WAR AGAINST HAZAEL KING OF SYRIA AT RAMOTH-GILEAD: AND THE SYRIANS SMOTE JORAM.

(6) "AND HE RETURNED TO BE HEALED IN JEZREEL BECAUSE OF THE WOUNDS WHICH WERE GIVEN HIM AT RAMAH, WHEN HE FOUGHT WITH HAZAEL KING OF SYRIA. AND AZARIAH THE SON OF JEHORAM KING OF JUDAH WENT DOWN TO SEE JEHORAM THE SON OF AHAB AT JEZREEL, BECAUSE HE WAS SICK."

The diagram is:

1. (Vs. 1) The king actually had three names: *"Ahaziah," "Azariah,"* and *"Jehoahaz."* All have the same meaning in Hebrew, *"Jehovah takes hold"*; however, Jehovah had no opportunity to take hold in the life of this wicked king.

As one reads these accounts, it becomes overly obvious that sin does not pay.

2. (Vs. 2) The *"leaven"* that was in the life of Jehoshaphat concerning his alliance with Ahab will now continue its rot. Athaliah, the mother of Ahaziah, was actually the daughter of Ahab and Jezebel, which made her the granddaughter of Omri. The Hebrew language had no designation such as *"granddaughter"* or *"grandson,"* etc.

3. (Vs. 3) Jehoahaz followed his wicked father, Jehoram, who had also walked in all the wicked ways of Ahab and Jezebel. His mother killed all of her grandsons except one and seized the throne of Judah, which she kept for six years.

4. (Vs. 5) Joram, the king of the northern confederacy of Israel, is the same as Jehoram. We have two kings here by the same name. The king of Judah had been named *"Jehoram,"* and the king of the northern confederacy of Israel was also named *"Jehoram."*

5. If it is to be noticed, the Holy Spirit removes from the name of *"Jehoram,"* the Jehovah syllable, leaving the name *"Joram."* His evil was so great that he could not be connected with the Lord.

THE RETRIBUTION OF AN ANGRY GOD

Pulpit said, *"It appears that Ahaziah was the only son left to the house of Jehoram; all the eldest had been slain by the invaders. Thus we find that the man who with shameful selfishness murdered his own brothers, had to suffer the loss, by violence, of his own sons. It was a fitting penalty – fitting that he who used the sword remorselessly should suffer from the sword; fitting that the man whose darkest crime was committed 'under his own roof' should bear his penalty in his own kindred."*[1]

What we sow we reap! The evil of Jehoram, king of Judah, will now increase, if possible, under his son, Ahaziah.

Verse 2 says that Ahaziah was *"Forty and two years old when he began to reign."* This evidently is an error by a copyist. II Kings 8:26 says that he was 22 years old, which is, no doubt, correct. He reigned one year in Jerusalem.

WICKED COUNSEL

His mother was either the daughter or the granddaughter of Ahab. Irrespective, she was as wicked as her forbearer. The terrible leaven that was brought into Judah by Jehoshaphat, his grandfather, is now spreading. When Jehoshaphat joined affinity with Ahab, even allowing his son Jehoram to marry the daughter (or granddaughter) of this wicked king of Israel, it resulted in a terrible, dark day for Judah. As we've already explained, sin is not a trifling business. It is a canker that eats away at the soul and will not stop until all is destroyed.

There is only one cure for sin, only one!

That cure is the shed Blood of the Lord Jesus Christ.

The world, which rejects God and His Way of Redemption, claims that other things can address this evil, such as education, proper environment, money, etc. Let it ever be understood that the only thing which can change the wicked heart of man is for that individual to be Born-Again, which can only be brought about as one expresses Faith in Christ and what Christ did for us at the Cross. That's the reason that Paul said, *"We preach Christ Crucified"* (I Cor. 1:23). To preach anything else as the answer and the solution is committing high treason against God, as should be overly obvious.

THE TERRIBLE PROBLEM OF SIN

Considering that sin is the cause of all death, all sickness, all war, all crime, all of man's inhumanity to man, etc., and considering that sin has soaked the Earth with blood from 10,000 battlefields, we should realize how horrible this monster actually is. It is the ruination of everything good, everything wholesome, and everything Divine. It has made the Earth a graveyard and has broken the heart of every human being, in one way or the other, who has ever lived.

WHAT IS SIN?

Pure and simple, sin is the disobedience of the Word of God. According to the Genesis account, original sin is a proud, loveless, rebellious, thankless, and destructive act of self-assertion, first against God Who gave man his reality, and, simultaneously, against both the self and every other form of created reality. Sin is the height of selfishness. In fact, Adam's sin was a declaration of self-sufficiency; in essence, he willed to go it alone. By that original, first sin of Adam, everything is alienated. Adam and Eve each hid from the other by donning clothes; Adam hid from God; Adam blamed God and Eve; Eve blamed the serpent; and the self is alienated from itself.

TOTAL DEPRAVITY

The Bible teaches total depravity. It says, *"And you has He quickened* (made alive), *who were dead in trespasses and sins"* (Eph. 2:1).

NOTES

Total depravity means that unconverted man is totally absent of anything that pertains to God. Whatever he thinks of God is wrong, and, in fact, he doesn't have, and cannot have, any right thinking as it regards God. So, any idea he has of God is twisted and perverted and, in fact, the total opposite of Who and what God really is.

The Scripture we quoted to you tells us that man is *"dead in trespasses and sins."* We must understand that *"dead is dead."* That means that man cannot have a correct moral comprehension of God. Neither can he have a desire for God, at least that is Scripturally legitimate. It also means that if he is to be converted, the initiation of such must begin with God because it cannot begin with man. As stated, *"He is spiritually dead."*

THE MANNER IN WHICH A PERSON IS BORN-AGAIN

Unconverted man cannot initiate any correct movement toward God. Any contact must be initiated by God Himself. For man to be Saved or Born-Again, in some way, the Word of God must come to him. It might be in the form of a Message, or written material, or in the form of a song, or someone witnessing over the backyard fence, etc. The Holy Spirit acts upon the Word, therefore, the Word must be given to the individual.

That's the reason that Satan fights Biblical preaching to the extent that he does. He doesn't care how many sermons are preached, just as long as they aren't Scriptural. He knows that if that's the case, man cannot be Saved.

When the Word is given to the sinner, the Holy Spirit quickens that Word to the person's heart. The individual then comes under conviction, even as Faith is imparted to that person by the Spirit.

At that time, the individual can say either *"yes"* or *"no"* to the tug of the Holy Spirit for that person to come to Christ.

To be frank, the unconverted person knows nothing about the Bible, nothing about God, and nothing about eternity. He only knows that he feels the weight of his sin. Through the administration of the Holy Spirit and the Word of God that's been given to him in some way, in a sense, he now knows there is an eternity without God, a place called Hell, and a place called Heaven. He feels his lostness. This is all initiated by the Holy Spirit.

And yet, in all of this, even though the Holy Spirit speaks to the person, deals with the person, and moves upon the person, still, He will not violate the person's free moral agency. As stated, the individual can say *"yes"* or *"no."* Regrettably, most say *"no"* and die eternally lost. But, thankfully, some do say *"yes,"* and when they do, Eternal Life is instantly given to them. In other words, they are *"Born-Again."*

THE EFFECT OF SIN

Sin effectively breaks man's relationship to all reality. This means that man cannot actually have an authentic relationship with himself, with God, with his fellowman, with nature, or, in fact, with anything. Sin is a form of insanity, which is the cause of all war, totalitarianism, poverty, superstition, want, etc.

Thus, original sin, as that act which breaks all of man's created God-relationships, is neither merely moral, intellectual, nor effective, but something deeper than all of these. It is, in essence, Spiritual. David said, *"Against You, You only, have I sinned, and done this evil in Your Sight"* (Ps. 51:4). It is this Divine reference that constitutes the essence of original sin and via this reference comes also man's sin against himself, his fellowman, and nature. The nature of sin is wholly destructive; sin, therefore, elicits those full realities which the Biblical concepts of death and the infinite Divine Wrath convey.

And yet, as it regards total depravity, such cannot be easily recognized in all men. In fact, man's moral behavior is often better than total depravity, and how do we account for that?

We account for that by the fact of God's Presence and His Dealings with man in this world. As well, the human race, even though it is loath to admit it, has been greatly influenced by the Gospel over the years. That's why Jesus said that converted man is the *"salt of the Earth"* and the *"Light of the world"* (Mat. 5:13-16). This preservative and illumination of the Gospel have provided whatever freedom that man has, whatever prosperity that man has, and whatever good relationships that man has. Even so, and as stated, man will never recognize this as being from God, but will attribute such to his own machinations, whatever they may be. Still, we, as Believers, know that all good comes from above, meaning that it certainly doesn't originate with man.

The Word of God has had a powerful effect upon the world, and because it is the Word of God. Someone has well said:
- No Bible, no freedom!
- A little Bible, a little freedom!
- Much Bible, much freedom!

THE ORIGIN OF SIN

Even though Adam and Eve brought sin into the world, at least as far as we know, still, they did not originate this monster.

Sin originated with Satan. Satan is a created being, actually, an Angel, originally, one of the most beautiful and wise Angels ever created by God. Concerning this, the Scripture says, and I quote from THE EXPOSITOR'S STUDY BIBLE:

"Moreover, the Word of the LORD came unto me, saying (the tenor of this Chapter will now change from the earthly monarch, the *'Prince of Tyre,'* to his sponsor, Satan, of which the earthly king was a symbol),

"Son of man, take up a lamentation upon the king of Tyrus, and say unto him, Thus says the Lord GOD; You seal up the sum, full of wisdom, and perfect in beauty. (As is obvious, even though the king of Tyrus is used as a symbol, the statements made could not refer to any mere mortal. In fact, they refer to Satan.

"'*You seal up the sum,*' means that Lucifer, when originally created by God, was the perfection of wisdom and beauty. In fact, the phrase intimates that Lucifer was the wisest and most beautiful Angel created by God, and served the Lord in Holiness and Righteousness for a given period of time.

"'*Perfect in beauty,*' means that he was the most beautiful of God's Angelic creation. The Holy Spirit even labeled his beauty as *'perfect.'*)

"*You have been in Eden the Garden of God; every precious stone was your covering, the sardius, topaz, and the diamond, the beryl, the onyx, and the jasper, the sapphire, the emerald, and the carbuncle, and gold: the workmanship of your tabrets and of your pipes was prepared in you in the day that you were created.* (The phrase, '*You have been in Eden the Garden of God,*' does not actually refer to the '*Eden*' of Gen., Chpt. 3, but rather to the '*Eden*' which existed on this Planet before Adam and Eve, which evidently was ruled by Lucifer before his rebellion.

"'*Every precious stone was your covering,*' presents itself as very similar to the dress of the High Priest of Israel [Ex. 28:19].

"'*The workmanship of your tabrets and of your pipes,*' has to do with music. There is every indication that Lucifer's leadership had something to do with the worship of God. As well, he is called, '*O Lucifer, son of the morning*' [Isa. 14:12]. When the Earth was originally created, the Scripture says, '*The morning stars sang together, and all the sons of God shouted for joy*' [Job 38:4-7]. So, if the idiom, '*son of the morning,*' can be linked to the '*morning stars,*' these Passages tell us that Lucifer, at least before his fall, was greatly used in leading the worship of God.

"In fact, this is the reason that Satan has done everything within his power to corrupt the music of the world and to corrupt the music of the Church above all. Inasmuch as the Book of Psalms is the longest Book in the Bible, we learn from this that music and singing are among the highest forms of worship of the Lord.)

"*You are the anointed Cherub who covers; and I have set you so: you were upon the Holy Mountain of God; you have walked up and down in the midst of the stones of fire.* ('*You are the anointed Cherub who covers,*' means that Lucifer was chosen and '*anointed*' by God for a particular task and service. This probably was the '*worship*' to which we have just alluded.

"'*You were upon the Holy Mountain of God,*' speaks of his place and position relative to the Throne [Rev. 4:2-11]. '*You have walked up and down in the midst of the stones of fire,*' has reference to his nearness to the Throne [Ezek. 1:26-27]. As well, the phrase, '*Walked up and down,*' seems to imply that not just any Angel would have been given such latitude.)

"*You were perfect in your ways from the day that you were created, till iniquity was found in you.* (Pride was the form of this iniquity [Lk. 10:17-18]; the rebellion of Lucifer against God probably caused the catastrophe which occurred between the First and Second Verses of Gen. Chpt. 1.)

"*By the multitude of your merchandise they have filled the midst of you with violence, and you have sinned; therefore I will cast you as profane out of the Mountain of God: and I will destroy you, O covering Cherub, from the midst of the stones of fire.* ('*Violence*' has been the earmark of Satan's rule and reign in the world of darkness [Jn. 10:10]. Lucifer being '*cast out*' of the '*Mountain of God*' refers to him losing his place and position, which he had held with God since his creation. It was because '*he had sinned,*' which spoke of pride that caused him to lift himself up against God.)

"*Your heart was lifted up because of your beauty, you have corrupted your wisdom by reason of your brightness: I will cast you to the ground, I will lay you before kings, that they may behold you.* ('*Your heart was lifted up because of your beauty,*' tells us the reason for his fall. As stated, it was pride. He took his eyes off of Christ, noticing his own beauty as it grew more and more glorious in his eyes. At some point in time, his '*heart*' was changed from Christ to himself. As far as we know, this was the origin of evil in all of God's Creation.

"'*You have corrupted your wisdom by reason of your brightness,*' does not refer to the loss of wisdom, but instead refers to wisdom corrupted, hence, the insidious design practiced upon the human family [Jn. 10:10].

"'*I will cast you to the ground,*' refers to his ultimate defeat [Rev. 12:7-12]. '*I will lay you before kings, that they may behold you,*' refers to him ultimately being cast into the Lake of Fire, where all the kings of the Earth who have died lost will behold him in his humiliation [Mat. 25:41; Rev. 20:10].)

"You have defiled your sanctuaries by the multitude of your iniquities, by the iniquity of your traffic; therefore will I bring forth a fire from the midst of you, it shall devour you, and I will bring you to ashes upon the earth in the sight of all them who behold you. (When Satan at long last will be thrown into the Lake of Fire [Rev. 20:10], all the billions he has duped, who also are in Hell because of him, will hate him with a passion that words cannot begin to express, and a hatred which will last forever and forever.)

"All they who know you among the people shall be astonished at you: you shall be a terror, and never shall you be anymore. (Then the prayer of Christ, 'Your Will be done in Earth, as it is in Heaven,' will finally be answered and brought to pass [Mat. 6:9-10])" (Ezek. 28:11-19).

THE CURE FOR SIN

Sin requires punishment. As an affront against the infinite Majesty of God, sin calls for infinite punishment, and that without limit, simply because of its terrible, destructive power. The Bible, therefore, speaks of the wages of sin being death and of eternal punishment in Hell. Such punishment is the reflex of the Holiness of God, whereby, He maintains Himself against man's sin. In responding to sin, God's Holiness takes the form of Justice expressing itself in infinite Wrath and unlimited Judgment.

The primary Divine response, however, takes place in history only at the Cross where the Son of God became the Object of God's Wrath—and dies. Otherwise, in human history God's Wrath and punishing Justice are always corrective, a form of Wrath for the sake of Grace, a form of Judgment which can be turned aside, averted, and repented of by God as men repent and respond to His Grace. The only Divine Judgment and Wrath God cannot withdraw or repent of in history is that which occurred at the Cross. The manner of God in this matter should portray to us that all other manifestations of Divine Judgment upon sin are contingent rather than absolute, and corrective rather than final, suggesting, thereby, that all justice, which society administers to its criminals, should be remedial and corrective,

NOTES

never merely punitive, and never final.

As stated, there is only one remedy for sin, and that is the Cross of Christ. Inasmuch as that is the only remedy, and that it came at great price, a price so staggering that it is beyond the comprehension of man, the greatest sin, therefore, is the rejection of Christ Crucified, Who shall judge every man according to the Gospel (Rom. 2:16).

All of this means that if the church is not preaching the Cross, then whatever it is preaching, as intellectual as it might be, and as educational as it might be, still, it's not the Gospel, and that means that it will really help no one.

Unfortunately, the church has pretty well adopted the ways of the world in dealing with sin. The world thinks, as we've also already stated, that sin can be dealt with, with education, with money, with a change of environment, and above all, with psychological counseling.

As we have already related in this Volume, in the late 1950's and the early 1960's, the Full Gospel side of the church, so-called, began its foray into humanistic psychology. That being done, the Cross, little by little, began to be laid aside. It is impossible to wed the two. If one is proclaimed, the other must go. Psychological counseling has been adopted and proclaimed by the modern church, covering almost the entirety of the spectrum of church bodies. As a result, the Cross of Christ is no more, and neither is forgiveness and cleansing from sin, and neither are bondages broken, which the Cross of Christ alone can accomplish (Rom. 6:1-14; 8:1-2, 11; I Cor. 1:17-18, 23; 2:2; Gal. 1:8; Chpt. 5; 6:14; Col. 2:14-15).

In fact, the Church as we know it, at least which has any semblance of New Testament principle, is in danger of being lost. We talk about the Church needing Revival, and, of course, that is true. However, first of all, it needs a Reformation, which means to return to Sound Doctrine, which is the Cross of Christ. Only then, can the Church truly have Revival.

(7) "AND THE DESTRUCTION OF AHAZIAH WAS OF GOD BY COMING TO JORAM: FOR WHEN HE WAS COME, HE WENT OUT WITH JEHORAM AGAINST

JEHU THE SON OF NIMSHI, WHOM THE LORD HAD ANOINTED TO CUT OFF THE HOUSE OF AHAB.

(8) "AND IT CAME TO PASS, THAT, WHEN JEHU WAS EXECUTING JUDGMENT UPON THE HOUSE OF AHAB, AND FOUND THE PRINCES OF JUDAH, AND THE SONS OF THE BRETHREN OF AHAZIAH, WHO MINISTERED TO AHAZIAH, HE KILLED THEM.

(9) "AND HE SOUGHT AHAZIAH: AND THEY CAUGHT HIM, (FOR HE WAS HID IN SAMARIA,) AND BROUGHT HIM TO JEHU: AND WHEN THEY HAD KILLED HIM, THEY BURIED HIM: BECAUSE, SAID THEY, HE IS THE SON OF JEHOSHAPHAT, WHO SOUGHT THE LORD WITH ALL HIS HEART. SO THE HOUSE OF AHAZIAH HAD NO POWER TO KEEP STILL THE KINGDOM."

The pattern is:

1. (Vs. 7) The Lord determined the destruction of Ahaziah because of his sins. It was brought about by Jehu, whom the Lord caused to be king of the Ten Tribes. Jehu killed both Jehoram (Joram), king of the Ten Tribes, and Ahaziah of Judah.

2. The last phrase of Verse 9 means that there was no one of the house of Ahaziah who could succeed him. The Hebrew Text does not say, *"no one left,"* simply because Joash was the son of Ahaziah, but he was an infant at the time.

3. As is here overly obvious, the wages of sin is death! But thank God, *"the Gift of God is Eternal Life through Jesus Christ."*

THE WRATH OF GOD

It must ever be understood that *"the Wrath of God* (God's Personal Emotion with regard to sin) *is revealed from Heaven* (this anger originates with God) *against all ungodliness and unrighteousness of men* (God must unalterably be opposed to sin), *who hold the truth in unrighteousness* (who refuse to recognize Who God is, and what God is)" (Rom. 1:18).

God's Wrath was poured out on His Only Son at Calvary's Cross, when our Saviour offered Himself in Sacrifice, and did so for the sins of man. So, men can accept Jesus Christ, and in doing so, escape the Wrath of God, but, if not, sooner or later they will face the Wrath of God. With many it may be at the time of death with eternal Hell as their due, but to be sure, and let all understand the following, it is either Jesus Christ or it is the Judgment of God.

Ahaziah had thumbed his nose at God, thereby, taking Judah deep into idol-worship and, as well, he patterned himself after the wicked *"house of Ahab."*

The Lord laid the path for his destruction.

The Scripture says, *"And the destruction of Ahaziah was of God by coming to Joram: for when he was come, he went out with Jehoram* (Joram) *against Jehu the son of Nimshi, whom the LORD had anointed to cut off the house of Ahab."*

Even though Ahaziah tried to escape the judging hand of Jehu, and did so by trying to hide in Samaria, to be sure, he was found and *"brought to Jehu,"* who killed him.

Man should learn that one cannot thumb one's nose at God and get by.

THE JUDGMENT OF AMERICA

This nation for many decades has been the envy of the world. It has all been because of the Blessings of God, and I speak of our prosperity, our freedoms, etc. Many of the powers that be in this nation, however, refuse to recognize God in any capacity. It is no longer the separation of Church and State, but it is now the separation of God and State. The latter will destroy us.

The terrible sin of homosexuality is an abomination in the Eyes of God (Ezek. 16:49-50).

Little children are being taught in public schools that homosexuality is a proper lifestyle. If the trend continues, very soon same sex marriages will be the law of the land.

Of every nation that has been brought to ruin, three sins of wickedness have proven to be predominant in these respective countries, wherever they may have been. They are:

1. Homosexuality;
2. Pedophilia; and,
3. Incest.

These three sins are pandemic in this nation presently and getting worse almost by the day.

I do not know who the author of the

following article is, so, all I can do is apologize for not giving him credit, whomever he or she might be, but I felt it needed to be printed. It is as follows:

"President Bush did make a bad mistake in the war on terrorism. But the mistake was not his decision to go to war in Iraq. His mistake came in his belief that this country is the same one his father fought for in WWII. It is not!

"Back then, America had just come out of a vicious depression. The country was steeled by the hardship of that depression, but they still believed fervently in this country. They knew that the people had elected their leaders, so it was the people's duty to back those leaders; therefore, when the war broke out the people came together, rallied behind, and stuck with their leaders, whether they had voted for them or not or whether the war was going badly or not.

"And war was just as distasteful and the anguish just as great then as it is today. Often there were more casualties in one day in WWII than we have in the entire Iraqi war. But that did not matter. The people stuck with the President because it was their patriotic duty. Americans put aside their differences in WWII and worked together to win that war. Everyone from every strata of society, from young to old pitched in. Small children pulled little wagons around to gather scrap metal for the war effort. Grade school students saved their pennies to buy stamps for war bonds to help the effort. Men who were too old or medically 4F lied about their age or condition trying their best to join the military. Women doubled their work to keep things going at home. Harsh rationing of everything from gasoline to soap, to butter was imposed, yet there was very little complaining.

"You never heard prominent people on the radio belittling the President. Interestingly enough in those days there were no fat cat actors and entertainers who ran off to visit and fawn over dictators of hostile countries and complain to them about our President. Instead, they made upbeat films and entertained our troops to help the morale of our fighting men. To be frank, many actors and actresses even enlisted.

NOTES

"And imagine this: teachers in schools actually started the day off with a Pledge of Allegiance, and with prayer for our country and our troops! But then, no newspaper would have dared point out certain weak spots in our cities where bombs could be set off to cause the maximum damage. No newspaper would have dared complain about what we are doing to catch spies. A newspaper would have been laughed out of existence if it had complained that German or Japanese soldiers were being 'tortured' by being forced to wear women's underwear, or subjected to interrogation by a woman, or being scared by a dog or did not have air conditioning.

"There were a lot of things different back then. We were not subjected to a constant bombardment of pornography, perversion and promiscuity in movies or on Radio or Television. We did not have legions of crack heads, dope pushers and armed gangs roaming our streets.

"No, President Bush did not make a mistake in his handling of terrorism. He made the mistake of believing that we still have the courage and fortitude of our fathers. He believed that this was still the country that our fathers fought so dearly to preserve.

"It is not the same country today. It is now a cross between Sodom and Gomorrah and the land of Oz. We did unite for a short while after 9/11/01, but our attitude changed when we found out that defending our country would require some sacrifices.

"We are in great danger. The terrorists are fanatic Muslims. They believe that it is okay, even their duty, to kill anyone who will not convert to Islam. It has been estimated that about one third or over three hundred million Muslims are sympathetic to the terrorists cause – Hitler and Tojo combined did not have nearly that many potential recruits. So . . . we either win it – or lose it – and if we lose it, to be sure, we're not going to like the position we will find ourselves in.

"America is not at war, the military is at war. America is at the mall. God help us!"

(10) "BUT WHEN ATHALIAH THE MOTHER OF AHAZIAH SAW THAT HER SON WAS DEAD, SHE AROSE AND

DESTROYED ALL THE SEED ROYAL OF THE HOUSE OF JUDAH.

(11) "BUT JEHOSHABEATH, THE DAUGHTER OF THE KING, TOOK JOASH THE SON OF AHAZIAH, AND STOLE HIM FROM AMONG THE KING'S SONS WHO WERE KILLED, AND PUT HIM AND HIS NURSE IN A BEDCHAMBER. SO JEHOSHABEATH, THE DAUGHTER OF KING JEHORAM, THE WIFE OF JEHOIADA THE PRIEST, (FOR SHE WAS THE SISTER OF AHAZIAH,) HID HIM FROM ATHALIAH, SO THAT SHE KILLED HIM NOT.

(12) "AND HE WAS WITH THEM HID IN THE HOUSE OF GOD SIX YEARS: AND ATHALIAH REIGNED OVER THE LAND."

The construction is:

1. (Vs. 10) Athaliah, the mother of Ahaziah, was one of the most wicked women ever!

2. (Vs. 11) Evidently, this bloody woman thought she had killed them all, not realizing that the infant Joash was not dead. From this bloodstained room, the daughter of Jehoram (Jehoshaphat's son) stole away baby Joash. He was the only one left in the lineage of Christ.

3. (Vs. 12) At this time, the Temple was not in use. The people were worshipping idols on the mountaintops and other places. So, the *"House of God"* was the logical place for him to be hidden, so he wouldn't be murdered by his grandmother.

ACUTE WICKEDNESS

The idea of a grandmother killing her grandchildren so there will be nothing to stand between her and the throne is unthinkable! But that was murderous, wicked, ungodly, reprobate Athaliah!

Satan had wreaked havoc with the throne of Judah. Jehoram had killed all of his brothers, so there would be no one to contest his place and position as king. And then it had come to pass that all of his sons had been slain by the Arabians. And now Athaliah, the mother of Ahaziah, killed all of her grandchildren—or so she thought she had!

How in the world could a grandmother kill her grandchildren, doing so in cold blood? The deeper that one goes into sin, the less feeling there is. As we have stated, there is a form of insanity about sin, and the worse that the sin gets, the more insane the individual becomes.

Athaliah destroyed all except baby Joash, one little boy whom they hid in the Temple so that the royal line of David might be continued to fulfill the Davidic Covenant which promised a king on the throne of Judah as long as they had a kingdom with any possibility of Righteousness. This was Satan's third attempt to destroy the royal line of David, so that God's Word could not be fulfilled.

The Eleventh Verse says, *"But Jehoshabeath, the daughter of the king, took Joash the son of Ahaziah, and stole him from among the king's sons who were killed. . . ."* Evidently, this bloody queen thought she had killed them all, not realizing that the infant was not dead. From this bloodstained room the granddaughter of Jehoshaphat stole away baby Joash. She *". . . hid him from Athaliah, so that she killed him not."*

She hid him in the Temple!

ISRAEL IN THE LAST DAYS

In a sense, this is a picture of Israel under the Antichrist in the days not too far ahead.

Wicked Athaliah was a type of the Antichrist, who will maltreat Israel terribly so in the coming Great Tribulation. In fact, in the latter half of that coming time, referred to as Jacob's trouble (Jer. 30:7), hundreds of thousands of Jews will, no doubt, die. As wicked Athaliah ruled at that time in Judah, likewise, the Antichrist, after a fashion, will rule in Israel, at least after a fashion.

As baby Joash was hidden in the Temple, likewise, Christ has been hidden in the heavens. However, as the hour came that Joash was crowned king of Judah, likewise, the hour will come that our Lord and Saviour Jesus Christ will be crowned King of kings and Lord of lords, for He is coming back.

As Athaliah was executed whenever Joash became king, likewise, the Antichrist will suffer the same fate when Jesus Christ comes back. Make no mistake about it, it will happen!

"Sound ye the trumpet-call;
"Heralds proclaim, Jesus is Lord of all,
"Sound forth His Fame:
"Tell of His great Renown,
"Lift high the kingly crown, let every
  knee bow down,
"At His blest Name."

"Who will go forth for Him?
"Who will arise?
"Though eyes with tears are dim,
"Severed love's ties:
"Counting all things but loss,
"Earth's highest gain but dross,
"And glorying in the Cross, Who will
  arise?"

"Go, for the crowning day,
"Draws ever near;
"Time will soon pass away, Jesus is
  here:
"Raise ye the Cross where now,
"Nations to idols bow;
"Dawn o'er the mountains brow,
"Tells He is near."

"Hark to the trumpet-blast!
"Jesus is King!
"He comes to reign at last,
"All conquering:
"Then the wide world shall own,
"Bending before His Throne,
"Jesus is King Alone, Jesus is King!"

CHAPTER 23

(1) "AND IN THE SEVENTH YEAR JEHOIADA STRENGTHENED HIMSELF, AND TOOK THE CAPTAINS OF HUNDREDS, AZARIAH THE SON OF JEROHAM, AND ISHMAEL THE SON OF JEHOHANAN, AND AZARIAH THE SON OF OBED, AND MAASEIAH THE SON OF ADAIAH, AND ELISHAPHAT THE SON OF ZICHRI, INTO COVENANT WITH HIM.

(2) "AND THEY WENT ABOUT IN JUDAH, AND GATHERED THE LEVITES OUT OF ALL THE CITIES OF JUDAH, AND THE CHIEF OF THE FATHERS OF ISRAEL, AND THEY CAME TO JERUSALEM.

(3) "AND ALL THE CONGREGATION MADE A COVENANT WITH THE KING IN THE HOUSE OF GOD. AND HE SAID UNTO THEM, BEHOLD, THE KING'S SON SHALL REIGN, AS THE LORD HAS SAID OF THE SONS OF DAVID.

(4) "THIS IS THE THING THAT YOU SHALL DO; A THIRD PART OF YOU ENTERING ON THE SABBATH, OF THE PRIESTS AND OF THE LEVITES, SHALL BE PORTERS OF THE DOORS.

(5) "AND A THIRD PART SHALL BE AT THE KING'S HOUSE; AND A THIRD PART AT THE GATE OF THE FOUNDATION: AND ALL THE PEOPLE SHALL BE IN THE COURTS OF THE HOUSE OF THE LORD.

(6) "BUT LET NONE COME INTO THE HOUSE OF THE LORD, SAVE THE PRIESTS, AND THEY WHO MINISTER OF THE LEVITES; THEY SHALL GO IN, FOR THEY ARE HOLY: BUT ALL THE PEOPLE SHALL KEEP THE WATCH OF THE LORD.

(7) "AND THE LEVITES SHALL COMPASS THE KING ROUND ABOUT, EVERY MAN WITH HIS WEAPONS IN HIS HAND; AND WHOSOEVER ELSE COMES INTO THE HOUSE, HE SHALL BE PUT TO DEATH: BUT YOU BE WITH THE KING WHEN HE COMES IN, AND WHEN HE GOES OUT.

(8) "SO THE LEVITES AND ALL JUDAH DID ACCORDING TO ALL THINGS THAT JEHOIADA THE PRIEST HAD COMMANDED, AND TOOK EVERY MAN HIS MEN WHO WERE TO COME IN ON THE SABBATH, WITH THEM WHO WERE TO GO OUT ON THE SABBATH: FOR JEHOIADA THE PRIEST DISMISSED NOT THE COURSES.

(9) "MOREOVER JEHOIADA THE PRIEST DELIVERED TO THE CAPTAINS OF HUNDREDS SPEARS, AND BUCKLERS, AND SHIELDS, THAT HAD BEEN KING DAVID'S, WHICH WERE IN THE HOUSE OF GOD.

(10) "AND HE SET ALL THE PEOPLE, EVERY MAN HAVING HIS WEAPON IN HIS HAND, FROM THE RIGHT SIDE OF THE TEMPLE TO THE LEFT SIDE OF THE TEMPLE, ALONG BY THE ALTAR AND THE TEMPLE, BY THE KING ROUND ABOUT.

(11) "THEN THEY BROUGHT OUT THE KING'S SON, AND PUT UPON HIM THE CROWN, AND GAVE HIM THE TESTIMONY, AND MADE HIM KING. AND JEHOIADA AND HIS SONS ANOINTED HIM, AND SAID, GOD SAVE THE KING."

The overview is:

1. (Vs. 1) Jehoiada was the High Priest of Judah.

2. The *"seventh year"* of Verse 1 refers to the length of time between Ahaziah's assassination through the reign of the wicked queen Athaliah. Joash was now seven years old. The *"covenant"* had to do with making Joash king, who was the rightful heir to the throne. He was the only one left at this time in the lineage of David.

3. *"Porters of the doors"* of Verse 4 were actually keepers of the doors of the Temple (I Chron. 9:19).

4. (Vs. 6) The distinction between *"the courts of the House of the LORD,"* which were outside the Temple, and *"the House of the LORD,"* is quite apparent. None but the Priests could enter the Temple.

5. (Vs. 7) The exception to the rule of no one entering the Temple but the Priests, at least at this time, was the boy king, Joash. He was to be surrounded by Priests and Levites when he was brought out of the Temple to the people.

6. (Vs. 8) Jehoiada the High Priest set about to set in motion once again the 24 courses of the Priests, which pertained to the time limit they would serve each year, and which was ordained originally by David.

7. Some think that the *"shields"* mentioned in Verse 9 may have been the shields of gold that king David took from the servants of Hadadezer (II Sam. 8:7, 11).

8. (Vs. 10) At the swearing in, so to speak, Joash was placed by the Altar of Burnt Offerings, which typified Calvary, with rows of guards bristling with weapons before, behind, and round about him.

9. The *"Testimony"* of Verse 11 was probably the Scrolls containing the Law— probably Exodus and Leviticus.

SONS OF DAVID

The phrase, *"And in the seventh year Jehoiada strengthened himself,"* refers, as stated, to the length of time between Ahaziah's assassination through the reign of the wicked queen, Athaliah. Joash was now seven years old.

No doubt, Jehoiada the High Priest had the mind of the Lord as he undertook this effort. In fact, if the Lord had not been leading him, every possibility existed that he could have been killed, plus all who sided with him. In fact, there was no limit to what this wicked queen, Athaliah, would do, as by now should be overly obvious.

Five men of the military are named in this First Verse, and only here. The Holy Spirit had them listed, no doubt, because of their faithfulness in throwing in their lot with Jehoiada in order that the boy, Joash, could be crowned king. The Holy Spirit overlooks nothing and forgets nothing and is careful to have listed those who embark upon a quest of Faith.

How much that Jehoiada told all of these people who made a covenant with him as it regards the making of Joash king, we aren't told; however, the implication is that he did not tell them his true intent and purpose until all had gathered in Jerusalem, actually at the Temple site. If, in fact, this is the way that this gathering took place, at the appointed time, Jehoiada *"said unto them, Behold, the king's son shall reign, as the LORD has said of the sons of David."*

The truth is, it was known only by a few in Judah that Joash was alive. In fact, Athaliah thought that she had killed all of her grandsons, and that there were no claimants to the throne. This secret had to be closely guarded, and for all the obvious reasons. But now, and, no doubt, according to the leading of the Holy Spirit, Joash would be revealed, with the Lord using Jehoiada to accomplish the task.

WHY WAS IT SO NECESSARY THAT A SON OF DAVID SIT ON THE THRONE OF JUDAH?

In II Samuel, Chapter 7, the Lord promised David that one in his lineage would ultimately come and would be the Messiah of Israel and the Saviour of the world. In effect, His Throne would last forever. To be frank, Israel understood this and did so plainly, inasmuch as Jesus was referred to time and time again as the *"Son of David,"* which, of course, was correct (Mk. 11:47; 12:35-37). Through Joseph, the foster father of Jesus, one might say, His Lineage went back to David through Solomon. Through His mother Mary, His Lineage went back to David through another son, Nathan. So, His Lineage was impeccable, which the religious leaders of Israel could easily have ascertained, if they had so desired.

THE INCARNATION

For man to be redeemed, God would have to become man, which is referred to as the *"Incarnation."* That's why Paul referred to Christ as the *"Last Adam"* and the *"Second Man"* (I Cor. 15:45-47).

The God-Man, Jesus Christ, has been debated from the times of the Early Church. He was and is Very Man and Very God. This means that He was not half Man and half God, but rather fully Man and fully God.

As a result, His essential Nature has been argued from the very beginning. Some have claimed that the Incarnation proved the absorption of the human nature into the Divine, or a fusion of the two natures making one new nature; however, if that were the case, Christ then would not have been true man, nor could He be man's true representative, substitute, or mediator. In fact, there are theories galore.

One must come to the conclusion that it's impossible to answer all possible questions as it regards the Incarnation. Whatever it is that God was pleased to reveal is that which He evidently wanted us to know. Thereby, one must unreservedly accept what is revealed in Scripture and then humbly acknowledge and accept the limitations of our understanding of this Divine Mystery.

Sufficient is revealed to constrain adoring worship of, and the fullest Faith in, the Lord of Glory, *"Who for us men, and for our Salvation, came down from Heaven, and was incarnate by the Holy Spirit of the Virgin Mary ... was crucified ... rose again ... ascended ... shall come again ... Whose Kingdom shall have no end."*

Man, even believing man, has to come to the conclusion sooner or later that there are some things the Lord did not see fit to reveal in His Word. Consequently, we must take the information given, believe what is said, understanding that God has revealed to us all that He desires that we know, and be satisfied with what is presented.

WHY DID GOD HAVE TO BECOME MAN?

For man to be redeemed, God would have to become a human being.

Man could not redeem himself because of his fallen condition. Angels could not redeem man because they were of another creation. So, if man was to be redeemed, God would have to become man. He would have to do for man what man could not do for himself.

He had to be born without sin, which means He could not be born by natural procreation. Consequently, if our Lord was to escape original sin, he would have to be born by decree of the Holy Spirit, using the Virgin Mary as a house for our Lord regarding the gestation period of some nine months. So, He was born without sin, meaning that He had no sin nature. He had to live a Perfect Life, not sinning in word, thought, or deed. This means that He had to keep the Law of Moses perfectly, which included all of that Law, but more specifically, the Moral Law of the Ten Commandments.

It must be understood that He did all of this for us and none at all for Himself, none at all for His Father, none at all for Angels, and none at all for Heaven. As stated, it was all for us. If man was to be redeemed, God would have to become man, thereby, becoming our Substitute, our Representative Man, so to speak, Who would do for us what we could not do for ourselves.

Even though He kept the Law of Moses perfectly, still, that within itself was not enough. The broken Law, which was incumbent upon every human being, had to be dealt with also. Man had broken this Law of God, and the penalty was death.

To answer the broken Law, Jesus would go to the Cross, that actually being His Destination from eternity past (I Pet. 1:18-20). In the giving of Himself as a Sacrifice, and a Perfect Sacrifice at that, which is all that

God would accept, the shedding of His Life's Blood and His Death on the Cross were accepted by God as payment in full, at least for all who will believe (Jn. 3:16).

Christ has made peace by the Blood of His Cross, reconciling man to God in the body of His Flesh through death (Col. 1:20-22). Christ suffered for all, bearing our sins in His Own Body on the tree, healing us by His Stripes (I Pet. 2:24; Isa., Chpt. 53).

Due to this, one can understand the saying of the Lord that the Son of Man came to give His Life a ransom for many (Mat. 20:28), making it possible for us to join with the Redeemed in the Book of Revelation in ascribing praise to Him *"Who loves us, and has freed us from our sins by His Blood"* (Rev. 1:5-6).

THE PLAN OF GOD

When Jehoiada said, *"Behold, the king's son shall reign, as the LORD has said of the sons of David,"* I wonder if he knew exactly what he had said, and above all, what it meant?

Jehoiada was dealing with the single most important thing on the face of the Earth, whether he realized it or not, the coming of the Redeemer.

Regrettably, when Jesus did come, Israel did not know him, despite the fact that His Healings and Miracles were astounding beyond belief, even to the raising of the dead. In other words, His Credentials in every respect were Perfect. But yet, they crucified Him, and as a result, destroyed themselves. They have wandered the world ever since A.D. 70 until finally becoming a Nation again in 1948. Yet, their hardest days are just ahead when they will be deceived by the Antichrist, as he will set out to completely destroy them and, in fact, would succeed but for the Second Coming of the Lord.

No people on Earth, and for all time, had the capacity to gain so much and then lost it all, as did Israel.

When they said, *"We have no king but Caesar,"* they were to find out that Caesar would be a terrible taskmaster (Jn. 19:15).

At His trial, Pilate said, *"I am innocent of the blood of this just person: see you to it."*

The Scripture then said, *"Then answered all the people, and said, His Blood be on us, and on our children"* (Mat. 27:24-25).

Concerning this, the notes from THE EXPOSITOR'S STUDY BIBLE read: *"The malediction they invoked upon themselves and upon their children rests upon them still, and was, and is, a malediction of appalling horror and suffering."*

But Israel will one day soon see the terrible mistake they made, a mistake which has caused untold suffering, and will then accept Christ as their Saviour, their Messiah, and their Lord. As stated, it will be at the Second Coming but after much, much suffering!

THE TESTIMONY

When Joash was brought out to stand before the people and to be crowned king, the people began to shout and say, *"God save the king."* Jehoiada then placed the *"Testimony"* in his hand, which was, no doubt, scrolls, more than likely of Exodus and Leviticus. In other words, it was a copy of the Law of Moses, signifying that from this day forward, Judah was going to do her best to obey the Law of God, which had been neglected for so long.

It is believed that when he was crowned, he was standing near, or at least not far away, from the great Brazen Altar, the Altar of Sacrifice, which was 30 feet wide and 30 feet long. Whether he understood it or not, holding the *"Testimony"* in his hand and standing somewhere near the Altar, he was standing on the Foundation of the Gospel.

(12) "NOW WHEN ATHALIAH HEARD THE NOISE OF THE PEOPLE RUNNING AND PRAISING THE KING, SHE CAME TO THE PEOPLE INTO THE HOUSE OF THE LORD:

(13) "AND SHE LOOKED, AND, BEHOLD, THE KING STOOD AT HIS PILLAR AT THE ENTERING IN, AND THE PRINCES AND THE TRUMPETS BY THE KING: AND ALL THE PEOPLE OF THE LAND REJOICED, AND SOUNDED WITH TRUMPETS, ALSO THE SINGERS WITH INSTRUMENTS OF MUSIC, AND SUCH AS TAUGHT TO SING PRAISE. THEN ATHALIAH RENT HER CLOTHES, AND SAID, TREASON, TREASON.

(14) "THEN JEHOIADA THE PRIEST

BROUGHT OUT THE CAPTAINS OF HUNDREDS WHO WERE SET OVER THE HOST, AND SAID UNTO THEM, HAVE HER FORTH OF THE RANGES: AND WHOSO FOLLOWS HER, LET HIM BE KILLED WITH THE SWORD. FOR THE PRIEST SAID, KILL HER NOT IN THE HOUSE OF THE LORD.

(15) "SO THEY LAID HANDS ON HER; AND WHEN SHE WAS COME TO THE ENTERING OF THE HORSE GATE BY THE KING'S HOUSE, THEY KILLED HER THERE."

The pattern is:

1. The latter phrase of Verse 12 should have been translated, *"Unto the House of the LORD."* Athaliah did not go into the Temple, but most definitely would have, had she not been restrained.

2. Verse 13 proclaims the fact that all of our music should be to render praise to the Lord.

3. Athaliah was executed exactly as she should have been. It is obvious from what was done that Judah was greatly sick of this bloody woman.

TO SING PRAISE UNTO THE LORD

It had been a long time since Jerusalem had heard praises to the Lord from the Temple Courts, but they were hearing it now.

Joash, a son of David, of course, several times removed, and who bloody Athaliah thought was dead, was now crowned king. The people were praising the Lord and worshipping God, and once again, this meant that the sun was rising on Judah.

As it regards Athaliah, they killed her, exactly as they should have done; consequently, three things took place at this time. They are:

1. Joash was crowned king, meaning that the Will of God was accomplished in Jerusalem and Judah. The Will of God was carried out.

2. There was great rejoicing, even as there should have been. Carrying out the Will of God brings about joy.

3. Bloody Athaliah was executed. When the Will of God is carried out, which elicits praise and rejoicing, at the same time, sin will be opposed.

NOTES

(16) "AND JEHOIADA MADE A COVENANT BETWEEN HIM, AND BETWEEN ALL THE PEOPLE, AND BETWEEN THE KING, THAT THEY SHOULD BE THE LORD'S PEOPLE.

(17) "THEN ALL THE PEOPLE WENT TO THE HOUSE OF BAAL, AND BROKE IT DOWN, AND BROKE HIS ALTARS AND HIS IMAGES IN PIECES, AND KILLED MATTAN THE PRIEST OF BAAL BEFORE THE ALTARS.

(18) "ALSO JEHOIADA APPOINTED THE OFFICES OF THE HOUSE OF THE LORD BY THE HAND OF THE PRIESTS THE LEVITES, WHOM DAVID HAD DISTRIBUTED IN THE HOUSE OF THE LORD, TO OFFER THE BURNT OFFERINGS OF THE LORD, AS IT IS WRITTEN IN THE LAW OF MOSES, WITH REJOICING AND WITH SINGING, AS IT WAS ORDAINED BY DAVID.

(19) "AND HE SET THE PORTERS AT THE GATES OF THE HOUSE OF THE LORD, THAT NONE WHICH WAS UNCLEAN IN ANYTHING SHOULD ENTER IN.

(20) "AND HE TOOK THE CAPTAINS OF HUNDREDS, AND THE NOBLES, AND THE GOVERNORS OF THE PEOPLE, AND ALL THE PEOPLE OF THE LAND, AND BROUGHT DOWN THE KING FROM THE HOUSE OF THE LORD: AND THEY CAME THROUGH THE HIGH GATE INTO THE KING'S HOUSE, AND SET THE KING UPON THE THRONE OF THE KINGDOM.

(21) "AND ALL THE PEOPLE OF THE LAND REJOICED: AND THE CITY WAS QUIET, AFTER THAT THEY HAD KILLED ATHALIAH WITH THE SWORD."

The construction is:

1. According to Verse 17, it seems that a building, dedicated to Baal, had been built alongside the Temple.

2. (Vs. 18) All of the 24 courses, as it regarded the activities of the Priests, ordained by David were reinstated, as well as all the ceremonies of the Law of Moses.

3. (Vs. 21) As the sword did rid Judah of this altogether evil influence, and we speak of Athaliah, likewise, the Sword of the Spirit, which is the Word of God, must, as well, rid every enemy of our souls from our

lives (Heb. 12:1; Eph. 6:17).

THE LORD'S PEOPLE

Israel was, in fact, ordained to be *"the LORD's People,"* however, as a whole, the Nation had been anything but that for the last few years.

But the tide has turned. Jehoiada the High Priest has been used of the Lord to bring about a Reformation, and in a sense, a Revival. Happy days are here again. What an honor to be referred to as *"the LORD's People."* And now, that they would be.

THE ETERMINATION OF IDOL WORSHIP

It is most probable that the *"house of Baal"* was actually reared alongside the very Temple itself. The people broke down this house, destroyed the altars of Baal and, as well, *"killed Mattan the priest of Baal before the altars."*

While our supposed sophistication will not allow such presently, still, it must ever be understood that anything and everything that's not strictly *"Jesus Christ and Him Crucified,"* whatever it is otherwise in which we have placed our Faith, can be construed as none other than an idol. In other words, it means that our Faith is entirely in Christ and the Cross, and that on a continuous basis. In the Eyes of God, there is very little difference in that and the Baal of Judah.

The Lord has one way of Salvation, one way of Sanctification, one way of Victory over sin, and one way of life and living, and that is Christ as the Source of all these things and the Cross as the Means, all superintended by the Holy Spirit.

God's Way is the Cross, and the Cross alone. If anything is substituted in its place, it becomes an idol, and to be sure, such idols must be broken down and destroyed exactly as they were in Judah so long, long ago.

THE PRIESTLY COURSES

In the last years of David, the Lord gave to him the means by which the Temple was to be operated, at least when it was built. All the Priests were assigned courses, which constituted so many days a year that they must serve. Regrettably, under wicked Athaliah all of this had been dispensed with. But now, Jehoiada the High Priest, a man who truly loved God, set all the courses in motion once again in order *". . . to offer the Burnt Offerings of the LORD, as it is written in the Law of Moses. . . ."* There was such joy in Judah when this was done, because it was in obedience to the Word of God, that the Scripture says it was done *"with rejoicing and with singing, as it was ordained by David."* While, in fact, it was ordained by David, still, the actual author of all this was the Holy Spirit.

Now begins with the reign of Joash one of the most prosperous times for Judah, at least while Jehoiada was alive. Sadly and regrettably, when he died, Joash went into deep sin, which ultimately instigated the Judgment of God, as unrepented sin always does.

"I lay my sins on Jesus,
"The Spotless Lamb of God;
"He bears them all, and frees us,
"From the accursed load.
"I bring my guilt to Jesus,
"To wash my crimson stains,
"White in His Blood most precious,
"Till not a spot remains."

"I lay my wants on Jesus,
"All fullness dwells in Him;
"He heals my diseases,
"He does my soul redeem,
"I lay my griefs on Jesus,
"My burdens and my cares;
"He from them all releases,
"He all my sorrows shares."

"I rest my soul on Jesus,
"This weary soul of mine;
"His Right Hand me embraces,
"I on His Breast recline.
"I love the Name of Jesus,
"Emmanuel, Christ the Lord;
"Like fragrance on the breezes,
"His Name abroad is poured."

"I long to be like Jesus,
"Meek, loving, lowly, mild;
"I long to be like Jesus,
"The Father's Holy Child.
"I long to be with Jesus,
"Amid the Heavenly throng;

*"To sing with Saints His Praises,
"To learn the Angels' song."*

CHAPTER 24

(1) "JOASH WAS SEVEN YEARS OLD WHEN HE BEGAN TO REIGN, AND HE REIGNED FORTY YEARS IN JERUSALEM. HIS MOTHER'S NAME ALSO WAS ZIBIAH OF BEER-SHEBA.

(2) "AND JOASH DID THAT WHICH WAS RIGHT IN THE SIGHT OF THE LORD ALL THE DAYS OF JEHOIADA THE PRIEST.

(3) "AND JEHOIADA TOOK FOR HIM TWO WIVES; AND HE BEGAT SONS AND DAUGHTERS."

The pattern is:

1. (Vs. 1) If it is to be noticed, the mother's name is given, as it regards these kings, because the father often had several wives.

2. (Vs. 1) Joash was the youngest king to reign in all Israel, and the fifth king to reign for 40 years. He is called *"Jehoash"* in II Ki. 12:2.

3. (Vs. 2) Joash did that which was right in the sight of the Lord during the lifetime of Jehoiada. Under the tutelage of this godly Priest, he had an excellent beginning; however, when Jehoiada died, Joash went into deep apostasy and sin. There is every indication that he died eternally lost.

AN UNPARALLELED OPPORTUNITY

Williams says, *"At the commencement of his reign Joash leaned on Jehoiada who was a good man, afterwards he leaned on the princes of Judah, who were wicked men. To lean on men, whether they be good or wicked, is disastrous. Had the king leaned only upon God (Ps. 62:5), how different would have been his history!"*[1]

As it stood at that time, considering that Joash became king when he was only 7 years old, and considering the help that he had, his reign could have been one of the most glorious ever experienced by Judah. He started out so well, and regrettably, ended so poorly.

The fires of consecration will soon cool in the hearts and lives of all unless the Believer is diligent in serving God as one should.

TAKE UP THE CROSS DAILY

This is one of the reasons Jesus said that if we were to come after Him, we would have to deny ourselves and take up the Cross daily and follow Him (Lk. 9:23).

If it is to be noticed, he used the word *"daily."* In essence, this means treating each new day with a desire to grow closer to the Lord and, thereby, each day accordingly.

What did Jesus mean by taking up the Cross daily?

He meant several things. They are:

• Everything the Believer receives from the Lord, and in whatever capacity, comes from Christ as the Source and the Cross as the Means. The Cross is the vehicle, one might say, that makes everything possible.

• When Jesus spoke of *"taking up the Cross,"* He was referring to the benefits applied by the Cross. Regrettably, Satan has made most Believers think that taking up the Cross is a very negative thing, when the very opposite is actually the truth.

• The benefits of the Cross, in other words, that for which Jesus paid such a price, include every single good thing that we receive from God. It does not refer to suffering as many have been led to believe.

• In order to do this, we have to *"deny ourselves,"* which refers to denying our own ability, strength, intellect, education, power, etc. In other words, we are to depend totally upon the Lord and what He did for us at the Cross. It does not refer to denying oneself of all things which are comfortable or pleasurable, which is another lie that Satan has made many believe.

• Taking up the Cross daily, in a sense, refers to renewing our Faith daily in that which our Lord has done for us.

• This great Verse given to us by Luke presents one of the greatest Blessings found anywhere in the entirety of the Word of God. It is the key to success, to prosperity, and Victory over the world, the flesh, and the Devil.

• The Believer is to place his Faith exclusively in Christ and what Christ has done for us at the Cross and not allow it to be moved elsewhere. As stated, this is the key to all Blessing and Victory.

If it is to be noticed, the Scripture says, *"And Joash did that which was right in the sight of the LORD all the days of Jehoiada the Priest."* Regrettably, he went into deep sin after the death of this great Man of God.

(4) "AND IT CAME TO PASS AFTER THIS, THAT JOASH WAS MINDED TO REPAIR THE HOUSE OF THE LORD.

(5) "AND HE GATHERED TOGETHER THE PRIESTS AND THE LEVITES, AND SAID TO THEM, GO OUT UNTO THE CITIES OF JUDAH, AND GATHER OF ALL ISRAEL MONEY TO REPAIR THE HOUSE OF YOUR GOD FROM YEAR TO YEAR, AND SEE THAT YOU HASTEN THE MATTER. HOWBEIT THE LEVITES HASTENED IT NOT.

(6) "AND THE KING CALLED FOR JEHOIADA THE CHIEF, AND SAID UNTO HIM, WHY HAVE YOU NOT REQUIRED OF THE LEVITES TO BRING IN OUT OF JUDAH AND OUT OF JERUSALEM THE COLLECTION, ACCORDING TO THE COMMANDMENT OF MOSES THE SERVANT OF THE LORD, AND OF THE CONGREGATION OF ISRAEL, FOR THE TABERNACLE OF WITNESS?

(7) "FOR THE SONS OF ATHALIAH, THAT WICKED WOMAN, HAD BROKEN UP THE HOUSE OF GOD; AND ALSO ALL THE DEDICATED THINGS OF THE HOUSE OF THE LORD DID THEY BESTOW UPON BAALIM.

(8) "AND AT THE KING'S COMMANDMENT THEY MADE A CHEST, AND SET IT WITHOUT AT THE GATE OF THE HOUSE OF THE LORD.

(9) "AND THEY MADE A PROCLAMATION THROUGH JUDAH AND JERUSALEM, TO BRING IN TO THE LORD THE COLLECTION THAT MOSES THE SERVANT OF GOD LAID UPON ISRAEL IN THE WILDERNESS.

(10) "AND ALL THE PRINCES AND ALL THE PEOPLE REJOICED, AND BROUGHT IN, AND CAST INTO THE CHEST, UNTIL THEY HAD MADE AN END.

(11) "NOW IT CAME TO PASS, THAT AT WHAT TIME THE CHEST WAS BROUGHT UNTO THE KING'S OFFICE BY THE HAND

NOTES

OF THE LEVITES, AND WHEN THEY SAW THAT THERE WAS MUCH MONEY, THE KING'S SCRIBE AND THE HIGH PRIEST'S OFFICER CAME AND EMPTIED THE CHEST, AND TOOK IT, AND CARRIED IT TO HIS PLACE AGAIN. THUS THEY DID DAY BY DAY, AND GATHERED MONEY IN ABUNDANCE.

(12) "AND THE KING AND JEHOIADA GAVE IT TO SUCH AS DID THE WORK OF THE SERVICE OF THE HOUSE OF THE LORD, AND HIRED MASONS AND CARPENTERS TO REPAIR THE HOUSE OF THE LORD, AND ALSO SUCH AS WROUGHT IRON AND BRASS TO MEND THE HOUSE OF THE LORD.

(13) "SO THE WORKMEN WROUGHT, AND THE WORK WAS PERFECTED BY THEM, AND THEY SET THE HOUSE OF GOD IN HIS STATE, AND STRENGTHENED IT.

(14) "AND WHEN THEY HAD FINISHED IT, THEY BROUGHT THE REST OF THE MONEY BEFORE THE KING AND JEHOIADA, WHEREOF WERE MADE VESSELS FOR THE HOUSE OF THE LORD, EVEN VESSELS TO MINISTER, AND TO OFFER WITHAL, AND SPOONS, AND VESSELS OF GOLD AND SILVER. AND THEY OFFERED BURNT OFFERINGS IN THE HOUSE OF THE LORD CONTINUALLY ALL THE DAYS OF JEHOIADA."

The pattern is:

1. (Vs. 4) Not having been used for years, the Temple had fallen into a state of disrepair. Presently, in the spiritual sense, there are many houses of the Lord which need repairing (I Cor. 3:16).

2. We are not told the reason for the delay mentioned in Verse 5; however, it seemed to rest in some way with Jehoiada.

3. (Vs. 6) A census was to be taken in Judah, with a half-shekel for each person levied against all the people of Judah (Ex. 30:13-16). This redemption money was to be used for the repair work. Organizing this, which was the responsibility of Jehoiada, seemed to cause the delay.

4. (Vs. 7) Most of the damage to the Temple came from wicked kings and, in this case, a wicked queen. Likewise, most of the damage done to the Work of God presently

is little done by the world, but, instead, by false doctrine in an apostate church.

5. That spoken of in Verse 9 is, again, the ransom money of a half-shekel for each person which was to be paid when a census was taken. This money was to go for the upkeep of the Temple, etc. This is why it was referred to as the *"shekel of the Sanctuary"* (Ex. 30:11-16).

6. (Vs. 10) When people start living right, people start giving. When people are not living right, people quit giving.

7. (Vs. 12) The *"House of the LORD"* presently (since the Cross) is the heart and life of each Believer (I Cor. 3:16). The Holy Spirit is the One Who does the repairing, which, from time to time, is needed!

8. (Vs. 14) Once again, the daily sacrifices were established; however, when Jehoiada died, this too would stop.

REPAIRING THE HOUSE OF THE LORD

The truth is, for some years now, the Temple was little used, if at all. The nation of Judah had gone deep into idol-worship, and especially under wicked Athaliah. Considering that the Temple was no longer used, and because the Lord was no longer worshipped, this would be, as we have seen, the perfect place to hide baby Joash until he would reach the age that he could be made king, which he was.

How old that Joash was at the time when he began to instigate the repair of the House of the Lord, we aren't told. More than likely, he was in his late teens or even early twenties.

Several good things can be said about this young man at this time.

• He seemed eager to get the work started.

• He began to send emissaries out over the entirety of Judah in order to *"gather of all Israel money to repair the House of God."*

• When the Levites did not carry out his instructions, the king immediately called for Jehoiada the High Priest. He demanded an explanation as to why the work was not going forward!

• The terminology that he used as he spoke to Jehoiada stating, *"according to the Commandment of Moses the servant of the LORD, and of the congregation of Israel,*

NOTES

for the Tabernacle of witness," tells us that he seemed to be very familiar with the Word of God.

How so much one grieves when we find that Joash did not continue to function accordingly. But, as of now, he has set out *"to repair the House of the LORD."*

Bringing all of this up to the present, what does it now take to repair the House of the Lord?

I think anyone who has a degree of spirituality knows that the House of the Lord needs repair. By that, we are speaking of the entirety of the Work of God in general, plus, and above all, the consecration and dedication of each Saint of God for, since the Cross, the *"House of the LORD"* is the individual Believer (I Cor. 3:16).

Pure and simple, repairing the House of the Lord refers to the Believer returning to Christ and the Cross, which, in essence, means to return to the Bible. And please understand, one cannot properly return to Christ unless one does so through the Cross. Please read the following carefully:

• The only way to God the Father is through the Lord Jesus Christ (Jn. 14:6).

• The only way to Jesus Christ is by the Cross (Lk. 9:23; Rom. 6:1-14).

• The only way to the Cross is by a denial of self (Lk. 9:23; Gal. 2:20).

WHY IS THE CROSS OF CHRIST
SO IMPORTANT?

It is important, and greatly so, for many and varied reasons.

It was there that Jesus atoned for all sin, past, present, and future, at least for all who will believe (Jn. 3:16).

It was at the Cross where Satan and all of his henchmen of darkness were totally and completely defeated. Sin is the legal right that Satan has to hold man captive. With that right removed, and because Jesus atoned for all sin, Satan can hold no one captive who knows and understands his place and position in the Lord.

With all sin removed, the Holy Spirit, Who works exclusively by and through the Cross of Christ, can do mighty things for the Believer. But if the Believer places his faith in something other than Christ and the

Cross, the Holy Spirit is then greatly limited as to what He can do.

This is so strong, the way the Holy Spirit works, without Whom we can accomplish nothing for the Lord, or be anything for the Lord, that it is referred to as *"Law,"* i.e., *"the Law of the Spirit of Life in Christ Jesus"* (Rom. 8:2).

BAALIM

The Hebrew noun *"Ba'al"* means *"master," "possessor"* or *"husband."* It is a proper name in the Old Testament and refers to a specific supposed deity. In fact, it was the most important deity in the Canaanite pantheon.

Actually, the name *"Baal"* was a general name used for all of the idols such as *"Melqart"* or *"Chemosh,"* etc.

The Baal cults effected and challenged the worship of the Lord throughout Israelite history.

The Lord was referred to as *"Master"* and *"Husband"* to Israel, and at times, they referred to Him as *"Baal,"* in all innocence. However, this practice led to confusion of the worship of Yahweh with the Baal rituals, and ultimately, it became essential to refer to the Lord by a different title.

With many Israelites referring to Jehovah as *"Baal,"* and because the name meant *"master"* and *"husband,"* the same as Jehovah, it became very easy for them to ultimately demand a material figure of Baal, which led them into idol-worship. It was as follows:

• *"Yahweh"* and *"Baal"* meant the same thing, *"master"* and *"husband."*

• The flesh likes to worship what it can see, and more specifically, this demanded an object of some kind; consequently, it was very easy for Israel to then shift over to the material idol, all the time referring to it as the Lord.

• With the idol being worshipped, claiming it was Jehovah, it was easy again to ultimately incorporate all the immoral rituals in their worship, the same as the heathen—grossly immoral.

God's Way is Faith, but it must be understood that it is Faith in Christ and what He did for us at the Cross. It has been that way actually from the very dawn of time. The Lord gave to the First Family the means by which they could have fellowship with Him and forgiveness of sins, even though they were fallen. The sacrifice of the lamb they were importuned to offer was a Type, a Symbol, if you will, of the coming Redeemer. While the ritual itself could not restore communion or forgive sins, what it symbolized, and we continue to speak of the sacrifice, most definitely could effect communion and forgiveness. It all pointed to Christ and what He would do at the Cross. Consequently, the Sacrificial system was incorporated as the means by which man could reach God, and the only means, until Jesus would come, which He did, and, thereby, give Himself on the Cross as a ransom for fallen humanity. If the Believer's Faith is placed in anything else, and no matter how Scriptural the other thing may be in its own right, in some way it will turn to idol-worship exactly as Israel and Judah of old.

This has always been the great conflict with the church. While the world seeks to produce another God, the church seeks to produce another sacrifice. But the fact remains, the Lord cannot be replaced and neither can the Cross.

If Judah had been informed that their worship of Baal was in reality a gross wickedness, they would have argued the opposite. In their minds they were worshipping Jehovah, and the material object in front of them, they would have argued, whatever that material object looked like, was only a point of contact for their Faith. But they were dead wrong!

Just this morning over television, immediately before our program came on, I happened to pass by another channel and observed a preacher who was giving away a *"green cloth,"* claiming that it would bring prosperity, blessing, healing, etc. He could have saved himself the trouble and referred to it as *"Baal."* Because that's exactly what it was. The people were encouraged to place their faith in that green cloth instead of Christ and what Christ did at the Cross.

Likewise, some preachers are encouraging Believers to place their faith in the Lord's Supper or the memorizing of certain Texts in the Bible, reciting them over and over, and claiming this will stir God to action.

As wonderful as the Lord's Supper is, and as wonderful as memorizing Scriptures is, still, it is misplaced faith, and it is the same as the worship of Baal because it's not the Cross. Let's make it easy to understand.

Anything in which the Believer places his or her faith other than the Cross of Christ, and the Cross of Christ exclusively, can be rendered as idol-worship, i.e., *"Baal."* As well, when we speak of the Cross of Christ, we aren't speaking of the wooden beam, but rather what Jesus there did. It's the Victory He there won, the price He there paid, and the ransom He satisfied in satisfying the demands of a thrice-Holy God. So, please understand that!

THE PROCLAMATION

The proclamation was, *"To bring in to the LORD the collection that Moses the servant of God laid upon Israel in the wilderness."*

This was probably the census money, which was a half shekel of silver for each man 20 years old and older. Silver was a type of Redemption in the Old Testament, which, of course, speaks of the Cross. Such proclaimed to Israel that her strength, her power, and her protection were all in the shed Blood of the Lamb, i.e., *"Christ."*

So, the *"proclamation"* levied by Joash did not constitute a request but, in effect, a command.

As to exactly how all of this was paid, and how it was brought to Jerusalem, we aren't told, only that when they brought it in, they *". . . cast it into the chest, until they had made an end."* This was for the repair of the Temple, and the need was great.

So the Scripture says, *"So the workmen wrought, and the work was perfected by them, and they set the House of God in his state, and strengthened it."*

In effect, what Joash demanded was that Judah return to the Cross, for this is what the poll tax represented.

If there is to be a Revival in this nation or any nation at any time, first of all, there has to be a Reformation, which means to return to correct Doctrine, which refers to the Cross of Christ. The church has drifted so far from Biblical concepts that anymore it hardly knows where it's been, where it is,

NOTES

or where it's going. Let it ever be understood, any and every Move of God must be based entirely on the premise of the Cross of Christ. The Lord will honor nothing else.

WHY THE CROSS?

The reason for the Cross is because everything in the Bible, the entirety of the Plan of God for the human race, and everything pertaining to Redemption, are all and without exception based on the Foundation of the Cross of Christ. In fact, the Cross as the Plan of Redemption was decided in the Mind of the Godhead from even before the foundation of the world (I Pet. 1:18-20). This means the following:

• The Cross of Christ is the very First Doctrine formulated by the Godhead, and done so before the foundation of the world.

• Every single doctrine in the Bible must be based entirely upon the Cross of Christ, or else, in some way, it will be specious.

• The principle of the Cross hasn't changed from the beginning unto now and, in fact, never will change. Paul referred to it as the *"Everlasting Covenant"* (Heb. 13:20).

• The Believer's Faith must be placed entirely in Christ and what He did for us at the Cross, or else it's faith that God will not recognize (Rom. 6:1-14; 8:1-2, 11; I Cor. 1:17-18, 21, 23; 2:2; Gal. 2:20-21; Chpt. 5; 6:14; Col. 2:14-15).

The Cross is where the price was paid. It's where Satan was defeated, and to be sure, it was a price that was paid in full and will never need to be repeated. In essence, that is the proclamation!

THE BURNT OFFERINGS

When the House of the Lord was repaired, in other words, made ready for service, the Scripture says, *"And they offered Burnt Offerings in the House of the LORD continually all the days of Jehoiada."*

In essence, the entire purpose for the *"House of the LORD,"* i.e., *"the Temple,"* was for the *"Burnt Offerings."* In today's dollars, when originally built, that Temple would have cost nearly one trillion dollars or more. And, as stated, it was all for but one purpose, and that was *"the sacrifice."*

How much more does the preacher need to know? How much more does he need to understand? How much more does the church need to know? It is the Cross, the Cross, the Cross!

(15) "BUT JEHOIADA WAXED OLD, AND WAS FULL OF DAYS WHEN HE DIED; AN HUNDRED AND THIRTY YEARS OLD WAS HE WHEN HE DIED.

(16) "AND THEY BURIED HIM IN THE CITY OF DAVID AMONG THE KINGS, BECAUSE HE HAD DONE GOOD IN ISRAEL, BOTH TOWARD GOD, AND TOWARD HIS HOUSE."

The pattern is:

1. (Vs. 15) Jehoiada was born in Solomon's reign. He, therefore, lived through the period of 8 kings, not counting the reign of that wicked woman, Athaliah.

2. (Vs. 15) As is obvious, the Lord allowed him to live far beyond the normal time, all in order to guide Joash.

3. What a Testimony, as it regards the Sixteenth Verse, given by the Holy Spirit to the faithfulness of this man.

4. The Holy Spirit said of him, *"Because he had done good in Israel, both toward God, and toward His House."* What is He saying about me? What about you?

HE HAD DONE GOOD

Jehoiada was the great High Priest of Judah.

Concerning Jehoiada, Pulpit says: *"This good man, husband of Jehoram's daughter, only comes to view in virtue of what his wife did in saving baby Joash, and what he did on behalf of Joash in protecting him until he was old enough to become king."*[2]

As long as Jehoiada was alive, Joash served the Lord; therefore, the Lord allowed this man to live far beyond the normal, some 130 years.

The expression *"full of days,"* as it regards Jehoiada, is used only of Abraham, Isaac, Job, and David. While Abraham, Isaac, and Job lived longer than Jehoiada, David passed away when only 70 years of age. The idea seems to be, as it regards David, that even though he wasn't aged when he died, still, he had accomplished so much in his lifetime that the Holy Spirit also labeled him as *"full of days."* In other words, he accomplished some three to four times what other great men were able to do.

The honor done to Jehoiada in his death well belonged to him, not only for his goodness, his greatness, and his practical services to the kingdom, but above all, his faithfulness.

How wonderful it was as it regards that which the Holy Spirit said about him when he died, and as we have previously asked, what will the Holy Spirit say about us?

(17) "NOW AFTER THE DEATH OF JEHOIADA CAME THE PRINCES OF JUDAH, AND MADE OBEISANCE TO THE KING. THEN THE KING HEARKENED UNTO THEM.

(18) "AND THEY LEFT THE HOUSE OF THE LORD GOD OF THEIR FATHERS, AND SERVED GROVES AND IDOLS: AND WRATH CAME UPON JUDAH AND JERUSALEM FOR THIS THEIR TRESPASS.

(19) "YET HE SENT PROPHETS TO THEM, TO BRING THEM AGAIN UNTO THE LORD; AND THEY TESTIFIED AGAINST THEM: BUT THEY WOULD NOT GIVE EAR."

The exegesis is:

1. (Vs. 17) At the commencement of his reign, Joash leaned on Jehoiada, who was a godly man. Afterwards, he leaned on the princes of Judah, who were wicked men. To lean on men, whether they be good or wicked, is disastrous. Had the king leaned *"only upon God,"* how different would have been his history!

2. (Vs. 18) It was the princes of Judah this time who led into sin and apostasy. Usually the king led the princes and the people astray, but not here. The *"wrath of God"* must always come upon sin. God cannot abide such in any form.

3. (Vs. 18) One can accept the wrath that came upon Christ at Calvary's Cross, which was for our sins, and definitely not His, for He had none, or one will experience the wrath of God upon oneself. There is no alternative!

JUDAH ABANDONS THE WORSHIP OF THE LORD

When Jehoiada died, evidently, there were

precious few men, if any, in places of authority, who would stand up for Jehovah. While evidently they paid lip service to the Lord while Jehoiada was alive, their hearts were far from God. Joash must have been now about 36 years of age.

We aren't told what these princes said to Joash, but evidently their words were those of flattery. At any rate, the Scripture says, *"Then the king hearkened unto them."*

Joash must have been a weak individual. As long as he was guided by Jehoiada, he functioned as he should. But with the influence of Jehoiada gone, he was now fodder for Satan's mill, and these wicked princes took full advantage of him. But it seemed to be an advantage that he desired that they take of him. In other words, whatever it was they proposed met with his desires. He will now abandon the worship of Jehovah and go into the most gross of idol-worship, which will ultimately bring Judah to ruin.

THEY SERVED GROVES AND IDOLS

"Groves" at times referred to the Asherah. This was one of the most hideous idols and was actually a replica of the man's reproductive organ. Every type of immorality was practiced as it regarded this particular idol, which was thought to be the god of fertility.

The idols were generally made of tree trunks and, thereby, carved into the shape desired.

The Scripture says, *"... and wrath came upon Judah and Jerusalem for this their trespass."*

God, as should be obvious, cannot abide sin in any form. When the believing sinner comes to Christ, the Holy Spirit comes into the heart and life of such a Believer, without which the Believer can little be what is demanded. But among all the things that the Spirit of God does for us and with us, ridding us of all sin is His primary Objective. That doesn't mean sinless perfection, for the Bible doesn't teach such; however, it does mean that the Believer is to be brought to the place that sin will no longer have dominion over him (Rom. 6:14). This refers to victory over the sin nature.

THE SIN NATURE

As we have already explained elsewhere in this Volume, the sin nature is that which Adam and Eve became after the Fall. In other words, their nature became that of disobedience to God, of sin, of transgression, and of failure, and constantly. That sin nature, due to the fact that all were in Adam's loins, came down to all who followed him, even to us at the present time. Before you came to Christ, the sin nature ruled you in every capacity, 24 hours a day, 7 days a week. Even the good that you tried to do, that is if you did, came from ulterior motives. It could not be any other way.

When you came to Christ, the sin nature was instantly made dormant, in other words, ineffective (Rom. 6:6). But, as with all Believers, we try to live for the Lord in all the wrong ways, thereby, depending upon self instead of depending fully on Christ and what He did for us at the Cross. This greatly hinders the Holy Spirit, and it gives occasion for the sin nature to be resurrected, so to speak, and even to begin to control us in some fashion.

DOMINION OF SIN

Satan desires to erect a stronghold in your life, as he attempts to do with every Believer, which will cause that Believer untold problems, in effect, getting worse and worse, dominating the individual, and despite everything he can do to conduct himself otherwise. Read carefully the following statement:

Every Believer in this world who doesn't have his Faith exclusively in Christ and what Christ did at the Cross is being dominated by the sin nature in some way. For a list of the ways that such can dominate, one only has to look at Galatians 5:19-21. Because this is so very, very important, please allow me to say it again:

God's way is *"Jesus Christ and Him Crucified"* (I Cor. 1:23). In other words, the Believer must place his Faith exclusively in Christ and what Christ did at the Cross, and not allow his Faith to be moved elsewhere, which Satan will constantly attempt to do. But the tragedy is, most Christians have a modicum of understanding as it regards the Cross as it pertains to Salvation but virtually none at all as it pertains to Sanctification.

THE CROSS AND SANCTIFICATION

Sanctification merely means to be set apart from something to something. In other words, the Believer is set apart from the world and unto God, and one might quickly add, unto God exclusively. This has to do with how we live for God. Regrettably, even though the word *"Sanctification"* is one of the great Biblical principles, the modern church has precious little knowledge of this all important Doctrine.

It is the task of the Holy Spirit to sanctify you, to get the world out of you, in order that you might altogether be unto God. He can only do that in one way:

That one way is that we place our Faith exclusively, as stated, in Christ and the Cross (Rom. 6:1-14; 8:1-2, 11; I Cor. 1:17-18, 23; 2:2).

When our Faith is properly placed, and we speak of Faith in the Cross of Christ exclusively, the Holy Spirit, Who works exclusively within the parameters, or in other words, the guidelines, of the Finished Work of Christ, will then work mightily on our behalf, giving us Victory over the world, the flesh, and the Devil (Rom. 8:1-2, 11). That is God's Way and, in fact, His only Way. If we try to live for the Lord by any other means or method, no matter how good it may seem to be on the surface, we will conclude every time by the sin nature dominating us in some way, making life miserable, to say the least, which could bring about the loss of the soul.

THE BELIEVER AND WILLPOWER

Most Believers are taught to live for God merely by the means of willpower. While the word *"willpower"* is not too often used, still, that's what it amounts to. Preachers tell individuals who are having problems, *"You've got to try harder,"* which simply means to use greater willpower.

Many Christians are led to believe that before they were Saved, Satan could force their will, thereby, causing them to do things they didn't want to do. But they now believe that since they have come to Christ,

NOTES

they have a stronger will and can, thereby, say *"no"* to Satan, etc.

No, that's not God's Way. There's nothing in the Bible that says that the Believer has some type of superhuman will. In fact, your will is really no stronger now than it was before you came to Christ. So, trying to live for God and trying to throw off the attacks by Satan by the means of willpower is a fruitless task. Let's go to the Word of God.

Paul addressed this thing, and I continue to speak of the subject of willpower, by saying, and I quote from THE EXPOSITOR'S STUDY BIBLE:

"For I know that in me, (that is, in my flesh,) dwells no good thing (speaks of man's own ability, or rather the lack thereof in comparison to the Holy Spirit, at least when it comes to spiritual things)*: for to will is present with me* (Paul is speaking here of his willpower; regrettably, most modern Christians are trying to live for God by means of willpower, thinking falsely that since they have come to Christ, they are now free to say 'no' to sin; that is the wrong way to look at the situation; the Believer cannot live for God by the strength of willpower; while the will is definitely important, it alone is not enough; the Believer must exercise Faith in Christ and the Cross, and do so constantly; then he will have the ability and strength to say 'yes' to Christ, which automatically says, 'no' to the things of the world)*; but how to perform that which is good I find not* (outside of the Cross, it is impossible to find a way to do good)" (Rom. 7:18).

Paul here plainly tells us that he tried his best to live for God by the means of willpower, but failed every time. Of course, this was before the Lord gave to the great Apostle the meaning of the New Covenant, which is the meaning of the Cross. When this great Revelation was given to the Apostle, then he knew the secret of Victory and was able to walk therein, and, in fact, he gave that secret to us in his Epistles, and more particularly, in Romans, Chapters 6, 7, and 8.

As we've already stated, while willpower is important, *"whosoever will. . . .,"* still, that within itself is not enough. We must have the help of the Holy Spirit, His Power, which is available to us on the premise of our Faith in Christ and what Christ did at the Cross. Satan is stronger than you and me, but he most definitely is not stronger than the Holy Spirit.

In fact, the Scripture says, *"You are of God, little children, and have overcome them* (some of the Christians of John's day were tempted to believe the doctrine that denigrated the Cross, but had overcome that temptation)*: because greater is He* (the Holy Spirit) *Who is in you, than he* (Satan) *who is in the world"* (I Jn. 4:4).

HOW THE HOLY SPIRIT WORKS

The nominal church world has little knowledge of the Holy Spirit. In those circles, He is somewhat taken for granted as just a part of the mix.

As it regards Pentecostals and Charismatics, who are supposed to major in the Moving and Operation of the Spirit, the situation is little better, if any at all. About as far as these groups (and I am Pentecostal) have ventured, as far as the Spirit is concerned, is limited to speaking with other Tongues and the Gifts of the Spirit manifested at times. Regrettably, even that is falling by the wayside. In other words, due to the fact that less than half of the people who belong to Full Gospel churches, so-called, even claim to be baptized with the Holy Spirit with the evidence of speaking with other Tongues, these denominations can little even claim anymore to be Pentecostal. Thank the Lord there are a few exceptions to this, but those exceptions are getting less almost by the day.

While speaking with other Tongues is of extreme significance, and while the Moving and Operation of the Spirit is vastly significant in any capacity, and while the Gifts are so very, very important, still, while that tells us a little bit as to what the Holy Spirit does, it does not at all tell us how He does it.

Concerning how the Holy Spirit works, the Scripture says, *"For the Law of the Spirit of Life in Christ Jesus has made me free from the Law of Sin and Death"* (Rom. 8:2). In essence, this Passage tells us how the Holy Spirit works within our hearts and lives. It is as follows:

• The Holy Spirit works exclusively within the parameters of the Finished Work of Christ. In other words, it is the Cross which has given the Holy Spirit the legal means and right to do all the things He does within our hearts and lives (Jn. 14:17).

• At the Cross Jesus atoned for all sin, past, present, and future, at least for all who will believe (Jn. 3:16). By Him atoning for all sin, which means that the sin debt was lifted from off all Believers, this made it possible for the Holy Spirit to come into the heart and life of the Believer, which He does at Conversion, and there to abide forever (Jn. 14:16). The Cross made all of this possible.

• It is required of the Believer that we place our Faith entirely in Christ and what He has done for us at the Cross, always understanding that Christ is the Source of all things, while the Cross is the Means by which these things are done, all superintended by the Holy Spirit (I Cor. 1:17-18; 2:2).

• The Sixth Chapter of Romans tells us how the Holy Spirit works and is given to us specifically in Verses 3 through 5. I quote from THE EXPOSITOR'S STUDY BIBLE:

"Know you not, that so many of us as were baptized into Jesus Christ (plainly says that this Baptism is into Christ and not water [I Cor. 1:17; 12:13; Gal. 3:27; Eph. 4:5; Col. 2:11-13]) *were baptized into His Death?* (When Christ died on the Cross, in the Mind of God, we died with Him; in other words, He became our Substitute, and our identification with Him in His Death gives us all the benefits for which He died; the idea is that He did it all for us!)

"Therefore we are buried with Him by baptism into death (not only did we die with Him, but we were buried with Him, as well, which means that all the sin and transgression of the past were buried; when they put Him in the Tomb, they put all of our sins into that Tomb as well)*: that like as Christ was raised up from the dead by the Glory of the Father, even so we also should walk in Newness of Life* (we died with Him, we were buried with Him, and His Resurrection was our Resurrection to a *'Newness of Life'*).

"For if we have been planted together (with Christ) *in the likeness of His Death* (Paul proclaims the Cross as the instrument through which all Blessings come; consequently, the Cross must ever be the Object

of our Faith, which gives the Holy Spirit latitude to work within our lives), *we shall be also in the likeness of His Resurrection* (we can have the *'likeness of His Resurrection,'* i.e., *'live this Resurrection Life,'* only as long as we understand the *'likeness of His Death,'* which refers to the Cross as the Means by which all of this is done)" (Rom. 6:3-5).

• The manner and way in which the Holy Spirit works, which is totally and completely by and through the Cross of Christ, meaning that He will function in no other manner, is referred to as a *"Law."* It's called *"The Law of the Spirit of Life in Christ Jesus"* (Rom. 8:2). In other words, one can be dead certain that the Holy Spirit is going to abide by this *"Law,"* which He devised Himself, and did so sometime in eternity past.

All of this means that the Holy Spirit works exclusively by and through the Cross of Christ, which gives Him the legal means to do all that He does, which requires Faith on our part as it regards the Finished Work of Christ. That's the way the Spirit works!

THE PROPHETS

Concerning Judah and the terrible spiritual declension under Joash, the Bible says, *"Yet He sent Prophets to them, to bring them again unto the LORD; and they testified against them: but they would not give ear."*

Prophets under the Old Covenant were, in effect, the Spiritual Leaders of Israel. They were meant to guide the Nation, whether positive or negative, with *"thus says the LORD!"*

So often, as here, the Message was not good and would incur the wrath of the leaders and the people, even as we shall see. This is what Jesus was talking about when He said, *"Oh Jerusalem, Jerusalem* (presents Jesus standing in the Temple when He gave this sorrowing account), *you who kill the Prophets, and stone them which are sent unto you* (presents the terrible animosity tendered toward these Messengers of God), *how often would I have gathered your children together, even as a hen gathers her chickens under her wings, and you would not!* (Proclaims every effort made by the Lord, and made *'often,'* to bring Israel back to her senses.)

"Behold, your house (the Temple or Jerusalem, are no longer God's habitation) *is left unto you desolate* (without God, which means they were at the mercy of Satan)" (Mat. 23:37-38).

As it concerns the Prophets sent to Judah at this time, the Scripture says, *"but they would not give ear."*

Once again we hear the words of Christ as He says, *"He who has ears to hear, let him hear"* (Mat. 11:15; 13:9, 43; Mk. 7:16).

False prophets, then as now, prophesied that which the people desired to hear, while true Prophets prophesied *"thus says the LORD,"* which oftentimes was not what the people wanted to hear. This was one of those times, and it would result in the death of the Prophet Zechariah, even as we shall see.

(20) "AND THE SPIRIT OF GOD CAME UPON ZECHARIAH THE SON OF JEHOIADA THE PRIEST, WHICH STOOD ABOVE THE PEOPLE, AND SAID UNTO THEM, THUS SAYS GOD, WHY TRANSGRESS YOU THE COMMANDMENTS OF THE LORD, THAT YOU CANNOT PROSPER? BECAUSE YOU HAVE FORSAKEN THE LORD, HE HAS ALSO FORSAKEN YOU.

(21) "AND THEY CONSPIRED AGAINST HIM, AND STONED HIM WITH STONES AT THE COMMANDMENT OF THE KING IN THE COURT OF THE HOUSE OF THE LORD.

(22) "THUS JOASH THE KING REMEMBERED NOT THE KINDNESS WHICH JEHOIADA HIS FATHER HAD DONE TO HIM, BUT KILLED HIS SON. AND WHEN HE DIED, HE SAID, THE LORD LOOK UPON IT, AND REQUIRE IT."

The composition is:

1. (Vs. 20) Zechariah was now, as well, the High Priest of Judah.

2. (Vs. 20) While a Believer who violates the Commandments of the Lord may occasionally prosper in the financial sense, he definitely cannot prosper in the spiritual sense.

3. The Spirit of the Lord spoke the words given in the Twentieth Verse through Zechariah, and they are easy to understand. If we forsake the Lord, He will forsake us. If

we uphold the Lord, He will uphold us!

4. (Vs. 21) This Zechariah who was stoned here was not the Prophet who wrote the Book of Zechariah, for the latter did not live until after the Babylonian captivities, which were over 150 years later (Zech. 1:1). Both men were stoned, one in the Court of the Temple, and the other between the Temple and the Altar, the latter being mentioned by Jesus (Mat. 23:35).

WHY DO YOU TRANSGRESS THE COMMANDMENTS OF THE LORD?

The Holy Spirit through the Prophet Zechariah, who was also the High Priest of Israel, asked them, in effect, as to the why of what they were doing? He plainly told them that transgressing the Commandments of the Lord would bring about poverty. He clearly said, *"You cannot prosper."*

The prosperity here mentioned spoke most of all of Spiritual Prosperity but, as well, spoke of every other facet of life and living.

Serving the Lord brings prosperity, while ignoring His Word brings poverty.

Tragically enough, Judah, and especially king Joash, didn't like what they heard. So they did what men have been attempting to do from the very dawn of time. They killed the Prophet.

Joash owed everything he had that was worth anything to Jehoiada, the father of Zechariah. But he seemed to forget that!

As the great Prophet was dying, he said, *"The LORD look upon it, and require it."* And that's exactly what happened!

Judah went further and further into decline, and Joash, even as we shall see, died an ignominious death.

(23) "AND IT CAME TO PASS AT THE END OF THE YEAR, THAT THE HOST OF SYRIA CAME UP AGAINST HIM: AND THEY CAME TO JUDAH AND JERUSALEM, AND DESTROYED ALL THE PRINCES OF THE PEOPLE FROM AMONG THE PEOPLE, AND SENT ALL THE SPOIL OF THEM UNTO THE KING OF DAMASCUS.

(24) "FOR THE ARMY OF THE SYRIANS CAME WITH A SMALL COMPANY OF MEN, AND THE LORD DELIVERED A VERY GREAT HOST INTO THEIR HAND, BECAUSE THEY HAD FORSAKEN THE LORD GOD OF THEIR FATHERS. SO THEY EXECUTED JUDGMENT AGAINST JOASH."

The pattern is:

1. The princes of Judah, who enticed Joash toward idolatry, are now killed by the army of Syria. The mills of God grind exceedingly slow, but they also grind exceedingly fine. In other words, they miss nothing.

2. (Vs. 24) This *"judgment"* was caused by the Lord. Even though Judah had a very large army, they were helpless to defeat the much smaller army of the Syrians, because the Lord decreed it so.

3. What we sow, that we reap!

THE JUDGMENT OF GOD

The army of Syria was very small, while the army of Joash was very large. Consequently, he, no doubt, thought that he would have no problem whatsoever defeating the Syrians; however, he reasoned without the Lord.

The Judgment of God was on Judah and on Joash, and it could not be deterred.

(25) "AND WHEN THEY WERE DEPARTED FROM HIM, (FOR THEY LEFT HIM IN GREAT DISEASES,) HIS OWN SERVANTS CONSPIRED AGAINST HIM FOR THE BLOOD OF THE SONS OF JEHOIADA THE PRIEST, AND KILLED HIM ON HIS BED, AND HE DIED: AND THEY BURIED HIM IN THE CITY OF DAVID, BUT THEY BURIED HIM NOT IN THE SEPULCHRES OF THE KINGS.

(26) "AND THESE ARE THEY WHO CONSPIRED AGAINST HIM; ZABAD THE SON OF SHIMEATH AN AMMONITESS, AND JEHOZABAD THE SON OF SHIMRITH A MOABITESS.

(27) "NOW CONCERNING HIS SONS, AND THE GREATNESS OF THE BURDENS LAID UPON HIM, AND THE REPAIRING OF THE HOUSE OF GOD, BEHOLD, THEY ARE WRITTEN IN THE STORY OF THE BOOK OF THE KINGS. AND AMAZIAH HIS SON REIGNED IN HIS STEAD."

The composition is:

1. The idea of Verse 25 is that Joash was greatly ill at the time the Syrians invaded the land.

2. (Vs. 25) It says, *"sons of Jehoiada"*; however, the Bible only records one son, Zechariah. There may have been other sons,

or other relations of Jehoiada covered by the word *"sons."*

3. (Vs. 26) The Holy Spirit emphasizes the fact that the two servants who killed him were heathen, which meant that his death was ignominious.

4. (Vs. 27) From all of this, we see how obvious it is that the Blessings of God come upon Righteousness; as well, how obvious it is that the Judgment of God comes upon unrighteousness.

DEATH

How different could have been the final years of Joash, and above all, his death. He had such an excellent beginning and such a sad, ignominious conclusion.

- He led Judah into gross idolatry.
- He ignored the Prophets sent to him by the Lord.
- He forgot the kindness of Jehoiada the High Priest, in effect, owing him everything that he had which was good.
- He murdered Zechariah the son of Jehoiada the High Priest, which proclaims the depth of his spiritual declension.
- He forsook the Lord and all that pertained to the Lord.
- By his actions, he invited the Wrath of God upon Judah and upon his person.

As a result, he incurred the following:

- He contracted great diseases.
- Two of his servants murdered him because of what he had done to Zechariah.
- While they buried him in the city of David, they did not bury him with the other kings.

And so this man died a terrible death, having forsaken God and, thereby, being forsaken of God.

"Tell me the Story of Jesus,
"Write on my heart every word;
"Tell me the Story most precious,
"Sweetest that ever was heard.
"Tell how the Angels, in chorus,
"Sang as they welcomed His Birth,
"Glory to God in the highest!
"Peace and good tidings to Earth."

"Fasting alone in the desert,
"Tell of the days that are past,
"How for our sins He was tempted,
"Yet was triumphant at last.
"Tell of the years of His Labor,
"Tell of the sorrow He bore,
"He was despised and afflicted,
"Homeless, rejected and poor."

"Tell of the Cross where they nailed Him,
"Writhing in anguish and pain;
"Tell of the grave where they laid Him,
"Tell how He lives again.
"Love in that Story so tender,
"Clearer than ever I see:
"Stay, let me weep while you whisper,
"Love paid the ransom for me."

CHAPTER 25

(1) "AMAZIAH WAS TWENTY AND FIVE YEARS OLD WHEN HE BEGAN TO REIGN, AND HE REIGNED TWENTY AND NINE YEARS IN JERUSALEM. AND HIS MOTHER'S NAME WAS JEHOADDAN OF JERUSALEM.

(2) "AND HE DID THAT WHICH WAS RIGHT IN THE SIGHT OF THE LORD, BUT NOT WITH A PERFECT HEART.

(3) "NOW IT CAME TO PASS, WHEN THE KINGDOM WAS ESTABLISHED TO HIM, THAT HE KILLED HIS SERVANTS WHO HAD KILLED THE KING HIS FATHER.

(4) "BUT HE KILLED NOT THEIR CHILDREN, BUT DID AS IT IS WRITTEN IN THE LAW IN THE BOOK OF MOSES, WHERE THE LORD COMMANDED, SAYING, THE FATHERS SHALL NOT DIE FOR THE CHILDREN, NEITHER SHALL THE CHILDREN DIE FOR THE FATHERS, BUT EVERY MAN SHALL DIE FOR HIS OWN SIN."

The pattern is:

1. Regarding Verse 2, one might say that Amaziah had a divided heart. It would lead to his ultimate ruin!

2. (Vs. 4) At the beginning of his reign, it seems that he tried to follow the Bible (Deut. 24:16).

3. As with Amaziah, so with many. He failed to seek the Lord, as it regarded direction, and found to his dismay that he did

not know the way. And neither does anyone else.

NOT WITH A PERFECT HEART

The phrase, *"Not with a perfect heart,"* seems to indicate that Amaziah knew the Ways of the Lord but did not want to follow the Ways of the Lord, but rather his own way. One might say that a divided heart is the cause of all spiritual declension. Such portrays the heart knowing the right way but self-will intruding and, thereby, gaining the upper hand. Such constitutes following *"self"* instead of the *"Spirit."*

THE DIVIDED HEART AND THE CROSS

At least one of the reasons that the Cross of Christ is such an offense, and the Holy Spirit through the Apostle Paul told us that it was (Gal. 5:11), is because it eliminates every other supposed object of faith.

The first step in the experience of the backslider is distaste for the Bible and a desire for the things of the world.

The next step is the substitution in the heart of a way other than the Cross—for the heart must have a religion. So, when Christ and the Cross are dethroned, an idol is of necessity enthroned. And to be sure, every single thing other than Christ and the Cross constitutes an idol.

The third step always follows the second in this moral sphere. It is fellowship with the world. That is spiritual adultery, for a way of salvation or victory other than the Cross of Christ is always the great rival of Christ for the affection of the heart. And when the rival is preferred, our marriage bond to Christ becomes defiled (II Cor. 11:1-4).

At the beginning, the great rival to the Cross of Christ is not necessarily the world. That comes later. It is a religious way of salvation and victory devised by man, which seems to be very desirable. It may be our good works, our religious denomination, or a particular church, or even a particular preacher. It might be one of the great Ordinances of the Church, such as the Lord's Supper, or Water Baptism, or any number of such things that we might name. Please understand, anything and everything that the human heart devises is always religious, and because it is religious, it fools people into believing that it's right. Let us say it again:

The divided heart cannot accept Christ and the Cross. It will always opt for the religious devices of men.

THE REJECTION OF THE CROSS IS NEVER THEOLOGICAL BUT RATHER MORAL

What do we mean by the statement of the heading?

If people rejected the Cross of Christ because of theological reasons, that would mean that it was too difficult to understand. But the truth is, the Message of the Cross is so easy to understand that it can be grasped even by a little child. So, the reason for rejecting the Cross is never theological but always moral.

What do we mean by moral?

We mean that men reject the Cross because of pride, because of self-will, because of arrogance, etc. And, as stated, whenever one accepts the Cross of Christ as the answer to man's dilemma and, in fact, the only answer, that means that everything else must drop off. While we continue to love our church, we now understand it for what it really is. While we cherish good works, we also understand them for what they really are.

If one watches Christian television to any degree at all, it quickly becomes obvious that scores of books, CD's, tapes, etc., are offered to the Christian public, with each and every one of them claiming to hold the key and the answer to man's dilemma, whatever that dilemma might be.

Do they?

Let me be as blunt as I know how to be.

Unless the preacher is proclaiming the Cross of Christ as the answer to man's dilemma, and the only answer to man's dilemma, then whatever it is he is promoting is not only useless, but, in fact, worse than useless. And the sad fact is, precious few preachers are proclaiming the Cross of Christ as the answer.

Show me in the Bible where there is another answer!

That's why Paul said, *"But God forbid that I should glory* (boast), *save in the Cross of our Lord Jesus Christ* (what the opponents of Paul sought to escape at the price of insincerity is the Apostle's only basis of exultation), *by Whom the world is crucified unto me, and I unto the world.* (The only way we can overcome the world, and I mean the only way, is by placing our Faith exclusively in the Cross of Christ and keeping it there)" (Gal. 6:14).

THE FAMILY CURSE

The Sacred Text says, *"But he killed not their children, but did as it is written in the Law in the Book of Moses, where the LORD commanded, saying, The fathers shall not die for the children, neither shall the children die for the fathers, but every man shall die for his own sin."*

There is a teaching referred to in Christian circles as the generational or the family curse. It is basically derived from a misinterpretation of Exodus 20:5 which says, *"You shall not bow down yourself to them, nor serve them: for I the LORD your God am a jealous God, visiting the iniquity of the fathers upon the children unto the third and fourth generation of them who hate Me."*

However, there are two qualifiers here. They are:

1. *"Of them who hate Me."* This means that if a man would commit some hateful crime, and with the third and fourth generation of that family continuing in that same direction, there most definitely would be a curse that would pass down. However, the moment that anyone in that family turns to Christ, the curse is broken. For the Scripture also says:

2. *"And showing mercy unto thousands of them who love Me, and keep My Commandments"* (Ex. 20:6).

Yes, there are all types of curses leveled at the human race because of sin. The greatest curse of all is the curse of the broken Law.

This means that all who break the Law of God, and regrettably, that includes every human being who has ever lived, comes under the sentence of death. For the Bible plainly tells us, *"The wages of sin is death"* (Rom. 6:23).

The remedy for all of this, however, is Jesus Christ and what He did for us at Calvary's Cross. Paul said, *"Christ has redeemed us from the curse of the Law* (He did so on the Cross), *being made a curse for us* (He took the penalty of the Law, which was death)*: for it is written, Cursed is everyone who hangs on a tree* (Deut. 21:23)*:*

"That the blessing of Abraham (Justification by Faith) *might come on the Gentiles through Jesus Christ* (what He did at the Cross)*; that we might receive the Promise of the Spirit through Faith.* (All sin was atoned at the Cross, which lifted the sin debt from believing man, making it possible for the Holy Spirit to come into the life of the Believer and abide there forever [Jn. 14:16-17])" (Gal. 3:13-14).

In other words, the Cross, at least for all who will believe, addressed it all. It addressed every curse, every sin, every power of darkness, the root cause of acts of sin, which is the sin nature, and, in fact, the entirety of the human dilemma. The Cross of Christ answered it all.

So, for any preacher to claim that the problems of a Believer are because of some type of family curse is doing a terrible injustice to Christ and what He did at the Cross. While it is definitely true that many Believers are having problems, it's not because of any family curse. It is because they do not understand the Cross as it regards their Sanctification, in other words, how they live for God. In effect, they are trying to live for the Lord in all the wrong ways. Their answer is not some preacher laying hands on them and rebuking the family curse, for that was done at the Cross, but rather that they learn and understand the truth, for our Lord said, *"You shall know the Truth, and the Truth shall make you free"* (Jn. 8:32).

The Text of our study (II Chron. 25:4), plainly tells us, *"The fathers shall not die for the children, neither shall the children die for the fathers, but every man shall die for his own sin."*

All false doctrine begins with a false interpretation, a misunderstanding, or an outright denial of the Cross of Christ. So, as a Believer, if you are, in fact, having problems, place your Faith squarely in Christ and what He did for us at the Cross, and do not allow it to be moved elsewhere, and you will find the Holy Spirit greatly helping you, bringing you in line with the Word of God and, thereby, giving you Victory over the world, the flesh, and the Devil. That is God's Answer, and there is no other, because no other is needed (Rom. 6:1-14; 8:1-2, 11; I Cor. 1:17-18, 23; 2:2; Gal., Chpt. 5; 6:14; Eph. 2:13-18; Col. 2:14-15).

John the Beloved wrote, *"And they overcame him by the Blood of the Lamb* (the power to overcome and overwhelm the kingdom of Satan is found exclusively in the Blood of the Sacrifice of the Son of God, and our Faith in that Finished Work [Rom. 6:3-5, 11, 14]), *and by the word of their testimony* (the *'testimony'* must pertain to the fact that the Object of our Faith is the Cross, and exclusively the Cross, which then gives the Holy Spirit latitude to work within our lives); *and they loved not their lives unto the death.* (This refers to the fact that the Believer must not change his testimony regarding the Cross to something else, even if it means death)" (Rev. 12:11).

(5) "MOREOVER AMAZIAH GATHERED JUDAH TOGETHER, AND MADE THEM CAPTAINS OVER THOUSANDS, AND CAPTAINS OVER HUNDREDS, ACCORDING TO THE HOUSES OF THEIR FATHERS, THROUGHOUT ALL JUDAH AND BENJAMIN: AND HE NUMBERED THEM FROM TWENTY YEARS OLD AND ABOVE, AND FOUND THEM THREE HUNDRED THOUSAND CHOICE MEN, ABLE TO GO FORTH TO WAR, WHO COULD HANDLE SPEAR AND SHIELD.

(6) "HE HIRED ALSO AN HUNDRED THOUSAND MIGHTY MEN OF VALOUR OUT OF ISRAEL FOR AN HUNDRED TALENTS OF SILVER.

(7) "BUT THERE CAME A MAN OF GOD TO HIM, SAYING, O KING, LET NOT THE ARMY OF ISRAEL GO WITH YOU; FOR THE LORD IS NOT WITH ISRAEL, TO WIT, WITH ALL THE CHILDREN OF EPHRAIM.

(8) "BUT IF YOU WILL GO, DO IT, BE STRONG FOR THE BATTLE: GOD SHALL MAKE YOU FALL BEFORE THE ENEMY: FOR GOD HAS POWER TO HELP, AND TO CAST DOWN.

(9) "AND AMAZIAH SAID TO THE MAN OF GOD, BUT WHAT SHALL WE DO FOR THE HUNDRED TALENTS WHICH I HAVE GIVEN TO THE ARMY OF ISRAEL? AND THE MAN OF GOD ANSWERED, THE LORD IS ABLE TO GIVE YOU MUCH MORE THAN THIS.

(10) "THEN AMAZIAH SEPARATED THEM, TO WIT, THE ARMY THAT WAS COME TO HIM OUT OF EPHRAIM, TO GO HOME AGAIN: WHEREFORE THEIR ANGER WAS GREATLY KINDLED AGAINST JUDAH, AND THEY RETURNED HOME IN GREAT ANGER.

(11) "AND AMAZIAH STRENGTHENED HIMSELF, AND LED FORTH HIS PEOPLE, AND WENT TO THE VALLEY OF SALT, AND SMOTE OF THE CHILDREN OF SEIR TEN THOUSAND.

(12) "AND OTHER TEN THOUSAND LEFT ALIVE DID THE CHILDREN OF JUDAH CARRY AWAY CAPTIVE, AND BROUGHT THEM UNTO THE TOP OF THE ROCK, AND CAST THEM DOWN FROM THE TOP OF THE ROCK, THAT THEY ALL WERE BROKEN IN PIECES.

(13) "BUT THE SOLDIERS OF THE ARMY WHICH AMAZIAH SENT BACK, THAT THEY SHOULD NOT GO WITH HIM TO BATTLE, FELL UPON THE CITIES OF JUDAH, FROM SAMARIA EVEN UNTO BETH-HORON, AND SMOTE THREE THOUSAND OF THEM, AND TOOK MUCH SPOIL."

The overview is:

1. The sum of Verses 7 and 8 may be translated, *"Under no circumstances join with Israel, and if you do join them, no matter how much you prepare, yet know that God will destroy you."*

2. (Vs. 9) It seems that Amaziah was much more concerned about the money lost than obeying God. If he had sought the Lord first, he would never have given the money to Israel to begin with. So, the loss was his fault and his fault alone!

3. (Vs. 10) The army of Israel anticipated plunder, which was now denied.

4. There is little doubt that Verses 11 and 12 pertain to Petra. It seems that he ruthlessly slaughtered 10,000 people.

5. (Vs. 13) The army of Israel satisfied their lust for plunder by ravaging Judah.

A FAILURE TO SEEK THE LORD

Once again, the imperfect heart of Amaziah is brought to the fore. In his war with Edom, he hired 100,000 mighty men of valor out of the northern kingdom of Israel. He paid them a hundred talents of silver.

The evidence is that he never sought the Lord as to what he should do about this matter but plunged ahead regarding his own desires. It was to be a costly mistake, even as all such forays are costly.

The Believer must seek the Lord as it regards the entirety of his life and living. Nothing is too small to take to the Lord, and nothing is too large. We should have His Leading and Guidance in all things. This means that we must seek His Face ardently, strongly desiring His Will, and not be satisfied with anything less.

To be sure, if the Believer evidences a desire for the Will of God, and ardently seeks that Will, the Lord will most graciously give His Leading and Guidance. This He desires to do, and this He will do, that is, if we will only seek His Face.

The problem is, most Christians do not have a prayer life at all. As a result, there is almost no relationship there, at least as it ought to be. Yes, they are Saved, but missing out on so very, very much of what they could have, if they only consecrated to the Lord.

So, Amaziah will strike out on his own and will fail to seek the Lord, which will prove to him to be very costly.

"A MAN OF GOD"

We aren't told who this *"Man of God"* actually is; nevertheless, he most definitely had the Message which he delivered to the king, without a doubt, directed by the Lord.

Even though the translation is less than perfect in Verse 8, the idea seems to be that the Man of God said to the king, *"If you will go, do it, make yourself as strong for the battle as you can; nevertheless, the LORD will make you fall."* In other words, if you go against God, you're going to find yourself in great trouble.

To the king's credit, he listened to the Man of God, dismissed the army of Israel, *"and they returned home in great anger."*

Why?

They had gotten their hundred thousand talents, so why would they be angry?

Actually, the State of Israel is, more than likely, what got the hundred thousand talents, and the men in the army were depending on plunder to enrich themselves. But being sent home, they were denied this plunder, so they left with great anger. On the way back to Samaria, in fact, they wreaked havoc on the cities of Judah as they passed through them.

All of this would have been avoided had Amaziah sought the Will of the Lord to begin with.

(14) "NOW IT CAME TO PASS, AFTER THAT AMAZIAH WAS COME FROM THE SLAUGHTER OF THE EDOMITES, THAT HE BROUGHT THE GODS OF THE CHILDREN OF SEIR, AND SET THEM UP TO BE HIS GODS, AND BOWED DOWN HIMSELF BEFORE THEM, AND BURNED INCENSE UNTO THEM.

(15) "WHEREFORE THE ANGER OF THE LORD WAS KINDLED AGAINST AMAZIAH, AND HE SENT UNTO HIM A PROPHET, WHICH SAID UNTO HIM, WHY HAVE YOU SOUGHT AFTER THE GODS OF THE PEOPLE, WHICH COULD NOT DELIVER THEIR OWN PEOPLE OUT OF YOUR HAND?

(16) "AND IT CAME TO PASS, AS HE TALKED WITH HIM, THAT THE KING SAID UNTO HIM, ARE YOU MADE OF THE KING'S COUNSEL? FORBEAR; WHY SHOULD YOU BE SMITTEN? THEN THE PROPHET FORBORE, AND SAID, I KNOW THAT GOD HAS DETERMINED TO DESTROY YOU, BECAUSE YOU HAVE DONE THIS, AND HAVE NOT HEARKENED UNTO MY COUNSEL."

The overview is:

1. (Vs. 15) How utterly ridiculous! Amaziah will now worship the gods of the people he has just defeated. If they were so great, why didn't these gods help the Edomites? A modern parallel concerns Believers who forsake the Presence of God for other things.

2. (Vs. 16) In essence, Amaziah says to the Prophet, *"If you keep this up, telling me what I should or should not do, I will kill you."*

3. The truth is, Amaziah had no heart for God. This is the conclusion of a divided heart!

THE GODS OF EDOM

Amaziah defeated the army of Edom and then adopted the Edomite gods, and *"set them up to be his gods."* He then *"bowed down himself before them, and burned incense to them."*

How stupid can one be! If the gods of the Edomites were so important and so powerful, how is it that Amaziah defeated the Edomite army in battle? How did Amaziah reconcile that?

I think it can be said without fear of contradiction, at least by true Believers, that any and every person who forsakes the Lord and follows their own counsel, in some way, functions in a form of insanity. The fear of God is the beginning of wisdom, and without such fear, which means to give God proper respect, man is left with no wisdom (Ps. 111:10). Even the people whom the world considers to be very intelligent function in such intelligence only in a very limited way.

The tragedy is, even the people who live for God only enjoy a partial potential of what they could have in Christ.

SPIRITUAL MATURITY AND THE CROSS OF CHRIST

The maturity of the Believer has to do solely with one's understanding of the Cross of Christ. Most Christians have little or no understanding at all as it regards the Cross. In those circles the Cross is relegated to the Salvation experience only. It is not understood at all as it regards Sanctification. When we come to the understanding that the Sanctification experience incorporates our total life and living for God, we then begin to realize the harm that's done by limiting the Cross to the Salvation experience.

While, of course, the Cross is all-important as it regards Salvation, as should be obviously understood, still, Salvation is a one-time experience. Sanctification involves our everyday life and living, which incorporates everything that we do and the way it's done. As stated, the modern church as a whole has absolutely no knowledge whatsoever of the Cross of Christ as it regards Sanctification. As a result, there is precious little Spiritual Maturity among most modern Believers. That's the reason false doctrine is eagerly accepted!

When one begins to understand the Cross of Christ, then the absurdities presented by most preachers, as to how the Believer is to live for God, become more and more pronounced. In fact, that's the reason for the manner in which the Apostle Paul wrote. That's why he said, *"But though we, or an Angel from Heaven, preach any other gospel unto you than that which we have preached unto you, let him be accursed"* (Gal. 1:8).

That's the reason he also said, *". . . if you be circumcised, Christ shall profit you nothing"* (Gal. 5:2).

And then, *"Christ is become of no effect unto you, whosoever of you are justified by the Law; you are fallen from Grace"* (Gal. 5:4).

That's the reason he also said, *"For I determined not to know anything among you, save Jesus Christ, and Him Crucified"* (I Cor. 2:2).

The great Apostle knew how absolutely absurd it was for Believers to make something other than the Cross of Christ the object of their faith. He knew the utter futility of such an effort. Please believe me, it hasn't changed from then until now. In other words, it is just as absurd now, or even more so, than it was then.

To be frank, there isn't that much difference in the stratagems presented by most modern preachers than Amaziah worshipping the gods of Edom!

THE ANGER OF THE LORD

Is the Lord any less angry today, as it regards unbelief toward the Cross of Christ, than He was as it regarded Judah worshipping the gods of Edom?

I maintain that the anger of the Lord must be even greater now than then. The way is presently clearer, plainer, and more understandable even than it was then. So, there is no excuse!

In fact, concerning these things, the Word of God says, *"And the times of this ignorance God winked at; but now commands all men everywhere to repent"* (Acts 17:30). In other words, the Lord expects more of us presently under the New Covenant than He did under the Old. Considering this, I think the anger of the Lord would be more now than ever!

Amaziah threatened to kill the Prophet! Nevertheless, the Prophet had one more word. He said, *". . . I know that God has determined to destroy you, because you have done this, and have not hearkened unto my counsel."*

With the counsel of the Lord ignored, the conclusion could not be that of victory!

(17) "THEN AMAZIAH KING OF JUDAH TOOK ADVICE, AND SENT TO JOASH, THE SON OF JEHOAHAZ, THE SON OF JEHU, KING OF ISRAEL, SAYING, COME, LET US SEE ONE ANOTHER IN THE FACE.

(18) "AND JOASH KING OF ISRAEL SENT TO AMAZIAH KING OF JUDAH, SAYING, THE THISTLE THAT WAS IN LEBANON SENT TO THE CEDAR THAT WAS IN LEBANON, SAYING, GIVE YOUR DAUGHTER TO MY SON TO WIFE: AND THERE PASSED BY A WILD BEAST THAT WAS IN LEBANON, AND TRODE DOWN THE THISTLE.

(19) "YOU SAY, LO, YOU HAVE SMITTEN THE EDOMITES; AND YOUR HEART LIFTS YOU UP TO BOAST: ABIDE NOW AT HOME; WHY SHOULD YOU MEDDLE TO YOUR HURT, THAT YOU SHOULD FALL, EVEN YOU, AND JUDAH WITH YOU?"

The construction is:

1. (Vs. 17) Amaziah took advice or counsel from some of his advisors. He definitely did not take it from the Prophet of God.

2. Regarding Verse 18, in this parable, Joash likens Israel to a cedar and Judah to a thistle. As well, he likens Israel to a *"wild beast"* that will ride roughshod over the thistle, i.e., *"Judah."*

3. The king of Israel read the situation well. Amaziah had defeated the Edomites, so his heart was lifted up as it regarded his proposed strength. In other words, he would have vengeance on Israel because of what their army had done in Judah by plundering a number of cities.

PRIDE

Amaziah has threatened the Prophet of God, so now he will threaten Israel as well. He has defeated the army of Edom, so it shouldn't be any trouble, or so he thinks, to defeat the army of Israel.

Concerning something like this, the Scripture says, *"Pride goes before destruction, and an haughty spirit before a fall"* (Prov. 16:18).

What is pride?

Probably the correct answer would be many faceted; however, in an abbreviated form, it could probably be said that *"pride is the exaltation of self."* It is the greatest obstacle between man and God.

Due to pride, man refuses to recognize what he is, and Who God is. He erroneously places himself in an exalted position and erroneously denigrates God. Or maybe in such a state he denies there is a God, and if he does admit there is a God, in his mind he places God outside the scope of involvement with man.

Jesus addressed this in His Sermon on the Mount. He said, *"Blessed* (happy) *are the poor in spirit* (conscious of moral poverty)*: for theirs is the Kingdom of Heaven* (the moral characteristics of the citizens of the Kingdom of the heavens; and so it is apparent that the New Birth is an absolute necessity for entrance into that Kingdom [Jn. 3:3]; this Kingdom is now present spiritually, but not yet physically).

"Blessed are they who mourn (grieved because of personal sinfulness)*: for they shall be comforted* (what the Holy Spirit will do for those who properly evaluate their spiritual poverty).

"Blessed are the meek (the opposite of the self-righteous; the first two Beatitudes guarantee the 'meekness')*: for they shall inherit the Earth* (speaks of the coming Kingdom Age, when the 'Kingdom of Heaven' will be brought down to Earth, when the Saints will rule, with Christ as its Supreme Lord).

"Blessed are they which do hunger and thirst (intense desire) *after Righteousness* (God's Righteousness, imputed by Christ, upon Faith in His Finished Work)*: for they shall be filled* (but first of all must be truly

empty of all self-worth)" (Mat. 5:3-6).

In these Beatitudes, I think it's easy to see man's problem. It is difficult for him to think of himself as *"poor in spirit,"* or to *"mourn over sinful failures,"* etc. But it's only that kind of person who can truly be helped by the Lord. In other words, such is the opposite of pride!

(20) "BUT AMAZIAH WOULD NOT HEAR; FOR IT CAME OF GOD, THAT HE MIGHT DELIVER THEM INTO THE HAND OF THEIR ENEMIES, BECAUSE THEY SOUGHT AFTER THE GODS OF EDOM.

(21) "SO JOASH THE KING OF ISRAEL WENT UP; AND THEY SAW ONE ANOTHER IN THE FACE, BOTH HE AND AMAZIAH KING OF JUDAH, AT BETH-SHEMESH, WHICH BELONGS TO JUDAH.

(22) "AND JUDAH WAS PUT TO THE WORSE BEFORE ISRAEL, AND THEY FLED EVERY MAN TO HIS TENT.

(23) "AND JOASH THE KING OF ISRAEL TOOK AMAZIAH KING OF JUDAH, THE SON OF JOASH, THE SON OF JEHOAHAZ, AT BETH-SHEMESH, AND BROUGHT HIM TO JERUSALEM, AND BROKE DOWN THE WALL OF JERUSALEM FROM THE GATE OF EPHRAIM TO THE CORNER GATE, FOUR HUNDRED CUBITS.

(24) "AND HE TOOK ALL THE GOLD AND THE SILVER, AND ALL THE VESSELS THAT WERE FOUND IN THE HOUSE OF GOD WITH OBED-EDOM, AND THE TREASURES OF THE KING'S HOUSE, THE HOSTAGES ALSO, AND RETURNED TO SAMARIA."

The composition is:

1. (Vs. 20) Because of idolatry, the Lord is now opposed to Judah.

2. (Vs. 22) With God against them, Judah couldn't win!

3. The Obed-edom of Verse 24 was a descendant of the Obed-edom of David's time (II Sam. 6:10; I Chron. 13:13), who was a custodian of the treasures in the House of God.

BECAUSE THEY SOUGHT AFTER THE GODS OF EDOM

The king of the northern confederation of Israel, Joash, warned Amaziah, but the Scripture says, *"Amaziah would not hear."* The Scripture further says, *"For it came of God, that He might deliver them into the hand of their enemies, because they sought after the gods of Edom."*

In any language, sin does not pay.

The following is the result of the worship of these heathen gods:

• In this battle, Judah was put to the worse before Israel.

• Joash, the king of Israel, broke down the wall of Jerusalem from the gate of Ephraim to the corner gate, four hundred cubits.

• He took all the gold and the silver.

• He took some of the sacred vessels from the Temple, most, if not all, which were made of gold.

• He, as well, took the treasures of the king's house, whatever that was.

• He took hostages, as well, which were probably some of the princes of Judah.

The sin of idolatry was the cause of all of this and was the sin that some years later finally led to the destruction of the nation.

(25) "AND AMAZIAH THE SON OF JOASH KING OF JUDAH LIVED AFTER THE DEATH OF JOASH SON OF JEHOAHAZ KING OF ISRAEL FIFTEEN YEARS.

(26) "NOW THE REST OF THE ACTS OF AMAZIAH, FIRST AND LAST, BEHOLD, ARE THEY NOT WRITTEN IN THE BOOK OF THE KINGS OF JUDAH AND ISRAEL?

(27) "NOW AFTER THE TIME THAT AMAZIAH DID TURN AWAY FROM FOLLOWING THE LORD THEY MADE A CONSPIRACY AGAINST HIM IN JERUSALEM; AND HE FLED TO LACHISH: BUT THEY SENT TO LACHISH AFTER HIM, AND KILLED HIM THERE.

(28) "AND THEY BROUGHT HIM UPON HORSES, AND BURIED HIM WITH HIS FATHERS IN THE CITY OF JUDAH."

The construction is:

1. According to Verse 27, the Holy Spirit pinpointed the exact *"time"* regarding the murder of Amaziah. Now he is at the mercy of Satan.

2. (Vs. 28) When the king turned away from the Lord, the Holy Spirit declined to call his burial place by the lofty titles of *"the city of David,"* or *"Jerusalem,"* but instead, called it *"the city of Judah."*

3. (Vs. 28) It seems that idol-worship and pride were the cause of Amaziah's fall.

II CHRONICLES 26:1-5

To be sure, idol-worship and pride are the cause of the fall of many Believers.

THE TIME

If it is to be noticed, the Holy Spirit catalogues the exact time that Amaziah turned away from following the Lord and the conspiracy against him that followed.

Success at times is dangerous. Victory over the Edomites was quickly followed by slavery to their idols.

What Satan fails to do by violence, he accomplishes at times by guile. The Edomites failed to destroy Judah, but Amaziah's worship of their gods provoked the wrath of Jehovah, and defeat, poverty, and death overtook Amaziah. His reign opened with sunshine but closed with darkest night. With God, there is prosperity; without God, ruin.

"'Twas Jesus my Saviour, Who died on the tree,
"To open a Fountain for sinners like me;
"His Blood is that Fountain which pardon bestows,
"And cleanses the foulest wherever it flows."

"And when I was willing with all things to part,
"He gave me His Blessing, His Love in my heart;
"So now I am joined with the conquering band,
"Who are marching to Glory at Jesus' Command."

"Though round me the storms of adversity roll,
"And the waves of destruction encompass my soul!
"And in vain this frail vessel the tempest shall toss,
"My hope is secure through the Blood of the Cross."

"And when the ransomed, by Jesus, my Head,
"From Fountain to Fountain I then shall be led;
"I'll fall at His Feet, and His Mercy adore,

NOTES

"And sing Hallelujah to God evermore."

———

CHAPTER 26

(1) "THEN ALL THE PEOPLE OF JUDAH TOOK UZZIAH, WHO WAS SIXTEEN YEARS OLD, AND MADE HIM KING IN THE ROOM OF HIS FATHER AMAZIAH.

(2) "HE BUILT ELOTH, AND RESTORED IT TO JUDAH, AFTER THAT THE KING SLEPT WITH HIS FATHERS.

(3) "SIXTEEN YEARS OLD WAS UZZIAH WHEN HE BEGAN TO REIGN, AND HE REIGNED FIFTY AND TWO YEARS IN JERUSALEM. HIS MOTHER'S NAME ALSO WAS JECOLIAH OF JERUSALEM.

(4) "AND HE DID THAT WHICH WAS RIGHT IN THE SIGHT OF THE LORD, ACCORDING TO ALL THAT HIS FATHER AMAZIAH DID.

(5) "AND HE SOUGHT GOD IN THE DAYS OF ZECHARIAH, WHO HAD UNDERSTANDING IN THE VISIONS OF GOD: AND AS LONG AS HE SOUGHT THE LORD, GOD MADE HIM TO PROSPER."

The diagram is:

1. (Vs. 1) Uzziah is named Azariah in II Kings.

2. The qualifier of Verse 4 is, Uzziah started well, but ended poorly.

3. The Zechariah mentioned in Verse 5 was not the *"Zechariah,"* the son of Jehoiada, who lived some years prior. That Zechariah was murdered by Joash, Uzziah's grandfather. Neither was he the Zechariah who wrote the Book of Zechariah. All we know about this Zechariah is what is said here.

4. The last phrase of Verse 5 is phenomenal to say the least. The words, *"sought the LORD,"* mean not only to desire what God desires, but to seek His Face incessantly. This is the secret of spiritual, domestic, financial, physical, and mental victory.

"AS LONG AS HE SOUGHT THE LORD, GOD MADE HIM TO PROSPER"

The statement regarding our heading was applicable to Uzziah, but, as well, is applicable to every single Believer on the face of the Earth, irrespective of the time frame in which they lived or do live.

The phrase, *"And as long as he sought the LORD,"* means that one wants the Will of God, the Way of God, and all that pertains to God. As stated, it applies to any and all who truly love the Lord.

Any and every Believer should serve the Lord with all of his strength and all of his might. This means to be totally consecrated to the Lord at all times, desiring His Perfect Will. At the same time, such a Believer should believe the Lord to prosper him and to bless him, which means to increase that which he has and desires. In other words, we shouldn't take such prosperity for granted. The Lord expects us to believe Him, to look to Him, and to expect Him to do great and mighty things for us.

Inasmuch as the Holy Spirit brought forward the Ministry of Zechariah, we have to believe that this man had a very positive influence on Uzziah. Unfortunately, the Holy Spirit did not give us any more information than we see here in the Sacred Text. But this we do know, the prosperity of Uzziah seemed to be linked with Zechariah, at least the Word of God seems to indicate such.

What a blessing it is for a Church to have individuals such as Zechariah in its midst. What a blessing to a city, a nation, etc. In fact, our Lord likened true Believers to *"the salt of the Earth,"* which is a preservative, and *"the Light of the world,"* which is illumination (Mat. 5:13-14).

(6) "AND HE WENT FORTH AND WARRED AGAINST THE PHILISTINES, AND BROKE DOWN THE WALL OF GATH, AND THE WALL OF JABNEH, AND THE WALL OF ASHDOD, AND BUILT CITIES ABOUT ASHDOD, AND AMONG THE PHILISTINES.

(7) "AND GOD HELPED HIM AGAINST THE PHILISTINES, AND AGAINST THE ARABIANS WHO DWELT IN GUR-BAAL, AND THE MEHUNIMS.

(8) "AND THE AMMONITES GAVE GIFTS TO UZZIAH: AND HIS NAME SPREAD ABROAD EVEN TO THE ENTERING IN OF EGYPT; FOR HE STRENGTHENED HIMSELF EXCEEDINGLY."

The diagram is:

NOTES

1. (Vs. 8) It evidently was the Will of God for Uzziah to war against these particular tribes, for the Bible says, *"And God helped him. . . ."*

Uzziah was able to strengthen himself, because *"God helped him."*

2. Unfortunately, Uzziah did not remain in a positive posture as it regarded the Lord but became lifted up in himself, even as we shall see.

"HE STRENGTHENED HIMSELF EXCEEDINGLY"

We find from the Sacred Text that the kings of Judah who served the Lord were blessed exceedingly by the Lord in every capacity. Why is it that so many of them started out well but ended so poorly?

Most, even presently, cannot stand prosperity. If the Lord blesses us, we very quickly, oftentimes, think that it's our wisdom or our cleverness that brings the prosperity, and then we credit ourselves. In doing so, we quit seeking the Lord, quit looking to Him, and quit depending on Him. Why should we do so, considering that we are so intelligent? Then we lose our way.

Why do we do such?

That's a good question!

As I dictate these notes, which, incidentally, is April 9, 2008, the Lord is beginning to bless Family Worship Center and, in fact, all that we are attempting for the cause of Christ, which includes radio and television, and especially THE EXPOSITOR'S STUDY BIBLE. This is something for which we have been seeking the Lord for many years. I personally believe that what we are going to see in the future will eclipse anything and everything that we've seen in the past.

And yet, at the same time, I realize how frail and how weak the flesh actually is, which refers to the tendency to depend upon ourselves instead of the Lord. Consequently, I'm seeking His Face constantly that His Spirit stay with us on an unending basis. We must not go in the wrong direction, and we must not get ahead of the Lord or behind Him. We must be led exclusively by Him. So, my prayers are, if I show the slightest tendency to go in the wrong direction, that the Lord will use whatever measures necessary to bring me back to the rightful place. I cannot afford to miss His Will, to go in the wrong direction, or to depend on the flesh. I must have His Leading and Guidance at all times. The more He blesses, the more I need that Leading and Guidance, the more I need His Presence, and the more I need His Spirit. I haven't learned much in the last few years, but I've learned enough to know that whatever has to be done, I must have the Leading and Guidance of the Holy Spirit, and in totality, to accomplish the task.

I believe the Lord is going to help us to see a tremendous Harvest of souls! I believe we're going to see many baptized with the Holy Spirit! I believe we're going to see many healed and many delivered by the Power of God.

THE MESSAGE OF THE CROSS

The Lord has given to us an understanding of His Redemption Plan, in other words, the meaning of the New Covenant. It's not something new but actually that which has already been given to the Apostle Paul and, no doubt, to many others down through the centuries. However, the Message of the Cross, which is the meaning of the New Covenant, is brand-new to the modern church because it has veered so far off course. The church must come back to the Cross. We must ever understand that the water, which was a Type of the Holy Spirit, did not come forth from the rock, which Rock was Christ, until that rock was smitten, which was a type of the Cross of Calvary (Ex. 17:1-7).

It has not changed from then until now. The Holy Spirit will not function, will not work, and will not do that which He Alone can do until our Faith is placed exclusively in the Cross of Christ, and the Cross of Christ Alone! This is the way and the manner in which the Holy Spirit works. And to be sure, He will not function in any other capacity. It is the Cross and what Jesus there did which gives the Spirit the legal means to do all the things which He is able to do. And to be sure, whatever it is we need from the Lord, the Holy Spirit Alone can accomplish the task.

The modern church does not have, as a whole, the help of the Spirit. It is because the church is looking to its own wisdom, thereby, excluding the Work and Ministry of the Holy Spirit. To be sure, and as stated, the Spirit will not function and will not work until our Faith has as its correct Object the Cross of Christ (Rom. 8:1-2, 11; I Cor. 1:17-18, 23; 2:2; Gal., Chpt. 5, 6:14; Eph. 2:13-18; Col. 2:14-15).

The strength of Uzziah was not in the military expertise, which he thought he had, but was rather in the Lord. Uzziah ultimately forgot that!

(9) "MOREOVER UZZIAH BUILT TOWERS IN JERUSALEM AT THE CORNER GATE, AND AT THE VALLEY GATE, AND AT THE TURNING OF THE WALL, AND FORTIFIED THEM.

(10) "ALSO HE BUILT TOWERS IN THE DESERT, AND DUG MANY WELLS: FOR HE HAD MUCH CATTLE, BOTH IN THE LOW COUNTRY, AND IN THE PLAINS: HUSBANDMEN ALSO, AND VINE DRESSERS IN THE MOUNTAINS, AND IN CARMEL: FOR HE LOVED HUSBANDRY.

(11) "MOREOVER UZZIAH HAD AN HOST OF FIGHTING MEN, WHO WENT OUT TO WAR BY BANDS, ACCORDING TO THE NUMBER OF THEIR ACCOUNT BY THE HAND OF JEIEL THE SCRIBE AND MAASEIAH THE RULER, UNDER THE HAND OF HANANIAH, ONE OF THE KING'S CAPTAINS.

(12) "THE WHOLE NUMBER OF THE CHIEF OF THE FATHERS OF THE MIGHTY MEN OF VALOUR WERE TWO THOUSAND AND SIX HUNDRED.

(13) "AND UNDER THEIR HAND WAS AN ARMY, THREE HUNDRED THOUSAND AND SEVEN THOUSAND AND FIVE HUNDRED, WHO MADE WAR WITH MIGHTY POWER, TO HELP THE KING AGAINST THE ENEMY.

(14) "AND UZZIAH PREPARED FOR THEM THROUGHOUT ALL THE HOST SHIELDS, AND SPEARS, AND HELMETS, AND HABERGEONS, AND BOWS, AND SLINGS TO CAST STONES.

(15) "AND HE MADE IN JERUSALEM ENGINES, INVENTED BY CUNNING MEN, TO BE ON THE TOWERS AND UPON THE BULWARKS, TO SHOOT ARROWS AND GREAT STONES WITHAL. AND HIS

NAME SPREAD FAR ABROAD; FOR HE WAS MARVELOUSLY HELPED, TILL HE WAS STRONG."

The composition is:

1. As the Sacred Text bears out, Uzziah ". . . *was marvelously helped, till he was strong."*

2. (Vs. 15) This means that God prospered him so greatly that the people marveled; however, when he became strong, he entered into the zone of extreme danger.

3. Once again let us state, Uzziah's strength was not in all of these things which the Text tells us that he did but rather was a result of his strength with God. All of this that was good came from the Lord, and the Lord exclusively!

MARVELOUS HELP

What Blessings Uzziah experienced! What prosperity came his way! How strong he became! In fact, he became so strong until his name spelled power throughout all the heathen nations which surrounded Judah. It was all because of the Blessings of God. It was the Lord Who helped him, Who strengthened him, Who prospered him, and Who gave him increase, which the Lord will always do for those who place their Faith and trust in Him.

WILL THE LORD BLESS UNDER THE NEW COVENANT AS HE BLESSED UNDER THE OLD COVENANT?

He will bless even more!

Paul plainly said, as it regards the Old Covenant and the New Covenant, and I quote from THE EXPOSITOR'S STUDY BIBLE: *"But now* (since the Cross) *has He* (the Lord Jesus) *obtained a more excellent Ministry* (the New Covenant in Jesus' Blood is superior, and takes the place of the Old Covenant in animal blood), *but how much also He is the Mediator of a Better Covenant* (proclaims the fact that Christ officiates between God and man according to the arrangements of the New Covenant), *which was established upon better Promises.* (This presents the New Covenant, explicitly based on the cleansing and forgiveness of all sin, which the Old Covenant could not do.)

"For if that First Covenant had been faultless (proclaims the fact that the First Covenant was definitely not faultless; as stated, it was based on animal blood, which was vastly inferior to the Precious Blood of Christ), *then should no place have been sought for the Second* (proclaims the necessity of the New Covenant)" (Heb. 8:6-7).

Our problem presently is, *"we have not, because we ask not."* Or if we do ask, we receive not at times because *"we ask amiss, that we may consume it upon our lusts"* (James 4:2-3).

Under the New Covenant we have opportunity for much greater Blessings than ever were given under the Old Covenant. We must understand this and believe this because it is true.

My grandmother taught me as a child, *"Jimmy, God is a big God, so ask big!"* I have never forgotten that, and it has helped me to touch this world for Christ.

(16) "BUT WHEN HE WAS STRONG, HIS HEART WAS LIFTED UP TO HIS DESTRUCTION: FOR HE TRANSGRESSED AGAINST THE LORD HIS GOD, AND WENT INTO THE TEMPLE OF THE LORD TO BURN INCENSE UPON THE ALTAR OF INCENSE.

(17) "AND AZARIAH THE PRIEST WENT IN AFTER HIM, AND WITH HIM FOURSCORE PRIESTS OF THE LORD, WHO WERE VALIANT MEN:

(18) "AND THEY WITHSTOOD UZZIAH THE KING, AND SAID UNTO HIM, IT APPERTAINS NOT UNTO YOU, UZZIAH, TO BURN INCENSE UNTO THE LORD, BUT TO THE PRIESTS THE SONS OF AARON, WHO ARE CONSECRATED TO BURN INCENSE: GO OUT OF THE SANCTUARY; FOR YOU HAVE TRESPASSED; NEITHER SHALL IT BE FOR YOUR HONOUR FROM THE LORD GOD.

(19) "THEN UZZIAH WAS WROTH, AND HAD A CENSER IN HIS HAND TO BURN INCENSE: AND WHILE HE WAS WROTH WITH THE PRIESTS, THE LEPROSY EVEN ROSE UP IN HIS FOREHEAD BEFORE THE PRIESTS IN THE HOUSE OF THE LORD, FROM BESIDE THE INCENSE ALTAR.

(20) "AND AZARIAH THE CHIEF PRIEST, AND ALL THE PRIESTS,

LOOKED UPON HIM, AND, BEHOLD, HE WAS LEPROUS IN HIS FOREHEAD, AND THEY THRUST HIM OUT FROM THENCE; YES, HIMSELF HASTED ALSO TO GO OUT, BECAUSE THE LORD HAD SMITTEN HIM.

(21) "AND UZZIAH THE KING WAS A LEPER UNTO THE DAY OF HIS DEATH, AND DWELT IN A SEVERAL HOUSE, BEING A LEPER; FOR HE WAS CUT OFF FROM THE HOUSE OF THE LORD: AND JOTHAM HIS SON WAS OVER THE KING'S HOUSE, JUDGING THE PEOPLE OF THE LAND."

The exegesis is:

1. (Vs. 16) The transgression of Uzziah was far more serious than we realize. For him to attempt to burn incense upon the Altar of Incense proclaims the fact that he, in essence, was saying that he did not need a Saviour. The Priest, who alone could offer Incense, stood as a Type of Christ, as a mediator between God and man.

2. (Vs. 16) As well, the sin of the modern church is the sin of ignoring, or else outright denying, the Cross. Christ must be worshipped as the Saviour, and He is the Saviour through the Cross (I Cor. 1:17-18, 23; 2:2). If Jesus is worshipped or sought after in any other manner, He becomes *"another Jesus,"* which God can never accept (II Cor. 11:4; Ex. 25:6; 30:1, 7-8, 34, 37-38; Lev. 16:13).

3. (Vs. 19) Because he attempted to worship God without the intervention of an ongoing Saviour, the Lord smote him with leprosy.

On the forehead of the High Priest was a golden plate with the words, *"Holiness to the Lord"*; on the forehead of Uzziah was *"sinfulness"* (leprosy). We must ever remember that Christ is the Source of all things, as it pertains to the Believer, and the Cross is the Means by which all of these things come to us. If we attempt to obtain anything from the Lord by means other than the Cross, we have, in effect, like Uzziah, claimed to be our own saviour.

4. (Vs. 20) To be frank, Uzziah was afraid that the Lord would kill him and, but for the Mercy of God, this is exactly what would have happened.

The leprosy started in his forehead, because, as stated, this was where the golden plate was worn by the High Priest, stipulating Holiness. Only Christ fits that designation. Man is holy only as he trusts Christ and what Christ did at the Cross. Upon proper trust in Christ, Righteousness and Holiness are instantly imputed to the individual. Otherwise, there is no Holiness!

THE LIFTED UP HEART

As pride lifted up Amaziah, the father of Uzziah, likewise, pride was the sin of this king. The blessings and prosperity, he thought, were the result of his own ingenuity and sagacity.

What possessed this man to think that he could go into the Temple and burn Incense upon the Altar of Incense is beyond comprehension? What did he think he was doing? Did he not know the Law? Or did he know the Law, but ignored the Law?

All of this, as he was to find out, had tremendous spiritual implications.

The Priests were Types of Christ. This meant that they alone could burn Incense upon the Altar of Incense.

The Altar of Incense represented the Intercession of Christ, all on our behalf. Every morning at 9 a.m., and every afternoon at 3 p.m., the Priests would take coals of fire from the Brazen Altar. This Altar typified the Cross of Calvary, with the fire typifying the Judgment of God. They would place the coals upon the Altar of Incense and then pour Incense over the coals, which would fill the Holy Place with smoke and a pleasant aroma, all typifying, as stated, the Intercession of Christ, all on our behalf.

As it should be understood, Christ Alone is the Mediator between God and men, which means that Uzziah, by his actions, in effect, was stating that he did not need a Mediator.

THE LEPROSY

As Uzziah tried to force his way to the Altar of Incense, despite the Priests admonishing him otherwise, all of a sudden, the Scripture says, *". . . the leprosy even rose up in his forehead."*

As previously stated, the High Priest had a golden plate around his forehead, which stated *"Holiness unto the Lord."* This signified the Holiness of Christ, Who Alone is Holy.

The leprosy coming up in the forehead of Uzziah was, in effect, the Lord stating to the king that he was a sinful man, typified by the leprosy. There was no way that he could offer up Incense. In fact, he was very, very fortunate to escape with his life. He feared that he would be smitten dead, and had it not been for the Mercy of God, this is exactly what would have happened.

THE FEAR OF GOD

In effect, Uzziah was stating, whether he realized it or not, that he did not need a Saviour, meaning that he did not need the Cross, and meaning that he could serve as his own saviour. Unfortunately, most of the world falls into this same category.

But Uzziah was different from most of the world. He was the king of Judah, God's Chosen People, and should have known better, as it regards all of these things. As stated, he was fortunate to have escaped with his life, even though the leprosy clung to him.

I have to wonder as to how much different the modern church is than Uzziah, considering that the Cross is given little shift, if any at all!

The only thing standing between mankind and eternal Hell is the Cross of Christ.

The only thing standing between the Church and total apostasy is the Cross of Christ!

But the Cross has been abandoned by the modern church in favor of humanistic psychology. And please understand, without the Cross of Christ, the leprosy is abundant!

(22) "NOW THE REST OF THE ACTS OF UZZIAH, FIRST AND LAST, DID ISAIAH THE PROPHET, THE SON OF AMOZ, WRITE.

(23) "SO UZZIAH SLEPT WITH HIS FATHERS, AND THEY BURIED HIM WITH HIS FATHERS IN THE FIELD OF THE BURIAL WHICH BELONGED TO THE KINGS; FOR THEY SAID, HE IS A LEPER: AND JOTHAM HIS SON REIGNED IN HIS STEAD."

The construction is:

1. (Vs. 22) Isaiah the Prophet asserts that his prophetic inspiration was during the time of Uzziah (Isa. 1:1, 6:1).

2. (Vs. 23) Hopefully Uzziah repented, but there is no evidence that he did.

3. (Vs. 23) The last thing the Holy Spirit said about him was, *"He is a leper"*—not *"was,"* but rather *"is."*

HE IS A LEPER

He began so wondrously and ended so poorly!

Considering, as stated, that the last thing said about this man by the Holy Spirit was, *"He is a leper,"* does not speak well of his closing days. As we also stated, it is hoped that he repented, but there is no proof that he did, and some small proof that he didn't.

The Scripture says, *". . . for he was cut off from the House of the LORD"* (Vs. 21). Of course, being a leper was the cause of his isolation.

Maybe he repented, and the Lord thought it necessary that the leprosy remain. But the Holy Spirit doesn't say that, but rather insinuates otherwise.

What a shame!

"O Breath of Life, come sweeping through us,
"Revive Your Church with life and power,
"O Breath of Life, come, cleanse, renew us,
"And fit Your Church to meet this hour."

"O Wind of God, come bind us, break us,
"Till humbly we confess our needs;
"Then in Your Tenderness remake us,
"Revive, restore, for this we plead."

"O Breath of Love, come breathe within us,
"Renewing thought and will and heart;
"Come, Love of Christ, afresh to win us,
"Revive Your Church in every part."

"O Heart of Christ, once broken for us,
"'Tis there we find our strength and rest;
"Our broken contrite hearts now solace,
"And let Your waiting Church be blessed."

"Revive us, Lord! Is zeal abating,
"While harvest fields are vast and white?
"Revive us, Lord, the world is waiting,
"Equip Your Church to spread the Light."

CHAPTER 27

(1) "JOTHAM WAS TWENTY AND FIVE YEARS OLD WHEN HE BEGAN TO REIGN, AND HE REIGNED SIXTEEN YEARS IN JERUSALEM. HIS MOTHER'S NAME ALSO WAS JERUSHAH, THE DAUGHTER OF ZADOK.

(2) "AND HE DID THAT WHICH WAS RIGHT IN THE SIGHT OF THE LORD, ACCORDING TO ALL THAT HIS FATHER UZZIAH DID: HOWBEIT HE ENTERED NOT INTO THE TEMPLE OF THE LORD. AND THE PEOPLE DID YET CORRUPTLY.

(3) "HE BUILT THE HIGH GATE OF THE HOUSE OF THE LORD, AND ON THE WALL OF OPHEL HE BUILT MUCH.

(4) "MOREOVER HE BUILT CITIES IN THE MOUNTAINS OF JUDAH, AND IN THE FORESTS HE BUILT CASTLES AND TOWERS."

The construction is:

1. (Vs. 2) The phrase, *"And he did that which was right in the sight of the LORD, according to all that his father Uzziah did,"* actually refers to the first ways of his father.

2. (Vs. 2) The meaning of the phrase, *"He entered not into the Temple of the LORD,"* probably refers to the fact that, terrified by the fate of his father, he did not associate with the Temple at all. If this is so, then Uzziah, Jotham, and Ahaz illustrate how incurably diseased is the natural heart.

• The first king boldly intrudes into the Temple.

• The second timidly stands away from it.

• The third shuts it up.

3. (Vs. 2) The short phrase, *"And the people did yet corruptly,"* means that they continued to worship idols.

4. (Vs. 4) If, instead of building all the things it says that Jotham built, he had broken down the high places at which the people did corruptly, quite possibly it would have brought revival to Judah. Regrettably, there has never been a perfect man. All, even when diligently trying to follow the Lord, are, it seems, freighted with failure. It is the Grace of God which gives us the victory, not our perfection.

"HE DID THAT WHICH WAS RIGHT IN THE SIGHT OF THE LORD"

It is the Holy Spirit through the sacred writer Who made the statement that the king *"did right in the sight of the LORD."* What a noble thing to be said about anyone, and especially if said by the Holy Spirit.

And yet, even as the Scripture bears out, Jotham was not perfect, not at all!

• His failure to enter the Temple for worship probably pertained to his fear because of what had happened to his father. If, in fact, this is the case, this means that he did not participate at all in the various Feasts during the year, such as Passover, etc. The failure to Worship the Lord in this capacity would have been very detrimental to him.

While it is true that his father contracted leprosy, and did so instantly, upon his intrusion into the very domain of Christ, still, it did not follow that the same thing would happen again, or something similar, to Jotham. In the face of something of this nature, the answer is not a withdrawal, but rather the opposite, of drawing closer to the Lord. So, Jotham missed out on very much by him taking the position that he did.

• The Scripture says, *"The people did yet corruptly,"* with the implication being that even though he was trying to do right, he seemed to have precious little influence on the people. It appears that he did not take a stand, which he should have done, against their idol-worship.

When we read these accounts in the Bible, we have to understand that our knowledge still is very limited. But yet, the manner and the way in which the Holy Spirit phrases the words lets us know what is right and what is wrong. For instance, it was not right for Jotham to neglect Temple worship, and neither was it right for him to not take a bold stand against the corruption of the people as it regarded their idol-worship. The Holy

Spirit didn't say much, but what little He did say lets us know, and unequivocally so, the Mind of the Lord.

It seems that Jotham felt that his construction of cities in the mountains of Judah, and the building of castles and towers in the forests, and above all, the repairs of *"the high gate of the House of the LORD,"* etc., made up for his lack in other ways.

It didn't!

Judah would have fared much better had Jotham set the example regarding Temple worship, and had he taken a bold stand against idol-worship. This is what the Holy Spirit wanted. The other things were merely window dressing and did not really help Judah in a Spiritual sense.

(5) "HE FOUGHT ALSO WITH THE KING OF THE AMMONITES, AND PREVAILED AGAINST THEM. AND THE CHILDREN OF AMMON GAVE HIM THE SAME YEAR AN HUNDRED TALENTS OF SILVER, AND TEN THOUSAND MEASURES OF WHEAT, AND TEN THOUSAND OF BARLEY. SO MUCH DID THE CHILDREN OF AMMON PAY UNTO HIM, BOTH THE SECOND YEAR, AND THE THIRD.

(6) "SO JOTHAM BECAME MIGHTY, BECAUSE HE PREPARED HIS WAYS BEFORE THE LORD HIS GOD."

The exegesis is:

1. Because of Jotham following the Lord, he prevailed against the Ammonites. Until we defeat the enemies within, we cannot defeat the enemies without.

2. Now, instead of Judah paying tribute to these heathen nations, the Ammonites were paying tribute to Judah. The Devil is to serve us; we are not to serve him.

3. (Vs. 6) The Holy Spirit said of Jotham, *"So Jotham became mighty, because he prepared his ways before the LORD his God."* What a beautiful statement!

"HE PREPARED HIS WAYS BEFORE THE LORD HIS GOD"

The Text means that Jotham worked diligently in his effort to obey the Lord. In other words, he took nothing for granted, but the indication is that he ardently sought the Lord. The words *"prepared his ways"* signify that.

NOTES

The idea seems to be that the king searched out the Scriptures in order that he might obey them. While very little is given to us about this man's reign, still, what little is given speaks so very highly of Jotham.

In this, we might possibly come to the conclusion that even though his father Uzziah suffered terribly, as it regarded the leprosy in the closing years of his life, still, his son turning out as he did for the good does lend credence to the idea that Uzziah repented at the last and tried to make up for what he did by training his son in the way that he ought to go. There is no Scriptural guarantee that this happened, but there is some small indication that it did. One would certainly hope so!

The last thing said by the Holy Spirit concerning Uzziah was, *"He was a leper,"* with no mention made by the Holy Spirit of Repentance. What Uzziah did was very, very wrong. As we have previously stated, it was only by the Mercy and Grace of God that he wasn't stricken dead on the spot. And yet, the Lord most definitely would have forgiven him had he truly repented.

At the same time, he could have truly repented, with the Holy Spirit allowing the leprosy to remain because of the gravity of his sin. As we've already stated, we pray this was the case.

Uzziah would have been immensely proud of his son, Jotham. While we are given precious little information concerning this man, still, what little is given is, for the most part, very positive. Of how many can it be said, *". . . he prepared his ways before the LORD his God?"*

(7) "NOW THE REST OF THE ACTS OF JOTHAM, AND ALL HIS WARS, AND HIS WAYS, LO, THEY ARE WRITTEN IN THE BOOK OF THE KINGS OF ISRAEL AND JUDAH.

(8) "HE WAS FIVE AND TWENTY YEARS OLD WHEN HE BEGAN TO REIGN, AND REIGNED SIXTEEN YEARS IN JERUSALEM.

(9) "AND JOTHAM SLEPT WITH HIS FATHERS, AND THEY BURIED HIM IN THE CITY OF DAVID: AND AHAZ HIS SON REIGNED IN HIS STEAD."

The pattern is:

1. (Vs. 8) Evidently, Jotham was forty-one when he died.

2. The Lord evidently cut his life short for a reason. Irrespective, the evidence is that he made the most of the years that God gave him.

3. Sadly, and as we shall see, Ahaz, his son, did not follow in the train of his father.

"A Lamp in the night, a song in time of sorrow,
"A great glad Hope which Faith can ever borrow,
"To guild the passing day with the glory of the morrow,
"Is the hope of the coming of the Lord."

"A Star in the sky, a Beacon bright to guide us;
"An Anchor sure to hold in storms betide us;
"A Refuge for the soul, where in quiet we may hide us,
"Is the hope of the coming of the Lord."

"A Call of command, like trumpet clearly sounding,
"To make us bold when evil is surrounding;
"To stir the sluggish heart, and to keep in good abounding,
"Is the hope of the coming of the Lord."

"A Word from the One to all our hearts the dearest,
"A parting word to make Him aye the nearest;
"Of all His precious Words, the sweetest, brightest, clearest,
"Is the hope of the coming of the Lord."

CHAPTER 28

(1) "AHAZ WAS TWENTY YEARS OLD WHEN HE BEGAN TO REIGN, AND HE REIGNED SIXTEEN YEARS IN JERUSALEM: BUT HE DID NOT THAT WHICH WAS RIGHT IN THE SIGHT OF THE LORD, LIKE DAVID HIS FATHER:

(2) "FOR HE WALKED IN THE WAYS OF THE KINGS OF ISRAEL, AND MADE ALSO MOLTEN IMAGES FOR BAALIM.

(3) "MOREOVER HE BURNT INCENSE IN THE VALLEY OF THE SON OF HINNOM, AND BURNT HIS CHILDREN IN THE FIRE, AFTER THE ABOMINATIONS OF THE HEATHEN WHOM THE LORD HAD CAST OUT BEFORE THE CHILDREN OF ISRAEL.

(4) "HE SACRIFICED ALSO AND BURNT INCENSE IN THE HIGH PLACES, AND ON THE HILLS, AND UNDER EVERY GREEN TREE."

The diagram is:

1. (Vs. 1) Ahaz was one of the most ungodly kings who ever ruled over Judah.

2. (Vs. 2) Worshipping Baalim was the characteristic sin of Israel, but Judah had not previously been guilty of making molten images during the recent past. This takes idolatry to a new level.

3. (Vs. 3) The short phrase, *"And burnt his children in the fire,"* refers to the sacrifice of little children to the heathen Moloch.

4. (Vs. 3) The intimation is, if Judah continued in this particular fashion, they would be cast out exactly as the heathen of old. In fact, that's exactly what ultimately happened!

5. (Vs. 4) The idea of all of this is, Ahaz engaged in idolatry to the hilt.

IDOLATRY

Concerning this terrible sin of idolatry, the Scripture says of Ahaz the following:

• *"For he walked in the ways of the kings of Israel"*;
• *"And made also molten images for Baalim"*;
• *"He burnt incense in the valley of the son of Hinnom"*;
• *"Burnt his children in the fire"* to Molech, which was human sacrifice; and,
• *"He sacrificed also and burnt incense in the high places, and on the hills, and under every green tree".*

The special enticements of idolatry, as entered into by the heathen nations and finally by Israel and Judah, consisted of any number of things. The primary appeal was that which was sexual, even as it involved temple prostitutes dedicated to the particular god in question. Baal and Astarte worship was closely associated with fornication and drunkenness (Amos 2:7-8; I Ki. 14:23). It also appealed greatly to magic and soothsaying (Isa. 2:6; 3:2; 8:19).

Sacrifices to idols were offered by fire with libations being poured out, along with tithes being presented. At times, tables of food were set before these idols with worshippers kissing the idols and throwing them kisses. They also stretched out their hands in adoration, and some knelt or prostrated themselves before the idols and, at times, danced about the altars, gashing themselves with knives.

MOLECH

As the national god of the Ammonites, Molech was sometimes known as *"Milcom,"* or *"Malcam."*

In the Levitical Ordinances delivered to the Israelites by Moses, there are stern prohibitions of Molech-worship (Lev. 18:21; 20:2-5). Parallel to these prohibitions, although the name of the god is not mentioned, are those of the Deuteronomic Code, where the abominations of the Canaanites are forbidden, and the burning of their sons and daughters in the fire to Molech is condemned as the climax of their wickedness (Deut. 12:31; 18:10-13).

Solomon, under the influence of his idolatrous wives, built high places for Chemosh, the abomination of Moab, and for Molech, the abomination of the children of Ammon. Because of this apostasy, it was intimated by the Prophet Ahijah that the kingdom was to be rent out of the hand of Solomon and ten tribes given to Jeroboam (I Ki. 11:31-33).

These high places, where this god was worshipped, survived to the time of Josiah, who, among his other works of religious reformation, destroyed and defiled them, filling their places with the bones of men (II Ki. 23:12-14). Molech-worship evidently received a great impulse from Ahaz, who, like Ahab of Israel, was a supporter of foreign religions (II Ki. 16:12). He also *"made his son to pass through the fire, according to the abominations of the nations, whom*

NOTES

Jehovah cast out from before the Children of Israel" (II Ki. 16:3).

His grandson, Manasseh, so far from following in the footsteps of Hezekiah, who had made great reforms in the worship, reared altars for Baal, and besides other abominations which he practiced, *"made his son to pass through the fire,"* i.e., *"sacrificed him"* (II Ki. 21:6).

The chief site of this worship, of which Ahaz and Manasseh were the promoters, was Tophet in the Valley of Hinnom, or as it is also called, *"the valley of the children,"* or where children were sacrificed to this heathen god. Of Josiah's reformation, it is said that *"he defiled Topheth . . . that no man might make his son or his daughter to pass through the fire to Molech"* (II Ki. 23:10).

Even Josiah's thorough reformation, however, failed to extirpate the Molech-worship, and it revived and continued till the destruction of Jerusalem, as we learn from the Prophets of the time. From the beginning, the true Prophets of God maintained against it a loud and persistent protest. Isaiah was acquainted with Tophet and its abominations (Isa. 30:33; 57:5). Over against his beautiful and lofty description of that which was truly of God, the Prophet Micah sets the exaggerated zeal of those who ask in the spirit of the Molech-worshipper, *". . . Shall I give my firstborn for my transgression, the fruit of my body for the sin of my soul?"* (Mic. 6:7). That Molech-worship had increased in the interval may account for the frequency and the clearness of the references to it in the later Prophets.

In Jeremiah we find the passing of sons and daughters through the fire to Molech associated with the building of *"the high places of Baal, which are in the valley of the son of Hinnom"* (Jer. 32:35; 7:31; 19:5). In his oracle against the children of Ammon, the same Prophet, denouncing evil against their land, predicts, almost in the very words of Amos above, that Molech shall go into captivity, his priests and his princes together (Jer. 49:1-3).

Ezekiel, speaking to the exiles in Babylon, refers to the practice of causing children to pass through the fire to heathen divinities as long established, and proclaims the Wrath of God against it (Ezek. 16:20; 20:26-31; 23:37).

Zephaniah, who prophesied to the men who saw the overthrow of the kingdom of Judah, denounces God's Judgments upon the worshippers of false gods (Zeph. 1:5).

The captivity in Babylon put an end to Molech-worship, since it weaned the people from all their idolatries.

THE MANNER OF THE SACRIFICE

The image of Molech was a human figure with a bull's head and outstretched arms, ready to receive the children destined for sacrifice. The image of metal was heated red hot by a fire kindled within, and the children were laid on its arms, and they then rolled off into the fiery pit below. In order to drown the cries of the victims, flutes were played, and drums were beaten by black-robed priests; and mothers stood by, without tears or sobs, to give the impression of the voluntary character of the offering.

Without God, the depths to which men will sink defy all description. In fact, the only reason that modern humanity has not destroyed itself is because of the influence of the Bible in the world and what Jesus did at Calvary's Cross.

(5) "WHEREFORE THE LORD HIS GOD DELIVERED HIM INTO THE HAND OF THE KING OF SYRIA; AND THEY SMOTE HIM, AND CARRIED AWAY A GREAT MULTITUDE OF THEM CAPTIVES, AND BROUGHT THEM TO DAMASCUS. AND HE WAS ALSO DELIVERED INTO THE HAND OF THE KING OF ISRAEL, WHO SMOTE HIM WITH A GREAT SLAUGHTER.

(6) "FOR PEKAH THE SON OF REMALIAH KILLED IN JUDAH AN HUNDRED AND TWENTY THOUSAND IN ONE DAY, WHICH WERE ALL VALIANT MEN; BECAUSE THEY HAD FORSAKEN THE LORD GOD OF THEIR FATHERS.

(7) "AND ZICHRI, A MIGHTY MAN OF EPHRAIM, KILLED MAASEIAH THE KING'S SON, AND AZRIKAM THE GOVERNOR OF THE HOUSE, AND ELKANAH WHO WAS NEXT TO THE KING.

(8) "AND THE CHILDREN OF ISRAEL CARRIED AWAY CAPTIVE OF THEIR BRETHREN TWO HUNDRED THOUSAND, WOMEN, SONS, AND DAUGHTERS, AND TOOK ALSO AWAY MUCH SPOIL FROM THEM, AND BROUGHT THE SPOIL TO SAMARIA."

The exegesis is:

1. (Vs. 5) Because of Ahaz's idol-worship, *"the LORD . . . delivered him into the hand of the king of Syria. . . ."* If it is to be understood, it is obvious here that the Lord controls all things. He can bless or He can curse, all because of obedience or disobedience.

2. Judah suffered terribly so at the hands of the Syrians at this time, as well as at the hands of Israel. The king of Israel slaughtered 120,000 of the men of Judah in one day.

3. (Vs. 6) All of this was *". . . because they had forsaken the LORD God of their fathers."*

"HAD FORSAKEN THE LORD GOD OF THEIR FATHERS"

Judah could not expect the Lord to help them, considering they had gone so deep into sin, but it seems they did not realize their plight. It seems they did not even understand the cause and the reason for their terrible defeat by the Syrians and the great slaughter which followed. Concerning Judah, the spiritual condition of such people, who have once known God but have turned their backs on Him, pushes such to deeper depths of evil than anyone else. Concerning this, our Lord said, *"But if your eye be evil, your whole body shall be full of darkness"* (if the spirit be evil, the entirety of the soul will be full of darkness). *If therefore the light that is in you be darkness* (the light is not acted upon, but rather perverted), *how great is that darkness* (the latter state is worse than if there had been no light at all)!" (Mat. 6:23).

So, Judah would go deeper into sin than even the heathen which surrounded her.

LIGHT TURNED TO DARKNESS

In the Twentieth Century, the Pentecostal Denominations touched this world for Christ. The Mission's activities, by the Leading and Guidance of the Holy Spirit, were miraculous, to say the least. I had the privilege, as well, to be a part of it.

It was all because of the Leading, the Guidance, and the Empowerment of the Holy Spirit.

At approximately the turn of the Twenty-first Century, however, these Pentecostal Denominations began to lose their way. It had not happened overnight. In fact, it began in the late 1950's and the early 1960's.

At approximately that time, these denominations began to embrace humanistic psychology. When this happened, the Cross was abandoned. As mentioned, it took place over a period of time with, little by little, humanistic psychology gaining the ascendancy, with the Cross, little by little, being phased out.

Presently, even as the little leaven leavens the whole lump, there is very little left of the Message of the Cross in modern Pentecostal circles, with almost all of its efforts being taken over by humanistic psychology. Please note carefully the following:

• The only thing standing between mankind and eternal Hell is the Cross of Christ.

• The only thing standing between the Church and total apostasy is the Cross of Christ.

Unfortunately, the world will not embrace the Cross of Christ, and most of the world, sadly and regrettably, has gone, or is going, to Hell.

Sadder still, the church, which is supposed to be under Christ, the Light of the world, has abandoned the Cross and has now become a depository for the wisdom of this world, which is earthly, sensual, and devilish (James 3:15-18).

Regrettably and sadly, I predict that these particular denominations, at least in America and Canada, will go to deeper depths of depravity than any of their nominal counterparts. The headlong plunge has already begun and will do nothing but accelerate.

The only answer, as it has always been the only answer, is that the church returns to the Cross. There is no other way.

Sin brings the Judgment of God, and the only thing that will stop that Judgment is the Cross of Christ and Faith evidenced in that Finished Work (Rom. 6:1-14).

NOTES

(9) "BUT A PROPHET OF THE LORD WAS THERE, WHOSE NAME WAS ODED: AND HE WENT OUT BEFORE THE HOST WHO CAME TO SAMARIA, AND SAID UNTO THEM, BEHOLD, BECAUSE THE LORD GOD OF YOUR FATHERS WAS WROTH WITH JUDAH, HE HAS DELIVERED THEM INTO YOUR HAND, AND YOU HAVE KILLED THEM IN A RAGE THAT REACHES UP UNTO HEAVEN.

(10) "AND NOW YOU PURPOSE TO KEEP UNDER THE CHILDREN OF JUDAH AND JERUSALEM FOR BONDMEN AND BONDWOMEN UNTO YOU: BUT ARE THERE NOT WITH YOU, EVEN WITH YOU, SINS AGAINST THE LORD YOUR GOD?

(11) "NOW HEAR ME THEREFORE, AND DELIVER THE CAPTIVES AGAIN, WHICH YOU HAVE TAKEN CAPTIVE OF YOUR BRETHREN: FOR THE FIERCE WRATH OF THE LORD IS UPON YOU.

(12) "THEN CERTAIN OF THE HEADS OF THE CHILDREN OF EPHRAIM, AZARIAH THE SON OF JOHANAN, BERECHIAH THE SON OF MESHILLEMOTH, AND JEHIZKIAH THE SON OF SHALLUM, AND AMASA THE SON OF HADLAI, STOOD UP AGAINST THEM WHO CAME FROM THE WAR,

(13) "AND SAID UNTO THEM, YOU SHALL NOT BRING IN THE CAPTIVES HITHER: FOR WHEREAS WE HAVE OFFENDED AGAINST THE LORD ALREADY, YOU INTEND TO ADD MORE TO OUR SINS AND TO OUR TRESPASS: FOR OUR TRESPASS IS GREAT, AND THERE IS FIERCE WRATH AGAINST ISRAEL.

(14) "SO THE ARMED MEN LEFT THE CAPTIVES AND THE SPOIL BEFORE THE PRINCES AND ALL THE CONGREGATION.

(15) "AND THE MEN WHICH WERE EXPRESSED BY NAME ROSE UP, AND TOOK THE CAPTIVES, AND WITH THE SPOIL CLOTHED ALL WHO WERE NAKED AMONG THEM, AND ARRAYED THEM, AND SHOD THEM, AND GAVE THEM TO EAT AND TO DRINK, AND ANOINTED THEM, AND CARRIED ALL THE FEEBLE OF THEM UPON ASSES, AND BROUGHT THEM TO JERICHO, THE CITY OF PALM TREES, TO THEIR

BRETHREN: THEN THEY RETURNED TO SAMARIA."

The composition is:

1. The particular language in which Verse 9 is set forth proclaims the inference of what Israel had done and was about to do to Judah as an abomination in God's Sight.

2. While the Lord will use certain things as a system of chastisement, woe be unto the one who carries that chastisement too far.

3. (Vs. 11) The Prophet Oded, in essence, said, *"The LORD is going to do to you what you have done to Judah, if you do not quickly make amends."*

4. (Vs. 13) For once, it seems that somebody heeded the Prophet of God!

THE PROPHET OF THE LORD

The northern confederation of Israel boasted some of the greatest Prophets of the Old Testament. Even though they did not have a single godly king, they did have some great Prophets, with Elijah and Elisha being but two. The Prophet "Oded" is mentioned only here. Another Oded, who was a Prophet, was mentioned in II Chronicles 15:1, 8; however, this particular Oded lived over 200 years before the Prophet of our present Text. So, whatever is known of the Prophet Oded, as it refers to Samaria at the time of Ahaz, is given to us only here.

Under the Old Covenant, the nations of both Judah and Israel were spiritually led by Prophets, and, of course, we speak of true Prophets. In fact, there was always an abundance of false prophets. Sometimes the Message of the true Prophet was welcome, even as it was here, but most of the time, it wasn't.

The modern Church is led by Apostles. While the Prophet retains his office as under the Old Covenant, the only change is his leadership.

An Apostle is known by the Message which God has given him. In other words, the Holy Spirit, knowing the need of the Church, will give a particular Apostle, or even several Apostles, the Message needed by the Church. While other Preachers may preach the same Message, the Apostle will do so with a greater strength and power.

NOTES

Apostles are not appointed by other men and, in fact, cannot be appointed. They are all Called by God and given their place and position strictly by the Holy Spirit.

There were no Apostles in the Old Testament, with that particular Office being reserved solely for the time of the New Covenant, and with the office actually having begun during the Ministry of Christ, which was, in fact, still the Old Covenant.

THE MESSAGE

As is obvious from the Text, Israel had won a tremendous victory over Judah in battle. In fact, they had slaughtered 120,000 valiant men, who, evidently, were the cream of the fighting forces of Judah. They had taken another 200,000 men, women, sons and daughters as captives, intending to make slaves of them in Israel. But now the Prophet Oded appears on the scene.

His first word to them was, *"Behold, because the LORD God of your fathers was angry with Judah, He has delivered them into your hand, and you have killed them in a rage that reaches up unto Heaven."*

And now he addresses the 200,000 who are to be used as slaves.

In effect, he tells the army of Israel that if they insist upon doing this thing, keeping these individuals as slaves, *". . . the fierce wrath of the LORD is upon you."* Thankfully, certain of the leadership of the Nation of Israel heard the statement given by the Prophet and immediately stepped in and took authority over the captives.

This was one time the Prophet of God was heeded, and as a result, *". . . took the captives, and with the spoil clothed all who were naked among them, and arrayed them, and shod them, and gave them to eat and to drink, and anointed them, and carried all the feeble of them upon asses, and brought them to Jericho, the city of palm trees, to their brethren: then they returned to Samaria."*

All of this proclaims the fact that the Lord was the Author of the defeat of Judah by both the Syrians and the army of Israel and, as well, was now the Author of the rescue of the 200,000 captives. As is obvious, the Lord controls all things.

(16) "AT THAT TIME DID KING AHAZ SEND UNTO THE KINGS OF ASSYRIA TO HELP HIM.

(17) "FOR AGAIN THE EDOMITES HAD COME AND SMITTEN JUDAH, AND CARRIED AWAY CAPTIVES.

(18) "THE PHILISTINES ALSO HAD INVADED THE CITIES OF THE LOW COUNTRY, AND OF THE SOUTH OF JUDAH, AND HAD TAKEN BETH-SHEMESH, AND AJALON, AND GEDEROTH, AND SHOCHO WITH THE VILLAGES THEREOF, AND TIMNAH WITH THE VILLAGES THEREOF, GIMZO ALSO AND THE VILLAGES THEREOF: AND THEY DWELT THERE.

(19) "FOR THE LORD BROUGHT JUDAH LOW BECAUSE OF AHAZ KING OF ISRAEL; FOR HE MADE JUDAH NAKED, AND TRANSGRESSED SORE AGAINST THE LORD.

(20) "AND TIGLATH-PILESER KING OF ASSYRIA CAME UNTO HIM, AND DISTRESSED HIM, BUT STRENGTHENED HIM NOT.

(21) "FOR AHAZ TOOK AWAY A PORTION OUT OF THE HOUSE OF THE LORD, AND OUT OF THE HOUSE OF THE KING, AND OF THE PRINCES, AND GAVE IT UNTO THE KING OF ASSYRIA: BUT HE HELPED HIM NOT.

(22) "AND IN THE TIME OF HIS DISTRESS DID HE TRESPASS YET MORE AGAINST THE LORD: THIS IS THAT KING AHAZ.

(23) "FOR HE SACRIFICED UNTO THE GODS OF DAMASCUS, WHICH SMOTE HIM: AND HE SAID, BECAUSE THE GODS OF THE KINGS OF SYRIA HELP THEM, THEREFORE WILL I SACRIFICE TO THEM, THAT THEY MAY HELP ME. BUT THEY WERE THE RUIN OF HIM, AND OF ALL ISRAEL.

(24) "AND AHAZ GATHERED TOGETHER THE VESSELS OF THE HOUSE OF GOD, AND CUT IN PIECES THE VESSELS OF THE HOUSE OF GOD, AND SHUT UP THE DOORS OF THE HOUSE OF THE LORD, AND HE MADE HIM ALTARS IN THE EVERY CORNER OF JERUSALEM.

(25) "AND IN EVERY SEVERAL CITY OF JUDAH HE MADE HIGH PLACES TO BURN INCENSE UNTO OTHER GODS, AND PROVOKED TO ANGER THE LORD GOD OF HIS FATHERS."

The composition is:

1. (Vs. 16) After all the problems of being defeated by both Syria and Israel, still, Ahaz will not seek the Face of the Lord, but, instead, will lean on the arm of man, and heathen man, at that.

2. (Vs. 19) *"Israel,"* as used in place of Judah, signifies the fact that the Lord looked at Judah as the legitimate Israel.

3. (Vs. 19) Judah was made naked by Ahaz to the Judgment of God.

4. (Vs. 19) Judgment brought by the Lord, and especially against His Own, is always redemptive in its application. It is intended to bring the person or the nation to Repentance. In this case, it would not.

5. (Vss. 20-21) The results of Ahaz getting the king of Assyria to help him only resulted in them walking on him, so to speak. Assyria took advantage of him, knowing that he could not do anything about it.

6. Regarding Verse 22, the Holy Spirit uses the phrase, *"This is that king Ahaz,"* in order to point him out. There are three other especially branded transgressors in the Word of God. They are: Cain (Gen. 4:15), Dathan, and Abiram (Num. 26:9).

7. (Vs. 23) When we read the account of Ahaz, his plight because of his rebellion seems to be so clear, and yet most of the world, and even the church, seek help from that other than God. I speak of witchcraft or humanistic psychology.

8. (Vs. 24) Tragically, the church is presently shutting the covers of the Bible, the only revealed Body of Truth in the world. Most preaching and teaching of that which professes to be the Word of God is, rather, psychology. Psychology places the emphasis on the person or the problem instead of Christ and the Cross. There is no profit in the victim or the symptom; there is only profit in the Victor, Who is Christ.

9. (Vs. 25) Anything that departs from the Bible, be it the obvious evil of Ahaz or the subtle proposed solution of psychology, angers the Lord of Glory.

FOR THE LORD BROUGHT JUDAH LOW

The Scripture says that it was "... *because of Ahaz king of Israel; for he made Judah naked* (naked to the Judgment of God), *and transgressed sore against the LORD."*

The leadership of a house, of a Church, and even of a nation, has an awful lot to do with the Spiritual condition of all concerned. It is believed that I Thessalonians was the First Letter written by the Apostle Paul. He wrote it to a Church, the Church at Thessalonica.

The Last Letter the great Apostle wrote, shortly before his death, was to Timothy, a Preacher. This was not without design.

As the Preacher, so much the Church. If the preacher isn't right, the church will not be right. If the Preacher is on fire for God, the Church will be on fire for God. If the Preacher is strong in the Word, the Church will be strong in the Word. Conversely, if the preacher is weak spiritually, the church will be weak spiritually. While some few Believers may serve God with fortitude and courage irrespective, the majority, however, will follow the Preacher, good or bad.

Unfortunately, most religious denominations give short shift to the preacher, placing their emphasis on the church. They fail to realize, as goes the preacher, so goes the church!

Ahaz, the king of Judah, was grossly ungodly. Judah, sadly and regrettably, and as usual, followed him. It would bring wreckage to the nation. The following is a score of that Judgment:

• *"Ahaz sent unto the kings of Assyria to help him."* He did not seek the help of the Lord because he had no regard for Jehovah.

• *"Again the Edomites had come and smitten Judah, and carried away captives."*

• *"The Philistines also had invaded the cities of the low country, and of the south of Judah...."*

• *"Tiglath-pileser king of Assyria came unto him, and distressed him, but strengthened him not."*

• Ahaz stripped the gold from the *"House of the LORD..."* and *"... gave it unto the king of Assyria: but he helped him not."*

NOTES

The following is the reason that the Lord allowed these things to happen.

THIS IS THAT KING AHAZ

Ahaz was one of the most ungodly kings to ever grace the throne of Judah. The Scripture says of him:

• *"And in the time of his distress did he trespass more against the LORD."*

• *"He sacrificed unto the gods of Damascus, which smote him ... that they may help me. But they were the ruin of him, and of all Israel."*

• He *"... cut in pieces the vessels of the House of God, and shut up the doors of the House of the LORD."*

• *"He made him altars in every corner of Jerusalem."*

• *"... He made high places to burn incense to other gods, and provoked to anger the LORD God of his fathers."*

The word *"naked"* means that he made Judah naked to the Judgment of God.

God cannot abide sin in any fashion or form. The Bible emphatically teaches the Wrath of God against disobedience. That is an infallible rule of Scripture. There is only one answer for that Wrath, only one thing that will stop that Wrath, and that is the Cross of Christ.

Unless there is Revival in America, which means that such Revival must begin with the church, America is going to face the Judgment of God and, in fact, such Judgment has already begun. Many of the leaders of this nation are shaking their fists in the Face of God and are advocating same-sex marriages, which is an abomination to God (Ezek. 16:49-50). As well, abortion has stained this nation with blood and is a grievous sin against God and against humanity. Also, for the sake of the dollar, the leadership of this nation has opened it up to gambling, which constitutes a tax against the poor, even the very poor, those who can least afford it. But yet, the blame for all of this is more so on the church than anything else. For as goes the church, so goes the nation.

Immediately after September 11, 2001 (9/11), two very prominent religious leaders were being interviewed by one of the News agencies. They were asked as to why the Lord had allowed this thing to happen to America?

Their answer laid the blame at the doorsteps of Congress, of our political leaders, etc. As I listened to them, however, I knew that the answer was far different.

The problem is with the church. It has denied the Power of God; it has compromised the Message; and, it has repudiated the Cross. What does the Word say about something like this?

I quote from THE EXPOSITOR'S STUDY BIBLE:

"For the time has come that Judgment must begin at the House of God (Judgment always begins with Believers, and pertains to their Faith, whether in the Cross or otherwise; the Cross alone is spared Judgment, for there Jesus was judged in our place)*: and if it first begin at us, what shall the end be of them who obey not the Gospel of God?* (If God will judge His Own, how much more will He judge the unredeemed? The Cross alone stays the Judgment of God. Let that ever be understood.)

"And if the Righteous scarcely be Saved (can be Saved only by trusting Christ and the Cross, and nothing else), *where shall the ungodly and the sinner appear?* (If the great Sacrifice of Christ is rejected and spurned, where does that leave those who do such a thing? There is no hope for their Salvation)*"* (I Pet. 4:17-18).

The tragedy is, the unredeemed place no confidence in the Word of God at all. There is a reason for that!

It is because the church has abandoned the Bible because it has abandoned the Cross. That is the reason for the terrible Judgment on this nation. It can be laid at the doorsteps of the church. While most definitely the political leaders of our nation will experience the Judgment of God, still, the acute blame must be laid at the doorsteps of those who call themselves Believers.

Ahaz was supposed to be at least one of the spiritual leaders of Israel. His place of leadership was prominent, as would be obvious. Instead of him using his high and holy office to lead the nation to God, he used it to lead the nation to idolatry, which was the ruin of everything.

ALTARS

Let me ask a question!

Ahaz forsook the great Altar of the Lord, which was a type of the coming Calvary, and instead, *"made him altars in every corner of Jerusalem,"* and we might quickly add, altars to heathen gods.

But is there any difference in that and the church presently abandoning the Cross and substituting other things to take its place?

I think not!

Bible Christianity is a very simple thing. It has no temples, no altars, no rules, no regulations, no ceremonies, and no rituals. It has only one thing, and that is Faith in Christ and what Christ has done for us at the Cross. It is just that simple.

So, whenever Believers leave the Cross and make something else the object of their faith, irrespective as to what that something else is, and no matter how holy it may seem to be in its own right, if it's not the Cross of Christ, they have abandoned the Faith. And that's exactly where the modern church is. Preachers are not preaching the Cross! Believers, consequently, are not looking to the Cross of Christ but rather something else altogether.

That's the reason the *"Purpose Driven Life"* book was so popular. The church has abandoned the Cross, therefore, whatever it has does not satisfy, even as it cannot satisfy. So, when this book came along, which appealed to the flesh, it was eagerly accepted by most in the church. Pure and simple, it, along with scores of other similar things, was just another altar, the same as the altars of Ahaz. I know that's strong, but I believe it to be true. The Scripture says that Ahaz *"made high places to burn incense unto other gods, and provoked to anger the LORD God of his fathers."*

ANOTHER JESUS

Do you realize the Apostle Paul stated that if we, in fact, do place our faith in the Lord Jesus Christ but omit the Cross, we are left with *"another Jesus"* (II Cor. 11:4)?

That's right, *"another Jesus."*

This means that it's a *"Jesus"* that God doesn't recognize, which is not Scriptural, and which can never be accepted by the Lord. But that's where the modern church is. It is proclaiming Jesus, but it's the intellectual Jesus, the Miracle-working Jesus, the prosperity Jesus, or even the healing Jesus. The truth is according to the following.

In fact, our Lord is all of these things, but He can be all of these things only if we place the Cross first of all. Jesus Christ is the Source of all things that come to us, but the Cross is the Means by which these things come. But the modern church has abandoned the Cross, which means the modern church doesn't understand, or else doesn't believe, what the true problem really is, which is sin. It has been so psychologized, in other words, it has bought into the psychological jargon to such a degree, that anymore, it doesn't know man's real problem and doesn't know the solution. So, the Jesus it serves and worships is not the Jesus of the Bible but a Jesus of their own fabrication.

Paul said, *"We preach Jesus Crucified"* (I Cor. 1:23). He said to the Church at Corinth, as well, *"I determined to know nothing among you save Jesus Christ and Him Crucified"* (I Cor. 2:2). He also said, *"God forbid that I should glory, save in the Cross of our Lord Jesus Christ, by Whom I was crucified to the world and the world unto me"* (Gal. 6:14). The great Apostle also said, *"Christ is become of no effect unto you, whosoever of you are justified by the Law; you are fallen from Grace"* (Gal. 5:4).

It's the Cross! The Cross! The Cross! Or else it's *"another Jesus!"*

(26) "NOW THE REST OF HIS ACTS AND OF ALL HIS WAYS, FIRST AND LAST, BEHOLD, THEY ARE WRITTEN IN THE BOOK OF THE KINGS OF JUDAH AND ISRAEL.

(27) "AND AHAZ SLEPT WITH HIS FATHERS, AND THEY BURIED HIM IN THE CITY, EVEN IN JERUSALEM: BUT THEY BROUGHT HIM NOT INTO THE SEPULCHRES OF THE KINGS OF ISRAEL: AND HEZEKIAH HIS SON REIGNED IN HIS STEAD."

The composition is:

1. (Vs. 27) It is with great relief that the Holy Spirit closes out the sordid history of Ahaz. Today he is in Hell, and will be there forever and forever!

2. What an opportunity this man had to do good for Judah, but he traded it all for idols made of wood, stone, etc.

3. Are the altars of the modern church, which is not the Altar of Calvary, any different than the altars of Ahaz?

ISRAEL

If it is to be noticed, Ahaz is entitled *"king of Israel"* (Vs. 19), and his fathers are named *"kings of Israel"* (Vs. 27). These are not errors, as some might suppose, but portray the fact that God would label Judah as the *"true Israel,"* even though the northern kingdom went under that name. In essence, he was recognizing a remnant in the nation as *"Israel,"* however feeble and fallen.

"I have such a wonderful Saviour,
"Who helps me wherever I go;
"That I must be telling His Goodness,
"That everybody should know."

"His Mercy and Love are unbounded,
"He makes me with gladness overflow;
"Oh, He is the Chief of ten thousands:
"That everybody should know!"

"He helps me when trials surround me,
"His Grace and His Goodness to show;
"Oh, how can I help but adore Him,
"That everybody should know."

"My life and my love I will give him,
"And faithfully serve Him below,
"Who brought me His wondrous Salvation,
"That everybody should know."

CHAPTER 29

(1) "HEZEKIAH BEGAN TO REIGN WHEN HE WAS FIVE AND TWENTY YEARS OLD, AND HE REIGNED NINE AND TWENTY YEARS IN JERUSALEM. AND HIS MOTHER'S NAME WAS ABIJAH, THE DAUGHTER OF ZECHARIAH.

(2) "AND HE DID THAT WHICH WAS

RIGHT IN THE SIGHT OF THE LORD, ACCORDING TO ALL THAT DAVID HIS FATHER HAD DONE."

The construction is:

1. (Vs. 2) David was always used as the yardstick or example.

2. (Vs. 2) That which is *"right in the sight of God"* is all that matters. Unfortunately, the church all too often cares little about what is right in God's Eyes, making their own eyes the yardstick.

3. Now will begin, thankfully, a time of Revival for Judah.

"THAT WHICH IS RIGHT IN THE SIGHT OF THE LORD"

The Scripture says that Ahaz was 20 years old when he began to reign, and that he reigned 16 years, which means that he was 36 years old when he died.

The Scripture also says that Hezekiah was 25 years old when he began to reign.

Some have concluded from that that Ahaz was only 11 years old when Hezekiah was born. That is not the case!

Even though the Scripture doesn't say, more than likely, Hezekiah was born when Ahaz was about 20 years old, or perhaps a little younger. And, as well, more than likely, and once again, even though the Scripture doesn't say one way or the other, it could have been several years after Ahaz died before Hezekiah actually took the throne, which is probably what happened.

The Scripture says that Ahaz, Hezekiah's father, *". . . did not that which was right in the sight of the LORD, like David his father"* (his father quite a few times removed) (II Chron. 28:1). And then it says concerning Hezekiah, *"And he did that which was right in the sight of the LORD, according to all that David his father had done."* How refreshing!

As we said previously, David was always used as the example.

Why?

Two reasons!

1. First of all, and foremost, David was chosen by God to be the man through whose lineage the Son of God, the Son of David would be born. That's the reason that the Gospel according to Matthew begins with the words, *"The Book of the generation of Jesus Christ, the Son of David, the Son of Abraham"* (Mat. 1:1).

Abraham was the titular leader of the family of Israel, having been chosen by God for that purpose (Gen. 12:1-3). So, the Nation of Israel came from the loins of Abraham and the womb of Sarah. But it was David in the Nation of Israel who was chosen by the Lord to be the lineage of Christ, the greatest honor that could ever be paid a human being. So, at the time of Christ, our Lord was often referred to as the *"Son of David"* (Mk. 10:47). Admittedly, the religious leaders of Israel did not refer to the Master in that capacity, but others did, such as Bartimaeus, proving that it was known that the Messiah would be the *"Son of David."* Tragically, the religious leadership of Israel did not recognize our Lord as their Messiah!

2. The second reason that David was chosen by the Lord to be in the lineage of the Messiah is because, even though he failed at times, and failed miserably, he would always be quick to repent and to take the blame personally for what had been done. Unfortunately, there are no perfect people, but fortunately, there is a Perfect Christ.

As well, when the Lord forgives someone, he is totally and completely forgiven. That means that the sin committed, no matter how dastardly it was, in the Mind of God, no longer exists and is completely taken away. It's called *"Justification by Faith."*

When David committed the horrible sin of adultery with Bath-sheba, and even worse than that, murdered her husband in cold blood, David could not go to the Law for Mercy, because there is no mercy in law. So, he had to reach back to the deliverance of the Children of Israel from Egyptian bondage, when the blood was applied to the doorposts of the homes of the Israelites in Egypt, meaning they were spared. For God had said, *"And the blood shall be to you for a token upon the houses where you are* (the blood applied to the doorposts meant that their Faith and trust were in the Pascal Lamb; the blood then applied was only a *'token,'* meaning that it was then but a symbol of One Who was to come, Who would redeem mankind by the shedding of His

Life's Blood): *and when I see the blood, I will pass over you* (this is, without a doubt, one of the single most important Scriptures in the entirety of the Word of God; the lamb had taken the fatal blow; and because it had taken the blow, those in the house would be spared; it was not a question of personal worthiness, self had nothing whatever to do in the matter; it was a matter of Faith; all under the cover of the blood were safe, just as all presently under the cover of the Blood are safe; this means that they were not merely in a savable state, but rather that they were *'Saved'*; as well, they were not partly Saved and partly exposed to Judgment, they were wholly Saved, and because there is no such thing as partial Justification; the Lord didn't say, *'When I see you,'* or, *'When I see your good works,'* etc., but, *'When I see the Blood'*; this speaks of Christ and what He would do at the Cross in order that we might be Saved, which pertained to Him giving Himself in Sacrifice, which necessitated the shedding of His Precious Blood [I Pet. 1:18-19]), *and the plague shall not be upon you to destroy you . . .* (Salvation from the *'plague'* of Judgment is afforded only by the shed Blood of the Lamb, and Faith in that shed Blood)" (Ex. 12:13).

In David's prayer of Repentance, he said the following.

DAVID'S PRAYER OF REPENTANCE

I continue to quote from THE EXPOSITOR'S STUDY BIBLE:

"Have mercy upon me, O God, according to Your Lovingkindness: according unto the multitude of Your tender Mercies blot out my transgressions. (This is a Psalm of David, written when Nathan the Prophet came unto him after the sin with Bath-sheba and the murder of her husband Uriah [II Sam., Chpt. 12]. This Psalm was given by the Holy Spirit to David when, his heart broken and contrite because of his sin against God, he pleaded for pardon through the Atoning Blood of the Lamb of God, foreshadowed in Exodus, Chapter 12. Thus, he was not only fittingly provided with a vehicle of expression in Repentance and Faith, but he was also used as a channel of prophetic communication.

NOTES

"David, in his sin, Repentance, and Restoration, is a forepicture of Israel. For as he forsook the Law and was guilty of adultery and murder, so Israel despised the Covenant, turned aside to idolatry [spiritual adultery], and murdered the Messiah.

"Thus the scope and structure of this Psalm goes far beyond David. It predicts the future confession and forgiveness of Israel in the day of the Messiah's Second Coming, when, looking upon Him Whom they pierced, they shall mourn and weep [Zech., Chpts. 12-13].

"As well, this is even more perfectly a vivid portrayal of the Intercessory Work of Christ on behalf of His People. Even though David prayed this prayer, the Son of David would make David's sin [as well as ours] His Own, and pray through him that which must be said.

"This means that this is the truest prayer of Repentance ever prayed, because it symbolizes the Intercessory Work of the Son of David.)

"Wash me thoroughly from my iniquity, and cleanse me from my sin (man's problem is sin, and man must admit that; the only remedy for sin is *'Jesus Christ and Him Crucified,'* to which David, in essence, appealed [Heb. 10:12]; the Blood of Jesus Christ alone cleanses from all sin [I Jn. 1:7]).

"For I acknowledge my transgressions: and my sin is ever before me (the acknowledgement of Verses 3 and 4 is the condition of Divine forgiveness; all sin, in essence, is committed against God; therefore, God demands that the transgressions be acknowledged, placing the blame where it rightfully belongs—on the perpetrator; He cannot and, in fact, will not, forgive sin that is not acknowledged and for which no responsibility is taken).

"Against You, You only, have I sinned, and done this evil in Your Sight: that You might be justified when You speak, and be clear when You judge. (While David's sins were against Bath-sheba, her husband Uriah, and all of Israel, still, the ultimate direction of sin, perfected by Satan, is always against God.

"All sin is a departure from God's Ways to man's ways.

"David is saying that God is always *'justified'* in any action that He takes, and His *'Judgment'* is always perfect.)

"Behold, I was shaped in iniquity; and in sin did my mother conceive me. (Unequivocally, this Verse proclaims the fact of original sin. This Passage states that all are born in sin, and as a result of Adam's Fall in the Garden of Eden.

"When Adam, as the federal head of the human race, failed, this means that all of humanity failed. It means that all who would be born would, in effect, be born lost.

"As a result of this, the Second Man, the Last Adam, the Lord Jesus Christ, had to come into this world, in effect, God becoming Man, to undo what the original Adam did. He would have to keep the Law of God perfectly, which He did, all as our Substitute, and then pay the penalty for the terrible sin debt owed by all of mankind, for all had broken the Law, which He did by giving Himself on the Cross of Calvary [Jn. 3:16].

"To escape the Judgment of original sin, man must be *'Born-Again,'* which is carried out by the believing sinner expressing Faith in Christ and what Christ did at the Cross [Jn. 3:3; Eph. 2:8-9].)

"Behold, You desire truth in the inward parts: and in the hidden part You shall make me to know wisdom (man can only deal with the externals, and even that not very well; God Alone can deal with the *'inward parts'* of man, which is the source of sin, which speaks of the heart; in other words, the heart has to be changed, which the Lord Alone can do [Mat. 5:8]).

"Purge me with hyssop, and I shall be clean: wash me, and I shall be whiter than snow. (The petition, *'purge me with hyssop,'* expresses a figure of speech. *'Purge me with the blood which on that night in Egypt was sprinkled on the doorposts with a bunch of hyssop'* [Ex. 12:13, 22] portrays David's dependence on *'the Blood of the Lamb.'*

"David had no recourse in the Law, even as no one has recourse in the Law. The Law can only condemn. All recourse is found exclusively in Christ and what He did for us at the Cross, of which the slain lamb and the blood on the doorposts in Egypt were symbols [Ex. 12:13])" (Ps. 51:1-7).

Everyone who is Saved is dependent solely and wholly on Christ and what **Christ** has done for us at the Cross and not at all upon our own personal merit, good works, etc. It has always been, it is, and it ever shall be, *"Jesus Christ and Him Crucified"* (I Cor. 1:23).

(3) "HE IN THE FIRST YEAR OF HIS REIGN, IN THE FIRST MONTH, OPENED THE DOORS OF THE HOUSE OF THE LORD, AND REPAIRED THEM.

(4) "AND HE BROUGHT IN THE PRIESTS AND THE LEVITES, AND GATHERED THEM TOGETHER INTO THE EAST STREET,

(5) "AND SAID UNTO THEM, HEAR ME, YOU LEVITES, SANCTIFY NOW YOURSELVES, AND SANCTIFY THE HOUSE OF THE LORD GOD OF YOUR FATHERS, AND CARRY FORTH THE FILTHINESS OUT OF THE HOLY PLACE.

(6) "FOR OUR FATHERS HAVE TRESPASSED, AND DONE THAT WHICH WAS EVIL IN THE EYES OF THE LORD OUR GOD, AND HAVE FORSAKEN HIM, AND HAVE TURNED AWAY THEIR FACES FROM THE HABITATION OF THE LORD, AND TURNED THEIR BACKS.

(7) "ALSO THEY HAVE SHUT UP THE DOORS OF THE PORCH, AND PUT OUT THE LAMPS, AND HAVE NOT BURNED INCENSE NOR OFFERED BURNT OFFERINGS IN THE HOLY PLACE UNTO THE GOD OF ISRAEL.

(8) "WHEREFORE THE WRATH OF THE LORD WAS UPON JUDAH AND JERUSALEM, AND HE HAS DELIVERED THEM TO TROUBLE, TO ASTONISHMENT, AND TO HISSING, AS YOU SEE WITH YOUR EYES.

(9) "FOR, LO, OUR FATHERS HAVE FALLEN BY THE SWORD, AND OUR SONS AND OUR DAUGHTERS AND OUR WIVES ARE IN CAPTIVITY FOR THIS.

(10) "NOW IT IS IN MY HEART TO MAKE A COVENANT WITH THE LORD GOD OF ISRAEL, THAT HIS FIERCE WRATH MAY TURN AWAY FROM US.

(11) "MY SONS, BE NOT NOW NEGLIGENT: FOR THE LORD HAS CHOSEN YOU TO STAND BEFORE HIM, TO SERVE

HIM, AND THAT YOU SHOULD MINISTER UNTO HIM, AND BURN INCENSE."

The construction is:

1. (Vs. 3) Immediately upon becoming king, Hezekiah began to institute reform. He wasted no time! Under his evil father Ahaz, the doors to the House of the Lord had been closed, meaning that this House was no longer in use. He began to repair things.

In our own spiritual lives, how much presently needs repairing?

2. The word *"sanctify"* (or *"Sanctification"*) of Verse 5, simply means in this case *"to set apart for the exclusive use of God."* In doing this, the *"filthiness"* would be carried out of the *"Holy Place."*

Regarding our lives, when given the opportunity, the Holy Spirit will always clean us up. Paul said, *". . . Let us cleanse ourselves from all filthiness of the flesh and spirit, perfecting holiness in the fear of God"* (II Cor. 7:1).

3. (Vs. 6) Repentance alone could reverse the situation of Judah. This means turning back to the Cross, for the Cross alone can address sin (Heb. 10:12).

4. (Vs. 7) The Golden Lampstand situated in the Holy Place of the Temple typified Christ as the Light of the world. It had long since gone out!

5. (Vs. 7) The burning of *"Incense"* typified the Intercession of Christ, all on our behalf.

6. (Vs. 7) The *"Burnt Offerings"* typified the Cross, where the Perfection of Christ is given to the believing sinner.

7. (Vs. 8) The Judgment was obvious! Because the Temple was symbolic of Christ and the Cross, when Christ and the Cross are forsaken, Judgment is inevitable! There can be no other way.

8. Sin puts people in captivity, even as Verse 9 proclaims, and it also kills.

9. The *"Covenant"* of Verse 10 meant simply to obey the Word of God.

THE REPAIRING OF THE DOORS OF THE HOUSE OF THE LORD

Hezekiah waited no time at all in getting started regarding the work that needed to be done. The Scripture says, *"He in the first year of his reign, in the first month, opened the doors of the House of the LORD, and repaired them."*

Work of this nature that must be done for the Lord cannot tolerate delay. It must begin immediately. The Scripture plainly tells us, *". . . Today if you will hear His Voice, harden not your hearts"* (Heb. 4:7).

Procrastination regarding the things of God proclaims a sure road to ruin. Hezekiah began immediately because the need was immediate, and he responded accordingly.

THE CONSECRATION OF HEZEKIAH

Considering that Hezekiah's father, Ahaz, was one of the most wicked men to grace the throne of Judah, and realizing that Ahaz surely did not steer his son toward the Lord, we have to wonder at this man's consecration.

Isaiah could very well have been instrumental in the direction taken by the young king. The Scripture says concerning Isaiah, *"The Vision of Isaiah the son of Amoz, which he saw concerning Judah and Jerusalem in the days of Uzziah, Jotham, Ahaz, and Hezekiah, kings of Judah.* (Isaiah was a contemporary of Jonah, Amos, Hosea, and Micah. It is thought that he began to preach at about 15 years of age and died at about 85. Tradition says that Manasseh placed Isaiah in a hollow log and cut him in two [Heb. 11:37]. This great Book which bears his name was written about 800 years before Christ.

"His Prophecies covered the entire or the partial reign of some four kings, as listed in the Text. [Every Message was primarily related to Judah, Jerusalem, or to the Jews and their Holy City.]

"He is called *'the Millennial Prophet,'* having given more Prophecies concerning that coming grand day than any other Prophet. As well, he was quoted by Christ more than any other Prophet.

"Of the four kings under whom Isaiah prophesied, *'Hezekiah' was* the godliest)" (Isa. 1:1).

One thing is certain, Ahaz gave no credence at all to the great Prophet Isaiah. Obviously, his son Hezekiah did!

Evidently the doors of the Temple were in a state of disrepair. Seemingly, this would be the first thing that would be repaired.

Incidentally, those *"doors"* were a Type of Christ. Jesus said concerning this, *". . . Verily, verily, I say unto you, I am the Door of the Sheep* (*'I am,'* exclusive of all others! there is only *'One Door,'* and that *'Door'* is Christ).

"All who ever came before Me are thieves and robbers (pertains to any and all before or after Christ, who claim to have the way of Salvation without Christ!)*: but the Sheep did not hear them* (True Sheep cannot be deceived).

"I am the Door (presents an emphatic statement; the Church is not the door to Christ, as the Catholics teach, but Christ is the Door to the Church)*: by Me if any man enter in, he shall be Saved* (as the *'Door,'* Jesus is the *'Saviour'*)*, and shall go in and out, and find pasture* (they went in for safety and went out for pasture)*"* (Jn. 10:7-9).

Everything about the Temple, in one way or the other, pointed to Christ in His Atoning, Mediatorial, or Intercessory Work.

This is so important, let us say it again.

Jesus Christ is the Door to all the things of God, and He is that Door by virtue of the Cross. In other words, He is the Source of all things from God, and the Cross is the Means by which these things are given to us, all superintended by the Holy Spirit (Rom. 8:1-2, 11).

JESUS CHRIST IS THE NEW COVENANT

Everything about the New Covenant, the greatest legislation, if one would refer to such in that capacity, that has ever been given to mankind, is all in Christ. It has no temples, no altars, that is, as it regards sacrifices, no ceremonies, and no rituals, only Christ.

A Covenant is always between two or more people. If either one or either side breaks the Covenant, the results are meant to be terrible.

Contrary to all other Covenants, even though the New Covenant is between God and Man, still, it cannot fail because it is all in Christ. Christ is Both God and Man, the Second Man, and as He is Both, it is all in Him, and it cannot fail. Man may fail, but Christ will never fail, and that means the Covenant will never fail; hence, it can be referred to as the *"Everlasting Covenant"* (Heb. 13:20).

So, if anything is going to truly be done for God, Jesus Christ had better be the First and the Last, the All in all, the King of kings, and Lord of lords!

SANCTIFY YOURSELVES

The word *"sanctify,"* or *"Sanctification,"* simply means, *"To be set apart from something to something, in this case, from the world unto God, and exclusively unto God."*

Sanctification before the Cross was little more than an external affair. It had to be that way, due to the fact that the Holy Spirit did not then abide in the hearts and lives of Believers. He was with Believers but not in Believers as He is presently (Jn. 14:17-18).

Before the Cross, Sanctification referred to anything and everything that was not strictly according to the Law of Moses. Such particulars, whatever they might have been, had to be addressed. That pretty much concluded the Sanctification process.

Since the Cross, the Holy Spirit comes into the heart and life of the Believer, there to abide forever (Jn. 14:16); consequently, Sanctification presently has nothing to do with the Law and everything to do with Grace.

Under the New Covenant, it's not possible for the Believer to sanctify himself, other than making himself available to the Holy Spirit.

The modern Believer, which refers to all since the Cross, is to place his Faith exclusively in Christ and what Christ has done for us at the Cross. The Holy Spirit, Who works exclusively within the parameters of the Finished Work of Christ, will then begin to develop His Fruit within one's heart and life, which means that one is then set apart from the world and unto God.

The Believer must understand that he can have the *"Fruit of the Spirit"* only as long as he places his Faith exclusively in Christ and the Cross, because the Holy Spirit works exclusively within the parameters of the Finished Work of Christ and, in fact, will work according to no other manner (Rom. 8:1-2, 11). If the Believer takes another tactic, he will come up with *"works of the flesh."* Actually, the *"Fruit of the Spirit"* and the *"works of the flesh"* are given by the Holy Spirit through Paul in the same Chapter of Galatians (Gal. 5:19-23). In effect, the Holy Spirit is saying that it's going to be one or the other as it regards the Believer. If the Believer tries to live this life by means other than the Cross of Christ, as stated, the works of the flesh will be the end result. If Faith is properly placed in the Cross of Christ, the end result will be the development of the Fruit of the Spirit.

The *"Fruit of the Spirit,"* as stated, is the result of Sanctification, while the *"works of the flesh"* are the result of self-will.

LAMPS, INCENSE, AND BURNT OFFERINGS

The Golden Lampstands in the Temple typified the Mediatorial Work of Christ. The burning of Incense, which was carried out twice a day, 9 a.m. and 3 p.m., was meant to typify the Intercessory Work of Christ, all on our behalf. Of course, the *"Burnt Offerings"* typified Calvary and, therefore, the Atonement. So, in these three particulars, we have the entirety of the Work of Christ, *"Atonement, Mediator, and Intercessor."*

Under Ahaz, all of this had ceased. As a result, *". . . the wrath of the LORD was upon Judah and Jerusalem. . . ."*

As we have said elsewhere in this Volume, the only thing standing between mankind and the Judgment of God is the Cross of Christ. That's why it is imperative that Preachers preach the Cross and that Believers place their Faith exclusively in the Cross of Christ. The Cross of Christ is as necessary to our Christian walk as oxygen is to our breathing. If the Cross of Christ is ignored or laid aside, or unbelief is tendered toward this greatest of the Work of Christ, Judgment in the form of the Wrath of God is the end result.

When Hezekiah instituted these reforms and cried to God for revival, Judah was in a terrible state; likewise, the present church is in a terrible state. It may even be that the modern church is in worse shape than Judah of old. At least Judah knew the difference in right and wrong. The modern church seems to have little understanding anymore as to what is right or what is wrong.

CHURCHES

One might say that there are basically four classes of churches in Christendom. They are as follows:

1. The modernist churches, which do not believe the Bible, or that Jesus is the Son of God, or that Calvary effected anything.

2. Churches that claim to believe in the Atoning Work of Calvary but completely ignore it.

3. Churches that claim to preach Calvary, but, instead, preach psychology, or the greed gospel, or something else.

4. Churches that preach *"Jesus Christ and Him Crucified"* as the Foundation of all Faith. These, sadly, are few and far between.

(12) "THEN THE LEVITES AROSE, MAHATH THE SON OF AMASAI, AND JOEL THE SON OF AZARIAH, OF THE SONS OF THE KOHATHITES: AND OF THE SONS OF MERARI, KISH THE SON OF ABDI, AND AZARIAH THE SON OF JEHALELEL: AND OF THE GERSHONITES; JOAH THE SON OF ZIMMAH, AND EDEN THE SON OF JOAH:

(13) "AND OF THE SONS OF ELIZAPHAN; SHIMRI, AND JEIEL: AND OF THE SONS OF ASAPH; ZECHARIAH, AND MATTANIAH:

(14) "AND OF THE SONS OF HEMAN; JEHIEL, AND SHIMEI: AND OF THE SONS OF JEDUTHUN; SHEMAIAH, AND UZZIEL.

(15) "AND THEY GATHERED THEIR BRETHREN, AND SANCTIFIED THEMSELVES, AND CAME, ACCORDING TO THE COMMANDMENT OF THE KING, BY THE WORDS OF THE LORD, TO CLEANSE THE HOUSE OF THE LORD.

(16) "AND THE PRIESTS WENT INTO THE INNER PART OF THE HOUSE OF THE LORD, TO CLEANSE IT, AND BROUGHT OUT ALL THE UNCLEANNESS THAT THEY FOUND IN THE TEMPLE OF THE LORD INTO THE COURT OF THE HOUSE OF THE LORD. AND THE LEVITES TOOK IT, TO CARRY IT OUT ABROAD INTO THE BROOK KIDRON.

(17) "NOW THEY BEGAN ON THE FIRST DAY OF THE FIRST MONTH TO SANCTIFY, AND ON THE EIGHTH DAY OF THE MONTH CAME THEY TO

THE PORCH OF THE LORD: SO THEY SANCTIFIED THE HOUSE OF THE LORD IN EIGHT DAYS; AND IN THE SIXTEENTH DAY OF THE FIRST MONTH THEY MADE AN END.

(18) "THEN THEY WENT IN TO HEZEKIAH THE KING, AND SAID, WE HAVE CLEANSED ALL THE HOUSE OF THE LORD, AND THE ALTAR OF BURNT OFFERING, WITH ALL THE VESSELS THEREOF, AND THE SHEWBREAD TABLE, WITH ALL THE VESSELS THEREOF.

(19) "MOREOVER ALL THE VESSELS, WHICH KING AHAZ IN HIS REIGN DID CAST AWAY IN HIS TRANSGRESSION, HAVE WE PREPARED AND SANCTIFIED, AND BEHOLD, THEY ARE BEFORE THE ALTAR OF THE LORD."

The exegesis is:

1. (Vs. 14) The names of the fourteen Levites given in these Passages have no interest for the historians of the world, but such an interest for the Holy Spirit that they are all set out here, and they have been read already by hundreds of millions of people for nearly 2,800 years.

2. The Words or Commands of the Lord mentioned in Verse 15 are such as are written in Exodus 19:22 and Leviticus 11:44. Nothing can be spiritually cleansed, unless it is done according to the Word of the Lord.

3. (Vs. 16) Only the Priests could enter the Temple, while the Levites' sphere of work and service lay in the courts and round about the Temple.

4. (Vs. 16) Spiritually, Revival must begin in the *"inner part,"* which means *"the heart."* It is unthinkable that the Temple was in this condition, but sadly, it was. Is it possible that the modern church is in the same condition now as the Temple of old?

5. The first thing that happens when Revival begins to take place is that things are cleaned up, as recorded in Verses 18 and 19.

TO CLEANSE THE HOUSE OF THE LORD

Under the New Covenant, the Believer is the *"House of the LORD."* Paul said, *"Know you not that you are the Temple of God (where the Holy Spirit abides), and that the Spirit of God dwells in you?* (That makes the Born-Again Believer His permanent Home)" (I Cor. 3:16).

The Old Covenant consisted, as is obvious, of carrying trash out of the Temple, and at the same time, setting up the sacred vessels so they could be put immediately to use. Presently, under the New Covenant, the *"cleansing of the House"* is totally different.

As already stated, the Temple is no more, and the House is now the Born-Again Believer. The Holy Spirit is the only One Who can do the cleansing that is now required.

THE HOLY SPIRIT AND THE CLEANSING OF THE TEMPLE

The Holy Spirit is God. Everything He does is done within the parameters, so to speak, of the Finished Work of Christ, i.e., *"the Cross."* In other words, it is the Cross of Christ which has given the Holy Spirit the legal means to do all that He does (Rom. 8:2).

The Holy Spirit comes into our hearts and lives to abide, and to do so permanently, to carry out a great Work. But the greatest of all that He does is to rid the Believer of the dominion of the sin nature.

DOMINION AND THE SIN NATURE

The sin nature is the human nature that has become corrupted. This took place at the Fall of Adam, when he fell from the lofty position of total God-consciousness down to the far, far lower level of total self-consciousness. All of this means that the very nature of the person, and we speak of one who is unredeemed, is altogether toward sin and transgression. In other words, the sin nature controls such a person 24 hours a day, 7 days a week. Everything that is done lends toward sin, iniquity, transgression, self-will, etc. Even the good things done, so-called, have an ulterior motive.

When the believing sinner comes to Christ, the sin nature is made dormant, i.e., *"ineffective"* (Rom. 6:6).

Sooner or later the new convert fails the Lord in some way. This comes as a shock, but it has happened to every one of us. This does not within itself reactivate the sin nature. What reactivates it is because of the following.

To try to keep from committing this sin again, whatever it may have been, the Believer, either through ignorance or rebellion, and it's almost always through ignorance, places his or her faith in something other than the Cross of Christ. When this is done, the Holy Spirit cannot function, and that means that the sin nature will be reactivated and will begin to control or rule the Believer in some way. That's what Paul was talking about when he said, *"Let not sin* (the sin nature) *therefore reign* (rule) *in your mortal body* (showing that the sin nature can once again rule in the heart and life of the Believer, if the Believer doesn't constantly look to Christ and the Cross; the *'mortal body'* is neutral, which means it can be used for Righteousness or unrighteousness), *that you should obey it in the lusts thereof* (ungodly lusts are carried out through the mortal body, if faith is not maintained in the Cross [I Cor. 1:17-18]).

"Neither yield you your members (of your mortal body) *as instruments of unrighteousness unto sin* (the sin nature): *but yield yourselves unto God* (we are to yield ourselves to Christ and the Cross; that alone guarantees Victory over the sin nature), *as those who are alive from the dead* (we have been raised with Christ in *'Newness of Life'*), *and your members as instruments of Righteousness unto God* (this can be done only by virtue of the Cross and our Faith in that Finished Work, and Faith which continues in that Finished Work from day-to-day [Lk. 9:23-24])" (Rom. 6:12-13).

If the Believer doesn't place his faith exclusively in the Cross of Christ, the sin nature is going to rule such a Believer in some way. This makes life miserable and is the very opposite of what the Holy Spirit intends (Rom. 7:19).

Virtually the entirety of the Body of Christ, and we speak of consecrated Christians, is being ruled by the sin nature in some way. And how do I know that?

I know that because the modern church is not preaching the Cross, and there is no other means or way of victory. It is the Cross of Christ, or it is law, and Paul said concerning this, *"But that no man is justified by the Law in the sight of God, it is evident"* (Gal. 3:11).

The great Apostle also said, *"For as many as are of the Works of the Law are under the curse* (the Believer can only be under Law or Grace; it is one or the other; one can only come to Grace through the Cross; if one is trusting in law, whatever kind of law, one is cursed)" (Gal. 3:10).

SIN AND DOMINION

The Bible does not teach sinless perfection; however, it does teach that sin is not to have dominion over us (Rom. 6:14).

Dominion of sin consists of a bondage or bondages of some sort that controls the individual. Regrettably, millions of Christians are plagued with the dominion of the sin nature.

The Believer can be free from the dominion of the sin nature only by the Believer placing his or her Faith exclusively in Christ and the Cross, which then gives the Holy Spirit latitude to work within their lives, bringing about the desired results.

But still, this does not mean that the Believer is totally free from committing acts of sin at times. The Scripture says, *"For all have sinned* (presents all men placed in the same category), *and come short of the Glory of God* (the Greek Text infers that even the most Righteous among us continue to come short of the Glory of God on a continuing basis)" (Rom. 3:23). Sinless perfection will not be reached until the Trump of God sounds. The Scripture says concerning that, *"For this corruptible* (sin nature) *must put on incorruption* (a Glorified Body with no sin nature), *and this mortal* (subject to death) *must put on immortality* (will never die)" (I Cor. 15:53).

As stated, it is the business now of the Holy Spirit to *"clean up"* the Child of God, and this He will do, if the Believer will only cooperate with Him by placing his Faith in the Finished Work of Christ and leaving it there.

THE ALTAR OF THE LORD

This Altar was the great Brazen Altar, some 30 feet wide and 30 feet long. It sat immediately in front of the Temple and was where the sacrifices of every nature were offered. It symbolized Calvary in all of its forms. In fact, one might say that the *"Altar of the LORD"* was the most significant vessel in the entirety of the Temple apparatus. Immediately, one may counter by saying that the Ark of the Covenant was the most important Vessel. In the strict sense of the word, that is probably correct. However, one, and we speak of the High Priest, for he was the only one who could enter the Holy of Holies, and then only once a year, could not do so unless a sacrifice was first offered on the *"Altar of the LORD."* The blood of that sacrifice was then taken and sprinkled on the Mercy Seat in the Holy of Holies, which was on the Great Day of Atonement. The great Altar was in use 24 hours a day, 7 days a week. In fact, it had four horns at each corner, symbolizing that Redemption was the same the world over. This means that the Gospel is not a white man's Gospel, or a red man's Gospel, etc., but is the Gospel for the entirety of the world.

The fires on the great Altar were to be kept burning 24 hours a day, 7 days a week, and for the simple reason that the people were constantly bringing sacrifices to be offered. In other words, the work of the great Altar was never finished and, as well, operated around the clock. And yet, the millions of sacrifices offered throughout some 15 centuries could not equal the one Sacrifice of Christ. The Scripture says, *"For by one Offering He has perfected forever them who are Sanctified"* (Heb. 10:14).

(20) "THEN HEZEKIAH THE KING ROSE EARLY, AND GATHERED THE RULERS OF THE CITY, AND WENT UP TO THE HOUSE OF THE LORD.

(21) "AND THEY BROUGHT SEVEN BULLOCKS, AND SEVEN RAMS, AND SEVEN LAMBS, AND SEVEN HE GOATS, FOR A SIN OFFERING FOR THE KINGDOM, AND FOR THE SANCTUARY, AND FOR JUDAH. AND HE COMMANDED THE PRIESTS THE SONS OF AARON TO OFFER THEM ON THE ALTAR OF THE LORD.

(22) "SO THEY KILLED THE BULLOCKS, AND THE PRIESTS RECEIVED THE BLOOD, AND SPRINKLED IT ON THE ALTAR: LIKEWISE, WHEN THEY HAD KILLED THE RAMS, THEY SPRINKLED THE BLOOD UPON THE ALTAR: THEY KILLED ALSO THE LAMBS, AND THEY SPRINKLED THE BLOOD UPON THE ALTAR.

(23) "AND THEY BROUGHT FORTH THE HE GOATS FOR THE SIN OFFERING BEFORE THE KING AND THE CONGREGATION; AND THEY LAID THEIR HANDS UPON THEM:

(24) "AND THE PRIESTS KILLED THEM, AND THEY MADE RECONCILIATION WITH THEIR BLOOD UPON THE ALTAR, TO MAKE AN ATONEMENT FOR ALL ISRAEL: FOR THE KING COMMANDED THAT THE BURNT OFFERING AND THE SIN OFFERING SHOULD BE MADE FOR ALL ISRAEL."

The diagram is:

1. (Vs. 21) After the cleansing of the Temple, which made it serviceable, the first thing that is now done, in essence, is that Judah went back to the Cross.

2. (Vs. 21) I must believe that the Holy Spirit urged Hezekiah to institute *"seven"* sacrifices each of the various animals. *"Seven"* signifies perfection, universality, and totality. It is God's Number.

It means that Israel was to have a complete cleansing. While the Temple could be cleansed of debris, it took the shed Blood of the Lamb to properly cleanse from sin. We as Believers can prepare the way, but only the Blood can cleanse (I Jn. 1:7).

3. (Vs. 22) The sprinkling of the blood marked the expiation of sin (Lev. 4:7, 18, 30; 5:9; 8:14-15; Heb. 9:12-14, 19-22).

4. (Vs. 23) The laying of the hands on the head of the animal signified the transferring of the sins of the person offering the sacrifice and, in this case, the entirety of the people of Judah, to the victim, which was a Type of Christ taking our sins on the Cross (Isa. 53:6). This is what Paul was speaking of when he mentioned the *"laying on of hands"* in Hebrews 6:2.

5. (Vs. 24) The Burnt Offering typified Christ giving His Perfection to the sinner. The Sin Offering typified the sinner giving his sin to Christ. He gives His Perfection to us; we give our sin to Him.

THE SIN OFFERING

Four particular animals were offered, seven each, *"seven bullocks, seven rams, seven lambs, and seven he goats."* All of these were for a *"Sin Offering."*

As we have stated, the *"Sin Offering"* portrayed the believing sinner giving his sin to Christ.

In this case, the Priests laid their hands on the heads of these animals and in doing so, confessed the sins of Judah, which were many.

After the hands were laid on the heads of these animals, *"the Priests killed them."* This, of course, typified the Death of Christ on the Cross. He gave up His Life, a Perfect Life, by the means of a Perfect Body, as a Sacrifice, which was accepted by God.

THE SPRINKLING OF THE BLOOD

When the animals were killed by their throats being slit, the blood was caught in a basin, and then it was *"sprinkled upon the Altar."* This was the first time in years this had been done. Now, that which typed the great price that Christ would pay at Calvary was once again instituted. True Revival always leads the Church back to Calvary—every time to Calvary.

Judah's protection was the shed Blood of the Lamb! Her prosperity was the shed Blood of the Lamb! Her healing was the shed Blood of the Lamb! All forgiveness of sins was by the shed Blood of the Lamb!

Please understand, it hasn't changed from then until now and, in fact, will never change. Every iota of Faith must be exclusively in the Cross of Christ. While other things have their place, the great Foundation principle of the Redemption Plan, i.e., the New Covenant, has always been, and is, and ever shall be, the shed Blood of the Lamb!

(25) "AND HE SET THE LEVITES IN THE HOUSE OF THE LORD WITH CYMBALS, WITH PSALTERIES, AND WITH HARPS, ACCORDING TO THE COMMANDMENT OF DAVID, AND OF GAD THE KING'S SEER, AND NATHAN THE PROPHET: FOR SO WAS THE COMMANDMENT OF THE LORD BY HIS PROPHETS.

(26) "AND THE LEVITES STOOD WITH THE INSTRUMENTS OF DAVID, AND THE PRIESTS WITH THE TRUMPETS.

(27) "AND HEZEKIAH COMMANDED TO OFFER THE BURNT OFFERING UPON THE ALTAR. AND WHEN THE BURNT OFFERING BEGAN, THE SONG OF THE LORD BEGAN ALSO WITH THE TRUMPETS, AND WITH THE INSTRUMENTS ORDAINED BY DAVID KING OF ISRAEL.

(28) "AND ALL THE CONGREGATION WORSHIPPED, AND THE SINGERS SANG, AND THE TRUMPETERS SOUNDED: AND ALL THIS CONTINUED UNTIL THE BURNT OFFERING WAS FINISHED.

(29) "AND WHEN THEY HAD MADE AN END OF OFFERING, THE KING AND ALL WHO WERE PRESENT WITH HIM BOWED THEMSELVES, AND WORSHIPPED.

(30) "MOREOVER HEZEKIAH THE KING AND THE PRINCES COMMANDED THE LEVITES TO SING PRAISE UNTO THE LORD WITH THE WORDS OF DAVID, AND OF ASAPH THE SEER. AND THEY SANG PRAISES WITH GLADNESS, AND THEY BOWED THEIR HEADS AND WORSHIPPED."

The exegesis is:

1. (Vs. 25) Music and joy always accompany proper Faith in the Cross, because all sins have been washed away.

2. (Vs. 25) The Bible does not distinguish between a *"Seer"* and a *"Prophet."* Sometimes both designations are used for the same individual (I Chron. 21:9; II Chron. 29:25).

3. (Vs. 27) When Faith is properly placed in Christ and the Cross, worship always follows, as it regards music and singing. Little Cross, little worship! Much Cross, much worship!

WORSHIP OF THE LORD WITH MUSIC AND SINGING

From all of this, it is obvious that Hezekiah was doing his very best to set the House in order exactly as the Lord had given it to David so long before. He called in the musicians and the singers, and it was Campmeeting time!

We learn from this just how significant that music and singing are as it regards the

Worship of the Lord. In fact, I think one could say, without fear of exaggeration, that it is the highest form of worship.

We learn this from the great Book of Psalms. It is the longest Book in the Bible, meaning that the Holy Spirit designated the longest Book to be about praise and worship with music and singing. That speaks volumes!

That's the reason that Satan has done everything within Hell's power to pervert the Worship of the Lord regarding music and singing. Regrettably, he has succeeded in many, if not most, cases. The Evil One knows how tremendously significant that proper music and singing actually are.

When I was eight years of age, I asked the Lord to give me the talent to play the piano. The Lord heard my prayer and not only gave me that talent but, as well, gave me an understanding as to what the Holy Spirit wants and desires as it regards the Worship of the Lord through music and singing. He has helped me to touch the world for Christ by the means of music and singing, for which we give the Lord all the praise and all the glory.

Seeing what Hezekiah has done and is doing, we can only say, *"Happy days are here again."*

(31) "THEN HEZEKIAH ANSWERED AND SAID, NOW YOU HAVE CONSECRATED YOURSELVES UNTO THE LORD, COME NEAR AND BRING SACRIFICES AND THANK OFFERINGS INTO THE HOUSE OF THE LORD. AND THE CONGREGATION BROUGHT IN SACRIFICES AND THANK OFFERINGS; AND AS MANY AS WERE OF A FREE HEART BURNT OFFERINGS.

(32) "AND THE NUMBER OF THE BURNT OFFERINGS, WHICH THE CONGREGATION BROUGHT, WAS THREESCORE AND TEN BULLOCKS, AN HUNDRED RAMS, AND TWO HUNDRED LAMBS: ALL THESE WERE FOR A BURNT OFFERING TO THE LORD.

(33) "AND THE CONSECRATED THINGS WERE SIX HUNDRED OXEN AND THREE THOUSAND SHEEP.

(34) "BUT THE PRIESTS WERE TOO FEW, SO THAT THEY COULD NOT FLAY ALL THE BURNT OFFERINGS: WHEREFORE THEIR BRETHREN THE LEVITES DID HELP THEM, TILL THE WORK WAS ENDED, AND UNTIL THE OTHER PRIESTS HAD SANCTIFIED THEMSELVES: FOR THE LEVITES WERE MORE UPRIGHT IN HEART TO SANCTIFY THEMSELVES THAN THE PRIESTS.

(35) "AND ALSO THE BURNT OFFERINGS WERE IN ABUNDANCE, WITH THE FAT OF THE PEACE OFFERINGS, AND THE DRINK OFFERINGS FOR EVERY BURNT OFFERING. SO THE SERVICE OF THE HOUSE OF THE LORD WAS SET IN ORDER.

(36) "AND HEZEKIAH REJOICED, AND ALL THE PEOPLE, THAT GOD HAD PREPARED THE PEOPLE: FOR THE THING WAS DONE SUDDENLY."

The overview is:

1. (Vs. 30) With the opening of the Temple, the people of Judah sang *"praises unto the LORD with the words of David, and of Asaph the Seer."*

2. (Vs. 35) The *"Drink Offerings"* poured out on the Altar signified Christ pouring out His Life on the Cross.

3. (Vs. 36) The Scripture says, *"The thing was done suddenly,"* meaning that Hezekiah felt a great urgency to cleanse the Temple in order that the sacrifices may begin, and rightly so!

THE CROSS OF CALVARY

As the people began to sing praises unto the Lord, thousands of animals would be offered up in sacrifice, proclaiming the fact that Judah's safety and protection, her power and her strength, her prosperity and, in fact, all good things, had their foundation in the Cross of Calvary. Of course, the blood of bulls and goats could never take away sins, but Faith registered in what it all represented guaranteed Salvation and the Blessings of God.

In 1997, the Lord began to give me a Revelation of the Cross, which has revolutionized my life, my Ministry, and all things that pertain to the Lord. No, it isn't new, having been given to the Apostle Paul nearly 2,000 years ago. However, as far as most of the modern church is concerned, it is most definitely new, because it has been decades since the Cross has been preached in most churches. As a result, the modern church hardly knows anymore as to exactly what the Gospel actually is.

The reason?

Very simply, they have little understanding of the Cross (I Cor. 1:17).

"Jesus has died and has risen again,
"Pardon and peace to bestow;
"Fully I trust Him; from sin's guilty stain,
"Jesus saves me now."

"Sin's condemnation is over and gone,
"Jesus Alone knows how;
"Life and Salvation my soul has put on:
"Jesus saves me now."

"Satan may tempt, but he never shall reign,
"That Christ will never allow;
"Doubts I have buried, and this is my strain,
"Jesus saves me now."

"Resting in Jesus, abiding in Him,
"Gladly, my Faith can avow,
"Never again need my pathway be dim:
"Jesus saves me now."

"Jesus is stronger than Satan and sin,
"Satan to Jesus must bow;
"Therefore I triumph without and within;
"Jesus saves me now."

"Sorrow and pain may beset me about,
"Nothing can darken my brow;
"Battling in Faith, I can joyfully shout:
"Jesus saves me now."

CHAPTER 30

(1) "AND HEZEKIAH SENT TO ALL ISRAEL AND JUDAH, AND WROTE LETTERS ALSO TO EPHRAIM AND MANASSEH, THAT THEY SHOULD COME TO THE HOUSE OF THE LORD AT JERUSALEM, TO KEEP THE PASSOVER UNTO THE LORD GOD OF ISRAEL.

(2) "FOR THE KING HAD TAKEN COUNSEL, AND HIS PRINCES, AND ALL THE CONGREGATION IN JERUSALEM, TO KEEP THE PASSOVER IN THE SECOND MONTH.

(3) "FOR THEY COULD NOT KEEP IT AT THAT TIME, BECAUSE THE PRIESTS HAD NOT SANCTIFIED THEMSELVES SUFFICIENTLY, NEITHER HAD THE PEOPLE GATHERED THEMSELVES TOGETHER TO JERUSALEM.

(4) "AND THE THING PLEASED THE KING AND ALL THE CONGREGATION.

(5) "SO THEY ESTABLISHED A DECREE TO MAKE PROCLAMATION THROUGHOUT ALL ISRAEL, FROM BEER-SHEBA EVEN TO DAN, THAT THEY SHOULD COME TO KEEP THE PASSOVER UNTO THE LORD GOD OF ISRAEL AT JERUSALEM: FOR THEY HAD NOT DONE IT OF A LONG TIME IN SUCH SORT AS IT WAS WRITTEN."

The pattern is:

1. (Vs. 1) The Passover is a Type of Calvary (Ex. 12:13).

2. (Vs. 3) The Passover was supposed to be kept the first month (Ex. 12:2-3), but, because of all the things that needed to be done, they would have to take the Passover a month late, i.e., *"the second month"* (Vs. 2).

3. (Vs. 5) Even though Israel is now divided, still, Hezekiah sends a message throughout both kingdoms, giving all an invitation to come and keep the Passover.

THE PASSOVER

The word *"Passover"* in the Hebrew is *"Pesah,"* and comes from a verb meaning *"to pass over,"* in the sense of *"to spare"* (Ex. 12:13, 27).

This affords excellent sense. There is no need to jettison the time-honored view that God literally passed over the blood-sprinkled Israelite houses while smiting the Egyptian ones. Of course, the Israelite houses had the blood applied to the doorposts as they were commanded to do.

Exodus 12:43-49 excluded Gentiles from partaking in the Passover unless they had become proselytes, who were expected, even obliged, to conform fully.

As it regards the particulars of the Passover, a lamb was roasted and then eaten with unleavened bread and bitter herbs. The lamb was typical of Christ and what He would do at the Cross. The *"unleavened bread"* typified His Perfection, and the *"bitter herbs"* typified the bitterness of the Cross. In the case of Israel, the *"bitter herbs"* typified the bitterness of Egyptian bondage.

The symbolism, *"Christ our Passover,"* as given to us by Paul, in effect, specifies that the Passover was a Type of Christ and what He would do at the Cross in order to deliver humanity. How much the Jews understood this is anyone's guess. I suspect that their thinking was mostly upon the deliverance from Egyptian bondage; nevertheless, the Passover ritual was, and was intended to be, a Type of the Sacrifice of Christ.

At the time that Hezekiah issued his decree, as it regarded the eating of the Passover, such had not been kept for *"a long time."* Consequently, it was imperative that Judah would keep this all-important ritual.

The only thing that stands between the fierce Anger of God and mankind is *"the Blood of Jesus Christ,"* i.e., the Cross. Self-righteousness tends to think that surely God looks at all of our good works. He doesn't. He looks only at the Precious shed Blood of Jesus Christ. If the church does not preach and proclaim the Blood, it preaches nothing that is of any value to its adherents. In fact, all the Feast Days of Israel, its sacrifices and rituals, had as its foundation *"the Passover."* Likewise, everything in the Church must be tied to Calvary. Calvary must be the Foundation, as it is truly the Foundation. Our worship must spring from Calvary. Our prosperity must spring from Calvary. Our preaching must be Calvary-centered. No wonder Paul would say, *"I determined to know nothing among you save Christ and Him Crucified"* (I Cor. 2:2). How many churches have the Cross as their Foundation? Sadly, precious few.

(6) "SO THE POSTS WENT WITH THE LETTERS FROM THE KING AND HIS PRINCES THROUGHOUT ALL ISRAEL AND JUDAH, AND ACCORDING TO THE COMMANDMENT OF THE KING, SAYING, YOU CHILDREN OF ISRAEL, TURN AGAIN UNTO THE LORD GOD OF ABRAHAM, ISAAC, AND ISRAEL, AND HE WILL RETURN TO THE REMNANT OF YOU, THAT ARE ESCAPED OUT OF THE HAND OF THE KINGS OF ASSYRIA.

(7) "AND BE NOT YOU LIKE YOUR FATHERS, AND LIKE YOUR BRETHREN, WHO TRESPASSED AGAINST THE LORD GOD OF THEIR FATHERS, WHO THEREFORE GAVE THEM UP TO DESOLATION, AS YOU SEE.

(8) "NOW BE YOU NOT STIFFNECKED, AS YOUR FATHERS WERE, BUT YIELD YOURSELVES UNTO THE LORD, AND ENTER INTO HIS SANCTUARY, WHICH HE HAS SANCTIFIED FOR EVER: AND SERVE THE LORD YOUR GOD, THAT THE FIERCENESS OF HIS WRATH MAY TURN AWAY FROM YOU.

(9) "FOR IF YOU TURN AGAIN UNTO THE LORD, YOUR BRETHREN AND YOUR CHILDREN SHALL FIND COMPASSION BEFORE THEM THAT LEAD THEM CAPTIVE, SO THAT THEY SHALL COME AGAIN INTO THIS LAND: FOR THE LORD YOUR GOD IS GRACIOUS AND MERCIFUL, AND WILL NOT TURN AWAY HIS FACE FROM YOU, IF YOU RETURN UNTO HIM."

The overview is:

1. (Vs. 6) The northern kingdom had by now fallen, and so the poorest of the poor had been left by Assyria in the land, with the elite taken out as captives; however, they were precious in God's Sight just the same. Regrettably, as we shall see, most would not take this opportunity offered by Hezekiah.

2. (Vs. 8) The only thing that assuages the Wrath of God is Calvary. *"His Wrath"* will either be turned toward the unrepentant Christian or Calvary. The price of sin must be paid. If we accept the price that He paid at Calvary, then His Wrath has already been expended toward His Son, the Lord Jesus Christ. If we do not accept the price that was paid at Calvary, then His Wrath is turned toward us.

3. The Ninth Verse proclaims the fact, no doubt, given to Hezekiah by the Holy Spirit, that restoration was possible, but only if Repentance was enjoined.

THE WRATH OF GOD

The only thing that assuages the Anger

of God and, thereby, the Judgment of God against sin is Calvary. Let us say it this way.

The only thing standing between mankind and the Wrath of God is the Cross of Christ. That's the reason the Church is to ever hold up the Cross as the beacon of light for a darkened world. Regrettably and sadly, however, the modern church has long since, as a whole, ceased to preach the Cross. It is mentioned once in awhile in some Churches as it regards Salvation, but understood not at all as it regards Sanctification. That is sad when one considers that it was to Paul that this great Truth was given, which is the meaning of the New Covenant, which is the meaning of the Cross. If we objectively look at Paul's writings, we find that virtually all of what he had to say, literally what was given to him by the Holy Spirit, was to Believers. In other words, telling Believers how to live for God.

HOW TO LIVE FOR GOD

Some time ago at Family Worship Center at our Wednesday night Bible Study, I made the simple statement, *"Most Christians simply do not know how to live for God."* It's a simple statement, as is obvious, but it came as a shock to those who heard it. You could feel the tension in the auditorium.

To not know how to live for God is tantamount to spiritual failure. But the sadness is, most Christians simply do not understand how to live for God. Functioning in that capacity, Believers go from one scheme to the other, in other words, the flavor of the month.

In brief, the following is God's Prescribed Order.

GOD'S PRESCRIBED ORDER OF VICTORY

The following was given to us by the Apostle Paul:

- The sin nature: Most of the problems which beset Believers are caused by the sin nature dominating the individual in some way, which brings on all types of problems. The entire Sixth Chapter of Romans deals with this subject. The first two Verses tell us, in one form or the other, that the problem is sin (Rom. 6:1-2).

NOTES

- The answer to the sin nature, and the only answer to the sin nature, is the Cross of Christ. Immediately after telling us the problem is sin, the next three Verses give us the cure for the problem, which is the Cross of Christ (Rom. 6:3-5). As well, the Holy Spirit in very abbreviated form again tells us how to live for God, as is recorded in the great Epistle of Paul the Apostle to the Galatians. Paul starts with the Cross by saying, *"I am Crucified with Christ. . . ."* He closes that one Verse by again going to the Cross, *"Who gave Himself for us"* (Gal. 2:20).

- Considering that the sin nature is the problem, and the Cross of Christ is the solution to the sin nature and, in fact, the only solution, the Object of our Faith must be the Cross of Christ (Rom. 6:11; I Cor. 1:17-18, 23; 2:2; Gal., Chpt. 5; 6:14; Col. 2:14-15). Our Faith, as should be obvious, is extremely important. The greater bulk in that significance lies in the correct Object of Faith, which must always be the Cross of Christ. It was there that the Victory was won, Satan was defeated, and all sin was atoned. So, that is where our Faith must be registered.

- The Holy Spirit: The Holy Spirit works exclusively within the framework of the Finished Work of Christ, i.e., *"the Cross"* (Rom. 8:1-2, 11). The Holy Spirit has the Power to do whatever is necessary, for He, as is obvious, is God. He stands ready to help us at all times and, in fact, can do anything, but His Help is greatly limited when we place our faith in something other than the Cross of Christ. Our Faith, without fail, must ever be registered in the Cross and must remain in the Cross.

Regrettably, the modern church has little idea as to how the Holy Spirit works. If they think of Him at all, they somewhat take Him for granted. When our Faith is correct, the Holy Spirit then works and does so grandly!

SPIRITUAL ADULTERY

If the Believer's Faith is in anything except the Cross of Christ, in the Eyes of God that Believer is functioning in a state of *"spiritual adultery"* (Rom. 7:1-4). Sadder still, most Believers have never even heard of spiritual adultery, much less understand what it actually is.

When we were Born-Again, in effect, we married the Lord Jesus Christ (II Cor. 11:1-4). Being married to Him, He is to meet our every need, which He Alone can do. He does so by the Means of the Cross, which then gives the Holy Spirit, as stated, liberty to work.

THE ADMONITION

As is obvious, Hezekiah had a burden for the northern kingdom of Israel, as well as his own country of Judah. No doubt, the Holy Spirit guided him in the information imparted to his northern neighbor. He said to them, *"You Children of Israel, turn again unto the LORD God of Abraham, Isaac, and Israel, and He will return to the remnant of you, who are escaped out of the hand of the kings of Assyria."*

He admonishes them to *"be you not stiffnecked, as your fathers were, but yield yourselves unto the LORD, and enter into His Sanctuary. . . ."* And then the Promise is given, *". . . for the LORD your God is gracious and merciful, and will not turn away His Face from you, if you return unto Him."*

GRACE AND MERCY

How right Hezekiah was. If anyone shows any inclination at all toward the Lord with any degree of Repentance, or if there is anyone with a broken and contrite spirit, even to a small degree, the Lord will be *"gracious and merciful, and will not turn away His Face from you."* What a beautiful promise!

As the Holy Spirit spoke through Hezekiah, the great promise, as well, was given that if those in the northern kingdom would serve God, Israel, which had been taken over by the Assyrians, would once again become a viable Nation. That never happened!

Some years later, because of her sin and shame, Judah fell to the Babylonians. They remained some 70 years in captivity with a remnant of them coming back from which the entirety of the nation was established. At any rate, Hezekiah tried.

(10) "SO THE POSTS PASSED FROM CITY TO CITY THROUGH THE COUNTRY OF EPHRAIM AND MANASSEH EVEN UNTO ZEBULUN: BUT THEY LAUGHED THEM TO SCORN, AND MOCKED THEM.

(11) "NEVERTHELESS DIVERS OF ASHER AND MANASSEH AND OF ZEBULUN HUMBLED THEMSELVES, AND CAME TO JERUSALEM.

(12) "ALSO IN JUDAH THE HAND OF GOD WAS TO GIVE THEM ONE HEART TO DO THE COMMANDMENT OF THE KING AND OF THE PRINCES, BY THE WORD OF THE LORD.

(13) "AND THERE ASSEMBLED AT JERUSALEM MUCH PEOPLE TO KEEP THE FEAST OF UNLEAVENED BREAD IN THE SECOND MONTH, A VERY GREAT CONGREGATION.

(14) "AND THEY AROSE AND TOOK AWAY THE ALTARS THAT WERE IN JERUSALEM, AND ALL THE ALTARS FOR INCENSE TOOK THEY AWAY, AND CAST THEM INTO THE BROOK KIDRON."

The pattern is:

1. The last two phrases of Verse 10 speak significant description of the exact moral state in which Israel's Tribes were now to be found. Sadly, far too many in the modern church meet the Message of the Cross with *"laughter, scorn, and mockery."*

2. (Vs. 11) While many, in fact, will laugh and mock, still, many, as well, will accept and receive. It is to the latter we look!

3. As it speaks of the *"Feasts of Unleavened Bread"* in Verse 13, in actuality, three Feasts were to be conducted at this time: *"Passover, Unleavened Bread, and Firstfruits."* That took seven days.

4. (Vs. 13) Passover commenced on the first day, Unleavened Bread was spread over the entire seven days, and Firstfruits took place the last day. Passover signified Calvary. Unleavened Bread signified the Perfect Life and Perfect Body of Christ, which would be offered in Sacrifice. Firstfruits typified His Resurrection.

THE MOCKING AND THE LAUGHING

Concerning this Passover, this great Feast ordained by Hezekiah was one of the ten great Passovers of the Bible.

Williams says, *"Certain facts connected*

with its observance prove that the Pentateuch was read, loved, and obeyed by Hezekiah. He invited all Israel; he kept the feast in the second month instead of the first (Num. 9); he ordained that it should be observed 'as it is written' (Lev. 23); he declared that their miseries were those predicted in Deuteronomy; that God would have compassion upon them if they turned unto Him, as promised in Deuteronomy; that all was to be regulated by the Word of the Lord, i.e., by the Bible; that the Priests should officiate according to the Law of Moses; he pointed out to the people that many of them were not ceremonially clean according to the Scriptures; learning that a great multitude ate the Passover 'otherwise than it was written', he prayed that they might be pardoned, thus showing his reverence for the Bible and his fear of disobeying it (Lev. 15:31); he believed the threatened plague to be a reality; he kept the Feast of Unleavened Bread seven days, because so the Book of God ordained; and, in a word, in the observance of the Feast, he confined himself within the leaves of the Bible."[1]

Irrespective of this great Move of God in Judah, still, many of the remnant, who were left in the northern Kingdom of what once had been Israel, had no heart for God. The Scripture says, when invited to the Passover, they *"mocked the messengers and laughed them to scorn."*

THE HEART OF MAN

Why is it that there is a terrible animosity in the hearts of men as it regards the Lord? This animosity is not found as it regards any other religion, no matter how base or how vile the other religion might be. Irrespective that untold millions of lives have been gloriously and wondrously changed by the Power of God, still, Jesus Christ is lampooned in so many circles, or at the least, simply ignored.

Why?

As far as I know, there is no profanity in any language of the world that lambastes, mocks, and profanes the religion of the land. It is only Christianity toward which such vituperation is enjoined.

The following constitutes some of the reasons for the vituperation against the Lord:

• The God of Israel given to us in the Bible is, in fact, the only True God. All else is a fake; consequently, Satan levels his attack against Jehovah.

• It all stems from the Fall in the Garden of Eden. From that moment, there has been an animosity in the heart of man against God. If man does not outright blaspheme God, at the very least, he tries to ignore Him.

• As it regards Jehovah, the Name, *"the Lord Jesus Christ,"* is hated by the powers of darkness and those who follow Satan, which constitutes the majority, as nothing else.

• Jesus Christ is the only Way to God (Jn. 14:6).

• To sum up, the animosity is in the heart of man against the Lord simply because the Lord of the Bible is the Lord, and despite all the claims, there is no other. To be sure, Satan will not lampoon and lambaste that which he has originated, and I speak of all the false religions and false gods.

THE ACCEPTANCE OF THE LORD

Despite those who laughed and mocked, the Scripture says, *"Nevertheless divers of Asher and Manasseh and Zebulun humbled themselves, and came to Jerusalem."*

That's the way it always has been. Many, if not most, laugh and mock, but some will accept, and all who do accept the Lord will prove to be a light in the darkness.

Why do some accept and some reject? Why will some few have a heart toward God if given the opportunity, while others, given the same opportunity, reject?

Why did Jacob love the Lord and Esau rebel against the Lord, considering they were brothers, even twins?

No one has the answer to that question.

One thing we do know, God does not force the issue. He will deal with man, speak to man, and move upon man, but He will not force man to do anything. Man is a free moral agent. He has the capacity to say *"yes"* or to say *"no,"* at least as it regards the acceptance or rejection of the Lord Jesus Christ.

THE WILL OF MAN

While Satan most definitely can override

the will of man, which he does constantly, there remains the capacity in the heart of all men to say *"yes"* to Jesus Christ. In other words, the Lord safeguards that capacity, and in every respect. There are millions at this moment in the world who try to say *"no"* to alcohol, drugs, or other evils, but are unable to do so because the powers of darkness are stronger than their wills. Still, those same individuals, if they so desire, can say *"yes"* to Jesus Christ, which then gives Him an opportunity to set them free from the terrible vices that darken their lives.

If my memory is correct, John Bunyan, who wrote *"Pilgrim's Progress,"* which influenced Christianity greatly, was a drunk before he gave his heart to Christ. He was not only a drunk but what is labeled as a mean drunk, a wife beater, the kind of individual that is despicable, to say the least.

He realized that his life was being totally wrecked, and besides that, he was destroying his wife and children. After a particular bout of drunkenness, it is said that he walked out into a field, fell down on his knees, and began to pray.

To be sure, his praying was very weak, to say the least. In fact, he did not know how to pray. But under Conviction because of the prayers of his wife, all he knew to do was to say the following:

"Gentle Jesus, meek and mild,
"Please have pity on a little child,
"Please suffer my simplicity,
"And allow me to come to Thee."

That was his prayer, actually, merely a little childhood prayer, but God heard it, and at that moment, Jesus Christ changed the heart and the life of John Bunyan.

If any man, woman, boy, or girl shows the slightest inclination toward the Lord, Mercy will always be forthcoming, and Grace will always be freely given. The Scripture plainly says to us, *"Whosoever shall call on the Name of the Lord shall be Saved"* (Rom. 10:13).

THE DESTRUCTION OF THE HEATHEN ALTARS

Whenever the Word of the Lord begins to be practiced, begins to take effect, and begins to be propagated among the people,

NOTES

the *"heathen altars"* have to go.

What would constitute a heathen altar at this present time, and we speak of modern times?

The answer is simple: any worship, any homage, that is paid to anything other than *"Jesus Christ and Him Crucified"* would be constituted in the Mind of God as a heathen altar. Paul said, *For whatsoever is not of faith is sin"* (Rom. 14:23).

The type of Faith addressed here is Faith in *"Jesus Christ and Him Crucified"*; any other type of faith in Believers is *"sin."*

The great Apostle also said, and I quote from THE EXPOSITOR'S STUDY BIBLE: *"Examine yourselves, whether you be in the Faith* (the words, *'the Faith,'* refer to *'Christ and Him Crucified,'* with the Cross ever being the Object of our Faith): *prove your own selves.* (Make certain your Faith is actually in the Cross, and not other things.) *Know you not your own selves, how that Jesus Christ is in you* (which He can only be by our Faith expressed in His Sacrifice), *except you be reprobates?* (Rejected)" (II Cor. 13:5).

Satan cannot stop the Gospel as the great Work of Calvary is already an historic fact. So, he seeks to pervert the Gospel, and he has been very successful at doing that.

THE NEW COVENANT

What is the meaning of the New Covenant?

The meaning of the New Covenant, as it was given to the Apostle Paul, is plain and simple, *"Jesus Christ and Him Crucified."* Perhaps the following statement will explain it better than ever:

Jesus Christ is the Source of everything we receive from God, while the Cross is the Means by which these things are given unto us, all superintended by the Holy Spirit (Rom. 6:1-14; 8:1-2, 11; I Cor. 1:17-18, 21, 23; 2:2; Gal., Chpt. 5; 6:14; Eph. 2:13-18; Col. 2:14-15).

It is all in Christ and what He did at the Cross. Unfortunately, the Evil One has been successful at making things other than the Cross of Christ the object of one's faith. Always remember the following:

Jesus Christ and what He did for us at the

Cross is to always be the Object of our Faith. If our Faith is in anything else, and I mean anything else, and no matter how Scriptural the other thing may be in its own right, such constitutes *"sin."*

So, unfortunately, the *"heathen altars"* continue to abound at the present time. God help us that the Church comes back to the Cross. If it does, and I might quickly say, the part of the modern church which does come back to the Cross, will, without doubt, eradicate the heathen altars. It had to be done in the days of Hezekiah, and it must be done presently.

(15) "THEN THEY KILLED THE PASSOVER ON THE FOURTEENTH DAY OF THE SECOND MONTH: AND THE PRIESTS AND THE LEVITES WERE ASHAMED, AND SANCTIFIED THEMSELVES, AND BROUGHT IN THE BURNT OFFERINGS INTO THE HOUSE OF THE LORD.

(16) "AND THEY STOOD IN THEIR PLACE AFTER THEIR MANNER, ACCORDING TO THE LAW OF MOSES THE MAN OF GOD: THE PRIESTS SPRINKLED THE BLOOD, WHICH THEY RECEIVED OF THE HAND OF THE LEVITES.

(17) "FOR THERE WERE MANY IN THE CONGREGATION WHO WERE NOT SANCTIFIED: THEREFORE THE LEVITES HAD THE CHARGE OF THE KILLING OF THE PASSOVERS FOR EVERYONE WHO WAS NOT CLEAN, TO SANCTIFY THEM UNTO THE LORD.

(18) "FOR A MULTITUDE OF THE PEOPLE, EVEN MANY OF EPHRAIM, AND MANASSEH, ISSACHAR, AND ZEBULUN, HAD NOT CLEANSED THEMSELVES, YET DID THEY EAT THE PASSOVER OTHERWISE THAN IT WAS WRITTEN. BUT HEZEKIAH PRAYED FOR THEM, SAYING, THE GOOD LORD PARDON EVERY ONE

(19) "WHO PREPARES HIS HEART TO SEEK GOD, THE LORD GOD OF HIS FATHERS, THOUGH HE BE NOT CLEANSED ACCORDING TO THE PURIFICATION OF THE SANCTUARY.

(20) "AND THE LORD HEARKENED TO HEZEKIAH, AND HEALED THE PEOPLE."

The pattern is:

NOTES

1. Verse 15 speaks of Repentance on the part of the Priests and the Levites. Judgment must begin at the House of God (I Pet. 4:17).

2. Verse 17 affirms that the original direction of Moses was that the person who brought the victim was to kill it; but, in this case, the Levites mostly officiated.

3. (Vs. 19) The reason all of this was so serious is simply because it all pointed to Christ and what He would do to redeem humanity, which all led to the Cross.

4. (Vs. 20) There is no *"healing"* other than Calvary. All other cisterns are broken and *"can hold no water"* (Jer. 2:13).

THE KILLING OF THE PASSOVER

The manner and the way in which this was to be carried out was according to the following:

The individual would bring the lamb to the Priest. The man would lay both hands on the head of the animal and then confess his sins, whatever they may have been. This constituted a transference of his sin to the innocent victim, which was a Type of Christ carrying the penalty of our sins upon Himself at the Cross.

When this was accomplished, the individual was to take a sharp knife and cut the jugular vein of the animal, with the hot blood then pouring into a basin, which was held by the Priest. This typified our Lord shedding His Blood on Calvary's Cross.

The individual bringing the lamb had to kill the animal because he was the one who had sinned and, therefore, must perform the deed. It was our sins which nailed Christ to the Cross, and certainly not sins that He had committed.

The type of Offering presented at the Passover was *"Sin Offerings."* This particular Offering portrayed the sins of the individual being transferred to Christ, as would be obvious. Conversely, the Whole Burnt Offering constituted the very opposite. It symbolized the Perfection of Christ being given to the sinner. So, we have in these two Offerings the sins of the sinner being given to Christ, and the Perfection of Christ being given to the sinner. All of this was a Type of Calvary.

Due to ignorance and the Passover being hastily instituted, there were many Israelites who were not properly sanctified. So, they could not kill the animal, that being left up to the Priests, who carried out the task.

THE SIGNIFICANCE OF THE PASSOVER

As is obvious, the Passover represented Christ and what He would do at the Cross. Hezekiah knew that many of the people had eaten unworthily, so the Scripture says that *"Hezekiah prayed for them, saying, The good LORD pardon every one who prepares his heart to seek God, the LORD God of his fathers, though he be not cleansed according to the purification of the Sanctuary."*

Then the Scripture says, *"And the LORD hearkened to Hezekiah, and healed the people."*

In a sense, the Lord's Supper is an outgrowth of the Passover. The Passover looked forward to something that was to come, namely the Lord Jesus Christ and what He would do at the Cross. The Lord's Supper looks backward to a work already finished, hence, the admonition, *"this do in remembrance of Me"* (I Cor. 11:24).

Concerning this, Paul said, and I quote from THE EXPOSITOR'S STUDY BIBLE: *"For as often as you eat this bread, and drink this cup* (symbolic gestures), *you do show the Lord's Death till He come.* (This is meant to proclaim not only the Atoning Sacrifice necessary for our Salvation but, as well, as an ongoing cause of our continued victory in life.)

"Wherefore whosoever shall eat this bread, and drink this cup of the Lord, unworthily (tells us emphatically that this can be done, and is done constantly, I'm afraid), *shall be guilty of the Body and Blood of the Lord* (in danger of Judgment, subject to Judgment).

"But let a man examine himself (examine his Faith as to what is its real object), *and so let him eat of that bread, and drink of that cup* (after careful examination).

"For he who eats and drinks unworthily, eats and drinks damnation to himself (does not necessarily mean the loss of one's soul, but rather temporal penalties, which can become much more serious), *not discerning the Lord's Body.* (Not properly discerning

NOTES

the Cross refers to a lack of understanding regarding the Cross. All of this tells us that every single thing we have from the Lord comes to us exclusively by means of the Cross of Christ. If we do not understand that, we are not properly *'discerning the Lord's Body.'*)

"For this cause (not properly discerning the Lord's Body) *many* (a considerable number) *are weak and sickly among you* (the cause of much sickness among Christians), *and many sleep.* (This means that many Christians die prematurely. They don't lose their souls, but they do cut their lives short. This shows us, I seriously think, how important properly understanding the Cross is.)

"For if we would judge ourselves (we should examine ourselves constantly, as to whether our Faith is properly placed in the Cross of Christ), *we should not be judged* (with sickness, and even premature death).

"But when we are judged (by the Lord, because we refuse to judge ourselves), *we are chastened of the Lord* (Divine discipline), *that we should not be condemned with the world* (lose our soul)" (I Cor. 11:26-32).

The Lord does not require sinless perfection in order for one to partake of that which is referred to as *"The Lord's Supper;"* however, He most definitely, as clearly given here in Scripture, demands that our Faith be exclusively in Christ and what Christ has done for us at the Cross. Unfortunately, at this present time, the faith of far too many Christians is placed in something other than Christ and Him Crucified. As a result, and exactly as the Word of God proclaims, if the truth be known, many Christians are physically ill because of not properly discerning the Lord's Body. And then, some even die prematurely. While the cause of death may be listed in any capacity, the truth is, it is because of this very thing which we have here addressed. Their faith is in something other than Christ and Him Crucified. Unfortunately, it's in their church, their religious denomination, their good works, the money they have given, religious activity, etc.

Please understand, as I think by now should be obvious, this is serious business.

We must treat it accordingly!

(21) "AND THE CHILDREN OF ISRAEL WHO WERE PRESENT AT JERUSALEM KEPT THE FEAST OF UNLEAVENED BREAD SEVEN DAYS WITH GREAT GLADNESS: AND THE LEVITES AND THE PRIESTS PRAISED THE LORD DAY BY DAY, SINGING WITH LOUD INSTRUMENTS UNTO THE LORD.

(22) "AND HEZEKIAH SPOKE COMFORTABLY UNTO ALL THE LEVITES WHO TAUGHT THE GOOD KNOWLEDGE OF THE LORD: AND THEY DID EAT THROUGHOUT THE FEAST SEVEN DAYS, OFFERING PEACE OFFERINGS, AND MAKING CONFESSION TO THE LORD GOD OF THEIR FATHERS."

The construction is:

1. Once again, even as we see in Verse 21, worship in the realm of music and singing always accompanies the Cross and our Faith in that Finished Work.

2. (Vs. 22) Part of the Peace Offering was the only Offering in part eaten by the offeror.

3. Almost always, Peace Offerings were offered with the Sin Offering, the Whole Burnt Offering, and the Trespass Offering. It signified that God had accepted the Offering, and that Peace, which had been interrupted, was now restored between God and man.

THE PEACE OFFERING

"Peace Offerings" almost always accompanied the Sin, Trespass, and Whole Burnt Offerings. In fact, it was the only Offering partaken of by both the Priests and the person bringing the Offering.

The idea was, now that the Sin, Trespass, or Whole Burnt Offering had been offered up to the Lord, which meant that the sin had been expatiated, it was now a time for rejoicing. In fact, the individual bringing the offering could take the part given to him, call in his friends and neighbors, if he so desired, and have a feast. It was to be a time of rejoicing before the Lord, and for all the obvious reasons. As stated, due to the sacrifice offered, peace has now been restored, hence, the *"Peace Offering."* That's the reason the Scripture says, *". . . the Feast of Unleavened Bread seven days with great gladness: and the Levites and the Priests praised the LORD day by day, singing with loud instruments unto the LORD."*

(23) "AND THE WHOLE ASSEMBLY TOOK COUNSEL TO KEEP OTHER SEVEN DAYS: AND THEY KEPT OTHER SEVEN DAYS WITH GLADNESS.

(24) "FOR HEZEKIAH KING OF JUDAH DID GIVE TO THE CONGREGATION A THOUSAND BULLOCKS AND SEVEN THOUSAND SHEEP; AND THE PRINCES GAVE TO THE CONGREGATION A THOUSAND BULLOCKS AND TEN THOUSAND SHEEP: AND A GREAT NUMBER OF PRIESTS SANCTIFIED THEMSELVES.

(25) "AND ALL THE CONGREGATION OF JUDAH, WITH THE PRIESTS AND THE LEVITES, AND ALL THE CONGREGATION THAT CAME OUT OF ISRAEL, AND THE STRANGERS WHO CAME OUT OF THE LAND OF ISRAEL, AND WHO DWELT IN JUDAH, REJOICED.

(26) "SO THERE WAS GREAT JOY IN JERUSALEM: FOR SINCE THE TIME OF SOLOMON THE SON OF DAVID KING OF ISRAEL THERE WAS NOT THE LIKE IN JERUSALEM.

(27) "THEN THE PRIESTS THE LEVITES AROSE AND BLESSED THE PEOPLE: AND THEIR VOICE WAS HEARD, AND THEIR PRAYER CAME UP TO HIS HOLY DWELLING PLACE, EVEN UNTO HEAVEN."

The construction is:

1. (Vs. 24) The conduits carrying the blood from these many sacrifices from the Temple Mount would have caused the Brook Kidron, which ran between the Temple Mount and Olivet, to run red with blood.

2. (Vs. 24) This is obnoxious and repulsive to the unspiritual eye, but, to those who know their God, Calvary is the greatest sight this side of Heaven. For it was there that man was liberated and set free (Col. 2:14-15).

3. (Vs. 26) Calvary alone brings *"great joy"*—nothing else will.

4. (Vs. 27) The only prayer that God will hear is that which is anchored in Calvary's Cross. In fact, as human beings, no matter what good we may think we do, such has no standing with God. Our standing with

Him, and exclusively, pertains to the Lord Jesus Christ and what He did at Calvary and our Faith in that Finished Work.

THE SACRIFICES

As is here glaringly obvious, the blessing, prosperity, and greatness of Judah all depended upon the shed Blood of the Lamb, of which all the sacrifices were a Type. It is no different presently. The blessings of the modern church, and especially each individual, are all predicated on Calvary, i.e., what Jesus there did. But let it ever be understood that the one Sacrifice of Himself given at Calvary's Cross was greater, far greater, than all the hundreds of thousands, and even millions, of animal sacrifices that had been offered up, even from the beginning of time. That's the reason that the entirety of the New Covenant is anchored in the Lord Jesus Christ and what He did at the Cross. In other words, the New Covenant is the Lord Jesus Christ. It has no altars, at least the kind on which sacrifices are made, no temples, no rituals, and no ceremonies, other than Water Baptism, which is a one-time affair, and the Lord's Supper, which should be taken at given times. All of this is symbolic of the Cross of Christ and, in fact, is to bring the Believer back to the Cross.

Concerning all of this which Hezekiah did, the Scripture says it was:
- *"With gladness";*
- *"Rejoicing";* and,
- *"Great Joy."*

I think it should be obvious by now that everything, as it relates to the Lord, is tied to the Cross.

As stated, no matter how good we might think we are, and no matter how many good works we might carry out, within ourselves, we have no standing with the Lord whatsoever. Any standing that we have is ours simply because the Lord Jesus Christ and what He has done for us at the Cross. We must never forget that. That must be the core, the central focus of our life and living for God. It is the Cross! The Cross! The Cross!

"Just as I am, without one plea,
"But that Your Blood was shed for me,

NOTES

"And that You bid me come to Thee,
"O Lamb of God I come!"

"Just as I am, and waiting not,
"To rid my soul of one dark blot,
"To Thee, Whose Blood can cleanse each spot,
"O Lamb of God I come!"

"Just as I am, though tossed about,
"With many a conflict, many a doubt,
"Fightings within and fears without,
"O Lamb of God I come!"

"Just as I am, poor, wretched, blind,
"Sight, riches, healing of the mind,
"Yea, all I need in Thee to find,
"O Lamb of God I come!"

"Just as I am, You will receive,
"Will welcome, pardon, cleanse, relieve;
"Because Your Promise I believe,
"O Lamb of God I come!"

"Just as I am, Your Love unknown,
"Has broken every barrier down;
"Now to be Thine, yea Thine Alone,
"O Lamb of God I come!"

"Just as I am, of that great love,
"The breadth, length, depth, the height to prove,
"Here for a season, then above,
"O Lamb of God I come."

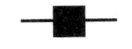

CHAPTER 31

(1) "NOW WHEN ALL THIS WAS FINISHED, ALL ISRAEL THAT WERE PRESENT WENT OUT TO THE CITIES OF JUDAH, AND BROKE THE IMAGES IN PIECES, AND CUT DOWN THE GROVES, AND THREW DOWN THE HIGH PLACES AND THE ALTARS OUT OF ALL JUDAH AND BENJAMIN, IN EPHRAIM ALSO AND MANASSEH, UNTIL THEY HAD UTTERLY DESTROYED THEM ALL. THEN ALL THE CHILDREN OF ISRAEL RETURNED, EVERY MAN TO HIS POSSESSION, INTO THEIR OWN CITIES."

The overview is:

1. The offering up of the great number

of sacrifices set the stage for all that would follow.

2. When the church comes back to the Cross, to be sure, the evil and the idols are cleaned out.

3. In fact, nothing can actually be made right until everything begins right, which again, refers to coming back to the Cross.

THE REVIVAL

A Revival necessitates several things.

Before there could be Revival, Judah had to come back to the Cross, typified by the sacrifices. Likewise, before there can be Revival in the church, or even in the heart and life of the individual, the church and the individual must come back to the Cross. Everything begins at the Cross. Any effort made without taking the Cross into account is a wasted effort.

WHY IS THE CROSS THAT NECESSARY?

The Cross of Christ is where all sin was atoned, and where Satan and all of his demon spirits and fallen Angels were defeated, thereby, making it possible for the Grace of God to be extended to believing man in an unprecedented manner. The Cross of Christ tells man what he is, tells man Who and what God is, and puts everything in proper perspective.

As we stated in the last Chapter, man, within himself, has absolutely no standing with God whatsoever, irrespective of how good he may think he is, or how good others may think he is. In other words, if we try to come to the Lord on our own merit, the door will be closed. Man has access to God, access to His Throne, and access to all that God is simply by and through the Cross of Christ, and no other way. This is a great Truth that we must ever understand (Eph. 2:13-18).

While man may admit that certain people of the human race may need the Cross, it is hard for those who consider themselves to be moral to admit their need for the Cross. However, it is like one leper claiming that he's better than another leper because he has only 142 leprous spots, while the other leper has 145 leprous spots. The moral is, all of mankind is constituted as sinful lepers, meaning that man desperately needs a Redeemer, and that Redeemer is the Lord Jesus Christ and, in fact, can only be the Lord Jesus Christ. There is no other! And Christ is the Redeemer by and through what He did at the Cross. The Cross is ever the catalyst for all things pertaining to the Lord and man.

DOES THE MODERN CHURCH BELIEVE THAT THE CROSS IS THE CATALYST?

In a word, *"No!"*

A great part of the church places no confidence in the Cross of Christ at all. Another part of the church claims to believe the Cross but projects a claim in name only. In other words, the Cross of Christ is very seldom mentioned. If it is mentioned, it is mentioned only in the capacity of the Salvation process. Thank the Lord for that; however, that is only a minor part of what the Lord gave to the Apostle Paul as it regards the meaning of the New Covenant, which is the meaning of the Cross. Only a small part of the modern church actually believes and understands that the Cross is the center of all things as it relates to the Lord and His Word.

CAIN AND ABEL

The stage is set in the Fourth Chapter of Genesis, as it regards that which God demands and man's reaction to that demand.

The Lord conveyed to the First Family that even though they were fallen, through the sacrifice of an innocent victim, namely a lamb, which would typify Christ, Who was to come, i.e., *"the Seed of the woman,"* they could have forgiveness of sins and fellowship with Him; however, it would be only by this Means that such could be attained.

It seems that Cain was the first of the two brothers to offer up a sacrifice. The Scripture says of this man, *". . . that Cain brought of the fruit of the ground an offering unto the LORD."* The Scripture also says, *"And Abel, he also brought of the firstlings of his flock and of the fat thereof."*

But then the Scripture tells us, *"And the LORD had respect unto Abel and to his offering: but unto Cain and to his offering He had not respect"* (Gen. 4:3-5).

It seems that Cain did not deny the need for an offering, but that he desired to offer up that which he had selected and not that which God had demanded.

These offerings, which were on the first page of human history, set the stage for all that would follow thereafter. The Lord accepted the offering of Abel because it was what He demanded, which was a lamb, an innocent victim, which would be typical of the coming Redeemer, the Lord Jesus Christ. He rejected the offering of Cain because it was *"the fruit of the ground,"* and not that which was necessary.

THE OFFERING WAS THE CATALYST

The Lord didn't even really look at the ones bringing the offering because it was obvious what they were. Both Cain and Abel were born outside of Eden, meaning they were born in original sin, and meaning they were both lost. He rather looked at the offering. If the offering met His Specifications, then the offerer was accepted also. If the offering was rejected, likewise, the offerer was rejected. This means that Abel was accepted, while Cain was rejected.

It has not changed from then until now. The Lord looks at our Faith, and more particularly, the Object of our Faith. The Object must be the Cross of Christ, that is, if it is to be accepted. If our Faith is in the proper Object, then we are automatically accepted as well. If it's not in the proper Object, namely the Cross of Christ, then the individual is instantly rejected.

THE FIRST MURDER

The first murder among the human family was because of religion.

Cain was angry because God had accepted the offering of Abel, his brother, and had rejected his, so he murdered his brother. Cain's religion was too refined to kill a lamb but not too cultured to murder his brother. God's Way of Salvation fills the heart with love; man's way of salvation inflames it with hatred. *"Religion"* has ever been the greatest cause of bloodshed.

Those who reject the Cross of Christ are not content to go their own way but feel they must, as Cain, eliminate those who believe

NOTES

in the one Sacrifice accepted by Lord. It hasn't changed, as stated, from then until now. The Cross was an offense to Cain, and it is an offense to millions at present.

HOW IS THE CROSS OF CHRIST AN OFFENSE?

Paul said, *"And I, Brethren, if I yet preach Circumcision, why do I yet suffer persecution?* (Any message other than the Cross draws little opposition.) *then is the offence of the Cross ceased.* (The Cross offends the world and most of the church. So, if the preacher ceases to preach the Cross as the only way of Salvation and Victory, then opposition and persecution will cease. But so will Salvation and Victory!)" (Gal. 5:11).

The Cross of Christ is an offense simply because it lays waste all of man's efforts to save himself or to sanctify himself. In other words, it shows what man really is, a poor, disconsolate, stumbling, and halting creature, who, because of the Fall, cannot even keep the slightest Commandment given by the Lord. But man does not like to admit that. He likes to think, and especially religious man, that whatever is necessary as it regards spiritual things, he can do. As a Believer, he is loath to admit that he cannot effect his own Sanctification, and that he cannot overcome the efforts by the Evil One to steal, kill, and destroy. So, when the Preacher stands up, even as Paul, and lays waste all of man's efforts, stating that the only way to Salvation, the only way to Victory, is by and through the Lord Jesus Christ and what He did at the Cross and our Faith in that Finished Work, which then enables the Holy Spirit to effect His great Work within our lives, that offends because it lays waste the flesh.

WHAT IS THE FLESH?

The flesh can actually be described in two parts. They are:

1. Man's personal ability, personal strength, education, knowledge, wisdom, efforts, talents, intellectualism, etc. While these things may or may not be wrong in their own right, the idea is, what we need to be in Christ, in fact, what we must be in Christ, cannot be effected by our own

personal efforts. Due to the Fall, man has been rendered incapable (Rom. 8:10).

2. Unholy and ungodly desires and passions, which are of this world, which are carnal and, thereby, unholy. The flesh will always gravitate toward that, hence, the reason the Scripture said, *"So then they who are in the flesh cannot please God"* (Rom. 8:8). That's the reason He also said, *"For they who are after the flesh do mind the things of the flesh; but they who are after the Spirit the things of the Spirit"* (Rom. 8:5). That's the reason we are emphatically told to not *"walk after the flesh"* (Rom. 8:1).

WHAT IS WALKING AFTER THE FLESH?

Of course, we are speaking of Believers. All unbelievers walk exclusively after the flesh because that's the only way they can function. The Spirit of God does not dwell in them, as is obvious, so the flesh is their only alternative, hence, the reason for all sin, man's inhumanity to man, ungodliness, crime, etc.

Walking after the flesh constitutes the Believer placing his faith in anything, irrespective as to what it might be, other than Christ and the Cross (Rom. 6:1-14; 8:1-2, 11; I Cor. 1:17-18, 21, 23; 2:2). Many Believers think that because their faith is in something religious that it is satisfactory with the Lord. It isn't! In fact, *"walking after the Spirit,"* which, of course, refers to the Holy Spirit, constitutes the Believer placing his Faith completely in Christ and the Cross (Rom. 8:2).

Many Christians think that the doing of spiritual things constitutes walking after the Spirit. While those things are commendable and should be done, that was not what Paul was talking about when he referred to *"walking after the Spirit."*

WHAT IS IT THAT THE SPIRIT DOES WHICH WE ARE SUPPOSED TO EMULATE?

The Holy Spirit, without Whom we can do nothing, works exclusively within the framework of the Finished Work of Christ, i.e., *"the Cross"* (Rom. 8:2).

Knowing and understanding how the Holy Spirit works is half the battle, so

NOTES

to speak. Unfortunately, so many in the Church take the Holy Spirit for granted, and that results in great difficulties. Most Christians, sad to say, are living in a state of *"spiritual adultery"* (Rom. 7:1-4). In fact, every single Believer who has ever lived, at one time or the other, has tried to function in the realm of *"spiritual adultery."* This is what the entirety of the Seventh Chapter of Romans is all about. It is a proclamation of the experience of the Apostle Paul after he was Saved, Spirit-filled, and preaching the Gospel. At that particular time, he did not know God's Prescribed Order of Victory, which is the Cross of Christ, and in his defense, no one else did either. In fact, it was to the Apostle Paul that this great Revelation was given (Gal. 1:12).

In the Seventh Chapter of Romans, the Apostle gives us the account of his life and experience after he was Saved on the road to Damascus. How long he was in this state of spiritual failure, we are not told; however, it must have been at least a year or two. Despite all of his efforts otherwise, he found he could not successfully live for the Lord, and if the Apostle Paul couldn't successfully live for the Lord in this capacity, neither can you nor I. (For a more detailed account of Romans, Chapter Seven, please see our Study Guide on that subject.)

The Holy Spirit works entirely within the framework of the Finished Work of Christ, and in view of this, we are expected to have our Faith anchored squarely in the Cross of Christ. In other words, the Cross of Christ is to ever be the Object of our Faith because that's where the Victory was won by Christ (Col. 2:14-15). When the Believer anchors his Faith exclusively in the Cross of Christ and doesn't allow it to be moved elsewhere, the Holy Spirit will then work mightily within his heart and life, developing His Fruit, which He Alone can do.

Incidentally, *"spiritual adultery"* constitutes the Believer placing his faith in something other than the Cross of Christ. Every Believer is married to Christ (Rom. 7:4; II Cor. 11:1-4). As such, and as should be obvious, Christ is to meet our every need, which, in fact, He Alone can do. But when we place our Faith in something other than Christ and what He has done at the Cross, this constitutes spiritual adultery. In effect, we are being unfaithful to Christ, which you can well imagine greatly hinders the Holy Spirit. Thank God that the Spirit does not leave us in those times because He loves us. He does everything He can do to help us, but the truth is, we greatly limit Him, as should be obvious, whenever our faith is misplaced.

FAITH

The Believer must understand that every single thing that we do, and the way that we live for the Lord, is all constituted by Faith. However, it must also be understood that the Object of our Faith must always be the Cross of Christ. This is where the problem comes in. We have Faith, but it's misplaced faith. It's faith in the wrong object, which the Holy Spirit can never honor.

Jesus said that when the Holy Spirit comes, and He most definitely has already come, *"He shall glorify Me* (will portray Christ and what Christ did at the Cross for dying humanity)*: for He shall receive of Mine* (the benefits of the Cross), *and shall show it unto you* (which He did, when He gave these great Truths to the Apostle Paul)" (Jn. 16:14).

Every Victory was won at the Cross, and as previously stated, Satan and all of his cohorts of darkness were defeated at the Cross. So that's where the Believer must anchor his Faith. That is the Word of God (Eph. 2:13-18; Col. 2:14-15; Gal., Chpt. 5; 6:14).

(2) "AND HEZEKIAH APPOINTED THE COURSES OF THE PRIESTS AND THE LEVITES AFTER THEIR COURSES, EVERY MAN ACCORDING TO HIS SERVICE, THE PRIESTS AND THE LEVITES FOR BURNT OFFERINGS AND FOR PEACE OFFERINGS, TO MINISTER, AND TO GIVE THANKS, AND TO PRAISE IN THE GATES OF THE TENTS OF THE LORD.

(3) "HE APPOINTED ALSO THE KING'S PORTION OF HIS SUBSTANCE FOR THE BURNT OFFERINGS, TO WIT, FOR THE MORNING AND EVENING BURNT OFFERINGS, AND THE BURNT OFFERINGS FOR THE SABBATHS, AND FOR THE NEW MOONS, AND FOR THE SET FEASTS, AS IT IS WRITTEN IN THE LAW OF THE LORD.

(4) "MOREOVER HE COMMANDED THE PEOPLE WHO DWELT IN JERUSALEM TO GIVE THE PORTION OF THE PRIESTS AND THE LEVITES, THAT THEY MIGHT BE ENCOURAGED IN THE LAW OF THE LORD.

(5) "AND AS SOON AS THE COMMANDMENT CAME ABROAD, THE CHILDREN OF ISRAEL BROUGHT IN ABUNDANCE THE FIRSTFRUITS OF CORN, WINE, AND OIL, AND HONEY, AND OF ALL THE INCREASE OF THE FIELD; AND THE TITHE OF ALL THINGS BROUGHT THEY IN ABUNDANTLY.

(6) "AND CONCERNING THE CHILDREN OF ISRAEL AND JUDAH, WHO DWELT IN THE CITIES OF JUDAH, THEY ALSO BROUGHT IN THE TITHE OF OXEN AND SHEEP, AND THE TITHE OF THE HOLY THINGS WHICH WERE CONSECRATED UNTO THE LORD THEIR GOD, AND LAID THEM BY HEAPS.

(7) "IN THE THIRD MONTH THEY BEGAN TO LAY THE FOUNDATION OF THE HEAPS, AND FINISHED THEM IN THE SEVENTH MONTH.

(8) "AND WHEN HEZEKIAH AND THE PRINCES CAME AND SAW THE HEAPS, THEY BLESSED THE LORD, AND HIS PEOPLE ISRAEL.

(9) "THEN HEZEKIAH QUESTIONED WITH THE PRIESTS AND THE LEVITES CONCERNING THE HEAPS."

The overview is:

1. (Vs. 2) Offering sacrifices and giving thanks to the Lord was thought of as so much foolishness by Ahaz. Likewise, the carnal mind sees no profit in such, but the Spiritual Mind understands its value. If we ignore the Bible, we lose our love for God. If we love the Bible, we will love God. Hezekiah loved the Bible, so he would obey the Bible.

2. (Vss. 3-4) Hezekiah did not evade his own responsibilities in the matter of contribution. His *"portion"* was the tithe, even as it should have been. The king meant to set an example, which he did!

3. (Vs. 5) Whenever the Church is on fire for God, money is given liberally to the

Work of God, otherwise, there is little giving.

4. (Vs. 6) When we give in *"heaps,"* the Lord gives it back to us even in *"greater heaps"* (Lk. 6:38).

5. (Vs. 7) In the *"third month"* the Feast of Pentecost was conducted, while in the *"seventh month"* was conducted the Feast of Tabernacles.

BURNT OFFERINGS AND PEACE OFFERINGS

If it is to be noticed, whenever Judah strayed from the Lord, the sacrifices ceased, or if they did continue, it was only a matter of ceremony. When Judah was on its way back to the Lord, the first thing that was re-instituted was always the Sacrificial system.

The Sacrificial system actually began at the very dawn of time. We find the first account given in the Fourth Chapter of Genesis as it regarded Cain and Abel. It continued to be conducted, more or less, even unto the flood and was picked up again by Noah after the flood (Gen. 8:20). We find by Noah offering up sacrifice that civilization, as it sprang from the sons of Noah, had as its foundation the Cross of Christ, i.e., *"the Altar."*

When this sacrifice was offered, the Scripture says, *"And the LORD smelled a sweet savor* (the burning of the sacrifice was sweet unto the Lord, because it spoke of the coming Redeemer, Who would lift man out of this morass of evil)*"* (Gen. 8:20-21).

The Sacrificial system continued under Abraham. In fact, Abraham built so many Altars on which to offer sacrifice that he was referred to as the *"Altar builder"* (Gen. 12:7-8; 13:4, 18; 22:9). When the Law was given, the very core or heartbeat of the Law was the Sacrificial system. Were it not for that system, Israel could not have survived. Their only recourse was the Altar, i.e., *"the Cross."*

As is obvious, the Altar typified the Cross of Calvary, and the offering up of the clean animals on that Altar previewed the coming Redeemer, Who would be the Lord Jesus Christ, Who would give His Life as a ransom for many.

When Jesus came, of course, the Altar and the Sacrificial system were no longer needed. The Sacrificial system was always a shadow of that which was to come, and now that the Substance has come, the Lord Jesus Christ, His one Sacrifice of Himself sufficed then and will suffice for all eternity. In fact, Paul referred to it as the *"Everlasting Covenant"* (Heb. 13:20).

It has not changed presently. The only thing standing between mankind and the Judgment of God is the Cross of Christ. In fact, the only thing standing between the Church and apostasy is the Cross of Christ. Whenever the church leaves the Cross, it always goes into apostasy. I'm afraid that I have to say at present, and certainly with no gladness of heart, that the church is not merely on the road of apostasy, it has already apostatized, and it's because it has left the Cross.

Hezekiah appointed the Priests their rightful courses in order that they may continually offer *"Burnt Offerings and Peace Offerings . . . and to give thanks, and to praise in the gates of the tents of the LORD."*

THE LAW OF THE LORD

The latter portion of the Third Verse says, as it regards Hezekiah and his obedience to the Word, *". . . as it is written in the Law of the LORD."* In other words, the king was doing everything within his power to abide by the written Word of God.

The Word of God is the single most important thing in the entirety of the world. In fact, the Bible is the only revealed Truth in the world and, in fact, ever has been.

I did not say that the Bible is the only thing that is true, but rather that it is the only *"Truth."* Concerning Truth, the Scripture says:

• Jesus is Truth. He doesn't merely have truth, He is Truth (Jn. 14:6).
• The Word of the Lord is Truth (Jn. 17:17).
• The Spirit is Truth (I Jn. 5:6).

IS ALL TRUTH GOD'S TRUTH?

Yes, it is!

However, one must first know what Truth actually is. As stated, just because something is true, doesn't mean at all that it is *"Truth."* For instance, it is true that if one drinks enough alcohol, one will be drunk, but that most definitely isn't *"Truth."*

One particular preacher claimed that it was God Who gave to Freud the rudiments of humanistic psychology. He claimed this on the basis of *"all truth is God's Truth."* Our dear brother evidently did not really know what Truth actually was or is.

We might say, Truth is not a philosophy, it is rather a Person, and we speak of the Lord Jesus Christ. The same thing can be said of the Holy Spirit. And, as well, the Word of God, which is Truth, is the written form of the Living Word, the Lord Jesus Christ. If it is to be noticed, everything that Jesus did in His earthly Ministry was backed up totally by the Word of God. In other words, He did nothing outside of the Word.

THE BIBLE

As we've said previously, Satan is presently making possibly his greatest attack against the Word of God; however, he is doing it in a subtle way. He's not making the attack from a frontal position, but rather, one might say, an end run. He is not directly opposing the Word of God, merely perverting the Word of God. He is doing that by bringing out scores of books which claim to be Bibles, such as the *"Message Bible,"* which is merely a collection of religious thoughts by some individual. Please read the next lines very carefully.

Unless your Bible is a word for word translation, then it's really not a Bible but merely a religious book. And most of the so-called Bibles at the present time come under the category of merely a *"religious book."* In other words, it's not the Bible because it's not a word for word translation.

The King James is a word for word translation, and there are one or two others as well. Concerning this, Jesus said, *". . . Man shall not live by bread alone, but by every Word that proceeds out of the Mouth of God"* (Mat. 4:4).

But, at the same time, Christians should understand that when the Word of God was originally given, actually covering a time span of approximately 1,600 years (from the time of Moses and concluding with John the Beloved, who closed out the Canon of Scripture by writing the Book of Revelation), the writers of the Gospels (Matthew, Mark, Luke, and John) did not write the Words of Christ in red. In fact, there was no red ink at that time.

As well, they did not write the Sacred Text in Elizabethan English. That type of English was given to us by the King James translators several hundreds of years ago. In fact, the King James translation has undergone two or three rewrites, and rightly so. I have a copy of the first King James translation, and it would be very difficult, if not nearly impossible, for anyone presently to read it.

I'm addressing this because some Christians have in their minds that if it's not Elizabethan English, then it's not the Bible. The Old Testament writers wrote in Hebrew, while the New Testament writers wrote in Greek. When the King James translators performed their great work, they used the English of that time, which is all they could do. From then until now, some of the words have changed meanings, and if the opportunity presents itself, we should effect that change of meaning in present printings, that is, if possible. For instance:

Peter said, *"Forasmuch as you know that you were not redeemed with corruptible things, as silver and gold, from your vain conversation received by tradition from your fathers"* (I Pet 1:18).

The word *"conversation"* translated thusly by the King James translators had an entirely different meaning then than it does now. Then, it meant one's lifestyle or the manner of one's behavior. Now, it refers to two or more people conversing with each other. As stated, some words through the centuries have changed meanings; however, in truth, not that many words in the King James have changed meaning.

I think it can be said, and without fear of contradiction, that when one holds the King James Version in his hand, he can understand that one is truly holding in his hand the Word of God.

THE ABUNDANCE

When the Spirit of the Lord is Moving, which always takes place when people adhere to the Word of God, then everything starts to move in a positive way, and there is an abundance. When people love the Lord, and they are trying to function according to the Word of God, their giving becomes automatic. They realize what the Lord has done for them, and they want to reciprocate as best they can. Of course, we cannot earn anything from the Lord, and neither can we pay for anything that we receive from the Lord. In fact, the Lord has nothing for sale. Everything He has, comes in the form of a Gift, and, in reality, there are no strings attached. He only asks that we love Him and strive to the best of our ability to obey Him. In fact, Jesus said as it regards this, *"My Yoke is easy, and My Burden is light"* (Mat. 11:28-30). In other words, the Lord doesn't demand very much of us. Actually, He demands almost nothing as it compares to what Satan demands of his followers. It's truly a pleasure to live for the Lord; it's truly a pleasure to follow Him; and it's truly a pleasure to know Him.

During the time of Judah's existence, they tithed their corn, their wine, their oil, their honey, etc. In other words, they brought in a tenth of their crop and deposited it at the Temple to be used by the Priests, for this was a part of the upkeep for the Priests. They brought so much that it was labeled as *"heaps,"* and rightly so!

Under the New Covenant, virtually all of the giving is in the form of money, as would be obvious. Actually, there are two things that are predominant as it regards giving. They are:

1. We are obligated as Believers to give to the Work of God. Paul said that we should give, *"to show the sincerity of our love"* (II Cor. 8:8). If we say we love the Lord and, in fact, actually do, we will give to His Work. It's that simple! People, who will not give to the Work of God, as far as I'm concerned, simply need to get Saved. Anyone who is truly Saved knows what the Lord has done for him, which constitutes an appreciation and a love for God that knows no bounds.

EVERY BELIEVER MUST GIVE

Any Believer that claims he cannot afford to give is cheating himself. The way to get out of poverty and, in fact, the only way for the Believer to get out of poverty, is to start giving to the Lord. The old adage is true that we simply cannot outgive God. In fact, giving to the Lord must be the first thing in our budget. Everything else must take second or third place, etc. Jesus plainly told us, *"But seek you first the Kingdom of God, and His Righteousness* (this gives the 'condition' for God's Blessings; His Interests are to be 'first'); *and all these things shall be added unto you* (this is the 'guarantee' of God's Provision)" (Mat. 6:33).

When the believing sinner comes to Christ, he enters into a brand-new culture, the culture of the Bible, and he enters into God's Economy. Yes, we are to use good sense in our daily walk, as should be obvious, but we are to look exclusively to the Lord for promotion. As well, as Believers and understanding His Word, we are to expect promotion. We are to believe Him for this. In turn, we will put the Kingdom of God first, even as Jesus demanded that we do. If that is done, and done with a spirit of expectation, the Blessings of God are guaranteed, providing the second point is correct, which we will now address. Incidentally, *"Blessings"* mean *"increase."*

2. Two things, as stated, pertain to giving. They are:

A. We must give; and,

B. *"Where"* we give is just as important as *"that"* we give. Biblical sense should tell us that if we're supporting that which is not of God, it cannot be blessed by the Lord. In fact, He doesn't even consider it as truly a gift to His Work, because it isn't His Work. Regrettably, most giving falls under that category. Let's use a New Testament example.

THE APOSTLE PAUL

As most Bible students know, Paul's greatest difficulty was the Judaizers who came into the Churches which he had planted, seeking to divert the people from Grace to Law. Actually, Paul didn't have much patience with these false apostles. He said of them, and I quote from THE EXPOSITOR'S STUDY BIBLE:

"Beware of dogs (the Apostle is addressing the Judaizers, who were Jews from Jerusalem who claimed Christ, but insisted

on Believers keeping the Law as well; all of this was diametrically opposed to Paul's Gospel of Grace, in which the Law of Moses had no part; as well, by the use of the word *'dogs,'* the Apostle was using the worst slur), *beware of evil workers* (they denigrated the Cross), *beware of the concision.* (This presents a Greek word Paul uses as a play upon the Greek word *'Circumcision,'* which was at the heart of the Law Gospel of the Judaizers)" (Phil. 3:2).

The great Apostle also said, *"For such are false apostles, deceitful workers* (they have no rightful claim to the Apostolic Office; they are deceivers), *transforming themselves into the Apostles of Christ.* (They have called themselves to this Office.)

"And no marvel (true Believers should not be surprised); *for Satan himself is transformed into an Angel of light.* (This means he pretends to be that which he is not.)

"Therefore it is no great thing if his ministers (Satan's ministers) *also be transformed as the ministers of righteousness* (despite their claims, they were 'Satan's ministers' because they preached something other than the Cross [I Cor. 1:17-18, 21, 23; 2:2; Gal. 1:8-9]); *whose end shall be according to their works* (that *'end'* is spiritual destruction [Phil. 3:18-19])" (II Cor. 11:13-15).

Now, I'll ask the question!

Is it permissible to support these false apostles, these whom the Holy Spirit through Paul labeled as *"dogs,"* etc.? I think the answer to that would be an obvious, *"No!"* And yet, most of what is being presently supported, and more than likely it's always been that way, is that which falls into the category of *"false."* The Lord does not label such as true giving, as ought to be obvious.

TO WHAT SHOULD WE GIVE?

The Holy Spirit through the Apostle Paul gave us implicit direction, as it regards that, as well.

When Paul was in prison in Rome, Epaphroditus came from the Church at Philippi, a distance of nearly 1,000 miles, bringing to Paul a very generous offering from that particular Church. Paul's Epistle known as *"Philippians,"* sent back

NOTES

to the Church, was, among other things, a *"thank you note"* for their generosity to him, which was very much needed. He said, *"Notwithstanding you have well done, that you did communicate with my affliction.* (They helped Paul with his needs, as it regards the offering they sent him.)

"Now you Philippians know also, that in the beginning of the Gospel (refers to the time when Paul first preached the Word to them, about ten years previously), *when I departed from Macedonia, no Church communicated with me as concerning giving and receiving, but you only* (proclaims the fact that the Philippians had always been generous).

"For even in Thessalonica (when he was starting the Church there) *you sent once and again unto my necessity* (proclaims their faithfulness).

"Not because I desire a gift (presents the Apostle defending himself against the slanderous assertion that he is using the Gospel as a means to make money): *but I desire fruit that may abound to your account.* (God keeps a record of everything, even our gifts, whether giving or receiving.)

"But I have all, and abound: I am full (proclaims the fact that the Philippian gift must have been generous), *having received of Epaphroditus the things which were sent from you* (Epaphroditus had brought the gift from Philippi to Rome), *an odour of a sweet smell* (presents the Old Testament odors of the Levitical sacrifices, all typifying Christ), *a Sacrifice acceptable, well-pleasing to God.* (For those who gave to Paul, enabling Him to take the Message of the Cross to others, their gift, and such gifts presently, are looked at by God as a part of the Sacrificial Atoning Work of Christ on the Cross. Nothing could be higher than that!)

"But my God shall supply all your need (presents the Apostle assuring the Philippians, and all other Believers, as well, that they have not impoverished themselves in giving so liberally to the Cause of Christ) *according to His Riches in Glory* (the measure of supply will be determined by the wealth of God in Glory) *by Christ Jesus* (made possible by the Cross)" (Phil. 4:14-19).

Pure and simple, the only giving that

God recognizes as such is that which is given to help proclaim the Message of the Cross, which is the meaning of the New Covenant, to a hurting, dying world.

THE HOLY SPIRIT

Two things are said here by the Holy Spirit as it regards the statements given by the Apostle.

1. He likened the gift given to him as *"an odour of a sweet smell."* What did he mean by that?

This statement, or one similar, was often used as it regarded sacrifices of clean animals offered up to the Lord. The Scripture says, *"And Noah built an Altar unto the LORD; and took of every clean beast, and of every clean fowl, and offered Burnt Offerings on the Altar. And the LORD smelled a sweet savor . . ."* (Gen. 8:20-21).

Ezra said, *"That they may offer sacrifices of sweet savors unto the God of Heaven . . ."* (Ezra 6:10).

And then, *"And you shall burn the whole ram upon the Altar: it is a Burnt Offering unto the LORD: it is a sweet savor . . ."* (Ex. 29:18).

How could an animal burning on an Altar, with greasy smoke going up toward Heaven, present itself as a *"sweet savor"* unto the Lord?

It could and did simply because it typified the Son of God giving Himself on the Altar of Sacrifice, i.e., *"the Cross,"* which would redeem fallen humanity from the terrible morass of evil. That's why it was a sweet savor, a sweet odor unto the Lord.

2. All of this, as should be obvious, pertained to the Cross. As we have repeatedly stated, the meaning of the New Covenant is the meaning of the Cross. It is the Gospel of Good News. It is the Means of Salvation for the sinner and Sanctification for the Saint. If the preacher is not preaching that, then whatever it is he is preaching is not the Gospel. Paul also stated as he wrote to the Galatians, *"I marvel that you are so soon removed from Him* (the Holy Spirit) *Who called you into the Grace of Christ* (made possible by the Cross) *unto another gospel* (anything which doesn't have the Cross as its Object of Faith):

NOTES

"Which is not another (presents the fact that Satan's aim is not so much to deny the Gospel, which he can little do, as to corrupt it); *but there be some who trouble you, and would pervert the Gospel of Christ* (once again, to make the object of Faith something other than the Cross).

"But though we (Paul and his associates), *or an Angel from Heaven, preach any other gospel unto you than that which we have preached unto you* (Jesus Christ and Him Crucified), *let him be accursed* (eternally condemned; the Holy Spirit speaks this through Paul, making this very serious).

"As we said before, so say I now again (at some time past, he had said the same thing to them, making their defection even more serious), *If any man preach any other gospel unto you* (anything other than the Cross) *than that you have received* (which Saved your souls), *let him be accursed* ('eternally condemned,' which means the loss of the soul)" (Gal. 1:6-9).

WHAT IS THE GOSPEL?

In fact, Paul also told us exactly what the Gospel of Jesus is. He said, *"For Christ sent me not to baptize* (presents to us a Cardinal Truth), *but to preach the Gospel* (the manner in which one may be Saved from sin): *not with wisdom of words* (intellectualism is not the Gospel), *lest the Cross of Christ should be made of none effect.* (This tells us in no uncertain terms that the Cross of Christ must always be the emphasis of the Message.)" As well, it tells us that the Gospel is the Message of the Cross (I Cor. 1:17.) Let me say it again: Unless one is supporting the Message of the Cross, whatever it is he is supporting, it's not the Gospel. It might be something about the Gospel, it might be pointing toward the Gospel, but unless one is preaching the Cross, one is not preaching the Gospel of Jesus Christ. And if it's not the Gospel, it should not be supported.

(10) "AND AZARIAH THE CHIEF PRIEST OF THE HOUSE OF ZADOK ANSWERED HIM, AND SAID, SINCE THE PEOPLE BEGAN TO BRING THE OFFERINGS INTO THE HOUSE OF THE LORD, WE HAVE HAD ENOUGH TO EAT, AND HAVE LEFT PLENTY: FOR THE LORD

HAS BLESSED HIS PEOPLE; AND THAT WHICH IS LEFT IS THIS GREAT STORE.

(11) "THEN HEZEKIAH COMMANDED TO PREPARE CHAMBERS IN THE HOUSE OF THE LORD; AND THEY PREPARED THEM,

(12) "AND BROUGHT IN THE OFFERINGS AND THE TITHES AND THE DEDICATED THINGS FAITHFULLY: OVER WHICH CONONIAH THE LEVITE WAS RULER, AND SHIMEI HIS BROTHER WAS THE NEXT.

(13) "AND JEHIEL, AND AZAZIAH, AND NAHATH, AND ASAHEL, AND JERIMOTH, AND JOZABAD, AND ELIEL, AND ISMACHIAH, AND MAHATH, AND BENAIAH, WERE OVERSEERS UNDER THE HAND OF CONONIAH AND SHIMEI HIS BROTHER, AT THE COMMANDMENT OF HEZEKIAH THE KING, AND AZARIAH THE RULER OF THE HOUSE OF GOD.

(14) "AND KORE THE SON OF IMNAH THE LEVITE, THE PORTER TOWARD THE EAST, WAS OVER THE FREEWILL OFFERINGS OF GOD, TO DISTRIBUTE THE OBLATIONS OF THE LORD, AND THE MOST HOLY THINGS.

(15) "AND NEXT HIM WERE EDEN, AND MINIAMIN, AND JESHUA, AND SHEMAIAH, AMARIAH, AND SHECANIAH, IN THE CITIES OF THE PRIESTS, IN THEIR SET OFFICE, TO GIVE TO THEIR BRETHREN BY COURSES, AS WELL TO THE GREAT AS TO THE SMALL:

(16) "BESIDE THEIR GENEALOGY OF MALES, FROM THREE YEARS OLD AND UPWARD, EVEN UNTO EVERYONE WHO ENTERED INTO THE HOUSE OF THE LORD, HIS DAILY PORTION FOR THEIR SERVICE IN THEIR CHARGES ACCORDING TO THEIR COURSES;

(17) "BOTH TO THE GENEALOGY OF THE PRIESTS BY THE HOUSE OF THEIR FATHERS, AND THE LEVITES FROM TWENTY YEARS OLD AND UPWARD, IN THEIR CHARGES BY THEIR COURSES;

(18) "AND TO THE GENEALOGY OF ALL THEIR LITTLE ONES, THEIR WIVES, AND THEIR SONS, AND THEIR DAUGHTERS, THROUGH ALL THE CONGREGATION: FOR IN THEIR SET OFFICE THEY SANCTIFIED THEMSELVES IN HOLINESS:

(19) "ALSO OF THE SONS OF AARON THE PRIESTS, WHICH WERE IN THE FIELDS OF THE SUBURBS OF THEIR CITIES, IN EVERY SEVERAL CITY, THE MEN WHO WERE EXPRESSED BY NAME, TO GIVE PORTIONS TO ALL THE MALES AMONG THE PRIESTS, AND TO ALL WHO WERE RECKONED BY GENEALOGIES AMONG THE LEVITES.

(20) "AND THUS DID HEZEKIAH THROUGHOUT ALL JUDAH, AND WROUGHT THAT WHICH WAS GOOD AND RIGHT AND TRUTH BEFORE THE LORD HIS GOD.

(21) "AND IN EVERY WORK THAT HE BEGAN IN THE SERVICE OF THE HOUSE OF GOD, AND IN THE LAW, AND IN THE COMMANDMENTS, TO SEEK HIS GOD, HE DID IT WITH ALL HIS HEART, AND PROSPERED."

The overview is:

1. (Vs. 10) Under the New Covenant, we have even greater Promises (Heb. 8:6). If the Work of the Lord is put first, the Lord has promised that a *"great store"* will accrue to us as well (Mat. 6:33).

2. The latter phrase of Verse 15 portrays the fact that the obligation had not always in the past been honestly discharged.

3. (Vs. 16) A picture of the little children being fed for the sake of their father's Sanctuary service is a pleasant glimpse.

4. (Vs. 19) All of the information given us in these Passages proclaims the fact that all the Priests and the Levites were remembered and carefully provided for, which is the way it was supposed to be.

5. (Vs. 21) True prosperity can only be found in faithfully following the Word of the Lord. This Hezekiah did!

WORKERS FOR THE LORD, HONORED

Concerning these individuals so named in the Sacred Text in their Work for the Lord, Williams says, *"Those who yielded themselves to God to be His instruments in this Reformation were enriched and glorified – enriched by the abounding tithes and glorified by their names being inscribed upon the Sacred Record. Such is God's way with His servants; that we enjoy the Blessing and share the glory."*[1] (I Cor. 9:13-14).

These are sample proofs of the record that God keeps as it regards all of His People, and our doings, whatever those doings might be. We should never forget this, understanding that the Lord sees, watches, observes, looks, and knows all things.

As well, every Believer should understand that one day each of us will stand at the *"Judgment Seat of Christ."*

THE JUDGMENT SEAT OF CHRIST

Paul said, *"Wherefore we labour* (are ambitious), *that, whether present* (with Christ) *or absent* (still in this world), *we may be accepted of Him* (approved by Him, which we will be if our Faith is in Christ and the Cross).

"For we must all appear before the Judgment Seat of Christ (this will take place in Heaven, and will probably transpire immediately before the Second Coming); *that every one may receive the things done in his body, according to that he has done, whether it be good or bad.* (This concerns our life lived for the Lord. Sins will not be judged here, but rather our motivation and faithfulness, for sin was judged at Calvary)" (II Cor. 5:9-10).

As we stated in the notes, no sins will be judged at the Judgment Seat of Christ, for that has been handled at Calvary. As well, only Believers, as should be obvious, will appear at this Judgment Seat. All unbelievers will appear at the Great White Throne Judgment (Rev. 20:11-15).

The Holy Spirit listed in this Chapter all of those who were in authority as it regarded the Work of the Lord respecting the Temple. And they are listed in a positive manner. As we've already stated, every single Believer is listed accordingly, respecting all that we do, in *"the Book"* (Rev. 20:12). Understanding that, and realizing that perpetually, we should desire to obey the Lord in all things.

HOLINESS

The holiness referred to in Old Testament times, as is referred to in Verse 18, was more ceremonial than anything else. In other words, the individual involved, whomever it may have been, was to do his best to adhere to the Law of Moses in every capacity as far as he was able to do so. Due to the blood of bulls and goats being unable to take away sins, the sin debt remained, meaning that the Holy Spirit, Who Alone can perfect holiness in one's heart and life, was unable to function in full capacity. So, as stated, holiness was basically ceremonial.

Holiness now, since the Cross, is entirely different. Because of what Jesus did at the Cross in taking our sin away (Jn. 1:29), the Holy Spirit can now live permanently in our hearts and lives, which He does in all Believers (Jn. 14:16-18).

Let's see what holiness isn't.

Holiness is not material things that we do or don't do. In other words, no human being, even the godliest among us can make himself or herself holy. In an attempt to do such, the only thing that will develop in one's life is self-righteousness.

Holiness is the Faith that the Believer has in Christ and what Christ did at the Cross. That being the case, and continuing to be the case, in other words, the Cross of Christ is ever the Object of our Faith, the Holy Spirit, Who Alone can develop His Fruit within our lives, can then accomplish His Work. So, one might say that holiness is a state of the heart, but the heart is right only because one's Faith is right, or rather has the correct Object.

The bane of the church is, and has always been, at least among some, that holiness is labeled according to material objects in which one does or does not engage. Please understand, one is not holy because one wears certain types of clothing, or cuts his hair in a certain way, or engages in particular practices. As stated, all that does is produce self-righteousness.

If the Holy Spirit can have His Way in one's life, He will develop holiness in such a heart and life, and He can have His Way if our Faith is properly placed in the Cross of Christ, which, at the same time, says it's anchored squarely in the Word. If the faith of the Believer is anchored in something other than the Cross of Christ, that means that such a Believer is living in a state of spiritual adultery. To be sure, even though that person is Saved, holiness most definitely is not being developed in such a life, as should be obvious.

The Believer must come to the place that he realizes that this tremendous attribute of God cannot be developed by his own personal efforts. It is impossible! Concerning this, Paul said, *"And if Christ be in you* (He is in you through the Power and Person of the Spirit [Gal. 2:20]), *the body is dead because of sin* (means that the physical body has been rendered helpless because of the Fall; consequently, the Believer trying to overcome by willpower presents a fruitless task); *but the Spirit is life because of Righteousness* (only the Holy Spirit can make us what we ought to be, which means we cannot do it ourselves; once again, He performs all that He does within the confines of the Finished Work of Christ)" (Rom. 8:10).

"Resting on the Faithfulness of Christ our Lord,
"Resting on the fullness of His Own sure Word,
"Resting on His Wisdom, on His Love and Power,
"Resting on His Covenant from hour to hour."

"Resting 'neath His guiding Hand for untracked days,
"Resting 'neath His Shadow from the noontide rays,
"Resting in the eventide beneath His Wing,
"In the fair pavilion of our Saviour King."

"Resting in the fortress while the foe is nigh,
"Resting in the lifeboat while the waves roll high,
"Resting in His Chariot for the swift, glad race,
"Resting, always resting, in His boundless Grace."

"Resting in the pastures and beneath the rock,
"Resting by the waters where He leads His Flock,
"Resting, while we listen, at His glorious Feet,

"Resting in His very Arms, Oh, rest complete!"

"Resting and believing, let us onward press;
"Resting on Himself, the Lord our Righteousness;
"Resting and rejoicing, let His Saved Ones sing,
"Glory, Glory, Glory, be to Christ our King!"

CHAPTER 32

(1) "AFTER THESE THINGS, AND THE ESTABLISHMENT THEREOF, SENNACHERIB KING OF ASSYRIA CAME, AND ENTERED INTO JUDAH, AND ENCAMPED AGAINST THE FENCED CITIES, AND THOUGHT TO WIN THEM FOR HIMSELF.

(2) "AND WHEN HEZEKIAH SAW THAT SENNACHERIB WAS COME, AND THAT HE WAS PURPOSED TO FIGHT AGAINST JERUSALEM,

(3) "HE TOOK COUNSEL WITH HIS PRINCES AND HIS MIGHTY MEN TO STOP THE WATERS OF THE FOUNTAINS WHICH WERE WITHOUT THE CITY: AND THEY DID HELP HIM.

(4) "SO THERE WAS GATHERED MUCH PEOPLE TOGETHER, WHO STOPPED ALL THE FOUNTAINS, AND THE BROOK THAT RAN THROUGH THE MIDST OF THE LAND, SAYING, WHY SHOULD THE KINGS OF ASSYRIA COME, AND FIND MUCH WATER?

(5) "ALSO HE STRENGTHENED HIMSELF, AND BUILT UP ALL THE WALL THAT WAS BROKEN, AND RAISED IT UP TO THE TOWERS, AND ANOTHER WALL WITHOUT, AND REPAIRED MILLO IN THE CITY OF DAVID, AND MADE DARTS AND SHIELDS IN ABUNDANCE.

(6) "AND HE SET CAPTAINS OF WAR OVER THE PEOPLE, AND GATHERED THEM TOGETHER TO HIM IN THE STREET OF THE GATE OF THE CITY, AND SPOKE COMFORTABLY TO THEM, SAYING,"

The overview is:

1. (Vs. 1) *"After these things"* means after the great Revival under Hezekiah. The king of Assyria then made war on Judah. He had already taken the Ten Tribes into captivity, and now his heart was lifted up to take Judah also. In this, he overstepped himself, for he had been commissioned by the Lord, although unknown to him, to destroy the Ten-Tribe kingdom only. God defeated the Assyrian's purpose and delivered Hezekiah after testing his Faith by permitting Judah to be tested.

2. (Vs. 2) According to II Kings 18:13-16, Hezekiah had already given Sennacherib great quantities of gold and silver to stop the invasion. These bribes were not pleasing to the Lord. Sennacherib came against Jerusalem anyway.

3. (Vs. 4) Hezekiah stopped the fountain, which is now known as the *"Virgin's Fount"* on the east of Ophel. Through the conduit he made (II Ki. 20:20), the water from this fount was brought down to the lower Gihon (Pool of Siloam). Now the upper Gihon was simply covered over and hidden from the enemy on the outside, making the water supply of Jerusalem safe by means of the two Gihons.

4. (Vs. 5) Hezekiah took all possible means to make himself, the people, and the city strong to withstand the invaders. Even though he, no doubt, did what he should have done, still, he would find that none of this was needed.

THE ONSLAUGHT OF SATAN

The short phrase, *"After these things,"* could be translated, *"After this faithfulness...."* It refers to faithfulness to the Bible. In the previous Chapter we find that Hezekiah did all he could to bring Revival to Judah, and he succeeded up to a point. As well, he had the Blessings of God. However, most of the time fidelity to the Bible meets with satanic hostility. Believers, therefore, should not think it a strange experience if they are suddenly confronted with sharp trials when seeking to fully follow the Lord. But, if we lean on the Lord, as did Hezekiah, we will find, as he did, that the Angel of Jehovah is *"mighty to save."* So,

NOTES

Sennacherib, the mightiest field general on the face of the Earth of that day, would come against Judah. In other words, Satan would send his very best with every intention of destroying the People of God and, in effect, taking the entirety of the land. He meant to lay it waste exactly as he had done previously with the northern confederation of Israel. He reasoned that both served the same God, and inasmuch as he had handily defeated Israel, he saw no danger with Judah either.

He completely misunderstood the situation. He didn't realize that Jehovah had allowed him to take the northern confederation of Israel captive because of their terrible sin and refusal to repent, even though He pleaded with them many times. So, the mighty Assyrian monarch thought that Judah, as Israel, would be a pushover. He was to find that he would come up against a Power such as he had never known before, a Power which would actually devastate his army. He had been commissioned by the Lord to destroy the Ten-Tribe kingdom only. God defeated his purpose and delivered Hezekiah after testing his Faith and permitting Judah also to be tested.

(7) "BE STRONG AND COURAGEOUS, BE NOT AFRAID NOR DISMAYED FOR THE KING OF ASSYRIA, NOR FOR ALL THE MULTITUDE THAT IS WITH HIM: FOR THERE BE MORE WITH US THAN WITH HIM:

(8) "WITH HIM IS AN ARM OF FLESH; BUT WITH US IS THE LORD OUR GOD TO HELP US, AND TO FIGHT OUR BATTLES. AND THE PEOPLE RESTED THEMSELVES UPON THE WORDS OF HEZEKIAH KING OF JUDAH.

(9) "AFTER THIS DID SENNACHERIB KING OF ASSYRIA SEND HIS SERVANTS TO JERUSALEM, (BUT HE HIMSELF LAID SEIGE AGAINST LACHISH, AND ALL HIS POWER WITH HIM,) UNTO HEZEKIAH KING OF JUDAH, AND UNTO ALL JUDAH WHO WERE AT JERUSALEM, SAYING,"

The pattern is:

1. (Vs. 7) Great Faith in a great God would come against a great enemy and win a great victory.

2. (Vs. 7) As ever, Faith is the ingredient.

Let all Believers know that whatever Satan brings against us, God has more for us than Satan has against us.

3. (Vs. 8) Our problem is that all too often we attempt to defeat the flesh by the flesh. It cannot be done. Our strength must be *"the LORD our God."*

THE MESSAGE FROM THE LORD

Even though Hezekiah is the one who delivered this Message, it was the Holy Spirit Who gave the Word to him. He said:
- Be strong;
- Be courageous;
- Be not afraid; and,
- Do not be dismayed.

The Holy Spirit through the king said this in the face of the mightiest field army on the face of the Earth which had vowed the destruction of Jerusalem. But let the reader understand, as that Message was viable at that time, it is just as viable presently, or even more. In other words, what the Holy Spirit said to Hezekiah and to Judah through Hezekiah, He is saying the same presently to modern Believers, at least for all who will believe.

THERE BE MORE WITH US THAN WITH HIM

How could Hezekiah make the statement, *". . . there be more with us than with him,"* considering the circumstances? Sennacherib had the mightiest field army at that time on the face of the Earth. That which was coming against Jerusalem was at least 200,000 strong. As well, they were men of war, meaning they were trained for the conflict and had, in fact, defeated nation after nation.

By comparison, the army of Judah was insignificant. In a face-to-face conflict, it could not hope to win such a battle.

The Believer must understand that what we can see with the eye, what is obvious to the flesh, or what circumstances show, does not constitute the true picture.

The Holy Spirit through the king says, *"With him is an arm of flesh; but with us is the LORD our God to help us, and to fight our battles."* In effect, one of the names of our God is, *"the LORD of Hosts."*

NOTES

This expression is used nearly 300 times in the Old Testament and is especially common in Isaiah, Jeremiah, Zechariah, and Malachi. It is a title of might and power used frequently in a military or apocalyptic context.

It is significant that the first occurrence of its use is found in I Samuel 1:3 in association with the Sanctuary at Shiloh. In fact, it could be translated, *"LORD of armies."*

The phrase, *"There be more with us than with him,"* was used, as well, by Elisha when the king of Syria sent an army to arrest him. The Scripture says, *"Therefore sent he thither horses, and chariots, and a great host: and they came by night, and compassed the city about"* (II Ki. 6:14).

When the servant of Elisha arose early the next morning and beheld the army that surrounded them, his question to Elisha was, *"Alas, my master! how shall we do?"*

Elisha answered, *"Fear not: for they who be with us are more than they who be with them"* (II Ki. 6:16).

Then the Scripture says, *"And Elisha prayed, and said, LORD, I pray You, open his eyes, that he may see. And the LORD opened the eyes of the young man; and he saw: and, behold, the mountain was full of horses and chariots of fire round about Elisha"* (II Ki. 6:17).

When Jesus was arrested in the Garden of Gethsemane, if it is remembered, Peter tried to defend him. *"Then said Jesus unto him, Put up again your sword into his place: for all they who take the sword shall perish with the sword. Thinkest thou that I cannot now pray to My Father, and He shall presently give Me more than twelve legions of Angels?"* (Mat. 26:52-53).

The idea is, there is a mighty host available to every single Child of God, and in every capacity. While we cannot see them, to be sure, they are there. At times they will intervene, even without us observing or seeing them, and will cause events to take place that will be to our good.

Simon Peter said, *"But you are a chosen generation* (a chosen or a new race, made up of all who have accepted Christ), *a Royal Priesthood* (Christ is King and High Priest; due to being *'in Him,'* we, as well, are *'kings and priests'* [Rev. 1:6]), *an Holy Nation* (a multitude of people of the same nature), *a Peculiar People* (each Saint is God's unique Possession, just as if that Saint were the only human being in existence); *that you should show forth the praises of Him Who has called you out of darkness into His marvelous Light* (He Saved us by virtue of what He did at the Cross, for which we should ever praise Him)" (I Pet. 2:9).

Wuest said, *"The word 'peculiar' here is used in a way not often seen today. The Greek word means literally 'to make round,' that is, to make something and then to surround it with a circle, thus indicating ownership. The same verb is used in the Septuagint translation of Isaiah 43:21 which reads, 'This people have I formed for myself.' The word 'peculiar' today usually means 'odd, strange.' But it is not so used here.*

"The Greek word speaks of the unique, private, personal ownership of the Saints by God. Each Saint is God's unique possession just as if that Saint were the only human being in existence."[1]

In essence, the Holy Spirit draws a circle around each and every Child of God and through Peter He is saying to Satan and his hoards of darkness, *"Satan, everything outside of that circle is one thing, but everything inside this circle is something else altogether. It is Mine, and you aren't to touch it, unless I give you permission to do so."*

There was a *"hedge"* around Job, which Satan could not penetrate unless the Lord gave him permission to do so (Job 1:10).

The idea is, there are tremendous resources available to the Child of God, if we only know how to use them.

HOW THE BELIEVER CAN USE THE RESOURCES OF HEAVEN

All the resources of Heaven, at least as it pertains to Believers on this Earth, are ensconced in the Cross of Christ. In other words, the answer is in the Cross! The solution is in the Cross! And the answer is found only in the Cross!

It was at the Cross where Satan and all of his minions of darkness were defeated, and defeated totally (Col. 2:14-15). It was at the Cross that all sin was atoned (Heb. 10:12). It was at the Cross that every Victory was won (Heb. 10:14). It was at the Cross that the door was opened (Heb. 10:19-20).

This means that our Lord is the Source of all things that we receive from God, and the Cross is the Means by which these things are given unto us, the Holy Spirit superintending it all (Eph. 2:13-18; Rom. 8:2).

The Believer, understanding this, is to place his Faith exclusively in Christ and what Christ did at the Cross, realizing that Christ and the Cross are to never be separated (I Cor. 1:17-18, 23; 2:2). That being done and maintained, the Holy Spirit, Who is God, and Who can do anything, will then begin to work mightily on our behalf, making available to us all the resources of Heaven. Please note the following:

• The way to God is through Jesus Christ and only through Jesus Christ (Jn. 14:6).

• The only way to Jesus Christ is through the Cross (Lk. 9:23; 14:27).

• The only way to the Cross is a denial of self (Lk. 9:23).

THE EFFORTS OF SATAN

The Ninth Verse says, *"After this did Sennacherib king of Assyria send his servants to Jerusalem. . . ."*

According to II Kings 18:14-16, this was after Hezekiah had already lost all the defense cities of Judah, except for Jerusalem, and had confessed his offense against the king of Assyria and had given him gold and silver. The Assyrian monarch, not being satisfied with this, replied that he wanted to take all the people captive. Thinking he had Judah to the point of absolute surrender, he sent servants to Jerusalem to announce the terms.

Hezekiah was wrong in the beginning to have submitted at all to Sennacherib. As well, Satan desires to take all that we as Believers have in Christ. We must understand, there is no way we can come to terms with the Evil One. He will not be satisfied with taking just a few cities in Judah; he wants Jerusalem, as well, to make all the people captive.

Faithfulness to the Word of God will always meet with satanic hostility. Believers, therefore, should not think it a strange experience if, when seeking to fully follow the Lord, they are suddenly confronted with sharp trials. If we lean only upon the Lord for deliverance, we will find that the Angel of Jehovah is *"mighty to save."* Let me say it again.

THE CROSS OF CHRIST IS GOD'S ANSWER TO SATAN

The Believer should read that heading over and over, in fact, any number of times. Victory is found in the Cross, and Victory is found only in the Cross. If the Believer attempts to find victory, to find power, to find solace, or to find help in any capacity other than the Cross, he will find to his dismay that no help is forthcoming.

Many would read these lines and boast that their confidence is in the Holy Spirit; however, each and every Believer should understand that the Holy Spirit works exclusively within the parameters of the Finished Work of Christ. In fact, He will not work outside of those parameters, not at all. Listen to Paul,

"For the Law (that which we are about to give is a Law of God, devised by the Godhead in eternity past [I Pet. 1:18-20]; this Law, in fact, is *'God's Prescribed Order of Victory') of the Spirit* (Holy Spirit, i.e., *'the way the Spirit works') of Life* (all life comes from Christ, but through the Holy Spirit [Jn. 16:13-14]) *in Christ Jesus* (any time Paul uses this term or one of its derivatives, he is, without fail, referring to what Christ did at the Cross, which makes this *'life'* possible) *has made me free* (given me total Victory) *from the Law of Sin and Death* (these are the two most powerful Laws in the Universe; the *'Law of the Spirit of Life in Christ Jesus'* alone is stronger than the *'Law of Sin and Death'*; this means that if the Believer attempts to live for God by any manner other than Faith in Christ and the Cross, he is doomed to failure)*"* (Rom. 8:2).

Even though the Cross was some 700 years into the future at the time of Hezekiah, if, at the very beginning, he had only placed his trust in the shed Blood of the Lamb, which was typified by the Sacrificial system, he would have found that Sennacherib would have made no headway in Judah at all. In other words, he would not have been able to take even one small village, much less almost the entirety of the country.

Any Believer in the modern church, whose Faith is not in Christ and what Christ did for us at the Cross, will not be able to live a victorious life, irrespective as to who that Believer might be, whether a pastor with the largest church in the world, or the evangelist drawing the biggest crowds. While one can certainly be Saved and not understand the Cross as it refers to Sanctification, one cannot live a victorious life without understanding this great Truth (Rom. 6:1-14; 8:1-2, 11; I Cor. 1:17-18, 23; 2:2; Gal., Chpt. 5; 6:14; Eph. 2:13-18; Col. 2:14-15).

(10) "THUS SAYS SENNACHERIB KING OF ASSYRIA, WHEREON DO YOU TRUST, THAT YOU ABIDE IN THE SIEGE IN JERUSALEM?

(11) "DOES NOT HEZEKIAH PERSUADE YOU TO GIVE OVER YOURSELVES TO DIE BY FAMINE AND BY THIRST, SAYING, THE LORD OUR GOD SHALL DELIVER US OUT OF THE HAND OF THE KING OF ASSYRIA?

(12) "HAS NOT THE SAME HEZEKIAH TAKEN AWAY HIS HIGH PLACES AND HIS ALTARS, AND COMMANDED JUDAH AND JERUSALEM, SAYING, YOU SHALL WORSHIP BEFORE ONE ALTAR, AND BURN INCENSE UPON IT?

(13) "KNOW YOU NOT WHAT I AND MY FATHERS HAVE DONE UNTO ALL THE PEOPLE OF OTHER LANDS? WERE THE GODS OF THE NATIONS OF THOSE LANDS ANY WAYS ABLE TO DELIVER THEIR LANDS OUT OF MY HAND?

(14) "WHO WAS THERE AMONG ALL THE GODS OF THOSE NATIONS THAT MY FATHERS UTTERLY DESTROYED, THAT COULD DELIVER HIS PEOPLE OUT OF MY HAND, THAT YOUR GOD SHOULD BE ABLE TO DELIVER YOU OUT OF MY HAND?

(15) "NOW THEREFORE LET NOT HEZEKIAH DECEIVE YOU, NOR PERSUADE YOU ON THIS MANNER, NEITHER YET BELIEVE HIM: FOR NO GOD OF ANY NATION OR KINGDOM WAS ABLE TO DELIVER HIS PEOPLE OUT OF MY HAND, AND OUT OF THE HAND OF MY FATHERS: HOW MUCH LESS SHALL YOUR GOD

DELIVER YOU OUT OF MY HAND?

(16) "AND HIS SERVANTS SPOKE YET MORE AGAINST THE LORD GOD, AND AGAINST HIS SERVANT HEZEKIAH.

(17) "HE WROTE ALSO LETTERS TO RAIL ON THE LORD GOD OF ISRAEL, AND TO SPEAK AGAINST HIM, SAYING, AS THE GODS OF THE NATIONS OF OTHER LANDS HAVE NOT DELIVERED THEIR PEOPLE OUT OF MY HAND, SO SHALL NOT THE GOD OF HEZEKIAH DELIVER HIS PEOPLE OUT OF MY HAND.

(18) "THEN THEY CRIED WITH A LOUD VOICE IN THE JEWS' SPEECH UNTO THE PEOPLE OF JERUSALEM WHO WERE ON THE WALL, TO AFFRIGHT THEM, AND TO TROUBLE THEM; THAT THEY MIGHT TAKE THE CITY.

(19) "AND THEY SPOKE AGAINST THE GOD OF JERUSALEM, AS AGAINST THE GODS OF THE PEOPLE OF THE EARTH, WHICH WERE THE WORK OF THE HANDS OF MAN."

The overview is:

1. Sennacherib, the king of Assyria, had laid siege to Jerusalem.

2. (Vs. 11) The emissaries of Sennacherib appealed to the people instead of to Hezekiah and his ministers of state, thinking to undermine their morale.

3. Verse 12 illustrates the fact that wherever there is obedience to the teaching of the Bible, it will be misinterpreted by people of the world. The written Word commanded that there should be only one Altar in Israel; man approves of many. The emissaries of Sennacherib didn't know what they were talking about.

4. Verse 13 portrays these emissaries of Sennacherib boasting that their god was more powerful than all others, so it was vain to expect Jehovah to rescue the people, especially since He did not rescue their brethren in Samaria (II Ki., Chpt. 17).

5. (Vs. 15) The mighty Sennacherib was soon to find out just Who the God of Judah actually was!

6. The Holy Spirit in Verse 16 shows us that the Lord is just as displeased with His Servants being spoken against as *"Himself."*

7. (Vs. 17) The emissaries of Sennacherib

NOTES

intended to intimidate the people of Jerusalem.

8. (Vs. 19) Over and over again, Jehovah is grossly insulted by Sennacherib! To be compared to the gods of other people, which were merely *"the work of the hands of man,"* not only showed the ignorance of Sennacherib but, as well, brought the blasphemy to a higher pitch.

INTIMIDATION

Sennacherib would intimidate Hezekiah and the people of Jerusalem by blow and bluster. And yet, many of the things he was saying, such as the strength and power of his army, were all too true and were overly obvious. This is one of Satan's favorite tactics against the Child of God. We should learn from this lesson.

Most of the other cities in Judah had already been taken by Sennacherib. And now he was purporting to lay siege against Jerusalem.

THEY KNEW WHAT WAS HAPPENING BUT THEY DIDN'T KNOW WHAT WAS GOING ON

What was happening was obvious. Everything in Judah had fallen to Sennacherib except Jerusalem, and now, at least according to circumstances, it was only a matter of days before Jerusalem would fall. The *"happening"* of the mightiest field army on the face of the Earth, the Assyrians, was obvious for all to see. At that time, Assyria was the mightiest power on the face of the Earth. Nation after nation had fallen to their advances. This is what was happening and, as stated, was obvious to all. But that was not what was going on.

What was going on?

What was going on that would decide the issue, and decide it totally and completely, was taking place in Heaven. Whatever Sennacherib said he would do, his brags and his boasts, had all been heard by Jehovah, and plans were underway at that very moment for Jehovah to intervene. That's what was going on.

We, as Believers, find ourselves in the same situation but, more than likely, on a lesser scale. We see what is happening, and it becomes very obvious and has an effect on us. But oftentimes, we do not stop to think as to what is going on.

Every single Believer in the world belongs to the Lord. We are bought with a price, and that price was high, the shed Blood of the Lord Jesus Christ. Satan does not have the latitude or leeway to do whatever he wants to do. In fact, he can only do what the Lord allows him to do. He might make his boast; he may blow and bluster; and he may tell us that he's going to do all types of things to us. But have you ever stopped to think of the following?

Despite all that Satan has told us in the last few years, even decades, have you noted that none of it has come to pass? Have you noted that you are still victorious, even stronger in the Lord than ever before? The truth is, if Satan could do all of these things, whatever it is he has threatened, he would have done it a long time ago. He hasn't done it simply because he can't do it unless we just give up and lose our faith, which gives him an open door. Whatever seems to be happening is one thing, but the Believer must understand that *"what is going on"* is that which is actual reality.

AGAINST GOD!

The nations of the world of that time were very religious, each having its god or gods. In fact, most nations, while having several gods at the same time, had a superior god. If one nation defeated another, it was surmised that the victor had a stronger god, etc.

Sennacherib felt very comfortable in his boasts inasmuch as he had recently defeated the northern kingdom of Israel, and surmising that they had the same God, Jehovah, he saw no difficulty with Judah.

He completely misunderstood Hezekiah's actions by removing the high places and the various altars scattered over Judah and Jerusalem. He thought it was a lack of confidence in Jehovah on the part of Hezekiah. Of course, what Hezekiah was doing was registering obedience to the Word of God. All of these *"high places"* were mostly used for idol worship and were opposed to the Word of God. So, Hezekiah had removed them in obedience to the Lord and His Word. But Sennacherib misunderstood all of this, thinking that it showed a vote of *"no confidence"* in Jehovah.

So, this heathen king boasts of his victories in other lands, asking the question, *"Were the gods of the nations of those lands in any way able to deliver their lands out of my hand?"* He reasoned that inasmuch as all of these gods had been defeated, likewise, Judah would be defeated also.

He had no way of knowing that all of these heathen gods were, in fact, nothing. If there was any power behind them at all, it was a nebulous power that was projected by demon spirits. But he knew none of this. As stated, he reasoned Jehovah to be helpless inasmuch as the northern kingdom of Israel had been defeated. They served the same God, so, how could Judah be of any difficulty?

PHARAOH

There was another monarch many centuries ago who boasted exactly as did Sennacherib.

The people of Israel were held as slaves in Egypt, actually being worked to death. The Lord had commissioned Moses to go into Egypt, then the mightiest nation in the world, and to demand of Pharaoh, *"Thus says the LORD God of Israel, Let My People go . . ."* (Ex. 5:1).

Pharaoh reasoned as to what kind of God Jehovah was, especially considering that His People were slaves in this land? In answer to the demand made by Moses, the Scripture says that Pharaoh replied, *"Who is the LORD, that I should obey His Voice to let Israel go? I know not the LORD, neither will I let Israel go"* (Ex. 5:2).

Pharaoh would find out as to Who Jehovah really was exactly as Sennacherib would many centuries later. When the Lord got through with Egypt, it was a wreck. When the Lord got through with Sennacherib, his army was a wreck, in fact, reduced down to almost nothing.

Sennacherib's answer to Hezekiah, exactly as Pharaoh's answer had been to Moses, proclaims him saying, *"As the gods of the nations of other lands have not delivered their people out of my hand, so shall not the God of Hezekiah deliver His People out of my hand."*

He was soon to be educated as to the might of the Power of God!

(20) "AND FOR THIS CAUSE HEZEKIAH THE KING, AND THE PROPHET ISAIAH THE SON OF AMOZ, PRAYED AND CRIED TO HEAVEN.

(21) "AND THE LORD SENT AN ANGEL, WHICH CUT OFF ALL THE MIGHTY MEN OF VALOUR, AND THE LEADERS AND CAPTAINS IN THE CAMP OF THE KING OF ASSYRIA. SO HE RETURNED WITH SHAME OF FACE TO HIS OWN LAND. AND WHEN HE WAS COME INTO THE HOUSE OF HIS GOD, THEY WHO CAME FORTH OF HIS OWN BOWELS KILLED HIM THERE WITH THE SWORD.

(22) "THUS THE LORD SAVED HEZEKIAH AND THE INHABITANTS OF JERUSALEM FROM THE HAND OF SENNACHERIB THE KING OF ASSYRIA, AND FROM THE HAND OF ALL OTHER, AND GUIDED THEM ON EVERY SIDE.

(23) "AND MANY BROUGHT GIFTS UNTO THE LORD TO JERUSALEM, AND PRESENTS TO HEZEKIAH KING OF JUDAH: SO THAT HE WAS MAGNIFIED IN THE SIGHT OF ALL NATIONS FROM THENCEFORTH."

The construction is:

1. (Vs. 20) Many, if not most, in the modern church no longer cry to God. Instead, they resort to psychology, which has the same source as witchcraft—Satan.

2. (Vs. 21) With only one Angel, the Lord struck down 185,000 Assyrians in one night (II Ki. 19:35). As a result, Sennacherib returned to Nineveh in shame. History records that he did not venture again even toward Judah. Some years later, he was murdered by his own sons.

3. (Vs. 22) What a beautiful statement! The Holy Spirit will lead and guide us into all truth (Jn. 16:13).

4. (Vs. 23) Judah at this time became one of the most powerful nations on the face of the Earth, all because of Hezekiah's Faith and the Blessings of God.

PRAYER

The Scripture beautifully and plainly tells us that both Hezekiah and the Prophet Isaiah, *"prayed and cried to Heaven,"* as it regarded these boasts of Sennacherib.

How many modern Christians have a prayer life?

How many take everything to the Lord in prayer?

How many look to Him for the answer that is needed?

Without a proper prayer life, the Believer simply cannot have a proper relationship with the Lord.

WHAT IS A PROPER PRAYER LIFE?

Every Believer ought to have a set time to go before the Lord each and every day, taking to Him all things which are needed, asking His Leading and Guidance. In fact, a Believer should have a spirit of prayer at all times. In other words, we should be praising Him and seeking His Guidance in all things, which can be done on a constant basis.

Most prayer should be in the context of thanking the Lord for all the things that He has done for us in the past, is doing for us in the present, and will do for us in the future. In fact, the Psalmist said, *"Enter into His Gates with thanksgiving, and into His Courts with praise: be thankful unto Him, and bless His Name"* (Ps. 100:4).

Of course, the part of that Psalm given was under the Old Covenant. In the New Covenant, which is our Lord Jesus Christ, there are no more *"gates"* or *"courts."* So, one could say and be correct, *"enter into His Presence with thanksgiving and into His Throne with praise."*

Due to what Jesus has done for us at the Cross, now the Believer has a far greater access to God than did Old Testament Saints. Then, the Tabernacle or Temple was as close as they could come, and even then, they could not actually enter into the confines of the building itself. As far as they could go were *"His Courts."* In fact, even those were segregated.

The Court nearest to the Temple was the *"Court of Men,"* sometimes referred to as the *"Court of Israel."* As would be obvious, only men could go into this Court.

The Court immediately behind the Court of Men was the Court of Women. As would be obvious, only women were allowed there.

Behind the Court of Women was the outer Court, actually, the Court of the Gentiles. The Gentiles who desired to come to the Temple to pray could only come to that outer Court. In fact, there was a barrier several feet high that separated the Court of Gentiles from the Court of Women. If that barrier was crossed, the Gentile who did such could be killed.

When Jesus died on the Cross, He atoned for all sin, making access to the very Throne of God possible, at least for those who have their Faith in Christ and what Christ has done for us at the Cross. That's the reason that Paul wrote,

"Let us therefore come boldly unto the Throne of Grace (presents the Seat of Divine Power, and yet the Source of boundless Grace), *that we may obtain Mercy* (presents that which we want first), *and find Grace to help in time of need* (refers to the Goodness of God extended to all who come, and during any *'time of need'*; all made possible by the Cross)" (Heb. 4:16).

THE CROSS OF CHRIST MADE ALL OF THIS POSSIBLE, AND IT IS THE CROSS OF CHRIST WHICH MAKES EVERYTHING POSSIBLE!

Unfortunately, far too many modern Believers little take advantage of the tremendous resources available to all of us.

In 1991, in the month of October, at a time of crisis for this Ministry, the Lord instructed me to begin having prayer meetings, actually two a day, morning and evening, which I immediately set out to do and, in fact, continued in that mode for some ten years. More or less, I continue the same regimen myself even until the present time.

The Lord said to me and, in fact, it was the only instruction I received, *"Do not seek Me so much for what I can do, but rather for Who I am."* Those were my instructions!

I gathered from that the Lord was speaking of relationship, and to be sure, those prayer meetings effected a tremendous relationship, which proved to be the greatest thing that ever happened to me.

I had always had a strong prayer life even before then. My grandmother taught me to pray. She taught me that God answers prayer. So, I have sought Him and believed Him all of my life. But this was different. It was something that He directly told me to do, and which has reaped astounding benefits.

PRAYER AND THE CROSS

But yet, from years of experience, I personally feel that a proper prayer life cannot really be had unless the Believer properly understands the Cross, and I speak of the Cross as it refers to Sanctification. Otherwise, the Believer is going to turn prayer into a law, which God can never accept. While the Lord is patient and kind with us and to us, and while He will do everything that He can to help us, still, without understanding the Cross as we should, our prayer life is hindered simply because the Holy Spirit, Who is our prayer helper, is greatly hindered.

The Holy Spirit works exclusively within the parameters, so to speak, of the Finished Work of Christ, i.e., *"the Cross."* So, if the object of our faith is something other than the Cross, this greatly hinders the Holy Spirit, and, to be frank, such a Believer is actually living in a state of *"spiritual adultery."*

I've been on both sides of the fence, so to speak, as it regards this of which I speak. As I have previously stated, I have always had a strong prayer life. However, I really did not know or understand what proper prayer actually was until I understood the Cross of Christ, and I continue to speak of the Cross as it refers to Sanctification.

So, Hezekiah the king and Isaiah the Prophet, *"prayed and cried to Heaven."*

THE MIRACLE WORKING POWER OF GOD

In answer to their prayer, the Scripture says, *"And the LORD sent an Angel, which cut off all the mighty men of valour, and the leaders and captains in the camp of the king of Assyria."* In fact, this one Angel of the Lord *". . . smote in the camp of the Assyrians 185,000"* (II Ki. 19:35).

Just how the Lord accomplished this through the Angel, we aren't told. At any rate, there were 185,000 Assyrian soldiers who went to bed the night before, but did not get up the next morning. So much for the god of Assyria and so much for the God of Abraham, Isaac, and Jacob.

As should be understood here, we are speaking of power that is beyond comprehension. One Angel inflicting this type of damage portrays to us the resources at the Command of our Lord, and this power is to be used on our behalf if necessary.

The Lord could easily have stricken Sennacherib, even as He did smite many of the *"mighty men of valour, and the leaders and captains,"* but He left the Assyrian monarch alive in order to consider what had happened.

The Scripture says, *"So he returned with shame of face to his own land."* No doubt, he concocted a story to relate to his people as to what had happened; nevertheless, the surrounding nations knew and understood what had happened, even though they were idol worshippers. As stated, when Israel, in this case Judah, was diligently serving the Lord, no nation or series of nations in the world could defeat them. The reason was because God was their Captain.

One of the Psalms portrays this happening. It is believed that Hezekiah could have written it, even though no such inscription is given at the heading. The Psalm says the following.

THE GREAT DELIVERANCE OF JUDAH

I am quoting this Psalm from THE EXPOSITOR'S STUDY BIBLE. It reads,

"When the LORD turned again the captivity of Zion, we were like them who dream. (This pictures the deliverance of Jerusalem from Sennacherib. It was so glorious that it all seemed like a dream [II Ki. 19:20-35].)

"Then was our mouth filled with laughter, and our tongue with singing: then said they among the heathen, The LORD has done great things for them. (The deliverance of Jerusalem was so outstanding that it was noticed by all the heathen round about, with them giving glory to God. The Lord sent one Angel and destroyed 185,000 Assyrians in one night [II Ki. 19:35].)

"The LORD has done great things for us; whereof we are glad.

"Turn again our captivity, O LORD, as the streams in the south. ('To turn again our captivity' is a figure of speech for the restoration of prosperity.)

"They who sow in tears shall reap in joy.

"He who goes forth and weeps, bearing precious seed, shall doubtless come again with rejoicing, bringing his sheaves with him. (Paul said, 'This Seed is Christ' [Gal. 3:16]. The 'sheaves' are symbolic of the harvest which, at long last, is Righteousness)" (Ps. 126:1-6).

One can well imagine the reaction of Judah when they were given the news.

They went to bed that night with the taunts of Sennacherib ringing in their ears. He would destroy Jerusalem, destroy the Temple, and take everyone captive, at least those he didn't kill.

But then early the next morning, the watchman on the wall must have seen a runner coming in the distance. He wondered what the news was that would require such haste because, no doubt, the runner was giving it his all.

The gate was open by the time the runner arrived, out of breath. He must have stopped and then began to blurt it out.

"The army of Assyria is defeated. Thousands are dead, victory is ours!"

The news rang throughout the city, going from street to street and even house to house, and soon the entire city was in jubilee, praising the Lord. The victory was so great that the surrounding nations knew what had taken place and gave God the glory, even though they did not really know or realize as to exactly Who Jehovah was.

The Lord must have spoken either to Isaiah or Hezekiah as it regarded the method of defeating this mighty army. To be sure, it is very doubtful that the Assyrians would have known it was one Angel who had caused all this destruction, so, the Holy Spirit had to reveal it, as stated, to either Hezekiah or Isaiah.

If it is to be noticed, the Scripture says, *"And many* (many surrounding nations) *brought gifts unto the LORD to Jerusalem, and presents to Hezekiah king of Judah: so that he was magnified in the sight of all nations from thenceforth."*

The idea is, considering the power that had been evidenced against the army of Assyria, at that time the mightiest field army on the face of the Earth, the surrounding nations wanted to make certain they stayed in the good graces of Judah, and rightly so! So, they brought gifts in order to show their allegiance to God's People.

(24) "IN THOSE DAYS HEZEKIAH WAS SICK TO THE DEATH, AND PRAYED UNTO THE LORD: AND HE SPOKE UNTO HIM, AND HE GAVE HIM A SIGN.

(25) "BUT HEZEKIAH RENDERED NOT AGAIN ACCORDING TO THE BENEFIT DONE UNTO HIM; FOR HIS HEART WAS LIFTED UP: THEREFORE THERE WAS WRATH UPON HIM, AND UPON JUDAH AND JERUSALEM.

(26) "NOTWITHSTANDING HEZEKIAH HUMBLED HIMSELF FOR THE PRIDE OF HIS HEART, BOTH HE AND THE INHABITANTS OF JERUSALEM, SO THAT THE WRATH OF THE LORD CAME NOT UPON THEM IN THE DAYS OF HEZEKIAH."

The exegesis is:

1. The *"sign"* mentioned in Verse 24 was the sundial going backwards ten degrees, which was a Miracle of unprecedented proportions. This means that the Earth literally went back on its axis, i.e., *"its rotation,"* which brought about a *"long day"* (II Ki. 20:8-11).

2. (Vs. 25) Someone has said that *"praise and prosperity are the greatest obstacles for a Christian to overcome."* Hezekiah did not overcome them, but rather succumbed to them. This probably referred to him showing all his material riches to the Babylonians (II Ki. 20:12-15) instead of the riches of the God of Israel.

3. (Vs. 26) Thankfully, Hezekiah repented, and the Lord healed him, giving him fifteen more years of life (II Ki. 20:1-7).

PRIDE

When men succeed in whatever it is they are attempting to do, so often, pride is the result. They give themselves credit; they boast of themselves; and they think of themselves as making the great contribution. In other words, God becomes less and less, and man becomes more and more. This is true in totality as it regards the unredeemed, but regrettably, it is also true oftentimes as it regards the Redeemed.

Hezekiah had been greatly blessed by the Lord. He had watched God answer prayer in defeating the mighty Assyrian host in such a way as to beggar description. The Miracle was so pronounced, especially considering that the mightiest field army on the face of the Earth had been totally decimated, and by one Angel at that, that the surrounding nations literally trembled at the mention of the name of Hezekiah and Judah. In fact, these surrounding nations did everything they could to ingratiate themselves to Judah. They had seen that mighty Power manifested, and they did not want it manifested against them.

So, the Scripture says in relation to all of this that the heart of Hezekiah was *"lifted up."* He did not *"render again according unto the benefit done unto him."*

Why?

That's a good question!

The truth is, we as Believers presently have less excuse now than did Hezekiah then. Why do we fail the Lord? Why do we go astray from the Word of God?

It's very easy to ask that question as it regards someone else such as Hezekiah, but another question altogether as the searchlight of Truth is turned on us.

Actually, the answer to that question is the same now as it was then. Whenever Believers take their eyes off of Christ and His Atoning Work at the Cross, automatically such eyes will rest upon ourselves. In other words, the only way we can stay true to God, the only way we can walk righteously before Him, and I mean the only way, is for the Cross of Christ to ever be the Object of our Faith. Otherwise, pride will be the result, and pride is always the result of self-righteousness. This is the cause of all sin, all failure, all disobedience, and all going astray. Regrettably and sadly, most Christians are trying to live for God in all the wrong ways. In other words, as sincere as they might be and as zealous as they might be, most modern Christians have little understanding as it regards the Cross of Christ respecting our Sanctification. As we've already said in this Volume, when most Christians think of the Cross, they speak of it in a past tense.

Not only is it spoken of in a past tense, but it remains there. In other words, they do not understand the Cross as it regards their present circumstances. As a result, the faith of such Christians is anchored somewhere else other than Christ and the Cross. Let us say it again.

That being the case, self-righteousness will always be the result, and pride is the outgrowth of self-righteousness.

HUMILITY

The Scripture says, *"Notwithstanding Hezekiah humbled himself for the pride of his heart, both he and the inhabitants of Jerusalem, so that the Wrath of the LORD came not upon them in the days of Hezekiah."*

It could be said that Hezekiah returned to the Cross. Of course, there was no thought of a Cross in the days of that monarch; however, the Sacrificial system pointed exclusively to the One Who was to come, and we speak of the Lord Jesus Christ.

Many Christians, and possibly we all have attempted such, try to bring about humility in their lives by their own machinations. Such cannot be done. Humility can only be experienced in the heart and life of the Believer as that Believer places his Faith exclusively in Christ and what Christ did at the Cross.

I suppose that the reader must think that we hold up the Cross as the answer to all things. If the reader thinks that, then the reader is thinking exactly right. There is no hope for man and no solution for man's dilemma other than Christ and the Cross. The Holy Spirit, Who Alone can develop in our lives what we need, works exclusively within the parameters of the Finished Work of Christ. So, if we want His Fruit, His Leading in our lives, and His Power manifested, the Cross of Christ must ever be the Object of our Faith (Rom. 6:1-14; 8:1-2, 11; I Cor. 1:17-18, 21, 23; 2:2; Gal., Chpt. 5; 6:14; Eph. 2:13-18; Phil. 2:14-15).

Actually, we are told in the body of the Text, as it regards Verse 26, that the *"Wrath of the LORD"* must be leveled against pride. Why?

Once again, pride places man in a position in which he does not rightly belong. It also places God in a position in which He doesn't rightly belong.

Man within himself is helpless. As it regards being what he ought to be and doing what he ought to do, due to the Fall, he simply cannot do such. But yet, he is loath to admit that, and religious man is loath most of all to admit that.

As serving God, we like to think that our consecration, our dedication, our zeal, and our efforts play a part in our life for the Lord. They don't! And it's hard for us to admit that. In fact, the Holy Spirit refers to it as *"works of the flesh"* (Rom. 8:1, 8).

That's the reason the Cross is so very, very important! It is only there that man can be reconciled to God and God to man. It cannot work any other way. Regrettably and sadly, the modern church has strayed from the Cross to such an extent that anymore, most of that which is presently being preached is not the Gospel at all. It is motivation, intellectualism, or some such similar effort. In fact, the modern gospel in no way places man in his true position. It admits that man has some problems, but it tells man that with a little change of habits, he can rectify the problem. It doesn't dare mention sin because, as many preachers put it, that might offend man.

Well, the problem is, it is God Who has been offended and has been offended by man's sin because man is a sinner. Not was a sinner, not shall be a sinner, but is a sinner presently, and the only answer, the only solution, and the only hope for man is the Cross of Christ. It was there that all sin was atoned and done so by the Lord Jesus Christ offering Himself as the Perfect Sacrifice, which was accepted by God. We accept that and be Saved, or we reject that and be lost! There is no alternative or in-between.

(27) "AND HEZEKIAH HAD EXCEEDING MUCH RICHES AND HONOUR: AND HE MADE HIMSELF TREASURIES FOR SILVER, AND FOR GOLD, AND FOR PRECIOUS STONES, AND FOR SPICES, AND FOR SHIELDS, AND FOR ALL MANNER OF PLEASANT JEWELS;

(28) "STOREHOUSES ALSO FOR THE INCREASE OF CORN, AND WINE, AND

OIL; AND STALLS FOR ALL MANNER OF BEASTS, AND COTES FOR FLOCKS.

(29) "MOREOVER HE PROVIDED HIM CITIES, AND POSSESSIONS OF FLOCKS AND HERDS IN ABUNDANCE: FOR GOD HAD GIVEN HIM SUBSTANCE VERY MUCH.

(30) "THIS SAME HEZEKIAH ALSO STOPPED THE UPPER WATERCOURSE OF GIHON, AND BROUGHT IT STRAIGHT DOWN TO THE WEST SIDE OF THE CITY OF DAVID. AND HEZEKIAH PROSPERED IN ALL HIS WORKS.

(31) "HOWBEIT IN THE BUSINESS OF THE AMBASSADORS OF THE PRINCES OF BABYLON, WHO SENT UNTO HIM TO ENQUIRE OF THE WONDER THAT WAS DONE IN THE LAND, GOD LEFT HIM, TO TRY HIM, THAT HE MIGHT KNOW ALL THAT WAS IN HIS HEART."

The exegesis is:

1. (Vs. 29) These Passages plainly tell us that the Lord was the Author of all the prosperity of Hezekiah and Judah.

2. (Vs. 31) Man, even the most dedicated and consecrated Believer, will invariably turn aside if *"God leaves us"* even for a moment.

3. (Vs. 31) Hezekiah would find that *"the heart is deceitful above all things, and desperately wicked: who can know it?"* (Jer. 17:9).

PROSPERITY

Whenever people, any people and any person, walk according to the Word of the Lord, such will always and without fail, bring prosperity, and we speak of prosperity in every capacity. However, such a Believer must believe the Lord and must expect God to bless him, even as the Word of God proclaims.

Some erroneously claim that while the Lord definitely did bless materially in Old Testament times, now our Blessings are all Spiritual.

While the greater Blessings most definitely now are Spiritual, still, God will bless and, in fact, desires to bless financially and materially as much and even more than He did in Old Testament times. We now have a better Covenant based on better Promises,

NOTES

all due to what Christ did at the Cross (Heb. 8:6). That *"better Covenant,"* to be sure, is better in every capacity, not merely in part. The problem is, we as Believers have not fully understood and, thereby, appropriated to ourselves the great Promises of God given to us in His Word.

Some time back, while preaching at Family Worship Center one Sunday morning, I was dealing with this very principle. I made the statement in preaching, *"If you need a better car, there is a car in the Cross. If you need a bigger house, there is a bigger house in the Cross. If you need a raise in pay, there is a raise in pay in the Cross."*

There were many people in the Service that morning who caught the spirit of what I was saying and began to believe God for certain needs to be met in their lives and in their families' lives. I watched the Lord work Miracles on behalf of some of these people because they began to believe for that which they needed. Let me say it again.

Whatever we need is in the Cross. Most definitely, Jesus went to the Cross in order to pay the terrible sin debt that we owed but could not pay. He suffered the penalty we should have suffered but, in fact, could not suffer. He became our Substitute, and in so doing, did for us in totality and in every capacity what we could never do for ourselves. Every problem, every question, every situation, every sin, everything, in fact, was answered at the Cross. The Believer is to understand that and look to the Cross in that capacity. Let us say it again.

Jesus Christ is the Source of all things that we receive from God, and the Cross is the Means by which these things are given to us, whatever they might be, all superintended by the Holy Spirit (Rom. 6:1-14; 8:1-2, 11; I Cor. 1:17-18, 23; 2:2; Mk. 11:24; Mat. 18:18; Jn. 15:7). While the Spiritual part of the Atonement was and is the primary objective of Christ, which should be overly obvious, still, this does not exclude everything else that we need as Believers.

THE TEST

After the great prosperity was given to Hezekiah, which included the tremendous victory over the Assyrians, the Scripture says, *"Howbeit in the business of the ambassadors of the princes of Babylon, who sent unto him to enquire of the wonder that was done in the land, God left him, to try him, that he might know all that was in his heart."*

In other words, the Lord engineered the situation with *"the princes of Babylon,"* in order to test Hezekiah. Of course, the Lord already knew what was in Hezekiah's heart. He knew that Hezekiah had become lifted up in his own pride, which means that he thought he had something to do with the great Blessings of the Lord. The Lord wanted Hezekiah to personally see what was in his heart, and it was not a pretty picture. Two things are involved in this. They are:

1. The first was the sickness and ultimate healing of Hezekiah, which is not carried in detail in II Chronicles, but it is mentioned. The Lord gave him a sign that He would heal him and that he would not die at that time, as the Lord had originally threatened.

This *"sign"* refers to the going back of the shadow on the sundial, which was so remarkable that even the Chaldean astronomers, who were famous in the world of that day, came to inquire about the God Who could turn the sun backward. Furthermore, several centuries later, Greek historians informed Alexander the Great that it was one of the great wonders recorded in their scientific books. This shows that the happening was not merely the moving of a shadow but the going backward of the Earth in its rotation. The matter was known in various lands, and the Chaldeans came to inquire about it when they learned that it was caused by Israel's God. Hezekiah was healed and actually given fifteen more years of life (II Ki. 20).

2. The second concerned the princes of Babylon.

Instead of Hezekiah showing *"these ambassadors"* the God of Israel, he, rather, showed them his riches and prosperity. Man, even the most dedicated and consecrated, will invariably turn aside if *"God leaves us"* even for a moment.

Had Hezekiah kept close to Jehovah, he would have spoken to the ambassadors of his unsearchable riches, not of his own poor treasures of silver and gold.

At that time, Babylon was not a kingdom of any note, actually being controlled by the Assyrian Empire. But a little over 100 years later, Babylon, having overthrown the Assyrian power, would sack Jerusalem, actually destroying the viability of Israel as a Nation.

(32) "NOW THE REST OF THE ACTS OF HEZEKIAH, AND HIS GOODNESS, BEHOLD, THEY ARE WRITTEN IN THE VISION OF ISAIAH THE PROPHET, THE SON OF AMOZ, AND IN THE BOOK OF THE KINGS OF JUDAH AND ISRAEL.

(33) "AND HEZEKIAH SLEPT WITH HIS FATHERS, AND THEY BURIED HIM IN THE CHIEFEST OF THE SEPULCHRES OF THE SONS OF DAVID: AND ALL JUDAH AND THE INHABITANTS OF JERUSALEM DID HIM HONOUR AT HIS DEATH. AND MANASSEH HIS SON REIGNED IN HIS STEAD."

The overview is:

1. (Vs. 33) Concerning his burial, and *"in the chiefest of the sepulchres of the sons of David,"* such was not said of any man before or after this. It must have meant that he was buried next to David's tomb. If, in fact, that were the case, there could have been no higher honor that Judah could have paid him.

2. (Vs. 33) Despite his failures, Hezekiah was one of the godliest kings who ever reigned over Judah.

"From every stormy wind that blows,
"From every swelling tide of woes,
"There is a calm, a safe retreat;
"'Tis found beneath the Mercy-Seat."

"There is a place where Jesus sheds,
"The oil of gladness on our heads,
"A place than all beside more sweet;
"It is the Blood-stained Mercy-Seat."

"There is a spot where spirits blend,
"And friend holds fellowship with friends;
"Though sundered far, by Faith they meet,
"Around one common Mercy-Seat."

"There, there on eagle-wing we soar,
"And time and sense seem all no more;

"And Heaven comes down our souls to greet,
"And Glory crowns the Mercy-Seat."

CHAPTER 33

(1) "MANASSEH WAS TWELVE YEARS OLD WHEN HE BEGAN TO REIGN, AND HE REIGNED FIFTY AND FIVE YEARS IN JERUSALEM:

(2) "BUT DID THAT WHICH WAS EVIL IN THE SIGHT OF THE LORD, LIKE UNTO THE ABOMINATIONS OF THE HEATHEN, WHOM THE LORD HAD CAST OUT BEFORE THE CHILDREN OF ISRAEL.

(3) "FOR HE BUILT AGAIN THE HIGH PLACES WHICH HEZEKIAH HIS FATHER HAD BROKEN DOWN, AND HE REARED UP ALTARS FOR BAALIM, AND MADE GROVES, AND WORSHIPPED ALL THE HOST OF HEAVEN, AND SERVED THEM.

(4) "ALSO HE BUILT ALTARS IN THE HOUSE OF THE LORD, WHEREOF THE LORD HAD SAID, IN JERUSALEM SHALL MY NAME BE FOREVER.

(5) "AND HE BUILT ALTARS FOR ALL THE HOST OF HEAVEN IN THE TWO COURTS OF THE HOUSE OF THE LORD.

(6) "AND HE CAUSED HIS CHILDREN TO PASS THROUGH THE FIRE IN THE VALLEY OF THE SON OF HINNOM: ALSO HE OBSERVED TIMES, AND USED ENCHANTMENTS, AND USED WITCHCRAFT, AND DEALT WITH A FAMILIAR SPIRIT, AND WITH WIZARDS: HE WROUGHT MUCH EVIL IN THE SIGHT OF THE LORD, TO PROVOKE HIM TO ANGER.

(7) "AND HE SET A CARVED IMAGE, THE IDOL WHICH HE HAD MADE, IN THE HOUSE OF GOD, OF WHICH GOD HAD SAID TO DAVID AND TO SOLOMON HIS SON, IN THIS HOUSE, AND IN JERUSALEM, WHICH I HAVE CHOSEN BEFORE ALL THE TRIBES OF ISRAEL, WILL I PUT MY NAME FOR EVER:

(8) "NEITHER WILL I ANY MORE REMOVE THE FOOT OF ISRAEL FROM OUT OF THE LAND WHICH I HAVE APPOINTED FOR YOUR FATHERS; SO THAT THEY WILL TAKE HEED TO DO ALL THAT I HAVE COMMANDED THEM, ACCORDING TO THE WHOLE LAW AND THE STATUTES AND THE ORDINANCES BY THE HAND OF MOSES.

(9) "SO MANASSEH MADE JUDAH AND THE INHABITANTS OF JERUSALEM TO ERR, AND TO DO WORSE THAN THE HEATHEN, WHOM THE LORD HAD DESTROYED BEFORE THE CHILDREN OF ISRAEL.

(10) "AND THE LORD SPOKE TO MANASSEH, AND TO HIS PEOPLE: BUT THEY WOULD NOT HEARKEN."

The composition is:

1. (Vs. 1) Manasseh was one of the most wicked of all the 42 kings of Israel and Judah, yet he reigned longer than any other—55 years.

2. (Vs. 1) Quite possibly the Lord allowed Manasseh to reign so long because He saw that this hard-riding monarch would repent. Everything that God does is an act of Mercy. Even His Judgment is redemptive, if only the individual or the nation will allow it to be so.

3. According to Verse 2, the Lord did cast out the heathen tribes which occupied Canaan because of their great evil, and not too many years from then, Judah would be cast out as well!

4. (Vs. 5) Manasseh built heathen altars in the *"Court of Israel,"* which was the closest to the Temple, and the *"Court of Women,"* which was immediately behind the Court of Israel.

5. (Vs. 6) This wicked king engaged in human sacrifice, even offering his own children in this horror.

6. (Vs. 7) The *"Asherah"* was actually a statue of the male reproductive organ. It was generally made of a tree trunk. Some believe that he put this in the very Holy of Holies, thereby, removing the Ark of the Covenant.

7. Sadly, the Tenth Verse is the story of untold millions. The Lord speaks in varied ways, but they will not hear, which refers to a willful rejection.

*"EVIL IN THE SIGHT
OF THE LORD"*

As the Scripture says, Manasseh was only 12 years old when he began to reign as king, and he reigned 55 years in Jerusalem.

The Scripture doesn't say when he began to carry out his wickedness. Considering his tender age, more than likely, he was helped along by certain individuals in Jerusalem encouraging him in this evil. Despite the tremendous reforms under his father Hezekiah, regrettably and sadly, it seems there was very little true spiritual depth in Judah as a whole.

Regarding Israel, there were always, one might say, two Israels. There was the Israel who truly served the Lord, and those who didn't. Sadly, those who served the Lord were always in the minority and, most of the time, greatly so.

It is the same in the modern church. There is what one might refer to as the true Church and then the apostate church. The dividing line between these two churches is the Cross of Christ, as the dividing line has always been the Cross of Christ. As well, the true Church is much smaller in number than the apostate church, even as it has always been.

Manasseh did not repent and serve God faithfully until after his captivity into Babylon. How many years his wickedness lasted is not known. There is this difference between him and Saul, Solomon, Uzziah, and others—he began his reign as a wicked king but ended it as a good one; they began as good kings and ended their rule as bad ones.

To the natural mind it would seem strange that Hezekiah, who was a blessing to his people, only reigned 29 years, but Manasseh, who was a curse to his people, reigned 55 years. And yet, the following may shed a small amount of light on the subject.

Why the Lord took Hezekiah when he was only 54 years old, we can only surmise. Quite possibly, the Lord looked down and saw that Hezekiah would lose his way if allowed to live longer. Manasseh lived until he was 67 years old. It is obvious that the Lord let him live so long because, looking into the future, He saw that Manasseh would humble himself and repent, thereby, serving God. In fact, everything that God does is an act of Mercy. Even His Judgment is redemptive, if only the individual or the nation will allow it to be so.

THE DEPTH OF EVIL

Verses 3 through 10, record the terrible acts of this wicked king. They are as follows:

1. *"For he built again the high places which Hezekiah his father had broken down, and he reared up altars for Baalim, and made groves, and worshipped all the host of heaven, and served them."* Consequently, Judah became a nation of idol worshippers, even worse than the heathen around her. They worshipped *"Baal"* and the *"groves,"* of which the latter consisted of the male reproductive organ that was fashioned, most of the time, out of a tree trunk. They also worshiped the stars of the heavens.

2. *"And he built altars in the House of the LORD. . . ."* He took away all the holy utensils and even the Ark of the Covenant, and in its place set up altars to Baal.

3. *"And he built altars for all the host of heaven in the two courts of the House of the LORD."* This means that he worshipped the sun, moon, stars, and planets of the heavens. These *"altars"* took the place of the great Brazen Altar built by Solomon and the great Brazen Laver, both of which had been designed by the Holy Spirit, and which pictured the Cross and the Word of God.

4. *"And he caused his children to pass through the fire in the valley of the son of Hinnom."* This pertains to the awful horror of the worship of the god *"Moloch."* This thing was made somewhat like a modern Buddha, which sat on the ground with its arms outstretched. A fire would be built in its bulbous belly; eventually, the entirety of this metal monster would grow red-hot. Before the fire was built, little children would be tied to the arms, and then gradually, as the metal arms grew red-hot, the priests would beat their drums to drown out the screams of the dying children. The awfulness of this, as should be obvious, defies all description. And this was from the people of God.

5. *"Also he observed times, and used enchantments, and used witchcraft, and dealt with a familiar spirit, and with wizards. . . ."* Under the wicked reign of Manasseh, the entire nation of Judah was actually led by demon spirits. Regrettably, much of the

world today falls into the same category.

6. *"And he set a carved image, the idol which he had made, in the House of God...."* This was probably the *"Asherah,"* which, in a sense, was the same as the *"groves,"* and was made out of a tree trunk. As stated, it was the male reproductive organ, supposed to be the god of fertility. The height varied anywhere from 3 feet to 20 feet tall. Most probably this terrible idol was set up in the Holy of Holies along with Baal in the place of the *"Ark of the Covenant."*

Why would a man, who had been raised by the godly Hezekiah, go into such depths of evil as did Manasseh? Every evidence is, which should be overly obvious, he knew what Judah was supposed to do, and that he was the titular leader. They were to follow the Law of God and do so without reservation. But yet, he forsook all that which his father had carried out, which took Judah to Spiritual Heights it had little known and, as well, had brought the Blessings of the Lord in an unprecedented fashion. None of that seemed to matter to this wicked man. Everything he did was bad, but when he offered up his own children in sacrifice to these heathen gods, that was an evil beyond compare.

There is really no answer as to why some people live for God, and some don't! Abel served the Lord; Cain, his brother, didn't! Jacob served the Lord; his twin brother, Esau, didn't! Joseph served the Lord; his brothers, at least at the beginning, didn't! What institutes some having a heart for God and some going in the opposite direction is known only to the Lord.

FREE MORAL AGENCY

There is what is referred to as free moral agency in the heart of every person. In other words, the person has the freedom to choose in the manner he so desires. There is no evidence that God tampers with one's free moral agency; however, Satan will most definitely do so, at least, within the limitations of his power. It's not so much that the Evil One can change this agency, but that he can apply pressure in the way of evil he so desires. However, the individual still has to make the final decision.

WILLPOWER

Willpower, which portrays the direction that one desires, is very important as it regards the individual. However, willpower within itself is unable to cope with the bondages of darkness, which incorporate alcohol, drugs, many types of sexual immorality, fear, emotional disturbances, depression, etc. In other words, the individual may desire to do something but be unable to carry it out. This is true with approximately 20 million alcoholics in this nation, who would desire to quit drinking but are unable to do so. The same could be said for drugs or any other type of bondage. The truth is, millions of Christians, and I speak of those who truly love the Lord, which means they are truly Born-Again, are being forced by a bondage of some nature to do things they don't want to do. The actual fact is, behind all of these bondages are the powers of darkness, i.e., Satan and demon spirits.

We are told that while it is possible for an individual to break a particular physical bondage in about three days, still, they are unable to break the mental bondage. All of this has to do with the sin nature. In other words, the sin nature is ruling such an individual, whether it's the unredeemed or even a Believer. The Apostle Paul spent almost the entirety of the Sixth Chapter of Romans addressing this situation. I quote from "THE EXPOSITOR'S STUDY BIBLE":

"Let not sin (the sin nature) *therefore reign* (rule) *in your mortal body* (showing that the sin nature can once again rule in the heart and life of the Believer, if the Believer doesn't constantly look to Christ and the Cross; the 'mortal body' is neutral, which means it can be used for Righteousness or unrighteousness), *that you should obey it in the lusts thereof* (ungodly lusts are carried out through the mortal body, if Faith is not maintained in the Cross [I Cor. 1:17-18]).

"Neither yield you your members (of your mortal body) *as instruments of unrighteousness unto sin* (the sin nature): *but yield yourselves unto God* (we are to yield ourselves to Christ and the Cross; that alone guarantees Victory over the sin nature), *as those who are alive from the dead* (we

have been raised with Christ in *'Newness of Life'*), *and your members as instruments of Righteousness unto God* (this can be done only by virtue of the Cross and our Faith in that Finished Work, and Faith which continues in that Finished Work from day-to-day [Lk. 9:23-24])" (Rom. 6:12-13).

As should be overly obvious, the unredeemed have no control over the sin nature. In fact, it controls them in one way or the other 24 hours a day, 7 days a week; however, the Believer most definitely does have control, but only in the following fashion.

THE CROSS OF CHRIST

The Believer is to place his Faith exclusively in Christ and the Cross, understanding that it was there that all Victory was won (Col. 2:14-15). That being maintained, the Holy Spirit, Who works exclusively within the framework of the Cross of Christ, will begin to work in the heart and life of the Believer, giving the power that is needed for the Believer to live the life that should be lived. Without this, Faith in Christ and the Cross, which gives latitude to the Holy Spirit to work, the Believer, although Saved, simply cannot live a victorious, overcoming, Christian life. No matter how hard one tries, no matter what type of effort one may put forth, and no matter how much one may fast or pray, even as wonderful as those things might be, still, such a Believer functioning outside of the Cross will be ruled in some way by the sin nature, which, to say the least, makes life miserable.

While all of us are complex creatures, still, God's Way for life and living is *"Christ and Him Crucified"* (I Cor. 1:23).

The Cross of Christ is the answer to man's dilemma and, in fact, the only answer. The world attempts every type of strategy that one can think, all to no avail. The tragedy is, the church is borrowing from the world, which means they are borrowing from a failed effort.

FIGHTING THE GOOD FIGHT OF FAITH

Let not the reader think, however, that once one places one's Faith exclusively in Christ and the Cross, which is exactly what should be done, that Satan will no longer try to cause problems. To be frank with you, Satan is going to continue his efforts, irrespective as to what the Believer does. He will try to discourage the Believer, intimidate the Believer, and lie to the Believer, all to get the Believer to place his faith in something other than Christ and the Cross. That's what Paul was talking about when he said, *"Fight the good fight of Faith* (in essence, the only fight we're called upon to engage; every attack by Satan against the Believer, irrespective of its form, is to destroy or seriously weaken our Faith; he wants to push our Faith from the Cross to other things), *lay hold on Eternal Life* (we do such by understanding that all Life comes from Christ, and the Means is the Cross), *whereunto you are also Called* (Called to follow Christ), *and have professed a good profession before many witnesses.* (This does not refer to a particular occasion, but to the entirety of his life for Christ)" (I Tim. 6:12).

As stated, the only actual fight that we are called upon to engage is *"the good fight of Faith."* It's good because it is the right fight. The *"Faith"* mentioned constitutes our Faith placed in Christ and what Christ has done for us at the Cross. This is where our Faith must reside, meaning that the Cross of Christ must ever be the Object of our Faith. But, as stated, Satan will do everything within his power to hinder us. In fact, that will never change.

But if the Believer keeps his Faith as it ought to be, victory in every capacity will be ours. The sin nature will not be able to rule over us; the Bible tells us so (Rom. 6:14).

As it regards unbelievers, the sin nature will rule more powerfully over some than it does others, with Manasseh being an excellent case in point. Of course, Manasseh did not know God and came under the category of the unredeemed, at least, until he repented before the Lord, which he did!

WORSE THAN THE HEATHEN

The Scripture says, *"So Manasseh made Judah and the inhabitants of Jerusalem to err, and to do worse than the heathen, whom the LORD had destroyed before the Children of Israel."*

Sadly, it is a fact that those who know the

Light, or know of the Light, can go deeper into darkness than those who have never known the Light. Again, Manasseh is an excellent example.

Another example is the Pentecostal or Full Gospel Denominations. These groups, and I am Pentecostal, touched the world with the Gospel, no doubt, with the greatest Move of God the world has ever known. It was done by the Power of the Holy Spirit. But, little by little, these denominations have ceased to follow the Moving and Operation of the Holy Spirit, rather adopting the ways of the world. If the trend continues, and we pray the Lord it doesn't, they will lose their way altogether. While there are still many godly Preachers and many godly people among them, regrettably, that number is diminishing almost by the day. In the late 1950's and early 1960's, these denominations, and I specifically speak of those in America and Canada, opted for humanistic psychology. When they did this, the Cross was abandoned. It didn't happen overnight but was a little by little process, with a little leaven corrupting the entirety of the lump, even as the Apostle Paul said.

At the present time, these denominations have opted entirely for humanistic psychology, which means that the Cross of Jesus Christ plays little or no part whatsoever in their efforts. I'm afraid that they are not merely on the road to apostasy but, in fact, have completely apostatized. Paul also said,

"Now the Spirit (Holy Spirit) *speaks expressly* (pointedly), *that in the latter times* (the times in which we now live, the last of the last days, which begin the fulfillment of Endtime Prophecies) *some shall depart from the Faith* (anytime Paul uses the term *'the Faith,'* in short, he is referring to the Cross; so, we are told here that some will depart from the Cross as the means of Salvation and Victory), *giving heed to seducing spirits* (evil spirits, i.e., *'religious spirits,'* making something seem like what it isn't), *and doctrines of devils* (should have been translated, *'doctrines of demons'*; the *'seducing spirits'* entice Believers away from the true Faith, causing them to believe *'doctrines inspired by demon spirits')"* (I Tim. 4:1).

In truth, most religious denominations

NOTES

do not survive spiritually the third generation. While Revival is desperately needed, the truth is, before Revival can come, Reformation is needed. In short, this refers to coming back to the Cross of Christ.

(11) "WHEREFORE THE LORD BROUGHT UPON THEM THE CAPTAINS OF THE HOST OF THE KING OF ASSYRIA, WHICH TOOK MANASSEH AMONG THE THORNS, AND BOUND HIM WITH FETTERS, AND CARRIED HIM TO BABYLON.

(12) "AND WHEN HE WAS IN AFFLICTION, HE BESOUGHT THE LORD HIS GOD, AND HUMBLED HIMSELF GREATLY BEFORE THE GOD OF HIS FATHERS,

(13) "AND PRAYED UNTO HIM: AND HE WAS INTREATED OF HIM, AND HEARD HIS SUPPLICATION, AND BROUGHT HIM AGAIN TO JERUSALEM INTO HIS KINGDOM. THEN MANASSEH KNEW THAT THE LORD HE WAS GOD.

(14) "NOW AFTER THIS HE BUILT A WALL WITHOUT THE CITY OF DAVID, ON THE WEST SIDE OF GIHON, IN THE VALLEY, EVEN TO THE ENTERING IN AT THE FISH GATE, AND COMPASSED ABOUT OPHEL, AND RAISED IT UP A VERY GREAT HEIGHT, AND PUT CAPTAINS OF WAR IN ALL THE FENCED CITIES OF JUDAH."

The diagram is:

1. (Vs. 11) Manasseh being taken by the king of Assyria, bound with fetters and carried to Babylon, was an act of Mercy on the part of God, as He attempted to bring Manasseh to his senses. It accomplished its purpose.

2. The Twelfth Verse proclaims at least one of the reasons, perhaps the overriding reason, that the Lord allowed Manasseh to rule as long as he did. It had the desired effect upon the monarch. Time and time again, the Lord brings Judgment in attempting to bring people to a place of Repentance.

3. (Vs. 13) There could be no more beautiful illustration of the Mercy and Grace of God than that which was extended to Manasseh. The great lesson learned here is that if the Lord would do that for this king, who had wrought more evil in Judah than any other king before him, He will do it for anyone. There are only two requirements:

to humble oneself, and to pray unto God.

AFFLICTION

Sometimes affliction works; sometimes it doesn't! This time it worked.

The Scripture says, *"And when he was in affliction, he besought the LORD his God, and humbled himself greatly before the God of his fathers, and prayed unto Him: and He was intreated of him, and heard his supplication, and brought him again to Jerusalem into his kingdom. Then Manasseh knew that the LORD He was God."*

Every evidence is that Manasseh truly repented. Had it been a halfhearted Repentance, the Lord would not have heard such, and Manasseh would not have been restored to his throne in Jerusalem.

In fact, this is one of the most remarkable illustrations of the Mercy and Grace of God found in the entirety of the Word of God. If the Lord would forgive this man after all the terrible and hideous sins committed by him, it should stand to reason that the Lord, upon proper sincerity and proper humility, will forgive anyone. What Grace! What Mercy! What Love!

But on the other hand, if there is no sincerity, meaning there is no true Repentance, the Judgment will continue, even as it ought to continue.

Man is an intractable, hard, obstinate, coarse, and stubborn creature. He is this way because of the Fall. It has warped and twisted every fiber of our being, making it very difficult for most to truly repent, even when Repentance is desperately needed.

For instance, had Judas sincerely repented, he would have been forgiven of the terrible betrayal of our Lord. But he did not repent, rather succumbing to despair, taking his own life.

Even as we shall see, the actions of Manasseh proved that his Repentance was sincere.

(15) "AND HE TOOK AWAY THE STRANGE GODS, AND THE IDOL OUT OF THE HOUSE OF THE LORD, AND ALL THE ALTARS THAT HE HAD BUILT IN THE MOUNT OF THE HOUSE OF THE LORD, AND IN JERUSALEM, AND CAST THEM OUT OF THE CITY.

(16) "AND HE REPAIRED THE ALTAR OF THE LORD, AND SACRIFICED THEREON PEACE OFFERINGS AND THANK OFFERINGS, AND COMMANDED JUDAH TO SERVE THE LORD GOD OF ISRAEL.

(17) "NEVERTHELESS THE PEOPLE DID SACRIFICE STILL IN THE HIGH PLACES, YET UNTO THE LORD THEIR GOD ONLY.

(18) "NOW THE REST OF THE ACTS OF MANASSEH, AND HIS PRAYER UNTO HIS GOD, AND THE WORDS OF THE SEERS WHO SPOKE TO HIM IN THE NAME OF THE LORD GOD OF ISRAEL, BEHOLD, THEY ARE WRITTEN IN THE BOOK OF THE KINGS OF ISRAEL.

(19) "HIS PRAYER ALSO, AND HOW GOD WAS INTREATED OF HIM, AND ALL HIS SINS, AND HIS TRESPASS, AND THE PLACES WHEREIN HE BUILT HIGH PLACES, AND SET UP GROVES AND GRAVEN IMAGES, BEFORE HE WAS HUMBLED: BEHOLD, THEY ARE WRITTEN AMONG THE SAYINGS OF THE SEERS."

The diagram is:

1. (Vs. 16) The repairing of the *"Altar of the LORD"* pertained to the Great Brazen Altar, on which the sacrifices were offered.

2. (Vs. 16) The *"Peace Offerings"* were generally offered after the Sin and Trespass Offerings, signifying that Peace with God had now been restored. This tells us that the Peace of God had now come to Manasseh.

3. (Vs. 16) To be sure, this king had much to be thankful for, hence, the *"Thank Offerings"* and the emphasis on this by the Holy Spirit.

4. The offering of sacrifices to the Lord in the high places, as mentioned in Verse 17, was contrary to the Word of God. There was to be one national worship in the one Temple, and the offerings and sacrifices on the one national Altar, which signified one Calvary.

STRANGE GODS

The Scripture says that Manasseh *"took away the strange gods, and the idol out of the House of the LORD. . . ."*

There is a great possibility that Manasseh set up the *"Asherah,"* which was a replica of the male reproductive organ, supposedly the god of fertility, in the very Holy of Holies. One thing is certain, he most definitely did set up an idol in the *"House of the LORD."* There was only one of two places it could have been placed, and that would be in the Holy Place, where were the Table of Shewbread, the Golden Lampstand, and the Altar of Incense, and then, the very Holy of Holies itself, which housed the Ark of the Covenant. While the Temple proper had many side rooms and porticos, and in reality was a huge affair, its actual workings consisted of two rooms, the Holy Place and the Holy of Holies. All of this tells us that he had greatly polluted the Temple of God, even the most holy part of the Temple, which was the Holy of Holies. That he and those who participated in such gross actions were not stricken dead on the spot was all because of the Mercy of God.

Undoubtedly, the priests of the idols carried on their rituals and ceremonies in the very heart of the Temple where God dwelt.

As well, it is quite possible their orgies between men and women or men and men took place in the very Temple itself, as it regarded the worship of these idols, which was generally accompanied by such.

Understanding all of this and, thereby, the terrible evil committed, when presently the Cross of Christ is ignored, which is the only way to God and, in fact, has always been the only way to God, how much different is this than that which took place so long ago? Anything that is not the Message of the Cross is a *"strange god."* Let us say it again.

If it's not the Cross of Christ and the Cross of Christ exclusively, then whatever it is, irrespective as to how religious it might seem to be, we have just turned it into a *"strange god."* I personally feel that the Lord looks at it with the same severity as He did long ago, and to be frank, even more so presently. Paul said this,

"And the times of this ignorance God winked at (does not reflect that such ignorance was Salvation, for it was not! before the Cross, there was very little Light in the world, so God withheld Judgment)*; but now commands all men everywhere to repent* (but since the Cross, the 'Way' is open to all; it's up to us Believers to make that *'Way'*

NOTES

known to all men)*:*

"Because He has appointed a day (refers to the coming of the Great White Throne Judgment [Rev. 20:11-15])*, in the which He will judge the world in Righteousness by that Man Whom He has ordained* (this Righteousness is exclusively in Christ Jesus and what He has done for us at the Cross, and can be gained only by Faith in Him [Eph. 2:8-9; Rom. 10:9-10, 13; Rev. 22:17])*; whereof He has given assurance unto all men, in that He has raised Him from the dead* (refers to the Resurrection ratifying that which was done at Calvary, and is applicable to all men, at least all who will believe!)*"* (Acts 17:30-31).

REPAIRING THE ALTAR OF THE LORD

The Altar then consisted of the Brazen Altar which had been designed by the Holy Spirit and built by Solomon. It was thirty feet long and thirty feet wide. Through lack of use and, no doubt, abuse, as well, it was in a state of disrepair. Manasseh repaired it, which means that it was put back into service.

The Altar of the Lord, i.e., *"the Message of the Cross," "Redemption through the Blood,"* speaking presently, desperately needs to be repaired. The modern church has opted for humanistic psychology. In doing this, they have abandoned the Cross, for it is impossible to mix the two. In fact, the church has become so psychologized that most preachers are preaching psychology and don't even realize they are doing so. At the same time, many realize they are doing so, and purposely. In other words, they no longer register faith in Christ and what He has done for us at the Cross. Irrespective as to what they say, their actions speak louder than words.

HOW DO WE REPAIR THE CROSS?

The first thing the Believer has to do, Preacher or otherwise, is to get to understand through the Word of God what the Cross of Christ actually means. The Cross of Christ, or one might say, *"The Message of the Cross,"* is the meaning of the New Covenant. In essence, the New Covenant is Jesus Christ, and Him in totality. But it's what He did at the Cross, which makes the

New Covenant viable and, in fact, a Covenant that will never need to be amended, hence, the Apostle Paul referring to it as the *"Everlasting Covenant"* (Heb. 13:20).

Many, if not most, Believers have at least a modicum of understanding as it regards the Cross respecting the Salvation experience; consequently, every time they speak of the Cross, it's always in the past tense. *"Jesus died for me"* is an excellent example and is one of the greatest statements that could ever be made; however, they stop there, not understanding the part the Cross plays in our everyday life and living.

About 99 percent of Paul's teaching concerned the Cross of Christ as it regards our every day life and living, in other words, our Sanctification (Rom. 6:1-14; I Cor. 1:17-18, 21, 23; Gal. 6:14; Col. 2:14-15). As should be obvious, it was to the Apostle Paul that the meaning of the New Covenant was given by the Lord (Gal. 1:12). So, we quote him often because he was the man to whom this great Truth was given.

If one properly understands the Cross of Christ, then one properly understands the Bible because the Bible is the Story of the Cross, i.e., *"Jesus Christ and Him Crucified"* (I Cor. 1:23). Even though we've already given the following in this volume, due to its great significance, please allow the repetition:

FOCUS: The Lord Jesus Christ (Jn. 14:6).

THE OBJECT OF FAITH: The Cross of Christ (Rom. 6:1-14; Gal. 6:14; Col. 2:14-15).

POWER SOURCE: The Holy Spirit (Rom. 8:1-2, 11).

RESULTS: Victory (Rom. 6:14).

In abbreviated form, which we have just given you, is the meaning of the New Covenant.

Now, let's look at it in a different way, actually, the way in which most people are trying to live for God, all to no avail.

FOCUS: Works (Rom. 4:4).

THE OBJECT OF FAITH: Performance (Rom. 4:1-2).

POWER SOURCE: Self (Rom. 4:4).

RESULTS: Defeat (Rom. 8:8).

The first diagram is God's Way, the second, that of man.

Perhaps everything can be summed up in a few words:

"Jesus Christ is the Source of all things we receive from God, and the Cross is the Means by which we receive these things, all superintended by the Holy Spirit" (Gal. 2:20-21).

If our Faith is anchored squarely in Christ and the Cross, which means it's anchored in the Word, that is the way and, in fact, the only way that one can repair the Altar. It is not a physical thing, as should be obvious, but rather that which is Spiritual, which refers to Faith in Christ and Him Crucified. It is not at all in doing but rather believing. And, when we get our believing right, to be sure, then we will do right. In fact, the Message of the Cross is the only Way, the only Means of getting Victory over the world, the flesh, and the Devil.

THE SACRIFICES

Immediately upon coming to God, Manasseh began to offer sacrifices, which means that he placed his Faith exclusively in the shed Blood of the Lamb. The Altar had been repaired, and proper Faith can now be exhibited.

As stated, under the Mosaic Law, when any one of the Whole Burnt Offering, the Sin Offering, or the Trespass Offering, was placed on the Altar, it was generally followed by the *"Peace Offering."*

The Peace Offering was the only sacrifice in which both the Priests and the individual bringing the sacrifice could participate. In other words, such a person could call his friends and relatives together and have a feast, and with great joy.

The reason?

Due to the Burnt, the Sin, or the Trespass Offering being tendered toward God, Peace with God had been restored because the sin was expiated. It was now a time of rejoicing, hence, the feast.

THE SEERS

The Seers were actually Prophets who ministered to Manasseh before he repented. In fact, it is believed that Manasseh murdered Isaiah the Prophet, one of the greatest Men of God who ever lived. Isaiah was quoted by Christ more than any other Prophet. He proclaimed more about the Cross and about the coming Kingdom Age than any other Prophet. The Book that bears his name is, without a doubt, one of the greatest works that's ever been offered to the general public, and because it is the Word of the Lord.

It is said that Manasseh placed aged Isaiah into a hollow log and sawed the log in twain, thereby, murdering this great Prophet. And yet, when he truly begged God for Mercy and Grace, which he ultimately did, the Lord forgave him even of these atrocious acts. As we have previously stated, we serve a wonderful, a glorious, and a merciful God!

(20) "SO MANASSEH SLEPT WITH HIS FATHERS, AND THEY BURIED HIM IN HIS OWN HOUSE: AND AMON HIS SON REIGNED IN HIS STEAD."

The construction is:

1. (Vs. 20) Unlike some of the other kings, Manasseh began his reign as a wicked king, but ended it as a good one.

2. He was buried in the garden of his own house, wherever it might have been in Jerusalem.

3. Amon his son now begins to reign, but sadly and regrettably, he followed in the footsteps of his father before his father's Repentance.

(21) "AMON WAS TWO AND TWENTY YEARS OLD WHEN HE BEGAN TO REIGN, AND REIGNED TWO YEARS IN JERUSALEM.

(22) "BUT HE DID THAT WHICH WAS EVIL IN THE SIGHT OF THE LORD, AS DID MANASSEH HIS FATHER: FOR AMON SACRIFICED UNTO ALL THE CARVED IMAGES WHICH MANASSEH HIS FATHER HAD MADE, AND SERVED THEM;

(23) "AND HUMBLED NOT HIMSELF BEFORE THE LORD, AS MANASSEH HIS FATHER HAD HUMBLED HIMSELF; BUT AMON TRESPASSED MORE AND MORE."

The overview is:

1. The Twenty-third Verse proclaims the fact that the Lord evidently chastised Amon, trying to get him to repent, but to no avail.

2. (Vs. 23) Actually, precious few humble themselves as did Manasseh, with most hardening themselves as did Amon, and that despite the appeal of the Lord.

3. The only thing that could be said about this man by the Holy Spirit was, ". . . but Amon trespassed more and more." What is the Lord saying about you and me?

AMON

Pulpit says, *"The long reign of Manasseh of 55 years – a signal and merciful instance of space given for repentance – ended, his death met him presumably at the age of 67. The son who succeeded him was 22 years old, born therefore not before his father was 45 years old. This may be an indication that it was indeed not only one son whom Manasseh 'caused to pass through the fire.' Amon emulated the sins of the former life of his father, but did not, like him, repent.*

"It is but very little we know or think of Amon: his name is unfamiliar, for his life was uneventful. And yet, he could have had a happy reign, a glorious reign, being useful to the Kingdom of God, and a blessing to his people, actually like David or Hezekiah, but he lost all of that by his own folly.

"He was heir to the throne of Judah, which within itself was of tremendous significance, and because he was a son of David, of course, many times removed. What a blessing he could have been!

"And yet, he deliberately chose the evil course. At 22 years old he did not have his father's excuse for being led astray. The stern discipline through which Manasseh had passed, and the mercy he had found in a forgiving God, surely should have affected Amon. But he disregarded and defied the lessons which were written in such large characters before his face, and as stated, chose the evil way. As a result, he only reigned two years, and was murdered."[1]

A MATTER OF CHOICE

Amon had a choice, and he chose evil. Which road are you choosing?

The little adage is true:

"One life will soon be past

"Only what's done for Christ will last!"

Do we realize that the choices we are making here will decide eternity? So many trade the eternal for the temporal. It is a sorry trade. It is said of Moses:

"By Faith Moses, when he was come to years (refers to him coming to the age of 40

[Ex. 2:11]), *refused to be called the son of Pharaoh's daughter* (in effect, he refused the position of Pharaoh of Egypt, for which he had been trained because he had been adopted by Pharaoh's daughter);

"*Choosing rather to suffer affliction with the people of God* (proclaims the choice Moses made; he traded the temporal for the Eternal), *than to enjoy the pleasures of sin for a season* (presents the choice which must be made, affliction or the pleasures of sin);

"*Esteeming the reproach of Christ greater riches than the treasures in Egypt* (he judged the reproach was greater than the throne of Egypt): *for he had respect unto the recompence of the reward.* (Moses habitually 'looked away' from the treasures in Egypt, and purposely fixed his eye on the Heavenly Reward.)

"*By Faith he forsook Egypt* (which, spiritually speaking, every Believer must do), *not fearing the wrath of the king* (Pharaoh tried to kill him at that time [Ex. 2:15]): *for he endured, as seeing Him Who is invisible.* (This speaks of Christ, Whom Moses saw by Faith)" (Heb. 11:24-27).

(24) "AND HIS SERVANTS CONSPIRED AGAINST HIM, AND KILLED HIM IN HIS OWN HOUSE.

(25) "BUT THE PEOPLE OF THE LAND KILLED ALL THEM WHO HAD CONSPIRED AGAINST KING AMON; AND THE PEOPLE OF THE LAND MADE JOSIAH HIS SON KING IN HIS STEAD."

The pattern is:

1. Amon took the throne at 22 years old, reigned two years, and was killed when he was 24 years old.

2. Beautifully enough, his son Josiah was one of the godliest kings to grace the Throne of Judah.

3. It is believed that the great Prophet Jeremiah was a great blessing and help to Josiah.

"Lord, to whom except to Thee
"Shall our wandering spirits go;
"The Whom it is light to see,
"And Eternal Life to know?
"Awful is that life of Thine
"Which the Spirit's Breath inspires;
"And the food must be Divine

NOTES

"Which each newborn soul desires."

"Israel on the heavenly seed
"Fed and died in days of yore;
"But the souls, that on Thee feed,
"Never thirst nor hunger more.
"Lord, to whom except to Thee
"Shall we go when ills betide?
"Who except Thyself can be
"Hope and help and strength and guide?"

"Who can cleanse the soul from sin,
"Hear the prayer, and seal the vow?
"Who can fill the void within,
"Blessed Saviour, who but Thou?
"Therefore evermore I'll give
"Laud and praise, my God to Thee;
"Evermore in Thee I live
"Evermore live Thou in me."

CHAPTER 34

(1) "JOSIAH WAS EIGHT YEARS OLD WHEN HE BEGAN TO REIGN, AND HE REIGNED IN JERUSALEM ONE AND THIRTY YEARS.

(2) "AND HE DID THAT WHICH WAS RIGHT IN THE SIGHT OF THE LORD, AND WALKED IN THE WAYS OF DAVID HIS FATHER, AND DECLINED NEITHER TO THE RIGHT HAND, NOR TO THE LEFT."

The synopsis is:

1. (Vs. 1) Josiah will be one of the most godly kings, and yet, Judah's sun is beginning to set.

2. (Vs. 2) The Holy Spirit saying of Josiah, "*. . . and declined neither to the right hand, nor to the left,*" presents a beautiful statement!

3. While Josiah definitely was godly, the truth is, the nation of Judah as a whole was going in the opposite direction. It was to be seen that despite Josiah's reforms, it could not be changed.

"*RIGHT IN THE SIGHT OF THE LORD*"

Williams says, "*The three events of this Chapter are the conversion of the king, the discovery of the Bible, and the reformation that resulted.*"[1]

Josiah was the seventeenth king of Judah. He was the son of Amon, the grandson of Manasseh, and the great grandson of Hezekiah.

When Josiah became king, the Assyrian Empire was weakening and actually dying. It would be taken over by the Babylonians shortly before Josiah was slain in a war against Necho, king of Egypt. With the advent of the Babylonian Empire, great changes would come about, changes which would affect the entirety of the world. The Prophecies and predictions concerning all of this are found in most all of the Books written by the great Prophets of the Old Testament, but especially by Daniel.

Under the leadership of Josiah and with the help of Jeremiah, it seemed that Judah would once again become a great nation, but the nation had drifted too far from God. As stated, while Josiah's heart was right with God, because *"he did that which was right in the sight of the LORD,"* still, Judah, as a whole, had no heart for God. The great Prophet Jeremiah would see this firsthand. It would result in the destruction of the land, the city of Jerusalem, and the Temple.

Of no other king of Judah was it said, *". . . and declined neither to the right hand, nor to the left,"* meaning that he did his very best to serve God with every capacity of his being.

(3) "FOR IN THE EIGHTH YEAR OF HIS REIGN, WHILE HE WAS YET YOUNG, HE BEGAN TO SEEK AFTER THE GOD OF DAVID HIS FATHER: AND IN THE TWELFTH YEAR HE BEGAN TO PURGE JUDAH AND JERUSALEM FROM THE HIGH PLACES, AND THE GROVES, AND THE CARVED IMAGES, AND THE MOLTEN IMAGES.

(4) "AND THEY BROKE DOWN THE ALTARS OF BAALIM IN HIS PRESENCE; AND THE IMAGES, THAT WERE ON HIGH ABOVE THEM, HE CUT DOWN; AND THE GROVES, AND THE CARVED IMAGES, AND THE MOLTEN IMAGES, HE BROKE IN PIECES, AND MADE DUST OF THEM, AND STROWED IT UPON THE GRAVES OF THEM WHO HAD SACRIFICED UNTO THEM.

(5) "AND HE BURNT THE BONES OF THE PRIESTS UPON THEIR ALTARS, AND CLEANSED JUDAH AND JERUSALEM.

(6) "AND SO DID HE IN THE CITIES OF MANASSEH, AND EPHRAIM, AND SIMEON, EVEN UNTO NAPHTALI, WITH THEIR MATTOCKS ROUND ABOUT.

(7) "AND WHEN HE HAD BROKEN DOWN THE ALTARS AND THE GROVES, AND HAD BEATEN THE GRAVEN IMAGES INTO POWDER, AND CUT DOWN ALL THE IDOLS THROUGHOUT ALL THE LAND OF ISRAEL, HE RETURNED TO JERUSALEM."

The construction is:

1. (Vs. 3) It seems that Josiah gave his heart to the Lord when he was 16 years old.

2. Burning the bones of the priests of Verse 5 is speaking of the ungodly priests who had burned incense on the altar at Beth-el nearly 350 years before.

3. (Vs. 5) A Prophet, at that time, came out of Judah and *"cried against the altar."* He prophesied at that time that a *"child shall be born unto the House of David, Josiah by name."* In other words, the Holy Spirit through him called Josiah's name about 320 years before Josiah was born (I Ki. 13:2).

4. (Vs. 6) Josiah extended his effort at reform even into what had been the northern kingdom.

5. He attended to this reformation personally, even as the Seventh Verse proclaims.

CONVERSION

There is a possibility that the Prophet Jeremiah was instrumental in bringing Josiah to a Saving Knowledge of the Lord. Jeremiah was probably several years older than the king, and some even conclude that the Prophet was related to him by marriage. If, in fact, Jeremiah was instrumental in guiding the young king, it would have been several years before he began his Prophetic Ministry.

THE PURGING

Josiah would have been twenty years old when he began the purging of Judah and Jerusalem. He had been serving the Lord now for some four years, having given his heart to the Lord when he was sixteen years old.

His father Amon had taken Judah to low depths of spiritual depravity, in fact, depravity of every kind. Thankfully, Amon only served as king for two years. Had he lived longer, only God knows what would have happened to Judah. But his son Josiah, completely unlike his evil father, now begins a purging process, which will include the entirety of the nation. To guarantee its success and that the reform was carried out as it should have been, he personally guided the effort. He did the following:

- He eradicated the high places.
- He tore down the groves, which was probably the Asherah, one of the most vile of heathenistic idols.
- He did away with the carved images.
- He did away with the molten images.
- He broke down the altars of Baal.

It seems he gathered all of these things together, broke them in pieces, *"and made dust of them."* He then scattered the dust of these images and idols *"on the graves of them who had sacrificed unto them."*

A PROPHECY FULFILLED

Some 320 years before Josiah was born (I Ki. 13:1-2), the Scripture says that *"A Man of God came out of Judah to Beth-el, and cried against the altar."* This was the altar built by Jeroboam in the northern kingdom of Israel, which was an abomination to the country.

The Man of God prophesied at that time that a *"child shall be born unto the House of David, Josiah by name."* In other words, and as stated, he called Josiah's name 320 years before Josiah was born.

Exactly as the Prophet had said so many years before, Josiah *"burnt the bones of the priests upon their altars, and cleansed Judah and Jerusalem."*

THE SIGNIFICANCE OF THIS EVENT

Why was this so important, Josiah burning the bones of these priests upon their altars, considering they had lived over three hundred years before? Sadly and regrettably, Judah and Israel had been filled with heathen altars any number of times. But yet, the Lord singled this out, this altar that was built by Jeroboam in the northern confederation of Israel, even specifying the name of the king in the distant future, Josiah, who would carry out this task. All heathen altars were despicable to the Lord, but this particular altar built by Jeroboam was hated by the Lord even to a greater degree.

Quite possibly, one of the reasons was, when the Nation of Israel split with Ten Tribes becoming the northern confederation and two Tribes, Judah and Benjamin, making up the southern kingdom, the altar built by Jeroboam started Israel down the long road of spiritual and physical destruction. In other words, it was the seedbed of all the idolatry which followed. It started the Nation on the road to destruction, which ultimately came to pass, as it was overrun by the Assyrians.

(8) "NOW IN THE EIGHTEENTH YEAR OF HIS REIGN, WHEN HE HAD PURGED THE LAND, AND THE HOUSE, HE SENT SHAPHAN THE SON OF AZALIAH, AND MAASEIAH THE GOVERNOR OF THE CITY, AND JOAH THE SON OF JOAHAZ THE RECORDER, TO REPAIR THE HOUSE OF THE LORD HIS GOD.

(9) "AND WHEN THEY CAME TO HILKIAH THE HIGH PRIEST, THEY DELIVERED THE MONEY THAT WAS BROUGHT INTO THE HOUSE OF GOD, WHICH THE LEVITES THAT KEPT THE DOORS HAD GATHERED OF THE HAND OF MANASSEH AND EPHRAIM, AND OF ALL THE REMNANT OF ISRAEL, AND OF ALL JUDAH AND BENJAMIN; AND THEY RETURNED TO JERUSALEM.

(10) "AND THEY PUT IT IN THE HAND OF THE WORKMEN WHO HAD THE OVERSIGHT OF THE HOUSE OF THE LORD, AND THEY GAVE IT TO THE WORKMEN WHO WROUGHT IN THE HOUSE OF THE LORD, TO REPAIR AND AMEND THE HOUSE:

(11) "EVEN TO THE ARTIFICERS AND BUILDERS GAVE THEY IT, TO BUY HEWN STONE, AND TIMBER FOR COUPLINGS, AND TO FLOOR THE HOUSES WHICH THE KINGS OF JUDAH HAD DESTROYED.

(12) "AND THE MEN DID THE WORK FAITHFULLY: AND THE OVERSEERS OF

THEM WERE JAHATH AND OBADIAH, THE LEVITES, OF THE SONS OF MERARI; AND ZECHARIAH AND MESHULLAM, OF THE SONS OF THE KOHATHITES, TO SET IT FORWARD; AND OTHER OF THE LEVITES, ALL WHO COULD SKILL OF INSTRUMENTS OF MUSIC.

(13) "ALSO THEY WERE OVER THE BEARERS OF BURDENS, AND WERE OVERSEERS OF ALL WHO WROUGHT THE WORK IN ANY MANNER OF SERVICE: AND OF THE LEVITES THERE WERE SCRIBES, AND OFFICERS, AND PORTERS."

The synopsis is:

1. (Vs. 8) In the eighteenth year of his reign, Josiah was 26 years old.

2. (Vs. 8) This reform took place approximately five or six years after Jeremiah the Prophet had begun to prophesy (Jer. 2:2). The great Prophet was, therefore, present at the time of these reformations and the great Passover Feast of these Chapters.

3. Josiah included the northern kingdom of Israel in this Reformation, at least, what few people were still in the land. As previously stated, the northern kingdom had been totally destroyed by the Assyrians some years before.

4. According to Verse 11, there had been much negligence of the Temple, and even outright destruction.

5. It seems from Verse 12 that the Levites played instruments and sang praises unto the Lord while the work on the Temple was being done. This was according to the Word of the Lord.

6. The Levites, according to Verse 13, had the general oversight of all the work and, thereby, filled the offices mentioned in this Verse.

THE REPAIRING OF THE HOUSE OF THE LORD GOD

First of all, Josiah had cleared the land of idols and idol worship, even as he should have done. Now, he would repair the House of the Lord, which evidently had fallen into a state of serious disrepair.

Does the House of the Lord presently need repairing?

As we have stated over and over again in this Volume and will continue to say so, if the Church is preaching the Cross, then it is abiding by the Word of God. If not, and regrettably, one must say that it isn't, then the House of the Lord, Spiritually speaking, needs repair.

This temple was referred to as *"the House of the LORD,"* simply because the Lord dwelt in that house, actually in the Holy of Holies, between the Mercy Seat and the Cherubim. When Jesus came and died on the Cross of Calvary, He atoned for all sin, past, present, and future, at least, for all who will believe (Jn. 3:16). With all sin being atoned, this means that the sin debt was paid for each and every individual who will believe. That being the case, the Holy Spirit can now come into the heart and life of the individual, which He does at conversion, there to abide forever (Jn. 14:16). Now, the House of the Lord is the physical body, soul and spirit, of the individual. Paul said,

"Know you not that you are the Temple of God (where the Holy Spirit abides), *and that the Spirit of God dwells in you?* (That makes the Born-Again Believer His permanent Home)" (I Cor. 3:16).

In regard to this, each individual is responsible for His *"House."* If the Faith of the person is strictly in Christ and the Cross, such being the key to all Life and Victory, the Holy Spirit in such a case will always see to it that the *"House"* is continually in a state of repair.

It is the desire of the Lord that each individual grow close enough to Him that the Holy Spirit can correct us, even to the raising of our voices, which possibly no one else would even notice. We are to be so close to the Lord that it can be easily ascertained if we have done something that He doesn't like. He will always reprimand us very gently, but it's a reprimand that tells us that whatever it might be, *"Don't do it again."*

The Holy Spirit desires to control every aspect of our life and living. However, it is control that we must voluntarily and freely give Him, for He will never take it by force, even though He most definitely, as would be obvious, has the Power to do so. He is in our hearts and lives as a gentle Dove, and as it regards His Action with us, He will always remain in that mode. But at the same time, if the need arises, He can most definitely chastise us, and to be sure, that He will do. In fact, if the Believer never experiences chastisement, that's a pretty good sign that such an individual is really not a Believer but is only posing as one. The Scripture plainly says, and concerning this very thing, *"For whom the Lord loves He chastens* (God disciplines those He loves, not those to whom He is indifferent), *and scourges every son whom He receives.* (This refers to all who truly belong to Him.)

"If you endure chastening, God deals with you as with sons (chastening from the Lord guarantees the fact that one is a Child of God); *for what son is he whom the father chastens not?* (If an earthly father truly cares for his son, he will use whatever measures necessary to bring the boy into line. If an earthly father will do this, how much more will our Heavenly Father do the same?)

"But if you be without chastisement, whereof all (all true Believers) *are partakers, then are you bastards, and not sons.* (Many claim to be Believers while continuing in sin, but the Lord never chastises them. Such shows they are illegitimate sons, meaning they are claiming faith on a basis other than the Cross. The true son, without doubt, will be chastised at times)" (Heb. 12:6-8).

(14) "AND WHEN THEY BROUGHT OUT THE MONEY THAT WAS BROUGHT INTO THE HOUSE OF THE LORD, HILKIAH THE PRIEST FOUND A BOOK OF THE LAW OF THE LORD GIVEN BY MOSES.

(15) "AND HILKIAH ANSWERED AND SAID TO SHAPHAN THE SCRIBE, I HAVE FOUND THE BOOK OF THE LAW IN THE HOUSE OF THE LORD. AND HILKIAH DELIVERED THE BOOK TO SHAPHAN.

(16) "AND SHAPHAN CARRIED THE BOOK TO THE KING, AND BROUGHT THE KING WORD BACK AGAIN, SAYING, ALL THAT WAS COMMITTED TO YOUR SERVANTS, THEY DO IT.

(17) "AND THEY HAVE GATHERED TOGETHER THE MONEY THAT WAS FOUND IN THE HOUSE OF THE LORD, AND HAVE DELIVERED IT INTO THE HAND OF THE OVERSEERS, AND TO THE HAND OF THE WORKMEN.

(18) "THEN SHAPHAN THE SCRIBE TOLD THE KING, SAYING, HILKIAH THE PRIEST HAS GIVEN ME A BOOK. AND SHAPHAN READ IT BEFORE THE KING.

(19) "AND IT CAME TO PASS, WHEN THE KING HAD HEARD THE WORDS OF THE LAW, THAT HE RENT HIS CLOTHES.

(20) "AND THE KING COMMANDED HILKIAH, AND AHIKAM THE SON OF SHAPHAN, AND ABDON THE SON OF MICAH, AND SHAPHAN THE SCRIBE, AND ASAIAH A SERVANT OF THE KING'S, SAYING,

(21) "GO, ENQUIRE OF THE LORD FOR ME, AND FOR THEM WHO ARE LEFT IN ISRAEL AND IN JUDAH, CONCERNING THE WORDS OF THE BOOK THAT IS FOUND: FOR GREAT IS THE WRATH OF THE LORD THAT IS POURED OUT UPON US, BECAUSE OUR FATHERS HAVE NOT KEPT THE WORD OF THE LORD, TO DO AFTER ALL THAT IS WRITTEN IN THIS BOOK.

(22) "AND HILKIAH, AND THEY WHOM THE KING HAD APPOINTED, WENT TO HULDAH THE PROPHETESS, THE WIFE OF SHALLUM THE SON OF TIKVATH, THE SON OF HASRAH, KEEPER OF THE WARDROBE; (NOW SHE DWELT IN JERUSALEM IN THE COLLEGE:) AND THEY SPOKE TO HER TO THAT EFFECT."

The structure is:

1. (Vs. 14) This was, no doubt, the original Book of the Pentateuch—the one actually personally written by Moses (II Ki. 22:8). The Hebrew should have been translated literally, *"The actual engraving of the Law of the Ever-Living in the hand of Moses."* The Scrolls were nearly 850 years old. They had been hidden in the Temple and were found somewhat by accident by Hilkiah the High Priest.

2. (Vs. 19) When Josiah heard the *"Words of the Law,"* he rent his clothes in grief, because the practice of the nation had diverged so terribly from the ever-to-be-venerated Law. Learning from it how defective his reformation was, he proceeded with a thorough one.

3. (Vs. 19) A cleansing of the heart and life under the searchlight of the Word of God differs vastly from a reformation

initiated by the feeble light of conscience or by tradition.

4. (Vs. 22) Even though Jeremiah was serving in the Office of the Prophet at that time, the Holy Spirit had the High Priest go to a woman, Huldah the Prophetess. In Christ, there is neither male nor female, and we speak of preference (Gal. 3:28).

THE LAW OF THE EVER-LIVING IN THE HAND OF MOSES

Hilkiah the High Priest came to king Josiah, bringing him something that was, without a doubt, the single most important work of writing in the world of that day. It was the actual Scroll on which the Law had been written by Moses as it was given to him on Mt. Sinai some 850 years earlier. To try to state the worth of such would be impossible! What the High Priest must have felt when he discovered this Scroll, and then found that it was not a copy but the actual autograph of the great Law-Giver, is anyone's guess. What king Josiah must have felt whenever he was told of this tremendous find, again, is anyone's guess.

To those of us who know the Lord and, thereby, love the Word of God, we can only imagine what went through the minds of these men as they held that Scroll in their hands.

There are two documents which have changed the history of mankind in every conceivable way possible, and we speak for the better. That is the Old Covenant of which we now speak, and then the New Covenant, which was given to the Apostle Paul. They are so special simply because they are the Word of the Lord.

THE PENTATEUCH

From the description given in the Sacred Text, it is not known exactly as to what was contained in this Scroll. Some say it was only the Book of Deuteronomy. Others say it was Exodus and Deuteronomy. And then, some say it was the entire five Books of Moses, Genesis through Deuteronomy.

Some say that it was not the entire Pentateuch because the Scripture says, *"And Shaphan read it before the king,"* implying that it would have been difficult to have

NOTES

read the entirety of all five Books of Moses; however, the Scripture gives no indication as to how long it took for this to be read. It could have been that Shaphan read a certain portion each day.

More than likely, this was the entire Pentateuch as originally written by Moses. As stated, it was not a copy.

It could have involved several Scrolls, or one gigantic Scroll, which meant that the skins would have been fastened together. At any rate, the value of this find was beyond compare.

To keep the matter straight, within itself, it was actually no more significant than the Copy that we have in our Bibles, Genesis through Deuteronomy. The wording and information are the same. However, as it regards its history and association, considering that Moses wrote these words down as God gave them to him, as stated, there is no way that its value could have been ascertained. In other words, it was priceless, as would be obvious.

As we previously mentioned, the two documents that have changed the world have served as the foundation of all things which are true, all things which are right, on that which all correct life and living are based, and we speak of the Old Covenant. The Old Covenant consisted of the first five Books of Moses, while the New Covenant consists of the fourteen Epistles written by the Apostle Paul. While there were many other Books in the Old Testament, all inspired by the Lord, in one way or the other, they related to the first five Books; likewise, all the Books of the New Testament in some way relate to that given to the Apostle Paul in his fourteen Epistles. Those fourteen Epistles are the embodiment of the New Covenant, that to which the Old Covenant ever pointed.

THE BIBLE

Regrettably and sadly, the great Scroll mentioned here in the Sacred Text was lost at some future point. As a result, there are no original autographs left of the Old Testament or the New Testament. But there are multiple thousands of copies, some going back to very near the original autograph.

Scholarship states that if there are ten

copies of the original, then it is looked at as authentic. The Bible has more copies of its 66 Books, or part copies, than any other work in the world many times over. Actually, there are over 10,000 copies or partial copies of all the Books of the Bible in existence.

The original Texts were written on Scrolls, which were animal skins, or upon a type of paper perfected in Egypt from a particular type of plant called the papyrus. It was not as durable as one would have liked. And yet, some of the copies, due to the dry climate of the Middle East, have been preserved even until now. The Dead Sea Scrolls are a case in point.

No Book in the world has been assailed as the Bible. Its critics have done everything to disprove its claims, all without success. As someone said, the hammers of opposition have beaten upon the anvil of the Word of God from the very beginning; however, the hammers always break, and the anvil remains.

Reading behind one Greek scholar just the other day, he said, *"When one holds the King James Version of the Bible in his hands, he can be certain beyond doubt that what he is holding in his hands is the Word of God."*

From the very beginning there were Scribes who copied the original autographs, actually making many copies, hence, the thousands of copies presently preserved. We are the beneficiaries presently of the work of those Scribes.

THE REACTION OF THE KING TO THE WORD OF GOD

When king Josiah heard the Word of God, the Law of the Lord, read to him, and knowing this was the Word of the Lord, the king was greatly disturbed. He knew, despite his best efforts, that what he had done regarding the Reformation had been in the right direction, but it was not exactly according to the Word of the Lord. Consequently, *"he rent his clothes,"* which was a sign in those days of great perturbance. In other words, he sincerely desired to obey the Word of the Lord in its entirety.

THE PROPHETESS

Why Josiah did not take this tremendous find, the actual autograph of the Law of Moses, to Jeremiah, we aren't told. Perhaps the great Prophet was elsewhere at that time, which well could have been the case; consequently, the implication is that they physically took this Sacred Scroll to *"Huldah the Prophetess,"* meaning that they knew the Lord had directed this great discovery.

(23) "AND SHE ANSWERED THEM, THUS SAYS THE LORD GOD OF ISRAEL, TELL YOU THE MAN WHO SENT YOU TO ME,

(24) "THUS SAYS THE LORD, BEHOLD, I WILL BRING EVIL UPON THIS PLACE, AND UPON THE INHABITANTS THEREOF, EVEN ALL THE CURSES THAT ARE WRITTEN IN THE BOOK WHICH THEY HAVE READ BEFORE THE KING OF JUDAH:

(25) "BECAUSE THEY HAVE FORSAKEN ME, AND HAVE BURNED INCENSE UNTO OTHER GODS, THAT THEY MIGHT PROVOKE ME TO ANGER WITH ALL THE WORKS OF THEIR HANDS; THEREFORE MY WRATH SHALL BE POURED OUT UPON THIS PLACE, AND SHALL NOT BE QUENCHED.

(26) "AND AS FOR THE KING OF JUDAH, WHO SENT YOU TO ENQUIRE OF THE LORD, SO SHALL YOU SAY UNTO HIM, THUS SAYS THE LORD GOD OF ISRAEL CONCERNING THE WORDS WHICH YOU HAVE HEARD;

(27) "BECAUSE YOUR HEART WAS TENDER, AND YOU DID HUMBLE YOURSELF BEFORE GOD, WHEN YOU HEARD HIS WORDS AGAINST THIS PLACE, AND AGAINST THE INHABITANTS THEREOF, AND HUMBLED YOURSELF BEFORE ME, AND DID REND YOUR CLOTHES, AND WEEP BEFORE ME; I HAVE EVEN HEARD YOU ALSO, SAYS THE LORD.

(28) "BEHOLD, I WILL GATHER YOU TO YOUR FATHERS, AND YOU SHALL BE GATHERED TO YOUR GRAVE IN PEACE, NEITHER SHALL YOUR EYES SEE ALL THE EVIL THAT I WILL BRING UPON THIS PLACE, AND UPON THE INHABITANTS OF THE SAME. SO THEY BROUGHT THE KING WORD AGAIN."

The exegesis is:

1. (Vs. 28) It seems from the pronouncement by the Lord against Judah that Josiah's reforms merely delayed the coming Judgment. It did not halt it.

2. (Vs. 28) In effect, the Lord told the monarch that it would not come in his lifetime. His death would be *"in peace,"* as it regards these Judgments.

3. The idea of all of this is that the Word of God had been ignored by Judah and its leaders. Now, or at least in the near future, Judgment would come because of this.

And yet, the Lord, through the great Prophets Jeremiah and Ezekiel, would over and over again warn Judah, promising respite if they would only repent; regrettably, it was all to no avail. Judah would not repent, and ultimately, Judah went to her doom.

*"THUS SAYS THE LORD
GOD OF ISRAEL"*

Even though the Word of God was obvious as to what it said, and when it was read, it brought great conviction to the heart of the king and others, still, and rightly so, they wanted to hear what the Prophetess would say as it regarded these things. As we have stated, Jeremiah was functioning at this time in the Office of the Prophet but more than likely, he was out of town. So, they went to *"Huldah the Prophetess."* The message was short and to the point and left absolutely no room for doubt. In essence, this is what the Holy Spirit said:

• Due to the great evil that had been practiced by Judah regarding idol worship, the Judgment was pronounced.

• Great wrath would be poured out upon Judah, Jerusalem, and even the Temple itself.

• However, as it regarded Josiah, because he had humbled himself before the Lord and had endeavored greatly to do exactly what the Lord wanted, this Judgment would be delayed and, in fact, would not come during Josiah's days.

We see from this what Repentance can do. In this case it delayed Judgment but did not stop it. The reason?

After the death of Josiah, Israel would go into deep sin despite the prophesying of Jeremiah and Ezekiel.

NOTES

When the Lord said that Josiah would be *"gathered to your grave in peace,"* that needs qualification. In fact, Josiah would be slain in battle at Charchemish.

The meaning is, the Judgment pronounced by God would be delayed until after the death of Josiah. It would not come to him or to Judah during his lifetime.

(29) "THEN THE KING SENT AND GATHERED TOGETHER ALL THE ELDERS OF JUDAH AND JERUSALEM.

(30) "AND THE KING WENT UP INTO THE HOUSE OF THE LORD, AND ALL THE MEN OF JUDAH, AND THE INHABITANTS OF JERUSALEM, AND THE PRIESTS, AND THE LEVITES, AND ALL THE PEOPLE, GREAT AND SMALL: AND HE READ IN THEIR EARS ALL THE WORDS OF THE BOOK OF THE COVENANT THAT WAS FOUND IN THE HOUSE OF THE LORD.

(31) "AND THE KING STOOD IN HIS PLACE, AND MADE A COVENANT BEFORE THE LORD, TO WALK AFTER THE LORD, AND TO KEEP HIS COMMANDMENTS, AND HIS TESTIMONIES, AND HIS STATUTES, WITH ALL HIS HEART, AND WITH ALL HIS SOUL, TO PERFORM THE WORDS OF THE COVENANT WHICH ARE WRITTEN IN THIS BOOK.

(32) "AND HE CAUSED ALL WHO WERE PRESENT IN JERUSALEM AND BENJAMIN TO STAND TO IT. AND THE INHABITANTS OF JERUSALEM DID ACCORDING TO THE COVENANT OF GOD, THE GOD OF THEIR FATHERS.

(33) "AND JOSIAH TOOK AWAY ALL THE ABOMINATIONS OUT OF ALL THE COUNTRIES THAT PERTAINED TO THE CHILDREN OF ISRAEL, AND MADE ALL WHO WERE PRESENT IN ISRAEL TO SERVE, EVEN TO SERVE THE LORD THEIR GOD. AND ALL HIS DAYS THEY DEPARTED NOT FROM FOLLOWING THE LORD, THE GOD OF THEIR FATHERS."

The overview is:

1. (Vs. 30) All of these people gathered in the Court in front of the Temple.

2. (Vs. 33) Every true Revival is always, and without exception, based on the Word of God.

3. (Vs. 33) The Bible is the only revealed Truth in the world and, in fact, ever has

been. There is not a spiritual problem that is not addressed in the Word. There is not a difficulty for which it does not have a solution. There is not a question that it cannot answer. There is not a life that the God of its pages cannot change. There is not a broken heart that its Words cannot mend. There is not a darkness that its Light cannot dispel; not a sin that the Blood of its pages cannot wash away (Ps. 119:105).

THE COVENANT BEFORE THE LORD

As it concerned all of Judah, the Covenant that Josiah made that day with the Lord was:
- To walk after the Lord;
- To keep His Commandments;
- To keep His Testimonies;
- To keep His Statutes;
- To do so with all his heart and with all his soul; and,
- To perform the Words of the Covenant which are written in this Book.

The idea is, he determined to obey the Word of the Lord. Our determination, consecration, and dedication presently should not be any less, as I think should be obvious.

Concerning this great Reformation based on the Word of God, the Thirty-third Verse says, *"And all his days they departed not from following the LORD, the God of their fathers."* What a testimony! This portrays Divine leadership evidenced through Josiah.

To be sure, every Preacher of the Gospel, and, of course, I speak of those who are truly Called of the Lord, must realize the tremendous responsibility we bear and the number of souls who actually lie within our hands. If the pulpit is on fire for God, likewise the pew. Conversely, if the pulpit is cold and lackadaisical toward the Lord and His Word, likewise the pew! Every Preacher will stand one day at the Judgment Seat of Christ and give account for his Ministry. All of us had best remember that.

REVIVAL

Every true Revival is based on the Word of God and, in effect, on the Cross. The Story of the Bible is the Story of the Cross, and one might say without fear of contradiction that the Story of the Cross is the Story of the Bible (Jn. 1:1-2, 14, 29). It is *"the Word of God."*

NOTES

When one considers the other religious books, such as the *"Koran"* and the *"Book of Mormon,"* plus the various other religious works that have come and gone down through the centuries, and compares them with the Bible, then the utter falsity of these other books causes them to pale into insignificance.

Also, when we realize that the Word of God is the only body of revealed Truth on the face of the Earth, then we should devote our time, our attention, and even our very lives to understanding its contents. It is the only *"Light"* in the world. That's the reason we strongly recommend THE EXPOSITOR'S STUDY BIBLE, which, incidentally, is King James.

Moses was the first of the great men of God in the Bible who had a portion of the written Word of God, the first five Books (the Pentateuch), actually written by him. When it was passed on to his understudy, Joshua, the warrior was told, *"This Book of the Law shall not depart out of your mouth; but you shall meditate therein day and night, that you may observe to do according to all that is written therein: for then you shall make your way prosperous, and then you shall have good success"* (Josh. 1:8).

Truly, *"Your Word is a Lamp unto my feet, and a Light unto my path"* (Ps. 119:105).

A PERSONAL EXPERIENCE

Frances and I began in the Ministry in 1956. Donnie was two years old. When I say, *"Began in the Ministry,"* to be sure, the beginning was unnoticed by practically everyone. It would have been impossible at the time to realize that the Lord would use us to touch much of this world for Christ, in effect, seeing literally hundreds of thousands brought to a Saving Knowledge of the Lord Jesus Christ. But yet, the illustration I desire to relate to you was in a sense a fore-picture of that of which I speak, with the great Promise given to me, at least, what little then I could understand, from the Word of God.

The year was 1958, and we were in a small town in northeast Louisiana preaching a meeting in a particular Church. After a couple of Services, that is, if I remember correctly, I came down sick, with the doctor telling me that I had pneumonia. Regrettably, we had to shut down the meeting.

Frances took me to a small hospital closer to home. The situation there was anything but good. The nurse was about as profane with her ungodly language as I had ever heard. I think I stayed one night. At any rate, she came in the next morning. I was doing my best to get dressed. I was very, very sick, so nauseous that I could hardly stand; nevertheless, I was trying to get dressed in order to leave.

She asked me as to what I was doing? I told her that I was going home.

She quickly retorted that I had not been released, and with a string of profanity, demanded that I get back in the bed.

I only weighed about 140 pounds in those days, but I stood 6 feet tall, and standing as tall as I could, even as sick as I was, I informed her that I was leaving that hospital forthwith. Her last words were, *"We'll not be responsible for you!"*

My thoughts were that they had not been too responsible previously, so I didn't think much would change. At any rate, Frances drove me home.

Since the Lord healed me in 1945, that is, if I remember the date correctly, I have been sick very, very little in my life, with this particular time being one of the few.

These were the days before television; at least, we didn't have a television set in our house at the time, only a radio.

Every once in a while Frances would turn on the radio, and almost invariably, one of my cousins' songs would be playing. At the time, Jerry Lee Lewis, my first cousin, had a song in the number one spot in the nation. Another cousin, Mickey Gilley, had a song in the top 40 and so did Carl McVoy, another first cousin. There were no Gospel stations in our part of the world at that time.

THE ATTACK BY SATAN

It was a Wednesday night. I had been home from the hospital three or four days. I was still too sick to even get up. Frances and Donnie went to prayer meeting that night, and I was left alone.

I will never forget this experience because of what it came to mean in my heart and life.

Not long after Frances and Donnie left, I was lying there contemplating my situation, which to be sure, was not good. And then it happened.

It was like everything in the room turned black, and the most awful oppressive feeling came over me. Then Satan began to speak to me.

"You claim to be a Preacher, and just exactly where is it that you're going to preach? You don't have any place to preach, and furthermore, no one wants to hear you preach. As well, you are so sick that you cannot walk, so where is your God?"

He then continued, *"Your cousins make more money in a week than you make all year. How are you going to pay the house note, the car note? Actually, how are you going to put food on the table for your family? You call yourself a Preacher. You are no more than a joke."*

I have experienced the attacks of Satan many, many times, but that was one of the most severe attacks that I've ever experienced. I look back now, and the reasons become more clear. But then, I didn't have the answer to many questions.

THE LORD SPOKE TO ME

As the attack by Satan became more and more furious, with the most awful oppression filling the room, I began to plead with the Lord to help me.

My Bible, which I had attempted to read off and on all day, even as I always did, was lying close by my side. Without premeditation, I reached and grabbed it to pull it to me, and it opened. I didn't open it; I didn't try to open it; I didn't even know what I was going to do with it. I just knew that this attack was so furious that I had to have help, and, therefore, I grabbed my Bible.

It opened, and I am positive it was by the Lord, to Joshua 1:9. That Scripture, even like it was capitalized, leaped out at me. It said,

"Have not I commanded you? Be strong and of a good courage; be not afraid, neither be thou dismayed: for the LORD your God is with you whithersoever you go."

Instantly, as I read that Passage, the

Power of God displaced the powers of darkness. It was as though one moment Satan had the upper hand, and the next moment he was gone.

The Presence of the Lord washed over me as I began to weep and praise the Lord. I remember sitting up on the side of the bed and thinking to myself, *"The Lord has given me a Promise, and, therefore, He, as well, can heal me."*

I stood to my feet and then began to walk, and when Frances and Donnie came home from prayer meeting a little later, I was not in the bed, but was walking from room to room in our little house (only four rooms), praising the Lord.

That January night in 1958, the Lord said several things to me. He said:

• *"Have not I commanded you?"* This was not a request; it was the command of a General, in this case, the Holy Spirit, and He was speaking to one of His Soldiers, even as weak as I was at the time.

• *"Be strong and of a good courage."* I came to understand that this meant to be strong and of a good courage in the Lord and in His Word, believing His Promises. What I saw around me might be what was happening, but it was not what was going on. What was going on was the Moving and Operation of the Holy Spirit to save, to heal, to deliver, and to do mighty things.

• *"Be not afraid, neither be thou dismayed."* In other words, don't fear and don't be discouraged.

• *"For the LORD your God is with you whithersoever you go."* The truth, which I came to learn, is that if the Lord is with us, nothing can stop us. In other words, if we don't quit, He won't quit, and that means He won't quit blessing us and helping us.

THE PROMISE

That was what the Lord gave me that January night in 1958, and I've never forgotten it. Time and time again through the years, even the many decades, I have had to go back to Joshua 1:9, and I've had to read those words carefully again and again, knowing that it was the Promise of God given to me, and knowing that the Lord cannot fail. As well, when He gives a Promise, that Promise will never be lifted. That is, if we will keep believing it, it will never fail. The old song says:

> *"Standing on the Promises of Christ my King,*
> *"Thro' eternal ages let His Praises ring;*
> *"Glory in the highest I will shout and sing,*
> *"Standing on the Promises of God."*

> *"Standing on the Promises that cannot fail,*
> *"When the howling storms of doubt and fear assail,*
> *"By the living Word of God I shall prevail,*
> *"Standing on the Promises of God."*

> *"Standing on the Promises I now can see,*
> *"Perfect, present cleansing in the Blood for me;*
> *"Standing in the liberty where Christ makes free,*
> *"Standing on the Promises of God."*

> *"Standing on the Promises of Christ the Lord,*
> *"Bound to Him eternally by love's strong cord,*
> *"Overcoming daily with the Spirit's Sword,*
> *"Standing on the Promises of God."*

> *"Standing on the Promises I cannot fall,*
> *"List'ning every moment to the Spirit's Call,*
> *"Resting in my Saviour, as my all in all,*
> *"Standing on the Promises of God."*

I have found through life, as stated, that those Promises never fail. They have never failed in the past; they will not fail in the present; and they cannot fail in the future. They are the Word of God.

CHAPTER 35

(1) "MOREOVER JOSIAH KEPT A PASSOVER UNTO THE LORD IN

JERUSALEM: AND THEY KILLED THE PASSOVER ON THE FOURTEENTH DAY OF THE FIRST MONTH.

(2) "AND HE SET THE PRIESTS IN THEIR CHARGES, AND ENCOURAGED THEM TO THE SERVICE OF THE HOUSE OF THE LORD,

(3) "AND SAID UNTO THE LEVITES WHO TAUGHT ALL ISRAEL, WHICH WERE HOLY UNTO THE LORD, PUT THE HOLY ARK IN THE HOUSE WHICH SOLOMON THE SON OF DAVID KING OF ISRAEL DID BUILD; IT SHALL NOT BE A BURDEN UPON YOUR SHOULDERS: SERVE NOW THE LORD YOUR GOD, AND HIS PEOPLE ISRAEL,

(4) "AND PREPARE YOURSELVES BY THE HOUSES OF YOUR FATHERS, AFTER YOUR COURSES, ACCORDING TO THE WRITING OF DAVID KING OF ISRAEL, AND ACCORDING TO THE WRITING OF SOLOMON HIS SON.

(5) "AND STAND IN THE HOLY PLACE ACCORDING TO THE DIVISIONS OF THE FAMILIES OF THE FATHERS OF YOUR BRETHREN THE PEOPLE, AND AFTER THE DIVISION OF THE FAMILIES OF THE LEVITES."

The overview is:

1. (Vs. 1) The *"Passover"* was the foundation of all Israel's worship and God's dealing with His People. It represents Israel's deliverance out of Egypt by the slain lamb and the shedding of innocent blood. Likewise, the entirety of the Foundation of Christendom is founded on Calvary, of which the Passover is a type (Ex. 12:13).

2. (Vs. 3) Evidently, the Ark of the Covenant had been taken out of the Holy of Holies, quite possibly by Josiah's wicked father, Amon. It was to be placed in the Holy of Holies and intended to be moved no more.

3. (Vs. 4) Josiah gave instructions as it regarded the Passover, that everything must be handled according to the Word of God.

THE PASSOVER

Three Verses in II Kings are given to Josiah's Passover—here, 19 Verses. This illustrates the difference between the two Books.

NOTES

Israel was commanded by the Lord that without fail they were to keep the Passover each year. Regrettably, due to the spiritual declension of many of the kings of Judah, at times, many years would go past without the Passover being conducted. This presented a tragic turn of events in Judah because Judah's blessing and prosperity, and her protection and security, all depended on the shed Blood of the Lamb, of which the Passover was a Type. So, what Josiah was now doing would guarantee that security and protection as well as blessing and prosperity of the nation. Tragically, after the demise of Josiah, the things of God fell by the wayside, and ultimately, actually just a few years later, Judah went to her doom.

Sadly, the modern church seems to follow suit. It is forgetting that the strength and power of the Church is not in its real estate, not in its educational structures, not in its numbers, or its wealth, but rather in the shed Blood of the Lamb. Do we know that? Do we understand that? Do we comprehend that?

The Cross of Christ is the Foundation of Christianity. Actually, it is the Story of the Bible. That's why the Apostle Paul said, *"We preach Jesus Crucified"* (I Cor. 1:23). Is the modern church preaching *"Jesus Christ and Him Crucified"*?

I think the answer is very obvious. The modern church as a whole is preaching anything but, *"Jesus Christ and Him Crucified."*

THE MODERN CHURCH

If the modern church continues to ignore the Cross of Christ, even in some circles to repudiate the Cross of Christ, what will be the end result?

I wish I could say that if the modern church continues on in its direction, it will result in apostasy. That would be bad enough! But the truth is, I'm afraid, the church has already apostatized. It's not merely traveling in that direction, it has already reached that place. The Apostle Paul also said,

"Now the Spirit (Holy Spirit) *speaks expressly* (pointedly), *that in the latter times* (the times in which we now live, the last of the last days, which begin the fulfillment of

Endtime Prophecies) *some shall depart from the Faith* (anytime Paul uses the term *'the Faith'*, in short, he is referring to the Cross; so, we are told here that some will depart from the Cross as the means of Salvation and Victory), *giving heed to seducing spirits* (evil spirits i.e., *'religious spirits,'* making something seem like what it isn't), *and doctrines of devils* (should have been translated, *'doctrines of demons'*; the *'seducing spirits'* entice Believers away from the true Faith, causing them to believe *'doctrines inspired by demon spirits'*)" (I Tim. 4:1).

Without the preaching of the Cross (I Cor. 1:21), there can be no Gospel. The Gospel of Jesus Christ, in effect, is the Cross of Christ. Paul also said,

"For Christ sent me not to baptize (presents to us a Cardinal Truth), *but to preach the Gospel* (the manner in which one may be Saved from sin)*: not with wisdom of words* (intellectualism is not the Gospel), *lest the Cross of Christ should be made of none effect.* (This tells us in no uncertain terms that the Cross of Christ must always be the emphasis of the Message)" (I Cor. 1:17).

As Josiah of old, the leaders of church denominations must do what they are called to do, that is to lead and take the church back to the Cross. But instead, they are taking it into humanistic psychology, into the Purpose Driven Life scheme, into the Government of Twelve scheme, etc. God help us!

Have you ever wondered why the modern church jumps from one fad to the other? If what they had was right, they wouldn't be wanting something else. Let me put it another way.

If the Church has its Faith anchored squarely in the Cross of Christ, in other words, the Cross is the Object of its Faith, and the Object of its Faith exclusively, there will be no need for anything else, and no desire for anything else, because, and to be sure, the Cross of Christ satisfies the longing of the soul, because it's there that Jesus paid the price for all things.

A MODERNISTIC APPROACH TO
THE OLD DOCTRINES?

Some time back, one large Pentecostal Denomination gathered its leaders together in order that they may learn how to *"modernize the old Doctrines."*

The modern church anymore little understands the old Doctrines. The truth is, it no longer believes the old Doctrines.

The church needs to anchor into the Cross of Christ. To be sure, the Cross is as old fashioned as yesterday and as modern as tomorrow. It is the answer for every generation, for every family, for every need, and for all time. That's why Paul referred to it as the *"Everlasting Covenant"* (Heb. 13:20). That means it will never have to be amended, never have to be replaced and, therefore, will never be outdated.

A resounding no! The old Doctrines do not need to be modernized. That's the trouble now. They've been too much modernized until there is nothing left of these great Doctrines. How the mighty have fallen!

The answer is, *"Back to the Cross!"* *"Back to the Cross!"* *"Back to the Cross!"*

THE ARK OF THE COVENANT

Verse 3 makes it clear that the *"Ark of the Covenant"* had been taken out of the Holy of Holies, for the Scripture says, *"Put the Holy Ark in the House which Solomon the son of David king of Israel did build."* Quite possibly, Josiah's wicked father Amon had it removed.

The question should be asked as to why God did not strike dead the wicked individuals who would have with impunity gone into the Holy of Holies and removed the Ark, as He did Uzza when he *"put forth his hand to hold the Ark"* (I Chron. 13:9-10)? There are a couple of answers that could be given in relationship to that question. They are:

1. When God's People turned their backs on Him, it seems the Lord withdrew from any participation at all. Uzza was stricken dead simply because David was trying to do the right thing before God, albeit in the wrong way, and the Presence of the Lord was obvious.

The Power of God cuts two ways. When it is present, it will save, it will heal, and it will deliver, etc. But, at such a time, if the people treat the Presence of God with disdain, whether out of ignorance or not, the end result will not be pleasant, even as it wasn't pleasant with Uzza.

Incidentally, only the High Priest was to go into the Holy of Holies where the Ark was, and that, only once a year, and then to offer up blood on the Mercy Seat.

2. Even though the Scripture is silent on the subject as it regards this incident, it may be that the Lord did strike those dead who came into the Holy of Holies, possibly during the time of Amon, but at a different time and in a different way. God seldom works the same way twice; however, the following should be noted:

The Jews in Jesus' day handled Him roughly, Him of Whom the Ark was a Type. These particular religious leaders were not immediately stricken by God but about A.D. 70, when Titus, the Roman General, invaded Jerusalem, over one million Jews were killed in that carnage. Let no man think that if God does not Move instantly, as in the case of Uzza, He will not Move at all. Someone has said:

"The mills of God grind slowly, but they grind exceedingly fine." In other words, they miss nothing.

So, the Ark of the Covenant at this time would be borne on the shoulders of the Priests, even as the Scripture demanded, and taken into the Holy of Holies. Such occasions were provided for in Scripture and would guarantee the safety of those bearing that sacred Vessel.

PREPARE YOURSELVES

The command by Josiah, *"prepare yourselves,"* was directed toward the Levites and Priests who attended to the duties of the Temple. They were to make certain, according to the Scriptures, always according to the Scriptures, that they did exactly what they were supposed to do, and in the way it was supposed to be done. The duties of the Priests and the Levites were divided into 24 courses, each course lasting for one week (II Chron. 23:8). To attend to all the duties of the Temple, which the Lord had commanded, such services required hundreds of Priests and Levites. While all Priests were Levites, all Levites were not Priests. All Levites, of course, were from the Tribe of Levi. Even though their services were in the Temple exclusively, still, Jerusalem was not their main place of residence, with Priests and Levites actually scattered all over Judah. They would come into Jerusalem at their appointed time in order to perform their services.

The reason for the warning given by Josiah is because for years, Temple duties had not been carried out according to the Word of God, and sometimes not carried out at all. For the many years that Manasseh, who was the grandfather of Josiah, lived in sin, the Temple was totally neglected, with even idols set up in its precincts. Even though Manasseh made things right with God at the last, no information is given us as it regards him repairing the Temple. One thing is certain, when his son Amon came in, even though he only ruled for two years, he once again desecrated the Temple and all therein. So, there was much work for Josiah to do, and he wanted to make certain that it was all done Scripturally.

THE NEW COVENANT

Everything in the Tabernacle, everything in the Temple, and I mean everything, plus all of its duties, the commands, the rituals, the ceremonies, all and without exception, pointed to Christ in His Atoning, Mediatorial, or Intercessory Work. When He came, with His Ministry on Earth being completed by His Sacrifice of Himself at Calvary, everything about the Tabernacle, the Temple, the Law, the Sacrificial system, etc., was all fulfilled in totality. Paul said, *"For Christ is the end of the Law for Righteousness"* (Christ fulfilled the totality of the Law) *to everyone who believes* (Faith in Christ guarantees the Righteousness which the Law had, but could not give)" (Rom. 10:4). As a result of what Christ did at the Cross, neither the Temple nor any of its appointments were needed anymore. Why the Shadow when one has the Substance?

As a result, it is hurtful to see preachers, who ought to know better, advocating the wearing of a Jewish prayer shawl, etc. This, whether they realize it or not, *"does despite to the Spirit of Grace"* (Heb. 10:29). In fact, through the Apostle Paul, the Holy

Spirit went into great detail concerning this very thing.

RESORTING TO JEWISH LAW

The following Passages that we will give from the Word of God need to be qualified. Paul was addressing Jews who knew the way. In other words, they understood the Message of the Cross, which was the Message of Grace, and were defecting from that which they knew. That's what was meant by the *"willful sin."* Those who are ignorant of the Message of the Cross would fall into another category. While they most definitely will cause themselves tremendous problems by placing their faith in something other than Christ and the Cross, still, as should be obvious, the Lord has much more patience with such people than with those who willfully reject His Way.

For instance, when we install a radio station in a given area of the nation, and we begin to preach and teach the Message of the Cross, which we've done scores of times and continue to do, every Preacher and person in the coverage area, whether they take the time to listen to the programming or not, are held accountable by the Lord from that moment on. In other words, the Light has been provided, and if they reject it or ignore it, the following Passages given in Hebrews most definitely apply. It says:

"For if we sin wilfully (the *'willful sin'* is the transference of Faith from Christ and Him Crucified to other things) *after that we have received the knowledge of the Truth* (speaks of the Bible way of Salvation and Victory, which is *'Jesus Christ and Him Crucified'* [I Cor. 2:2]), *there remains no more sacrifice for sins* (if the Cross of Christ is rejected, there is no other sacrifice or way God will accept),

"But a certain fearful looking for of judgment and fiery indignation (refers to God's Anger because of men rejecting Jesus Christ and the Cross), *which shall devour the adversaries.* (It is Hellfire, which will ultimately come to all who reject Christ and the Cross.)

"He who despised Moses' Law died without mercy under two or three witnesses (there had to be these many witnesses to a capital crime before the death sentence could be carried out, according to the Old Testament Law of Moses [Deut. 17:2-7])*:

"Of how much sorer punishment, suppose you, shall he be thought worthy, who has trodden under foot the Son of God (proclaims the reason for the *'sorer punishment'*), *and has counted the Blood of the Covenant, wherewith he was sanctified, an unholy thing* (refers to a person who has been Saved, but is now expressing unbelief toward that which originally Saved him), *and has done despite unto the Spirit of Grace?* (When the Cross is rejected, the Holy Spirit is insulted.)

"For we know Him Who has said, Vengeance belongs unto Me, I will recompense, says the Lord (is meant to imply that every single thing is going to be judged by the Lord, Who Alone is the righteous Judge). *And again, The Lord shall judge His People* (chastise His People [Deut. 32:35-36]).

"It is a fearful thing to fall into the hands of the Living God. (This refers to those who have once known the Lord, but now express no faith in the Cross)*" (Heb. 10:26-31).

(6) "SO KILL THE PASSOVER, AND SANCTIFY YOURSELVES, AND PREPARE YOUR BRETHREN, THAT THEY MAY DO ACCORDING TO THE WORD OF THE LORD BY THE HAND OF MOSES.

(7) "AND JOSIAH GAVE TO THE PEOPLE, OF THE FLOCK, LAMBS AND KIDS, ALL FOR THE PASSOVER OFFERINGS, FOR ALL WHO WERE PRESENT, TO THE NUMBER OF THIRTY THOUSAND, AND THREE THOUSAND BULLOCKS: THESE WERE OF THE KING'S SUBSTANCE.

(8) "AND HIS PRINCES GAVE WILLINGLY UNTO THE PEOPLE, TO THE PRIESTS, AND TO THE LEVITES: HILKIAH AND ZECHARIAH AND JEHIEL, RULERS OF THE HOUSE OF GOD, GAVE UNTO THE PRIESTS FOR THE PASSOVER OFFERINGS TWO THOUSAND AND SIX HUNDRED SMALL CATTLE, AND THREE HUNDRED OXEN.

(9) "CONANIAH ALSO, AND SHEMAIAH AND NETHANEEL, HIS BRETHREN, AND HASHABIAH AND JEIEL AND JOZABAD, CHIEF OF THE LEVITES, GAVE UNTO THE LEVITES FOR PASSOVER

OFFERINGS FIVE THOUSAND SMALL CATTLE, AND FIVE HUNDRED OXEN.

(10) "SO THE SERVICE WAS PREPARED, AND THE PRIESTS STOOD IN THEIR PLACE, AND THE LEVITES IN THEIR COURSES, ACCORDING TO THE KING'S COMMANDMENT."

The structure is:

1. (Vs. 6) These Passages record the fact that Josiah believed that Moses wrote the Pentateuch, and Verse 12 shows his acquaintanceship with the Book of Exodus.

2. (Vs. 7) All of these tremendous numbers of animals named were to be offered up as sacrifices according to the Word of the Lord, and it seems the animals were given to the people free of charge.

3. Once again, all of these sacrifices, as should be overly obvious, point to the Cross. This was the safety, the security, the protection, the prosperity, and the glory of Judah.

THE SACRIFICES

Josiah knew the necessity of the people offering up the Passover sacrifice, so he made it possible that no one would have an excuse. He would provide the animals for those who could not afford to pay for a lamb, etc.

Yes, the slaughter of multiple thousands of animals presented a gruesome situation. In fact, it was meant to present a gruesome situation.

Sin is an awful business, much more awful than anyone dare realize. To address this monster, man has no solution, and I mean none. Education is no answer, money is no answer, environment is no answer, and religion is no answer. There is only one answer for sin, and that is the Cross of Christ. But tragically, the modern church seems to have forgotten that.

Jesus was placed on the Cross a day before the Passover Sabbath. In fact, He died at approximately 3 p.m. At approximately 6 p.m., the Passover Sabbath would begin. Actually, it was a Thursday.

Josephus, the Jewish historian, stated that during that Passover week, some 250,000 lambs were offered up. The blood ran down the conduits into the brook Kedron below, actually running red for some days.

The one Sacrifice of Christ was of much greater value, actually, infinite value, than all the sacrifices of animals put together. Paul said in relationship to this:

"So Christ was once offered to bear the sins of many (the Cross was God's answer to sin and, in fact, the only answer); *and unto them who look for Him shall He appear the second time without sin unto Salvation.* (This refers to the Second Coming. 'Without sin' refers to the fact that the Second Coming will not be to atone for sin, for that was already carried out at the Cross at His First Advent. The Second Coming will bring all the results of Salvation to this world, which refers to all that He did at the Cross. We now only have the *'Firstfruits'* [Rom. 8:23])" (Heb. 9:28).

To properly understand how bad that sin actually is, we only have to look at the price that was paid to address this monster, and that price was the Cross of Christ. So, when religious man thinks that he can address sin by any other means than Christ and the Cross, he has just stepped outside the Plan of God for the human race.

(11) "AND THEY KILLED THE PASSOVER, AND THE PRIESTS SPRINKLED THE BLOOD FROM THEIR HANDS, AND THE LEVITES FLAYED THEM.

(12) "AND THEY REMOVED THE BURNT OFFERINGS, THAT THEY MIGHT GIVE ACCORDING TO THE DIVISIONS OF THE FAMILIES OF THE PEOPLE, TO OFFER UNTO THE LORD, AS IT IS WRITTEN IN THE BOOK OF MOSES. AND SO DID THEY WITH THE OXEN.

(13) "AND THEY ROASTED THE PASSOVER WITH FIRE ACCORDING TO THE ORDINANCE: BUT THE OTHER HOLY OFFERINGS SOD THEY IN POTS, AND IN CALDRONS, AND IN PANS, AND DIVIDED THEM SPEEDILY AMONG ALL THE PEOPLE.

(14) "AND AFTERWARD THEY MADE READY FOR THEMSELVES, AND FOR THE PRIESTS: BECAUSE THE PRIESTS THE SONS OF AARON WERE BUSIED IN OFFERING OF BURNT OFFERINGS AND THE FAT UNTIL NIGHT; THEREFORE THE LEVITES PREPARED FOR THEMSELVES, AND FOR THE PRIESTS THE SONS OF AARON.

(15) "AND THE SINGERS THE SONS OF ASAPH WERE IN THEIR PLACE, ACCORDING TO THE COMMANDMENT OF DAVID, AND ASAPH, AND HEMAN, AND JEDUTHUN THE KING'S SEER; AND THE PORTERS WAITED AT EVERY GATE; THEY MIGHT NOT DEPART FROM THEIR SERVICE; FOR THEIR BRETHREN THE LEVITES PREPARED FOR THEM.

(16) "SO ALL THE SERVICE OF THE LORD WAS PREPARED THE SAME DAY, TO KEEP THE PASSOVER, AND TO OFFER BURNT OFFERINGS UPON THE ALTAR OF THE LORD, ACCORDING TO THE COMMANDMENT OF KING JOSIAH."

The exegesis is:

1. The Levites flaying the little animals, as portrayed in Verse 11, means that they pulled the skin from their bodies.

2. Verse 15 proclaims the fact that as the sacrifices were offered, they were accompanied by music, singing, and worship. When Calvary is held up as the Foundation of the Faith, it always elicits joy.

3. (Vs. 15) As well, the porters made certain that the Law of the Lord was adhered to regarding the sacrifices. All of this shows Josiah's adherence to the Word of God.

THE KILLING OF THE PASSOVER

The killing of the Passover took place at the Temple. The individual man, whomever he may have been, among many, many thousands, brought his animal to the Temple, actually to the Priests. It could be either a lamb or a goat, but it had to be a male that was over two years of age.

When the people brought their lambs to be offered, it was to the Outer Court. The Priests stood in two rows. In one row each man had a golden basin, in the other a silver basin. The basin which caught the blood of the expiring victim was passed from hand to hand in continuous exchange to the end of the line where the last Priest tossed the blood in ritual manner on the Altar. All of this was done to the singing of the *"Hallel"* (Ps. 113-118).

As the lamb was offered, no bone of the Passover victim was to be broken. This small detail was fulfilled when it was reverently

NOTES

applied to the Crucified One (Jn. 19:36).

After the *"killing of the Passover,"* we now have the *"eating of the Passover"*. It included the symbolic elements of roasted lamb, which was the sacrifice, eaten with unleavened bread and bitter herbs.

At that time, the story of the Egyptian Passover and Exodus was rehearsed.

THE LORD'S SUPPER

As it regards Bible Christianity, the *"Lord's Supper"* came out of the Passover. The bread symbolizes His broken Body given at Calvary's Cross in Sacrifice, while the cup represents His shed Blood, which, again, was carried out at the Cross.

As should be obvious, the Lord's Supper points totally and completely to the Cross of Calvary, the price there paid, actually, the substitutionary element of the Sacrifice of Christ.

There is no time limit as it regards the frequency of the Lord's Supper being taken. The Scripture merely says, *"As oft as you drink it,"* speaking of the cup (I Cor. 11:25).

It is meant to be taken as Jesus said, *"in remembrance of Me."* He further said, when it is taken, *"you do show the Lord's Death till He come"* (I Cor. 11:25-26).

He then stated that we must not *"drink this cup of the Lord, unworthily"* (I Cor. 11:27).

What did He mean by that?

While it is not required that the person be sinlessly perfect in order to take the Lord's Supper, it most definitely requires that our Faith be placed exclusively in Christ and what Christ has done for us at the Cross. When this is done, He further said that we aren't, *"discerning the Lord's Body"* (I Cor. 11:29).

That refers to not properly discerning the Cross. It means that every single thing we have from the Lord comes to us exclusively by means of the Cross of Christ. If we do not understand that, we are not properly *"discerning the Lord's Body."*

The penalty for such is sickness and even premature death (I Cor. 11:30). We should consider that very carefully because it is certain that the Lord says exactly what He means and means exactly what He says.

Faith in Christ and the Cross is the requirement, and that requirement will never be changed.

Unfortunately, of the millions of Christians who partake of the Lord's Supper, and do so constantly, the Cross of Christ is not their object of faith but something else entirely. The church desperately needs to understand how serious this is. Let me say it again:

To do so invites sickness and even premature death. It doesn't mean the person will lose his soul, but it does mean his life will be cut short. It's something we should think about!

(17) "AND THE CHILDREN OF ISRAEL WHO WERE PRESENT KEPT THE PASSOVER AT THAT TIME, AND THE FEAST OF UNLEAVENED BREAD SEVEN DAYS.

(18) "AND THERE WAS NO PASSOVER LIKE TO THAT KEPT IN ISRAEL FROM THE DAYS OF SAMUEL THE PROPHET; NEITHER DID ALL THE KINGS OF ISRAEL KEEP SUCH A PASSOVER AS JOSIAH KEPT, AND THE PRIESTS, AND THE LEVITES, AND ALL JUDAH AND ISRAEL WHO WERE PRESENT, AND THE INHABITANTS OF JERUSALEM.

(19) "IN THE EIGHTEENTH YEAR OF THE REIGN OF JOSIAH WAS THIS PASSOVER KEPT."

The composition is:

1. Three Feasts were to be kept during the seven days of Verse 17. The Passover was to be kept on the first day of the seven. The *"Feast of Unleavened Bread"* lasted for the entire seven days. The *"Feast of Firstfruits"* was on the last day of the seven. It is not mentioned here.

2. Concerning the greatest Passover ever as recorded in Verse 18, this was also said of Hezekiah's observance of the Passover. The statement is true in both cases, for Hezekiah kept the Passover such as had never been kept up unto his day (II Chron. 30:26), and here Josiah kept one that was greater than Hezekiah's.

3. (Vs. 19) Josiah was 26 years old at the time of this Passover.

THE FEAST OF UNLEAVENED BREAD

The Passover was meant to be a Type of the Cross of Calvary and the price that Jesus would there pay and, in fact, did pay.

NOTES

The *"Feast of Unleavened Bread"* was meant to portray His Perfect Life, thereby, a Perfect Sacrifice. Bread was to be eaten with no leaven, for leaven represented that which pushed toward rot or putrification. There was no sin in Christ, so the bread partaken at this time was to have no leaven.

Did the Jews properly understand what all of this meant as it referred to Christ?

Some few possibly did, and, if so, it had to have been revealed to them by the Lord. It would not have been obvious otherwise. The truth is, most did not understand it beyond what they could see with their eyes at the present time. To them, these were Feasts which had been demanded by the Lord, and that's about as far as their knowledge went.

Considering that the Holy Spirit now fills the hearts and lives of Believers, and considering that our understanding is after the fact, things become much more clear to modern Believers than they did in those days of long ago.

The Nineteenth Verse says, *"In the eighteenth year of the reign of Josiah was this Passover kept."* This was five or six years after Jeremiah began his Ministry. There is a possibility that Jeremiah was Josiah's father-in-law.

(20) "AFTER ALL THIS, WHEN JOSIAH HAD PREPARED THE TEMPLE, NECHO KING OF EGYPT CAME UP TO FIGHT AGAINST CHARCHEMISH BY EUPHRATES: AND JOSIAH WENT OUT AGAINST HIM.

(21) "BUT HE SENT AMBASSADORS TO HIM, SAYING, WHAT HAVE I TO DO WITH YOU, YOU KING OF JUDAH? I COME NOT AGAINST YOU THIS DAY, BUT AGAINST THE HOUSE WHEREWITH I HAVE WAR: FOR GOD COMMANDED ME TO MAKE HASTE: FORBEAR YOU FROM MEDDLING WITH GOD, WHO IS WITH ME, THAT HE DESTROY YOU NOT.

(22) "NEVERTHELESS JOSIAH WOULD NOT TURN HIS FACE FROM HIM, BUT DISGUISED HIMSELF, THAT HE MIGHT FIGHT WITH HIM, AND HEARKENED NOT UNTO THE WORDS OF NECHO FROM THE MOUTH OF GOD, AND CAME TO FIGHT IN THE VALLEY OF MEGIDDO.

(23) "AND THE ARCHERS SHOT AT

KING JOSIAH; AND THE KING SAID TO HIS SERVANTS, HAVE ME AWAY; FOR I AM SORE WOUNDED.

(24) "HIS SERVANTS THEREFORE TOOK HIM OUT OF THAT CHARIOT, AND PUT HIM IN THE SECOND CHARIOT THAT HE HAD; AND THEY BROUGHT HIM TO JERUSALEM, AND HE DIED, AND WAS BURIED IN ONE OF THE SEPULCHRES OF HIS FATHERS. AND ALL JUDAH AND JERUSALEM MOURNED FOR JOSIAH."

The structure is:

1. (Vs. 20) Josiah was 39 years old at the time of this battle with Necho king of Egypt, in which Josiah lost his life.

2. Verse 21 presents quite a statement considering that it comes from a heathen, but yet, the Holy Spirit would ultimately say that he was right.

3. (Vs. 22) Every evidence is that Josiah was wrong in contesting Necho.

4. (Vs. 24) It has been argued from then until now as to why Josiah did this. Other than the information given here, the Scriptures are silent.

Every evidence seems to point to the fact that the Lord tried to warn him; however, we can certainly understand Josiah paying no attention at all to a heathen who claimed to hear from God. He didn't and neither would we; therefore, with so little information given, we can only venture an opinion:

5. (Vs. 24) Despite Josiah's reforms, Judah, at heart, had little turned to the Lord; consequently, the Lord would take Josiah away, simply because it was time for Judgment to come. In other words, He would allow such to happen at this time, even though it may not have been His Perfect Will. Isaiah said, possibly concerning such as this: *"The righteous perish, and no man lays it to heart: and merciful men are taken away, none considering that the righteous is taken away from the evil to come"* (Isa. 57:1).

THE GREAT QUESTION

That great question is, *"Did Necho, king of Egypt, truly hear from God?"* Secondly, *"Was king Josiah in the Perfect Will of God as it regarded what he did in fighting Necho?"*

As it regards these questions, we have no evidence given us in Scripture as to what the answers would be except what is obvious.

From the time of the great Passover of Verse 19, when Josiah was 26 years old, to the time of his death, was a period of some 13 years. He died at 39 years old. During that time, it is most probable that Josiah kept the Passover faithfully each year as instructed in the Word of God.

As well, during this interval of some 13 years, Babylon was making its debut against the Assyrian Empire, in which it would be successful. It is believed by some scholars that Babylon had exerted authority over Judah but perhaps only in a nominal way. At any rate, Necho, king of Egypt, marched into Syria to assist Assur-uballit the II, the last king of Assyria, against Babylon. But Josiah intercepted Necho at Charchemish and forced a battle with him. In fact, this delay of the Egyptian force helped seal the fate of the Assyrians but at the cost of Josiah's own life.

After Necho defeated Josiah, he took Josiah's son Jehoahaz captive and appointed instead another son, Jehoiakim, as vassal king in Jerusalem, which was then obliged to pay tribute to Egypt, which it did (II Ki. 23:31-35).

Egypt then claimed Judah as her share of the former Assyrian Empire; however, Nebuchadnezzar stormed the Egyptian outpost and defeated them, with the Egyptian forces returning home to Egypt. Judah thus exchanged an Egyptian for a Babylonian master (II Ki. 24:1).

Necho wisely desisted from any further adventures into Judah. But the Babylonian Chronicles show that in 601 B.C., Nebuchadnezzar marched against Egypt. Necho met him in open battle, with both sides suffering heavy losses. Nebuchadnezzar, therefore, had to spend the next year at home in Babylon to refit his army. The Egyptian rebuff for the Babylonians perhaps tempted Jehoiakim to revolt against Babylon, as recorded in II Kings 24:1, but no help came to him from neutral Egypt.

We do know that the battle waged by Josiah against Necho sealed the doom of the Assyrian Empire, thereby, ushering in the Babylonian Empire. It is also Scripturally obvious that it was now time for the

Babylonian Empire to make its ascendancy. How all of this figured into the death of Josiah, on that the Scriptures are silent.

We do know that the Lord controls all things, meaning that He could easily have diverted the arrow that took Josiah's life. So, considering world events at that time, quite possibly, the Lord intended for Josiah to pass from the scene at that given time. If that, in fact, is the case, the Lord desired that the king enter the battle, which he did! Irrespective as to what Necho, Pharaoh of Egypt, said, I do not for a moment think that the Lord spoke to him. While the Lord most definitely can use anything, even the heathen, still, it is highly unlikely that the Lord did so in this case.

(25) "AND JEREMIAH LAMENTED FOR JOSIAH: AND ALL THE SINGING MEN AND THE SINGING WOMEN SPOKE OF JOSIAH IN THEIR LAMENTATIONS TO THIS DAY, AND MADE THEM AN ORDINANCE IN ISRAEL: AND, BEHOLD, THEY ARE WRITTEN IN THE LAMENTATIONS.

(26) "NOW THE REST OF THE ACTS OF JOSIAH, AND HIS GOODNESS, ACCORDING TO THAT WHICH WAS WRITTEN IN THE LAW OF THE LORD,

(27) "AND HIS DEEDS, FIRST AND LAST, BEHOLD, THEY ARE WRITTEN IN THE BOOK OF THE KINGS OF ISRAEL AND JUDAH."

The diagram is:

1. The Lamentations mentioned in Verse 25 is not the Book of Lamentations later written by Jeremiah.

2. The statement of Verse 26 pictures Josiah as a careful, loving student of the Word, to the end that he might become a *"doer"* of it.

3. The Holy Spirit does not ascribe *"goodness"* to many people, as He did Josiah.

LAMENTATIONS

The loss of Josiah was a great loss indeed!

Jeremiah knew the worth of this man to the nation of Judah and to the Kingdom of God in general. So, as it regards the battle at Charchemish, with the news of his death, the blow must have been telling regarding Jeremiah. He was to find out shortly as to how severe this loss actually was when he attempted to carry out the Work of God under the kings who followed Josiah. These sons of Josiah had no heart for God!

"A Debtor to Mercy alone,
"Of Covenant Mercy I sing;
"Nor fear to draw near to Your Throne
"My person and offerings to bring."

"The wrath of sin—hating God
"With me can have nothing to do;
"My Saviour's Obedience to Blood
"Hides all my transgressions from view."

"The Work which His Goodness began,
"The Arm of His Strength will complete;
"His Promise is Yea and Amen,
"And never was forfeited yet."

"Things future, nor things that are now,
"Not all things below or above,
"Can make Him His Promise forego,
"Or sever my soul from His Love."

"My name from the palms of His Hands
"Eternity will not erase:
"Impressed on His Heart it remains,
"In marks of indelible Grace."

"And I to the end shall endure,
"As sure as the earnest is given;
"More happy but not more secure,
"When glorified with Him in Heaven."

CHAPTER 36

(1) "THEN THE PEOPLE OF THE LAND TOOK JEHOAHAZ THE SON OF JOSIAH, AND MADE HIM KING IN HIS FATHER'S STEAD IN JERUSALEM.

(2) "JEHOAHAZ WAS TWENTY AND THREE YEARS OLD WHEN HE BEGAN TO REIGN, AND HE REIGNED THREE MONTHS IN JERUSALEM."

The diagram is:

1. (Vs. 2) Jehoahaz reigned for a shorter period of time than any other king of Judah.

2. (Vs. 2) In II Kings 23:32, we read

that he did that which was evil in the sight of God.

3. Josiah was the last godly king to grace the throne of Judah.

UNGODLY KINGS

Concerning this Chapter, it has been said, *"As the kingdom of Judah after Josiah's death advanced with swift steps to its destruction by the Chaldeans, so the author of the Chronicles goes quickly over the reigns of the last kings of Judah, who by their Godless conduct hastened the ruin of the kingdom. As to the four kings remaining, who reigned between Josiah's death and the destruction of Jerusalem, he gives, besides their ages at their respective accessions, only a short characterization of their conduct towards God, and a statement of the main events which, step by step, brought about the ruin of the king and the burning of Jerusalem and the Temple."*

This Chapter, even as we shall see, contains first, very brief accounts of the four reigns of *"Jehoahaz"* (Vss. 1-4), *"Jehoiakim"* (Vss. 4-8), *"Jehoiachin"* (Vss. 9-10), and *"Zedekiah"* (Vss. 10-13).

(3) "AND THE KING OF EGYPT PUT HIM DOWN AT JERUSALEM, AND CONDEMNED THE LAND IN AN HUNDRED TALENTS OF SILVER AND A TALENT OF GOLD.

(4) "AND THE KING OF EGYPT MADE ELIAKIM HIS BROTHER KING OVER JUDAH AND JERUSALEM, AND TURNED HIS NAME TO JEHOIAKIM. AND NECHO TOOK JEHOAHAZ HIS BROTHER, AND CARRIED HIM TO EGYPT."

The exposition is:

1. (Vs. 3) Now Judah will become a vassal state of Egypt for a short period of time.

2. It would seem, would it not, that the people of Judah could see where they were heading; unfortunately, they couldn't! Spiritual deficiency falls out to spiritual blindness.

3. All of the time, Jeremiah was prophesying, attempting to turn the nation around, all to no avail!

JEHOIAKIM

Since the death of Josiah, Pharaoh-Necho now takes over Judah. He now levies a tribute or fine on Judah and, as well, takes Jehoahaz captive and puts his brother Jehoiakim in his place. Jehoiakim means *"Jehovah sets up."* More than likely, this Egyptian king, not recognizing Jehovah at all, seeks to insult Him. He, no doubt, reasons in his mind that inasmuch as he has defeated Judah, and has done so handily, this proves that Judah's God is of little consequence, or so he thinks!

(5) "JEHOIAKIM WAS TWENTY AND FIVE YEARS OLD WHEN HE BEGAN TO REIGN, AND HE REIGNED ELEVEN YEARS IN JERUSALEM: AND HE DID THAT WHICH WAS EVIL IN THE SIGHT OF THE LORD HIS GOD."

The construction is:

1. (Vs. 5) The words, *"his God,"* mean that God fervently dealt with him to bring him to the true way. Nevertheless, despite the heavy dealings by the Holy Spirit, Jehoiakim continued to *"do evil."*

2. He had seen the great Blessings of the Lord upon Judah under the reign of his father, Josiah; however, that seemed to have no effect on him, for the Bible says, *". . . he did that which was evil in the sight of the LORD his God."*

3. His eleven year reign was marked by disobedience to the Lord and resulted in Judgment, even as we shall see. It could have been different.

(6) "AGAINST HIM CAME UP NEBUCHADNEZZAR KING OF BABYLON, AND BOUND HIM IN FETTERS, TO CARRY HIM TO BABYLON.

(7) "NEBUCHADNEZZAR ALSO CARRIED OF THE VESSELS OF THE HOUSE OF THE LORD TO BABYLON, AND PUT THEM IN HIS TEMPLE AT BABYLON.

(8) "NOW THE REST OF THE ACTS OF JEHOIAKIM, AND HIS ABOMINATIONS WHICH HE DID, AND THAT WHICH WAS FOUND IN HIM, BEHOLD, THEY ARE WRITTEN IN THE BOOK OF THE KINGS OF ISRAEL AND JUDAH: AND JEHOIACHIN HIS SON REIGNED IN HIS STEAD."

The construction is:

1. (Vs. 6) At this stage, Egypt begins to wane in power, which now sees the advent

and rise of mighty Babylon.

2. (Vs. 7) The sacred Vessels of the Temple were taken by Nebuchadnezzar and put in the temple of the god Bel in Babylon. Incidentally, *"Bel"* is a derivative of Baal.

3. (Vs. 7) This was the first deportation, which included Daniel and the three Hebrew children (II Ki. 24:14; Dan. 1:1-3).

THE SACRED VESSELS

The holy Vessels that Nebuchadnezzar took, no doubt, consisted of the *"Tables of Shewbread."* There were ten. Also, he would have taken the *"Golden Lampstands,"* of which there were ten of them as well. Quite possibly, he also took the *"Altar of Incense,"* which sat immediately in front of the veil which hid the Holy of Holies. As stated, he placed these Vessels in the temple of the god Bel. The various heathenistic gods of countries defeated by Babylon were also placed in the temple of Bel as a sign of the superiority of Bel.

There was no idol god in the Temple in Jerusalem when Nebuchadnezzar sacked the House of God. So, he took *"the Vessels"* at hand.

There is no record that the Ark of the Covenant was taken by Nebuchadnezzar. No doubt, had it been in the Holy of Holies, he would have taken it, as well, to Babylon.

Some claim that Jeremiah, before Nebuchadnezzar entered the city, took the Ark of the Covenant and hid it in a cave. At any rate, it has never been found from then until now.

THREE DEPORTATIONS

There were actually three deportations to Babylon by the Babylonians. In fact, the 70 year captivity of Judah began with the first deportation. They are as follows:

1. The one under Jehoiakim: During this deportation, as stated, Daniel and the three Hebrew children were taken to Babylon with an indefinite number of others (II Ki. 24:14; Dan. 1:1-3).

2. The one under Jehoiachin: In this, Mordecai and Esther, as well as Ezekiel, were taken to Babylon, no doubt, with others also (II Ki. 24:10-16).

3. The one under Zedekiah: With this last deportation, Jerusalem, as well as the Temple, were completely destroyed.

Up to the destruction of Jerusalem by Nebuchadnezzar, Jeremiah was continuing to prophesy, begging Judah to repent. His efforts were not met with success, and, in fact, they would have killed him but for the protection of the Lord.

Nebuchadnezzar now comes into view. He was the second king of Babylon and was the son of Nabopolassar. The father of Nebuchadnezzar took Ninevah in 625 B.C., destroying the Assyrian Empire, and reigned a little bit above 40 years.

The Scripture says that Nebuchadnezzar took Jehoiakim and *"bound him in fetters, to carry him to Babylon"*. For some reason, however, he put him to death at Jerusalem (Jer. 22:18-19; 36:30; Ezek. 19:8-9).

Nebuchadnezzar set out for Jerusalem, which was in the year 605-4 B.C. During his journey, his father died and, therefore, he succeeded him to the throne. He will figure very prominently in Bible history.

(9) "JEHOIACHIN WAS EIGHT YEARS OLD WHEN HE BEGAN TO REIGN, AND HE REIGNED THREE MONTHS AND TEN DAYS IN JERUSALEM: AND HE DID THAT WHICH WAS EVIL IN THE SIGHT OF THE LORD.

(10) "AND WHEN THE YEAR WAS EXPIRED, KING NEBUCHADNEZZAR SENT, AND BROUGHT HIM TO BABYLON, WITH THE GOODLY VESSELS OF THE HOUSE OF THE LORD, AND MADE ZEDEKIAH HIS BROTHER KING OVER JUDAH AND JERUSALEM."

The composition is:

1. Verse 9 should have been translated, *"Jehoiachin was 18 years old when he began to reign."* It is that way in II Kings 24:8. No doubt, the error was made by a copyist.

2. (Vs. 10) Nebuchadnezzar now instigates the second deportation, taking Jehoiachin to Babylon, along with Mordecai and Esther, as well as Ezekiel, as stated!

3. During all of these periods, Jeremiah continued to prophesy, but again, to no avail!

(11) "ZEDEKIAH WAS ONE AND TWENTY YEARS OLD WHEN HE BEGAN TO REIGN, AND REIGNED ELEVEN YEARS IN JERUSALEM.

(12) "AND HE DID THAT WHICH WAS EVIL IN THE SIGHT OF THE LORD HIS GOD, AND HUMBLED NOT HIMSELF BEFORE JEREMIAH THE PROPHET SPEAKING FROM THE MOUTH OF THE LORD."

The exegesis is:

1. (Vs. 12) Once again, the words, *"his God,"* refer to the fact that the Holy Spirit through Jeremiah the Prophet dealt strongly with Zedekiah, but all to no avail!

2. Under the reign of Zedekiah, the city of Jerusalem would be totally destroyed, along with the Temple, and all because of sin!

3. (Vs. 12) Millions presently fall into the same category of destruction, refusing to humble themselves before God.

JEREMIAH

Zedekiah is mentioned 48 times in the Book of Jeremiah. He had ample opportunity to turn to God and to obey Him, but he *"hardened his heart."* It is terrible to sin in any case, but it is more terrible than all to sin against Light, and this, Zedekiah did!

Despite the prophesying of Jeremiah, in other words, attempting to bring Judah back to God, they yet sinned more and more, even as we shall see, until, as we also shall see, *"there was no remedy."*

(13) "AND HE ALSO REBELLED AGAINST KING NEBUCHADNEZZAR, WHO HAD MADE HIM SWEAR BY GOD: BUT HE STIFFENED HIS NECK, AND HARDENED HIS HEART FROM TURNING UNTO THE LORD GOD OF ISRAEL.

(14) "MOREOVER ALL THE CHIEF OF THE PRIESTS, AND THE PEOPLE, TRANSGRESSED VERY MUCH AFTER ALL THE ABOMINATIONS OF THE HEATHEN; AND POLLUTED THE HOUSE OF THE LORD WHICH HE HAD HALLOWED IN JERUSALEM.

(15) "AND THE LORD GOD OF THEIR FATHERS SENT TO THEM BY HIS MESSENGERS, RISING UP BETIMES, AND SENDING; BECAUSE HE HAD COMPASSION ON HIS PEOPLE, AND ON HIS DWELLING PLACE:

(16) "BUT THEY MOCKED THE MESSENGERS OF GOD, AND DESPISED HIS WORDS, AND MISUSED HIS PROPHETS, UNTIL THE WRATH OF THE LORD AROSE AGAINST HIS PEOPLE, TILL THERE WAS NO REMEDY.

(17) "THEREFORE HE BROUGHT UPON THEM THE KING OF THE CHALDEES, WHO KILLED THEIR YOUNG MEN WITH THE SWORD IN THE HOUSE OF THEIR SANCTUARY, AND HAD NO COMPASSION UPON YOUNG MAN OR MAIDEN, OLD MAN, OR HIM WHO STOOPED FOR AGE: HE GAVE THEM ALL INTO HIS HAND.

(18) "AND ALL THE VESSELS OF THE HOUSE OF GOD, GREAT AND SMALL, AND THE TREASURES OF THE HOUSE OF THE LORD, AND THE TREASURES OF THE KING, AND OF HIS PRINCES; ALL THESE HE BROUGHT TO BABYLON.

(19) "AND THEY BURNT THE HOUSE OF GOD, AND BROKE DOWN THE WALL OF JERUSALEM, AND BURNT ALL THE PALACES THEREOF WITH FIRE, AND DESTROYED ALL THE GOODLY VESSELS THEREOF.

(20) "AND THEM WHO HAD ESCAPED FROM THE SWORD CARRIED HE AWAY TO BABYLON; WHERE THEY WERE SERVANTS TO HIM AND HIS SONS UNTIL THE REIGN OF THE KINGDOM OF PERSIA:

(21) "TO FULFILL THE WORD OF THE LORD BY THE MOUTH OF JEREMIAH, UNTIL THE LAND HAD ENJOYED HER SABBATHS: FOR AS LONG AS SHE LAY DESOLATE SHE KEPT SABBATH, TO FULFILL THREESCORE AND TEN YEARS."

The synopsis is:

1. Considering Verse 13, the criticism by the Prophet Ezekiel concerning this oath violation on the part of Zedekiah is to be found in his Book (Ezek. 17:12-20; 21:25).

2. Verses 14 through 16 may be regarded as the formal and final indictment of the people of Judah. This Passage tells us that even the Priests practiced abominations!

3. (Vs. 15) As we shall see, God's Compassion can be exhausted. The *"Messengers"* addressed here could very well have been Isaiah, Jeremiah, and Ezekiel, with the emphasis on Jeremiah.

4. (Vs. 16) It is one thing for man to say that there is no remedy, but quite something

else altogether for the Lord to say, *"Till there was no remedy."* In these very words, one can feel the sob of the Holy Spirit!

5. This, as recorded in Verse 18, was the last deportation, with Jerusalem, as well as the Temple, being completely destroyed.

6. By the Lord allowing the happenings of Verse 19, in effect, He is saying that Judah was no longer His People. Now they belonged to the Babylonian king.

7. (Vs. 21) The Law of Moses had demanded that every seventh year the entirety of the land of Israel should rest. It was called *"a Sabbath of rest unto the land."* On the seventh year, the Lord said, *"You shall neither sow your field, nor prune your vineyard"* (Lev. 25:3-4).

For some 490 years, Israel ignored this Law of God; consequently, Israel *"owed"* the Lord 70 years of Sabbaths as it regarded the land. Her deportation to Babylon would be for 70 years, thereby, guaranteeing that the land would then lay fallow and would *"enjoy her Sabbaths."* God says what He means and means what He says.

ABOMINATIONS

With Babylon breathing down their neck, you would think that Judah would cry to God; however, they did the very opposite. They sinned more and more with even the Priests going deep into sin, and quite possibly the High Priest as well.

In the midst of all of this, the Lord sent Prophets to them, which included the great Ministry of Jeremiah. But the Scripture says, *"But they mocked the Messengers of God, and despised His Words, and misused His Prophets. . . ."*

They did not want to hear the truth, so the Lord allowed them to believe a lie. They did not want freedom, so they were made captives. They spurned Mercy, so they were given wrath.

I have to wonder as to how much different the modern church is presently than Judah of old!

"TILL THERE WAS NO REMEDY"

No remedy!
What a statement!
It would be bad enough if man made such

NOTES

an announcement, but, considering that these are Words which came from the Lips of the Lord Himself, then the awful finality of such hits us in the face. In other words, there was nothing else that God could do. He had sent Prophet after Prophet, all to no avail! He had tried everything that could be tried, all to no avail!

As there came a time for Judah that Mercy could no longer be extended, likewise, there comes a time for individuals who fall into the same category. But yet, something must be said about this.

When people such as those in Judah, or even the modern variety, come to this place, they have no desire to come to the Lord, no care about His Word, and no regard at all for what He wants. They have spurned the Holy Spirit so long until there is no twinge of conscience left.

As long as people want to come to the Lord, irrespective as to what they have done in the past, if they come sincerely, they will always be met with Mercy and Grace. We serve a good God, as ought to be overly obvious.

Whatever happened to Judah was caused by Judah herself. Whatever happens to millions of others who fall into the same category can only be blamed by their own actions.

The destruction of Jerusalem is not here recorded, that being given in II Kings, Chapter 25.

When Zedekiah rebelled against Nebuchadnezzar, in essence, giving allegiance to Egypt, because he thought the Egyptians would come to his rescue, Nebuchadnezzar then sent an army against Jerusalem.

Jeremiah pleaded with the leaders of Jerusalem to surrender, but they would not heed. Consequently, Nebuchadnezzar grew very angry, and when he finally did breach the walls of the city, he spared no one, meaning that he showed no mercy.

He killed the sons of Zedekiah before the king's eyes and then put out the eyes of Zedekiah. He then bound him with fetters of brass and carried him to Babylon.

When he took the city, the Scripture says, *"He burnt the House of the LORD, and the king's house, and all the houses of*

Jerusalem, and every great man's house burnt he with fire" (II Ki. 25:9).

During the siege before the city fell, untold thousands died of starvation and plague. The horror of this knew no bounds. The Holy Spirit had said, *"Till there was no remedy."*

In essence, the Lord was saying that Judah no longer desired His Land or His House, so He would give it to the king of Babylon, which He did! The Temple had stood for over 400 years, and now there was nothing left but a smoking ruin.

THE SABBATH OF REST UNTO THE LAND

The Scripture says, *"To fulfill the Word of the LORD by the mouth of Jeremiah, until the land had enjoyed her Sabbaths: for as long as she lay desolate she kept Sabbath, to fulfill threescore and ten years."*

In the Levitical Law, the Lord had decreed that the land would lay fallow every seventh year, in effect, letting it rest. For 490 years, Israel had ignored this Law, continuing to plant and harvest on the Sabbath year. She was to learn that the Lord said what He meant and meant what He said.

In that 490 years, there were 70 Sabbath years, in effect, 70 Sabbath years which were owed to God.

When Israel was taken captive by the Babylonians, the period lasted for some 70 years; therefore, the Lord collected His Sabbaths.

TITHING

The Lord has decreed that 10 percent of our income belongs to Him, in other words, is to be dedicated to His Service. In fact, all that we have belongs to Him.

Tithing was instituted long before the Law, actually, with the first mention of it concerning Abraham paying tithe to Melchizedek (Gen. 14:20).

Inasmuch as we presently are children of Abraham, and inasmuch as we have been justified by Faith, with the rudiments of that great Doctrine given to Abraham (Gal. 3:6), the great Patriarch set the standard for us all. As he paid tithe to Melchizedek, who was a Type of Christ, we are to pay tithes as it regards the Work of Christ. As Abraham did, so must we (Gal. 3:7).

I maintain that every single Believer on Earth pays tithes. They may do so willingly or unwillingly, nevertheless, they pay tithes. In other words, if we do not voluntarily give that to God which belongs to Him, He will collect it in other ways, but collect it, He will. He will do so exactly as He collected His Sabbaths of so long ago.

So, I think it would stand to reason that it would be far better for the Believer to give to God that which belongs to Him, and reap the great Blessings which follow, than for Him to have to take it from us by force, which He definitely will do, and we receive no blessing whatsoever.

The Prophet Haggai said, *"You looked for much, and, lo, it came to little; and when you brought it home, I did blow upon it. Why? says the LORD of Hosts. Because of My House that is waste, and you run every man unto his own house.* (God first is the secret of Spiritual and temporal prosperity. The phrase, *'You looked for much, and, lo, it came to little,'* is one step further than the first phrase of Verse 6. There they sowed much and brought in little; here, they expect much and get little.

"The phrase, *'And when you brought it home, I did blow upon it,'* signifies that what little harvest they did get was cursed by the Lord, because they were not attending to His Work. Please understand; this was for all the people, and not just the Priests, etc.)" (Hag. 1:9).

As I think should be obvious, God collects in one way or the other! So, why not obey Him and, thereby, receive all the wonderful benefits which obedience brings!

(22) "NOW IN THE FIRST YEAR OF CYRUS KING OF PERSIA, THAT THE WORD OF THE LORD SPOKEN BY THE MOUTH OF JEREMIAH MIGHT BE ACCOMPLISHED, THE LORD STIRRED UP THE SPIRIT OF CYRUS KING OF PERSIA, THAT HE MADE A PROCLAMATION THROUGHOUT ALL HIS KINGDOM, AND PUT IT ALSO IN WRITING, SAYING,

(23) "THUS SAYS CYRUS KING OF PERSIA, ALL THE KINGDOMS OF THE EARTH HAS THE LORD GOD OF HEAVEN

GIVEN ME; AND HE HAS CHARGED ME TO BUILD HIM AN HOUSE IN JERUSALEM, WHICH IS IN JUDAH. WHO IS THERE AMONG YOU OF ALL HIS PEOPLE? THE LORD HIS GOD BE WITH HIM, AND LET HIM GO UP."

The composition is:

1. (Vs. 22) A period of about 50 years had elapsed between the last date of the foregoing Verses and the date signalized here. As well, Cyrus was Esther's son.

2. (Vs. 23) The Medo-Persian Empire had defeated the Babylonian Empire. No doubt, Cyrus had been greatly influenced by his godly mother, Esther, in that he now recognizes that it is the Lord Who has raised up the Persian Empire.

3. Verse 23 pertains to the rebuilding of the Temple under Ezra. All the Israelites were now free to go back to the Land of Israel. Chapter 2 of Ezra gives us a list of the first group returning from captivity.

BUILD THE HOUSE

The great Babylonian Empire has now fallen with the Medo-Persians taking its place. Beautifully and strangely enough, Cyrus is the king of Persia. He is the son of Esther, who, no doubt, informed him of Israel's place in the Plan of God. At any rate, the Scripture says, *"The LORD stirred up the spirit of Cyrus king of Persia."* As a result, he made a proclamation throughout all his kingdom, actually putting it in writing, saying that the God of Heaven had charged him to build Him a House in Jerusalem, which was in Judah. As a result, with the 70 years now finished, he gave freedom to all the captive Israelites, giving them the latitude to return to their homeland, if they so desired.

Beautifully enough, over 200 years before, Isaiah had prophesied, *"Who says of Cyrus, He is My shepherd, and shall perform all My Pleasure: even saying to Jerusalem, You shall be built; and to the Temple, Your foundation shall be laid.* (Amazingly enough, the Lord called Cyrus by name approximately 150 years before he was born, and about 200 years before these things came to pass)" (Isa. 44:28).

The Prophet went on to say,

"Thus says the LORD to His Anointed,

NOTES

to Cyrus, whose right hand I have held, to subdue nations before him; and I will loose the loins of kings, to open before him the two leaved gates; and the gates shall not be shut (this Chapter gives us a direct address of God to a heathen king, which is without parallel in Scripture.

"'*His Anointed,*' as it pertains to Cyrus, refers to what Cyrus would do, and not to holiness and character.

"The '*two leaved gates*' refer to the great gates which went down into the Euphrates River, built to keep out intruders. They were left unlocked, which made it possible for the army of Cyrus to take Babylon. As stated, these predictions were given about 200 years before they actually happened);

"I will go before you, and make the crooked places straight: I will break in pieces the gates of brass, and cut in sunder the bars of iron (on the night that Belshazzar was slain, these gates, by a strange oversight, were left open; the Medes had diverted the course of the river, and so the soldiers marched up its dried bed and entered the city through the open gates, thus becoming masters of Babylon after a siege of two years. Belshazzar and his government had thought the city impregnable, but God said differently!):

"And I will give you the treasures of darkness, and hidden riches of secret places, that you may know that I, the LORD, which call you by your name, am the God of Israel. (This pertained to the treasures and riches of Babylon.)

"For Jacob My Servant's sake, and Israel My Elect, I have even called you by your name: I have surnamed you, though you have not known Me. (The conqueror's name was Agradetes, but God surnamed him Cyrus; and, as predicted in these Verses, he has ever since been known by this name.

"Josephus said that this Prophecy was pointed out to Cyrus on his conquest of Babylon, and he thereupon determined to fulfill what was written; however, he probably already knew about it from his mother, Esther.)

"I am the LORD, and there is none else, there is no God beside Me: I girded you, though you have not known Me (the Holy

Spirit is calling to attention the fact that none but *'the LORD'* could forecast such minute detail concerning something that would happen approximately 200 years in the future):

"That they may know from the rising of the sun, and from the west, that there is none beside Me. I am the LORD, and there is none else. (The phrase, *'From the rising of the sun, and from the west,'* is meant to call attention to all the world, from the extreme east to the extreme west, to these wonderful occurrences, so that Jehovah's Hand in them would be perceived and His sole Godhead would be acknowledged; for only Jehovah could do such a thing!)" (Isa. 45:1-6).

> "See where our great High Priest before the Lord appears,
> "And on His loving Breast the Tribe of Israel bears;
> "Never without His People seen,
> "The head of all believing men."
>
> "With Him, the Cornerstone, the living stones conjoin;
> "Christ and His Church are one, one Body and one Vine;
> "For us He uses all His Powers,
> "And all He has, or is, is ours."
>
> "The path of Christ our Head the members all pursue,
> "By His good Spirit led to act and suffer too:
> "Like Him, the toil, the Cross, sustained,
> "Till, glorious all, like Him we reign."

CONCLUSION

It is May 19, 2008, as I conclude my efforts as it regards the Commentary on I and II Chronicles. Having begun this work in September of 2007, I have spent approximately eight months in this endeavor. In fact, and in truth, I have spent a lifetime, for anything now done draws from all the many, many years of study as it regards the Word of God.

As always, I am indebted to so many who have gone before me from whom I have gleaned, as it regards their thoughts, their work, their efforts, and their labor. It is only my hope that others, as well, can glean from me, for such is the Gospel.

I love the Word of God even more than I have words to express. In writing these Commentaries, the pleasure of such knows no bounds. I think that I am blessed more than those who will survey my efforts.

If there is any blessing in these efforts, we give all the glory to the Lord. And, if our efforts open up the Scriptures to you to a greater degree, then our labor has not been in vain.

As well, I owe so very much to many who make this Commentary possible. I speak of typing the many hundreds of pages, the many corrections of punctuation and grammar, of which we never quite seem to catch them all, of the typesetting, all, a monumental effort of labor, but yet a labor of love. My thanks go to these individuals. If I tried to call their names, I would miss some, and that I must not do.

If you have purchased this Volume, or else you have been the recipient of it as a gift, I believe if you will study its pages, you will learn more about the Word of God. If, in fact, that is the case, then it will have been well worth your time. There is nothing in the world more important than the Bible.

May the greatest Blessings of the Lord ever rest upon you,
Jimmy Swaggart.

BIBLIOGRAPHY

CHAPTER 4

George Williams, *The Student's Commentary on the Holy Scriptures*, Grand Rapids, Kregel Publications, 1949, pgs. 20-21, 915-916.

CHAPTER 7

George Williams, *The Student's Commentary on the Holy Scriptures*, Grand Rapids, Kregel Publications, 1949, pg. 244.

The New Bible Dictionary, Second Edition, Wheaton, Tyndale House Publishers Inc., 1962, pg. 761.

CHAPTER 9

George Williams, *The Student's Commentary on the Holy Scriptures*, Grand Rapids, Kregel Publications, 1949, pg. 245.

CHAPTER 13

George Williams, *The Student's Commentary on the Holy Scriptures*, Grand Rapids, Kregel Publications, 1949, pg. 247.

CHAPTER 20

George Williams, *The Student's Commentary on the Holy Scriptures*, Grand Rapids, Kregel Publications, 1949, pg. 250.

CHAPTER 21

H.D.M. Spence, *The Pulpit Commentary: Vol. 6*, Grand Rapids, Eerdmans Publishing Company, 1978, pg. 258.

CHAPTER 22

H.D.M. Spence, *The Pulpit Commentary: Vol. 6*, Grand Rapids, Eerdmans Publishing Company, 1978, pg. 264.

CHAPTER 24

George Williams, *The Student's Commentary on the Holy Scriptures*, Grand Rapids, Kregel Publications, 1949, pg. 252.

H.D.M. Spence, *The Pulpit Commentary: Vol. 6*, Grand Rapids, Eerdmans Publishing Company, 1978, pgs. 284-285.

CHAPTER 30

George Williams, *The Student's Commentary on the Holy Scriptures*, Grand Rapids, Kregel Publications, 1949, pg. 254.

CHAPTER 31

George Williams, *The Student's Commentary on the Holy Scriptures*, Grand Rapids, Kregel Publications, 1949, pgs. 254-255.

CHAPTER 32

Kenneth S. Wuest, *Wuest's Word Studies from the Greek New Testament: Vol. 2*, Grand Rapids, Eerdmans Publishing Company, 1973, pgs. 56-57.

CHAPTER 33

H.D.M. Spence, *The Pulpit Commentary: Vol. 6*, Grand Rapids, Eerdmans Publishing Company, 1978, pgs. 403, 407.

CHAPTER 34

George Williams, *The Student's Commentary on the Holy Scriptures*, Grand Rapids, Kregel Publications, 1949, pg. 256.

REFERENCE BOOKS

Atlas Of The Bible — Rogerson
Notes On Exodus — C.H. Mackintosh
Strong's Exhaustive Concordance Of The Bible
The Complete Word Study Dictionary
The Interlinear Greek — English New Testament — George Ricker Berry
The International Standard Bible Encyclopedia
New Bible Dictionary — Tyndale
The Pulpit Commentary — H.D.M. Spence
The Student's Commentary On The Holy Scriptures — George Williams
The Zondervan Pictorial Encyclopedia Of The Bible
Vine's Expository Dictionary Of New Testament Words
Webster's New Collegiate Dictionary
Word Studies In The Greek New Testament, Volume I — Kenneth S. Wuest
Young's Literal Translation Of The Holy Bible

INDEX

The index is listed according to subjects. The treatment may include a complete dissertation or no more than a paragraph. But hopefully it will provide some help.

As well, even though extended treatment of a subject may not be carried in this Commentary, one of the other Commentaries may well include the desired material.

"A MAN OF GOD", 400
ABOMINATIONS, 499
ABUNDANCE, 447
ACCEPTANCE OF THE LORD, 436
ACCORDING TO THE WORD OF THE LORD, 102
ACTIONS OF THE LORD, 369
ADAM, 3
ADMONITION, 435
"AFFECTION TO THE HOUSE OF MY GOD", 191
AFFLICTION, 472
AGAINST GOD!, 459
ALL HER DESIRE, 263
ALL SHOULD BE GUARDIANS, 177
ALL THE KINGS OF THE EARTH, 265
ALTAR, 149, 238, 419
ALTAR OF THE LORD, 257, 428
AMALEK, 10
"AMBUSHMENTS", 360
AMERICA AND THE BIBLE, 92
AMON, 475
AN ANSWERED PRAYER, 20
AN ILLUSTRATION, 77
AN OLD SIN IS AN EASY SIN, 363
AN UNPARALLED OPPORTUNITY, 385
"AND THE LORD WAS WITH JEHOSHAPHAT", 326
ANGER OF THE LORD, 401
ANOINTED, 240
ANOTHER JESUS, 281, 419
ANSWER IS THE CROSS OF CHRIST, 274
ANSWER OF THE LORD, 155
APOSTATE CHURCH, 70
APOSTLE PAUL, 159, 448
ARGENTINA, 276
ARK OF GOD, 80

ARK OF THE COVENANT, 106, 231, 488
"AS LONG AS HE SOUGHT THE LORD, GOD MADE HIM TO PROSPER", 404
ASK WHAT I SHALL GIVE YOU, 203
ATTACK AGAINST THE CROSS, 249
ATTACK BY SATAN, 485
AUTHORITY OF THE BELIEVER, 61
BAALIM, 388
BACK TO THE CROSS, 346
BAROMETER OF SPIRITUALITY, 38
"BATTLE IS NOT YOURS, BUT GOD'S", 355
BECAUSE THEY HAD TRANSGRESSED AGAINST THE LORD, 286
BECAUSE THEY SOUGHT AFTER THE GODS OF EDOM, 403
BEGINNING OF CONSTRUCTION, 211
BEGINNINGS OF THE EXPOSITOR'S STUDY BIBLE, 331
BELIEF SYSTEM, 347
BELIEVE HIS PROPHETS AND PROSPER, 359
BELIEVE WHAT?, 301
BELIEVER AND WILLPOWER, 392
BIBLE, 447, 481
BIRTHRIGHT, 23
"BLESSED BE THE LORD YOUR GOD", 263
BLESSED FOREVER, 125
BLESSING, 19, 109
BLESSING AND THE CURSE, 88
BLESSING OF THE LORD, 87, 176, 353
BOASTING IN THE CROSS, 32
BRAZEN ALTAR, 216
BRAZEN LAVER, 217
BREAD, THE FLESH, THE WINE, 110
BROUGHT THE PEOPLE BACK TO THE LORD GOD

OF THEIR FATHERS, 346
BUILDING OF THE HOUSE, 123, 159, 206, 501
BURNING OF THE IMAGES, 99
BURNT OFFERINGS, 117, 241, 389
BURNT OFFERINGS AND PEACE OFFERINGS, 446
BURNT OFFERINGS, PEACE OFFERINGS, AND MEAT OFFERINGS, 246
BURNT SACRIFICES AND PEACE OFFERINGS, 109
CAIN AND ABEL, 442
CARNAL PLAN SUCCEEDS!, 321
CAUSE WAS OF GOD, 271
CHASTISEMENT, 311
CHERUBIM, 214
CHOICE THAT WAS NOT THE WILL OF GOD, 364
CHRIST AND THE CROSS, 224
CHRISTIAN AND SIN, 287
CHRONOLOGY, 2
CHURCH AND AMERICA, 92
CHURCH AND THE CROSS, 163
CHURCHES, 426
COME OUT FROM AMONG THEM AND BE SEPARATE, 343
COMING KINGDOM AGE, 255
CONCLUSION, 502
CONDITIONS, 253
CONFIRMATION OF THE LORD, 89
CONSECRATION OF HEZEKIAH, 424
CONSTRUCTION, 256
CONSULTING MAN, 80
CONVERSION, 477
CORRECT KNOWLEDGE OF THE CROSS OF CHRIST, 177
CORRECT OBJECT OF FAITH, 335
COUNSEL, 270
COUNTERFEITS, 120
COURSES OF THE PRIESTS, 258
COURTS, 225
COVENANT, 319
COVENANT BEFORE THE LORD, 484
COVENANT OF SALT, 294
CREATION OF EVE, 3
CREATION OF MUSIC, 38
CROSS AND SANCTIFICATION, 392
CROSS AND THE HOLY SPIRIT, 98
CROSS AS THE MEANS, 61
CROSS OF CALVARY, 431
CROSS OF CHRIST, 31, 51, 81, 82, 137, 194, 289, 327, 350, 354, 470
CROSS OF CHRIST AND THE POWERS OF DARKNESS, 278
CROSS OF CHRIST IS GOD'S ANSWER TO SATAN, 457
CROSS OF CHRIST MADE ALL OF THIS POSSIBLE, AND IT IS THE CROSS OF CHRIST WHICH MAKES EVERYTHING POSSIBLE!, 461
CROSS OF CHRIST, SATAN'S PLACE OF DEFEAT, 279
CURE FOR SIN, 375
DAUGHTER OF PHARAOH, 256
DAVID, 16, 238, 270
DAVID AND MUSIC, 38
DAVID AND SOLOMON, BOTH TYPES OF CHRIST, 158
DAVID'S PRAYER OF REPENTANCE, 422
DEATH, 84, 396
DEATH AND RESURRECTION, 228
DEATH OF SOLOMON, 266
DECEPTION, 262
DEFENSE, 278
DEPTH OF EVIL, 468
DESTRUCTION, 253
DESTRUCTION OF THE HEATHEN ALTARS, 437
DEVIL WORSHIP, 282
DIARY KEPT BY GOD, 2
DISGUISE, 341
DISOBEDIENCE, 50
DISPENSATION OF GRACE, 170
DISPLEASURE OF GOD, 145
DIVIDED HEART AND THE CROSS, 397
DIVINE PROCESSION, 107
DO WE MAKE TOO MUCH OF THE CROSS?, 318
DOES THE MODERN CHURCH BELIEVE THAT THE CROSS IS THE CATALYST?, 442
DOES THE NEW GOSPEL PRODUCE DESIRED RESULTS?, 273
DOMINION, 128
DOMINION AND THE SIN NATURE, 427
DOMINION OF SIN, 391
DREAM, 306
DRINK OF THE WATER OF THE WELL OF BETHLEHEM, 66
DWELLING PLACE OF GOD, 241
EATING OF THE PEACE OFFERING, 247
EATING THE BREAD, 225
EFFECT OF SIN, 373
EFFORTS OF SATAN, 456
ELEMENTS, 252
ELIJAH THE PROPHET, 368
ENEMY COMES YET AGAIN, 99
ENLARGE MY COAST, 20
ESAU AND JACOB, 9
ESTABLISHING THEIR OWN RIGHTEOUSNESS, 162
ETERMINATION OF IDOL WORSHIP, 384

EVERY BELIEVER MUST GIVE, 448
"EVIL IN THE SIGHT OF THE LORD", 467
EVIL SPIRITS IN HEAVEN, 339
EXAMPLE GIVEN BY OUR LORD, 229
EXPOSITOR'S STUDY BIBLE, 330
EXPRESSED BY NAME, 77
EYES AND EARS OF GOD, 253
"EYES OF THE LORD", 322
FAILURE TO HEED THE WORD, 36
FAILURE TO SEEK THE LORD, 400
FAITH, 29, 43, 301, 445
FALL OF ADAM AND EVE, 3
FALSE MESSAGE, 337
FALSE PROPHETS!, 337
FAME OF DAVID, 100
FAMILIAR SPIRITS, 55
FAMILY CURSE, 398
FAMOUS, 77
FATE OF MICAIAH, 340
FEAR OF THE LORD, 333, 409
FEAST OF UNLEAVENED BREAD, 493
FELLOWSHIP, PLENTY, JOY, 78
FIGHTING THE GOOD FIGHT OF FAITH, 470
FINISHED WORK OF CHRIST, 167
FIRE CAME DOWN FROM HEAVEN, 241
FIRE FROM HEAVEN, 152
FIRST MURDER, 443
FIRST PRINTING, 333
FIVE WORDS, 111
FLESH, 292
FLESH AND THE SPIRIT, 274
FOOLISHNESS OF SIN, 145
FOR THE LORD BROUGHT JUDAH LOW, 418
FORGIVENESS, 138
FORMULA, 250
FORNICATION, 367
FORSAKING THE LORD, 366
FOUNDATION, 179
FREE MORAL AGENCY, 469
FRUSTRATING THE GRACE OF GOD, 96, 128
GENTILES, 240, 256
GERSHONITES, 34
GIANTS, 140
GIVE THANKS, 112
GLAD AND MERRY IN HEART, 248
GLORY IN HIS HOLY NAME, 112
GLORY OF THE LORD, 212, 233
GLORY OF THE LORD FILLED THE HOUSE, 242
GOD'S CHOICE, 26
GODS OF EDOM, 401
GOD'S PEOPLE GOING ASTRAY, 269
GOD'S PRESCRIBED ORDER OF VICTORY, 163, 167, 201, 274, 300, 434
GOLDEN ALTAR, 217
GOOD AND RIGHT IN THE EYES OF THE LORD, 299
GOOD THINGS FOUND IN YOU, 344
GOVERNMENT OF GOD, 182
GRACE AND MERCY, 435
GREAT DELIVERANCE OF JUDAH, 462
GREAT HOST, 74
GREAT IS THE LORD, 115
GREAT PROMISE OF GOD, 188
GREAT QUESTION, 494
GREAT RELIGIOUS FERVOR, 82
GREAT SIGNIFICANCE OF ALL THIS, 69
GREAT STRAIT, 147
GREAT VEXATIONS, 314
GREAT WHITE THRONE JUDGMENT, 369
GUARDING THE GATES, 177
"HAD FORSAKEN THE LORD GOD OF THEIR FATHERS", 414
HAND OF THE LORD, 20
HAPPY!, 262
"HE DID THAT WHICH WAS RIGHT IN THE SIGHT OF THE LORD", 410
HE HAD DONE GOOD, 390
HE IS A LEPER, 409
"HE PREPARED HIS WAYS BEFORE THE LORD HIS GOD", 411
HE STOOD IN THE MIDST OF THE GROUND, AND DEFENDED IT, 65
"HE STRENGTHENED HIMSELF EXCEEDINGLY", 405
HEART OF MAN, 436
HEART OF THE UNREDEEMED, 108
HEBRON, 58
HELP US, O LORD OUR GOD, 305
HELPERS OF THE WAR, 68
HIGH PLACES, 362
HINDRANCES, 72
HIRAM, THE KING OF TYRE, 208
HISTORICAL SIGNIFICANCE, 1
HOLINESS, 115, 452
HOLY OF HOLIES, 214
HOLY SPIRIT, 156, 187, 214, 332, 450
HOLY SPIRIT AND THE CLEANSING OF THE TEMPLE, 427
HOLY SPIRIT AND THE CROSS OF CHRIST, 167, 355
HOMEBORN SLAVE, 279
HOMOSEXUALITY, 92
HONORABLE, 18
HOUSE OF AHAB, 365
HOUSE OF GOD, 320
HOUSE OF SACRIFICE, 251

HOUSE OF THE LORD, 153
HOW CAN MAN RESIST GOD?, 368
HOW DO WE LET THE LORD FIGHT FOR US?, 356
HOW DO WE OBTAIN THIS REST?, 302
HOW DO WE REPAIR THE CROSS?, 473
HOW IS THE CROSS OF CHRIST AN OFFENSE?, 443
HOW IS THIS WAR OF THE LORD?, 31
"HOW SHALL I BRING THE ARK OF GOD TO ME?", 86
HOW THE BELIEVER CAN USE THE RESOURCES OF HEAVEN, 456
HOW THE COMMANDMENTS ARE KEPT, 159
HOW THE HOLY SPIRIT WORKS, 344, 393
HOW TO LIVE FOR GOD, 288, 434
HOW WAS JUDAH ANY BETTER THAN REUBEN, OR SIMEON OR LEVI?, 26
HOW WE ARE TO FIGHT THIS WAR, 30
HUMANISTIC PSYCHOLOGY, 323
HUMANISTIC PSYCHOLOGY AND THE CROSS OF CHRIST, 345
HUMILITY, 287, 464
I'VE LEFT THIS PEA PATCH MY LAST TIME, 65
IDOLATRY, 33, 412
"IN CHRIST JESUS", 352
IN THE WORLD BUT NOT OF THE WORLD, 344
INCARNATION, 381
INCARNATION OF CHRIST, 125
INNER FOES AND THE OUTER FOES, 51
"INQUIRE OF THE LORD?", 337
INQUIRING OF GOD, 97
INSPIRATION, 190
INTIMIDATION, 458
INWARD AND OUTWARD ENEMIES, 127
IS ALL TRUTH GOD'S TRUTH?, 446
IS HIS OPERATION AUTOMATIC?, 73
IS IT POSSIBLE FOR THE BELIEVER TO BE TAKEN OUT OF CHRIST?, 223
IS IT WHO HE IS OR WHAT HE DID?, 162
IS IT WHO JESUS WAS OR WHAT HE DID?, 210
IS THE CROSS THE ANSWER FOR EVERYTHING?, 324
IS THE HELP OF THE HOLY SPIRIT AUTOMATIC?, 95
ISHMAEL, 8
ISLAM, 133
ISRAEL, 113, 420
ISRAEL IN THE LAST DAYS, 378
IT IS FINISHED, 129
JEHOIAKIM, 496
JEHOSHAPHAT, 339
JEREMIAH, 498
JERUSALEM, 147

JESUS CHRIST IS THE NEW COVENANT, 425
JESUS CHRIST THE SON OF GOD, 369
JESUS PAID IT ALL, 54
JOSEPH, 24
JOY OF THE LORD, 104
JUDAH, 269
JUDAH ABANDONS THE WORSHIP OF THE LORD, 390
JUDGMENT OF AMERICA ACUTE WICKEDNESS, 378
JUDGMENT OF GOD, 395
JUDGMENT SEAT OF CHRIST, 452
JUSTIFICATION BY FAITH, 138, 158
KEEP AND SEEK THE COMMANDMENTS OF THE LORD, 186
KEEP ME FROM EVIL, 20
KEEPING RANK, 78
KILLING OF THE PASSOVER, 438, 492
KINDNESS REWARDED?, 132
KING SOLOMON, 162
KINGDOM AGE, 119
KOHATHITES, 35
LABOR AND LOVE, 165
LAMENTATIONS, 495
LAMPS, INCENSE, AND BURNT OFFERINGS, 426
LAMPSTANDS, 222
LAST ASSEMBLY, 185
LAW!, 97
LAW AND THE MODERN CHRISTIAN, 187
LAW OF THE EVER-LIVING IN THE HAND OF MOSES, 481
LAW OF THE LORD, 446
"LAW OF THE SPIRIT OF LIFE IN CHRIST JESUS", 351
LEBANON AND ISRAEL, 89
LEPROSY, 408
LIFTED UP HEART, 408
LIGHT TURNED TO DARKNESS, 414
LIST OF NAMES, 171
LORD CHOSE JERUSALEM THAT HIS NAME MIGHT BE THERE AND DAVID TO BE OVER HIS PEOPLE, 235
LORD GAVE THEM REST, 319
LORD GOD OF ISRAEL, 238
LORD HELPED HIM, 341
LORD HELPED ME, 332
LORD HIS GOD WAS WITH HIM, 200, 319
LORD IS GOOD, HIS MERCY ENDURES FOREVER, 243
LORD IS OUR GOD, 296
LORD JESUS CHRIST AND THE PSALMS, 39
LORD SPOKE TO ME, 315, 485
LORD WILL NEVER ALLOW HIS WORD TO BE USED

AGAINST HIMSELF, 203
LORD'S PEOPLE, 384
LORD'S SUPPER, 492
MAKE THE MOST OF THE TIME WE HAVE, 194
MAN OF GOD, 277
MAN RULES AND GOD OVERRULES, 2
MANNER IN WHICH A PERSON IS BORN-AGAIN, 372
MANNER IN WHICH SATAN KEEPS BELIEVERS IN BONDAGE, 279
MANNER OF THE ARK, 88
MANNER OF THE RULE OF GOD, 351
MANNER OF THE SACRIFICE, 414
MANNER OF VICTORY, 127
MARVELOUS HELP, 407
MATTER OF CHOICE, 475
MATURE BELIEVERS, 29
MEANT TO BE NOTICED, 18
MEAT OFFERINGS, 247
MEN OF WAR, 69
MERARITES, 35
MESSAGE, 146, 416
MESSAGE FROM THE LORD, 455
MESSAGE OF THE CROSS, 280, 406
MESSAGE OF THE TRUE PROPHET, 339
MIGHTY MEN OF VALOR, 181, 304
MINISTRY OF MUSIC, 37
MIRACLE WORKING POWER OF GOD, 461
MOCKING AND THE LAUGHING, 435
MODERN CHURCH, 283, 312, 487
MODERN IDOLS, 367
MODERNISTIC APPROACH TO THE OLD DOCTRINES?, 488
MOLECH, 413
MONEY, 29, 328
MORAL, NOT THEOLOGICAL, 292
MORE ABUNDANT LIFE, 54
MOST PROFITABLE STUDY, 2
MOVING OF THE HOLY SPIRIT, 73
MUSIC AND SINGING, 103, 111
MUSIC HAS THREE CHARACTERISTICS, 173
MUSIC, SINGING, WORSHIP, AND PROPHECY, 173
MUSLIM WORLD, 235
"MY EYES HAVE SEEN IT", 262
NAME JABEZ, 18
NAME OF JESUS, 306
NEW CART, 81
NEW COVENANT, 437, 489
NIMROD, 7
NOT WITH A PERFECT HEART, 397
NUMBERING OF ISRAEL, 142
OBED-EDOM, 88, 104

OBJECT OF FAITH, 29
OFFERED WILLINGLY, 191
OFFERING WAS THE CATALYST, 443
ONLY ANSWER IS, *"JESUS CHRIST AND HIM CRUCIFIED"*, 324
ONSLAUGHT OF SATAN, 454
OPPOSITION OF THE ENEMY, 349
OPPRESSION, 248
OPPRESSION AND THE CROSS OF CHRIST, 248
ORDER OF EVENTS, 169
ORIGIN OF SIN, 373
OUR WALK BEFORE GOD, 219
OVERSEERSHIP, 173
PASSOVER, 432, 487
PASSOVER, PENTECOST, AND TABERNACLES, 258
PATTERN OF ALL THAT HE HAD BY THE SPIRIT, 188
PEACE OFFERING, 440
PENTATEUCH, 481
PERFECT HEART, 78, 323
PERFECTION OF THE HOUSE OF THE LORD, 259
PERSONAL, 199
PERSONAL EXPERIENCE, 28, 73, 113, 206, 276, 295, 305, 484
PERSONAL PRIDE?, 143
PERSONAL REVELATION, 149
PHARAOH, 459
PILLARS IN THE TEMPLE OF GOD, 129
PLACE FOR ISRAEL, 122
PLAN OF GOD, 382
PLANS WHICH WERE NOT OF GOD, 275
POLYGAMY, 91
POSSESSION OF THE CHILDREN OF GOD, 353
POSSESSIONS LOST, 53
POTENTIAL OF THE BELIEVER, 82
PRAISE THE BEAUTY OF HOLINESS, 360
PRAYER, 28, 351, 460
PRAYER AND THE CROSS, 461
PRAYER OF JABEZ, 19
PRAYER OF REPENTANCE, 252
PREACHING OF THE CROSS AS IT REGARDS OUR LIFE AND LIVING, 209
PRECIOUS STONES, 212
PREPARATION, 154
PREPARATION FOR THE ARK OF GOD, 101
PREPARATION OF THE HEART, 292
PREPARE YOURSELVES, 489
PRESENCE OF GOD, 87
PRESERVATION OF THE LORD, 131
PRESUMPTION, 121
PRICE, 151
PRIDE, 402, 463
PRIESTLY COURSES, 384

PRIESTS AND THE LEVITES, 282
PROBLEM IS SIN, 303
PROBLEM WITH THE MODERN CHURCH, 105
PROCLAMATION, 389
PROMISE, 353, 486
PROPHECY FULFILLED, 478
PROPHET, 145, 394
PROPHET OF GOD, 322, 342, 416
PROPHET SHEMAIAH, 287
PROPHETESS, 482
PROPHETS AND APOSTLES, 120
PROSPERITY, 158, 193, 204, 285, 465
PROSPERITY OF SOLOMON, 259
PROVISION MADE AT CALVARY, 53
PROVOCATION OF SATAN, 142
PULLING DOWN STRONGHOLDS, 60
PURE GOLD, 212
PURGING, 477
PUT AWAY THE IDOLS, 317
QUEEN OF SHEBA AND THE FAME OF SOLOMON, 261
QUEEN OF SHEBA CAME, 261
QUEEN OF SHEBA GAVE . . ., 263
REACTION OF THE KING TO THE WORD OF GOD, 482
RECIPIENTS OF MERCY, 244
REJECTION OF THE CROSS IS NEVER THEOLOGICAL BUT RATHER MORAL, 397
REMEMBER HIS MARVELOUS WORKS, 112
REPAIRING OF THE DOORS OF THE HOUSE OF THE LORD, 424
REPAIRING THE ALTAR OF THE LORD, 473
REPAIRING THE HOUSE OF THE LORD, 387, 479
REPENTANCE, 312
RESORTING TO JEWISH LAW, 490
RESORTING TO THE WAYS OF THE WORLD, 321
RESTORATION, 255
RESURRECTION LIFE, 249
RETRIBUTION OF AN ANGRY GOD, 371
REVELATION, 156
REVELATION OF THE CROSS, 156
REVIVAL, 442, 484
"RICHES AND HONOR IN ABUNDANCE", 326
RICHES AND PROSPERITY, 264
"RIGHT IN THE SIGHT OF THE LORD", 476
ROBE OF RIGHTEOUSNESS, 107
SABBATH OF REST UNTO THE LAND, 500
SACRED VESSELS, 497
SACRIFICE OF SHEEP AND OXEN WITHOUT NUMBER, 232
SACRIFICES, 105, 246, 441, 474, 491
SADNESS OF DAVID, 85

SANCTIFICATION, 136
SANCTIFICATION OF THE HOUSE, 253
SANCTIFY YOURSELVES, 425
SATAN CAN DO NOTHING TO THE CHILD OF GOD BUT THAT WHICH IS ALLOWED BY THE LORD, 290
SATAN'S RESPONSE TO THE ANOINTING, 94
SEEK THE LORD, 112, 350
SEEKING THE LORD OR MAN, 323
SEERS, 474
SEPARATION, 71
SERIOUSNESS OF THE MATTER, 343
SERVANTS OF SATAN, 290
SEVENTH CHAPTER OF ROMANS, 136
SHEPHERD, 122
"SHIELDS OF GOLD", 291
SHOUT OF VICTORY, 298
SIGNIFICANCE OF THE PASSOVER, 439
SIGNIFICANCE OF THIS EVENT, 478
SIMEON AND LEVI, 25
SIN, 105, 239
SIN AND DOMINION, 428
SIN AND ITS CONSEQUENCES, 287
SIN NATURE, 391
SIN NATURE AND THE CHILD OF GOD, 289
SIN OFFERING, 430
SING UNTO HIM, 112
SINLESS PERFECTION?, 96
SIX STEPS TO THE THRONE, 265
SO THEY BUILT AND PROSPERED, 302
SO WHY IS MOST OF THE WORLD STILL IN SPIRITUAL CAPTIVITY?, 32
SOLOMON, 195
SOLOMON, THE HORSE TRADER, 266
SONS OF DAVID, 380
SOUND, 100, 297
SPIRIT OF THE LORD, 308, 355
SPIRIT WORLD, 71
SPIRITUAL ADULTERY, 434
SPIRITUAL AUTHORITY, 86
SPIRITUAL CONSTRUCTION, 123
SPIRITUAL DEFEAT, 300
SPIRITUAL MATURITY AND THE CROSS OF CHRIST, 401
SPIRITUALITY, 265
SPOILS, 361
SPOILS WON IN BATTLE, 180
SPRINKLING OF THE BLOOD, 430
"STAND STILL, AND SEE THE SALVATION OF THE LORD", 356
STEPPINGSTONES TO THE FINISHED WORK, 199
STRANGE GODS, 472

STRENGTH, 291
TABERNACLE, 201
TABERNACLE SERVICE, 34
TABLES OF SHEWBREAD, 224
TAKE UP THE CROSS DAILY, 100, 385
TEACHING THE PEOPLE THE WORD OF GOD, 329
TEMPLE OF THE LORD, 186
TEN COMMANDMENTS, 233
TERRIBLE PROBLEM OF SIN, 372
TEST, 465
TEST OF FAITH, 58
TESTIMONY, 19, 382
"THAT WHICH IS RIGHT IN THE SIGHT OF THE LORD", 421
THAT WHICH THE CHILD OF GOD FACES, 140
THE ANOINTING, 64, 59, 93
"THE LAW OF SIN AND DEATH", 351
THERE BE MORE WITH US THAN WITH HIM, 455
THEY CRIED UNTO THE LORD, 297
THEY KNEW WHAT WAS HAPPENING BUT THEY DIDN'T KNOW WHAT WAS GOING ON, 458
THEY SERVED GROVES AND IDOLS, 391
THINE IS THE KINGDOM, 193
THIS IS THAT KING AHAZ, 418
THORN IN THE FLESH, 349
THREE CHOIRS, 110
THREE DEPORTATIONS, 497
THREE MIGHTIES, 65
THREE PARTICULARS OF THE TEMPLE, 207
THREE THINGS SAID BY OUR LORD, 87
THRESHINGFLOOR, 84
THUS SAYS THE LORD . . ., 278
"THUS SAYS THE LORD GOD OF ISRAEL", 483
"TILL THERE WAS NO REMEDY", 499
TIME, 404
TITHING, 500
TO CLEANSE THE HOUSE OF THE LORD, 427
TO MINISTER CONTINUALLY, 117
TO SEE BY FAITH, 69
TO SING PRAISE UNTO THE LORD, 383
TO STEAL, TO KILL, AND DESTROY, 134
TO WHAT SHOULD WE GIVE?, 449
TOTAL DEPRAVITY, 372
TOWARD JERUSALEM, 239
TRANSGRESSION, 55
TREASURES OF THE DEDICATED THINGS, 178
TREASURES OF THE HOUSE OF THE LORD, 290
TRIBES OF CANAAN, 6
TRUE REPORT, 262
TRUST IN THE LORD, 28
TRYING OF THE HEART, 194
TWO PILLARS, 215

TWO STATEMENTS BY CHRIST, 31
TWO TYPES OF SIN, 146
TYPE OF REDEMPTION, 143
TYPES OF CHRIST, 119
UNBELIEF, 347
UNDERSTANDING OF THE TIMES, 77
UNGODLY KINGS, 496
VALLEY OF BLESSING, 361
VALLEY OF THE GIANTS, 95
VERY MUCH SPOIL, 307
VICTORY, 98, 136
VISION, 339
WAITING ON THE LORD, 57
WALKING AFTER THE FLESH, 219
WALKING AFTER THE SPIRIT, 219
WAR?, 255
WAR IS OF GOD, 30
WAS GOD CRUEL FOR DOING SUCH A THING?, 85
WASHING OF THE FEET, 218
WASHING OF THE HANDS AND THE FEET, 218
WAY OF DAVID AND SOLOMON, 283
WAY OF THE CROSS, 180
WAY OF THE SPIRIT, 90
WAY TO VICTORY, 140
WAYS OF GOD, 310
WE HAVE NEED OF NOTHING, 87
WEAPONS OF OUR WARFARE, 60
WHAT ARE THE EARMARKS OF AN APOSTLE?, 120
WHAT DID PAUL MEAN BY ANOTHER JESUS?, 318
WHAT DID THE DREAM MEAN?, 307
WHAT DO WE MEAN BY A WORD FOR WORD TRANSLATION?, 330
WHAT DO WE MEAN BY THE TERM *"FAITH"*?, 224
WHAT DOES IT MEAN TO PREACH THE CROSS?, 150
WHAT EXACTLY WERE THE HIGH PLACES?, 363
WHAT IF ADAM HAD NOT JOINED EVE IN PARTAKING OF THE FORBIDDEN FRUIT?, 5
WHAT IS A PROPER PRAYER LIFE?, 460
WHAT IS A WORD FOR WORD TRANSLATION?, 221
WHAT IS FAITH?, 335
WHAT IS INSPIRATION?, 221, 330
WHAT IS IT THAT THE SPIRIT DOES WHICH WE ARE SUPPOSED TO EMULATE?, 444
WHAT IS JUSTIFICATION BY FAITH?, 301
WHAT IS MERCY?, 243
WHAT IS RIGHTEOUSNESS?, 300
WHAT IS SIN?, 372
WHAT IS THE ANOINTING?, 93
WHAT IS THE AUTHORITY OF THE BELIEVER?, 305
WHAT IS THE FLESH?, 274, 443
WHAT IS THE GOSPEL?, 450
WHAT IS THE SIN NATURE?, 136, 289

WHAT IS THE TRUE WORK OF GOD PRESENTLY?, 209
WHAT IS TRUE REPENTANCE?, 312
WHAT IS WALKING AFTER THE FLESH?, 444
WHAT PORTION HAVE WE IN DAVID?, 272
WHAT PORTION HAVE WE IN THE WORD OF GOD?, 273
WHAT TYPE OF HOUSE DOES THE LORD HAVE NOW?, 122
WHAT TYPE OF PREPARATION?, 155
WHAT WAS THE GOSPEL THAT PAUL PREACHED?, 283
WHAT WAS THE SIN OF NADAB AND ABIHU?, 170
WHO AM I?, 193
WHO WILL WEAR THE CROWN?, 139
WHOLE ARMOR OF GOD, 60
WHOLE BURNT OFFERINGS, 201
WHY ARE OUR PERSONAL EFFORTS INSUFFICIENT?, 220
WHY DID GOD HAVE TO BECOME MAN?, 381
WHY DID THE LORD HAVE ME TO DEVELOP THE EXPOSITOR'S STUDY BIBLE?, 332
WHY DIDN'T THE LORD STOP THE SITUATION?, 365
WHY DO YOU TRANSGRESS THE COMMANDMENTS OF THE LORD?, 395
WHY DOES THE CHURCH HAVE A PROBLEM WITH THE CROSS?, 62
WHY DOESN'T THE MODERN CHURCH WANT TO KNOW ABOUT THE CROSS REGARDING SANCTIFICATION?, 151
WHY IS THE CROSS OF CHRIST SO IMPORTANT?, 32, 336, 387
WHY IS THE CROSS THAT NECESSARY?, 442
WHY ISN'T THE CROSS RELATIVE TO OUR DAILY WALK BEFORE GOD TAUGHT IN MOST CHURCHES?, 151
WHY ISRAEL AND NOT DAVID ALONE?, 146
WHY THE ANIMOSITY TOWARD THE LORD?, 132
WHY THE CROSS?, 389
WHY WAS IT SO NECESSARY THAT A SON OF DAVID SIT ON THE THRONE OF JUDAH?, 380
WICKED COUNSEL, 371
WILL GOD DWELL ON THE EARTH?, 239
WILL OF GOD, 52, 57, 164
WILL OF MAN, 436
WILL THE LORD BLESS UNDER THE NEW COVENANT AS HE BLESSED UNDER THE OLD COVENANT?, 407
WILLPOWER, 288, 469
WISDOM AND KNOWLEDGE, 203
WITHOUT BEING DESIRED, 370
WITHOUT THE LORD, 310

WORD OF GOD, 220, 282
WORD OF GOD AND THE CROSS OF CHRIST, 295
WORD OF THE LORD, 64, 75, 270
WORK FOR THE LORD AND PRAISE TO THE LORD, 165
WORK OF THE HOLY SPIRIT, 94
WORK OF THE HOLY SPIRIT IN OUR HEARTS, 102
WORK OF THE HOUSE OF THE LORD IS FINISHED, 230
WORK OF THE PRIESTS, 166
WORK OF THE SPIRIT WITHIN OUR LIVES, 228
WORKERS FOR THE LORD, HONORED, 451
WORLD, THE FLESH, AND THE DEVIL, 143
WORSE THAN THE HEATHEN, 470
WORSHIP, 118, 233
WORSHIP OF THE LORD WITH MUSIC AND SINGING, 430
"WORSHIPPING THE LORD", 357
WRATH OF GOD, 183, 376, 433
"YOUR WORK SHALL BE REWARDED", 314

For information concerning the *Jimmy Swaggart Bible Commentary,* please request a Gift Catalog.

You may inquire by using Books of the Bible.

- Genesis (639 pages) (11-201)
- Exodus (639 pages) (11-202)
- Leviticus (435 pages) (11-203)
- Numbers
  Deuteronomy (493 pages) (11-204)
- Joshua
  Judges
  Ruth (329 pages) (11-205)
- I Samuel
  II Samuel (528 pages) (11-206)
- I Kings
  II Kings (560 pages) (11-207)
- I Chronicles
  II Chronicles (528 pages) (11-226)
- Ezra
  Nehemiah
  Esther (288 pages) (11-208)
- Job (320 pages) (11-225)
- Psalms (672 pages) (11-216)
- Proverbs (311 pages) (11-227)
- Ecclesiastes
  Song Of Solomon (238 pages) (11-228)
- Isaiah (688 pages) (11-220)
- Jeremiah
  Lamentations (456 pages) (11-070)
- Ezekiel (508 pages) (11-223)
- Daniel (403 pages) (11-224)
- Hosea
  Joel
  Amos (496 pages) (11-229)
- Obadiah
  Jonah
  Micah
  Nahum
  Habakkuk
  Zephaniah (545 pages) (11-230)
- Haggai
  Zechariah
  Malachi (449 pages) (11-231)

- Matthew (888 pages) (11-073)
- Mark (606 pages) (11-074)
- Luke (626 pages) (11-075)
- John (532 pages) (11-076)
- Acts (697 pages) (11-077)
- Romans (536 pages) (11-078)
- I Corinthians (632 pages) (11-079)
- II Corinthians (589 pages) (11-080)
- Galatians (478 pages) (11-081)
- Ephesians (550 pages) (11-082)
- Philippians (476 pages) (11-083)
- Colossians (374 pages) (11-084)
- I Thessalonians
  II Thessalonians (498 pages) (11-085)
- I Timothy
  II Timothy
  Titus
  Philemon (687 pages) (11-086)
- Hebrews (831 pages) (11-087)
- James
  I Peter
  II Peter (730 pages) (11-088)
- I John
  II John
  III John
  Jude (377 pages) (11-089)
- Revelation (602 pages) (11-090)

For telephone orders you may call 1-800-288-8350 with bankcard information. All Baton Rouge residents please use (225) 768-7000.

For mail orders send to:
Jimmy Swaggart Ministries
P.O. Box 262550
Baton Rouge, LA 70826-2550

Visit our website: www.jsm.org

NOTES

NOTES

NOTES

NOTES

NOTES

NOTES

NOTES

NOTES

NOTES